The Oxford Guide to
LITERARY BRITAIN
& IRELAND

The Oxford Guide to
Literary Britain
& Ireland

THIRD EDITION EDITED BY
DANIEL HAHN AND NICHOLAS ROBINS

FIRST EDITION COMPILED AND EDITED BY
DOROTHY EAGLE AND HILARY CARNELL

SECOND EDITION EDITED BY
DOROTHY EAGLE AND MEIC STEPHENS

OXFORD
UNIVERSITY PRESS

OXFORD

UNIVERSITY PRESS

Great Clarendon Street, Oxford OX2 6DP

Oxford University Press is a department of the University of Oxford.
It furthers the University's objective of excellence in research, scholarship,
and education by publishing worldwide in

Oxford New York

Auckland Cape Town Dar es Salaam Hong Kong Karachi
Kuala Lumpur Madrid Melbourne Mexico City Nairobi
New Delhi Shanghai Taipei Toronto

With offices in

Argentina Austria Brazil Chile Czech Republic France Greece
Guatemala Hungary Italy Japan Poland Portugal Singapore
South Korea Switzerland Thailand Turkey Ukraine Vietnam

Oxford is a registered trade mark of Oxford University Press
in the UK and in certain other countries

Published in the United States
by Oxford University Press Inc., New York

First and second editions published as *The Oxford Illustrated Literary Guide
to Great Britain and Ireland* 1981, 1992

First published in 2008

British Library Cataloguing in Publication Data

Data available

Library of Congress Cataloging in Publication Data

Data available

Typeset by Graphicraft Limited, Hong Kong
Printed in China through Asia Pacific Offset

ISBN 978-0-19-861460-9

10 9 8 7 6 5 4 3 2 1

PREFACE

The writer has for a long time been beneath the notice of many university literature departments: the text is the thing, and authors—the conditions in which they wrote and the sites upon which their imaginations have fed—were long ago shown the door to their own creations. Many readers, however, remain cheerfully and untidily oblivious to this austere dispensation. Literary lives continue to be written in abundance, a few lucky ones forming the basis for film and television scripts, and since the publication of the 1991 edition of the *Oxford Guide*, a public appetite for places of literary interest has shown no sign of abatement. Some major, if very different, new sites have appeared or are about to do so—Shakespeare's Globe in London, the Writers' Museum in Dublin, Dickens World in Chatham; and many old favourites—the Burns properties in Alloway, the Dylan Thomas Boat House at Laugharne—have been greatly developed or improved. These signs have indicated that, even with the seismic impact of the Internet on reading habits and attitudes to information, an updated version of a book first published over thirty years ago deserved reissue.

This edition includes a generous selection of places associated with writers who have died since 1991, but in a departure from the principles of the earlier editions, it also includes a selection of sites associated with living writers. The difficulty we had in keeping this list to a manageable length (the list of writers added finally stands at close to 300) is a testimony to the abundance of good literature still being written in the British Isles and, reassuringly, to the excellent contemporary writing these islands continue to inspire. We have also included eleven essays by expert contributors on writers whose work demonstrates a particularly strong sense of place, and ten maps of cities with a particularly great density of literary sites.

We have taken the opportunity to correct a (very) few errors, address some omissions, and remove descriptions of ephemera (such as businesses and signage) we could not—or could not persuade others to—verify. Like our predecessors, we can make no claim for comprehensiveness and beg the indulgence of those who do not find a cherished writer, book or place represented here.

DANIEL HAHN
NICHOLAS ROBINS

June 2007

From the Preface to the First and Second Editions

There is a fascination about places associated with writers that has often prompted readers to become pilgrims; to visit a birthplace and contemplate the surroundings of an author's childhood, to see with fresh eyes places that inspired poems or books, to pay homage at a graveside or public memorial. Many books have described such pilgrimages and this one has had some admirable predecessors, in particular John Freeman's admirable work *Literature and Locality* (1963) and the Great Britain and Ireland volume of Margaret Crosland's *A Traveller's Guide to Literary Europe* (1966).

The Oxford Literary Guide was originally planned to refer only to those places where something relevant to literature—a house, a school, a garden—could be seen, but so many buildings have been demolished or replaced that it has been necessary to add the word 'gone' after the description of an author's home or workplace and leave the rest to the reader's imagination.

DOROTHY EAGLE
HILARY CARNELL

October 1976

Dorothy Eagle was working on the second illustrated edition of the *Guide* when she died in January 1990. It then fell to me to complete the work of revision left unfinished at her death and to prepare this new, enlarged edition for the press. In so doing, I have tried to respect her wishes to the fullest possible extent, following the style and spirit of the work that she did so much to create. Dorothy was a distinguished editor and, during the eight years that I worked under her supervision on *The Oxford Companion to the Literature of Wales* (1986), I came to think of myself as one of her most devoted apprentices. Although her name is associated with *The Oxford Companion to Art* (1970) and with the fourth edition of Sir Paul Harvey's *Oxford Companion to English Literature* (1967), the *Literary Guide* was the book of which Dorothy was the most proud, and I can only hope that she would have approved of my part in the preparation of this edition.

As before, the *Guide* is primarily intended for the literary pilgrim. The main part of the book consists of entries for places in England, Scotland, Wales, and Ireland which have associations with writers and their work. There is a fascination about such places that the informed reader, whether out and about or seated in an armchair, will find clearly reflected here in the description of cities, towns, villages, districts, and houses where writers have been born, educated, or buried, or where they have lived, worked, and drawn inspiration for their writing. The location of commemorative plaques, monuments, and museums is also noted, as are the mountains, lakes, and rivers featured in literature.

Like my predecessors, I have visited many of the places for which I have made entries, in a bid to check the locations at first hand, but for others I have had to rely on advice kindly supplied by readers and correspondents. The number of new entries for places in the second edition is 105, bringing the total to 1337.

The second part of the book is an Index of Authors designed to enable the reader to follow a writer's career from place to place and to discover which of his or her works are linked to specific localities. Living authors are still excluded from the purview of the *Guide*.

Although most of the writers included are English and were domiciled in England, I have gone some way towards improving the representation of Scotland, Wales, and Ireland in the gazetteer, in order to correct an imbalance noted by readers and reviewers of earlier editions; this, too, was one of Dorothy Eagle's intentions. I have taken the further step, in the cases of certain Scottish, Welsh, and Irish writers, of providing biographical and bibliographical details which the general English reader may find illuminating.

April 1991   Meic Stephens

ACKNOWLEDGEMENTS

The editors would like to thank the following for their assistance checking on-the-ground bits of information in various more or less awkward bits of the country: Lyn Williams; Joanna Eley, Sarah Eley and Jeremy Osborn; Lorna Hutchings; Abigail Anderson; Yzanne and Neil Mackay; Sarah Gristwood; Susan and Anthony Reuben; John Darcy; Tim Jones; Antonia Honeywell; Jane Darcy; Carol Robinson; Jenny Mayhew; Caroline Ellwood, Gina Bryson, and Jane Martin; Leonie Flynn and Laura Hutchings; Sean Moore; Brian Posner and Pat Lowery; Amanda Hopkinson; Victoria Le Poidevin; Suzannah Purslow; and Paul Ryan. John Jones, Heather Neill, and Jane Ashley helped with matters of Welsh translation; and Lavinia Greacen advised on J. G. Farrell.

Thanks too to all the writers who contributed author features: Margaret Drabble (Thomas Hardy); Glyn Hughes (the Brontës); Kathryn Hughes (George Eliot); Andrew Lycett (Dylan Thomas; also for the photo of Ian Fleming); Christopher MacLachlan (Walter Scott); Lawrence Manley (Shakespeare); Robert Nicholson (Joyce—and also for considerable assistance on the Joyce entries); David Nokes

(Jane Austen); John Sutherland (Charles Dickens); Jenny Uglow (Elizabeth Gaskell); and Duncan Wu (William Wordsworth).

At Oxford University Press, many thanks are due—of course—to the team who actually made this rather complicated book happen: to our picture editor Carrie Hickman and designer Nick Clarke; to our commissioning editor Judith Wilson; to our hugely diligent copy-editor Laurien Berkeley and proof-readers Bernadette Mohan and Penny Trumble, who all fulfilled their taxing roles (all the more taxing in a large and intricate volume such as this) with the greatest patience and care; to our production editors Sarah O'Connor and Clare Jenkins who bore uncomplainingly with our last-minute changes (and some even after the last minute); and of course to our editors, Joanna Harris and Ruth Langley, who looked after the whole thing, and kept us (and all of the above) in order.

If this book should prove useful, it will be because it has represented the lasting work of the editors who have preceded us: Dorothy Eagle, Hilary Carnell, and Meic Stephens; our final and greatest debt is to them.

CONTENTS

Contents

East of England

Midlands

North of England

Wales

Scotland

Ireland

ABBREVIATIONS

AV	Authorized Version (of the Bible)	*fl.*	flourished	pr.	pronounced		
Ave.	Avenue	Gdns	Gardens	prob.	probably		
b.	born	Gt	Great	pub.	published		
BBC	British Broadcasting Corporation	m.	marries	Rd	Road		
		m.	mile(s)	S	south		
Bldg(s)	Building(s)	Mt	Mount	SE	south-east		
c.	circa, about	N	north	ser.	series		
c.	century	n.d.	no date	Sq.	square		
cc.	centuries	NE	north-east	SSE	south-south-east		
ch.	chapter	N.G.S.	National Gardens Scheme	SSW	south-south-west		
CI	Church of Ireland	NM	National Monument	St	Saint		
Co.	County	NNE	north-north-east	St.	Street		
Cres.	Crescent	nr.	near	SW	south-west		
Ct	Court	NT	National Trust	Ter.	Terrace		
d.	died, dies	NTS	National Trust for Scotland	trans.	translated		
E	east	NW	north-west	TV	television		
ed.	edited, editor	OS	Ordnance Survey	US	United States		
edn.	edition	p.	page	vol.	volume		
educ.	educated	Ⓟ	plaque	W	west		
ENE	east-north-east	PEN	Poets, Playwrights, Editors, Essayists, Novelists	WNW	west-north-west		
ESE	east-south-east	Pk	Park	WSW	west-south-west		
est.	established	Pl.	Place	yd(s)	yard(s)		

PRONUNCIATION

Occasionally where a place name has an unexpected pronunciation this is given in parentheses after the headword, using the following symbols:

ă	as in bat	ō	as in bold
ā	as in make	ŏo	as in book
ĕ	as in red	ōo	as in roof
ē	as in feet	ow	as in now
ĭ	as in bit	ŭ	as in nut
ī	as in kind	ū	as in mute
ŏ	as in hot	χ	as in loch

The guidance given in this book on how to pronounce Welsh place names is only approximate. In order to avoid frequent repetition it may be said here that the double 'l', as in the prefix 'Llan-', is aspirated, with a sound roughly corresponding to 'hl-'.

NOTE TO THE READER

The Oxford Guide to Literary Britain and Ireland makes connections between places in Britain and Ireland and writers and their works. Some of the connections are biographical (a place where a writer lived, or a tavern where a writer drank), while others relate to the work itself (a scene in a novel is set in a particular town square, a particular lake in spring is described in a poem). The way that the *Guide* is structured makes it possible for you to approach the variety of information it contains by a number of routes.

The places and how they are arranged geographically

Most of the book consists of entries on places—cities, towns, villages, houses, parks—which detail that place's literary connections. The places are grouped within regions, so that you can plan trips to, or simply read about the literary connections of, the part of the British Isles you are interested in.

The nine regions included in the *Guide* are South-West England, South-East England, London, East of England, Midlands, North of England, Wales, Scotland, and Ireland. Three of these—the North of England, the Midlands, and Ireland—are subdivided into smaller areas either based on historical divisions or because they are relatively densely populated, and boast a particularly large number of sites of literary interest. London is classified both as a single entry and as a region in its own right because of the huge concentration of literary sites to be found there.

A list of the regions, and the counties that belong within them, can be found in the Contents on pp. vii–ix. The entries appear in A–Z order within the regions and sub-regions (although please note that 'Mc' and 'St' are treated as if spelled 'Mac' and 'Saint'). They are not divided by county although each place name is followed by the name of the county in which it is situated.

Please note that the county names used do not always follow the current administrative divisions. This is because the local government boundary changes of 1974 and 1996, based on present-day population densities, are often inappropriate as a source of reference in a historical context. For example, the former metropolitan areas such as West Midlands, Greater London, and Greater Manchester have been retained because to single out current unitary authority areas would have introduced an unnecessary and unhelpful degree of detail. In Scotland, larger historical county and regional names have been used in preference to the council areas established in 1996. In Wales, the current divisions in use since 1996 have been used with the exception of Cardiganshire, Monmouthshire, and Glamorgan which are the historic counties. In Ireland, the historic provinces of Ulster, Connacht, Leinster, and Munster have been used in preference to the current division

between the Republic of Ireland and the UK province of Northern Ireland: Northern Ireland is included within Ulster.

Note also that the mileages provided within entries are approximate.

Index of Writers

Following the nine regional sections you will find an Index of Writers, which details the places associated with that writer: all the places mentioned in the Index have entries in the *Guide*. You can use this Index to track down all the places associated with a particular writer.

Index of Places

If you have trouble finding the place you are looking for there is a complete alphabetical listing of places, the Index of Places, on page 361. All the areas of London that are included as subheadings in the London entry are listed in the Index. It also includes fictional places, pointing you to the entry on the real places that inspired them, for example if you look up Christminster you will be directed to Oxford.

City Maps

A number of the city entries are complemented by illustrated maps showing some of the sites of literary interest to be found in that city; these are schematic and not intended to be used on the ground, but should help to give a general idea of what the major sites are, and where they are to be found.

Author features

Some authors, such as Thomas Hardy, Walter Scott, and Jane Austen, have particularly significant relationships to places. The *Guide* includes special features charting these relationships, which allow you to see, for instance, how the different Wordsworth—Lake District links fit together. You will find these features close to the places with which the writer is associated; they are also listed in the Index of Writers.

Site details

Buildings that are no longer standing are described as '(gone)'. The existence of a plaque is indicated by 'Ⓟ'.

Cross references

Cross references within entries to other places that have their own entries are indicated by an asterisk or small capitals.

Websites

A number of website addresses appear within entries. These are provided for your convenience and are current at the time of going to press, but we cannot guarantee that they will remain so.

South-West England

South-West England

ADLESTROP *Gloucestershire*

Stone village 1 m. N of the A44 and A436, 6 m. W of Chipping Norton. Jane Austen stayed at the rectory in August 1806 with her uncle. Edward Thomas (1878–1917) remembered the station by the main road:

> because one afternoon
> Of heat the express train drew up there
> Unwontedly. It was late June.
> No one left and no one came
> On the bare platform. What I saw
> Was Adlestrop—only the name . . .

This nameplate has been moved from the station (now closed) to the village bus shelter. Dannie Abse's poem 'Not Adlestrop', about the poet's appreciation of a 'very, *very* pretty girl' leaning out of a carriage window at another, anonymous station, pays a direct compliment to Thomas's poem.

ADSCOMBE *Somerset*

Village 1 m. W of Over (Upper) Stowey, off the A39, well known to Coleridge, who hoped to rent a cottage here before he found one at Nether Stowey (1796). The family of his friend Thomas Poole lived at Marshmills, Over Stowey. In 'The Foster-Mother's Tale' in the *Lyrical Ballads* (1798), Coleridge mentions 'the hanging wall of that old chapel' which stood in a field near Adscombe Corner. The ruined Norman chapel, in which occasional services were held, was demolished in the 1960s.

ALDERNEY *Channel Islands*

T. H. White lived at 3 Connaught Sq. from 1947 until the end of his life (he died during a visit to Greece in Jan. 1964). Here he completed *The Age of Scandal* (1950) and *The Book of Beasts* (a translation from a 12th-c. Latin bestiary, 1954), and wrote *The Scandalmonger* (1952), *The Master* (1957), the last volume of the Arthurian cycle *The Once and Future King* (1958), and *The Godstone and the Blackymor* (1959). While he was living here the typescript of *The Goshawk*, written 1936/7, was discovered under a cushion by his publisher and subsequently published (1951).

ALFOXTON (or ALFOXDEN) PARK *Somerset*

House, later a hotel, off the A38 near Holford, rented by the Wordsworths on their visit (1797) to Coleridge at *Nether Stowey. Dorothy Wordsworth's *Alfoxden Journal* records her impressions of the area from the Quantocks to the Culbone Hills, which inspired *The Lyrical Ballads* (1798) on which Wordsworth and Coleridge collaborated. 'There is everything here; sea, woods wild as fancy ever painted, brooks clear and pebbly as in Cumberland, villages so romantic.' But 'Our principal inducement was Coleridge's society.' Coleridge himself said Alfoxden dell 'is rather a place to make man forget there is any necessity for treason'. Lamb and Hazlitt were also among the visitors. The only drawback was the local people's suspicions. The Wordsworths' north country accents and Dorothy's brown complexion, as well as the long walks they took, often at night, with camp stools, telescopes, and notebooks, led to an investigation of spying for the French revolutionaries. After a year here, the Wordsworths left with Coleridge for Germany.

ALL CANNINGS *Wiltshire*

Village off the A342, 4 m. N of Chirton. In 1817 Coleridge stayed at the Old Rectory opposite the church with the Revd Anthony Methuen.

ALLINGTON *Wiltshire*

Village on the A338, 9 m. NE of Salisbury. Jane Austen's sister Cassandra became engaged to Tom Fowle, the vicar, who died in 1797 of yellow fever in the W Indies before they could be married. The two sisters had known Tom Fowle since he had been their father's pupil at Steventon. A copy of a marriage certificate, witnessed by Jane Austen at Steventon, is in the church.

ALPHINGTON *Devon*

Village on the Plymouth road 1½ m. out of Exeter, now almost a suburb. On the W side of the road, opposite the post office, is Mile End Cottage ℗, once the home of Dickens's parents and interesting as a record of his care for his improvident father. Early in 1839 this Micawber-like character, who had previously been imprisoned for debt, was again in serious financial difficulties and Dickens decided that it would be better for his parents to live in the country, remote from London. He found 'a little white cottage with . . . a splendid view of Exeter', signed the agreement for its modest rent, arranged its furnishings, and installed his father and mother, their youngest child, Augustus, and the dog, Dash. For a few years they seemed contented with their country life, but when Dickens returned from a visit to America in 1843 he found his parents tired of being immured in the 'little doll's house' and reluctantly agreed to their return to London.

AMESBURY *Wiltshire*

Town on the A345, 8 m. N of Salisbury. In *Guinevere* (1859), Tennyson describes the Queen's flight from the court of King Arthur to the 'holy house of Almesbury', where she dies. Lancelot is said to have led her funeral cortège over the hills to Glastonbury for burial. The early abbey at Amesbury was destroyed by invaders and the Saxon foundation which replaced it was given by King Alfred to his biographer Asser (d. 909?), the scholar from St David's. The *Amesbury Psalter*, a mid-13th-c. illuminated manuscript, is now in All Souls Library, Oxford. Joseph Addison (1672–1719) went to school here before going to Charterhouse. In the early 18th c. Amesbury Abbey (now a nursing home) was a home of the Duke and Duchess of Queensberry, who befriended Gay. He often stayed here and wrote *The Beggar's Opera* (1728), from an idea of Swift's, in the Diamond Room.

ANSFORD *Somerset*

Village on the A371, N of Castle Cary. James Woodforde (1740–1803), the diarist, was born at the rectory at the corner of Tucker's Lane. When he became his father's curate he lived at Lower Ansford Manor (burnt down 1892), called the Lower House in his *Diary*. His niece Nancy, who kept house for 24 years at his rectory at Weston Longville, is buried in the church, since rebuilt.

ASHBURTON *Devon*

Market town on the A38, 20 m. SW of Exeter, birthplace of William Gifford, the shoemaker's apprentice who became a poet and satirist, translator of Juvenal, and first editor of the *Quarterly Review*. With the help of the local physician William Cookesley, who had noticed his early efforts at writing poetry, Gifford was able to leave his apprenticeship and attend Ashburton Grammar School (whose old gateway and Tower Room—the oldest schoolroom in England—are still preserved). The Ashburton Museum has an engraved portrait of Gifford in middle age and a framed cutting from an old journal (n.d.) giving the story of his life and a picture of him as a youth at the shoemaker's bench.

ASHTON *Devon*

Village c. 8 m. SW of Exeter, on a minor road off the B3193. Lady Mary Chudleigh (1656–1710) lived here after her marriage to Sir George Chudleigh and caused a stir by the publication of her poem *The Ladies' Defence* (1701) in answer to a sermon preached locally on 'Conjugal Duty'. Her *Poems on Several Occasions* (1703) was dedicated to Queen Anne, and her last work, *Essays upon Several Subjects* (1710), to the Electress Sophia. She was buried at Ashton without a monument or inscription.

BARNSTAPLE *Devon*

Town in N Devon of importance since Saxon times (formerly a seaport), on the A39 and the A361, at the head of the Taw Estuary. Around Michaelmas 1605, and again in 1607, Shakespeare's company, the King's Men, performed in the town.

John Gay was born (1685) at 35 High St. (supermarket on site on Joy St. corner; Ⓟ on Joy St. side) and educated at the Grammar School (formerly St Anne's Chapel) near the parish church; the 14th-c. building, a school from 1547 to 1908, is now a museum. The playwright John Osborne was educated at St Michael's School from 1943. His stay at the school was cut short in 1945 by an unfortunate incident in which the headmaster was moved to strike him, whereupon the 15-year old hit him back; Osborne was expelled.

BATH *Somerset*

City on the Avon, the Roman Aquae Sulis, rebuilt in Palladian style in the 18th c., frequented by the fashionable and the ailing who came to drink the waters. Chaucer's Wife of Bath in *The Canterbury Tales* (c. 1387–1400) probably lived in the parish of St Michael without the Walls, today the area around Northgate St. Evelyn in 1654 and Pepys in 1668 comment in their diaries on the fine stone houses and narrow streets. Joseph Glanvill was appointed rector of the Abbey church the year his book on witchcraft was published, generally known as *Sadducismus Triumphatus* (1666). He died here in 1680 and is buried in the Abbey. Celia Fiennes, who visited in 1687, describes in her *Journeys* (1947) the stiff canvas garments worn by men and women in the baths to conceal their 'shape', a refinement on the earlier nude mixed bathing.

Congreve was here with Gay and Arbuthnot in 1721 and spent the season in the second Duchess of Marlborough's train in 1722. Arbuthnot and Gay came again in 1724. Samuel Richardson, whose wife's family lived here, visited in the 1740s.

Burke stayed at Circus House in 1756 with his physician, whose daughter he married. Sterne, never robust, put up at Three Black Birds Inn (gone). Goldsmith visited Bath in 1762 for his health and wrote his *Life of Richard Nash, of Bath, Esquire* ('Beau Nash'). Catharine Macaulay, author of a popular *History of England* (8 vols, 1763–83), and a friend of Dr Johnson, lived at 2 Alfred St. for a short time. Horace Walpole stayed in Chapel Court Ⓟ in 1766, when he met the Millers of *Batheaston. He wrote that he was tired of the place and only came for his health.

Anstey, whose satirical *New Bath Guide* (1766) describes the fashionable round in verse, lived (1770–1805) at 5 Royal Cres. at the top of the town. His contemporary Thomas Whalley, whose wife's fortune enabled him to devote himself to poetry and travel, exchanged views on sensibility with Anna Seward when she visited his house in the centre of Royal Cres.

(now a hotel) where, he said, 'the wind blew in a manner, really frightful'.

In 1772 Sheridan, living with his father at 9 New King St. Ⓟ, escorted the singer Elizabeth Linley to France from 11 Royal Cres. (to evade her persistent suitor Major Matthews) and became engaged to her in Calais. Foote's play *The Maid of Bath* (1771) satirizes another of the singer's suitors, a sexagenarian, and Sheridan's comedy *The Rivals* also takes place here. One of the duels Sheridan fought with Matthews took place on Lansdown Hill. He revisited the scene years later, when taking his wife, dying of consumption, to Bristol Hotwells. Goldsmith stayed with his patron Lord Clare at 11 North Parade in 1771. Smollett, who had earlier tried to practise medicine here, often came to drink the waters. He stayed in Gay St. in the 1760s. In his *Humphry Clinker* (1771), Matthew Bramble stays on the Parade.

Dr Johnson came with his friends the Thrales in 1776 and Boswell at his invitation put up at the Pelican (gone). In 1780 the Thrales brought Fanny Burney, delighted to be recognized as the author of *Evelina*, published anonymously in 1778. They stayed at 14 South Parade Ⓟ, and Elizabeth Carter, Mrs Montagu, and Christopher Anstey called. In 1783 Mrs Thrale, then a widow, lived in Russell St. She married Mr Piozzi at St James's Church (gone) early in the next year. Some years after his death she settled (1814–20) at 8 Gay St. Ⓟ. A large party gathered in the Lower Assembly Rooms (gone) for her eightieth birthday—at which she danced. Lady Miller of Batheaston died in 1781 and her memorial in the Abbey was written by Anna Seward, whom she had first encouraged to write. Gibbon, who had benefited from the waters as a youth, stayed at 10 Belvedere Ⓟ in 1793, a few months before his death. William Lisle Bowles, recovering from ill health on the Parade in 1795, wrote 'Elegiac Stanzas' within the sound of the 'river rapids', now a weir.

Southey, who as a boy stayed with an aunt at 108 Walcot St. Ⓟ, spent his vacations from Balliol (1792–5) with his mother at her boarding house at 9 Duke St. De Quincey lived at 6 Green Park Bldgs while at the Grammar School (c. 1796–9). Mary Martha Butt (Mrs Sherwood) lodged in South Parade with her sister and widowed mother in 1801. She sold her successful novel *Susan Grey* (1802) while here. She attended a *bas bleu* evening at the lodgings of Elizabeth Hamilton, author of *Memoirs of Modern Philosophers* (1800), and used the experience in a later novel. Her detailed memoirs describe her meeting with Hannah More at 76 Gt Pulteney St.; the future author of *The Fairchild Family* (1818–47) was not pleased by the condescension in her welcome.

Jane Austen, who had often spent holidays here with members of her family, lived with her parents after her father's retirement (1801) at 1 The Paragon, then at 4 Sydney Pl. Ⓟ, previously Sydney Ter. She wrote *Lady Susan* there and began *The Watsons*. In *Persuasion* (1818), largely set in Bath, Lady Dalrymple

takes a furnished house in Laura Pl. nearby. *Northanger Abbey* (1818) (like *Persuasion* written earlier but not published until after her death) satirizes Bath society as well as the Gothic novel. Both have scenes in the Pump Room and in the Assembly Rooms in Alfred St. (interior rebuilt), then known as the Upper Rooms. Elizabeth Inchbald's *Lovers' Vows* (1798), which caused such problems when rehearsed by the amateur actors in *Mansfield Park* (1814), was a popular play at the old Theatre Royal in Orchard St. Sarah Siddons, who often acted there, lived at 33 The Paragon Ⓟ. Jane Austen was living at 27 Green Park Bldgs, continuing *The Watsons*, when her father died (1804). It remained unfinished. She moved with her mother and sister to 25 Gay St. and her last lodgings here were in Trim St. (1806). The Jane Austen Centre, with a permanent exhibition on her relationship with Bath, can be visited at 40 Gay St. (www.janeausten.co.uk). There are also displays relating to Austen, Dickens, and bookbinding at the Book Museum on Manvers St.

Christopher Anstey, who died in 1805, was buried in St Swithin's, Walcot St. Shelley and Mary Godwin lodged at 4 Roman Pavement and 6 Queen Sq. briefly in 1816 while waiting until a house at *Marlow was ready for them. T. L. Beddoes attended the Grammar School before going to Charterhouse in 1817.

Fanny Burney came back to Bath with her husband General D'Arblay. They lived for a short time in Rivers St. before moving to 23 Gt Stanhope St. (1815–18), where he died. They and their son, who predeceased his mother, are buried in a vault in the Old Burial Ground of St Swithin's Church, Walcot, but the Portland stone memorial was moved in 1955 to the recently cleared churchyard. The lines on the General's monument were composed by his wife. Harrison Ainsworth spent part of his honeymoon at 7 South Parade in 1826. Crabbe, who later spent many holidays with Mrs and Miss Hoare, was first introduced to them during his stay at 26 Brock St. in 1826. For many years he carried on a sentimental correspondence from Trowbridge Rectory with Elizabeth Charter of 11 Gt Pulteney St.

Landor married Julia Thullier in 1811, falling in love at first sight at a ball here. After their separation in 1835, he lived at 35 St James Sq. Ⓟ, where he was visited by Dickens, who created the character of Little Nell there in 1840, and had his host in mind when creating Boythorn in *Bleak House* (1852–3). The much-travelled Mr Pickwick spent some time in Bath, first at the White Hart (gone) and then in Royal Cres., site of 'a most extraordinary Calamity that befell Mr Winkle'. Longfellow, Hawthorne, Carlyle, and Wordsworth also visited Landor here. Wordsworth and his sister Dorothy were guests of Miss Fenwick, their friend from Ambleside, at 9 North Parade in 1841 for his daughter's wedding. Wordsworth had opposed the match for some time as he distrusted Quillinan's ability to provide for Dora. He was too overwrought to attend the service, but gave

35 St James Square
A plaque marks the address where Walter Savage Landor lived; he was visited by Dickens (who created Little Nell here), as well as by Longfellow, Carlyle, and Wordsworth

← 16 Lansdowne Place East
Novelist Thackeray stayed here in 1857

9 Royal Crescent
Novelist Edward Bulwer-Lytton stayed here in 1866

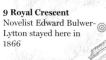

Royal Crescent

6 Queen Square
Shelley and Mary Godwin stayed here briefly in 1816

Circus House
Edmund Burke stayed here in 1756 with his physician. He would later marry the physician's daughter

BROCK ST

GAY STREET

GEORGE ST

MILSOM ST

BROAD ST

Assembly Rooms

40 Gay Street
Commemorating Bath's favourite literary resident, this is the Jane Austen Centre

Queen
SQUARE

N

LANSDOWN ROAD

WALCOT STREET

RIVER AVON

HENRIETTA STREET

4 Sydney Place →
(formerly Sydney Terrace) This was one of Jane Austen's many Bath addresses; here she wrote *Lady Susan* and *The Watsons*

Laura Place
In Jane Austen's *Persuasion*, Lady Dalrymple takes a house here. Both *Persuasion* and *Northanger Abbey* include scenes that take place at the Pump Room

LAURA PLACE

BRISTOL ROAD

6 Green Park Buildings
Thomas De Quincey lived here while he was studying at the Grammar School

Theatre Royal

Northgate Street
This is the area where Chaucer's Wife of Bath probably lived

UNION ST

Abbey

NORTH PARADE

9 New King Street
Playwright Sheridan lived here with his father (there's a plaque commemorating this). He would later set his *Rivals* in Bath

Roman Baths & Pump Room

GREEN PARK ROAD

11 North Parade
Oliver Goldsmith stayed here with his patron Lord Clare in 1771. Novelist Tobias Smollett (who'd recently lived in Bath) wrote of the Parade in *Humphry Clinker*

9 Duke Street
Robert Southey stayed here with his mother during his holidays from university

Bath Spa Station

14 South Parade
The Thrales came to Bath with Fanny Burney and stayed here (there's a plaque here today)

Jane Austen and Bath

JANE Austen's first trip to Bath was not auspicious. She spent a month here in 1797, when the family were invited by her aunt and uncle the Leigh-Perrots to spend the late autumn with them in Paragon Buildings. The streets were dirty, it rained a lot, and altogether she was *not* impressed. She returned a few years later in a party led by her brother Edward, now the squire of Godmersham, took rooms in Queen Square, and decided it really was quite fine. Living in Bath, she concluded, was all a matter of being in the right location and associating with the right people. She was gratified to observe that 'Mr and Mrs E. Austen' were listed as new arrivals in the city by the *Bath Chronicle* and need have no fear of languishing, like Catherine Morland in *Northanger Abbey*, alone and unregarded in the Upper Rooms, lamenting how uncomfortable it was 'not to have a single acquaintance here'.

There were fashionable public breakfasts to be had each morning in Sydney Gardens ('we shall not be wholly starved', she noted), and gala evening concerts, with illuminations and fireworks. The location was even sufficiently large for her 'to get pretty well beyond' any disagreeable sounds. She took to perambulating the Pump Room dressed in all her finery, paying particular attention to hats: 'Flowers are very much worn, & fruit is still more the thing,' she wrote to her sister Cassandra; 'I have seen grapes, cherries, plumbs & apricots,' but she could not help observing it was 'more natural to have flowers grow out of the head than fruit. What do you think?'

Her aunt Mrs Leigh-Perrot was also addicted to such accessories and went to shop in Bath Street for some black lace to trim a cloak. Alas! She became entrapped in a conspiracy and was indicted for grand larceny. At her eventual trial the jury acquitted her in less than ten minutes, but the expense of seven months' incarceration amounted to over £1,000. Jane Austen, who had reluctantly volunteered to share her aunt's prison room (and been thoroughly relieved when the offer was declined), was delighted when the family's brief stay in Bath was over. She was frankly astonished to learn, on returning from a brief holiday, that the family had decided to quit Steventon and go to Bath for good; so astonished, indeed, that she immediately fainted.

Living in Bath on a modest income was a very different thing from visiting the city as part of her brother Edward's entourage. The question of location was vital. Mrs Leigh-Perrot recommended Axford Buildings, but all the Austens joined in a 'particular dislike of that part of the town'; Cassandra was averse to Trim Street; Mr Austen favoured the streets near Laura Place though Jane thought them 'above our price'. She herself voiced a preference for Charles Street, whose nearness to Kingsmead Fields 'would be a pleasant circumstance'. Failing that, she thought it might be 'very

JANE AUSTEN AFTER CASSANDRA AUSTEN, PUBLISHED 1870

pleasant' to be near Sydney Gardens. The matter of servants, how many, and which ones, was hotly contested, as were furnishings, of which all but their own bed ('My father & mother, wisely aware of the difficulty of finding in all Bath such a bed as their own, have resolved of taking it with them') were sold.

Jane decided as a matter of policy to *like* Bath, but her decision did not last. She was soon grumbling to Cassandra that she could not 'continue to find people agreeable', complaining of stupid people attending one another's stupid parties: 'I hate tiny parties,' she exclaimed; 'they force one into constant exertion.' Staying with the Leigh-Perrots, they pursued their search for a decent but modest home: Seymour Street was too poky; New King Street was 'quite monstrously little', and Green Park Gardens had dampness in 'the offices'. When Cassandra arrived, Jane commented, she would have the delight 'of examining some of these putrifying houses again'. The owner of Green Park Buildings offered to raise the floor, but such efforts would be 'fruitless', concealing but not excluding the damp.

The family eventually decided upon Sydney Place from where, in summer, Jane could take herself out striding across Sion Hill, content herself with walking in Sydney Gardens, or stroll around the city's other handsome squares and elegant crescents. Over 40,000 visitors came to Bath each year and the arrival of notables such as Richardson or Sterne was announced in the *Bath Chronicle*. Burke and Goldsmith had lived in the North Parade, Sheridan in the Royal Crescent, and the young Horatio Nelson had a house in Pierrepont Street. Visitors might perambulate the Lower Rooms, whose commanding views were reckoned among 'the pleasantest in the kingdom', or promenade the Pump Room where Beau Nash's 'Rules of Etiquette' were posted for all to see. They might attend the Theatre Royal and see Kemble playing *Macbeth*, gather in the Lower Rooms for Mr Wilkinson's lectures on galvanism, or go to Mr Rauzzini's subscription concerts in the New Assembly Rooms. And yet, for all that, Jane Austen did not *like* Bath. In 1808 she wrote to Cassandra that it would be 'two years tomorrow since we left Bath for Clifton, with what happy feelings of escape!'

In her works the reputation of Bath depends upon the feelings of her heroines. Naive young Catherine Morland in *Northanger Abbey* is all 'eager delight;-her eyes were here, there, everywhere . . . She was come to be happy, and she felt happy already.' The rather older Anne Elliot in her last novel, *Persuasion*, dreads the 'white glare' of Bath on a hot summer's day and enters the family's rented house in Camden Place 'with a sinking heart, anticipating an imprisonment of many months, and anxiously saying to herself, "Oh! When shall I leave you again?"' Yet it is Anne's final 'senseless joy' on receiving, and assenting to, Captain Wentworth's written note of proposal that gives the final lift to the variety of Bath, which is presented as a kaleidoscopic picture of 'sauntering politicians, bustling house-keepers, flirting girls', from half-pay officers and elegant beaux to nursery maids and children.   DAVID NOKES

her his blessing. Froude in 1848 and Thackeray in 1857 stayed at 16 Lansdown Pl. East. William Beckford lived at 20 Lansdown Cres. (1822–44) and linked this by an arched bridge with 1 Lansdown Pl. West, where many of his books from *Fonthill were housed. He built a tower on the top of Lansdown Hill and it was from there that he is said to have seen Fonthill Tower crash to the ground 25 m. away. He had a secluded path built by his gardener (who transplanted well-grown trees) from the stables to the tower, where he spent most of his days. He revised *Dreams, Waking Thoughts and Incidents* in 1834 and wrote another book about his travels, *Recollections of an Excursion to the Monasteries of Alcobaça and Batalha* (1835). He wished to be buried near the tower but this was not possible until some time after his death, when his daughter bought back the tower in its surrounding gardens, and part of the ground was consecrated. His tomb there has the inscription

> Eternal Power
> Grant me through obvious clouds one transient gleam
> Of Thy bright essence in my dying hour.

There is a small museum of Beckfordiana in two rooms at the base of the tower (www.bath-preservation-trust.org.uk).

Bulwer-Lytton stayed at 9 Royal Cres. in 1866 and George Saintsbury lived from his retirement in 1915 to his death (1933) at no. 1. As well as *History of Criticism* he wrote the entertaining *Notes on a Cellar Book* and *A Scrap Book*.

During the Second World War the Bath Royal Literary and Scientific Institution at 16–18 Queen Sq. (www.brlsi.org) was requisitioned by the Admiralty, and John Betjeman worked in 'P' Branch here. The city features in a number of his poems, including 'In a Bath Teashop':

> Let us not speak, for the love we bear one another—
> Let us hold hands and look.
> She such a very ordinary little woman;
> He, such a thumping crook.

More recently the novelist Angela Carter was resident in Bath upon her return from Japan; the town appears in her 'Bristol Trilogy' novels.

BATHEASTON *Somerset*

Former village, now a suburb, NE of Bath on the A4. Horace Walpole in 1766 mentions in his *Letters* dining with the agreeable Miller family in their 'new built house' (Bath Easton Villa), now 172 Bailbrook Lane, a steep turning up a hill N of the A365. He describes the view across the Avon from their bow window and their pretty garden with several small rivulets. In 1773 Lady Miller returned from a tour of Italy and France, where she had acquired a Tuscan vase and a passion for bouts-rimés. These she connected into a ceremony for the poetical assemblies at her fashionable breakfasts (on one occasion four duchesses were present and the line of coaches stretched back to Bath). Fortified by chocolate and macaroons the guests put their verses in the vase, which stood in the bow window, and the author of those judged the best was crowned with laurel. Fanny Burney, who found that 'the business of the vase' was 'over for this season' when she visited, said that Lady Miller was 'an ordinary woman in very common life, with fine clothes on' but was flattered when the 10-year-old Miss Miller talked to her of Evelina as if she were a real person. The minor poets of Bath often visited the villa and William Hayley sent a poem with his wife, who found Batheaston no more ridiculous than other assemblies.

BATSFORD *Gloucestershire*

Cotswold village 1½ m. from Moreton-in-Marsh. Nancy Mitford's family lived at Batsford Park from 1916 and the mock-Tudor house, cold, vast, and surrounded by elaborate gardens and an arboretum, is the original of 'Alconleigh', the home of the Radlett family and its paterfamilias, the comically 'violent, uncontrolled', and xenophobic Uncle Matthew in her novel *The Pursuit of Love* (1945).

> The Radlett daughters did practically no lessons. They were taught by Lucille, the French governess, to read and write, they were obliged, though utterly unmusical, to 'practise' in the freezing ballroom for one hour a day each, their eyes glued to the clock, they would thump out the 'Merry Peasant' and a few scales, they were made to go for a French walk with Lucille on all except hunting days, and that was the extent of their education.

The house was used in the BBC adaptation *Love in a Cold Climate*.

BEAMINSTER (pr. 'Bĕminster) *Dorset*

Village on the A3066 and the B3162, 6 m. N of Bridport. It is celebrated in the lines by William Barnes, the Dorset dialect poet:

> Sweet Be'mi'ter that bist a bound
> By green an' woody hills all round.

The Manor House, off North St., has a painted ceiling from *Fonthill.

BECKHAMPTON *Wiltshire*

Village on the A4, 7 m. W of Marlborough. The Wagon and Horses, though slightly altered, is thought to be the inn where the bagman tells his story in *Pickwick Papers* (1837). He describes his arrival 'in the snug, old parlour before the roaring fire' after his journey across the bleak, windswept Marlborough Downs, the pleasure of successive glasses of hot punch, and the consequences of the extremely odd behaviour of his bedroom chair.

BECKINGTON *Somerset*

Village on the A36 and the A361. Samuel Daniel returned to live (1610–19) in his native county. He is thought to have built a farmhouse on the right bank of the Frome and called it Cliffords after his former pupil Lady Anne. As well as farming he continued to write masques which were acted in London and Bristol. Some time before his death (1619), he moved to Rudge (then called Ridge), 2 m. W, where he made his will. He was buried in St George's Church here, where the Lady Anne, then Dowager Countess of Pembroke, erected a memorial, renovated in 1778 by the poet William Mason.

BEMERTON *Wiltshire*

Former village, now a suburb of Salisbury, where George Herbert was rector (1630–2) of the little church of St Andrew. He supervised the repair of the rectory and the verse he placed over his hearth is now above the door of the Victorian addition. Izaak Walton and John Aubrey mention his love for his garden and tradition credits him with the planting of the medlar-tree by the Nadder, along whose bank he walked to Salisbury Cathedral services. Herbert died of consumption and is buried in the church ℗. The W window commemorates him and his friend Nicholas Ferrar of the Little Gidding community, to whom he sent his religious verse, entitled *The Temple* (1633), which contains 'Teach me, my God and King'. Charles I, in prison, and Cowper, recovering from depression, found solace in these poems and through Ferrar's connection with the Virginia Plantation they were well known there.

BERE REGIS *Dorset*

Village on the A35, halfway between Bournemouth and Dorchester. The fine church contains the Turberville window and vault referred to in *Tess of the D'Urbervilles* (1891). The village is Hardy's 'Kingsbere-sub-Greenhill', Woodbury Hill rising behind being 'Greenhill'.

BERKELEY *Gloucestershire*

Norman castle overlooking the river Severn. Marlowe's Edward II was murdered in Berkeley Castle and the castle also features in Shakespeare's *Richard II* (1595) as a mustering place for the forces of the Duke of York.

BERRY HILL *Gloucestershire*

Small village in the Forest of Dean, N of Coleford. The playwright Dennis Potter was born at Berry Hill in 1935, where he attended the local Salem Chapel; he would retain an attachment to the Forest of Dean throughout

his life, including working on a *Panorama* documentary about closure of the area's coal-pits.

BERRYNARBOR *Devon*

Village *c.* 3 m. E of Ilfracombe, just S of the A399. John Jewel, Bishop of Salisbury (1560–71) and author of the celebrated defence of the Church of England *Apologia Ecclesiae Anglicanae* (1562), which Queen Elizabeth I ordered to be read in churches throughout the kingdom, was born (1522) at Bowden, a farmhouse in the parish.

BIBURY *Gloucestershire*

Village on the B4425, 7 m. NE of Cirencester. Pope writing to Swift in 1726 recalls their recent visit: 'I shall never more think of . . . the woods of Ciceter, or the pleasing prospect of Byberry, but your Idea must be join'd with 'em.'

John Byng mentions his stay here in 1794 (*Torrington Diaries*, 1934):

> After breakfast and two fine basins of snail tea which always is of sovereign use to my lungs, we walked down the village, by the side of a pastoral trout stream full of fish, (for this place is a famous spot for fly-fishing . . .). We procured the key of the church (a key the size of Dover Castle), and admired it as lightsome, and well-glazed.

BIDEFORD (pr. 'Biddyford') *Devon*

Ancient seaport on the estuary of the Torridge, where the A39 crosses the river by a bridge of 24 arches (built 1460; widened 1925). The Royal Hotel embodies, at its N end, the original town house of John Davie, a merchant (1688), and Kingsley is said to have written part of *Westward Ho!* (1855) when staying here in 1854. He is commemorated by a statue at the N end of the promenade.

Edward Capern, the postman-poet, lived in Bideford for 17 years. His *Poems* (1856) were compared by W. S. Landor with those of Burns, and Wordsworth admired his work. He was buried in the churchyard at Heanton Punchardon, 4 m. NW of Barnstaple, where his tombstone is inscribed with some verses by Alfred Austin.

BLAGDON *Somerset*

Village on the A368, 14 m. SW of Bristol. In 1795 Hannah More started a school in Church St. (now Hannah More Cottage), for which she wrote moral tales. The popularity of these then led to the start of the Religious Tract Society, which aided mass literacy. Resistance by some clergy and farmers to the education of the poor resulted in the action known as the Blagdon Controversy (1800–2), which accused Hannah More of allowing her school to be used for Nonconformist meetings.

BLISLAND *Cornwall*

Village on Bodmin Moor. Charles Causley wrote of the famous church at Blisland, 'a stack of granite harvested | From Bodmin Moor' in 'St Proteus & St Hyacinth, Blisland'; and of its setting

> Above a valley loud with water, rocks,
> Voices of bald-faced rooks that lurk and strut
> High shelves of ash and sycamore.

BODINNICK *Cornwall*

Village across the river Fowey from the town of Fowey. Daphne du Maurier's parents bought Ferryside, the house at Bodinnick where at the end of 1929 she came, escaping London, to write the novel *The Loving Spirit* (1931). *Jane Slade*, the schooner which lay in nearby Pont Creek, the boatyard at nearby Polruan ('Plyn' in the novel) and Castle Point in Fowey all appear in the novel.

BODMIN *Cornwall*

County town, on the A30, on the SW edge of Bodmin Moor. Sir Arthur Quiller-Couch was born here (21 Nov. 1863) in Pool St. (gone). The area is now known as Church Square and a free-standing pillar there, erected on the centenary of his birth, commemorates the site of the house. St Petroc's Church contains, in the W end, a replica of part of the Bodmin Gospels as a memorial to Joseph Frank Trewarne Warne, a sub-deacon (d. 1949). This consists of a leather cover holding two pages of written manuscript and one page of illuminated manuscript of the 9th-c. Gospels, now in the British Museum, thought to have been produced by Frankish monks.

Jamaica Inn (1938), Daphne du Maurier's historical romance of 18th-c. smuggling, takes its name from the 'old, granite-faced' coaching inn on Bodmin Moor. She had sought refuge here after getting lost while out riding in fog. The inn makes much of its associations, offering a smugglers museum and a Daphne du Maurier Room, containing memorabilia.

BOSCASTLE *Cornwall*

Small village on the NW coast, on the B3263. The little harbour at the foot of the steep main street, and the surrounding cliffs are NT property. It figures in Hardy's *A Pair of Blue Eyes* (1873) as 'Castle Boterel'. In Howard Jacobson's *Peeping Tom* (1984), Barney Fugelman abandons his Finchley life to go on a Thomas Hardy quest to 'Castle Boterel'. Boscastle is also the setting for the opening of H. G. Wells's novel *The Sleeper Awakes* (1899), which he calls the first of a series of 'fantasies of possibility'. In the story Mr Isbister, a young artist lodging at Boscastle, walks over to the picturesque cove of Pentargon, ½ m. NE, and encounters a melancholy insomniac about to commit suicide. He takes him back to Boscastle, where the man falls into a trance which lasts for 203 years.

BOSCOMBE *Wiltshire*

Village on the A338, 7 m. NE of Salisbury. Richard Hooker, rector from 1591 to 1595, was said to have written the first four books of *Laws of Ecclesiastical Polity* in the former vicarage near the Close. However, it is thought that he was resident as a minor prebend in Salisbury at this time.

BOTALLACK *Cornwall*

Old tin-mining village on the extreme W coast, just over 1 m. N of St Just, on the B3306. Wilkie Collins visited the mines during a summer holiday in 1851 and made use of this experience as well as impressions of the surrounding country in his stories (see *Rambles Beyond Railways, or, Notes in Cornwall taken A-foot*, 1851). The mines also feature in *Deep Down* (1868), a story by R. M. Ballantyne, who visited in 1868. The village is the subject of D. M. Thomas's poem 'Botallack'.

BOURNEMOUTH *Dorset*

Large seaside resort on the A35, set among gardens, pine trees, and steep ravines, where the Bourne enters Poole Bay. The town only came into being in the early 19th c.; when Southey was living at *Burton in 1797 he used to walk on Poole Heath, where the town was later built, 'through desolation', but as it began to develop it attracted visitors and residents, who came to enjoy the beautiful scenery and benign climate.

John Keble, author of *The Christian Year* (1827), came here for his wife's health in the winter of 1865–6 and stayed at Brookside, a boarding house in Exeter Lane, from which he used to walk daily across the Pleasure Gardens to morning service at St Peter's. He died here in March 1866 and is commemorated by a memorial window in the S transept (now Keble Chapel) of St Peter's.

Sir Henry Taylor spent his later years in Bournemouth and is buried here.

Disraeli came for a visit (Nov. 1874–Jan. 1875) on Queen Victoria's recommendation of 'the very salubrious air' and stayed at the Bath Hotel. Here he considered the New Year's Honours and wrote to the Queen recommending a baronetcy for Tennyson and the Grand Cross of the Bath, with a pension, for Carlyle, then 'old and childless and poor . . . but very popular and respected by the nation'. The Queen agreed, but Tennyson and Carlyle both declined (the former was persuaded by Gladstone to accept a peerage 10 years later).

Francis Kilvert visited in the winter of 1875, but unfortunately the volume of his *Diary* (1870–9) for this period is missing. Later he wrote of 'wild sad sweet trysts in the snow and under the pine trees, among the sandhills on the East Cliff and in Boscombe Chine'.

In September 1876 Paul Verlaine came to teach French and Latin at St Aloysius' School, a small Catholic school run by the Revd Frederick Remington. He lived with Mr Remington and his wife and sister at 2 Westburn Ter. and out of school hours he wrote much poetry, notably 'La mer est plus belle . . .' (originally 'La Mer de Bournemouth') and 'Bournemouth', the impression of the town which appeared later in *Amour* (1888). Many other poems written at this time were published in *Sagesse* (1881), *Amour*, *Bonheur* (1891), and *Liturgies intimes* (1892). He left at Easter 1877, with a 'splendid testimonial' (see his account of the time in the *Fortnightly*

Review, July 1894). Max Beerbohm drew a cartoon of him (1904) with his scholars as he imagined them in 1877.

Galsworthy was at a prep school (1876–81) called Saugeen, near St Swithun's Church, where he sang in the choir. He travelled to and from his home in Surrey with Joseph Ramsden, his father's confidential clerk, the original of Soames Forsyte's clerk, Thomas Gradman, in *To Let* (1921).

R. L. Stevenson came to Bournemouth in August 1884 and after staying at various addresses finally (Apr. 1885–Aug. 1887) dug himself in 'like a weevil in a biscuit' at Skerryvore in Alum Chine Rd. The site of the house (demolished by enemy bombing in 1940) is now a memorial garden, opposite the end of R. L. Stevenson Ave., containing a model of the Skerryvore Lighthouse, copied from the original built by the Stevenson family firm on the Argyll coast. During his three years in Bournemouth, Stevenson published *A Child's Garden of Verses*, *More Arabian Nights*, and *Prince Otto* (1885); *The Strange Case of Dr Jekyll and Mr Hyde* and *Kidnapped* (1886); and *The Merry Men* and *Underwoods* (1887). In 1887 he left for the South Seas and made his home in Samoa for the rest of his life.

Olive Schreiner, whose best-known work, *The Story of an African Farm*, was published in 1883, stayed here from February to April 1886, but her visit was clouded by illness.

John Eglinton (pseudonym of William Kirkpatrick Magee, 1868–1961), friend and intended biographer of George Moore, was closely associated, with Joyce, Yeats, and 'AE' (George William Russell), with the Irish literary movement. While living at Bournemouth he wrote *Irish Literary Portraits* (1935) and edited *Letters of George Moore* (1942). He also wrote a memoir of 'AE' (1937), who came here in his last years and died on 17 July 1935. John Eglinton appears in Moore's autobiographical *Hail and Farewell* (1911–14) and in Joyce's *Ulysses* (1922).

In St Peter's churchyard an impressive tombstone marks the grave of Mary Shelley (author of the enduringly popular *Frankenstein* (1818), a horror story written while on holiday in Switzerland), buried with Shelley's heart, which had been saved from the funeral pyre after his drowning at Viareggio, and with her parents, William Godwin, author of *Political Justice* (1793) and Mary Wollstonecraft Godwin, author of *A Vindication of the Rights of Women* (1792), their bodies having been brought here from St Pancras churchyard in 1851.

In Hardy's *Tess of the D'Urbervilles* (1891), Bournemouth figures as 'Sandbourne', a 'fashionable watering-place, with its eastern and western stations, its piers, its groves of pine, its promenades, and its covered gardens'.

Born in India, Gerald Durrell moved to England with his family in 1931, settling in Bournemouth, where they remained for four years (and where Gerald briefly attended a local prep school). In 1935 the family moved to Corfu (the setting for his most famous book, *My Family and Other Animals*, 1956),

returning to Bournemouth in 1939 to pass the war years there.

BOWERCHALKE *Wiltshire*

Village 12 m. E of Shaftesbury. The novelist William Golding moved to the village in 1940 after talking up a post at Bishop Wordsworth's School, Salisbury. His family remained here during the Second World War (while Golding was in the Royal Navy), moving to Salisbury in 1946. He returned in 1958, living at Ebble Thatch, where he wrote, among other books, *The Spire* (1964), *Darkness Visible* (1979), and *Rites of Passage* (1980). He is buried at Holy Trinity Church.

BREMHILL *Wiltshire*

Village off the A4, 4 m. E of Chippenham. The poet William Lisle Bowles, vicar from 1804 to 1850, lived at the 17th-c. vicarage, now the Old Vicarage. Thomas Moore, a frequent visitor, wrote that Bowles 'had frittered away its beauty with grottos, hermitages, and Shenstonian inscriptions'. Lamb and Wordsworth stayed with Bowles at the house which he Gothicized. His verse included epitaphs on some of the parishioners, and a poem on the planting of the two cedars in the churchyard.

BRIDGWATER *Somerset*

Market town on the A38 and the A39, where Coleridge often stayed with John Chubb, a merchant, whose house (gone) was on the riverside. Coleridge preached in 1797 and 1798 at Christ Church, the Unitarian Chapel in Dampiet St. The (Admiral) Blake Museum nearby has paintings of the town by John Chubb. In 1807 De Quincey, who had expected to find Coleridge at Tom Poole's house in Nether Stowey, rode to Bridgwater and met Coleridge in the main street. He gave him a rare Latin pamphlet when they arrived at Chubb's house. Coleridge talked far into the night, dwelling on the horror of the opium habit. De Quincey thought it a strange conversation for a first meeting, and on his ride back through the night decided to arrange for £300 to be given to Coleridge from 'an unknown friend'.

BRIDPORT *Dorset*

Small town on the A35, 15 m. W of Dorchester and 2 m. N of its little harbour at West Bay. It appears as 'Port Bredy' in Hardy's Wessex novels.

BRISTOL *Somerset*

Cathedral and university city, and port on the Avon:

> a street of masts
> And pennants from all nations of the earth,
> Streaming below the houses, piled aloft
> Hill above hill . . .

wrote William Bowles in *Banwell Hill* (1829) when both the Avon and the Frome were crowded city waterways.

Pepys's *Diary* tells of his visit in 1668 with his wife and her servant Deb (born in Marsh St.).

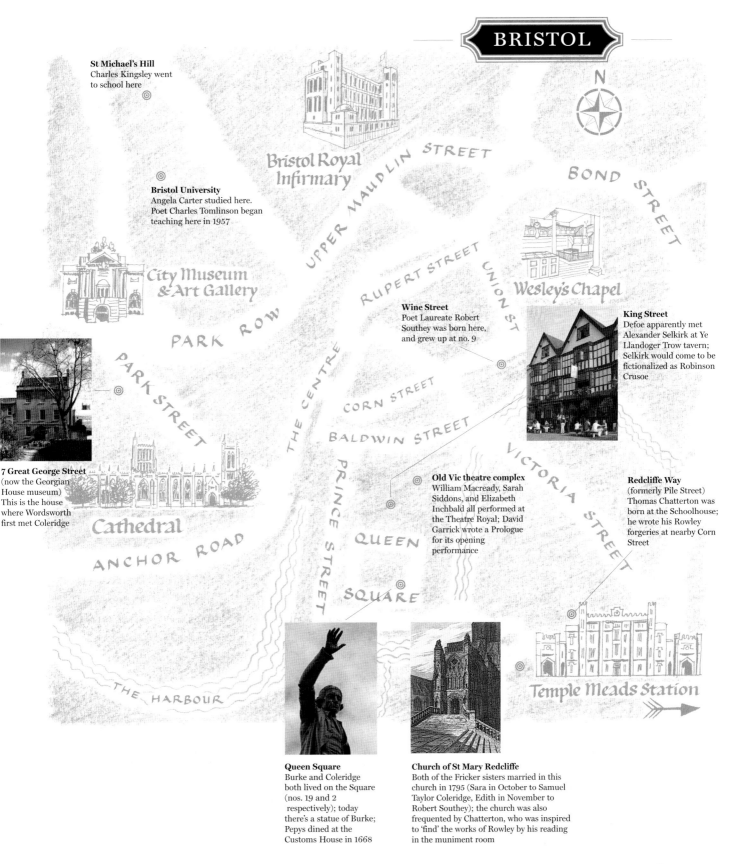

St Michael's Hill
Charles Kingsley went to school here

Bristol University
Angela Carter studied here. Poet Charles Tomlinson began teaching here in 1957

Bristol Royal Infirmary

City Museum & Art Gallery

UPPER MAUDLIN STREET

RUPERT STREET

UNION ST

BOND STREET

Wesley's Chapel

Wine Street
Poet Laureate Robert Southey was born here, and grew up at no. 9

King Street
Defoe apparently met Alexander Selkirk at Ye Llandoger Trow tavern; Selkirk would come to be fictionalized as Robinson Crusoe

PARK ROW

THE CENTRE

CORN STREET

BALDWIN STREET

PARK STREET

7 Great George Street
(now the Georgian House museum) This is the house where Wordsworth first met Coleridge

Cathedral

ANCHOR ROAD

PRINCE STREET

QUEEN SQUARE

Old Vic theatre complex
William Macready, Sarah Siddons, and Elizabeth Inchbald all performed at the Theatre Royal; David Garrick wrote a Prologue for its opening performance

VICTORIA STREET

Redcliffe Way
(formerly Pile Street) Thomas Chatterton was born at the Schoolhouse; he wrote his Rowley forgeries at nearby Corn Street

THE HARBOUR

Temple Meads Station

Queen Square
Burke and Coleridge both lived on the Square (nos. 19 and 2 respectively); today there's a statue of Burke; Pepys dined at the Customs House in 1668

Church of St Mary Redcliffe
Both of the Fricker sisters married in this church in 1795 (Sara in October to Samuel Taylor Coleridge, Edith in November to Robert Southey); the church was also frequented by Chatterton, who was inspired to 'find' the works of Rowley by his reading in the muniment room

9

Deb's uncle, a merchant, took Pepys to the Custom House in Queen Sq. and entertained them afterwards with venison, strawberries, and Bristol Milk. Burke, whose statue stands in the Centre, stayed in 1774 during his successful month-long election campaign at 19 Queen Sq., the house built by Captain Rogers, commander of the ships *Duke* and *Duchess*. Rogers's *Voyage Round the World* (1712) relates the rescue of Alexander Selkirk from his 'Robinson Crusoe' existence. Coleridge lodged at 2 Queen Sq. when lecturing. The Custom House and half Queen Sq. were burnt in the 1831 riots and rebuilt. Crabbe in Clifton, and Charles Kingsley at school in St Michael's Hill, witnessed the great fires. Kingsley came back in 1858 and gave a graphic account to the Mechanics' Institute. Coleridge and Southey lectured at the Assembly Rooms Coffee House (gone) in Prince St.

Defoe, whose *Tour Through Great Britain* (1724–7) brought him to Bristol, is said to have met Selkirk in Ye Llandoger Trow, the old tavern in King St., and to have based *Robinson Crusoe* (1719) on his adventures. The Almshouses for Merchant Seamen was the home for some years of a Mr Williams, whose manuscript about the experiences of a young sailor marooned on a W Indian island for 27 years was published after his death as *The Journal of Llewellin Penrose* (1815). Byron wrote that Penrose 'kept me up half the night, and made me dream of him the other half. It has all the air of truth, and is most entertaining.'

The Theatre Royal in King St. opened in 1766 with Steele's *The Conscious Lovers*, for which Garrick wrote the Prologue. Sarah Siddons often acted here and Elizabeth Inchbald, novelist and dramatist, made her debut as an actress in 1772 as Cordelia. Combe's *The Flattering Milliner* played here in 1775. Macready, whose father leased the theatre in 1819, often acted here, his last performance being in 1850. It is now the Bristol Old Vic, the interior having been altered. The former Bristol Library in King St. was where Coleridge, Southey, and Landor read, and the registers they signed can be seen at the newer Central Library. Maria Edgeworth was unable to get a ticket, though her father was a reader, as 'No ladies go to the Library'.

Thomas Chatterton (1752–70), 'the Marvellous Boy', was born at the Schoolhouse in Pile St., now Redcliffe Way. He spent many hours in St Mary Redcliffe Church, where his uncle was sexton, reading in the muniment room over the N porch the old manuscripts which inspired his medieval-style poems. He started writing these while still at school and is said to have sold some under the name of a fictitious 15th-c. monk, Thomas Rowley. At 15 he went to Corn St. as a scrivener and, as his indentures allowed him only one hour's absence in the day, it was there that he wrote the Rowley poems. But the recognition he craved never came. His satirical Will written after a dispute with his employer caused the

cancelling of his indentures and at 17 he set out for London with a small subscription from his friends. A memorial was put up in the church in 1967 but his statue in the long gown of a Colston schoolboy is no longer on the green. The Colston Hall now stands on the site of his old school. More attention was paid to the question of the authenticity of Rowley's poems (1777) than to their merit. Johnson and Boswell made a special visit to look into the matter 'upon the spot' six years after Chatterton had died in poverty. Cottle and Southey published the *Collected Works* (1803) to help Chatterton's family.

Two sisters married in St Mary Redcliffe in 1795, Sara Fricker to Coleridge in October, and Edith to Southey in November. After some months in Clevedon the Coleridges rented rooms in Redcliffe Hill, where Sara had lived before her marriage.

Southey was born (1774) in Wine St. and spent his boyhood at no. 9 (gone). A plaque is fixed where the new buildings join Christ Church. The Plume of Feathers, where Coleridge gave lectures, has also gone. The narrow junction here was once the main crossroads and Pepys mentions the old cross there, now at Stourhead, being 'like the one at Cheapside'.

Lloyds TSB on Corn St. is on the site of the Bush Inn, where Burke's election day celebrations took place and where Dickens's Mr Winkle stayed while searching for Arabella Allen.

Richard Savage, befriended by Johnson, who wrote his life, died (1743) in poverty in the prison (gone; ℗ on site) in Newgate, and was buried in the churchyard of St Peter's nearby. His instability thwarted his well-wishers, as Pope complained to him in a letter in 1742.

Joseph Cottle, poet, publisher, and friend of Southey, Coleridge, and Wordsworth, had his bookshop (gone) on the corner of Corn St. and High St., where they all visited him. He gave Southey and Coleridge advances on their poems, which enabled them to marry, and when Southey sailed for Portugal he left his wife with Cottle and his sisters. Coleridge often used Cottle's address for his correspondence and tickets for his and Southey's lectures could be bought at Cottle's shop. Southey never forgot Cottle's kindness and years later recalled how he was indebted to him even for his wedding ring. Wordsworth, whose 'Tintern Abbey' lines were not written down until he and Dorothy reached Bristol, took them at once to Cottle and finished them in his parlour. After the failure of the Pantisocracy scheme (a utopian community was planned), Coleridge planned *The Watchman*, his short-lived periodical, from the Rummer Tavern near the flower market entrance in High St.

The Bishop's Palace near the Cathedral, where Addison stayed with his old schoolfriend Bishop Smallridge in 1718, was burnt down in the 1831 riots; only a 14th-c. doorway near the Chapter House remains.

Hakluyt was made a prebend of the Cathedral in 1586, having already published

two books of his Voyages (1582 and 1587). His *Principall Navigations* followed (1589 and 1598). Sydney Smith occupied the same prebendal stall in 1828. His house (gone) in Lower College Green, he wrote to Lady Holland, was large enough to take her entourage as he had a seven-stall stable and room for four carriages. He could see the masts of the East Indiamen from his window.

In the Cathedral the silver candlesticks in the E Lady Chapel were a thanksgiving gift after the safe return in 1711 of the two ships *Duke* and *Duchess*. In the E cloister is the memorial stone to Sterne's correspondent Eliza Draper (d. 1778). When William Mason's wife died in 1767, their friend Thomas Gray added the last lines to her epitaph in the N aisle. Lady Hesketh, Cowper's cousin, to whom he wrote many of his *Letters* (1803), is buried in the Cathedral. Southey wrote the inscription for the memorial to Bishop Butler in the N transept. His own bust, to which his friend Landor contributed, stands in the N choir aisle near the tablet to Hakluyt.

No. 48 College St., where Coleridge and Southey lodged before their marriages, is now a garage (the plaque once there has gone). De Quincey refers to the unsolved murders of Mrs Ruscombe and her maid on College Green in his essay 'Murder Considered as One of the Fine Arts' in *Blackwood's* (1827).

St Mark's, the Lord Mayor's chapel, at the foot of Park St. has some French and Flemish glass from *Fonthill Abbey, collected by Beckford on his travels. The large window at the E of the S aisle was designed by Benjamin West for the Becket room.

Hannah More, whose first school, which she ran with her sisters, started in Trinity St., moved in 1762 when Park St. was being built, into no. 43, where the new shop on the site has a commemorative inscription over the doorway. She helped Burke, who visited her there, with his election campaign. One pupil was 'Perdita' Robinson, the actress and novelist, who was born at the Old Minster House (gone).

Wordsworth first met Coleridge at 7 Gt George St., now the Georgian House museum. This was the home of John Pinney, a W Indies sugar merchant, who lent the Wordsworths *Racedown Lodge and with whom they often stayed.

F. J. Fargus, author (under the pen-name Hugh Conway) of many songs and the popular novel *Called Back* (1885), was born in Bristol in 1847. Ambrose Bierce lived here during 1872, writing the sardonic sketches published in *The Fiend's Delight* and *Nuggets and Dust* in 1873.

From 1962 to 1965 Angela Carter was at Bristol University studying English (and especially medieval English); bohemian Bristol life features in her novels *Shadow Dance* (1966), *Several Perceptions* (1968), and *Love* (1971), now sometimes known as her 'Bristol Trilogy'.

The bells of the city are evoked in John Betjeman's 'Bristol' (1945). The poet Charles Tomlinson taught at the University of Bristol from 1957 to 1992, becoming Professor of English Poetry in 1982.

CLIFTON, to the W, was considered a health resort in the 18th and 19th cc. Maria Edgeworth lodged in Princes Bldgs in 1791 with her family as her young brother Lovell was consumptive. They walked on the Downs nearby, hunting for fossils. She came again in 1799 and some of her children's stories in *The Parent's Assistant* (1796–1800) and *Moral Tales* (1806) were set in Bristol. Her nephew Thomas Lovell Beddoes was born (1803) at 3 Rodney Pl., where a plaque also commemorates Humphry Davy's stay in the house. Lady Hesketh (d. 1807) wrote some of her last letters to her cousin Cowper (d. 1800) from Clifton Hill, where she spent many months during the last decade of her life. Harriet and Sophia Lee, authors of popular romances, lived in Clifton for many years. Sophia came here after retiring from her school in Bath in 1803. The last stories in their joint *Canterbury Tales* (1805) were written by her. They were buried in the parish church of St Andrew's on Clifton Hill (bombed and later demolished) and commemorated by wall tablets.

York Hotel (gone) in Gloucester Pl., overlooking the Downs and Leigh Woods, was where the exploring party in *Northanger Abbey* (1818) dined on their abortive visit to Blaise Castle. It was closed by 1819. Mrs Piozzi stayed for some months before her death in 1821 at 10 Sion Row near the Avon Gorge. This house was one belonging to Mrs Rudd, mother of the young actor William Conway, whom Mrs Piozzi was befriending during his unhappy love affair. His situation was made more appealing by his belief that he was the son of a lord. Mrs Rudd was having 36 Royal York Cres., a larger house with fine views, prepared for Mrs Piozzi but it was not ready in time. Her will was, however, read there to her daughters, who were with their mother when she died.

The frail Hannah More (d. 1833), imposed on by her servants at Barley Wood, came to spend her last years in Windsor Ter. Macaulay stayed at 16 Caledonia Pl. Ⓟ in 1832, and Frances Trollope, mother of Anthony Trollope and herself author of over 100 books, lived at no. 7 in 1843. Dickens, in 1851, brought a group of friends including Douglas Jerrold, John Forster, Mark Lemon, and Wilkie Collins to the Victoria Rooms, where they acted Lytton's *Not So Bad As We Seem* and *Mr Nightingale's Diary* to such an enthusiastic audience that they repeated the performance. J. Addington Symonds, born (1840) at 7 Berkeley Sq., moved to Clifton Hill House (built 1749) as a boy and it remained his family home until 1880. He spent an increasing time abroad as he was consumptive but he was at 7 Victoria Sq. for some time after giving up his London home in 1868 until he moved back to Clifton Hill House after his father's death in 1871. He left finally in 1880 and wrote (*Letters*, 1907) of the difficulty of clearing up accumulations of family papers. He wrote of his home in his essay 'Clifton and a Lad's Love', published in *In the Key of Blue* (1893). Clifton Hill House is now a university residential hall.

The Manx poet T. E. Brown was a housemaster at the new Clifton College from 1864 to 1893, and it was here that he wrote the tales of Manx men and women, *Betsy Lee* (1873) and *Fo'c's'le Yarns* (1881). The lines in 'Clifton'

I'm here at Clifton grinding at the mill
My feet for thrice nine barren years have trod,
But there are rocks and waves at Scarlett still,
And gorse runs riot in Glen Chass—thank God

show that his native island had strong ties for him, but one of the three places he asks a friend to visit for him after his death is the Avon Gorge. In 'Epistola ad Dakyns' he writes:

There come, and pause upon the edge,
And I will lean on every ledge,
And melt in grays and flash in whites,
And linger in a thousand lights;
And you shall feel an inner sense,
A being kindred and intense;
And you shall feel a strict control,
A something drawing at your soul,
A going out, a life suspended,
A spirit with a spirit blended.
And you shall start as from a dream,
While I, withdrawing down the stream,
Drift vaporous to the ancient sea,
A wraith, a film, a memory . . .

Brown had retired to the Isle of Man but died here on a visit in 1897 and he was buried in the cemetery at Redland Green Chapel (1 m. NE), where the tombstone also commemorates his wife and his young son. Quiller-Couch, Newbolt, who wrote the poem 'Clifton Chapel', and Robert Hichens, who also lived in Bristol, were pupils at Clifton in the 1870s, and Joyce Cary in the early years of the 20th century.

The novelist Barbara Pym lived at The Coppice (now Leigh House), near Clifton Suspension Bridge, from 1941 to 1943. She worked as a postal censor at the Royal West of England Academy (converted for the purpose) during the Second World War.

FISHPONDS, to the NE. Hannah More, whose popular poems and dramas provided the money for her philanthropy, was born in the house Ⓟ near the church, facing the park. Her father was a schoolmaster, and she and her elder sisters opened a successful school in the centre of the town.

HENBURY, to the NW. Blaise Castle, an 18th-c. Gothic ruin in the grounds of Blaise Castle House (built 1795), now a Folk Museum, was the place the young people in Jane Austen's *Northanger Abbey* hoped to visit but lacked time. In 1774 Burke stayed with Richard Champion here during the election campaign. He admired the view from the dining room so much that it was afterwards called Burke's window.

HOTWELLS, to the W, where the curative spring was discovered at the foot of St Vincent's Rocks on the N bank of the Avon, and the Pump and Assembly Rooms rose dramatically from the water. The diarist Evelyn described climbing about on the rocks in 1654 looking for Bristol diamonds, the crystals that Spenser called adamants. Addison wrote to Swift of his visit in 1718, and Pope came in November 1739 and described the 'vast rock of an hundred feet of red, white, green, blue and yellowish marble' in his *Letters* to Martha Blount.

William Combe (1741–1823) was born in Bristol and often visited Hotwells. He wrote a poem to Clifton and *The Philosopher in Bristol* (1775). He was known as Count Combe for his ostentatious living, which resulted in many years spent in a debtors' prison.

Fanny Burney on a visit with her father in 1767 walked down the zigzag path from Clifton Hill to the Well, below where she set some scenes in *Evelina* (1778). Lydia Melford in *Humphry Clinker* (1771) described 'the enchanting variety of moving pictures' to be seen when the ships passed 'close under the windows'. The building was destroyed in the 19th c. to continue the road but the colonnade remains. Here Ann Yearsley, a milkwoman, set up her Circulating Library with the money from her *Poems*, which Hannah More had got published with her friends as subscribers. Ann Yearsley resented being given the proceeds as an annuity; Hannah More regarded this as ingratitude. The feud ended in the failure of the library and Ann Yearsley's insanity. The spring was excavated back into the rock, making a grotto until 1912, when river water seeped through and it was closed. De Quincey was staying in the district in 1807, writing to Cottle to arrange his first meeting with Coleridge. Soon after, he wrote to his sister that he and Hartley Coleridge had gone walking in Leigh Woods, endangering their necks on the tangled paths.

The small Dowry Square Chapel was built to save the invalids the climb up Granby Hill to the parish church in Clifton. Hannah More wrote the epitaph there on Sir John Stonhouse (d. 1795), her 'Shepherd of Salisbury Plain', who was ordained after being cured by the waters. This chapel was demolished in 1878. Dowry Sq. was the home of the Pneumatic Institute founded in 1799 by Dr Beddoes, who married Maria Edgeworth's sister Anna. He brought the young Humphry Davy to be its superintendent, whose use of nitrous oxide so impressed Southey and Coleridge. A young doctor helping Beddoes with the outpatients was Peter Mark Roget, later author of the *Thesaurus* (1852). Sheridan's *Letters* (1966) recount his tragic visits in 1787 and 1792 when his wife and her sister died from consumption. Bowles, staying here in 1789, wrote an 'Elegy' on his dead friends.

In 1845 the ailing R. H. Barham came to stay at 9 Dowry Sq. but died a month later.

KINGSDOWN, to the N, where Coleridge and his wife took lodgings in Oxford St., when they found *Clevedon too isolated. Hartley, their first child, was born here (1796), while Coleridge was visiting his friend Charles Lloyd in Birmingham.

STOKE BISHOP, to the NW. Katharine Bradley and her niece Edith Cooper moved here in 1878, writing *Bellerophon* (1881) as Arran and Isla Leigh. Their joint pseudonym 'Michael Field' came into being in 1885 with *Callirrhoë*.

The Portuguese novelist Eça de Queiroz lived at 38 Stoke Hill from 1878 to 1888 after his marriage when consul in Bristol. While he was here, *O Primo Basilio* (Cousin Basilio), *Os Maias* (The Maias), *A Reliquia* (The Relic), and *Letters from England* were published. It was known that he lived away from the consulate in Queen Sq. but the exact house then called Vashni was only located after a long search for the original of a contemporary sketch. A commemorative plaque was unveiled by the Portuguese Ambassador in 1963 and the sketch and a page in manuscript were presented to the owner of the house by the novelist's son.

WESTBURY ON TRYM, to the NW. In 1798 Southey settled with his wife in a one-time alehouse, which they called Martin Hall because of the birds nesting under the eaves. Supported by advances from his publisher, Cottle, he devoted himself to writing; he completed the first draft of *Madoc* (1805), prepared the 2nd edition of *Letters from Spain and Portugal* (1797), and wrote 'The Holly Tree', 'Ebb Tide', and the sonnet 'Winter'. He wrote later, 'I have never before or since produced so much poetry in the same space of time.' The house (gone) had large rooms, a productive garden, and splendid views. During this time he was also preparing the *Annual Anthology* (1799–1800) by getting poems from Coleridge, Lamb, 'Perdita' Robinson, Amelia Opie, and Cottle. He thought the year here one of the happiest of his life. Iris Murdoch was awarded a scholarship to Badminton School in Westbury on Trym, which she attended as a boarder from 1932.

BRIXHAM *Devon*

Fishing port that became a pioneer of deep-sea trawling, S of Tor Bay, on the A3022. Henry Francis Lyte came here in 1824 as curate-in-charge of All Saints' Church and was instituted as first incumbent in 1826. The church, built 1814–16 as a chapel of ease to accommodate the growing population of Lower Brixham, or 'Brixham Quay', was enlarged in 1825–7 and 1872 and finally rebuilt (1884–1907) in memory of Lyte. When he arrived with his wife and family they lived in Burton St., at a house now called Whitegates, until 1833, when they moved to Berry Head House (later a hotel). It was at Berry Head, a short time before his death from tuberculosis, that he wrote 'Abide with Me' after watching the sun set over Tor Bay in the late summer of 1847 (he died in Nice on 20 Nov.). The carillon of All Saints' plays his three best-known hymns daily: 'When at Thy footstool, Lord, I bend', 'Praise, my soul, the King of Heaven', and 'Abide with Me', at 8 a.m., noon, and 8 p.m. respectively.

Francis Brett Young had his first medical practice here (1907–14), when he lived at Cleveland House. His first novel, *Deep Sea* (1914), makes Brixham its background. It was followed by *The Dark Tower* (1914).

Flora Thompson came here in 1940, when her husband retired from the post office in Dartmouth, and lived in Higher Brixham until her death in 1947 at a house called Lauriston, in New Rd. It was here that she wrote *Candleford Green* (1943) and *Still Glides the Stream* (1948), with difficulty, as her heart had become affected by a serious illness. She was not much moved by her success as a writer as she said it had come too late.

BROAD CHALKE *Wiltshire*

Village between the A30 and the A354, 8 m. SW of Salisbury. John Aubrey lived here in the Old Rectory, part of a former nunnery, which has a 15th-c. entrance arch. He was churchwarden and described the church as having 'one of the tunablest ring of bells in Wiltshire'. Maurice Hewlett lived in the Old Rectory, where he was visited by Ezra Pound at Christmas in 1911. His verse epic *The Song of the Plow* (1916) and *Wiltshire Essays* (1921) were written here. He died in 1923 and is commemorated by a tablet in the church.

BROAD CLYST *Devon*

Village on the B3181, 6 m. NE of Exeter. Eden Phillpotts, prolific writer of novels and plays, mainly of the West Country, spent his last years at his home, Kerswell, dividing his time between writing and gardening.

BROADHEMBURY *Devon*

Small village 5 m. NW of Honiton, off the A373. A tablet on the S wall of the church chancel records that Augustus Montague Toplady, author of the hymn 'Rock of Ages', was vicar here 1768–78.

BROMHAM *Wiltshire*

Village off the A342, 5 m. NW of Devizes. Thomas Moore lived at Sloperton Cottage, now on the B3102 S of the junction with the A342, from 1818 to 1852. It was then thatched and smaller with a pretty garden and a gravelled walk, and was within walking distance of Bowood. He was visited here by Samuel Rogers and Washington Irving, who wrote later to say he was living near Sleepy Hollow, which would amuse Moore's wife, who used to laugh at his habit of falling asleep after dinner. William Lisle Bowles came from Bremhill to baptize the children, Sydney Smith and Captain Marryat called, and William Napier walked from Battle House in the village to read them chapters of his *History of the Peninsular War*. Moore himself collected his popular songs and ballads and wrote *Captain Rock* (1824) and lives of Sheridan (1825) and Byron (1830). He spent musical evenings and accompanied his wife to archery picnics. He died here in 1852, having outlived all his children, and a large Celtic cross marks his grave in the churchyard. The W window of the church commemorates him and the E window by William Morris and Burne-Jones is dedicated to Elizabeth Morris. Moore's grave is the subject of John Betjeman's 'Ireland's Own, or, The Burial of Thomas Moore'.

BRYANSTON *Dorset*

N Dorset village on the river Stour, known for the independent school (Bryanston School), whose alumni include the poet Kevin Crossley-Holland.

BUCKLAND *Gloucestershire*

Village off the A44, 2 m. SW of Broadway. Mrs Delany describes in her *Autobiography* (1861–2) the dramatic start to her journey in 1715 to the manor, which she calls The Farm. She was 15 and her uncle Lord Lansdowne was in the Tower for his Jacobite sympathies. Government officers arrived early in the morning before the family was dressed to prevent their leaving the capital. Her mother fainted, her father was distracted, the children cried, and only the arrival of her indomitable aunt set the cavalcade rumbling on its five-day journey here. The medieval Buckland Rectory was visited by John Wesley.

BURRINGTON COMBE *Somerset*

Limestone gorge on the B3134, where Augustus Toplady (1740–78), sheltering in a cave from the storm, was inspired to write 'Rock of Ages, cleft for me' (1775).

CALLINGTON *Cornwall*

Quiet market town on the A390 and the A388, 8 m. NE of Liskeard. It has been traditionally claimed as one of the sites of King Arthur's palace.

CALNE *Wiltshire*

Market town on the A4. Coleridge lodged (1814–16) with the Morgan family, friends of Charles and Mary Lamb, who also stayed here for a month in 1816. Coleridge, who was taking laudanum, was working intermittently on *Biographia Literaria*. 'Calne is a sepulchre in a desert,' he wrote to a friend in Devizes asking for a good brewer. When John Morgan became insolvent, Lamb and Southey contributed an allowance.

CAME *Dorset*

Hamlet 2 m. SE of Dorchester, on the A352. The thatched rectory (now Old Came Rectory), set back from the road in a pleasant garden, was the home of William Barnes when he was rector of the combined parish of Whitcombe and Winterborne Came. The little church of Whitcombe can be seen from the main road; that of Winterborne Came is hidden among trees and not signposted, but can be reached by the road to Came House, a turning W between Whitcombe and the old rectory, and it is here that Barnes is buried, his grave marked by a high cross of Celtic design.

CAMELFORD *Cornwall*

Busy little town on the A39, between the NW edge of Bodmin Moor and the sea. According to tradition it was the site of King Arthur's

William Barnes in the garden of Came Rectory, 1885

Camelot, and Slaughter Bridge, 1 m. N, is said to be the scene of his last battle.

CHAGFORD *Devon*

Little market town on the edge of Dartmoor, 4 m. NW of Moretonhampstead, reached by the B3206 and several minor roads W of the A382 or N of the B3212. Sidney Godolphin was killed (1643) during the Civil War in a skirmish here, traditionally at the Three Crowns Inn, an early 16th-c. building facing the churchyard.

Evelyn Waugh wrote *Brideshead Revisited* (1945) while staying at Chagford in the spring and summer of 1944.

CHALDON HERRING (or EAST CHALDON) *Dorset*

Little village on a minor road in a fold of the downs, S of the A352 from a turning *c.* 9 m. SE of Dorchester and 1 m. N of the sea. Theodore Francis Powys (1875–1953), after farming for a time in Suffolk, settled here in 1905 for much of his life, at a red-brick Victorian house called Beth Car. His writing, almost all published between 1923 and 1935, consists of novels and short stories with allegorical themes of love and death, God, and evil, mostly set in a Dorset rural background. Chaldon Herring is portrayed as 'Folly Down' in *Mr Weston's Good Wine* (1927) and Chaldon Hill as 'Madder Hill'. His other titles include *Black Bryony* (1923), *Mr Tasker's Gods* (1925), and *Unclay* (1931) (novels), and 'The Left Leg' (1923), 'The House with the Echo' (1928), and 'Penitent' (1931) (short stories). He moved to *Mappowder in 1940. His brother Llewelyn (1884–1939), after living abroad for health reasons, came to Chaldon Herring with his wife in 1925 and lived at Chydyok Farm, sharing the property with two of his sisters. While here he published *The Pathetic Fallacy* (a study of Christianity, 1930), *Dorset Essays* (1935), and the novels *Apples Be Ripe* (1930) and *Love and Death*

(an imaginary autobiography, 1939). Finally, illness made it necessary for him to move to Switzerland, where he died in December 1939. After the war his ashes were brought to Dorset as he had wished, and scattered on the cliff top near Chaldon, where a Portland stone memorial, carved by Elizabeth Muntz, now stands.

In 1922 the novelists Sylvia Townsend Warner and David Garnett visited Chaldon Herring and were instrumental in getting Theodore Powys's novels and short stories published. Garnett wrote *The Sailor's Return* (1925) and Townsend Warner *Mr Fortune's Maggot* (1927) while living here. Sylvia Townsend Warner also met the poet Valentine Ackland at Chaldon, who was to be her partner until Ackland's death in 1959. They are both buried under one stone in the churchyard.

CHARLES *Devon*

Village 6 m. NW of S Molton, off the A399. In the small church a tablet commemorates R. D. Blackmore's holidays in the village where his grandfather was curate-in-charge.

CHARLTON *Wiltshire*

Village on the B4040, 2 m. NE of Malmesbury. Dryden stayed at the Jacobean Charlton Park (burnt down 1962), seat of his wife's father, during 1665–6 to escape the plague. He wrote *Annus Mirabilis* and *Essay of Dramatic Poesy* while here with friends including his brother-in-law Robert Howard, the dramatist, and Charles Sedley.

CHARLTON ST PETER *Wiltshire*

Small village on the A342 near the junction with the A345. Stephen Duck, a self-educated farm labourer, was born (1705) here, and became known as the thresher-poet from his long poem on the labourer's work which includes the lines:

From the strong planks our crab-tree staves rebound,
And echoing barns return the rattling sound. . . .

In briny streams our sweat descends apace,
Drops from our locks, or trickles down our face.
No intermission in our work we know;
The noisy threshal must for ever go.

He married here and six years later, in 1730, his wife was buried in the churchyard. In the same year Joseph Spence recommended him to Pope. The village remembers him at the June Duck feast at the Charlton Cat (Ducks are married farm workers who have lived in the village for at least a year). Costs are met from the rent of Duck's Acre, a field given to the threshers by the first Lord Palmerston, to whom a toast is also drunk at the feast. The Chief Duck's tall silk hat, adorned with feathers and a picture of a thresher, has traditionally been kept on view in the pub.

CHEDDAR *Somerset*

Small town on the A371. In 1788 Hannah More and her sisters, determined to open a school for the illiterate of the wild Mendip Hills, stayed at the George Hotel (gone). They found 'an old vicarage house, empty for years', and in spite of opposition from farmers who thought education would unsettle their labourers, opened the school (now Hannah More Cottage, Lower North St., an Old People's Club), writing their own instructional tracts to resemble the popular penny tales sold by pedlars. In 1794 Coleridge and Southey, walking to Huntspill to visit George Burnett and Tom Poole, were locked in the garret of the inn as though they were footpads, but Southey said, 'the cliffs amply repaid us'.

CHELTENHAM *Gloucestershire*

Regency spa town on the A40 and the A46, 9 m. NE of Gloucester, made popular as a spa after George III's visit in 1788. Fanny Burney, whose official post in the royal household made her part of the entourage, wrote a lively account in her *Diary* of their five weeks at Fauconberg House (rebuilt).

Adam Lindsay Gordon, who became known as the 'National Poet of Australia', came here from the Azores with his parents *c.* 1840 and lived at 3 (renumbered 4) Pittville Villas, Prestbury Rd, for four years, and later (1847–53) at 25 (renumbered 28; Ⓟ) Priory St. He was one of the first boys to enter Cheltenham College, which opened in July 1841, but left after a year and from 1843 to 1847 attended a private school at Dumbleton, 12 m. NE of Cheltenham. In 1853 he emigrated to Australia to join the South Australian mounted police. His sense of adventure and his love of horses are expressed in his poetry, but he took his own life in 1870, the year that his *Bush Ballads and Galloping Rhymes* was published. His poem 'Of Myself' was published in the *Cheltenham Examiner* (14 Oct. 1885).

Tennyson stayed for a short time in 1843, while taking a cure for his nervous illness, at 6 Belle Vue Place and 10 St James's Sq., part of the terraces, crescents, and squares, waspishly called by Cobbett 'white tenements with green balconies', which give the town its Regency flavour. At this time Tennyson was writing the elegies later called *In Memoriam* (1850).

Sydney Dobell leased (1848–53) Coxhorne House at Charlton Kings (2 m. SE), a square Georgian house in a large garden. He finished the dramatic poem *The Roman* (1850), published under the name 'Sydney Yendys', and began *Balder* (1854), the tragedy of a poet who kills his wife when she becomes mad after the death of their son.

A. C. Bradley, the Shakespearian scholar, was educated at Cheltenham College in Bath Rd in the 1860s.

James Elroy Flecker lived from 1886, when he was 2, at Dean Close School, where his father was the first headmaster. He spent his vacations from Uppingham and Oxford here and his room, at first his nursery and then his study, looked S across the roses and elms in the garden to the Cotswolds in the distance. In 'November Eves' he remembers the damp evenings that

> Used to cloak Leckhampton Hill . . .
>
> And send queer winds like Harlequins
> That seized our elms for violins
> That struck a note so sharp and low
> Even a child could feel the woe . . .

Flecker, who died (1915) in Davos, is buried in the cemetery here near two 'gossip pines'. A granite cross marks the grave on which an Alexandrian laurel and an *Olearia haastii* were planted to represent the trees of his poem 'Oak and Olive' in *The Old Ships* (1915). His parents erected a plaque over the door of the school chapel, which has since been moved to the new War Memorial Chapel.

Margaret Kennedy, who made her name with her novel *The Constant Nymph* (1924), was educated at Cheltenham Ladies' College just before the First World War. Phyllis Bentley, author of novels with Yorkshire settings, was also at Cheltenham Ladies' College (1910–14) and went to London to take an external BA degree during her last term.

C. Day-Lewis, who was English master at Cheltenham College from 1930 to 1935, lived (1932–8) at Box Cottage, in Charlton Kings, which joins Cheltenham to the SE. He published the revolutionary poem *The Magnetic Mountain* in 1933. In 1935 he wrote a detective story, *A Question of Proof*, under the pseudonym 'Nicholas Blake', to pay for the repair of the roof. The school in the story is based partly on Cheltenham Junior School. He gave up teaching the same year. *Collected Poems 1929–36* was published in 1938.

Since 1949 Cheltenham has hosted the Cheltenham Festival of Literature, the oldest event of its kind in the country, bringing hundreds of writers for adults and children together in mid-October, to take part in events held over a week at venues around the town.

In Howard Jacobson's *No More Mr Nice Guy* (1998), TV critic Frank Ritz takes himself off on a nostalgic road trip, and ends up spending much of it in Cheltenham, where he takes a room at the Queens, tries to resist the temptation to phone Kurt and Liz, picks up a comedian, and reminisces fondly about his experiences with prostitutes. Then on to *Gloucester.

CHESIL BEACH *Dorset*

18-m. beach on the Jurassic coast of S Dorset. Ian McEwan's novel *On Chesil Beach* (2007) describes the disastrous honeymoon of Edward and Florence at a hotel here on the Dorset coast; a crucial parting scene takes place on the beach itself. The beach distinguishes itself by the gradation of the pebbles by size, coarser at one end and finer at the other; in A. S. Byatt's novel *The Virgin in the Garden* (1978) Alexander has collected a handful of Chesil Beach stones as a souvenir of his Dorset home.

CHICKSGROVE *Wiltshire*

Hamlet 11 m. W of Salisbury off the A30. Sir John Davies (1569–1626), barrister and poet, was born at the manor house (rebuilt).

CHILTON FOLIAT *Wiltshire*

Village on the banks of the Kennet, 1 m. from Hungerford. Auberon Waugh lived at the Old Rectory.

CHIPPING CAMPDEN *Gloucestershire*

Small Cotswolds town, home since 1610 to the Cotswolds 'Olympicks', and, more recently, to the novelist Susan Hill.

Graham Greene lived at Little Orchard on Mud Lane on the edge of the village from 1931 to 1933. He drew an unflattering comparison in *A Sort of Life* (1971) between the vivid observations of local life made in his diary and the lifeless quality of his largely unpublished early fiction.

T. S. Eliot visited his friend Emily Hale in Chipping Campden, herself a guest of the Perkins family, several times a year between 1934 and 1938 (except for 1936). He felt at home here and would go on long rambles with Emily, one of which is described in his poem 'The Country Walk'. The poem describes his nervousness of cows, which may have arisen in part from his having been chased by a bull into some blackberry bushes. In 1934 they also walked to Burnt Norton, Viscount Sandon's large 18th-c. manor house built on top of another that had burnt down in the 17th c., situated 1 m. E of Aston Subedge. The garden, then derelict, provides an abstract setting for 'Burnt Norton', the first of the *Four Quartets*:

> To be conscious is not to be in time
> But only in time can the moment in the rose-
>   garden,
> The moment in the arbour where the rain beat,
> The moment in the draughty church at smokefall
> Be remembered.

CHRISTCHURCH *Dorset*

Town on the A35, at the head of Christchurch Harbour, between the Avon and the Stour.

John Marston, playwright and poet, who renounced the theatre *c.* 1607 and took holy orders, was rector here 1616–31: his name can be seen on the list of incumbents in the magnificent priory church. Under the tower of the church there is an elaborate sculptured monument to Shelley, erected by his son Sir Percy Florence Shelley, who lived at Boscombe, nearby.

A very different literary figure is remembered in connection with the Catholic church in Purewell Rd. F. W. Rolfe ('Baron Corvo'), author of *Hadrian the Seventh* (1904), stayed in Christchurch in 1889 and 1891 and, according to A. J. A. Symons in *The Quest for Corvo* (1934), executed a number of frescoes in the Roman Catholic church of St Michael's, and as recently as 1960 a letter in *Country Life* states 'Corvo's fresco is still at St Michael's.' But there are two discrepancies to confuse the story: the church is named after the Immaculate Conception and St Joseph, and the painting at the E end is a mural, on canvas, not a fresco. The painting, *The Assumption*, was restored in 1965, but there is considerable doubt as to whether the original was the work of the strange, enigmatic man who was author, schoolmaster, artist, and failed priest.

CHRISTCHURCH *Gloucestershire*

Small village 2 m. E of the Welsh border at Monmouth. The playwright Dennis Potter, born nearby at *Berry Hill (just to the S of Christchurch), was educated here at Christchurch Junior School. In January 1959 he would marry Margaret Morgan at Christchurch parish church.

CHUDLEIGH *Devon*

Village on the A38, *c.* halfway between Exeter and Ashburton. Ugbrooke Park, formerly the seat of Lord Clifford, contains a grove of beech trees known as 'Dryden's Walk'. There is a tradition that Dryden, who was a close friend of the first Lord Clifford, completed his translation of Virgil's *Aeneid* while staying here, or, alternatively, that he may have written part of *The Hind and the Panther* here in the winter or spring of 1686–7.

CIRENCESTER *Gloucestershire*

Roman Corinium and market town on the Fosse Way, A419, and Ermine Way, A417. In 1718 Gay and Pope spent the summer at Oakley House in the absence of Lord Bathurst, the owner. His old house had been demolished and the new Cirencester Park not yet built. Pope wrote that Oakley Wood was inspiring Gay 'like the cave of Montesinos'. His letter to Martha Blount said, 'we draw plans for houses and gardens, open avenues, cut glades, plant firs, contrive water-works, all very fine and beautiful in our imagination'. He was there again in 1719 and in 1726 visited with Swift. They lodged with a tenant farmer and walked 2 m. to dinner, as Swift reminded Bathurst in a letter in 1735. Mrs Delany, writing to Swift, recalled seeing the cottage rebuilt after it had 'burst with pride . . . after entertaining so illustrious a person'. Some of Pope's plans were used when the House in the Wood or Alfred's Hall was renovated and Gothicized. Mrs Delany later wrote, 'it is now a venerable castle and has been taken by an Antiquarian for one of King Arthur's'. She was referring to a translation (in reality a fabrication) by Charles Bertram in 1757 of an 11th-c. monk's history of Roman antiquities.

The 18th-c. theatre in Gloucester St., now Barton Hall, was dismantled in the 1850s. It stood behind the old Volunteer Inn, now no. 27; Mrs Siddons, Kean, and Kemble acted there, and Cobbett lectured there.

CLAVERTON *Somerset*

Village 2 m. E of Bath on the A36. Richard Graves, rector here from 1749 to his death in 1804, was the author of *The Spiritual Quixote* (1772), a gentle satire on the Methodists, in which Whitefield and Shenstone, with whom he was at Oxford, are depicted. He also wrote *Columella, or the Distressed Anchoret* (1776), in which Shenstone again appears, *Eugenius, or Anecdotes of the Golden Vale* (1785), and *Plexippus, or, the Aspiring Plebian* (1790).

CLEVEDON *Somerset*

Coastal town 12 m. W of Bristol on the B3130. Coleridge and his wife, Sara, set up house here after their marriage in 1795, and a two-storey stone cottage ℗ in Old Church Rd, near the junction with Coleridge Vale Rd North, is claimed as his. He was soon writing to his publisher for further help in equipping it and Cottle drove from Bristol with a cartload of necessities. Many years later he recalled that the cottage was only one storey high. The town was then secluded and peaceful and Coleridge liked the walk along Dial Hill, but he and Sara returned to Bristol before the birth of their first child. Thackeray, who often stayed at the 14th-c. Clevedon Court (NT), and wrote part of *Vanity Fair* (1847) there, portrayed it as 'Castlewood' in *Henry Esmond* (1852), but set it in Hampshire.

A commemorative tablet to Arthur Hallam, Tennyson's friend, whose early death inspired the long poem 'In Memoriam', is in the parish church of St Andrew's. Tennyson and his wife, who had suggested the title of the poem, visited the church on their honeymoon (1850). The seashore here is traditionally the setting for 'Break, break, break, | On thy cold grey stones, O Sea!' The vicarage in Coleridge Rd is thought to be the one rented by Rupert Brooke's parents in 1909 where he invited his friends from Cambridge for the summer vacation.

CLOUDS HILL *Dorset*

T. E. Lawrence's cottage (NT), on an unclassified road N of Bovington Camp, reached either from the B3390, from Bere Regis on the A35, or from East Burton on the A352. Lawrence rented the cottage first in 1923 when he was stationed at the camp as Private Shaw, and later bought it, to be a retreat where he could come to read or write or play the gramophone, and it was here that he worked on

T. E. Lawrence's music room, with his desk and gramophone, at Clouds Hill, Dorset. It was his retreat when he was stationed at Bovington Camp and finally his permanent home

Seven Pillars of Wisdom (1926). He finally retired to live here in 1935.

CLOVELLY *Devon*

Picturesque village on the NW coast, at the end of the B3237. Charles Kingsley lived here as a boy when his father was rector (1830–6) and is commemorated by a tablet in the church. He describes the village in *Westward Ho!* (1855). Dickens came here in 1861 with Wilkie Collins and wrote about it in 'A Message from the Sea', a story written in collaboration with Collins, first published in *Household Words* (later in *Christmas Stories*). Clovelly appears as 'Steepway'.

COATE *Wiltshire*

Hamlet off the A419, 3 m. SE of Swindon. Richard Jefferies, a farmer's son, was born (1848) and spent his early life in the house ℗ above the inn, which he describes in *The Old House at Coate* (1948). Cuttings from the russet apple and mulberry trees planted there by his father were taken in 1973 by the Richard Jefferies Society to perpetuate those trees he mentioned. Two of the naturalist's favourite walks were to Barbury Camp (5 m. S) on the Marlborough Downs and to Burderop Park (2 m. S), the subject of *Round About a Great Estate* (1880) and the location of many scenes in *Bevis* (1882), a novel about his boyhood. Coate Reservoir, where he skated and idled hours away, also features in *Bevis*. The house is now Richard Jefferies' House and Museum, containing information about the writer, his work, and the places that influenced him. It is occasionally open to the public.

COLEFORD *Gloucestershire*

Market town in the Forest of Dean, 4 m. E of the Welsh border, where the playwright Dennis Potter attended Bell's Grammar School.

COMBE (pr. Cōom) FLOREY *Somerset*

Village off the A358, 8 m. NW of Taunton. Sydney Smith was rector here (1829–45) and wrote that his Georgian house (now the Old Rectory) was 'like the parsonages described in novels'. 'My neighbours look very much like other people's neighbours; their remarks are generally of a meteorological nature.' The church has a memorial E window to him. The manor house, rebuilt on the site of an Elizabethan house in the park, was the home (1956–66) of Evelyn Waugh, who wrote here *Unconditional Surrender* (1961), the last volume of his war trilogy *Sword of Honour* (1965). Waugh is buried in the churchyard. His son Auberon Waugh spent part of his childhood here and returned to live in the house after he bought it from his widowed mother in 1971. Paul Durcan regrets his ignorance of the birds around the manor house in his poem 'Combe Florey'.

COMBE (pr. Cōom) MARTIN *Devon*

Village on the A399, stretching 1 m. down the Umber valley to the sea. Marie Corelli is reputed to have written *The Mighty Atom* (1896) when she was staying at the Pack of Cards inn. The characters in the story are believed to have been based on local people. A panelled room on the first floor is named after

Miss Corelli and the old built-in desk at which she wrote is still there.

CORSTON *Somerset*

Village on the A39, near the junction with the A4, 5 m. W of Bath. Southey's first school kept by a Mr Flower was at the Manor Farm. 'The Retrospect', written at Oxford after his return in 1793 to find the school had closed, contains the lines:

Silent and sad the scene: I heard no more
Mirth's honest cry, and childhood's cheerful roar
No longer echo'd round the shout of glee . . .

COWSLIP GREEN *Somerset*

Hamlet at the Butcombe turn off the A38 near the Paradise Motel. Hannah More lived here (1785–1802) (house now called Brook Lodge) after her successful dramas provided the money for her Sunday schools for the poor. She designed the house herself, sending the 'plan and drawing' to her friends. Horace Walpole wrote that he thought Cowslip Green sounded a sort of cousin to Strawberry Hill. Anna Seward visited in 1791. When Southey visited with his publisher and friend Cottle, the Misses More wrote that 'he was brimful of literature, and one of the most elegant and intellectual young men they had seen'.

CREDITON *Devon*

Town 8 m. NW of Exeter, on the river Creedy. The novelist Jean Rhys moved to nearby Cheriton Fitzpaine in 1960, where her husband died six years later. In spite of ongoing tensions with her neighbours (some of whom accused her of witchcraft) she remained here for the rest of her life, dying in the County Hospital in Exeter in 1979.

CULMSTOCK *Devon*

Village on the B3391, off the A38, situated in the Culm Valley below the Black Down Hills. R. D. Blackmore, who had been brought up by his aunt after his mother's death, came to live here when his father married again and accepted the curacy in 1831. He grew to love the surrounding country and referred to Devon as 'my (almost) native land'.

DARTINGTON *Devon*

Village in the Dart valley, 2 m. NW of Totnes, on the A384. J. A. Froude, the historian, was born (1818) at his father's rectory, now the Old Postern, at the entrance to Dartington Hall School, of which it has become a part. The Ways with Words literature festival has been held here annually since 1991.

DARTMOOR *Devon*

High tract of open country over 300 sq. m. in area, of which the main part, anciently the royal Forest of Dartmoor, is a National Park. The scenery is wild and hilly, with numerous streams among the moors, and occasionally wooded. In 1826 a poem entitled 'Dartmoor' by N. T. Carrington, a schoolmaster and poet of Plymouth, narrowly missed a prize (offered by

the Royal Society of Literature and won by Mrs Hemans) because it was late, but it pleased George IV, who awarded the author 50 guineas. R. D. Blackmore gives an excellent description of the country in one of his lesser-known novels, *Christowell: A Dartmoor Tale* (1881), and Conan Doyle makes the most of its wildness and mystery in his detective thriller *The Hound of the Baskervilles* (1902). Eden Phillpotts, the most prolific and versatile of Devon writers, wrote 18 Dartmoor novels, a cycle planned to cover the whole area, begun with *Children of the Mist* (1898) and completed with *Children of Men* (1923). Of these, the tragic tale *The Secret Woman* (1905) is probably the best known.

DARTMOUTH *Devon*

Ancient seaport on the W bank of the beautiful Dart estuary, reached by the A379 from Torquay and the ferry from Kingswear or by the B3205 from the Plymouth road. In the chancel of St Saviour's Church is the brass of John Hawley (d. 1408), the chief shipowner in Dartmouth in his day and possibly the model for Chaucer's Shipman in *The Canterbury Tales* (c. 1387–1400) ('For aught I woot, he was of Dertemouthe'). Certainly Chaucer was here on business during Hawley's lifetime, and the description of the Shipman in the Prologue could fit the type of man he was.

Defoe, in his *Tour* (1724–7), describes the sight of many small fish skipping and playing on the surface of the water and was told it was a school of pilchards. His servant bought 17 on the quay for ½*d.* and he, a friend, and the servant had them for dinner, dressed by the cook for ¼*d.* Defoe recorded, 'We really din'd for three farthings, and very well too.'

Flora Thompson lived here from 1928 to 1940 at The Outlook, 126 Above Town, a semi-detached house on the high side of a narrow street running S from just above the church. She began *Lark Rise* (1939) in 1937 and followed it by *Over to Candleford* (1941). She is buried in Long Cross cemetery.

DAUNTSEY *Wiltshire*

Village off the B4069, 8 m. NE of Chippenham. In 1628 George Herbert, who suffered from consumption, went to recuperate at Dauntsey Park, the home of Lord Danby, elder brother of Herbert's mother's second husband. Here he met Jane Danvers, a young relative of his host, and according to Izaak Walton he married her after a three-days' acquaintance.

DAWLISH *Devon*

Seaside resort on the A379. Jane Austen spent a holiday here in 1802. In *Sense and Sensibility* (1811), Robert Ferrars, on meeting Elinor Dashwood, presumes that as she lives in a cottage in Devonshire it must be near Dawlish. When she sets him right (the Dashwoods' cottage was 4 m. N of Exeter), 'it seemed rather surprising to him that anybody could live in Devonshire, without living near Dawlish'. In Dickens's *Nicholas Nickleby* (1838–9), Nicholas is born on a small farm near Dawlish, the

inherited property of his unworldly father, which is sold up at his death, and bought again by Nicholas at the very end of the story, as his first act when he becomes rich and prosperous.

In Keats's 'Poems Written at Teignmouth' is 'Dawlish Fair':

Over the hill and over the dale,
    And over the Bourne to Dawlish,
Where ginger-bread wives have a scanty sale,
    And ginger-bread nuts are smallish.

DEAN PRIOR *Devon*

Small village on the A38, a few miles S of Ashburton. Robert Herrick, a Londoner who regarded himself as an exile in Devon, was vicar here from 1629 to 1647 and from 1662 to the end of his life (having been ejected by Parliament and reinstated after the Restoration). Most of his poetry—over 1,000 poems of great diversity and charm—was written during the first period and published under the title *Hesperides* (1648), a tribute to the West Country in spite of his avowed dislike of Devon, and although he missed the literary circles of London he wrote contentedly of simple things, as in *Noble Numbers*, a collection of devotional verse published with *Hesperides*:

Lord, Thou hast given me a cell
    Wherein to dwell;
A little house, whose humble roof
    Is weather-proof;
Under the spars of which I lie
    Both soft and dry.

He wrote many love lyrics, but never married, being cared for by his servant Prudence Baldwin ('faithful Prew'), who, like himself, was buried in the churchyard. He is commemorated by a tablet, a stained-glass window, and an inscribed window. Parts of the old vicarage are incorporated in the back of the present building.

Herrick figures in Rose Macaulay's novel *They Were Defeated* (1932), the first part of which is set in Dean Prior.

Robert Herrick, vicar of Dean Prior, Devon. Frontispiece to his *Hesperides*

DEVIZES *Wiltshire*

Market town on the A361 and the A342. Fanny Burney and her friend Mrs Thrale stayed at the Bear Hotel on their way to Bath in 1780. They were interested in Mrs Lawrence, the innkeeper's wife, who seemed 'something above her station'. They heard singing and the piano, and met her two accomplished daughters and 'the wonder of the family' Thomas, her 10-year-old son, whose skill in drawing was so impressive. They planned to return but their fear of mobs increased by tales of riots in London led them to avoid the towns.

DINTON *Wiltshire*

Village on the B3089, 9 m. W of Salisbury. It is thought that the Old Rectory, near the church, was built (1725) on the site of the house where Edward Hyde, later Lord Clarendon, was born (1609). His family is said to have lived in other houses in the area, including the 14th-c. Wardour Castle, blown up after the siege of 1643. A tradition also arose that Edward Hyde lived for a time in the Elizabethan house which is now called Little Clarendon (NT). This is next to the birthplace of Henry Lawes (1596–1662), the musician who suggested to Milton the idea of the masque *Comus* (1637) and who wrote the music for it.

DITTISHAM *Devon*

Village 2 m. N of Dartmouth, by the SW bank of the river Dart. It is the setting for the 'cottage in the lane' described in the poem by Brian Patten (unsurprisingly called 'A Cottage in the Lane, Dittisham'). It is a devastating picture of a woman in the house, just a 'ghost-in-waiting', about to leave the place to its new tenants, and to the animals who have always been there:

> The squirrels nesting in the roof,
> The mice in the cellar, and in the eaves
> The birds that came each spring
> And nested there and sang . . .
> For all they knew the house was theirs,
> So quietly had she lived in one small room . . .

Liverpool-born Patten is himself now a part-time Devonian.

DORCHESTER *Dorset*

County town overlooking the valley of the Frome. William Barnes, the Dorset poet, is remembered by a statue outside St Peter's Church in High West St. with a dialect rhyme below it:

> Zoo now I hope his kindly face
> Is gone to vind a better place
> But still wi'vo'k a left behind
> He'll always be a-kept in mind.

Barnes spent much time in Dorchester. He ran a little school in Durngate St., which later moved to South St. When he was rector of *Came during the last 24 years of his life he frequently walked to and from the town and was greatly respected as a local historian. He was one of the founders of the County Museum, run by the Dorset Natural History and Archaeological Society, which now has a

Statue of Thomas Hardy by Eric Kennington, at Dorchester. It was unveiled by Sir James Barrie, who is standing at the base

Thomas Hardy Memorial Room, with a reconstruction of Hardy's study and a collection of material concerning his life and work. A bronze statue of Hardy seated, hat on knee, looks westward from a grassy bank in Colliton Walk. He was educated at the village school, and after an apprenticeship as an architect and a period in London he lived in various places in the county, finally settling in 1885 at Max Gate, a house of his own design, about a mile out of Dorchester on the Wareham Road. Hardy, one of Siegfried Sassoon's heroes, was visited by the latter at Max Gate, and described thus:

> Old Mr Hardy, upright in his chair
> Courteous to visiting acquaintance chatted
> With unaloof alertness while he patted
> The sheepdog whose society he preferred.
> He wore an air of never having heard
> That there was much that needed putting right.
> Hardy, the Wessex Wizard, wasn't there.
> Good care was taken to keep him out of sight.

Opposite this house a field path leads to Old Came Rectory, the home of William Barnes when he was rector of Whitcombe and Winterborne Came. Dorchester figures as 'Casterbridge' in Hardy's *The Mayor of Casterbridge* (1886) and other Wessex novels. Tour guides to *The Mayor of Casterbridge* and all the other Hardy novels can be obtained from www.hardysociety.org.

Llewelyn Powys was born in Dorchester in 1884 when his father was curate of St Peter's, and his brother Theodore Francis was educated at the Grammar School. After his return from

America in 1934 the eldest brother, John Cowper Powys, stayed for a short time in the town working on his novel *Maiden Castle* (1937), before moving to *Corwen.

David Edgar's play *Entertaining Strangers* (1985) is set in 19th-c. Dorchester, during a great cholera outbreak; based on research into the lives of real people in Dorchester at the time, it was written as a community play for the people of contemporary Dorchester to perform themselves; the first performance took place at St Mary's Church on 18 November 1985.

DOVER'S HILL *Gloucestershire*

Hill (NT) W of Chipping Campden, the scene of the Cotswold Games revived by Robert Dover in 1612, held every Whitsun until stopped by enclosures in 1852, and revived again in the 1960s. Endymion Porter (1587–1649) of Mickleton Manor 2 m. N, friend and patron of many poets, brought a party of courtiers to the games, and *Annalia Dubriensia* (1636) was a collection of poems by Ben Jonson, Drayton, Randolph, Heywood, and Marmion in their praise. Richard Graves was born (1715) at Mickleton Manor, and the first exploit of Wildgoose in his novel *The Spiritual Quixote* (1772) is about the games. A memorial to Dover, with a relief portrait, stands in the car park.

DOZMARY POOL *Cornwall*

Lonely expanse of water, high on Bodmin Moor, reached by a minor road *c.* 2 m. SE of Bolventor, a tiny hamlet on the A30, 11 m. NE of Bodmin. By some accounts this is the lake

Thomas Hardy and Wessex

Thomas Hardy's Wessex is one of the best known of literary landscapes. He described and mapped a region that is at once full of topographical detail, and charged with mythical resonance. So familiar are the fictional names he gave to his towns, villages, heaths, and valleys that they have sometimes confused themselves with their originals—Budmouth and Weymouth, Casterbridge and Dorchester, Abbot's Cernel and Cerne Abbas, Mellstock and Stinsford, merge in the reader's memory, and Egdon Heath takes on an independent imaginative life. Hardy's Wessex includes much of Dorset, Devon, Cornwall, Somerset, Wiltshire, and Hampshire, but cannot be defined by the specific counties most closely associated with it. To use his own phrase, he 'disinterred' the old name for an extinct kingdom for a series of novels 'of the kind called local', and found his adoption of the term so successful that it could not be confined to 'the horizons of a partly real, partly dream-country'. It was taken up by the public, and became a 'utilitarian region'. Fiction created fact.

Hardy was born in 1840 in Higher Bockhampton in Dorset, not far from Dorchester, the historic town that became the central point of his fictional space. His birthplace was a thatched 'mudwall' cottage, once known simply as 'Hardy's', and had been built by his great-grandfather. It was bordered on one side by a woodland plantation, which supplied fuel, and on the other by the heathland that he was to name Egdon. The cottage seemed part of the natural world around it: bats flew in and out of the windows, sparrows rustled in the eves, and snakes slept in the porch. The interpenetration of outdoor and indoor life was to be one of Hardy's lasting themes, and it is easy to see where his sense of man's closeness to the animal and vegetable kingdoms was born. Here too in his childhood he learned about the hard lives and traditional customs and pleasures of neighbouring villagers. He lived very close to his subject for most of his long life.

Bockhampton, in the parish of Stinsford, was the primal source of his sense of landscape, and it appeared in many of his poems and novels. But he also ranged further afield, into strikingly different territories. Each of the novels has its own sense of place, its own location. His first major work, *Far from the Madding Crowd* (1874), written while he was still living at his parents' home, draws largely on the immediate neighbourhood, and on the comfortable village of Weatherbury, based on Puddletown, a few miles to the north. But the novel also evokes the bleaker landscape of Norcombe Hill, not far from lonely Toller Down, a 'featureless convexity' of ancient chalk and soil, half-wooded and half-naked, and fringed by a decaying plantation of beech trees: it is here that Gabriel Oak minds his lambs in his

Thomas Hardy by Walter William Ouless, 1922

shepherd's hut, and here that tragedy strikes his flock. Place is plot, in Hardy.

The Return of the Native (1878) is his novel of Egdon, which is the name he gave to the barren stretch of uninhabited land between Dorchester and Bournemouth. It is dominated, in his version, by the prehistoric hill of Rainbarrow, 'the pole and axis of this heathery world', and it is crossed by an 'aged highway, dry, empty and white', that 'bisected that vast dark surface like the parting-line on a head of black hair'. The lives of the heath dwellers are bound up with the changing aspects of the heath, described in minute detail: the itinerant Reddleman, peddling ochre and dyed red by his trade, seems hardly separate from the earth that colours him. The heath brings loneliness and madness, drama and death, to its inhabitants. *The Mayor of Casterbridge* (1886) is the least rustic of Hardy's works, as it is based largely in Dorchester itself, and deals with trade rather than agriculture, with corn and flour and commerce rather than growing things, but its protagonist, Henchard, dies alone and outcast in a hut on Egdon.

The Woodlanders (1887) is set in the Hintocks, the villages of Hardy's mother's youth, and it evokes a life of forestry, sawmills, hurdle-making, and plantations: the trees—forked old elms and ashes, beeches with 'hectic leaves, that rustled in the wind with a sound almost metallic'—are known and named. Nature in Hardy is often sinister, but at times the novel has a memorably lush fecundity: some of its finest passages describe spring in the cider country of Blackmoor Vale with its 'blaze of pink blossom', followed by autumn 'now bossed, nay encrusted, with scarlet and golden fruit, stretching to infinite distance under a luminous lavender mist'. The crafts of the woodland are recorded with the affectionate respect of incipient nostalgia: Hardy knew they would soon perish.

Rural change is also a dominant theme in *Tess of the D'Urbervilles* (1891), which leads its tragic heroine through many different landscapes, each taking on a spiritual significance in her long and painful journey. She is introduced at a May Day dance as a village maiden in Marnhull (Marlott), with a peeled willow wand and flowers in her hand: after her seduction in sinister Cranborne Chase, she is allowed a period of happiness at 'green, sunny, romantic' Talbothays in the Valley of the Great Dairies, 'that green trough of sappiness and humidity', but is soon expelled to the harsh dry swede field of Flintcomb-Ash, to the only work she can find. Mechanization and the railways are destroying a way of life. Geographically, she is only a few miles away from the Froom Valley and paradise, but she can never return, and fate drives her relentlessly on to Stonehenge and sacrifice.

Hardy's evocations of place are so powerful that he has inspired generations of readers with the desire to follow in his footsteps, and to identify his locations. Some of his sites are disputed, and he admitted that he had sometimes shifted scenes by 'a witch's ride' of a mile or more, but many of them may still be recognized. He wrote of a world that was changing rapidly and inexorably, but the spirit of his Wessex remains. We see his landscape through the eyes that he gave us.   MARGARET DRABBLE

into which Sir Bedivere threw King Arthur's sword Excalibur (see 'The Passing of Arthur' in Tennyson's *The Idylls of the King*, 1869).

DULVERTON *Somerset*

Small Exmoor town near the Devon border. The journalist, editor, and novelist Auberon Waugh was born at Pixton Pk on 17 November 1939, the first six years of his life being spent, as he records in his autobiography, *Will This Do?* (1991), with an 'exotic countess and others who made up the extended household-aunts, cousins, retired nannies and household servants in various states of physical disarray'.

DYMOCK *Gloucestershire*

Village on the B4215, 5 m. S of Ledbury. John Kyrle, the 'Man of Ross', was born (1637) at the White House. In 1911 Lascelles Abercrombie settled at Gallows, two cottages joined together (gone) at Ryton (2 m. E). 'Ryton Firs' in *Emblems of Love* (1913) describes the daffodils:

> tumbling in broad rivers
> Down sloping grass under the cherry trees
> And birches.

In 1913 Rupert Brooke and John Drinkwater joined him for a time at Gallows, and Wilfrid Gibson came to stay at the Old Nail Shop at Greenway Cross, a red-brick cottage with exposed timbers which then had a thatched roof. The four poets contributed to *New Numbers*, a quarterly published from Ryton in 1914. It contained some of Brooke's poems on the Pacific, also 'The Great Lover' and the prophetic 'The Soldier', and Gibson's 'The Old Nail Shop'. In the summer the American poet Robert Frost rented the black-and-white labourer's cottage Little Iddens, then in the middle of a vegetable garden, which his wife and children cultivated. Edward Thomas came to Old Fields, a cottage in a field nearby, where Frost persuaded him to try writing verse as well as the essays he had written formerly. Although the group dispersed at the end of the year, Gibson still remembered in *The Golden Room* (1928) the friends who had met in the Old Nail Shop. When Frost returned to England for honorary degrees in 1957, he visited the four cottages. *Dymock Down the Ages* (1951) by Canon J. E. Gethyn-Jones contains a chapter on the poets and has photographs of their homes.

EAST BUDLEIGH *Devon*

Village 3 m. N of Budleigh Salterton on the B3178. Sir Walter Ralegh's birthplace, the thatched Tudor farmhouse of Hayes Barton, can be reached by Hayes Lane, a narrow turning on the W side of the village.

EAST COKER *Somerset*

Village off the A37, 3 m. SW of Yeovil. The ashes of T. S. Eliot (d. 1965), whose ancestors left the village for America, are buried as he requested in the church (tablet). The second section of his *Four Quartets* (1944) is named after the village.

EASTON *Dorset*

Village on the E side of the Isle of Portland. On the Wakeham Rd, near the turning down to Church Ope, is the Hardy and Portland Museum, housed in Avice's Cottage, a low thatched building made famous by Hardy as the home of Avice in *The Well-Beloved* (1897). Dr Marie Stopes, who lived at the Old Lighthouse, restored the cottage from a state of disrepair and founded it as a museum in 1929.

EAST STOUR *Dorset*

Village on the A30, *c.* 4 m. W of Shaftesbury. Henry Fielding came here at the age of 3 with his family and lived at the Manor House, which stood on the site of the farm by the church, formerly known as Fielding's Farm, later Church Farm. After an education at Eton and at Leiden, where he studied law, he supported himself in London for a few years by writing for the stage, and then in 1734 married Charlotte Cradock, his model for Sophia Western in *Tom Jones* (1749), and brought her to East Stour. They lived here for a short time and he then decided to take up the study of law again and returned to London, where he was called to the Bar in 1740. Parson Adams, the amiable curate of Fielding's *Joseph Andrews* (1742), is thought to have been modelled on the Revd William Young, rector of the adjoining parish of West Stour, with whom Fielding collaborated in the translation of the *Plutus* of Aristophanes.

ELKSTONE *Gloucestershire*

Village 6 m. S of Cheltenham. P. J. Kavanagh has lived near the village for many years and much of his poetry and prose reflects his detailed and affectionate response to the local country. Of the destruction of a wall he writes in 'News from Gloucestershire':

> they are done
> That were my passion. Foxes' navigation, weasels'
> run,
> Skilful catchers of every light, they open
> Like graves, a jumble of yellow bone
> That tractors tidy away. Visitors from the town
> May vaguely remark an absence, travel on.

Hayes Barton Manor, East Budleigh, Devon. Birthplace of Sir Walter Ralegh

EXETER *Devon*

Cathedral and university city and county town of Devon, on the NE bank of the Exe, the Isca Dumnoniorum of the Romans and the Escancestre of the Saxons. Defoe in his *Tour Through the Whole Island of Britain* (1724–7) describes the city as 'famous for two things which we seldom find united in the same town, viz., that it is full of gentry and good company, and yet full of trade and manufactures also'. Its distinguished natives include Sir Thomas Bodley (1545–1613) and Richard Hooker (1553/4–1600, born in Heavitree, now an E suburb). Thomas Fuller (1608–61) came here with the Royalists when they moved from Oxford in 1643 and was made chaplain to Charles I's infant daughter the next year. During his time here he was a popular preacher and was working on *The Worthies of England* (1662). Thomas D'Urfey (1653–1723), a poet and dramatist of Huguenot descent, was born here and went to London to make his name, his most popular work being *Wit and Mirth, or, Pills to purge Melancholy* (1719), a collection of songs and ballads. Sabine Baring-Gould (1834–1924), theologian and prolific writer in many fields, was born in Exeter, but spent a great part of his life as rector of *Lew Trenchard. Patrick Sheehan came to work in Exeter shortly after he was ordained in 1875 and stayed until 1877, when he returned to his native Mallow. George Gissing came in 1891 for two years, staying first at 24 Prospect Pk and then at 1 St Leonard's Ter. He enjoyed the peace after London: 'Every morning when I wake', he said, 'I thank heaven for silence.' *Born in Exile* (1892) is set partly in the city and its environs, and part of the setting of *The Private Papers of Henry Ryecroft* (1903) also derives from his knowledge of the surrounding countryside. The Dominican-born novelist Jean Rhys,

long resident in Devon, died at the County Hospital in Exeter on 14 May 1979; shortly after her death a posthumous autobiography appeared, entitled *Smile Please* (1979). The poet Patricia Beer studied English at Exeter University in the late 1930s; and Harry Potter author J. K. Rowling took her degree in French and Classics here too, graduating in 1986.

The Turk's Head in the High St. is a 15th-c. inn where Dickens found the original of his Fat Boy for *Pickwick Papers* (1837). In Thackeray's *Pendennis* (1848–50), Exeter is portrayed as 'Chatteris'.

The Cathedral, dating from Norman times, was substantially rebuilt between *c.* 1270 and *c.* 1360. Miles Coverdale was bishop in 1551–3 and John Gauden in 1660–2. Just inside the W entrance there is a memorial tablet to R. D. Blackmore, unveiled by Eden Phillpotts in 1904. A statue of Richard Hooker stands on the N side of the Close.

The Cathedral Library, now housed principally in the Bishop's Palace adjoining, claims a history of over 900 years, beginning with the gift of 66 books from Leofric, the first Bishop of Exeter, between 1050 and his death in 1072. These include the 10th-c. Exeter Book, the largest known collection of Anglo-Saxon poems, including 'The Wanderer', 'The Seafarer', and 'Deor'. There are also the Exeter Domesday Book, and many medieval manuscripts, including the beautiful 13th-c. Psalter probably written for the church of St Helen at Worcester, and the 14th-c. manuscript of the *Polychronicon* of Ranulf Higden of Chester. An interesting example of early printing (1492) is a fragment of Chaucer's *Canterbury Tales*, the opening of the 'Franklin's Tale'. The Library is usually open on weekday afternoons (www.exeter-cathedral.org.uk).

EXMOUTH *Devon*

Port and resort on the E side of the mouth of the river Exe. The childhood of the poet Patricia Beer was spent at Withycombe Raleigh, a village now part of Exmouth. The family lived on Bradham Lane, 'in a small red-brick house called Petitor, on the front door of which my sister Sheila chalked almost as soon as she could write: MRS BEERS HOUSE'. Her Plymouth Brethren upbringing, education in Exmouth Grammar School, and holidays in Torquay are recalled in her memoir *Mrs Beer's House* (1968).

FALMOUTH *Cornwall*

Port and holiday resort at the end of the A39, overlooking a sheltered harbour opening off the Carrick Roads. Kenneth Grahame stayed here in May 1907 at the Green Bank Hotel and wrote to his young son Alistair about the misdeeds of Toad, part of the story that became *The Wind in the Willows* (1908). Copies of two letters (the originals are at the Bodleian Library, Oxford) can be seen at the hotel.

Howard Spring moved here from *Mylor in 1947 and settled at the White Cottage, Fenwick Rd. Here he finished *There Is No Armour* (1948), a novel which begins in Didsbury and moves on to Falmouth and the neighbouring country, and continued writing until the end of his life. His last novel was *Winds of the Day* (1964).

In 1929 the poet and editor Alan Ross was sent from Calcutta to Belmont House, a school with 20 pupils. When he arrived, his Hindustani was better than his English. It is now occupied by the Falmouth School of Art, where Peter Redgrove was resident poet from 1966 to 1983. Redgrove met a retired Jungian psychotherapist with whom he studied dream analysis—an experience which affected his outlook on life and attitude to his first marriage. He married the novelist Penelope Shuttle and the couple pursued an unusually close literary collaboration on poems, novels, and works of psychology and socio-sexuality. Much of his work was written in celebration of the Cornish landscape and one of Falmouth's local beaches, 'where the mud spatters with rich seed and raging pollens', is the subject of perhaps his best-known poem 'The Idea of Entropy at Maenporth Beach'. His late poem 'Elderhouse' takes as its subject the pouring of a glass of tap water in a Falmouth café. Redgrove's ashes were scattered at Maenporth in 2003. Penelope Shuttle's moving collection of poems *Redgrove's Wife* (2006) express her response to the last stages of her husband's life.

FLEET *Dorset*

Village consisting of East and West Fleet: a few scattered cottages, a church, and Moonfleet House (now the Moonfleet Manor Hotel), lying between Chesil Beach and the B3157 from Weymouth to Bridport. The house, formerly Fleet House, belonging to the Moone, or Mohun, family and dating from the 17th c.,

Godrevy Lighthouse from St Ives, Cornwall. Virginia Woolf spent childhood holidays in St Ives and had Godrevy in her mind when she came to write *To the Lighthouse*

'The Wanderer' as it appears in the Exeter Book (or Codex Exoniensis). The book preserves the largest collection of Anglo-Saxon literature and has been kept in the library at Exeter Cathedral since 1072

stands on the edge of the water at the end of a minor road, *c.* 1½ m. from Chickerell, and was the setting for Meade Falkner's *Moonfleet* (1898), a novel of adventure and smuggling, based on local tradition.

FONTHILL ABBEY *Wiltshire*

The remains of William Beckford's extravagant and fantastic mansion are in private grounds in Fonthill Abbey Wood, Fonthill Gifford, on a minor road *c.* 1 m. S of Fonthill Bishop on the B3089, 15 m. W of Salisbury. Beckford, a man of vast wealth, remembered for his oriental romance *Vathek* (1787, reprinted 1970), inherited the house from his father and in 1790 employed James Wyatt to rebuild it in the Gothic style, complete with a high wall round

the grounds to keep out unwanted visitors. Here he housed his great collection of curios, works of art, and books, and spent visits between his tours of the Continent. The building took nearly 20 years to complete (the Great Tower was too hurriedly erected in 1799 and collapsed soon after), but Nelson and Sir William and Lady Hamilton were entertained there in 1800, and in 1807 Beckford moved into the S wing. Eventually his fortune dwindled and in 1822 he sold the Abbey and moved to *Bath. In October 1823 Thomas Moore, who was staying nearby, walked over for the sale and brought back a cup and saucer as a memento for his wife, Bessy. Today all that remains is some 60 ft of the Lancaster Tower, the dismantled Duchess's Bedroom, the

Oratory, and the Steward's Room with adjoining bedrooms.

FORTHAMPTON *Gloucestershire*

Village near Tewkesbury. The novelist Henry Green (Yorke) was born and brought up at Forthampton Court. He writes evocatively about the servants and others with whom he was brought up in his memoir *Pack My Bag* (1940). The house and its staff—particularly the butler—also found its way into his novel *Loving* (1945).

FOWEY (pr. Foy) *Cornwall*

Picturesque seaport situated near the mouth of the Fowey, at the end of the A3082. The road comes steeply down into the narrow ways of the town and it is advisable to leave a car at the top of the hill and walk down the paths and steps to the waterfront. Celia Fiennes, visiting in 1698, wrote of the road 'dropping at breakneck speed' and that

> Near the road were many holes and sloughs wherever there was clay ground, and when, by the rain, these were filled with water it was difficult to sheer danger. My horse was quite down in one of these holes, head and all, but by the good hand of God's providence, I giving him a sharp strap, he floundered up again, and retrieved his feet and got clear of the place with me on his back.

A short way along the Esplanade, just above Polruan Ferry, is The Haven ℗, the home of Sir Arthur Quiller-Couch ('Q') from 1892 to 1944. Here he wrote many of his novels and short stories, immortalizing Fowey as 'Troy Town' in *The Astonishing History of Troy Town* (1888). He also edited *The Oxford Book of English Verse* (1900) and other anthologies. He was mayor of Fowey in 1937–8 and is commemorated by a memorial on Hall Walk, overlooking the harbour. Kenneth Grahame, who became friends with 'Q' in 1899, used to come and stay and they enjoyed sailing together. Grahame married Elspeth Thomson at St Fimbarrus's Church on 22 July 1899, with his cousin Anthony Hope Hawkins as best man. *The Wind in the Willows* (1908), begun as bedtime stories for his young son Alistair, *c.* 1904, was continued in letters to him during visits to Fowey, which inspired much of the idyllic river setting of 'messing about in boats'.

Daphne du Maurier lived in her parents' holiday house at *Bodinnick on the other side of the river. She rented the nearby houses *Menabilly and Kilmarth near *Par and the landscape around Fowey features often in her best-known novels and stories. The Tourist Information Office provides a display about her life in the area, details of the Daphne du Maurier literary festival, books, and walking guides.

The travel writer and novelist Jonathan Raban finds *Gosfield Maid* here, the small ketch that in silhouette resembled 'a cracked army boot' and which was to take him on a journey around the British coast recorded in his travel book *Coasting* (1986).

FROME (pr. Froom) *Somerset*

Historic market town near the Mendip Hills. The novelist Anthony Powell lived at The Chantry from 1952 until his death in 2000.

FROME ST QUINTIN *Dorset*

Village off the A37, 11 m. NW of Dorchester. George Crabbe occasionally visited here after he had been presented to the living together with Evershot (3 m. NW) in 1783. He brought his wife in 1784 and stayed at Frome St Quintin House. His host was George Baker, who had just completed the classic portico (with 'Geo. Baker A.D. 1782' cut in the stone above).

FROME VAUCHURCH *Dorset*

Village in the Frome valley, 7 m. NW of Dorchester. The novelist Sylvia Townsend Warner and the poet Valentine Ackland came to live in the village, settling at Riverside in 1937. Townsend Warner wrote many novels here, including *The Corner That Held Them* (1948) and many of her short stories are set in the village. Items from their house and an archive of their diaries, letters, and other manuscripts are kept at the Dorset County Museum, *Dorchester.

GALMPTON *Devon*

Suburban village on Torbay between Brixham and Paignton. Robert Graves lived with his second wife, Beryl, at Vale House Farm from 1940 to 1946.

GEORGEHAM *Devon*

Village on the B3231, N of the estuary of the rivers Taw and Torridge. Henry Williamson took a labourer's cottage here in 1921, where he produced the first fruits of his talent as a naturalist. *Tarka the Otter* was published in 1927. He also wrote *The Pathway* (1928), which completed his tetralogy of novels *The Flax of Dream*. In 1930 he left to farm in Norfolk, but returned to Georgeham in 1947 to spend the rest of his life in Ox's Cross, a hut in a hilltop field which he had bought with the Hawthornden Prize money for *Tarka the Otter*. The hut, which he built with two local boys, consists of overlapping planks of untrimmed elm fastened to an oak frame, and on the walls are grim photographs of Passchendaele as a reminder of his war experiences. Here he wrote *Salar the Salmon* (1935) and the 15-volume *roman-fleuve* entitled *A Chronicle of Ancient Sunlight* (1951–69).

GLASTONBURY *Somerset*

Town on the A39, 6 m. SW of Wells. Legends of King Arthur, whose Isle of Avalon is traditionally placed here, were a favoured theme of medieval poets and chroniclers including Layamon, Geoffrey of Monmouth, Huchoun, and Malory. Their works inspired Tennyson's *Idylls of the King* (1859), John Masefield's novel *The Badon Parchments* (1947), and J. C. Powys's *A Glastonbury Romance* (1933) with its modern setting. The site ⓟ where the monks claimed to have found (1191) the remains of Arthur and Guinevere

and where the reinterment took place in 1278 is S of the Lady Chapel in the ruined monastery.

GLOUCESTER *Gloucestershire*

County town on the A40, the A38, and the A417. The poet and traveller John Taylor (1580–1653), who later became one of the King's Watermen in London, was born here and educated at the Grammar School before being press-ganged for the Cadiz expedition. William D'Avenant, poet and dramatist, was knighted during the Gloucester siege of 1643 for his services in importing arms from France for the Royalists. William Lisle Bowles wrote the sonnet 'On Hearing the Messiah Performed in Gloucester Cathedral' in 1835. The Manx poet T. E. Brown (1830–97) was headmaster of the Crypt School for a short time when W. E. Henley (born in 1849 at 2 Eastgate St., now rebuilt), who edited his *Collected Poems* in 1900, was a pupil. The illustrations in Beatrix Potter's *The Tailor of Gloucester* (1901) show the little house (later an antiques and curios shop) in College Ct off Westgate St., where the tailor lived.

The poet and composer Ivor Gurney was born in 1890 at 3 Queen St. (now Queen's Way) (gone). Soon after his birth the family moved to a more spacious house at 19 Barton St. He attended the National School in London Rd from *c.* 1896, won a place in the Cathedral Choir in 1900, and became a pupil at the King's School, where he began to write music. After studying at the Royal College of Music in London, he volunteered at the outbreak of the First World War and served on the Western Front, where he was wounded and gassed. Committed to a mental institution in 1922, suffering from the effects of war, he died in the City of London Mental Hospital in 1937. Many of the poems in his *Severn and Somme* (1917) and *War's Embers* (1919) evoke his native county.

The Centre for Cognitive Science at the fictional University of Gloucester is the setting for David Lodge's novel *Thinks . . .* (2001).

GODOLPHIN HOUSE *Cornwall*

Mansion 1 m. NW of Godolphin Cross, a village on a minor road between Breage (A394) and Townshend (B3280). It was a former home of the earls of Godolphin and the birthplace of Sidney Godolphin (1610–43), a poet of promise who was killed at *Chagford in the Civil War. He was the 'little Sid' of Sir John Suckling's works.

GOLANT (pr. Gō'lănt) *Cornwall*

Small village on the W bank of the Fowey, 2 m. N of Fowey town, reached by car from a turning off the B3269, the Lostwithiel road. This was traditionally the setting of the romance of Tristram and Iseult of Arthurian legend, and the ancient grass-grown mound of Castle Dore, 1 m. inland, is reputedly the palace of King Mark, legendary king of Cornwall.

GOLSONCOTT *Somerset*

Country house set between the Brendon Hills and Exmoor, just N of Roadwater, this is the old family home of the writer Penelope Lively;

her collection of autobiographical stories centred around this house where her grandparents lived is *A House Unlocked* (2001). Her grandmother came from St Albans to Golsoncott in 1923, 'a Lutyens-style house built some ten or fifteen years earlier at the foot of the Brendon Hills, and set about creating a large Gertrude Jekyll-style garden to complement it'.

GOONHILLY *Cornwall*

A telecommunications site near Helston. Goonhilly Downs' twin nature as an Iron Age burial ground and a satellite station inspires Anne Stevenson's poem 'Earth Station'.

GREAT TORRINGTON *Devon*

Village situated above the Torridge, 7 m. SSE of Bideford, on the A386. William Johnson (who later assumed the surname Cory) was born (7 Jan. 1823) at Palmer House. He was a great-nephew of William Johnson, who was three times mayor of Torrington and brother-in-law of Sir Joshua Reynolds. Reynolds and his friend Dr Johnson visited Palmer House together in 1762.

GWENNAP PIT *Cornwall*

A stepped amphitheatre, *c.* 300 yds in circumference, perhaps originally caused by mining subsidence, *c.* 1 m. W of Redruth, reached by a minor road opposite the junction of the B3297 and the A393, in the direction of St Day. John Wesley preached here on several occasions to large congregations of miners, first in 1762 and lastly 29 years later, in his 85th year.

HAM *Wiltshire*

Small village off the A338, 4 m. S of Hungerford. Lytton Strachey lived from 1924 to the end of his life at Ham Spray House, a pleasant Georgian building sheltered by trees at the end of a long avenue and looking S to the Newbury Downs. The Mill House at *Tidmarsh had become too damp for him in winter and after the move to higher ground his health improved. In December 1925 he began work on *Elizabeth and Essex* (1928), and followed this with collections of shorter writings in *Portraits in Miniature* (1931) and *Characters and Commentaries* (1933). The devoted Carrington kept house as before, and her husband, Ralph Partridge, completed the strange trio. When Strachey died in 1932 Carrington took her own life.

HARDENHUISH (pr. 'Harnĭsh') *Wiltshire*

Village formerly *c.* 1 m. NW of Chippenham, now engulfed by that ever-expanding town. Francis Kilvert, the diarist, was born (1840) at the vicarage when his father was vicar here.

HELFORD *Cornwall*

Riverside village 5 m. E of Helston. *Frenchman's Creek* (1942), Daphne du Maurier's historical romance set during the reign of Charles II, takes its name from one of the creeks off the Helford River.

HERM *Channel Islands*

Sir Compton Mackenzie purchased the tenancy of Herm and of the smaller neighbouring island of Jethou in 1920. He lived in the sombre, granite 18th-c. Manor House on Herm from 1920 to 1923 and on Jethou from 1923 to 1930. During this time he wrote *The Altar Steps* (1922), *The Parson's Progress* (1923), *The Heavenly Ladder* (1924), *Fairy Gold* (which makes use of local scenes, 1926), *Vestal Fire* (1927), *Extremes Meet* (1928), and *April Fools* (1930). D. H. Lawrence's short story 'The Man Who Loved Islands' is about Mackenzie on Herm.

HEYTESBURY (pr. 'Hātisbry) *Wiltshire*

Village on the A36, *c.* 4 m. SE of Warminster, on the edge of Salisbury Plain. At the E end of the village a drive leads from the main road through informal parkland to Heytesbury House, the home for many years of Siegfried Sassoon. In 'Awareness of Alcuin' (*Collected Poems 1908-1956*, 1961), he wrote:

At peace in my tall-windowed Wiltshire room
(Birds overhead from chill March twilight's close)
I read, translated Alcuin's verse, in whom
A springtide of resurgent learning rose.

T. E. Lawrence (remembered in the village as T. E. Shaw) used to come over for visits when he was stationed at Bovington Camp. Sassoon died here and was buried at Mells, *c.* 3 m. W of Frome.

HIGHER BOCKHAMPTON *Dorset*

Hamlet 4 m. NE of Dorchester, 1 m. S of the A35, along Cuckoo Lane. A turning at the top of the hill leads to Hardy's Cottage (NT), but cars must be left in the Thorncombe Wood car park and the rest of the way made on foot up the lane or through the wood (*c.* 10 minutes). Thomas Hardy was born in the cottage on 2 June 1840 and lived there for most of the first 30 years of his life. His earliest-known poem, 'Domicilium', written in his early teens, describes the cottage as he knew it:

It faces west, and round the back and sides
High beeches, bending, hang a veil of boughs,
And sweep against the roof. . . .
Red roses, lilacs, variegated box
Are there in plenty, and such hardy flowers
As flourish best untrained. Adjoining these
Are herbs and esculents; and farther still
A field; then cottages with trees, and last
The distant hills and sky.
Behind the scene is wilder. Heath and furze
Are everything that seems to grow and thrive
Upon the uneven ground. . . .

and as his grandmother described it when she first lived there:

Our house stood quite alone, and those tall firs
And beeches were not planted. . . .
　　　　　　Heathcroppers
Lived on the hills, and were our only friends;
So wild it was when we first settled here.

Another poem, 'The Self-Unseeing' (1901), describes a return visit and childhood memories.

A detailed picture of the cottage, as Tranter Dewy's House, appears in *Under the Greenwood Tree* (1872), written in the deep window-seat of Hardy's bedroom, where he also wrote *Far From the Madding Crowd* (1874). (Tour guides to these and all the other Hardy novels can be obtained from www.hardysociety.org.) A gate near the cottage leads to 'Egdon Heath', Hardy's 'untamed and untameable wild', now considerably modified by forestry plantations. Nearby is a stone memorial to Hardy, erected by 'a few of his American admirers' (1931). The garden can be seen from the lane. Appointments to visit the cottage should be made by telephoning 01305-262366.

HOLNE *Devon*

Little village high above the Dart valley, 3 m. SW of the medieval Holne Bridge on the A38 and 4 m. NW of Buckfastleigh on the A384. Charles Kingsley was born (12 June 1819) at the old vicarage, a short way from the village, off the Hexworthy road, while his father was curate-in-charge for a few months. A memorial window in the N transept of the church includes a portrait medallion of Kingsley in middle age.

HUCCLECOTE *Gloucestershire*

Village 2 m. E of Gloucester on the A38. Sydney Dobell, having spent the first two years after his marriage in 1844 in *Gloucester, moved to Lark Hay to recuperate from rheumatic fever. He started his most popular poem, *The Roman* (1850), here, published under the pseudonym 'Sydney Yendys', after he left in 1848.

ILCHESTER *Somerset*

Village on the A303 and the A37, 5 m. NW of Yeovil. A brass tablet, erected in the church to commemorate the 700th anniversary of Roger Bacon's birth here (1214), calls him 'Doctor Mirabilis' and 'a free enquirer into true knowledge'. Though his scientific experiments led people to believe him a necromancer and his Franciscan colleagues kept him under surveillance for years, the Pope commissioned his treatises, which led him to be called the founder of modern philosophy.

ILSINGTON *Devon*

Village on the E edge of Dartmoor, *c.* 3 m. SW of Bovey Tracey, on a minor road off the A382. John Ford, the dramatist, was born at the Manor of Bagtor, 1 m. SW, and baptized in the village church (22 Apr. 1586). Little is known of his life, though after living and working in London he probably spent his last years in Devon. His plays, some of which were written in collaboration with Dekker and Rowley, include the tragedies *'Tis Pity She's a Whore* (1633) and *The Broken Heart* (1633).

KELSTON *Somerset*

Village on the A431, 4 m. NW of Bath. Sir John Harington, godson of Queen Elizabeth I, inherited the manor built by James Barozzi of Vignola for his father. He translated *Orlando Furioso* (1591) at the Queen's suggestion and entertained her at Kelston (1592) when he was Lord Lieutenant of Somerset. His collection of anecdotes *Nugae Antiquae* (1769), which contains information about Queen Elizabeth I's last illness, was published by a descendant. The house, on the site of Tower House gardens, was demolished after the 18th-c. Kelston Park was built. It is said that the perfumed water closet Harington invented was erected in the garden.

KINGSBRIDGE *Devon*

Busy little market town on the A379 and the A381 at the head of the Kingsbridge Estuary. Pindar Lodge, at the beginning of the Promenade, is the house where John Wolcot (the satirist 'Peter Pindar') was born. The house, which has been largely rebuilt, is in the parish of Dodbrooke and originally faced on to Ebrington St., now its back entrance. Wolcot attended Kingsbridge Free School before going to Bodmin Grammar School.

KINGTON ST MICHAEL *Wiltshire*

Village *c.* 3 m. NW of Chippenham, off the A350. A memorial window in the church commemorates two natives of the parish, distinguished by their writings on the antiquities of Wiltshire: John Aubrey (1625–97), whose works include the unfinished manuscripts of *Topographical Collections of Wiltshire, 1659–70*, with illustrations (corrected and enlarged by J. E. Jackson, 1862), and John Britton (1771–1857), author of *Beauties of Wiltshire* (1801) and other works. John Aubrey was born at Easton Piers (now Easton Piercy or Percy), a hamlet in the parish of Kington St Michael to the NW of the village. He inherited the house Lower Easton Piers (illustrated in the *Collections of Wiltshire*) from his mother's family, but pecuniary troubles compelled him to sell it in 1671 and from then on he had no settled home. The site of the house (long demolished) was later occupied by Easton Percy Farm, opposite the site of the old Priory Chapel.

KNOWSTONE (pr. 'Nowston) *Devon*

Small village 10 m. ESE of South Molton, on a minor road between the A361 and the B3227. Parson Froude, the infamous, bad-tempered vicar here for nearly 50 years, died in 1853 in a fit of rage and is buried in the churchyard. He is portrayed as Parson Chowne in R. D. Blackmore's *Maid of Sker* (1872).

LANGLEY BURRELL *Wiltshire*

Village on the B4069, 1 m. N of Chippenham. Francis Kilvert was curate to his father here from 1872 to 1876 after leaving his curacy at *Clyro. His parents' house, later called Kilvert's Parsonage, has been restored. Among the entries in the notebooks that he kept from 1870 to 1877 (*Diary*, 3 vols, 1938–40; new edn, 1969), he records his parish work, his pleasure in the countryside, and the election at Chippenham, when a secret ballot was used for the first time. The pages of his notebooks were ornamented with his own drawings. The church is on the A420 (½ m. NW).

LANGPORT *Somerset*

Small town on the A372 and the A378, 13 m. W of Taunton. Walter Bagehot (1826–77) was born at a stone house Ⓟ near the Langport Arms. He was editor of *The Economist* from 1860 to the end of his life. He died at Herds Hill, a large house on the hill W of the town on the A378. His critical essays *Literary Studies* (1879) were published posthumously.

LAUNCESTON *Cornwall*

Market town and ancient county capital. The poet Charles Causley was born in the town and, apart from six years in the Royal Navy, he spent his life there. His first home was in his grandmother's cottage by the river Kensey. Later he lived with his mother in a slate-hung tenement higher up in the town. He was educated at a local elementary school and at Launceston College, and taught for 30 years at Launceston County Primary School on Windmill Lane. His career in the classroom provided the inspiration for 'Timothy Winters':

> When teacher talks he won't hear a word
> And shoots down dead the arithmetic-bird,
> He licks the patterns off his plate
> And he's not even heard of the Welfare State.

A portrait of Causley hangs in the Lawrence House Museum, Castle St. He is buried beside his mother in St Thomas' churchyard.

LECHLADE *Gloucestershire*

Small market town where the A361 joins the A417, 12 m. NE of Swindon. In 1815 Shelley, with Peacock, Mary Godwin, and Charles Clairmont, rowed up the Thames from

Charles Causley outside St Thomas' Church, Launceston, in 1968

Windsor and stayed at the inn here. Shelley had been listless on the journey, which Peacock put down to a diet of bread and butter. He recommended 'three mutton chops, well peppered', which so raised Shelley's spirits that he made exuberant plans to row the length and breadth of Britain. But, unable to get the boat to the source of the river, they stayed another night at the inn before rowing back. Shelley wrote 'Stanzas in a Summer Evening Churchyard', and a stone set in the churchyard wall in 1968 at the beginning of Shelley's Walk, leading from the church to the river, quotes from the poem.

LEW TRENCHARD *Devon*

Village *c.* 10 m. SW of Okehampton, just S of the A30. The Revd Sabine Baring-Gould, antiquarian and expert on West Country folklore and legend, theologian, hymn writer, novelist, and musician, was rector and squire here from 1881 until his death in 1924. He is buried in the churchyard. His numerous works include *The Gaverocks: A Tale of the Cornish Coast* (1887), *In the Roar of the Sea* (1892), *A Book of the West* (1899), and *A Book of Dartmoor* (1900). His best-known hymn is 'Onward, Christian Soldiers'.

LONGLEAT *Wiltshire*

Country house off the A362, 6 m. SW of Warminster. In 1717 Mary Granville stayed with Lord and Lady Lansdowne, who arranged her marriage (which took place here) to their friend Mr Pendarves of Roscrow, very much against her will. Later, as Mrs Delany, she wrote a number of journals. George Crabbe dined here in 1824, a guest of the Marquess of Bath. He had recently met Scott in Edinburgh and told Thomas Moore, a fellow guest, about his visit.

LOWER INGLESHAM *Wiltshire*

Village on the A361, 2 m. S of Lechlade. The small parish church was repaired in 1888-9 by William Morris, and the old pews remain. A commemorative brass to Morris is to the right of the entrance.

LYME REGIS *Dorset*

Old fishing town picturesquely situated on Lyme Bay, on the A3052, a seaside resort which began to be fashionable in the late 18th c. In 1725 Henry Fielding (aged 18½) fell in love with Sarah Andrew (aged 15), whose guardian frowned on the match. Fielding tried to abduct her from a house near the church (now the Tudor House Hotel), lurking in Long Entry just opposite, to carry her off on her way to church. However, he was thwarted and left the town, later using the episode in his first play, *Love in Several Masques* (1728), the old squire, Sir Positive Trap, being a caricature of Sarah's guardian, Andrew Tucker.

On the N side of Broad St. a plaque records that Mary Russell Mitford stayed for some months in 1796-7 in what was originally known as the Great House of Lyme Regis, formerly on the present site. Jane Austen, in a

letter to her sister Cassandra of 14 September 1804, describes a visit here with her parents, James the coachman, and Jenny the maid, and gives an account of an evening spent at the weekly ball at the Assembly Rooms (site later a car park) at Cobb Gate, at the E end of the Marine Parade, and of her enjoyment of sea-bathing. Eleven years later she drew on her memories of this and possibly other visits to the town when she was writing *Persuasion* (finished in 1816 but not published until 1818) and planned the expedition to Lyme of the young people. The famous Cobb (the long, curving harbour wall) is probably familiar to more people than have ever seen it as the place of Louisa Musgrove's dramatic fall, and Bay Cottage (later a café) at the W end of the Marine Parade as the place where Captain Harville had taken rooms for the winter season and where Louisa stayed to convalesce. On the cliff-side above the cottage a pleasant little garden Ⓟ commemorates Jane Austen's association with Lyme, its opening on 23 April 1975 being the occasion of the performance of a short play, *Miss Austen at Lyme*, by Henry Chessell, the mayor.

In 1867 William Allingham and Alfred Tennyson stayed at The Cups and called on F. T. Palgrave, who was in lodgings near the Cobb. Palgrave bought Little Park, Haye Lane, in 1871 and lived there until his death. Tennyson, who had helped him to plan *The Golden Treasury of Songs and Lyrics* (1861), was a frequent visitor.

'Henry Handel Richardson' (Mrs J. G. Robertson) used to spend vacations with her husband at Westfield in Cobb Rd. She describes the town in *The Fortunes of Richard Mahony*, Part II (1925), where Mahony and his wife make their home 'in the ancient little town of Buddlecombe' until society repulses them and they return to their native Australia.

Somewhere in the country behind the town, in the direction of Beaminster, the anonymous hero, sportsman, and would-be assassin of Geoffrey Household's *Rogue Male* (1939) digs the woodland burrow in which he lies low with the wild cat he names Asmodeus, and from which he kills his sinister adversary 'Major Quive-Smith'. The coast nearby is the setting for the novel *Queen of Stones* (1982), Emma Tennant's response to William Golding's *Lord of the Flies* (1954), an account of the so-called 'Isle of Portland tragedy'. The harbour at Lyme inspired Patricia Beer's 1967 poem 'On the Cobb at Lyme Regis':

> Dangerous the sea is; for all I know
> It is even now, underneath the skin,
> Battering the sea-wall with drowned sailors
> Or countrymen who carelessly fell in.

The novelist John Fowles moved to Lyme Regis in 1968, and would remain until his death in 2005. His best-known novel, *The French Lieutenant's Woman* (1969), is set here; it is the story of the disgraced Sarah Woodruff, and her relationship with Charles Smithson. The novel is full of detail of Victorian Lyme Regis, the town and the natural environment around it. Sarah herself spends a great deal of time standing on the Cobb staring out to sea, and it is here that the novel opens:

> An easterly is the most disagreeable wind in Lyme Bay—Lyme Bay being that largest bite from the underside of England's outstretched south-western leg—and a person of curiosity could at once have deduced several strong probabilities about the pair who began to walk down the quay at Lyme Regis, the small but ancient eponym of the inbite, one incisively sharp and blustery morning in the late March of 1867 . . .

LYNMOUTH *Devon*

Holiday resort on the N coast, where the East and the West Lyn meet before flowing into the sea. The twin village of Lynton, situated near the edge of the cliff, 430 ft above, is reached by a steep road and a funicular railway. Coleridge took many walks here with Wordsworth when he was living (1797–8) at *Nether Stowey. Dorothy Wordsworth, who often walked with them, mentions the two men 'laying the plan of a ballad' which became 'The Ancient Mariner', published in the *Lyrical Ballads* (1798). Hazlitt also walked here with Coleridge, who was impressed with the desolate Valley of the Rocks near Lynton.

In June 1812 Shelley and his wife, Harriet, then 17, stayed at Mrs Hooper's cottage here. Shelley's pleasure in sailing makeshift 'boats' and launching bottles containing messages led him to be looked upon with suspicion. He and Harriet left after nine weeks and returned to Wales. The cottage was rebuilt after a fire in 1907.

MADRON *Cornwall*

Village in West Penwith, near Penzance. Not far from the village stands the Men-an-Tol. The prehistoric arrangement of stones has a disturbing effect on the pair of couples who crawl through the hole in the central stone in D. H. Thomas's novel *Birthstone* (1983).

MAIDENCOMBE *Devon*

District overlooking Babbacombe Bay, 4 m. N of Torquay. Kipling and his wife came here in September 1896 to Rock House, Rock House Lane, a place that he said seemed 'almost too good to be true . . . with big rooms each and all open to the sun, the grounds embellished with great trees and the warm land dipping southerly to the clear sea under the Marychurch cliffs'. But gradually they were overcome by depression—'a gathering blackness of mind and sorrow of heart'—caused by 'the Feng-shui—the Spirit of the house itself' a 'Spirit of deep, deep Despondency', described by Kipling in *Something of Myself* (1937), that drove them away the following June. But while he was there Kipling first had the idea of writing 'tracts or parables on the education of the young', which developed into the series of tales called *Stalky & Co.* (1899). Rock House was the subject of a psychoanalytical story, 'The House Surgeon', written somewhat in the manner of Henry James.

MALMESBURY (pr. 'Mahmzbŭri) *Wiltshire*

Small town on the A429, 16 m. W of Swindon. William of Malmesbury (d. *c.* 1143) the historian, was librarian at the Abbey here. Thomas Hobbes was born (1588) while his father was minister of Westport church, though the house has gone. An old acacia tree in the garden of Abbey House is said to have been planted by him. Addison was MP for Malmesbury from 1710 to 1719.

MANATON *Devon*

Quiet village on the A382, 4 m. S of Moretonhampstead. John Galsworthy spent his honeymoon (1904) at Wingstone, a house beside a farm, down an avenue off the road a little N of the village, which he had discovered on a walking tour earlier that year. He and his wife loved the place so much that they became summer tenants of the main part of the house for 15 years. Part of the novel *The Country House* (1907) and most of *Fraternity* (1909) were written here. In August and October of 1914 Galsworthy recorded visits from Bernard Shaw and his wife, and 'much talk'. The pleasure Galsworthy felt in living in the county of his ancestors in the peace of an unspoilt country is described in his letters (H. V. Marrot, *Life and Letters*, 1935, which also has photographs of the house).

MAPPOWDER *Dorset*

Village on the N side of the North Dorset Downs, on an unclassified road opposite the junction of the B3143 from Dorchester and the B3146. It was the home of T. F. Powys, who lived for the last 10 years of his life near the church in the little lodge at the entrance to Newleaze House (the Old Rectory) and is buried in the churchyard. There is a detailed account in the church of other distinguished members of the Powys family.

MARLBOROUGH *Wiltshire*

Town on the A4 and the A346. In 1728 James Thomson wrote *Spring*, part of *The Seasons* (1730), while a guest of the Countess of Hertford. Her house later became one of the most splendid of the coaching inns and was described by Stanley Weyman in his novel *The Castle Inn* (1898). In 1843 it became the main building of the new Marlborough College, and her grotto, where she and Thomson often sat, is by the Mound in the school grounds. C. S. Calverley, William Morris, J. Meade Falkner, A. Hope Hawkins, E. F. Benson, Siegfried Sassoon, and Charles Sorley were educated at the College.

F. W. Farrar, author of *Eric, or, Little by Little* (1858), and an assistant master in 1854, was master from 1871 to 1876. E. F. Benson's school story *David Blaize* (1915) is about Marlborough College. Charles Sorley, who was killed at the battle of Loos in 1915, wrote of local places such as Barbary Camp and Liddington Castle (the favourite places of Richard Jefferies, whom he admired) in *Marlborough and Other Poems* (1916). Writing

from France in 'I have not brought my Odyssey' he thinks of his return here:

> And soon, O soon, I do not doubt it,
> With the body or without it,
> We shall all come tumbling down
> To our old wrinkled red-capped town.
> Perhaps the road up Ilsley way,
> The old ridge-track, will be my way.

Many of his poems had appeared in the College magazine, *The Marlburian*.

John Betjeman was an unhappy pupil at Marlborough College in the early 1920s. His contemporary Louis MacNeice remembered him as 'a mine of useless information and a triumphant misfit. 'Thank God I'll never have to go through that again,' he wrote when he left. He was followed some decades later by the travel writer and novelist Bruce Chatwin.

William Golding's father taught at Marlborough Grammar School, which is where Golding himself was educated in the 1920s. They lived at 29 The Green.

MELLS *Somerset*

Stone-built village on a minor road 3 m. NW of Frome. The Tudor Manor House, formerly the property of the Benedictine abbey of Glastonbury, was acquired by the Horner family on the dissolution of the monasteries in 1539. John Horner, bailiff to the last abbot, is said to be the original of 'Little Jack Horner' of the nursery rhyme. Canon J. O. Hannay ('George A. Birmingham') was rector here from 1924 to 1934 and is commemorated in the church by a bust over the choir vestry door. Evelyn Waugh took rooms in the village in the 1930s while he was writing the biography *Edmund Campion* (1935). His friend Christopher Hollis lived here at Little Claveys for many years until his death in 1977. His writings include *Foreigners Aren't Fools* (1936), *Foreigners Aren't Knaves* (1939), *Death of a Gentleman* (1943), *A Study of George Orwell* (1956), *The Seven Ages* (autobiography, 1974), and *Oxford in the Twenties* (1976).

Monsignor Ronald Knox lived at the Manor House from 1947 until his death in 1957 as chaplain to the Asquith family. Here he completed his translation of the Old Testament (1949) (the translation of the New Testament having been published in 1945), and finished *Enthusiasm: A Chapter in the History of Religion with a special reference to the XVII and XVIII Centuries* (1950). He also prepared his Romanes Lecture 'On English Translation' (1957) and translated the autobiography of St Theresa of Lisieux. He is buried on the E side of the churchyard, his gravestone inscribed 'Priest, Scholar, Preacher, and Writer'. Siegfried Sassoon, who died in 1967, is buried nearby.

MENABILLY *Cornwall*

17th-c. seafront house on St Austell Bay. In 1943, escaping the war, Daphne du Maurier and her children moved to Cornwall, taking the house called Menabilly, just around the bay from *Par. The house was the inspiration for a number of her novels. In the neglected state in which she first found it, Menabilly was the basis for 'Manderley' in the opening dream passage of *Rebecca* (1938): 'Last night I dreamt I went to Manderley again.' The discovery in the 19th c. of the skeleton of a cavalier, walled up in a hiding place near the old kitchen since the English Civil War, gave her the idea for *The King's General* (1946). The house was also the main setting for her mystery-romance *My Cousin Rachel* (1951). The sight of gulls following a plough nearby gave du Maurier the idea for her famous story 'The Birds' (1952).

MERE *Wiltshire*

Village on the A303, 10 m. SW of Warminster. The Dorset poet William Barnes was a schoolmaster here from 1823 to 1835. He married Julia Miles in 1827 and transferred his school to the old Chantry House, adjoining the churchyard, which was their home until they went back to Dorchester.

MEVAGISSEY *Cornwall*

Village, fishing port, and tourist destination. The little town gives its name to Charles Causley's visionary poem in which 'The seagulls came in through the ceiling | The fish flew up through the floor.' Susan Cooper holidayed in Mevagissey as a child, and based Trewissick (in her *Dark is Rising* fantasy sequence) on it.

MILSTON *Wiltshire*

Village off the A345, 4 m. N of Amesbury. Joseph Addison was born (1652) at his father's vicarage (rebuilt, now Addison House) and baptized in the old flint church.

MINSTERWORTH *Gloucestershire*

Village on the right bank of the river Severn, 5 m. W of Gloucester. The folk poet Frederick William Harvey (1888–1957) was brought up here at The Redlands, a house set back from the road opposite the Apple Tree inn. His best-known poem, 'Ducks', was written in a prison camp in Germany during the First World War. By profession a solicitor in Lydney, he lived from 1926 at High View in Yorkley in the Forest of Dean. He was buried in the graveyard of Minsterworth parish church and there is a commemorative tablet in Gloucester Cathedral. *Collected Poems of F. W. Harvey* was published in 1983.

MORETON *Dorset*

Little village in the Frome valley, 1 m. E of the B3390. T. E. Lawrence is buried in the new cemetery, on the opposite side of the road from the turning to the church. He had been living at *Clouds Hill and died (May 1935) after a motorcycle accident.

MORWENSTOW *Cornwall*

Large parish comprising the scattered hamlets of Woodford, Shop, Crosstown, and others, *c.* 6–7 m. N of Bude, reached by minor roads from the A39. Robert Stephen Hawker, the eccentric parson-poet, was vicar here from 1835 to 1874. He restored the church, which had had no resident incumbent for over 100 years, and

built the vicarage, with an inscription in Old English lettering over the door:

> A House, a Glebe, a Pound a Day,
> A Pleasant Place to Watch and Pray;
> Be true to Church, Be kind to Poor,
> O Minister, for evermore.

His great poetic achievement was *The Quest of the Sangraal* (1863), which he is thought to have written in the hut which he built of timber from wrecks, dragged up from the rocks below, on the edge of the 450-ft Vicarage Cliff (NT). But his best-known work is 'The Song of the Western Men', which he wrote as an undergraduate, staying on vacation (1825) at Coombe Cottage on the S border of the parish. He said that he wrote it 'under a stag-horned oak in Sir Bevil's Walk in Stowe Wood'. It was printed anonymously in the *Royal Devonport Telegraph and Plymouth Chronicle*, where it was noticed by Davies Gilbert, President of the Royal Society, and sent to the *Gentleman's Magazine* as a supposedly ancient traditional ballad. Scott referred to it, Macaulay quoted it, and Dickens reprinted it in *Household Words*, but the author long remained 'unnoted and unknown'.

Patricia Beer's poem 'Parson Hawker's Farewell' imagines the old poet's defiant leave-taking of life. In 'Morwenstow', Charles Causley asks of the ravenous sea:

> When will you rest, sea?
> *When moon and sun*
> *Ride only fields of salt water*
> *And the land is gone.*

MUDEFORD (pr. 'Mŭddiford) *Dorset*

Village on the coast 2 m. E of Christchurch. The last house in the road to Avon Beach, no. 175, was built in the style of a Persian tent by William Stuart Rose (1775–1818), MP for Christchurch and a poet. It is part of a complex of houses called Gundimore, and Rose lived there on and off for 18 years, during which time it was a focal point for poets, artists, and politicians. The round house was named after Sir Walter Scott, who stayed there briefly in 1807 while he was writing *Marmion*. Coleridge and Southey were also visitors.

MUSBURY *Devon*

Village on the A358, 4 m. NE of Seaton Bay. Cecil Day-Lewis moved in 1938 from *Cheltenham to Brimclose here. In *The Buried Day* (1960), he describes his pleasure in the countryside. He was on the edge of Hardy country here and his pastoral poems show an affinity with Hardy. As the Second World War progressed Day-Lewis resigned from the Communist Party (which he had joined in 1936) and left the area to spend most of the war years in London, where he worked for the Ministry of Information.

MYLOR *Cornwall*

Little village on Mylor Creek, off the Truro estuary, *c.* 2 m. ENE of Penryn. Katherine Mansfield and John Middleton Murry took a cottage here in 1916 after leaving D. H. Lawrence and Frieda at *Zennor. It was a

pleasant and peaceful place, with a kitchen garden running down to the water's edge, but Katherine was restless and made frequent trips to London as well as visiting Lady Ottoline Morrell at *Garsington. Murry spent much time on his own, reading and reviewing French books for *The Times Literary Supplement*. Later in the year he was taken on as a translator in a department of the War Office in London and Katherine went to live in *Chelsea, not far from where he had rooms.

Howard Spring came to live at Mylor in 1939, in a bungalow on Hooper's Hill, looking down the creek. Here he finished *Fame Is the Spur* (1940) and wrote the second part of his autobiography, *In the Meantime* (1942), and *Hard Facts* (1944), a novel set mainly in Manchester. His funeral service was held in the Church of St Mylor (after his death in Falmouth, 1965) and his ashes were laid in the N side of the churchyard where an ancient sundial has been restored in his memory.

NAILSWORTH *Gloucestershire*

Market town on the A46, 5 m. S of Stroud, the final home of the 'super-tramp' W. H. Davies, where, in his own words, he could be 'near to Wales but . . . not haunted by any sort of trail from his past'. He came here in 1931 and, after one or two moves, settled for the rest of his days in Glendower ℗, a low, two-storey cottage overlooking the valley on the narrow road to Watledge.

NETHERAVON *Wiltshire*

Village off the A345, 5 m. N of Amesbury. In 1794 Sydney Smith obtained the curacy of Netheravon, and became tutor to the son of the squire, Michael Hicks-Beach, whom he subsequently accompanied to Edinburgh. The house became a barracks.

NETHER STOWEY *Somerset*

Village on the A39, 8 m. W of Bridgwater. In the winter of 1796 Coleridge, his wife, Sara, and their son, moved to a small thatched cottage in Lime St. (now tiled, enlarged, and called Coleridge Cottage; NT) found for him by his friend Thomas Poole, whose garden joined the cottage garden. Coleridge visited Wordsworth at Racedown and in deciding to rent the house at Alfoxden, Dorothy Wordsworth wrote in her *Journal* that their 'principal inducement was Coleridge's society'. Wordsworth and Coleridge agreed to combine to publish a collection of their verse, the former providing simple subjects such as 'Simon Lee the Old Huntsman' and 'Lines Composed Above Tintern Abbey' and the latter providing the 'supernatural or at least romantic' characters with 'The Ancient Mariner' and 'The Foster Mother's Tale'. Joseph Cottle, who published the collection as *The Lyrical Ballads* (1798), mentions his visit in *Early Recollections of Southey and Coleridge* (1837). During Lamb's stay in 1797, Sara spilled boiling milk over Coleridge's foot, and while incapacitated he wrote 'This Lime Tree Bower My Prison' in the garden as Lamb and Wordsworth were out walking; the lime tree is no longer there. Hazlitt first met Wordsworth here. The Wordsworths and Coleridge were regarded with suspicion locally because of their nocturnal walks with camp stools and notebooks. Unusual northern accents and Dorothy's brown complexion led to the belief that they were French spies, and an investigator from the Home Office arrived at The Globe inn (later Globe House) next to Poole's house. Servants gave evidence of talk about 'Spy Noza' when the friends gathered at table, but at length the investigator told his superiors he thought them harmless cranks. The poets left Stowey in 1798 to tour Germany. Thomas Poole is commemorated in the church, where a tablet states he was a friend of Coleridge, Wordsworth, and Southey. Coleridge called Poole his 'anchor'.

NEWQUAY Cornwall

Fishing village turned tourist resort and Britain's surfing capital. William Golding was born in 1911 at 47 Mount Wise, now the Blenheim Hotel.

NEWTON ABBOT Devon

Market town and tourist centre at the junction of the A380 and several other main roads, *c.* 5 m. from the coast. Sir Arthur Quiller Couch was educated at Newton Abbot College before going to Clifton College, *Bristol.

NEWTON TONEY Wiltshire

Village off the A338, 9 m. NE of Salisbury. Celia Fiennes was born at the Manor House (gone), from where she set off on many of the rides recounted in her journal, of which an incomplete version was published in 1888 under the title *Through England on a Side Saddle in the Time of William and Mary*. A definitive edition, *The Journeys of Celia Fiennes*, edited by Christopher Morris, was published in 1947.

NORTH NIBLEY Gloucestershire

Village 8 m. SW of Nailsworth, on the A4135, which honours William Tyndale, who was a native of Gloucestershire. A tower, from which a good view can be had of the Severn estuary, was erected on the hill overlooking the village in 1866, commemorating his first translation of the Bible into English and his death at the stake in Vilvorde in 1536. The path to the tower climbs through beech woods to the level turf above.

NORTH TAWTON Devon

Small town on the river Taw. The end of 1961 saw Ted Hughes and Sylvia Plath living here, at Court Green—it was here that their son Nicholas was born. Hughes's poem 'Error' begins:

> I brought you to Devon. I brought you into my
>   dreamland.
> I sleepwalked you
> Into my land of totems. Never-never land:
> The orchard in the West.

During this period Plath was beginning the work that would come to be her collection *Ariel*. Hughes and Plath would separate in

1962. After Plath's suicide in London (Fitzroy St., *Chalk Farm) in February 1963, Hughes returned to Court Green, to be joined in 1965 by Assia Weaver and their daughter Shura. The following year Hughes's parents moved into the house too.

Hughes's ashes were scattered on Dartmoor, and a memorial stone erected above the Taw near Belstone (there is a memorial walk today).

OARE Somerset

Village off the A39, midway between Lynton and Porlock. The small church has a tablet with a relief portrait commemorating the centenary of the birth (1825) of R. D. Blackmore, author of the novel *Lorna Doone* (1869). Blackmore, whose grandfather was the rector (1809–42), set scenes in the novel in the neighbourhood. 'Plovers Barrows Farm', home of the hero John Ridd, is said to be Oareford. Farmer Snow is based on the 17th-c. Nicholas Snow of Oare Farm (now Manor), who is buried in Oare church ℗, where Lorna Doone was shot at her wedding. Blackmore is said to have written part of the novel at Parsonage Farm where, as well as at Yenworthy Farm, he set one of the Doone raids. A path from Malmsmead along Badgworthy (pr. Badgery) Water, passes a plaque erected in 1969 to commemorate the centenary of the publication of *Lorna Doone*, and leads to the combe now known as Doone Valley. Nearby Hoccombe Combe has ruins of houses said to have been occupied in the 17th c. by Doones.

ODCOMBE Somerset

Village off the A3088, 4 m. W of Yeovil. The church has a vivid modern E window and a facsimile of the title page of Thomas Coryate's *Crudities* (1611), the story of his travels, mainly on foot, through Europe. An account of his life hangs under the tower where the shoes he wore hung until their decay in 1702. Coryate (1577?–1617) was born in the Elizabethan rectory which stood near the church. His last journey in 1612 took him through Mesopotamia to India, where he died.

ORCHARDLEIGH PARK Somerset

Mansion, home of the Duckworth family, N of Frome. The entrance is on the A362, *c.* 5 m. NW of Frome, just beyond the railway bridge. Sir Henry Newbolt is buried in the churchyard of the small island church, which is situated in a lake in the grounds. The church, probably dating from the 13th c. (restored 1879), is reached by a bridge at the W end of a sheltered lake and contains stone carvings and 15th–16th-c. stained glass of great interest. A poem by Geoffrey Swain pays tribute to Sir Henry Newbolt:

> Most English Poet of our Poets' Race!
> A son of Clifton's School, where lives his fame;

and there is a memorial tablet on the N wall to him and his wife, Margaret (née Duckworth) of Orchardleigh. At the E end of the churchyard, overlooking the water, two simple stones mark their graves. Orchardleigh is described in his

historical romance *The Old Country* (1906), where it is called 'Gardenleigh'. Cars are not admitted, but the 2 m. walk along public footpaths to the church is rewarding, although sometimes muddy.

OTTERY ST MARY Devon

Market town on the Otter, S of the A30 between Exeter and Honiton. Alexander Barclay (1475?–1552), poet, scholar, and divine, probably of Scottish origin, translated Sebastian Brandt's *Narrenschiff* (1494) into English as *The Ship of Fools* (1509) when a priest at the college founded by Bishop Grandison in 1337. His version was a free adaptation of the original, which had been written first in Swabian dialect and then in Latin, and he intended it as a satire of contemporary English life and its corruptions and abuses.

William Browne of Tavistock spent his last years and died here (1645), though no memorial of him remains. According to Southey, who visited the church in 1796, two epitaphs in St Stephen's Chapel are by Browne.

Samuel Taylor Coleridge was born on 21 October 1772 at the schoolhouse, the 13th and youngest child of the Revd John Coleridge, vicar 1760–81, and master of the Grammar School. After his father's death the 9-year-old boy went to Christ's Hospital, London (see LONDON: CITY). He wrote a sonnet 'To the River Otter' and remembered his birthplace and the music of the church bells in 'Frost at Midnight' (Feb. 1798). A memorial plaque on the churchyard wall has a low-relief bust and portrays the albatross from 'The Rime of the Ancient Mariner' (1798).

A. W. Kinglake went to the Grammar School before going to Eton. Ottery St Mary appears as 'Clavering St. Mary' in Thackeray's *Pendennis* (1848–50).

PADSTOW Cornwall

Picturesque resort, formerly a port, on the A389, on the estuary of the Camel. On South Quay is Ralegh's Court House, where Sir Walter Ralegh held court when he was Warden of Cornwall (from 1585).

D. H. Lawrence came here after leaving London in December 1915 and stayed at his friend J. D. Beresford's house, Porthcothan, St Merryn (2 m. W, on the B3276), until the following March. He had plans (which never materialized) to settle in Florida with a group of like-minded people, and this was meant to be the first step on the way. 'The wind blows very hard,' he wrote; 'the sea all comes up the cliffs in smoke.' In January they had a visit from Dikrān Kouyoumdjian, the Bulgarian novelist who became a naturalized British citizen in 1922 and changed his name to Michael Arlen. In *Women in Love* (1920) Arlen is lampooned as a minor character.

PAIGNTON Devon

Seaside resort, with a small harbour, overlooking Tor Bay, on the A379 and the A3022. The 14th-c. Coverdale Tower, which was part of the palace belonging to the bishops of Exeter, was once thought to be where Miles Coverdale stayed while working on his translation of the Bible, but this is now regarded as an exploded myth, originating in some anonymous guidebook. Coverdale was appointed by Edward VI, on account of 'his extraordinary knowledge of divinity and his unblemished character', to be assistant to Vesey, the last Bishop of Exeter to hold Paignton, but it is doubtful whether he ever visited the town.

PAINSWICK *Gloucestershire*

Village on the A46, 3 m. NE of Stroud. Sydney Dobell, who died in 1874, spent the last years of his life at Barton End House, Horsley (8 m. SW) and his grave in the churchyard here has a Celtic cross. James Elroy Flecker, whose home was in *Cheltenham, mentions Cranham (3 m. NE), where he spent some months in a sanatorium in 1910 after the diagnosis of tuberculosis, and Painswick Hill in the poem 'Oak and Olive' from *The Old Ships* (1915).

PAR *Cornwall*

Fishing village 4 m. E of St Austell. In 1969 Daphne du Maurier moved from *Menabilly down the road to Kilmarth on the Par seaside, where she remained for the rest of her life. The 14th-c. foundations of the house which had previously occupied the site gave her the idea for her novel *The House on the Strand* (1969). The house of the title was in fact Tiwardrai, a vanished manor house close to *Tywardreath near Par. She died at Kilmarth on 19 April 1989, was cremated, and her ashes scattered on the cliffs nearby.

PENRYN *Cornwall*

Ancient town at the head of Penryn Creek, on the A39. Shortly after her marriage in 1817 Mrs Pendarves (later Mrs Delany) came to live at her husband's home, the manor of Roscrow (demolished 1890), overlooking Falmouth harbour and Pendennis Castle. Her marriage was not happy and the house, which she called 'Averno' because its situation made her think of Italy, was 'old, damp, and poorly furnished, with floor boards pulled up to get at the rats', but she enjoyed the company of her brother Bunny, with whom she explored the neighbourhood on horseback. They rode together on the sands and gathered shells—a pastime which led to the making of the 'shell-pictures' for which she became renowned.

PENZANCE *Cornwall*

Seaport and holiday resort situated on the NW of Mount's Bay, on the A30. In July 1820 Mrs Piozzi, having recently celebrated her 80th birthday in Bath, came here to recoup her depleted finances, hoping to enjoy warm sea bathing and economical living. Accommodation was hard to find and she was obliged to take a little 'nutshell of a cottage'. Although she missed the social amenities of Bath, she achieved her object of settling her debts: '*No Milliner's Shop*,' she wrote, '*no

Rooms, *no* Theatre, *no* Music Meeting—*no* Pleasure, but *no* Expence. I had too much of *both* the last Winter at Bath.' The following spring she decided to return to civilization and reached Clifton (see BRISTOL) on 18 March.

John Davidson, Scottish poet and schoolmaster, spent his last years here. Depressed by poverty and ill health he drowned himself near Penzance and when his body was recovered he was buried at sea.

In a house on the Cornish coast near Penzance the young cousins of Mary Wesley's *The Camomile Lawn* (1984) meet for their last innocent summer before the outbreak of war:

> Waiting for the midnight train, which was late, Calypso shivered as she walked along the platform. She remembered Polly's suggestion that this might be their last holiday. She and her cousins had been coming every summer for ten years, ever since Helena married Richard and bought the house, square and ugly but in a marvellous position. Every August since she was Sophy's age she had come with Polly, Walter and Oliver to bathe, climb cliffs and over-eat at Helena's expense, treating the house as their own, then vanish like a flock of starlings . . .

The Morrab Library on Morrab Rd, one of only 19 independent libraries in the UK, has a collection of rare Cornish books and prints; day tickets available.

PERRANARWORTHAL *Cornwall*

Village halfway between Truro and Falmouth. Two years after winning the Nobel Prize for Literature in 1983 the novelist William Golding moved to Tullimaar, a large regency house situated in the woods above the road as you approach the village from Truro. He wrote *Close Quarters* (1987) and *Fire Down Below* (1989), the sequels to *Rites of Passage* (1980), here. He died here in 1993.

PHILLACK *Cornwall*

Village off the A30, *c.* 1 m. NE of Hayle. Compton Mackenzie lived at Rivière House with his parents from 1908 to 1913, during which time he published his first novel, *The Passionate Elopement* (1911), which was followed by *Carnival* (1912). He also finished the last chapter of vol. I of *Sinister Street* (2 vols, 1913–14).

PICKWICK *Wiltshire*

Village on the A4 between Bath and Chippenham, consisting of one main street, now part of NW Corsham. Dickens stayed at the historic Hare and Hounds while he was writing *The Pickwick Papers* (1836) and the inn has several items of 'Pickwickiana'.

PILTON *Devon*

Village 1 m. N of Barnstaple. Hector Hugh Munro ('Saki') was brought up here from the age of 2. His mother had died soon after his birth in Burma, and his father, an Inspector-General of Police, took a house, Broadgate Villa, where Hector and his brother and sister lived with his paternal grandmother and two

aunts. The grandmother was gentle and dignified, but Aunt Augusta and Aunt Tom, vividly described in the biography of Saki by his sister in *The Square Egg* (1924), dominated the house with their fierce quarrels and jealousies. Aunt Augusta, the autocrat, was a woman of ungovernable temper and a moral coward, the last person who should have been in charge of children. She is depicted, 'more or less', according to her niece, in 'Sredni Vashtar' (*Chronicles of Clovis*, 1911), and 'to the life' in 'The Lumber-Room' (*Beasts and Super-Beasts*, 1914). Broadgate Villa, now two houses, Fairmead and Fairfield, is on the corner of Bellaire and Bellaire Drive, NW of the church, a pleasant building with a balcony over a pillared veranda, no longer shut in by the high walls of Saki's time.

PIMPERNE *Dorset*

Village on the A354, 2 m. NE of Blandford Forum. Christopher Pitt, a minor 18th-c. poet whom Dr Johnson included in his *Lives of the English Poets* (1779–81), was rector here from 1722 until his death in 1748.

PLYMOUTH *Devon*

One of the chief seaports of England, known as Sutton in the Domesday Book and by its present name since 1439, situated at the head of Plymouth Sound, at the mouths of the Plym and the Tamar. The adjacent towns of Stonehouse and Devonport were combined with Plymouth in 1914 and the three became a city in 1928. It suffered extensive bombing in the Second World War and rebuilding has replaced many buildings of historic interest.

The theologian Joseph Glanvill (1636–80) was born here (site unrecorded), the son of a merchant. He became rector of the Abbey Church, *Bath.

N. T. Carrington (1777–1830), a Devon poet, was born in Old-Town St. (gone). His first names have sometimes been given as Noel Thomas, but according to local records he was named Nicholas Toms after his father's stepfather. Soon after his birth his parents moved to Plymouth Dock (now Devonport) and here he spent his boyhood. After he left school he became a dockyard apprentice, but found it uncongenial and ran away to sea. He was present at the Battle of Cape St Vincent and then returned to his parents, settled down as a schoolmaster, and in 1809 established his own academy. He wrote poetry as a leisure occupation and contributed occasional pieces to magazines and annuals. His poem 'Dartmoor' narrowly missed the Royal Society of Literature prize in 1826, but he was awarded 50 guineas by George IV. His popular *Teignmouth, Dawlish and Torquay Guide* (1810) has been frequently reprinted.

Robert Stephen Hawker, author of 'The Song of the Western Men', was born (3 Dec. 1803) at 6 Morley St., the vicarage of Charles Church (now only a shell since the bombing), where his grandfather was incumbent, and baptized (29 Dec. 1803) in the parish of Stoke Damerel (now part of the city, to the NW), when his father was curate there. He spent most of his life as vicar of *Morwenstow, but was buried at Plymouth, in Ford Park cemetery, off Ford Park Rd. His grave, near the northern end of the cemetery, is marked by a granite cross.

Henry Austin Dobson, poet and essayist, was born (18 Jan. 1840) at Plymouth, the son of an engineer, and educated at Beaumaris Grammar School and at Strasbourg before entering the Board of Trade. Plymouth was the native town of Hardy's first wife, Emma, and he had a great affection for it. His poem 'The West-of-Wessex Girl' (begun in Plymouth, Mar. 1913, four months after her death) laments the fact that they were never there together:

> Yet now my West-of-Wessex girl,
> When midnight hammers slow
> From Andrew's, blow by blow,
> As phantom draws me by the hand
> To the place—Plymouth Hoe—
> Where side by side in life, as planned,
> We never were to go!

Other natives include J. C. Squire (1884–1958), who was educated at the Grammar School before going to Blundell's at *Tiverton, and L. A. G. Strong (1896–1958), whose Devon upbringing inspired *Dewer Rides* (1929), a Dartmoor story whose success encouraged him to give up teaching for novel-writing.

Charles Causley's nautical years lay behind his sailors' poem 'Plymouth'. A similar background inspired his ballad 'Devonport':

> Blithely O blithely the casual morning
> Burned life away as the leaf on a tree,
> Rolling the sun like a mad hoop beside me,
> And down at the end of the alley, the sea.

POLPERRO *Cornwall*

Fishing village on the S coast. Hugh Walpole rented The Cobbles, a cottage overlooking the harbour, from 1913 to 1921. His good friend Henry James expressed his interest in 'a very pleasant and convenient and solid old Desk, with capacious table and drawers and pigeon-holes etc.', followed shortly by a little mirror, from which he hoped the donor's 'battered old mug' would glimmer out in some dim benefaction. During some of his frequent visits to The Cobbles, Walpole planned and worked on *The Green Mirror* (1918).

PORLOCK *Somerset*

Former port, now a resort, on the A39, visited by William and Dorothy Wordsworth and Coleridge in 1797, and in 1799 by Southey, who stayed at The Ship and wrote some lines by the alehouse fire. A road off the A39 at the top of Porlock Hill leads to Ash Farm, where tradition says Coleridge, after a dream, wrote 'Kubla Khan' until interrupted by a 'person . . . from Porlock' (Broomstreet Farm off the A39 also has a claim). In the novel *Lorna Doone* (1869) by R. D. Blackmore, John Ridd and his father, who was later ambushed and killed at the top of Porlock Hill, often came here.

PORTHCURNO *Cornwall*

Coastal village 3 m. from Land's End. Bertrand Russell spent long periods in the mid-1920s at Carn Voel, an isolated house not far from the village. They were, as a letter to Lady Ottoline Morrell suggests, among the happiest of his life:

> It is lovely here—the birds sing all day—there are larks & thrushes & blackbirds & cuckoos & curlews & seagulls all round the house & ships sail by, & at night one hears the sea in the distance booming on the rocks, & there is blackthorn & whitethorn & bluebells & buttercups, & green fields & gorse moors, all without stirring from the house.

PORTLAND, ISLE OF *Dorset*

Rocky limestone peninsula, 4 m. long by 1 m. wide, reached by the A354 S of Weymouth. Hardy called it 'the Gibraltar of Wessex' and in *The Well-Beloved* (1897) it figures as 'the Isle of Slingers'. Off the rocky headland of Portland Bill in the south William Wordsworth's brother John, captain of the East Indiaman *Abergavenny*, was lost when it went down in February 1805. Wordsworth was deeply affected by the tragedy, which seems to have been one of the heaviest blows of his life. His poems 'Character of the Happy Warrior' and 'Elegiac Stanzas' commemorate his brother.

POXWELL *Dorset*

Village on the A353, 7 m. NE of Weymouth. Poxwell Manor, a stone-mullioned house built in 1654, may be seen from the churchyard gate (the church has been demolished). It was possibly Hardy's model for Squire Derriman's 'Oxwell Hall' in *The Trumpet-Major* (1880).

PRIOR PARK *Somerset*

Palladian mansion 1 m. SE of Bath, built (1743) by John Wood for Ralph Allen. Pope, a lifelong correspondent and a guest here, advised Allen on his pictures and statues, and wrote:

> Let humble Allen with an awkward shame
> Do good by stealth, and blush to find it fame.

Fielding, who also visited, was an early recipient of Allen's good will and made him a model for Squire Allworthy in *Tom Jones* (1749). In 1833 Tom Moore visited the house (now a Catholic school) with his wife and sister.

PUDDLETOWN *Dorset*

Village on the A35 and the A354, 5 m. NE of Dorchester. This was the 'Weatherbury' of Hardy's *Far From the Madding Crowd* (1874), though the village is much changed since the date of the novel and it is rash to try to identify all the features in the story. Bathsheba Everdene's farmhouse, described as on a hill west of the church, 'not more than a quarter of a mile' away, is regarded as being modelled on Waterston Manor, Lower Waterston, an Elizabethan house nearly 2 m. NW in the Piddle valley, on a minor road off the B3134 to Druce.

RACEDOWN LODGE *Dorset*

Three-storey Georgian house (now a farmhouse) near the village of Bettiscombe on the B3165 Crewkerne-Lyme Regis road, on high ground facing westward below Pilsdon Pen (909 ft, the highest hill in Dorset). It was the property of John Pinney, a retired sugar merchant, who settled in Bristol in the 1780s and rebuilt and furnished it (it was previously called Pilsmarsh, or Pylemarsh, Lodge). His son John Frederick, a friend and admirer of Wordsworth, offered it, with his father's approval, as a home for William and his sister Dorothy. The Wordsworths arrived in September 1795 and stayed until June 1797 and here for the first time realized their longed-for idea of living together and sharing the experiences of daily life. They had with them Basil Montagu, the young son of a London friend of Wordsworth, whose wife had lately died. The child, who was under 3 when he arrived, benefited from Dorothy's affectionate and sensible management and after six months she wrote that he was her 'perpetual pleasure . . . quite metamorphosed from a shivering half-starved plant, to a lusty, blooming, fearless boy'.

Wordsworth's time at Racedown was a vitally important stage in his career. Here, while living on money bequeathed to him by his friend Raisley Calvert, and sustained by Dorothy's faith in him, he recovered his own belief in himself as a poet, after a period of doubt and lack of self-confidence. In London he had been unsettled and had written little; now he came back to Nature, his 'first love'. In Book XI of *The Prelude* he looks back to the Racedown years and Dorothy,

> the beloved woman in whose sight
> Those days were pass'd . . .
> She, in the midst of all, preserv'd me still
> A Poet, made me seek beneath that name
> My office upon earth, and nowhere else.

and the renewal of his communion with Nature:

> And lastly, Nature's self, by human love
> Assisted, through the weary labyrinth
> Conducted me again to open day,
> Revived the feelings of my earlier life,
> Gave me that strength and knowledge full of
>   peace,
> Enlarged, and never more to be disturbed.

His first writing at Racedown was the revision of 'Salisbury Plain', a long narrative poem about war and poverty, a bitter indictment of social injustice. In the autumn of 1796 he began his blank-verse tragedy *The Borderers*, a play which was rejected as unsuitable for acting. By the following spring he was steadily writing poetry, including 'Lines Left Upon a Seat in a Yew-Tree', and 'The Ruined Cottage'. There was a visit from Mary Hutchinson, who shared Dorothy's excitement and helped to copy out poems. After she left (in June) Coleridge arrived and the two poets spent much time in reading aloud each other's work. Then the Wordsworths went back with Coleridge to his cottage at *Nether Stowey, from which they moved to *Alfoxton Park.

REDRUTH *Cornwall*

Former copper-mining and market town. The poet, novelist, and translator D. M. Thomas was educated at Redruth Grammar School in the 1950s.

RINGMORE *Devon*

Small village *c.* 4 m. S of Modbury, on a minor road off the A379. R. C. Sherriff wrote *Journey's End*, his play about the First World War, produced in 1929, while here. The village pub, where he stayed, is named after the play.

ROZEL *Jersey*

Fishing port on the N Jersey coast. The dictionary maker John Lemprière was born and brought up here in a house at Rozel; so it features in Lawrence Norfolk's novel based on his life, *Lemprière's Dictionary* (1991).

RUSH-HAY *Dorset*

Smallholding in the parish of Bagber, a hamlet 2 m. W of Sturminster Newton, on the A357 at the Bagber Common turn. This was the birthplace of William Barnes, the Dorset poet, schoolmaster, and clergyman. He attended the village dame school until he was old enough to go to the church school at *Sturminster Newton and make the daily walk there and back across the common.

ST AUSTELL *Cornwall*

China clay mining and brewing town. The historian, poet, and man of letters A. L. Rowse was born at Tregonissey in 1903, the son of a china clay worker. He describes his escape from humble origins via St Austell Grammar School to a scholarship to Christ Church, *Oxford, and a Fellowship at All Souls, in his autobiography *A Cornish Childhood* (1942). In 1973 he retired to his Cornish home at nearby Trenarren, where he continued to write a flow of books, articles, and poetry. A memorial stone to Rowse stands at Black Head, overlooking St Austell Bay.

The poet Jack Clemo was born at Goonamaris, St Stephen, in 1916. The industrial landscape around the town, excavated for china clay, provided the inspiration for many of his poems, including 'Tregargus', 'The Flooded Clay-Pit', and 'The Water Wheel':

> The plashy ground turns white
> With clay-silt from the wheel,
> And still the trough pours on to smite
> Both wood and iron, to seal
> The dream-world with the real.

ST ENODOC *Cornwall*

Hamlet on the E side of the Camel estuary, *c.* 5 m. SE of the village of Rock, reached by ferry from Padstow, or from Wadebridge by a turning off the B3314. It is the setting for Sabine Baring-Gould's novel *In the Roar of the Sea* (1892), a tale about wreckers on the Cornish coast. The little 15th-c. church, near the golf course, now recovered from the sand dunes which once enveloped it, is described in

The grave of Sir John Betjeman at St Enodoc

the opening chapter. Peter Trevisa, the rector, dies exhausted after his unavailing efforts to clear away the sand which restricts entry to the church to a hole in a window. Sir John Betjeman is buried in the churchyard. He spent his holidays locally and stayed in nearby *Trebetherick. The place prompted him to write 'Sunday Afternoon Service in St Enodoc Church, Cornwall' and 'By the Ninth Green, St Enodoc'.

Justin Cartwright's novel *The Promise of Happiness* (2004) begins on just this spot, with Charles Judd on the beach looking out to sea, watching a fishing boat coming up the Camel estuary towards Bray Hill; before heading on, though, he stops to relieve himself, and notices that he's standing beside a gravestone reading 'John Betjeman, 1906–1984'. 'He doesn't like the fancy-curlicued, arty script of the headstone. It seems to him to contain volumes of smugness; of taste; of self-congratulation.'

ST HELIER *Channel Islands*

Port and resort in Jersey. Edward Hyde, later 1st Earl of Clarendon, stayed (1646–8) in Elizabeth Castle with the young Prince Charles, whom he had brought here for safety. The Prince was soon sent to France and Hyde continued writing his *History of the Rebellion*, which he had begun in the *Scilly Isles.

Karl Marx visited Jersey many times between the 1850s and 1880s. In 1879 he stayed at the Hôtel de l'Europe, having forsaken the Trafalgar Hotel in St Aubin, which he abandoned because of the constant diet of mutton.

ST IVES *Cornwall*

Holiday resort and haunt of artists, formerly a pilchard-fishing town, situated on the W side of St Ives Bay, at the end of the A3074. Virginia Woolf (née Stephen) spent her summers here

as a child, at Talland House, a large white house in Talland Rd overlooking the harbour. Godrevy Lighthouse, on an island at the far side of the bay, was probably in her mind when she wrote *To the Lighthouse* (1927). Henry James stayed at the Tregenna Castle Hotel in August 1894 to be near the Stephens, 'the silent Stephen, the almost speechless Leslie', with whom he walked over the moors, and his beautiful wife, Julia. He visited Talland House and was struck by Virginia's delicate beauty.

Dorothy Richardson came here in 1912 at the invitation of John and Beatrice Beresford, who gave her the use of the chapel next to their cottage to write in. She met Hugh Walpole and they all went for walks on the cliffs. She wrote *Pointed Roofs* (1915), a novel at first rejected, but published later with the support of Edward Garnett.

ST JULIOT *Cornwall*

Church, known locally as St Jilt, 3 m. E of Boscastle, in the Valency valley, reached by a minor road (signposted to Lesnewth W of the A39) and up a steep hill N of the river. Thomas Hardy came here as a young architect in March 1870 to advise on the restoration of the church (which dates from 1450), and some of his drawings are still there. A little further on, a grassy road leads down to the Old Rectory (later a private house), where Hardy met Emma Gifford, the rector's sister-in-law, and fell in love with her. They married in 1874 and there is a memorial plaque to her in the church. The valley and the country around are recognizable, with a few minor alterations, as the Cornish scene of *A Pair of Blue Eyes* (1873): the church becomes 'St. Agnes's' in the parish of 'West Endelstow', and Lesnewth 'East Endelstow' (although it is in fact to the S).

ST LUKE'S *Channel Islands*

District near St Helier, the capital of Jersey, where Victor Hugo lived from 1852 to 1855 to escape the regime of Louis Napoleon. *Les Châtiments*, his verse satirizing the Second Empire, was published in 1853, and his house, Maison Victor Hugo, was subsequently converted into a hotel.

ST PETER PORT *Channel Islands*

Capital of Guernsey. Victor Hugo, an opponent of Louis Napoleon's regime in France, moved here from Jersey in 1855 and lived at 20 Hauteville. He then lived (1856–70) at Hauteville House (open to the public, www.victorhugo.gg), where he wrote his greatest and most popular novel, *Les Misérables* (1862), *Littérature et philosophie mêlées* (1864), *Chansons des rues et des bois* (1865), and *Les Travailleurs de la mer* (1866), an epic of the sea set in Guernsey. He is commemorated by a statue in Candie Gdns. In May 1876 Swinburne accompanied his friend John Nichol to Guernsey and *Sark. He came again to Guernsey in September 1882 and stayed here with Theodore Watts-Dunton, enchanted by all he saw, though disappointed by the absence of the Master (Hugo) for the

Statue of Victor Hugo by Jean Boucher in St Peter Port. It was given by France to Guernsey in 1914

second time. Swinburne's series of Channel Island poems includes 'In Guernsey' and 'The Statue of Victor Hugo' (both 1883).

ST STEPHEN *Cornwall*

Village on the A3058, 5 m. W of St Austell. The brothers Joseph Hocking (1850–1935) and Silas Hocking (1860–1937) were born here, the sons of a mine owner. Both were Methodist ministers and prolific novelists. Silas, whose first story, *Alec Green*, was published in 1878, achieved immense popularity with his novels, mainly on religious themes, and after holding pastorates in Liverpool, Manchester, and Southport, retired from the ministry in 1895 to devote himself to writing. Joseph spent some time in the Near East as a young man before settling as pastor in Woodford Green, Essex. He wrote about 50 novels between 1891 and 1936, some with Cornish settings, others with historical and religious themes.

SALCOMBE *Devon*

Resort and yachting centre at the end of the A381, beautifully situated on the steep W side of the wooded estuary of the Avon. J. A. Froude rented The Moult as a summer residence for many years, when he was living and working in London, and built a small yacht, which he sailed himself. Later he took Woodville (later Woodcot), where he retired in 1894 and died (20 Oct.) the same year. Both houses stand in

extensive grounds, between North and South Sands, on the road to Bolt Head. Froude is buried in the cemetery, on the other side of the town.

Tennyson's poem 'Crossing the Bar' is traditionally associated with his visit to Salcombe in May 1889. He was convalescing after an illness, cruising in a friend's yacht, which put in to the harbour so that he might stay with Froude. When he left, sitting on deck on a fine Sunday evening, the church bell was ringing for evensong, and he noticed how as the yacht reached the sandy bar the waves 'gave forth a surfy, slow, deep, mellow voice, and with a hollow moan crossed the bar on their way to the harbour'. The haunting impressions of the scene are recorded in the poem written the following October at *Farringford.

SALISBURY (pr. 'Sawlzbry) *Wiltshire*

Cathedral city 25 m. W of Winchester. John Foxe, who returned to England after Queen Elizabeth's accession, published his *Book of Martyrs* (1563) in the year he was made Canon of Salisbury. Philip Massinger, whose father was employed by the Herberts of *Wilton, was baptized in November 1583 at St Thomas's Church, but the record does not survive in the Diocesan Office in The Close. In 1668 Pepys, who was guided 'all over the plain by the sight of the steeple' of the Cathedral, was given a silk bed at The George inn (gone). He thought the town 'a very brave place' and noted that the 'river runs through every street' (a system of canals for water and drainage), before going sightseeing to *Stonehenge and Wilton. The heavy old timbers of The George inn now form the entrance to Old George Mall, where a plaque commemorating Pepys's visit is affixed. The Cathedral contains the diamond-shaped stone with William Browne's epitaph to the Countess of Pembroke (d. 1631), 'Sidney's sister, Pembroke's mother', and also a bust of Richard Jefferies (d. 1887), a native and a lover of Wiltshire. In the cathedral library there survives the sole autograph manuscript of Book III of William Browne's *Britannia's Pastorals*, bound in the back of a volume containing printed copies of Book I (1613) and Book II (1616), but which remained unpublished until the 19th c.

Trollope in his *Autobiography* (1883) recalls how, when 'wandering one midsummer evening round the purlieus of Salisbury Cathedral', he 'conceived the story of *The Warden*, from whence came the series of novels of which Barchester . . . was the central site'. Although Barchester was Winchester and the county of Barset was imaginary, *The Warden* was certainly inspired by his view of the city from the 'little bridge' near the Cathedral. Hardy called Salisbury 'Melchester' in his novels of Wessex.

William Golding taught at Bishop Wordsworth's School Ⓟ from 1940 to 1962 (with a break during Golding's period in the Royal Navy during the Second World War) under the shadow of the Cathedral, a formative influence on his novel *The Spire* (1964), which

tells the story of the obsessional Dean Jocelin and the building of the church's great phallic spire, 'springing, projecting, bursting, erupting from the heart of the building'. His teaching experience contributed to his knowledge of boys and to the writing of *Lord of the Flies* (1954), written while he taught at the school. He lived in the city from 1946 to 1958.

Kazuo Ishiguro's novel *The Remains of the Day* (1989) takes the butler Stevens on a driving tour across the south-west, from his home at Darlington Hall; his first stop, and the first part of the novel, takes place at Salisbury.

> I would suppose it was shortly after four o'clock that I left the guest house and ventured out into the streets of Salisbury. The wide, airy nature of the streets here give the city a marvellously spacious feel, so that I found it most easy to spend some hours just strolling in the gently warm sunshine. Moreover, I discovered the city to be one of many charms; time and again, I found myself wandering past delightful rows of old timber-fronted houses, or crossing some little stone footbridge over one of the many streams that flow through the city. And of course, I did not fail to visit the fine cathedral, much praised by Mrs Symons in her volume . . .

SALTRAM HOUSE *Devon*

Mansion (NT) built *c.* 1750, incorporating the remains of a Tudor house, in a landscaped park 4 m. E of Plymouth city centre, between the A38 and the A379. Dr Johnson sometimes visited here when he came with Sir Joshua Reynolds, who was a native of Plympton St Maurice nearby. Fanny Burney was also a visitor, and wrote (1789), 'the house is one of the most magnificent in the kingdom, its view is noble'.

SAPPERTON *Gloucestershire*

Village off the A419, 6 m. W of Cirencester. In 1933 John Masefield and his wife, who was recovering from a serious illness, came to live at

Fanny's Bower, Saltram House, Devon. Fanny Burney visited Saltram in 1789

Pinbury Park, an old Cotswold manor house, which had once been a nunnery. He loved living in the country, but did not find the local gentry and hunting set congenial and they on their part resented his unsympathetic portrayal of them in his novels *Eggs and Baker* (1935) and *The Square Peg* (1937). He and his wife left in early 1939.

SARK *Channel Islands*

Small island *c.* 8 m. E of Guernsey. Swinburne visited Sark in May 1876 while staying in Guernsey and wrote ecstatically to his mother, describing the landscape in rapturous terms and adding that among it all, 'we had a day and a half of the best scrambling I *ever* had in my life'. 'A Ballad of Sark' and 'Les Casquets' (both 1884) belong to his series of Channel Island poems.

Mervyn Peake fell in love with Sark on his first visit in 1933 with a group of young artists, who founded a colony and built the Sark Gallery, where each had a studio and shared a common life. After an interval in London he returned in 1938, with his wife, Maeve, for a delayed honeymoon, to find the Gallery closed and the members dispersed. After the war he and his family came to live in a large rented house called The Chalet, while he was writing *Gormenghast*, the successor to *Titus Groan* (1946). Although they were very happy, they had to return to London in 1949 in order to make ends meet. His comic allegory *Mr Pye* (1953) is set on the island.

SCILLY ISLES *Cornwall*

Group of *c.* 150 islands, five of which are inhabited, 28 m. SW of Land's End. Traditionally they are the remnants of the legendary Arthurian land of Lyonesse, supposed to be lying under the sea between them and the mainland.

Edward Hyde, later 1st Earl of Clarendon, came here on 4 March 1646 with the young Prince Charles and his council and stayed until 17 April, when they moved to *St Helier in Jersey because the Parliamentary fleet was threatening their safety. On 18 March, Hyde began *The History of the Rebellion and Civil Wars in England* (first published after his death by his son, 1702–4), which he continued at St Helier.

George Eliot and George Lewes visited St Mary's, the largest island, from March to May 1857 and lodged at the post office. She was writing *Mr. Gilfil's Love-Story* (published in *Scenes of Clerical Life*, 1858) and he was studying marine life for his *Seaside Studies at Ilfracombe, Tenby, the Scilly Isles, and Jersey* (1858).

The island of Samson, now uninhabited, was the setting for Sir Walter Besant's *Armorel of Lyonesse* (1890).

Sir Arthur Quiller-Couch gives a graphic account of the islands in the second half of the 19th c. in his romantic novel *Major Vigoureux* (1907).

Christopher Isherwood and Edward Upward holidayed in Hugh Town in 1926, where, as

Isherwood noted in his autobiography *Lions and Shadows* (1938), 'there was a good hotel with excellent beer and a waiter with discreet Mortmere tones, who murmured: 'Plenty of young *ladies* on this island, sir.'

The rocks of the Scillies, submerged in a darkness,

> where no comparisons are possible
> Miles below the fields
> That raise flowers like tissue paper
> And gorse like lions,

inspired Patricia Beer's poem 'Group of Islands'. These 'islands of dead hope' also moved Geoffrey Grigson to write his poem 'The Isles of Scilly'.

The Scilly Isles can be reached by boat or helicopter from *Penzance.

SEVENHAMPTON *Wiltshire*

Small village NE of Swindon. In 1960 the novelist Ian Fleming bought the demolished Warneford Place, moving in on the completion of the house in 1963. He died the following year and is buried at Sevenhampton church.

SHAFTESBURY *Dorset*

Ancient town on the A30 and the A350, situated on the edge of a 700–ft plateau, with extensive views over Blackmoor Vale. The town is well described in Hardy's *Jude the Obscure* (1895), where it appears under its old name of 'Shaston'. The railway station at Semley, *c.* 2 m. N of the town, is now closed.

SHARPHAM *Somerset*

Hamlet N of the A39 at Walton, 3 m. N of Street. Sharpham Park, an old manor house (with garden walls remaining from a demolished wing), now an organic farm, was the birthplace of Edward Dyer (1543), a friend of Philip Sidney. Dyer, who wrote elegies, was for a time regarded as the author of the lyric on contentment 'My mind to me a Kingdom is'. He held an official post in the county and died in 1607. A century later Henry Fielding was born in the same house (his mother's home) but spent only a short time there before his parents moved to East Stour.

SHAUGH PRIOR *Devon*

Village on a minor road, *c.* 5 m. NE of the centre of Plymouth. The church has a memorial in white marble, an inscription set in a Gothic arch, commemorating the Devon poet N. T. Carrington, a native of *Plymouth who loved this district. One of his favourite haunts was Shaugh Bridge, *c.* 1 m. NW, where the Plym and the Meavy meet, and shortly after his death some of his admirers had his name carved on the Dewerstone, a commanding rock overlooking the Plym just above the bridge.

SHEPTON MALLET *Somerset*

Small town near the Mendip Hills, 6 m. E of Wells. Auberon Waugh attended the preparatory school at Cranmore Hall and recalled its cruel and eccentric headmaster in his autobiography *Will This Do?* (1991):

He would insist . . . on being present at the weighing which occurred at the beginning of term. The whole school would be required to sit, naked, one by one on a red velvet weighing machine under the direction of the matron, while the headmaster smoked his pipe ruminatively above.

SHERBORNE *Dorset*

Ancient stone-built town on the A30, 6 m. E of Yeovil. It was the seat of a bishopric from 705 to 1078 and the chronicler Asser (d. 909?) was bishop here. During his episcopate he wrote a life of King Alfred in Latin (*c.* 893). In the N transept of the Abbey Church (the church of the former Benedictine abbey, which dates from the 15th c.) is a stone which is believed to mark the grave of the poet Sir Thomas Wyatt, who died of a fever here in the summer of 1542, when on his way to bring the imperial ambassador from Falmouth to London.

The old castle, now ruined, at the E end of the town, was leased by Queen Elizabeth I to Sir Walter Ralegh in 1592 and given to him in 1599. He attempted to modernize the building, but abandoned it in order to build the existing castle. A will made by Ralegh in July 1597 was discovered in the Digby estate office in Sherborne in the 1970s and reveals something of his style of living and his concern for his wife and heirs. The castle is mentioned in Hardy's *The Woodlanders* (1887) and is a central feature of Dame the Seventh in his *A Group of Noble Dames* (1891). Sherborne appears as 'Sherton Abbas'.

Sherborne School (founded 1550) incorporates the 15th-c. Abbot's Hall and other monastic buildings formerly belonging to the Abbey. Its distinguished pupils include Lewis Morris, the brothers John Cowper and Llewelyn Powys, and Cecil Day-Lewis. The school is featured in J. C. Powys's novel *Wolf Solent* (1929) and his *Autobiography* (1934).

The novelist John le Carré attended the school in the 1940s, but persuaded his father to let him complete his schooldays in Switzerland.

SIDMOUTH *Devon*

Seaside resort 10 m. NE of Exmouth, approached by the A3052 or the A375. Elizabeth Barrett came here with her family in 1832 after the sale of Hope End, her father hoping that the warm climate would help to dispel her cough. They took a house at 7–8 Fortfield Ter., previously occupied by the Grand Duchess Helena of Russia and described by Elizabeth as 'not at all *grand*, but extremely comfortable and cheerful, with a splendid sea view in front, and pleasant green hills and trees behind'. The house is now flats, but a replica of the original Russian Eagle still stands above it. The family moved to Belle Vue (later a hotel) in All Saints Rd in 1833 and stayed there until they left for London two years later. While she was in Sidmouth, Elizabeth translated Æschylus' 'Prometheus Bound'. She also became acquainted with the Revd George Hunter, minister of a Nonconformist chapel, in whom she seemed to find a kindred spirit as they walked beneath the trees and talked about poetry and literature. But he fell in love with her and became embittered by her inability to respond to his devotion, which persisted for 13 years—until he realized that Browning had won her heart (see the *Cornhill Magazine*, Spring 1951, 'Miss Barrett and Mr. Hunter'). Sidmouth is the 'Baymouth' of Thackeray's *Pendennis*.

SLAD *Gloucestershire*

Village in the Slad valley, 2 m. NE of Stroud. Laurie Lee's family moved to a rented cottage in Slad from nearby Stroud when he turned 3; he wrote about his secluded childhood, the disappearing countryside, and many local Cotswold characters in his much-loved *Cider with Rosie* (1959).

> I was set down from the carrier's cart at the age of three; and there with a sense of bewilderment and terror my life in the village began. The June grass, amongst which I stood, was taller than I was, and I wept. I had never been so close to grass before. It towered above me and all around me, each blade tattooed with tiger-skins of sunlight. It was knife-edged, dark, and a wicked green, thick as a forest and alive with grasshoppers that chirped and chattered and leapt through the air like monkeys. . . . That was the day we came to the village, in the summer of the last year of the First World War. To a cottage that stood in a half-acre of garden on a steep bank above a lake; a cottage with three floors and a cellar and a treasure in the walls, with a pump and apple trees, syringa and strawberries, rooks in the chimneys, frogs in the cellar, mushrooms on the ceiling, and all for three and sixpence a week.

From the ages of 4 to 12 Lee attended the Slad village school. *Cider with Rosie* was followed by *As I Walked Out One Midsummer Morning* (1969), which begins with Lee's departure from Stroud and takes him down to London and Spain. When *Cider with Rosie* appeared to such success in 1959, Lee bought himself Rose Cottage, and remained in Slad—at home there and at The Woolpack pub—for the rest of his life. He died there on 13 May 1997, and a week later was buried in the graveyard at Holy Trinity Church, under the epitaph 'He lies in the valley he loved'.

SOUTH CADBURY *Somerset*

Village off the A303, 6 m. N of Sherborne. Charles Churchill was curate here (1754–6) until he left for Rainham, London.

SOUTH MARSTON *Wiltshire*

Village off the A361, 4 m. NE of Swindon. Alfred Williams lived most of his life in this village, where he was born (1877) and buried (1931). He worked in the railway works at Swindon and his knowledge of the classics in *Nature and Other Poems* (1912) caused the reviewers great surprise. He was living at Dryden Cottage when he described rural life in *A Wiltshire Village* (1912).

Evelyn Waugh in front of his home, Piers Court, Stinchcombe

STINCHCOMBE *Gloucestershire*

Village on the B4060, 2 m. E of Dursley. Evelyn Waugh lived (1937–56) at Piers Court after his second marriage. He wrote here *The Loved One* (1948), *Helena* (1950), and *Men at Arms* (1952) and *Officers and Gentlemen* (1955), the first two volumes of his trilogy about the war, in which he served first in the Royal Marines and then in the Royal Horse Guards. He also experienced here the mental disturbances that preceded the hallucinations he suffered on a voyage to Ceylon, recounted in *The Ordeal of Gilbert Pinfold* (1957). His son Auberon recorded (as did Evelyn himself in his diaries) that when the children were in the house his father generally took his meals in the library.

STINSFORD *Dorset*

Village off the A35, just over 2 m. E of Dorchester. There is a memorial window to Hardy in the church, where he sang in the choir as a boy. His heart is buried in the churchyard, near the graves of his parents, and Cecil Day-Lewis, his devoted admirer, is buried close by. Stinsford is the 'Mellstock' of *Under the Greenwood Tree* (1872) and of the poems 'A Church Romance' (1835) and 'Afternoon Service at Mellstock' (1850).

STONEHENGE *Wiltshire*

Prehistoric circle of standing stones on Salisbury Plain. Towards the end of Thomas Hardy's *Tess of the D'Urbervilles* (1891), Tess and her lover Angel Clare spend the night at Stonehenge, Tess sleeping on one of its stone 'altars'. As dawn rises, Stonehenge is surrounded by police, who take Tess into custody for the murder of Alec D'Urberville. Penelope Lively's *Treasures of Time* (1979) centres on an archaeologist in Wiltshire. Kate brings Tom home to meet her archaeologist father in (says Tom)

> the cradle of British archaeology. Stonehenge. Avebury. Stukeley's stamping ground—right up my street. Immemorial landscapes. And I'd like to know more about your father, anyway. I suppose the house is stuffed with axe-heads and bits of broken pot . . .

STOURHEAD *Wiltshire*

Country house (NT) on the B3092, 3 m. NW of Mere, with grounds and gardens landscaped in the 18th c. for the Hoare family. The changing of the landscape into *le jardin anglais* needed the combination of philosopher, patron, poet, and architect. Locke's philosophy of Man 'in a state of Nature' appealed to patrons who, after a war against France, wished to break away from Le Nôtre's geometric designs which they saw as the embodiment of despotism. This wish led to the softening of line under the architects Kent and Wyatt and to the removal of whole hillsides under 'Capability' Brown. Under their influence water meandered in serpentine ways, fell into grottoes embellished with statues and overhung with shrubs, and was crossed by eye-catching bridges half hidden by trees. Temples stood out on knolls, cast reflections in lakes, or nestled in dells. The chief architect of the temples at Stourhead is Flitcroft. Pope's lines embellish the curb of the basin in the grotto which has a statue of a sleeping nymph:

> Nymph of the Grot these sacred springs I keep
> And to the murmur of these waters sleep;
> Ah! spare my slumbers, gently tread the cave,
> And drink in silence or in silence lave.

The Bristol Cross, of which Pepys remarked on his visit there that it reminded him of the one at Cheapside, and which the citizens later asked to have removed as it obstructed the road, was re-erected here in 1765.

Alfred's Tower, a red-brick triangular tower, with a statue of King Alfred, was erected in 1772 on Kingsettle Hill (2 m. NW) and commemorates his fight against the Danes in 879. 'Parson' Woodforde wrote in his *Diary* of his visit.

STROUD *Gloucestershire*

Cotswolds town, where Laurie Lee was born, at 2 Glenview Ter., Slad Rd, Uplands, on 26 June 1914. The family moved away from Stroud (down the road to *Slad) when he turned 3, but Lee spent much of his childhood in the town, both as a pupil at Stroud Central Boys' School and discovering the great writers at Stroud Public Library.

STURMINSTER NEWTON *Dorset*

Market town on the Stour, *c*. 10 m. SW of Shaftesbury, on the B3091. William Barnes, who spent his early years at *Rush-Hay, in the nearby parish of Bagber, attended the church school, and the eagle lectern in the church is a memorial to him. Robert Young, the tailor and poet who wrote as 'Rabin Hill', was born here (1811). He left school at the age of 11 and, after working in London and Poole, returned to his native town, succeeded in business, and built his own house, The Hive, where he lived for most of the rest of his life. His poems, in Dorset dialect, include 'Rabin Hill's Visit to the Railway', composed on the opening of the Somerset and Dorset line in 1861. Young also owned Riverside Villa, at the end of Rickett's Lane, on a bluff overlooking the Stour, which Hardy rented when he was writing *The Return of the Native* (1878). Young ended his days at Riverside Villa (1908) and was buried in the cemetery.

Sturminster Newton appears as 'Stourcastle' in *Tess of the D'Urbervilles* (1891).

SUTTON COURT *Somerset*

Elizabethan house on the A368, 1 m. N of Bishop's Sutton, enlarged in the 19th c. John Locke (1632–1702) visited it, as did John Addington Symonds, who wrote about the house, his sister's home, in *In the Key of Blue* (1893).

TAUNTON *Somerset*

County town in the valley of Taunton Deane, on the A38 and the A358. It was founded *c*. 705 by Ine, King of the West Saxons, as a stronghold against the Celts. The castle (much restored) dates from the 12th c. and houses the County Museum. It is probable that Samuel Daniel was born (1562) near Taunton, though the exact location is not known. He was the son of a music master, was educated at *Oxford, and after a career in London (he was Spenser's 'new shepherd late up sprong' in *Colin Clout*), returned to Somerset and rented a farm near *Beckington.

In May 1798, when Coleridge was living at *Nether Stowey, he walked 11 m. to conduct the service for the Unitarian minister at the Mary St. Chapel in Taunton, Dr Toulmin. He continued to preach at the chapel from time to time, at this period of his life when he was an ardent Unitarian. A. W. Kinglake, historian and author of *Eōthen* (1844), a narrative of his travels in the Near East, was born (5 Aug. 1809) at Wilton House, Upper High St. (now a home for the elderly). Kinglake lived here until he was sent to the Grammar School at *Ottery St Mary, and subsequently to *Eton.

A. P. Graves was an inspector of schools when he came to Taunton from *Huddersfield in the spring of 1882. His district was West Somerset, with headquarters at Taunton, and he and his wife and their four children settled at Haines Hill and spent three happy years there. They had as a near neighbour Arthur Kinglake, the eccentric brother of A. W.

Kinglake, and they enjoyed the friendship of Juliana Horatia Ewing and her husband, who were living at *Trull, and gave Graves encouragement in the publication of *Songs of Old Ireland*, which was going through the press at that time. He lived for a time at West Hay in the village of Kingston St Mary, 2 m. N of Taunton, and in 1895 was transferred to *Southwark.

The poet Peter Porter reflects on the preservation of England in his poem 'At the Castle Hotel, Taunton'.

TAVISTOCK *Devon*

Market town on the A384 and the A390, traditionally regarded as the western capital of Dartmoor. It was the birthplace (house not traced) of William Browne (1591–1645), whose narrative poem *Britannia's Pastorals* (Book I, 1613; Book II, 1616; Book III, 1852) contains some of the earliest topographical poetry, concerning the surrounding countryside:

> My muse for lofty pitches shall not roam,
> But homely pipen of my native home.

Among various epitaphs he wrote the well-known lines on the Dowager Countess of Pembroke, 'Sidney's sister, Pembroke's mother'. He was educated at Tavistock Grammar School before going to *Oxford. The church (restored 1845) has a window designed by William Morris.

Tavistock's October 'Goose Fair' inspired Charles Causley's poem which recalls his childhood memory of the fair when

> I heard the frightened geese in wicker pen.
> Out of his mouth an Indian man blew fire.
> There was a smell of beer; cold taste of rain.

TEIGNMOUTH (pr. 'Tĭnmuth) *Devon*

Seaside resort and fishing and shipbuilding centre, situated on the N shore of the mouth of the Teign, on the A379. Fanny Burney came here on three occasions: as a young woman in 1773; in attendance on Queen Charlotte in 1778; and in 1791, shortly before her marriage. She was delighted with the country and tried sea bathing, when her bathing machine was pushed into the sea by two sturdy women and the plunge into the water gave her a shock 'beyond expression great!'

Jane Austen may have visited here during her Devon holiday in 1802, and in March 1818 Keats came to stay with his brother Tom (Ⓟ at 35 The Strand, but it is doubtful whether this was the actual house). While he was here he completed *Endymion*, wrote the Preface, and sent it to his publishers. It rained a great deal and in a letter to B. R. Haydon he called Devon 'a splashy, rainy, misty, snowy, foggy, haily, floody, muddy, slipshod County'.

Keats's visit was the subject of Charles Causley's poem 'Keats at Teignmouth':

> Then I saw the crystal poet
> Leaning on the old sea-rail;
> In his breast lay death, the lover,
> In his head, the nightingale.

TEWKESBURY *Gloucestershire*

Old town where the Severn and the Avon meet. The great Norman abbey was saved by the town at the Dissolution on the plea that it was the parish church. The Milton organ is said to have been played by John Milton while secretary to the Council of State when Cromwell installed it in Hampton Court; the town bought it in 1727. Nearby is the marble memorial to Mrs Craik, author of *John Halifax, Gentleman* (1857), the fame of which turned the Abbey Mill into 'Abel Fletcher's Mill', now converted into apartments. The Pickwick Club dined at the Royal Hop Pole (now closed and to be reopened as part of a pub chain). The Tudor House Hotel, the mayor's house in *John Halifax, Gentleman*, was the boyhood home of John Moore, whose amusing novels are about the local countryside. A small countryside museum, the John Moore Museum, commemorates him.

TINTAGEL *Cornwall*

Village on the Atlantic coast, on the B3263, *c*. 4½ m. NW of Camelford. On Tintagel Head, a rocky promontory ½ m. away, jutting into the sea across a narrow causeway, are the fragmentary ruins of a castle, built partly on the mainland and partly on the so-called 'Island' and traditionally the birthplace of King Arthur. The castle, a stronghold of the earls of Cornwall from *c*. 1145 until the 15th c., was thought to have been built on the site of Arthur's castle (*c*. 5th–6th cc.), but excavations have uncovered remains of a Celtic monastery probably occupied from *c*. 500 to *c*. 850. A path leads down to a shingle beach, on the W side of which is Merlin's Cave, where, according to Tennyson's *Idylls of the King* (1859), Arthur appears to Merlin after his secret upbringing. King Arthur's Hall in the village was put up between the First and Second world wars by the Fellowship of the Round Table. It has stained-glass windows picturing Arthur's knights, and a library of Arthurian literature.

Swinburne stayed at Tintagel in 1864 from the end of August to the end of October with his friend J. W. Inchbald, and wrote of visits to 'lone Camelford and Boscastle divine'. While he was here he finished *Atalanta in Calydon* (1865). A century later the poet Brian Patten would write his poem 'In Tintagel Graveyard':

> Who brought flowers to this grave?
> 'I,' said the wren.
> 'I brought them as seeds and then
> Watched them grow.'

TIVERTON *Devon*

Old market and lace-making town situated on the Exe, 15 m. N of Exeter, on the A361 and the A396. Mrs Hannah Cowley (1743–1809), the daughter of a bookseller, Philip Parkhurst, was born here. She was a prolific writer for the London stage, after her first success with *The Runaway* at Drury Lane in 1776. Other plays included *A Bold Stroke for a Husband* (1783) and *The Belle's Stratagem* (1780). She also wrote sentimental verses as 'Anna Matilda'. She died at Tiverton and is buried here.

R. D. Blackmore went to Blundell's School (founded 1604), as did John Ridd, the hero of his *Lorna Doone* (1869). Old Blundell's School (NT) was converted into dwelling houses when the new school was built in 1882. The forecourt of the school is usually open.

The science-fiction novelist John Wyndham attended the school briefly (and unhappily) during the First World War. Geoffrey Willans was educated at Blundell's School from 1924 to 1929, storing up experience for the *Molesworth* books. Stephen Spender taught at the school in 1940, as did the poet Laurence Sail in the 1970s and 1980s.

TORQUAY (pr. Tor'kē) *Devon*

Large seaside resort 22 m. S of Exeter on the A380 (or 24 m. on the A379 coast road), situated on seven hills where two valleys meet. Tennyson, who stayed here in 1838, called it 'the loveliest sea-village in England', and it was the inspiration for his poem 'Audley Court'.

Elizabeth Barrett came here from London in 1838 in the hope that the mild climate would improve her health. She stayed at the Bath House, 1 Beacon Ter. (now the Hotel Regina; Ⓟ), sheltered by the hills and overlooking the harbour, but the good results of her visit were ruined by the death of her favourite brother, Edward, in a sailing accident in Babbacombe Bay, in July 1840. She was so devastated that although she longed to leave the sea and its painful associations she was too ill to travel until September 1841, when she went in an invalid carriage by easy stages back to Wimpole St. In the summer of 1840 she wrote in a letter that she had 'written lately (as far as manuscript goes) a good deal, only on all sorts of subjects, and in as many shapes . . . I lie here weaving a great many schemes.' After the tragedy, when she was unable to write, books were her great solace, especially the Greek classics, in spite of the doctor's advice not to tire herself with studying.

Charles Kingsley came over from Eversley in the winter of 1853–4 with his wife, who had been ill, and stayed until the following spring. His house, Livermead Cottage, at the entrance to Livermead Beach, was burnt down and replaced by a villa residence called Livermead Cliff. Kingsley enjoyed the scientific society he met in Torquay, 'a place', he wrote, 'which should be as much endeared to the naturalist as to the patriot and the artist', and he described his wanderings among rocks and pools and 'happy evenings spent over the microscope . . . examining the wonders and labours of the day'. In the spring of 1854 he wrote the Preface to *Theologia Germanica*—the book which Martin Luther said he owed more to than any other 'saving the Bible and St. Augustine'—which was published in its first English translation (by Susan Winkworth) that year. He returned to Torquay in 1858, when his friend Philip Henry Gosse, the marine biologist, was living nearby.

Edmund Gosse in *Father and Son* (1907) describes how he moved from London in 1857,

aged 8, with his father and governess, to Sandhurst, a villa in the Manor Park, St Marychurch (now private apartments in Manor Rd, Babbacombe), and gives a picture of the dominating personality of his father, the narrowness of their life as members of the Plymouth Brethren, of whom Philip Henry was a leading figure, and the absorbing study of marine biology. Kingsley was a frequent visitor, 'always a jolly presence that brought some refreshment to our seriousness'. Edmund attended school locally from 1860 to 1863, when he went to boarding school, and on his walks there and back he met an old gentleman with whom he became friends. This was the former dramatist James Sheridan Knowles, who had come to Torquay as a Baptist minister, causing a great stir by his change of profession. He talked to the boy about his stage experiences in his 'unconverted days' and inspired him with a love of Shakespeare. Knowles died in Torquay in 1862.

Edward Bulwer-Lytton first came to Torquay in August 1856 and, like his friend Disraeli, who was a frequent visitor, grew much attached to the place. He stayed for a time at the old Union Hotel before buying Argyll Hall in Warren Rd, where he used to come each winter to relax, write, and entertain his friends. He died there on 18 January 1873, just after reading the proofs of his last work, having, it is believed, caught a chill while watching a burning brig which had drifted onto the rocks below the hill on which his villa stood.

Henry James loved Torquay, to which he came as to a refreshing bath of quietness. He used to stay at the Osborne Hotel and it was here that he began writing *The Spoils of Poynton* (1897) in May 1895. He was still at work on it in October, when he made a note that was to lead to *The Ambassadors* (1903).

Eden Phillpotts, prolific author of novels and plays, especially of the West Country, lived at Eltham, Oak Hill Rd, from *c*. 1901 until 1929. During this time he wrote much of the work for which he is best remembered, including the Dartmoor novels, such as *The Secret Woman* (1905, dramatized 1912), *The Thief of Virtue* (1910, probably his own favourite), and *Widecombe Fair* (1913); also the immensely popular plays *The Farmer's Wife* (1917) and *Yellow Sands* (with his daughter Adelaide, 1926). He was made a Freeman of Torquay in 1921. An account of his friendship with Arnold Bennett during these years is given in his autobiography, *From the Angle of 88* (1951).

Margaret Fairless Barber, author of *The Roadmender* (1901) and an invalid for most of her life, lived here for some years before her death (1901). Sean O'Casey came from *Totnes in 1955 and lived, with his wife, Eileen, to the end of his life in a flat in a large white Victorian house, Villa Rosa, 40 Trumlands Rd, St Marychurch, just off the Torquay–Teignmouth road. His last plays, *The Bishop's Bonfire* (1955), *The Drums of Father Ned* (1960), and *Behind the Green Curtains* (3 plays, 1961), and essays and stories entitled *The Green Crow* (1956), were published at this time.

A less certain literary association is that of Sir Richard Burton, travel writer (especially of his *Pilgrimage to Mecca*, 1855–6) and translator from the Arabic of *The Thousand and One Nights* (1885–8). According to his own account he was born at his maternal grandparents' home, Barham House, near Elstree, Hertfordshire, but, although the Elstree parish register records his baptism on 2 September 1821, a marginal note in the same handwriting reads 'born 19th March, 1821, Torquay, Devon', so it is reasonable to regard him as a native of Torquay, although the exact place and circumstances of his birth are not known.

The queen of crime novelists Agatha Christie was born in Torquay on 15 September 1890. She was brought up in Ashfield, a large house (complete with gardens, tennis courts . . .) the sort of home that she would later come to use frequently as a setting for her novels. Her observation of refugees coming into Torquay—these foreigners with their surprising mannerisms—is said to have come in useful when modelling her creation of the Belgian detective Hercule Poirot.

TOTNES *Devon*

Old town situated on a steep hill above the Dart, on the A381 and the A385. In 1938 Sean O'Casey came here from London with his wife and family so that the children could go to Dartington Hall School. They rented Tingrith, a Victorian house in Ashburton Rd, which became their home until they moved to *Torquay 17 years later.

TREBETHERICK *Cornwall*

Coastal village on the NW bank of the river Camel. John Betjeman died at Treen, Daymer Lane. He celebrated youthful holidays around here in 'Trebetherick':

> But when a storm was at its height,
> And feathery slate was black in rain,
> And tamarisks were hung with light
> And golden sand was brown again,
> Spring tide and blizzard would unite
> And sea came flooding up the lane.

TREEN *Cornwall*

Village 3 m. from Land's End. The nearby Logan Rock, 'obsequious to the gentlest touch | Of him whose breast is pure', features in 'Caractacus', William Mason's dramatic poem of 1759, and is the subject of a concrete poem by D. M. Thomas.

TRETHOSA *Cornwall*

China clay mining village near St Austell. The poet Jack Clemo was taught at the local school and baptized and married at the Methodist Chapel, which contains a room dedicated to his memory.

TREVONE *Cornwall*

Village 2 m. W of Padstow, on a minor road N of the B3276. Dorothy Richardson, pioneer of the 'stream-of-consciousness' novel, lived here after her marriage to the painter Alan Odle in

1917. They rented Rose Cottage in the village and later other cottages in the *Padstow area, spending the winters here when rents were low and letting their room in Queen's Ter., London. Dorothy Richardson's novels, written between 1917 and 1938, either in Cornwall or in London, form a single sequence entitled *Pilgrimage*.

TRINITY *Jersey*

Parish to the NE of the island, home to the manor house and grounds of Les Augrès. When Gerald Durrell returned to England from Cameroon in 1957, hoping to realize his lifelong dream of running his own zoo (nurtured in his experience working at *Whipsnade), he took a lease on Les Augrès, which he opened up to the public with his collection in March 1959, followed in 1963 by the founding of the Jersey Wildlife Preservation Trust. Durrell was based on Jersey for the rest of his life, working on Jersey Zoo and the Trust; he died there on 30 January 1995. The Trust, managed by Durrell's widow, has since been renamed the Durrell Wildlife Conservation Trust.

TROWBRIDGE *Wiltshire*

Market town on the A363, 12 m. SE of Bath. In 1814, soon after the death of his wife, George Crabbe moved to the vicarage here (demolished in the 1960s) and eventually met his neighbouring poets William Lisle Bowles and Tom Moore. Crabbe's married son John came as his curate in 1816, and in 1819 Crabbe published *Tales of the Hall*, followed the next year by his *Collected Works*. In *Romance of an Elderly Poet* (1913) A. M. Broadley and W. Jerrold tell of Crabbe's proposal of marriage to Charlotte Ridout and later his sentimental correspondence with Elizabeth Charter of Bath. Crabbe died here in 1832 and there is a memorial tablet in the chancel.

Maureen Duffy was evacuated from London to the town during the Second World War. Her experience as a child evacuee provides the basis for her first, most autobiographical, novel, *That's How It Was* (1962).

TRULL *Somerset*

Village 2 m. SW of Taunton. Mrs Ewing settled here in 1883, when her husband returned from military duties in Ceylon. She was happy here, wrote *Mary's Meadow* (1883–4) and *Letters from a Little Garden* (1884–5), and cultivated her garden, but two years later, after an illness that necessitated two spinal operations, she died. She is buried in the churchyard and a memorial window on the N wall of the church testifies to the affection in which she and her husband were held. The beautiful alms dish was the gift of their nephews and godchildren.

TRURO *Cornwall*

Cathedral city and administrative centre on the A39, situated on the river Truro. Samuel Foote (1720–77), dramatist, actor, and humorist, was born at Johnson Vivian's House (gone), formerly on the S side of Boscawen St., and was baptized in St Mary's Church, of which only the S aisle survives, now forming the S aisle of the choir of the Cathedral. Foote grew up in the town residence of the Footes of Lambesso, a house on the N side of Boscawen St., which was later destroyed by a lorry. A Co-op store is now on the site. He was educated at *Worcester Grammar School and *Oxford and made his name in London as a wit and writer of short topical sketches.

Sir Hugh Walpole wrote a series of novels in a Cornish setting, which include *The Cathedral* (1922), *The Old Ladies* (1924), and *Harmer John* (1926), in which the town of 'Polchester' represents Truro. In the N aisle of the Cathedral (built 1880–1910) a tablet commemorates Sir Arthur Quiller-Couch as one who 'kindled in others a lively and discriminating love of English literature'.

Kenneth Grahame's marriage certificate, bearing the signatures of Anthony Hope Hawkins and Sir Arthur Quiller-Couch as witnesses to his marriage (22 July 1899) at *Fowey, may be seen at the County Archivist's Office.

Malpas (pr. Mōpus), 1½ m. SE, can be reached by a pleasant road on the E bank of the river. The ferry here is mentioned in the Tristram and Iseult stories, when Iseult had to make her way across the water to the palace of King Mark at Blandreland (in the parish of Kea).

An exhibit in the Royal Cornwall Museum on River St. inspired Penelope Shuttle's poem 'Three Lunulae, Truro Museum'. The poet and editor Alan Ross records in his memoir *Blindfold Games* (1986) holidays from Belmont School in Falmouth spent on a farm near Truro.

TRUSHAM *Devon*

Village between Exeter and Newton Abbot. Charles Causley's family originated from the village, and its churchyard and war memorial inspire the melancholy poem 'Trusham':

> Beyond those pale disturbances of sky
> Another year assembles its vast floe.
> Ice lines the turning air. It softens. Soon
> Advances from the west the carrion snow.

TYWARDREATH *Cornwall*

Small village to the NW of Fowey, E of Par. The manor of Tywardreath was known as 'the house on the strand', and became the model for Daphne du Maurier's 1969 novel of that name.

ULEY *Gloucestershire*

Village in a wooded valley between Stroud and Dursley. The poet and novelist John Burnside lived in S Gloucestershire in the 1980s. A number of the poems in his first collection, *The Hoop* (1988)—including 'Only the Rain', 'A Calendar for the Parish of Bagpath', 'Uley, Glos', and 'At Owlpen', quoted here—respond to the country around Uley:

> Pigeons stand for angels in this dream
> of England. Sunday stones and windfalls
> are chapters in a book of Revelation
> left open on the altar after mass.

UPOTTERY *Devon*

Village in the Blackdown Hills. Patricia Beer lived in a Tudor farmhouse here from the mid-1960s until her death in 1999. She described the surrounding country in poems such as 'Mist in the Otter Valley' and set her novel *Moon's Ottery* (1978) in Elizabethan Devon.

WAREHAM *Dorset*

Market town on the Frome, on the A351 and the A352. In St Martin's Church there is a recumbent statue by Eric Kennington of T. E. Lawrence in Arab dress, his head resting on a camel saddle. Lawrence was living at *Clouds Hill at the time of his death.

WEST DEAN *Wiltshire*

Village 9 m. SE of Salisbury, off the A36, whence Lady Mary Pierrepoint eloped to marry (1712) Edward Wortley Montagu. Nothing remains of her grandfather's house, where she spent her childhood, but his ornate tomb has been restored in the 14th-c. Borbach Chantry, once used as the family chapel.

Gilbert White was curate here for a short time and mentions how lonely he felt away from *Selborne.

WESTON-SUPER-MARE *Somerset*

Seaside resort on the A370, 21 m. SW of Bristol. Mary Webb lived at 6 Landemann Circus after her marriage in 1912. The first act of 'Nothing On', the bad bedroom farce parodied in Michael Frayn's farce *Noises Off* (1982), is performed at the fictional Grand Theatre.

WESTWARD HO! *Devon*

Bathing resort, named after Kingsley's novel (1855), on Barnstaple or Bideford Bay, 3 m. NW of Bideford, on the B3236. Rudyard Kipling, who was born and had spent his childhood in India, was educated at the United Services College here from January 1878 to July 1882. He described it as 'largely a caste school . . . some 75 per cent of us had been born outside England, and hoped to follow their fathers into the army'. Kipling drew on memories of his schooldays for *Stalky & Co.* (1899), stories about the exploits of Beetle (himself) and his friends, Stalky and M'Turk, which he dedicated to Cormell Price, the headmaster. The verses which form the introduction to the book include the evocative lines:

> Western wind and open surge
> Took us from our mothers;
> Flung us on a naked shore
> (Twelve bleak houses by the shore!)
> Seven summers by the shore!
> 'Mid two hundred brothers.

The twelve houses still survive, as Kipling Ter. Ⓟ, now let off as flats and guest houses, and the school gymnasium is now an entertainment centre. The rough land to the south of the school buildings was the scene of much of the action in *Stalky & Co.* and is described in the opening of the first story, 'In Ambush'.

Clevedon Court, Somerset, where Thackeray wrote part of *Vanity Fair* and on which he based the 'Castlewood' of *Henry Esmond*

In summer all right-minded boys built huts in the furze-hill behind the College—little lairs whittled out of the heart of the prickly bushes, full of stumps, odd root-ends, and spikes, but, since they were strictly forbidden, palaces of delight. And for the fifth summer in succession, Stalky, M'Turk, and Beetle (this was before they reached the dignity of a study) had built, like beavers, a place of retreat and meditation, where they smoked.

This area, 18 acres of gorse-covered hill, now called Kipling Tors, was given to the National Trust in 1938 by the Rudyard Kipling Memorial Fund.

WEYMOUTH *Dorset*

Coastal town, port, and royal watering place, overlooking Weymouth Bay and Portland Harbour, on the A353. Thomas Love Peacock was born here (18 Oct. 1785), but soon after his father's death in 1788 his mother took him to live in her father's house in *Chertsey. George III used to stay at Gloucester Lodge, the Duke of Gloucester's home on the seafront, and Fanny Burney records in her *Diary* her visits there in attendance on Queen Charlotte in the summer of 1789. 'The King bathes,' she wrote, 'and with great success.'

G. A. Henty, writer of adventure stories for boys, died (1902) on board his yacht *The Egret*, which was moored in the harbour. His body was taken to London and buried in Brompton cemetery.

Weymouth is the 'Budmouth' of Hardy's *The Trumpet-Major* (1880), a novel set in the time of the Napoleonic wars.

In Kazuo Ishiguro's *The Remains of the Day* (1989), Stevens's journey across the south-west concludes here at Weymouth:

> This seaside town is a place I have thought of coming to for many years. I have heard various people talk of having spent a pleasant holiday here, and Mrs Symons too, in *The Wonder of England*, calls it 'a town that can keep the visitor fully entertained for many days on end'. In fact, she makes special mention of the pier, upon which I have been promenading for the past half-hour . . . I have a good view from here of the sun setting over the sea, and though there is still plenty of daylight left—it has been a splendid day—I can see, here and there, lights starting to come on all along the shore. Meanwhile, the pier remains busy with people; behind me, the drumming of numerous footsteps upon these boards continues without interruption.

It is here where he describes his meeting with Miss Kenton at the Rose Garden Hotel in the nearby (and fictional) Dorset village of Little Compton, and sets off on the road back home to Darlington Hall.

WIDCOMBE *Somerset*

Former village 1½ m. SW of, and now joining, Bath. Henry Fielding stayed for some time in 1748 at Widcombe Lodge while writing *Tom Jones* (1749). He is said to have modelled 'Squire Western' on his neighbour at Widcombe Manor. This 18th-c. house was the home (1927–52) of H. A. Vachell, author of *The Hill* (1905), a story of Harrow School, novels, plays, including *Quinney's* (1914) about an antique dealer who appears in subsequent novels, and autobiographical works including *Fellow Travellers* (1923) and *Methuselah's Diary* (1950).

WILSFORD *Wiltshire*

Village on Salisbury Plain, near Amesbury. In the 1980s V. S. Naipaul lived in the grounds of the decaying Wilsford Manor, not far from *Stonehenge, where his landlord was the eccentric writer and recluse Stephen Tennant. His time spent describing with meticulous care 'the country life, the slow movement of time, the dead life, the private life, the life lived in houses close to one another' furnished him with the material for his meditative autobiographical novel *The Enigma of Arrival* (1987):

> But that idea of changing life was wrong. Change was constant. People died; people grew old; people changed houses; houses came up for sale. That was one kind of change. My own presence in the valley, in the cottage of the manor, was an aspect of another kind of change . . . Everything was ageing; everything was being renewed or discarded.

WILTON *Wiltshire*

Village on the A30, 3 m. W of Salisbury. Wilton House, begun in Tudor times and added to in the 17th and 18th cc., was the home after her marriage of Mary Herbert, the Countess of Pembroke, sister of Sir Philip Sidney (open, www.wiltonhouse.co.uk). She is thought to have suggested the prose romance *The Arcadia*, which he began (*c.* 1580) during one of his many visits, and to have played some part in its composition, and in its revision for publication in 1590, after his early death. It is illustrated in a frieze by De Critz in the Single Cube Room. The Countess, who was the 'Urania' of Spenser's *Colin Clout* (1595), was the patron of many poets including Nicholas Breton, Ben Jonson, and two local men, the Somerset-born Samuel Daniel, who tutored her son, and Philip Massinger, whose father was a member of the household. Shakespeare visited in 1603, when *As You Like It* was performed before James I. Mary Herbert's son Philip, the 4th Earl, who built the classical front of the house and laid out the gardens, was the patron of Massinger and William Browne, who lived here for some years.

A. G. Street began writing while farming at Ditchampton Farm, where he was born (1892) and which he wrote about in 1946. His first two popular novels were *Farmer's Glory* (1932) and *Strawberry Roan* (1932).

WIMBORNE (or WIMBORNE MINSTER) *Dorset*

Ancient town on the Allen at its confluence with the Stour, on the A31. The splendid old Minster of St Cuthburga (dating from the 12th c.) possesses a chained library, founded in 1686 for the free use of the citizens of Wimborne. It contains some 185 works in 240 volumes, mainly theological, including the beautiful *Regimen Animarum* (The Direction of Souls), written on vellum in 1343. The earliest printed book is a copy of Anselm's *Opuscula* (Lesser Works) of 1495. A copy of Sir Walter Ralegh's *History of the World* (1634) has 104 pages which have been damaged by apparently deliberate burning and neatly repaired with the missing words rewritten. Both the damage and the repair have been attributed to Matthew Prior, the poet and diplomat, who was the son of a Wimborne joiner.

Thomas Hardy stayed at Wimborne from 1881 to 1883 (the house is not known) and describes it as 'Warborne' in *Two on a Tower* (1882). In his poem 'Copying Architecture in an Old Minster (Wimborne)' he refers to the passage of time marked by the Quarter Jack or Jackman, the figure of a Grenadier who stands high on the wall of the West Tower and wields his hammer each quarter-hour when the bells of the ancient astronomical clock in the baptistery are struck:

> How smartly the quarters of the hour march by
> That the jack-o'-clock never forgets;
> Ding-dong; and before I have traced a cusp's eye
> Or got the true twist of the ogee over
> A double ding-dong ricochetts.

WINCHCOMBE *Gloucestershire*

Cotswold town near Tewkesbury. Sudeley Castle to the SE has been proposed, notably by Norman Murphy, as P. G. Wodehouse's model for Blandings Castle, the seat of Clarence Threepwood, 9th Earl of Emsworth, father of Freddie, and devoted keeper of his pig the Empress of Blandings.

WINTERSLOW *Wiltshire*

Village off the A30, 8 m. NE of Salisbury. Hazlitt and Sarah Stoddart lived at Middleton Cottage, which she owned, after their marriage in 1808. Sarah was a friend of Mary Lamb, who came with Charles to stay in the summers of 1809 and 1810. They walked to *Wilton, *Stonehenge, and *Salisbury, and Hazlitt mentions in 'Farewell to Essay Writing' how they had walked out 'to look at the Claude Lorraine skies over our heads . . . to gather mushrooms that sprung up at our feet, to throw into our hashed mutton at supper'. Hazlitt edited the *Memoirs of Thomas Holcroft* (1816) here. Winterslow was a favourite place of his and after his divorce in 1823 he stayed at the Winterslow Hut (now The Pheasant inn) on the main road (2 m. N). The essays written here were collected by his son (born at Middleton Cottage) and called *Winterslow* (1839).

WOOL *Dorset*

Village on the Frome, 5 m. W of Wareham, on the A352. Woolbridge Manor (formerly the home of the Turbervilles) on the N side of the main road, approached by a fine 17th-c. bridge (closed to traffic), was Hardy's 'Wellbridge Manor-house' in *Tess of the D'Urbervilles*

Hay Tor from Hound Tor, Dartmoor. Arthur Conan Doyle made the most of the moor's wildness and mystery in *The Hound of the Baskervilles*

(1891), where Tess and Angel Clare spent their wedding night. S of the main road and E of the village a minor road leads to the ruins of Bindon Abbey, where, in the NE corner, there is the empty stone coffin where the sleepwalking Angel laid Tess. In the story Hardy places the Abbey and the adjacent mill nearer to the manor house than they are in fact. Wool itself appears as 'Wellbridge'.

WOTTON-UNDER-EDGE
Gloucestershire

Cotswold market town. The poets U. A. Fanthorpe and Charles Tomlinson both live in or near the village. Tomlinson, who lives in the Ozleworth valley, has taken inspiration from the local landscape: 'for the last half century I have lived in Gloucestershire, a setting which enriches and reinforces my sense of nature'.

WRINGTON *Somerset*

Village off the A38, 12 m. SW of Bristol. John Locke was born (1632) at the house of his mother's brother, which he later inherited. He stayed here occasionally, perhaps between 1680 and 1690, and is commemorated by a plaque on the churchyard wall. Hannah More lived at Barley Wood from 1802 until a short time before her death in 1833. She and her sisters wrote tracts for the schools they were starting in the neighbourhood. Coleridge and Cottle, his friend and publisher, visited them in 1814, and the young De Quincey, whose mother lived at Westhay on the Congresbury road, first read 'The Ancient Mariner' in the library here. Hannah More corresponded with many of the intellectuals of her day; her *Letters* were published in 1834. She is buried in the churchyard.

YEALMPTON (pr. Yampton) *Devon*

Village 7 m. E of Plymouth, on the A379. 'Mother Hubbard's Cottage' (now a restaurant) on the main road is said to have belonged to the original of the nursery rhyme, a housekeeper at Kitley, 1 m. W, which was the home of the Pollexfens in Henry VIII's day, and later of the Pollexfen Bastards. The house, situated in a large park and not visible from the road, has been considerably altered and rebuilt. The library contains the only known copy of the first edition of the 'Mother Hubbard' rhyme (1805), which was written by Sarah Martin (1768–1826), who lived here for a time with her sister, who had married Squire Bastard.

ZELAH *Cornwall*

Village halfway between Truro and Newquay. The legend of St Michael shooting down the demon's boulder is retold by Charles Causley in his ballad 'Zelah':

> Angel and stone and demon-claw,
> These I did see, though never saw.
> All these I saw but did not see
> As I went down by Zelah Tree
> And found beside the fading grass
> The sharp, sweet flowers of Michaelmas.

ZENNOR *Cornwall*

Small village 5 m. W of St Ives, on the B3306. W. H. Hudson stayed here in December and January 1906–7 while gathering material for his book *The Land's End: A Naturalist's Impressions in West Cornwall* (1908). A plaque on the top of the hill near the old quarry commemorates the place where he used to sit and watch the seabirds and wildlife around him.

D. H. Lawrence came here in 1916 with his wife, Frieda, and stayed at the Tinners' Arms while looking for a cottage to rent. They found Higher Tregerthen, one of a pair of small cottages in farmland near the sea, down a stony lane c. 1½ m. NE of the village, and moved there in March, for an annual rent of £5. They asked Katherine Mansfield and John Middleton Murry to come and live in the other cottage, with the object of forming 'a tiny settlement', but though the two did come they found the place uncongenial (Katherine was haunted by the crying of the gulls) and soon left. Lawrence stayed on, working on the sequel to *The Rainbow* (1915), published later as *Women in Love* (1920), but gradually he and Frieda—the bearded anti-war intellectual and his German wife—became objects of suspicion to the local people and on 12 October 1917 their cottage was searched by the police and they were told to leave (see his *Collected Letters*, ed. H. T. Moore, 1962). The bitterness of this experience is recorded in 'The Nightmare' chapter of the semi-autobiographical novel *Kangaroo* (1923). Lawrence's wartime experiences in the village were the inspiration for Helen Dunmore's novel *Zennor in Darkness* (1993), with its account of the mermaid carved on a bench-end in the church: 'She floats, round-bellied, arms raised, innocent above the curve of her tail. Her fins flick and scull. He traces the carving of breast and navel. How fine she is.' John Heath-Stubbs lived for a while in the same cottage occupied by Katherine Mansfield. The mermaid—'half fish, half fallen angel'—appears in his poem 'To the Mermaid at Zennor'. Emma Tennant's novel *Strangers and Sisters* (1990) is set in part in Zennor.

South-East England

South-East England

ABINGDON *Oxfordshire*

Old town on the Thames, once the county town of Berkshire, 7 m. S of Oxford on the A34. It was the birthplace of Edward Moore (1712–57), a minor dramatist who lived and died in poverty, author of the comedy *Gil Blas* (1751) and the tragedy *The Gamester* (1753). Ruskin, who had been appointed the first Slade Professor of Art at *Oxford in 1869, moved to the Crown and Thistle at Abingdon in the New Year of 1871. He stayed here some months, coming to Oxford almost daily to work on illuminated manuscripts at the Bodleian Library, and then moved to rooms at Corpus Christi College. Abingdon was also the birthplace of the novelist Dorothy Miller Richardson.

ABINGER HAMMER *Surrey*

Village on the A25, 5 m. SW of Dorking. West Hackhurst, the house on the brow of the steep hill N of the village, was E. M. Forster's home from 1902 to 1945, though he spent some years in Italy, which provided him with the background for two novels, and he made two visits to India, which gave him material for *A Passage to India* (1924), thought by many to be his finest novel. Many of his essays collected as *Abinger Harvest* (1936), and his short stories *The Celestial Omnibus* (1914) and *The Eternal Moment* (1928), were written here. Piney Copse, near the house, which he describes buying in 'My Wood', was bequeathed by him to the NT.

ACOL (pr. 'Aycole) *Kent*

Village on the B2048 in the Isle of Thanet, NE of the county. The chalk-pit here features in R. H. Barham's 'The Smuggler's Leap' from the *Ingoldsby Legends* (1840–7). Baroness Orczy, who leased (1908–9) Cleve Court, on the Minster road, after finishing *Beau Brocade* (1908), set her next adventure story, *Nest of the Sparrowhawk*, here. She and her husband, the painter Montagu Barstow, imported three horses from her home in Hungary and drove them abreast in their carriage.

ADDERBURY *Oxfordshire*

Village 4 m. S of Banbury on the A361. The dark ironstone Adderbury House (built 1624) was inherited by John Wilmot, 2nd Earl of Rochester, who lived there intermittently after his marriage (1667) to the heiress Elizabeth Malet. Pepys records that she was expected to be the bride of the son of his patron Lord Sandwich. Wilmot, who wrote to Elizabeth,

When wearied with a world of woe,
To thy safe bosom I retire,
Where love, and peace, and truth does flow,
May I contented there expire,

spent much time at the profligate court hoping for an appointment from the King. He was portrayed by Etherege as Dorimant in *The Man of Mode* (1676). Pope stayed here in 1739, when the house belonged to the Duke of Argyll, and wrote 'Verses left by Mr Pope, on his lying in the same bed which . . . Rochester slept in'. The narrow entrance to the drive is on the E side of the road opposite the green and immediately above the steep hill S of the village. It has now been converted into private homes.

ALDERMASTON *Berkshire*

Since 1958 the Atomic Weapons Research Establishment, S of the village, has been the final destination of the Campaign for Nuclear Disarmament's annual march from Trafalgar Square. The critic and poet William Empson joined the march every year, providing the subject for Alan Brownjohn's protest poem 'William Empson at Aldermaston'.

ALDERSHOT *Hampshire*

Town some 35 m. SW of London, best known for its long-standing association with the army, whose presence here has been continuous since the establishment of a base in the 1840s. The novelist Ian McEwan was born here in 1948, the son of an army officer.

ALDINGTON *Kent*

Small village off the B2067, 5 m. W of Hythe. Thomas Linacre was rector in 1509, the year he became one of Henry VIII's doctors, and probably spent some time at the parsonage, later a farm, S of the church. Erasmus followed as rector in 1511 but is not thought to have lived here, preferring *Cambridge, where he was Greek Reader from 1511 to 1514. Reproductions of old portraits of both men are in the tower. Aldington Knoll, a small farmhouse overlooking Romney Marsh, was the home of Ford Madox Hueffer (later Ford Madox Ford), who collaborated with Conrad at *Postling on *The Inheritors* (1901) and *Romance* (1903). From 1909 to 1910 Conrad took over another house in the village and, restless with overwork on *Under Western Eyes* (1909), suffered a nervous breakdown.

ALLINGTON *Kent*

Village off the A20, 1½ m. NW of Maidstone. The poet Sir Thomas Wyatt was born (1503?) at Allington Castle beside the Medway. He and the Earl of Surrey were the first in England to write sonnets in the Italian form, and many of these were published in *Tottel's Miscellany* (1557). The castle, now a conference centre, has been restored.

ALTON *Hampshire*

Market town at the junction of the A31 and the A339. A plaque of uncertain date records that Edmund Spenser lived at 1 Amery St., near the market place, in 1590. This may have been his home for a short time after he returned from Ireland with Sir Walter Ralegh to visit the court and to arrange for the publication of the first three books of *The Faerie Queene*. According to A. C. Judson (*Life of Spenser*, 1945) he probably spent the later months of 1590 writing, revising, and assembling material for *Complaints, containing sundrie small poems of the worlds vanitie* (1591), and perhaps did some of this work in Hampshire, visiting during the same period his friend Sir Henry Wallop at Farleigh Wallop, 6 m. from Alton. When Cardinal Newman was an undergraduate at *Oxford he stayed at Swarthmore, 59 High St. Ⓟ.

Compton Mackenzie, who stayed at *Beech as a young man, knew Alton well and in 1925 he presented the Curtis Museum, High St., with the manuscript of his story for children, 'Mabel in Queer Street'. Alton is the 'Galton' of his novels *The Altar Steps* (1922), its sequel *The Parson's Progress* (1923), and *Buttercups and Daisies* (1931).

ANNINGSLEY PARK *Surrey*

Country house off the Castle Inn turn on the A320, 1 m. S of Ottershaw. When Thomas Day moved here in 1781 it was a small, remote, early 18th-c. farmhouse in the middle of desolate heathland. Day had legal training but had inherited money and married a rich wife, and therefore was able to lead a frugal life as a disciple of Rousseau, bent on improving the lot of the poor. *The History of Sandford and Merton*, a humourless tale depicting his ideal of manliness, by which he is best remembered, was written here (1783–9). His friends the Edgeworths (he had hoped to marry Honora), whose methods of education he admired and used in bringing up two orphans, visited him here.

ARUN *West Sussex*

River which runs from the N of the county through Arundel to Littlehampton on the coast. Charlotte Smith's sonnet in its praise recalls that Otway, Collins, and Hayley were all inspired in its vicinity. In Hilaire Belloc's *The Four Men* (1912), it was 'a valley of sacred water'.

ASHEHAM (pr. 'Asham) *East Sussex*

Hamlet 4 m. SE of Lewes on the B2109. The Regency–Gothic Asham House was leased (1912–17) by Virginia and Leonard Woolf after they saw it on a walk from *Firle along the Ouse. The front of the house was 'flat, pale, serene, yellow-washed' and it was said locally to be haunted. Virginia Woolf describes the ghostly couple who restlessly open and shut doors in *A Haunted House* (1943), a collection of short pieces. The Woolfs drew water from the well and used oil lamps on their weekend and holiday visits, often with other members of the Bloomsbury Group.

ASTHALL *Oxfordshire*

A small village on the river Windrush. Nancy Mitford's family moved from *Batsford to the rambling Jacobean manor house at Asthall in 1919. The annual visit of the 'chub fuddler', who strewed the local river with a mysterious substance to bring the chub to the surface during mayfly time, is described in *Love in a Cold Climate* (1949). The garden and ballroom are occasionally open (www.onformsculpture.co.uk).

ASTON CLINTON *Buckinghamshire*

Large village on the A41 between Aylesbury and Tring. Evelyn Waugh was a schoolmaster here from September 1925 to April 1927. He had previously taught in North Wales, where he sets the school in his first satirical novel *Decline and Fall* (1928), begun here. The master in Wales, on whom he bases his character 'Captain Grimes', visited him here.

BABLOCKHYTHE *Oxfordshire*

Hamlet of caravan homes off the B4449 Eynsham–Standlake road, 2 m. SE of Stanton Harcourt. A ferry used to ply across the river and it was there that Matthew Arnold in his poem 'The Scholar-Gipsy' (1853) said the Scholar had been seen

In hat of antique shape, and cloak of grey
Crossing the stripling Thames at Bab-lock-hithe,
Trailing in the cool stream thy fingers wet
As the slow punt swings round.

BANBURY *Oxfordshire*

Market town on the river Cherwell. Anthony Burgess taught at the Grammar School in the early 1950s, a period in his life he recalled in his autobiography, *Little Wilson, Big God* (1987):

In the lower A stream I could ask the question: 'Why don't we place a centralisation diacritic on a schwa?', to which the answer was choroused: 'Because schwa is already a central vowel.' On Friday afternoons I would read aloud to 3A from Evelyn Waugh's *Decline and Fall*, Ray Bradbury's *The Silver Locusts*, and Orwell's *Nineteen Eighty-Four*. 'Sir, does Julia become an unperson?' asked a wide-eyed girl, tremulous. These children could write a passable pastiche of Joycean interior monologue.

BEACON HILL *Surrey*

Bertrand and Dora Russell ran an experimental school at Telegraph House, a former Admiralty semaphore station. The school opened in 1927, with 12 boarders and five day-children and for some 10 years attempted, with mixed success, to implement Russell's ideas on education.

BEACONSFIELD (pr. 'Bĕconsfield) *Buckinghamshire*

Old town on the B474. The poet Edmund Waller, who became an MP in his youth, inherited (1624) the estate of Hall Barn (rebuilt) and it was his main home until his death. After being detected in a Royalist plot, for which, having betrayed his friends, he was fined and banished, he managed to steer a safe course between Cromwell and Charles II, writing poems to both. Many of his early poems are addressed to 'Sacharissa', Lady Dorothy Sidney, whom he courted unsuccessfully after becoming a widower at 25. Waller died in 1687 and his ornate tomb is in the churchyard.

Edmund Burke, who bought (1768) the two-storey house with a pedimented front called Gregories, invited the impoverished poet George Crabbe there in 1781. Burke entertained many literary friends here, including Sheridan, Garrick, and Murphy. Dr Johnson was brought by Mrs Thrale, who commented on the dust and the cobwebs. The house was rebuilt after a fire in 1813. Burke's memorial is in the parish church. In 1809 William Hickey, the son of one of Burke's friends, took 'a pretty cottage called Little Hall Barn' near Hall Barn, then the seat of a descendant of Edmund Waller. Hickey, who brought with him his elderly sisters, an Indian servant, and a large dog, decided to fill the vacuum surrounding him after returning from his exciting life in India by 'setting his memories in order and writing down his life-story'. *The Memoirs of William Hickey* (ed. A. Spencer, 1913–25; ed. P. Quennell, 1960, 1975) tell of the uproarious escapades of his youth, both amorous and felonious, his banishment to a cadetship in the East India Company, and his success at the Indian Bar, which gained him a small fortune.

St Teresa's Catholic church commemorates G. K. Chesterton, who lived (1909–36) at Overroads, Grove Rd Ⓟ, and wrote his best work there, including the Father Brown crime stories, *The Innocence of Father Brown* (1911), *The Wisdom of Father Brown*, and others, *Collected Poems* (1915), which includes 'Lepanto', and the critical study *George Bernard Shaw* (1909; enlarged edn, 1935).

Robert Frost lived at The Bungalow, Reynolds Rd, most of the time he was in England (Sept. 1912–Feb. 1915). Here he assembled his first book of poems, *A Boy's Will* (1913), and wrote most of his second volume, *North of Boston* (1914).

BEARSTED *Kent*

Large village off the A20, on the eastern outskirts of Maidstone. Edward Thomas lived (1901–4) at two cottages here; the first, Rose Acre, damp and ugly and with no roses until he planted them, was 1 m. from the village at the foot of the N Downs, and the second, which he also called Rose Acre, was on the village green next to a wheelwright's shop. He published two volumes of essays, *Horae Solitariae* (1902) and *Rose Acre Papers* (1904), and some reviews, but his financial position, with a wife and son to support, was precarious. In 1921 Sinclair Lewis spent two months at the Bell House at the end of the green. He was writing *Babbitt* (1922), and he left for Paris at the end of September. (For Leeds Castle, see MAIDSTONE.)

BECKLEY *Oxfordshire*

Village 6 m. NE of Oxford. It figures in R. D. Blackmore's story *Cripps the Carrier* (1876). The carrier's home, Cripps Cottage, is on the road leading to Otmoor.

Beckley Park, with its three gables, is said to be a model for the house in Aldous Huxley's *Crome Yellow* (1921), which has 'three projected towers'. Evelyn Waugh wrote much of *Rossetti: His Life and Works* (1928) in the village at the Abingdon Arms. He also spent his honeymoon there after his marriage in June 1928 to Evelyn Gardner.

BEDHAMPTON *Hampshire*

Town on the B2150 adjoining Havant. Mill Lane, near the parish church in Old Bedhampton, leads to the Old Mill House facing the wide stream. Keats and his friend Charles Armitage Brown spent some time here after visiting Chichester in January 1819. They were present at the consecration of the much discussed new Gothic chapel at *Stansted built by Lewis Way. Robert Gittings's *John Keats: The Living Year* (1967) describes how Keats used his experience there in 'The Eve of St Agnes' (1820), begun in Chichester but finished here when his stay was extended because of illness. A plaque on the back of the house, placed there in 1959 by the Keats–Shelley Memorial Associations of England and America, records also that Keats spent his last night in England in the mill house when his ship put into Portsmouth because of a storm.

BEECH *Hampshire*

Village just off the A339, 2 m. W of Alton. Sir Compton Mackenzie lived at Canadian Cottage (demolished in the 1960s) in the holidays and at weekends from 1896 to 1900. Although he said this was 'long, long before I wrote anything', he drew on his memories of the place for three of his novels: *The Altar Steps* (1922) and its sequel, *The Parson's Progress* (1923), are partly founded on Alton Abbey, Beech, which is run by Benedictines; *Buttercups and Daisies* (1931), written with lively humour, contains thinly veiled portraits of local characters of recent memory.

BEMBRIDGE SCHOOL *Isle of Wight*

School on the B3395, on the E coast, where John Howard Whitehouse (Warden 1919–54) established the Ruskin Galleries, which contain the largest single collection of Ruskin's work. The collection is now housed at the Ruskin

Foundation, University of *Lancaster. Whitehouse, who edited (with J. Evans) *The Diaries of John Ruskin* (1956–9), also helped establish Ruskin's home, *Brantwood, as his national memorial.

John Heath-Stubbs was educated at Bembridge School, chosen for him, as he wrote in his autobiography *Hindsights* (1993), 'mainly because of the injunctions of the oculist that I should not read too much and should be encouraged to do things with my hands'. The school was not academic enough for his tastes and Heath-Stubbs, whose sight was failing, had to try and teach himself Greek by huddling away in the library with Dr Smith's Greek Grammar.

BENTWORTH *Hampshire*

Village on a minor road S of the A339, 5 m. W of Alton. George Wither, one of the most famous of Hampshire poets, was born here (11 June 1588), the son of a well-to-do farmer. He received his 'grammatical learning' from a local schoolmaster and went to Magdalen College, *Oxford, when he was 16. Many years later he wrote of his carefree boyhood days when 'hounds, hawks and horses were at my command', and at the age of 79 he wished to return to his birthplace but died instead 'in streaming London's central roar'.

BEXHILL-ON-SEA *East Sussex*

Town and seaside resort. The novelist Angus Wilson was born at Dunscore, on Dorset Road, in 1913, but his childhood was peripatetic because of the fluctuating circumstances brought about by his father's habitual gambling. The lives of his parents are the basis of those of the Calverts in his novel *Late Call* (1964).

BIGNOR PARK *West Sussex*

Country house, 2 m. W of the A29 at Bury, not visible from the road. Charlotte Smith (*née* Turner) spent her childhood here at her father's house and her family arranged her unhappy marriage to Benjamin Smith, the spendthrift son of a West India merchant. Her sonnets 'Bignor Park' and 'To the Arun' recall the pleasures of her childhood and her love for the county where she spent most of her life.

BINFIELD *Berkshire*

Village on the B3034, *c.* 3 m. NE of Wokingham, on the edge of Windsor Forest, now widely developed on both sides of the main road. A house called Pope's Manor is thought to be an extension of a 17th-c. brick house bought by Pope's father in 1698 and known successively as Whitehill House, Binfield Lodge, Pope's Lodge, The Firs, and Arthurstone, before its present name. Pope was brought here from London at the age of 12 (1700) and stayed until the house was sold in 1713. During this time he planned his own method of study and began his literary career, his first published work being *Pastorals*, written when he was 16 (published in Tonson's

Poetical Miscellanies, pt. VI, 1709); followed by *An Essay on Criticism*, a didactic poem in heroic couplets (1711), which introduced him to Addison's circle; *The Messiah*, a sacred eclogue, published in *The Spectator* (May 1712); *The Rape of the Lock*, a mock-heroic poem (published in Lintot's *Miscellanies*, 1712; enlarged 1714); and *Windsor Forest*, a pastoral poem (1713). By the time he left Binfield, Pope had begun the translation of Homer's *Iliad* (6 vols, 1715–20). The row of fine Scots firs from which one of the modern names of the house was taken probably existed in Pope's time and it has been thought that he alludes to the house and its surroundings in the lines:

> My paternal cell,
> A little house, with trees a-row,
> And like its master very low.

The original house could well have been 'little' and 'low' before the extensive 19th-c. alterations and additions were made.

BINSEY *Oxfordshire*

Small Thames-side village reached from the Botley Rd in Oxford, or on foot, from the towpath. The poem by G. M. Hopkins 'Binsey Poplars, felled 1879' describes his sense of loss in the lines:

> My aspens dear, whose airy cages quelled,
> Quelled or quenched in leaves the leaping sun,
> All felled, felled, are all felled;
> Of a fresh and following folded rank
> Not spared, not one
> That dandled a sandalled
> Shadow that swam or sank
> On meadow and river and wind-wandering
>   weed-winding bank.

A. E. Coppard, when working (1907–19) at the Eagle Ironworks in Walton Well Rd, *Oxford, often visited the Perch during the midday break. Dylan Thomas, Louis MacNeice, and W. R. Rodgers also used to come here on weekend visits to Oxford.

In the churchyard of St Margaret's Church, ½ m. along a sequestered lane from the village green, is St Frideswide's well, believed to be the prototype of the treacle well in *Alice in Wonderland* (1865). C. L. Dodgson ('Lewis Carroll') used to visit Binsey, perhaps with Alice Liddell, whose nanny, Miss Prickett, came from the village. He would know its local name, 'Binsey treacle mine', in which 'treacle' is used in its original sense of 'curative fluid' or 'balm', the well being renowned for its therapeutic qualities.

BIRCHINGTON *Kent*

Seaside resort on the A28, adjacent to Margate. Dante Gabriel Rossetti, who spent the last months of his life as an invalid in a bungalow (gone) lent by the architect J. P. Seddon, was buried (1882) near the porch of the parish church, where a large Celtic cross marks the grave. Hall Caine looked after him and Watts-Dunton was at his deathbed. Inside the church is a Pre-Raphaelite memorial window.

BISHOPSBOURNE *Kent*

Quiet village off the A2 S of Canterbury, where Richard Hooker became rector in 1595. Much of *Ecclesiastical Polity* was written here, book V being published in 1597. A memorial on the S side of the chancel states he was buried in 1600. The 12-ft-long stone slab over his remains is thought to have been the old altar. He left £3 in his will for a 'newer and sufficient pulpit'. His rectory has gone but the old yew hedge is still called Hooker's Hedge. Near the church is a late Georgian successor to Hooker's rectory (now called Oswalds); it was Conrad's home from 1920 until his death in 1924.

Jocelyn Brooke spent his childhood summers in Forge Cottage and returned to the village to live at Ivy Cottage later in life. His autobiographical novel *The Military Orchid* (1948) shows that the village occupied a central place in his childhood botanizing, 'where Mr Bundock lurked like a wood-spirit in the warm, tree-muffled evenings'.

BISHOPSGATE *Berkshire*

Hamlet on a minor road just W of the B4447, 10 m. NW of Windsor. Shelley and Mary Godwin stayed here in the summer of 1815, in a low-roofed cottage near the Rhododendron Walk of Windsor Park, 'so secluded that even the tax-collector didn't know it'. Bishopsgate Heath lay in front and Chapel Wood and Virginia Water to the W. A garden provided flowers. Shelley loved walking in the forest, and Peacock, whom he later joined at *Marlow, was a frequent visitor. During this time Shelley wrote *Alastor, or, The Spirit of Solitude* (1816), his first important work.

BISHOPSTONE *East Sussex*

Village off the A259 N of Seaford. James Hurdis (1763–1801) was born here, spent his vacations from Oxford here, and in 1791 became the vicar. He lived at Hallands, a long, low, flint house with Gothic windows, in the hamlet of Norton (½ m. N), where he set up a printing press in the cellar and produced *The Favourite Village* (1800). He was a friend and correspondent of Cowper, and of Hayley, who wrote memorial verses on his sudden death in 1801. He is buried in the church with his sister Catherine, whose gradual decline and early death he lamented in a long poem. Memorial tablets to them both are in the church together with Hayley's lines.

BLACK BOURTON *Oxfordshire*

Little village *c.* 5½ m. N of Faringdon, on a minor road off the B4095. Maria Edgeworth was born (1 Jan. 1768) at her mother's family home, the old hall, which once stood just NW of the church, but of which no trace remains.

BLEWBURY *Oxfordshire*

Village in the downs, a few miles S of Didcot, off the A417. Kenneth Grahame, who lived here at Boham's, a Tudor brick farmhouse, from 1910 to 1924, described it as 'the heart of King Alfred's country', hardly changed since Saxon times except for William the Conqueror's Curfew bell, which still rings during the winter.

BOGNOR REGIS *West Sussex*

Coastal resort. Julian MacLaren-Ross sold vacuum cleaners door-to-door in the town in the mid-1930s. The experience furnished material for *Of Love and Hunger* (1947), his novel of doorsteps, dingy boarding houses, unrequited love, and novel-writing under the shadow of the approaching Second World War.

BOLDRE *Hampshire*

Village just N of Lymington, off the A337. Its most celebrated vicar was William Gilpin, whose travels in the New Forest, the Lakes, and Scotland were recorded in *Picturesque Tours* (1782), illustrated by his own drawings. The proceeds of his *Remarks on Forest Scenery* (1791), illustrated by scenes of the New Forest, enabled him to found a school for poor children. He was vicar from 1777 until his death in 1804 and there is a tablet to his memory in the N chapel and an engraving of his only known portrait at the W end of the S aisle. His tomb in the churchyard bears an inscription composed by himself.

Southey married his second wife, Caroline Bowles, in Boldre church (1839).

BONCHURCH *Isle of Wight*

Coastal resort on the A3055, 1 m. E of Ventnor. In 1849 Dickens rented Winterbourne (now a hotel, residents only), a large house on the side of the steep hill overlooking the sea. He had first seen this when staying with his friend the Revd James White at Woodlynch (now a private home). Dickens wrote part of *David Copperfield* here and the story of the donkeys and some incidents from the later novel *Great Expectations* are thought to have originated here (see *Dickens on an Island*, 1970, by Richard J. Hutchings). Dickens's sons played with 'the golden haired lad of the Swinburnes', who lived at East Dene (now a children's environmental education centre), a little way up the hill. Swinburne spent his childhood and many vacations here until his parents moved in 1868 when he was 31. In his *Letters* he mentions being revived from a faint by a sheep licking his face, after succeeding at the second attempt in scaling the steep Culver Cliff (3 m. NE). Henry de Vere Stacpoole (1863–1951), who lived at Cliff Dene, donated the pond to the village in memory of his wife. He made his name as a novelist with *The Blue Lagoon* (1909). A collection of his poems is called *In a Bonchurch Garden* (1937). Stacpoole and Swinburne are buried in the new church (built 1847). In 1910 Hardy wrote 'A Singer Asleep' by Swinburne's grave.

BOROUGH FARM *Surrey*

18th-c. farmhouse, later in a nature reserve, N of the A3, 1 m. SW of Milford. Mrs Humphry Ward saw the house when staying at *Peper Harow and rented the major part of it (1883–90). Here she wrote her most famous novel, *Robert Elsmere* (1888), which Gladstone reviewed.

BOTLEY *Hampshire*

Large village on the A334 and the A3051, just E of Southampton. William Cobbett lived from 1804 to 1817 at Botley House with 4 acres of productive garden, and he acquired Fairthorn Farm in 1807, and Raglinton the next year. He thought Botley, where he organized single-stick matches, 'the most delightful village in the world', and here he, as the epitome of an Old English yeoman, was a generous host to his many visitors. Cobbett's *Weekly Political Register* was published from 1802 to his death in 1835 and when addressing meetings, he frequently asked the company to drink to it, raising his glass to 'Trash', the name given it by his opponents.

BOUGHTON MALHERBE *Kent*

Small village on a high ridge 2 m. S of the A20 at Lenham. The early 15th-c. manor (often called Bocton in the past) was the birthplace (1568) of the poet Henry Wotton, younger son of the retired diplomat who was visited here by Queen Elizabeth I when his son was 5. Wotton left to attend Winchester College but later visited his niece and her children here. Walpole mentions the manor in his letters when his friend Galfridus Mann bought the estate in 1750.

BOURNE END *Buckinghamshire*

A village near the confluence of the Wye and the Thames. In 1901 the novelist Rosamond Lehmann was born at Fieldhead, a rambling, large-gabled, red-brick, Arts and Crafts house surrounded by a large, handsome garden. Lehmann looked back on the place as a lost Eden, and took the house and garden as a major setting for her first novel, *Dusty Answer* (1927).

BOX HILL *Surrey*

Wooded down (NT) E off the A25, 4 m. NE of Dorking, named from the box trees once prevalent there. Jane Austen, who probably visited from *Great Bookham, chose the hill for the scene in *Emma* (1816) of one of Mrs Elton's 'exploring parties'. This was even more unsuccessful than the picnic at Donwell as everyone was upset by someone and Emma was unkind to Miss Bates. In a letter from *Burford Bridge, Keats wrote that he 'went up Box Hill this evening after the moon'.

BRADENHAM *Buckinghamshire*

Village with a large green off the A4010, where Isaac D'Israeli wrote *Curiosities of Literature* (1791). His son Benjamin Disraeli described the Manor and 'the glade-like terrace of yew trees' in the gardens with poetic licence in *Endymion* (1880).

BREDE *East Sussex*

Village on the A28, 6 m. N of Hastings. The church, which was presented with Swift's cradle by the vicar in 1895, is opposite the lane to Brede Place (1 m.), a 14th-c. manor with Elizabethan alterations. The American Stephen Crane, author of *The Red Badge of Courage* (1895), and Lady Stewart (Cora), rented it in January 1899 after his visit to Cuba. The rambling house was damp and unmodernized and Crane, who was consumptive, became gravely ill. Visitors, who included Conrad and Henry James, found Cora cheerful until the end of the year, when she took Crane abroad. He died soon after and was buried in the family grave in New Jersey.

BRIGHTON AND HOVE *East Sussex*

Large resort city on the S coast, formerly the fishing village of Brighthelmstone, which became fashionable in the mid-18th c. for its bracing air and sea-bathing. Dr Johnson was so much a part of the Thrale household that he usually accompanied them in the 1770s to their seaside home in West St. Their house was replaced by a concert hall (where Dickens gave some of his readings), which lost favour when the Dome was opened, and later became a dance hall (Ⓟ erected by the Regency Society). Dr Johnson worked on the *Lives of the Poets* here and Mrs Thrale read the proofs. Fanny Burney also stayed with the Thrales and her *Diary* records her visits to Shergolds or the New Assembly Rooms in the Castle inn (gone) in Castle Sq. (site later the electricity showroom). They also went to the Assembly Rooms, known as Hicks, attached to the Old Ship in Ship St. Mr Thrale played cards and his wife and Fanny Burney danced. In the mornings they patronized Mr Thomas's bookshop on the Steine. The Thrales and their guests attended St Nicholas's Church, where a tablet to Dr Johnson is on a N wall window-ledge.

George IV, when Prince of Wales, visited Brighton in 1783 and later added to its attractions by building the Royal Pavilion, completed when he was Regent.

In 1791 Wordsworth, waiting for a boat to France, called on Mrs Charlotte Smith, whose nostalgic descriptions of the countryside he had admired in her *Elegiac Sonnets* bought at Cambridge two years before. Her last volume, *Beachy Head and Other Poems* (1807), appeared posthumously. One of Robert Anderson's sonnets in *Poetical Works* (1820) was addressed to her.

Charles and Mary Lamb spent a holiday here in 1817 'in sight of the sea' with their friends the Morgans. Dickens stayed here many times from 1837, at the Old Ship, at 148 Kings Rd, and at 62 East St. He also stayed at the Bedford Hotel Ⓟ in 1848, when writing *Dombey and Son* (1847–8), where he lodged Captain Cuttle and other characters. Dr Blimber's school is said to have been at Chichester House, Chichester Ter. His friend Harrison Ainsworth spent many months here with his family in the 1840s, first at 38 Brunswick Ter., then at 25 Oriental Pl. He and Dickens visited Horace Smith at 12 Cavendish Pl., where the Misses Smith welcomed their father's literary friends, including Thackeray, Thomas Hood, and Samuel Rogers. Smith was contributing to

Ainsworth's *New Monthly Magazine*. Thackeray gave his lecture on 'The Four Georges' at the Town Hall in 1851. Ainsworth was at 6 Brunswick Sq. while alterations were made to Kensal Manor. Then (1853–67) he moved to 5 Arundel Ter. Ⓟ, where he wrote *Cardinal Pole* (1863) and *Constable de Bourbon* (1866).

Robert Surtees, whose sporting Cockney grocer John Jorrocks enjoyed himself on the Downs, died in Brighton (1864) but was buried near *Hamsterley Hall. Richard Jefferies lived here for a short time (1885) at 5 (now 87) Lorna Rd, Hove, adjoining Brighton to the W. Lewis Carroll paid regular Christmas holiday visits between 1874 and 1887, staying with an old Oxford friend at 11 Sussex Sq. Ⓟ. He also came to Brighton in 1887 to see a stage version of *Alice in Wonderland* at the Theatre Royal, acted by his young friends Isa, Maggie, and Emsie Bowman. Thomas Hughes died here in 1896 and Herbert Spencer died at 5 Percival Ter. in 1903.

A. E. Coppard (1872–1957), who went to the Board School in Fairlight Pl., leaving at the age of 9, lived with his parents in lodgings in Melbourne St. and Gladstone Pl. When he worked as a bookkeeper at the Engineering Works near the barracks, he educated himself at the former Public Library. He married here in 1906. The short stories 'Ninepenny Flute' and 'Pomona's Babe' are about Brighton, although written after he left in 1907. John Cowper Powys taught at a girls' school in the W of the town for a short time. Conan Doyle's *Rodney Stone* (1896) and Thackeray's *Vanity Fair* (1847–8) have scenes of Regency Brighton; Henry James's short story 'Sir Edmund Orme,' Arnold Bennett's *Clayhanger* (1910) and its sequel *Hilda Lessways* (1911), Maugham's *Of Human Bondage* (1915), and A. S. M. Hutchinson's *If Winter Comes* (1920) also have scenes set here.

Ivy Compton-Burnett lived in Hove from 1892 to 1916. In 1897 her parents and their large family moved to 20 The Drive, a mid-Victorian double-fronted house. She published her first novel, *Dolores*, in 1911 and five years later moved to the first of her London flats.

Behind the 'cream houses [which] ran away into the west like a pale Victorian water-colour' the underworld of the 1930s is unforgettably evoked in Graham Greene's *Brighton Rock* (1938). Nelson Place, where the boy gangster Pinkie and his confederates Spicer and Dallow hole up, was cleared away after the war. It is on the Palace Pier where Pinkie makes the cruel sixpenny recording for his deceived teenage wife, Rose, and where, earlier in the novel, he articulates his bleak faith:

> 'These atheists, they don't know nothing. Of course there's Hell. Flames and damnation,' he said with his eyes on the dark shifting water and the lightning and the lamps going out above the black struts of the Palace Pier, 'torments.'

Greene stayed in the Royal Albion Hotel opposite the pier on his visits to the town.

Less well known, but highly praised by Greene himself (he called it 'the best book written about Brighton'), is Patrick Hamilton's *The West Pier* (1951), which follows the activities of the heartless Ernest Gorse, seducer and con artist, along the front and pier and in and out of the Metropole Hotel in Brighton during the 1920s. The city also appears in a humiliating episode in Hamilton's novel *Hangover Square* (1941), when the schizophrenic hero stays at a hotel off Castle Sq. Hamilton was born at 12 First Ave. and brought up in Hove.

The poet and editor Alan Ross trained for a naval commission here in 1943. His wartime experience on Arctic destroyers is the substance of his collection *Open Sea* (1975) and his two volumes of memoir, *Blindfold Games* (1986) and *Coastwise Lights* (1988). Anthony Burgess lived in Hove in 1959–60 and it was here, in 1959, that he was diagnosed with the 'inoperable brain tumour' that was supposed to give him only a year to live. His determination to write enough books in the time remaining to him in order to support his wife in her 'widowhood' launched his writing career in earnest. Hove itself, with its pubs, 'gull-clawed air, New Year blue, the tide crawling creamily in', is an inspiration for his *Enderby* novels (1960s and 1980s). Some locations, such as the Neptune on Kingsway, 'the sort of pub in which any of the three parts—saloon, public, outdoor—is visible from any other', can be identified; others, such as no. 81 Fitzherbert Avenue, containing Enderby's flat and famous lavatory, cannot (although it could be imagined in the Poets' Corner district, not far from the Town Hall). The interior of Enderby's flat was modelled on Burgess's own furnished lodgings.

The autumn of 1967 saw the novelist-to-be Martin Amis at Sussex Tutors, a crammer on the waterfront at 55 Marine Parade—his 'last-gasp saloon', he wrote:

> a ramshackle warren that seemed to be all attic, stood on an urban cliff above the pier and the pebbly beach where the breakers flopped and trawled. It was said that the building had once been a nursing home, and it was adjacent to a nursing home and surrounded by other nursing homes. Brighton itself was a nursing home; and on warm days the elderly would be helped or wheeled out on to the terraces and fenced rooftops, tier after tier of candyfloss hair and vague, freckled, upturned faces, enjoying the sun and the unvaryingly barbarous wind.

Perhaps unknown to the young Amis, one of his older neighbours was the playwright Terence Rattigan, who spent the 1960s in a house just a few doors along the seafront, Bedford House, at 79 Marine Parade Ⓟ, which he had bought in 1961.

Alan Brownjohn's poem 'A Brighton' makes engaging use of the town's reputation as a secret bolthole for Londoners:

> 'Brighton': not far, a lie or an excuse
> Like dental checks or grandmothers' funerals.
> 'Did you have a nice day at Brighton?' asks the master
> Receiving a boy's forged note about his cold.

The two coastal journeys of the travel writers Paul Theroux (made by land) and Jonathan Raban (made by sea) converge at Brighton. Their meeting is recorded, in rather different ways, in Theroux's *The Kingdom by the Sea* (1983) and Raban's *Coasting* (1986). A lively description of the city opens Michael Smith's *The Giro Playboy* (2006), set in this 'Beverley Hills of the Georgian era'.

BRIGHTWALTON *Berkshire*

Small village 10 m. N of Newbury. In 1985, after the death of her husband, the novelist Monica Dickens moved to Brightwalton, to the thatched cottage where she lived for the rest of her life. She died in a Reading hospital on Christmas Day in 1992.

BROADSTAIRS *Kent*

Coastal resort on the A255, in the NE of the county, popular since the 19th c. Charles Dickens spent holidays here between 1836 and 1850. He wrote part of *Pickwick Papers* (1836) while lodging at 12 High St. (gone, but Ⓟ on the site of no. 31). *Nicholas Nickleby* (1839) was written at 40 Albion St., now the Royal Albion Hotel Ⓟ. *The Old Curiosity Shop* (1840) and *Barnaby Rudge* (1841) were written at Lawn House, now called Archway House, which spans the walk leading from Bleak House on the cliff above to 'the Old Curiosity Shop'. Bleak House (open to the public, www.bleakhouse.info), where the study, bedroom, and dining room are furnished with Dickens's possessions, was originally called The Fort and was where he completed *David Copperfield*. The original Betsey Trotwood is said to have lived at the end of Victoria Parade; this is now the Dickens House Museum, and commemorates Dickens's association with the town (www.dickenshouse.co.uk) Ⓟ.

In July 1914 John Buchan was staying in lodgings with his wife and daughter Alice, who was recovering from a mastoid operation, when he fell ill and had to stay in bed. To relieve the boredom he began writing the spy story *The Thirty-Nine Steps* (1915), linking the title to a wooden flight of steps (now replaced by a more solid structure) leading to a small cove on the North Foreland.

The beginning of the chapter 'A Summer's Day' in Elizabeth Bowen's novel *Eva Trout* (1969) has a description of the study of Bleak House with the lantern window, which hangs out in the air overlooking the sea and, in Dickens's day, the cornfields all around.

BROCKENHURST *Hampshire*

Village on the A337, halfway between Lymington and Lyndhurst. Roydon Manor, a house of mellowed brick among the trees, can be seen from a bridle path which leads off an unclassified road to the SE. W. H. Hudson lodged here when he wrote *Hampshire Days* (1903), an account of local natural history and people, 'Inscribed to Sir Edward and Lady Grey, Northumbrians with Hampshire written in their hearts'.

BUCKLEBURY *Berkshire*

Village 8 m. from Newbury, between the B4009 and the A4. Richard Aldington's novel *The Colonel's Daughter* (1925) had its origins in this village, where he lived (*c.* 1921) before going to France.

BURFORD *Oxfordshire*

Picturesque little Cotswold market town 20 m. W of Oxford, on the A40. John Wilmot, 2nd Earl of Rochester, who was born at *Ditchley, was educated at the old Grammar School before going to Wadham College, *Oxford.

Across the bridge over the Windrush, at the foot of the wide main street, there are one or two old houses on the river bank. Compton Mackenzie stayed in one of these from 1904 to 1911 and drew a delightful portrait of Burford as 'Wychford' in his novel *Guy and Pauline* (1915). John Meade Falkner, author of *Moonfleet* (1898), contributed to the restoration of the church, and is buried in the churchyard.

C. E. Montague came to Burford when he retired from the *Manchester Guardian* in 1925. He lived at Kitt's Quarries, ½ m. W of the town, a house built by Christopher Kempster, a mason who worked for Sir Christopher Wren in the rebuilding of St Paul's. In 1927 Montague published *Right off the Map*, an anti-militarist novel originally written as a play. The following year he was working on a long new novel about the 20 years preceding the First World War when he died suddenly on a visit to *Manchester. He was cremated there and his ashes were buried in Burford churchyard.

BURFORD BRIDGE *Surrey*

Bridge over the Mole, 1 m. N of Dorking. Anna Barbauld, in her poem on the bridge, wrote in 1796:

From the smoke and the din, and the hurry of town
Let the care wearied cit to this spot hasten down.
Here may Industry, Peace, Contentment reign still
While the Mole softly creeps at the foot of the hill.

In late November and early December 1817 Keats spent two weeks in a small back room of the Fox and Hounds (now the larger Burford Bridge Hotel) consistently writing about 80 lines a day to finish *Endymion* (1818). He climbed *Box Hill by the path behind the inn. During the second week he composed the song 'In a drear-nighted December'. Stevenson also stayed at the hotel, once when walking in the hills nearby and again in 1878 when he visited Meredith at *Mickleham. He wrote part of *The New Arabian Nights* (1882) here.

BURITON (pr. 'Berriton) *Hampshire*

Quiet village on an unclassified road, 3 m. S of Petersfield. The historic manor house on the N side of the church was the home of Edward Gibbon, when he returned from Switzerland in 1758, where he spent as much time as possible in the library, 'although occasionally compelled to visit horse races, entertain country squires, or canvas at elections'. He joined the South Hampshire Militia and was called out for active service—'most disagreeably active', he recorded, '—a wandering life of military servitude', which ended at Christmas 1762, but which proved useful experience of military matters when he came to write the *History of the Decline and Fall of the Roman Empire* (1776–88).

BURPHAM (pr. 'Burfam) *West Sussex*

Quiet village on the Arun, 2 m. N of Arundel. Mervyn Peake and his wife, Maeve, stayed for a weekend honeymoon at his father's newly built house, Reed Thatch. Two years later they came again before the arrival of their first baby and then found a small house at Lower Warningcamp nearby. It was here that Titus Groan, the central character of the *Titus Groan* trilogy, was conceived. When Mervyn's call-up papers brought him a spell of desultory war service, Burpham was his home base, and where he lived from 1942 to 1944 on indefinite sick leave after a nervous breakdown. He will probably be remembered best for *Titus Groan* (1946), *Gormenghast* (1950), and *Titus Alone* (1959), and for the poems *The Glassblowers* (1950). He died in 1968 after a long illness and was buried in the churchyard at Burpham.

BURTON *Hampshire*

Village off the B3347, 1 m. N of Christchurch. Southey and his wife found lodgings here in 1797 for the summer while he was studying law in London and pining for country air. He delighted in the sea and the rivers of the New Forest—'the clearest you ever saw'—and returned to London in September with reluctance. Two years later he came back to Burton and acquired a pair of adjoining cottages, which he converted into the thatched house as it exists today, 'small . . . and somewhat quaint', with a fishpond and a garden and a book room 'that, like the Chapter House at Salisbury . . . requires a column to support the roof'. He was working at the time on *Thalaba the Destroyer* and his letters sounded cheerful, but no sooner was the work on the house finished than he became ill and had to leave. The house, called Burton Cottage, is at the S end of the green, shielded from the road by trees and bushes.

BURWASH *East Sussex*

Village on the A265, 7 m. SW of Hawkhurst. James Hurdis, who lived at The Friars (Burwash Place) was a correspondent of William Cowper, and William Hayley, who, when Hurdis was in distress at the death of his sister, persuaded him to visit *Eartham. Hurdis's long poem *The Village Curate* (1788) stems from the years (1785–91) of his curacy here.

The tall-chimneyed, 17th-c. house called Bateman's (NT), ½ m. S of the village, was the home (1902–36) of Rudyard Kipling, who, on first looking over the house, felt 'her Spirit—her Feng Shui—to be good'. *Puck of Pook's Hill* (1906) (the hill of the title is visible from the house), *Rewards and Fairies* (1910), and the unfinished autobiography *Something of Myself* (1937) are among the books written in the study, which remains as he left it. He redesigned the garden, planted yew hedges, and had plans for further alterations. The lines from his poem 'Sussex' show his pleasure in the county:

God gives all men all earth to love,
But since man's heart is small,
Ordains for each one spot shall prove
Beloved over all.
Each to his choice, and I rejoice
The lot has fallen to me
In a fair ground—in a fair ground—
Yea, Sussex by the sea!

BURY *West Sussex*

Village off the A29, 4 m. N of Arundel. John Galsworthy bought Bury House, the Tudor-style stone house at the top of the village, at first sight in 1920, and divided his time between Bury and his *Hampstead home. The house has extensive views across farmland to the South Downs, where he used to ride and where, after his death in Hampstead in 1933, his ashes were scattered.

BYFLEET *Surrey*

Large village off the A245, 5 m. NE of Woking. In 1749 Joseph Spence, author of the well-known *Anecdotes* about Pope and others, was given a house here by his former pupil Lord Lincoln. Spence in turn obtained the living for Stephen Duck, brought to prominence by his poem 'The Thresher's Labour'. Duck moved here in 1752 (rectory rebuilt) and in 1755 published *Caesar's Camp, or, St George's Hill*, which contains the lines:

Remote from giddy crowds and noisy strife
Yet near the few whose converse sweeten life
Here let me live. Be mindful of my end,
Adore my Maker and enjoy my friend.

However, Duck, who began to suffer from depression after his second wife's death in 1749, enjoyed Spence's company for a few years only, before drowning himself on *Reading on returning from a visit to his native *village in 1756. Spence suffered a similar fate, though his death in a pond in his grounds was accidental. A memorial tablet is in the church, and Spence's Point on St George's Hill, marked by the firs he planted, perpetuates his name.

CAMBERLEY *Surrey*

Town SW of London situated at the intersection of Surrey, Hampshire, and Berkshire. The voice of Sir John Betjeman's 'Camberley' advises her listener to

Make for Posnah Punkah Park,
And by the Monument to Clive
You'll come to Enniscorthy Drive,
Coolgreen is the last of all,
And mind the terrier when you call.

The novelist Simon Raven was educated (and seduced) at Cordwalles School in the 1930s.

CANTERBURY *Kent*

Cathedral city on the Roman roads, the A2, A28, and the A290. Chaucer stayed here (1360–1) as part of the royal household, and he makes *The Canterbury Tales* a collection of stories to beguile the journey of pilgrims, coming to do penance at the ornate shrine of St Thomas Becket, originally to the E of the High Altar, in the Trinity chapel of the Cathedral, but wrecked in 1538. Becket's murder was the subject of dramas by George Darley in 1840, by Tennyson in 1884, and of Eliot's *Murder in the Cathedral* (1935), first staged in the Chapter House.

John Bale, whose persecution after leaving the Catholic Church sent him abroad during Mary's reign, was made a prebend by Elizabeth I and spent his remaining years here, where he wrote *King John* (1548) and morality plays. The poet Alexander Barclay wrote the *Life of St Thomas* (1520) and joined the Franciscans here before becoming a rector in London in 1552. Part of their Grey Friars buildings can still be seen and the dorter (built 1267) was for a time the home of Richard Lovelace, who, though heir to estates in the county, fell on hard times during the Commonwealth after presenting the Kentish Petition. The birthplace of John Lyly (1569) is unknown, and that of Christopher Marlowe (1564) in St George's St. was destroyed in 1942. Like the playwright Stephen Gosson in 1554, Marlowe was baptized in St George's Church, of which only the tower remains ℗ in the new shopping area. A Victorian tribute representing the four main characters in his plays acted by Irving, Forbes Robertson, Alleyn, and James Hackett stands in Dane John gardens by the old city wall. Nearby, off the busy Rheims Way, is the church (locked) of St Mildred with St Mary de Castro, where Izaak Walton married in 1626. Anne Finch, Countess of Winchilsea, lived at The Moat (gone) off the Littlebourne road, where she was visited by Celia Fiennes. In their verses Pope addressed her as 'Ardelia' and Rowe as 'Flavia'.

Richard Barham was born (1785) in the Burgate at the corner of Canterbury Lane (℗ on site of former house). Some of his *Ingoldsby Legends* (1840) are set in the city, where the sisters Harriet and Sophia Lee chose to keep their travellers snowbound long enough to recount their improbable *Canterbury Tales* (1797–1805). Dickens set many scenes in *David Copperfield* (1850) here and the House of Agnes Hotel in St Dunstan St. is said to have been Agnes Wickfield's home. The Sun (built 1503), later a shop near the Cathedral, has a plaque listing Dickens's associations with the inn. Conrad (d. 1924) was buried in the cemetery (memorial stone) after a service in St Thomas's Roman Catholic Church, attended by many of his friends including Cunninghame Graham, who described the scene in 'Inveni Portum', published in *Redeemed* (1927).

Linacre, Marlowe, Hugh Walpole, and Maugham were at King's School in the cathedral precincts. Walpole and Maugham left bequests to the school. In 1961 Maugham returned to open the Maugham Library, which houses his own books, and manuscripts of *Liza of Lambeth* (1897) and *Catalina* (1948), his first and last novels. In *Of Human Bondage* (1915), his autobiographical novel, Philip Carey goes to school in 'Tercanbury', his name for Canterbury. Maugham's ashes were placed in the wall of the Maugham Library, where there is a simple plaque.

Lawrence Durrell spent a little over a year at St Edmund's College in Canterbury, dropping out in December 1927. Forty-five years later the novelist Kazuo Ishiguro studied at Canterbury too, taking his degree at the University of Kent.

The remains of Canterbury—known as 'Cambry' in the book—play an important part in the post-Armageddon world of Russell Hoban's *Riddley Walker* (1980). The four protagonists of Graham Swift's novel *Last Orders* (1996) stop and visit the Cathedral with the ashes of their friend Jack Dodds.

CARISBROOKE *Isle of Wight*

Village on the B3323, just SW of Newport. In 1648, when Charles I was imprisoned in the castle, ½ m. S, Dorothy Osborne and her brother, who had just met William Temple on the journey, stayed at the inn nearby. Young Osborne, who had Royalist sympathies, scratched a biblical quotation on the window which was considered seditious, and they were taken before the Governor. Dorothy Osborne, trusting his chivalry, confessed that she was the culprit and they were released, to Temple's admiration. Dorothy Osborne's *Letters* to Temple during their long courtship were published in 1888 and 1928.

John Keats stayed here in April 1817. In a letter to his friend John Reynolds from 'Mrs Cook's new village' (now Canterbury House, Castle Rd) he writes that he has unpacked his books, pinned up the picture by their friend Haydon, but is apprehensive as he has not yet written a word of the long poem he has planned. His room has a view of the castle (now obscured by trees) and he has walked about the island, 'which should be called Primrose Island', and found just the place where they can read their poems aloud when Reynolds comes. He has been reading *King Lear* and he includes the sonnet 'On the Sea', which he wrote as a result. Keats visited the island again but he and Reynolds never met here though Reynolds lived in *Newport later.

The castle figures in Meade Falkner's *Moonfleet* (1898).

CATERHAM *Surrey*

Town on the North Downs. Liam O'Flaherty, having enlisted in the Irish Guards, was trained at Caterham Barracks.

CAVERSHAM *Berkshire*

Suburb of Reading, 2 m. NE on the Henley road. Caversham Park is on the site of Lord Knollys's house (originally Cawsome-House), where Queen Anne of Denmark, wife of James I, was entertained by revels and a masque by Thomas Campion in April 1613. The house, which has since been twice rebuilt, was then 'fairly built of brick, mounted on the hillside of a Parke within view of Redding', and the Queen was so pleased with her entertainment that after supper 'she vouchsafed to make herselfe the head of their revels and graciously to adorn the place with her personall dancing'. A full description of the masque is given in *The Works of Thomas Campion*, ed. W. R. Davis (1967). The house became the headquarters of the BBC Monitoring Service.

CHALFONT ST GILES *Buckinghamshire*

Large village off the A413. Milton's Cottage, where he came with his family in 1665 to escape the plague, was found for him by a former pupil, the Quaker Thomas Ellwood. Now a museum, it contains many relics of the poet and rare editions of *Paradise Lost*, completed here before he returned to London in 1666. The popular novel *Deborah's Diary* (1859) by Anne Manning is an account of Milton's life here as told by his daughter.

CHALK *Kent*

Village on the E outskirts of Gravesend, on the A226. Charles Dickens spent his honeymoon (1836) here in a house at the end of the village on a corner of the lane leading to Shorne and Cobham. He often passed the house, when he was living at *Gad's Hill, on his extensive walks. The house has gone and a plaque has been fixed to a weatherboard house nearby. The forge in the village is traditionally that of Joe Gargery in *Great Expectations* (1860–1), which is set in the neighbourhood. A photograph of the honeymoon cottage is at the Dickens House, Doughty St. (see LONDON: HOLBORN).

CHATHAM *Kent*

One of the Medway towns off the M2. Cobbett arrived here in 1784 intending to enlist as a marine but found himself a foot soldier on sixpence a day instead. He spent the year here educating himself in grammar, which earned him a corporal's extra twopence a day, before he embarked for Nova Scotia.

Many scenes in Dickens's works stem from his early years when he lived (1817–21) with his parents in Ordnance Ter. ℗, now opposite the station but then covered with Virginia creeper and surrounded by fields. Later (1821–3), owing to money troubles which so often embarrassed his father, they moved to the smaller House on the Brook, St Mary's Pl. (gone), off Military Rd. Dickens went to Mr Giles's School in Clover Lane and spent many hours at the genial parties in the Mitre Inn and Clarence Hotel in the High St., which he describes in 'The Holly Tree' from *Christmas Stories*. In *David Copperfield* (1849–50), the young hero spends a night listening to the sentries' feet after selling his jacket to buy food. Members of the Pickwick Club attended a military review, and the fields about Fort Pitt, a naval hospital, were to be the scene of Mr Winkle's duel until it was so happily avoided.

Milton's Cottage, Chalfont St Giles

Jane Austen's House, Chawton

In *The Uncommercial Traveller* (1860), Dickens describes his arrival at the railway station, which had swallowed up the 'departed glories' of the fields where he had played the imaginative games of his youth. Dickens World, 'an indoor visitor complex themed around the life, books and times' of Dickens, has recently opened on Leviathan Way.

The obelisk at Chatham forms part of the itinerary of the four friends in Graham Swift's novel *Last Orders* (1996).

CHAWTON *Hampshire*

Village 1 m. S of Alton, now bypassed by the A31, but well signposted. Jane Austen and her sister Cassandra came with their mother, following their father's death in 1805, to Chawton in July 1809 after several moves and settled in the house then known as Chawton Cottage:

> Our Chawton Home, how much we find
>   Already in it to our mind:
> And now convinced, that when complete
>   It will all other houses beat
> That ever have been made or mended,
>   With rooms concise or rooms distended.

Thus Jane wrote to her brother Captain (later Admiral) Francis Austen RN, while they were still settling in. She wrote the final versions of her six novels here and lived here until her last move, to *Winchester in 1817. Now called Jane Austen's House Museum (www.jane-austens-house-museum.org.uk), it is beautifully cared for by the Jane Austen Memorial Trust, and has many treasures to delight her admirers: furniture, clothes, pictures, and books (including an American 1st edition of her novels, 1832).

CHERTSEY *Surrey*

Town on the A317. Abraham Cowley, who, as Evelyn records in his *Diary*, was considered the best poet of his day, was given an estate here by the Duke of Buckingham. His house in Guildford St. (altered in 1883) was an irregular, gabled, Tudor building with a room above the porch which jutted out into the road. This porch, with a plaque reading 'Here the last accents flowed from Cowley's tongue', was taken down in the 18th c. and the plaque has gone. The low-gabled shops in front of the Victorian building are all that remain.

Thomas Peacock lived at Gogmoor Hall with his widowed mother and grandfather Thomas Love. In *Recollections of Childhood* (1837), he gives an idealized description of Abbey House (gone), the home of a schoolfriend. After working in a merchant's office in London, he returned here and in 1807 met Fanny Faulkner at *Newark Priory. Opposite Cowley House was Beomonds, an 18th-c. house visited by Dickens, who used the Black Swan (gone) near Chertsey Bridge in *Oliver Twist* (1838) and modelled Mr Pecksniff in *Martin Chuzzlewit* (1843) on a local resident. The car park and Public Library are on the site of Beomonds, which was later the home of Ernest Coleridge, who edited extracts from his grandfather's notebooks, *Anima Poetae* (1895). Dickens was a friend of Albert Smith, the son of a doctor, born (1816) in a house opposite the church. He was a journalist and wrote the play *Blanche Heriot, or, The Chertsey Curfew* (1842) and many humorous novels, some illustrated by Phiz, which were popular in the 1850s. J. Maddison Morton, son of the creator of Mrs Grundy, wrote the popular farce *Box and Cox* (1847) at his home Laburnum Cottage in Bridge Rd.

CHICHESTER *West Sussex*

Cathedral city on the A27 and the old Stane St. Reginald Pecock when Bishop (1450) wrote three works in English instead of the usual Latin, which united the differing sections of church opinion against him. These, *The Repressor of over much blaming of the Clergy* (1455), *Book of Faith* (1456), and *Provoker*, resulted in his resigning the bishopric and being sent into retirement. The Gateway and the Bishop's Palace itself date from the 14th c. The Prebendal (choir) School later used part of the palace, as well as its original flint building and adjoining 18th-c. houses in West St. John Selden (b. 1584), who later disputed the legality of Charles I's privileges, was educated there by the lawyer Hugh Barker (d. 1632). Then known as the Free Grammar School, it had been reformed by Bishop Story (d. 1503), who built the ornate market cross. Poet James Hurdis was a pupil in the 1770s. Defoe mentions the 'great hole big enough for a coach and six' made when the cathedral spire was struck by lightning.

William Collins, whose father was three times mayor, was born (1721) at 21 East St. (now a bank). He lived, after returning from London, at 11 Westgate St., which he had inherited, but he became mentally ill and was cared for by his sister until his death at the Royal Chantry in the cloisters. He is buried in St Andrew Oxmarket, reached by a passage from East St., which has a memorial. There is a marble monument by Flaxman with lines by William Hayley, also a native, in the SW tower of the Cathedral. This shows Collins, head on hand, reading the Bible. The Cathedral Library contains a book with Thomas Cranmer's signature, and three books signed by John Donne, which had belonged to Bishop Henry King.

Charlotte Smith, who had been sent to school here at the age of 6, rented a house in the town after separating from her husband (*c*. 1787). Her sonnets had been printed in the town at her expense in 1784, five editions following in as many years. Her novels, which were admired by Sir Walter Scott, who wrote her biography, were so popular that she was able to keep her 12 children on the proceeds.

Blake, who had been arrested in *Felpham, was tried for high treason and acquitted in 1804 at the Guildhall in Priory Park (later an archaeological museum), once the choir of the Greyfriars.

A plaque on no. 11, one of the remaining houses in Eastgate Sq. (formerly Hornet Sq.), commemorates Keats's stay in 1819 with the Dilkes. 'Hush, hush! tread softly!' was written at this time, perhaps in the coach on his way down from London. He visited the old Vicar's Close with its crypt, then a wine store, and Robert Gittings's *John Keats: The Living Year* gives this as the source of the imagery of 'The Eve of St Agnes', which he started to write here.

Charles Crocker (1797–1861) was born here and apprenticed to a shoemaker. He then worked for a bookseller and his first poem appeared in the *Brighton Herald*. A collection

was published by subscription. Crocker became sexton at the Cathedral in 1845 and then Bishop's verger. He was buried in the Subdeanery graveyard. Cobbett, in his *Rural Rides*, was pleased with the well-attended meeting he addressed at The Swan.

In January 1956 Philip Larkin visited the Cathedral and saw the 'pre-Baroque' tomb of the Earl and Countess of Arundel, 'his hand withdrawn, holding her hand'. It became the subject of his moving meditation on time and tenderness, 'An Arundel Tomb', in which

> Time has transfigured them into
> Untruth. The stone fidelity
> They hardly meant has come to be
> Their final blazon, and to prove
> Our almost-instinct almost true:
> What will survive of us is love.

The poet, dramatist, and short-story writer Ted Walker taught at Chichester High School in the 1960s.

CHOLSEY *Oxfordshire*

Small town 2 m. S of Wallingford. Agatha Christie (who spent her last years at Wallingford) was buried in the churchyard here on 16 January 1976.

CHRIST'S HOSPITAL *West Sussex*

Public school off the A24, S of Horsham, which moved from Newgate St. in the City (see LONDON) in 1902. Middleton Murry mentions having a year at the old site in *Between Two Worlds* (1934). Edmund Blunden, who won an entrance scholarship here and also in 1914 a scholarship to The Queen's College, *Oxford, published two short collections of verse in his last year, *Poems* and *Poems Translated from the French*. Keith Douglas came here in 1931 and at 16 had one of his poems accepted in *New Verse*. He won a scholarship to Oxford in 1938.

CLIFTON HAMPDEN *Oxfordshire*

Village on the A415, 8 m. S of Oxford. The Thames-side inn the Barley Mow (badly damaged by fire in 1975) was one of the halts chosen by the characters in *Three Men in a Boat* (1889) by Jerome K. Jerome, who had also stayed there himself.

John Masefield lived at Burcote Brook from 1939 to the end of his life. His prolific writing included *New Chum* (1944) and *The Badon Parchments* (1947). After his death (1967) the house was burnt down and a home for the disabled, the Masefield Leonard Cheshire Home, was built on the site.

COBHAM *Kent*

Village off the A2, 5 m. W of Rochester. One of Dickens's favourite walks from *Gad's Hill was through Cobham Park (now a girls' school; occasionally open to the public, www.cobhamhall.com). The owner, Lord Darnley, who had given him a key, arranged for the small Swiss chalet, used by Dickens as a study at Gad's Hill, to be re-erected in the grounds of the park after Dickens's death. In

Pickwick Papers (1837), the disappointed Mr Tupman retires to the Leather Bottle Inn, but when his friends arrive after a hot walk, they manage to persuade him to rejoin them. Part of the inn was damaged by a fire in the 1880s but it has many mementoes of Dickens.

COBHAM *Surrey*

Large village on the A3 and the A245, 5 m. NW of Leatherhead. Matthew Arnold lived from 1873 until his death in 1888 at Pain's Hill Cottage (gone), now commemorated by Matthew Arnold Close on the site near the bridge over the Mole. While here he published collections of essays including a second volume of literary criticism. His letters refer to the country around and to the lake in the ornamental park of Pain's Hill, where he used to skate, and to the family pets who died here, including the canary Matthias, the subject of a short poem.

From 1920 to 1925 Terence Rattigan (soon to be a distinguished playwright) was a pupil at Sandroyd prep school here. Christina Stead lived from 1958 to 1961 in a cottage in the grounds of Foxwarren Park. She finished writing her novel *Miss Herbert: The Suburban Wife* (1976) here.

COLEMAN'S HATCH *East Sussex*

Village S of the B2110, 6 m. SE of East Grinstead. Yeats spent December and January of 1913–14 at Stone Cottage, 'four rooms . . . on the edge of the heath and our backs to the woods'. When he returned again the next year for January and February, Ezra Pound and his wife were with him.

COLESHILL *Buckinghamshire*

Village off the A355, 3 m. N of Beaconsfield. Edmund Waller was born at the manor house (gone). Foundations of an old house thought to be the manor were uncovered when a garage was built at Stock Place, a privately owned timber and plaster house known locally as his birthplace. In the next-door garden is 'Waller's Oak', under which he is reputed to have sat.

COMBE (*pr.* Cōom) *Oxfordshire*

Village 1 m. N of the A4095 at Long Hanborough. The short-story writer A. E. Coppard moved here *c*. 1914 from *Islip, to return to writing. In his autobiography (1957), he says that 'Piffing Cap' from *Pearson's Magazine* and *Clorinda Walks in Heaven* (1922) have 'vague traces of Combe'.

COOKHAM DEAN *Berkshire*

Village in the Thames valley between Marlow and Maidenhead, where Kenneth Grahame stayed with his maternal grandmother ('Granny Ingles') at The Mount after his mother's death in 1864. He used to go on the river with his uncle the Revd David Ingles, who probably first inspired his passion for 'messing about in boats'. Later, when he was Secretary of the Bank of England and famous for *The Golden Age* (1895) and *Dream Days* (1898), he came back with his wife and son Alistair

('Mouse') and lived at Mayfield from 1906 to 1910. *The Wind in the Willows*, begun as bedtime stories for Alistair, gradually took shape as a book and was published in 1908.

COOLING *Kent*

Village off the B2000, in the marshes, N of Rochester. The castle, once the home of Sir John Oldcastle (d. 1417), though ruined, still has a 14th-c. gatehouse. The play *The First Part of Sir John Oldcastle* (1600), though included in the 3rd and 4th folios, is not by Shakespeare. The opening scenes of *Great Expectations* (1860–1) are set in the area, and Dickens is said to have written of Pip's little brothers and sisters in the churchyard after seeing the coffin-shaped stones above the graves of 13 children here.

COTTISFORD *Oxfordshire*

Village off the A43, 6 m. S of Brackley. In the 1880s Flora Thompson (then Timms) walked with the other children from Juniper Hill to school here, which she depicted as Fordlow in her trilogy *Lark Rise to Candleford* (1945). The school, later a private house, is on the triangle at the crossroads.

COWES *Isle of Wight*

Town on the N coast, divided by the estuary of the Medina. West Cowes is noted for the Royal Yacht Squadron built on the site of the castle where in 1650 William D'Avenant was imprisoned. A staunch Royalist, active in Charles I's cause, he left France for Virginia on Queen Henrietta Maria's behalf but was intercepted by a Parliamentarian ship. While in prison he continued his poem of chivalry *Gondibert* (1651), which, when he was taken to the Tower, he said was 'interrupted by so great an experiment as dying', though this fate was happily delayed and he was released on bail in 1652. Charles and Mary Lamb spent a holiday here in 1803 with Fanny Burney's nephew Martin. 'We do everything that is idle, such as reading books from the circulating library, sauntering, hunting little crabs among the rocks, reading churchyard poetry, which is as bad at Cowes as any churchyard in the Kingdom can produce.'

CRANBROOK *Kent*

Village off the A229, 14 m. S of Maidstone. Phineas Fletcher (1582–1650) and his brother Giles (1585?–1623), who both became poets and who were the cousins of the dramatist John Fletcher (1579–1625), were perhaps both born at their grandfather's rectory (site later part of Cranbrook School). Phineas was certainly baptized here, but Giles's birthplace, which some think was in London, has not been confirmed. In 1760 Edmund Gibbon, then in the militia, was billeted at the George Inn while guarding French prisoners of war at *Sissinghurst Castle (2½ m. N). Sydney Dobell was born here in 1824, but his father, a wine merchant, moved to *Cheltenham shortly afterwards. One of this extensive family erected the Union Mill (restored).

CROWBOROUGH *East Sussex*

Small town on the A26, 7 m. SW of Tunbridge Wells. Richard Jefferies spent the winter of 1885–6 at Downs Cottage Ⓟ in London Rd, where he wrote his last essays, *Field and Hedgerow* (1889). Sir Arthur Conan Doyle lived at Windlesham Manor in Sheep Plain (later a nursing home) and died (1930) there. He was buried in the garden but his body was later moved to Minstead. Edwin Muir and his wife, Willa, who brought Franz Kafka's novels to English readers with their translations, lived (1929–32) at The Nook, Blackness Rd, where they translated *Das Schloss* (The Castle, 1930). Novelist A. S. M. Hutchinson's last home was New Forest Lodge in Beacon Rd, where he died in 1971.

CUCKFIELD (pr. Coŏkfield) *West Sussex*

Small town on the A272, 2 m. NW of Haywards Heath. The physician and traveller Andrew Boorde (or Borde) was born near here (*c.* 1490) but the family who built the 17th-c. Borde Hill is not thought to be his. Harrison Ainsworth stayed at Cuckfield Park in 1830 with his friend William Sergison, who had changed his name and been ordained on marrying the Sergison heiress. In 1831 Ainsworth started *Rookwood* (1834), modelling the house of that name on Cuckfield Park, which has a 16th-c. wing, and describing it in the language of the Gothic novelist Mrs Radcliffe. The 'omen' tree that he mentions, which foretells the death of a member of the family by shedding a branch, has since been felled. Henry Kingsley lived at Attrees (later Kingsleys), a half-timbered house in the High St. named after a 17th-c. churchwarden. He died (1876) here and is buried in the churchyard on the slope below the church, where his grave is marked by a tall obelisk.

CUMNOR *Oxfordshire*

Village WSW of Oxford. The site of the medieval Cumnor Place, where in 1560 Amy Dudley was found dead at the foot of 'a paire of staires', is W of the church. The first written account of rumours of her murder, *The Secret Memoirs of Robert Dudley*, published on the Continent, accused Dudley of poisoning not only her but his second wife's husband too. Aubrey in *Brief Lives* and Anthony à Wood in *Athenae Oxonienses* (1691–2) drew on the *Memoirs*, and Ashmole told the story in *Antiquities of Berkshire*, where Scott saw it. Scott also read Mickle's ballad 'Cumnor Hall' (1784), the title he preferred for his novel but changed to *Kenilworth* (1821) at his publisher's wish.

The church has a small collection relating to Amy Dudley, and the ornate tomb of Anthony Foster, her host, who was suspected as her husband's agent in her murder. A few heavy stones in the churchyard wall are all that remain of the house, but 3 m. N at Wytham some windows and doorways of the ruin it had become were put in when the church was renovated in 1810.

CURTISDEN GREEN *Kent*

Village on the B2079, 4 m. NW of Sissinghurst. Richard Church, poet and novelist, lived (1939–65) near the post office at the Oast House, converted by his wife and near a large cherry orchard. *The Solitary Man and Other Poems* (1941), some essays, two volumes of autobiography, *Over the Bridge* (1955) and *The Golden Sovereign* (1957), and a guidebook, *Kent* (1948), were all published during his time here.

DARTFORD *Kent*

Old manufacturing town where the A2 crosses the Darent. Jane Austen stayed twice at the Bull and George (later the premises of a chemist) in the High St. She shared a room with her mother 'up two pairs of stairs' as they wanted 'a sittingroom and chambers' on the same floor. They dined on 'beef steaks and a boiled fowl but no oyster sauce'. They were going to *Godmersham Park.

Sidney Keyes, the young poet who died (1943) as a prisoner of war in North Africa, was born (1922) at The Dene in Dene Rd, his grandfather's home. Keyes, orphaned early, lived with his grandfather, a mill owner who wrote a history of the town, and went (1931–4) to the Grammar School until leaving for Tonbridge.

DEAL *Kent*

E coast resort 8 m. N of Dover. Elizabeth Carter, whose father was perpetual curate, was born in South St. Ⓟ. A linguist, she published her early poems in 1738, but it was her translation of *Epictetus* (1758) which brought her a wide public, friendship with Samuel Richardson and Dr Johnson, and entry to the select band of bluestockings. The £1,000 she received enabled her to buy a property on the S outskirts of the town, where she took her father on his retirement, and to spend every winter in London. She was one of the last women to assume the customary title of 'Mrs' though unmarried.

Cobbett hurried through the town in 1823 and wrote in *Rural Rides* (1830) that he found it a 'villainous' place, 'full of filthy-looking people'.

Simon Raven moved to Deal in 1961 and lived at 134 Manor Rd and at two different addresses on London Rd, returning later to a clapboard cottage on Manor Rd. He stayed in the town for 34 years (it was a condition of his publisher that he live at least 50 m. from London) and wrote much of his novel sequence *Alms for Oblivion* here in the 1960s and 1970s.

DENHAM *Buckinghamshire*

Quiet village off the A40, 3 m. E of Gerrard's Cross. John Dryden stayed (1692) with his wife's relatives, the Bowyers, at Denham Court, down a mile-long avenue leading from the church. He wrote *Alexander's Feast* (1697) under the cedar tree by the river.

DENTON *Kent*

Village 9 m. SE of Canterbury on the A260. Gray stayed here with his Cambridge friend William Robinson, who rented Denton Court (rebuilt). After his visit in 1768 some verses on Lord Holland's villa at *Kingsgate were found in his dressing table drawer and returned to him. Egerton Brydges, brought up at Wootton (1 m. SE), married Robinson's daughter and bought the Court in 1792, spending large sums to repair and enlarge it. He was able to entertain the troop of yeomanry he had raised against an invasion, in the galleried great hall. His *Censura Literaria* (1805) was started here before he moved to Littlebourne in 1810. The house fell into disrepair while Brydges was on the Continent and in 1822 it was demolished and replaced by a smaller building. The inn, formerly the Red Lion, changed its name to the Jackdaw after one of Barham's *Ingoldsby Legends* (see TAPPINGTON HALL FARM).

DITCHLEY *Oxfordshire*

Country house of the Lee family built by Gibbs in 1722, now a conference centre, 1 m. SW of the A44 at Kiddington. A print of the earlier house, described by Thomas Hearne (1678–1735) shortly before it was pulled down, is in the library. The poet John Wilmot, 2nd Earl of Rochester, was born in 1648 and spent his childhood there—his mother's first husband was a Lee. The Velvet Room has a Gheeraerts portrait of an Elizabethan Sir Henry Lee, with his faithful hound Bevis, who both appear in *Woodstock* (1826), a novel by Scott set in the Civil War. A series of prints illustrating Saint-Pierre's *La Chaumière Indienne* (1791) is upstairs.

DITCHLING *West Sussex*

Village on the B2112 *c.* 9 m. N of Brighton. William Hale White was minister of the Unitarian Chapel here in 1856–7 and describes his experiences in chapter 7 of *The Autobiography of Mark Rutherford* (1881). This has been considered as one of the major descriptions of Nonconformist life in the 19th c.

DONNINGTON *West Sussex*

Village off the A286, 2 m. S of Chichester. Ellen Nussey hoped her brother Henry, curate-in-charge of Earnley (4 m. S) and settled in the rectory (later the Old Rectory) here, would marry her friend Charlotte Brontë, but when he proposed in 1839 after first offering for another woman, he received a 'decided negative'. Charlotte wrote to Ellen, 'I had not, and could not have, that intense attachment that would make me willing to die for him; and, if ever I marry, it must be in that light of adoration that I will regard my husband . . .'

DORKING *Surrey*

Town on the A24 and the A25. Anna Barbauld, who came to live with her brother John Aikin in 1796, wrote of her delight in the countryside in her poem on *Burford Bridge. Disraeli dedicated *Coningsby* (1844) to Henry Hope, owner of Deepdene, as it was 'conceived and partly executed amid the glades and galleries' there. The house on the eastern outskirts, which was later a hotel, has been replaced by a modern office block but the wooded terrace on the hill behind the house is NT (footpath only). George Gissing lived at 7 Clifton Ter. in 1895, the year that *Eve's Ransom*, *Paying Guest*, and *Sleeping Fires* were published. Meredith, whom Gissing visited, was buried in the cemetery in 1909.

DOVER *Kent*

Chief of the Cinque Ports on the SE coast, where Watling Street, the A2, starts. On the E cliff, the castle was visited by Celia Fiennes, whose ancestors had been Hereditary Constables. To the W is Shakespeare's Cliff, over which the blind Gloucester in *King Lear* tried to jump.

The parish church of St Mary's has a wall tablet to the actor and dramatist Samuel Foote, who died (1777) here on his way to recuperate in France. Another tablet commemorates the poet and satirist Charles Churchill, who died at Boulogne and was brought back for burial in the old churchyard. Byron, waiting for a

favourable wind to escape from his creditors, spent two days here, his last in England. He visited the churchyard with his friend Hobhouse and measured himself against the grave of Churchill, 'who blazed | The comet of a season', afterwards paying the sexton to turf it. His tombstone is inscribed with the words 'Life to the last enjoyed, here Churchill lies'.

Many 18th- and 19th-c. visitors stayed at the Ship Inn (gone), sometimes called the Shipwright, near the harbour. Chateaubriand was given a very respectful reception when he arrived in 1822 as the new ambassador, in contrast to his previous visit as a penniless émigré. Fenimore Cooper, author of *The Last of the Mohicans* (1826), remarked on the 'solid unpretending comfort' of the hotel and 'the perfect order in which everything was kept' in *England, with Sketches of Society in the Metropolis* (1837). Another American, the journalist and poet N. P. Willis, also listed the comforts of the place, adding that 'a greater contrast than this to the things that answer to them on the Continent could scarcely be imagined'. He also noted with relief that as well as being 'kind and civil' his landlady 'spoke English' (*Pencillings by the Way*, 1835). The Ship Inn was demolished *c.* 1907.

In 1851 Matthew Arnold spent some days here after his marriage in June, and 'Dover Beach', with the lines

> on the French coast the light
> Gleams and is gone; the cliffs of England stand,
> Glimmering and vast, out in the tranquil bay,

was probably written then, though he also spent a night here on his way back from his Continental honeymoon in October. In 1852 Wilkie Collins stayed with Dickens at 10 Camden Cres. (within a few minutes' walk of baths and bathing machines). Dickens read *Bleak House* here to Collins and Augustus Egg. In 1884 Henry James lodged on Marine Parade, where he wrote the first part of *The Bostonians*. In the dedication to his *Cruelle Énigme* (1885), Paul Bourget mentions staying here with James.

DOWNE *Kent*

Village 8 m. NW of Sevenoaks. Downe is the setting for Down House, Charles Darwin's house (on the North Downs). Darwin would spend 40 years at his quiet Kent home ('the extreme verge of the world'), during which time he wrote prolifically, including his *On the Origin of Species by Means of Natural Selection, or, The Preservation of Favoured Races in the Struggle for Life*, which was published in 1859. Samuel Butler twice visited Charles Darwin at Down House. In *Unconscious Memory* (1880), Butler describes the disagreement between them, which prevented further visits. Charles Darwin's grandchild Gwen Raverat, born (1885) three years after his death, describes the idiosyncrasies of her five Darwin uncles and captures the flavour of family holidays here in the 1890s in *Period Piece* (1952). Although

Ditchley House, Oxfordshire, *c.* 1674. John Wilmot, 2nd Earl of Rochester, was born here in 1648

when she 'was eleven Grandmamma died and it all came to an end', Down House (English Heritage) remains much as it was in Darwin's lifetime and one room is devoted to exhibits relating to his work.

DUNCTON HILL *West Sussex*

Hill on the N of the South Downs, one of the many places in Sussex mentioned by Hilaire Belloc in *The Four Men* (1912). The four, Grizzlebeard, Sailor, Poet, and Belloc as Myself, converse as they walk through the county. Belloc then sets off for his home at Terra Regis or King's Land at *Shipley, certain that after his death

> The passer-by shall hear me still,
> A boy that sings on Duncton Hill.

DUNSDEN *Oxfordshire*

Village just NE of Reading, on a minor road N of the A4155. Wilfred Owen lived at the vicarage from October 1911 until February 1913 as lay assistant to the vicar, while studying in the hope of going to a university. He worked hard in the parish, but he also found time to read—Keats, Shelley, Ruskin, Milton—and to write poetry, constantly experimenting and developing his powers as a poet, as can be seen in his letters and early poems (*Wilfred Owen: Collected Letters*, ed. H. Owen and J. Bell, 1967; *The Collected Poems of Wilfred Owen*, ed. C. Day-Lewis, 1963). A memorial to Wilfred Owen was dedicated in the village church in November 1978.

EARTHAM *West Sussex*

Village E of the A285, 8 m. NE of Chichester. Eartham House (rebuilt 1904 and now Great Ballard School) was the home of William Hayley, a popular poet, though Southey wrote, 'everything about the man is good except his poetry'. In 1792 Cowper and the invalid Mrs Unwin were brought by John Johnson, with his servants and Beau his dog, to spend a holiday with Hayley with whom he had corresponded over his life of Milton. The scheme that Cowper should live at Eartham after Mrs Unwin's death came to nothing as 'the melancholy wildness of the scenes' nearby soon became more than he could bear. He enjoyed the company of Mrs Charlotte Smith, then writing *The Old Manor House* (1793, reprinted 1969), and another frequent visitor, Romney, who drew sketches of them both to hang either side of the fireplace in the billiard room. Cowper met here his correspondent of many years, James Hurdis, whom Hayley invited when, after his sister's death at Burwash, Hurdis felt he could no longer live in the house there. Anna Seward also visited that year. Hayley had praised her *Louisa* (1782) but offended her with his *Essay on Old Maids*. However, she came again in 1796 and was also painted by Romney, who after hints presented the portrait to her father. The red-brick and flint orangery remains. The church has a marble tablet to Hayley's son Thomas by Flaxman, whose pupil he had been.

EASTBOURNE *East Sussex*

Resort on the A259. Lewis Carroll spent his summer vacations from Oxford (1877–87) at 7 Lushington Rd, where a plaque 'to perpetuate his memory with gratitude' as the author of *Alice in Wonderland* was placed by the Eastbourne Literary Society in 1954.

Edna Lyall lived at 6 Osbourne Rd, in Old Town, from 1884 to her death in 1903. Her reputation had been made with *We Two* (1884) and after moving here she showed sympathy with Irish Home Rule and the Boers in her later novels *Doreen* (1889) and *The Hinderers* (1902).

Angela Carter was born at 12 Hyde Gdns on 7 May 1940.

Susan Hill's *A Change for the Better* (1969) is set around the esplanade at 'Westbourne', 'a town of old, selfish and dying people', according to Deirdre Fount.

In the essay 'Such, Such Were the Joys', published posthumously in the *Partisan Review* (1952), George Orwell discusses the guilt and bewildering incomprehension he felt at the crimes, often nameless, of which he was accused at his local preparatory school.

Cyril Connolly, a friend of Orwell's at St Cyprian's (which Connolly called St Wulfric's), describes his time here in *Enemies of Promise* (1938). In 1970 he returned to the town and lived at 48 St John's Rd until his death in 1974.

EASTBURY *Berkshire*

Little village in the Lambourn valley, 12 m. NW of Newbury on the B4000. In the S wall of the church there is a window by Laurence Whistler, provided by people from all over the world, in memory of Edward Thomas and his wife, Helen, who spent the last years of her life here. The window is of clear glass engraved with scenes of hills and sea and trees, interspersed with lines from Thomas's poetry.

EASTHAMPSTEAD *Berkshire*

Village on the A3095, just S of Bracknell. There is an epitaph in the church by Pope on his friend Elijah Fenton, a minor 18th-c. poet (recorded in Dr Johnson's *Lives of the Poets*), who assisted him in the translation of *The Odyssey*. Reeds Hill Farm, near Church Hill House Hospital, is thought to be the house rented by Shelley and his first wife, Harriet, in 1814.

EAST HOATHLY *East Sussex*

Village on the A22, *c.* 6 m. NE of Ringmer. Thomas Turner was a shopkeeper and general dealer here and kept a diary from 1754 to 1765, in which he recounts his personal affairs and the day-to-day life of the villagers. He supplied the needs of a large county area as well as the great banquets of Thomas Pelham, 1st Duke of New-castle, at nearby Halland Hall (gone). The repercussions of the Seven Years War form a distant background, as news of battles and victories come slowly through. The diary ends with Turner's second marriage, in June 1765, and the prospect, he says, that 'I begin once

more to be a little settled, and am happy in my choice.' The second edition of the diary, under the title *The Diary of a Georgian Shopkeeper*, is a concise and readable selection (1979). Turner was buried in the churchyard, and his cottage in the village bears a plaque.

EGHAM *Surrey*

Town on the A30. Sir John Denham (1615–68), the poet who became Surveyor-General over Wren, lived in the family home (gone) near the church (rebuilt 1817) in which one of the few memorials transferred from the old building is to his father, and another, which shows him kneeling, holding a book, is to his mother. His lines on the Thames,

> O, could I flow like thee, and make thy stream
> My great example as it is my theme,
> Though deep, yet clear, though gentle yet not dull,
> Strong without rage, without o'erflowing full,

from *Cooper's Hill* (1642), the topographical poem by which he is best remembered, were inspired by the view from the local hilltop of that name, where the Commonwealth Air Forces Memorial now stands, which overlooks the meadow of Runnymede. Dr Johnson wrote of Denham's translations of Virgil, which influenced Dryden and Pope, that he was 'one of the first that understood the necessity of emancipating translation from the drudgery of counting lines and interpreting single words'.

F. J. Furnivall was born (1825) at Great Fosters, the Tudor house (now a hotel). He founded the Early English Text Society (1864).

Ivy Compton-Burnett was educated at Royal Holloway College, Englefield Green. In 1911 a 20-year-old Richmal Crompton won a scholarship to study at Royal Holloway College.

ELSFIELD *Oxfordshire*

Small village 4 m. N of Oxford off the A40. One of the earliest visitors to the fine old Manor House was Dr Johnson, who walked up to visit Francis Wise with Thomas Warton from *Oxford in the summer of 1754. Johnson greatly enjoyed the library. Wise, the antiquary, lived here when he was Librarian at the Bodleian in Oxford (1748–67).

R. D. Blackmore, who lived as a child with his aunt at the vicarage, used many local scenes in his woodland tale *Cripps the Carrier* (1876).

John Buchan lived at the Manor House from 1919 to 1935, when he was appointed Governor-General of Canada. Many of his novels were written here, including *Midwinter* (1923), which opens with a scene on Otmoor nearby. His grave is in the churchyard.

EMSWORTH *Hampshire*

Small town on the N side of Chichester Harbour. P. G. Wodehouse lived periodically between 1904 and 1914 at Threepwood, Record Rd Ⓟ. The house gave its name to the earls of Emsworth, residents of Blandings Castle. A section of the Emsworth Museum is dedicated to Wodehouse.

ENGLEFIELD GREEN *Surrey*

Village in northern Surrey between Egham and Windsor Great Park. The novelist Mary Wesley was born at Red Gables, Englefield Green, on 24 June 1912.

EPSOM *Surrey*

Former spa whose therapeutic waters were first discovered *c*. 1639, according to John Aubrey, who tried them in 1654. In a letter to her future husband Dorothy Osborne mentions staying here for three weeks to take the waters, which 'agreed' with her. Pepys, whose failing eyesight was causing concern, got leave to come here in 1668. He stayed at the King's Head (site now entrance to shopping precinct) in the High St. In his *Diary* he says, 'Lord Buckhurst and Nell are lodged in the next house, and Sir Charles Sedley with them; and keep a merry house. Poor Girl! I pity her.' This house, formerly Nell Gwynne's Café, later became a jeweller's. Shadwell's comedy *Epsom Wells* (1673) mentions the 'impertinent, ill-bred City wives', who flocked to the well on the Downs, which Celia Fiennes on her travels described as 'unpaved', 'dirty', and 'the wooden building, dark'. This old well Ⓟ still stands in a small railed enclosure, reached by a footpath at the end of Wells Rd (off the A24 Dorking Rd). Wells House nearby stands on the site of a later well.

Hugh Walpole was a schoolmaster in Epsom in 1908 and based his novel *Mr. Perrin and Mr. Traill* (1911) on Epsom College, though he set it in Cornwall as a disguise.

The racecourse on Derby Day is the setting for *Epsom Downs* (1977), Howard Brenton's satirical play attacking the British class system, in which even the course itself has a voice: 'I am the Derby Course. Don't be fooled by lush green curves in the countryside. I am dangerous. I am a bad-tempered bastard. I bite legs.'

ESHER *Surrey*

Town on the A244 and A307, just S of the Thames. The sisters Jane and Anna Maria Porter lived (1823–32) at Alderlands, a house with a pillared porch, at 85 High St. The historical novels *The Hungarian Brothers* (1807) by the latter and *The Scottish Chiefs* (1810) by Jane were very popular both in English and in translation.

William and Mary Howitt lived (1835–40) at West End Cottage (West End Gardens later on the site), which had a 'well-stocked orchard, and a meadow to the Mole with rights of fishing and grazing'. William wrote *Rural Life in England* (1836) and *Visits to Remarkable Places*. They also lived (1866–70) at The Orchard, Hare Lane (on the corner of Rayleigh Drive), Claygate.

In 1859 Meredith, on the advice of his friend Captain Maxse, the original of the Radical parliamentary candidate in *Beauchamp's Career* (1876), became the tenant of Fairholme, once the Bunch of Grapes, an old posting inn, later The Grapes, a private house. By chance he met again the Duff Gordons of Belvedere House, which their hospitality led to his calling the Gordon Arms. They were the originals of Lady Jocelyn and Rose in *Evan Harrington* (1861), the novel he finished after his move to Copsham Cottage on the Oxshott Rd, Esher Common. The gypsies he met on the common appear in *Poems of the English Roadside* (1862). Swinburne visited him and read *The Rubáiyát of Omar Khayyám* (1859), newly published, and wrote 'Laus Veneris' on the Round Hill behind the cottage, a favourite place of Meredith's, which he dubbed the Mound. Meredith divorced his first wife, and he explores the 'dusty answer' to the question why in the poems in *Modern Love* (1862). Meredith moved soon after his happy marriage (1864) to Marie Vulliamy, whom he met here.

R. C. Sherriff lived at Rosebriars from 1929, when he wrote the final part of *Badger's Green* (1930), until his death in 1975. Here all his subsequent work (apart from film scripts in Hollywood) was written, including the plays *Windfall* (1933), *Home at Seven* (1950), and *A Shred of Evidence* (1960), the novels *The Fortnight in September* (1931), *King John's Treasure* (1954), and *The Wells of St Mary's* (1962), and his autobiography, *No Leading Lady* (1968). He bequeathed Rosebriars to the local council.

ETCHINGHAM *East Sussex*

Village 12 m. NW of Hastings. Anthony Burgess lived here in a semi-detached house called Applegarth in the late 1960s and 1970s, drinking a great deal of gin and moving a cage of guinea pigs around the lawn to keep the grass down. The village is reflected in the *Enderby* novels (1960s and 1980s). Burgess found the villagers hostile and it was not a happy period of his life, as the second part of his autobiography, *You've Had Your Time* (1990), reveals.

ETON *Berkshire*

Small town to the N of Windsor, dominated by Eton College, the public school founded in 1440 by Henry VI. One of the earliest headmasters was Nicholas Udall (or Uvedale, 1534–41). He was notorious for flogging and he was also dismissed for misconduct in 1541. His play *Ralph Roister Doister*, the earliest English comedy, may have been acted by the boys during his time here, but was not printed until *c*. 1566. John Harington, translator of *Orlando Furioso* (1591), and the ingenious inventor of a perfumed water closet, was a pupil in the 1570s.

Sir Henry Wotton became Provost in 1624 after many years of being 'an honest man sent to lie abroad for the good of his country'. He died here in 1639 and is buried in the chapel. Giles Fletcher the Elder left in 1565, his son Phineas in 1600, and Edmund Waller in 1620. Henry Fielding was here *c*. 1720 and Horace Walpole and Thomas Gray were contemporaries (1727–34). Gray's *Ode on a Distant Prospect of Eton College* was written *c*. 1742 and contains the lines:

> Alas! regardless of their doom
> The little victims play!
> No sense have they of ills to come

> Nor care beyond to-day
> Yet, ah! why should they know their fate,
> Since sorrow never comes too late,
> And happiness too swiftly flies?
> Thought would destroy their paradise.
> No more—where ignorance is bliss
> 'Tis folly to be wise.

Christopher Anstey was a pupil 1738–42, and John Hookham Frere was here 1784–8.

Shelley, who arrived in 1804, was considered an eccentric, attracted to scientific experiments. He had started to write at home and before he left in 1810 had published two novels in the style of 'Monk' Lewis, *Zastrozzi* and *St Irvyne*. John Cornewall Lewis and Alexander Kinglake were contemporaries *c*. 1820, and Kinglake later gave a portrait of their Provost, Dr Keate, in *Eōthen* (1844). William Johnson, who assumed the name Cory on his retirement in 1872, became an assistant master here at his old school in 1845. One of his best-remembered poems is the translation of the epitaph to Heraclitus by his friend Callimachus, which begins: 'They told me, Heraclitus, they told me you were dead.' He also wrote the 'Eton Boating Song', published in 1865. Cory writes in *Letters and Journals* (1897):

> I could not get to sleep last night, being engaged in making a half-humorous, half-sentimental boating song for the 4th of June . . . I do a song with a tune in my head, or perhaps two; last night it was 'Waiting for the Wagon' and 'A health to the outward-bound'.

Swinburne came here in 1849, overlapping with Robert Bridges, who came in 1854. Bridges became a friend of D. M. Dolben, whose poems, some written here, he edited years later in 1915. Dolben was drowned in 1867 soon after leaving Eton. Edward Plunkett (Lord Dunsany) and Percy Lubbock were pupils in the 1890s. Lubbock published *Shades of Eton* in 1929. Julian Grenfell, Ronald Knox, and G. H. Tyrwhitt-Wilson (Lord Berners) were pupils at the turn of the century. Lord Berners's *A Distant Prospect* (1945), an account of his childhood, includes the story of his leaving the College in a high fever to be treated at home.

Aldous Huxley was at Eton from 1908 to 1911, when he left because of serious eye trouble. After Oxford he returned to teach from the autumn of 1917 until April 1919, while working on *Leda and Other Poems* (1920).

M. R. James became Provost in 1918, while Eric Blair ('George Orwell') was a scholar. Cyril Connolly gives a picture of his years here (1918–21) at the end of *Enemies of Promise* (1938), an appraisal of writers and the pitfalls awaiting them. He sums up with his 'Theory of Permanent Adolescence', in which he claims that public schools intensify 'the glories and disappointments' of experiences so that they dominate boys' lives and arrest their development. Eric Parker, later a writer on natural history and sport, gives an account of his years here in *Eton in the Eighties* (1914) and in the novel *Playing Fields* (1922). Like Connolly he discusses the all-important election to the society 'Pop'.

Thomas Hardy's cottage, Higher Bockhampton, Dorset. Hardy spent the first 30 years of his life here and left a detailed portrait of the cottage in his novel *Under the Greenwood Tree*

The travel writers Robert Byron and Peter Fleming, and Fleming's brother the novelist Ian, all studied here in the 1920s. Henry Yorke (Green) began his first novel, *Blindness* (1926), while still at the school. The first chapters of the book, before the schoolboy protagonist is blinded in a railway carriage, take the form of a diary: 'Read a little Carlyle to a few of the House. What else could it be but incomprehensible to them? "Mad," they called it. Anything of genius is "mad" in a Public School. And rightly so, I suppose.' His contemporary Anthony Powell also attended the College and it provided the basis for the school in *A Question of Upbringing* (1951), the first volume of his 12-volume novel *A Dance to the Music of Time*, in which the reader is introduced to the ludicrous and doggedly ambitious Widmerpool, first emerging from the mist after a long-distance run and then later in Le Bas's boarding house 'in a setting of brown-paper parcels, dog-eared school books and crumbs'.

The poet and essayist Hugo Williams went to Eton in the 1950s and recalled his time here in some of the poems in his collection *Writing Home* (1985). The poet, novelist, playwright, and actor Heathcote Williams (no relation) was a contemporary. John le Carré (then David Cornwell) taught for two years at Eton in the mid-1950s.

The College is open to visitors in the spring and summer (www.etoncollege.com).

EVERSLEY *Hampshire*

Village SE of Reading where the A327 crosses the Blackwater. Lying back from a minor road a little to the S is the church where Charles Kingsley was rector from 1844 to 1875. Most of his books, including *The Water Babies* (1863), were written in the rectory. Inside the church there is a plaque of Kingsley in high relief below a Latin inscription, and a memorial window in the chancel shows St Elizabeth of Hungary (the subject of one of his poems) and two water babies. Kingsley's grave in the churchyard is marked by a marble cross, with the inscription 'Amavimus, Amamus, Amabimus'.

EWELL *Surrey*

Town joined with Epsom on the SW fringe of Greater London. The playwright, novelist, and philosopher Michael Frayn was brought up here and it is a residential close in suburban South London—for which Frayn has shown affection in other works—that provides the setting for *Spies* (2002), his novel about a Second World War childhood.

EWELME *Oxfordshire*

Village off the B4009, NE of Wallingford. Chaucer is traditionally said to have visited his granddaughter Alice (effigy in the church), wife of William de la Pole, 1st Duke of Suffolk (1396–1450), who built the almshouses. Jerome K. Jerome, after the success of *Three Men in a Boat* (1887), lived at Gould's Grove (or Troy), an old farmhouse on the hill (1½ m. SE)

near the junction with the A423. He worked in a summerhouse called The Nook, which was surrounded by a thick yew hedge. Israel Zangwill, on a visit, wrote *Children of the Ghetto* (1892) here in between digging up worms with his pen to feed a young blackbird. H. G. Wells, W. W. Jacobs, and Eden Phillpotts were other visitors. Jerome worshipped at Ewelme church, where he was buried (1927).

FALMER *East Sussex*

Village 5 m. NE of Brighton, and now home to the University of Sussex, where the novelist Ian McEwan did an English degree. The library holds the papers of Rudyard Kipling.

FARINGDON *Oxfordshire*

Market town on the A417 and the A420, between Oxford and Swindon. Faringdon House, an elegant 18th-c. house replacing the former Elizabethan building, standing in beautiful grounds to the N of the church, was built by George III's Poet Laureate, Henry James Pye, *c.* 1770—a more lasting memorial to his good taste than his undistinguished poetry. Having been dedicated to writing poetry from the age of 10, when he read Pope's translation of the *Odyssey*, he published his first poem when he was 17 and continued to write for the rest of his life, combining this occupation with the affairs of a country gentleman and election as an MP in 1784. Election expenses together with inherited debts compelled him to sell the estates and leave Faringdon some time in the 1780s. He was made Poet Laureate by Pitt in 1790 and, according to Southey (his successor in the office), went on rhyming 'doggedly and dully'. There is a copy of his supposed self-portrait in the Pye Chapel in the church. The grounds of the house are said to be haunted by the headless ghost of Hampden Pye, an earlier member of the family, who was serving abroad as a midshipman when his stepmother, in collusion with the ship's captain, arranged for his death so that her own son could become heir. His head was blown off during an action at sea, seemingly by accident, but his ghost came back to haunt his stepmother. The story, told to Richard Barham by Mrs Mary Ann Hughes (grandmother of Thomas Hughes of Uffington), was the source of 'The Legend of Hamilton Tighe' in his *The Ingoldsby Legends* (1840).

In the 1930s Faringdon House became the home of Lord Berners, musician, author, painter, and wit. He wrote some whimsical novels, including *The Camel* (1936) and *Far from the Madding War* (1941). *First Childhood* (1934) and *A Distant Prospect* (1945) are two volumes of autobiography. He was Nancy Mitford's 'Lord Merlin' in *The Pursuit of Love* (1945), with his telegraphic address 'Neighbourtease'. Across the road to the E is Faringdon Hill, celebrated in verse by Henry Pye and planted by him (or by his successor, William Hallet) with clumps of Scots pine. On top of this Lord Berners built a folly tower, culminating in a Gothic octagonal lantern, in 1935, the last large folly built in England.

FARNBOROUGH *Berkshire*

Village on the Berkshire Downs. Sir John Betjeman lived in the rectory from 1945 to 1951. There is a memorial window to him designed by John Piper in the church.

FARNHAM *Surrey*

Old town on the A31 and the A325. The castle, on a hill to the N, was garrisoned in swift succession by the Parliamentarian George Wither and the Royalist John Denham in 1642. Wither, a convert to puritanism, raised a troop of horse for the cause. In 1643 he wrote *De Defendendo* to refute charges of cowardice at the Royalist onslaught. The keep is maintained by English Heritage. The domestic buildings, now occupied by the International Briefing and Conference Centre, were a residence of the bishops of Winchester, including William of Wykeham and William Waynflete. Izaak Walton, who had been George Morley's steward in his previous see, accompanied him here in 1662 and is thought to have written part of the lives of Hooker (1665) and Herbert (1670) in the palace.

Waverley Lane, by the station, leads to an entrance to the ruins in the fields of Waverley Abbey, the first Cistercian house in England, from which Scott is said to have taken the title of his series of novels. The Abbey figures in Conan Doyle's *The White Company* (1891) and *Sir Nigel* (1906). Opposite the lodge, along Moor Park Lane, is the much altered 17th-c. house, bought in 1680 by Sir William Temple, the diplomat, and his wife, Dorothy Osborne. He renamed the house (previously Compton Hall) after *Moor Park in Hertfordshire, and replanned the gardens on similar lines (site later a field below the house). Swift, whose mother is thought to have been a family connection of Temple's, came here (*c.* 1690), acting as secretary while waiting for a post in Ireland which he hoped Temple would secure for him. While he was here, Swift met the young Esther Johnson (a daughter of a servant or companion to Temple's sister), later the recipient of many of his intimate letters (collected as *Journal to Stella*, 1948). Disappointed in the extent of Temple's patronage, Swift returned to Ireland in 1694 but came back in 1696 and again stayed here. He wrote in 1696 and 1697 *A Tale of a Tub* and *The Battle of the Books*, satires on 'corruptions in religion and learning' published together in 1704. When Temple died in 1699, Swift returned to Ireland.

Cobbett, who described his first reading of *A Tale of a Tub* as the 'birth of intellect', was born (1762) at his father's inn, the Jolly Farmer, in Bridge Sq. (now the William Cobbett with a plaque erected by the Farnham Society). A column with his bust in the riverside Gostrey Meadow nearby calls him the 'champion of Democracy, master of English Prose and enemy of cant in public affairs'. He left Farnham when 11 to walk to Kew to find work but he often visited the town, as he relates in *Rural Rides*. In 1835 he was buried at the parish church,

Lyme Regis, Dorset, visited by Jane Austen and home from the late 1960s to John Fowles, much of whose novel *The French Lieutenant's Woman* is set in the town which has a tablet with his portrait in relief on the S wall of the tower. The museum, 38 West St., has mementoes of him.

Augustus Toplady, author of 'Rock of Ages' (1775), was born (1740) at 10 West St., which has a plaque of stone from *Burrington Combe. Ada Ellen Bayly, who wrote as 'Edna Lyall', spent her holidays from the age of 4 (1861) with her cousins in West St., where she began *We Two* (1884). *To Right the Wrong* (1894), a novel about the Civil War, which has scenes in the town, came to her mind in the church.

George Sturt, who wrote as 'George Bourne', was born (1863) at 18 The Borough and was at the Grammar School (1876–84), where he became a pupil-teacher. He describes the family business, which he entered after his father died (1884), in *The Wheelwright's Shop* (1923). His family lived on the premises at 84 East St. but in 1891 he moved to Vine Cottage in a large garden at Lower Bourne (now a suburb). The old man he engaged as gardener and handyman there provided the subject of *The Bettesworth Book* (1901) and *Memoirs of a Surrey Labourer* (1907), and often appears in *The Journals of George Sturt* (ed. E. D. Mackerness, 1967). Sturt, who was looked after by his unmarried sisters, was disabled by strokes and he died at Vine Cottage in 1927. A commemorative tablet in the church records that he 'wrote with understanding and distinction of the wheelwright's craft and English peasant life'.

J. M. Barrie wrote *Peter Pan* (1904) in the pinewoods behind his country home Blacklake Cottage (now Lobs Wood Manor) in Tilford Lane (1 m.), where his Newfoundland dog, the original of Nana, is buried.

The castle, 'not one of the great castles of the world', is the venue for the huge wedding between the Seton and Fairley families in Jane Gardam's novel *Faith Fox* (1996).

FARRINGFORD *Isle of Wight*

Georgian house (now a hotel), off Bedbury Lane, Freshwater, leased by Alfred Tennyson in 1853 and bought with the proceeds from *Maud* (1855). It was then ivy-covered, secluded from the village by its park and farmland, and had a view across the sea. Tennyson's many visitors included Charles Kingsley, Edward FitzGerald, Arthur Hugh Clough, Edward Lear, and Swinburne. It is possible that Charles Dodgson got the idea of the Mouse's Tale in *Alice's Adventures in Wonderland* (1865) from a dream Tennyson related on his visit. Works written here include 'The Charge of the Light Brigade' (1854), 'Maud' (1855), *The Idylls of the King* (1859), and 'Enoch Arden' (1864). Some were written in the attic, which he called the 'fumitory', some in the garden arbour, or in his study in the newly added west wing, where his later poems were written, including *Locksley Hall Sixty Years After*. Tennyson started to build Aldworth (see HASLEMERE) in 1868 and then usually spent the winters here. Freshwater church, where his wife is buried, has a stone commemorating him with the lines:

Speak, living voice, with thee death is not death;
Thy life outlives the life of dust and breath.

Much of Tennyson's life was spent out of doors and his favourite walk was along the Downs to the Needles. This is now called Tennyson Down, where a large memorial cross has been erected on the site of the beacon 'by the People of Freshwater and other friends in England and America'.

FAVERSHAM *Kent*

Old town off the A2, 10 m. NW of Canterbury. The timber and plaster 80 Abbey St. ℗, with its overhanging storeys, once part of the abbey buildings, was the home of Richard Arden, mayor in 1547. Holinshed in his *Chronicles* (1577) records the murder in 1559 on which the unknown author, thought by some to be Shakespeare, bases his play *The Tragedy of Mr. Arden of Feversham* (1592). In this, Arden, after many attempts, is murdered by his wife and her lover, who are both caught and executed. George Lillo also used this subject for his play *Arden of Feversham*, published posthumously in 1762.

FAWLEY *Berkshire*

Village off the A338, 5 m. S of Wantage. Thomas Hardy, whose maternal grandmother came from the village, calls it 'Marygreen' in *Jude the Obscure* (1895), which is partly set here. Aunt Drusilla's house cannot be identified but the large green with the school and the rectory are still there.

FELPHAM *West Sussex*

Resort on the A259 adjoining Bognor Regis. Limmer Lane by the post office leads to the site of Turret House, where the poet Hayley lived when Felpham was a small village. He gave up his estate at Eartham in the 1790s and called the house his marine cottage. Flaxman, the sculptor, who had designed the memorial to Hayley's son, may have introduced him to Blake as an illustrator for his *Ballads, Founded on Anecdotes of Animals* (1805). Hayley in 1800 provided Blake with a cottage (later Blake's House, behind the Thatch Inn). Blake enjoyed this at first and wrote that 'the voices of winds, trees and birds . . . make it a dwelling for immortals'. He began the poem *Milton* (1804) and composed *Jerusalem* for the preface, and made some illustrations for Hayley's life of Cowper (1803). But the local people, and even Hayley too, thought him strange and his ideas incomprehensible. In August 1803 a disturbance in his garden led him to eject a drunken soldier, who retaliated by accusing him of sedition. He was arrested and later (Jan. 1804) tried at Chichester, accused of high treason, but found not guilty. Hayley is buried in the churchyard.

FERNHURST *West Sussex*

Wealden village 3 m. S of Haslemere. Bertrand Russell moved to Millhanger, a 16th-c. workman's cottage a mile or so SE of the village in 1895. He wrote *Principia Mathematica* there.

FINSTOCK *Oxfordshire*

Village between Witney and Chipping Norton. The novelist Barbara Pym kept Barn Cottage from 1972, living here permanently from 1974 until her death in 1980. It provides the setting for her last novel, *A Few Green Leaves* (1980). There is a plaque to her on the wall near the place where she sat in the church and she is buried in the churchyard.

FIRLE *East Sussex*

Village 6 m. E of Lewes. In 1916 Virginia Woolf found Charleston Farmhouse (www.charleston.org.uk) as a country home for her sister Vanessa Bell:

It is about a mile from Firle, on that little path which leads under the downs. It has a charming garden, with a pond, and fruit trees, and vegetables, all now rather run wild, but you could make it lovely . . . The house wants doing up—and the wallpapers are awful. But it sounds a most attractive place—and 4 miles from us, so you wouldn't be badgered by us.

Vanessa Bell and Duncan Grant created what is the most remarkable example of Bloomsbury taste to have survived. Virginia and Leonard Woolf, Lytton Strachey, and E. M. Forster were among the regular visitors. Other Bloomsbury figures—Maynard Keynes, Clive Bell, and David Garnett—lived at the house for significant periods.

FLETCHING *East Sussex*

Village off the A272, 4 m. NW of Uckfield. Edward Gibbon first met his friend John Baker Holroyd in Lausanne. In 1793, though in ill health, he again made the journey to England to be with his friend after his wife's death. Holroyd was then Lord Sheffield and had inherited Sheffield Park, just outside the village (Garden, NT; 1½ m. W on the A275). Gibbon spent the rest of the year there but went to London in the New Year and died suddenly a few days later. Sheffield, who had Gibbon's body interred in his family mausoleum in the parish church, collected his friend's memoirs, which were published with his *Miscellaneous Works* in 1796.

FOLKESTONE *Kent*

SE coast resort 7 m. W of Dover. Dickens rented 3 Albion Villas (now Copperfield House) from mid-July to October 1855. He was at first unable to concentrate on the writing of *Little Dorrit* as his sons made such a noise on the wooden staircase during their holidays. His exercise was in climbing 'a precipitous cliff in a lonely spot overhanging the wild sea-beach'. Wilkie Collins, who often joined Dickens on his holidays, visited him here.

H. G. Wells and his wife, Catherine, moved into their new home, the Spade House, looking over the terraced garden to Sandgate Bay in 1900. He wrote here *Mankind in the Making* (1903), *The Food of the Gods* (1904), *Kipps* (1905), *Tono-Bungay* (1909), and *The History of Mr. Polly* (1910), using first a small study, then enlarging it and later building a garden study where he could be undisturbed. He entertained his friends, among them Shaw, Conrad, Henry James, and Kipling, and played exciting floor games with his sons.

A. E. Coppard was born in lodgings here in 1878 and he recalls his childhood in *It's me, O Lord!* (1957).

In 1961 Samuel Beckett was secretly married in Folkestone to Suzanne Deschevaux-Dumesnil. They had met in 1938 when Beckett was stabbed in a Paris street. They remained together until her death in July 1989. The town is known as 'Fork Stoan' in the post-nuclear society of Russell Hoban's novel *Riddley Walker* (1980).

FOREST HILL *Oxfordshire*

Small village on the E outskirts of Oxford, off the A40. Milton, whose grandfather had lived at Stanton St John, came here in 1643 possibly to collect a debt from Richard Powell of the manor house. A month later he returned to London married to the 17-year-old Mary Powell. Many scenes in Robert Graves's novel *Wife to Mr. Milton* (1943) are set in the village, and the novelist Anne Manning wrote a popular account, *Mistress Mary Powell* (1851). The house they describe has been rebuilt; the ornate gateway seen over the churchyard wall, and the mounting block now outside the main gate, were there in Milton's time.

William Mickle, who lived at the old manor and married here, was a corrector at the Clarendon Press (1765–71), translator of the *Lusiads* (1775), and author of 'Cumnor Hall' (1784) among other ballads. His gravestone is in the church vestry.

FRIMLEY *Surrey*

Town on the A325, 4 m. SW of Bagshot. Francis Bret Harte (known as 'Bret Harte'), the American author of *The Luck of Roaring Camp* (1870), was buried (1902) in St Peter's churchyard. The low red-marble tombstone surrounded by chains is near the churchyard wall.

FRINGFORD *Oxfordshire*

Village off the A4421, 4 m. NE of Bicester. In 1890, when she was 14, Flora Thompson (then Timms) was driven by her father in a borrowed cart to take up work as assistant to Mrs Whitton, the postmistress, who also kept the forge (later a private house called The Forge) on the large green. She stayed until she was nearly 20, when she chose the more varied positions offered as a relief clerk, for which she was thought flighty by her family. Later she drew on her life here for her autobiographical novel *Candleford Green* (1943), in which Mrs Whitton appears as Miss Lane.

GAD'S HILL *Kent*

Hamlet on the A289, 4 m. NW of Rochester, haunt of robbers who preyed on travellers on the old Dover road. The coaching inn is named after Falstaff, who robbed with his cronies and was robbed in turn in Shakespeare's *1 Henry IV*. Dickens, who had looked with envy at the 18th-c. Gad's Hill Place when a boy, realized his ambition to buy the house in 1856. The owner was Eliza Lynn (later Mrs Lynn Linton, the novelist) who had spent her girlhood there. The main road runs through the property and Dickens had a tunnel made to link the garden with the wilderness and shrubbery in which he set the little Swiss chalet given him by the actor Fechter (removed to Rochester). *Great Expectations* (1860), *The Uncommercial Traveller* (1860), *Our Mutual Friend* (1865), and the unfinished *Edwin Drood* (1870) were largely written in the chalet or in the study on the ground floor, which was the setting for the drawing *The Empty Chair* by Fildes after Dickens's death here in 1870. The house is now a school, but open for occasional tours (www.gadshill.org).

GARSINGTON *Oxfordshire*

Village 5 m. SE of Oxford, on a minor road off the B480 from Cowley. Rider Haggard was sent to the Revd H. J. Grahame's school at the rectory when he was 10 (1866), as he seemed to be learning nothing from his day schools in London. He made friends with a farmer called Quatermain, who let him help to feed the pigs and gave him walnuts, from whose shells the boy made little boats. Haggard used the name in *King Solomon's Mines* (1885) and other romances with African settings.

The Manor was the home of Lady Ottoline and Philip Morrell from 1915 to 1928, and a place of unflagging hospitality to young writers and artists, though sometimes regarded with suspicion as a pacifist centre during the war. Aldous, Huxley, then an undergraduate at Balliol, *Oxford, described his first visit in a letter to his father (8 Dec. 1915): 'out to Garsington for luncheon to the Philip Morrells, who have bought a lovely Elizabethan manor there. Lady Ottoline . . . is a quite incredible creature—arty beyond the dreams of avarice and a patroness of literature and the modernities.' Later, as a frequent guest, he was writing that the household was among the most delightful he knew: 'always interesting people there and v. good talk'. He stayed for an amusing Christmas, when Middleton Murry and Katherine Mansfield, Lytton Strachey, Carrington, and Clive Bell were of the party. 'We performed a superb play invented by Katherine, improvising as we went along.' Other visitors included Siegfried Sassoon, on leave in 1916, who found it 'enchanting', D. H. Lawrence, who discovered a keenly sympathetic friend in Lady Ottoline, Virginia Woolf, Edmund Blunden, and T. S. Eliot. When the conscientious objectors became too many for The Manor they overflowed into the bailiff's house across the road. A portrait of a typical house party is given in Aldous Huxley's first novel, *Crome Yellow* (1921), and the house is possibly a model for Breadalby in D. H. Lawrence's *Women in Love* (1920). Lady Ottoline's own account of The Manor appears in volume ii of her memoirs, *Ottoline at Garsington* (1974). There is a memorial to Lady Ottoline in the church.

Virginia Woolf at Garsington Manor in 1924

GAYHURST *Buckinghamshire*

Village on the B526, 3 m. NW of Newport Pagnell. The mansion, which was given by Queen Elizabeth I to Francis Drake, was the birthplace, in 1606, of Kenelm Digby, whose father was hanged for his part in the Gunpowder Plot. The initials KD appear on columns in the main hall. The house, which underwent major repairs in 1973 and can be seen from the church (1728), was owned by the Wrighte family in the 18th c. In 1779 Cowper drove over with Mrs Unwin from *Olney and praised the gardens with the hothouse and orange trees. He also walked here (it took him 55 minutes) to discuss plants and seeds which he exchanged with the gardener.

GERRARD'S CROSS
Buckinghamshire

Village on the border of Greater London. John Betjeman taught at Thorpe House School after his rustication from Oxford.

GODALMING *Surrey*

Old market town on the A3100, situated on the Wey, once a centre of the wool industry. Charterhouse School, on the NW, removed here from the City of London in 1872 to imposing buildings designed by Hardwick, Blomfield, and others. An old archway, carved with the names of former Carthusians, was brought from London, and the library houses the manuscript of Thackeray's *The Newcomes* (1853–5). Max Beerbohm and Richard Hughes were pupils here. Aldous Huxley, whose father was a master at Charterhouse, was born (1894) at Laleham (one of several houses now converted into flats), Peperharow Rd.

Robert Graves suffered an 'oppression of spirit' at the school, where he felt himself 'a potato out of a different sack from the rest'. His period at the school is memorably described in *Goodbye to All That* (1929). The novelist Simon Raven was also educated at Charterhouse, where he was distinguished for classics, cricket, and sex. He was expelled in 1945 for 'the usual thing' (a sexual relationship with another boy)—a fate he shared with Fielding Gray, the main character in his satirical novel sequence *Alms for Oblivion*. He recorded his mixed feelings about public school life in the memoir *Shadows on the Grass* (1982). His own moral attitude he described in *Boys Will Be Boys* (1963) as 'a worldly, weary de-Christianised version of the public school code'.

GODMERSHAM *Kent*

Small village off the A28, 8 m. SW of Canterbury. Jane Austen's brother Edward, adopted by the Knights, inherited the estate here in 1797. Jane and her sister Cassandra often stayed here and many of Jane's letters were written from the 18th-c. Godmersham Park. The church has a wall memorial to Edward and Elizabeth Knight.

GOODNESTONE (pr. 'Gŏoneston) *Kent*

Village off the A257, 1 m. S of Wingham. Jane Austen spent holidays with her brother Edward when, after his marriage (1791) to the daughter of Sir Brook Bridges of Goodnestone Park, he lived at Rowling House (1 m. E). She mentions in her *Letters* leading the dancing at the evening parties at the Park, and also that Edward has changed his name to that of his aunt Knight, who had made him her heir, an expedient that Frank Churchill was to use in *Emma* (1816). The Edward Knights left Rowling for their aunt's estate at *Godmersham. Montague Rhodes James, author of *Ghost Stories of an Antiquary* (1905), was born at the rectory and baptized in the church.

GORING-BY-SEA *West Sussex*

South coast resort W of Worthing on the A259. The southbound side of the dual Sea Lane, by the parish church, leads to Jefferies Lane, a short cul-de-sac, where Jefferies House has a plaque stating that 'Richard Jefferies, Naturalist and prose writer lived and died here'. When Jefferies died (1887) the house was called Sea View House, but later development has blocked the view.

GRAVESEND *Kent*

Thames-side town on the A226. Dr R. Austin Freeman settled (1902–21) at 2 Woodville Ter. (site now of the Woodville Halls) where he started to write the detective stories solved by Dr Thorndyke, the expert on medical jurisprudence. *The Red Thumb Mark* (1907) features the then new technique of fingerprint identification. He lived most of his life in Gravesend, at 94 Windmill St. from 1930 until his death in 1943. He is buried in the cemetery.

Conrad's story *Heart of Darkness* is told on board a ship lying off Gravesend.

The poet Thom Gunn was born in Gravesend in 1929.

GRAYSHOTT *Hampshire*

Village on the B3002, just W of Hindhead. Flora Thompson (then Timms) worked here as post office assistant from 1896 until her marriage to John Thompson, a post office clerk, in 1900. She lived first in the postmaster's house and then in a single, sparsely furnished, rented room, where she embarked on her 'long haphazard self-education', based on reading books from public libraries and second-hand shops. Grayshott at that time was becoming a popular resort of writers, and she was impressed by seeing Conan Doyle, Richard Le Gallienne, and the newly married Bernard Shaw, as they came to the post office to buy stamps or send telegrams. Later, after the publication of *Lark Rise* and its sequels (1939–43), she wrote an account of her years at Grayshott, disguised as 'Heatherley', with herself as 'Laura', but never offered the book to her publisher. *Heatherley* was first published in 1979 in *A Country Calendar and Other Writings*, edited by Margaret Lane.

GREAT BOOKHAM *Surrey*

Village on the A246, 4 m. SW of Leatherhead. Fanny Burney and her husband, General D'Arblay, lived at The Hermitage, on the corner of East St., after their marriage in 1793. She wrote her third novel, *Camilla* (1796), here, with 'no episode' as she told the King, 'but a little baby'. They had lived frugally, as the General was in exile and had no money, but they were able to build their own house from the proceeds of this novel.

Jane Austen's *Letters* show she spent holidays at the vicarage (gone, a cedar tree marks the site), where her cousin Cassandra was married to the Revd Samuel Cooke (tablet in the chancel of the church), Jane Austen's godfather. One of her visits was in 1814, the year she began *Emma* (1816), which has a scene on the nearby *Box Hill.

GREATHAM (pr. 'Grettam) *West Sussex*

Hamlet E of the A29, 8 m. NE of Arundel. Shed Hall, the long low cottage adapted from cowsheds at Humphreys Homestead on the Rackham road, was lent by Viola Meynell to Padraic Colum for his honeymoon in 1912, and to D. H. Lawrence in 1915, when he was finishing *The Rainbow*. Shed Hall was the setting for the title story in Lawrence's *England, My England* (1922).

GREAT HAMPDEN *Buckinghamshire*

Village on a minor road 3 m. W of Great Missenden, where in 1909 John Masefield and his wife took a small house, Rectory Farm, which became a treasured retreat for holidays until 1913. It was here that Masefield had the inspiration for *The Everlasting Mercy* (1911), the narrative poem 'about a blackguard who becomes converted', which marked the turning point in his career.

GREAT MISSENDEN
Buckinghamshire

Village in the Chilterns, off the A413. It was the final home of children's writer Roald Dahl (d. 1990), who is buried in the churchyard. The Roald Dahl Museum and Story Centre opened in 2005 (www.roalddahlmuseum.org).

GREAT TEW *Oxfordshire*

Sheltered Cotswold village on the B4022, between the A4260 from Oxford and the A361 from Banbury. When Lucius Cary, 2nd Viscount Falkland (1610?–43), lived at the manor house in the 1630s he kept open house for his friends and his home became a cultural centre for scholars and poets. His many guests included Ben Jonson, Abraham Cowley, Edward Hyde, Earl of Clarendon, Sidney Godolphin, and Thomas Hobbes.

GROOMBRIDGE *Kent*

Village off the A26, 5 m. SW of Tunbridge Wells. A public footpath from St John's Church passes in front of the moated 17th-c. Groombridge Place, where Evelyn helped the owner Philip Packer design the gardens. W. Hale White lived (1903–13) at The Cottage, set back in its gardens from the road, N of the village. He wrote here a biography of John Bunyan (1904), under whose influence he grew up in Bedford, and, as a tribute to Dr Johnson, *Selections from the Rambler* (1907). In the same year he met Dorothy Horace Smith, the young author of a first novel, and they were married in the parish church in 1911 after his recovery from an operation. He was buried in the churchyard there in 1913.

Sir Arthur Conan Doyle frequently used to walk over from his home at *Crowborough, and Groombridge Place became the inspiration for Birlstone Manor House in his novel *The Valley of Fear* (1914–15).

GUILDFORD *Surrey*

Large town, on the A3, thought by Malory to be the Astolat of Arthurian legends. The 12th-c. poem *The Owl and the Nightingale* refers to a Nicholas of Guildford in terms suggesting that he was the author. The popular Gothic novelist Charlotte Smith was buried (1806) in St John's Church, Stoke, where her family erected a monument in the chancel to her 'talents and virtues'. Cobbett in *Rural Rides* (1830) thought this 'the most agreeable and happy looking town'.

C. L. Dodgson ('Lewis Carroll') often stayed at his family home with his sisters at The Chestnuts Ⓟ in Castle Hill, a three-storey house with a birdcage-like trellis over the front steps. He occasionally preached at St Mary's, which he always attended when staying here. He died here (1898) and his grave under a pine tree in the cemetery at the top of the Mount has a marble cross. Some of his letters and other relics are in the Museum and Muniment Room, Castle Arch.

P. G. Wodehouse was born (1881) at 1 Vale Pl., Epsom Rd (Ⓟ on 59 Epsom Rd).

HALSTEAD *Kent*

Village off the A21, 6 m. NW of Sevenoaks. E. Nesbit spent the years 1871 to 1877 at The Hall, 'a long low red-brick house, that might have been commonplace but for the roses and the ivy that clung to the front of it, and the rich, heavy jasmine that covered the side', as she described it later. The games that she and her brothers and sisters played on the new railway line at Knockholt probably gave her the idea for her novel *The Railway Children* (1906). Family fortunes deteriorated and the Nesbits moved to London, where Edith married in 1880.

HARBLEDOWN *Kent*

Village to the NW of Canterbury, 1 m. outside the city walls. The first Englishwoman to become a professional writer, Aphra Behn, was baptized at St Michael's Church on 14 December 1640 (her name in the register appearing as 'Eaffry'). She sailed to Suriname with her father (who died on the voyage to take up his appointment of lieutenant-governor) and remained there long enough to make the territory the background for her novel *Oroonoko, or, The Royal Slave*, dramatized by her friend Thomas Southerne in 1695. Swinburne wrote, 'This improper woman of genius was the first literary abolitionist—the first champion of the slave in the history of fiction.' Her husband is thought to have been a city merchant who died in 1665, perhaps of the plague. She became a spy for Charles II's government, who were so dilatory in paying her that she was put in a debtors' prison. Her novels and plays, written in the robust style of the times, were very popular and she herself was a friend of Dryden, Otway, and other Restoration wits, who celebrated her in their verses.

HARTFIELD *East Sussex*

Village off the A264, between Tunbridge Wells and East Grinstead. On the S side of the village, *c.* 1 m. along the B2026, a lane turns off on the right hand to Cotchford Farm, the much-loved country home of A. A. Milne, which he bought in 1925 and finally settled in after leaving London in 1940. His son Christopher Milne in *The Enchanted Places* (1974) describes his childhood there, in a private world shared by chosen companions, especially the now immortal Winnie-the-Pooh. Many of the places can still be seen, including Poohsticks Bridge, by way of the path to Posingford (no parking for cars nearer than the main road); Gills Lap ('Galleon's Lap' in *The House at Pooh Corner*), a clump of pines on the top of a hill in Ashdown Forest, 1½ m. S; Five Hundred Acre Wood ('Hundred Acre Wood') on the E side of the main road, and the group of pine trees that became 'Six Pine Trees'. The books that became children's classics, *Winnie-the-Pooh* (1926), *The House at Pooh Corner* (1928), and a book of verses, *Now We Are Six* (1927), were conceived and mainly written here. A. A. Milne and E. H. Shepard, whose illustrations are an inseparable part of the Pooh stories, are commemorated by an inscribed stone *c.* 200 yds N of Gills Lap, approached by a narrow footpath and commanding a fine view towards Cotchford.

HASLEMERE *Surrey*

Town on the A286 and the A287. In 1868 Tennyson started to build Aldworth, his new home, situated on a heather-covered ledge near the top of Blackdown (NT, 1 m. SE). The house has stone-mullioned windows, a balustraded projecting central bay, tall pinnacled dormers, and a large hall. The name came from his wife's family home in Berkshire, and he describes her pleasure in the view eastward over the Weald in the lines

You came, and looked and loved the view
Long known and loved by me,
Green Sussex fading into blue
With one gray glimpse of sea.

One of his favourite walks was to Chase Pond, and another to the Temple of the Four Winds, his name for a group of firs on the exposed SE corner of Blackdown, where a stone seat was placed in 1954 to commemorate him. The road along the crest of the down (now tree-covered) is called Tennyson's Lane. He wrote many of the Arthurian poems here, including *The Holy Grail* (1869) and *Gareth and Lynette* (1872), and his collection *Ballads* (1880). After refusing many honours, he accepted a barony in 1883. He died here in 1892 and was buried in Westminster Abbey. Friends in the town erected a stained-glass window depicting Sir Galahad (from a design by Burne-Jones) in the parish church of St Bartholomew in 1899. Another window in the N aisle commemorates Gerard Manley Hopkins, who died (1889) in *Dublin and is buried in Glasnevin cemetery. Hopkins used to visit his parents, who lived after 1885 at Court's Hill Lodge.

HASSOCKS *East Sussex*

Village 8 m. N of Brighton. Patrick Hamilton went to school at Dale House.

HASTINGS *East Sussex*

Resort on the A21 and the A259. Leigh Hunt started the long poem *The Story of Rimini* when on holiday here with his wife and first child in 1812. Two years later Byron stayed with his half-sister Augusta near All Saints' Church at Hastings House (gone). He swam, drank smuggled Hollands, and ate the local turbot. Keats spent short holidays here in 1815 and 1817. He was a friend of Haydon the painter, who lodged on his visit at the New England Bank, a weatherboarded tavern at the hamlet of Bo-Peep (site now West St Leonard's station), where Keats may also have stayed. The 'lively Lady from Hastings' was Isabella Jones, whose friendship inspired 'The Eve of St Agnes' (1820) and other poems.

The first scheme for a new resort adjoining Hastings, later carried through (1828–34) by James and Decimus Burton and called St Leonard's, is thought to have influenced Jane Austen's unfinished novel *Sanditon*. Charles and Mary Lamb lodged at 4 York Cottages near the Priory (gone) in 1823. They bathed and Charles was dipped three times by the attendants before his stutter enabled him to say 'once'. They also tried the local turbot and the smuggled Hollands. They walked to Lovers' Seat (footpath from Fairlight Rd), Mary's favourite place, and to Hollington church, which Charles preferred. His description of this 'protestant Loretto' led his friend Thomas Hood (1799–1845) to honeymoon here on his marriage (1825) to John Reynolds's sister. Hood wrote that 'the small Christian dovecote' gave him the sentimental desire to be buried there. Hollington Wood, where he killed an adder, he thought romantic enough for even the lovers in Boccaccio. Like the Lambs they enjoyed walking and a sprained ankle on the shingle brought on a fit of punning. The elderly George Crabbe was knocked down by a phaeton as he got out of the coach to stay at 34 Wellington Sq. in 1830, causing his friends the Hoares great concern.

Thomas Campbell took a house and stayed for almost a year in South Colonnade (site near Marine Court) from the summer of 1831; he wrote to his sister that his 'small neat house hung over the sea almost like the stern of a ship'. He also visited Lovers' Seat and 'Lines on a View from St Leonards' and 'Lines on the Camp Hill' were written at this time.

In 1854 Rossetti took rooms in the Old Town at 12 East Parade (now the saloon bar of the Cutter Hotel) on the front, while Elizabeth Siddal, the model for many Pre-Raphaelite portraits, stayed at 5 High St. She was lodging at 12 Beach House (now probably East Beach St.) when they were married in 1860 at St Clement's Church. The sanctuary light and the framed sonnet on the W wall are donations in Rossetti's memory. In 1857 George Macdonald lived with his wife at Providence House on East Hill, once a rope-walk called the Tackleway. He renamed the house Huntly Cottage Ⓟ after his birthplace. His friendship with Lewis Carroll, who was having treatment for a stammer, started here. A plaque on no.2 Wellington Sq. records that 'Lewis Carroll (1832–1898), Writer and Scholar, was a frequent visitor to this house, the home of his aunts, the Misses Lutwidge'. Macdonald, whose health was precarious, returned to the town in 1871 after the publication of *At the Back of the North Wind* and stayed at Halloway House (next to Huntly Cottage).

Carlyle spent some months in 1864 at 117 Marina Ⓟ. In the same year John Addington Symonds married Catharine North at St Clement's Church. Her family, with whom they stayed during the early years of their marriage, lived in a red-brick Queen Anne house, Hastings Lodge (gone), in Old London Rd.

Coventry Patmore lived in the Mansion House between High St. and Old London Rd (1875–91). He had liked the house when he visited the resort with his young family and his pleasure in settling there was increased as his daughter was in a convent nearby. Patmore was the chief contributor to the Catholic church St Mary Star-of-the-Sea, dedicated in memory of his second wife in 1883. His house was renamed Old Hastings House in 1892. Olive Schreiner spent some winters in Hastings during her years in England (1882–9).

Matilda Betham-Edwards (1838–1919) lived at 1 High Wickham Ⓟ. Author of the popular novel *Kitty* (1870) and many others, she was visited by Henry James and Mrs Humphry Ward and she was a friendly neighbour of Hale White, who lived at 9 High Wickham from 1892 and in 1895 moved to the larger no. 5 until 1900. There he wrote *Catharine Furze* (1893), which has many scenes taken from his childhood home of *Bedford, and *Clara Hopgood* (1896). He spent many hours in the observatory he had had constructed in the garden (1896). Henry James gives his view of Hastings as a place to retire to in *Portraits of Places* (1883):

> There amid the little shops and the little libraries, the bath-chairs and the German bands, the Parade and the long Pier, with a mild climate, a moderate scale of prices, and the consciousness of a high civilisation, I should enjoy a seclusion which would have nothing primitive or crude.

In 1860 Augustus Hare (1834–1903) moved to Little Ridge, Ore, with the aunt who had adopted him. He called her 'the Mother' and

wrote her biography, *Memorials of a Quiet Life* (1872–6). The house, which overlooked the sea, they renamed Holmhurst. Soon after the 1914–18 war, Rider Haggard bought North Lodge on Maze Hill. He spent the winters there, writing in the room above the archway spanning the road.

Robert Noonan was the author under his pen-name 'Robert Tressell' of *The Ragged Trousered Philanthropists* (1914; 1955, ed. F. C. Ball from original maunscript), written while he lived in Hastings (from *c.* 1902), working as a house painter. The novel describes a year in the lives of a group of workmen like himself, their families, and their employers, the poverty, greed, and hypocrisy, and the lack of hope for improving their lot. Hastings appears as 'Mugsborough'. In 1982 a 5-ft-square mural was unveiled at the museum, part of a larger work by Noonan for St Andrew's Church (demolished 1970) and the only bit saved. Mary Webb died at a nursing home in West Hill in 1927. 'Henry Handel Richardson' wrote *The Young Cosima* while living (1930–46) at Green Ridges, Tilekiln Lane, Fairlight, a modern house looking over the Old Town to the sea. Leaving her native Tyneside, the novelist Catherine Cookson moved down to Hastings, where she ran a lodging house with her mother; Cookson was married at St Mary's Star-of-the-Sea on 1 June 1940.

HAWKLEY *Hampshire*

Village, 3 m. N. of Petersfield. V. S. Pritchett stayed in the village in 1935 and wrote much of *Dead Man Leading* (1937), his novel of Amazonian exploration here. He had never visited Brazil and created a small model of a stretch of the river in the garden.

HAYWARDS HEATH *West Sussex*

Town on the A272, 15 m. N of Brighton. Daisy Ashford, author of *The Young Visiters* (written in 1890 but not published until 1919), had her only year of formal education at the Priory in the 1890s.

HENLEY *Oxfordshire*

Thames-side town on the A4155. The Red Lion Hotel, an old coaching inn by the bridge, put up the poet Shenstone in 1750 and Johnson and Boswell in 1776. Bedrooms have been named after these three visitors and a replica of the verse said to have been scratched on a window-pane by Shenstone can be seen in the room he occupied. John Betjeman celebrates the town in 'Henley-on-Thames':

> And pink on white the roses cling,
> And red the bright geraniums swing
> In baskets dangling down.

Henley is the basis for Thames Lockdon in Patrick Hamilton's boarding house novel *Slaves of Solitude* (1947).

HIGH WYCOMBE *Buckinghamshire*

Industrial and market town. The novelist Penelope Fitzgerald was educated at Wycombe Abbey in the 1930s.

HINDHEAD *Surrey*

Village high among commons of heather and pine trees, situated where the A287 crosses the A3. Sir Arthur Conan Doyle built his house, Undershaw, opposite the Royal Huts Hotel and lived there from 1896 to 1907, as it was hoped that the air would benefit his first wife. The house, later a private hotel, has a wrought-iron gate with the monogram ACD. The name 'Undershaw' is believed to have been a tribute to Bernard Shaw. *The Hound of the Baskervilles* (1902) was written here.

W. H. Auden attended St Edmund's preparatory school in the town, as did Christopher Isherwood, later to become his friend, playwriting collaborator, and, occasionally, lover. Isherwood, Auden's senior by three years, left a vivid picture of his schoolfellow in his autobiographical novel, *Lions and Shadows* (1938):

> To several of us, including myself, he confided the first naughty stupendous breath-taking hints about the facts of sex. I remember him chiefly for his naughtiness, his insolence, his smirking tantalising air of knowing disreputable and exciting secrets. With his hinted forbidden knowledge and stock of mispronounced scientific words, portentously uttered, he enjoyed among us, his semi-savage credulous schoolfellows, the status of a kind of witch-doctor.

HOLYBOURNE *Hampshire*

Village off the A31, 2 m. NE of Alton. In 1865 Elizabeth Gaskell bought The Lawns, a large house still in the main street here. She was writing *Wives and Daughters*, which was being published in instalments in *The Cornhill*, and she intended to give the house to her husband, a Unitarian minister in Manchester, as a present on completion of the novel. However, she died suddenly here in November and the novel remained unfinished.

HORTON *Berkshire*

Small village off the B376, now within the sound of Heathrow though once 'far from the city's noise'. In the partly Norman church is the memorial window to John Milton, who lived here from 1632, after leaving Cambridge, until 1640. In the chancel is the tomb of his mother, Sara (d. 1637). The traditional site of the Milton home is Berkin Manor, but the building is later. Milton wrote 'L'Allegro' and 'Il Penseroso' here, also the sonnets 'Now the Bright Morning-Star . . .' and 'O Nightingale . . .', and 'Lycidas', the elegy on his Cambridge friend Edward King.

HOTHFIELD *Kent*

Village S of the A20, 4 m. W of Ashford. Alfred Austin, editor (1883–94) of the *National Review*, lived (1867–1913) at Swinford Old Manor, ½ m. S. He recounts in *The Garden That I Love* (1894) how he found the house and restored the neglected garden. A prolific writer, he produced 20 volumes of verse between 1871 and 1908. He became Poet Laureate in 1896.

HUGHENDEN *Buckinghamshire*

Small village off the A4128, 2 m. N of High Wycombe. The Manor House (NT) was Gothicized by Benjamin Disraeli, whose home it was from 1848 to his death in 1881. He bought Hughenden the year after the publication of *Tancred* (1847), the third novel in the trilogy publicizing his 'Young England' policy, which he hoped would impress the rich with the necessity of caring for the poor, 'the two nations' of the country. *Lothair* (1870) and *Endymion* (1880), written here, though about political circles, have no political purpose. He was buried in the church in the grounds, which has a large memorial donated by Queen Victoria.

HUNSTON *West Sussex*

Rural village 1½ m. S of Chichester. The poet, dramatist, and short-story writer Ted Walker lived in the village from the early 1960s, and taught at Chichester High School. Much of his poetry—especially that in his first and best-known collection, *Fox on a Barn Door* (1965)—reflects his love for the local Sussex countryside.

HURSLEY *Hampshire*

Village on the A3090, 5 m. SW of Winchester. Thomas Sternhold (d. 1549), who with John Hopkins made metrical translations of the Psalms, lived here and was buried in the churchyard. There is a brass on the W wall of the church tower in memory of his wife. John Keble, founder of the high Anglican Oxford Movement, was vicar 1836–66 and was responsible for the building of the present church on the old foundations, chiefly from the proceeds of *The Christian Year* (a volume of sacred verse published in 1827). He is buried in the churchyard and there is a memorial brass on the chancel floor.

HURSTBOURNE TARRANT *Hampshire*

Village on the A343, 5 m. N of Andover. William Cobbett, who rode about the countryside recording the worsening plight of the agricultural workers, often came here. In *Rural Rides* (1830), he writes that Uphusband, the local name of the village, is 'a great favourite' with him 'not the less so certainly on account of the excellent free quarter that it affords'. His host was a Mr Blount, who lived in the red-brick farmhouse by the bridge. Cobbett's initials (WC 1825) are still to be seen where he scratched them on the brick wall to the left of the front gate.

HURSTPIERPOINT *West Sussex*

Large village W of the A23, 9 m. N of Hove. Harrison Ainsworth lived (1869–78) at Little Rockley, a house then on the edge of the village, with his unmarried daughter. He occasionally visited his mentally ill brother, whom he had installed in a house in Reigate, but compared with former times his life was a solitary one.

Novels written here include *Boscobel* (1872), and *The Manchester Rebels* (1874) about the 1745 rebellion, which proved one of his most popular.

HYTHE *Kent*

Coastal market town and Cinque Port near Romney Marsh. The novelist Colin MacInnes lived and died at 74 Marine Parade. Peter Porter reflects upon 'the brilliant and disgusting skulls' in his poem 'The Charnel House, St Leonard's, Hythe'.

IBSTONE *Buckinghamshire*

Chiltern village 2 m. S of Stokenchurch, on the Oxfordshire boundary. Rebecca West moved with her husband into the surviving wing of Ibstone House in 1941, the same year in which *Black Lamb and Grey Falcon*, her account of Yugoslav culture under the threat of Nazi Germany, was published. They raised pigs and cattle, market gardened, entertained in style, and during the Second World War sheltered Jewish and Yugoslav refugees.

IFIELD *West Sussex*

Former village, 1 m. E of Crawley, now part of the town. Mark Lemon moved from London in 1858 to Vine Cottage (demolished 1970s), which later, because of boundary changes, became part of Crawley High St. He was a close friend of Dickens and was known as 'Uncle Porpoise' to the Dickens children, who sometimes visited with their mother. When John Tenniel was illustrating *Through the Looking-Glass*, he used the 8-year-old Kate Lemon as a model for Alice. She disliked having to wear striped stockings for the occasion. Lemon, who was editor of *Punch*, entertained the contributors at Vine Cottage. He and his family attended St Margaret's Church, Ifield, where he was buried in 1870. His grave, SE of the church, has a plain stone border. Crawley church has a window, donated by his family, commemorating his charitable works in the town.

IPSDEN *Oxfordshire*

Small village on the Icknield Way, 4 m. SE of Wallingford, on a minor road off the A4074. Charles Reade was born (8 June 1814) in Ipsden House, a Queen Anne manor house on the S side of the village. The novelist Rosamond Lehmann came to live in the same house in 1930. The Fleming brothers, Ian and Peter, were born at Braziers Park, a manor house remodelled in the Strawberry Hill Gothick style on the outskirts of the village. Their father was MP for South Oxfordshire. The Flemings stayed for five years. The building is now a residential college.

ISLIP *Oxfordshire*

Village on the river Ray, 6 m. SW of Bicester. In the early 1920s Robert Graves lived with Nancy Nicholson, at first renting, later buying, a cottage called The World's End. He describes his four years here in *Goodbye to All That* (1929).

JUNIPER HILL *Oxfordshire*

Hamlet 3 m. S of Brackley, off the A43. Flora Thompson (née Timms) was born here in 1876 and grew up in 'the end house' ℗ of a lane in this still largely unchanged village. The thatched cottage (now slated) looked out over the field called Lark Rise, from which she took the title of her first autobiographical novel, or social history, about the hard life of country working people, observed and written as one of them. The village children walked 3 m. to the school at *Cottisford, which she left at 14 to work in the post office at *Fringford. Her three novels, based mainly on her life in the neighbourhood, published in one volume as *Lark Rise to Candleford* (1945), were written in Devon but their success came too late for her to enjoy it.

KELMSCOTT (or KELMSCOT) *Oxfordshire*

Small village off the A361 about 3 m. E of Lechlade. The Manor, a gabled Cotswold stone house dating from the late 16th c., was the home of William Morris from 1871 until his death in 1896 and contains relics of his work as writer, artist, and designer. In his Utopian story *News from Nowhere* (1891), the travellers end their journey here, and Morris's woodcut frontispiece depicts the house. At first he shared the tenancy with Dante Gabriel Rossetti, but a lack of sympathy between the two, exacerbated by Rossetti's love for Morris's wife, Jane, gradually made the situation intolerable and Rossetti left in 1874. W. T. Watts-Dunton wrote part of the once-popular novel *Aylwin* (1898) here, portraying Kelmscott as 'Hurstcote' and Rossetti as the painter. The house is now owned by the Society of Antiquaries and is usually open on a weekly basis in the summer months. Closed at the time of writing for flood repairs (www.sal.org.uk). Morris died at his London home, Kelmscott House, *Hammersmith, but is buried in the village churchyard.

KIDDINGTON *Oxfordshire*

Village off the A44, 15 m. NW of Oxford. Thomas Warton, the rector here from 1771 to his death in 1790, wrote a *History of Kiddington* (1783). He combined his duties here with a Fellowship at Trinity College, *Oxford.

KINGSCLERE *Hampshire*

Large village halfway between Basingstoke and Newbury. Between Kingsclere and the neighbouring village of Sydmonton lies Watership Down, the site of the rabbit warren in Richard Adams's novel (1972).

KINGSGATE *Kent*

Village 3 m. E of Margate, N of North Foreland, where Lord Holland built a villa in 1760 (later divided into flats). It was an imitation of Cicero's villa at Baiae and had a vast Doric portico with 12 columns of Portland stone. Thomas Gray wrote some satirical lines about it and the sham ruins built in the gardens:

Now mould'ring fanes and battlements arise
Arches and turrets nodding to their fall,
Unpeopled palaces delude his eyes
And mimick desolation covers all.

The steps from the castle to the beach at
Kingsgate Gap are thought locally to be the
origin of the steps in John Buchan's novel *The
Thirty-Nine Steps* (1914).

KNOLE *Kent*

Country house (NT) approached by the road
opposite St Nicholas Church in Sevenoaks. It is
the setting for *Orlando* (1928), the novel by
Virginia Woolf, who gave the manuscript to
Victoria Sackville-West ('Vita'), born here in
1892. She bequeathed it to the house as she 'felt
there was so much about Knole in it, that it was
the right place'. The manuscript is now shown
in the Great Hall. The house is 'Chevron', the
background for the family in Victoria Sackville-
West's own novel, *The Edwardians* (1930).
In *Knole and the Sackvilles* (1923), she tells
how her ancestor Thomas Sackville (later 1st
Earl of Dorset), part author of *The Mirror for
Magistrates* (1559) and *Gorboduc* (1565), was
given the house by his cousin Queen Elizabeth
I in 1566. The 3rd Earl was a friend of Jonson,
Fletcher, Drayton, and Donne, who preached in
the chapel (not open) on his annual visits to his
parish church of St Nicholas ℗ in Sevenoaks,
where he was rector (1616–31). The countess
moved to tears by Donne's sermons was the
unhappily married Anne Clifford, a pupil, as a
girl, of the poet Samuel Daniel, and the subject
of many poems. The 6th Earl (1638–1706),
author of some satires and the lyric 'To all you
ladies now at land', was a friend and
companion of Charles Sedley at Charles II's
court. He was also a friend and patron of
Dryden, who dedicated his *Essay upon Satire*
and *Of Dramatick Poesie* (1668) to him, and
of Prior, who owed his years at Cambridge to
him. Prior also wrote that 'A freedom reigned
at his table which made every one of his guests
think himself at home.' The dining room
became known as the Poets' Parlour (not open)
because it had portraits of the poets on the
wall.

LACEY GREEN *Buckinghamshire*

Village off the A4010, 3 m. S of Princes
Risborough. Pink Rd, a left turn at the
beginning of the village by the Whip, leads to
the Pink and Lily, an inn where Rupert Brooke
spent weekends with his friends. There are
photographs of him and a copy of one of his
poems over the old fireplace.

LALEHAM *Surrey*

Village on the B377 and the B376, 2 m. NE of
Chertsey. Matthew Arnold was born here in
1822, but the house, where his father tutored
before becoming headmaster of Rugby, has
been demolished. He spent his last years at
Cobham (6 m. SW), but was buried (1888)
in the churchyard here. A brass tablet
commemorates him in the church where he
worshipped.

LANCING *West Sussex*

Coastal downland village on the W edge of the
Adur valley, near Shoreham-by-Sea. Evelyn
Waugh, who was at Lancing College from 1917
to the end of 1921, gives an account of his years
here in his autobiography *A Little Learning*
(1964). Other students at the College have
included the novelist Tom Sharpe. The poet,
dramatist, and short-story writer Ted Walker
was born (in 1934) and brought up near the
beach at Lancing. The poems in his first and
best-known collection of poems, *Fox on a Barn
Door*—'On the Sea Wall', 'The Skate Fishers',
'Breakwaters'—show the influence of the local
scenes of early years. His childhood here is also
evoked in the first volume of his autobiography,
The High Path (1983).

LANGLEY *Berkshire*

Expanding town off the A4, merging with the
suburbs of Slough. The beautifully restored
parish church is in the old village centre.
Prominent treasures are the unusual
Kedermister pew and library. An early reader
of the old leather-bound ecclesiastical books
was John Milton, who often walked over from
*Horton; some of the marginal annotations are
said to be in his hand. The founder, Sir John
Kedermister, whose portrait hangs near his
books, was descended from his namesake,
Edward IV's Ranger of Langley Forest. The
poet Waller's daughter married into the family.

LEATHERHEAD *Surrey*

Old town on the A24 and the A245. The
Running Horse, part of which dates from the
15th c., is thought to be the inn of the ale-wife
in Skelton's poem *The Tunning of Elynour
Rummyng*, written *c.* 1517, which describes the
brewing (tunning) of 'noppy ale' for 'travellers
and tynkers, for sweters and swynkers, and all
good ale drynkers'. Skelton was attached to
Prince Henry's household and may have been
staying at the royal palace at Nonsuch, 5 m. NE
(stone columns mark the groundplan of the
palace).
In 1808 Sheridan rented Randall's Farm
(opposite the cemetery entrance) from his
friend Richard Iremonger for 15 months.
Sheridan wrote inviting a friend to a fishing
party 'on our river Mole' nearby.
Sir Anthony Hope Hawkins, author, as
'Anthony Hope', of *The Prisoner of Zenda*
(1894), was buried (1933) in the parish
churchyard.

LETCOMBE BASSETT *Oxfordshire*

Village in a fold of the Berkshire Downs, on
a minor road off the B4001, *c.* 3 m. SW of
Wantage. Jonathan Swift, a friend of the rector,
the Revd John Geree, came to visit him in June
1714 as a respite from the political turmoil at
the end of Queen Anne's reign. Swift's devoted
'Vanessa' (Esther Vanhomrigh) attempted to
join him, but seems to have been put off by his
meeting her at *Wantage and turning her back
to avoid scandal at the Rectory. During this
quiet interlude Swift wrote the 'Verses on

Himself' and the tract 'Some Free Thoughts on
the Present State of Affairs', reputedly sitting
under the great mulberry tree in the Rectory
(later Old Rectory) garden, where it still
flourishes.
In Hardy's *Jude the Obscure* (1895), Jude is
seduced by Arabella in the thatched cottage
opposite the church on the edge of the stream.
In the story Letcombe Bassett is called
'Cresswell'.

LEWES *East Sussex*

Town on the A27. Evelyn in his *Diary*
mentions staying here with his grandparents,
the Stansfields, for his schooldays, first with Mr
Potts in the Cliffe and then at the Grammar
School. He records laying one of the stones at
the foundation of the church his grandfather
was building at South Malling (1 m. N) and the
solemnity of his grandfather's funeral in 1627 at
All Saints' Church (monuments). When Evelyn
attended the Grammar School, in 1630, it
adjoined the grounds (now public gardens) of
Southover Grange, his new home after his
grandmother's remarriage. This house, now
owned by the Council, can be rented for
receptions and meetings. One room is called
after Evelyn and another after Harrison
Ainsworth, who portrays the house as 'Mock
Beggars' Hall' in *Ovingdean Grange* (1860), a
novel set in the Civil War.
Thomas Rickman was born (1761) in the
Cliffe at the bottom of the town; his forceful
satires written under the pseudonym 'Clio'
appeared in the *Black Dwarf* and other
periodicals. An early friend of his was Tom
Paine, who lodged at the Bull House near the
former Westgate in the High St. Paine drew up
a petition about the grievances over pay and
conditions of his fellow excisemen. This was
circulated in London and, when the demand
failed, he lost his post. He had married the
daughter of his landlord, a tobacconist, and
helped run the business for a time, but he
separated from his wife and set out for America
in 1774. Rickman, who became a bookseller in
London, sold Paine's works and the two met
again at his shop.
Daisy Ashford came here at the age of 5 to
live at Southdown House, 44 St Anne's Cres.
(now residential). She was one of a large, merry
family—'We weren't at all what you call stuffy,'
she remembered. She enjoyed writing, a ready
occupation for a wet day, and completed *The
Young Visiters* when she was 9 (though it was
not published until 1919). The story of Mr
Salteena, self-admittedly 'not quite a
gentleman', and his initiation into high society
is an entertaining account of the adult world as
seen by a child.

LIMPSFIELD *Surrey*

Village on the A25. Edward Garnett (reader for
the publisher T. Fisher Unwin) and his wife,
Constance, translator of many Russian classics,
built in 1896 The Cearne, a house in the woods
overlooking the valley, off the B269 at
Limpsfield Chart. They entertained many
writers here including Hudson, Cunninghame

Graham, Belloc, Edward Thomas, W. H. Davies, and Galsworthy, whose character Bosinney in *The Man of Property* was partly based on Garnett. In 1898, when Conrad visited, he met F. M. Hueffer (later Ford) and his wife, who lived nearby. Hueffer introduced D. H. Lawrence to the hospitable Garnett, and many of Lawrence's dialect poems, including the long 'Whether or Not', were written by the log fire at The Cearne. A young generation, including Rupert Brooke, used to meet at Champions, the home of their neighbours the Oliviers, where Shaw, E. V. Lucas, and other friends were at one time the audience for Garnett's play *Robin Hood*, which the young people acted.

Florence Barclay (née Charlesworth), born (1862) at the vicarage, was the author of the popular novel *The Rosary* (1909). She was buried in the churchyard (1921).

Richard Church married in 1916 and rented a Georgian cottage in the High St. of Limpsfield village, next door to a grocer's shop (now a bookshop opposite the Bull Inn), which features in his first novel, *Oliver's Daughter*, written 10 years later, where the heroine is a grocer's daughter. In 1927 Church leased the 14th-c. Comfort's Cottage in a clearing in Staffhurst Wood for a year before moving to London. W. H. Davies, who met Church there, bought a cottage in the High St. near the parish church.

LITTLEBOURNE *Kent*

Village on the A257, 4 m. E of Canterbury. Lee Priory, on the E of the village over the bridge, was rebuilt in the Gothick style for Thomas Barrett, a friend of Horace Walpole, who after a visit in the summer of 1790 wrote to Mary Berry, 'I think that if Strawberry were not its parent, it would be jealous.' On Barrett's death in 1803 the ownership of the Priory passed through Samuel Egerton Brydges's wife to his eldest son. After his wife's death Brydges lived at the Priory from 1810 to 1818, when he went abroad. The printers Johnson and Warwick set up a press here to print poems of Breton, Browne, Ralegh, and other Elizabethans, which had been collected by Brydges from many sources. Jane Austen was one of those unimpressed by his novels, but his many bibliographical works have been highly regarded, including *The British Bibliographer* (1810–14), and *Restituta* (1814–16). He became an MP in 1812 and was made a baronet in 1814. After alterations to the house, one of the rooms was re-erected at the Victoria and Albert Museum as an example of neo-Gothic architecture.

LITTLE CHART *Kent*

Village off the A20, 6 m. NW of Ashford. H. E. Bates in his autobiography, *The Vanished World* (1969), *The Blossoming World* (1971), and *The World in Ripeness* (1972), describes how in 1931 he found the barn, which he and his wife converted to The Granary, in a garden made from a wilderness, that was his home until his death in 1974. He wrote here *The Fallow Land* (1932) and *The Poacher* (1935), which, like the later *Love for Lydia* (1952), stem from his youth in the Nene valley in Northamptonshire; the war novels, which include the first part of *Fair Stood the Wind for France* (1944), written while on leave, *The Purple Plain* (1947), and *The Jacaranda Tree* (1949); also the 'Chaucerian' tales of the Larkin family. He is the author of the short stories written by 'Flying Officer X'.

LITTLEHAMPTON *West Sussex*

South coast resort at the mouth of the Arun. John Galsworthy often spent working holidays at the Beach Hotel. At Christmas in 1918, when writing *Saint's Progress* (1919), he received the offer of a knighthood. His letter of refusal was somehow delayed and he found his name in the New Year's honours list and had to write again to correct the mistake.

LONG WITTENHAM *Oxfordshire*

Thames-side village on the A415, 5 m. SE of Abingdon. Robert Gibbings, whose *Sweet Thames Run Softly* (1940) and *Till I End My Song* (1957) were illustrated with his own woodcuts, lived at Footbridge Cottage, by the Cross. He was buried (1958) in the churchyard.

LONGWORTH *Oxfordshire*

Little village near the Thames, on a minor road N of Kingston Bagpuize on the A420. The Old Rectory was the birthplace of Dr John Fell (1625–86), Dean of Christ Church, Oxford, and Bishop of Oxford. He contributed greatly to the development of the Oxford University Press, for which he procured matrices and punches of the best available types (from which the 'Fell types' were cast), and every year he arranged for the publication of a different classical author. It seems unfair that the most familiar association with his name should be Thomas Brown's lines: 'I do not like thee, Dr. Fell . . .'.

The Old Rectory was also the birthplace of Richard Doddridge Blackmore, author of *Lorna Doone* (1869), whose father was curate there for a short time, but it was not a home to remember as his mother died when he was 4 months old and he was taken away to live with an aunt during the years before his father remarried.

LYMINGTON *Hampshire*

Old port and yachting station on the A337, at the mouth of the Lymington on the W side of the Solent. Henry Francis Lyte, author of 'Abide with me', was curate here from *c.* 1820 until he went to *Brixham in 1824. Frederick Marryat (1792–1848) lived for a time in the Brockenhurst Rd, just N of the town, the house where he stayed being portrayed as 'Wolverley Lodge' in *The Children of the New Forest* (1847).

William Allingham was stationed here as a Customs Officer, 1863–70. He describes the office in his *Diary* (ed. H. Allingham and D. Radford, 1907) as

a small first-floor room over the Coastguard Station [demolished], looking upon the little Harbour (muddy at low water, occupied chiefly by pleasure-yachts), and the woods of Walhampton beyond. . . . in the evening after my arrival . . . I heard four nightingales.

While he was here he edited *The Ballad Book* (1864) and wrote *Laurence Bloomfield in Ireland*, a poem of over 5,000 lines (published in book form 1864), which he regarded as his most important work and which was quoted by Gladstone in the House of Commons.

Coventry Patmore (1823–96) came to Lymington in 1891 and stayed for the rest of his life.

LYNDHURST *Hampshire*

Village in the heart of the New Forest, 10 m. SW of Southampton on the A35. In the churchyard is the grave of Mrs Reginald Hargreaves, née Alice Liddell, who inspired Lewis Carroll's *Alice's Adventures in Wonderland* (1865). The graves of the 'Two yeomen . . . and a maiden fair' of Kingsley's 'A New Forest Ballad' cannot now be located.

MAIDENHEAD *Berkshire*

Boating and commuter town on the Thames. George Harvey Bone, the central character of Patrick Hamilton's novel *Hangover Square* (1941), longs in his schizophrenic periods to 'get to Maidenhead'. Peter Templer, schoolfriend of Nicholas Jenkins, the narrator of Anthony Powell's *A Dance to the Music of Time* (1951–75), lives in the town in an expensive ugly house in 'a settlement of prosperous businessmen'.

MAIDSTONE *Kent*

Market and manufacturing town on the Medway. In 1605–6 the King's Men, Shakespeare's company, acted in Maidstone. The account books record that there was 'paid to the King's players by Mr Mayor and to the trumpeters two pounds five shillings'. It is not known which play they performed.

From October 1665 to August 1667 John Evelyn was in charge of 500–600 French and Dutch prisoners of war (mainly sick and injured) at Leeds Castle, 5 m. E. In his *Diary* he shows his sympathy for his 'flock' and in the second winter orders them more food, clothes, and fuel.

Christopher Smart attended the Grammar School when it was housed in the medieval Corpus Christi Hall in Earl St. William Hazlitt was born (1778) in Rose Yard, between Earl St. and High St. (Ⓟ on building in latter), near his father's Unitarian Chapel Ⓟ in Dullock Lane (now called Market Buildings). There is a Hazlitt Theatre on Earl St., and a substantial collection of Hazlitt material, including a self-portrait and other paintings, a death mask, his writing slope, and a range of publications, is kept at Maidstone Museum. Some items may be on display; any may be viewed by appointment (www.museum.maidstone.gov.uk).

61

Dickens modelled 'Dingley Dell', Mr Wardle's house in *Pickwick Papers*, on Cobtree Manor on the Chatham Rd. Part of Tennyson's poem *The Princess* (1853) is set at Park House, Invicta Pk (Barracks), which belonged to his brother-in-law Edward Lushington.

William Golding began teaching at the Grammar School for Boys in 1938. He married Anne Brookfield in a registry office in the town. Muriel Spark rented a cottage in the grounds of Allington Castle, described in her autobiography *Curriculum Vitae* (1992) as 'a Carmelite stronghold of tertiary nuns'. She wrote her first novel, *The Comforters* (1957), here. The story was based on the hallucinatory word games which arose from the doses of Dexedrine she took as an appetite suppressant.

MAPLEDURHAM HOUSE
Oxfordshire

Elizabethan manor house off the B481, 6 m. NW of Reading, built beside the Thames for the Blount family. Pope, who was a friend and correspondent of Teresa and Martha Blount throughout his life, wrote some lines 'To Miss Blount, On her leaving the Town after the Coronation':

> She went, to plain-work, and to purling brooks,
>   Old-fashion'd halls, dull aunts, and croaking
>   rooks.
> She went from Op'ra, park, assembly, play,
> To morning-walks, and pray'rs three hours a day;
> Or o'er cold coffee, trifle with the spoon,
> Count the slow clock, and dine exact at noon;
> Divert her eyes with pictures in the fire,
> Hum half a tune, tell stories to the squire;
> Up to her godly garret after sev'n
> There starve and pray, for that's the way to
>   heav'n.

Pope visited the house in 1713 and 1714, and in 1717 the sisters moved from the family home, which their brother had inherited, to live in London.

MARGATE *Kent*

Resort on the NE coast, on the A28. Gray, staying at Denton in 1766, visited 'Margate, which is Bartholomew Fair by the seaside'. Keats, lodging here in 1816 and 1817 for a few weeks while working on *Endymion*, found it bare and treeless. Lamb, who came first when 15, returned 'with Mary, to drink seawater and pick up shells' in 1821. One of his *Essays of Elia* (1820–3) is about 'The Old Margate Hoy', the coaster which took visitors from London to Margate.

'On Margate Sands I can connect nothing with nothing,' wrote T. S. Eliot in 'The Waste Land' (1922). He came here to recuperate in October 1921, staying at the Albemarle Hotel at 47 Eastern Esplanade in the Cliftonville area of town, drawing people, playing scales on the mandolin, and writing part of 'The Waste Land'. Betjeman reflects on the defence of England in his poem 'Margate, 1940'. The pier represents the end of the journey for the four protagonists in Graham Swift's novel *Last Orders* (1996), and they commit the ashes of

Beachcombers at Margate, where T. S. Eliot recuperated and wrote parts of 'The Waste Land'

their friend Jack Dodds to wind and water here.

MARLOW *Buckinghamshire*

Town where the A404 crosses the Thames. Thomas Love Peacock wrote *Nightmare Abbey* at 47 West St. (once Peacock's restaurant, now renamed). Shelley stayed with him here on returning with Mary Godwin from Switzerland in September 1816. When, three months later, Shelley's wife, Harriet, drowned herself in the Serpentine it was Peacock who advised him to marry Mary as soon as possible. After their wedding on 30 December the couple moved into Albion House, a two-storey building with Gothic windows, early in 1817. Leigh Hunt on a visit found Mary transcribing *Laon and Cythna*, published later as *The Revolt of Islam* (1818), and preparing her own *Frankenstein* for publication. The friends walked, rowed, and dined in the local inns together. Shelley sold the house in 1818 before leaving England for

ever. It is now divided, and not shown to the public.

In Sarah Waters' *Fingersmith* (2002), Sue Trinder is sent off from her London home to work (and to set up a little scam) at a wealthy household near Marlow.

MARTIN *Hampshire*

Village near the Hampshire, Wiltshire, and Dorset borders, *c.* 11 m. SW of Salisbury on the A354. Although W. H. Hudson never disclosed its name, it is believed to be the original of 'Winterbourne Bishop', the 'favourite village' of his book *A Shepherd's Life* (1910), in which he recounts the characters and ways of the people of the Wiltshire Downs and the wildlife of the region.

MATFIELD *Kent*

Village on the B2160, 6 m. NE of Tunbridge Wells. In *The Old Century* (1938) and *The Weald of Youth* (1942), the poet and writer

Siegfried Sassoon describes his life at Weirleigh, the tall red-brick house where before the First World War he learned to ride and arranged for his first poems to be published.

MEDMENHAM (pr. 'Mĕdn'm) ABBEY *Buckinghamshire*

An 18th-c. mansion on the site of a Cistercian abbey, 4 m. SW of Marlow. Here Sir Francis Dashwood founded the Hell-Fire Club, whose members, sometimes called the Monks of Medmenham, adopted as their motto 'Fay ce que voudras' after that of the community at Rabelais's Abbey of Thelema in *Gargantua* (1534). There it was expected that a carefully selected band of virtuous people with the highest qualities would need no rules to live a virtuous life, but Charles Johnstone's description of the activities of the club in *Chrysal, or, The Adventures of a Guinea* (1760–5) suggests that a virtuous life was not one of the aims here.

MEREWORTH *Kent*

Village on the A228, 8 m. SE of Maidstone. *The Torrington Diaries* (1934), 24 volumes about the leisurely rural rides made (1781–94) by John Byng, 5th Viscount, were left at Yotes Court (E of Seven Mile Lane), but an auction dispersed them. Byng, a nephew of the Admiral, had stayed there in 1790 with cousins.

MICKLEHAM *Surrey*

Village off the A24, 3 m. N of Dorking. Fanny Burney often visited Norbury Park, the home of her friend Mrs William Lock. In 1793 she made the acquaintance of a group of French émigrés who had taken Juniper Hall (NT; altered, now let to the Field Studies Council; appointments to visit should be made with the Warden). These included Talleyrand, Mme de Staël, and General D'Arblay. Many visits took place between the two households, Fanny Burney improving D'Arblay's English and he, her French, and their marriage took place at Mickleham church in 1794. The impecunious couple took rooms at Phenice Farm, Bagdon Hill (rebuilt), and, after living at *Great Bookham, returned to build (1797) their own house (gone, site near the railway station). This, called Camilla Cottage by Fanny's father, Dr Charles Burney, after her novel *Camilla* (1796), which provided the money, was their home until D'Arblay returned to France in 1802.

Marie Corelli lived (1865–83) at Fern Dell, on the old London–Dorking road now bypassed by the A24, but her success as a popular novelist came later. The house above, on the winding Box Hill road below Juniper Hall, is Flint Cottage (NT, but not open to the public), the home of George Meredith, and his second wife (d. 1885), from 1867. One of his most popular novels, *Diana of the Crossways* (1885), was written here. The little chalet high up in the steep garden was furnished as a study bedroom, where he could work undisturbed. There was also a shed for Picnic, the donkey.

Meredith was visited by George Gissing, whose work he was one of the first to praise, Stevenson, who appeared as Woodseer in *The Amazing Marriage*, Barrie, and James Russell Lowell, the American poet. In 1895 Henry James accompanied Alphonse Daudet, who describes his host and himself, both then suffering from paralysis, as two wounded seagulls. Meredith died in 1909.

MIDDLETON STONEY *Oxfordshire*

Village on the A430, 3 m. W of Bicester. The mansion in the park is on the site of the house where John Gay stayed with his patrons, the Duke and Duchess of Queensberry, who financed the production of his play *The Beggar's Opera* (1728), which is said to have made Gay rich, and Rich (the producer) gay.

MIDHURST *West Sussex*

Old market town on the Rother, 9 m. S of Haslemere, on the A286. H. G. Wells was briefly at the Grammar School in 1881, where he learnt Latin from Horace Byatt, the headmaster, having previously been apprenticed to a chemist in the town. In 1883, after two unhappy years apprenticed to a drapery establishment in *Portsmouth, he returned at Mr Byatt's invitation as a student assistant teacher, and the following year won a scholarship to the Normal School of Science in London. Midhurst figures as 'Wimblehurst' in *Tono-Bungay* (1909).

MILLAND *West Sussex*

Village E of the A3, 3 m. S of Liphook. Thomas Otway was born (1682) at the rectory (rebuilt), near the church on the A3. His father was curate of Trotton (4 m. S), where the church has a memorial to Thomas Otway, but they moved to *Woolbeding while he was still a child.

MINSTEAD *Hampshire*

Little village in the New Forest, 2½ m. NNW of Lyndhurst, on a minor road between the A31 and the A337. Sir Arthur Conan Doyle is buried on the S side of the churchyard, near open fields, in a simple grave inscribed 'Steel true, blade straight' and, under his name, 'Patriot, physician and man of letters'. Conan Doyle knew and loved the New Forest from early days. His novel *The White Company* (1891), set in the 14th c., when Beaulieu Abbey dominated life in the area, was written while he was staying at a cottage on Emery Down, 2 m. S. A few years before his death he bought the half-timbered house of Bignell Wood in the parish of Minstead.

MINSTER *Kent*

Village E of Sheerness in the Isle of Sheppey. The partly Saxon church of St Mary and St Sexburga contains the late 13th-c. monument to Sir Robert Shurland, whose adventures were told in 'The Grey Dolphin' in Richard Barham's *Ingoldsby Legends* (1840).

MORETON *Oxfordshire*

Village 2 m. SSW of Thame, off the B4013. William Basse (or Bas) (1583?–1653) lived in a cottage here at one time. He was retainer to his patron Sir Richard (later Lord) Wenman of Thame Park. His first published work was *Sword and Buckler, or, Serving Man's Defence* (1602), followed in the same year by *Three Pastoral Elegies*. He also wrote 'Epitaph on Shakespeare' and 'Angler's Song', which was included in *The Compleat Angler*.

NETLEY ABBEY *Hampshire*

Ruined Cistercian abbey, built *c*. 1239, 3 m. SE of Southampton, on the A3025. Pope and Lord Peterborough, his host at Bevis Mount, set out in August 1734 to sail round the Isle of Wight. They lunched in the woods at Netley and sketched the ruins. Pope writes of this visit to Martha Blount in his *Letters*. Gray, who went by ferry, describes his two visits in 1755 and 1764 to his friends James Brown and Norton Nicholls. The ferryman told him he would never venture there at night. William Lisle Bowles wrote 'Sonnet to Netley Abbey' after his visit, and N. P. Willis crossed from Ryde to picnic among the ruins with a party of friends in the 1830s. He describes, in *Loiterings of Travel* (1840), how a young man sketched the scene of 'gaily dressed ladies' and 'bright wines on the mossy grass'. He thought that the ivy enhanced the beauty of the ruins.

NETTLEBED *Oxfordshire*

Village, 5 m. NW of Henley, on the A4130. Karl Moritz, a German schoolmaster, stayed here (1782) while walking from London to Dovedale, with a change of linen and the works of Milton in his pocket. He found travellers on foot were received with suspicion but he was given a carpeted bedroom, a very good bed, and supper in the kitchen. It reminded him of Fielding's novels, which he found had given him an accurate idea of English manners. There were pewter dishes round the walls and hams, black puddings, sugar loaves, and sausages hung from the ceiling. Next morning he wore clean linen and at once was shown into the parlour. At church he noticed the Ten Commandments (which are still there), written above the altar, and was pleased at the instrumental accompaniment given by the villagers. Writing home he mentioned the blacksmith's tombstone in the churchyard, because of the verse:

> My sledge and anvil be declined,
> My bellows too have lost their wind;
> My fire's extinct, my forge decayed,
> And in the dust my vice is laid;
> My coals are spent, my iron's gone,
> My nails are drove: my work is done.

The travel writer and foreign correspondent for *The Times* Peter Fleming lived at Merrimoles estate.

NEW ALRESFORD (pr. 'Allsford) *Hampshire*

Small market town on the A31, 8 m. NE of Winchester. The parish church has specimens of cuneiform inscriptions on two ancient bricks from Ur of the Chaldees (birthplace of Abraham) and Babylon: the first from the ziggurat at Ur dedicated to the moon god Nannar, *c.* 2150 BC; the other from Nebuchadnezzar's palace at Babylon, *c.* 604–562 BC.

At 27 Broad St. a plaque marks the house where Mary Russell Mitford was born on 16 December 1787 and where she lived until she was 10, when her winning of a £20,000 lottery prize enabled her father to move the family to a new house at Reading.

Alresford Pond, to the N of the town, was created by Bishop Lucy in the early 13th c. in order to make the Itchen navigable from Alresford to Southampton and is celebrated by George Wither in his pastoral poem *Fair Virtue* (1622): 'For pleasant was that pool . . .'. There is a handsome memorial window to Wither in the church of Old Alresford, 1 m. N.

Many literary men of the mid-19th c. were guests of Lady Ashburton at The Grange, an imposing mansion in a park (*c.* 3 m. NW). On one occasion she was mockingly taken to task by Henry Taylor, author of *Philip van Artevelde*, for the heartless way previously honoured guests were displaced in favour of new writers. Lady Ashburton's hurried excuses caused wry smiles by others in the house party, which at various times included Tennyson, and Carlyle, with whom she conducted 'an affair of the heart and head' for 14 years, until her death (1857).

NEWARK PRIORY *Surrey*

Ruins of an Augustinian priory (*c.* 1190) visible from the B367 S of Pyrford. Thomas Love Peacock fell in love with Fanny Faulkner and used to meet her here in 1807, when he was living at Chertsey, but through a misunderstanding the engagement was broken off, and she, thinking herself deserted, married another. She died in the following year. 'Revisiting Newark Abbey' (1842), 'Remember Me' (1809), and 'Al mio primiero amore' (1813) all relate to her and she was partly the model for Miss Touchandgo of *Crotchet Castle* (1831).

NEWBURY *Berkshire*

Racing and county town on the river Kennet and the Kennet and Avon Canal. The environs provide the setting for John Betjeman's 'Indoor Games Near Newbury':

Spingle-spangled stars are peeping
At the lush Lagonda creeping
Down the winding ways of tarmac to the leaded
lights of home.

Certain aspects of the fictional village described in Adam Thorpe's novel *Ulverton* (1992) lie in the downland somewhere to the W of Newbury.

NEWPORT *Isle of Wight*

Administrative capital on the Medina, 5 m. S of Cowes. In 1846 John Hamilton Reynolds was appointed clerk to the newly formed County Court, but his health was undermined and he died in 1852. He was buried in the old churchyard, now a rose garden adjoining the public park on Church Litten, where his tombstone has been preserved. The inscription 'Friend of Keats' was added during renovations in 1917. Reynolds was the recipient of many of Keats's letters.

NORMANDY *Surrey*

Village 7 m. NE of Farnham, on the A323. William Cobbett farmed at Normandy Farm near the manor from 1831 to his death in 1835, when the hamlet was part of the parish of Ash. He published *Rural Rides* in 1830, an account of journeys taken from 1821 to refute the landlords' policy towards agricultural labourers with a first-hand account of the distress and mismanagement. There is a tradition, recounted in Ralph Wightman's *Rural Rides* (1957), that Cobbett brought Tom Paine's bones here instead of leaving them in *Liverpool and that the young daughter of Cobbett's friend at the manor was frightened to pass the room where they lay. Cobbett died here and was buried at *Farnham.

NUNEHAM COURTENAY
Oxfordshire

Village on the A4074, 5 m. S of Oxford. The regularity of the matching pairs of cottages facing each other across the main road was the result of a planned removal of the entire village in 1760–1, when the 1st Earl of Harcourt required the site for his landscape garden. The mid-18th-c. vogue for creating magnificent gardens at the cost of destroying villages which spoilt the view roused Goldsmith to take a lone stand against the practice. In *The Deserted Village* (1770), he expressed his fears that it would lead to the ruin of the peasantry, and it has been thought that he had Nuneham Courtenay in mind when he wrote the poem. The Revd T. Mozley, referring to the time when J. H. Newman, his brother-in-law, was staying at the schoolhouse (1828, then the officiating clergyman's residence), speaks of the tradition that the village was 'the true Auburn of Goldsmith's "Deserted Village"' (*Reminiscences Chiefly of Oriel College and the Oxford Movement*, 1882). In an essay 'The Revolution in Low Life' (*New Essays*, 1927), Goldsmith says that he had actually witnessed in the summer of 1761 the removal of a village and the destruction of its farms to make a new 'seat of pleasure' for a wealthy landowner, 50 m. from London, and it seems almost certain that Nuneham Courtenay was this village, and that the subject of the essay corresponds with the theme of the poem:

The man of wealth and pride
Takes up a space that many poor supplied;
His seat, where solitary sports are seen,
Indignant spurns the cottage from the green.

The solitary widow of 'sweet Auburn' left after the houses of the other villagers had been destroyed:

She only left of all the harmless train,
The sad historian of the pensive plain,

is paralleled by a real old woman at Nuneham called Barbara Wyatt, the 'Mopsa' of a poem ('The Removal of the Village at Nuneham Courtenay') by the Poet Laureate, William Whitehead, who extolled the kindness shown to her by the 'indulgent' Earl in leaving her to end her days in her 'clay-built cot'. A memorial to her can be seen on a seat on the terrace near the site of her cottage in Nuneham Park. The site of the old village is beside the present estate road. In spite of the poignancy of 'The Deserted Village' there is no evidence that (at Nuneham at any rate) any real hardship was suffered, and many villagers may have been better off after their removal, as Whitehead suggests:

The careful matrons of the plain
Had left their cots without a sigh,
Well pleased to house their little train
In happier mansions warm and dry.

Goldsmith may have woven several strands into his poem: his general concern over the practice of destroying villages to make private parks, his experience of witnessing such an occurrence at Nuneham in 1761, and his idealized childhood memories of *Lissoy.

The 2nd Earl of Harcourt was an admirer of Rousseau, who is said to have stayed in the village in 1767 and to have planted seeds of many foreign wild flowers in Nuneham Park— his favourite, the periwinkle, grows up the banks and, as in *La Nouvelle Héloïse*, trailing garlands of clematis, bryony, and creepers twine among the trees 'negligently, as they do in the forest'. A garden seat bears a quotation from Rousseau's concept of nature. Lord Harcourt entertained artists and writers, including Mason, Whitehead, Walpole, Gilpin, and Fanny Burney, who, on her visit in 1786 with George III and Queen Charlotte, recorded in her *Diary* that she was lost for a quarter of an hour in the 'straggling, half-new, half-old, half-comfortable, half-forlorn' house which the Earl was remodelling. He encouraged Mason to lay out the flower garden, with carefully irregular beds and inscriptions and memorial urns placed in flowery glades, embodying the theories expressed in his poem 'The English Garden'. Much is now altered and overgrown, but a fine view of the mansion and the park can be had from the river.

OLNEY *Buckinghamshire*

Small market town on the A509, 13 m. SE of Northampton. William Cowper and Mrs Unwin came here in 1767, at the Revd John Newton's suggestion, to live at Orchard Side in the Market Place (now the Cowper and Newton Museum). Cowper and Newton collaborated on the *Olney Hymns* (1779) in a household, described by David Cecil in *The Stricken Deer* (1929), where time was divided between irregular piety and unrestrained philanthropy, where masters and servants alike were liable at any time to burst out with intimate revelations about the state of their souls.

Cowper helped with parish work and taught in the Sunday school. He continued to suffer

Cowper's parlour at Orchard Side, Olney, showing the sofa of *The Task*

from depression and during one bout was cared for at the rectory by Newton. On his return to Orchard Side, the villagers gave him a leveret, the first of three. These, Puss, Tiney, and Bess, who had a special door from the hall to the parlour, were the subject of many of Cowper's *Letters*, considered 'divine chit-chat' by Coleridge and Lamb, two recipients. The house is furnished with much of Cowper's furniture, including the sofa of *The Task*.

> Now stir the fire, and close the shutters fast,
> Let fall the curtains, wheel the sofa round,
> And, while the bubbling and loud-hissing urn
> Throws up a steamy column, and the cups,
> That cheer but not inebriate, wait on each,
> So let us welcome peaceful ev'ning in.

Poems (1782) contains the satires written at Mrs Unwin's suggestion when Cowper was

Joseph Conrad with his wife and son in the study at Capel House, Orlestone

unable to garden: 'Table Talk', 'The Progress of Error', 'Truth', 'Expostulation', 'Hope', 'Charity', 'Conversation', and 'Retirement'. The ballad *John Gilpin* (1782) came from a story that Lady Austen, who lived at the rectory of Clifton Reynes, ½ m. E, told him in order to divert his depression. *The Task* (1784), also written at her suggestion, was an immediate success. The library at the Museum contains many of Cowper's works. The garden contains the 'Bouderie' or the 'nutshell of a summerhouse which is my verse manufactory'. In 1786 Orchard Side needed repairs and Cowper and Mrs Unwin moved to *Weston Underwood. A window in the Memorial Chapel (now known as the Lady Chapel) of the parish church portrays Newton, Cowper, and the hares.

ORLESTONE *Kent*

Village on the B2070, 6 m. S of Ashford. Capel House, an old farmhouse on the Bonnington road, was where Conrad lived (1910–19) and recovered from ill health and low spirits. He found the place 'sympathetic', and his writings here included the long short story 'A Smile of Fortune' and the novels *Chance* (1913) and *Victory* (1915).

OTTERBOURNE *Hampshire*

Village on the M3, 5 m. S of Winchester. Charlotte Mary Yonge was born (1823) and brought up at Otterbourne House, a solid late Georgian house set back from the main road, opposite the church. After her father's death she moved with her mother in 1862 to Elderfield, nearby, and stayed there for the rest of her life. She came under the influence of John Keble (rector of Otterbourne with the neighbouring parish of *Hursley), who encouraged her to expound her religious views in her fiction. She wrote over 150 books, including novels, of which *The Heir of Redclyffe*

(1853) first brought her popular success, historical romances, and a biography of Hannah More (1888). She is buried near the S porch of the church which her father and Keble designed together.

OVINGDEAN *East Sussex*

Village on the B2123. Harrison Ainsworth often walked over the Downs to church here, when living in *Brighton (1853–67) 3 m. W. In his novel *Ovingdean Grange* (1860), Prince Charles spends his last night in England at the Grange (near the church in the lower village) before escaping to France. The red-brick Tudor front has been stuccoed and the oak panelling and stained glass have disappeared.

OXFORD *Oxfordshire*

University and cathedral city, which grew up around the Saxon priory of St Frideswide at the confluence of the Thames and the Cherwell. The settlement was first mentioned as Oxnaforda in the Anglo-Saxon Chronicle of 911. The priory church, of which Walter Map (or Mapes) was archdeacon in 1197, now serves as the cathedral and as the chapel of Christ Church, the college built by Cardinal Wolsey on the site of St Frideswide's.

Geoffrey of Monmouth, creator of King Arthur as a romantic hero, is thought to have studied at Oxford *c*. 1129. Grosseteste, first rector (1224) of the Franciscan Order in Oxford, who became first Chancellor of the University, made translations from Greek and wrote the long poem *Le Chasteau d'amour*. The philosopher and man of science Roger Bacon lived in the Franciscan House (site now a housing estate in Paradise Sq.) after his return from Paris *c*. 1250 until *c*. 1257, when his researches alarmed the religious community and he was sent away. While here he is said to have studied astronomy from the roof of the New Gate, built to control the long bridge over the marshes known as Grandpont. Bacon, after writing his three major works under surveillance in Paris, is thought to have died in Oxford (1294) and to have been buried in the Franciscan burial ground. Pepys visited in 1668 and writes in his *Diary* that he climbed the tower to 'Roger Bacon's study'. The gate had then become a house and had an ornamented second storey. This folly (demolished in 1779) gave to the bridge its present name, Folly Bridge.

Chaucer shows some knowledge of the town and gown, and especially of the district of Osney, in 'The Miller's Tale' in *The Canterbury Tales* (*c*. 1387–1400). John Skelton is thought to have been made 'poet laureate' (before the official post existed) in Oxford *c*. 1490 and he himself claimed to have received the honour from Henry VII. William D'Avenant was born (1606) at The Crown inn in Cornmarket (now no. 3), where his father was innkeeper. The Painted Room on the second floor (now part of an office: occasional tours; contact the tourist office), so called when 16th-c. paintings were restored on the walls in 1927, is said to be where Shakespeare stayed on his way each year

Eagle and Child
The pub of choice for the Inklings, a group of writers that included Tolkien, C. S. Lewis, and others

Jericho
Thomas Hardy's Jude lodged in Jericho, and Inspector Morse made his first foray into television here in 'The Dead of Jericho'. St Barnabas' Church appears in both *Jude the Obscure* and *Inspector Morse*, is mentioned in *Brideshead Revisited*, and is the subject of a poem by Betjeman

Railway ← Stn

Martyrs' Memorial
In 1556, at the height of Bloody Queen Mary's reign, Thomas Cranmer (who developed the Book of Common Prayer) was burnt alive on this spot

Bus Station

N

Oxford Castle

New Road

Ashmolean Museum

BEAUMONT STREET

St Giles

Walton Street

78 Banbury Road
From 1885 James Murray lived here, and worked on the first edition of *The Oxford English Dictionary*. The postbox you see outside the house was installed specially to cope with the resulting correspondence

University Museum

Parks Road

Balliol College
Alumni include Gerard Manley Hopkins, Aldous Huxley, Adam Smith, John Evelyn, Robert Southey, Matthew Arnold, and Algernon Swinburne

Balliol College

Sheldonian Theatre

Bodleian Library

BROAD STREET

Cornmarket

HIGH STREET

Bodleian Library
The Library of the University, but also one of the country's five copyright libraries, and by some five centuries its oldest

University College
Percy Bysshe Shelley spent a year here and distributed his anonymous pamphlet *The Necessity of Atheism*, for which he was sent down. Visit the striking sculpture by Onslow Ford in the NW corner of the quad

Magdalen College
Alumni include Oscar Wilde and C. S. Lewis

Botanic Garden
The Garden features in Philip Pullman's *The Amber Spyglass*, where there is an almost-meeting on a bench here on Midsummer's Day . . .

Oriel College
Matthew Arnold was a Fellow here—and it was he who famously referred to the city's 'dreaming spires'. Alumni include Thomas Hughes, who wrote *Tom Brown's Schooldays*

Pembroke College
Samuel Johnson studied here, sharing modest rooms above the gatehouse on the second floor

Oriel College

Alice's Shop
The shop at 83 St Aldates was the model for the Old Sheep Shop in Lewis Carroll's *Through the Looking Glass*

Christ Church
Alumni include Philip Sidney, and W. H. Auden (below), and Charles Lutwidge Dodgson (Lewis Carroll) was Professor of Maths here

The Painted Room, in what was once The Crown inn, where Shakespeare is thought to have stayed

to and from Stratford. The antiquaries John Aubrey and Anthony Wood vary in their accounts of Shakespeare's relationship to young D'Avenant; they imply that though he admitted to being his godfather, he might perhaps have been his natural father too.

Alexander Pope often passed through Oxford. His friend Joseph Spence mentions meeting him at the Cross Inn (the Golden Cross) in 1735 looking 'quite fatigu'd to death'. He had walked from Bagley Hill (3 m. S) after giving up his coach to a young woman whose arm had been broken in an accident.

Karl Moritz, a German schoolmaster savouring the land of his favourite poet John Milton in spite of constant rebuffs from suspicious innkeepers, was taken to The Mitre by a young chaplain, who had accompanied his walk from *Nuneham Courtenay. In *Travels in England* (1795), Moritz mentions the sightseeing tour he took with this guide next day. They saw the elderly Thomas Warton, whom Moritz knew as the editor of Milton's poems, and who the young chaplain said was partial to duck-shooting. Moritz thought the buildings were 'much over loaded with ornaments' and deplored their 'dingy, dirty, and disgusting appearance'.

Charles Lamb's 'Oxford in the Vacation' from his *Essays of Elia* (1833) was written during his visit to *Cambridge in 1820 and is a conflation of his memories of the two universities. Jane Austen and her elder sister Cassandra were sent to school here, for a short time, to the widow of a Principal of Brasenose. Jane Austen often mentions Oxford, where her father and brothers were educated, in her novels and she depicts three very different undergraduates in *Northanger Abbey* (1818), and in *Mansfield Park* (1814), in which the serious-minded Edmund Bertram is destined for the Church. Edward Bradley, author, as 'Cuthbert Bede', of *The Adventures of Mr. Verdant Green, an Oxford Freshman* (1853–7), is thought to have been studying here during 1849 to enter the Church, though he was not a member of the University.

Wordsworth, a Cambridge man, wrote two sonnets on Oxford during his visit in May 1820. One ends with praise of the High St.:

I slight my own beloved Cam, to range
Where silver Isis leads my stripling feet;
Pace the long avenue, or glide adown
The stream-like windings of that glorious street.

William Cobbett was uncomplimentary about the University and lashed out in *Rural Rides* (1830): 'Upon beholding the masses of buildings at Oxford, devoted to what they call "*learning*", I could not help reflecting on the drones that they contain and the wasps they send forth.'

Mrs Humphry Ward lived (1872–81) at 5 (now 17) Bradmore Rd immediately after her marriage. In 1888 she was nursing her dying mother at 2 Bradmore Rd when she heard that Gladstone wished to discuss her recently published novel *Robert Elsmere*. She met him twice at the Warden's lodgings at Keble and defended the novel, which he said was an attack on Christianity. Gladstone's review appeared in the *Nineteenth Century* in May 1888.

Hardy set many scenes of *Jude the Obscure* (1895) in Oxford, his 'Christminster'. Jude Fawley had lodgings in Jericho, the area near Walton St., and 'St Silas's Church' in the novel is really St Barnabas', whose architect, Arthur Blomfield, employed Hardy for five years from 1862. Christ Church becomes 'Cardinal College' and St Aldates, 'Cardinal St.'.

In *Portraits of Places* (1883), Henry James writes that Oxford

typifies to an American, the union of science and sense—of aspiration and ease. A German university gives a greater impression of science, and an English country house or an Italian villa a greater impression of idle enjoyment; but in these cases, on the one side, knowledge is too rugged, and on the other, satisfaction is too trivial. Oxford lends sweetness to labour and dignity to leisure.

Part of the title story of James's *A Passionate Pilgrim* (1875) has scenes in Oxford and describes the cloisters of Magdalen and the gardens of New College, St John's, and Wadham. 'The Altar of the Dead' (1895) was sketched out while James was lodging at 15 Beaumont St. in 1894.

In 1885 Sir James Murray moved to Oxford from Mill Hill Boys' School, where he had been assistant master for 15 years and where he first became involved with the editorship of the *Oxford English Dictionary*. He and his family lived at Sunnyside, 78 Banbury Rd, where he worked on the Dictionary to the end of his life. He is buried in Wolvercote cemetery. (See his biography *Caught in the Web of Words*, by Elizabeth Murray, 1977.)

William de Morgan's novel *Joseph Vance* (1906) describes a row from Binsey upstream to Godstow.

In his autobiography *It's Me, O Lord!* A. E. Coppard tells of his life in Oxford (1907–19), and his first lodgings in Iffley (2 m. SE). An episode there, when he was charged with poaching while exercising his two whippets, was the origin of his story 'The Poor Man', written 15 years later. Coppard moved many times before giving up his job at the Eagle Ironworks on Walton Well Rd (gone) to devote himself to writing. He and his wife lived for a time in a fourth-floor flat in Cornmarket, the setting for 'Arabesque' and 'The Quiet Woman'. During the First World War, Ronald Firbank rented rooms at 66 High St., where he wrote the novels *Inclinations* (1916), *Caprice* (1917), and *Valmouth* (1919). He chose black decor with exotic designs; cushions on the floor served as seats.

Yeats, with his wife and child, lived for some years on the corner of Broad St. opposite Balliol in a tall narrow house (gone), where many literary friends visited him. He moved to *Shillingford in April 1921 to save money by letting the house. The view of Oxford from Boars Hill inspired Matthew Arnold's 'The Scholar Gypsy' (1853) and 'Thyrsis' (1866).

Robert Bridges, Edmund Blunden, and John Masefield all lived here after the end of the First World War. Masefield lived at Hill Crest (now Masefield House) from 1919 to 1933. His writings at this time included the narrative poem *Reynard the Fox* (1919) and the novels *Sard Harker* (1924) and *Odtaa* (1926). He became an honorary D.Litt. at Oxford in 1922 and Poet Laureate in 1933. Masefield had a small, intimate private theatre in his house, used for productions of verse plays, and Robert Graves lived at Dingle Cottage at the bottom of Masefield's garden in the 1920s. His first wife, Nancy, ran a shop for the community of numerous local artists and writers—too numerous, Graves complained—while her husband wrote poetry and studied for the degree he had been prevented from reading for by the First World War.

Kenneth Grahame was educated at St Edward's School from 1868 to 1875, and there is a memorial window to him in the school chapel. He is buried in St Cross churchyard in the same grave as his son, for whom he wrote *The Wind in the Willows*. His epitaph was written by his cousin Anthony Hope Hawkins.

John Drinkwater and T. E. Lawrence were pupils at the Oxford Boys High School. Lawrence lived at his family home, 2 Polstead Rd Ⓟ from 1896 to 1921. He made his study in an outhouse in the garden.

Charles Williams came to Oxford in 1940. He worked for the Oxford University Press and was the author of many poems on the Arthurian legend, including *Taliessin in Logres* (1938) and the unfinished *The Arthurian Torso* (1948), which has a commentary by his friend C. S. Lewis of Magdalen. They and other cronies, including J. R. R. Tolkien, drank in the back bar of the Eagle and Child in St Giles', where they were known as 'the Inklings'. A plaque marks their presence there; in Colin Dexter's novel *The Secret of Annexe 3* (1986) Morse and his sidekick Lewis meet here, and Lewis reads the Inklings' plaque, imagining that some day a plaque might commemorate other patrons of this establishment: Chief Inspector Morse, with his friend and colleague Sergeant Lewis, sat in this back room one Thursday, in order to solve . . .'.

Williams also wrote religious works, biographies, and metaphysical thrillers, his name for *War in Heaven* (1930), *The Place of the Lion* (1931), and others. He is buried in St Cross churchyard, as is H. W. Garrod of Merton (d. 1960). St Cross Church, described by a character in Dorothy Sayers's *Busman's Honeymoon* (1936) as 'an obscure little church in a side street', was the scene of Lord Peter Wimsey's marriage to Harriet Vane.

George Santayana lodged in Beaumont St. during the First World War. In *My Host the World* (1953) he describes a visit to Robert Bridges and to Lady Ottoline Morrell at *Garsington. His novel *The Last Puritan* (1935) has scenes in Oxford and Iffley. Thomas Wolfe, the American novelist, who visited Oxford briefly, set here some scenes of his novel *Of Time and the River* (1935).

Dylan Thomas and his family spent Christmas 1945 at Holywell Ford, off St Cross Rd, with A. J. P. Taylor and his wife. In March the Thomases moved into a summerhouse on the water's edge in the Taylors' garden for a short stay which lengthened to a year. Dylan Thomas had just published *Deaths and Entrances* (1946) and he was suffering from exhaustion. While here he wrote many of the scripts for his BBC broadcasts, which proved popular and brought his name to a wider audience. Thomas was one of the group of poets, including Louis MacNeice, who met at the Port Mahon in St Clement's and The George (closed), on the corner of Cornmarket and George St., which had a restaurant upstairs cooled by punkahs. The crime novelist P. D. James was born in Oxford in 1920 and spent some of her childhood here, though her family moved away when she was 11.

Elizabeth Bowen lived in Old Headington after her marriage to Alan Charles Cameron in 1923, the year she published her first volume of short stories, *Encounters*. She wrote her first four novels here and another volume of short stories, *Joining Charles* (1929). She inherited her father's house in Ireland in 1928 and after living there for a few years following the death of her husband, returned here in 1960 for a short time before leaving for *Hythe, where she had spent her childhood. She was made an honorary D.Litt. at the University in 1957.

Jonathan Coe's *An Accidental Woman* (1987) is set largely in Oxford:

> When Maria came to look back on her days at Oxford, which, to her credit, she did very seldom, it seemed to her that it had all taken place in bright sunshine. We can safely assume, I think, that this was in reality not the case, but then who said our concern was with reality, or hers, for that matter. If Maria's memories were of an Oxford bathed in sunlight, we might as well respect them, except perhaps for parts of the third chapter, where the mood will be rather more autumnal . . . It was in any case autumn by the time she got there, bright blue autumn, and Maria's college, we won't name names, looked very pretty, even to her.

In 1999 Paul Muldoon was appointed Professor of Poetry at the University, a post that had been held between 1989 and 1994 by Seamus Heaney.

ALL SOULS COLLEGE (1438). Graduate college which refused a fellowship to William Camden in 1571 because of his Protestantism. Jeremy Taylor, who became a Fellow on the recommendation of Archbishop Laud, who had heard him preach at Cambridge, preached many of his outstanding sermons at St Mary's, the University Church, nearby in the High St. John Evelyn inspected the new painting over the plastered reredos in the college chapel in 1664 but wrote in his *Diary* that it 'seemes too full of nakeds for a Chapell'. Christopher Codrington, who had rich sugar estates in Barbados, was made a Fellow in 1690. The College inherited his books and a large sum of

money for the rebuilding of the library, which in spite of losses at the Reformation, contains many manuscripts, including the 13th-c. Amesbury Psalter. Edward Young, who became a Law Fellow in 1708, was a friend of Thomas Tickell of Queen's and like him a member of Addison's circle in London. Richard Graves, a friend and contemporary of Shenstone at Pembroke, was made a Fellow in 1736. Francis Doyle, a Fellow from 1835 to 1844, who succeeded to the baronetcy in 1839, was Professor of Poetry (1867–77). He wrote many poems extolling courage and patriotism including 'The Private of the Buffs', and was made an honorary DCL in 1877.

T. E. Lawrence was elected a Fellow in 1919 and lived in the College for a time. He started to write here *Seven Pillars of Wisdom* (1926), about his experiences in the Middle East, which earned him the name 'Lawrence of Arabia'.

The philosopher Isaiah Berlin took his degree at Corpus Christi College, where he won a scholarship in 1928; in 1932 he was elected to a fellowship at All Souls College (as the College's first Jewish fellow), where he remained until 1938; 12 unsatisfying years at New College followed, whereupon he returned (in 1950) to All Souls; he left again in 1966 to be founding President of Wolfson College, returning (again) to his proper home at All Souls in 1975. Upon his marriage in 1956 to Aline Halban, Berlin and his new wife settled into her house outside town—Headington House—where he was to spend the rest of his life. He died in a nursing home on the Banbury Rd on 5 November 1997.

BALLIOL COLLEGE (1263). John Wycliffe, a Fellow who became the Master in 1361, was forbidden to teach here in 1381 after rejecting the doctrine of transubstantiation. John Evelyn, an undergraduate (1637–40), describes in his *Diary* his years here, uneventful except for the time he was so entranced with watching a play that he fell off a table and injured his leg. He visited Oxford again in 1654, when he was made welcome at Balliol, and he showed his wife the rarities of the Bodleian.

Adam Smith came from *Glasgow University as Snell Exhibitioner and graduated *c.* 1744. He stayed on for two years and went home to *Kirkcaldy.

Robert Southey, who came up from Westminster in 1792, met Edward Seward here, after whose death he wrote, 'I loved him with my whole heart, and shall remember him with gratitude and affection, as one who was my moral father, to the last moment of my life.' It was to Seward, who graduated in 1793 and died suddenly in 1795, that Southey wrote the poem 'To a Dead Friend'. Southey was visited by Coleridge in 1794 and with other friends planned to form a community on the banks of the Susquehanna in America. This, which they called a Pantisocracy, would give the minimum time to manual labour and the maximum to the improvement of the mind. While at Balliol, Southey was engaged on his epic *Joan of Arc* (1796).

The Palace Pier, Brighton. The city's dark side is vividly evoked in novels by Graham Greene and Patrick Hamilton

J. G. Lockhart came from Glasgow with a Snell Exhibition in 1809 and graduated in Classics in 1813. He was a friend of H. H. Milman of Brasenose.

Matthew Arnold, son of Thomas Arnold of *Rugby, came up with a classical scholarship in 1841, and gained a reputation for a lack of seriousness and a tendency to practical jokes, indolence, and affectation, although he won the Newdigate Prize with his poem 'Cromwell' in 1843. He was a contemporary of F. T. Palgrave and intimate friend of Arthur Hugh Clough, who had also been at Rugby, and whom he followed to *Oriel as a Fellow. C. S. Calverley, after two years here, left for Cambridge in 1852.

Algernon Swinburne, who was an undergraduate 1856–9, became acquainted with the Pre-Raphaelites when they decorated the Union with illustrations from the Arthurian legends, which inspired his poem 'Queen Yseult'. He wrote the first draft of his play *Rosamond* here, and was kindly treated by Benjamin Jowett, Professor of Greek (later Master of Balliol), whose translations of Plato he read in draft.

T. H. Green, the idealist philosopher on whom Mrs Humphry Ward based Mr Gray in *Robert Elsmere* (1888), was a Fellow here from 1860. He is buried in St Sepulchre's cemetery in Walton St.

J. A. Symonds, Andrew Lang, and Gerard Manley Hopkins were undergraduates in the 1860s. Symonds won the Newdigate Prize with his poem 'The Escorial' in 1860. Gerard Manley Hopkins came up in 1863 with an exhibition to read Classics. He became a friend of Robert Bridges and fell under the influence of Walter Pater of Brasenose and the writings of J. H. Newman. It is thought that his Platonic dialogue 'On the Nature of Beauty' was written for Pater. In his letters to his mother he describes his first rooms and writes, 'Balliol is the friendliest and snuggest of colleges, our inner quad is delicious and has a grove of fine trees and lawns, where bowls are the order of the evening'. The *Journal*, which he began here, describes his walks to the surrounding villages. His poem 'Duns Scotus's Oxford' opens with the lines:

Towery city and branchy between towers;
Cuckoo-echoing, bell-swarmèd, lark-charmèd,
    rook-racked, river-rounded,

and closes with strictures on the town's 'brickish skirt'. In 1866 Hopkins wrote 'Heaven-Haven' and having had instruction, which he kept from his family, high Anglicans, was finally received into the Catholic Church. After leaving Oxford for a course of study to become a Jesuit he returned in 1878 to be a curate at St Aloysius', the Catholic church at the S end of Woodstock Rd, and it was at this time that he wrote the poem 'Binsey Poplars'. The Holy Water stoup in the church was given in his memory.

A. C. Bradley, an undergraduate from 1869 to 1872, was elected a Fellow in 1874 and Professor of Poetry in 1901. He is chiefly remembered as a Shakespearian critic by

Shakespearean Tragedy (1904) and *Oxford Lectures* (1909). He is buried in St Cross churchyard.

Anthony Hope Hawkins was elected President of the Union when an undergraduate (1881–4), as was Hilaire Belloc, a contemporary here of George Douglas Brown in the 1890s. Belloc's poem 'To the Balliol Men Still in Africa' contains the lines:

Balliol made me, Balliol fed me,
Whatever I had she gave me again;
And the best of Balliol loved me and led me,
God be with you, Balliol men.

Owen Morgan Edwards entered in 1884 and had a brilliant career, winning the three chief history prizes and graduating with first-class honours in 1887.

C. E. Montague entered as a classical exhibitioner in 1885 and graduated in 1889. Oxford streets and buildings appear in his novel *Rough Justice* (1926), where St Giles' is 'a forested street, a Cathedral-like street', with a 'broad, roofless nave'. Julian Grenfell, who graduated in 1909, is remembered for the poem 'Into Battle', about the First World War, in which he was killed in 1915. L. P. Hartley and Aldous Huxley were undergraduates during the war. Part of Huxley's novel *Eyeless in Gaza* (1936) describes life in North Oxford. He lived (1915–16) with the Haldanes at Cherwell (now the site of Wolfson College). Dorothy L. Sayers's detective hero Lord Peter Wimsey, an officer in the war, was a Balliol man. Ronald Knox, an undergraduate 1906–10, wrote sermons, essays, and detective stories. He was an honorary Fellow from 1953 to his death in 1957. Logan Pearsall Smith describes his memories of Oxford in his autobiography *The Unforgotten Years* (1938).

Michael Sadleir (1888–1957), author and publisher, was a native of Oxford and an MA of Balliol. His best-known novel is *Fanny by Gaslight* (1940).

N. S. Norway, aircraft engineer who achieved popularity as a novelist under the name Nevil Shute, was an undergraduate just before serving in the First World War (1918). *Pied Piper* (1940) and *A Town Like Alice* (1949) are among his best-known titles.

Arnold Toynbee, author of *A Study of History*, was Fellow and Tutor (1912–15) and honorary Fellow from 1957. He includes some mention of his Oxford friends in *Acquaintances* (1967). Cyril Connolly's undergraduate years in the early 1920s are encapsulated in the letters he wrote to Noel Blakiston, a friend at Eton, who went to Cambridge. These, which show the very high goals he set for himself, were published as *A Romantic Friendship* (1975).

Graham Greene came up in 1922 to read History, where it was felt he took a poor view of his fellow undergraduates. He published a book of poems while still a student. He returned to Oxford in 1933 and lived at 9 Woodstock Close.

Greene was followed the next year by Anthony Powell, who also read History, and also found university life disappointing, describing it in *A Dance to the Music of Time*

(1951–75) as 'the crushing melancholy of the undergraduate condition'. In his third year he moved out of college and shared digs with Henry Yorke (later the novelist Henry Green).

BODLEIAN LIBRARY (1490). The University Library as we now know it was started by a collection of manuscripts bequeathed by Duke Humphrey of Gloucester (d. 1447). Much of this collection had been dispersed when Thomas Bodley refounded the Library in 1602. He devoted the rest of his life and most of his fortune to enlarging it, and arranged (1610) that the Stationers' Company should give a free copy of every book printed in England to the Library. Bodley, who was knighted in 1604, left his own collection to the Library. Further volumes and a large number of oriental manuscripts were given by the jurist John Selden. Anthony Wood, who helped carry Selden's books into the Library in 1659, found several pairs of spectacles left between the pages. Wood was allowed to have a pair and he kept them in memory of Selden until his death. A large marble plaque on the stairs gives a list of the many benefactors to the Library. Many books and manuscripts can be seen in the 15th-c. Divinity School below, including *Tottel's Miscellany* (1557), Shakespeare's *Venus and Adonis* (1593), an autograph of a poem by Donne, Shelley's notebook containing 'Ode to the West Wind', Kenneth Grahame's original manuscript of *The Wind in the Willows*, the third manuscript of *Seven Pillars of Wisdom* by T. E. Lawrence, and Joyce Cary's papers and manuscripts.

BRASENOSE COLLEGE (1509). John Foxe was an undergraduate here from 1533 to 1537 and then became a Fellow of Magdalen. Barnabe Barnes, who joined the Earl of Essex's expedition in 1591 after graduating, may have written here some of the sonnets, madrigals, elegies, and odes which he published in 1593 as *Parthenophil and Parthenope*. Robert Burton was an undergraduate here from 1593, and in 1599 was elected a Student (Fellow) of Christ Church. Both John Marston, BA 1594, and Thomas Traherne, BA 1656, graduated here and later were ordained. Elias Ashmole, whose collection of curiosities, originally made by John Tradescant and his son, formed the nucleus of the Ashmolean Museum and who bequeathed his library to the Bodleian, studied Physics and Mathematics here after joining the Royalists. Jeremy Taylor was created DD by Royal Mandate from Brasenose in 1642.

Reginald Heber, remembered for his hymn 'From Greenland's Icy Mountains', R. H. Barham, and H. H. Milman were undergraduates in the early years of the 19th c. Milman won the Newdigate Prize in 1812 with the poem 'Apollo Belvedere', which was later considered the 'most perfect' prize poem by Dean Stanley, himself a winner of university prizes. Milman was made a Fellow in 1814 and a year later published *Fazio*, a drama, in which the main part of Bianca was acted by the

Bateman's, Burwash, East Sussex, the home for over 30 years of Rudyard Kipling. Pook's Hill is visible from the house

principal actresses of the time. *Samor, the Lord of the Bright City* (1818), a poem about Vortigern written in a style resembling Southey's *Madoc* (1805), was considered by Southey rather 'too full of power and beauty' for anything less than a dramatic rendering. Milman, who became vicar of St Mary's, Reading, in 1818, was elected Professor of Poetry in 1821.

Walter Pater, who became a Fellow in 1864, had a long association with Oxford. His first critical study, 'Winckelmann', published in the *Westminster Review* in 1867, was included in *Studies of the History of the Renaissance* (1873), which established his reputation. *Marius the Epicurean* (1885), a philosophic romance, *Imaginary Portraits* (1887), and *Appreciations* (1889), literary criticism, were followed by posthumous publications including the unfinished *Gaston de Latour* (1896), which has portraits of Montaigne and Ronsard. Pater lived for many years at 2 Bradmore Rd, and then at 64 St Giles', where he died (1890). He is buried in St Cross churchyard.

John Buchan came here (1895–9) from Glasgow University and won the Stanhope Prize with an essay on Walter Ralegh, and the Newdigate Prize with a poem on the Pilgrim Fathers. Later he lived at *Elsfield, and he wrote in his autobiography, *Memory Hold-the-Door* (1940), that 'Oxford has a cincture of green uplands and a multitude of little valleys. It is only from her adjacent heights that her charms can be comprised into one picture and the true background found to her towers.'

John Middleton Murry describes his years here (*c*. 1909–12) in *Between Two Worlds* (1934). His fear of ordeals at the hands of the 'hearties' was dispelled by his friendly reception. His rooms looked across to the roof of the Radcliffe Camera. In 1911 he was editing the illustrated quarterly *Rhythm* with Michael Sadleir, financed by Joyce Cary, and he wrote to Katherine Mansfield for a contribution. He left Oxford in 1912 uninterested in further examinations.

Charles Morgan came up in 1919 after serving in the Navy in the war, which gave him the theme for his first novel, *The Gunroom* (1919). He became President of the University Dramatic Society, and left in 1921 to join the staff of *The Times*. He returned as Zaharoff Lecturer (French Studies) in 1948.

The novelist James Gordon Farrell came up in the early 1950s to read Law but, after a serious attack of poliomyelitis in his first term, he was advised to give up the prospect of too strenuous a career, and so changed to Modern Languages.

Novelist Edward Bradley's hero Mr Verdant Green was an undergraduate here.

William Golding came to read Natural Sciences here in 1930, later changing to English; the barrister and novelist John Mortimer studied at Brasenose 1940–2.

The (Cambridge-educated) Oxford resident Colin Dexter is the creator of Inspector Morse of the Thames Valley Police; the grumpy, opera-loving, crossword-solving detective was

introduced in 1975 in the book *Last Bus to Woodstock*, and popularized in another dozen books and a series of successful TV adaptations. The books drift in and out of real Oxford settings, many of which were used as locations for filming the TV series. In a number of the books Brasenose stands in for 'Lonsdale College'. Other local settings include the Pitt-Rivers Museum (an African knife in the Pitt-Rivers collection is the murder weapon in *The Daughters of Cain*, 1994), and room 310 of the Randolph Hotel, where an American woman is found dead and a valuable jewel goes missing, in *The Jewel That Was Ours* (1991).

CHRIST CHURCH (1525). This college is often called 'the House' and includes the former Canterbury Hall (site now Canterbury Quad). Thomas More studied Greek here under Linacre from 1492 to 1494, soon after Linacre and Grocyn had returned from a visit to Italy. The three scholars often met later in London. Richard Edwards, a Student (Fellow) here from 1547, composed *Palamon and Arcite* to entertain Queen Elizabeth on her visit in 1566. William Camden was at Magdalen then but transferred here soon after. His contemporary Philip Sidney was an undergraduate from 1568 to 1571, when he left on account of the plague. Richard Hakluyt, who later chronicled the English voyages of exploration, was another contemporary. George Peele, who graduated in 1577, was much admired as a poet while here.

Richard Corbett lived here from 1598, when he became a Student. He was Dean of the Cathedral (Head of the College) in 1620 and then Bishop of Oxford until he was transferred to *Norwich. In 1613 Corbett gave the funeral oration for Sir Thomas Bodley, benefactor of the University Library, and in 1619 as Senior Student was host to Ben Jonson, who graduated MA 'by their favour not his studie', by which he probably means he made no effort to get the honour. Corbett's verses, collected as *Certain Elegant Poems* (1647), include 'The Fairy's Farewell' with the line 'Farewell rewards and fairies', 'Iter Boreale', a traveller's tale, and a poem to his son Vincent on his third birthday.

Robert Burton spent 53 years in Oxford, as an undergraduate, a Student (1599–1640), and as rector of St Thomas the Martyr, a parish in the W near the present railway station. He built the S porch of the church, which has his arms over the door. His *Anatomy of Melancholy* (1621) on the causes, symptoms, and varieties of melancholy, written as a medical treatise, is illuminated by examples from classical and contemporary literature. Dr Johnson said it was 'the only book that ever took him out of bed two hours sooner than he wished to rise'. Burton was buried (1640) in the Cathedral, where a monument, erected by his brother, on a pillar contains a bust and lines in Latin composed by himself.

William Cartwright, who became a Student in 1628, was a dramatic preacher. His play *The Royal Slave* was acted before Charles I on his visit in 1636. He became a Proctor in 1643 and

died later that year. His *Comedies, Tragi-Comedies, with Other Poems* was published in 1651. John Fell became Dean in 1660 and Bishop of Oxford in 1676. Thomas Brown, who was an undergraduate 1678–82, is remembered as the author of the lines: 'I do not like thee, Dr. Fell | The reason why I cannot tell.'

John Locke, who graduated in 1658, returned to live in college in 1680 but was expelled reluctantly by Dean Fell for his alleged complicity in 1684 in Shaftesbury's plot. Thomas Otway left in 1672 without taking the degree examination. Richard Steele stayed one year only before going to Merton in 1691, and John Philips, author of *The Splendid Shilling* (1705), a mock-heroic poem in Miltonic blank verse, was an undergraduate in the 1690s.

John Boyle, 5th Earl of Orrery, a friend of Swift, Pope, and Dr Johnson, who was an undergraduate in the 1720s, wrote to his son when he came up about Swift. These letters were published as *Remarks on the Life and Writings of Dr. Jonathan Swift* (1751).

George Colman, a barrister on the Oxford circuit until he became an established dramatist and a friend of David Garrick, was an undergraduate in the 1750s. His son George Colman the Younger spent a few years here before going to *Aberdeen to study Medicine in 1781. Matthew Gregory Lewis was an undergraduate from 1791 to 1794, when he became an attaché at The Hague.

John Ruskin became a gentleman commoner with rooms in Peckwater Quad in January 1837. His mother rented rooms at 90 High St. and he visited her for tea and again after dinner on most days. He won the Newdigate Prize in 1839 with his third entry, but soon after, a haemorrhage necessitated recuperation abroad. He returned to graduate in 1842. His publications include *Modern Painters* (1843–60) and *The Stones of Venice* (1851–2), and his Oxford memorial is the University Museum in Parks Rd, built in Venetian Gothic with pillars and capitals ornamented with animals and flowers. The story of the difficulties Ruskin faced to get the building of the Museum accepted by the authorities is told in *The Oxford Museum* (1859, reprinted 1893), by Sir Henry Acland and John Ruskin. Not least of his troubles was the prevailing thought that science was 'adverse to religion'. Ruskin's enthusiasm ensured that the workers were provided with books and started their day with 'simple prayers'. His desire to promote the dignity of manual labour led a group of undergraduates, including Oscar Wilde, to improve the road at North Hinksey in 1874, a project commemorated by a plaque on the wall of Ruskin Cottage, in the village. Ruskin, who established the Ruskin School of Drawing, was twice appointed Professor of Fine Art (1870–9 and 1883–4) and many of his lectures were published. North Oxford has houses built with stained-glass windows, Romeo balconies, pointed turrets, and castellated roofs that show the influence of his architectural doctrine.

T. E. Brown, a servitor here from 1850 to 1853, found himself, because of his lowly status, ineligible for a Studentship in spite of his academic attainments. He was later elected to a Fellowship at Oriel, then considered 'the blue riband' of the University.

Charles Dodgson, an undergraduate from 1851 to 1855, became a Student and mathematics lecturer. He suffered from a stammer and lived a retired life, carrying on friendships chiefly by correspondence. He was, however, able to communicate with children and *Alice's Adventures in Wonderland* (1865) and its sequel, *Through the Looking Glass* (1872), were written as a result of a story he made up for Alice Liddell, the young daughter of the Dean, during afternoon excursions in a punt up the river to Godstow (2 m. N). He used the pseudonym 'Lewis Carroll'. Alice Liddell is said to have bought sweets at a little shop ('Alice's Shop') with stone mullions (opposite what is now the Memorial Gardens). The photographs that Dodgson took of many of his contemporaries at 'the House' survive.

Edward Martyn, who came from Dublin in the 1870s and found himself almost the only Catholic here, contributed £10 to the new organ at St Aloysius' Church.

W. H. Auden, an undergraduate (1925–8), was one of the poets, including Louis MacNeice and Cecil Day-Lewis, who were grouped together as left-wing in the 1930s. He worked harder on his poems than his studies and cultivated an eccentric persona, keeping a starting pistol in his rooms, wearing a green eyeshade, and keeping his curtains drawn (chiefly because his eyes were morbidly sensitive to light).

The travel writer Peter Fleming, author of *Brazilian Adventure* (1933), was educated here. He later ran across Auden in China (the subject of another travel book, *One's Company*, 1934) and was admitted, at first rather warily, into Auden and Isherwood's account of their visit, *Journey to a War* (1939).

Auden edited *Oxford Poetry* in 1926 with Charles Plumb and with Day-Lewis in 1927. A limited edition of his *Poems* (1928) was hand-printed in Oxford. In 1939 he went to the US and became an American citizen. He was elected Professor of Poetry (1956–60) and an honorary Student in 1961. He came back to England in 1972 and lived in the Brew House, on the S side of Christ Church Hall, by the cobbled walk to the meadow. He died on a visit to Vienna in 1974.

Auden was a contemporary of the Cornish historian and man of letters A. L. Rowse, who describes his rise to academic fame in his vivid autobiography *A Cornish Childhood* (1942). The poet and translator Michael Hamburger came up to the college in the 1940s. He describes his undergraduate life, and the lives of such Oxford contemporaries as Philip Larkin and John Heath-Stubbs, in his 'intermittent memoir' *A Mug's Game* (1973). Auberon Waugh was an undergraduate at Christ Church and did no work. He was rusticated in 1959 and chose not to return.

CLARENDON BUILDING. The Oxford University Press was housed from 1713 to 1829 in this building by Nicholas Hawksmoor (1661–1736) in Broad St. Profits from *The History of the Rebellion*, Clarendon's great work (1702–4), partly paid for the building. Edward Hyde, Earl of Clarendon, whose statue is in a niche at one end, was chief minister under Charles II and Chancellor of the University 1660–7. The Press moved from here to its present premises in Walton St. in 1829.

CORPUS CHRISTI COLLEGE (1517), usually known as Corpus. Nicholas Udall (or Uvedale), a scholar here in 1520, became a Fellow in 1524 and was suspected of nonconformity in religious matters two years later.

Richard Edwards was here for seven years, as undergraduate and Fellow (1544–7), before migrating to Christ Church in 1547. Richard Hooker and Stephen Gosson were both ordained in the 1570s.

Thomas Day, author of *Sandford and Merton* (1783–9), studied here in the 1760s. In 1871 Ruskin, an honorary Fellow, had rooms in college overlooking the garden. Robert Bridges, a friend who was an undergraduate here of Gerard Manley Hopkins of Balliol, whose collected poems he edited in 1918, lived (1907–30) at Chilswell House (now occupied by a religious community), Boars Hill (3 m. SW). He became Poet Laureate in 1913 and his long philosophical poem *The Testament of Beauty* (1929), written there, was published when he was 85, the year before his death.

Henry Newbolt, some of whose poems, including 'Vitaï Lampada' and 'Drake's Drum', have remained popular for over a century, was an undergraduate here in the 1880s. Bernard Spencer, an undergraduate (1927–30), edited *Oxford Poetry* (1929–30). Many of his early poems were published in *New Verse* in the late 1930s when he was working with Geoffrey Grigson. The novelist Vikram Seth was later educated at Corpus, where he read PPE (Philosophy, Politics, and Economics).

EXETER COLLEGE (1314) has associations with the West Country. John Ford studied here (*c.* 1601–2) and was followed by another Devonian, William Browne of *Tavistock, who became a tutor in 1624. Joseph Glanvill, who graduated in 1655, returned in 1659, engaged on *The Vanity of Dogmatizing* (1661). This contains the first reference to the story of the scholar who left the University to join a band of gypsies, which inspired Matthew Arnold's poem 'The Scholar-Gipsy' (1853). William Gifford, a shoemaker's apprentice from *Ashburton, rewarded for his industry by the opportunity to study here (BA 1782), left benefactions to help other students. J. A. Froude became Devon Fellow in 1842, but resigned after a copy of his *Nemesis of Faith* (1849) was publicly burned by a former Professor of Moral Philosophy. Froude, a friend of Carlyle and Kingsley, became Regius Professor of Modern History in 1892 and lived at Cherwell Edge (now Linacre College). Three

volumes of his lectures were published between 1894 and 1896. In 1846 F. T. Palgrave (best known as the compiler of *The Golden Treasury*, 1861) became a private secretary to Gladstone, then out of office, and in 1847 was elected a Fellow. When Gladstone became Oxford's MP later in the year, Palgrave joined the Civil Service. He was Professor of Poetry from 1885 to 1895.

R. D. Blackmore, who spent his childhood nearby at *Elsfield and then in Devon, was a classical scholar here (1844–7). William Morris, a student from 1853 to 1855, became interested in the Pre-Raphaelites and with Burne-Jones painted scenes from Arthurian legends at the Union. A Morris tapestry from a painting by Burne-Jones is in the chapel.

Alfred Noyes published his first collection of poems, *The Loom of Years* (1902), while an undergraduate. Noyes wrote in 1907 in 'Oxford Revisited':

> And still in the beautiful City, the river of life is no duller,
> Only a little strange as the eighth hour dreamily chimes.
> In the City of friends and echoes, ribbons and music and colour,
> Lilac and blossoming chestnut, willows and whispering limes . . .

He mentions in *Two Worlds for Memory* (1953) his surprise when he found his initials added to those of Ford and Morris on the windows of the dining hall, where those members of the College who have obtained merit are commemorated. J. R. R. Tolkien was an undergraduate just before the First World War, in which he served from 1915 to 1918. He was later made an honorary Fellow. R. M. Dawkins, Professor of Modern Greek and Fellow (1920–39), wrote *Forty-Five Stories from the Dodecanese* (1950), *Modern Greek Folk Tales* (1952), and a study (1952) of his friend Norman Douglas. He also befriended Frederick Rolfe. He was made an honorary Fellow in 1939 and spent much of his time here until his death in 1955.

The playwright Alan Bennett went up to Exeter in 1951, and even spent a brief period at Oxford lecturing.

> I never deceived myself that I was that unappealing entity 'a first-class mind'. I no more had a first-class mind than I had a first-class body (which I would at that time much have preferred). I worked hard, it's true, and took copious notes but for most of my undergraduate career never had the first idea how to organise them into an essay. I must have been a dull pupil to teach, tutorials tentative and awkward affairs, punctuated by long silences—exactly the kind of tutorials I was later to give myself when I taught pupils as a postgraduate.

One of Bennett's most successful plays, *The History Boys* (2004), follows a group of sixth-formers preparing for their Oxbridge entrance exams.

The novelist Philip Pullman graduated from Exeter in 1968, followed shortly by Martin Amis, who had been born in Oxford (in 1949), who gained his first-class degree in English here at Exeter; later novelist students would include Will Self, who would set a scene in his 1997 novel *Great Apes* in the college Hall. Pullman would go on to teach English at Westminster College, and still lives in Oxford. An alternative version of the city would provide the backdrop for his best-known series of novels 'His Dark Materials', beginning with *Northern Lights* (1995), set in part at the fictional 'Jordan College'. In 2003 Pullman published a little companion to his alternative city, *Lyra's Oxford*.

In the final book of Colin Dexter's 'Inspector Morse' series, *The Remorseful Day* (2000), Morse collapses on the lawn in the front quad here at Exeter, and is rushed to the John Radcliffe Hospital where he dies.

HERTFORD COLLEGE (1874), including the former Hart Hall. Samuel Daniel entered Hart Hall in 1579 and later became tutor to William Herbert at Wilton. John Donne, who came up in 1584, became acquainted with Henry Wotton and John Davies of Queen's, who remained his lifelong friends. John Selden, who like Donne went on to the Inns of Court, was an undergraduate at the turn of the 17th c.

John Meade Falkner, who graduated here in 1882, wrote *The Lost Stradivarius* (1895), a mystery novel in which an undergraduate finds a violin hidden behind the panelling in his room in the older part of the College, overlooking New College Lane. Falkner became an honorary Fellow in 1927.

Evelyn Waugh, an undergraduate at Hertford in the 1920s, who became a Catholic in 1930, wrote, as well as his satirical novels, a life of the Jesuit martyr Edmund Campion, which received the Hawthornden Prize in 1936, and a life of his friend Ronald Knox (1959). In *Brideshead Revisited* (1945), a novel with many scenes in Oxford, Waugh describes Oxford as 'the city of aquatint' and mentions the café in Broad St. where Balliol and Trinity men shuffle in their bedroom slippers to breakfast, Dollbear and Goodall, chemists in the High famous for their pick-me-ups, and The George. His autobiography, *A Little Learning* (1964), gives an account of his years here.

JESUS COLLEGE (1571) has a strong Welsh connection. Henry Vaughan, from Brecknock (now part of Powys), was an undergraduate from 1638. Ellis Wynne, Welsh cleric and author, entered in 1692. It used to be thought that he left without graduating, but recent evidence suggests that he became a BA and later an MA.

Lewis Morris, who later helped to establish the University of Wales, won the Chancellor's Essay Prize in 1858. He was made a Fellow after the publication of *The Epic of Hades* (1876–7), an account in blank verse of his supposed encounter with some characters of Greek mythology. John Morris-Jones, Welsh-language poet and critic, matriculated as a scholar in 1883 and graduated with honours in Mathematics in 1887. He spent much time

reading Welsh books and manuscripts in the Bodleian, and attended the lectures of John Rhys, Professor of Celtic, thus preparing the way for an appointment at University College, *Bangor, in 1889. William John Gruffydd entered in 1899 as a Meyrick Classical Exhibitioner and graduated first in Classics (1901) and then in English Literature (1903).

Frederick Rolfe spent part of 1906–7 here as secretary to Dr Hardy. T. E. Lawrence entered as an exhibitioner in 1907. He graduated in 1910 (Ⓟ in Lodge).

After taking his degree at *Aberystwyth, T. H. Parry-Williams came here in 1909 as a research graduate student in Celtic. He was made an honorary Fellow in 1968. D. J. Williams was also a graduate student (1916–18) from Aberystwyth. Thomas Rowland Hughes was awarded a University of Wales Fellowship in 1928 and came here to study under Edmund Blunden. He obtained a B.Litt. for his thesis 'The London Magazine from 1820 to 1829'.

The novelist William Boyd came up to Jesus College in 1975 and completed a Ph.D. thesis on Shelley (as did Logan Mountsuart in his novel *Any Human Heart*, 2002).

KEBLE COLLEGE (1870). The poet Geoffrey Hill was educated at Keble College.

LADY MARGARET HALL (1878). The novelist Gillian Tindal read English here.

LINCOLN COLLEGE (1427). William D'Avenant was an undergraduate in the 1620s, and his first play, *The Tragedy of Albovine*, was produced in 1629. D'Avenant was a Royalist like Thomas Fuller, who came here in 1643, lived in college, and preached to Charles I.

Mark Pattison, author of the life of Isaac Casaubon (1875), was Rector (1861–84). Marian Evans (George Eliot) visited him when she was writing *Middlemarch* (1871–2), though whether her portrait of the elderly pedant Mr Casaubon owes anything to him has been doubted. Pattison is certainly thought to be the origin of Professor Forth in Rhoda Broughton's novel *Belinda* (1883). She was a prolific novelist and was a welcome guest of Pattison's at the Rector's Lodgings. She lived at 51 Holywell St. from 1894 to 1900 and at Riverview, Headington Hill, from 1900 until her death in 1920. Owen Morgan Edwards was elected Fellow in 1889 and remained in Oxford as history tutor until 1907. Edward Thomas, who lodged at 113 Cowley Rd in 1898 as an external student, won a scholarship here later in the year, and married before leaving the University. *Oxford* (1903) was one of the first topographical books he wrote in an effort to make a living from writing.

John le Carré (then David Cornwell) read Modern Languages at Lincoln in the 1950s. The priest and historian Vivian H. H. Green, then Rector of Lincoln, is reputed to have been a model for le Carré's famous spymaster George Smiley. The poet Tom Paulin studied at Lincoln College, and in 1994 was appointed to a Fellowship at Hertford College.

MAGDALEN (pr. 'Mawdlin) **COLLEGE** (1458). John Foxe, an undergraduate in the 1530s, was elected a Fellow in 1539 but resigned in 1545 over his religious beliefs. He went abroad after the martyrdom of his friend Latimer. The English version of his long account of religious persecution, *Actes and Monuments* (1563), became known as *The Book of Martyrs*. John Lyly, who was here from 1567 to 1575, went on to Cambridge. Though in *Euphues* (1578) he thought Oxford colleges 'more stately for the building' and Cambridge 'much more sumptuous for the houses in the town', he writes that they are equal in learning 'for out of them both do dayly proceed men of great wisdom'.

Thomas Bodley came here after some years in Geneva, where his parents had gone to escape religious persecution. He graduated BA in 1563 before becoming a Fellow of Merton.

John Florio, son of a refugee from religious persecution, entered the College in 1581. His great work, an Italian–English dictionary (1598), led to his appointment as a reader in Italian to Queen Anne in 1604.

George Wither, an undergraduate from 1603 to 1605, writes in 'A Love Sonnet':

> In summer time to Medley,
> My love and I would go;
> The boatman there stood ready,
> My love and I to row.

Medley ferry (1 m. W), now replaced by a bridge, was the nearest river crossing to *Binsey. Wither also gives snatches of his life here in his pastoral poem *Fair Virtue* (1622). In *Abuses Stript and Whipt* (1613), he says that he was called back to his father's farm 'to learne to hold the plough' before he could 'take the lowest degree'.

Joseph Addison became a Fellow here at his own college in 1698. He was a noted classical scholar and his Latin poems were admired by Dryden. He travelled on the Continent (1699–1703) with a scholarship to enable him to embark on a diplomatic career and, though he became an Under-Secretary of State in 1706, did not resign his Fellowship until 1711. His favourite walk by the mill where there was a ford, and along the bank of the Cherwell, then known as the Water Walk, is now called Addison's Walk after him. A young girl at the mill was later the subject of T. E. Brown's poem 'An Oxford Idyll'.

William Collins, who came up in 1741, was a friend of Gilbert White of Oriel. *Persian Eclogues* (1742), his first volume of verse, was well received, but his health was poor and he suffered a mental breakdown while he was here. Edward Gibbon became a Catholic after some 'unprofitable' months here (1752–3) and his father sent him to Lausanne. He poured much scorn on the Fellows, who he said 'had absolved their conscience' from 'the toil of reading, or thinking, or writing'. H. J. Pye, an undergraduate in the 1760s, was later Poet Laureate and a constant butt of ridicule. James Hurdis, who graduated in 1782 and was made a Fellow in 1786, tried to vindicate academic life here from Gibbon's gibes. His long poem *The Village Curate* (1788) was written here but it is based on his years at *Burwash. He was made Professor of Poetry in 1793 and took a house at Temple Cowley (2 m. E) with his two sisters during terms and lived also at *Bishopstone, East Sussex.

R. S. Hawker, whose studies at Pembroke had been interrupted by his marriage, transferred here in 1824. 'The Song of the Western Men', published anonymously and usually referred to by the first line 'A good sword and a trusty hand', was written in the vacation in 1825 and many critics, including Scott and Dickens, thought it a 17th-c. song. Hawker won the Newdigate Prize in 1827 with 'Pompeii'. On a later visit to Oxford he was the object of a practical joke, which gave him a poor opinion of Matthew Arnold, the perpetrator.

Charles Reade, an undergraduate from 1831 to 1835, became a Fellow in 1838 but spent much of his time in London. *Masks and Faces* (1851), a popular play which he rewrote as the novel *Peg Woffington* (1852), and *The Cloister and the Hearth*, his novel about 15th-c. Europe, preceded others which he wrote to promote social change. He entertained Marian Evans (George Eliot) in his rooms, painted deep blue to simulate tropical sea and sky, though it was thought he admired her more for her unconventional life than for her writing. J. A. Symonds was elected a Fellow in 1862 and the next year won the Chancellor's Essay Prize with 'The Renaissance', but he was soon forced by ill health to go abroad, where he spent most of his life.

Oscar Wilde, an undergraduate from 1874 to 1878, who lived in rooms close to the kitchens, won the Newdigate Prize with his poem 'Ravenna'. He was the founder of an aesthetic cult whose members were caricatured as those who were 'anxious for to shine in the high aesthetic line' in the Gilbert and Sullivan opera *Patience* (1881).

A. D. Godley, who was a Fellow (1883–1912) and Public Orator (1910–25), translated Horace's *Odes* (1898) and Herodotus' *Works* (1921–3). He wrote much light verse, including *Verses to Order* (1892), *Lyra Frivola* (1899), *Second Things* (1902), and *The Casual Ward* (partly in prose; 1912). Many poems are about life in the University. T. E. Lawrence first travelled to the Middle East when he was a Senior Demy (1910–14). Compton Mackenzie, in his novel *Sinister Street* (2 vols, 1913–14), describes life in the first decade of the 20th c. when he was an undergraduate.

C. S. Lewis, a Fellow here (1924–54) until he became a Professor at Cambridge, wrote here *The Allegory of Love: A Study in Medieval Tradition* (1936) and *English Literature in the Sixteenth Century*, volume III in the *Oxford History of English Literature* (1954). As well as literary criticism he wrote works on religious and moral themes including *The Pilgrim's Regress* (1933), *The Problem of Pain* (1940), and *The Screwtape Letters* (1942). His versatility was also shown by science-fiction novels, one of which, *That Hideous Strength*

(1945), gives an account of a college meeting, and the very popular stories for children which include *The Lion, the Witch and the Wardrobe* (1950). He lived in college and also had a house in Kiln Lane, Headington Quarry. He is buried in Headington Quarry parish churchyard.

Parts of John Betjeman's autobiographical *Summoned by Bells* (1960) describe his life at Oxford, which, putting aside his prep school years at the Dragon School, started for him in 1925. He came across the group of poets led by Auden, but was more at home with Harold Acton and other members of the Aesthete set. He wrote a good deal of poetry and articles on architecture (including Victorian, on which he was becoming an authority) but his undergraduate career was undistinguished and he did not get on well with his tutor, the newly appointed C. S. Lewis, who considered him a dilettante. He was rusticated for failing his Divinity examination (which he successfully resat) and eventually left with a Pass degree in English. Henry Yorke (later Green), who also got on badly with Lewis, came up to Magdalen in 1924 to study Classics and English. *Blindness* (1926), his first novel, started when he was at Eton, was published while he was still an undergraduate. James Fenton studied English here and two poems about Oxford appear in early collections of his work: 'South Parks Road', 'both wilderness and formal garden', and 'The Pitt-Rivers Museum, Oxford', which describes the Museum's miscellaneous collection, 'the fabled lands where myths | Go when they die'.

Julian Barnes studied here in the 1960s; then before embarking on his novel-writing career he worked from 1969 to 1972 at Oxford University Press as a lexicographer on the supplement to the *Oxford English Dictionary*.

Philip Pullman's 'His Dark Materials' trilogy concludes with *The Amber Spyglass* (2000), which ends with a heartbreaking parting in Oxford's Botanic Garden, just across the road from Magdalen.

MAGDALEN HALL (*c.* 1487). William Tyndale, first translator of the Bible into English, studied here from 1510 to 1515. Thomas Hobbes, author of *Leviathan* (1651), was an undergraduate 1603–8. Edward Hyde, author of *The History of the Rebellion*, graduated BA in 1626.

In September 1817 John Keats shared his friend Benjamin Bailey's rooms for a fortnight. He worked each morning on *Endymion* and in the afternoons he and Bailey took a punt on the Isis and tied up among the rushes. They named one secluded spot 'Reynolds's Cove' after their friend John Reynolds, whose sister Bailey was hoping to marry. Keats enjoyed his visit and enclosed a poem on Oxford, a parody of Wordsworth's 'The cock is crowing', in his letter to Reynolds. George Gleig, who had fought in the Peninsula and in America, was a contemporary of Bailey here. Gleig, ordained in 1820, was the author of *The Subaltern* (1826). Bailey later married his sister. Magdalen Hall was burnt down after a party in 1820 (site now

St Swithun's Quad, Magdalen College) and the student body was later incorporated in Hertford College.

MARTYRS' MEMORIAL (1841), St Giles'. This Gothic pinnacled memorial commemorates the Protestant martyrs Thomas Cranmer, Hugh Latimer, and Nicholas Ridley. They were held in Bocardo, a prison over Cornmarket by the North Gate in the city wall (a restored bastion of the wall can be seen behind shops at the SW corner of Broad St.). Latimer and Ridley were burnt alive in the ditch outside the wall in 1555 and Cranmer was burnt the next year. An inscription on the wall of the Master's Lodgings at Balliol College faces the site of their martyrdom, which is marked by a concrete cross let into the surface of Broad St.

MERTON COLLEGE (1264), incorporating St Alban Hall. Thomas Bodley became a Fellow in 1564 and MA in 1566. He was buried in the chapel with great ceremony according to instructions in his will. A memorial by Nicholas Stone was erected in 1615. Philip Massinger was followed by Thomas Carew, as undergraduates, in the first decade of the 17th c. Anthony Wood, who was born (1632) at his father's house near the College and attended New College School (1641–4), was an undergraduate from 1647 to 1652, when he was given a bible clerkship. He collected much information on Oxford for *Historia et Antiquitates Universitatis Oxoniensis* (1674). He spent most of his time shut away in his father's house in a closet-like room he constructed by the chimney in the garret. There he maintained a long correspondence with John Aubrey on, as well as other topics, his biographical dictionary of Oxford scholars, *Athenae Oxonienses* (1691–2), which contained such unfavourable judgements on Lord Clarendon that his son brought an action and Wood was expelled from the University. *The Life and Times* was even more bitter and Wood complains of the vice and the 'decay of learning', the 'multitudes of ale-houses' and the 'harlots, pimps and panders, bawds and buffoons, lechery and treachery, atheists and papists' with which the place abounded. Wood, who called himself à Wood towards the end of his life, died in the garret which his father had bequeathed him and is buried in the antechapel, which contains his memorial as well as Bodley's, which was moved from the chapel.

Richard Steele, who had been at Christ Church, transferred here in August 1691 but did not stay long. He left in March 1692 and the next year he was commissioned in the Duke of Ormonde's Regiment of Life Guards.

Andrew Lang, best known for his collections of fairy stories such as the *Blue Fairy Book*, was a Fellow (1868–75). George Saintsbury, an undergraduate from 1863 to 1866, who became a literary critic and historian, was elected an honorary Fellow in 1909. Max Beerbohm, who was an undergraduate from 1891 to 1894, contributed some essays to *Isis* and other university publications. Many of his drawings, letters, and books are now on show in the Beerbohm Room in Mob Quad. His novel *Zuleika Dobson* (1911) describes the disastrous effect that his beautiful heroine has on all the undergraduates in Oxford, before she asks her maid to look up the next train to Cambridge. H. W. Garrod, who educated himself and won the Newdigate Prize, was elected a Fellow in 1901 and remained here until his death in 1960. He published *Oxford Poems* in 1912, and was Professor of Poetry 1923–8. Many of his lectures were published. T. S. Eliot came here in 1914–15 after Harvard and was made an honorary Fellow in 1949.

Robert Byron attended the College in the early 1920s and provided inspiration for some of the outrageous episodes in Evelyn Waugh's *Brideshead Revisited* (1945).

Louis MacNeice describes his years as an undergraduate (1926–30) in *The Strings Are False* (1965), his unfinished autobiography. His first volume of poems, *Blind Fireworks* (1929), was published the year before his marriage at Carfax Registry Office (gone), and his acceptance of a lectureship at *Birmingham. Cantos 12 and 13 of *Autumn Sequel* (1954) are set in Oxford.

Edmund Blunden, formerly an undergraduate at Queen's, was a Fellow from 1931 to 1943 and an honorary Fellow from 1964 to 1974. He published *Poems 1930–40* (1940) and *Shells by a Stream* (1944) while here. John Mulgan, the New Zealand novelist, read English Literature under Blunden from 1933 to 1935 and then joined the Clarendon Press in Walton St. He compiled an anthology, *Poems of Freedom* (1938), published a novel with a New Zealand background, *Man Alone* (1939), and joined the Oxfordshire and Buckinghamshire Light Infantry in 1939. *Report on Experience* (1947), an autobiographical work, was published after his death in Cairo in 1945. Keith Douglas, an undergraduate who also had Blunden as tutor from 1938 until called up in 1940 for war service, wrote many poems in Oxford, most of them published in the wartime Oxford magazine *Kingdom Come*. He edited *Cherwell*, the undergraduate journal, and helped to prepare *Augury*, an Oxford miscellany of verse and prose. He was killed in Normandy in 1944.

J. R. R. Tolkien was a Fellow and Merton Professor of English Language and Literature from 1945 to 1959. His epic story *The Lord of the Rings* was published in three parts: *The Fellowship of the Ring* (1954), *The Two Towers* (1954), and *The Return of the King* (1955). He lived at 3 Manor Rd (1947–50), 99 Holywell St. (1950), and 76 Sandfield Rd (1953–68; ℗). He is buried in Wolvercote cemetery.

Angus Wilson studied here, as did, in the early 1950s, the poets Alan Brownjohn and P. J. Kavanagh. Kavanagh described the resilient beauty of Oxford in his memoir *The Perfect Stranger* (1966) and, sitting on

> this meaningful,
> Ancient, uncomfortable,
> Breeze-petalled seat,

J. R. R. Tolkien in his rooms at Merton College, Oxford

confronts a more troubled history of the College in his poem 'Merton Garden'.

NEW COLLEGE (1379). William Grocyn studied here and became a Fellow in 1467. He was one of the scholars who introduced the study of Greek to the University. Henry Wotton left after two years (1584–6) to go to The Queen's College. William Somerville, who became a Fellow when he graduated in 1693, joined the Middle Temple three years later. He is remembered for *The Chace* (1735), a long poem in blank verse on various aspects of hunting and management of hounds. William Harrison was elected a Fellow here at his own college in 1706 and it was probably soon after that he wrote the poem 'Woodstock Park' (see WOODSTOCK). Harrison died young of a fever while still a Fellow and Thomas Tickell of Queen's wrote of him as 'that much lov'd youth'.

James Woodforde, an undergraduate from 1759 to 1763, was ordained deacon at Christ Church Cathedral. In *Diary of a Country Parson* (5 vols, 1924–31) he writes that he played cricket on Port Meadow, the 300-acre open space NW of the city, and that he went to shoot in Stanton Woods (NE) with the 'Masters'. Woodforde returned in 1773 as Fellow and Sub-Warden. His hope for a college living was answered when he was made rector of *Weston Longville. When on the annual journeys from his rectory to holidays in his native Somerset, he stayed at The Angel inn (site now the Examination Schools in the High St.) or at the Blue Boar (site now the Town Hall).

Sydney Smith, an undergraduate from 1789, became a Fellow in 1791 but left no witty sayings about his time here. Thomas Warton, Fellow of Trinity and Poet Laureate, wrote in 1789 'Verses on Sir Joshua Reynolds's Painted Window at New College'. This window, in the

antechapel, has a painting of the Nativity in the upper lights, and a row of figures representing the Virtues in the lower.

Lionel Johnson and John Galsworthy were undergraduate contemporaries in the 1880s. Johnson's poem 'Oxford' from *Poems* (1895) has the lines:

> There, Shelley dreamed his white Platonic
>   dreams;
> There, classic Landor throve on Roman thought;
> There, Addison pursued his quiet themes;
> There, smiled Erasmus, and there, Colet taught.
>
> That is the Oxford, strong to charm us yet:
> Eternal in her beauty and her past.
> What though her soul be vexed? She can forget
> Cares of an hour: only the great things last.

Galsworthy is commemorated by a plaque in the cloisters. R. C. Sherriff, author of the play *Journey's End* (1929), who spent two years here (1932–4) as a mature student, founded a scholarship in English Literature at the College. The poet George MacBeth came here in 1951 with an open scholarship in Classics. The poet, novelist, and translator D. M. Thomas came up to read English in 1955. The novelist John Fowles studied French and German here; and in 1956 the playwright Dennis Potter matriculated here too, with a scholarship to study PPE; in 1987 Potter would be made an honorary Fellow at the College.

ORIEL COLLEGE (1326), including St Mary's Hall. Walter Ralegh was a member of the College (1568–9) but though Anthony Wood, the antiquary, wrote that he was 'worthily esteemed', little is really known of his life here. John Taylor, 'the water-poet', lived in college during the plague in 1625 and was here again in the Civil War, when he saw the surrender of the city in 1645.

Gilbert White, an undergraduate from 1740 to 1743, was elected to a Fellowship (1744–55) and he became a Proctor and Dean of the College. His friend Mulso introduced him to his sister Hester (later Chapone), to whom he proposed marriage but was refused. White was also a friend of William Collins of Magdalen.

J. H. Newman, who became a Fellow in 1822, was one of the founders of the Oxford, or Tractarian, Movement. In 1828 he was appointed vicar of St Mary's parish, which included Littlemore (3 m. E), where, until his new parsonage was built, he stayed in a cottage which later became The George inn. From 1842 until 1846 he lived at 'The College', converted farm buildings (now in private occupation) used as a place of retirement, study, and prayer. Newman was received into the RC Church in 1845, and is commemorated by a bust (by Miss R. Fletcher) in the garden. His sermons at St Mary's have been published and his *Apologia pro Vita Sua* (1864), which gives an account of his spiritual history, in answer to Charles Kingsley's charges, is considered a masterpiece. His novel *Loss and Gain* (1848) contains an account of an Oxford breakfast at a tutor's, formerly a well-established institution but now generally discontinued.

J. A. Froude, who won the Chancellor's Essay Prize here and graduated in 1842, later became a Fellow of Exeter. T. E. Brown, who was elected a Fellow in 1854 after being considered ineligible at his own college (Christ Church), stayed here only five years before returning to his native Isle of Man. Arthur Hugh Clough,

who had been a friend of Matthew Arnold at Rugby, and who preceded him as an undergraduate at Balliol, was a Fellow here from 1841 to 1848. His poem *The Bothie of Tober-na-Vuolich: A Long Vacation Pastoral*, written in 1848, was considered by many, perhaps those satirized in it, as 'indecent and profane, immoral and (!) communistic', as Clough himself recorded to a friend. Thomas Hughes, who also came from Rugby, was an undergraduate (1842–5) who can hardly be separated from his novel *Tom Brown at Oxford* (1861), a sequel to the hero's schooldays at Rugby. Arnold, son of the headmaster eulogized in Hughes's school story, was a Fellow here from 1845 to 1847. *Poems* (1853) contains 'The Scholar-Gipsy', based on the tale of an Oxford scholar, whom poverty 'forced to leave his studies', first recounted in Glanvill's *The Vanity of Dogmatizing* (1661). Arnold's poem describes the peaceful rural haunts of the scholar who wandered nearby in North Hinksey and on Cumnor Hill in a former golden age:

O born in days when wits were fresh and clear,
And life ran gaily as the sparkling Thames;
Before this strange disease of modern life,
With its sick hurry, its divided aims
Its heads o'ertaxed, its palsied hearts, was rife.

Arnold gives another nostalgic description in his preface to *Essays in Criticism* (1865):

Beautiful city! so venerable, so lovely, so unravaged by the fierce intellectual life of our

century, so serene! . . . whispering from her towers the last enchantments of the Middle Age. . . . Home of lost causes, and forsaken beliefs, and unpopular names, and impossible loyalties!

Arnold's poem 'Thyrsis' in *New Poems* (1867) was written to commemorate his friend Clough, who died in Florence aged 42, and contains many references to the places they had visited together.

Richard Hughes came here in 1919 as a scholar and graduated in 1922. His first play, *The Sisters' Tragedy* (1922), was produced in London while he was still an undergraduate. He became an honorary Fellow in 1975.

PEMBROKE COLLEGE (1624). This college, which includes the earlier Broadgates Hall and Beef Hall, retains a connection with Abingdon School. Francis Beaumont, the dramatist, entered Broadgates Hall in 1597, but left a year later, after his father's death. Thomas Browne studied medicine here and became an MA in 1629. He practised for a short while in the county, was made an MD in 1637, and then settled in *Norwich.

Samuel Johnson came up in 1728 and had rooms on the second floor over the gateway. He had hoped to eke out the small amount of money he had by sharing the rooms of a friend. This friend left Oxford before Johnson could benefit and, after 14 months, he was forced to leave the University. Johnson always thought of

Oxford from the 'Childsworth Farm', North Hinksey, as recalled by Arnold in his poem 'Thyrsis', written in memory of his friend Clough

Oxford with pleasure and often returned. In 1754 he came with Hannah More, whom he showed over the College, and he stayed with his friend Thomas Warton of Trinity. He came again in 1755. It was a college tutor here whom he afterwards quoted as saying, 'Read over your compositions, and where ever you meet with a passage which you think is particularly fine, strike it out.' The College still has his desk, some of his books, a portrait by Reynolds, and his teapot.

Richard Graves was a friend and contemporary of William Shenstone in the 1730s. Shenstone appears in Graves's novels *Columella* (1776) and *The Spiritual Quixote* (1772), in which another contemporary, George Whitefield, the Methodist, is satirized. Thomas Lovell Beddoes, who came up in 1820, wrote *The Improvisatore* (1821), tales in verse, followed by *The Bride's Tragedy* (1822), a drama, which like his other works has an obsession with death. Beddoes graduated in 1825, the year he began *Death's Jest Book*, a play which features such Gothic elements as a sepulchre, a charnel-house, a poisoned goblet, and a spectre. Beddoes spent most of the last 25 years of his life revising the play, mainly in Zurich. The lyrics and some of the blank-verse passages are very fine.

R. S. Hawker came up in 1823 but his studies here ended when he married. The woman of his choice was 20 years older than himself, and their marriage proved a happy one. Hawker transferred to Magdalen in 1824. J. R. R. Tolkien, Professor of Anglo-Saxon and a Fellow (1926–45), wrote during this time, as well as critical works on *Beowulf* and Beorhtnoth, the novel *The Hobbit* (1937), the first of a series which has a strange mythology invented by himself.

THE QUEEN'S COLLEGE (1341). This college elected many of its early scholars and Fellows from the old counties of Cumberland and Westmorland. Henry Wotton came to Queen's from New College in 1586. The play *Tancredo*, which he wrote for a performance in the College, was based on Tasso's *Gerusalemme Liberata* (1581), and brought him to the notice of Alberico Gentile, the Professor of Civil Law, a connection of use to him in his future diplomatic career.

John Davies from Wiltshire, a student from 1585 to 1590, returned to Oxford in 1598 after attacking a colleague in the Middle Temple. He composed *Nosce Teipsum* (1599) here, a philosophical poem discussing the vanity of acquiring knowledge without also cultivating the mind and the soul.

Thomas Middleton entered in 1598 and his early poems *The Wisdom of Solomon Paraphrased* (1597), *Micro-Cynicon* (1599), and *The Ghost of Lucrece* (1600), were written here, but have none of the power of his later plays. Little is known of his life here but later he described, perhaps from his own experience, a poor scholar who, while servant to a rich Londoner, 'kept his study warm' while he was playing tennis 'and sucked the honey of wit

from the flowers of Aristotle' by reading his employer's books.

William Wycherley, who came in 1659, stayed a short time only and left before passing the entrance requirements. Joseph Addison spent a short time here before obtaining a demyship at Magdalen in 1689. Thomas Tickell became an MA in 1709 after publishing his poem 'Oxford' in 1707, and in 1711 was elected Professor of Poetry over the heads, it was thought, of more worthy candidates. His *On the Prospect of Peace* (1712) was noticed by Addison and Pope, and led to his contributing to *The Guardian* and *The Spectator* and to his getting a post in Ireland under Addison. William Collins spent a short time here in 1740 before going as a demy to Magdalen. William Gilpin became an MA here in 1748 and later wrote lives of Latimer (1755), Wycliffe (1765), and Cranmer (1784), though he is chiefly remembered for his popular illustrated tours.

Walter Pater graduated BA in 1862 before becoming a Fellow of Brasenose.

Louis Golding, author of several novels set in his native Manchester, was an undergraduate before serving in the First World War.

Edmund Blunden was an undergraduate (1919–23) after serving in the First World War. He published three volumes of verse before becoming Professor of English Literature at Tokyo University (1924–7). Thomas Hardy was made an honorary Fellow here in 1922. He had visited Oxford for a performance of *The Dynasts* by OUDS in 1920, when he was made an honorary D.Litt.

Sidney Keyes, an undergraduate from 1940 to 1942, who had started to write poetry at school, published *Iron Laurel* (1942) and *Cruel Solstice* (1943) before his death in the North African campaign in 1943. These volumes were then published as *Collected Poems* (1945).

John Heath-Stubbs was awarded the Barker Exhibition for a student who was blind or in danger of losing his sight and studied English here in the late 1930s. In 1972 he accepted a tutorial post at Merton College, a position he held for some 20 years.

ST ANNE'S (1878). The Cairo-born novelist Penelope Lively took a history degree here. In 1974 she published her novel *The House on Norham Gardens*, a book for young readers set in the eponymous house in North Oxford (off the Banbury Rd).

> Belbroughton Road. Linton Road. Bardwell Road. The houses there are quite normal. They are ordinary sizes and have ordinary chimneys and roofs and gardens with laburnum and flowering cherry. Park Town. As you go south they are growing. Getting higher and odder. By the time you get to Norham Gardens they have tottered over the edge into madness: these are not houses but flights of fancy. . . . People live in these houses. Clare Mayfield, aged fourteen, raised by aunts in North Oxford.

The poet Elizabeth Jennings, born in Lincolnshire, moved to Oxford with her family when she was 6 years old, and studied at Oxford High School before matriculating for

her degree at St Anne's. She would remain in Oxford for the rest of her life; she died in Bampton in 2001.

In 1948, after some years away from Oxford—studying in Cambridge and working in London, Iris Murdoch returned to Oxford and took up a teaching post at St Anne's, where she taught Philosophy for 15 years. She remained in Oxford for the rest of her life, living first out in Steeple Aston (from 1956), then in 1986 moving back to the north of the city, to Hamilton Rd, then in 1989 to Charlbury Rd, where she remained until her death from Alzheimer's in 1999.

ST CATHERINE'S (1963). The novelist Jeanette Winterson studied English here.

ST EDMUND HALL (13th c.). Thomas Hearne, the antiquary, was educated here (BA 1699, MA 1703) through the influence of Francis Cherry, a nonjuror, who had the similar interests of a bibliophile. Hearne became a Keeper at the Bodleian Library but lost his post when he, as a Jacobite, refused to take the oath of allegiance to George I. He published *Reliquiae Bodleianae* (1703) and a large number of medieval texts and chronicles. His diaries contain diatribes on the decay of learning. His tombstone can be seen in the nearby churchyard of St Peter in the East (now the college library). More recently the poet Kevin Crossley-Holland studied here.

ST HILDA'S COLLEGE (1893). Barbara Pym came up to study English in 1931. Many of her stories and novels—including *A Few Green Leaves* (1980) and *An Academic Question* (1986)—have Oxford associations. William Boyd returned to Oxford for three years in the early 1980s as an English lecturer teaching the contemporary novel at St Hilda's College. It was while he was here that his first novel, *A Good Man in Africa* (1981), was published.

ST HUGH'S COLLEGE (1886). The poet Patricia Beer came up to St Hugh's and graduated B.Litt. in 1941. Six years later the novelist Brigid Brophy won a scholarship to read Classics at the College. She was sent down at the end of her fourth term for unspecified sexual misdemeanours.

ST JOHN'S COLLEGE (1555). James Shirley came here in 1612 from the Merchant Taylors' School but soon transferred to Cambridge. Abraham Cowley, who had been at Cambridge, migrated here in the Civil War. During his two years here (1644–6) his friend the physician William Harvey was made Warden of Merton.

A. E. Housman, who came up with a scholarship in 1877, took a First in Honour Moderations, but failed in his hopes of getting a good degree in 1881. Housman's time here was dramatized by Tom Stoppard in his *The Invention of Love* (1997): 'I was eighteen when I first saw Oxford, and Oxford was charming then, not the trippery emporium it has become. There were horse-buses at the station to meet

Iris Murdoch at home on the Charlbury Rd, Oxford, in the house she shared with her husband and fellow academic John Bayley

Verse (1973). At the beginning of Larkin's third term he met Kingsley Amis, with whom he shared tastes in poetry, fiction, film, jazz, and jokes. They wrote parodies and travesties together, including the Willow Gables stories, a scurrilous send-up of the schoolgirls' adventure story genre. Amis was at St John's from 1941. The life and libido of an Oxford don would form the subject of his 1978 novel *Jake's Thing*.

The poet and critic John Wain and the poet, editor, cricket writer, and memoirist Alan Ross were also contemporaries of Larkin and Amis at St John's. For Ross, as he records in the first part of his autobiography *Blindfold Games* (1986), the sense of literary talent at the College was not obvious:

> In retrospect, the years 1940–42 might seem to have constituted a dazzling period in the literary life of the college, but this was far from apparent at the time. Philip Larkin arrived the same term as I to read English, and Kingsley Amis two terms later, to be followed by John Wain. None of them, however, was, in terms of literary talent, notably precocious.

ST MARY THE VIRGIN (13th–14th c.). St Mary's, the University Church in the High St., has a tablet in the sanctuary to Amy Dudley, who died (1560) at *Cumnor. She was the wife of Lord Leicester, Queen Elizabeth's favourite. All three are characters in Scott's novel *Kenilworth* (1821). The martyrs Cranmer, Latimer, and Ridley were condemned as heretics after a long interrogation by the university clergy in this church in 1554.

SOMERVILLE COLLEGE (1879). Rose Macaulay was the first of a group of writers who were up *c.* 1910 to 1915. Her satirical novel *Potterism* (1920) was the first of her successes. Dorothy L. Sayers, who was born (1893) in Oxford, where her father was headmaster of the Cathedral School, came up with a scholarship in 1912. Her detective novel *Gaudy Night* (1935), set in an imaginary women's college, which she places apologetically on Balliol's cricket ground, has the two main characters Oxford-educated with first-class degrees like herself. The sequel, *Busman's Honeymoon* (1936), in which the two characters marry, also has some scenes in Oxford. Dorothy Sayers, who became a publisher's reader at Blackwell's, published two volumes of poetry, and edited *Oxford Poetry* from 1917 to 1919, when she left Oxford.

Vera Brittain, who described Dorothy Sayers as an 'exuberant young female' who always seemed to be preparing for parties, mentions her own years here in *Testament of Youth* (1933) and *Testament of Friendship* (1940), the latter a tribute to the friend Winifred Holtby whom she met here. Winifred Holtby, who is chiefly remembered by *South Riding* (1936), a novel about her native Yorkshire, also wrote the earlier novels *The Land of Green Ginger* (1927) and *Poor Caroline* (1931), as well as short stories and a study of Virginia Woolf (1932). Another contemporary was Margaret Kennedy, who made her name with *The Constant Nymph*

the Birmingham train; and not a brick to be seen . . .'.

Robert Graves, newly released from the trenches, was admitted to read Classics (later English) at St John's in 1919. He found, as he recorded in *Goodbye to All That* (1929), a quiet Oxford: 'The returning soldiers did not feel tempted to rag about, break windows, get drunk, or have tussles with the police and races with the proctors' "bulldogs", as in the old days.' He lived 5 m. out, on Boar's Hill.

Philip Larkin studied here in the 1940s, and set his first novel, *Jill* (1946), and part of his

second, *A Girl in Winter* (1947), in Oxford. *Jill*, whose hero finds himself wretchedly out of place in wartime Oxford, seems to bear out Larkin's own admission that 'Oxford terrified me. Public schoolboys terrified me. The dons terrified me. So did the scouts'. He revisited his undergraduate past in 'Dockery and Son', and in 'A Poem About Oxford' expresses no regret at having attended Oxford rather than Cambridge (or anywhere else). He came back to Oxford in 1970 on a visiting Fellowship at All Souls College to select the poems for *The Oxford Book of Twentieth-Century English*

(1924), which was also very popular when dramatized. Helen Waddell, whose novel *Peter Abelard* (1933) brought her medieval scholarship before a wide public, was a Research Fellow here (1920–2).

Penelope Fitzgerald (then Knox) pursued a brilliant student career here, taking a First in English in 1939. The novelists Iris Murdoch and Nina Bawden studied at Somerville too. Murdoch (whose 1938 scholarship to Somerville would win her a First in 1942) would go on to teach Philosophy at Oxford.

TRINITY COLLEGE (1555). Thomas Lodge, an undergraduate from 1573 to 1577, left to enter Lincoln's Inn. He returned to study medicine and became an MD in 1603. John Denham entered in 1631 but left soon after to study Law, and 10 years later John Aubrey spent a short time here, but left in 1643 because of smallpox and civil war. In June 1697, passing through Oxford to stay with his friend Lady Long, he died suddenly and was buried in the church of St Mary Magdalen (tablet in the S chapel). Aubrey's short biographies of his contemporaries, first published in 1813 and now known as *Brief Lives*, were written to be used by Anthony Wood of Merton.

Elkanah Settle came up in 1666 but left without taking a degree. Shortly afterwards his version of the historical tragedy *Cambyses, King of Persia* was performed in London. After success there it was acted in Oxford.

Thomas Warton, younger son of Thomas Warton, Professor of Poetry (1718–28), came up in 1744 and was made a Fellow in 1751. He wrote *The Pleasures of Melancholy* and other verses while an undergraduate. *The Triumphs of Isis* (1749), which made his name, was a reply to the aspersions William Mason of Cambridge had made on the University in *Isis* (1748). Warton contributed poems to many Oxford periodicals, wrote an ode for the Encaenia ceremony which was set to music, and edited the Oxford anthologies *The Union* (1753) and *The Oxford Sausage* (1764). He also wrote an amusing satire on guide books, *A Companion to the Guide* (1760). His friendship with Dr Johnson began after the publication of *Observations on the 'Faerie Queene' of Spenser* (1754), which Johnson thought outstanding. Warton was Johnson's host on his visit that summer and was helpful in getting him made MA the next year. Johnson and Boswell both came in 1776 when Johnson was made an LL D. Warton was one of the earliest to appreciate Gothic architecture again and led the way for the Romantic movement's admiration. He wrote the life of Dr Ralph Bathurst, a President of the College, and that of Sir Thomas Pope, the founder, though this latter was thought tedious by Horace Walpole. He died (1790) in a chair in the Senior Common Room and is buried in the antechapel. The chair and his portrait, painted by his friend Sir Joshua Reynolds, are in the Old Library.

William Lisle Bowles, who graduated in 1792, wrote one of his many sonnets to the river Cherwell with its 'willow'd edge'. Walter Savage Landor came up in 1793 but quarrelled with the authorities and was rusticated for a year, by which time his father had died and he could not return.

J. H. Newman was an undergraduate here (1816–20) and was made an honorary Fellow in 1877. He is commemorated by a bust by Thomas Woolner in the college garden. Richard Burton, Arabic scholar and explorer, came up in 1840 after having spent many years abroad with his parents. He left without graduating and joined the Indian Army in 1842. Sir Arthur Quiller-Couch, an undergraduate here from 1882 to 1886, became a lecturer in Classics (1886–7). He edited *The Oxford Book of English Verse* (1900) and *The Oxford Book of Ballads* (1910) and then became a Professor of English Literature at Cambridge. Laurence Binyon was here from 1887 to 1890. His first volume of verse, *Lyric Poems* (1894), was published when he took up an appointment at the British Museum.

James Elroy Flecker came up with a scholarship in 1902. Some of his poems, including 'Oxford Canal', 'I Have Sung All Love's Great Songs', and 'Roses and Rain', were included in *The Best Man*, a paperback volume published in 1906. Some were also included in *Bridge of Fire* (1907). He was disappointed at getting a third-class degree. Joyce Cary, an undergraduate here from 1909 to 1912, returned to Oxford after resigning from the Colonial Service because of ill health in 1920. He settled at 12 Parks Rd, where he wrote a succession of novels including *Aissa Saved* (1932), *The African Witch* (1936), *Mr. Johnson* (1939), *Charley Is My Darling* (1940), *The Horse's Mouth* (1944), and *Not Honour More* (1955). Cary, who became paralysed, died in 1957 and is buried in Wolvercote cemetery.

Ronald Knox was a Fellow and lecturer here from 1910 to 1917. After ordination in 1912 he was chaplain until his conversion to Catholicism (1917). He was Catholic chaplain to the University from 1926 to 1939, and lived in the Old Palace in St Aldates. He wrote *Essays in Satire* (1928), *Let Dons Delight* (1939), other essays, and a number of detective stories. He became an honorary Fellow in 1941.

The playwright Terence Rattigan matriculated at Trinity in 1930, but ended up spending most of his university career at OUDS instead of going to lectures, and left without taking a degree. His plays *First Episode* (1934), and *French Without Tears* (1936), which was to be his first great success at the West End, both drew on his time at Oxford. The novelist Justin Cartwright was also later at Trinity.

UNIVERSITY COLLEGE (1249), commonly known as Univ., was reputedly founded by Alfred the Great. Dr Johnson dined here with Boswell in 1776 on visiting Oxford, when he was made an honorary LL D, and later said that he drank three bottles of port without feeling the worse for it.

Percy Bysshe Shelley's year here in 1810 was described by Thomas Jefferson Hogg, his contemporary, in the *New Monthly Magazine* in 1832. As undergraduates they had written together 'Posthumous Fragments of Margaret Nicholson' and taken part in a number of hair-raising experiments, which left Shelley's hands and clothes marked with chemicals. They walked about Shotover Hill (3 m. E), and Shelley indulged in his habit of sailing paper boats. He was sent down when he sent a copy of his pamphlet *The Necessity of Atheism*, to the Master and other heads of colleges and refused to admit it was his. Hogg protested and was also expelled. Shelley's death near Spezia in Italy in 1822 is commemorated in the NW corner of the quad by the Shelley Memorial, a domed structure containing the marble figure of the drowned poet by Onslow Ford (1894).

Edwin Arnold, an undergraduate from 1851 to 1854, won the Newdigate Prize in 1852 with 'Belshazzar's Feast', which was published in his *Poems Narrative and Lyrical* (1853). He went to India as Principal of the College of the Deccan in 1856, and his long poem *The Light of Asia* (1879), on the life of Buddha, coincided with a popular interest in Eastern religious thought, and proved very popular. After his death in 1904 his ashes were deposited in the chapel. C. S. Lewis came up in 1917 and enlisted within a short time. He resumed his studies after he was demobilized in January 1919.

Stephen Spender studied here. In the summer of 1928 he first met W. H. Auden, then in his last year at Christ Church, and subsequently Christopher Isherwood. His first proper, disconcerting meeting—or appointment—with Auden 'in a darkened room with the curtains drawn' is described in Spender's autobiography *World Within World* (1951). He published *Twenty Poems* (1930) in May of his third year, before, like Isherwood at Cambridge, failing his finals in spectacular fashion. V. S. Naipaul came from Trinidad to University College in 1950 having won an 'Island Scholarship' to study English.

A few years later Shiva Naipaul, the novelist and travel writer, followed in the footsteps of his elder brother to the same college.

WADHAM COLLEGE (1610). Shakerley Marmion, a young dramatist patronized by Ben Jonson, graduated MA in 1624, and then fought in the Netherlands. Charles Sedley came up in 1656 and John Wilmot, 2nd Earl of Rochester, entered in 1660. They became intimate friends at court later. Rochester gave the College four silver tankards. John Gauden came to Wadham after being at St John's, Cambridge. He was made a DD in 1641.

Francis Kilvert came up in 1859 and graduated BA in 1862, MA in 1866. He returned to Oxford to stay with friends in 1874 and found it much altered, recording in his *Diary* (1938–40; new edn, 1969): 'New College extending itself into Holywell, a new and beautiful walk planted with elms from Christ Church to the barges, and a new College, Keble, red brick relieved with white, which disappoints me at present.'

L. A. G. Strong, a classical scholar during the First World War, left in 1917, before taking his degree, to join the staff of Summer Fields, a prep school in North Oxford, to replace the men who had enlisted. He graduated after the war but returned to the school to teach. During his time here he met many writers who were in Oxford, including L. P. Hartley, A. E. Coppard, Roy Campbell, and Yeats, who was living opposite Balliol. Strong was able to leave teaching when his novel *Dewer Rides* (1929) was accepted and proved successful. C. Day-Lewis came up in 1923 already writing verse and in 1927 edited *Oxford Poetry* with W. H. Auden, and published his own poems, *Country Comets*, the next year. He describes his time here in *The Buried Day* (1960). He taught (1927–8) at Summer Fields (Strong had told him of the vacancy) and lived in a room over the gate lodge. He was elected Professor of Poetry (1951–5). The novelist and broadcaster Melvyn Bragg also took a history degree at Wadham, and the novelist Monica Ali read PPE here.

WORCESTER COLLEGE (1714), which includes the earlier Gloucester Hall, is the only college with a lake. Thomas Coryate came here in 1596 but little is known of his life until he was appointed court jester to Prince Henry's household. Kenelm Digby, whose father had been executed for treason in 1606, spent two years (1618–20) here before he went to Paris. Richard Lovelace, who came up in 1634, was made much of by the courtiers on Charles I's stay in 1636, and was made an MA by the Chancellor, Archbishop Laud, before he had finished his studies. Lovelace joined Sir John Suckling's troop to fight in Scotland in 1639. Samuel Foote, who came up in 1737, managed to dissipate a large fortune here before leaving to read for the Bar.

Thomas De Quincey, who spent his time wandering about the country and almost starved in London after running away from school, decided to study at Oxford and arrived to choose a college in December 1803. He settled on Worcester after trying Christ Church, as he found the 'caution money', a sum of money demanded as a surety of good behaviour, was lower here, and his allowance was meagre. He led an isolated life here, reading German philosophy and learning the language, and buying the latest works in English. He wrote to Wordsworth, whose *Lyrical Ballads* (with Coleridge) were 'so twisted with my heart strings'. De Quincey's health was poor, however; he felt himself doomed by consumption and while low-spirited over the disappearance of his brother he bought some opium in London to relieve the pain of neuralgia. The dreams that resulted he later recorded in *Suspiria de Profundis* (1847). He left Oxford without a degree before his viva, in spite of his belief that he had written well in the examination, in May 1808.

Henry Kingsley, younger brother of Charles, led an exuberant life as an undergraduate in 1850, left the College without a degree, and

spent some years in the Australian goldfields and in the mounted police in Sydney. An early chapter of his *Ravenshoe* (1862) describes the process of rustication from an Oxford college.

The family press run by Dr Charles Daniel, Fellow from 1863 and Provost (1903–19), was active here intermittently from 1874 to 1906.

The Russian émigré novelist William Gerhardie read Russian at Worcester in the early 1920s. While still an undergraduate he wrote the first study of Chekhov in English and *Futility*, the novel for which he is best known. 'What I was really doing while there', he wrote in *Memoirs of a Polyglot* (1931),

> was to write my *Futility*. I was fortunate in having Mr Nichol Smith as my tutor. He said that my accent was not un-English, but my intonation was, largely owing to the speed with which I spoke, and he advised me to talk more slowly. I rejoined that if I talked quickly it was because I did not wish to take up too much of the time of so eminent a scholar. He replied that by talking too rapidly I often failed to convey my meaning clearly, and, in the repetition which ensued, wasted more of his time than if I had spoken slowly.

A few years later the novelist Jocelyn Brooke came up to Worcester. His contribution to the short-lived literary periodical *Flux* was considered sexually offensive by the university proctors and he was sent down. The poet Glyn Maxwell was educated here from 1982 to 1985.

OXTED *Surrey*

Small town on the A25, 8 m. E of Redhill. In 1897 the American novelist Stephen Crane and Lady Cora Stewart lived at Ravensbrook House (now flats) at the foot of Snats Hill, to the N of the town. Crane, who had made his name with *The Red Badge of Courage* (1895), a realistic novel of the American Civil War, published two volumes of short stories, *The Open Boat* (1898) and *The Monster* (1899).

PANGBOURNE *Berkshire*

Village on the Thames, on the A329. Kenneth Grahame spent his last years here and is commemorated by a decorative sign at the N end of the main street. *The Wind in the Willows* (1908) shares the sign with the 9th-c. granter of Pangbourne's charter, Berhtulf, King of Mercia. Church Cottage, where Grahame lived, is withdrawn from traffic, and its pleasant garden, with the old village roundhouse now a toolshed, and a stretch of grass ending in a tree-shaded amphitheatre, may be seen by courtesy of the present owner. E. H. Shepard came here to plan the illustrations for *The Wind in the Willows*, with such success that Pangbourne and its stretch of river became for many readers the veritable home of Rat and Mole.

Jerome K. Jerome's heroes of *Three Men in a Boat* (1889) visited the riverside Swan Hotel. D. H. Lawrence spent part of the summer at Myrtle Cottage on Reading Rd. He didn't stay long, finding the village 'repulsive'.

PENSHURST PLACE *Kent*

Country house open to the public (www. penshurstplace. com) 6 m. SW of Tonbridge, off the A26. The Great Hall, which has a 60-ft-high roof of chestnut beams, was begun in 1339 and added to in the 15th c. One of the owners was Humphrey of Gloucester (d. 1447), the Duke Humphrey who bequeathed his library to *Oxford University. Later the estate was given by the young Edward VI to Sir William Sidney, grandfather of Philip and Robert Sidney, who were born and spent part of their youth here. As a boy Philip accompanied his father to Ireland and Wales and later attended Queen Elizabeth's court in the hope of employment, but between whiles spent his time at Penshurst or Wilton, his sister's home. He inherited the estate while he was Governor of Flushing in the Netherlands, and died soon afterwards from wounds received in an attack on the Spaniards at Zutphen. His younger brother Robert, also employed at court and on foreign missions, spent more time here and added the Long Gallery and the Nether Gallery to the house. In 'To Penshurst' from *The Forest* (1616), Ben Jonson, a frequent visitor, describes the groves, the mount, the river, and the oak tree planted when Philip Sidney was born, and then comes nearer the house:

> Then hath thy orchard fruit, thy garden flowers,
> The early cherry with the later plum,
> Fig, grape and quince, each in his turn doth come:
> The blushing apricot and woolly peach
> Hang on thy walls, that every child may reach.

Jonson writes that the informal hospitality of Sir Robert and his wife made Penshurst a pleasure to visit. Their eldest daughter, Mary, married here in 1604 the newly knighted Sir Robert Wroth of *Loughton. Robert Sidney is thought by some to have written the words for *A Musicall Banquet* (1610) of his godson, Robert Dowland, and he is now known to be the author of a notebook containing songs, sonnets, and longer poems dedicated to his sister, which has recently been found to be in his handwriting. Robert Sidney's granddaughter Dorothy was courted here by Edmund Waller after the death of his first wife in 1634. He called her Dorothea, or Sacharissa, in the poems he wrote to her, addressed to her portrait, to her sister Lucy, and to her maid. While walking about the estate he wrote:

> Ye lofty beeches, tell this matchless dame,
> That if together ye fed all one flame,
> It could not equalise the hundredth part
> Of what her eyes have kindled in my heart!

However, in 1639 she married Lord Spencer, later Earl of Sunderland.

John Evelyn visited in the summer of 1652 and wrote in his *Diary* (1955) that the place was

> famous once for its Gardens and excellent fruit: and for the noble conversation which was wont to meete there, celebrated by that illustrious person Sir Phil. Sidny, who there composed divers of his pieces. It stands also in a park, is

finely water'd: and was now full of Company, upon the marriage of my old fellow-collegiate, Mr. Robert Smith, who married my Lady Dorothy Sidny, widdow of the Earle of Sunderland.

There are many portraits in the house, including those of Philip Sidney, Robert Sidney and his wife, their sister, the Countess of Pembroke, and Dorothy, Countess of Sunderland. Philip Sidney's helm, carried at his funeral in St Paul's, is displayed in the Nether Gallery. Monuments to other members of the family are in the small parish church nearby.

PEPER (pr. 'Pepper) HAROW *Surrey*

Village off the A3, 5 m. SW of Guildford. Mrs Humphry Ward stayed at the rectory (later Mulberry House, Shackleford) in 1882. It became the 'Murewell Rectory' of her most famous novel, *Robert Elsmere* (1888). Henry James visited her here.

PETERSFIELD *Hampshire*

Market town on the South Downs. The science-fiction novelist John Wyndham enjoyed a comparatively stable and happy three years of education at Bedales from 1918 to 1921. In 1963 he returned to live nearby, spending the last six years of his life at Oakridge, Mill Lane, Steep. The novelist Jocelyn Brooke went to school at Bedales in the 1920s. He hunted for orchids around the school and conceived the idea of writing a book about the British orchid with his friend Gavin Bone. This eventually bore fruit in the 'autobotonography' *The Military Orchid*.

PIDDINGTON *Oxfordshire*

Village on a minor road 1 m. off the B4011, *c.* 14 m. NW of Aylesbury. The poet and playwright John Drinkwater is buried in the churchyard as he requested 'in the quiet and peaceful village' of his childhood memories, where he used to spend his school holidays with his great-uncle at the manor house.

PILTDOWN *East Sussex*

Small village near Uckfield. The Piltdown skull hoax was an inspiration for the faked evidence introduced into the excavation of the tomb of Bishop Eorpwald at 'Melpham' in Angus Wilson's novel *Anglo-Saxon Attitudes* (1956).

POLESDEN LACEY *Surrey*

Regency house 2 m. S of the A246 at Great Bookham, built on the site of the house which Sheridan bought (1796) for his second wife. He wrote, 'it shall be a seat of health and happiness—where she shall chirp like a bird, bound like a fawn and grow fat as a little pig'. He also bought Yew Trees Farm nearby. In 1798 he was still enjoying 'nature and retirement' but in 1802, when his wife, son, servants, and labourers, including his washerwoman's family, caught scarlet fever so badly that he feared for their lives, he wished he had never seen the place.

PORTSMOUTH *Hampshire*

City and naval base, occupying Portsea Island, N of Spithead. Charles Dickens was born at 1 Mile End Ter., Portsea, now the Dickens Museum, 393 Commercial Rd, his father being a clerk in the Navy Pay Office. The family moved to a smaller house in Hawke St. (gone), and in 1814 to London. Dickens came back to Portsmouth in 1838 to collect local colour for *Nicholas Nickleby* (1838–9).

George Meredith was born in a house (gone) on the corner of Broad St. and High St. (though for many years his biographers have been misled by his own reference to his birthplace as simply 'near Petersfield'), and baptized in St Thomas's Church (now the Cathedral). His grandfather Melchisedek Meredith was a prosperous tailor and naval outfitter, immortalized as Melchisidec Harrington, 'the Great Mel', in the novel *Evan Harrington* (1861), and his father, Augustus, who carried on the business, was the original of Evan Harrington. Portsmouth is the 'Lymport' of the novel and many of the characters are drawn from Meredith's relations and contemporaries. He attended St Paul's School, Southsea (a private school which existed 1825–50), before going to boarding school at Lowestoft in 1840.

Sir Walter Besant was born in St George's Sq., Portsea (the house has gone). His novel *By Celia's Arbour* (1878) gives a description of the old town of his boyhood. Rudyard Kipling, who was born in India, was sent as a boy (1874–7) to live with relatives in Campbell Rd, Southsea, and went to school at Hope House. It has been thought that some of the descriptions in his novel *The Light That Failed* (1890) belong to this period of his life.

H. G. Wells served two years (1881–3) of an uncongenial apprenticeship at Hyde's Drapery Establishment, on the corner of St Paul's Rd and King's Rd (gone), the misery of which is reflected in the early part of his novel *Kipps* (1905).

Sir Arthur Conan Doyle first set up in practice as a doctor at 1 Bush Villas, Elm Grove, Southsea (gone), in September 1882, and married in August 1885. It was here that the character of Sherlock Holmes was conceived and first appeared in the detective novel *A Study in Scarlet* (1887). Holmes was modelled on Dr Joseph Bell, under whom Doyle had studied medicine at Edinburgh University (1876), and Dr Watson, the narrator and Holmes's foil, on Doyle's friend Dr James Watson, the president of the Portsmouth Literary and Scientific Society. Other novels written at Portsmouth were *Micah Clarke* (1888), *The Sign of Four* (1890), and *The White Company* (1891). Doyle left for Vienna, to study the eye, in 1889.

Portsmouth appears frequently in the seafaring novels of Captain Marryat and also as the home of Fanny Price in Jane Austen's *Mansfield Park* (1814).

Simon Armitage studied Geography here at Portsmouth Polytechnic; his poem 'True North' describes the journey home from college:

George Meredith's birthplace, on the corner of Broad St. and High St., Portsmouth, *c.* 1920

It's not much to crow about,
the trip from one term at Portsmouth Poly,
all that Falklands business still to come.

And in 'The Stern' he writes of a Falklands widow, and ships leaving Portsmouth Harbour:

Portsmouth Harbour in '82, an afterthought.
The fleet making its way, sharp end first, trailing
a wake in its wake, setting out for the south.
The shape and the taste of the heart in its mouth.

POSTLING *Kent*

Village off the A20, 4 m. N of Hythe. Visible from the road between the village and the junction with the B2068, Stone St., is Pent Farm, rented from 1898 to 1907 by Conrad from Hueffer, with whom he collaborated on *The Inheritors* (1901) and *Romance* (1903). Conrad also wrote *Lord Jim* (1900), *Youth* and *Typhoon* (1902), *Nostromo* (1904), and *The Mirror of the Sea* (1906) while living here.

PYRFORD *Surrey*

Village on the B367, 1 m. SW of West Byfleet. Pyrford Place (rebuilt) in Warren Lane was the home of a lady-in-waiting to Queen Elizabeth, who, after being widowed, became the second wife of the Lord Keeper, Sir Thomas Egerton. They used the house as their country home. On Lady Egerton's death (1600) the house passed to her son Francis Wolley, who gave refuge to his cousin Anne More and Egerton's secretary John Donne after their rash marriage in 1601. Evelyn wrote that 'the house is timber, but commodious, and with one ample dining room, and the hall adorned with paintings of fowle and hunting'. Donne's first two children, Constance and John, were born and probably christened here, but the records of the small Norman church on the hill are missing for that period.

RAMSGATE *Kent*

Coastal resort on the A253. Wickham's attempted elopement with Darcy's sister in Jane Austen's *Pride and Prejudice* (1813) was set here, and here Tom Bertram in *Mansfield Park* (1814) experienced the difficulties of knowing whether young ladies were 'out' or not. Jane Austen herself visited the town, probably in 1803 when her brother Frank was stationed here. Egerton Brydges, a former neighbour in Steventon, last saw her in Ramsgate. Coleridge, an enthusiastic bather, was a regular summer visitor from 1816 when he lived in Highgate.

Karl Marx visited the town on several occasions in the 1850s and 1860s, staying at Hardras St. His holiday pleasures were sometimes confined by troublesome boils.

R. M. Ballantyne, author of *Coral Island* (1858), stayed here researching for his stories *The Lifeboat* (1864) and *The Floating Light of the Goodwin Sands* (1870). The coxswain Isaac Jarman let him sail in the tug accompanying the lifeboat.

Known as the Ram, and detached from the mainland, Ramsgate is the seat of government for what remains of Kent in Russell Hoban's post-Armageddon novel *Riddley Walker* (1980).

READING *Berkshire*

County town, noted for its industries and its university (1926), situated on the Kennet near its confluence with the Thames, 38 m. W of London. Jane Austen and her elder sister Cassandra went to the Abbey School (1785–7), run by Mrs Latournelle, a French émigrée. The school occupied two rooms (now used for plays and lectures) over the Gateway of the ruined Benedictine abbey in Forbury Rd and eventually overflowed into a nearby house (gone). Jane's contemporary Mary Martha Sherwood (remembered especially for *The History of the Fairchild Family*, 1818–47) was also a pupil, as was Mary Russell Mitford, when she came with her parents from *New Alresford to Reading in 1797. A £20,000 lottery prize won when she was 10 had enabled Mary's father, Dr Mitford, a man of extravagant tastes and improvident ways, to move to a larger house, 39 London Rd Ⓟ. This, a substantial red-brick building of the late 18th c., may not have been built for the Mitfords (as has been supposed), though it must have been quite new when they moved in. In 1802 Dr Mitford bought Grazeley Court, a mid-16th-c. farmhouse *c.* 3 m. from Reading, which he pulled down and replaced with a building which he named Bertram House (gone). The Mitfords moved here some time between 1804 and 1806 (the dates are disputed) and stayed until 1820, when they went to *Three Mile Cross.

Oscar Wilde was imprisoned in Reading jail (rebuilt) in Forbury Rd, after being moved from Wandsworth prison in November 1895. He served a two-year sentence of hard labour after a London court found him guilty of homosexual practices, and left prison in 1897,

bankrupt and ruined in health. While in prison he wrote a long, bitter letter to Lord Alfred Douglas (the son of the Marquess of Queensberry, whose denunciation had initiated the proceedings against him), published in part as *De Profundis* (1905) and in full in the *Letters* (ed. R. Hart-Davis, 1962). *The Ballad of Reading Gaol* (1898), written in Paris, where he spent his last few years, is a moving account of his experience in prison:

> I never saw a man who looked
>   With such a wistful eye
> Upon that little tent of blue
>   Which prisoners call the sky . . .
>
> All that we know who lie in gaol
>   Is that the wall is strong;
> And that each day is like a year,
>   A year whose days are long.

In Hardy's *Jude the Obscure* (1895), where Reading becomes 'Aldbrickham', Jude and Arabella are reported to have stayed at the George Hotel.

While living (1936–7) with Wilma Gregory at Padworth 6 m. W, Laurie Lee studied art at the University of Reading.

REDHILL *Surrey*

Town S of London, in 1959 the birthplace of the novelist Nick Hornby. Domestic life in suburban Redhill—with its smells of beer, toast, perfume, and cut grass—is sensuously rendered in Shena MacKay's comic novel *Redhill Rococo* (1986).

REIGATE (pr. 'Rīgate) *Surrey*

Old town on the A25. John Foxe, the martyrologist, was made tutor, by the Duchess of Richmond, to the three children of Henry, Earl of Surrey, the poet beheaded in 1547. They lived in the castle (earthworks now a public garden) until Foxe fled to the Continent on the accession of Queen Mary in 1553.

Harrison Ainsworth often stayed with his invalid brother at Hill View Lodge, now in Glovers Rd, where he wrote *Boscobel* (1872). In 1878 he moved to Belvedere, St Mary's Rd (both houses E of Bell St.), where he died (1882). Katharine Bradley and her niece Edith Cooper lived here in retirement from 1888. They contributed to the American journal *The Dial* as 'Michael Field'.

RINGMER *East Sussex*

Village off the A26, 3 m. NE of Lewes. From 1745 onwards Gilbert White made annual visits to his aunt Rebecca, who lived at Delves House (rebuilt), set among the trees across the common. Many details in *The Natural History of Selborne* (1789) were observed here, including Timothy, his aunt's tortoise. He had written under Timothy's name to his friend 'Heckey Mulso' (later Mrs Chapone), and he took Timothy, inherited with the rest of the property, to *Selborne after his aunt's death in 1780.

RIPE *East Sussex*

Village N of the A27, 6 m. E of Lewes. The 17th-c. weather-boarded White Cottage, in

a lane by The Lamb, was the last home of Malcolm Lowry, author of *Under the Volcano* (1947). His wife found the place, in January 1956, the 'dream cottage' of his doctor's orders, remote yet within reach of fortnightly therapy for manic depression and alcoholism. Here Lowry was able to write again and worked on *October Ferry to Gabriola*, short stories collected later as *Hear Us O Lord from Heaven Thy Dwelling Place*, poems, and the essay on the encroachments on freedom made by McCarthyism, before he died in June 1957. He is buried in the churchyard.

ROCHESTER *Kent*

Cathedral town on the Medway and the A2. Dickens, who spent his youth in neighbouring *Chatham, his honeymoon at *Chalk, and his last years at *Gad's Hill, made many references to the city. The poetic fervour of Mr Pickwick and his friend Snodgrass at their first sight of the Norman castle is tempered by Jingle's 'Ah, fine place! . . . glorious pile—frowning walls— tottering arches—dark nooks—crumbling staircases—.' The Royal Victoria and Bull remembers that it is the Bull Hotel where Pickwick and his creator stayed, and Eastgate House Ⓟ resembles Westgate House. The Charles Dickens Centre at Eastgate House closed in 2004, but the writing chalet removed from Dickens's house at *Gad's Hill may be seen in the garden. *Great Expectations* (1861) opens on the nearby marshes, Miss Havisham's house is modelled on Restoration House in Maidstone Rd, and Uncle Pumblechook's on one of the black-and-white Tudor houses in the High St. 'The Seven Poor Travellers' in *Christmas Stories* features Richard Watts's Hospital, also in the High St. The city becomes 'Dullborough' in *The Uncommercial Traveller* (1860), and the 'Mudfog' of *Mudfog Papers* (1880). It is also 'Cloisterham' of the unfinished *Edwin Drood* (1870), where Eastgate House is again the model for Miss Twinkleton's seminary at the Nun's House, and Uncle Pumblechook's house doubles as the house Ⓟ of Mr Sapsea, auctioneer and mayor. The sinister John Jasper lives over the College Gate and Edwin and Rosa sit under the trees in The Vines to discuss their future. Dickens, who wished to be buried here, has a memorial in the Cathedral.

The four men carrying the remains of their friend Jack Dodds stop at the Bull on their way to *Margate in Graham Swift's novel *Last Orders* (1996).

RODMELL *East Sussex*

Village on the A275, 4 m. S of Lewes. Leonard and Virginia Woolf bought Monk's House (NT), near the church, in 1919. Thought to have been a retreat for the monks of Lewes Priory it was in fact early 18th c. At first they used oil lamps and well water, hardships mitigated by an acre of garden and a view across the Ouse to the hills that Leonard Woolf describes in his autobiography as unchanged since Chaucer's day. One of their earliest visitors was T. S. Eliot, whose 'The Waste Land' they were publishing at their Hogarth Press. They divided their time between Monk's House and their London home until that was bombed in 1940. In 1941 Virginia Woolf drowned herself in the Ouse on the recurrence of her manic-depressive illness. Her ashes are buried in the garden.

ROLVENDEN *Kent*

Village on the A28, 3 m. SW of Tenterden. Frances Burnett, author of *Little Lord Fauntleroy* (1886), came from America and rented Great Maytham Hall, on the Rolvenden Layne road, throughout the 1890s. It is thought she based the overgrown wilderness in *The Secret Garden* (1911) on the high-walled garden here. The house was altered by Lutyens in 1910 and is now flats in carefully tended grounds. A tablet in the church commemorates her.

ROTHERFIELD *East Sussex*

Village to the E of Crowborough, where George du Maurier (who had been born in Paris) was baptized in May 1935.

ROTTINGDEAN *East Sussex*

Coastal resort on the A259, 4 m. E of Brighton. Kipling stayed with his uncle, Edward Burne-Jones, at North End House Ⓟ, and wrote 'Recessional' there. He then lived (1897–1902) at The Elms, across the Green, where a commemorative plaque was placed on the long garden wall by the Kipling Society. Here he wrote *Stalky & Co.* (1899), *Kim* (1901), and the *Just So Stories* (1902). Conrad was one of his visitors. The Grange, built as the vicarage in the early 19th c. and now the Public Library and Art Gallery, has a Kipling room with portraits, letters, and early editions of his works. In 1909 D. H. Lawrence bicycled over the Downs from Croydon, where he was teaching, and lodged in the High St.

ROUSHAM (pr. 'Rausham) HOUSE *Oxfordshire*

Country house E of the A4260, 15 m. N of Oxford, home of the Cottrell-Dormer family and open to the public (www.rousham.org). This 17th-c. house was visited by Pope, Gay, and Horace Walpole, guests of the Dormers and admirers of the gardens, terraces, and temples designed by William Kent about the Cherwell, which runs through the grounds. Walpole wrote that 'The whole is as elegant and antique as if the emperor Julian had selected the most pleasing solitude about Daphne to enjoy a philosophic retirement.' Literary treasures include autograph letters of Gay, Swift, and Pope, Mrs Caesar's copy of Pope's *Works* (1735), inscribed 'from her most obliged and faithful servant', and her volumes of Pope's translation of the *Odyssey*. Mrs Caesar, Pope's patron and friend, whose daughter married into the family, undertook to find subscribers for this work. Portraits of the Caesars and Pope are among those here.

RYDE *Isle of Wight*

Resort on the NE of the island. The American writer Nathaniel Parker Willis, who visited the town in the early days of its popularity (*c.* 1830), wrote:

> Ryde is the most American-looking town I have seen abroad; a cluster of white houses and summery villas on the side of the hill, leaning up from the sea. It is a place of baths, boarding-houses and people of damaged constitutions, with very select society, and quiet and rather primitive habits. The climate is deliciously soft, and the sun seems always to shine there.

RYE *East Sussex*

Port on the Rother and the A259. John Fletcher, the dramatist, Beaumont's collaborator, was born (1579), while his father was priest-in-charge, probably in the Tudor building superseded by the Old Rectory in 1703, but traditionally in the half-timbered Ancient Rectory Ⓟ refronted in 1701, now a shop serving luncheons and tea.

In 1896 Henry James rented Point Hill in Playden (1 m. N) as a change from his London flat. The house, almost covered by a large ash tree, looked across the red roofs of the town to the church. Here he finished *The Spoils of Poynton*, published in 1897 after serialization in the *Atlantic Monthly* as *The Old Things*. In October he moved to the Old Rectory for a short tenancy and then in 1898 bought Lamb House (NT) in West St., his home until his death (1916). *The Wings of the Dove* (1902), *The Ambassadors* (1903), and *The Golden Bowl* (1904) were written in the Garden Room (destroyed 1940) or the upstairs study. He often bicycled in the district and was visited by many writers including Conrad, Chesterton, Stephen Crane, and Wells, who wrote in his autobiography that the house was 'one of the most perfect pieces of suitably furnished Georgian architecture imaginable'. After James's death in London, Lamb House became the home of E. F. Benson, author of the popular Lucia books, which have many scenes in Rye, and two volumes of reminiscences, *As We Were* (1930) and *As We Are* (1932). He was mayor of Rye (1934–7) and gave the W window in the church in memory of his parents; another window commemorates his brother A. C. Benson.

The Mermaid inn, which features in many smuggling stories, was bought by Richard Aldington's mother in 1913. It became a club, used by servicemen in the First World War, and Aldington's wartime experiences produced his novel *Death of a Hero* (1929).

Jeake's House was the home of the American poet and novelist Conrad Aiken during the Depression. Malcolm Lowry, whose first novel,

The Garden Room, Lamb House, Rye, home of Henry James and, later, E. F. Benson. Drawing given to Henry James by Edward Warren

Ultramarine (1933), owed much to Aiken's *Blue Voyage* (1927), spent his Cambridge vacations (1929–32) with Aiken and his family. Ford Madox Ford's *The Half Moon* (1909), the early chapters of his *Some Do Not* (1924), and Thackeray's unfinished *Denis Duval* (1864–7) are set in Rye.

St Lawrence *Isle of Wight*

Village 2 m. W of Ventnor, with the cliffs above and the sea below. Alfred Noyes lived (1929–58) at Lisle Combe, a house he describes in *Orchard's Bay* (1939), and where he planted a cedar from *Swainston and a yew from *Farringford. His *Collected Poems* were published in 1950, and a further volume of verse, *Letter to Lucian*, in 1956. His autobiography, *Two Worlds for Memory* (1953), was written here.

St Mary Bourne *Berkshire*

Downland village NE of Andover. The short-story writer, novelist, and critic V. S. Pritchett, encouraged by the success of his novel *Mr Beluncle* (1951), moved to Wadwick House with his wife, Dorothy, in 1952.

St Mary in the Marsh *Kent*

Small village 3 m. SW of Dymchurch. E. Nesbit, who died at the Long Boat, Jesson St Mary, near Dymchurch, where she had spent many happy holidays with her family and friends, was buried in the churchyard here. Her second husband, whom she called the Skipper, carved the wooden name plate over her grave. John Davidson describes a visit to Dymchurch in 'In Romney Marsh', where

> Masts in the offing wagged their tops:
> The winging waves peal'd on the shore;
> The saffron beach, all diamond drops
> And beads of surge, prolonged the roar.

Sandgate *Kent*

Coastal village now in the Hythe and Folkestone urban area. Jocelyn Brooke spent his childhood autumns and winters in a family house on the Undercliff and lovingly evokes the place and its local flora in his Proustian memoir-cum-*Bildungsroman*-cum-travel-book-cum-botanical-textbook *The Military Orchid* (1948)—'bathed in the keen, windy light of spring mornings, a seaside gaiety and brilliance haunted by the thud of waves on the shingle and the tang of seaweed'. The lifeboat station at Sandgate, 'that extraordinary Gothic structure, more like a chapel than a boathouse', forms a central motif in *The Goose Cathedral* (1950), the last volume in Brooke's semi-autobiographical trilogy:

> We called it the 'Goose Cathedral' on account of the geese which, at that period, waddled about the shingle patch surrounding it . . . Anything less like one's idea of a lifeboat station it would have been hard, indeed, to imagine. Seeing it from a passing bus, one would have supposed it to be some kind of Nonconformist tabernacle—a spiky and ornate affair in pseudo-Ruskinian

Gothic. Yet who, after all, would build a chapel just here, on this desolate stretch of coast, within a few yards of the sea itself?

Sandhurst *Berkshire*

Small town 3 m. SW of London. The novelist Ian Fleming proved a not very successful cadet at the Royal Military Academy in 1926.

Sandwich *Kent*

Old town on the A256 and the A257, 12 m. E of Canterbury, once the premier Cinque Port. Tom Paine, who set up business as a staymaker in 1759, married Mary Lambert at St Peter's Church and lived at 20 New St. Ⓟ. His business failed and he moved to Dover, where his wife died in 1760. Sandwich is the 'Sunwich Port' of W. W. Jacobs's comic stories of longshoremen.

The novelist Ian Fleming owned a house at St Margaret's Bay nearby. He played golf at the Royal St George's Golf Club at Sandwich Bay. The club was the basis for the famous match between James Bond and Auric Goldfinger in his novel *Goldfinger* (1959). He died in Kent on 12 August 1964.

Selborne *Hampshire*

Village on the B3006, 5 m. S of Alton. Gilbert White, 18th-c. naturalist and writer, was born at the vicarage and lived at The Wakes (now the Oates Memorial Library and Museum and the Gilbert White Museum), from 1729 until his death in 1793. The Museum contains personal relics and editions of *The Natural History and Antiquities of Selborne* (1789), which he wrote at The Wakes, and in the grounds can be seen the pathway which he laid down to enable him to reach his bird-watching arbour, the ha-ha which he dug, and his famous sundial. He is buried in the churchyard, his grave, to the N of the chancel, marked by a

simple headstone with only his initials and the date of his death.

Sevenoaks Weald *Kent*

Village off the A21, 3 m. S of Sevenoaks. Edward Thomas, with his wife and children, rented (1904–6) Else's Farm above the railway, opposite the inn still known locally as The Shant. He often spent 16 hours a day on reviews and other commissions but was always short of money. He made fortnightly journeys to London to find work, and his friends, including Edward Garnett and his young son David, came at weekends. Thomas rented Stidolph's Cottage in Eggpie Lane to write in and wore a path across the fields to its door. There he installed W. H. Davies to write *The Autobiography of a Super-Tramp* (1908), which Davies recounted to him through tobacco fumes by the fire at the farmhouse. Davies broke his wooden leg there and the village carpenter made a makeshift replacement from Thomas's design.

Beyond the village green stands the ancient timber-framed house of Long Barn. The small manor house, dating from the second half of the 14th c., was reputedly the birthplace of Caxton, and used to be known locally as Caxton's House. After years of neglect and dilapidation it was restored by Mrs Gilchrist Thompson, wife of a local vicar, and sold in 1915 to Harold Nicolson and his wife, Victoria Sackville-West. They lived there until 1930, during which time they created a delightful garden and extended the house by the addition of a 16th-c. barn taken down in the grounds and reconstructed as an L-shaped wing. They were visited by numerous political, literary, and artistic friends, including members of the Bloomsbury Group, especially Virginia Woolf while she was writing *Orlando* (1928). She recorded her love of the place and her devotion to Vita Sackville-West in her *Letters* (1929–31).

Watercolour by S. H. Grimm, 1776, of Selborne, with Gilbert White's house to the right

After the Nicolsons moved to *Sissinghurst Castle in 1930 Long Barn changed hands several times, but so far has remained unaltered in character and tranquillity.

SHAMLEY GREEN *Surrey*

Village halfway between Guildford and Cranleigh. T. S. Eliot stayed in the village with his friend Hope Mirrlees for much of the Second World War, commuting into London for meetings at Faber and Faber and taking country walks with hat and stick. He wrote 'Burnt Norton' from *Four Quartets* here.

SHANKLIN *Isle of Wight*

Resort on the SE coast adjacent to Sandown. John Keats lodged at Mrs Williams's house, Eglantine Cottage, 76 High St. Ⓟ, in July and August 1819. He completed the first book of *Lamia*, and with Charles Armitage Brown started the drama *Otho the Great*.

H. W. Longfellow, the American author of the poems *Hiawatha* (1855) and *Tales of a Wayside Inn* (1863), which contains 'Paul Revere's Ride', stayed at The Crab inn in the Old Village in July 1868. He wrote to a friend that he was staying in 'a lovely little thatch-roofed inn, all covered with ivy'. The inscription that he was asked to write now embellishes the fountain outside:

> O traveller, stay thy weary feet;
> Drink of this fountain pure and sweet;
> It flows for rich and poor the same.
> Then go thy way, remembering still
> The wayside well beneath the hill,
> The cup of water in His name.

SHEPPERTON *Surrey*

Large village 3 m. E of Chertsey. The satirical novelist T. L. Peacock bought (1823) a riverside house Ⓟ at the entrance to Walton Lane in Lower Halliford (then a separate hamlet) for his mother, where he could spend weekends and holidays from his post in the India Office. After his marriage to Jane Griffith, whom he had met eight years before in Wales, he bought the house adjoining his mother's and turned them into one (later known as Elmbank). After his retirement (1856) he settled here permanently. *Memoirs of Shelley* (1858) and *Gryll Grange* (1860) were written here. His daughter married the novelist George Meredith, who joined him (1853) for a while but, after disagreements, moved to Vine Cottage across the green. Meredith was deserted by his wife in 1858. She died in 1861 and is buried in the churchyard, where her tombstone has lines written by her father, who was buried (1866) in the cemetery.

As a boy the hymn writer J. M. Neale was tutored at the rectory, which he often revisited after his ordination. Author of 'Jerusalem the Golden', 'Good King Wenceslas', and many other hymns as well known, he also wrote the novel *Shepperton Manor* (1844), about the village in the 17th c. Part of this was written at the rectory.

J. G. Ballard, who has lived in the town since the 1960s, has set a number of his novels here, including, in part, the controversial and disturbing *Crash* (1973), whose narrator (named Ballard) lives here, and the surrealist fantasy *The Unlimited Dream Company* (1979), in which Shepperton is strangely transformed after a young pilot crashes his plane into the Thames:

> The once immaculate lawns and flower-beds were overrun with tropical plants. Palmettos, banana trees and glossy rubber plants jostled for a place in the vivid light. Lilies and bizarre fungi covered the grass like marine plants on a drained sea-bed. The air was filled with the racket of unfamiliar birds.

SHERMANBURY *West Sussex*

Hamlet 2 m. N of Henfield, on the A281. A tree-lined drive S of the bridge over the Adur leads to Mock Bridge House, where Margaret Fairless Barber spent her last two summers (1900–1). She took the name of Dowson, the family by whom she was 'adopted' and who nursed her during her prolonged illness. She continued to write here, under the pseudonym 'Michael Fairless', the essays started in Chelsea and later published as *The Roadmender*. 'There is a place waiting for me under the firs in a quiet churchyard,' she wrote, 'and her grave with a tall wooden cross is in Ashurst churchyard, 2 m. W.

SHILLINGFORD *Oxfordshire*

Little village 10 m. SE of Oxford, on the A4074. W. B. Yeats stayed here with his wife and child between April and June 1921, having let their house in Oxford for the summer months. They rented Minchen's Cottage, a modest two-storey cottage on the W side of the road to Warborough, hoping to go to Ireland, as Yeats said in a letter, 'at the first sign of a lull in the storm there as George [his wife] pines for Ballylee'. (The 'storm' was the outbreak of violence that had followed the meeting of the Dáil in 1919 and its subsequent suppression.) While he was in Shillingford, Yeats began writing 'Meditations in Time of Civil War', the first of a series of poems finished at *Thoor Ballylee in 1922, *Seven Poems and a Fragment*, which he described as 'a lamentation over lost peace and hope'. From Shillingford the Yeats family moved over to *Thame.

SHIPBOURNE (pr. 'Shibbon') *Kent*

Village on the A227, 5 m. SE of Sevenoaks. The poet Christopher Smart was born (1722) at Fairlawn, the country house ½ m. N of the church, where his father was steward.

SHIPLAKE *Oxfordshire*

Village on the A4155, 6 m. NE of Reading. Tennyson married Emily Sellwood here. The reconciliation after their broken engagement occurred after he had sent a copy of the elegies on the death of Arthur Hallam to his friend Rawnsley, the vicar whose wife was a cousin of Emily's and in favour of the marriage. Doubts Emily and her parents had felt about his religious beliefs were dispelled and they were married a fortnight after *In Memoriam* (1850), the title chosen by Emily for the elegies, was published. Before her wedding Emily stayed at Holmwood, the Georgian house 1 m. W. In the coach to *Pangbourne, the first stop on their honeymoon, Tennyson wrote a poem to Rawnsley, who had performed the ceremony, and whose three children were bridesmaids.

The church, on a knoll above the Thames, has a memorial to James Granger, vicar from 1746 to his death in 1776, whose *Biographical History of England* (1769) included blank pages to be filled with illustrations to suit the owner's taste. To 'Grangerize' became a popular pastime.

Swinburne made many visits to Holmwood, his parents' home from 1865–79, usually to recuperate from his intemperate life in London. He was working on *Tristram of Lyonesse* in 1869 and wrote 'On the Cliffs' in the summer of 1879 after a longer illness than usual had prevented his writing from the November of the previous year. The novelist Watts-Dunton visited Holmwood that summer, and an arrangement for the tenancy of 2 The Pines (see LONDON: PUTNEY) jointly with Swinburne was agreed upon. Eric Blair ('George Orwell') lived as a boy at Roselawn, Station Rd.

SHIPLEY *West Sussex*

Village off the A272, 7 m. SW of Horsham. Hilaire Belloc lived from 1906 to his death in 1953 at King's Land, a house dating from the 15th c. Much of his work, including light verse, essays, novels (some illustrated by his friend G. K. Chesterton), and studies of the French Revolution, was written here. His love of Sussex is shown in the lines from 'The South Country':

> I never get between the pines
> But I smell the Sussex air;
> Nor I never come on a belt of sand
> But my home is there.

Shipley Mill Ⓟ near his house has been restored as a memorial to him.

SHOREHAM *Kent*

Village off the A225, 5 m. N of Sevenoaks. William Blake was often visited in London by a group of young painters including Samuel Palmer, whom he most influenced, and when Palmer moved here to the Water House in 1826 Blake, although in poor health (he died in 1827), came to stay with him. The group, known locally as the Extollagers, roamed day and night over the countryside, reciting poetry and carrying painting equipment and camp stools. Blake accompanied them on a ghost hunt to the ruined castle and demonstrated his telepathic powers by foretelling Palmer's unexpected appearance well before it occurred.

The Regency Dunstall Priory with its round tower was the childhood home of Lord Dunsany. He inherited the house in 1916 and lived here intermittently. He died at his Irish home, Dunsany Castle in Co. Meath, but was buried at his request in the churchyard here, where there is a memorial. His short stories,

Pilgrims at the Shrine of St Thomas Becket, Canterbury. The city's status as a pilgrimage centre features in the poetry of Chaucer, and Beckett's murder in plays by Tennyson and T. S. Eliot

plays, and verse are largely myth and fantasy but *The Curse of the Wise Woman* (1935) is partly autobiographical.

The novelist and short-story writer Shena Mackay spent much of her childhood in the village in the 1950s. *Old Crow* (1967) is set in Shoreham and, with its 'hop pickers, painters, ramblers and cyclists', it is also the 'Stonebridge' of her novel *The Orchard on Fire* (1995).

SHOREHAM-BY-SEA *West Sussex*

Port and sailing resort on the Adur, W of Hove. Woodview, the house in George Moore's novel *Esther Waters* (1894), is said to be modelled on Buckingham House (gone). The grounds are now a public park. Esther visits the entertainments at Swiss Gardens and undergoes many disasters before finding peace with her former employer, widowed and impoverished, and living in a corner of the old house.

SHOTTERMILL *Surrey*

Residential district, 1 m. SW of Haslemere, on the A287. George Eliot rented a furnished house called Brookbank here with George Lewes from May to August in 1871. The house, not far from the railway, was later divided in two, Brookbank and Middlemarch, and the yew tree under which George Eliot sat while writing *Middlemarch* (1872) is just visible in the garden behind. Tennyson first met her here, and used to come over from Aldworth and read his poems to her. She liked being here so much, where 'there were no interruptions except welcome ones', that on leaving Brookbank she decided to prolong her stay and moved across the road to Cherrimans before returning to London in September.

SISSINGHURST CASTLE *Kent*

Part of an Elizabethan manor house (NT) off the A262, 3 m. N of Cranbrook, restored from 1930 by Victoria Sackville-West and her husband, Harold Nicolson, who also planted the gardens together. They made their home in the 15th-c. South Cottage, where Harold Nicolson wrote biographies including *King George V* (1953), and the essay *The English Sense of Humour* (1947). He died there in 1968. Victoria Sackville-West had her study in the Elizabethan tower Ⓟ, where she wrote the novels *The Dark Island* (1934) and *Pepita* (1937), and the biographical study *Saint Joan of Arc* (1936). An oast house on the premises now houses the printing press used by Virginia and Leonard Woolf to print the first edition of *The Waste Land* (1922) and other early works of the Hogarth Press. The Turret houses diaries, letters, and a series of pictures showing the restoration of the house and gardens. Victoria Sackville-West died (1962) in the 16th-c. Priest's House by the White Garden, which was also the last home of the poet and novelist Richard Church (d. 1972).

In 1760, when the house was still intact, Edward Gibbon in the Hampshire Militia was appointed to guard the 1,750 French prisoners of war held there. He complained in his *Journal* of 'the inconceivable dirtiness of the season' in which his few men walked from their 'wretched barracks' to undertake guard duty of so many.

SLOUGH *Berkshire*

Town and business centre W of London. The town is famously vilified in John Betjeman's 'Slough'.

SOULDERN *Oxfordshire*

Quiet village off the B4100, 8 m. SE of Banbury. Wordsworth wrote the sonnet 'On a Parsonage in Oxfordshire' when staying in 1820 with his friend Robert Jones at the rectory (gone, site below the garden of the present one).

SOUTHAMPTON *Hampshire*

Historic city, seaport, and university town, situated at the head of Southampton Water, the estuary of the Test, on a peninsula bounded on the E side by the Itchen. Isaac Watts was born here (17 July 1674), of Puritan stock. A plaque near the back entrance of a chain store in Above Bar St. records that 'On this site stood the Above Bar Congregational Church founded in 1662 and destroyed by enemy action in 1940. Among those who worshipped here was Isaac Watts, author and hymn writer.' Watts was born in the first Meeting House on this spot, though shortly after his birth his family moved to 41 French St. (also bombed, and later demolished). He attended King Edward VI School and went on to the Nonconformist Academy at Newington Green (London). His writings include sermons, philosophical treatises, poems, and educational manuals, but he is chiefly remembered for his hymns, especially 'Our God, our help in ages past', 'When I survey the wondrous cross', and 'Jesus shall reign where'er the sun'. His statue, carved by a local sculptor, R. C. Lucas, stands in Watts Park, N of the Civic Centre, and has panels on three sides of the pedestal, showing him as a young poet, a teacher, and a philosopher. The last panel depicts a terrestrial globe and a telescope, with a quotation from Dr Johnson: 'He has taught the art of reasoning and the science of the stars.' The Church of the Ascension, Bitterne Park, has four memorial windows illustrating seven of his best-known hymns, and St Andrew's Church in Brunswick Pl. contains his sculptured head and shoulders, rescued from the ruin of the Above Bar Congregational Church. The modern Isaac Watts Memorial Church (dedicated 1960) stands at the junction of Winchester Rd with Luccomb Rd.

Charles Dibdin, dramatist and songwriter, was also a native of Southampton (born 15 Mar. 1745) and lived here until he was 11, when he became a chorister at Winchester Cathedral. After his father's death he went to London, where he wrote songs (including 'Tom Bowling', 'Poor Jack', and other sea songs), plays, and novels. He is commemorated by a stone tablet erected (1814) by the Southampton Literary and Philosophical Society on the W front of Holy Rood Church (ruined) in Bernard St., on the E side of High St.

In the 18th c. Southampton became fashionable as a spa, assembly rooms were built, and many distinguished visitors came and went, including Pope, who stayed in 1734 with his friend Lord Peterborough at Bevis Mount (outside the city gates, 1 m. N, the estate now occupied by suburban houses), from which he visited *Netley Abbey; and Gray, who also stayed at Bevis Mount (1755 and 1764) and went over to Netley.

In 1806 Jane Austen came from Bath with her mother and sister Cassandra, and stayed in lodgings with her brother Frank. They moved in 1807 to 3 Castle Sq., a roomy, comfortable house (gone), which stood near the Juniper Berry public house in modern Upper Bugle St., with a pleasant garden, bounded on one side by the city walls, on the top of which it was possible to walk and enjoy extensive views. The Austens stayed here until the spring of 1809 and during part of this time Jane looked after her two young nephews, who came to stay after their mother's death. On one occasion they had a little water party on the Itchen and the boys rowed part of the way from the ferry to Northam, where they landed and walked home. In the evening Jane introduced them to the card game Speculation.

Robert Pollok (1795–1827), a Scottish poet born at the little farm of Moorhouse, 10 m. S of Glasgow, is commemorated by a red granite obelisk in the old churchyard of St Nicholas, Millbrook. He qualified as a minister, but ill health prevented his taking a regular appointment. On 1 September 1827, suffering from consumption, he came to stay with his sister at Shirley Common in the hope of recuperating, but died a fortnight later. His religious–philosophical poem *The Course of Time* was published in 10 books in 1827 and went through many editions in Britain and America. There is another monument to him at Logan's Well on the road from Glasgow to Kilmarnock, 3 m. S of Newton Mearns.

The centenary of the death of another writer was celebrated on 5 March 1967 when a brass plate was unveiled on the London Hotel, Terminus Ter., recording that 'Charles Browne, known to the world as Artemus Ward, died in the hotel which formerly stood opposite this spot, March 6th, 1867'. The former hotel, Radley's, is now the Royal Mail House. Browne was a popular American humorous writer, well known for his comments on life in the character of Artemus Ward, the travelling showman. He was taken ill on the boat from Jersey and brought to Southampton, where he died. His body was eventually taken back to his birthplace, Waterford, Maine.

George Saintsbury, literary historian and critic, was born (23 Oct. 1845) in a house (gone) which stood at the corner of Briton St. and Orchard Pl. After his retirement from the chair of Rhetoric and English Literature at Edinburgh in 1915 he spent a few months in

The Botanic Garden, Oxford. The garden provided inspiration to Lewis Carroll and J. R. R. Tolkien, and figures in Philip Pullman's novel trilogy 'His Dark Materials'

Southampton before settling in Bath, where he died (1933). He is buried in the Old Cemetery at Southampton.

Southampton is the 'Bevishampton' of Meredith's *Beauchamp's Career* (1876).

SOUTH HARTING *West Sussex*

Village on the B2146, 4 m. SE of Petersfield. Alexander Pope used to stay at Ladyholt Park (now gone), the home of his friend John Caryll. Anthony Trollope lived at the Grange Ⓟ for 18 months during 1880–2. It is said that he wrote standing at a desk upstairs, rode every morning before breakfast, and shocked the village with his weekend parties. Trollope relics may be seen in the church.

SOUTHWATER *West Sussex*

Village off the A24, 5 m. S of Horsham. In 1895 Wilfrid Scawen Blunt took possession of Newbuildings Place, which came into his family in 1757, and commissioned a tapestry illustrating Botticelli's *Spring* from William Morris. He entertained his many friends here, including Yeats, who read his poems aloud, and Belloc, a good neighbour at *Shipley. In 1907 Francis Thompson visited and Blunt remarked in *My Diaries* (1920) that he was not long for this world. Padraic Colum also visited from *Greatham, where he was spending his honeymoon. Cunninghame Graham's essay on his friend in *Redeemed* (1927) mentions the ride in the woods behind the house, where Blunt chose to be buried, and the great grass mound of the grave between the row of new yew trees that he had planted under the oaks. Today the tomb, inscribed with lines from Blunt's *Collected Poems* (1914), is overshadowed by these tall yews. The essay also mentions the Arab horses bred here, and in the house 'the newelled staircase . . . the priest's secret

chamber, the prints of horses . . . from the Godolphin Arab down to his own Messaud'.

SPELSBURY *Oxfordshire*

Village on the B4026, 9 m. NW of Woodstock. John Wilmot, 2nd Earl of Rochester, after the deathbed repentance avowed by Bishop Burnet, was buried (1680) in the vault beneath the church. There are memorials here to the Lees of Ditchley, into which family his mother married.

STANSTED *West Sussex*

Hamlet 2 m. NE of Havant off the B2149 at Westbourne. Stansted Chapel was rebuilt (1817) in the Gothic style from a 15th-c. core by the owner of Stansted House, Lewis Way, who wished to found a college to convert the Jews and then settle them in a permanent homeland. Keats attended the impressive service of dedication, driving over from *Bedhampton, and used descriptions of carvings, tapestries, and carpets in the 18th-c. house, and the stained glass of the chapel, in 'The Eve of St. Agnes' and 'The Eve of St. Mark'. Anglican services are held here and the E window is unusual in having Jewish emblems. Lord Bessborough's *A Place in the Forest* (1958) gives the history of the house.

STANTON HARCOURT *Oxfordshire*

Village on the B4449, 10 m. W of Oxford. Near the church is a 15th-c. building known as Pope's Tower, which was part of the former manor house belonging to the Harcourt family. Alexander Pope was lent a room on the top floor by the first Viscount Harcourt, so that he could write his translation of the *Iliad* in peace, and here he finished the fifth volume in 1718. The tower is not open to the public. In a letter to Martha Blount (Aug. 1718) Pope tells the story of John Hewet and Sarah Drew, young

rustic lovers who were killed by lightning in the harvest field and buried together in the churchyard. Pope and John Gay were both touched by the story and persuaded Lord Harcourt to erect a little monument over the grave, with an epitaph by Pope engraved on it. Goldsmith introduces Gay's version of the story into *The Vicar of Wakefield* (1766), where Sophia Primrose says, 'There is something so pathetic in the description that I have read it an hundred times with new rapture.' But Lady Mary Wortley Montagu was less touched by pathos. In reply to a letter from Pope enclosing two versions of his proposed epitaph she remarked, 'I must applaud your good nature in supposing that your pastoral lovers . . . would have lived in everlasting joy and harmony, if the lightning had not interrupted their scheme of happiness,' and offered a more cynical epitaph of her own, ending:

> For had they seen the next year's sun,
> A beaten wife, and cuckold swain
> Had jointly curs'd the marriage chain;
> Now they are happy in their doom,
> FOR POPE HATH WROTE UPON THEIR TOMB.

On the N side of the church is Wesley's Cottage, where John and Charles Wesley and their sister Kezia used to stay when they visited the vicar.

STANTON ST JOHN *Oxfordshire*

Village on the B4027, 5 m. NE of Oxford, where Milton's grandfather lived. A. E. Coppard rented (1919–22) Shepherd's Pit, Bayswater, a small cottage with a barn in a grassy hollow off the road to Oxford. He used to write at an old table outside his 'yaller door' that the locals laughed at, and on fine nights slept out and was awakened by whitethroats. He once played in a cricket match between Stanton and Islip, watched by *Garsington Manor guests, and occasionally went to The Star and The George. Few people called except the postman until Harold Taylor arrived on a bicycle to offer to publish his collected stories *Adam and Eve and Pinch Me* (1921) as the first volume for the Golden Cockerel Press. His verse *Hips and Haws*, and the stories *Clorinda Walks in Heaven*, followed in 1922.

STEEP *Hampshire*

Village at the foot of Stoner Hill on an unclassified road 2 m. N of Petersfield. Edward Thomas lived (1913–16) at Yewtree Cottage, one of a group of semi-detached cottages on the road to the church. He had previously lived (1906–9) at Berryfield Cottage, c. 1 m. from Ashford, near Steep, so that his son Mervyn could go to school at nearby Bedales, and then at Wick Green (also spelt Week Green) at the top of the hill, where a house was built for him by Geoffrey Lupton, a master at Bedales and a disciple of William Morris. The house (later the Bee House, Cockshutt Lane) was the work of local craftsmen and commanded a splendid view: 'Sixty miles of South Downs at one glance', but Thomas and his family never felt at home in it, as he explains in the poem

Wilfrid Scawen Blunt (centre) and fellow poets at Newbuildings Place, Southwater, West Sussex, in 1914. Yeats is on his right and Pound on his left

'Wind and Mist'. Rupert Brooke, many of whose friends had been at Bedales, spent some days at Wick Green, in the summer of 1910, reading his poems to Thomas. After Thomas moved to Yewtree Cottage he kept on the study, where he could house his books and have solitude for writing. Half the room was used as an apiary and when Ernest Rhys visited him he remarked: 'The bees seemed a natural part of his equipment on a hot day, and you could smell the honey in his own hive.' A large sarsen stone in a clearing on the slope of the Shoulder of Mutton Hill records the dedication of the hillside to Thomas's memory. The place can be found by following Cockshutt Lane as far as Old Litten Lane and then turning down the footpath to Steep. On the S wall of the church two lancet windows, with glass engraved by Laurence Whistler, commemorate the centenary of Thomas's birth.

Thomas Sturge Moore, poet and art critic, lived (1922–32) in the village at Hillcroft Ⓟ, not far from Yewtree Cottage.

STEEPLE ASTON *Oxfordshire*

Village 8 m. W of Bicester, the home from 1956 of Iris Murdoch and her husband, John Bayley. Their famously chaotic house there, Cedar Lodge, would be their home for 30 years.

STEVENTON *Hampshire*

Small village *c.* 8 m. SW of Basingstoke, between the A30 and the B3400. Jane Austen was born in the rectory, the seventh child of George Austen, the rector of this and the neighbouring parish of Deane for over 40 years. The site of the house (demolished in the 19th c.) is marked by a metal pump, the successor of an old family pump, which stands in a field by the lane leading to the church. Jane Austen lived here for the first 25 years of her life, as recorded in a memorial in the church, and by the time she was 23 had written *Sense and Sensibility*, *Pride and Prejudice*, and *Northanger Abbey*, although they were not published until many years later. A reproduction of a drawing of the rectory can be seen at her home at *Chawton. Ashe House, about 2 m. N of Steventon, off the B3400, was the rectory of Ashe and home of the Lefroys, friends of the Austens. Mrs Lefroy was the sister of Sir Egerton Brydges, who describes in his *Autobiography* (1834) the 'small parsonage-house' in the adjoining parish, where he lived for two years after his marriage in 1786. Jane Austen's niece Anna married Benjamin Lefroy, youngest son of the rector and later his successor.

STEYNING (pr. 'Stenning) *West Sussex*

Village on the A283, 5 m. from the S coast. Yeats often stayed at the Chantry House Ⓟ above the small green in Church St. in the 1930s, the home of Miss Shackleton Heald. He began his play *Purgatory* here and a new Crazy Jane poem.

The poet and playwright Ted Walker was educated at Steyning Grammar School in the 1940s and 1950s.

STOKE POGES *Buckinghamshire*

Large village on the B416. Thomas Gray often visited his mother, who in 1742 came to live with her sister at West End (now Stoke Court). Gray wrote 'Ode on a Distant Prospect of Eton College' here and is thought to have begun *c.* 1742 the 'Elegy in a Country Churchyard', finished here in 1750 and inspired in part by the death of Richard West, his friend at Eton. Gray's poem 'A Long Story' is set in the Manor House, where he visited Lady Cobham and Henrietta Speed. Near the church is a solid monument (NT) erected in 1799 inscribed with lines from his poems. Gray, who wrote the inscription on his mother's tomb in the churchyard, is buried with her.

STORRINGTON *West Sussex*

Small town on the A283, 10 m. NW of Worthing. The Norbertine monks of Storrington Priory, beyond the parish church, cared for Francis Thompson after he had been rescued from vagrancy and destitution in London by Alice and Wilfred Meynell. Many of his poems, including 'The Hound of Heaven', were written here.

STOWE *Buckinghamshire*

Former ducal seat, now a public school, off the A422, NW of Buckingham. The landscaped gardens here derive from the early 18th-c. desire to free design from the geometric bonds of the former age and to develop gardens similar to Milton's description in *Paradise Lost* where Man (as hoped for by Locke) would be ennobled by Nature. Charles Bridgeman's design for an octagonal lake was changed, by the ideas of Sir Richard Temple and his friends at the Kit-Cat Club, into a serpentine channel. Kent developed the ha-ha (introduced by Bridgeman) to enable wilder country to appear in vistas unbroken by hedges, and created the Elysian Fields and the Grecian Valley. The Temple of Ancient Virtue and the Temple of British Worthies are also by Kent. In the latter are busts including those of Bacon, Shakespeare, Locke, and Milton. Pope, who was a frequent visitor, addressed the first of his *Moral Essays* (1733) to his host, then Lord Cobham. He describes the aims of the designers in his *Epistle to Lord Burlington*:

Consult the Genius of the Place in all;
That tells the Waters or to rise, or fall,
Or helps th'ambitious Hill the heavens to scale,
Or scoops in circling theatres the Vale,
Calls in the Country, catches opening glades,
Joins willing woods, and varies shades from shades,
Now breaks, or now directs, th'intending Lines;
Paints as you plant, and, as you work, designs.
Still follow Sense, of ev'ry Art the Soul.
Parts answering parts shall slide into a whole,
Spontaneous beauties all around advance,
Start ev'n from Difficulty, strike from Chance;
Nature shall join you, Time shall make it grow
A Work to wonder at—perhaps a STOW.

Congreve spent many summers here and Cobham commemorated his wit by a statue,

designed by Kent, showing Comedy in the guise of a monkey holding up a mirror to life.

T. H. White's novel *Mistress Masham's Repose* (1947) is set at Stowe. He was a master at the school from 1932 to 1936 and then lived for three years in Stowe Ridings, a cottage on the estate, where he wrote *The Goshawk* (1951), an account of how he trained a hawk.

SUNNINGWELL *Oxfordshire*

Small village on the road between Abingdon and Cumnor. Roger Bacon, 13th-c. philosopher and scientist, who came to Oxford *c.* 1250, is believed to have frequented the church tower to study astronomy and test his theories about making telescopes. A model of the church in its 13th-c. setting stands in the unique seven-sided Jewel Porch (built *c.* 1550–2, when John Jewel was rector) and shows Bacon at the top of the tower in the habit of a Franciscan friar, with an astrolabe in his hand.

SUTTON COURTENAY *Oxfordshire*

A large, straggling village on the B4016, between Abingdon and Didcot. A simple headstone in the churchyard near the end of an avenue of yews marks the grave of Eric Blair (1903–50), author, under the pen-name 'George Orwell', of the political satires *Animal Farm* (1945) and *Nineteen Eighty-Four* (1949), and other novels and essays.

SWAINSTON MANOR *Isle of Wight*

18th-c. house (burnt in a 1941 air raid; now a hotel) off the B3401, with a 13th-c. oratory, home of Sir John Simeon. Tennyson often came over from *Farringford (6 m. W) and *Maud* (1855) evolved from a conversation the two men had here and the poem is set in the garden with the cedars. Tennyson called Sir John 'the prince of courtesy' in the lines 'Swainston', which he wrote after his death.

SWALLOWFIELD *Berkshire*

Village on the A33 a few miles S of Reading. This was the last home of Mary Russell Mitford, who moved here from Three Mile Cross in 1851 and published her *Recollections of a Literary Life* the following year. She died on 10 January 1855 and was buried in the churchyard, where a tall stone cross, erected by public subscription, marks her grave. The church, peacefully withdrawn from the main road, is described in 'The Visit' in *Our Village* (1824–32), 'peeping out from amongst magnificent yew-trees'. Miss Mitford's cottage has been enlarged and altered out of recognition.

SWANBOURNE *Buckinghamshire*

Village on the B4032, 2 m. E of Winslow. Swanbourne House, not to be confused with the newer house, now a school, was the home of Lady Fremantle (née Elizabeth Wynne), the chief contributor to the *Wynne Diaries* (3 vols, 1935–40). She and her sisters spent their early lives on the Continent and Elizabeth married Captain Thomas Fremantle in 1797 at Lady Hamilton's house in Naples. The diaries

Detail from a photograph by Lady Ottoline Morrell of a group at Tidmarsh Mill House, 1923, with Dora Carrington (left) and Lytton Strachey (centre)

include accounts given by the three sisters of their lives between 1789 and 1820, and some letters and the journal of Captain, later Admiral, Sir Thomas Fremantle, a friend of Nelson.

SWINBROOK *Oxfordshire*

Stone village on the Windrush, 3 m. E of Burford. Nancy Mitford's father built a house in the village, to which the family moved after leaving the Jacobean manor at *Asthall (1 m. SE) in 1926. Nancy disliked the house, but its heating system provided the inspiration for the 'Hons' Cupboard'—the linen cupboard to which the children resort to swap secrets and discuss the conduct of their elders—in her satirical novel *The Pursuit of Love* (1945). She is buried in the churchyard.

TANGMERE *West Sussex*

RAF station, off the A27, 4 m. NE of Chichester, where H. E. Bates was stationed in 1942. He wrote the popular collections of short stories of Air Force men and women under the pseudonym 'Flying Officer X'. He also finished here the novel *Fair Stood the Wind for France* (1944).

TAPPINGTON HALL FARM *Kent*

Remaining part of an Elizabethan mansion off the A260, 2 m. SW of Denton, inherited by R. H. Barham's father. Barham's *Ingoldsby Legends* (1840), first published in *Bentley's Miscellany* and the *New Monthly Magazine*, are humorous and grotesque verses based on old legends. Many ghost stories and anecdotes are about the county and two are set in Tappington itself. 'The Spectre of Tappington' recalls a murder committed in the Hall, and

Tappington Moor in 'The Hand of Glory' is Barham Downs to the N.

TEMPLE GROVE *East Sussex*

Country house at Heron's Ghyll, 3 m. NE of Maresfield, now a school. Coventry Patmore, who had completed the four parts of his long poem on married love, *The Angel in the House*, in 1862, bought the 400–acre estate, which he named Heron's Ghyll, and moved here with his family and his second wife in 1865. He was most successful in improving the estate but wrote no poetry while here. The house has stained-glass medallions representing the heroines lauded in verse throughout the ages, including Eve, Helen of Troy, Guinevere, Laura, and Beatrice. Patmore sold the estate in 1875 and moved to *Hastings.

THAME *Oxfordshire*

Market town on the A418, between Oxford and Aylesbury. John Fell (b. 1625) and Anthony Wood (b. 1632) were pupils at the Grammar School then in the Tudor building next to the church. Yeats, with his wife and child, rented the three-storey Cuttlebrook House, 42 High St., in 1921. He found the furniture pleasing, especially the guns and swords on the top floor. They noticed an unseasonal smell of roses, and the doctor attending the birth of their son commented on it.

John Fothergill's *An Innkeeper's Diary* (1931) describes the Spread Eagle in the High St., where he was 'Pioneer Amateur Innkeeper' from 1922 to 1932. The inn was frequented by writers. Carrington, friend of Lytton Strachey and the 'Mary Bracegirdle' of Aldous Huxley's *Crome Yellow* (1921), painted the inn sign for Fothergill.

THREE MILE CROSS *Berkshire*

Village in the parish of Shinfield, on the A33, just S of Reading. On the E side of the main road stands a humble cottage, later called The Mitford, where Mary Russell Mitford spent most of her writing life. She moved here with her parents in 1820, when her father's extravagance prevented the upkeep of their larger house near *Reading. The village and surrounding neighbourhood were the source of her delightful sketches of rural life, contributions to the *Lady's Magazine* later published in five volumes as *Our Village* (1824–32). Miss Mitford's devotion to her father is reflected in the dedication to her 'most cherished friend, her beloved and venerable father' of 'recollections of the beautiful scenery where they have so often wandered, and of the village home where for so many years they have dwelt together'.

TIDMARSH *Berkshire*

Village on the Pang, 1 m. S of Pangbourne, on the A340. Lytton Strachey lived with his devoted friend Carrington at the Mill House, built on the end of a large weatherboarded water mill E of the crossroads, from December 1917 to July 1924. The house stood in 1½ acres of ground, which included a small orchard and a sunken Roman bath, supplied with water from the millstream, and was an ideal headquarters for Strachey, where Carrington did the housekeeping and he could rest between excursions in the outside world. Strachey had just finished *Eminent Victorians* and was busy with proof-reading for the first months of 1918. Its publication suddenly brought him success and fame and encouraged him to set about his classic biography of Queen Victoria (published in 1921). In spite of its attractions the situation of the Mill House proved too damp in the winter and in 1924 Strachey and Carrington moved to a house at *Ham.

TILFORD *Surrey*

Village off the B3001, 3 m. SE of Farnham. Charlotte Smith, who, after her husband's bankruptcy, supported her family by writing novels, which proved very popular, spent her last year here. She died in 1806 and is buried at Guildford. The village was well known to William Cobbett from his youth at *Farnham. In *Rural Rides* (1830) he mentions stopping on the green to show his son Richard the oak he had seen as a boy, which he said was 30 ft in circumference (Ⓟ on seat).

Sir Arthur Conan Doyle stayed with friends at The Spinney (*c.* the 1880s) and played cricket for Tilford. He mentions the village in *The White Company* (1891) and *Sir Nigel* (1906).

The Old Kiln Museum in Reeds Rd, which has a collection of farm implements and machinery of the past, contains an exhibition of the work of George Sturt, wheelwright and author, who lived at Farnham.

Titchfield Abbey, Hampshire, home of the 3rd Earl of Southampton, where Shakespeare visited

TITCHFIELD *Hampshire*

Little town 10 m. SE of Southampton, S of the A27. Titchfield Abbey, dissolved in 1536, was rebuilt as a mansion by Thomas Wriothesley, 1st Earl of Southampton, in 1542. John Florio, lexicographer and translator of Italian descent, stayed here (1590–1) as tutor to the young 3rd Earl, who lived under the care of his widowed mother. Florio's brother-in-law Samuel Daniel also stayed, and Thomas Nash and Shakespeare visited. It is believed that the majority of Shakespeare's sonnets were written here, most of them in the Abbey itself, as well as several of the *Passionate Pilgrim* collection (1599), *Love's Labour's Lost* (1595), and the neglected poem 'A Lover's Complaint'. The Abbey is open to the public (www.english-heritage.org.uk).

TONBRIDGE *Kent*

Old market town on the Medway and the A227, 7 m. SE of Sevenoaks. Among the pupils of Tonbridge School (founded 1553) were E. M. Forster in the 1890s and Sidney Keyes in the late 1930s. Some of the poems Keyes wrote here were included in *Iron Laurel* (1942), published while he was at Oxford. The Calcutta-born novelist and poet Vikram Seth was a later pupil at Tonbridge School; the novelist Shena Mackay attended Tonbridge Girls' Grammar School in the 1950s.

TUNBRIDGE WELLS *Kent*

Inland spa, on the A26 and the A264, which grew up round the chalybeate spring discovered in 1606. The church of King Charles the Martyr has the names of Pepys and Evelyn, who both visited here, on the list of subscribers whose money paid for the building.

Defoe gives a picture of the resort in *A Tour Through the Whole Island of Great Britain* (1724–7). He arrived when the Prince of Wales was visiting, which drew a larger crowd than usual to the place:

> The Ladies that appear here, are indeed the glory of the Place; the coming to the Wells to drink the Water is a meer matter of custom; some drink, more do not, and few drink Physically: But Company and Diversion is in short the main business of the Place; and those People who have nothing to do any where else, seem to be the only People who have any thing to do at Tunbridge . . . As for Gaming, Sharping, Intrieguing; as also Fops, Fools, Beaus, and the like, Tunbridge is as full of these, as can be desired, and it takes off much Diversion of those Persons of Honour and Virtue, who go there to be innocently recreated: However a Man of Character, and good behaviour . . . may single out such Company as may be suitable to him.

Defoe left Tunbridge because he was short of money, the one thing no one could do without here, he wrote. John Gay escorted the Countess of Burlington here in 1723. He had been staying with Lord Burlington in London, working on his play *The Captives*, and he continued with it here. It was performed at Drury Lane the next year.

Edward Young, rector of Welwyn, who never received the preferment his friends thought he merited, often came here for health and exercise. He believed that 'steel water', as the chalybeate spring was called, and riding were his 'only cure'. His long poem *Night Thoughts on Life, Death, and Immortality* (1742–5), with its vision of eternity, was a popular solace to his contemporaries. Richard Cumberland, whose sentimental comedies had introduced him to Garrick and his circle, often visited with his family, and after losing his post as Secretary to the Board of Trade through a change in government, chose to settle in a house (gone) on Mt Sion. Fanny Burney, who stayed at the Sussex Hotel (now divided between the Tunbridge Wells Arts Society and an Indian restaurant) on The Pantiles with Mrs Thrale soon after the publication of her novel *Evelina* (1778), mentions in her *Journal* the airs his wife and daughters assumed. She was warned that he would refuse to speak to her as, now that his new plays were no longer acceptable, he hated to meet successful authors. She set some scenes from *Camilla* (1796) on Mt Ephraim.

The Pantiles, a paved walk shaded by trees, and sometimes called The Walks or The Promenade, contains the Bath House (ⓟ, built 1804), now without its Victorian crenellations, and the site of the Assembly and Gaming Rooms (ⓟ on 40–6).

Horace Smith spent the last years of his life here with his daughter Elizabeth. He died in 1849 and is buried in Holy Trinity churchyard. Thackeray, who spent part of his childhood (1825) at Bellevue, on the Common, recalls reading the Gothic novel *Manfroni, or, The One-Handed Monk*, alone in the drawing room while his parents were out and being too frightened to move. This was one of the books from 'the well-remembered library on the Pantiles' that he mentions in 'Tunbridge Toys' from *Roundabout Papers* (1863), written when he was living (1860) at another house on the Common (now Thackeray House, ⓟ).

A train from Central Station conveys Betjeman's 'Eunice' from her weekend retreat in Kent and back to London. To help fund a trip to Russia in 1961, Anthony Burgess bought two suitcases' worth of polyester dresses in Marks and Spencer in Tunbridge Wells and sold them in the basement of a hotel in Leningrad. His other preparations for the trip included learning Russian, an acquisition that stood him in good stead when he came to write *A Clockwork Orange* (1962). The town also gives its name rather unfortunately to a TV play by John Osborne, *God Rot Tunbridge Wells* (1985).

TURVILLE HEATH *Buckinghamshire*

Small village in the Chilterns, 7 m. W of High Wycombe. In 1932, novelist John Mortimer's father built a house there, where Mortimer still lives. Describing the village of 'Rapstone' that appears in his *Paradise Postponed* (1985) and *Titmuss Regained* (1990), Mortimer wrote that while it is a fictional village yet in essence it is precisely that 'highly prosperous part of southern England where I have spent my life'. Edward Mayhew, the protagonist of Ian McEwan's novel *On Chesil Beach* (2007), is from this village too.

TWYFORD *Hampshire*

Village on the B3335, 4 m. S of Winchester. Alexander Pope came here at the age of 8 for his first schooling away from home, and was apparently unhappy. According to a 19th-c. magazine, *Merry England*, he 'was dismissed in consequence of writing a lampoon on his tutor, and was transferred to a Roman Catholic school situated close by Hyde Park Corner, kept by another priest, where he lost nearly all that he had gained under Mr. Banisher [the headmaster]'. His schoolhouse, a beautiful old house called Seagers Buildings which stood in a quiet corner, was pulled down in the 1960s to make room for a housing estate. In 1771 Benjamin Franklin stayed at Twyford House, at the top of the hill, while he was writing the first part of his autobiography. His host was Jonathan Shipley, Dean of Winchester and later Bishop of St Asaph.

UFFINGTON *Oxfordshire*

Village in the Vale of the White Horse (formerly in Berkshire), *c.* 6 m. S of Faringdon, reached by minor roads off the B4508 and the B4507. Thomas Hughes, author of *Tom Brown's Schooldays* (1857), was born (20 Oct. 1822) in an old farmhouse in the village (pulled down in the later 19th c. to make way for the new school) and was baptized in the church, where his grandfather was vicar. He spent his early years here before going to a prep school at Twyford, Hampshire (1830), and the opening chapters of *Tom Brown's Schooldays* describe the village and the features of the Vale which he knew so well: White Horse Hill (NT), with its white chalk galloping horse (374 ft long) revealed by the cut turf; Uffington Castle above on the Ridgeway, the ancient track running along the crest of the Downs; the Blowing Stone, on the way from the Hill to Kingston Lisle, nearly 4 ft high and pierced with holes, which was said to have been used long ago to sound the alarm at the approach of an enemy; and, 1½ m. W, a burial place of great antiquity, known as Wayland's Smithy, whose legends Scott adapted for his novel *Kenilworth* (1821). Tom Brown's early days are set in Uffington and before going to Rugby he attends the old schoolhouse, a small stone building dated 1617, just outside the churchyard on the corner of the Faringdon road, now a museum (usually open weekend afternoons, www.uffingtonmuseum.members.beeb.net).

Thomas Hughes returned to Uffington in 1857, after a long absence, for the scouring of the White Horse, recorded in his *The Scouring of the White Horse, or, The Long Vacation Ramble of a London Clerk* (1859). There is a memorial plaque to him in gunmetal with a portrait in low relief in the church, on the N wall of the N transept. The organ was dedicated to his memory on 24 January 1918. A new village hall, the Thomas Hughes Memorial Hall, was opened on 29 November 1975 by Mrs L. Akroyd, a great-grandniece. The foyer contains a brass plaque with an engraving of the Uffington White Horse to commemorate the 150th anniversary (1972) of his birth.

After the death of his grandfather (1833) his grandmother, Mrs Mary Anne Hughes, moved to Kingston Lisle, 1½ m. SE, where her house (probably Kingston Lisle House) still stands. She was a friend of Scott, Dickens, Richard Barham, and Harrison Ainsworth, and, when she lived in London, had regaled them with an immense fund of legends and folklore, which frequently served as source material for novels and poems. Ainsworth stayed with her on many occasions at Kingston Lisle, and wrote the last chapters of *Jack Sheppard* (1839) and *Guy Fawkes* (1841) here. Ainsworth, who was offered every comfort, including 'your own hours for every meal; your own sitting room; your great chair', dedicated *Guy Fawkes* to his hostess. In his story *Old St Paul's* (1841), some of the scenes are based on White Horse country, including an account of the Blowing Stone, and Mrs Hughes is portrayed as 'Mrs. Compton'.

In the 1930s John Betjeman lived at Garrard's Farm ⓟ, which provided the inspiration for his poem 'Uffington'. Mementoes of his time in the village can be found in Tom Brown's School Museum on Broad St.

UPHAM *Hampshire*

Village on a minor road off the A335, *c.* 9 m. SE of Winchester. Edward Young, author of *Night Thoughts on Life, Death, and Immortality* (1742–5), was born (1683) at his father's rectory (later the Old Rectory). The plaque recording his birth has been moved to the New Rectory. Young grew up in Upham and was educated at *Winchester before going to *Oxford.

UPPARK *West Sussex*

Mansion built *c.* 1685–90 (NT) on the B2146, 6 m. SE of Petersfield. After leaving Bromley at the age of 13, H. G. Wells lived here for a time when his mother was housekeeper to Miss Fetherstonhaugh. He read voraciously from the library and a hidden store of books discovered in the attic, which included Thomas Paine's *The Rights of Man* (1791–2). The house figures as 'Bladesover' in the partly autobiographical *Tono-Bungay* (1909).

The house was devastated by fire in August 1989, but has been beautifully restored (NT).

UPPER LAMBOURN *Berkshire*

Village N of Lambourn and home of the prehistoric Seven Barrows. Its reputation for horse-breeding is hauntingly evoked by John Betjeman in his poem 'Upper Lambourn':

> Leathery limbs of Upper Lambourn,
> Leathery skin from sun and wind,
> Leathery breeches, spreading stables,
> Shining saddles left behind—
> To the down the string of horses
> Moving out of sight and mind.

VENTNOR *Isle of Wight*

S coast resort on the A3055. Ivan Sergeyevich Turgenev spent three weeks here in August 1860, staying first at Rock Cottage, Belgrave Rd, and then at Belinda House, Esplanade (both houses have gone), and it was here that he conceived the idea for his novel *Fathers and Sons* (1862). He also drew up a programme for a 'Society for the Propagation of Literacy and Primary Education', which he presented to a group of compatriots staying in Ventnor, but it lacked the necessary practical sense to carry its ideals into action.

Pearl Craigie ('John Oliver Hobbes') wrote her first novel, *Some Emotions and a Moral* (1891), here after separating from her husband. She lived with her father in London and in Steephill Castle (house gone; garden now built over), W of the town, where she wrote many other novels and some less successful dramas, the most popular being *The Ambassador* (1898). In 1900 she moved to St Lawrence

The Housekeeper's Room at Uppark, West Sussex. H. G. Wells lived here as a boy (his mother was housekeeper) and the house figures in his novel *Tono-Bungay*

Lodge, a small cottage nearby, where she wrote *Robert Orange* (1902), whose hero is based on Disraeli. After her death in 1906 her father renamed the cottage Craigie Lodge.

WALLINGFORD *Oxfordshire*

Country town on the Thames, at the junction of the A329 and the A4130. From 1914 to 1917 John Masefield had a country retreat *c.* 3 m. SW, off the A417 at Lollington Farm below Lollington Hill on the edge of the Berkshire Downs. Here he wrote his only war poem, 'August 1914', and published *Lollington Downs and Other Poems, with Sonnets* (1917). Agatha Christie spent much of her later life at Winterbrook House (NT), by the Thames at Wallingford; she died at Winterbrook on 12 January 1976.

WALMER *Kent*

Coastal resort, adjoining Deal, which grew up round Henry VIII's castle. This became the official residence of the Warden of the Cinque Ports, where Benjamin Robert Haydon spent a short stay when invited to paint a portrait of the Duke of Wellington. Haydon gives an account of his visit in his *Autobiography* (1853). Robert Bridges was born (1844) at Roselands. P. J. Kavanagh records a visit here in his poem 'Walmer Castle'.

WALTHAM ST LAWRENCE *Berkshire*

Village on the B3024, 3 m. E of Twyford. John Newbery, the original of Goldsmith's 'philanthropic publisher of St. Paul's Churchyard, who has written so many little books for children' in *The Vicar of Wakefield* (1766), was born here, educated at the village school, and, after a prosperous career in London, buried in the churchyard at his own request. He was the first bookseller to provide books for the very young on a large scale and he probably wrote many of the stories himself, although *Goody Two Shoes* (1765) has generally been attributed to Goldsmith. As well as Goldsmith (whom he frequently helped financially), his friends included Dr Johnson, Christopher Smart, and Smollett, and the epitaph on his imposing tombstone was written by Smart's biographer the Revd C. Hunter.

WALTON-ON-THAMES *Surrey*

Town on the A244, 5 m. E of Chertsey. In 1717 and 1719 Congreve stayed at Ashley Park (gone), the seat of Viscount Shannon, whose large memorial by Roubiliac is in the church. William Maginn, whose intemperance dissipated the rewards of a long association with *Fraser's Magazine*, died (1842) of consumption soon after retiring here. He is buried in an unmarked grave in the parish churchyard.

WALTON ON THE HILL *Surrey*

Village on the B2220, 5 m. E of Leatherhead. Sir Anthony Hope Hawkins ('Anthony Hope') lived at Heath Farm, Deans Lane, where he

wrote *Memories and Notes* (1927), a volume of reminiscences. He died here in 1933.

WANTAGE *Oxfordshire*

Market town in the Vale of the White Horse, on the A338 and the A417. Alfred the Great, King of the West Saxons, was born here (849) and is commemorated by a statue (1877) in the marketplace. There was probably a royal palace, but no trace of it survives. Alfred is distinguished in the history of English literature for the revival of letters that he effected in the West of England. He translated Pope Gregory's *Cura Pastoralis* and the *Historia adversus Paganos* of Orosius, a Spanish disciple of St Augustine; and he is believed to have inspired and possibly written the earlier part of the Anglo-Saxon Chronicle, a record of events in England from the Christian era to the middle of the 12th c.

Wantage appears as 'Alfredstown' in Hardy's *Jude the Obscure* (1895).

John Betjeman moved into 'The Mead' in 1951 and the town inspired 'Wantage Bells' and the elegiac 'On Leaving Wantage 1972':

> From this wide vale, where all our married lives
> We two have lived, we now are whirled away
> Momently clinging to the things we knew—
> Friends, footpaths, hedges, house and animals—
> Till, borne along like twigs and bits of straw,
> We sink below the sliding stream of time.

Near Betjeman's house and the church lies the Betjeman Millennium Park, with a stone poetry trail.

WAREHORNE *Kent*

Small village in Romney Marsh, off the B2067, SW of Hamstreet. R. H. Barham was curate of Snargate (3 m. S) and Warehorne, living here in the red-brick rectory (later Church Farm) next to the church. In his *Life* (1870) his son tells of his acceptance by the smugglers of Snargate, 'Good night,' they'd say; 'it's only parson.'

WARGRAVE *Berkshire*

Village on the E bank of the Thames, 3 m. S of Henley, on the A321. Thomas Day, author of *The History of Sandford and Merton* (1783–9), is buried in the churchyard. He died on 28 September 1789, after a fall from his horse when he was visiting his mother at Bear Hill, nearby. A memorial erected on the wall of the S aisle of the church contained an epitaph thought to have been written by his friend Richard Lovell Edgeworth, father of Maria Edgeworth, who used to live at Hare Hatch, *c.* 1 m. SE. The memorial, however, is not to be seen today and it was probably destroyed in 1914 when the church was burned down by suffragettes (rebuilt 1916). The epitaph declared that Day had promoted by the energy of his writings, and encouraged by the uniformity of his example, the unremitting exercise of every public and private virtue.

WARNHAM *West Sussex*

Village off the A24, 3 m. NW of Horsham. Field Place (1 m. S) was the birthplace of

Shelley, who as a boy fished and shot in the park and made up fantastic stories to tell his sisters during his holidays from Syon House Academy and *Eton. *Original Poetry* (1810) by 'Victor and Cazire' contains his early poems with those of his sister Elizabeth. His expulsion from Oxford and his runaway marriage caused a permanent break with his father, although he later undertook the custody of Shelley's children after the marriage failed. Shelley's son Charles, who died aged 11, shares a memorial in the church with Elizabeth (d. 1831), in the Field Place Chapel. A facsimile of Shelley's certificate of baptism (1792) can be seen in the S aisle.

WATERINGBURY *Kent*

Village on the A26, 5 m. SW of Maidstone. In 1931 George Orwell, who had been sleeping in London doss-houses to share the lives of down-and-outs, set off with two tramps to find work in the hop fields. He describes his 18 days at Home Farm here, where they lodged on straw in a barn, in the essay 'Hop Picking', and used his experience in the novel *A Clergyman's Daughter* (1935).

WATLINGTON *Oxfordshire*

Market town in the Chilterns, between Reading and Oxford. In the Vale of Oxford, near Watlington, just off the Ridgeway Path, a hot-air balloon comes free of its moorings, precipitating some unexpected and rather alarming consequences, in Ian McEwan's novel *Enduring Love* (1997).

WEST GRINSTEAD *West Sussex*

Village off the A24, 7 m. S of Horsham. Pope used to stay at West Grinstead Park (house gone) with his friend John Caryll and while here in 1712 wrote the satirical *The Rape of the Lock* about the origin of a family feud mentioned by his host. Pope's Oak, under which according to tradition he wrote the poem, can be seen from the public footpath through the park. The tree is also shown in the background of a stained-glass window in the parish church. Hilaire Belloc, who died at *Shipley, is buried in the Catholic churchyard here. A tablet by the church door indicates the site of the grave.

WESTON UNDERWOOD *Buckinghamshire*

Small village 13 m. SE of Northampton, a favourite walk of William Cowper when he was living (1767–86) at *Olney. He was often accompanied by Mary Unwin, with whom he had shared a house since her husband's death. Sometimes he came alone:

> When winter soaks the field and female feet
> Too weak to struggle with tenacious clay
> Or ford the rivulets, are best at home.

Their goal was Weston Park (gone), the home of their friends the Throckmortons, who gave them a key to the gardens and to the wilderness or spinney opposite the house. The gardens (now made into the Flamingo Gardens and Zoological Park) contain Cowper's epitaphs to the spaniel Fop and the pointer, cut on stone columns surmounted by urns, which stand under the trees housing exotic birds whose plumage casts our native 'jay, the pie and e'en the boding owl' into the shade. The little temple where he used to rest is still there and ½ m. away, along the lane skirting the gardens, is the Alcove, a rather larger temple still crowning the summit and embracing the view of 'Square tower, tall spire' among other 'beauties numberless'. Behind the Alcove is a large pit where the clay is still tenacious. In 1786, at the suggestion of his cousin Lady Hesketh, Cowper and Mary Unwin moved into the Lodge, a house in the main street. His quiet life here was interrupted by Mrs Unwin's illness, when Lady Hesketh came to look after them and solace his depression. His lines 'To Mary' were written at this time. In 1795 Cowper and Mrs Unwin left to stay with 'Johnny of Norfolk', a younger cousin, in East Dereham. The poem 'The Yardley Oak', about a tree in Yardley Chase, gives its name to the village inn, Cowper's Oak. The church contains an inscription to Dr Gregson, the Throckmorton's chaplain, with whom Cowper, who nicknamed him Griggy, discussed his translations of Virgil.

WHITSTABLE *Kent*

Seaside resort and old fishing port, famous for oysters, on the A290, 7 m. N of Canterbury. After his parents died, Somerset Maugham was brought up at the rectory in Canterbury Rd by his uncle, easily recognizable as the Revd William Carey in the novel *Of Human Bondage* (1915), in which the town is called Blackstable. *Cakes and Ale* (1930) is also said to have some scenes based on Maugham's life here. He made two visits to the Old Rectory in 1948 and in 1951 when he stayed at the Bear and Key. There is a photograph of the house in *Somerset and All the Maughams* by R. Maugham (1966).

WIGHT, ISLE OF

The Isle of Wight provides a retreat and a place in which to gather resources against the monstrous mobile plants in John Wyndham's science-fiction classic *The Day of the Triffids* (1951).

In Julian Barnes's *England, England* (1998), the tycoon Jack Pitman decides to create the ultimate tourist attraction by reproducing every popular aspect of Englishness (cups of tea, beefeaters, Buckingham Palace, Stonehenge) on the Isle of Wight—or 'The Island', as it will come to be known. Why the Isle of Wight? Relevant factors had included 'size, location and accessibility of the island, plus the extreme unlikelihood of it being spot-listed by UNESCO as a World Heritage Site. Access to labour pool, elasticity of planning regulations, malleability of locals . . .'. (See also entries for specific places on the Isle of Wight.)

WINCHESTER *Hampshire*

Historic county town and cathedral city, situated on the Itchen and the hillside above it, on the A31 and the M3. The British settlement of Caer Gwent was developed by the Romans as Venta Belgarum, the fifth-largest town in Britain, and became the Saxon Wintanceaster, capital of Wessex, in 519. King Alfred made it his capital, and his statue (by Hamo Thornycroft, erected in 1901 to commemorate the thousandth anniversary of his death) stands at the E end of High St., dominating the Broadway. Near West Gate, at the top of High St., stands the Great Hall of the former Norman castle. Sir Walter Ralegh was tried here and condemned to death in 1603. At the W end, above the remains of the royal dais, hangs a representation of the Round Table of King Arthur's Knights, probably made in Tudor times or even earlier.

Izaak Walton came to Winchester in his last years and lived with his son-in-law Prebendary Hawkins at 7 The Close (down Dove Alley). He died here (15 Dec. 1683) and was buried in Prior Silkstede's Chapel in the S transept of the Cathedral. At the end of the 19th c. the fishermen of England added the figure of Izaak Walton to the Great Screen at the E end, and in 1914 the fishermen of England and America gave the memorial window in the chapel, above his tomb.

Jane Austen came to Winchester at the end of May 1817. She had been suffering from ill health for some time and had decided to place herself in the care of a Winchester doctor, Giles King Lyford. But her illness, now thought to be Addison's disease, did not yield to treatment and on 18 July she died at the house, 8 College St. (now owned by Winchester College; ⓟ), where she was staying with her sister Cassandra. She died with her faculties unimpaired and three days before her death she wrote a lighthearted poem for St Swithun's Day, entitled 'Venta' (published in a booklet available in the Cathedral). She was buried in the Cathedral in the N aisle of the nave, where an inscribed stone marks her grave, above which are a brass tablet and a memorial window. The City Museum nearby contains a few of her personal belongings. The memorial inspired Anne Stevenson's poem 'Re-reading Jane'.

In 1819 Keats stayed from 12 August until early October with his friend Charles Armitage Brown (house demolished). He wrote 'Ode to Autumn' and revised 'The Eve of St. Agnes'. He was impressed with the neatness of the town: 'The side streets here are excessively maiden-lady-like,' he wrote. He also gave a description of his daily walk:

> I take a walk every day for an hour before dinner and this is generally my walk. I go out at the back gate across one street, into the Cathedral yard, along a paved path, past the beautiful front of the Cathedral, turn to the left under a stone doorway—then I am on the other side of the building—which leaving behind me I pass on through two college-like squares seemingly built for the dwelling place of Deans and Prebendaries—garnished with grass and shaded with trees. Then I pass through one of the old city gates and then you are in College Street.

The Hospital of St Cross, *c.* 1 m. S of the city centre, reached by St Cross Rd, was founded by Bishop Henry of Blois for 13 poor brethren in 1136 and extended by an 'Almshouse of Noble Poverty' by Cardinal Beaufort in 1446. It is believed that Trollope based *The Warden* on St Cross, and the scandal concerning the abuse of the Mastership in 1808.

Charlotte M. Yonge, who lived all her life at *Otterbourne, is commemorated by the reredos in the Lady Chapel of the Cathedral.

The cathedral library is housed in the oldest book room in Europe, which was added to the Cathedral in the 12th c. During the Reformation and again in Cromwell's time many manuscripts and books were taken into private custody and some were probably lost, but there are many treasures to be seen, notably the beautiful Winchester Bible, written *c.* 1150 in two volumes (rebound in 4 vols, 1948), and the private library of Bishop Morley, first offered by him to the Dean and Chapter in 1667. Other items of interest include a copy of Ralegh's speech from the scaffold, an unrecorded edition of *Eikon Basilike*, and a copy of the first edition of Gilbert White's *Natural History and Antiquities of Selborne* (1789).

Winchester College in College St. was founded by William of Wykeham in 1382 and is one of the oldest public schools in England. Distinguished literary men who were pupils include Nicholas Udall (or Uvedale, 1505–56), who became headmaster of *Eton; Sir Henry Wotton (1568–1639); Sir John Davies (1569–1626); Thomas Coryate (1577/9–1617); Sir Thomas Browne (1605–82); Thomas Otway (1652–85; ⓟ erected by William Collins and Thomas and Joseph Warton); John Philips (1676–1709); Edward Young (1683–1765); William Somerville (1675–1742); William Whitehead (1715–85); William Collins (1721–59), who later returned to live in Winchester, where he wrote *Persian Eclogues* (1742); Sydney Smith (1771–1845); Anthony Trollope (1815–82), who was here for a short time before moving to Harrow in 1827 as a 'home boarder' (day boy); Matthew Arnold (1822–88), who was here before going to Rugby in 1837; Arnold Toynbee (1889–1975), historian and the critic; and the poet William Empson (1906–1984) soon after the First World War.

Charles Wolfe (1791–1823) was educated at Hyde Abbey School before going to Trinity College *Dublin.

In Hardy's *Tess of the D'Urbervilles* (1891), Tess is hanged in the city jail. Winchester is the 'Wintoncester' of the novel. Basil Bunting, who refused military service when he left school in 1918, spent a term in the jail. He was released in 1919. Norman MacCaig, a conscientious objector during the Second World War, spent a brief period in 1941 in Winchester prison.

The travel writer and novelist Jonathan Raban attended Peter Symonds School on Owens Rd in the 1950s.

WINDLESHAM *Surrey*

Village on Surrey Heath. Geoffrey Willans was a master at Woodcote House School in the 1930s, an experience which contributed to the creation of the 'utterly wet and weedy' St

Custard's of the *Molesworth* books, home of 'grabber', 'fotherington tomas', and Molesworth himself.

WINDSOR *Berkshire*

Royal Borough on the A308 and the S bank of the Thames, dominated by Windsor Castle, chief residence of the sovereign since Norman times. Geoffrey Chaucer is thought to have lived in the Winchester Tower while Clerk of the Royal Works, *c.* 1390. The Scottish King James I, captured (*c.* 1406) as a youth by the English, spent the later years of his exile imprisoned in the castle by Henry V, a few years his senior. While here James courted Jane Beaufort, daughter of the Earl of Somerset, and married her in 1424 shortly after his release. His poem *The Kingis Quair*, first printed in 1783, is about their courtship.

In 1786 Fanny Burney obtained the post of Second Keeper of the Robes to George III's queen through the help of Mrs Delany. However, this independence from her stepmother was dearly bought and her health suffered, as she recounts in her *Diary and Letters*.

Monica Dickens's work as a nurse at the Edward VII Hospital in Windsor led to her writing the successor to *One Pair of Hands* (1939), *One Pair of Feet* (1942).

In Beryl Bainbridge's novel *The Bottle Factory Outing* (1974), the eponymous outing takes the bottle factory workers (from Paganotti's wine-bottling factory) out to Windsor Great Park, with shocking consequences.

WITHYHAM *East Sussex*

Village on the B2110, 9 m. SE of East Grinstead. Thomas Sackville, 1st Earl of Dorset, author with Thomas Norton of the blank-verse tragedy *Gorboduc* (1561), was born here. Charles Sackville, Lord Buckhurst, was a companion of Charles Sedley in his early days. His poems, including the lyric 'To all you ladies now on land', were published with Sedley's in 1701. He became the 6th Earl, died in 1706, and is buried in the Sackville Chapel in the parish church, where there are many family memorials. Also buried in the Chapel are the ashes of Victoria Sackville-West, who died at *Sissinghurst Castle in 1962. Old Buckhurst, a family home of the Sackvilles, is now flats.

Penns in the Rocks, an 18th-c. house in gardens with rocky outcrops, was the home in the 1930s of Dorothy Wellesley. Through Lady Ottoline Morrell she met W. B. Yeats and their letters on poetry were published in 1940. Yeats included many of her poems in *The Oxford Book of Modern Verse* (1936). He stayed here in 1938 and enjoyed sitting in The Folly, a small classical temple in the glade in front of the house.

WITLEY *Surrey*

Village on the A283, 4 m. SW of Godalming. Mr and Mrs George Lewes (as George Lewes and George Eliot were called), after many holidays in hotels and furnished houses, bought in 1877 The Heights (Ⓟ, later Roslyn Court in Wormley, ½ m. S), which was to be their country home. Delays in the arrival of their furniture made their bedroom look as if there had been a distraint on the house, George Eliot wrote, but the view and the country walks made up for the initial discomforts. John Cross, who came from Weybridge, set up tennis equipment and taught her to play. They met their neighbours Alfred Tennyson and William Allingham, and Henry James visited. The next summer George Eliot worked on *Theophrastus Such*, but soon George Lewes became fatally ill. After his death George Eliot married John Cross, and in 1880 the couple spent the autumn here before her death in December.

WOKING *Surrey*

Dormitory town approximately 25 m. SW of central London. The Martians in H. G. Wells's science-fiction novella *The War of the Worlds* (1898) land in a cylinder on Horsell Common in Woking and much of the action takes place in the town. Statues by Michael Condron of one of the Martians' 'fighting machines' and of their crashed cylinder stand in the town centre.

WOKINGHAM *Berkshire*

Busy market town on the A329 between Reading and Bracknell. The Olde Rose inn in the Market Place (now the New Rose) was famous as a meeting place of 18th-c. wits, and tradition has it that one wet afternoon in 1726 Pope (who had lived nearby at *Binfield) and his friends Gay, Swift, and Arbuthnot amused themselves by composing a ballad in praise of pretty Molly Mog, the landlord's daughter. The ballad attained great popularity when published in the contemporary *Mist's Weekly Journal*.

WOODSTOCK *Oxfordshire*

Old town on the A44, 10 m. N of Oxford, once surrounded by the royal forest which survives today in the old oaks in Blenheim Park. Henry II tried to conceal his mistress Rosamond Clifford here and Deloney in his *Garland of Good Will* (1631) lists the precautions he took:

> Most curiously this Bower was built of stone and
>   timber strong,
> An hundred and fifty doores did to that Bower
>   belong,
> And they so cunningly contriv'd with turnings
>   round about,
> That none but with a clew of thread could enter
>   in or out.

But all the 'labyrinthine brickwork maze in maze', as Tennyson describes it in his play *Becket* (1884), was unable to save her. Her exact fate is uncertain; Deloney has the Queen poison her while the King is in France, where Drayton places him in *England's Heroicall Epistles* (1597) writing to tell Rosamond that his heart remains with her in 'Sweet Woodstock'; Tennyson, who makes her Henry's morganatic wife in *Becket*, has her banished to the nunnery at Godstow, where she is said to be buried.

Another bower, this time covered with green ivy, was made for Queen Elizabeth I's visit when *The Queen's Majestie's Entertainment at Woodstock* (1575), the play by George Gascoigne, which tells of a princess giving up her lover for reasons of state, was acted before the Queen and Leicester. Pope, who came to see Fair Rosamond's Well in 1717, 'toasted her shade in the cold water' and noted that only one wall of Henry's manor remained standing. Scott tells how this destruction came about in his novel *Woodstock* (1826), set in the Civil War, when the manor was the home of the Cavalier Sir Henry Lee, Ranger of Woodstock Forest, whose daughter loved a Roundhead. The site of this old manor near Vanbrugh's bridge is marked by a stone pillar. So when John Wilmot was made Ranger by Charles II, more as a reward for his father's virtue than his own, he had to live in High Lodge near the Combe gate. When Nathaniel Hawthorne visited this battlemented tower (later private flats), he described in *Our Old Home* (1863) seeing the canopied bed in the ground-floor room where Rochester made his deathbed repentance. Vanbrugh designed Blenheim Palace in 1705, the year his plays *The Country House* and *The Confederacy* were published. 'Woodstock Park', the poem by William Harrison, protégé of Addison and Swift, was included by Dodsley in his *A Collection of Poems by Several Hands* (1748–58).

Chaucer's House in Park St. is probably on the site of the Gothic house where John Aubrey, the antiquary, said Chaucer stayed with his son.

WOOLBEDING (pr. Woŏbeeding) *West Sussex*

Village off the A272, 1 m. NW of Midhurst. Thomas Otway (1652–85), the dramatist, spent his youth here; his father was rector until 1670. Charlotte Smith made the decision to leave her improvident husband after living here (*c.* 1786) in the 17th-c. colonnaded Woolbeding Hall. When in France, she had translated *Manon Lescaut* (1785), which was withdrawn as offensive, but her *Elegiac Sonnets* (1784), although Anna Seward thought their best lines plagiarisms, were as popular as the novels she wrote later, which gave her financial independence.

WOOTTON *Oxfordshire*

Quiet village 2 m. N of Woodstock, on a minor road E of the A44. Here Francis Kilvert, the diarist, married Elizabeth Rowland of Holly Bank on 20 August 1879 in St Mary's Church. A tablet commemorating the marriage can be seen in the NE corner of the nave, adjacent to the tower arch. Sadly, Kilvert died at *Bredwardine just over a month later. His widow returned to her father's house and is believed to have destroyed those parts of his *Diary* which she considered too personal for publication.

Blenheim Palace, Woodstock, Oxfordshire, designed by the playwright Sir John Vanbrugh in 1705

WORTH *East Sussex*

Village off the B2036, 2 m. E of Crawley. Cobbett, riding round the countryside to catalogue the abuses of the 'jobbers' and landlords, often stayed at Worth Lodge (gone), the farm where his friend Samuel Brazier used Cobbett's methods and grew maize, known as Cobbett's corn. Old Mrs Brazier, who could 'neither write nor read, understood well the making of bread, the brewing of beer, the keeping of cows, the rearing of pigs, the salting of meat, the rearing of poultry, the obtaining of honey', so that it is not surprising that Cobbett wrote *Cottage Economy* (1821) here.

Crabbet Park (now a school of equitation) on the B2036 was inherited by Wilfrid Scawen Blunt in 1872 soon after he had retired from the Diplomatic Service and married Lady Anne Noel, the Arabic scholar. Blunt, who continued to travel in the Arab world, wrote *Sonnets and Songs of Proteus* (1875) and *Esther* (1892).

WORTHING *West Sussex*

Resort on the A259 and the A24. A turn S off the A27, 1 m. W of the A24 roundabout, leads to The Lamb at Durrington, from which Salvington road runs to the former village of Salvington, now a suburb. Near the inn that bears his name is the site of the birthplace (1595) of John Selden in Selden's Way. This was a small, square, brick and flint house with a thatched roof, donated to the Council in 1941,

but burnt down *c.* 1957. A plaque is on the gatepost of the bungalow which replaced it. West Tarring church (just S of Salvington) has replicas in the porch of his will and his dying testimony.

In 1894 Oscar Wilde took rooms for himself and his family at The Haven, 5 The Esplanade, for August and September. He wrote the greater part of *The Importance of Being Earnest* (1895) here, remarking in a letter, 'I find farcical comedies admirable for style, but fatal to handwriting.'

In a NE suburb, not far from the parish church, is the Broadwater and Worthing cemetery where Richard Jefferies (d. 1887), 'Prose Poet of England's Fields and Woodlands', is buried. The naturalist W. H. Hudson (d. 1922) was buried by his own wish in the same cemetery as the man he admired.

In 1920–1 Stephen Spender spent an unhappy year at Charlcote School, where he was bullied for being a 'Hun' (his mother's family, whose name was Schuster, was German).

WOTTON (pr. Wŏóton) *Surrey*

Village on the A25, 4 m. SW of Dorking. John Evelyn was born (1620) at his father's home, Wotton House, a large, rambling house (now rebuilt) surrounding a courtyard. He writes in his *Diary* that 'it was sweetly environ'd with those delicious streames and venerable Woods, as in the judgment of strangers, as well as Englishmen, it may be compared to one of the most tempting and pleasant seates in the

Nation'. He would have written about 'the Gardens, Fountaines and Groves' but that everyone knew about their magnificence. Evelyn's love of gardens led him to visit the best examples on the Continent, and on his return to plan and plant the garden of his home at Sayes Court (see LONDON: DEPTFORD). In 1694 he returned to Wotton to live in the apartment his brother assigned to him as heir of the estate, and his prayer to God that 'this solemn Remove may be to the Glory of his mercy, & the good of my family' was a timely intercession because his nieces and their husbands threatened to go to law about the entail. Evelyn spent some time with his son in London to avoid the quarrel. His brother died in 1699 and two years later Evelyn finished planting 'the Elm walke at the back of the Meadow'. On his 80th birthday he thanked God that he was in full possession of his faculties but asked pardon that during the sermons he was 'apt to be surprised with sleepe'. He died aged 86 in London and was buried in the parish church here, where a long epitaph commends him.

YALDING *Kent*

Village on the B2010, *c.* 6 m. SW of Maidstone. The poet Edmund Blunden came here with his parents in 1900 and spent his early years in what he felt to be the rural world of his ancestors. His father was the village schoolmaster and church organist and his mother the headmistress of the infants' school. He attended Cleave's Grammar School from 1907 to 1909, before going to *Christ's Hospital at Horsham. There is a memorial window to him in the chancel of the church, engraved by Lawrence Whistler (1979).

YARNTON *Oxfordshire*

Village off the A44, 5 m. N of Oxford. A. E. Coppard's poem 'The Sapling' commemorates the acacia he gave Agnes Evans for the garden of her new house (built 1907 by Ashbee and

now called Byways) where he stayed and set the title story of *Adam and Eve and Pinch Me* (1921). In *It's Me, O Lord!* (1957) he regrets that the acacia, chosen because it was William Cobbett's favourite tree, didn't thrive.

YATTENDON *Berkshire*

A village of quiet charm, off the B4009, 6 m. SW of Streatley. Robert Bridges, Poet

Laureate 1913–30, lived in the Manor House 1882–1904. His work of this period includes the long narrative poem *Eros and Psyche* (1885) and the Yattendon Hymnal (1899), produced in collaboration with H. Ellis Woodbridge and printed by the Oxford University Press. Bridges is buried in the churchyard and has a memorial tablet in the church.

London

London

LONDON

The capital of the United Kingdom (situated on the tidal Thames), consisting, since 1965, of an area of 610 sq. m., known as Greater London, and including parts of Essex, Kent, Surrey, Hertfordshire, and most of the former county of Middlesex.

The historic centre from which the great metropolis has grown is the City of London, known as 'the square mile', which maintains its independence under the control of the Corporation entitled 'The Mayor and Commonalty and the Citizens of the City of London'.

The City, established by the Romans in AD 43 as Londinium and described by Tacitus as 'a busy emporium for trade and traders', remained an outpost of the Roman Empire for nearly 400 years, until the Romans finally left Britain. During the Middle Ages it began to expand beyond the City walls and by the 16th c. men of wealth and influence were building great houses on the river banks all the way to the village of Westminster, where the court was, and to quiet country places further out.

The literary associations of London from Chaucer's time to the 20th c. are so dense that only a selection can be given here. These are listed alphabetically under the names of recognizable areas, such as Chelsea or Highgate, and references from the index of authors indicate the relevant headings.

ADELPHI, area S of the Strand developed (1768–74) by the Adam brothers, Scottish architects and designers.

Adelphi Ter. (rebuilt 1938, ⓟ), which overlooked the river, was the home of David Garrick, actor–manager and dramatist, who lived at no. 5, the centre house, until his death in 1779. He was visited here by Dr Johnson and other members of the Literary Club and by the young Hannah More. Thomas Hardy was employed (1862–7) in an architect's office at no. 8, where he found the marble fireplaces useful to make quick sketches on. Bernard Shaw lived from 1899, soon after his marriage, until 1927 at his wife's flat at no. 10. *Man and Superman* (1903) and *Major Barbara* (1905) were written here. After 1906 he divided his time between this apartment and his house at *Ayot St Lawrence.

Thomas Hood, who married his friend John Reynolds's sister Jane in 1825, moved two years later to 2 **Robert St.** ⓟ, their first real home together. Their friend Charles Lamb wrote 'On an Infant Dying As Soon As Born' about their daughter:

Riddle of destiny, who can show
What thy short visit meant, or know
What thy errand here below.

The plaque on nos 1–3 (rebuilt) also commemorates John Galsworthy, who lived here from 1912 to 1918, and J. M. Barrie, who had an apartment on the top floor. It was here, on 4 June 1919, that Barrie received the adult Daisy Ashford, who as a child of 9 had written *The Young Visiters*, for which her publisher then hoped Barrie would write a foreword. His appreciation of the child's unerring eye for the quirks of her characters led some people to think he himself was the author. (See also STRAND.)

ANERLEY, district in the SE. Walter de la Mare lived (1899–1908) at 195 **Mackenzie Rd** when working in London for an oil company. He wrote here *Songs of Childhood* (1902) and a novel, *Henry Brocken* (1904), under the name 'Walter Ramal'. He then lived (1908–12) in **Worbeck Rd**, where he wrote more novels and *The Listeners and Other Poems* (1912), which combines images of dreams and childhood. From 1912 to 1925 he lived at 14 **Thornsett Rd**, where he published two other collections of poems and *Memoirs of a Midget* (1921), the novel that won (1922) the James Tait Black Memorial Prize.

BARNES, district to the SW. Abraham Cowley lived (1663–5) in the old mansion where Walsingham had entertained Queen Elizabeth I, in **Barn Elms Park**. Philip Sidney married Walsingham's daughter Frances in 1583 and lived here until he sailed for the Netherlands (1585). Jacob Tonson (1656–1736), publisher of Addison and Steele, had a house (gone) in the park where he entertained the Kit-Cat Club, whose members also included Congreve and Vanbrugh, when he was its secretary and moving spirit. The promenade in the park, fashionable in the 17th and 18th cc. and mentioned by Congreve in *Love for Love* (1695), was also the scene of duels.

Henry Fielding lived (1748–53) in failing health at Milburne House (altered) on **Barnes Green**. Matthew Lewis, nicknamed 'Monk' from his successful Gothic novel, bought in 1798 Hermitage Cottage (gone) in Goodenough's Lane (site now at the head of **Nassau Rd** near the church). He was living there in 1801 and he owned the cottage throughout his life but was not a permanent resident.

William Cobbett, who leased (1828–30) the home farm on the Barn Elms estate, continued to edit his *Weekly Political Register* while he was living there, and wrote *Advice to Young Men* (1830).

The travel writer Eric Newby was born in Barnes in 1919. The novelist Barbara Pym lived at 47 Nassau Rd from 1949 to 1961. Sporting life on this part of the Thames is touched upon in her novel *Less Than Angels* (1955). Gavin Ewart reflects on the passing of time and tide in his 1964 poem 'Tennysonian Reflections at Barnes Bridge'.

BARNET, a district to the NW. The defeat and death of Richard Neville, Earl of Warwick ('the Kingmaker') at Barnet, whose demise puts an end to the Lancastrian resurgence, was dramatized by Shakespeare in *3 Henry VI*:

My parks, my walks, my manors that I had,
Even now forsake me, and of all my lands
Is nothing left me but my body's length.

BATTERSEA, district to the S. William Blake married Catherine Boucher, daughter of a market gardener in Battersea, at the parish church in 1782. G. A. Henty, whose roving life as a war correspondent led him over many of the scenes he used in his adventure stories, lived at 33 **Lavender Gdns** ⓟ. His many stories include *With Clive in India* (1884), *With Moore at Corunna* (1898), and *With Buller in Natal* (1901).

Edward Thomas and his wife lodged at 61 **Shelgate Rd** ⓟ for a short time in 1900 before moving into the country at *Bearsted. The Happy-Go-Lucky Morgans* (1913), his only novel, is partly set in the area.

Graham Greene lived at 141 **Albert Palace Gdns**, Battersea Park, from 1926 to 1931 and marked his first, in retrospect premature, successes as a writer while living here and working as a sub-editor on *The Times*. The novelist Paul Bailey was born and brought up in Battersea and went to Walter St John's Grammar School in the 1940s and 1950s. He has recorded episodes from his early life in his memoir *An Immaculate Mistake: Scenes from Childhood and Beyond* (1990). **Battersea Reach** is the setting for Penelope Fitzgerald's *Offshore* (1979), her novel about a community of London houseboats, 'creatures of neither firm land nor water'. The barge life is brilliantly evoked:

On every barge on the Reach a very faint ominous tap, no louder than the door of a cupboard shutting, would be followed by louder ones from every strake, limber and weatherboard, a fusillade of thunderous creaking, and even groans that seemed human. The crazy old vessels, riding high in the water without cargo, awaited their owner's return.

In Sarah Waters's *The Night Watch* (2006), Kay lodges above Mr Leonard's 'treatment room' on **Lavender Hill**, close to Clapham Junction station. From her window she watches the patients come and go, including Duncan, escorting his 'uncle' Mr Mundy; as she sits at her window, though, she hasn't realized that Duncan has noticed her too.

In his novel *Mr Phillips* (2000), John Lanchester's eponymous hero goes uncharacteristically AWOL from his respectable life as an accountant and spends his day wandering London instead; while in **Battersea Park** he finds himself confiding in a pornographer he meets on a park bench, and soothes himself (after the excitement of all his new experiences) by drawing up an imaginary double-entry account for the park's operations. Assets: car park fees; fees for tennis courts, football pitches, etc.; park benches; fees from people willing to pay to shoot geese. Liabilities: car park upkeep; upkeep of pavements; insurance for trips and falls; cost of geese damage. Meanwhile, in a flat at the back of a block that faces onto Battersea Park, hack writer Michael Owen is living, working on his history of the extraordinary Winshaw dynasty, in Jonathan Coe's *What a Carve Up!* (1994).

BAYSWATER, district NW of Hyde Park. Sir James Barrie lived (1902–9) at 100 **Bayswater Rd** Ⓟ, one of a pair of pleasant Regency houses standing in their own gardens above the main road, on the corner of Leinster Ter. It was here that he wrote the plays *Peter Pan* (1904; also partly written at *Farnham) and *What Every Woman Knows* (1908).

In Bernice Rubens's *Madame Sousatzka* (1962), the eponymous eccentric piano teacher lives at (the fictional) 132 Vauxhall Mansions W2, on a square off the Bayswater Rd, where she teaches her child prodigies.

> It wasn't the isolated castle Marcus had envisaged. It wasn't in any way different from any of the other houses in the square. It had its equal share of dry rot, damp, bitumen-patched walls; like the others, it shivered on a diminishing leasehold.

Monica Dickens, who like her great-grandfather Charles would grow up to be a novelist, was born at 52 **Chepstow Villas**, Bayswater, on 10 May 1915.

In **Hyde Pk Pl.**, Bayswater Rd, behind a group of flats (St George's Fields) is a disused graveyard, later the playground of the Hyde Park Nursery School. This was the burial place of Laurence Sterne, whose bones were twice disturbed: the first time apparently by body-snatchers for dissection purposes, but recognized and reinterred; the second time (1969) removed more reverently, by the Sterne Trust for reburial at *Coxwold. Ann Radcliffe, author of Gothic novels, was buried here (1823) and her tombstone is one of those lining the walls.

Lytton Strachey came at the age of 4 to 69 **Lancaster Gate**, just N of the Lancaster Gate entrance to Kensington Gdns, when his parents moved from Clapham Common in 1884. The house, later part of Douglas House (nos 66–71), was his home for the next 25 years.

Ivy Compton-Burnett lived (1916–29) at 59 **Leinster Sq.**, where she wrote *Pastors and Masters* (1925) and *Brothers and Sisters* (1929), set between 1885 and 1910.

Alice Meynell was a daughter of T. J. Thompson, a friend of Dickens, who visited the family in Italy, where she spent her childhood. She lived (1890–1905) at 47 Palace Ct Ⓟ and her first volume of poems was published before her marriage to Wilfrid Meynell in 1877. The Meynells rescued Francis Thompson from destitution and were friends of Meredith and Coventry Patmore. Alice Meynell published three volumes of poems here and the essays *The Rhythm of Life* (1893), *The Colour of Life* (1896), and *The Spirit of Peace* (1898).

Edith Sitwell moved into a shabby fourth-floor flat at **Pembridge Mansions** on Moscow Rd in 1912, where she entertained Wyndham Lewis to tea and excited his unwanted attentions. Lewis later lampooned her in *The Apes of God* (1930), his satirical crawl through the 'Ape-world' of London's literary bohemia.

In 1849 Harriet Martineau, then highly esteemed for her novel *Deerbrook* (1839), was staying at 17 **Westbourne St.** She mentions in her *Autobiography* (1877) receiving a copy of *Shirley* (1849) and a short letter from the new author 'Currer Bell' hoping that a meeting might be arranged. Charlotte Brontë's usual nervousness had been increased when she had been introduced to Thackeray at her publisher's house, 4 **Westbourne Pl.** (gone), where she was staying, but her meeting with Harriet Martineau passed without any awkwardness, and she had easily distinguished her from the other women present, by her ear-trumpet. It was on this visit to London, where she met again a family she had known in Brussels, that the idea came for her next novel, *Villette* (1853).

Thomas Hardy lived at 16 **Westbourne Pk Villas** from 1863 to 1867. Peter Porter reflects on his time here in his poem 'Thomas Hardy at Westbourne Park Villas'. The novelist, critic, and journalist Rebecca West was born at 28 **Burlington Rd**, Westbourne Park.

The Ufford, a private hotel near the **Queen's Rd**, was the principal residence of Uncle Giles, a shady relative of Nicholas Jenkins in Anthony Powell's *A Dance to the Music of Time* (1951–75). Its battleship grey walls and angular, top-heavy aspect, 'suggested a large vessel moored in the street . . . riding at anchor on the sluggish Bayswater tides'.

Leamas, the hero and victim of John le Carré's novel *The Spy Who Came in From the Cold* (1963), builds up his cover as a failed and embittered agent while living and working near the Bayswater Rd.

The novelist Muriel Spark lived overlooking Kensington Gdns at the top of 82 Lancaster Gate, the Helena Club, founded for 'Ladies from Good Families of Modest Means who are

Obliged to Pursue an Occupation in London'. It was the original for the 'May of Teck Club' in her novel *The Girls of Slender Means* (1963).

BELGRAVIA, district between Buckingham Palace Rd and Knightsbridge. Margaret Oliphant, novelist and biographer, spent her last years at 85 **Cadogan Pl.**, on the E side of Sloane St. Her *Autobiography*, published posthumously (1899), describes her efforts to provide for an education for her own and her brother's children by writing novels.

Dickens lived at 1 **Chester Row** in 1846, the year he founded, and was for a short time the editor of, the *Daily News*.

Shelley's second wife, Mary (née Godwin), spent her last years at 24 **Chester Sq.**, and died there in 1851. Matthew Arnold lived at no. 2 Ⓟ for 10 years until 1868. *Schools and Universities on the Continent* (1868) was written after visits made in connection with his post as Inspector of Schools (1851–83). *New Poems* (1867) contains 'Rugby Chapel', and 'Thyrsis' in memory of Arthur Hugh Clough, who died in Florence in 1861.

Algernon Charles Swinburne was born at 7 **Chester St.** in 1837.

Edward Trelawny, author of *Adventures of a Younger Son*, and *Records of Shelley, Byron, and the Author* (1858), lived at 17 **Eaton Sq.** during 1838. Sir W. S. Gilbert lived (1907–11) at no. 90 and, after a successful series of operas in collaboration with Sir Arthur Sullivan, wrote *Fallen Fairies* (1909) with Edward German and a serious sketch, *The Hooligans* (1911).

The charlady in Brian Patten's poem 'The Song of the Grateful Char' is lucky enough to work on the Square too, and for a most sympathetic employer:

> 'Sweetheart,' said the banker's wife,
> 'I too know of despair,
> I think about it often
> In my house in Eaton Square.'

George Meredith lived (1849) at 153 **Ebury St.** (gone). George Moore lived from 1911 to his death in 1933 at no. 121 Ⓟ. He was visited here by many literary friends including Yeats and Shaw. He wrote the novels *The Brook Kerith* (1916) and *Ulick and Soracha* (1924) here, also the autobiographical *Hail and Farewell* and *Conversations in Ebury St*. Victoria Sackville-West and her husband, Harold Nicolson, lived for a short time at no. 182 (gone) in the 1920s.

Ian Fleming lived at 22 Ebury St. from 1936 to 1939 Ⓟ. In 1953 he bought 16 **Victoria Sq.**, which he used when not in Jamaica. High earnings from his novel sequence *Strangers and Brothers* (1940–70) allowed C. P. Snow to move with his wife, the novelist Pamela Hansford Johnson, into 85 Eaton Sq. in 1968. He completed the series here in 1970, and continued to write both fiction and non-fiction here until his death in 1980.

No. 17 **Gerald Rd** was the London home of Noël Coward from the mid-1930s to the mid-1950s. As well as his earlier plays, which caught the mood of the 1920s, Coward wrote *Cavalcade* (1931), and *This Happy Breed*

British Library
This is the nation's supreme repository of knowledge; the John Ritblat Gallery displays a Shakespeare First Folio, a Magna Carta, the Lindisfarne Gospels, and countless remarkable literary manuscripts—among them the only page of drama written in Shakespeare's hand

British Library

King's Cross
A trolley disappearing into the brickwork marks the site of Platform 9¾, from which the Hogwarts Express takes Harry Potter and his friends to school. Adjacent St Pancras Station hosts a statue of poet John Betjeman

Platform 9¾ King's Cross Stn

Gordon Square
No. 46 was an early Bloomsbury Group HQ; and Lytton Strachey would later live at no. 51

Tavistock Square
Dickens lived at Tavistock House (now the home of the British Medical Association) from 1841; here he wrote *Bleak House*, *Hard Times*, *Little Dorrit*, and *A Tale of Two Cities*

Mecklenburgh Square
Virginia and Leonard Woolf ran the Hogarth Press from what was then no. 37

Foundling Hospital

Fitzroy Square
...he first to Bernard Shaw, ... wrote *Mrs Warren's ...ssion* here, and ...sequently to Virginia Woolf, ... hosted meetings of the ...omsbury Group here. In ...3 a house towards the north ... of the square was also home ...eurosurgeon Henry ...wne, the protagonist of Ian ...wan's *Saturday*

University College London
This university, at which A.E. Housman taught Latin, was partly founded by philosopher Jeremy Bentham, whose preserved body is still there on permanent display

Jeremy Bentham University College

13 Coram Street
Thackeray lived here, and it was in this house that his daughter Anne was born

Bedford Way
When this was still called Upper Bedford Place, no. 18 was home to Peter Mark Roget, compiler of the famous thesaurus, published during his time here

Russell Square
Famous residents of the Square include Thomas Gray, William Cowper, Ralph Waldo Emerson, and (fictionally) several characters from *Vanity Fair*. T. S. Eliot worked at the offices of Faber and Faber, at no. 24

Great Ormond Street Hospital

British Museum
The old round Reading Room has been the research home of writers ranging from Marx and Lenin to Oscar Wilde and Gandhi. Keats's 'Ode on a Grecian Urn' was inspired by a visit to the Museum too

Telecom Tower

44 Bedford Square
Home to society hostess Ottoline Morrell, and setting for her famous salons; she (and they) would later move round the corner to 10 Gower Street

Centrepoint
Meepers, the lonely, eccentric, and homeless amateur archaeologist of Maureen Duffy's experimental novel about London's ancient past and present, *Capital*, finds shelter on the 11th floor of an unoccupied high-rise based on the recently built Centrepoint

99

(1943), whose patriotism was popular in wartime, and two volumes of autobiography, *Present Indicative* (1937) and *Future Indefinite* (1954).

Swinburne lived at 18 **Grosvenor Pl.** for a short time (1860–1) while working on *The Queen Mother and Rosamond* (1860; chiefly written at Oxford). Mrs Humphry Ward lived (1891–1919) at no. 25, while engaged in her many philanthropic works. Her novels were written in the country.

The narrator of the stories in Paul Theroux's collection *The London Embassy* (1982), sequel to *The Consul's File* (1977), works as a diplomat at the American Embassy in **Grosvenor Sq.**

During a lunch hour in the spring of 1956 the travel writer Eric Newby, then working in the fashion business at a firm in **Grosvenor St.**, sent a cable from the post office on Mount Street (gone) to a friend in the British Embassy in Rio de Janeiro. It read, 'Can you travel Nuristan June?' The adventure that followed was recorded in *A Short Walk in the Hindu Kush* (1958) and launched Newby's career as a travel writer.

James Russell Lowell, American poet and essayist, lived at 37 **Lowndes St.** in 1880 and at nos 10 and 31 **Lowndes Sq.** (1881–5), when an American Minister (ambassador) in England.

T. S. Eliot's play *The Family Reunion* was first performed at the Westminster Theatre on **Palace St.** (gone) in 1939.

Walter Bagehot, editor of *The Economist* from 1860, lived at 12 **Upper Belgrave St.** Ⓟ for many years. *Literary Studies* was a posthumous collection of articles which had appeared first in the *National Review*.

Swinburne lived at 36 **Wilton Cres.** in 1865 when *Atalanta in Calydon*, a drama with Greek-style choruses, and *Chastelard*, a romantic drama about Mary Queen of Scots, were published.

Henry Green lived at 30 **Wilton Pl.** The gigantic hotel beside **Victoria Station** (originally the Grosvenor, now the Thistle Victoria) is the likely setting for the fog-bound bright young things of his novel *Party Going* (1939).

> Fog was down to ground level outside London, no cars could penetrate there so that if you had been seven thousand feet up and could have seen through you would have been amused at blocked main roads in solid lines and, on the pavements within two miles of this station, crawling worms on either side.

Bob, the hero of Patrick Hamilton's novel *The Midnight Bell* (1929), waits at the station in vain for his unrequiting lover, the prostitute Jenny, and comes to realize that 'he had never made any impression on her, and never would have done so'.

BERMONDSEY, district to the SE. The area was once the centre of the leather trade and as an adolescent V. S. Pritchett worked for four years in a leather factory not far from London Bridge station beside 'the malodorous yet lively air peculiar to the river of Bermondsey'. His

professional experience is vividly described in his early novel *Nothing Like Leather* (1935) and the first volume of his autobiography, *A Cab at the Door* (1968):

> The thing I liked best was being sent on errands in Bermondsey . . . I had a special pleasure in the rank places like those tunnels and vaults under the railway: the smells above all made me feel importantly a part of this working London. Names like Wilde's Rents, Cherry Garden Street, Jamaica Road, Dockhead and Pickle Herring Street excited and my journeys were not simply street journeys to me: they were like crossing the desert, finding the source of the Niger.

Somewhere in Bermondsey stands the Coach and Horses, the fictional starting point for the journey of Ray, Lennie, Vince, and Vic with their friend Jack Dodds's ashes in Graham Swift's novel *Last Orders* (1996).

Lorimer Black, hero of William Boyd's novel *Armadillo* (1998) and a man who takes a 'perverse pleasure' in the traditional British 'caff', visits the fictional St Mark's café on the **Old Kent Rd**:

> The windows facing the Old Kent Road were fogged and teary with condensation and the display unit contained only three ingredients for sandwiches—ham, tomato and chopped boiled eggs. Tea was served from an aluminium teapot, coffee was instant, the crockery was Pyrex, the flatware plastic.

Boyd's researches into these diehard institutions are described in his essay collection *Bamboo* (2006).

BETHNAL GREEN, a parish in the East End. This former village just outside London was the home of the heroine of the ballad 'The Blind Beggar's Daughter of Bednall-Green' (1600). Israel Zangwill, journalist, novelist, and playwright, prominent in Jewish cultural circles, is commemorated by a plaque at 288 **Old Ford Rd**. He published his first novel in 1881. *Children of the Ghetto* (1892), written at the invitation of the Jewish Publication Society of

America, and dramatized by him in 1899, was followed by other humorous and realistic stories of Jewish life. His play *The Melting Pot* (1908) is about immigrants to America. He was a friend of Jerome K. Jerome and W. W. Jacobs.

BEXLEYHEATH, district to the SE. From 1860 to 1865 William Morris lived at The Red House in **Red House Lane**, off Upton Rd, formerly in the village of Upton in Kent. Morris met the architect Philip Webb, who designed the house, when he himself was studying to be an architect in *Oxford. The two, who were lifelong friends, became partners in a firm to establish good decoration and design as a fine art. The only poetry Morris wrote here was the unfinished 'Scenes from the Fall of Troy'.

BLACKHEATH, district to the SE. Nathaniel Hawthorne, who gives an account of his Puritan ancestors in the introduction to *The Scarlet Letter* (1850), lived at 4 **Pond Rd** Ⓟ during his visit in 1856. He describes Blackheath in 'A London Suburb' in *Our Old Home* (1863).

In the spring of 1928 Malcolm Lowry's father made him an allowance of £7 a week and found him a room at 5 **Woodville Rd**, later 20 Rochester Way (gone, site at the junction of Rochester Way and Annesly Rd, at Shooters Hill Rd roundabout). Lowry started writing *Ultramarine* (1933) here.

BLOOMSBURY AND FITZROVIA, districts N of St Giles High St., between the City and Marylebone. When Carlyle and his wife first came to London they lodged (1831–2) at 33 (formerly 4) **Ampton St.** Ⓟ, on the E side of Gray's Inn Rd.

The science-fiction novelist John Wyndham lived at the Penn Club, 21–3 **Bedford Pl.**, for over 30 years, and wrote his best-known novels here: *The Day of the Triffids* (1951), *The Kraken Wakes* (1953), *The Midwich Cuckoos* (1957), and *The Trouble with Lichen* (1960).

The Red House, Bexleyheath, the home of William Morris from 1860 to 1865

Sir Anthony Hope Hawkins (author, as 'Anthony Hope', of *The Prisoner of Zenda*, 1894) lived at 41 **Bedford Sq.** from 1903 to 1917.

Dr Peter Mark Roget, physician and scholar, came to London in 1808 and lived at 39 **Bernard St.** (gone) until 1843. He did not begin to devote his time to the compilation of the *Thesaurus* (his best-known work) until he retired from medical practice in 1840. Two of his autograph letters, dated 4 June 1825 and 23 May 1859, can be seen at the Holborn Central Library in Theobald's Rd.

The **British Museum** (built 1823–1938 on the site of Montagu House), main entrance in Gt Russell St., houses Greek, oriental and other antiquities in its many galleries, and was formerly home to the British Library. The Museum, founded in 1753 and opened in Montagu House (gone) in 1759, had as its nucleus the collection of Sir Hans Sloane and the Cottonian Library, state papers and other manuscripts collected by Sir Robert Bruce Cotton (d. 1631) and presented to the nation by his grandson in 1702. The Harleian manuscripts, added in 1754, were the collections of the 1st and 2nd earls of Oxford. George II's and George III's bequests were housed in the King's Library. Keats wrote a sonnet on the Elgin Marbles, the sculptures from Athens which Robert Haydon persuaded the nation to buy for the Museum. Keats's 'Ode on a Grecian Urn' was also written after he had seen the sculptures. During its time here, the British Library would attract Karl Marx, who retreated from personal and political miseries to its Reading Room, where he wrote *Das Kapital* (1867). The Reading Room now holds a public reference library. The British Library collection, formerly held and displayed here, is now housed in the Library's new, purpose-built home on Euston Rd (see St Pancras). Garrick donated the statue of Shakespeare by Roubiliac long displayed in the Museum and now also removed to the new Library premises.

From 1852 George du Maurier, newly arrived in London, was a regular visitor to the British Museum, where he would go to sketch the sculptures.

Richard Garnett was an official here from 1875 to 1899, as was Laurence Binyon for 40 years until his retirement in 1933. Binyon's *Collected Poems* (two vols, 1931) contains 'For the Fallen', first published in *The Times* on 21 September 1914. Lines from the poem are carved on the wall at the entrance to the Museum as a war memorial to the staff. In the late 1920s the novelist Laurence Durrell moved to London and determined to become a poet and a bohemian, and spent a lot of his time at the British Library Reading Room.

Angus Wilson worked in the British Library after leaving Oxford in 1935; he returned after the Second World War and rose to become Deputy Superintendent of the Reading Room. Life in the great institution provided material for his satirical novel *The Old Men at the Zoo* (1961). Bernard Sands, the Grand Old Man of letters in Wilson's first novel, *Hemlock & After*

(1952), keeps a flat near Gordon Sq. looking down onto a Bloomsbury 'embalmed in its Sunday death'.

While doing his postgraduate studies at Queen Mary College, the novelist Malcolm Bradbury used to work at the British Library Reading Room too. Adam Appleby, the chief character in David Lodge's comic novel *The British Museum Is Falling Down* (1965), is another frequent user of the Reading Room, but spends too much time there worrying whether his wife might unfortunately be pregnant and not quite enough concentrating on writing his thesis.

> He would sit slumped at his desk in the British Museum, a heap of neglected books before him, while his mind reeled with menstrual cycles and temperature charts and financial calculations that never came right . . .

His one consolation is that as a sufficiently regular visitor to the Library he is no longer asked to show his card on arrival, which makes him feel at least a little bit important.

The famous 1970s 'Tutankhamun' blockbuster exhibition at the Museum provided the cue for Penelope Fitzgerald's first novel, *The Golden Child* (1977):

> The enormous building waited as though braced to defend itself, standing back resolutely from its great courtyard under a frozen January sky, colourless, cloudless, leafless and pigeonless. The courtyard was entirely filled with people. A restrained noise rose from them, like the grinding of the sea at slack water. They made slight surges forward, then back, but always gaining an inch.

In Sue Townsend's *Secret Diary of Adrian Mole* (1982), the British Museum is the unfortunate recipient of a visit from Adrian's class, 4–D (who 'run beserk, laughing at nude statues and dodging curators'), a visit ending with a teacher drafting her resignation and the coach driver being led off by police. The next day's diary entry begins, 'Keep having anxiety attacks every time I think about London, culture or the M1.'

Described as 'not far from the British Museum', in an institute of art history perhaps modelled on the Warburg Institute in Gordon Sq., Jacques Austerlitz, the subject of W. G. Sebald's last novel, *Austerlitz* (2001), teaches and conducts his endlessly ramifying research into the underlying principles of 19th-c. architecture.

Brunswick Sq., N of Guildford St. and now mainly occupied by university buildings, was the home of Virginia Stephen shortly before her marriage to Leonard Woolf. She and her brother Adrian moved in 1911 into no. 38 (gone), a four-storey house which they shared with J. M. Keynes, Duncan Grant, and Leonard Woolf. She and Leonard left when they married in 1912. Their friend E. M. Forster came here later and lived at no. 26 from 1929 to 1939.

Isabella, in Jane Austen's *Emma* (1816), gives a spirited defence of the healthiness of Brunswick Sq., after her father's complaint of the general sickliness and bad air of the capital.

Our part of London is so very superior to most others. You must not confound us with London in general, my dear sir. The neighbourhood of Brunswick Square is very different from all the rest. We are so very airy. I should be unwilling, I own, to live in any other part of the town; there is hardly any other that I could be satisfied to have my children in; but we are so remarkably airy. Mr Wingfield thinks the vicinity of Brunswick Square decidedly the most favourable as to air.

Charles Dibdin, dramatist and songwriter, lived at 30 **Charlotte St.** (now the Étoile restaurant) from 1805 to 1810. The Fitzroy Tavern was a well known literary rendezvous, particularly in the 1930s, 40s, and 50s, when patrons included Dylan Thomas, George Orwell, Julian Maclaren-Ross, and Brendan Behan. The bars are decorated with literary photographs of the period.

In a 'sordid spot' off Charlotte St. lived Mr Deacon, the enthusiastic and disreputable painter of Anthony Powell's novel sequence *A Dance to the Music of Time* (1951–75).

George Gissing lived at 22 **Colville Pl.**, near the S end of Tottenham Ct Rd, from January to September 1878. His days of poverty and hardship here are described in *The Private Papers of Henry Ryecroft* (1903).

Thackeray brought his young wife to live at 13 **Coram St.** (then Gt Coram St.), which runs from Woburn Pl. to Brunswick Sq., in 1837 and it was here that their first child, Anne Isabella, was born. After the birth of a third child, in 1840, Mrs Thackeray suffered a mental breakdown from which she never recovered and a few years later Thackeray gave up the house. Mr Todd, the junior partner in the firm of Osborne & Todd in *Vanity Fair*, lived in Gt Coram St.

In 1896 to 1906 Dorothy Richardson had a top-floor room at a lodging house kept by a Mrs Baker at 7 **Endsleigh St.** She was working as the assistant to a Harley St. dentist and in her spare time reading at the British Museum. She came back to a room here from 1907 to 1911. The young Jewish friend who became her fiancé for a short time becomes 'Michael' in *Pilgrimage* (1915–38), her long autobiographical novel, begun after she left Endsleigh St., which she calls Tansley St.

No. 29 **Fitzroy Sq.** Ⓟ, was the home of Bernard Shaw from 1887, when he moved in with his mother from 36 Osnaburgh St., to 1898, when he married Charlotte Payne-Townshend. He was music and drama critic for several papers, writer of political and economic tracts for the Fabian Society, which he had joined in 1884, and the author of several unsuccessful novels, when in 1892 he began to make his name as a dramatist with the production of *Widowers' Houses*, written in collaboration with William Archer, his friend and neighbour at no. 27. This play was followed by *Mrs. Warren's Profession* (1893), *Arms and the Man* (1894), and *Candida* (1894). In May 1898, when he was suffering from a foot injury and general debilitation, he received a visit from Charlotte Payne-Townshend, the fellow Fabian whom he had first met at the house of Sidney and Beatrice Webb in 1896 and whom

Brendan Behan at The Fitzroy tavern, Charlotte St., Fitzrovia. The pub was a meeting place for writers from the 1920s to the 1950s

he gradually became deeply attached to. Charlotte, his 'green-eyed Irish millionairess', who had called at Beatrice Webb's suggestion, was shocked at his poor state of health and invited him to her home at *Haslemere to be looked after. Shaw liked the idea but considered it outside the bounds of propriety, so he promptly arranged for their marriage, which took place on 1 June at the Strand Register Office, he still hobbling on crutches. He was restored to health and, after visits to Surrey and Cornwall and a Mediterranean cruise, he settled at 10 Adelphi Ter. (see Adelphi) for the next 28 years.

Virginia Woolf (née Stephen) lived at no. 29 with her brother Adrian from 1907 to 1911, when her sister Vanessa, married to Clive Bell, took over their former family house at 46 Gordon Sq. Virginia and Adrian began to entertain and to revive the 'Thursday evenings' started by Thoby Stephen and interrupted by his untimely death. Their circle of friends expanded to include Cambridge contemporaries of Thoby's and by the end of 1907 they had embarked on regular Friday evening readings—of authors ranging from the Restoration dramatists and Shakespeare to Swinburne and Ibsen. In 1909 Lytton Strachey proposed to Virginia Stephen and was accepted. But the engagement was short-lived and was broken to the relief of both parties. When their lease expired, Virginia and Adrian moved to 38 Brunswick Sq.

Ian McEwan's novel *Saturday* (2005) describes a day in the life of Henry Perowne, a neurosurgeon; as the novel opens, early in the morning of 15 February 2003, Perowne wakes up at his home on the NE corner of Fitzroy Sq. and looks out of his window onto the Square,

the passers-by crossing towards Cleveland St., a plane, an ambulance turning into Charlotte St., the mock-Regency façade, and, behind it, the Post Office Tower, 'municipal and seedy by day, but at night, half-concealed and decently illuminated, a valiant memorial to more optimistic days'. And he ventures out into the London streets. The third part of Edwin Morgan's poem 'London' is inspired by the **Post Office Tower**.

Gordon Sq., in the heart of London University buildings, was once the centre of the Bloomsbury Group, whose members lived in or near the Square in the early 20th c. The prime movers of the Group were the children of Sir Leslie Stephen, Thoby (who died young), Vanessa and her husband, Clive Bell, Virginia and her husband, Leonard Woolf, their brother Adrian, and their friends Lytton Strachey, E. M. Forster, Roger Fry, J. M. Keynes the economist, and G. E. Moore the philosopher, among many others in the world of art and letters who met 'for the pleasures of human intercourse and the enjoyment of beautiful objects'. Their headquarters was at no. 46, which became the home of the Stephen brothers and sisters in 1905 after the death of their father. The Thursday evening 'at homes', which soon became an institution, were started by Thoby, and his friend Leonard Woolf was one of the first to be invited. Others who soon became regulars included Clive Bell, Desmond MacCarthy, and Lytton Strachey. Thoby died in 1906 and soon afterwards Vanessa married Clive Bell. Virginia and Adrian left for Fitzroy Sq. in 1907, but kept in close touch with the others.

Lytton Strachey made no. 51 Ⓟ his London base when his family moved there in 1909 after his father's death, and it was here that he wrote

Queen Victoria (1921). The house is now part of University College London.

Norman Lewis lived at 4 **Gordon St.**, with the Corvajas, his Sicilian in-laws, their aggressive and smelly dog, an incontinent cat fed on pickled mushrooms and tagliatelle, a small owl, and a kestrel who liked to perch on a copy of Donatello's David. His association with the family excited his interest in Sicily, which led to a number of travel books written about the island.

Swinburne lived in rooms at 3 **Gt James St.**, running N off Theobald's Rd, from 1872 to 1875 and from 1877 to 1878. Edmund Gosse has described taking Mallarmé there in 1875 to effect a much-desired introduction, 'where that extraordinary man of genius lived in a dignified mediocrity'. Swinburne, for his part, was quick to praise 'the almost miraculous beauty' of Mallarmé's translation of Poe's *The Raven*.

Theodore Watts-Dunton, who later took Swinburne to live with him at *Putney, first got to know him when he was living nearby, at no. 15, in 1872–3.

Dorothy L. Sayers took a first-floor flat at no. 24 in 1921 and kept it on until the 1940s, when she settled in *Witham. When she married Arthur Fleming in 1926 they took the upper flat as well.

Gt Russell St. runs from Tottenham Ct Rd to Southampton Row, past the main entrance to the British Museum. The poet Harold Monro, founder of the quarterly *Poetry Review* (1912–), opened the Poetry Bookshop at no. 38 in 1913 and ran it until the end of his life (1932) as a centre for anyone interested in poetry and a place for poetry readings. It was here that Edward Marsh introduced W. H. Davies to him. Davies, a poet and wanderer, had made his name with *The Autobiography of a Super-Tramp* (1908) and had been granted a civil pension in 1911. He lived at no. 14 from 1916 to 1922.

Arthur Rowe, the central character of Graham Greene's wartime novel *The Ministry of Fear* (1943), lives on a bombed-out **Guilford St.** Its focus on London during the Blitz, with fireplaces suspended against walls above the streets and the sound of glass being swept up 'like the lazy noise of the sea on a shingled beach', was sharpened by Greene's experience as an air raid warden.

Anthony Trollope was born (1815) at 6 **Keppel St.**, N of the British Museum. The house, believed to have been no. 6 (though unnumbered when his father was living there), was demolished for university development.

Virginia Woolf's last London home was at 37 **Mecklenburgh Sq.** (gone), where she and Leonard Woolf ran the Hogarth Press from 1939 until the bombing in September 1940 necessitated its evacuation and it was moved to Letchworth until the end of the war.

Russell Sq., one of London's largest squares, off Southampton Row, was once an exclusive residential area, with an uninterrupted view of the Hampstead hills. Thomas Gray had lodgings (the Imperial Hotel occupies the site) in 1759–61 so that he could be within easy reach of the Reading Room of the newly opened British Museum. William Cowper lodged at no. 62 when he was a law student in the early 1750s. Henry Crabb Robinson, whose *Diary* is a remarkable source of facts and anecdotes about his literary contemporaries, lived at no. 30 (gone) from 1839 until his death in 1867, as the householder. Mary Russell Mitford lived at no. 56 in 1836 and left an account of a literary dinner party that she gave:

> Mr. Wordsworth, Mr. Landor and Mr. White dined here. I like Mr. Wordsworth, of all things, Mr. Landor is very striking-looking and exceedingly clever. Also we had a Mr. Browning, a young poet . . . and quantities more of poets.

Ralph Waldo Emerson, American philosopher and poet, stayed at no. 63 when he visited England in 1833. Mrs Humphry Ward and her husband lived at no. 61 from 1881 until 1891, when they moved to Grosvenor Pl.

T. S. Eliot used no. 24, where he worked in the editorial office of Faber and Faber, as his London address. Lawrence Durrell's first significant volume of poetry, *A Private Country*, was published in 1943 by Faber, where Eliot was his editor.

During the Second World War Eliot would often stay in a flat in the office and perform fire-watching duties on the roof. In June 1944 a bomb hit the premises and the flat became uninhabitable. These experiences are reflected in 'Little Gidding' in *Four Quartets*:

> Between three districts whence the smoke arose
> I met one walking, loitering and hurried . . .

In Thackeray's *Vanity Fair* the Osbornes lived at no. 96 and the Sedleys at no. 62.

Centrepoint, the tower at **St Giles Circus**, is selected as a temporary squat by the homeless archaeologist Meepers in Maureen Duffy's novel *Capital* (1975). Alan Brownjohn's poem 'Ode to Centre Point' derides the tower's 'hive of empty | Cells' and laments the useful buildings swept away to make room for it.

St Giles-in-the-Fields Church (rebuilt 1731–3 by Henry Flitcroft, the third since its foundation in 1101) is on the S side of **St Giles High St.**, which leads from St Giles Circus to High Holborn. The dramatist James Shirley died after shock and exposure in the Great Fire and is buried with his wife in the church. George Chapman, translator of Homer, is buried in the S side of the churchyard and has a monument by Inigo Jones. Andrew Marvell is also buried here and there is a memorial tablet to him on the N wall.

In Michel Faber's novel of Victorian London *The Crimson Petal and the White* (2002), the prostitute Sugar begins her career in the streets around St Giles, 'where even the cats are thin and hollow-eyed for want of meat'.

Colley Cibber, actor, playwright, and Poet Laureate, was born (1671) in **Southampton Pl.**, facing Southampton House (later Bedford House, which Evelyn says he saw being built in 1664). Pope made him the hero of the last edition (1743) of his satirical poem *The Dunciad*.

Jerome K. Jerome lodged at 33 (gone) **Tavistock Pl.** with his friend George Wingrave in 1889. Wingrave was the 'George' of *Three Men in a Boat* (1889). Jerome's *Idle Thoughts of an Idle Fellow* (1889) was written here. His play *The Passing of the Third Floor Back* (1907) is set in a Bloomsbury boarding house.

Tavistock House (rebuilt; now BMA House) in **Tavistock Sq.**, was Dickens's home from 1851. He wrote *Bleak House* (1852–3), *Hard Times* (1854), *Little Dorrit* (1855–7), and *A Tale of Two Cities* (1859), and started *Great Expectations* (1860–1) here. He was also able to stage the theatrical entertainments he loved in the schoolroom at the back of the house, where he used a platform outside the window as a prop for the scenic effects. Friends taking part included Mark Lemon, Wilkie Collins, and Alfred Ainger, and the plays included Collins's *Frozen Deep* and *The Lighthouse*, Lemon's and Dickens's *Mr. Nightingale's Diary*, and a farce, *Tom Thumb*, by Henry Fielding. Hans Andersen was a guest in 1857. Dickens moved to *Gad's Hill in 1860.

Virginia and Leonard Woolf took the lease of no. 52 in 1924 and ran the Hogarth Press there until 1939. The site is now occupied by the Tavistock Hotel.

Samuel Beckett underwent psychotherapy at the Tavistock Clinic, then on Tavistock Sq., in 1934–5. The experience was reflected in his novel *Murphy* (1936) in allusions to the Magdalene Mental Mercyseat, an institution 'on the outskirts of London' that provided for 'the better class mentally deranged'. Anthony Powell lived at 33 Tavistock Sq. from 1929 to 1932 and at 26 Brunswick Square (1932–5) and 47 Gt Ormond Street (1935–6). He set the publishing offices of the feuding brothers Hugh and Bernard Judkins 'in one of the Bloomsbury Squares' in his early novel *What's Become of Waring* (1939). In his novel sequence *A Dance to the Music of Time* (1951–76), the publishing firm of 'Quiggin and Craggs' acquires a lease near the Square after the Second World War, a place of 'sad streets and squares, classical façades of grimy brick, faded stucco mansions long since converted into flats'. Like his original, Julian Maclaren-Ross, Powell's hand-to-mouth man of letters X. Trapnel also haunts the local residential hotels and boarding houses. When in very low funds, Maclaren-Ross would spend the night in the Turkish baths at Russell Sq. The statue of Gandhi and a birch tree planted in memory of Hiroshima appear in Hugo Williams's poem 'Tavistock Square'.

Edmund Blunden was born at 54a **Tottenham Ct Rd** in November 1896. In Jean Rhys's *After Leaving Mr Mackenzie* (1930), Julia Martin leaves the eponymous Mr M in Paris and returns to London, to Bloomsbury, where she had lived ten years earlier. She lives in the fictional 33 Arkwright Gdns, and spends some time walking the local streets, through Woburn Sq. to Tottenham Ct Rd:

> She walked on through the fog to Tottenham Court Road. The people passing were withdrawn, nebulous. There was only a grey fog shot with yellow lights, and its cold breath on

her face, and the ghost of herself coming out of the fog to meet her.

The three children of Karl and Jenny Marx, lost while the family lived in Soho, were buried in the grounds of Whitefield's Tabernacle, which formerly stood at the site now occupied by the American Church in London and the London Chinese Lutheran Church.

University College London, in Gower St., founded in 1826, opened in 1828 as the University of London. Thomas Campbell and Crabb Robinson were among the group who first advocated a university for London and saw the project through. The library has a James Joyce centre and letters and manuscripts of George Orwell. A. E. Housman was Professor of Latin from 1892 to 1911. Stella Gibbons was educated at UCL. The Senate House of the University on nearby Malet St. was the home of the Ministry of Information during the Second World War; Dylan Thomas wrote propaganda film scripts for the Ministry, and John Betjeman worked here, as did Arthur Koestler and George Orwell. The building was the inspiration for the 'Ministry of Truth' in his novel *Nineteen Eighty-Four* (1949). The novelist and critic A. S. Byatt lectured at UCL from 1972 to 1983. Rebecca West studied at the Academy of Dramatic Art (later Royal) on Gower Street from 1910 to 1911.

Dr Peter Mark Roget lived at 18 **Upper Bedford Pl.**, now Bedford Way, to the N of Russell Sq., from 1843 until his death in 1869. His *Thesaurus of English Words and Phrases* was published in 1852 and has been through many subsequent editions.

A plaque at 5 **Woburn Pl.** commemorates Yeats's lodgings from 1895 to 1919 at what was then 18 Woburn Bldgs. His many visitors included Lady Gregory, Arthur Symons, Ernest Rhys, Laurence Binyon, and John Masefield. During this time he published the poetry collections *The Wind Among the Reeds* (1899), *The Green Helmet and Other Poems* (1910), and the plays *Cathleen ni Hoolihan* (1902), *On Baile's Strand* (1904), and *Deirdre* (1907). He married Georgie Hyde-Lees in 1917 and moved to Oxford two years later. Dorothy Richardson, while living (1906) at 2 Woburn Bldgs, often saw him working by candlelight across the street.

BRIXTON, district to the SW. Bertrand Russell began a six-month sentence in **Brixton prison** in 1918 for supporting conscientious objectors during the First World War. He was provided with books and writing materials, and allowed three visitors a week and his own food sent from outside the prison. He read and wrote uninterruptedly. He served a second, very brief sentence at the prison hospital in Brixton in 1961.

Billy Whispers in Colin MacInnes's novel *City of Spades* (1957), the earliest in his London trilogy, lives in a solitary house amid a corner of Brixton's wartime ruins, 'like one tooth left sticking in an old man's jaw'. Mr Stone, head librarian at Excal and the central character of V. S. Naipaul's novel *Mr Stone and the Knight's*

Companion (1963), lives in Brixton. The underground station, the Ritzy cinema, and nearby Streatham and Herne Hill all appear in the South London pages of Shena Mackay's *Dunedin* (1992). At her death in 1992, the film lover (and novelist) Angela Carter was commemorated with a memorial event at the Ritzy cinema.

Brixton today is home to dub poet Linton Kwesi Johnson, who came over to England from Jamaica in 1963. Much of his poetry is about this area, including 'Five Nights of Bleeding'; 'Yout Scene':

> last satdey
> I nevah deh pan no faam,
> so I decide fi tek a walk
> doun a Brixton
> an see wha gwaan,

and 'Di Great Insohreckshan' about the Brixton riots of the early 1980s:

> it woz in april nineteen eighty wan
> doun inna di ghetto af Brixtan
> dat di babylan dem cauz such a frickshan
> dat it bring about a great insohreckshan
> an it spread all owevah di naeshan
> it woz truly an historical occayshan . . .

BROMLEY AND BECKENHAM, district to the SE. Dr Johnson's wife, Tetty, is buried in the graveyard of the parish church of St Paul's. The church was destroyed by a flying bomb in the Second World War and the gravestone bearing Johnson's Latin inscription, which he composed in the last year of his life, has been moved to the ambulatory of the new building.

H. G. Wells was born (1866) above his father's crockery shop at 47 **High St.** Ⓟ. Wells first went to school at Morley's Academy (gone), also in the High St., but later went on to the Grammar School at *Midhurst. His father became bankrupt and his mother, who had been in service, became the housekeeper at *Uppark. In Wells's novel *The New Machiavelli* (1911), Bromley appears as 'Bromstead'. Dinah Mulock lived at Chilchester Lodge, **Wickham Rd**, Beckenham, after her marriage in 1865 to George Craik, and in 1870 they moved to the Corner House, Shortlands, nearby. She attended St Mary's Church there and a brass commemorating her as the author of *John Halifax, Gentleman* was put up after her death (1887).

In 1917 Richmal Crompton moved to Kent and taught Classics at Bromley High School for Girls, where she remained for seven years; during her time at the school she wrote her first story about the immortal William Brown, who would burst into the world in 1922 in *Just William*. Crompton lived at Bromley Common through the Second World War (when she volunteered with the Bromley Fire Service), only leaving eventually in 1953.

A later part of V. S. Pritchett's childhood and adolescence was spent in Bromley. It was the inspiration for the 'pink suburban fat' of 'Boystone', stamping ground of that domestic tyrant and monster of sanctimonious self-regard, the central character of his novel *Mr*

Beluncle (1951). Alan Brownjohn's poem 'Snow in Bromley' welcomes the 'white informal fantasies' that cover for a while the local proprieties and obsessions.

After the death of her husband in 1945, the novelist Jean Rhys moved in with his cousin Max Hamer at Beckenham, where she lived from 1946; conflict with her neighbours landed her in court on more than one occasion, and briefly in Holloway prison too. This ill welcome notwithstanding, she remained at Beckenham until 1960, when she finally moved down to Devon.

The novelist Hanif Kureishi was born in Bromley in 1954 and grew up there; it formed the setting for his novel *The Buddha of Suburbia* (1990), a tale of coming of age in the 1970s, against a backdrop of mixed communities and racial tension.

CAMBERWELL, district to the SE. Robert Browning, who was born (1812) in Southampton St. (gone), is commemorated by a plaque at 179 **Southampton Way**, adjacent to the house where he next lived with his parents. His father, who worked as a clerk at the Bank of England, amassed a library of 6000 books. Robert was educated at home, where he read voraciously and precociously. 'I was studying the grammar of music when most children are learning the multiplication table.' He was baptized in the Congregational Chapel at Walworth and is commemorated there by Browning St. (formerly York St.).

John Ruskin lived (1842–72) at 163 **Denmark Hill**, an imposing house, with a veranda and portico, standing in 7 acres. In his autobiography *Praeterita* (1885–9), he writes that there was 'a stable, and a farmyard, and a haystack and a pigstye and a porter's lodge, where undesirable visitors could be stopped before startling us with a knock'. Ruskin wrote *Modern Painters* (1843, later volumes 1846–60), and *The Stones of Venice* (1851–3) in his study on the first floor, though from 1852 to 1854 he was married and officially living elsewhere. In 1854, after the breakdown of his marriage, he made his home again here with his parents. After the death of his father (1864) and mother (1871) he moved (1872) to *Brantwood. No. 163 became a hotel, called Ruskin Manor, and was demolished in 1947. Ruskin is commemorated by **Ruskin Pk**, almost directly opposite the site of his house. A drawing of the house can be seen at *Brantwood.

V. S. Pritchett lived for a period as a child 'in a street off **Coldharbour Lane** in which the smell of vinegar from a pickle factory hung low, a street of little houses . . . and little shops that sent out such a reek of paraffin and packages that one's nostrils itched' (*A Cab at the Door*, 1968). The family later lived on Denmark Hill. The area is obliquely evoked in his celebrated short story about the antiques trade 'A Camberwell Beauty'.

Christopher Isherwood spent an inglorious year as a medical student at **King's College Hospital** in 1928–9, feeling, after having spent some six years studying at Cambridge and

teaching and writing in London, like 'the backward, overgrown boy who finds himself left behind in the infants' class'. He left to pursue the homosexual and literary life in Berlin described in *Christopher and His Kind* (1976), *Mr Norris Changes Trains* (1935), and *Goodbye to Berlin* (1939). The poet, novelist, and memoirist Dannie Abse continued his medical training at King's. He subsequently pursued a twin career as poet and doctor.

Muriel Spark lived for many years in digs at 13 **Baldwin Cres.**, spending some of her time here writing *The Ballad of Peckham Rye* (1960), whose action takes place in Camberwell and Peckham. Julia Langdon, the narrator of Anita Brookner's novel *Brief Lives* (1990), is brought up in Camberwell in 'one of those narrow Georgian houses' resembling those on **Camberwell Grove** and **Grove Lane**. King's College Hospital, Ruskin Pk, and Denmark Hill feature in Shena Mackay's novel *Dunedin* (1992).

Peter Ackroyd's *Dan Leno and the Limehouse Golem* (1994) is a tale of East End murder (and Victorian music hall), which begins in 1881 with a woman being hanged in the fictional Camberwell prison.

CAMDEN TOWN, district to the N. Christina Rossetti lived for a time with her mother in **Albany St.** (house demolished). There is a memorial to her in Christ Church in this street where she worshipped for many years. There was a funeral service for Eric Blair ('George Orwell') in Christ Church before his burial at *Sutton Courtenay.

Charles Dibdin, who published a *History of the Stage* (1795) and produced several plays at the Lyceum Theatre, lived in **Arlington Row** (gone). He is best remembered by his nautical songs, of which 'Tom Bowling' was the most popular. His last songs, including 'The Round Robin', were written here.

> But the standing toast that pleased the most
> Was—The wind that blows, the ship that goes,
> And the lass that loves a sailor!

Charles Dickens lived (1823–4) at 16 **Bayham St.** (gone) when his father was transferred to Somerset House from Chatham. The family were often in financial difficulties and Charles was sent to work in 1824 at Warren's Blacking Factory in the City, just before his father was arrested for debt. Camden Town and its neighbourhood feature in his novels as the homes of Bob Cratchit, Jemima Evans, Traddles, and Micawber. After John Dickens's release from jail, the family moved to Little College St. and then to Somers Town to the N.

V. S. Pritchett lived at **Parkhill Rd** in the 1940s. A remark from his cleaning woman here in 1948 gave him the idea for his celebrated short story of post-war London, 'When My Girl Comes Home'.

Theodore Fontane, a leading 19th-c. novelist and poet, stayed at 52 **St Augustine's Rd** with his wife and children from September 1855 to January 1859. He commemorated the house in a poem for his wife's birthday, 'Zum 14, November 1859'.

Alan Bennett, a long-time Camden resident, has written a play about an elderly woman who lives in a van which she has decided to park in his driveway for 15 years—a van which he is forced on one occasion to push up **Albert St.** for her. She describes to Bennett her sightings of a large grey snake ('it was keeping close to the wall and seemed to know the way') and Nikita Khrushchev, both apparently on the loose on **Parkway** (*The Lady in the Van*, 2002).

CARSHALTON, district to the S. William Hale White, who wrote as 'Mark Rutherford', lived in three houses here. The first was demolished to make way for a railway; he lived (1865–6) then at Stream or Spring House (now Honeywood). His sons liked the stream which ran through the garden and under the kitchen, but White was concerned about the damp. He wrote to *The Telegraph* in reply to Ruskin's letter about poor standards, asking where good, simple styles of houses could be found cheaply. This led to an introduction to Ruskin and through him to Philip Webb, who designed a new house for White on **Park Hill** (now no. 19). It was red-brick, tile-hung, dry, and soundproof, and had interior designs by William Morris. White lived here for 21 years (1868–89) while working at the Admiralty, and moved only when his wife's paralysis made more ground-floor rooms necessary. He wrote here *The Autobiography of Mark Rutherford* (1881), *Mark Rutherford's Deliverance* (1885), and *The Revolution in Tanner's Lane* (1887).

CHALK FARM, district to the NE of Regent's Park. In Jean Rhys's *Voyage in the Dark* (1934), Anna Morgan leaves Dominica to live in England; the book describes her life as a chorus girl in London and on tour. When she arrives in London she takes rooms on **Adelaide Rd** ('not far from Chalk Farm Tube station'), and wanders up the road to sit on Primrose Hill. She subsequently moves south to *Camden. (Rhys also explores the world of London theatre people in her story 'Before the Deluge'.)

Dodie Smith, who lived in a black and white flat on Regent's Park, set *The One Hundred and One Dalmations* (1956) in the district. Its canine hero, Pongo, barked on Primrose Hill, which is also where H. G. Wells concluded *The War of the Worlds* (1898).

In February 1960 Ted Hughes and Sylvia Plath took a flat in 3 **Chalcot Sq.**; their daughter Frieda was born in April.

W. B. Yeats came to London with his family in 1867 and lived at 23 **Fitzroy Rd** Ⓟ until 1874, when they moved to West Kensington. Sylvia Plath lived in the same house from 1962 to 1963 with her two children after separating from Hughes. In her *Letters Home* (ed. Aurelia S. Plath, 1975), she describes how she came to rent the flat:

[I] had the uncanny feeling I had got in touch with Yeats' spirit . . . I opened a book of his plays . . . as a joke for a 'message' and read 'Get

Chelsea Reach, where Penelope Fitzgerald lived on a barge in the early 1960s

wine and food to give you strength and courage, and I will get the house ready.'

She published a novel, *The Bell Jar*, in 1963 under the pen-name Victoria Lucas (reprinted under her own name, 1966), and wrote some of her best poetry here (*Ariel*, 1965). She suffered from severe fits of depression and took her own life in the flat.

'Henry Handel Richardson' (Ethel Florence Richardson) lived (1910–34) at 90 **Regent's Pk Rd**, where she wrote the trilogy *The Fortunes of Richard Mahony* (1930).

CHELSEA, district between Kensington and the river.

Karl Marx lived for a few months at 4 **Anderson St.** in 1849. The property proved beyond their means. The bailiffs removed everything they could and the family was forcibly evicted, to the amusement of the local crowds.

Quentin Crisp lived at 129 **Beaufort St.** in spectacular squalor, providing Harold Pinter with material for his first play, *The Room* (1957).

Arnold Bennett spent his latter years (1923–30) at 75 **Cadogan Sq.** Ⓟ, on the W side of Sloane St. *Riceyman Steps* (1923), set in Clerkenwell, has been considered the best novel of his later period.

In 1928, during her first stay in England, Christina Stead lived at 33 **Cartwright Gdns**.

Jerome K. Jerome wrote *Three Men in a Boat* (1889) when he was living in **Chelsea Gdns**, in a block of flats at the corner of Chelsea Bridge Rd and Ebury Bridge Rd. He described his 'little circular drawing-room' on the top floor as 'nearly all windows, suggestive of a lighthouse', from which he looked down upon the river and over Battersea Park to the Surrey hills beyond.

Penelope Fitzgerald and her family lived on a houseboat at **Chelsea Reach**, a period in her

life that yielded material for her novel *Offshore* (1979). The barge eventually sank.

Thomas Carlyle came to Chelsea with his wife, Jane, when they left Scotland for London in 1834, and lived at 5 (now 24) **Cheyne Row** (NT) until the end of his life. His two most famous works, *The French Revolution* (1837) and *Frederick the Great* (1857–65), were written in his 'soundproof' study at the top of the house. The house contains the original furnishings and many personal relics. His dog Nero is buried in the garden. There is a statue of Carlyle, 'Sage of Chelsea', between the foot of Cheyne Row and Chelsea Embankment, sheltered by trees and shrubs. The statue figures in Gavin Ewart's 1964 poem 'Chelsea in Winter'.

Thomas Carlyle in his garden at 5 (now 24) Cheyne Row, Chelsea

Cheyne Walk is an irregular street of houses overlooking the river, running from Royal Hospital Rd to Lots Rd Power Station, W of Battersea Bridge. No. 4 Ⓟ was George Eliot's last home, where she lived with her husband, John Cross, a few weeks only until her death. D. G. Rossetti lived at no. 16 Ⓟ from 1862 to 1882 and his house became a meeting place for artists and writers. Swinburne stayed there intermittently (1862–4), writing poetry in the first-floor drawing room, and other visitors included George Meredith, William Morris, and Oscar Wilde, coming and going in a house filled with immense collections of furniture and bric-à-brac and a garden inhabited by all manner of exotic birds and beasts. A memorial to Rossetti stands in the shrubbery between Cheyne Walk and the Embankment, a bust in high relief showing him with quill pen and palette, carved by Ford Madox Brown, on a base designed as a drinking fountain by John Seddon.

No. 18, called 'Don Saltero's', stands on the site of Don Saltero's Coffee House, which was originally opened by James Salter *c.* 1695 at the corner of Lawrence St. Salter had been valet to Sir Hans Sloane (1660–1753) on his travels abroad and acquired from him a strange assortment of unwanted curiosities from the collection which became the nucleus of the British Museum. These exhibits added to the fame of the establishment, which he finally moved to no. 18 *c.* 1717, describing it as 'My Museum Coffee-House', and which became a meeting place for literary men from London as well as local Chelsea people: Addison, Steele, Goldsmith, Sterne, Dr Johnson. Steele, who is believed to have nicknamed him 'Don Saltero', gave him welcome publicity in the *Tatler*, 1709–10. Fanny Burney refers to 'Saltero's Coffee House' in *Evelina* (1778).

Carlyle Mansions, on the E corner of **Lawrence St.**, is a block of flats where Henry James had his winter quarters from 1912 until his death there in 1916 (a bust of him, carved in 1914, is in the Public Library in King's Rd). The opening scene of David Lodge's novel *Author, Author* (2005) describes James's death.

London, December 1915. In the master bedroom (never was the estate agent's epithet more appropriate) of Flat 21, Carlyle Mansions, Cheyne Walk, Chelsea, the distinguished author is dying—slowly, but surely. In Flanders, less than two hundred miles away, other men are dying more quickly, more painfully, more pitifully—young men, mostly, with their lives still before them, blank pages that will never be filled.

On the other corner of Lawrence St. is the site of no. 59 Cheyne Walk, where the Welsh poet Ernest Rhys lived for a time from 1886.

The elite precincts of **Chelsea Harbour**— hardly disguised as 'Chelsea Marina'—is the setting for J. G. Ballard's radical black comedy *Millennium People* (2003):

For reasons no one understood, the inhabitants of Chelsea Marina had set about dismantling their middle-class world. They lit bonfires of

books and paintings, educational toys and videos. The television news showed families arm in arm, surrounded by overturned cars, their faces proudly lit by the flames.

Chelsea Old Church (mainly rebuilt after bomb damage in the Second World War) is at the corner of **Old Church St**. In the More Chapel (which escaped the bombing) is a tomb designed by Sir Thomas More, but there is no evidence that he was buried there. John Donne preached here at the funeral of Magdalen Herbert, mother of George Herbert, and his friend Izaak Walton was among those who attended. Thomas Shadwell, 17th-c. Poet Laureate and dramatist, who lived in the vicinity, was buried in the churchyard, but the exact site is unknown. On the S wall there is a memorial plaque to Henry James. Between the church and the Embankment there is a statue of Sir Thomas More, whose manor house, once situated in extensive grounds a little further W, was a centre of learning and culture from *c.* 1524 until 1534, when he was committed to the Tower on a charge of high treason.

At no. 91 Margaret Fairless Barber ('Michael Fairless') lived for a time with her friends the Dowsons and began the essays later published as *The Roadmender* (1901). William Bell Scott, poet and artist, lived at no. 92, celebrated in his poem 'Bellevue House', and Elizabeth Gaskell, née Stevenson, was born at no. 93 Ⓟ, but only lived there just over a year before being taken to *Knutsford after her mother's death. No. 104 Ⓟ was the home of Hilaire Belloc and his wife from *c.* 1900 to 1906.

Laurie Lee, author of *Cider with Rosie* (1959) kept his Chelsea flat even after moving back to the Cotswolds; he was a keen member of the Chelsea Arts Club (at 143 Old Church St.), and a regular visitor in his later years.

Logan Mountstuart, hero of William Boyd's novel *Any Human Heart* (2002), lives in a flat on the 'darkly anonymous' **Draycott Ave**.

Bram Stoker, author of *Dracula* (1897), lived at 4 **Durham Pl.**, a dignified row of houses dated 1790, lying back from Ormonde Gate, near the corner of St Leonard's Ter.

Bearing letters of introduction from Matthew Arnold, Leo Tolstoy, 'a Russian gentleman interested in public education', visited, among other educationally advanced schools in the capital, St Mark's Practising School (later the Octagon School, 1994–6) on **Fulham Rd** in March 1861. The essays he was presented with by the children are preserved in the Tolstoy Museum in Moscow.

Fay Langdon, the narrator of Anita Brookner's *Brief Lives* (1990), lives in a house on **Gertrude St.**, 'a handsome street, filled with handsome houses', but which 'merely feeds into other streets exactly like itself'. Nancy Mitford was born at 1 **Graham St.** (now Ter.) in 1904.

George Meredith lived at 8 **Hobury St.** Ⓟ for a time (1858–9) after being separated from his first wife. Here he wrote *The Ordeal of Richard Feverel* (1859) and the first chapters of *Evan Harrington* (1861). He often came across Carlyle in his walks and longed to speak

to him, a wish that was fulfilled when Carlyle himself made contact with him through his publisher and encouraged him to call at Cheyne Row.

The Gateways Club ('the Gates'), which stood just off the **King's Rd**, was the original for the House of Shades, the lesbian club in Maureen Duffy's novel *The Microcosm* (1966). Also off the King's Rd, on Bywater St., lived John le Carré's spymaster George Smiley behind, as described in *Tinker, Tailor, Soldier, Spy* (1974), 'two locks, a Banham deadlock and a Chubb Pipekey, and two splinters of his own manufacture, splits of oak each the size of a thumbnail'.

John Gay was secretary to the Duchess of Monmouth when she lived at the 'great house' *c.* 1714, on the site of 16 **Lawrence St.** Tobias Smollett lived (1750–62) in apartments in the present house Ⓟ, where he wrote *Peregrine Pickle* (1751), *Ferdinand Count Fathom* (1753), and the less successful *Sir Launcelot Greaves* (1760–2). Among his visitors were Goldsmith, Sterne, and Dr Johnson (whom he called 'the Great Cham of Literature').

A. A. Milne lived at 11 (now 13) **Mallord St.** Ⓟ from the 1920s until 1940. He had previously been assistant editor of *Punch* (1906–14) and had published several successful plays, including *Mr. Pim Passes By* (1919), *The Truth About Blayds* (1921), and *The Dover Road* (1922), before he made his name as a children's writer with the enduringly popular verses in *When We Were Very Young* (1924) and *Now We Are Six* (1927) and the stories (based on his son's childhood) of *Winnie-the-Pooh* (1926) and *The House at Pooh Corner* (1928). Much of his writing was done here, as well as at *Hartfield.

Percy Wyndham Lewis studied at the Slade School of Fine Art on **Manresa Rd** in the late 1890s, as did the novelist and playwright David Storey in the 1950s. Storey, who was under a 15-year contract to Leeds Rugby League Club, was obliged to return to the north every weekend to play rugby.

P. G. Wodehouse lived at **Markham Sq.** while working at the Hong Kong and Shanghai Bank in the City. He also lived briefly at 23 Walpole St.

George Gissing lived at 33 **Oakley Gdns** Ⓟ from 1882 to 1884.

The novelist Brigid Brophy lived on **Old Brompton Rd** from the mid-1960s until 1991.

Between 1933 and 1935 Samuel Beckett lived at 48 **Paultons Sq.** He wrote much of *Murphy* (1936) here, and the area is recalled in an episode involving the novel's heroine, Celia:

She walked to a point about halfway between Battersea and Albert bridges and sat down on a bench between a Chelsea pensioner and an Eldorado Hokey-Pokey man . . . A tug and barges coupled abreast, foamed happily out of the reach. The Eldorado man slept in a heap, the Chelsea pensioner tore at his scarlet tunic, exclaiming 'Hell roast this weather, I shall niver fergit it.' The clock of Chelsea old church ground out grudgingly the hour of ten.

Sir Thomas More, his father, his household, and his descendants at Chelsea. A painting after Hans Holbein by Rowland Lockey (1593)

She also meets Murphy in the vicinity:

> She had turned out of Edith Grove into Cremorne Road, intending to refresh herself with a smell of the Reach and then return by Lot's Road, when chancing to glance to her right she saw, motionless in the mouth of Stadium Street, considering alternately the sky and a sheet of paper, a man, Murphy.

In the 1940s the poet and critic Kathleen Raine installed herself at 47 Paultons Sq. In 1949 she met Gavin Maxwell here, with whom she was to have a famously unhappy relationship for seven years.

Ranelagh Gardens, formerly belonging to the Earl of Ranelagh (site now part of the Chelsea Royal Hospital grounds), were opened to the public in 1742 for entertainments of singing and dancing known as *ridottos*. Many of Christopher Smart's songs were sung here, some set to music by Thomas Arne (employed at Ranelagh from 1745), whom Smart had probably met through Charles Burney, his friend at Cambridge. Gray, who refused to desert Vauxhall Gardens at first, spent many evenings here later, as did Lord Chesterfield and Horace Walpole. Matthew Bramble and Lydia Melford in Smollett's *Humphry Clinker* (1771) give, as usual, widely divergent views on the entertainments. Karl Moritz, visiting

England in 1782, compared the gardens unfavourably with Vauxhall at first, but was entranced on entering the Rotundo (gone) to be reminded of his childhood idea of fairyland. Robert Bloomfield's poem 'A Visit to Ranelagh' comments on the visitors incessantly walking round and round. The gardens closed in 1803, and were completely remodelled in 1860.

The **Royal Court Theatre** (formerly the Court Theatre, rebuilt 1888 after an earlier theatre) stands on the E side of Sloane Sq. In the foyer was a bust (which has disappeared) of Bernard Shaw (by Michael Werner, 1955), commemorating the production of eleven of his plays from 1904 to 1907. These included *Candida, John Bull's Other Island* (which had a 'special evening performance for H.M. the King' on 11 March 1905), *Man and Superman*, and *The Doctor's Dilemma* (which has a programme note saying, 'The Doctor's Dilemma is the title of a story by Miss Hesba Stretton, who has been kind enough to allow the Author to use it for his tragedy'). The plays, produced by Harley Granville-Barker (1877–1946), ran to 701 performances. Since 1956 the theatre has been the home of the English Stage Company. Upon the establishment in 1955 of the Company, which hoped to seek out and promote the best new writing for the theatre,

the young playwright John Osborne submitted his play *Look Back in Anger*, which he had written that summer; the play was chosen for the first season in the Royal Court Theatre under the auspices of the ESC, opening on 8 May 1956. The play earned Osborne the epithet of 'angry young man' and divided critics sharply.

St Luke's Church in Sydney St., between the King's Rd and Fulham Rd, is the parish church of Chelsea (built in Gothic Revival style, 1820–4). Dickens married Catherine Hogarth here in 1836, and Charles Kingsley served for a short time as curate to his father (who was rector, 1836–60) before going to *Eversley.

A number of distinguished playwrights would be associated with the theatre's first half-century, from Osborne in 1956 (and his *Epitaph for George Dillon*, co-written with Anthony Creighton, two years later) running through premières of work by Samuel Beckett (*Endgame*, 1957; *Krapp's Last Tape*, 1958), John Arden (*Live Like Pigs*, 1958; *Serjeant Musgrave's Dance*, 1959), David Storey (*The Changing Room*, 1971; *Home*, 1972; *The Farm*, 1973; *Life Class*, 1974), and Hanif Kureishi as writer in residence (1982), right though to a new play by Tom Stoppard (*Rock 'n' Roll*) and performances by Harold Pinter (in Samuel Beckett's *Krapp's Last Tape*) in 2006.

Sloane St., a long, straight thoroughfare which runs from Knightsbridge to Sloane Sq., was named after Sir Hans Sloane (1660–1753), the physician and naturalist whose collection of books, manuscripts, prints, coins, and other treasures formed the nucleus of the British Museum. Edgar Allan Poe, who was brought to England from Boston, Massachusetts, in 1815, went to a boarding school at no. 146 in 1816–17 before going to *Stoke Newington. Mrs Mary Louisa Molesworth, author of children's books, lived in Sloane St. for the last 20 years of her life (1901–21). On 6 April 1895 Oscar Wilde was arrested in room 118 of the Cadogan Hotel for 'committing acts of gross indecency'. The incident is the subject of John Betjeman's 'The Arrest of Oscar Wilde at the Cadogan Hotel':

> He rose, and he put down *The Yellow Book*.
> He staggered—and, terrible-eyed,
> He brushed past the palms on the staircase
> And was helped to a hansom outside.

Mark Twain lived at 23 **Tedworth Sq.** Ⓟ in 1897. He describes in his autobiography how the publishing firm of Webster & Co., New York, which he had founded, had failed in the early 1890s, its liabilities exceeding its assets by 66 per cent. Feeling morally bound to repay the debts, he decided to write a book and return to the lecture platform, with the result that he set off on a world tour in 1895, wrote *Following the Equator* (1897) while staying in London, and paid off the debts in full at the end of 1898 or the beginning of 1899.

No. 34 **Tite St.** Ⓟ was Oscar Wilde's home from the time of his marriage in 1884 until his disastrous trial and imprisonment brought his career to an end in 1895. His principal work was written here, including *The Happy Prince* (fairy tales, 1888), *The Picture of Dorian Grey* (novel, 1891), and the social comedies *Lady Windermere's Fan* (1892), *A Woman of No Importance* (1893), *An Ideal Husband* (1895), and the brilliant and enduring *The Importance of Being Earnest* (1895).

Leigh Hunt lived with his wife and seven children (1833–40) at 22 **Upper Cheyne Row** Ⓟ.

Thomas Wolfe, the American novelist, lodged in a room at 32 **Wellington Sq.** in 1926 when writing his first book, *Look Homeward, Angel*, published, after being rejected many times, in 1929.

CHESSINGTON, district to the SW. Chessington Hall (site in **Garrison Lane**, near the church) was often visited by Fanny Burney in the 1770s. Her host was her father's friend the embittered author of the unsuccessful tragedy *Virginia* (1754), whom she called 'Daddy Crisp'. She was staying here when Mrs Thrale reported Dr Johnson's praise of *Evelina* (1778) and she danced with joy round the mulberry tree on the lawn. The epitaph to Samuel Crisp, on the N wall of the church, with its rhyming tribute to his 'enchanting powers of brightening social and convivial hours', was written by Dr Burney. The house, partly 16th-c., which Fanny Burney called 'Liberty Hall', was rebuilt (1830–40) and this was in turn demolished in the 1960s.

CHISLEHURST, district to the SE. Ronald Firbank's parents bought the 18th-c. house Coopers (now part of a school) in **Hawkwood Lane** in 1886. The artificial romance *Lady Appledore's Mésalliance* (1907), in which someone sits up all night with a sick orchid, was written when 'dear Home', as Firbank called the 100-acre estate, had to be sold.

Just William author Richmal Crompton spent the last 15 years of her life, from 1953, at Chislehurst.

Harold Pinter's *The Caretaker* (1960), though not specific in its setting, is peppered with references to places in London; most insistent of these is Davies's concerns about whether he'll be able to get to **Sidcup** (think of the Three Sisters and Moscow, but laced with added anxiety), which punctuate all three acts of the play, through to the very closing lines; he absolutely must go to Sidcup to get his papers—'a man I know has got them'.

CHISWICK, riverside district to the W of Hammersmith. Pope came here with his parents in 1716 and lived at the corner house of Dr Matthias Mawson's New Bldgs in Chiswick Lane, now the Fox and Hounds (or the Mawson Arms), **Chiswick Lane South**. While he was here he wrote 'Elegy on the Death of an Unfortunate Lady' and 'Epistle of Eloisa to Abelard'. He moved to *Twickenham in 1718.

Rousseau stayed in Chiswick as an exile from France in 1765–6 and lodged with 'an honest grocer', probably in Church St., before going to *Wootton, Staffordshire, in early 1766.

Thackeray received his early education at the Preparatory School for Young Gentlemen, at Walpole House in Chiswick Mall, and later turned it into Miss Pinkerton's Seminary for Young Ladies, attended by Becky Sharp and Amelia Sedley in *Vanity Fair* (1847–8).

In 1879, when he was 13, W. B. Yeats moved with his family to 8 **Woodstock Rd**, one of the new houses in Bedford Park built by Norman Shaw under the influence of William Morris. He went to the Godolphin Boys' School in *Hammersmith. After two years the family returned to Ireland, but came back to Bedford Park in 1888, Yeats living with them at 3 Blenheim Rd Ⓟ until 1895.

John Betjeman, who campaigned to preserve Bedford Park, set his poem 'Narcissus' here—'that sweet flower which self-love takes its name from | Nodding among the lilies in the garth'.

Jenny, later to become the prostitute who makes the life of Bob a misery in Patrick Hamilton's early 1930s trilogy *Twenty Thousand Streets Under the Sky*, works as a housekeeper in the elderly household of Dr Chingford in Chiswick.

Nancy Mitford moved into Rose Cottage, 84 **Strand on the Green**, on the corner of Hearne Rd in 1934. Her third novel, *Wigs on the Green*, was published that year and sent up the British Union of Fascists. It went down badly with her sisters Unity (an admirer of Hitler) and Diana, who had recently married the Fascist leader Sir Oswald Mosley.

Gabriel Harvey, the tragicomic narrator of Paul Bailey's novel *Gabriel's Lament* (1986), lives in a 'miniature mansion' overlooking the river at Strand on the Green.

A young Iris Murdoch lived at 4 **Eastbourne Rd** from 1926.

The playwright John Osborne and his friend the actor Anthony Creighton lived on a barge in Chiswick, where some of *Look Back in Anger* (1956) was written.

CITY, district from the Tower to Holborn and the Strand, including the old City of London. The garden at the corner of **Aldermanbury** and Love Lane replaces the Church of St Mary Aldermanbury, bombed in the Second World War and removed in 1966 to Westminster College, Fulton, Missouri, as a memorial to Sir Winston Churchill. The foundations of the church showing the round pillars of the nave remain.

Shakespeare, who lived nearby in Silver St. (gone), has a memorial bust on a pedestal which also commemorates his friends and fellow actors Henry Condell and John Heminge. They edited the First Folio (1623) of his plays (the book is depicted open showing their foreword) and are buried here.

At **Aldersgate** John Betjeman mourned the passing of the underground station in 'Monody on the Death of Aldersgate Street Station'.

A plaque on the post office at 2 **Aldgate High St.** records that Geoffrey Chaucer lived in 1374 in the rooms over Aldgate, a medieval gate into the City (removed 1760). Chaucer is thought to have lived here from 1374 to 1386 except when his duties in the King's service took him to embassies abroad or to oversee customs at the ports. Chaucer wrote *Troilus and Criseyde* during the time he was living here, and one of the two men named in the dedication was Ralph Strode, the philosopher, who at one time was living over Aldersgate (*c*. 1 m. W).

On a site now occupied by the Great Eastern Hotel (see also Liverpool St. Station) once stood the **Bethlehem Hospital**, or Bedlam Ⓟ, a hospital for the mentally ill. Shakespeare's Edgar impersonates a 'Bedlam beggar' in *King Lear*:

> The country gives me proof and precedent
> Of Bedlam beggars who with roaring voices
> Strike in their numbed and mortified bare arms
> Pins, wooden pricks, nails, sprigs of rosemary . . .

Shakespeare's first London lodgings (gone) were in the parish of St Helen's **Bishopsgate**, where he is recorded as living in October 1596. It was then a well-to-do area approximately halfway between the two theatre districts of *Shoreditch and Bankside (see SOUTHWARK). His parish church, which survived the Great Fire of 1666, has the finest Elizabethan monuments in the City.

Blackfriars, an area between Queen Victoria St. and the river, was the site of Blackfriars' Monastery, rented out after the Dissolution as apartments, houses, and shops. In 1596 James Burbage adapted some of the buildings, including the Frater, for the second Blackfriars' Theatre (Playhouse Yard now on the site). This was a small indoor theatre seating about 700 and intended for performances in the winter months. Disputes between Burbage and the City authorities resulted in the theatre being used by another company, the Children of Paul's, boy actors from the Cathedral School, but in 1608 Burbage's company, the King's Men (formerly the Lord Chamberlain's Men), were granted a lease. Shakespeare had a profitable share in this company, which also played in Southwark. *Cymbeline* (1610) was one of many plays performed at both theatres. Ben Jonson lived in Blackfriars from 1607 to 1616 and in 1613 Shakespeare bought the gatehouse to the old priory near the river at Puddle Wharf. It was the first and only property he ever bought in London. He seems never to have lived there and by 1616 he was renting it out. Part of *Richard III* is set at Baynard's Castle, which once stood on the river near the area now occupied by Blackfriars station.

Dickens's David Copperfield spends a miserable time as a boy in Blackfriars after his mother's death when he is sent to wash and label bottles at Murdstone and Grinby's warehouse, 'a crazy old house with a wharf of its own, abutting on the water when the tide was in, and on the mud when the tide was out, and literally overrun with rats'. His first day there is not auspicious:

No words can express the secret agony of my soul as I sunk into this companionship; compared these henceforth everyday associates with those of my happier childhood—not to say with Steerforth, Traddles, and the rest of those boys; and felt my hopes of growing up to be a learned and distinguished man crushed in my bosom.

He makes the acquaintance of Mr Micawber and lodges at his house. After Micawber's arrest for debt, David decides to run away.

The offices of *The Times* stood at Printing House Sq. before the paper's removal to Gray's Inn Rd and later Wapping. Graham Greene worked as a sub-editor on the paper from 1926 to 1930 and remembered in *A Sort of Life* (1971) peaceful times there, 'the slow burning fire in the sub-editors' room, the gentle thud of coals as they dropped one by one in the old black grate'. He left before he had fully established himself as a writer and, for a few years, bitterly regretted his decision.

The travel writer Peter Fleming was a foreign correspondent for *The Times* in the 1930s. His career as a writer had been launched earlier with an advertisement placed in the agony column of the paper:

Exploring and sporting expedition, under experienced guidance, leaving England June, to explore rivers Central Brazil, if possible ascertain fate Colonel Fawcett; abundance game, big and small; exceptional fishing; ROOM TWO MORE GUNS; highest references expected and given.— Write Box X, *The Times*, E.C.4.

Fleming's account of this expedition resulted in *Brazilian Adventure*.

Harrison Ainsworth wrote most of *The Tower of London* (1840) at the Sussex Hotel in **Bouverie St.**, off Fleet St., where on completion of the novel he gave a large dinner for friends including Dickens, Forster, and Barham, and he sang the popular ballad 'Lord Bateman'. In the 1840s and 1850s the contributors to *Punch* (founded 1841) met at no. 10 and dined at a large deal table known as the Mahogany Tree. Mark Lemon, founder and editor (to 1870), first published Hood's 'The Song of the Shirt' (1843) in *Punch*.

The Mermaid tavern stood on the E side of **Bread St.** near the junction with Cheapside. It was frequented by Marlowe (d. 1593), Shakespeare, Donne, Beaumont, Fletcher, Drayton, Selden, Browne, and Coryate, most of whom were members of one of the earliest clubs, established by Sir Walter Ralegh *c.* 1603, which met here on the first Friday of the month. Beaumont, writing to Ben Jonson, exclaims:

What things have we seen,
Done at the Mermaid! heard words that have been
So nimble, and so full of subtle flame,
As if that every one from whence they came,
Had meant to put his whole wit in a jest,
And had resolv'd to live a fool, the rest
Of his dull life.

And Keats in 'Lines on the Mermaid Tavern' asks the dead poets whether even Elysium can compare with the place. The houses where Donne (1571/2) and Milton (1608) were born are gone.

After completing his studies a young George du Maurier was set up in his father's lab in Barge Yard, **Bucklersbury**, to analyse deposits in a Devon gold mine. But as it turned out there wasn't any gold, so the job did not last long. But at least he could write about it, in 'Recollections of an English Goldmine' (1861).

London Stone on **Cannon St.** figures in Shakespeare's *2 Henry VI* when Jack Cade strikes his staff on it and declares:

Now is Mortimer Lord of this city. And here, sitting upon London Stone, I charge and command that the Pissing Conduit run nothing but claret wine this first year of our reign.

The 14th-c. Carthusian priory in **Charterhouse Sq.** was re-established in 1611 as a school for boys and a refuge for old lay brothers. Elkanah Settle, whose dramas had vied in popularity with Dryden's, spent his last years from 1718 here and died in 1724. Pupils at **Charterhouse** include Crashaw, Lovelace, Joseph Addison, and his contemporary Richard Steele, John Wesley, Thomas Day, T. L. Beddoes, F. T. Palgrave, and Thackeray. In *The Newcomes* (1853–5), Thackeray's Colonel Newcome, a pupil in his youth, has a last refuge here in old age. The school moved to new buildings in *Godalming in 1872. The Charterhouse, restored after Second World War damage, is now a home to 40 male pensioners, known as Brothers. The novelist Simon Raven, a pupil of the school, spent his last years here.

Cheapside, the City of London's old high street and in Shakespeare's time famous for its goldsmiths, was the setting for Thomas Middleton's comedy *A Chaste Maid in Cheapside* (1612). Shakespeare refers to the figure of Diana which stood atop one of the conduits on Cheapside in *As You Like It* (*c.* 1600) and probably set the important scene he contributed to *Sir Thomas More* here.

At the end of 1816 Keats moved into lodgings with his brothers at 76 Cheapside, where their sitting room overlooked the street. He was still working as a dresser at Guy's Hospital but, stimulated by his friendship with Charles Cowden Clarke, which led to his meeting Leigh Hunt, John Reynolds, and the painter Benjamin Robert Haydon, he was writing more. His first collection of *Poems* (1817) contained the sonnet on Chapman's Homer, which he had looked at with Clarke, that on the Elgin Marbles, which he had seen with Haydon, others addressed to Hunt, Reynolds, and his brothers, and also the longer 'Sleep and Poetry' suggested by the Chaucer lent him by Clarke. Keats and his brothers moved to Hampstead in the summer of 1817.

F. W. Rolfe ('Baron Corvo') was born (1860) at no. 112 (rebuilt). The family moved to *Camden Town when he was a young child.

Clifford's Inn, Fetter Lane, is a block of flats built on the site of the oldest of the Inns of Chancery, to which Selden was admitted in 1602. George Dyer, the myopic subject of one of Charles Lamb's essays, 'Amicus Redivivus', lived here (1792–1841). Samuel Butler settled at no. 15 after his return from New Zealand in 1864. He wrote the satirical novel *Erewhon* (1872) and its sequel, *Erewhon Revisited* (1901), which contains the professors Hanky and Panky. The autobiographical novel *The Way of All Flesh* (1903), published the year after Butler's death, gives an embittered account of paternal tyranny.

Anthony Powell worked at Duckworth publishers at New Fetter Lane from 1926 to 1936. His years in publishing are evoked in *What's Become of Waring* (1939) and while working here he wrote his early comic novels *Afternoon Men* (1931), *Venusberg* (1932), *From a View to a Death* (1933), and *Agents and Patients* (1936).

After the Second World War the novelist Barbara Pym spent most of her working life as the assistant editor for the journal *Africa* at the International African Institute at St Dunstan's Chambers, Fetter Lane. The business of moving office from here to the School of Oriental and African Studies near Russell Sq. at the end of her career provided material for her novel *Quartet in Autumn* (1977).

Horace Smith, parodist and novelist, was a clerk in a merchant's office at 39 **Coleman St.**, near Moorgate. He had published some novels when he made his name with *Rejected Addresses* (1812), parodies written with his brother James.

Thomas Gray was born (1716) at 39 **Cornhill** (rebuilt), near St Michael's Church, where his father is buried. One of the carved panels on the door at no. 32 (site of former no. 65) commemorates the first visit of Charlotte and Anne Brontë to their publishers in 1848 and shows them meeting Thackeray, though this meeting took place the next year. 'We found 65 Cornhill to be a large bookseller's shop, in a street almost as bustling as the Strand,' Charlotte Brontë wrote in her letter home, and after managing to accost and ask one of the 'many young men and lads' in the shop if she might see Mr Smith, she allayed her nervousness during the interval by looking 'at some books on the counter'. Mr Smith, who had not met 'Currer Bell', showed sharp surprise for a moment when Charlotte Brontë advanced with his opened letter to Currer Bell in her hand. She said they had come to give him 'ocular proof' that Currer and Acton Bell were different people, to refute the rumour that the pseudonyms hid merely one writer. Another panel at no. 32 shows Garraway's Coffee House (gone) established at 3 Exchange Alley, off Cornhill, in 1670 and mentioned in *The Tatler* (1709–10), in *Amelia* (1751), and in many novels by Dickens, whose Mr Pickwick writes the short letter requesting 'chops and tomato sauce' from there. Garraway's (demolished *c.* 1873) is thought to have been built over an old monastery, whose crypt made a fine cellar. Mr Pickwick, attended by Sam Weller, stayed on many occasions at the George and Vulture, an inn in Castle Ct, Birchin Lane, another alley off Cornhill.

T. S. Eliot found employment in 1917 in the Colonial and Foreign Department of Lloyds Bank at 17 Cornhill, where his job was to evaluate the balance sheets of foreign banks. When I. A. Richards, the author of *Practical Criticism*, visited him, he described a man

> very like a dark bird in a feeder, over a big table covered with all sorts and sizes of foreign correspondence. The big table almost entirely filled a little room under the street. Within a foot of our heads when he stood were the thick, green glass squares of the pavement on which hammered all but incessantly the heels of the passers-by.

A colleague described him as often

> living in a dreamland . . . he would often in the middle of dictating a letter break off suddenly, grasp a sheet of paper and start writing quickly when an idea came to him . . .
>
> (quoted in Peter Ackroyd, *T. S. Eliot*)

He worked at the bank until 1925, immaculately dressed in sponge-bag trousers and tortoiseshell glasses, lunching at Baker's Chop House and visiting a wine shop in Cowper's Ct. He published *Prufrock and Other Observations* while working here and the images of London in 'The Waste Land' derive from his period as a bank official.

Crane Ct, Fleet St., is a narrow entry leading to the hall (gone) where the Philosophical Society invited Coleridge to give a series of lectures on Shakespeare in 1813. Byron, Rogers, and Godwin were among the audience, which Crabb Robinson reported was usually about 150. Mark Lemon helped to inaugurate *Punch*

at no. 9 in 1841. Douglas Jerrold, who wrote as 'Q', and Thackeray, who wrote *Jeames's Diary* and *The Snobs of England*, were both contributors.

Crosby Sq., Bishopsgate, was the site of Crosby Place, built in the 1460s for a rich merchant and then the home of Richard III, mentioned by Shakespeare in his play on the King. Thomas More lived here soon after returning from Flanders, where he started *Utopia* (1516), until he moved to his riverside house in *Chelsea (*c.* 1524). *Utopia* had been translated from Latin into German, French, and Italian before an English version was made in 1551. Crosby Place, home of the Countess of Pembroke in 1609, was demolished *c.* 1908 except for the timbered Hall, which was re-erected near the site of More's Chelsea home in 1910; it was later the dining hall of the British Federation of University Women and is now a private residence. Stephen Gosson, author of *Schoole of Abuse* (1579), was rector of **St Botolph without Bishopsgate**, from 1600 until his death in 1624.

The site of the Fleet prison, from medieval times until its demolition in 1846, was near the entrance to Fleet Lane in **Farringdon St.** Thomas Nash was imprisoned here after his play *The Isle of Dogs* (1597) caused a furore by exposing abuses. John Donne spent a short time here in 1601, when it became known that he had secretly married a minor. While John Cleland was imprisoned for debt (1748–52), he wrote *Fanny Hill: Memoirs of a Woman of Pleasure* (1748–9), which caused a further rift with his family. Charles Churchill made a Fleet marriage dispensing with licence or banns, but this practice, whereby imprisoned clergy officiated, was stopped by the Marriage Act of 1753. Walter Besant's novel *The Chaplain of the Fleet* (1881) is about the abuses of the marriages.

Dickens sets scenes in the Fleet in *Pickwick Papers* (1837), when Mr Pickwick, incarcerated after refusing to pay his fine, treats Mr Jingle with charity and secures his release from poverty and squalor.

Fleet St. is a street of publishers, printers, booksellers, and journalists. No. 1 ⓟ marks the site of The Devil tavern, where Ben Jonson and his friends established the Apollo Club, which had the rules engraved in marble over the chimneypiece. Thomas Randolph is said to have made Ben Jonson's acquaintance here after writing some verses about having no money. The verses were accepted as payment for his bill. No. 10 is the site of Richard Tottel's printing house at the sign of the Hand and Bar, where the *Songs and Sonnets* of Wyatt and Surrey, which came to be known as *Tottel's Miscellany* (1557), were published. Later, rooms above became Dick's Coffee House, which Addison and Steele, who gathered there, mention in *The Tatler*. Dryden lived (1673–82) in this street. His best-known play, *All for Love* (1678), and the poem *Absalom and Achitophel* were written at this time. John Murray founded the *Quarterly Review* in 1809 at his publishing offices (site of no. 32).

Christina Stead lived in a flat at Red Lion Ct off Fleet St. in 1936. It provided the basis for the apartment in her autobiographical novel *For Love Alone* (1944).

William Tyndale was a preacher at **St Dunstan-in-the-West** (rebuilt in 1833 and restored after bomb damage in 1950) before he went to the Continent in 1524. John Davies of Hereford (d. 1618), Thomas Campion (d. 1620), and Thomas Carew (d. 1639?) were buried there. John Aubrey in *Brief Lives* records that Michael Drayton lived at 'the bay-window house next the east end of St Dunstan's', and Izaak Walton, who was a vestryman (or parish officer), lived 'two doors west of Chancery Lane'. He is commemorated by a tablet on the wall outside the church and by a stained-glass window (behind the Romanian icon screen), donated by 'Anglers and other admirers' in 1895. Walton's *Compleat Angler* (1653) was published by the press at St Dunstan's churchyard. John Donne was rector here from 1624 to his death in 1631. Dickens is said to have written *The Chimes* (1844) about St Dunstan's.

Two Mitre taverns have disappeared from the street: the Elizabethan tavern frequented by Shakespeare, Ben Jonson, and their circle, was at the corner of Old Mitre Ct; the Mitre that became the special haunt of Dr Johnson and Boswell was farther west. Goldsmith was often at the latter Mitre, and Boswell, who wrote that Fleet St. was Dr Johnson's favourite street, records that Johnson also said here that 'Goldsmith should not be for ever attempting to shine in conversation.'

Cobbett lived in Fleet St. during the time he was a journalist with Tory leanings. He started the *Weekly Political Register* (1802–35) here. The publishers Taylor and Hessey had their offices at no. 93. This was the rendezvous for Hazlitt, William Cary, John Reynolds, Lamb, De Quincey, and Landor. Keats stayed here, and Clare, who first came to London in 1821 in the company of Taylor's cousin, stayed here then and on his later visit. In the winter of 1833 Dickens posted his first story 'in a dark letter-box in a dark office in a dark court in Fleet Street'. Ye Old Cocke tavern at no. 22 is said to have been Dickens's favourite tavern.

St Bride's Church, just S of the E end of Fleet St., was rebuilt 1670–84 by Wren and again in 1956–7 to Wren's plans after bomb damage. Thomas Sackville, co-author of *Gorboduc*, was buried in the old church in 1608. Samuel Pepys, born (1633) in Salisbury Ct ⓟ nearby, was baptized in St Bride's, and Richard Lovelace, who died in Gunpowder Alley (now Shoe Lane), was buried in the old church in 1658. Samuel Richardson, who employed Goldsmith for some months in his printing works in Salisbury Sq., was buried in the Wren building in 1761.

Oliver Goldsmith had two rooms (1760–2) in Mrs Carnan's house, 6 Wine Office Ct, Fleet St. (bombed and rebuilt as the House of Goldsmith), where Dr Johnson visited him for the first time in 1761. Thomas Percy, who went with him, was surprised into commenting on his unusual neatness and Johnson replied that Goldsmith defended his own slovenliness by quoting Johnson's, and so he intended to set a better example. Goldsmith, whose *Memoirs of M. Voltaire* was being serialized in the *Ladies' Magazine*, and whose income was precarious, asked Johnson for help when he became seriously in debt. Johnson sold the manuscript of a novel of Goldsmith's that he had laid aside, the landlady was paid, and some years later *The Vicar of Wakefield* (1766) was published. Newbery, the publisher, then made plans to help Goldsmith with his finances by paying him an allowance and housing him near his own country apartments in *Islington.

Ye Olde Cheshire Cheese (or the Cheese) in Wine Office Ct was rebuilt after the Fire of London in 1666 and claims associations with Johnson, Boswell, and Goldsmith, though Boswell does not mention the name. The seat in the restaurant on the ground floor where it is said they sat is marked with a plaque and a copy of Reynolds's portrait of Johnson hangs above it. In the 1890s the Rhymers' Club met here. It was founded in 1891 by Yeats and Ernest Rhys; Lionel Johnson, Ernest Dowson, John Davidson, and Richard Le Gallienne used to drink and read their poems aloud here. Davidson published a collection of poems as *Fleet Street Eclogues* in 1893. A second volume followed in 1896. Le Gallienne's *The Romantic Nineties* (1926, reprinted 1951) gives a first-hand account of the literary and artistic scene.

The novelist and playwright Michael Frayn began his career as first a reporter and then a columnist for *The Guardian* and then a columnist for *The Observer*. *Towards the End of the Morning* (1967), his comic novel of journalistic life, is set in the fictional Hand and Ball Ct off Fleet St.

Grub St., which Dr Johnson in his *Dictionary* said was 'much inhabited by writers of small histories . . . whence any mean production is called Grub St.', used to lead N from **Fore St.** It was renamed Milton St. (Milton died nearby) and disappeared in the redevelopment in the 1960s. George Gissing's novel *New Grub Street* (1891) has powerful descriptions of a writer struggling to make his way in London.

John Foxe (d. 1587) and Milton (d. 1674) are buried in **St Giles Cripplegate Church**, Fore St. Milton's grave is marked by a tablet near the pulpit. The Barbican Centre opposite the church was the home of the Royal Shakespeare Company from 1982 to 2002.

Dr Johnson's House, 17 **Gough Sq.** (spelt 'Goff' by Dr Johnson), on the N side of Fleet St., is reached by the narrow alleyway off Johnson's Ct (well signposted). Dr Johnson lived here from 1749 to 1759, the only one of his many London residences to have survived. In 1750 he began *The Rambler*, a twice-weekly periodical, written almost entirely by himself, which ran until 1752, the year his beloved wife, Tetty, died. By this time he was fully occupied on the *Dictionary* (1755), which had been commissioned by a syndicate of booksellers and was compiled in the garret, a room running the full length of the house, where he employed six clerks—five of whom were Scots. In 1758 he began *The Idler*, a series of papers contributed over two years to *The Universal Chronicle, or, Weekly Gazette*, and it is possible that he wrote *Rasselas* (1759) here, although he may have done so after moving to Staple Inn (see HOLBORN).

The house, now the property of Dr Johnson's House Trust (www.drjohnsonshouse.org), contains portraits of Johnson and his contemporaries, personal relics, and two copies of the first edition of the *Dictionary*. In the parlour there is a copy of 'In the Shades—1915', an imaginary conversation by Max Beerbohm (one of the original governors of the Trust), with portraits of Johnson and Boswell, celebrating the opening of the house after its restoration in 1911. After several other moves Johnson lived in Johnson's Ct (rebuilt, P on E side) from 1765 to 1776, and finally at Bolt Ct (gone) nearby, where he died (1784). The last house had a garden which, though no gardener, he delighted to water. 'I have three bunches of grapes', he wrote to a friend, 'on a vine in my garden.' This home features in Beryl Bainbridge's 2001 novel *According to Queeney*.

Green Arbour Ct, Old Bailey, was a small enclosed square formerly at the corner of Seacoal Lane and Green Arbour Lane. Oliver Goldsmith lodged (1759–60) here with Mrs Martin and he was popular with her children and with the other poor families in the court. When Thomas Percy visited he was surprised to find only one chair so that his host was obliged to sit on the windowsill. Goldsmith finished *Enquiry into the Present State of Polite Learning* (1759) here and was writing regularly for *The Bee*, the *Ladies' Magazine*, and the *Critical Review*. The publisher and philanthropist John Newbery also interested him in his new *Public Ledger*, for which Goldsmith wrote his 'Chinese Letters'. By the middle of 1760 he had found new lodgings, probably through Newbery, whose wife had been a connection of the new landlady, but Goldsmith still continued to help Mrs Martin and the children. Nathaniel Hawthorne described the 'miserable houses' in the square in *Our Old Home* (1863) and commented on the washing hanging from every window.

Guildhall, centre of the administration of the City, has a 15th-c. crypt although much of the building suffered in the Fire of London in 1666 or in the Second World War and has been rebuilt. The trial of Henry Howard, Earl of Surrey, was held in the Great Hall in 1547. He was condemned to death for treason on slender evidence. Buckingham, in Shakespeare's *Richard III*, is dispatched by Richard to the Guildhall to 'infer the bastardy of Edward's children' before the citizens, at which

> They spake not a word,
> But, like dumb statues or breathing stones,
> Stared on each other and looked deadly pale.

The Guildhall is open to visitors (www.cityoflondon.gov.uk).

Pepys in his *Diary* mentions attending a banquet in 1663 when the French Ambassador was 'in a discontent', and being present at a trial later in the year about a ship's insurance. Elkanah Settle, as City poet from 1691, wrote plays and pageants for the Lord Mayor's Show. Dickens sets the Bardell and Pickwick trial here in *Pickwick Papers* (1836–7). The Guildhall Library has many books and manuscripts relating to the City, including Stow's *Chronicles* and *A Survey of London*. It also has the deed signed by Shakespeare in 1613 for the purchase of a house in Blackfriars. The stained-glass window depicts Stow and Milton and there are busts of Chaucer and Tennyson on the stairs.

Stained-glass windows in **St Lawrence Jewry Church**, by Guildhall, commemorate William Grocyn (d. 1519), the scholar who introduced Greek studies to Oxford University, and Thomas More, his pupil, author of *Utopia* (1516). The church was rebuilt by Wren after the Fire of London in 1666, and restored after bomb damage in the Second World War.

The statue of William IV on **King William St.** occupies the approximate site of the Boar's Head (gone), the Eastcheap tavern of Falstaff, Hal, and their companions in Shakespeare's *Henry IV*.

Thomas Kyd was baptized (1558) at the **Church of St Mary Woolnoth**. John Newton, author with Cowper of the *Olney Hymns*, was rector from 1780 to his death in 1807. He was buried here beside his wife and their remains were moved to *Olney in 1893. T. S. Eliot, who worked nearby at Cornhill, observed in 'The Waste Land' the crowds of office workers who

> Flowed up the hill and down King William Street,
> To where St Mary Woolnoth kept the hours
> With a dead sound on the final stroke of nine.

Hawksmoor's polygonal black and gold clock is still there.

In **Leadenhall St.** an early 16th-c. church, **St Andrew Undershaft**, possibly derives its name from the large maypole which used to be put up at the church on May Day. John Stow, born nearby in the parish of Cornhill, has a memorial erected by his wife at the end of the N aisle. He published many chronicles as *The Annales of England*, the second edition of Holinshed's *Chronicles* (1585–7), and the fascinating *Survey of London* (1598) with its details of the customs of the day. At the annual church service commemorating him the quill pen in his memorial is renewed.

The East India House, which stood on the corner of **Lime St.** and Leadenhall St., was where Charles Lamb worked as a clerk for over 30 years. In a letter to Crabb Robinson at the end of March 1825 he wrote, 'I have left the d——d India House for Ever.'

The concluding, apocalyptic vision of W. G. Sebald's *Vertigo* is half dreamt by the narrator as his train draws out of **Liverpool St. Station**,

> past the soot-stained walls the recesses of which have always seemed to me like part of a vast system of catacombs that comes to the surface there. In the course of time a multitude of buddleias, which thrive in the most inauspicious

conditions, had taken root in the gaps and cracks of the nineteenth-century brickwork.

In the bar of the Great Eastern Hotel, next door to the station (see also Bethlehem Hospital), the narrator of *Austerlitz* (2001), Sebald's last fiction, while regarding 'the toilers in the City gold-mines', meets Jacques Austerlitz again after a space of 20 years.

The certainty of the bet 'All Lombard Street to a China orange' shows the riches of **Lombard St.**, named after the medieval merchant bankers from Lombardy. Alexander Barclay became rector of All Hallows Church (site at entrance to Ball Alley) in 1552, the last year of his life. Joseph Addison married the Dowager Countess of Warwick and Holland in **St Edmund's Church** in 1716.

Pontacks (gone), the fashionable eating house of the late 17th and early 18th cc., is mentioned in Evelyn's *Diary* and in plays by Congreve, Southerne, and Susannah Centlivre.

From 1900 to 1902 P. G. Wodehouse worked at the Hong Kong and Shanghai Bank (then on Lombard St.). The work did not suit him and in the evenings he worked on his stories, novels, parodies, lyrics, and humorous journalism. The experience contributed to the success of *Psmith in the City* (1910).

Bible translator Miles Coverdale, rector of **St Magnus the Martyr** in **Lower Thames St.** from 1563 until his resignation in 1566, is buried near the altar. The church was rebuilt by Wren in 1666. T. S. Eliot remarked the church's 'inexplicable splendour of Ionian white and gold' in *The Waste Land* (1922).

At the NW corner of **Ludgate Circus** a bronze plaque records the nearby site where the young Edgar Wallace sold newspapers outside Cook's travel agency, playing truant from afternoon school to earn 2 or 3 shillings a week.

The Stationers' Hall, off **Ludgate Hill**, is the home of the Stationers' Company, founded in 1403 and incorporated by royal charter in 1557, which decreed that all work intended for publication had to be registered here. The registers contain titles and dates of works from the middle of the 16th c. The Hall was rebuilt after the Fire of London and refronted in 1800, and the Stationers' Company is now joined by the Newspaper Makers' Company.

Samuel Purchas was rector of **St Martin within Ludgate**, rebuilt by Wren after the Fire of London, from 1614 to his death in 1626. He wrote *Purchas his Pilgrim, Microcosmus, or, The Histories of Man* (1619), and *Hakluytus Posthumus, or, Purchas his Pilgrimes, containing a History of the World in Sea Voyages and Land Travell by Englishmen and Others* (1625), partly based on papers which came to him after the death of Richard Hakluyt. Richard Barham, who died at Amen Corner (see St Paul's) in 1845, is commemorated by a tablet in the porch.

On her first visit to England, in 1928, Christina Stead worked at Strauss & Co., a grain exchange on **St Mary Axe**. Her manager, the cosmopolitan New Yorker and Marxist

William Blech (later Blake), gave her a job on the strength of her seriousness and shyness and for carrying a book by Bertrand Russell into the interview. She and Blech became lovers and later married. He was the basis of a number of characters in Stead's novels, notably of James Quick in *For Love Alone* (1944), the sequel to her best-known novel, *The Man Who Loved Children* (1940).

John Keats was born (1795) on the site of 85 **Moorgate** ℗, then a prosperous livery stable owned by his father at the Swan and Hoop at Finsbury Pavement (gone). Keats went to school from the age of 8 at Enfield and his parents both died while he was there. He and his brothers and sister were put in the charge of a guardian and at 16 he was apprenticed to a surgeon.

The Central Criminal Court on the corner of **Newgate St.** and Old Bailey stands on the site of Newgate prison. Sir Thomas Malory, imprisoned for murder as well as other crimes, is thought to have written *Le Morte D'Arthur* to while away the many years spent here. He was perhaps allowed to read in the fine library of Grey Friars Monastery (gone) opposite, and he finished (1469–70) the work which was printed by Caxton in 1485. He is said to have died (1471) in prison and been buried in Grey Friars.

Shakespeare, in *1 Henry IV*, remarks on the marching of prisoners, 'two and two, Newgate fashion'. The playwright John Marston was imprisoned in Newgate in 1608 for writing a play, now lost, which was offensive to James I.

George Wither, the Puritan, was imprisoned here 1660–3 after his manuscript *Vox Vulgi* was considered seditious. Defoe's *The Shortest Way with Dissenters* (1702) led to his being imprisoned here after being pilloried, when he was cheered by the passers-by, and wrote *Hymn to the Pillory* (1704) as a result. He also started *The Review* in prison, a thrice-weekly paper about foreign and commercial affairs which lasted until 1713. Richard Savage spent one of his many periods of imprisonment here, this time (1727) not for debt, but for killing a man in a brawl. He was pardoned soon afterwards. *The Newgate Calendar* (1774) is an account of the inmates' crimes from 1700 and a later series was edited in 1826. Borrow mentions the chronicles of Newgate in *Lavengro* (1851).

The original building of **Christ's Hospital**, often called the Bluecoat School, was on the site of Grey Friars. Camden, Richardson, George Dyer, Coleridge, Lamb, and Leigh Hunt were pupils here, and Middleton Murry had a year here before the school moved in 1902. A plaque formerly on the E wall of the school and now on the E wall of **St Sepulchre's Church** in Giltspur St. (leading N from Newgate St.) commemorates Charles Lamb, 'Perhaps the most loved name in English Literature, who was a Bluecoat boy here for 7 years'. *Lamb's Essays* recount his impressions of Coleridge at Christ's Hospital, and his *Letters* mention the evenings he spent with the adult Coleridge and Southey at the Salutation and Cat, a coaching inn (burnt 1883) opposite the school where

they drank egg-hot, a hot drink made from beer, eggs, sugar, and nutmeg, and smoked oronooko, a Virginian tobacco. The **Old Bailey** is the professional home of Rumpole, the much-loved barrister created by the novelist (and himself a barrister) John Mortimer, in *Rumpole of the Bailey* (1978) and its many sequels.

Paternoster Row was a street famous for its booksellers and publishers until its destruction in the Second World War. The Chapter Coffee House stood at the entrance to Paul's Alley (gone), an opening off Paternoster Row. Thomas Chatterton, who in 1770 when 17 had come to London to make his literary fortune, wrote to his mother from here sending trifling gifts, saying, 'I am quite familiar at the Chapter Coffee House and know all the geniuses there,' but within three months he was dead. In 1848 Charlotte and Anne Brontë made an overnight train journey to visit their publishers. They stayed at the Chapter Coffee House, where they had been with their father, as they knew nowhere else.

A plaque at the entrance to **Plough Ct**, Lombard St., states that Alexander Pope was born (1688) here. The house (gone) faced up the alley. His father was a prosperous linen-draper and Pope a precocious child, who suffered a crippling illness when he was 12.

Thomas Hood was born (1799) at 31 **Poultry**, now the Midland Bank ℗, near Queen Victoria St. His family moved shortly afterwards, so it is more likely that his poem 'I remember, I remember | The house where I was born' refers to *Islington. Sir John Vanbrugh was buried (1726) at **St Stephen Walbrook**, near the Mansion House. Facing onto Queen Victoria St. is **City of London School**, whose past pupils (when the school was on former premises in nearby Blackfriars) include the novelists Kingsley Amis and Julian Barnes.

In 1731 Defoe died 'of lethargy' in lodgings in Ropemaker's Alley, now **Ropemaker St.**

The Post Office in **St Martin's le Grand** stands on the site of the old Northumberland House, home of Shakespeare's 'Hotspur', where Thomas Percy lodged when in London in the late 1760s and 1770s. Boswell recalls that he and Dr Johnson 'passed many an agreeable hour' there with Percy, who was also a frequent companion when they dined at the nearby taverns. Percy's antiquarian interests led him to publish *The Northumberland Household Book of 1512* (1768). A fire in 1780 burned £100-worth of Percy's clothes and movables but did not cause him a 'literary loss'.

St Paul's Cathedral, at the top of Ludgate Hill, was built (1675–97) by Wren on the site of the church destroyed in the Fire of London, 1666.

The old church, which once had the tallest spire in Christendom, dominated the Elizabethan city, and in Shakespeare was a byword for conspicuousness. Hal says of Falstaff that 'This oily rascal is known as well as Paul's.' Falstaff himself picked up Bardolph on Paul's Walk, a thoroughfare and meeting place which ran through the old church. Paul's Boys, the most celebrated children's theatre company of Shakespeare's time, had their playhouse beside the Cathedral. John Lyly and John Marston were company playwrights.

Sir Philip Sidney, who died of wounds at Zutphen in 1586, was buried with great pomp in Old St Paul's. The monument in the S choir aisle to John Donne, Dean of St Paul's from 1621 to his death in 1631, is one of the few surviving. He modelled himself for it in his shroud to the sculptor Nicholas Stone. (One of the best known of Harrison Ainsworth's historical novels is *Old St Paul's*, 1841.) There are statues in the Wren church of Dr Johnson (in a toga) and his friend Joshua Reynolds under the dome to the N. The S choir aisle has a monument to H. H. Milman, dean from 1849 to his death in 1868 and author of *Annals of St*

John Donne depicted in his shroud at St Paul's. The monument survived the destruction of the old Cathedral in the Great Fire

Paul's Cathedral (1868). The crypt contains memorials to William Blake (d. 1827), R. H. Barham (d. 1845), Charles Reade (d. 1884), Walter Besant (d. 1901), W. E. Henley (d. 1903), and T. E. Lawrence (d. 1935). Sydney Smith was a canon from 1831 to his death in 1845. The ashes of Max Beerbohm (d. 1956) and Walter de la Mare (d. 1956) are buried here.

At Paul's Cross in **St Paul's churchyard**, where public pronouncements were made, the indictment of Lord Hastings is given out in *Richard III*. In Shakespeare's time the churchyard was the centre of London's book trade. Many of the original, quarto, editions of his plays were sold here.

John Newbery, a bookseller and publisher, remembered especially for his publications for children, established himself at the Bible and Sun at no. 65 in 1744 (building destroyed by enemy action, 1940). A memorial plaque, presented by the Pennsylvania Library Association, was unveiled on a wall near the site in 1978.

Richard Barham, who had been appointed a minor canon of St Paul's in 1821, came to know Mary Ann Hughes, the wife of a canon residentiary who lived in Amen Corner, a precinct near the Cathedral. She was a mine of information on legends, ghost stories, and ballads and she encouraged him to write verse. Barham himself lived (1824–39) at 4 St Paul's Churchyard (gone) and much of his collection *The Ingoldsby Legends* (1840–7), which first appeared in periodicals, originated from her. She was also visited by Harrison Ainsworth, and Scott, who wove her account of Wayland's Smithy into *Kenilworth* (1821). Mrs Hughes moved to *Kingston Lisle in the 1830s after her husband died. In 1839 Barham himself moved into Sydney Smith's house in Amen Corner, as he was leaving for Green St. Barham's comic description of his garden, which contained 'eight broken bottles' and 'a tortoiseshell cat asleep in the sunniest corner', appears in his *Life* (1870), written by his son. He wrote 'As I lay a thinking', his last poem, shortly before his death (1845), and he was buried at St Mary Magdalene, Old Fish St., where he had been rector. After the church was burnt down in 1885, the commemorative tablet was re-erected in St Martin within Ludgate. Under the dome of the Cathedral the two First World War veterans, Victor Harker and Eric Talbot (alias Captain Standish, alias Julian Borrow, alias Tommy), first meet in Paul Bailey's novel *Old Soldiers* (1980).

St Paul's School was founded by Dean Colet in 1509 with William Lily as first High Master. They collaborated on a book to help the pupils and this became known later as the *Eton Latin Grammar*. Literary Old Paulines include William Camden, Milton, Pepys, J. H. Reynolds, R. H. Barham, L. Binyon, G. K. Chesterton, E. C. Bentley, Edward Thomas, and Compton Mackenzie. The school moved to new buildings in West Kensington in 1884, and to Barnes in 1968 (see HAMMERSMITH). Other distinguished alumni of St Paul's School and St Paul's Girls' School include (respectively) the

philosopher Isaiah Berlin and the novelist Monica Dickens. (The unruly Dickens was expelled.)

All books for publication were first registered at the Stationers' Company in **Stationers' Ct**, a trade guild chartered in 1557. The company regulated the trade practices of publishers, printers, bookbinders, and booksellers. The publishing fortunes of, for instance, Shakespeare's plays and poems between the 1590s and the Restoration period can be traced in the entries of the Stationers' Register.

Merchant Taylors' School (founded 1561), in **Suffolk Lane** until 1875, had Edmund Spenser, Thomas Kyd, Thomas Lodge, James Shirley, and John Byrom among its pupils.

A plaque on Kent House in **Telegraph St.**, across Moorgate on the E side, marks the site of a house where Robert Bloomfield lived. In 1781 he came from a farm in his native Suffolk to be apprenticed to his uncle, a tailor in Pitcher's Ct (gone), off Bell Alley (now **Gt Bell Alley**). He read the newspaper to the men as they worked and one, seeing his interest in literature, lent him *Paradise Lost* and *The Seasons*. He married in 1790 and continued to work in Bell Alley, where he wrote *The Farmer's Boy* (1800), a long poem which proved popular, about the life he was not strong enough to follow.

The Temple consists of the Inner Temple and the Middle Temple, two of the four *Inns of Court, situated between the Victoria Embankment and Fleet St., which have occupied the site of the buildings of the Order of Knights Templar since the 14th c. Many of the buildings suffered from bombing in the Second World War, but much restoration has been carried out, as far as possible with the use of the original materials.

Middle Temple Hall, an assembly hall on the S side of Fountain Ct, opened by Elizabeth I in 1576, was the setting for the first recorded performance of *Twelfth Night*. It was acted before the Queen by Shakespeare's company in 1602. One of the stained-glass windows contains the coat of arms of Sir Walter Ralegh. John Evelyn, the diarist, lived in Essex Ct (off Fountain Ct) in 1640, but stayed less than a year. Oliver Goldsmith took a room in Garden Ct (also off Fountain Ct), above the Middle Temple Library, for a short time in 1764, when he was living in the country at Canonbury. This year saw the publication of *The Traveller*, a long poem begun years before in Scotland, which established him as a poet. In 1765 he took more comfortable rooms on the second floor of 2 Brick Ct (gone) and after the death of his friend John Newbery in 1767 he lived there, except for intervals in the country, for the rest of his life. He was able to furnish his rooms very well from the proceeds of his successful comedy *The Good Natur'd Man* (1768). He was writing *The Deserted Village* (1770) when he heard of the death of his brother, to whom he dedicated the poem, in which many references to their childhood in Ireland can be detected.

Middle Temple Hall, where the first recorded performance of Shakespeare's *Twelfth Night* took place on 2 February 1602

Anthony Hope Hawkins ('Anthony Hope') was called to the Bar in 1887. The story of *The Prisoner of Zenda* (1894) came to him as he was walking back to his chambers in Brick Ct after winning a case at Westminster county court.

Fountain Ct is described by Dickens in *Martin Chuzzlewit* (ch. xlv) as the accustomed meeting place of Tom Pinch and his sister Ruth, where for once Tom is late and it is the ardent John Westlock instead who encounters Ruth and overtakes her in the sanctuary of Garden Ct.

The **Temple Church**, which takes its name from the crusading Order of Knights Templar (founded 1118), has belonged to the lawyers of the Inner Temple and the Middle Temple since 1608, when the Benchers secured the freehold by charter from James I. John Marston, playwright and divine, who was a student at the Middle Temple but apparently found legal studies distasteful, returned to London after giving up his living at Christchurch, Hampshire, and was buried (26 June 1634) beside his father in the church. His gravestone, which bore the inscription 'Oblivioni sacrum', has disappeared. On the left of the entrance from the S porch, the gravestone of John Selden, jurist, legal antiquary, and scholar, may be seen through a glass panel on the floor. The basement apartment under the S aisle containing his coffin is reached by a stair in the porch. Beside the W porch there once stood the music shop of John Playford, Clerk of the Temple Church, whom Pepys used to visit to buy the latest songs. On the upper level of the graveyard on the N side an inscribed stone

marks the vicinity of Goldsmith's grave. Charles Lamb, like the rest of his brothers and sisters, was baptized in the church.

Members of the Middle Temple (in addition to those already mentioned) include: Sir Walter Ralegh (1552?–1618); Sir John Davies (1569–1626), barrister and poet, who entered in 1587 and after returning to Oxford to take his BA (1590) was called to the Bar in 1595, but was expelled the following year for attacking his friend Richard Martin at dinner in Hall (he was restored to his position and reconciled to Martin six years later); John Ford (1586?–1640?), who entered in 1603 but was never called to the Bar; Thomas Carew (1598?–1639?), who entered in 1612; John Evelyn (1620–1706); John Aubrey (1626–97), who entered in 1646 but was not called to the Bar; Thomas Shadwell (1642?–92); Thomas Southerne (1660–1746), who came from Trinity College *Dublin to study Law and spent the rest of his life in London; William Congreve (1670–1729), who entered in 1691 and stayed three years, but made little progress towards the Bar, preferring the playhouse and the literary society of Will's Coffee House; Nicholas Rowe (1674–1718); William Somerville (1675–1742), who entered in 1696; Henry Brooke (1703–83), who entered in 1724 but was recalled to Ireland by the death of an aunt, who made him guardian of her daughter Catherine, whom he later married; Henry Fielding (1707–54), who was called to the Bar in 1740; Edmund Burke (1729–97), who entered in 1750; William Cowper (1731–1800), who entered in 1748, but spent more time

visiting his cousins Theodora and Harriet Cowper in Southampton Row than studying Law; he was called to the Bar in 1754, but never practised; William Hayley (1745–1820), who entered in 1766, when he was still at Cambridge, but preferred poetry to law; Thomas Moore (1779–1852), who entered in 1799, after being at Trinity College Dublin; and W. M. Thackeray (1811–63), who entered in 1831, but soon abandoned the legal profession.

The red and white roses of the rival houses of Lancaster and York were plucked in **Temple Gardens** (usually open weekdays 12.30–3pm), a doom-laden episode dramatised by Shakespeare in *1 Henry VI* which would send 'between the red rose and the white, | A thousand souls to death and deadly night.' A border of red and white roses along Paper Buildings represents the later union of the two houses.

Charles Lamb was born (10 Feb. 1775) at 2 Crown Office Row (rebuilt; Ⓟ), opposite the garden gates. His father was confidential clerk to Samuel Salt, one of 'The Old Benchers of the Inner Temple' portrayed in Lamb's *Elia* essay of that name (1821), which also has an affectionate portrait of his father as 'Lovel'. It was in Mr Salt's chambers, remembered by Lamb as the 'place of my kindly engendure' in 'cheerful Crown Office Row', that he and his elder sister Mary grew up and 'tumbled into a spacious closet of good old English reading, and browsed at will on that fair and wholesome pasturage'. They lived there until Mr Salt's death in 1795. Near the Embankment end of the Gardens there is a fountain commemorating Lamb and a stone figure of a boy inscribed with a quotation from one of his Essays: 'Lawyers were children once.'

Members of the Inner Temple include: Francis Beaumont (1584–1616), who entered in 1600 but does not seem to have pursued his legal studies; William Browne (1591–1645), who entered in 1611, wrote an elegy on Prince Henry (printed 1613), and superintended the masque here of *Ulysses and Circe* in 1615; William Wycherley (1640–1716), who entered in 1659, but found the fashionable and literary circles of London more attractive than the study of Law; James Boswell (1740–95), who, after studying Law at *Edinburgh, *Glasgow, and Utrecht, came to the Inner Temple in 1775 and was called to the English Bar in 1786; Sir Francis Doyle (1810–88), who entered in 1832 and was called to the Bar in 1837, but found that his marriage in 1844 required him to take a more remunerative job—in Customs and Excise; John Forster (1812–76), who entered in 1828, was called to the Bar in 1843, but gave up law for literature; Thomas Hughes (1822–96), who was called to the Bar in 1848, and became a QC in 1869 and a Bencher in 1870; and Compton Mackenzie (1883–1972), who studied Law for a time, and then turned to writing.

The Inner Temple is an old haunt of Sir Edward Feathers, the ancient lawyer of Jane Gardam's novel *Old Filth* (2005). At his death, the bell of the Temple Church tolls once for every year of his long life.

The Tower of London, from a mid-16th-century panorama of London by Anthony van Wyngaerde

Charles Lamb remembers in *Essays of Elia* the idiosyncrasies of the clerks, who toiled at 'worm-eaten tables . . . with tarnished gilt-leather coverings' at the South-Sea House (gone), **Threadneedle St.**, 'a melancholy looking, handsome brick and stone structure to the left where Threadneedle Street abuts upon Bishopsgate'. Here Lamb himself, when 17, was a clerk for a short time. Kenneth Grahame, while working (1898–1908) at the Bank of England, wrote *The Wind in the Willows* (1908), which began as stories for his young son.

William, the hero of Jonathan Coe's *The Dwarves of Death* (1990), lives on an estate (the fictional Herbert Estate) near **Tower Hill** station; he is inspired to use it for a piece of music he is working on.

> Tower Hill. It suddenly struck me as an appropriate title for a piano piece I was in the process of writing. It was meant to have a weary and melancholy feel to it—like you feel at the end of a long day, with maybe the hope of better to come . . .

The **Tower of London** was built as a fortress and a palace by William the Conqueror on the N bank of the river. Among those imprisoned here were James I of Scotland, a political prisoner for many years, and author of *The Kingis Quair*; Sir Thomas More in 1534–5 for refusing to recognize Henry VIII as the Pope's superior; Thomas Wyatt in 1536 for complicity in Anne Boleyn's adultery: he was released on that charge, and was imprisoned again (1540–1) as an ally of Thomas Cromwell, and again released. Sir Walter Ralegh was imprisoned briefly by Elizabeth I (1592) for his courtship of, and marriage to, one of her maids of honour, Elizabeth Throckmorton, and by James I for treason (1603–16). During the latter time he wrote the *History of the World* (1614), a copy of which is kept in the Bloody Tower. He was released in 1616 to lead the

unsuccessful expedition to Guiana in search of gold, and was executed on his return in Palace Yard, Westminster. William D'Avenant was transferred to the Tower (1650–2) from *Cowes after being captured by the Parliamentarians. John Wilmot, 2nd Earl of Rochester, was imprisoned for a short time in 1665 by Charles II for abducting the heiress Elizabeth Malet, who later became his wife. The site on Tower Hill where More was executed is commemorated by a plaque on the pavement to the last victims to die here in 1746. More was buried in St Peter ad Vincula within the Tower. Scenes from Shakespeare's *Richard III* (1594), Scott's *Peveril of the Peak* (1823) and Harrison Ainsworth's *The Tower of London* (1840) are set in the Tower. A three-centuries-old legend says that when the resident ravens leave the Tower, the kingdom will crumble. In Sue Townsend's satirical novel *The Queen and I* (1992), they do. 'The Yeoman Raven Master passed the White Tower, then retraced his steps. Something was wrong . . .'.

All Hallows Barking, NW of the Tower, has the grave of William Thynne (d. 1546), friend of Skelton and first editor of Chaucer's works.

Pepys lived for many years N of the church in **Seething Lane** near the Navy Office, where he was employed from 1659 to 1673. His *Diary*, written from 1660 to 1669, and given up because of failing eyesight, describes the plague, the Fire of London, and intrigues at court, as well as political and domestic events. During the Fire, having got his wife, her servant, and his gold safely away, he climbed 'to the top of Barking Steeple and there saw the saddest sight of desolation that I ever saw'. He and his wife went to church at St Olave's in Seething Lane where, after her death (1669), he set up a bust that he could see from his pew. He died at *Clapham Common and is buried in the crypt at St Olave's in the same grave as his wife.

The Mermaid Theatre in Puddle Dock, **Upper Thames St.**, opened in 1959 (now a conference centre), was the first theatre to be built in the City for 300 years.

Chaucer, the son of a vintner, was born (1345?) on the site of this street.

Dante Gabriel Rossetti lived (1852–62) at 14 Chatham Pl. (gone), at the Blackfriars Bridge end of the **Victoria Embankment**. Elizabeth Siddal, whom he married in 1860, was the subject of his poems as well as the model for his paintings. Grief at her death, from an overdose of chloral some months after the birth of a stillborn child, led Rossetti to bury with her the manuscript of these poems (which he later retrieved).

Robert Herrick was apprenticed for 10 years (c. 1604–14) to his uncle, the goldsmith Sir William Herrick (or Hericke), who lived in **Wood St.**, Cheapside.

Wordsworth in 'Reverie of Poor Susan' mentions the old clump of trees where 'At the corner of Wood Street, when daylight appears, | Hangs a thrush that sings loud, it has sung for three years.' A single plane tree in a small paved courtyard is all that remains now of the churchyard of St Peter Westcheap, destroyed in the Fire of London, 1666.

CLAPHAM, district to the S. A plaque on The Elms, 29 **North Side**, **Clapham Common**, commemorates Sir Charles Barry, the architect whose house is on the site of Pepys's last home (1700–3). Pepys lived at the house of William Hewer, his former clerk at the Navy Office. In 1700 Evelyn writes in his *Diary*, 'I went to visit Mr. Pepys, at Clapham, where he has a very noble and wonderfully well-furnished house, especially with India and China curiosities. The offices and gardens well accommodated for pleasure and retirement.' Pepys died here in 1703 and was buried in the City.

Harriet Westbrook was at a school in Clapham run by Miss Hawkes. Her fellow pupils included the sisters of Shelley, who introduced her to their brother, with whom she eloped to Scotland in 1811.

A plaque at 5 **The Pavement** commemorates Zachary Macaulay, the philanthropist, and his son Thomas Babington, later Lord Macaulay. T. B. Macaulay grew up here, rambled over the Common, and attended Mr Greaves's day school. He frequently visited Hannah More, who started his library by her presents of books. Macaulay went to Cambridge in 1818 and his father moved to Gt Ormond St. in 1823.

Lytton Strachey was born (1880) at Stowey House, but his family moved to Lancaster Gate when he was 4.

Kingsley Amis was born on 16 April 1922 at 102 **South Side**, on the edge of the Common; he was brought up in Norbury, and educated at Norbury College. Graham Greene lived at 14 **North Side**. In 1938 the young Julian Maclaren-Ross met Greene at his house for an alcoholic lunch to discuss a radio version of Greene's thriller *A Gun for Sale* (1936), an episode described in Maclaren-Ross's *Memoirs of the Forties* (1965). In Greene's novel *The End of the Affair* (1951), Maurice Bendrix makes his way from 'the wrong—the south—side of the Common' to the north side of Sarah and Henry Miles. The story was based in part on the author's affair with Dorothy Glover—a liaison which probably saved Greene's life, since he was out with Glover when his house was badly bombed. The Common is also the imagined location of 'Blenheim', the pretentious house of the monstrous and irrepressible Oswald Harvey, father to Gabriel, in Paul Bailey's novel *Gabriel's Lament* (1986).

Penelope Fitzgerald taught at the Italia Conti Theatrical School, which retains its old premises at 72 **Landor Rd**. It provided the inspiration for the 'Temple School', otherwise known as 'Freddie's' after its formidable founder, in her novel *At Freddie's* (1982):

> Everyone who knew the Temple School will remember the distinctive smell of Freddie's office. Not precisely disagreeable, it suggested a church vestry where old clothes hang and flowers moulder in the sink, but respect is called for just the same. It was not a place for seeing clearly. Light, in the morning, entered at an angle, through a quantity of dust.

CLERKENWELL, area to the N of the City. The gatehouse to the old Priory of St John on St John's Lane (now occupied by the Museum of the Order of St John) was in Shakespeare's day the office of the Master of Revels, a unit of the Lord Chamberlain's office responsible for approving and where necessary censoring plays and other entertainments for court and public performance. The censor's hand can be detected on the manuscript fragment of Shakespeare's *Sir Thomas More* in the British Library. The best-known Master of the Revels in Shakespeare's day was Sir Edmund Tilney.

The dingier streets of Clerkenwell are memorably evoked in the pages of Arnold Bennett's novel *Riceyman Steps* (1923).

In Peter Ackroyd's *The House of Doctor Dee* (1993), Matthew Palmer inherits a house just off Clerkenwell Green, and discovers that it used to belong to the astrologer John Dee. In 2003 Ackroyd published *The Clerkenwell Tales*, set at the start of the 14th c. beside the river Fleet.

COVENT GARDEN, area to the NE of Trafalgar Sq. The offices of *The Lady* magazine stand at 39–40 **Bedford St.** Stella Gibbons worked as a reporter at the magazine in the 1930s, while writing her parody of the rural novel *Cold Comfort Farm* (1932),

> sometimes on the backs of some of those envelopes which have played their part in many writers' lives; sometimes on office paper, in office time, in a dark little den at the back of *The Lady* premises, to which I had been gently relegated because I made the other two in the main office laugh so much that we couldn't work.

The title of the farm and the book was suggested to her by her friend and colleague at the magazine Elizabeth Coxhead.

The Poetry Café and home to the Poetry Society are at 22 **Betterton St.**

A plaque on the Broad Ct side of 19–20 **Bow St.** mentions Sackville, Wycherley (who died here in 1716), and Fielding among others who lived here. This is the site of the Magistrates' House, where Fielding officiated. Nearby was The Cock tavern frequented (*c.* 1670) by Sedley and Sackville. At no. 1 Will Urwin or Unwin established Will's Coffee House *c.* 1660 and it was probably 'the Great Coffee House' that Pepys looked into in 1668, commenting, 'there I perceive is a very witty and pleasant discourse', but he could not stay long as he had to collect his wife. Here, a few years before Samuel Butler's death in 1680, a Dr Yonge saw 'the famous old Mr. Butler, an old paralytick claret drinker, a morose surly man except elevated with claret, when he becomes very brisk and incomparable company'. Dryden frequented Will's, having his own seat by the fireside in winter and by the window in summer. Wycherley, Addison, Steele, Congreve, and the young Pope were all visitors. Addison forsook Will's for Button's *c.* 1712 and the name the Wits' Coffee House, by which Will's had been known, went with him. Will's closed in 1739 and the site was then used as 20–1 Russell St. Boswell, who wrote that in 1763 he drank at the Will's mentioned in *The Spectator*, must have visited one of the many other Will's Coffee Houses.

The Theatre Royal in **Catherine St.** is the fourth on the site; it took the name Drury Lane as it originally opened onto that street. Dramatists who have been associated with the management include D'Avenant, Killigrew, Dryden, Hill, Cibber, and Sheridan. Adjoining the theatre on the corner of Russell St., and in 1766 overrun by its extensions, was The Rose tavern (established 1651), where Pepys dined alone in 1668 'on a breast of mutton off the spit'. The duel in 1712 between Lord Mohun and the Duke of Hamilton, which ended fatally

for both, and which Thackeray in *Henry Esmond* (1852) uses to deprive Beatrix of a coronet, was actually arranged here by the seconds. The Rose tavern is often mentioned in Restoration plays, in *The Tatler*, and in Gay's song 'To Molly Mog of The Rose', though The Rose at *Wokingham claims her as the landlord's daughter there.

On his second visit to London, in 1821, Marie-Henri Beyle (Stendhal) saw Edmund Kean play Othello at Drury Lane. On an earlier visit in the summer of 1817 he stayed at the Tavistock Hotel, approving of the city's wide streets, handsome shop windows, the freedom of its women, and the relative (to Paris) lack of soldiers.

Covent Garden itself was once a convent garden developed by Inigo Jones (1573–1652) as a colonnaded square. **St Paul's Church** (W side), rebuilt after a fire in 1795 to Jones's designs, is the burial place of Samuel Butler (d. 1680), author of *Hudibras* (1663–78), Wycherley (d. 1716), and John Wolcot (d. 1819). Lady Mary Wortley Montagu was baptized there (1689). The churchyard is now a garden with seats. The opening scene of Shaw's *Pygmalion* (1916) is set outside St Paul's, where Professor Higgins meets the flower seller Eliza Doolittle.

In the 16th and 17th cc. the fruit and flower market (removed 1974) was surrounded by fashionable houses. William Alexander (d. 1640) and Thomas Fuller (d. 1661) both died in the square. Aubrey in *Brief Lives* writes that after 1660 Sir Kenelm Digby (d. 1665) 'lived in the last fair house westward in the north portico . . . I think he died in this house.' Thomas Killigrew lived 1636–40 on the N side. At the W end of this N side was the Great Piazza Coffee House where Boswell dined in 1773, where in 1809 Sheridan drank 'a glass of wine at his own fireside' (after the fire at his Drury Lane theatre nearby), and where the lonely Jos Sedley 'dined with nobody' in *Vanity Fair*. Dickens stayed at the Great Piazza Hotel in 1844 and 1846, and characters in Thackeray's *The Newcomes* (1855) join a supper club in the Tavistock Hotel. This end of the N side was rebuilt in the 1890s and became part of the market.

At the N of the E side the Shakespeare's Head tavern (gone), frequented by Boswell, stood next to the Bedford Coffee House (*fl.* 1730–1837) haunt of actors, dramatists, and their audiences: Pope, Collins, Fielding, who met Arthur Murphy here and made him his assistant on *The Covent Garden Journal* (1752), Charles Churchill, Horace Walpole, and Sheridan. Hummums Hotel (established 1699), S of **Russell St.**, was visited by Dr Johnson and Boswell. Gibbon, however, in his *Autobiography* (first published in 1796 as *Memoirs of My Life and Writings*), remembers that, as a young man, he was 'too bashful to enjoy, like a manly Oxonian in town, the taverns and bagnios of Covent Garden'.

The young Hannah More stayed in **Henrietta St.** on her first visit to London with her sisters in 1774. She was introduced to Dr Johnson by Sir Joshua Reynolds. Jane Austen,

who often visited her brother Henry, stayed with him at no. 10 in 1813. He helped her in dealings with her publisher.

Rules Restaurant in **Maiden Lane** was patronized by Dickens. One of his *Sketches by Boz* is called 'Covent Garden'. Maurice Bendrix first kisses Sarah in Rules in Graham Greene's *The End of the Affair* (1951). It is also where the couple are later observed by the private detective Parkis. The dilapidated Temple School in Penelope Fitzgerald's novel *At Freddie's* (1982) is placed in a fictional Baddeley St. near **Covent Garden piazza**, from which at midday break many pupils 'ran, like little half-tame animals on the scavenge, through the alleys of the great market'.

Samuel Butler spent his last years in Rose Alley (now **Rose St.**), which led from the NE corner of Covent Garden piazza. He died there and Aubrey was one of the pallbearers at his funeral in St Paul's Church nearby. Dryden, on his way in 1679 from Will's Coffee House to his home in Long Acre, was assaulted in Rose Alley by a masked gang thought to have been in the pay of the Earl of Rochester, who supposed Dryden responsible for the *Essay on Satire* (written by the Earl of Mulgrave, but published anonymously) in which Rochester was derided.

Addison and his friends Steele, Philips, and Cibber visited Button's Coffee House (gone) established near the SW end of **Russell St.**, in 1712. Pope, who derided Philips's 'namby-pamby' verses and Addison's rule over his 'little senate', came with Gay, Swift, and Arbuthnot. Button's, also called the Wits' Coffee House, was closed by 1751, and Elizabeth Inchbald wrote the successful play *Such Things Are* (1788) in lodgings on the floor above.

Tom's Coffee House (gone) was established at no. 8 in 1700 above a bookshop. It was a rendezvous of Dr Johnson and the following 'clubbable' men: Arthur Murphy and Goldsmith, who first met Johnson in the 1760s; George Colman the Elder, who collaborated with Garrick in 1766 and dramatized Fielding's *Tom Jones* as *The Jealous Wife* (1761); and Fielding, who in his *Covent Garden Journal* (1752) attacked Smollett over *Peregrine Pickle* (1751). The existing coffee house now called Boswell's Coffee House is on the same site at no. 8 Ⓟ. It was erected 1759–60 and owned by Thomas Davies, a bookseller and publisher, formerly an actor. The first meeting here of Boswell and Dr Johnson (16 May 1765) is recorded in detail inside the coffee room.

Charles and Mary Lamb lived (1817–21) at '20 Russell Ct, Covent Garden East, half way up, next the corner, left hand side' (now 20–1) as he replied to a letter from the painter Haydon, who had given him similar directions to a dinner. Many of the *Essays of Elia* (1820–3) were written here and Wednesday evening parties of 'not silent whist' were attended by their 'many friends.

Simon Gray's play *Cell Mates* (1995) was first performed at the Albery Theatre on **St Martin's Lane**. Its run was cut short, largely as a result of the disappearance of one of its leading men,

Stephen Fry. Gray's memoir, *Fat Chance* (2005), records his account of the experience.

Tavistock St. was the site of York St., where at no. 4 De Quincey lodged for some years until 1824 and wrote *Confessions of an English Opium Eater* (1822).

Agatha Christie's play *The Mousetrap*, based on her own radio play *Three Blind Mice*, began its run at the Ambassadors Theatre on **West St.** on 25 November 1952. In March 1974 it transferred to the St Martin's Theatre (also West St.), where it can still be seen; the 55 years and more than 22,000 performances it has notched up to date make it the longest-running production in the world.

CRANFORD, parish to the W. Thomas Fuller, whom Pepys called a 'great cavalier parson', became rector of the village of Cranford in 1658, combining this after the Restoration with again resuming the lectureship at the Savoy Chapel. In 1661 Pepys mentions in his *Diary* that Fuller had talked to him about his 'last and great new book', which was to be 'the History of all the Families of England'. However, when Pepys read 'England's Worthys' (*The Worthies of England*, 1662) after Fuller's death and burial here (1661), he found that 'he says nothing at all, nor mentions us either in Cambridgeshire or Norfolke'.

CRAYFORD, parish to the SE. Algernon Blackwood, the novelist interested in the occult, was born (1869) at the Manor House (now an adult education college). He is best remembered for *John Silence* (1908), a collection of five short stories with the same interlinking character. His most successful novel was probably *A Prisoner in Fairyland* (1913), on which the original musical drama *Starlight Express* (1915) was based, with music by Elgar. A collection of short stories, *Tales of the Uncanny and Supernatural*, was published in 1949.

CROYDON, district to the S. John Ruskin's mother was brought up at the King's Head inn, and Ruskin visited the town often as a child, writing fondly of it in his autobiography, *Praeterita* (1899):

> it is evident to me in retrospect that . . . the personal feeling and native instinct of me had been fastened, irrevocably, long before, to things modest, humble, and pure in peace, under the low red roofs of Croydon, and by the cress-set rivulets in which the sand danced and minnows darted above the Springs of Wandel.

His parents are buried in St John's Church, Shirley, and the headquarters of Croydon's Labour Party are at Ruskin House on **Coombe Rd.**

D. H. Lawrence taught (1908–12) at the newly built **Davidson High School** in East Croydon, from where he could see the 'fairy-like . . . blue bubble of the Crystal Palace'. His pupils, 'my pack of unruly hounds', are mentioned in his few poems on the school written at his lodgings with the Jones family at

12 **Colworth Rd**. They all lived in the kitchen, 'small bare, and ugly, because the electric isn't connected up—all too poor to have it done'. 'Jones', he wrote to an Eastwood friend, 'is just jawing me how to make my fortune in literature.' He often 'worked all night at verse' published by Hueffer in the *English Review* and he was able to give his mother a copy of his first novel, *The White Peacock* (1911), but she died before she could read it. He also entered into his short-lived engagement to Louie Burrows on one of his vacations. After an absence through ill health Lawrence resigned from the school in 1912.

The Eastbourne-born novelist Angela Carter attended a school in south London before taking a job as a reporter on the local *Croydon Advertiser*. She would later set her novel *Wise Children* (1991) in south London.

John Horne Tooke's treatise on philology *The Diversions of Purley* (1786) is named in recognition of the fact that the country house of Horne Tooke's patron was in **Purley**, but otherwise the title has nothing to do with the work at all. In turn the title was borrowed by Peter Ackroyd for his collection of poetry *The Diversions of Purley* (1987).

DEPTFORD (pr. 'Detford), parish to the SE. **St Nicholas's Church** (rebuilt in 1697 and, after bombing, in 1957) contains a new tablet to Christopher Marlowe, who died in 1593. He was thought to have been killed as a result of an argument over the bill in a tavern here, but is now said to have been deliberately murdered for political reasons while employed as a government agent. He is buried in the churchyard. Marlowe's plays include *Tamburlaine* (1590), *The Tragedy of Dr. Faustus* (1604), and *Edward II* (1594), and he wrote the lyric so often parodied 'Come live with me and be my love' in *The Passionate Pilgrim* (1599). He influenced Shakespeare, who pays tribute to him in *As You Like It*, written after Marlowe's death, and he is said to have written part of Shakespeare's *Titus Andronicus*. Michael Drayton praises him in the lines:

> Next Marlow, bathed in the Thespian Springs,
> Had in him those brave translunary things,
> That the first poets had.

An Elizabethan dockland milieu is faithfully evoked in Anthony Burgess's fictionalized account of Marlowe's death in *Dead Man in Deptford* (1993):

> Morning Deptford and the shipbuilders early awork. The chandlers' shops busy. Hounds from the Queen's kennels howled bitterly. A faint stink from the Queen's slaughterhouse. A firmer stink from the tanneries. Inland gulls wove over the waters and crarked. Sails, sails, a wilderness of them.

The crime is also the subject of Charles Nicholl's investigative account *The Reckoning* (1995).

John Evelyn settled at **Sayes Ct** (site now Sayes Ct Gdns, off Evelyn St.) in 1653 after many years of Continental travel on which he was Edmund Waller's companion. His *Diary* (1818; new edn, 1955) gives details of his life here, the visit of his friend Samuel Pepys, the beginnings of the Royal Society, and in 1694 his removal to the family home at *Wotton on becoming his brother's heir.

Edgar Wallace moved with his wife and children to 6 **Tressillian Cres**. Ⓟ, Brockley, near the district in Greenwich where he spent his early years. Here he wrote a series of West African stories for *The Weekly Tale-Teller*, under the collective title of *Sanders of the River*, followed by a second series called *People of the River*, and then *Bones* (published in book form 1911). At the outbreak of the 1914–18 war he became a military correspondent for the duration.

In one of Deptford's 'plump-fronted houses' with their look of 'iron closets clamped against thieves' live Hood and his confederates in Paul Theroux's novel *The Family Arsenal* (1976).

The 1981 'New Cross Massacre' was a fire at 439 New Cross Rd that killed 13 people, and which was believed by some to have been a racially motivated arson attack; it was commemorated in a poem by Linton Kwesi Johnson, 'New Craas Massakah':

> fi know seh dem kine a ting deh
> couda happn to wi
> inna disya Great Britn
> inna Landan tiddey . . .

DULWICH (pr. 'Dullidge), district to the S. Edward Alleyn (1566–1622), the actor-manager, bought the manor here in 1605 and in 1619 founded **Dulwich College**, rebuilt in 1870 on the edge of the common. The school possesses the *Diary* of his stepfather-in-law, Philip Henslowe, manager of the Rose and Fortune theatres. The *Diary*, kept between 1592 and 1609, gives miscellaneous information and the accounts of the actors and playwrights employed by Henslowe. Alleyn is buried in the chapel, between College Rd and Gallery Rd, where the Old College stood.

The new school was built in 1870 on the edge of the common: an imitation in red brick of Milanese 14th-c. architecture.

P. G. Wodehouse, author of the 'Jeeves' novels, was educated at Dulwich and had a lifelong affection for his old school. His Memorial Study, containing his desk and personal belongings bequeathed by him, can be seen in the library. A number of other well-known writers who were pupils at the College include A. E. W. Mason, Raymond Chandler, Richard Church, Dennis Wheatley, and C. S. Forester (Cecil Lewis Troughton Smith). The novelist Graham Swift went to Dulwich College in the 1960s. Other schools in the Dulwich foundation have been attended by the short-story writer, critic, and novelist V. S. Pritchett (who was at Alleyn's School during the First World War) and the novelist and art historian Anita Brookner (who attended James Allen's Girls' School in the 1940s).

EALING, district to the W. The biographer, novelist, and historian of London Peter Ackroyd was educated in Ealing, at St Benedict's School.

EARLS COURT, district to the W. George Harvey Bone, the unfortunate schizophrenic hero of Patrick Hamilton's novel *Hangover Square* (1941), pursues his pointless infatuation with the disdainful actress Netta in the pubs, bedsits, and residential hotels of Earls Court, drinking heavily with Netta's horrible friends at the 'Rockingham' (imagined opposite the underground station). The story was based in part on Hamilton's own unrequited passion for the actress Geraldine Fitzgerald. He suffered near-fatal injuries in a road accident in Earls Court in 1932, an experience which left him with a scarred face and damaged arm, but which he turned into material for the dramatic traffic accident in *Twenty Thousand Streets Under the Sky* (1935).

The narrator of V. S. Naipaul's autobiographical novel *The Enigma of Arrival* (1987), newly arrived from Trinidad, settles in a boarding house in Earls Court in the 1950s. The novelist Brigid Brophy lived at 23 **Earls Ct Rd**. Gavin Ewart called the area 'the country of the single room, | The two-room flat, three single girls who share' in his 1964 poem 'Earls Court'. Shena Mackay lived in Earls Court in the 1960s, moving from job to job. Her literary career took off when she showed the manuscript of her novella *Toddler on the Run* (1964) to Frank Marcus, the author of *The Killing of Sister George*, then working in an antiques shop on Chancery Lane. The flat-share world of Earls Court provides the background for her novel of bisexual rites of passage *Music Upstairs* (1965). A few years later the travel writer Jonathan Raban lived in a square in Earls Court, and contemplated its provisional nature in his personal portrait of London, *Soft City* (1974):

> Earls Court people . . . are temporary; no-one asks where they come from or go to; they leave no places behind them when they move, only unpaid bills and unopened circulars. For many of them, Earls Court has been a place to disappear into, and their brief showing here has left an unexplained gap somewhere else.

In 1960 Harold Pinter's play *The Dwarfs* had its first performance, on BBC radio. In it, Mark and Len discuss Earls Court, where Mark has just come from; Len describes the place mysteriously as 'a mortuary without a corpse'.

EDGWARE, district to the N. The poet Stevie Smith and the novelist Stella Gibbons, author of *Cold Comfort Farm* (1929), were both educated at North London Collegiate School at Canons Drive.

EDMONTON, parish to the N. After his mother's death in 1810 Keats was articled to a surgeon and lived with his grandmother in a house on the site of **Keats Parade**, a row of shops at the SE end of **Church St.**, near the railway. At no. 7 a plaque over a florist commemorates the former cottage belonging to the surgeon Thomas Hammond, where Keats served his apprenticeship (1811–15). Some of his early poetry written at this time was published in *Poems by John Keats* (1817).

A short distance further W, near the corner of Lion Rd and up a narrow garden path, is Lamb's Cottage Ⓟ, formerly Bay Cottage, where Charles Lamb brought his sister Mary in May 1833, when she was suffering from severe and prolonged depressions, to be in the care of a Mr and Mrs Walden, who took in patients. This year saw the publication of *Last Essays of Elia*, the work that marked the end of his literary life. He died on 27 December 1834, following a fall that bruised his face and led to a fatal attack of erysipelas. He was buried in the churchyard nearby, where Mary, as they had both wished, was buried beside him, 13 years later. Much of the churchyard has been grassed over and the headstones removed to the sides, but the Lambs' tombstone still stands in its place, in a paved enclosure SW of the church. Inside the church, near the entrance, there are two mural tablets side by side, each with a portrait medallion; the first in memory of Lamb, 'the gentle Elia', bearing Wordsworth's lines:

> At the centre of his being lodged
> A soul by resignation sanctified.
> O, he was good, if e'er a good man lived,

and the second in memory of William Cowper, whose *Diverting History of John Gilpin* (1782) immortalized The Bell at Edmonton.

ELTHAM, parish to the SE. The 18th-c. red-brick Well Hall (gone) in **Well Hall Rd**, covered with Virginia creeper, was the home (1899–1922) of E. Nesbit. She wrote here the stories for children which appeared regularly in the *Strand Magazine*, *The Wouldbegoods* (1901), *Five Children and It* (1902), *The Phoenix and the Carpet* (1904), and *The Railway Children* (1906). The old moat, part of the Tudor house of Sir Thomas More's daughter Margaret Roper (who tradition says buried her father's head here after his execution), gave its name to the Moat House, home of E. Nesbit's fictitious family the Bastables. She and her husband, both founder members of the Fabian Society, entertained many literary friends here including Wells, Chesterton, and Frederick Rolfe, some of whom played her favourite games of charades and hide-and-seek. Extra participants made from clothes padded with paper came to life as the Ugly Wuglies in *The Enchanted Castle* (1907). E. Nesbit, who married again in 1917, found the house too large after her family had grown up, and left in 1922. The site of the house is now Well Hall Pleasaunce, a public garden.

Mervyn Peake, writer and artist, the second son of a medical missionary in China, came to England in 1923 and entered Eltham College as a boarder. The school, founded in 1842 for the sons of missionaries, had moved from Blackheath in 1912 to Mottingham, *c.* 1 m. from Eltham (then open country). Mervyn enjoyed six happy years here and later drew on memories of school characters for *Titus Groan* (1946).

Richmal Crompton, author of the William Brown books, died at Farnborough Hospital on 11 January 1969; on 16 January she was buried here at Eltham.

ENFIELD, district to the N. Captain Frederick Marryat, author of novels about the sea, was at school at Holmwood (gone), at the NW corner of Baker St. by the turning into Clay Hill. He often tried running away, with the idea of going to sea.

Chase Side is a road running N and S from Windmill Hill and Church St. to Lavender Hill and Lancaster Rd. Charles and Mary Lamb moved here from Islington in 1827, having previously made excursions and visits ever since Charles first came with Crabb Robinson to see friends in 1814. They lived first at a house originally called The Manse (later The Poplars), now Clarendon Cottage Ⓟ, no. 85. Lamb had hoped they were settled for life, but housekeeping proved too heavy a burden for Mary and in 1829 they moved next door, to a house now called Westwood Cottage, to lodge with a retired haberdasher and his wife, where they stayed until they moved to *Edmonton in 1833. These were not happy years. Lamb missed his friends, though Hazlitt, Leigh Hunt, and Thomas Hood came occasionally and the faithful Crabb Robinson often walked over for tea or a stroll, on one occasion, as he records in his *Diary*, bringing with him 'the mighty Walter Savage Landor'. Lamb did little serious literary work during this period, apart from the completion of the *Last Essays of Elia* (1833), but some of his best writing appears in his *Letters* (ed. E. V. Lucas, 3 vols, 1935). Clarendon Cottage and Westwood Cottage are part of Gentleman's Row, a group of houses lying back from the main road.

A plaque in the booking hall of Enfield Town station, **Southbury Rd**, commemorates Keats's first school, which occupied a house built on the site in the late 17th c. In 1849 it became the station house and was demolished in 1872.

Norman Lewis lived at Forty Hill as a child, on the borders of **Enfield Chase**. In the years before the First World War the village was, as Lewis recalls in his essay 'God Bless the Squire', still isolated, 'never quite released . . . from the previous century', and owned and ruled by Colonel Sir Henry Ferryman Bowles, 'a sporadically benevolent tyrant who would not have been out of place in Tsarist Russia'. Lewis was educated at Forty Hill Church School and at Enfield Grammar School, where he was badly bullied. His father, as he recorded in his autobiography *Jackdaw Cake* (1984; reissued as *I Came, I Saw*, 1995), was a 'spiritless and lackadaisical' pharmacist, displaying in his shop window on Southbury Rd 'perhaps a hundred books on pharmacology and allied subjects, grouped round a box of Beechams Pills, and a card which said, "I read all these, to sell this"'. His parents put more enthusiasm into spiritualism, but the young Lewis was consistently unimpressed by the spiritual manifestations: 'I soon discovered that the spirits of the dead had no sense of humour, and there was a terrible flatness, a lack of enthusiasm in their communications suggestive of convalescence, fatigue, even boredom.'

ERITH, parish S of the river to the E. William Thynne (d. 1546) was granted a house and tithes here by Henry VII. Thynne, an admirer of Chaucer, is thought to have been host to John Skelton, when he was writing his satirical attack on Cardinal Wolsey *Why Come ye nat to Courte*. Both men had court appointments and, after Skelton's death, Thynne edited *Chaucer's Works* (1532).

FINSBURY, district to the N. **Bunhill Fields**, City Rd, a burial ground, called the 'Campo Santo of Nonconformity' by Southey, was used from 1685 to 1852. It contains the graves of John Bunyan (d. 1688), Daniel Defoe (d. 1731), marked by an obelisk erected by the boys and girls of England in gratitude for their enjoyment of *Robinson Crusoe* (1719), Isaac Watts (d. 1748), and William Blake (d. 1827).

After going into hiding at the Restoration, Milton lived (1662–74) in a house (gone) in **Bunhill Row**, then called Artillery Row, where he finished *Paradise Lost* (1667) and wrote the sequel *Paradise Regained* (1671). He left London with his family during the plague years.

Fortune St. commemorates the Fortune Theatre built outside the City wall here by Henslowe and his stepson-in-law Edward Alleyn in 1600 for performances by the Lord Admiral's Men. The building and design are described in Henslowe's *Diary*. Alleyn took the chief parts in Marlowe's *Tamburlaine the Great*, *The Jew of Malta*, and *The Tragedy of Doctor Faustus*. The theatre gained a reputation for barnstorming revivals of old favourites such as *The Spanish Tragedy* (c. 1586). The Fortune was square rather than round and, until a disastrous fire in 1621, when 'all the apparels and playbooks [were] lost', commercially successful. Alleyn's diary entry for that evening was terse: 'this night at 12 of clock ye Fortune was burnt'.

FULHAM, parish N of the river to the SW. **Elysium Row**, between 128 and 154 (Ⓟ above nos 144–6) **New King's Rd**, was Horace Smith's home after his second marriage. He lived here from 1818 to 1821.

Samuel Richardson, 'the father of the English novel', had already had a successful career as a printer in Fleet St. before he turned to writing. He came to 40 **North End Cres.**, North End Rd, in 1739 and developed an idea of making a novel based on a series of letters, which he published in 1740, with immediate success, under the title *Pamela, or, Virtue Rewarded*. He wrote this and its successors, *Clarissa* (1747–8) and *Sir Charles Grandison* (1753–4), in a little grotto in the garden. He moved to Parson's Green in 1754.

As a boy, Kipling used to spend his holidays here with his aunt Lady Burne-Jones.

In 1922 J. B. Priestley and his new wife, Pat Tempest, moved to **Walham Green**, where their children were born.

The playwright John Osborne was born in Fulham, at 2 **Cookham Rd**, on 12 December 1929; his childhood is described in his autobiography, *A Better Class of Person* (1981).

GOLDERS GREEN, district to the NW. Golders Green appears in the poems of Dannie Abse, including 'Here' (a comic vision) and 'Odd':

It's a nice, clean, quiet, religious place.
For my part, now and then, I want to scream:
thus, by the neighbours, am considered odd.

GREENWICH (pr. 'Grenidge'), district on the S bank of the river to the E. The Tudor palace,

The Grange, North End, Fulham (now gone), Samuel Richardson's first country home

predecessor of Charles II's palace, which became Greenwich Hospital, was the scene of performances before Queen Elizabeth I of two Shakespeare plays in the winter of 1594.

In 1851 Harrison Ainsworth gave a whitebait dinner for his friends at The Trafalgar inn at the N end of **Park Row** near the Royal Naval College. This was to celebrate the completion of his novel *Mervyn Clitheroe*. Dickens and Ainsworth often attended each other's completion dinners.

The Royal Observatory in Greenwich Park was the objective of the anarchist who blew himself up there in 1894. Conrad is said to have admitted that this incident was the source of his novel *The Secret Agent* (1907).

C. Day-Lewis lived (1958–72) in **Crooms Hill**, W of Greenwich Park. He was made Poet Laureate in 1968. He published *The Buried Day* (1960), his autobiography, *The Gate and Other Poems* (1962), *The Room and Other Poems* (1965), *Whispering Roots* (1970), and many detective stories, under the pseudonym Nicholas Blake, during this time. He died in 1972 while visiting friends.

Edgar Wallace was born at 7 **Ashburton Grove**, the illegitimate child of a small-part actress at the old Greenwich Theatre. He was adopted by a Billingsgate fish porter who lived with his wife and 10 children at nearby Norway Ct behind **Bridge St**. After leaving school at 12 he tried various unskilled jobs before enlisting as a private in the Royal Kent Regiment.

HACKNEY, district N of Bethnal Green. William Hazlitt attended the New College for Protestant Dissenters at Hackney (founded in 1786 in a mansion in Lower Clapton and closed *c*. 1797), site between Tresham Ave. and Urswick Rd at the S of **Lower Clapton Rd**, 1½ m. SE.

The subject of Betjeman's 'Cockney Amorist' is a past denizen of the old music hall theatre here:

> No more the Hackney Empire
> Shall find us in its stalls
> When on the limelight crooner
> The thankful curtain falls,
> And soft electric lamplight
> Reveals the gilded walls.

The Playwright Harold Pinter was born in Hackney in 1930, and educated at the Hackney Downs Grammar School. The novelist Jane Rogers has taught at the Hackney College of Further Education; and the area is now home to Iain Sinclair, whose 1997 collection of London walks *Lights Out for the Territory* (subtitled '9 Excursions in the Secret History of London') begins here.

Marcus Crominski, the piano-playing child prodigy at the centre of Bernice Rubens's *Madame Sousatzka* (1962), lives with his family in the Jewish community in Stamford Hill.

HAM, riverside parish to the SW. Sarah Smith, author, as 'Hesba Stretton', of *Jessica's First Prayer* (1866), the popular tale of a waif finding Christianity, lived (1890–1911) at Ivy Croft. She is buried in the churchyard.

HAMMERSMITH, district N of the river to the W. Coleridge lived at 7 **Addison Bridge Pl.** Ⓟ from 1811 to 1812. It was at this time that he was working on *The Friend*, 'a literary, moral, and political weekly paper' which was subsequently rewritten and published as a book (1818).

Rider Haggard lived at 69 **Gunterstone Rd** from mid-1885 until *c*. April 1888. He completed *King Solomon's Mines* (published in September 1885), his first, and immensely successful, African romance.

The playwright Dennis Potter spent much of his childhood in Hammersmith, at the home of his maternal grandfather; parts of his most famous work *The Singing Detective* (1986) are set around Hammersmith and at the river by **Hammersmith Bridge**.

> The Thames at Hammersmith slip-slaps and glistens and blobs in the moonlight, and, in stages, the moon itself is half glimpsed, breaks up, and then is fully seen, floating mysteriously in the oily-black water. . . . Unexpectedly, there *is* someone on the bridge after all. The Singing Detective, in his 1945 garb, is on the pedestrian walk, a hand on the wooden-topped rail, looking at the slow, dark river, and smoking a cigarette. The music dips under, and he is talking straight at us, in his best, sardonic, 'Side-of-the-mouth' delivery—'The thing about the moon is, it gives you the creeps with a capital K. Am I not right?'

Arthur Murphy, playwright, actor, and friend of Dr Johnson, lived from 1795 to 1799 at 16 **Hammersmith Ter.** after leaving the Bar. He is buried in the churchyard of St Paul's, but the commemorative tablet has disappeared.

When W. B. Yeats was living with his family in Chiswick he attended the **Godolphin Boys' School** (founded 1856) in **Iffley Rd** as a day-boy. Yeats described the school, which catered for the sons of struggling professional men, as 'a Gothic building of yellow brick, with a separate house for boarders, all built *c*. 1860 or 1870'. He found it 'rough' and 'cheap' and disliked being teased for his 'Irishness'. He was there from 1876 to 1880, when the family returned to Ireland. The school was closed in 1900 and from 1906 the premises have housed the **Godolphin and Latymer School**.

Patrick Hamilton went to school at St Paul's Preparatory School, Colet Ct, on **Lonsdale Rd** in the years before the First World War. In the 1940s the novelist Brigid Brophy also attended St Paul's, a boys' school, because her mother was head teacher. The novelist Emma Tennant attended St Paul's Girls' School at **Brook Green** in the 1950s.

Marie Louise de la Ramée, who achieved international fame as a romantic novelist under the name 'Ouida' (a childish pronunciation of 'Louisa'), came to London from *Bury St Edmunds in 1857, when she was 18, and after a short stay at 41 Lansdowne Rd, Kensington Park, moved to Bessborough House, 11 **Ravenscourt Sq.** Ⓟ. Here she lived with her mother, Mme de la Ramée, and her grandmother Mrs Sutton, who had bought the house, until the latter's death in 1866. After the house was sold Ouida and her mother took apartments at 51 Welbeck St. before moving to the Langham Hotel. In 1870 they left England and finally settled in Italy.

Ouida first made her name in 1859 when Harrison Ainsworth, her doctor's cousin, arranged for a series of her short stories to be published in *Bentley's Miscellany*, a periodical which introduced many notable writers to the public. Ouida's first long novel, *Granville de Vigne*, was published in 1863 and was followed in rapid succession by many others, of which the best known is probably *Under Two Flags* (1867). Her stories dealt with high life and stirring action, her style was flamboyant, and her popularity immense. A parody in *Punch* of her novel *Strathmore* (1865) helped to establish her reputation.

Leigh Hunt spent his last years (1853–9) at 7 (now 16, Ⓟ) **Rowan Rd**, formerly Cornwall Rd. Nathaniel Hawthorne describes in *Our Old Home* (1863) how he visited him here, 'a beautiful and venerable old man, buttoned to the chin in a black dress-coat', occupying 'a very plain and shabby little house'. The plaque was unveiled in September 1973 by his great-great-grandson, Mr John Leigh Hunt.

The poet and novelist Robert Graves lived at 35 **St Peter's Sq.** with his wife, the American poet and novelist Laura Riding, and they set up a small press here in 1927. Laura Riding attempted suicide by jumping out of the window in 1929.

Kelmscott House, 26 **Upper Mall**, stands 100 yds upstream of the river creek which formerly separated the Upper and Lower Malls. George Macdonald, poet and novelist, came to live here in 1868, the house then being known as The Retreat, and wrote *Robert Falconer* (1868), a novel of the Aberdeenshire countryside, and the fairy tales *At the Back of the North Wind* (1871) and *The Princess and the Goblin* (1872). His wide circle of friends included Browning, Ruskin, Tennyson, the Carlyles, and Morris, and it was to the last-named that he sold the house in 1878. Morris moved in with his family at the end of October and renamed the property Kelmscott House after his country home at *Kelmscott. His utopian story *News from Nowhere* (1891) begins in Kelmscott House, as he envisaged it as a guest house of the 21st c. In 1890 he set up the Kelmscott Press, for which he designed founts of type and ornamental letters and borders, and from which he published his own works, reprints of the English classics, and various smaller books. The coach house, which bears an inscription over the lintel, taken from *News from Nowhere*, was used for weaving Morris Hammersmith carpets. Morris was happy to think of his country home up the river and twice rowed the 130 m. upstream to visit it. He died in Hammersmith and was buried in Kelmscott churchyard. Kelmscott House is now a private house. The basement and coach house are the headquarters of the William Morris Society.

Charles Reade lived at 3 Blomfield Villas, **Uxbridge Rd**, from 1882 to 1884 and died here.

HAMPSTEAD, district to the N on the W of Hampstead Heath. Hampstead plays a crucial role in Will Self's *The Book of Dave* (2006); in this story a book written by a London taxi driver, written as a useful volume of advice to his son, is buried in Hampstead and reappears many centuries later (on what is then the Island of Ham), where it becomes the basis of a new religion.

John Galsworthy lived at Grove Lodge, **Admiral's Walk** Ⓟ, a secluded, tree-lined street off Hampstead Grove, from 1918 until his death in 1933. He wrote much of *The Forsyte Saga* (1922) and its sequel, *A Modern Comedy* (1929), here, and his study overlooking the garden can be seen from Windmill Hill, at the other side of the house. He was awarded the Nobel Prize for Literature in 1932.

Christina Stead spent 1949 at 6 Downside Cres., **Belsize Park**. Charles Cleasby, the hero-worshipping narrator of Barry Unsworth's novel *Losing Nelson* (1999), lives in a large Victorian house in Belsize Park, where upstairs he writes a biography of Nelson and in the basement obsessively re-enacts with models on a glass table the admiral's great naval victories.

Joanna Baillie, poet and dramatist, came to Hampstead in 1802 from her native Scotland with her mother and sister. After her mother's death in 1806 she and her sister moved to **Bolton House** Ⓟ, one of a group of four tall houses between the S end of Hampstead Grove and the S end of Windmill Hill, facing Holly Bush Hill, and lived here until her death in 1851. Scott was introduced to her in 1806 by Southey, at his own request, and became a good friend, and Wordsworth used to walk over from London across the fields to stroll on the Heath with the lady he considered 'the ablest authoress of the day'. She wrote three volumes of *Plays on the Passions* (1798, 1800, and 1812), the most successful drama being *The Family Legend* (1810), and collections of poems published as *Fugitive Verses* (1790) and *Metrical Legends* (1821).

Aldous Huxley lived with his father and stepmother at 16 **Bracknell Gdns**, between Frognal Lane and Heath Drive, in 1917, while a clerk at the Air Board. He began work on his second collection of wartime poems, published the following year as *Defeat of Youth*.

In September 1899 Frederick Rolfe rented an attic room at 69 **Broadhurst Gdns**, West Hampstead (demolished in the Second World War), which appears in *Hadrian the Seventh* (1904), the work by which he is best known—part autobiography, part fantasy, written while he lived here.

Downshire Hill runs from Rosslyn Hill to the edge of Hampstead Heath, lined on its N side with pleasant early 19th-c. houses. Olive Schreiner lived at no. 30 in 1885, and Anna Wickham from 1909 to 1919 at no. 49, a house with a large and beautiful garden, where she

wrote some of her best-known poetry, including *The Contemplative Quarry* (1915) and *The Man with a Hammer* (1916). Edwin Muir lived at no. 7 from 1932 to 1935. His *Autobiography* (1954) gives a description of the contemporary literary set in Hampstead, which 'was filled with writing people and haunted by young poets despairing over the poor and the world, but despairing together, in a sad but comforting communion'. He also describes how he and his wife, Willa, were still translating from the German, mainly from Hermann Broch and Franz Kafka: 'At one stage Kafka's stories continued themselves in our dreams, unfolding into slow serpentine nightmares, immovably reasonable.'

Katherine Mansfield and John Middleton Murry lived at 17 **East Heath Rd** Ⓟ after their marriage in 1918. They called it The Elephant. In an entry in her *Journal* (1927), headed *October, Hampstead: Geraniums*, she writes, 'I went to London and married an Englishman, and we lived in a tall grave house with red geraniums and white daisies in the garden at the back.'

The novelists Monica Dickens and Paul Bailey and the playwright Harold Pinter (for two terms in 1951) are among the writers who have studied at the Central School of Speech and Drama on **Eton Ave** in Swiss Cottage. Bailey (here in the 1950s) worked as an actor until 1967. Dickens was asked to leave; she later said this was simply because she couldn't act . . .

From the summer of 1976 Kingsley Amis lived with his wife, the novelist Elizabeth Jane Howard, at Gardnor House on **Flask Walk**. After the breakdown of this marriage Amis spent his last year living with his first wife and her new husband down the road in Primrose Hill, where his funeral service was held in 1995, at St Mark's Church.

In **Frognal**, just N of the Frognal Way turning, opposite Frognal Lane (formerly West End Lane), stood Priory Lodge (demolished 1925), sometimes called Dr Johnson's House. In 1745 Dr Johnson used to come out from London and stay with his wife, who lodged here for a time for the sake of her health, and it was here that he wrote most, if not all, of *The Vanity of Human Wishes* (1749). Dion Boucicault, Dublin-born 19th-c. playwright, was educated at University College School (founded 1830).

Stephen Spender lived for much of his childhood at 10 Frognal, 'an ugly house in the Hampstead style', he wrote in his autobiography, *World Within World* (1951), 'as if built from the box of bricks of a nineteenth-century German child'. He lost his parents while living here and suffered rheumatic fever. After some unhappy and unsuccessful years at boarding schools, he attended University College School as a day-boy. At the age of 20 he entertained W. H. Auden at Frognal, who, at that time, 'was extremely particular about food, grumbled outrageously if everything was not arranged as he wished, sometimes carried a cane and even wore a monocle'. From 1942 to

1944 he lived in a flat beside the fire station in Maresfield Gdns, where he and the writer William Sansom worked as firemen.

At 18 **Frognal Gdns**, a secluded road leading from Church Walk to Frognal, is a private drive to Frognal End Ⓟ, the house where Sir Walter Besant spent his last years (1896–1901). He died here and was buried close by in the cemetery N of the parish church.

Coming to England at the start of 1962, Clive James took a room at Swiss Cottage; he wrote about this period of his life in his memoir *Falling Towards England* (1985), in which he wanders **Hampstead Heath** in winter ('Hampstead Heath was a slush curry of dead leaves but lent itself readily to the creative meanderings of young writers with high expectations and cold hands stuffed into duffel-coat pockets').

In the garden of **Kenwood House**, an 18th-c. mansion in the N part of Hampstead Heath, converted into an art gallery and museum, entered from Hampstead Lane, it is a pleasant surprise to come upon Dr Johnson's summerhouse, in which he and Mrs Thrale used to sit and talk in the garden at *Streatham Park. After the house was demolished, the summerhouse was moved to Ashgrove, Knockholt, Kent, and in 1968 was refurbished and transferred to its present site. The final scene of John Fowles's novel *Daniel Martin* (1977) is a walk on Hampstead Heath too, up into Kenwood, and a visit to the self-portrait by Rembrandt on display in Kenwood House.

> He walked round the place, not really looking at anything, until, by chance in the last room he came to, he stood before the famous late Rembrandt self-portrait. The sad, proud old man stared eternally out of his canvas, out of the entire knowledge of his own genius and the inadequacy of genius before human reality. Dan stared back.

Aldous Huxley rented a flat from June 1919 to December 1920 at 18 **Hampstead Hill Gdns**, a quiet street curving round from Rosslyn Hill to Pond St. Here he completed *Leda and Other Poems*, his third collection of wartime poems, and *Limbo*, short stories, both published in 1920. The critic and poet William Empson lived from 1952 until the end of his life at The Studio, 1 Hampstead Hill Gdns. It was a meeting point for many of the well-known figures of literary London of the 1950s and 1960s—including T. S. Eliot, Louis MacNeice, Kathleen Raine, and Elias Canetti. Canetti paints an unsparing portrait of that literary scene in his posthumously published memoir *Party in the Blitz* (2005). He had moved to Hampstead in 1939, living for a period at 19 South Hill Pk Gdns, and wrote *Crowds and Power* (1960) while in Hampstead, where he lived until the early 1970s.

Hampstead parish church has near the lectern a marble bust of Keats, erected (1894) by a group of American admirers. There is also a memorial tablet to Joanna Baillie, whose grave is in the SE corner of the churchyard.

The Load of Hay at 94 **Haverstock Hill** was rebuilt (1863) on the site of an old coaching inn where Addison used to alight from the London coach to visit Steele, who, in the summer of 1712, was living in a cottage beyond a high bank at the other side of the road. Steele had come here to find a rural retreat, partly to escape the attention of his creditors, and he described the cottage (the last home of Sir Charles Sedley, d. 1701) as 'in a solitary spot between London and Hampstead'. The cottage was the subject of many paintings, notably by Constable, and reproductions from these illustrate Steele's *Correspondence* (ed. R. Blanchard, 1941), *Annals of Hampstead* (ed. T. J. Barratt, 1912), *Northern Heights of London* (ed. W. Howitt, 1869), etc.; it was demolished in 1867, the site being commemorated by **Steele's Rd** (not by the Sir Richard Steele further up the Hill).

Heath House, a handsome Georgian house at the junction of North End Way and Spaniards Rd, was once the home of Sir Samuel Hoare, a 19th-c. Quaker banker and hospitable friend of many poets. His frequent guests included Crabbe, Cowper, Campbell, and Wordsworth.

Heath St. is one of the two principal streets of the old village running from the top of the High St. to Whitestone Pond and the Heath. The Kit-Cat Club, said by Vanbrugh to have been the best club that ever was, held its summer meetings in the early 18th c. at the Upper Flask tavern, which stood on the site of no. 124 (now occupied by Queen Mary's Hospital). Members (each of whom had his portrait painted for the Club) included Steele, Addison, Congreve, and Vanbrugh, as well as artists and leading society figures. These portraits are now in the National Portrait Gallery, north of Trafalgar Sq (*Soho).

The General, an old ally of the spymaster George Smiley, is murdered on Hampstead Heath in John le Carré's novel *Smiley's People* (1980).

Evelyn Waugh, whose first novel was the satirical *Decline and Fall* (1928), was born (1903) at 11 **Hillfield Rd**, West Hampstead. His father was Arthur Waugh, publisher and man of letters.

Jack Straw's Castle, an old coaching inn on North End Way (rebuilt in 1964), was patronized by Wilkie Collins, Thackeray, and Dickens. Karl Marx's housekeeper would buy flagons of beer here when the family made Sunday picnics on Hampstead Heath. Thom Gunn named a dreamlike poem after the place. Gunn was brought up in Hampstead, attended, like Stephen Spender, University College School, and warmly recalled in his autobiographical essay of 1977 'My Life Up To Now' a childhood in a bookish house and of playing with friends on the Heath. Its great chestnut trees did, and did not, bring memories of his childhood:

> without regret
> hardening tender green
> to insensate lumber.

Keats Grove is a road near the SE corner of Hampstead Heath. Keats lived (1818–20) with Charles Armitage Brown in one of a pair of semi-detached houses built in 1815 by Brown and Charles Wentworth Dilke and known as Wentworth Place. Keats's fiancée, Fanny Brawne, lived next door with her widowed mother. A nightingale that sang in the garden inspired his 'Ode to a Nightingale' written in May 1819. Wentworth Place is now a museum containing relics of Keats and his friends. Next door is the Heath Branch Library housing the Keats Memorial Library.

Having arrived in London in the summer of 1938, Sigmund Freud first took up residence at 39 **Elsworthy Rd** (where he began work on his *Outline of Psychoanalysis*), before moving (on 27 September) to 20 **Maresfield Gdns**, where he also did clinical work. While at Maresfield Gdns, Freud was visited by, among others, H. G. Wells and Leonard and Virginia Woolf. In July 1939 he would write to Wells, 'since I first came over to England as a boy of eighteen years, it became an intense wish phantasy of mine to settle in this country and become an Englishman'. Freud would have only slightly over a year in his adopted home country; he died in his study on 23 September 1939. A statue by Oscar Nemon stands outside the Tavistock Clinic at the bottom of Fitzjohn's Avenue, and the house on Maresfield Gdns is now the Freud Museum.

George Orwell lived at 10a **Mortimer Cres.**, South Hampstead, from 1942 to 1944, when he was bombed out. The newly completed manuscript of *Animal Farm* (1945) was sent to the publishers somewhat crumpled and dusty, but otherwise unscathed.

Wilfrid Gibson, whose early work was published in *Georgian Poetry* (ed. Edward Marsh, 1912–22), lived at 26 **Nassington Rd**, off Parliament Hill, from 1934 to 1939. His volume of *Collected Poems* (1905–25) was published in 1926 and he continued to publish other volumes of poetry throughout the war and up to 1950, the last title being *Within Four Walls*.

New End Hospital, between Rosslyn Hill and Pond St., was built (as the Hampstead General Hospital) on the site of The Green, 'the pretty, old-fashioned house at Hampstead' which was Francis Turner Palgrave's boyhood home.

In 1869 the novelist and cartoonist George du Maurier moved to Hampstead, living at Church Row and then in 1874 settling at **New Grove House**. He would remain in Hampstead until 1895, and the area (Hampstead Heath in particular) would feature in many of his cartoons. His ashes are buried in Hampstead parish church. In his novel *Author, Author* (2004), the novelist Henry James comes to Hampstead to visit du Maurier at New Grove House and the two men walk together on the Heath.

Off they would go together, perhaps with some of the children, perhaps with another visitor, certainly with a dog—Chang, or his diminutive successor the terrier, Don—down the hill and on to the Heath, past the ponds, past the place where in summer the donkeys waited patiently to give rides to children, and then wander as their inclination, or the dog's wagging tail, took them, perhaps towards the Spaniard's Road, where Du Maurier, in obedience to some superstitious private ritual, had to touch the last tree with his stick before turning home, or perhaps to Parliament Hill, where they would look down on the London plain, picking out the landmark buildings of Westminster and the City piercing the haze of coal smoke.

Dinah Mulock came in 1857 to **North End**, formerly a village N of Hampstead, and settled at Wildwood Cottage, where she became the centre of a large literary coterie. The work by which she is chiefly remembered, *John Halifax, Gentleman*, was published the year she arrived and was immensely successful, 250,000 copies being sold in her lifetime. Abel Fletcher, the mill owner, is believed to have been based on a Hampstead resident. In 1865 she married George Lillie Craik, a partner in Macmillan's publishing house, and soon after went to live at Beckenham (see BROMLEY).

Parliament Hill runs up from South End Rd to Hampstead Heath. John Betjeman was born at 52 Parliament Hill Mansions in 1906. The Betjemans (or Betjemanns—the family modified its name to something less Germanic during the First World War) lived here for three years, moving to Highgate in 1909.

No. 68 was the home of the poet Anna Wickham (Mrs Patrick Hepburn) and her family from 1919 to 1947 and a meeting place for many writers and painters, who enjoyed her hospitality and the stimulation of her lively personality. *The Little Old House* (1921) and *Thirty-Six New Poems* (1936) were published during this period. *Selected Poems* was published in 1971, with an introduction by David Garnett. Her eldest son, James Hepburn, was a friend of Malcolm Lowry's and in the autumn of 1932, soon after Lowry had left *Cambridge, invited him home, where he was made welcome and became a frequent visitor. His first novel, *Ultramarine*, begun in 1928 and written mainly during his Cambridge years, was accepted about this time and (after a series of misadventures) published in 1933. Dylan Thomas was another visitor of the 1930s and immortalized the bathroom, which contained an aviary, in *Adventures in the Skin Trade* (1955), the beginning of a partly autobiographical novel which was never finished.

At **South End Green** a pizzeria on the corner of Pond St. and South End Rd stands on the site of a bookshop where George Orwell worked in return for his lodging (1934–5) and wrote *Keep the Aspidistra Flying* (1936). He is commemorated by a plaque with a portrait bust.

The Vale of Health is a cul-de-sac in Hampstead Heath on the N side of East Heath Rd, overlooking a pond where Shelley used to sail paper boats. Leigh Hunt lived here in 1815, possibly in one of the three villas on the Heath

(Hunt Cottage; Ⓟ) or, now thought more probably, at Vale Lodge, and was visited by Keats and Shelley. Ernest Rhys stayed at Hunt Cottage in the 1880s, believing it to have been Hunt's home. The Indian poet and dramatist Rabindranath Tagore (1861–1941) lived in one of the villas Ⓟ in 1912, the year he published *Gitanjali*, a collection of poems for which he was awarded the Nobel Prize (1913). D. H. Lawrence and his wife took a ground-floor flat at **1 Byron Villas** Ⓟ in 1915. They were full of plans for forming a community of like-minded people, such as Katherine Mansfield and John Middleton Murry, and when Lawrence's newly published novel *The Rainbow* was suppressed in November as obscene, they decided that they must emigrate to America. 'It is the end of my writing for England,' said Lawrence bitterly, and he posted a pack of his manuscripts (including *The Rainbow*) to his friend Lady Ottoline Morrell, at *Garsington, for her to keep until they were worth selling. He and Frieda gave up the flat in December, hoping (though vainly) to sail for Florida.

The novelist Stella Gibbons, who was born in nearby *Kentish Town, lived in and around Hampstead throughout her life at a number of different addresses, including **Vale Cottage** on the Vale of Health from 1927 to 1930, 67 Fitzjohn's Ave. from 1930 to 1932, and, from 1933 until her death in 1989 at 19 Oakeshott Ave., Highgate.

Well Walk, off East Heath Rd, took its name from the chalybeate spring which was a source of health-giving waters drunk by the fashionable in the 18th c. Keats had lodgings here before moving to Wentworth Place (Keats Grove) in 1818. John Masefield lived at no. 14 from 1913 to 1916. Thomas Sturge Moore lived from *c.* 1914 to 1919 in Constable's house, no. 40, which became a meeting place for artists and writers and their friends.

HAMPSTEAD GARDEN SUBURB, district N of Hampstead. Old Wyldes Ⓟ, **Hampstead Way**, a 17th-c. farmhouse owned by Sir Raymond Unwin, the Suburb's architect and 'father of British town planning', from 1907 until his death in 1940, was once a retreat and a meeting place for artists and writers. William Blake was a frequent visitor when his friend John Linnell, a successful landscape and portrait painter, rented the house from 1824 to 1830. Linnell commissioned Blake to engrave illustrations to the book of Job and to produce a new series of illustrations from Dante. Dickens spent some time here in 1832, and later visitors included Walter Besant and Bernard Shaw.

HAMPTON, riverside district to the SW. Richard Steele bought a house in Hampton Wick, 2 m. E, in 1707. It is thought he lived here for a short time only, with his wife, the 'dear Prue' to whom he apologizes so often in his letters. The house, which he called The Hovel, is thought to be the place Addison had sold to get repayment for a loan he made Steele.

Garrick's Villa (later flats), which he bought in 1754, with the Grecian temple in the garden of 'syringas and lilacs' sloping to the Thames, was visited by his many friends, including Hannah More and Dr Johnson. Garrick discussed details here for the first night of Richard Cumberland's *The West Indian* (1771), a successful play for many years.

HAREFIELD, parish to the NW. The parish church has the painted, canopied tomb of Alice, Dowager Countess of Derby, who seems to have retained this title when she came to Harefield Place (gone, site near the church) with her second husband, Sir Thomas Egerton (later Lord Ellesmere). He was Jonson's 'grave and great orator' and was also eulogized by Samuel Daniel. In *Colin Clouts come home againe* Spenser, who calls her Amaryllis, reminds her that he is a member of her 'noble familie'. Sir John Davies (1569–1626) wrote *The Lottery* as part of the entertainment given by the newly married couple to Queen Elizabeth I in 1602. Milton is thought to have met the Dowager Countess here, perhaps through an introduction by his friend Henry Lawes, who was attached to the household of her stepson (who was also her son-in-law), the Earl of Bridgewater. Lawes wrote the music for 'Arcades', the masque Milton wrote to entertain the Dowager Countess here. It was probably performed in 1633 with some of her grandchildren among the actors. Entertainments for the Dowager Countess and her family were also given at *Ashby-de-la-Zouch and *Ludlow.

HARROW ON THE HILL, parish to the NW. Harrow School (founded 1572) has had many distinguished literary men among its pupils. R. B. Sheridan was there from 1762 to 1768 and left his name carved on a panel of the old Fourth Form Room. He came back to live in Harrow at the end of 1781, a married man and a successful playwright (*The Rivals* had been produced in 1775 and *The School for Scandal* in 1777), and his house, The Grove, by the N side of the churchyard, is now a school boarding house. Byron was a pupil from 1801 to 1805 and his name can also be seen on the same panel as Sheridan's. He used to spend many hours in the churchyard near the tomb of John Peachey (now protected with iron casing), which he mentions in a letter from Italy in 1822 as 'my favourite spot'. A marble plaque near the tomb is engraved with a verse from his 'Lines Written Beneath an Elm' (2 Sept. 1807), in which he considers being buried there:

> Here might I sleep where all my hopes arose,
> Scene of my youth, and couch of my repose;
> For ever stretch'd beneath this mantling shade,
> Press'd by the turf where once my childhood
>   play'd.

Anthony Trollope came in 1827 and stayed until he was nearly 19, but he was looked down on by the other boys because he was a day-boy. His home from 1817 to 1827 had been at

Julians, a big house (now altered) S of the Hill, and then a farmhouse (demolished *c.* 1901) nearby called Julians Hill (which appears in *Orley Farm*, 1862). A later move was to a farmhouse at Harrow Weald, from which Trollope had to tramp 3 m. of muddy lanes to school. This was believed to be Durrant's Farm, at the corner of Weald Lane and High Rd (demolished in the 1930s).

Other literary Harrovians include C. S. Calverley, R. B. Cunninghame Graham, J. A. Symonds, H. A. Vachell, author of *The Hill* (1905), a novel about the school, John Galsworthy, G. M. Trevelyan, and L. P. Hartley. The playwright Terence Rattigan won a scholarship to the school, which he took up in 1925; from 1937 to 1940 John Mortimer was a pupil here.

F. W. Farrar was a master here (1855–70) and wrote *Eric, or, Little by Little* (1858, about schooldays in the Isle of Man), and *Julian Home: A Tale of College Life* (1859, about Cambridge).

Byron House, at the foot of **Byron Hill** on the right-hand side going up, was the home of Matthew Arnold (1868–73) when he was Inspector of Schools for a country area including Harrow, as well as for Westminster. The grounds have been broken up for housing development. Charles Kingsley lived for a few months in 1873 in a large Victorian house (now flats) in **London Rd**, known as Kingsley House. A little further south R. M. Ballantyne spent the later part of his life (1880–93) at Duneaves Ⓟ, **Mount Pk Rd**, not far from South Harrow underground station.

The poet and artist David Jones lived in Harrow from 1946 until his death in 1974, first at Northwick Lodge (gone), Peterborough Rd (1946–63), then at Monksdene Hotel, 2 Northwick Pk Rd (1963–70), and finally, after suffering a bad fall, at Calvary Nursing Home, Sudbury Hill (1970–4). During this time he published *The Anathemata* (1952), a religious poem relating to the Catholic Mass and his personal life, and other works, including *The Wall* (1955), *Epoch and Artist* (1959), and *The Tribune's Visitation* (1969).

John Betjeman imagines the town as an island in a sea of 'Wealdstone turned to waves' in 'Harrow-on-the-Hill'.

HARROW WEALD, district N of Harrow on the Hill. Sir W. S. Gilbert bought a house and estate (now a country hotel) on the edge of the common in 1890 and lived there until his death from heart failure, after rescuing a young woman from the lake. His ashes are buried in the churchyard at Great Stanmore.

HAYES, former village in Middlesex on the A4020 *c.* 2½ m. SW of Northolt. Eric Blair taught at the Hawthorns High School for Boys, Station Rd—now a hotel, 116 Church Rd Ⓟ—from April 1932 to December 1933. During this time he finished *Down and Out in Paris and London* (1933), in which he first used the pen-name 'George Orwell', and began *Burmese Days* (1934).

HEATHROW, district to the W. The flyover at Heathrow Airport—still called London Airport in the book—is the site of Vaughan's car accident in J. G. Ballard's surrealistic novel *Crash* (1973).

HENDON, parish to the NW. Church Farm House Museum, the oldest surviving dwelling house in the ancient parish or manor of Hendon, is next to the church and The Greyhound inn. Mark Lemon, editor of *Punch* and friend of Dickens, lived at the 200-acre farm with his grandparents after the age of 8, and local people and incidents inspired some of his *Tom Moody's Tales* (1863), which were often autobiographical.

HERNE HILL, area to the S. John Ruskin lived (1823–42) at 28 **Herne Hill** Ⓟ, a large semi-detached villa, from the age of 4 until his parents moved to Denmark Hill to the N. Ruskin writes of the house, its garden, the almond blossom, the country walks, and views in his autobiography *Praeterita* (1885–9). In 1852, four years after his marriage, his father bought no. 30, adjacent to their former home, for his son and daughter-in-law. Ruskin's mother, who was excessively possessive about her only child and worried about his health, wished to have him near her. He was able to work in his old study at Denmark Hill every day, and his wife was expected to drive over to join the family for dinner. But in 1854 Ruskin's wife, who was in love with the painter Millais, got an annulment of her marriage. Ruskin, after travelling abroad, rejoined his parents at Denmark Hill. No. 28 was let from 1852 and was demolished in 1906. A drawing of the house can be seen at *Brantwood.

J. R. Ackerley was born at 4 **Warmington Rd** on 4 November 1896.

HIGHGATE, district to the N on the NE of Hampstead Heath. Coleridge lived for 19 years in Highgate including at 3 **The Grove** Ⓟ with his friends James and Ann Gillman from 1823 until his death. Lamb visited him in 1831 and put up at the Gate House inn nearby. No. 3 was the home of J. B. Priestley from 1935 to 1939.

Highgate cemetery is in two parts, the principal gates opposite each other in Swain's Lane. The older part, to the W, can only be seen by guided tour. It is a fantastic and beautiful place on the hillside below St Michael's Church. The newer part is more formal, though its regularity is pleasantly broken by glades and shaded paths. Here George Eliot's obelisk (not far from Karl Marx's monument) is easily found, but the graves of Crabb Robinson, Christina Rossetti, and Leslie Stephen take time to discover. Mrs Henry Wood's massive family tomb is in the old part. In the catacombs is an elaborate vault where Radclyffe Hall is buried. She was the author of eight novels, of which the most famous is *The Well of Loneliness* (1928), banned in England (until 1949) on account of its study of lesbianism. It was, however, published abroad and has

continued to sell worldwide in numerous translations. An account of her remarkable life and writings is given in *Our Three Selves*, by Michael Baker (1985), the title being her own dedication to herself and the two women who successively shared her life.

Highgate School was founded by Sir Roger Cholmeley in 1565. The senior school and chapel (buildings mostly dating from *c.* 1866) stand between Southwood Lane and North Rd, with a new block (Dyne House, 1967) on the S side of the lane. Former pupils include W. W. Skeat, Gerard Manley Hopkins, who won the school Poetry Prize in 1860 and boarded at Elgin House (later commercial premises) in the **High St.**, and John Betjeman. T. S. Eliot taught here for a time.

A. E. Housman wrote *A Shropshire Lad* (1896) while he was living at 17 **North Rd** Ⓟ from 1886 to 1905. The house (formerly Byron Cottage) is one of a row set back from the road behind sycamore trees and has been little altered since Housman's day.

St Michael's Church was built on the site of Arundel House (parts of the cellar are incorporated in the undercroft), which was demolished in 1825, the place where Francis Bacon died from a chill after stuffing a chicken with snow to test the preservation of meat by refrigeration.

Coleridge was reburied here, after having been removed from a grave in Old Highgate Chapel. A fine memorial to the 'poet, philosopher and theologian' was erected on the N wall of the nave by his friends James and Ann Gillman, whose own memorial of similar design accompanies it.

On the outside wall of **Waterlow Park** on the W side of Highgate High St., just N of Lauderdale House, a weather-beaten plaque records the site of the cottage where Andrew Marvell once lived. The inscription reads:

Four feet below this spot is the stone step formerly the entrance to the cottage in which lived

ANDREW MARVELL

poet, wit and satirist

colleague with John Milton in the Foreign or Latin Secretaryship during the Commonwealth and for about twenty years MP for Hull. Born at Winstead, Yorkshire, 31st March 1621. Died, in London, 18th August 1678, and buried in the church of St.-Giles-in-the-Fields.

As a child, John Betjeman lived at **Highgate West Hill**, which he remembers in his long autobiographical poem *Summoned by Bells*. Highgate cemetery did much to foster his affection for Victoriana.

Keats's encounter with Coleridge prompted Thom Gunn's poem 'Keats at Highgate', the younger poet pressing 'the famous hand with warmth' and sauntering home 'in his own state of less dispersed | More passive consciousness'. Gunn, brought up in *Hampstead, was a passionate reader of Keats as an adolescent.

Howard Baker's absent-mindedness at a junction on **Highgate Hill** causes the accident

that opens Michael Frayn's afterlife novel *Sweet Dreams* (1973).

HOLBORN (pr. 'Hōbern), district between the City and Bloomsbury. In 1770 the 17-year-old Thomas Chatterton lodged in the attic at 39 **Brooke St.** (Ⓟ erected in 1928 on site) kept by Mrs Angel, a sack maker. He wrote a burletta (a musical farce) for the entertainments in Marylebone Gdns and spent some of the money he received on presents for his mother and sister in *Bristol. A letter to them boasts of the amount of work he has had accepted and that he has 'a deal of business now'. However, the works that he mentioned never appeared, his second burletta was not performed, and his money ran out. His death from arsenic poisoning was thought to be due to poverty and despair; his landlady had offered him food but a baker had refused him a loaf on credit and Chatterton might have thought his landlady, to whom he owed rent, would expect payment too. The possibility that he died as a result of trying to cure himself of a venereal disease has also been put forward. He was buried in the workhouse cemetery (gone) in Shoe Lane on the day his second burletta was performed.

Sydney Smith, having arrived with his wife from Edinburgh, lived (1803–6) at 14 (formerly 8) **Doughty St.** Ⓟ. In March 1837 Dickens, with his wife, Catherine, and their baby son Charles, came to live at no. 48 Ⓟ, now the Dickens House Museum (open daily, www.dickensmuseum.com). Here he finished the last five monthly numbers of *The Pickwick Papers* (Apr.–Oct. 1837) and wrote *Oliver Twist* (1837–8) and *Nicholas Nickleby* (1838–9). He also began *Barnaby Rudge*, but its publication did not begin until 1841. This pleasant 18th-c. house, where his reputation became established, was the scene of the lively dinner parties that he delighted to give, where the guests included many literary and artistic celebrities, notably Harrison Ainsworth, Leigh Hunt, and John Forster, who became Dickens's lifelong friend and biographer. By October 1839 Dickens had become the father of two more children, both daughters, and as the family needed a larger house they moved to 1 Devonshire Ter. (see MARYLEBONE).

The Dickens House Museum is owned by the Dickens Fellowship (founded 1902) and contains a library and museum of wide-ranging interest. Pages of the original manuscripts of Dickens's early books are on view, as well as a large collection of his letters and personal relics. Of particular interest is the velvet-topped portable desk designed by himself, from which he gave dramatic readings from his works in many parts of Britain and America.

The Bishop of Ely's palace (gone) stood at **Ely Pl.** In Shakespeare's *Richard III*, Richard sends the Bishop to fetch from here the strawberries he had admired in his garden.

Gray's Inn, one of the four *Inns of Court, and known to have existed as a school of law since the 14th c., is situated between High Holborn and Theobalds Rd and is bounded on the E by Gray's Inn Rd. The main entrance is through the 17th-c. gateway in High Holborn and leads to South Sq., where the statue of Sir Francis Bacon, Lord Verulam (by F. W. Pomeroy, 1912), stands at the E end of the lawn. Bacon, regarded by many as the Inn's greatest figure, entered as a student in 1576, became a Bencher in 1586, and treasurer in 1608. He retained his chambers here, on the site of the present Verulam Bldgs on the NE corner of Gray's Inn Sq., until his death in 1626, and laid out the gardens, entered from Field Ct. At least one ancient catalpa tree which he planted there is alleged to have been grown from a slip brought by Sir Walter Ralegh from America. The gardens and walks were once fashionable places for meeting and talking; Pepys mentions strolling there, Bacon and Ralegh paced arm-in-arm, Sir Philip Sidney, Addison, Macaulay, all knew them well, and Charles Lamb called them 'the best gardens of any in the Inns of Court, my beloved Temple not forgotten'.

The Hall, on the N side of South Sq., was built in 1556–60, bombed in 1941, and rebuilt in its original style in 1951. It was the scene of many royal occasions and the setting for the first production of Shakespeare's *The Comedy of Errors* in 1594. The 16th–17th-c. stained glass includes the arms of Bacon. T. B. Macaulay, called to the Bar in 1826, took chambers in 1829 at 8 South Sq. (library on site). Dickens, aged 15, worked as a clerk for Ellis and Blackmore, solicitors, at 1 South Sq., then Holborn Ct. The desk he used here is preserved at the Dickens House in Doughty St.

Other distinguished members include: George Gascoigne (1525?–77), who entered before 1548; Thomas Campion, who entered in 1586 but withdrew before 1595, was probably connected with the Gray's Inn masque of 1594–5, which included some of his songs (he was an authority on music and published some books of airs); Thomas Middleton (1570?–1627), who probably entered 1593; James Shirley (1596–1666), who was a resident *c.* 1625 and compiled the text for the Inns of Court masque *The Triumph of Peace* (1634); Robert Southey (1774–1843), who entered in February 1797, but found the study of Law 'laborious indulgence' and gave it up. He published *Minor Poems* the same year, completed *Madoc*, and planned *Thalaba the Destroyer*.

Edward Marsh, classicist and patron of modern poetry, lived at 3 **Gray's Inn Pl.** (1899–1903) and then at 5 **Raymond Bldgs** (1903–40) nearby, where he was visited by his many friends, including Rupert Brooke (whose literary executor he was), W. W. Gibson, W. H. Davies, Edmund Blunden, Walter de la Mare, and Harold Monro, among numerous others. He edited *Georgian Poetry*, a series of contemporary verse (1912–21), and wrote *A Memoir of Rupert Brooke* (1918). He was knighted in 1922.

Ian Fleming secured congenial terms of employment with the *Sunday Times* (whose offices once stood on **Gray's Inn Rd**), which allowed him periods of the year to live in Jamaica, where the James Bond novels were

written. In 1959 he proposed to the paper's travel writer Norman Lewis that he go to Cuba 'to find out all [he] could about the charismatic revolutionary called Castro who had established himself in the mountains of that island'. Lewis's subsequent journey to Cuba brought him in contact with not only Castro but also Hemingway (drinking neat Dubonnet in half-pints) and Ed Scott, the model for James Bond. His meeting with Scott was observed by Graham Greene, and formed the basis of a scene in Greene's *Our Man in Havana*. In 1968 Lewis wrote a 12,000-word article for the *Sunday Times* about the genocide of the Amazonian Indians, the longest ever published by the paper. It provided the basis for his book *The Missionaries* (1988). In 1972 Bruce Chatwin was hired by the paper to write on art and architecture, famously disappearing in 1974 and sending the telegram 'Gone to Patagonia'. The trip resulted in *In Patagonia* (1977), which made his name as a travel writer. The children's hospital at **Great Ormond St.** was in 1929 granted by J. M. Barrie perpetual copyright in his *Peter Pan* and continues to receive royalties.

William Hayley, who studied Law at the Middle Temple, lived (*c.* 1770) at 55–6 **Gt Queen St.**, off Kingsway (near Lincoln's Inn Fields). William Blake, who became his friend, served his apprenticeship as an engraver with James Basire at no. 31 from 1771 to 1778, and R. H. Barham, who was appointed a minor canon of St Paul's in 1821, lived at no. 51 from 1821 until 1824.

Henry Crabb Robinson moved to 56 **Hatton Garden** in 1810 when his landlord changed houses. Dorothy Wordsworth, one of the many literary friends mentioned in Robinson's *Diary*, dined with him here when he accompanied her in the coach from *Bury St Edmunds to stay with the Lambs.

On the N side of **Holborn**, between Brooke St. and Leather Lane, the Holborn Bars Bldg (now a De Vere Conference Venue) occupies the site of Furnival's Inn (demolished 1897; Ⓟ), where Dickens lived in 1836. Inside the covered entrance on the left is a bust of Dickens by Percy Fitzgerald, commemorating the writing of *The Pickwick Papers*, which first appeared in 20 monthly instalments beginning in April 1836. Thackeray met Dickens here for the first time, having called with the idea that he might illustrate Dickens's stories. The drawings that he offered, however, were unsuitable and this disappointment (so he said) caused him to direct his attention to another form of art. John Macrone, who published Dickens's sketches in book form, *Sketches by Boz* (1836–7), brought N. P. Willis, the American littérateur, to call on Dickens here. Willis described the poverty of 'the young paragraphist' in his rooms, his 'three-pair-back' as Dickens called them.

Hazlitt married Sarah Stoddart in 1808 at **Holborn Circus** at **St Andrew's**. Charles and Mary Lamb were groomsman and bridesmaid and Charles wrote that he was nearly turned out of the church during the ceremony as 'anything awful makes me laugh'.

John Ruskin was born (1819) at 54 **Hunter St.** (demolished 1969) and lived there until his parents moved to *Herne Hill in 1823. The drawing-room door and shutter knobs and the front-door chain were preserved and can be seen in Ruskin's study at *Brantwood.

Holy Trinity Church Ⓟ, **Kingsway**, was built in 1910, replacing the former church built (1831) on the site of Little Queen St., where Charles and Mary Lamb and their family had lodgings when they left the Temple in 1795. It was here in the following year that Mary, in a fit of insanity, stabbed her mother to death and was temporarily confined to an asylum at Hoxton. Charles, who had moved with his father after the tragedy to 45 Chapel St. (gone), Pentonville, was determined that Mary should not stay in hospital, and for the rest of his life took the responsibility of caring for her and helping her over the recurrent attacks of her congenital mental illness.

Lincoln's Inn, one of the Inns of Court, is situated between Chancery Lane and Lincoln's Inn Fields. It was named after Henry de Lacy, Earl of Lincoln (d. 1311), whose house stood in the vicinity and whose lion crest is on a shield over the Gothic gateway in Chancery Lane. The Old Hall (1506), opposite the gatehouse, was for centuries the centre of the Inn's communal life, where the members took their meals, performed masques, and danced, activities conducive 'to the making of gentlemen more fit for their books at other times'. The New Square (17th c.), which has housed many eminent members of the Bar and legal profession, is reached through an archway between the Hall and the Chapel. Arthur Murphy, dramatist and actor and friend of Dr Johnson, lived at no. 1 from 1757 to 1788, having been accepted by Lincoln's Inn after being refused at Gray's Inn and the Middle Temple because he had been an actor at Covent Garden and Drury Lane. He was called to the Bar in 1762. Dickens worked as a clerk in a solicitor's office here for a short time when he was 14. On the N side of the Square are the Inn gardens, mentioned by Pepys in his *Diary* and by Steele in *The Tatler*, and the 19th-c. Hall and Library, the latter containing the oldest collection of books in London (founded 1497).

Distinguished members of the Inn include: Sir Thomas More (1478–1535), who entered in 1496; Richard Edwards (1523?–66), who entered after leaving Oxford in 1547, but does not appear to have followed the legal profession; Thomas Lodge (1558?–1625), who entered in 1576; John Donne (1571/2–1631), who entered in 1592 and shared chambers with Christopher Brooke, another poet; later he was the Chapel's first chaplain; George Wither (1588–1667), who entered in 1606, but preferred to be a writer; Sir John Denham (1615–69), who entered in 1634 after leaving Oxford, and was called to the Bar in 1639; Lord Macaulay (1800–59), who was called to the Bar in 1826 and in 1829 took chambers in 8 South Sq. (demolished to make room for the library); Benjamin Disraeli (Lord Beaconsfield) (1803–81), who entered in 1824 and kept nine terms, but removed his name in 1831. He began his literary career by writing poetry, but made his name with his successful first novel, *Vivian Grey* (1826–7); Charles Reade (1814–84), who entered in 1835 and was called to the Bar in 1842; Thomas Hughes (1822–96), who entered in 1845 and migrated to the Inner Temple in 1848; Rider Haggard (1856–1925), who was called to the Bar in 1884 but left after his success as a novelist; Sir Henry Newbolt (1862–1938), who was called to the Bar in 1887 and practised for 12 years, gradually spending more time on writing. He spoke of his 'real claim to immortality' as having contributed largely to the *Law Digest*. His first novel, *Taken from the Enemy*, a tale of the Napoleonic wars, appeared in 1892; and John Galsworthy (1867–1933), who was called to the Bar in 1890, but did not practise for long.

Lincoln's Inn Fields, a spacious square, laid out by Inigo Jones in 1618, between Lincoln's Inn and Kingsway. The poet Thomas Campbell lived at no. 61 from *c.* 1828 to 1832. John Forster, biographer and critic, moved into chambers at no. 58 in 1832 after studying Law at the Inner Temple. He was called to the Bar in 1843, but gave up a legal career for literature and became a close friend of Lamb, Leigh Hunt, and Dickens. His works include biographies of Goldsmith, Landor, and Dickens, and the first volume of a life of Swift. Dickens portrays Forster's house as the home of Mr Tulkinghorn in *Bleak House* (1852–3).

William Cowper worshipped at the **Church of St George the Martyr, Queen Sq.**, when he was a law student. Frederick Walker's picture *Thanksgiving* was drawn here, showing the family in church, to illustrate Thackeray's novel *The Adventures of Philip* (1861–2). Ted Hughes and Sylvia Plath were married here on 16 June 1956, less than four months after their first meeting. The date—16 June—was chosen to coincide with Joyce's Bloomsday. (Queen Sq. would later be home to Hughes's publisher Faber and Faber.)

William Morris and his family lived in the upper part of no. 26 from 1865 to 1872, above the workshops of the manufacturing and decorating firm of Morris, Marshall, Faulkner & Co. He published the poems *The Life and Death of Jason* (1867) and *The Earthly Paradise* (1868–70) while he was living here.

Charles Churchill taught for a short time at a boarding school at no. 24 run by a Mrs Dennis and known as the 'Ladies' Eton'. Fanny Burney was a pupil here, and after her father's second marriage in 1770, she lived with him and her stepmother for the next four years at a house in the Square with a pleasant prospect of Hampstead and Highgate.

After graduating from *Cambridge in 1954, Ted Hughes divided his time between Cambridge and 18 **Rugby St.**, where Plath would visit him: 'So there in Number Eighteen Rugby Street's | Victorian torpor and squalor I waited for you . . .'.

Staple Inn in Holborn, opposite the end of Gray's Inn Rd, was a former Inn of Chancery and consists of sets of chambers round two courtyards erected in 1545–89, and largely rebuilt in the 18th c. The Inn suffered extensive bomb damage in the Second World War and has been faithfully restored. Dr Johnson stayed at no. 2 in the first court in 1759–60 and is believed to have written *Rasselas* here, in the evenings of a single week, in order to pay the expenses of his mother's funeral. Alternatively, he may have written it before leaving Gough Sq. (see CITY).

Benjamin Disraeli was born (1803) at 22 **Theobalds Rd** (Ⓟ, formerly 6 King's Rd, Bedford Row).

HOLLOWAY, district to the N. **Bowman's Mews** turns off the SW end of Seven Sisters Rd near its junction with Holloway Rd. A plaque there records that in Elizabethan times it was a favourite spot for archery contests and that nearby Bowman's Lodge (gone) was the birthplace and childhood home (1812–22) of Edward Lear.

Mr Pooter, hero of the Grossmiths' *Diary of a Nobody* (1892) lives at The Laurels, Brickfield Ter., Holloway.

Rob, the narrator of Nick Hornby's *High Fidelity* (1995), runs Championship Vinyl, a record shop on a quiet street in Holloway,

carefully placed to attract the bare minimum of walk-past punters; there's no reason to come here at all, unless you live here, and the people that live here don't seem terribly interested in my Stiff Little Fingers white label (twenty-five quid to you—I paid seventeen for it in 1986) or my mono copy of *Blonde On Blonde*.

I get by because of the people who make a special effort to shop here Saturdays—young men, always young men, with John Lennon specs and leather jackets and armfuls of square carrier bags—and because of the mail order: I advertise in the back of the glossy rock magazines, and get letters from young men, always young men, in Manchester and Glasgow and Ottawa, young men who seem to spend a disproportionate amount of their time looking for deleted Smiths singles and 'ORIGINAL NOT RE-RELEASED' underlined Frank Zappa albums. They're as close to being mad as makes no difference.

After a confrontation with her Beckenham neighbours, who made her unwelcome in their town, Jean Rhys spent time in **Holloway prison**, which features in her story 'Let Them Call It Jazz'.

HORNSEY, district to the N. In 1817 Thomas Moore took a furnished cottage at the foot of *Muswell Hill** in order to be near London while he was correcting the proofs of *Lalla Rookh* (1817), a series of oriental tales in verse connected by a prose narrative. At first he disliked the cottage because it abounded in rats and the chimneys smoked, but later the family was happy enough until the tragic death, after a fall, of his little daughter Barbara. He left Muswell Hill in the autumn, returning only to visit Barbara's grave in Hornsey churchyard. The house, later called Lalla Rookh Cottage, has gone (site behind the houses in Etheldene Ave.) and its garden has been incorporated in Alexandra Park. Moore's friend Samuel Rogers is also buried in Hornsey churchyard.

HOUNSLOW, borough in West London, to the W of Richmond. Gautam Malkani attended school here, and set his debut novel, *Londonstani* (2006), in the area. *Londonstani* reveals the world of Hounslow teenagers, mainly second- and third-generation South Asian immigrants. Narrated by Jas, new recruit to the gang, it is told in a dynamic mixture of languages, street slangs, and text-message-speak, and explores a culture defined by enthnicity and machismo, all taking place around this cluster of roads that feed traffic between London and Heathrow Airport.

HYDE PARK, 360-acre public park to the W of Mayfair and N of Belgravia. The bird sanctuary in the NW part is a memorial to W. H. Hudson, author of *Birds in London* (1898), *Birds and Man* (1901), and *Adventures Among Birds* (1913), and Epstein's sculpture *Rima* portrays the heroine of *Green Mansions* (1904), the spirit of the forest.

Ezra Pound remembers 'our London, my London, your London' in *Pisan Cantos* LXXX (1949):

and the Serpentine will look just the same
and the gulls be as neat on the pond
and the sunken garden the same unchanged.

During his visit to London in 1924 the Czech novelist Karel Capek saw Speakers' Corner and described his experience—beside which 'nothing pleased me so much'—in his *Letters from England*. Sean O'Casey's speculation about the lives and afterlives of the people who speak here is inscribed at the beginning of Heathcote Williams's novel *The Speakers* (1964).

In 1974 a short ceremony at Byron's statue at Hyde Pk Corner celebrated the 150th anniversary of his death.

In Vikram Seth's *An Equal Music* (1999), Michael takes to swimming in the Serpentine, a habit that rather bemuses his fellow characters.

In Jeanette Winterson's *Sexing the Cherry* (1989), the Dog Woman spends her time and makes her money by fighting her dogs in Hyde Park. She wants to escape from the city, 'a foul place, full of pestilence and rot', to take her son Jordan (whom she fished out of the Thames as a baby) somewhere cleaner, but can't afford to be too far from Hyde Park, 'so I can enter my dogs in the faces and the fighting. Every Saturday I come home covered in saliva and bitten to death but with money in my pocket . . .'. Eventually she and Jordan come to know John Tradescant, who takes them down to lovely rural *Wimbledon.

Charles Reade lived (1869–79) at 2 **Albert Ter.** (later 19 Albert Gate, gone), opposite Sloane St. The American actress Rose Eytinge, who played in the stage version of Reade's *Griffith Gaunt* (1866), described the house on her visit in the late 1870s as

distinguished from its neighbours by the courtyard, which is full of foliage, underbrush, and a 'rockery' and 'fernery', while an arbor covers the walk leading up to the doorway. Inside the house is a perfect treasure house of objects. . . . Mr. Reade's study is at the back of the house in a room on the first floor, which he had built himself. It extends clear across the house, some thirty or forty feet, and has an enormous window in the centre, which commands a view of the gardens and Hyde Park . . .

Reade's novel *A Terrible Temptation* (1871), written like the earlier *Hard Cash* to highlight the need for reform of the laws regarding lunacy, also shows how the author assembled the evidence needed in all his novels advocating change.

ILFORD, district to the E. The poet Kathleen Raine was born at 6 Gordon Rd in 1908 and educated at Highlands Elementary School. The novelist Nina Bawden, born in 1925, was educated at Ilford County High School.

INNS OF COURT. Groups of buildings belonging to the four legal societies having the exclusive right to admit persons to practise at the English Bar: the Inner Temple and Middle Temple (see CITY), Lincoln's Inn, and Gray's Inn (see HOLBORN). These societies, formed in the 14th and 15th cc., became wealthy and powerful, and governed themselves by elected bodies of Benchers (senior members). Students training to become barristers used to receive a general education at the Inns, including subjects such as history and music as well as law.

ISLINGTON, former riverside village to the N. In 1683 Thomas Sadler built a music hall and entertainment centre round a medicinal spring which became a popular spa, called Sadler's Wells (now in Rosebery Ave.). 'The Morning Ramble', a burlesque of 1684, though praising Epsom and Tunbridge Wells, says: 'Those are but good for one disease, | To all distempers this gives ease.' In 1753 the wooden building became a theatre with a regular company and in 1765 a new stone theatre was built.

In Nina Bawden's *Family Money* (1991), Fanny Pye is being encouraged by her children to move out of her large home in (the fictional) Sickert Terrace, just behind the **Angel**:

'Home' was a five-floored terrace house, jobbing-builder's Georgian, built in the 1840s. It had been slum property when Daniel had bought it for his young bride in the Fifties; a base for home leave and a store for belongings unwanted abroad. Now Sickert Terrace had been largely yuppified; bright paint and window-boxes, Volvos and BMWs lining both sides of the narrow street. Behind the houses the small gardens that went down to the Regent's Canal were prettily landscaped, furnished with mock-Victorian iron furniture, romantic stone statues of suitable size, plant pots and amphoras brought home from holiday raids on Provence, Tuscany, Greece.

Bawden herself still lives in Islington.

In Smollett's *Humphry Clinker* (1771), Winifred Jenkins, who had been enchanted by the tumbling and dancing upon ropes and wires, was molested in a dark passage by 'a fine gentleman' who began to show 'his cloven futt'. She hardly knew how she was rescued, 'being in such a flustration'. The actor-manager Samuel Phelps, who lived at 8 **Canonbury Sq.** Ⓟ, made Shakespeare's plays popular at Sadler's Wells for nearly 20 years. The theatre was rebuilt in 1931. Evelyn Waugh was living in Canonbury Sq. when his first satirical novel, *Decline and Fall* (1928), was published. George Orwell lived at no. 27 Ⓟ from 1944 to early 1946, his last London home.

Canonbury Tower (now the Canonbury Masonic Research Centre), built originally as part of the country house of the priors of St Bartholomew's, was rebuilt in Queen Elizabeth I's reign and later (1616–25) leased to Sir Francis Bacon. In the 1760s the first floor of this tower with its two wings became the country home of the publisher John Newbery and his family, and he installed (1762) Oliver Goldsmith in one of the apartments above. Goldsmith, who wrote *The Traveller* (1764) here, often took a room in the city for short periods until Newbery's death in 1767.

Charles and Mary Lamb lived (1823–7) at Colebrook Cottage (now 64 **Duncan Ter.**, Ⓟ), 'a detached, whitish house, close to the New River, end of Colebrook Terrace, left hand from Sadler's Wells'. Lamb, who retired from the India Office in 1825, mentions in his *Letters* the pleasure of his first garden with his vegetables and his vine. They were visited by a large number of friends including Crabb Robinson, Mary Russell Mitford, Mary Shelley, Barry Proctor, the young Harrison Ainsworth, and their near neighbour Thomas Hood. Their publisher Edward Moxon helped carry books into their new quarters and later married their adopted daughter Emma Isola. Their friends left safely except the myopic George Dyer, who walked straight into the New River (now safely under the gardens dividing Duncan Ter. from Colebrook Row). His rescue gave Lamb the subject for 'Amicus Redivivus', in *Essays of Elia* (1823). Lamb's friend Thomas Hood moved to 5 Lower St. (now 50 **Essex St.**) as a child and it

Sketch by Daniel Maclise of Charles Lamb when he was living in Islington

Charles Dickens and London

IF the whole of Dickens's œuvre could be shrunk down to a single verbal tablet it would be the one-word sentence that opens *Bleak House* (1852–3): 'London.' If Dickens's standpoint—or characteristic angle of observation—could be summarized in twenty or thirty words, it would be the sentences that follow:

> London. Michaelmas term lately over, and the Lord Chancellor sitting in Lincoln's Inn Hall. Implacable November weather. As much mud in the streets as if the waters had but newly retired from the face of the earth.

Dickens's first success as an author was not, as is commonly supposed, *The Pickwick Papers* (1836–7), but the preceding miscellany, *Sketches by Boz*. This series of snapshot articles he contributed to the *Morning Chronicle* in the early to mid-1830s were his breakthrough.

The Boz papers are still delightful and rich in what Henry James called 'solidity of specification'. One also sees the author's insatiably curious eye for the passing urban world. 'Shops and their Tenants', for example, opens, 'What inexhaustible food for speculation do the streets of London afford!' Dickens's art would feed on that nourishment for a quarter of a century.

Much has changed in London. For Boz, as for us, it changes even as one watches. But there is also something timeless in the city. In sketches like 'Meditations in Monmouth Street', Dickens penetrates to the heart of one of the city's distinctive pedestrian thoroughfares—a distinctiveness which is still evident today as one strolls, meditatively, down its length to Covent Garden.

Dickens was born in Portsmouth and died in Rochester, Kent. As regards his art, these are entirely accidental locations. Like his best-known juvenile creation, Oliver Twist (born in 'Mudfog'), the young Dickens was sucked, as by magnetism, towards London. Oliver could as reasonably, like his fellow waif David Copperfield, have made for green fields. But the capital's pull was irresistible.

Once arrived, Oliver, with his jovial Virgilian guide, the Artful Dodger, is plunged into the miry depths of the 'abyss'. Think *Oliver Twist*, and most readers will think Fagin's den: the filth, the smell of frying sausages (and worse), the child-pickpockets and doxies; and yet, for all the filth and fug, a warmer, friendlier place than the Benthamite workhouse in Mudfog.

Dickens's supercharged emotional feelings about the city can be traced, like much else in his art, to his childhood. His naval clerk father moved to London, while Charles was just 10 (Oliver's age). The dozen-strong Dickenses pigged it in lodgings in Camden (that region which is immortalized in the soon-to-be-destroyed Staggs's Gardens, in *Dombey and Son* (1848)). Here it was Dickens came to consciousness.

CHARLES DICKENS IN A PHOTOGRAPH OF C. 1868

The family thereafter had a dizzying series of ups and downs. Dickens, while still a boy, was exposed to the very different milieux of respectable Bloomsbury, rural Hampstead, and Westminster's newly reconstructed palaces. There are many Londons in the novels, as there were in his life. He knew St James's as well as St Giles. He knew Dulwich, among whose fields and gentle cows Mr Pickwick retires, and the route there via Walworth, where Wemmick lives in his absurd 'Castle' with The Aged P.

At the lowest point of the family fortunes, Dickens's father found himself in the Marshalsea debtors' prison—a scorching shame, recalled in Pickwick's Fleet Prison sojourn, and the 'father of the Marshalsea' subplot in *Little Dorrit* (1855–7).

Charles himself had his lowest moment, aged just 12, when he was put to work washing bottles and sticking on labels in Warren's blacking family, on the bank of the Thames—a fetid stream to whose stench and pollution Warren's added. The psychic wound of that childhood labour remained with

Dickens throughout his life. 'Until Old Hungerford Stairs were destroyed,' he told Forster, 'I never had the courage to go back to the place where my servitude began.' He would take lengthy detours rather than see it.

It was typically the dirt which interested him. The epithet 'Dickensian' recalls those particles of soot the size of snowflakes in *Bleak House*'s London. That peculiar compound 'mudfog' swirls mephitically throughout the narratives. Nonetheless, as he everywhere insists, Dickens was an indomitable and effective fighter for the sanitary cause. Clean air, clean water, and a clean city. If the soot-flakes are Dickensian, so is Bazalgette's monumental sewerage system, laid beneath the capital in the 1850s.

Dickens's London was fluidly changing around him, and is as fluid in his fiction. 'Scotland Yard', for example, in *Sketches by Boz*, is a tiny back alley: a 'yard' indeed. In *Bleak House* it is 'the Yard'—the police headquarters of intrepid crime-fighters like Inspector Bucket.

The largest change to London (and England generally) was steam-driven. The railway jerked mid-Victorian Britain, and its capital, into a new age. It is as symbolic as Caesar's riding in triumph through Rome when, in *Dombey and Son*, Bagstock and Dombey pass in their carriage under the majestic arch of Euston's railway station, raised on the ruins of Staggs's slum 'gardens'. The railway is the future: the stagecoach (on which Pickwick conducts his peregrination) is the past.

Meanwhile, amid all this turmoil of change, the Thames rolls on, timelessly. There are many depictions of the river that divides the two great sectors of London. The most vivid is that in one of the great 'dark' novels of Dickens's late period, *Our Mutual Friend* (1864–5). The novel opens with:

> a boat of dirty and disreputable appearance, with two figures in it, floated on the Thames, between Southwark Bridge which is of iron, and London Bridge which is of stone, as an autumn evening was closing in.

Old Father Thames is the great life-giver: the inland access it gave shipping is the reason for its being. In its waters, John Harmon is reborn. But, as Dickens portrays it in his opening scene, the Hexams, in their rowing boat, are fishing for corpses. It gives life and death, even-handedly. There is no better metaphor for Dickens's London. All life is there. And the other thing. Both fascinate.   JOHN SUTHERLAND

❖

is probably this house that he was thinking of in his poem beginning 'I remember, I remember, | The house where I was born.' A plaque on 3 **Terrett's Pl.**, off Upper St., mentions 'A Singular Little Old Fashioned House' where Tom Pinch in Dickens's *Martin Chuzzlewit* (1843–4) goes looking for lodgings.

In 'Sursum Corda' in *Success* (1902), Cunninghame Graham tells of his two months' imprisonment in Pentonville prison following his arrest during a demonstration in Trafalgar Sq. in 1887.

The travel writer Jonathan Raban lived in a square on the borders of Islington and Holloway in the early 1960s and 1970s, observing in his portrait of London life *Soft City* (1974) a transient population, where the most rooted inhabitants are the local cats:

> They were the real permanent residents of the square, these animals for whom the rest of London, and the wheels of changing social fortune, were not even rumours. The landlord could tear the cat's owner away from the place he had lived in as long as he could remember; but the cat stayed, like the name on the disconnected bell, and the dead-pigeon smell in the front-area—mortal remains, of the kind preserved in old photographs . . .

Jonathan Coe's *The Dwarves of Death* (1990) begins with William in a north Islington street:

> a handsome, sad sort of road, with high Georgian terrace on either side. It was that hour of the evening when the lights are on but the curtains are not yet drawn, and through the windows, bathed in a golden glow, I could see families and couples preparing their suppers, pouring their drinks. You could almost smell the basil and the bolognese sauce. We were in North Islington.

But the apparent domestic bliss is interrupted by a rather gruesome murder . . .

Fever Pitch (1992) is Nick Hornby's study of obsession; in particular obsession with football, and—more exactly—obsession with Arsenal. It all begins with young Nick being taken to Highbury by his father to watch the team play, and a father–son routine settles in:

> We could talk when we wanted, the football gave us something to talk about (and anyway the silences weren't oppressive), and the days had a structure, a routine. The Arsenal pitch was to be our lawn (and, being an English lawn, we would usually peer at it mournfully through driving rain); the Gunners' Fish Bar on Blackstock Road our kitchen; and the West Stand our home.

It was only when Gillian Tindall bought a 17th-c. print of an Islington view—'I bought it because I liked it and because I enjoyed thinking that this rugged, stream-crossed landscape was what lay below the streets about the Angel tube station'—that she first came across the name of the engraver Wenceslas Hollar. This began her attempt to write his biography—or rather, half-biography and half-novelization of his life; this is the book that would become *The Man Who Drew London* (2002).

KENSAL GREEN AND WILLESDEN, district to the NW. Harrison Ainsworth lived (1835–41) at Kensal Lodge, Harrow Rd, a white, two-storeyed house overlooking woods and fields to Willesden. He describes the view as 'A superb panorama . . . a vast and beautiful prospect' in *Jack Sheppard* (1839), the story of a young criminal, John Sheppard (1702–24), subject of many 18th-c. plays and ballads, who was hanged at Tyburn. Ainsworth's book, set mainly in the Willesden area nearby, started the myth that Sheppard was buried in Willesden cemetery, whereas he had a pauper's grave in St Martin-in-the-Fields. Ainsworth also wrote the major parts of *Crichton* (1837) and *The Tower of London* (1840) here. He lived next door (1841–53) at the larger Kensal Manor to make a home for his daughters. He entertained his many friends at both these houses, including John Macrone his publisher, Francis Mahony, William Maginn, Daniel Maclise, who painted his portrait, Cruikshank, who illustrated his novels, Richard Barham, John Forster, Dickens, who brought his 'conjuring apparatus' for the winter evenings, and Mrs Hughes, Thomas Hughes's grandmother, who brought her fund of ghost stories and legends. Thackeray walked across the fields with the family to Willesden church, where Harrison Ainsworth was churchwarden. In the summer the guests sat on the seat round the old oak tree in the garden, where they could hear nightingales. *Windsor Castle* (1843), *The Lancashire Witches* (1848), and *Mervyn Clitheroe* (1851) were mainly written here.

The main entrance to **Kensal Green cemetery** is in Harrow Rd, near its junction with Ladbroke Grove. It contains the graves of many distinguished writers, including Thomas Hood (d. 1845: 'He sang the Song of the Shirt'), Sydney Smith (d. 1845), Douglas Jerrold (d. 1857), Leigh Hunt (d. 1859), Thackeray (d. 1863), Samuel Lover (d. 1868), John Forster (d. 1876), Harrison Ainsworth (d. 1882),

Trollope (d. 1882), Wilkie Collins (d. 1889), and Francis Thompson (d. 1907), in the Roman Catholic cemetery. The playwright Terence Rattigan, who died in Bermuda in November 1977, was cremated and his ashes buried at Kensal Green. The area of the cemetery is extensive and a newcomer would find it best to consult a guide, obtainable from the Main Gate.

The cemetery is the subject of a poem by Tony Harrison:

> The void may well be cheated by a voice,
> composer's quill, the artist's brush or pen,
> but memory might only have one choice:
> a stone in Kensal Green—£11.10 . . .

Zadie Smith's debut novel, *White Teeth* (2001), is a portrait of three families in multicultural north London; it begins with a suicide attempt in a car on Cricklewood Broadway. Smith herself grew up in nearby Willesden.

KENSINGTON, district W and SW of Hyde Park.

Nicholas Jenkins, the narrator of Anthony Powell's *A Dance to the Music of Time* (1951–75), falls in love with Barbara Goring on a June Sunday afternoon at the **Albert Memorial**, where 'beside the kneeling elephant, the Bedouin forever rests on his haunches in hopeless contemplation of Kensington Gardens'.

Sir Edwin Arnold, author of *The Light of Asia* (1879), a poem in eight books of blank verse about the life and philosophy of the Buddha, made his last home at 31 **Bolton Gdns**, South Kensington, Ⓟ and died there (1904). Beatrix Potter was born at no. 2 and lived there, apart from visits to Scotland and the Lake District, until her marriage to William Heelis in 1913. The house (together with many of its neighbours) has been demolished, and the site is occupied by Bousfield Primary School. Beatrix Potter's *Journal, 1881–97* (ed. L. Linder, 1966) gives an insight into her conventional middle-class upbringing which nevertheless allowed scope for the growth of her vigorous and independent mind.

Brompton cemetery, N of Fulham Rd, has the graves of Lady Morgan, author of *The Wild Irish Girl* (1806), George Borrow, who died at Oulton in 1881 and is buried with his wife, and G. A. Henty, who died on his yacht in Weymouth in 1902.

Brompton Oratory, or the London Oratory of St Philip Neri, a Roman Catholic church founded (1849) principally by the efforts of Cardinal Newman, was built on its present site in Brompton Rd in 1854. A statue of Newman stands at the W end. Frederick Faber, author of many hymns and devotional books, was its first head.

Stéphane Mallarmé, at the age of 21, married Marie Gherard here on 10 August 1863, and in 1927 Alfred Noyes married his second wife, Mary Weld-Blundell.

Mallarmé, who had come to London in the autumn of 1862 in order to improve his English

and study the life and works of Edgar Allan Poe, stayed at 6 **Brompton Sq.** Ⓟ, on the N side of Brompton Rd, from April to the end of August in the following year. He later made French translations of Poe's poems that delighted Swinburne (whom he addressed as 'Cher Monsieur et Maître').

Lord Macaulay spent his last years (1856–9) at Holly Lodge (gone), at the upper end of **Campden Hill**, near the narrow way to Holland Walk. The original plaque commemorating his death was placed there in 1903 and re-erected in 1968.

The poet Stephen Spender was born at 47 Campden House Ct, off Campden Hill, in 1909.

Ford Madox Hueffer lodged at South Lodge, 80 **Campden Hill Rd** Ⓟ, the home of the novelist Violet Hunt, from *c.* 1912 until he enlisted in the army. He changed his name to Ford Madox Ford after joining up.

The smart, scheming, and oversexed teenager who narrates Martin Amis's debut novel, *The Rachel Papers* (1973), Charles Highway, spends most of the book living at his sister's home in **Campden Hill Sq.**

In the later part of her life, the novelist Rosamond Lehmann lived at 30 **Clareville Grove** until her death in 1990.

Terence Rattigan, who would become a playwright celebrated for work like *The Winslow Boy* (1946) and *The Browning Version* (1948), was born on **Cornwall Gdns**, on 9 June 1911.

Ivy Compton-Burnett lived (1934–69) at 5 Braemar Mansions, Cornwall Gdns, at first with Margaret Jourdain, but alone after her death in 1951. Most of her novels, including *Daughters and Sons* (1937), *Parents and Children* (1941), and *Mother and Son* (1955), which won the James Tait Black Memorial Prize, were written here. After the Second World War, Compton-Burnett invited her friends to Saturday afternoon tea parties, formal meals where unpunctuality was censured. She was made a DBE in 1957 and given an honorary degree by Leeds University in 1960. She died in 1969 and after cremation her ashes were buried at Putney Vale cemetery.

The novelist C. P. Snow lived with his wife and fellow novelist Pamela Hansford Johnson at 199 **Cromwell Rd** from 1957 until 1968. He wrote a number of the later volumes of his novel sequence *Strangers and Brothers* (1940–70) here.

Henry James lived at 34 **De Vere Gdns** Ⓟ from 1886 to 1896. It was here that he wrote the novels *The Tragic Muse* (1890) and *What Maisie Knew* (1897), and here in 1894 that he made the first notes for *The Wings of the Dove* (1902). He spent the winters here from 1896 to 1902. No. 22 Ⓟ was Robert Browning's last home (1888–9) in England before he returned to Italy, where he died (1889).

W. B. Yeats stayed with his family at 14 **Edith Rd**, West Kensington, from 1874 to 1876, when they moved to Bedford Pk (see Chiswick).

G. Lowes Dickinson, pacifist, critic, and Fellow of King's College, *Cambridge, is commemorated at 11 **Edwardes Sq.** Ⓟ, his London home.

J. M. Barrie lived (1895–8) at 133 **Gloucester Rd**. He wrote here *Sentimental Tommy* (1896) and *Margaret Ogilvy* (1896), the life of his mother, both set in his home town of *Kirriemuir.

After the collapse of his first marriage T. S. Eliot lived from 1933 to 1940 at the presbytery of St Stephen's Church on **Grenville Pl.**, Gloucester Rd. He served as a churchwarden, lectured at church meetings and conferences, and attended communion with great diligence. A plaque at the church commemorates his duties there from 1934 to 1959. He later lived at 3 Kensington Ct Gdns, dying there on 4 January 1965.

W. S. Gilbert lived (1883–90) at 39 **Harrington Gdns** Ⓟ, a house designed for him by Ernest George and Peto. His operas, containing satires on topics of the day and with music by Arthur Sullivan, include *Princess Ida* (1884), *The Mikado* (1885), *Ruddigore* (1887), *The Yeomen of the Guard* (1888), and *The Gondoliers* (1889).

George Borrow, after many travels, lived at 22 **Hereford Sq.** Ⓟ, on the W side of the Old Brompton Rd end of Gloucester Rd, from 1860 until his return to *Oulton in 1874. *Wild Wales*, an account of his wanderings in Wales, was published in 1862. His wife, Mary, died in 1869.

Holland House (Ⓟ on site), a 17th-c. mansion, was famous under the 3rd Lord Holland as a centre of influence in the Whig Party. Addison, who married the Dowager Countess of Warwick and Holland in 1716, lived here until his death in 1719. The 1st Lord Holland, who acquired the house in 1767, often entertained Horace Walpole.

The imperious wife of the 3rd Lord Holland (1773–1840), Carlyle's 'proud old dame', welcomed men of promise in political and literary circles so long as they reached her exacting standards of wit and worldly knowledge. Sheridan, Thomas Campbell, Sydney Smith, Tom Moore, Samuel Rogers, Crabbe, Washington Irving, Fenimore Cooper, James Mackintosh, Monckton Milnes, Dickens, and Macaulay succeeded in entertaining her.

The house was demolished after damage in the Second World War. One wing has been rebuilt and is now part of a Youth Hostel.

Crime novelist P. D. James has since 1991 been titled Baroness James of **Holland Park**.

Ford Madox Hueffer (later Ford) lived (1908–10) at 84 **Holland Pk Ave.**, where he edited the *English Review*.

Dickens had lodgings in 1862 (gone) at 16 **Hyde Pk Gate**, off Kensington Rd, when he came to London from *Gad's Hill.

Sir Leslie Stephen, scholar and original editor of *The Dictionary of National Biography*, lived at no. 22 Ⓟ, from 1879 until his death in 1904. His daughter Virginia (later Virginia Woolf) was born here in 1882.

Muriel Spark lived at 1 Vicarage Gate, a rooming house near **Kensington Church St.**, in the 1950s. 'I had a small single-bed room, a gas ring and a wash basin.' It provided the scene for her novel *Loitering with Intent*

(1981). A number of her novels are set to a greater or lesser degree in and around Kensington, including *The Bachelors* (1960), *A Far Cry from Kensington* (1988), where the narrator is imagined as living near South Kensington underground, and *The Girls of Slender Means* (1963), where the 'May of Teck Club' stands obliquely opposite the Albert Memorial, in one of a row of tall houses that had endured—for most of the novel at least—the Second World War bombs. The Club existed 'for the Pecuniary Convenience and Social protection of Ladies of Slender Means below the age of Thirty Years, who are obliged to reside apart from their Families in order to follow an Occupation in London'.

Ezra Pound rented the first-floor front room at 10 **Kensington Church Walk**, a paved cul-de-sac off Holland St., near St Mary Abbott's Garden, from Mrs Langley, his 'unique and treasured landlady'. It had 'a cast-iron fireplace with a hob either side of the bars and a pair of good windows looking south'. His bath, which he used to supply with cans of hot water from the kitchen boiler, was kept under his bed—see his poem 'The Bathtub'. He lived here from 1909 until his marriage with Dorothy Shakespear in 1914.

Gore House in **Kensington Gore** (site now the Royal Albert Hall) was the home of Lady Blessington, whose salon, first at Seamore Pl. (gone), Mayfair, and here after 1836, was the scene of brilliant gatherings. The American N. P. Willis wrote, in *Pencillings by the Way* (1835), that she was 'one of the most lovely and fascinating women I have ever seen'. After her husband's sudden death she turned to writing to augment her income. Her first novel, *Grace Cassidy, or, The Repealers* (1833), was followed by *Conversations with Lord Byron* (1834), first published in the *New Monthly Magazine*. She wrote other novels and edited *The Keepsake* for 10 years from 1841. *The Belle of the Season* (1840) was in verse. She was acquainted with many of the literati of her day and among those who frequented her salon at Gore House, where she was living with Count D'Orsay, were Samuel Rogers, Landor, Thomas Campbell, Horace and James Smith, joint authors of *Rejected Addresses* (1812), Tom Moore, Disraeli, Harrison Ainsworth, Dickens, Monckton Milnes, John Forster, Dickens's first biographer, and Thackeray.

Though Lady Blessington's income from her writing was considerable, she became bankrupt in 1849 and fled to Paris, whither D'Orsay had preceded her. Gore House was sold and in 1851 it became the restaurant attended by the thousands of visitors to the Great Exhibition (1851). Thackeray described the scene in an article in *Punch*.

When Sir James Barrie lived in Bayswater Rd (1902–9) he used to walk in **Kensington Gdns** with his Newfoundland dog Luath, the prototype of Nana in *Peter Pan, or, The Boy Who Wouldn't Grow Up* (the popular play for children, produced 1904). The Peter Pan statue, near the Westbourne Gate entrance, was designed by Sir George Frampton in 1912

at Barrie's expense. The nearby stretch of the Serpentine, the Long Water, was the place where Shelley's first wife, the tragic young Harriet, drowned herself (1816).

In a boarding house near **Kensington High St.** lives Ralph Singh, the Caribbean narrator of Indian heritage in V. S. Naipaul's novel *The Mimic Men* (1967). The locale does not live up to his expectations:

> And looking out from that room to the thin lines of brown smoke rising from ugly chimneypots, the plastered wall of the house next to the bombsite tremendously braced and buttressed, looking out from that empty room with the mattress on the floor, I felt all the magic of the city go away and had an intimation of the forlornness of the city and of the people who lived in it.

Naipaul's London experiences also contributed to the story of the two West Indian brothers which forms part of his novel *In a Free State* (1971).

Rebecca West lived at 48 **Kingston House North** from 1969 until her death in 1983.

The Kensington museums, the Brompton Oratory, and Holy Trinity, Brompton, all feature in parts of Gavin Ewart's poem 'South Kensington'. Martin Clay, narrator of Michael Frayn's novel *Headlong* (1999), spends time researching Bruegel in the library of the Victoria and Albert Museum. Ruth Fainlight has lived near **Ladbroke Sq.** since the 1970s and she has explored her relationship with it in the short cycle of poems 'Time and Ladbroke Square'. She has also been a regular visitor to Kensington Gdns, where a bench near the pond is the context for her poem 'Launching',

> where
> I've watched the seasons change
> for twenty years.

Marie Corelli lived at 47 **Longridge Rd** ⓟ from 1883 to 1900. After her father had a stroke she moved with him from their home at *Mickleham and began her writing career. Her first novel, *A Romance of Two Worlds*, was published in 1886 and was followed by the successful *Barabbas* (1893) and the immensely popular *The Sorrows of Satan* (1895). In 1900 she decided to settle in *Stratford-upon-Avon.

Andrew Lang lived from 1875 at 1 **Marloes Rd** ⓟ. He wrote here the poems *Ballades in Blue China* (1880) and *Helen of Troy* (1882), the anthropological *Custom and Myth* (1884), some historical works, essays, including *Letters to Dead Authors* (1886), *Books and Bookmen* (1887), and the *Life and Letters of J. G. Lockhart* (1896). Lang returned to *St Andrews at the end of his life.

The historian J. A. Froude lived from 1862 to 1892 at 5 **Onslow Gdns** ⓟ, leading off Onslow Sq. W. E. H. Lecky, another historian, lived at no. 38 ⓟ after his marriage in 1871, and died here. No. 36 **Onslow Sq.** ⓟ, just S of South Kensington Station, became Thackeray's home in 1853 after his return from his first American lecture tour. His daughter Anne Ritchie described the house as 'a pleasant, bowery sort of home, with green curtains and carpets,

looking out upon the elm trees'. They lived there for seven years, next door to Thackeray's friend Baron Marochetti, who subsequently made his bust for Westminster Abbey. Here Thackeray completed *The Newcomes* (1853–5), and wrote *The Virginians* (1857–9), *The Adventures of Philip* (his last complete novel, 1861–2, published serially in the *Cornhill Magazine*, of which he was the first editor in 1860), and many of *The Roundabout Papers* (also published in the *Cornhill Magazine*, 1860–3).

No. 57 **Palace Gdns Ter.** ⓟ, off Bayswater Rd, a little W of Kensington Gdns, was the birthplace of Sir Max Beerbohm, essayist and caricaturist. The tree-lined terrace is known as 'Cherry Mile'. At the S end of Kensington Palace Gdns, a quiet private road shaded by tall trees, is **Palace Green**. Thackeray lived at no. 2 ⓟ, designed by himself, for the last two years of his life (1861–3) and died there.

Kenneth Grahame lived (1901–8) at 16 **Phillimore Pl.** ⓟ when he was Secretary to the Bank of England (he retired in 1908). It was here that he wrote most of *The Wind in the Willows* (1908).

No. 40 **St Luke's Rd**, North Kensington, was the home from 1886 to 1922 of W. H. Hudson, naturalist and writer, whose best-remembered work is *Green Mansions* (1904), a romance of the South American forest. A plaque placed on the house by the Hudson's Friends Society of Quilmes, near Buenos Aires, has a bronze low relief showing the house where he was born.

G. K. Chesterton was born (1874) at 32 **Sheffield Ter.** ⓟ, between Campden Hill Rd and Kensington Church St. He spent his early years (1879–99) at 11 **Warwick Gdns** ⓟ, S of Kensington High St. His first book of poems, *The Wild Knight* (1900), was written here. In 1904 he published *The Napoleon of Notting Hill*.

The poet Alan Ross edited *London Magazine* at 7 **Thurloe Pl.** from 1961 until his death in 2001, for much of the time working in a shed at the end of his garden. Writers who have worked at the magazine include the poet Hugo Williams and the writer and biographer Jeremy Lewis.

On the S side of Kensington High St., nearly opposite the end of Kensington Church St., is **Young St.**, where Thackeray lived at no. 13 (now no. 16, ⓟ) from 1846 to 1853. He wrote *Vanity Fair* (1847–8), *Pendennis* (1848–50), and *The History of Henry Esmond* (1852) here, and began *The Newcomes* (1853–5). In May 1850 he met Charlotte Brontë again at her publisher's house and she discussed his literary shortcomings with 'decent amity'. Though George Smith, her publisher, had told Thackeray that she was shy and did not wish to be recognized as the author of *Jane Eyre*, he arranged an evening party for her to meet a large gathering including the Carlyles and Adelaide Procter. Thackeray's daughter, then aged 13, observed that Charlotte Brontë 'enters in mittens, in silence, in seriousness'. The evening was insipid and Thackeray left for his club in the middle of the party.

KENTISH TOWN. Karl Marx moved in to 9 **Grafton Ter.** in 1855. Jenny Marx found it

a princely dwelling compared with the holes we lived in before, and although it was furnished from top to bottom for little more than £40 (in which second-hand rubbish played a leading role), I felt quite grand at first in our snug parlour.

They moved further up in the world in 1864 when, having received two legacies, the family moved to a substantial detached house at 1 Modena Villas, **Maitland Pk**. They lived a bourgeois life here, hosting dinners, setting off on family holidays, and walking their dogs on the heath while Marx took to speculating on the Stock Exchange. In 1875 they downsized, moving a few doors along to the cheaper 44 **Maitland Pk Rd**. Marx lived here for the rest of his life, following a general routine of *The Times* over breakfast, a day in his study, and an evening walk through the London streets in cloak and hat.

The novelist Stella Gibbons was born at **Malden Cres.** in 1902. The household was turbulent and noisy (her self-dramatizing father had a succession of mistresses) and as a child she would withdraw to the attic to write stories and play solitary games.

Tom Paulin's poem 'An Ulster Unionist Walks the Streets of London' describes arriving in Kentish Town:

then walked the streets
like a half-foreigner
among the London Irish.
What does it feel like?
I wanted to ask them—
what does it feel like
to be a child of that nation?

For Gillian Tindall, author of *The Fields Beneath*, a 1977 study of the area, Kentish Town is archetypal 'of a million other ancient villages gradually absorbed into metropolises; not just round London but in many parts of England, and not just in England either. Paris, too, has its Kentish Towns.'

KESTON, district to the SE. Mrs Craik, author of the popular *John Halifax, Gentleman* (1856), was buried (1887) in Keston churchyard, on the A233, 1¼ m. S of the junction with the A232. Her grave with a tall Celtic cross is near the hedge bordering the triangular green.

KEW, riverside district to the SW. Stephen Duck, whose long poem 'The Thresher's Labour', later included in *Poems on Several Occasions* (1736), found favour with Queen Caroline, was consequently made a Yeoman of the Guard. In 1733 he married the Queen's housekeeper at Kew and lived in the Palace, but his life there was not happy. He became librarian in 1735 and, after taking orders, was made preacher at Kew Palace Chapel. He may have met James Thomson, author of *The Seasons*, at Richmond as they exchanged volumes of their verse. Duck left on becoming rector of *Byfleet in 1752.

In 1773 Cobbett, aged 11, worked in Kew Gardens after walking here from *Farnham.

Fanny Burney, through Mrs Delany, became (1786) Second Keeper of the Robes to Queen Charlotte and she describes her unhappy life at Kew and the other royal palaces in her *Journal*. She was able to resign only because of a breakdown in health. Walpole commented on the menial task of folding muslins and Macaulay wondered that a writer of her calibre should have accepted such a post.

KILBURN, area to the NW of London, N of Paddington. Julian Barnes's *Metroland* (1980) explores Metropolitan Line suburbia; one particular favourite spot, on the long stretch between Finchley Rd and Wembley Park, is the high viaduct system the trains cross at Kilburn:

Below, as far as you could see, lay cross-hatched streets of tall, run-down Victorian terraces. Half a dozen television aerials interwoven on every roof implied a honeycomb of plasterboard partitioning beneath. There were few cars in that sort of area at that time, and no visible greenery. A huge, regular, red-brick Victorian building stood in the middle: a monster school, infirmary, lunatic asylum. I never knew, nor wanted that sort of precision. The value of Kilburn depended on not knowing particularities, because it changed by the eye and the brain according to yourself, your mood and the day.

KINGSBURY, district to the NW. In 1771, when **Edgware Rd** still led from village to village, Oliver Goldsmith first spent the summer at a cottage, belonging to a farmer called Selby, on a hill between the villages of *Edgware and Hyde. He wanted to be uninterrupted while writing and also to save himself the expenses of the city. He was here when *The History of England* (1771) was published and when he mentioned that he was writing a new comedy. This, when the difficulty of deciding on a title was resolved, became *She Stoops to Conquer* (1773). He also wrote part of *History of the Earth and Animated Nature* (1774) here and friends, finding him away, were amused to see that he had drawn subjects for this on the walls of his room. He was making plans to retire here but was taken ill in London and died in 1774.

KINGSTON UPON THAMES, district S of Richmond Park to the SW. John Galsworthy was born (1867) at Parkfield, **Kingston Hill**, where his parents were waiting for their new house to be finished on the 24 acres they had bought. This was Coombe Warren (gone), the first of their houses on Coombe Hill. The best-remembered home of his childhood was Coombe Leigh, where he lived from 1875 to 1878, and again from 1881 to 1886 when the family returned to London. The estate with its spinney, cricket field, and large garden was the model for the surroundings of 'Forsyte House' in *The Forsyte Saga* (1922). The area has been developed and Coombe Leigh is now Holy Cross, a school in **George Rd**.

The poet and novelist Peter Redgrove was born (1932) at 9 Lanherne, Kingston Hill, Kingston upon Thames.

The playwright and novelist Michael Frayn was educated at Kingston Grammar School in the 1940s.

KNIGHTSBRIDGE, district S of Hyde Park. Gerald Middleton, the medieval historian of Angus Wilson's novel *Anglo-Saxon Attitudes* (1956), lives in comfortable isolation in **Montpelier Sq**. At no. 8 in the same square the novelist Arthur Koestler lived from 1952. He never lost the consciousness of being an exile from his native Hungary. Looking down on the Square he remarked 'it is all I hoped for . . . Yet I shall always remain the stranger in the square.' After being diagnosed with leukaemia, he committed suicide here with his wife, Cynthia, in 1983. The novelist Henry Green lived at 16 **Trevor Pl.** in the 1940s and 1950s. Gavin Ewart's 1961 poem 'Harrods' remembers how

My mother, with myself, two sisters and a dog
Would walk across Hyde Park from Albion Street
To shop at Harrods. Bringing her small convoy in
As sheepdogs worry home the wandering sheep.

LAMBETH, district S of the river. William Blake and his wife lived from 1790 to 1800 at 13 Hercules Bldgs, a terraced house formerly on the E side of **Hercules Rd**, where a block of flats called Blake House Ⓟ now stands. At the end of the little garden a vine (Blake's favourite symbol) veiled an arbour where he and his wife were discovered one day, reading *Paradise Lost*, 'freed from "those troublesome disguises" which have prevailed since the Fall'. 'Come in!' cried Blake; 'it's only Adam and Eve, you know!' The Lambeth years were a time of great productivity for Blake, with the publication of *Visions of the Daughters of Albion* (1793), *Songs of Innocence and of Experience* (1794), *The First Book of Urizen* (1794), *The Book of Los* (1795), and *The Four Zoas* (1797).

When Arthur Rimbaud and Paul Verlaine came back to London in early 1874 (after their first visit in 1872–3) they shared a room in a boarding house at 178 **Stamford St.**, near Waterloo station. They were both hard up and lived in considerable squalor, ready to take any available job (such as employment in a cardboard box factory) to make ends meet. Rimbaud probably composed the poem *Jeunesse* during this time. He left London, possibly for Scotland, at the end of July, was briefly in *Reading in November, and finally returned to his home at Charleville at the end of the year.

The site of Astley's Amphitheatre (est. 1794 and given the prefix Royal in 1798), the most popular equestrian entertainment of the showman Philip Astley, was at 225 **Westminster Bridge Rd**. Jane Austen herself visited in 1796 and in *Emma* (1816) tells how Harriet Smith and Robert Martin, at last, come to an understanding here, well out of reach of Emma's interference. A spectacle based on the ride in Byron's *Mazeppa* (1819) was one of

Wentworth Place, Hampstead, London, where John Keats lived from 1818 to 1820 and in whose garden he heard the bird that inspired 'Ode to a Nightingale'

the popular events taken on tour after the Amphitheatre was burned down. It was often performed by the actress Ada Menken, author of the poems *Infelicia* (1868) and a friend of Dickens, who mentions Astley's in *Sketches by Boz* and in *The Old Curiosity Shop* (1841), ch. 39, when Kit goes to an entertainment there.

On his second visit to England in 1821 Marie-Henri Beyle (Stendhal) enjoyed evenings at a miniature brothel on Westminster Bridge Rd. His experiences are reflected in *Souvenirs d'égotisme*.

Just on the eastern end of Westminster Bridge is **St Thomas's Hospital**, where Briony Tallis works as a nurse during the Second World War, in Ian McEwan's *Atonement* (2001).

Doris Lessing's *Briefing for a Descent into Hell* (1971) begins with the discovery of a man wandering on the **Embankment** near Waterloo Bridge, described by the police as 'Rambling, Confused and Amenable'. The novel pieces together how he came to be there.

The first professional production of a Tom Stoppard play came in 1967 with the National Theatre's production of *Rosencrantz and Guildenstern Are Dead*, which opened on 11 April at the **Old Vic**; the company's literary manager Ken Tynan had spotted the show at the Edinburgh fringe. In 1976 the National Theatre moved from the Old Vic to its newly built home on the south bank of the Thames. The last play to be produced in the old theatre, and one of the first played in the new one, was John Osborne's *Watch It Come Down*. Osborne referred to the new building as 'Colditz-on-Thames'.

The playwright Howard Brenton has also had a number of plays premièred at the National Theatre, including *Weapons of Happiness*, which inaugurated the Lyttelton Theatre in 1976, *The Romans in Britain* (1980), *Pravda*, with David Hare (1985), and *Paul* (2005). On level 5 of the adjacent **Royal Festival Hall** building is the Poetry Library.

In 1997 the dub poet Linton Kwesi Johnson was appointed the Borough of Lambeth's writer in residence.

LEE, district to the SE. Ernest Dowson was born (1867) at The Grove, **Belmont Hill** (site now occupied by small blocks of flats, of which one is called Dowson Ct), in Lee, then a village. After Oxford, which he left after a short time without a degree, and some years in the 1890s when he was a member of the Rhymers' Club, he went abroad. 'Non sum qualis eram . . .', the poem with the refrain 'I have been faithful to thee, Cynara! in my fashion', was published in *Poems* (1896). In 1900 he was found destitute by a friend who cared for him at 26 Sandhurst Gdns (now 216 Sangley Rd), Catford (a few miles SW). He died six weeks later and was buried in the Catholic cemetery at Lewisham to the NW. David Jones, who died in 1974, is buried in the same cemetery.

LEYTONSTONE, district to the NE. John Drinkwater, Georgian poet and author of the play *Abraham Lincoln* (1918), was born (1882) at Dorset Villa, 105 **Fairlop Rd**, the son of a schoolmaster who became an actor. Drinkwater Towers in Browning Rd, a tower block of flats, is called after him.

MARYLEBONE (or St Marylebone) (pr. 'Mărlĭb'n), district between Regent's Park and Oxford St. Edward Bulwer, later Lord Lytton, was born (1803) at 31 **Baker St**.

Sherlock Holmes, the 'consulting detective' whose amazing powers of deduction solved the crimes in the ingenious stories of Sir Arthur Conan Doyle, lived at 221B Baker St., though no such number can now be found. The Abbey National Bank, whose head office still stands in the place where 221B should be, once employed a clerk to answer correspondence from members of the public posted to Holmes during and after his 'lifetime'. Here hansom cabs deposited the clients who called for his help, and from here, fuelled by the tremendous fare served up by the long-suffering Mrs Hudson and aided by the faithful Dr Watson, he strode energetically into the foggy, gaslit streets of late Victorian and Edwardian London. The Sherlock Holmes Museum, located at no. 239, just up from 'the world's most famous address', displays a range of Holmesiana, including a reconstruction of the famous sitting room and a range of waxwork tableaux illustrating scenes from some of the most famous stories (www.sherlock-holmes.co.uk).

A bronze statue of Holmes by John Doubleday stands outside Baker Street station. Sir John Betjeman, who began his train journey through 'Metro-land' for a 1973 television programme from Baker St., also set his melancholy satirical poem 'The Metropolitan Railway' in the station buffet.

Arnold Bennett moved to 97 Chiltern Ct, a large block of flats on the Baker St. corner, in 1930 and died here (1931) a few months later. William Gerhardie, pausing outside the flat while Bennett lay dying, noticed in *Memoirs of a Polyglot* (1931) the straw spread 'lavishly' across the road to quieten the carriage wheels and remarks on the obsolete practice in an age of pneumatic tyres: 'Presently, I hoped, he would come to and expose the archaism in an article in the *Evening Standard*. When I passed again the straw had been removed, and Arnold Bennett was dead.' H. G. Wells also lived here from 1930 to 1937, during which time he wrote the science-fiction novel *The Shape of Things to Come* (1933).

In his *Letters from England* (1924), the Czech writer Karel Capek records how, during his visit to London in 1924, at Madame Tussaud's he

> stopped next to one particularly effective figure in a top hat and looked in my catalogue to see who it was. Suddenly the gentleman with the top hat moved and left. It was ghastly. After a while two young ladies looked in their catalogue to see who I represented.

Gavin Ewart's poem 'Madame Tussaud's' conducts a guided tour around the waxworks,

'a heaven of Top People'. In the 1960s Paul Durcan, while trying to establish himself as a poet in London, was employed as a stellar manipulator at the London Planetarium.

Gibbon, after disposing of his Buriton estate and putting up with lodgings including that over 'a stinking apothecary's', leased (1773–83) 7 **Bentinck St**. (rebuilt, Ⓟ). He wrote to his mother of the comfort of his library, '*my gardens at Kensington*', and the friends 'who are chained to London'. These included Goldsmith, Joshua Reynolds, and his friends in the House of Commons, one of whom wrote, 'I have seldom met with a more agreeable party or more profitable subjects of conversation' than at Gibbon's house. In February 1773 Gibbon wrote in his *Autobiography*:

> No sooner was I settled in my house and library than I undertook the composition of the first Volume of my history. At the outset all was dark and doubtful . . . and I was often tempted to cast away the labour of seven years.

Dickens lived (1833–4) at no. 18 (rebuilt) while writing *Sketches by Boz* (1835–6).

Coleridge lodged at 17 **Berners St**. (rebuilt, Ⓟ) for 18 months (1812–13) with his friends the Morgan family. His tragedy in blank verse *Remorse*, set in the time of the Spanish Inquisition and written in 1797 as *Osorio*, was produced at Drury Lane in 1813. Charles Lamb was a frequent visitor.

Henry Taylor, who worked in the Colonial Office, lived for some years in **Blandford Sq**. In 1828 he started to write the play *Philip van Artevelde* (1834), after a suggestion by Southey, with whom he had made a tour of Belgium and France (1824–5).

From the late 1840s to 1850 Wilkie Collins lived with his mother and brother at no. 38. He wrote here a *Memoir* (1848) of his father, a painter and a friend of David Wilkie, and also his first novel, *Antonina* (1850).

George Eliot and George Lewes took the lease (1860–3) of no. 16. It was here that George Eliot heard that Queen Victoria had praised her novel *Adam Bede* (1859), and that she wrote *Silas Marner* (1861). After a visit to Italy to research into the background of her new novel, she began *Romola*, set in the Italy of Savonarola, in January 1862.

George Gissing lived from 1884 to 1890 at 7k **Cornwall Residences**, a block of flats near Baker St. Station, behind Madame Tussaud's. While he was here he published *The Unclassed* (1884), *Isabel Clarendon* (1886), *Demos: A Story of English Socialism* (1886), *Thyrza* (1887), *A Life's Morning* (1888), *The Nether World* (1889), and *The Emancipated* (1890).

T. S. Eliot lived at 18 **Crawford Mansions** from 1916 to 1920 and in various apartments at **Clarence Gate Gdns** from 1920 to 1932. In his final two years at Clarence Gate were enacted the last unhappy scenes of his marriage to Vivien Eliot.

Conan Doyle moved with his wife in 1890 from *Southsea to London and he then found a consulting room at 2 **Devonshire Pl.**, where he set up his plate as an oculist. Every day he walked from Montagu Pl. and waited from ten o'clock until four, but as no patients appeared and the conditions were ideal he used the time to write. The 'first fruits of a considerable harvest' enabled him to give up the surgery and, as he wrote in *Memories and Adventures* (1930), 'to trust for ever to my power of writing'.

Ferguson House stands on the site of 1 **Devonshire Ter.**, Charles Dickens's home from 1839 to 1851. The villa with a double bow-front and dormer windows above had a walled garden. Ferguson House has a panel with Dickens's characters in low relief. Dickens wrote here part of *The Old Curiosity Shop* (1841), *Barnaby Rudge* (1841), *American Notes* (1842), and *Martin Chuzzlewit* (1843–4), written after his visit to America, *A Christmas Carol* (1843), the first of his Christmas books, and *Dombey and Son* (1848), which has many scenes in Marylebone. Longfellow was among Dickens's visitors in 1842. Dickens kept ravens here, prototypes of Grip in *Barnaby Rudge*.

Graham Greene lived at 15 Devonshire Ter. for six months in 1921 with the psychiatrist Kenneth Richmond, a formative period he describes in *A Sort of Life* (1971).

Swinburne lived (1865–70) at the two-storey 22 **Dorset St.**, where *Poems and Ballads* (1866), including 'Laus Veneris', 'Dolores', and 'A Litany', and *A Song of Italy* (1867) were written. His irregular life at this time often resulted in illness, when he was cared for at Shiplake by his mother. Elizabeth and Robert Browning spent 1855 at no. 13 (rebuilt), where she was writing *Aurora Leigh*, her major work, a long romance in blank verse (1857). This was her last home in England.

Rose Macaulay, author of the satirical novels *Potterism* (1920), *Dangerous Ages* (1921), and *Told by an Idiot* (1923), lived in St Andrew's Mansions here for many years after 1926. She also wrote the historical novel *They Were Defeated* (1932) and the novel of London at the end of the war *The World My Wilderness* (1950).

John Byng (later Lord Torrington), who summed up his military service and civilian appointment in the lines:

> His early days were spent in camps
> His latter days were passed at stamps,

lived at 29 **Duke St.**, near Manchester Sq., after retiring from the army and becoming a Comptroller of Stamps. He set out from here, sometimes accompanied for part of the journey by his wife, on the sightseeing tours he describes in the *Torrington Diaries* (1934, reprinted 1970).

Patrick Hamilton located the Midnight Bell on the **Euston Rd**, the pub at the centre of *Twenty Thousand Streets Under the Sky* (1935), his trilogy of heartache and wasted dreams. It is there, between the 'spotless, tidy, bright, and a little chilly' saloon and the 'dreary, seatless and bareboarded' public bar, that the barman Bob conceives his unrequited infatuation for the prostitute Jenny. The story was inspired by Hamilton's own hopeless relationship with the prostitute Lily Connolly.

Colin MacInnes studied at the **Euston Road School of Drawing and Painting** in the late 1930s.

Sir John Betjeman succeeded in helping to save St Pancras station from demolition, but not Euston.

Thomas Moore lodged at 44 **George St.** on coming from Dublin in 1799 to the Middle Temple, and later at no. 85. He dedicated *Anacreon* (1800), a verse translation of 6th-c. BC odes, to the Prince of Wales, and was dubbed 'Anacreon Moore' by Byron, whose friend he became. A plaque from Moore's lodgings in Bury St. was re-erected on no. 85 in 1963.

Henry Green spent his working life at his family firm of Pontifex & Son on George St., early in his career writing novels during his lunch break. Life in the office is brilliantly captured in *Back* (1946), with its flirtations, sense of routine, business letters, and bureaucratic jargon.

Charles and Mary Lamb, Wordsworth, Coleridge, Tom Moore, and Samuel Rogers were guests of the MP Thomas Monkhouse at 34 **Gloucester Pl.** in 1823. Lamb wrote that he 'dined in Parnassus'. Elizabeth Barrett, one of a large family, lived at no. 99 (Ⓟ; previously no. 74) from 1835 to 1838. Dickens lodged at no. 57 in 1865.

Wilkie Collins lived at no. 65 (Ⓟ; previously no. 90) from 1867 to 1888. *The Moonstone* (1868), written here, was dictated as he was being given laudanum to relieve pain. Sergeant Cuff, one of the earliest detectives in fiction, appears in this novel.

Nancy Mitford was educated at Francis Holland School at 39 **Graham Ter.** She was removed from the school when the family moved to Victoria Rd in 1910 and subsequently (to her disgust) taught by a governess.

James Boswell lived from 1790 until his death in 1795 at 122 **Gt Portland St.** Ⓟ. He had outlived the friends who enliven the pages of his *London Journal*.

Rossetti House Ⓟ at 106–10 **Hallam St.**, is on the site of 38 Charlotte St., where Dante Gabriel Rossetti, poet and painter, was born in 1828, and his sister Christina (author of *Goblin Market and Other Poems*, 1862) in 1830. Six years later the family moved to no. 50.

The novelist William Gerhardie, author of some of the most admired novels of the 1920s, including *Futility* (1922) and *The Polyglots* (1925), lived an increasingly hermit-like existence, writing less and less, at Rossetti House from 1931 to 1977. For many years he was thought to have been working on a huge tetralogy, but after his death only a card index relating to this work was discovered. He records more outgoing times, and especially his friendships with H. G. Wells, George Bernard Shaw, and Arnold Bennett, in his *Memoirs of a Polyglot* (1931).

Barry Cornwall (pseudonym of Bryan Procter, the friend of Lamb and Dickens) lived with his daughter the poet Adelaide Procter at 38 **Harley St.** in the 1840s and 1850s. Katherine Mansfield lived (1903–6) at no. 41

while at Queen's College (founded 1848) nearby. At this time she was hoping to make music her career. Arthur Pinero, whose plays *The Second Mrs. Tanqueray* (1893) and *Trelawny of the Wells* (1898) are still revived, lived at no. 115a Ⓟ for some years after 1910.

George Gordon Byron was born (1788) in **Holles St.**, off Cavendish Sq.

Marie Louise de la Ramée ('Ouida') lived at the Langham Hotel, in **Langham Pl.**, 1867–70. She was visited by a number of writers and painters, including Millais, Browning, and Lord Lytton. The hotel was also a favourite of many Americans, including the poet H. W. Longfellow and the novelist Samuel Clemens ('Mark Twain'). It became part of the BBC in the 1930s (until 1986) and it was here that Max Beerbohm arranged his broadcasts, collected as *Mainly on the Air* (1946, 1957), that were such a feature of wartime Britain.

Edmond Malone, a member of Dr Johnson's Club, lived from 1779 to his death in 1812 at 40 **Langham St.** Ⓟ. He edited Shakespeare's *Works* in 1790 and gave his friend Boswell scholarly assistance with the *Life of Samuel Johnson* (1791). Boswell spent many days with Malone here, though there were occasions when he wrote, 'Malone was busy with his Shakespeare, so I could not get any of his time.' The Malone Society (founded 1906), which publishes early dramatic texts and other documents, is named after him.

Ezra Pound took lodgings next to the Yorkshire Grey in 1908. He wrote 'Night Litany', 'The Goodly Fere', and 'Sestina Altaforte'. He was also working on a 'damn bad novel' which he burnt here.

Leigh Hunt lived at 15 **Lisson Grove** (gone), *c*. 1815–17, and was visited by Byron, Wordsworth, and Shelley. In 1817 the painter Haydon gave a dinner at no. 116 Ⓟ for friends, including Charles Lamb, and Keats, who wished to be introduced to Wordsworth. The company talked of their favourite poets and Keats had asked a young surgeon, who was about to explore the Niger, to fling a copy of his *Endymion* into the Sahara, when they were joined by a Comptroller of Stamps who said he was a correspondent of Wordsworth. Lamb, who took exception to the interruption and became impolite, was led out to the next room but his protests remained audible and the pleasant atmosphere was ruined. Haydon painted Amelia Opie here.

Jerome K. Jerome was educated (1869–73) at **Marylebone Grammar School** (then called the Philological School).

Near the N end of **Marylebone High St.** a little garden marks the site of the 15th-c. **Marylebone parish church**, where Francis Bacon was married in 1606. In the church built on the site in 1741, displaced as the parish church by the new building (see below), and destroyed by bombs in the Second World War, Sheridan married the beautiful singer Elizabeth Linley in 1773, the year after he had escorted her to France from *Bath, where she had been plagued by an unwanted suitor. In 1788 Byron was baptized here. Thomas

Holcroft, actor, novelist, and playwright, friend of Tom Paine and Charles Lamb, who lived in **Marylebone St.** during the 1780s, died in 1809 in Clipstone St. and was buried here. There are memorials to Allan Ramsay and Charles Wesley, who were buried in the churchyard.

In Margaret Drabble's *The Millstone* (1965), Rosamund lives in her parents' flat near Marylebone High St.; 20 years later another Drabble heroine, Liz Headleand, would live just a few blocks away on Harley St. A New Year's Eve party at Liz's Harley St. home (celebrating the end of the 1970s) would open Drabble's *The Radiant Way* (1987), the first in a trilogy about Liz and her two friends Alix Bowen and Esther Breuer (who in contrast lives 'at the wrong end of Ladbroke Grove').

Wilkie Collins lived at 9 **Melcombe Pl.**, between Marylebone Rd and Marylebone station, from the end of 1864 to 1867, and wrote his novel *Armadale* (1866).

Anthony Trollope lived (1872–80) at 39 **Montagu Sq.** Ⓟ, W of Gloucester Pl. *The Eustace Diamonds* (1873), which appeared first in the *Fortnightly Review*, was written here. John Forster, friend of Harrison Ainsworth and Dickens and the latter's first biographer, lived at no. 46 in the 1850s.

Sheridan lived at 22 **Orchard St.**, the S end of Baker St., after his marriage in 1773, and wrote *The Rivals* and *The Duenna*, comedies acted in 1775. Sydney Smith lived (1806–9) at no. 18 while he was lecturing on moral philosophy to a large audience, which needed the addition of a gallery in the lecture room. The witty *Letters of Peter Plymley* (1807–8) were written here. The letters purport to be written by one Peter Plymley in favour of Catholic Emancipation to his brother Abraham, an Anglican clergyman.

Motor boats make their way up **Oxford St.** after the landing of interstellar invaders on the earth's seabed in John Wyndham's science-fiction novel *The Kraken Wakes* (1953). Dorothea May, the reclusive widow of Anita Brookner's novel *Visitors* (1996), makes a trip to a department store on Oxford Street, 'carried along like a dry stick on a stream'.

In Vikram Seth's *An Equal Music* (1999), Michael is on a bus on Oxford St., beside Selfridge's department store, and he sees Julia—a former lover from whom he has been apart for 10 years—passing on a no. 94; he races down Oxford St. after it. Failing to find her, he sits down at Piccadilly Circus, under the statue of Eros, and cries.

Coventry Patmore, author of poems collectively called *The Angel in the House*, and an assistant in the Printed Books Department of the British Museum (1848–62), is commemorated by a plaque at 14 **Percy St.**

John Buchan, who lived until 1919 in the house he bought, 76 **Portland Pl.**, in 1913, wrote the spy story *The Thirty-Nine Steps* (1915) while recuperating from an illness.

Penelope Fitzgerald's wartime experience working at Broadcasting House on Portland Pl. furnished the material for her novel *Human Voices* (1980). In an atmosphere of confusion,

'urgency and worry', and where the 'pungent rankness' of the old 78 records constitute the 'true smell of the BBC's war', the Corporation dedicated itself to 'the strangest project of the war, or of any war, that is, telling the truth . . . droning quietly on, at intervals from dawn to midnight, telling, as far as possible, exactly what happened'. Other writers who worked at Broadcasting House during the war included George Orwell, Louis MacNeice, and William Empson.

In 1781 the fashionable Mrs Elizabeth Montagu moved to her new house, now 22 **Portman Sq.**, designed by 'Athenian' Stuart. It had a room decorated with 'roses and jessamine', the delight of Cowper and Mrs Delany, and another adorned with the feathers of brightly coloured birds. Mrs Montagu's salon was attended by other 'blue stockings' and by Burke, Horace Walpole, Dr Johnson, and Boswell. She was the author of three of Lord Lyttelton's *Dialogues of the Dead* (1760) and an essay on Shakespeare which attacked Voltaire's views. She was the patron of London's chimney sweeps and gave them an annual dinner.

The French poet André de Chénier lived (1787–90) at no. 31 while Secretary to the Ambassador. He made few friends in England but visited Richard and Maria Cosway, the miniature-painters whom he had known in Paris. He was working on his *Bucoliques* and he bought many English editions of the classics while here. He was guillotined shortly before the fall of Robespierre.

Boswell worked on his *Life of Samuel Johnson* (1791) in **Queen Anne St.** Richard Cumberland lived at the corner of Wimpole St. and Queen Anne St. when finishing *The West Indian* (1771), begun at his father's house in Clonfert. His later work did not enjoy the same high degree of success as this play.

Edward Lear lived at 30 **Seymour St.** Ⓟ. He needed to be near the Regent's Park Zoo in order to study parrots for his commission from the Royal Zoological Society.

Plaques at 3 **Spanish Pl.** commemorate both Captain Marryat (author of numerous sea stories, including *Mr. Midshipman Easy*, 1836), who wrote *Masterman Ready* (1841) when living here, and the comedian George Grossmith. George and his brother Weedon were joint authors of *The Diary of a Nobody* (1894), which catalogues with poignant irony the domestic and social gaucheries of Mr Charles Pooter of The Laurels, Holloway, an assistant in a mercantile business.

Mervyn Peake married Maeve Gilmore at the Catholic church of St James's in December 1937. At that time he was teaching at the Westminster School of Art, where Maeve was a sculpture student.

St Marylebone parish church (built 1813–17), in Marylebone Rd, opposite York Gate, has a window commemorating Robert Browning and Elizabeth Barrett, who were married here secretly in 1846 a week before their elopement. A bronze tablet to Browning was erected on the W wall in 1887.

Letitia Elizabeth Landon, who lived at 28 **Upper Berkeley St.**, wrote, as 'L.E.L.', novels and poems, including her first poem, 'Rome', published in the *Literary Gazette* in 1820, *The Fate of Adelaide* (1821), another poem, *Ethel Churchill* (1837) considered her best novel, and *Traits and Trials of Early Life* (1837), which may be autobiographical. She died (1838) from poisoning soon after her marriage to George MacLean, a provincial governor, and her arrival in West Africa.

Max Beerbohm lived at no. 48 with his family from the early 1890s, when he was at *Oxford, to 1910, when he married and went to live in Italy. He wrote here the essays collected as *The Works of Max Beerbohm* (1896), *More* (1899), and *Yet Again* (1909), and also *Zuleika Dobson* (1911), the fantasy about Oxford which he began in 1898.

The **Wallace Collection** (open daily, www.wallacecollection.org) at Manchester Sq. contains Poussin's 'A Dance to the Music of Time', the painting Anthony Powell felt described the relationships in the novel sequence he named after it, and a description of which opens its first volume.

The Brownings spent part of the summer of 1852 at 58 **Welbeck St.**, later a hotel. Marie Louise de la Ramée ('Ouida') lived with her mother at no. 51 for a short time in 1867, when her popular novel *Under Two Flags* was published. Trollope died (1882) at no. 33, now part of the rebuilt Welbeck Mansions, where he was being nursed after a stroke.

In Ian McEwan's *On Chesil Beach* (2007), Florence dreams of her quartet one day playing at the **Wigmore Hall**:

> Florence and Edward arrived well before the others so that she could give him a tour of the Hall. The green room, the tiny changing room, even the auditorium and the cupola could hardly account, he thought, for her reverence for the place. She was so proud of the Wigmore Hall, it was as if she had designed it herself. . . . She told him that one day it would happen, she had made up her mind: the Ennismore Quartet would perform here, play beautifully and triumph.

As indeed they do. In Vikram Seth's *An Equal Music* (1999), the Maggiore Quartet also realize their ambitions when they make it onto the Wigmore stage, 'the sacred shoe-box of chamber music', to play quartets by Haydn, Mozart, and Beethoven.

Elizabeth Barrett, who was a semi-invalid perhaps as a result of a fall from her pony, lived at 50 **Wimpole St.** (rebuilt, Ⓟ) from 1838 to 1846. The publication of her poems and *Prometheus Bound* (1833) began a correspondence with Robert Browning which resulted in his offer of marriage. The ceremony took place in secret in 1846 to prevent her father from banning the marriage because of her precarious state of health. The popular play by Rudolph Besier (1878–1942) *The Barretts of Wimpole Street* (1930) presents Mr Barrett as a parent whose zealous care of his daughter becomes a tyranny. On her elopement to Italy,

Elizabeth Barrett took with her the spaniel that Mary Mitford had given her. The dog's story is told in *Flush: A Biography* (1933), by Virginia Woolf.

Wilkie Collins spent the last months of his life at no. 82 (rebuilt) and died there in 1889.

MAYFAIR, district between Oxford St. and Piccadilly. **Albany**, just E of Burlington House, is a private enclave (Ⓟ nearby) where in 1802 the mansion of the Duke of York and Albany was divided into fashionable sets of rooms or chambers. Byron lived here for a short time and Matthew Gregory Lewis, known as 'Monk Lewis' after his Gothic novel, lived here from *c*. 1812. Lewis made two journeys in 1815–16 and 1817–18 to look into the running of his plantation in Jamaica, and his *Journal of a West Indian Proprietor* (1834) was published after his death from a fever on the voyage home in 1818. Edward Bulwer-Lytton had a pied-à-terre here when he was living at *Knebworth and Lord Macaulay lived here from 1841 to 1856.

Soon after moving to new offices at 50 **Albemarle St.**, John Murray published Byron's successful *Childe Harold* (1812), and introduced the young author to Scott here. The *Quarterly Review*, founded by Murray in 1809 and edited by Gifford, contained the article on Keats's *Endymion* (1812) to which Byron replied with the lines:

> Who killed John Keats?
> 'I' says the Quarterly,
> So savage and Tartarly,
> ''Twas one of my feats.'

Scott, who tried to temper Gifford's bitterness to new-style authors, praised Jane Austen's *Emma* (1816) and reviewed his own *Tales of My Landlord* (1817). Murray recounts in his *Autobiography* how the booksellers' messengers filled the streets and made 'obstreperous demands' for copies of Byron's *Don Juan* on publication day in 1819. It was at no. 50 that Murray angrily refused to jeopardize Byron's reputation by publishing his memoirs. Tom Moore, to whom the memoirs had been bequeathed, reluctantly acquiesced, and the manuscript was burnt in the grate in 1824.

Berkeley Sq., a residential square built in the 1740s, is now chiefly office blocks. Colley Cibber, a popular actor-turned-dramatist, who became Poet Laureate in 1730, and was satirized by Pope in *The Dunciad*, died here (in a house on the site of no. 19) in 1757. Horace Walpole stayed (1779–97) at his town house, no. 11 (gone), when visiting from Strawberry Hill (*Twickenham), and he died here. Thackeray called the Square, then the finest in London, 'Buckley Square' in *Yellowplush Papers* (1837) and 'Gaunt Square' in *Vanity Fair* (1847–8).

Charles Reade lodged (1856–68) with Laura Seymour, an actress, who with her husband kept a boarding house at 6 **Bolton Row** (gone, formerly at the end of Bolton St.). Reade's novel *It Is Never Too Late to Mend* (1856), part of which is set in the goldfields of Australia, exposes the harshness of the penal system. Its realism was also popular when dramatized. *The Cloister and the Hearth* (1861), a historical novel often considered his best work, *Hard Cash* (1863), propaganda against the lunacy laws, and *Griffith Gaunt* (1866), which raised a storm because of its alleged immorality, were also written here. Reade spent part of the year in *Oxford where he was a Fellow of Magdalen.

A plaque on 11 **Bolton St.** commemorates Fanny Burney, who lived here (1818–28) after the death of her husband, General D'Arblay. Here she completed her *Diary and Letters* (1778–1840), which include an interesting account of her life at court.

Henry James, the American who called himself an 'observant stranger', moved into lodgings on the first floor at no. 3 in December 1876 and stayed until 1885. *The Europeans* (1878), *Daisy Miller* (1879), *Washington Square* (1881), and *The Portrait of a Lady* (1881) are among the works he wrote partly here and partly on visits to Italy and the south coast of England. He said that *The Princess Casamassima* (1886) originated in his habit of walking through the London streets.

Bruce Chatwin worked at Sotheby's on **Bond St.** from 1958 to 1965, becoming an expert on antiquities and Impressionism. His experience in the world of connoisseurship bore literary fruit in his last novel, *Utz* (1988).

Somerset Maugham lived from 1911 to 1919 at 6 **Chesterfield St.** Ⓟ. His plays include *The Circle* (1921), *The Breadwinner* (1930), and *For Services Rendered* (1932). He made his own selection of his works, *Complete Short Stories* (3 vols, 1951); *Collected Plays* (3 vols, 1952), and *Selected Novels* (3 vols, 1953).

Ronald Firbank, author of novels that are mainly conversations, was born (1886) at 40 **Clarges St.** (site later a hotel).

Bruce Chatwin in the Antiquities Department at Sotheby's, Bond St., where he worked from 1958 to 1965

Benjamin Disraeli's last novel, *Endymion*, was published in 1880, the year he resigned as Prime Minister. He died at 19 **Curzon St.** Ⓟ in 1881.

Heywood Hill's bookshop, which stands at 10 Curzon St., employed Nancy Mitford. She corrected the proofs of *The Pursuit of Love* (1945) here and the shop became a resort for her friends. She subsequently became a partner in the business.

When the Second World War threatened, Henry Green joined the Auxiliary Fire Service and was based at Sub-Station 34A5V 'A' Division, 79 **Davies St.** His experience assisted him in the writing of *Caught* (1943), his atmospheric novel of the London Blitz:

At that period the Fire Service came next after pilots with the public . . . Street cleaners called Richard 'mate'. Girls looked him straight, long in the eye as never before, complicity in theirs, blue, and blue, and blue. They seemed to him to drag as they passed.

Evelyn's town house (gone) was 'nine doors up' in **Dover St.** and he died there in 1706. Dr Arbuthnot, Queen Anne's physician, lived in Dover St. (1714–21) after her death. His friends, including Swift, Pope, Gay, and Congreve, formed (*c.* 1713) the Scriblerus Club, whose memoirs, written mainly by Arbuthnot, were published in 1741. Edward Moxon, who helped his friend Lamb move books to his Islington cottage and who married Lamb's adopted daughter, moved to new premises in this street in 1832. Later he became Wordsworth's publisher. Brown's Hotel, nos 17–24, has a Kipling room to commemorate his frequent visits. Mark Twain stayed at Brown's when on his lecture tour (*c.* 1895), and Alphonse Daudet was also staying there on his short visit (1895) to meet Henry James and Meredith.

According to Norman Murphy, P. G. Wodehouse, who lived at 17 **Dunraven St.** (formerly Norfolk St.) from 1924 to 1934, modelled the awe-inspiringly grand and expensive 'Barribault's Hotel', which appears in a number of his stories, on Claridge's, **Brook St.** In a fictional mansion block on nearby Berkeley St., Jeeves ministered to Bertie Wooster. The 'Drones'—Wodehouse's most famous fictional club—was, as a letter of the author's makes clear, based on Buck's Club, still thriving at 18 **Clifford St.** On Curzon St., not far from the Drones, was situated Jeeves's own club, the 'Junior Ganymede', for butlers and gentlemen's gentlemen. It features prominently in *Much Obliged, Jeeves* (1971).

Sydney Smith lived at 56 **Green St.** from 1839 to his death in 1845. He was made a canon of St Paul's in 1831 and held a country living but he is better known for his droll wit, which made him a popular dinner guest and an amusing letter writer and reviewer, than for his interest in religious dogma. His *Letters* (ed. Nowell C. Smith, 2 vols) were published in 1953.

The travel writer Peter Fleming was born at 27 Green St. in 1907. His brother, the novelist Ian, was born in the same house the following year.

During a lunch hour in the spring of 1956 the travel writer Eric Newby, then working in the fashion business at a firm in **Grosvenor St.**, sent a cable from the post office on Mount St. (now gone) to a friend in the British Embassy in Rio de Janeiro. It read, 'Can you travel Nuristan June?' The adventure that followed was recorded in *A Short Walk in the Hindu Kush* (1958) and launched Newby's career as a travel writer.

Fleming's Hotel on **Half Moon St.** would be the model for Agatha Christie's 'Bertram's' in *At Bertram's Hotel* (1965).

General John Burgoyne, whose home when he was not on active service was at 10 **Hertford St.** Ⓟ, near the S end of Park Lane, wrote the comedies *The Maid of the Oaks* (1774) and the very successful *The Heiress* (1786). He and Sheridan were prominent in the impeachment of Warren Hastings (*c.* 1788) and after the death here of Burgoyne, the 'Gentlemanly Johnny' of Shaw's *The Devil's Disciple* (1900), Sheridan bought (1795) the house Ⓟ, soon after the opening of the newly built theatre in Drury Lane of which he was manager. Edward Bulwer-Lytton wrote the popular historical novels *The Last Days of Pompeii* (1834) and *Rienzi* (1835) at no. 36. His son the poet who wrote as 'Owen Meredith' was born there (1831).

Contributors to *Bentley's Miscellany* (founded 1837), who included Dickens, Tom Moore, Richard Barham, and Harrison Ainsworth, met for dinners in the Red Room at the publisher's house (gone) in **New Burlington St.** Dickens, as editor, had an uneasy time with Richard Bentley and wrote that the magazine had always been Bentley's in deed as well as in name. His 'A Familiar Epistle from a Parent to a Child Aged Two Years, Two Months' appeared on his handing over the editorship to his friend Harrison Ainsworth in 1839.

Mark Akenside had a prosperous medical practice in Burlington St., now **Old Burlington St.**, from 1760 until his death in 1770. He is said to have died in the bed, given him by a friend nine years before, in which Milton had died. He was buried in St James's Church, Piccadilly.

John Gay died (1729) at the home of the Duke and Duchess of Queensberry (site at the corner of Old Burlington St. and Burlington Gdns).

The Café Royal, near **Piccadilly Circus**, with red-plush seats, gilded mirrors, and chandeliers, was a haunt of literary and artistic coteries in the decades at the turn of the 19th c. In the 1880s and 1890s it was the special rendezvous for Oscar Wilde and others in the Aesthetic Movement who believed in 'Art for Art's sake'. Ernest Dowson and some of his friends from the Rhymers' Club also came here. In 1913–14 Ronald Firbank, one of the later aesthetes, dined here. It provided the inspiration for John Betjeman's 'On Seeing an Old Poet in the Café Royal'.

Simon Gray's play *Butley* (1971) was first performed at the Criterion Theatre on Piccadilly Circus, directed by Harold Pinter.

Contributors to *Fraser's Magazine* (1830–82) formed a literary club, the Fraserians, which met for dinners at the publisher's at 215 **Regent St.** Maclise's sketch of the diners shows Maginn (co-founder with Hugh Fraser), Coleridge, Southey, Carlyle, Hogg, Egerton Brydges, Mahony, Ainsworth, and Thackeray. R. M. Ballantyne spent some time at a fire station in Regent St. when collecting material for his novel *Fighting the Flames* (1867).

St George's Church, Hanover Sq., is an early 18th-c. church where the following were married: Shelley to Harriet Westbrook in 1814 after a ceremony in Scotland following their elopement, Disraeli to Mrs Wyndham Lewis in 1839, Marian Evans (George Eliot) to John Cross in 1880, John Galsworthy to Ada Galsworthy in 1904, and John Buchan to Susan Grosvenor in 1907.

Sheridan, author of *The Rivals* and *The School for Scandal*, lived for five years until his death in 1816 at 14 **Savile Row** Ⓟ. His speech of nearly six hours at Warren Hastings's trial and that upholding the freedom of the Press are among his collected *Speeches* (1816).

Nicholas Jenkins, the narrator of Anthony Powell's *A Dance to the Music of Time* (1951–75), has rooms in **Shepherd Market** between a sandwich bar, a garage, and a block of flats inhabited by rowdy prostitutes. Powell himself lived at 9 Shepherd St. from 1926 to 1929.

Thomas Holcroft worked in his father's cobbler's shop in **South Audley St.** as a boy. He acted at Covent Garden as Figaro in his translation of Beaumarchais's *Le Mariage de Figaro*, which he had seen in Paris in 1784. Ambrose Philips (d. 1749), a member of Addison's circle, and Lady Mary Wortley Montagu, a toast as a child of the Kit-Cat Club, letter writer, and an early advocate of vaccination, are buried in the Grosvenor Chapel in South Audley St. Also buried here are David Mallet (d. 1765), author of the ballad 'William and Margaret' (1723); William Whitehead (d. 1785), dramatist and Poet Laureate; and Elizabeth Carter (d. 1806), a friend of Dr Johnson, who admired her puddings as well as her excellent classical translations.

The poet Gavin Ewart, who spent much of his working life in the copywriting departments of London's West End advertising agencies, included in his collection *Londoners* (1964) poems dedicated to 'The Marble Arch', 'Park Lane', and 'Hyde Park Corner', that 'nest of monuments'. He also wrote affectionately of the Grosvenor Chapel and Thos Goode & Co., 'a paradise of china, glass', in his two poems 'South Audley Street I' and 'South Audley Street II'.

William Blake and his wife lived (1803–21) in one room at 17 **South Molton St.** Ⓟ. He engraved the plates, with illustrations surrounding the text, for his poem *Milton*, for Young's *Night Thoughts*, and Blair's *The Grave*.

The novelist Simon Raven was born in 1927 at 27 **Welbeck Street**.

MITCHAM, district to the S. John Donne lived (1606–10) in a two-storey house (gone) in **Whitford Lane**, with overhanging gables and a row of yews in the garden. His letters from his 'hospital' and sometimes his 'prison' show his anxiety at his lack of a place at court to provide for his increasing family, and his reluctance to accept the only alternative, ordination. *Pseudo-Martyr* (1610), *Biathanatos* (written 1607–8), and *Ignatius His Conclave* (1611) were written here.

Michael Moorcock's vast, multi-voiced novel *Mother London* (1988) tracks the stories of four psychiatric outpatients through four decades; the book begins with David Mummery,

> born in Mitcham, famous for its lavender, between the aerodromes of Croydon and Biggin Hill. . . . In the summer there was the endless and verdant Mitcham Common, with her ponds on which oildrum rafts and army inflatables were sailed, especially after the destruction of the Luftwaffe in the Battle of Britain, a soft green golf-course, copses, unthreatening marshes, stands of poplars, cedars and, of course, her elms. She had pedestrian bridges of wood and iron spanning a railway, sandy bunkers and depressions where all day long I sprawled and read and ate unseen. I do not remember ever learning the limits of Mitcham Common . . .

MUSWELL HILL, district W of Hornsey. W. E. Henley lived from 1896 to 1899 at Grange Lodge, Tetherdown, which had originally been built as a public house and then refronted (see also HORNSEY).

NEWINGTON, district S of Southwark. Thomas Middleton, author of *A Chaste Maid in Cheapside* (1613), *Women Beware Women* (1621), and many other plays, some in collaboration with other dramatists, lived in **Newington Butts** (site unknown) from 1609 to his death in 1627. He was buried in the parish church, demolished in 1720.

NORTHOLT, former village in Middlesex, on the A310, *c*. 3 m. SSW of Harrow-on-the-Hill. Goronwy Owen, Welsh poet, obtained the curacy here in 1755, through the good offices of the Cymmrodorion, and continued to write his poetry, including the best of all, 'Cywydd yn ateb Huw'r Bardd Coch' (Cywydd in Answer to Huw the Red Poet). A memorial tablet to Owen can be seen in the church. The vicar of Northolt obtained an appointment for him as headmaster of the grammar school attached to William and Mary College, Virginia, and he emigrated there in 1758.

NORWOOD, district to the SE. Julian MacLaren Ross was born at 18 Whitworth Rd in 1912.

NOTTING HILL, district W of Bayswater. Julian MacLaren Ross lived at 16 Chepstow Pl. The less fashionable part of Notting Hill, with its cracked asphalt, broken milk bottles, 'strange number of male urinals', and, later,

riots, is the 'London Napoli' depicted by Colin MacInnes in his novel *Absolute Beginners* (1959).

In Doris Lessing's *The Sweetest Dream* (2001), Johnny, Frances, and the children live in 'a wretched flat in Notting Hill, then a run-down and poor part of London' on 'a dreary street that had a house sagging to its knees in ruins'.

NUNHEAD, district to the SE. The character of the district is deftly caught in Blake Morrison's 'Nunhead Motors':

> But at night the frost-skinned cars inside the yard
> have the sadness of cattle at a bidding-gate,
> blotchy and big-eyed, silent as the guard
> dealing hearts to himself over a stove-light,
> the low-burning patience of this lot
> *Everything will work out if we just wait.*

PADDINGTON, district W of Marylebone. In his poem 'Brendon Street', Hugo Williams watched the life behind the casinos of the Edgware Rd, its croupiers barging their shoulders 'against the evening like a ball and chain'.

Thomas Hardy married Emma Lavinia Gifford at St Peter's Church, **Elgin Ave.**, in September 1874, 4½ years after they had first met at *St Juliot.

X. Trapnel, the hand-to-mouth man of letters of Anthony Powell's *A Dance to the Music of Time* (1951–75), discovers the manuscript of his unpublished novel *Profiles of Spring* in the canal at **Maida Vale**, dumped there by his lover Pamela Widmerpool. In despair, he flings his beloved prop, a swordstick with a death's-head handle, Excalibur-like into the water. The beginning of 1968 saw a teenage Martin Amis living in London, at 108 Maida Vale.

The poet Gavin Ewart was born at 25 **Norfolk Cres.** in 1916.

George du Maurier moved from his long-standing *Hampstead home to Paddington in 1895, settling into 17 **Oxford Sq.** But he died soon afterwards—on 8 October 1896—and his ashes were returned to Hampstead to be buried there.

Agatha Christie would begin her novel *The 4.50 from Paddington* (1957) with a woman (a friend of Miss Marple's) witnessing a murder taking place on an adjacent train as they are both pulling out of **Paddington station**.

Olive Schreiner, author, under the pseudonym 'Ralph Iron', of *The Story of an African Farm* (1883), lived at 16 **Portsea Pl.** Ⓟ from 1885 to 1887. This is a quiet corner near the SW end of Edgware Rd, between Connaught St. and Kendal St.

When Robert Browning returned from Italy in 1861 after the death of his wife, he lived until 1887 at 19 **Warwick Cres.** (site later a block of flats), overlooking the stretch of the Grand Union Canal called Little Venice. His sister-in-law Arabella lived close at hand, at 17 Delamere Ter., and he used to call there every evening. His long poem *The Ring and the Book* (4 vols, 1868–9), based on the story of a Roman murder case, was written while he was living here.

PALMER'S GREEN, district to the N. Florence Margaret Smith (Stevie Smith) lived (1907–71) at 1 **Avondale Rd** from the age of 5, when her parents moved from Hull, until just a few months before her death. She went to Palmer's Green High School and later worked as secretary to a publisher. She wrote three novels: *Novel on Yellow Paper* (1936), *Over the Frontier* (1938), and *The Holiday* (1949). She attended St John's Church and her poems reflect her desire to believe in a just God free from High Anglican dogma. She died in 1971 and after a service at Holy Trinity, Buckfastleigh, was cremated at *Torquay. *Selected Poems* was published in 1972 and *Collected Poems* in 1975.

PECKHAM, district to the SE. At the age of 8 or 9, William Blake saw his first recorded vision, a tree filled with angels, their 'bright angelic wings bespangling every bough like stars'. He narrowly avoided a thrashing from his father for this 'lie' when he got home. There is a mural depicting the vision at Goose Green in East Dulwich. Muriel Spark lived in nearby Camberwell in the 1950s, and Dougal Douglas, anti-hero of her novel *The Ballad of Peckham Rye* (1960), lives in Peckham, near the Rye.

PIMLICO, district S of Victoria. Joseph Conrad took rooms (1889–90) in **Bessborough Gdns**, near Vauxhall Bridge, after returning from two years at sea in the merchant navy. Soon afterwards he had the idea of writing a novel and he had begun *Almayer's Folly* when he sailed for the Congo in May 1890.

Marian Evans (George Eliot), after boarding with the publisher John Chapman, moved in September 1853 into lodgings on her own at 21 **Cambridge St.** She was translating Feuerbach's *Essence of Christianity* (1854) and editing the *Westminster Review*. By July 1854 she and George Lewes had decided to live together and they left for a holiday in Germany.

Barbara Pym lived at 108 Cambridge St. in the late 1940s, and Pimlico features in her novels *Excellent Women* (1952)—in particular St Gabriel's Church, Warwick Sq., the inspiration for 'St Mary's'—and *A Glass of Blessings* (1958).

Lorimer Black, the insurance loss adjuster in William Boyd's novel *Armadillo* (1998), owns a flat at 11 Lupus Cres., a fictional road off the real **Lupus St.** Logan Mountstuart, the narrator of Boyd's novel *Any Human Heart* (2002), lives in obscurity around the corner at 10a **Turpentine Lane**.

Sarah Waters's novel *Affinity* (1999) is set in the Millbank penitentiary, a Victorian panopticon prison that used to be on **Millbank**, where Tate Britain now stands.

> The prison, drawn in outline, has a curious kind of charm to it, the pentagons appearing as petals on a geometric flower—or, as I have sometimes thought, they are like the coloured zones on the chequer-boards we used to paint when we were children. Seen close, of course, Millbank is not charming. Its scale is vast, and its lines and angles, when realised in walls and towers of yellow brick and shuttered windows, seem only

wrong or perverse. It is as if the prison had been designed by a man in the grip of a nightmare or a madness—or had been made expressly to *drive* its inmates mad.

Paintings and drawings by Blake, Rossetti, Ruskin, Morris, and Wyndham Lewis form part of the national collection of British art at **Tate Britain**. The gallery also includes many paintings of literary subjects, including Millais' 'Ophelia'. (www.tate.org.uk)

In P. D. James's *Innocent Blood* (1980), Philippa lives happily with her adopted family in Pimlico, at (the fictional) 68 Caldecott Ter.; but the first step in tracing her biological parents takes her away from home, east to Seven Kings in Essex, where she has a dreadful surprise . . .

PINNER, district to the NW. Bulwer-Lytton wrote *Eugene Aram* (1832) while he was living at Pinner Wood House, **Albury Drive**, in 1831–2.

A. E. Housman lived at 1 Yarborough Villas (gone), **Devonshire Rd**, after his landlady moved from 17 North Rd, *Highgate. When he left in 1911 to take up his appointment as Kennedy Professor of Latin at *Cambridge, his landlady is reported to have told him that, though sorry to lose him, she could not entirely regret his going, as she understood that by living in a college he would have other men's society forced upon him and 'would be taken out of himself, shaken up, made to chatter like the rest of the world'.

Howard Spring lived at the White Cottage, **East End Way**, in the 1930s and contributed to the local residents' association magazine, *The Villager*. His best-selling novel *Oh Absalom* (later retitled *My Son, My Son!*) was published in 1938 while he was here.

On the wall of the S aisle of the parish church there is a monument to Henry James Pye, Poet Laureate in the reign of George III. His poetry has not endured and he was subject to ridicule by his contemporaries.

POPLAR, district to the E. Arthur Morrison, author of *A Child of the Jago* (1896), was born (1863) in one of the two John Streets here. These, rebuilt and now renamed **Grundy St.** and **Rigden St.**, N of East India Dock Rd, may have been those depicted in his introduction to *Tales of Mean Streets* (1894).

Jerome K. Jerome was 4 years old when he came with his family to live in a small house in **Sussex St.** They stayed here from 1863 to 1870, and although they had great financial difficulties, the boy seems to have been unaware of poverty. A poignant picture of this time is shown in extracts from his mother's diary, quoted in his autobiography, *My Life and Times* (1926).

PUTNEY, district to the N of Wimbledon Common. Edward Gibbon, born in Putney in 1737, is commemorated by **Gibbon Walk**. As a child he was cared for by his aunt Catherine Porten, and he mentions, in his *Autobiography*, 'that the house, near Putney bridge and

churchyard, of my maternal grandfather, appears in the light of my proper and native home'. Leigh Hunt died at a friend's house in **Putney High St.** in 1859.

The Russian émigré writer Alexander Herzen lived at Laurel House, Putney High St.

J. R. Ackerley lived at 17 Star and Garter Mansions, 6 **Lower Richmond Rd**, with 'three bitches', including his dog Queenie, the subject of his 1960 novel *We Think the World of You*. He wrote about his relationship with his Alsatian in his frank memoir *My Father and Myself* (1968): 'She offered me what I had never found in my sexual life, constant, single-hearted, incorruptible, uncritical devotion, which it is the nature of dogs to offer.' A walk in Putney moved Gavin Ewart to write his sonnet 'Intimations of Mortality in the Lower Richmond Road'.

In 1879 a joint tenancy was agreed between Watts-Dunton and Swinburne for 2 The Pines at the foot of **Putney Hill** (now no. 11, Ⓟ). Swinburne's health improved under Watts-Dunton's care but his last volumes of verse, *Astrophel* (1894), *A Tale of Balem* (1896), and *A Channel Passage* (1904), show a loss of power. Swinburne wrote monographs on *Shakespeare* (1880), *Ben Jonson* (1889), and other Elizabethans and also on more modern writers including Dickens and the Brontës. Max Beerbohm visited him in 1899 and describes the tamed Swinburne in his essay 'No. 2 The Pines'.

In 1934 Laurie Lee came down to London, and lodged here in Putney, trying to combine his earnest desire to live like a proper bohemian with the fact that he was working as a labourer.

QUEEN'S PARK, district to the NW. The novelist Barbara Pym lived at 40 Brooksville Ave. from 1961 to 1972 Ⓟ. The district features in her novel *An Unsuitable Attachment*, written in the 1960s but not published until 1982.

REGENT'S PARK, district enclosing one of the largest open spaces in London. In Jonathan Coe's *An Accidental Woman* (1987), Maria works in the offices of a women's magazine in Baker Street, and in her lunch hour would often go to sit in Regent's Park:

> She would find a vacant bench in one of the most secluded parts of the park and sit there for nearly an hour, sometimes thinking, sometimes looking around her, sometimes dozing and sometimes feeding the birds. For this last purpose she would bring with her a paper bag full of stale crumbs. Today she also had a packet of sandwiches, egg and cress, bought at a take-away in Baker Street. These turned out to be disgusting. She ended up eating the stale crumbs and throwing the sandwiches to the birds. That soon got rid of them.

Elizabeth Bowen lived at 2 **Clarence Ter.** from 1935 until the death of her husband in 1952. She wrote here the novel *The House in Paris* (1935), two volumes of short stories, *Look at All Those Roses* (1941) and *The Demon Lover* (1945), and the two major novels set in London, *The Death of the Heart* (1938) and the

wartime story *The Heat of the Day* (1949). She worked in the Ministry of Information during the day and was an air raid warden at night, and *The Heat of the Day* is considered a realistic evocation of London in wartime. The novelist Anthony Powell lived at 1 Chester Gate from 1936 to 1952, and began his 12-volume novel sequence *A Dance to the Music of Time* (1951–75) while living here.

The novelist Daphne du Maurier was born on 13 May 1905 at 24 **Cumberland Ter.**, Regent's Park, where she spent most of her childhood.

William Wilkie Collins lived at 17 **Hanover Ter.** with his mother and brother Charles from 1850 to 1859. He first met Dickens soon after coming here and he contributed many travel sketches and short stories to his *Household Words*, including the eerie tale 'A Terribly Strange Bed' in the April number of 1852. He joined the staff of this periodical in 1856, and wrote *The Woman in White* (1860), the first English crime detection novel, for its successor, *All the Year Round*, where it shared a place with Dickens's *A Tale of Two Cities*. Wilkie Collins, whose father was a popular Royal Academician, was often visited by his friends of the Pre-Raphaelite Brotherhood here and he and Edward Lear were among those at the dinner before Millais left for his marriage to Effie Gray. Dickens frequently invited Collins to join him on his holidays, and shared his love of amateur theatricals, and the families were further united when Dickens's daughter Kate married Charles Collins.

Edmund Gosse lived at no. 17 from 1901. His *Father and Son* (1907), first published anonymously, depicts the tyrannies of family relationships in an exclusive sect. Alfred Noyes, who had visited Gosse here, lived at no. 13 after his second marriage in 1928, but soon afterwards found the Isle of *Wight home where he gradually spent more time. When he finally gave up the house, H. G. Wells moved in (1937) and it was at no. 13 Ⓟ that he died in 1946. His last work, *Mind at the End of its Tether* (1945), reflects his disillusion at yet another war.

Marian Evans (George Eliot) lived with George Lewes as his wife at The Priory, 21 North Bank, a road (gone) formerly curving S off **Lodge Rd**. They moved into the house, secluded in its garden full of roses by the Regent's Canal, in November 1863 after an interior designer had made 'an exquisite thing of it'. Hampstead Heath was a favourite place for long walks together. The play George Eliot was writing, set in Spain, was put aside for *Felix Holt* (1866), the novel about a Radical and the Reform Bill, but it appeared later as the dramatic poem *The Spanish Gypsy* (1868). Lewes, who called her Polly, wrote for the *Pall Mall Gazette*, became editor of *The Fortnightly*, and made hard bargains with her publishers. George Eliot began *Middlemarch* here in January 1869 but this was interrupted by the illness of Lewes's son, at whose deathbed she wrote the first part of her poem *The Legend of Jubal* (1870). Emanuel Deutsch, a friend who taught her Hebrew, inspired her novel *Daniel*

Deronda (1874–6). These like her other works were partly written elsewhere. Though George Eliot's situation was considered immoral, an increasing number of literary friends came to her parties, including Wilkie Collins, Trollope, Browning, Tennyson, Henry James, and in 1878 Turgenev. George Lewes died here in 1878 and George Eliot married their friend John Cross in May 1880, and moved to *Chelsea in November.

Christina Stead refreshed herself with visits to **London Zoo** when she lived at Primrose Hill for three months in 1947. The sound of the 'hippos mating and roaring . . . and the parrots, monkeys, seals . . . screaming with love' at London Zoo was within the earshot of V. S. Pritchett, who lived at 12 **Regent's Pk Ter.** Brigid Brophy also lived near the Zoo in the 1950s, and it provided the inspiration for her novel *Hackenfeller's Ape* (1953), at the centre of which is an imaginary animal 'the same size as a gorilla, but in appearance and character nearer the chimpanzee'. The narrator of Colin MacInnes's novel *City of Spades* (1957) lives in a high, narrow house overlooking the Zoo, which is also the scene for Angus Wilson's satirical fantasy *The Old Men at the Zoo* (1961).

After graduating from university, Ted Hughes took a job in the Zoo cafeteria to fund his fledgling poetry habit. The release of two sea turtles from the aquarium here is the subject of Russell Hoban's novel *Turtle Diary* (1975). The Zoo is also the setting for an exciting lion escape (which spells bad news for a hapless city trader) in Justin Cartwright's 1990 novel *Look At It This Way*.

Cyril Connolly, founder and editor (1939–50) of *Horizon*, lived at 25 **Sussex Pl.**

The revolutionary and memoirist Alexander Herzen lived at Orsett House, **Westbourne Ter.**, gradually reconciling himself in his exile from Russia to the city's fogs and solitudes and eventually 'coming to love this fearful ant-heap, where every night a hundred thousand men know not where they will lay their heads' (*My Past and Thoughts*, 1862).

RICHMOND, riverside district to the SW. In 1736 James Thomson, with a government sinecure, moved into a small cottage in **Kew Foot Lane**. He was in love with 'Amanda' (Elizabeth Young, who refused his offer of marriage), for whom he had described the view from **Richmond Hill** in the lines beginning 'Which way, Amanda, shall we steer our course,' which he added to *Summer* when it was published in *The Seasons* (1744). Thomson was often visited by William Collins, who sometimes lodged at The Castle inn where Thomson was to be found when not at his cottage. Collins said this was Thomson's real Castle of Indolence. In 1739 Thomson moved to a larger cottage in the same lane, which became known as Rossdale, then Rosedale, and was incorporated into the Royal Hospital. (Fanny Burney was a visitor and saw the garden alcove where Thomson wrote.) He collaborated with Thomas Arne on the masque *Alfred* (1740), which contains 'Rule Britannia'.

Thomson died in August 1748 after contracting a chill on a river trip.

Virginia and Leonard Woolf moved to 17 **The Green** in 1914, and then lived (1915–24) at Hogarth House, Paradise Rd, from which they took the name of their hand-printing press. Virginia Woolf, recovering from depression when she first arrived, contributed 'The Mark on the Wall' to the first publication, *Two Stories* (1917). Other Hogarth Press works were T. S. Eliot's *The Waste Land* (1922) and Virginia Woolf's *Kew Gardens* (1919). The house, which was divided during their occupation, has been restored to its original appearance but is now offices.

Richard Burton boarded at Charles de la Fosse's school on **Little Green** for a short time in his youth. His last years were spent in translating *The Lusiads* (1880–4), *The Arabian Nights* (1885–8), and the *Pentamerone*, published posthumously. He was buried (1890) in the cemetery of St Mary Magdalen at Mortlake (1½ m. NE) in a large tomb resembling an Arab tent (restored 1975). Many of his papers were burnt by his wife, but some books can be seen at the Richmond Local Studies Library, and artefacts can be seen at the Orleans House Gallery in Twickenham.

Marian Evans and G. H. Lewes lived at 7 **Clarence Row**, East Sheen (probably the site once occupied by The Bull inn, now shops and offices), during the summer of 1855, and after a short holiday settled (1855–9) at 8 **Parkshot** (site now The Courthouse) where Marian first used the pseudonym George Eliot when writing *Amos Barton* (1857), the first part of *Scenes of Clerical Life*. The house was ivy-clad and secluded though near the railway. A long, narrow, walled garden was at the back. She started *Adam Bede* (1859) here.

John Gay, who from 1720 became part of the Duke and Duchess of Queensberry's household, often lived with them at Douglas House, off **Petersham Rd**, Petersham, to the S.

Dickens was on holiday here in 1836. His address, Mrs Denman's, was probably the Dysart Arms, whose proprietor had that name. He returned in 1839 to rent Elm Cottage (later Elm Lodge) in Petersham Rd, where he was visited by the artist Maclise, and John Forster, whose biography of Dickens comments on his prowess at athletic games performed in the extensive grounds, and his frequent swims from the cottage to Richmond Bridge. Both *Pickwick Papers* and *Oliver Twist*, which he was writing on these visits, have scenes in the vicinity.

Daisy Ashford, author of *The Young Visiters* (1919), was born at Elm Lodge, 230 Petersham Rd. Her family moved to nearby Park Gate, 137 Petersham Rd, the following year and it was here that Daisy, aged 4, dictated her first story, *The Life of Father McSwiney*, to her father and mother. She also dictated *Mr. Chapmer's Bride* (which did not survive to be published) and *A Short Story of Love and Marriage* in this house. In 1889 the Ashford family moved to *Lewes.

From 1838 Dickens frequently stayed at the old Star and Garter Hotel on **Richmond Hill**, to celebrate his birthday, a new novel, or, as in

1844, the birth of his third son. In 1850 Tennyson and Thackeray were his guests there when *David Copperfield* was published. The Misses Berry, in their youth friends of Horace Walpole, spent the summer months at Devonshire Lodge after 1820. They invited Dickens to dine and when he declined, they called upon Sydney Smith to add weight to their invitation. Dickens had just finished *Nicholas Nickleby* and Sydney Smith wrote that the Misses Berry and their other guests would have 'not the smallest objection to be put into a Number, but on the contrary would be proud of the distinction; and Lady Charlotte, in particular, you may marry to Newman Noggs'.

The critic and novelist Rebecca West attended Richmond High School from 1900 to 1901. The short-story writer Sean O'Faolain lived on Queen's Rd, on the northern side of Richmond Hill, in the early 1930s.

Katharine Bradley (1848–1914) and her niece Edith Cooper (1862–1913) wrote poetry and plays under the pen-name 'Michael Field'. After publishing *Bellerophon* (1881) and *Callirrhoë* (1885) they came to Richmond in 1899 and lived at The Paragon.

Richmond Park is the remaining part of royal lands surrounding Henry VII's palace, which replaced the earlier palace at Sheen. James Thomson's favourite walks are commemorated by a board, at the entrance to Pembroke Lodge here, which has a verse by the historical writer John Heneage Jesse (1815–74). Jeanie Deans, in Scott's *The Heart of Midlothian* (1818), meets Queen Caroline here and obtains her sister's pardon.

During one of his visits to England in the 1820s, Marie-Henri Beyle (Stendhal) admired the trees in the park and in their shade read *Memoirs of the Life of Colonel Hutchinson*, which was to exercise a pervasive influence upon his 1839 novel *La Chartreuse de Parme*.

Harriet Beecher Stowe (1811–96), author of *Uncle Tom's Cabin*, paid a short visit to Byron's widow in 1859, and was invited to meet Lord John Russell (1st Earl Russell) at Pembroke Lodge. She thought the household 'so New England-like'.

Bertrand Russell spent his childhood at Pembroke Lodge, a grace-and-favour house in Richmond Park, under the stern attention of his grandmother, where days began with a cold bath and half an hour's piano practice before morning prayers. 'I lived', wrote Russell of his years here, 'wholly in the past. [Lady Russell] would call me by mistake by the names of people who were dead.'

Thomson was buried (1748) near the font in **Richmond parish church**, where a tablet was erected in 1792. Other tablets commemorate Norton Nicholls (d. 1809), with whom Gray stayed at Blundeston, and Mary Braddon (d. 1915), author of the popular *Lady Audley's Secret* (1862). She lived at Lichfield House (demolished in the 1930s and the site later occupied by a block of flats named Lichfield Ct), **Sheen Rd**, where most of her novels were written. She married the publisher John

Maxwell in 1874, but they had lived together for some years and had a child, which helped her critics dub her and her novels sensational. Many of her novels, including *The Conflict* (1903), have scenes set in the neighbourhood. She died at Lichfield House.

George Colman the Elder, manager of Covent Garden and the Haymarket, lived in **The Vineyard** (house gone). Soon after 1764, when he inherited money from the Earl of Bath, he built Bath House, a villa by the river, a short distance from Garrick at *Hampton, with whom he was collaborating on *The Clandestine Marriage* (1766). Bath (later Northumberland) House was demolished in 1968. It was in a bookshop in the town that the 11-year-old William Cobbett, on the way to find work in Kew Gardens, bought Swift's *Tale of a Tub* (1704) with his last threepence. Reading that work, he said, was 'the birth of intellect'.

ST JAMES'S, district between Piccadilly and St James's Park. Horace Walpole, who was born (1717) in **Arlington St.** (Ⓟ on no. 22 commemorates his father, Robert Walpole), wrote many of the vast collection of his *Letters* from a house (gone) opposite, which his father bought in 1742 and bequeathed to him at his death in 1745. Walpole stripped it of all but the essentials to furnish Strawberry Hill, *Twickenham, in 1766, but continued to use it as his town house until 1779, when he moved to Berkeley Sq.

Byron lodged (1813–14) at 4 **Bennet St.** In January 1813 he started to write *The Giaour*, published in June, and he also wrote here *The Bride of Abydos* and *The Corsair* before moving to Albany.

Steele lived (1707–12) in **Bury St.**, 'at the third door, right hand, turning out of Jermyn Street', with his second wife, 'dear Prue', while writing for *The Tatler* and *The Spectator*. He was troubled by debts and was indignant to find his wife upset after the landlady had approached her for payment. Swift lodged here on his visits to London in 1710, 1713, and 1726. Tom Moore often lodged here and after his marriage he and Bessy lived here for a short time (1811–12). The plaque at no. 28, where he also stayed when he visited from *Bromham, has been moved to George St. Crabbe lodged at no. 37 while arranging publication of *Tales of the Hall* (1819). Sinclair Lewis stayed at no. 10 for a short time in 1922 when writing *Babbitt*, and on his visits in 1924 and 1927.

Thomas Campbell lived (1832–40) on the top floor of the site of 10 **Duke St.**, above the headquarters of the Polish refugees from the 1831 revolution. Campbell's patriotic verses gave him the introduction to Niemcewicz, the poet and former aide-de-camp to their national hero Kościuszko, whom he met here.

In July 1966 William Burroughs moved into 8 Duke St. He wrote four books (including *The Wild Boys*, 1971) while living in London from 1966 to 1973.

Colm Tóibín's *The Master* (2004) weaves a novel around the life of Henry James, beginning with the disastrous première of

James's play *Guy Domville* at the St James's Theatre on **King Street** (the theatre closed in 1957), which ends his theatrical career. (While the opening is taking place, James himself needs to take his mind off the proceedings so goes to the Haymarket nearby to watch Oscar Wilde's *An Ideal Husband*.) George du Maurier's 1894 novel *Trilby*, about an Irish model and Svengali (the original Svengali figure), who hypnotizes her and makes her a great singer, was adapted for the stage and produced by Herbert Beerbohm Tree at the Haymarket in 1895, with Tree in the role of Svengali.

Pall Mall was a street associated with chocolate houses, taverns, and clubs. The Cocoa Tree, established in the 1690s as a chocolate house, was frequented by Steele, Swift, and his friend Rowe, who was made Poet Laureate in 1715, three years before he died. It became a private club in 1745 and Gibbon, who lodged at 'Mr Taylor's Grocers' at no. 29 during 1769, found the Cocoa Tree 'served now and then to take off an idle hour'. He also frequented White's and Boodle's, clubs which are still in being. Byron, who fell in love with his cousin Mary Chaworth, wrote 'The Duel' about the fatal quarrel at the Star and Garter tavern (gone) where his great-uncle killed her grandfather in 1769. The miniature-painters Richard and Maria Cosway held musical evenings at their home, Schomberg House, Pall Mall (the W wing survives at no. 80). André de Chénier, who had known them in Paris, frequented their salon while he was at the French Embassy (1787–90). Horace Walpole, who also attended the salon, wrote slightingly of Richard Cosway. Lockhart, who married Scott's elder daughter in 1820, lived for the next decade at no. 25, where he wrote several novels including *Adam Blair* (1822), and his adaptations of *Ancient Scottish Ballads* (1823). He was the first biographer of his father-in-law, who visited them here. Richard Monckton Milnes gave fashionable parties for literary and political figures at no. 26, where he lived from 1837. *Tribute*, which he inaugurated in 1836 as a Christmas annual, contained his friend Tennyson's verses which were later included in *Maud* (1855). Monckton Milnes published the *Life and Letters of Keats* (1848) using material from the poet's friend Charles Armitage Brown.

St James's Church, **Piccadilly**, with modern wrought-iron gates, was rebuilt to Wren's original plan after being burnt out in the Second World War. Charles Cotton (d. 1687), Thomas D'Urfey (d. 1723), Dr Arbuthnot (d. 1735), and Mark Akenside (d. 1770) are buried here. The white marble font and the Grinling Gibbons altarpiece were saved after the bombing.

On 14 March 1861 Tolstoy heard Dickens reading *A Christmas Carol* at St James's Hall, Piccadilly. Tolstoy's enthusiasm for Dickens survived undiminished into old age. The subject of Anne Stevenson's poem 'Cashpoint Charlie' crouches by the ATM at the HSBC bank on Piccadilly and regards the shoes and trousers as they pass.

In J. G. Ballard's prescient science-fiction novel *The Drowned World* (1962), the solidly built **Ritz Hotel** stands isolated in the tropical lagoon that has inundated the city and which accommodates the scientist Kerans in its 'huge high-ceilinged state-rooms'.

During the Second World War, Graham Greene worked at **Ryder St.** in the Iberian Department of MI6 under Kim Philby. He learned from Philby how the sewerage system in Vienna was used by an underground socialist movement and used the information when he came to write *The Third Man* (1950). He wrote a sympathetic introduction to Philby's memoir *My Secret War* and parodied the activities of the service in his novel *Our Man in Havana* (1958). He drew on Philby's experiences again when he wrote *The Human Factor* (1978) and made use of his time as a local resident—his flat at 5 St James's St. was the basis for Captain Daintry's 'very discreet' home in that book. Castle, its central character, shops locally: 'he bought the Yardley's at the chemist in St James's Arcade, the Earl Grey at Jackson's, a Double Gloucester there too to save time, although he usually went to the cheese shop in Jermyn Street'.

St James's Palace in **The Mall** was built by Henry VIII. Thomas Coryate, who came to London after his father's death in 1607, became part of Prince Henry's household here, perhaps as a court buffoon. It is thought that the distinguished foreigners he met at court first gave him the ambition to travel. Dr John Arbuthnot, physician (1709–14) to Queen Anne, was a member with Pope, Gay, Swift, Congreve, and Atterbury of the Scriblerus Club (formed *c.* 1713) which met in his rooms here.

Edwin Morgan placed the first, dreamlike, part of his poem 'London' in **St James's Park**.

Addison had lodgings in **St James's Pl.** in 1710 when he was contributing to his friend Steele's *Tatler*. William Whitehead, Poet Laureate and dramatist who became Garrick's reader of plays, lived (1768–72) at no. 3. In 1769 Gibbon, who was slowly preparing his long *History of the Decline and Fall of the Roman Empire*, had 'an indifferent lodging' at Miss Lake's at no. 2. The widowed Mrs Delany lived in this street from 1770 until her move to Windsor *c.* 1785. She mentions in her *Autobiography and Letters* (1861–2) that her friends Mrs Carter and Mrs Chapone called her house The Dove and Olive Branch from the painted window there which she had brought from Ireland. Samuel Rogers, who inherited his banker father's fortune, moved to no. 22, which backed on St James's Park, in 1803 and instituted here the famous breakfasts to which the majority of the literary figures for the next 50 years were invited. His *The Pleasures of Memory* (1792) and his verse tales were popular and he was offered the Laureateship in 1850 but declined. *Recollections of the Table Talk of Samuel Rogers* (1856), edited by Dyce, and his own *Recollections* (1859) were both published after his death in 1855.

The publisher John Macrone had his office at 3 **St James's Sq.** He met Dickens at

Ainsworth's house in *Kensal Green after having published Ainsworth's first novel, *Rookwood* (1834), which became immediately popular, and he later published Dickens's sketches in book form, *Sketches by Boz* (1836–7). Thackeray sketched Dickens, Maclise, Mahony, and himself in Macrone's office in 1837.

The **London Library** at 14 St James's Sq. is the world's largest independent library and one of London's great literary institutions. Founded in 1841 by Thomas Carlyle, who was dissatisfied with the reading arrangements at the British Library, it had Thackeray as its first auditor and founder members in George Eliot and Dickens. Past presidents and vice-presidents of the Library include Tennyson, Kipling, T. S. Eliot, Rebecca West, and Isaiah Berlin. At the time of writing its President is Tom Stoppard. Membership is open to all, for a fee.

The Library is affectionately described in Maureen Duffy's *Londoners* (1983):

> The notice on the door about members makes it the only club I belong to, and each time I push through the swing doors I get this faint frisson of exclusivity. I hang up my plastic bag on the hat rack because bags must be deposited: even paid-up scholars pilfer.

In A. S. Byatt's *Possession* (1990), it is in the London Library that Roland Michell does his literary detective work:

> The London Library was Roland's favourite place. It was shabby but civilised, alive with history but inhabited also by living poets and thinkers who could be found squatting on the slotted metal floors of the stacks, or arguing pleasantly at the turning of the stair.

Byatt also features the Library in her short story 'On the Day that E. M. Forster Died', about Mrs Smith settling in to embark on the writing of a long novel. And the Library appears in a more sinister context in Ian McEwan's *Enduring Love* (1997), for it is here, in the Reading Room, that Joe sees his stalker, just a momentary glimpse of his shoe, a white trainer with red laces . . .

Martin Clay, the young art historian of Michael Frayn's novel *Headlong* (1999), pursues some of his research on Bruegel in the Library, his back turned against 'the real spring in St James's Square'.

Many of the taverns and chocolate houses in **St James's St.** eventually became private clubs. Steele (knighted in 1714) lodged (1714–16) next to White's Chocolate House, where in 1709 he had written many numbers of the thrice-weekly *Tatler*, which set out to record acts of 'Gallantry, Pleasure and Entertainment' in the house. Steele wrote the weekly *Town Talk* (1715–16) here but his authorship was sometimes disputed. Letitia Pilkington, abandoned by her husband and with no income, managed to set up a bookshop in this street. Swift, who had helped her husband before their separation, became severely critical of them both and she retaliated in her *Memoirs* (1748), which Colley Cibber arranged to get

published. Steele and Swift patronized the Thatched House tavern (gone), on the W of the street, which was popular into the 19th c., when Scott attended meetings there of the Literary Club, founded by Dr Johnson. After the death (1768) of Dr Delany, who had introduced the Pilkingtons to Swift, Mrs Delany took lodgings (1769) in Thatched House Ct (gone).

Gibbon, who was in poor health, stayed at the house of his friend Elmsley (site of no. 74) during the Christmas and New Year of 1793–4. The surgeons recommended an operation and he was thought, at first, to be recovering but he died after two more operations. The first cantos of *Childe Harold* were published in March 1812, when Byron was lodging at no. 8 (rebuilt and later Byron House), near his friend Hobhouse. He said later, 'I awoke one morning, and found myself famous.' Thackeray lived at no. 88 when he assumed the character of Fitz-Boodle to contribute *The Luck of Barry Lyndon* (1844) to *Fraser's Magazine*.

ST JOHN'S WOOD, district NW of Regent's Park. Katherine Mansfield and John Middleton Murry rented a house at 5 **Acacia Rd** in July 1915, partly to be near D. H. Lawrence, who had just arranged to live in *Hampstead and with whom they were planning to launch a magazine called *The Signature*. The house had a gracious atmosphere that suited Katherine, and a garden with a lovely pear tree, and Lawrence and Frieda both liked it. Katherine's brother 'Chummie', to whom she was deeply attached, had just finished his military training and was a frequent visitor. It was from here that he left for the front in September. A few days later the news came that he had been killed and Katherine felt that she could not go on living in the house. She and Murry gave it up and went to the South of France in November.

Thomas Hood lived (1841–5) at 17 **Elm Tree Rd** (rebuilt), where he edited (1841–3) the *New Monthly* and his own *Hood's Magazine* (1843–4). The poem *The Song of the Shirt*, a powerful description of the sweated labour of seamstresses, was published in *Punch* in 1843. Hood's health gave way under the constant worry over money and he died soon after the efforts of his friends to get him a pension were successful. He had just moved to Devonshire Lodge, 28 **Finchley Rd** ℗.

Louis Golding lived at 16 **Hamilton Ter.** and died there in 1958.

Stephen Spender settled at 15 **Loudoun Rd** in 1945, living there until his death in 1995.

Dorothy Richardson lived (1916–38) in a top-floor room at 32 **Queen's Ter.** (rebuilt). When writing *Honeycomb* (1917), the third of her autobiographical novels, collectively called *Pilgrimage*, she married the painter Alan Odle, a fellow lodger, who a medical board said was dying of tuberculosis. Her Impressionist novels, to which the critics first applied the term 'stream of consciousness', were written partly here and partly in cottages in Cornwall.

In Howard Jacobson's *The Making of Henry* (2004), Henry Nagel suddenly inherits a luxury flat in a mansion block behind St John's Wood

Church, opposite **St John's Wood Church Gdns**.

> Prior to NW8, Henry had lived postcodeless and with the semi-permanent headache of the never quite settled anywhere, with one dry foot on the cobblestones of the town and one wet one in the drains and delfs of a moor so dour it was a miracle a single flower could find the will to bloom there, and few did.

But now, he thinks, his life will never be the same again.

ST PANCRAS, district to the W of Islington. Mary Wollstonecraft Godwin, author of *A Vindication of the Rights of Women* (1792), was buried (1797) in the churchyard of **Old St Pancras Church**, in **Pancras Rd**. Her daughter Mary used to come and sit by her grave to read and dream, and it was here, in June 1814, that she and Shelley first acknowledged their love. In a letter to his friend Hogg, Shelley wrote:

> 'The sublime and rapturous moment when she confessed herself mine, who had so long been hers in secret, cannot be painted to mortal imaginations.'

Long afterwards Mary expressed the wish to be buried next to her parents under the gravestone that had witnessed 'the momentous pledge of undying love between herself and her own Shelley'. Her father, William Godwin, author of *Enquiry Concerning Political Justice* (1793) and *The Adventures of Caleb Williams* (1794), was buried in the same grave in 1836, but both bodies were removed in 1851 to *Bournemouth. The churchyard and the adjoining burial ground of St Giles-in-the-Fields were made into a public garden in 1877 and a stone pedestal to the NE of the church records the names of the Godwins.

A statue of John Betjeman in **St Pancras station** recognizes his role in saving the building from demolition.

The **British Library** is the UK's national library; as a copyright library it receives a copy of every publication produced in the UK and Ireland. Faced with pressures of space at the British Museum (*Bloomsbury), in 1998 the Library moved to a new, purpose-built home on Euston Rd, between St Pancras and Euston stations. Designed by Colin St John Wilson, the building houses the Library's collections of early and modern books and manuscripts (a total of 150 million items, on 388 m. of shelves), with a number of reading rooms and a public exhibition (the Sir John Ritblat Gallery) showcasing some of the treasures of the collection including: the Anglo-Saxon Chronicle, Magna Carta, the Lindisfarne Gospels (from the Cotton collection), an early manuscript copy of Chaucer's *Canterbury Tales*, a Shakespeare First Folio and a page from the play *Sir Thomas More* believed to be in Shakespeare's hand (from the Harley collection), Charlotte Brontë's manuscript copy of *Jane Eyre*, and Lewis Carroll's manuscript of *Alice in Wonderland*, all the way through to manuscript lyrics by the Beatles.

J. K. Rowling began to write her phenomenally successful Harry Potter series while on a train between Manchester and **King's Cross station**; the London station was commemorated in the books as the place where students board the Hogwarts Express, the train to take them to the Hogwarts School of Witchcraft and Wizardry. The train leaves from Platform 9¾ (reached by hurtling with your luggage trolley at a bit of wall between platforms 9 and 10); the spot is marked in the real King's Cross station with a sign beside platform 9, and a trolley half-submerged in the brickwork. The series ends here, too.

SHADWELL, district in the East End. Colley Cibber was buried in the family vault at the Danish Church, **Wellclose Sq.**, built by order of the King of Denmark for Danes in the Port of London. Cibber's father, the sculptor Caius Cibber, who had worked on the church, was also buried there. The building was demolished in 1870 and St Paul's Whitechapel School is now on the site. Dickens visited Shadwell to see the emigrant Mormons in their ship the *Amazon*. His essay 'Bound for the Great Salt Lake' describes them and life along the waterfront.

The crime writer P. D. James took a break from fiction-writing to investigate the 1811 'Ratcliffe Highway Murders' in her book *The Maul and the Pear-Tree* (1971, co-written with T. A. Critchley). Peter Ackroyd's novel *Dan Leno and the Limehouse Golem* (1994) also draws on the Ratcliffe murders.

SHEPHERD'S BUSH, district to the W. In the mid-1930s Christopher Isherwood worked as a screenwriter for the Gaumont-British Studios at Lime Grove (subsequently converted for television use by the BBC). The scripts he wrote were unremarkable and Isherwood had a low opinion of the work, but the experience furnished him with material for his satirical novel *Prater Violet* (1945), in which the Gaumont studios are thinly disguised as 'Imperial Bulldog', where

> beneath a firmament of girders and catwalks, out of which the cowled lamps shine coldly down, like planets, stands the inconsequent, half-dismantled architecture of the sets; archways, sections of houses, wood and canvas hills, huge photographic backdrops, the frontages of streets; a kind of Pompeii, but more desolate, more uncanny, because this is, literally, a half-world, a limbo of mirror-images, a town which has lost its third dimension.

SHOREDITCH, district in the East End. In 1576 James Burbage, one of Lord Leicester's players, leased a site (now 86–8 **Curtain Rd**, Ⓟ) for the first building to be used specifically for play acting. It was called the Theatre (opened 1577) and was next door to the Priory of St John the Baptist, Holywell. Burbage lived with his sons in Holywell Lane nearby. Shakespeare, a friend of the Burbages, acted at the Theatre and the Curtain and lodged near Norton Folgate, S of Shoreditch High St. Theatres were closed in 1592 because of the

Brick Lane, the setting for Monica Ali's 2003 novel

plague and he is thought to have written *Venus and Adonis* and *The Rape of Lucrece* at this time. In 1594 he joined the Lord Chamberlain's Company as actor and playwright with Burbage as manager. After Burbage's death in 1597, his son Richard dismantled the Theatre and rebuilt it in *Southwark with Shakespeare as one of eight partners, or 'sharers', in the company.

Brick Lane. In Monica Ali's *Brick Lane* (2003), Nanzeen, recently arrived in London from Bangladesh for an arranged marriage, finds herself isolated and lonely in Tower Hamlets, living in a tower block and shopping on the Bethnal Green Rd . . .

In Peter Ackroyd's novel *Hawksmoor* (1985), the architect Nicholas Dyer is a 17th-c. East-Ender:

> I was born in Black-Eagle-Street in the parish of Stepney, close by Monmouth Street and adjoining Brick Lane, in a wooden house which was tottering to the last degree and would have been pull'd down but for the vast Quantity of wooden dwellings on either side . . .

He has been commissioned to build seven churches for the cities of London and Westminster, but he hides a secret in each— and now, three centuries later, a series of inexplicable murders is taking place on their sites. The book is inspired by Iain Sinclair's *Lud Heat* (1975), an alternative exploration of the mythical patterning behind the building of eight Hawksmoor churches. An attic room above a synagogue in 19 **Princelet St.**, just off Brick Lane (now a museum dedicated to immigration to London), was the home of the reclusive David Rodinsky, whose story the artist Rachel Lichtenstein began to explore while looking into her own family's history; she and Iain Sinclair collaborated on a book, *Rodinsky's Room* (1999).

White Chappell, Scarlet Tracings (1997) is Sinclair's investigation of the area's

'psychogeography'; his first novel, it is a fictional inquiry into Jack the Ripper.

St Leonard's, the parish church, whose steeple and columned portico remain from the 18th-c. rebuilding, was restored after bomb damage and the churchyard became a garden. James and Richard Burbage, William Sly (another of Shakespeare's actors and a man who appears as himself at the beginning of Marston's *The Malcontent*), the Elizabethan clown Richard Tarleton, and George Lillo, playwright and friend of Fielding, are buried here.

Also buried in St Leonard's is the actor Gabriel Spencer, whom, on 22 September 1598, Ben Jonson killed in a duel at Hoxton Fields, now **Hoxton Sq.** Jonson, when brought before the Old Bailey, pleaded guilty but claimed benefit of clergy. He escaped the gallows, but his property was confiscated and his thumb branded.

Old Nichol St., off Shoreditch High St., was the setting for Arthur Morrison's novel *A Child of the Jago* (1896). He came to stay with Arthur Osborne Jay, vicar of Holy Trinity parish (which included Old Nichol St.), who had been impressed with the realism of his *Tales of Mean Streets* (1894). In this area, with the highest incidence of crime and infant mortality, Morrison found the setting for which he had been searching. *A Child of the Jago* was 'the story of a boy who, but for his environment, would have been a good citizen'. Jay's work led to the building of a church, a social club, and a gymnasium, and eventually to large slum clearance. When the new housing estate was opened (1900), the publicity given by Jay's writings and *A Child of the Jago* led to the ceremony being performed by the Prince of Wales.

At the 'Church of St Andrew Upchance', a fictional Inigo Jones building created by Alan Bennett 'on the borders of Shoreditch and the City', the funeral takes place of Clive Dunlop; and it is a funeral that goes astray somewhat.

The story is Bennett's *The Laying On of Hands* (2001). After the service some of the mourners go on to a café at nearby *Smithfield where they serve excellent tripe.

SILVERTOWN, dockland district to the E. Lorimer Black, the main character in William Boyd's novel *Armadillo* (1998), buys a flat in Silvertown and records the alterations made to the Docklands:

> Everything old was going here, or being transformed, cast out by the new. It seemed a different, pioneering city out here in the east, with its emptiness and flatness, its chill refulgent space, its great unused docks and basins—even the air felt different, colder, uncompromising, tear-inducing . . .

SMITHFIELD, district in the N of the City. This large open space ('smooth field'), just outside the medieval walls, was used for tournaments, pageants, cattle markets, and fairs from the 12th c. Stow describes the main way there, Giltspur St., getting its name from the knights passing by. It was also used as a place of execution. William Wallace (d. 1305) and Wat Tyler (d. 1381) were killed here. Rahere, a prebendary of St Paul's and a counsellor of Henry I, founded (1123) the Augustinian priory dedicated to St Bartholomew, and became its first prior. The Priory's hospital was refounded by Henry VIII after the Dissolution and has become the teaching hospital familiarly called 'Barts' today. A plaque (erected 1956) on the wall commemorates William Wallace and the Protestant martyrs. Robert Bridges became a medical student in 1869 and held appointments there after qualifying but retired because of ill health in 1881. During this time he published three volumes of *Poems*.

Smithfield was also the site of the **Cloth Fair**, instituted by Rahere, the largest fair for clothiers and drapers in the country. It attracted entertainers, and Ben Jonson in his play *Bartholomew Fayre* (1614) depicts these and the bawds, cutpurses, and tricksters, who preyed on the stallholders and their customers. Evelyn and Pepys were visitors and Pepys writes in his *Diary* of the reintroduction of the old custom of wrestling. He also saw Jonson's play 'with puppets'. Elkanah Settle, whose changes of allegiance left him with little support after the revolution, wrote farces and other short pieces for the Fair. In 1707 his play *The Siege of Troy* was staged at the booth of Mrs Mynn, a show-woman. The Fair, which continued as an entertainment until 1855, appealed to rich and poor, as George Stevens's lines in *Songs* (1772) state: 'While gentle folks strut in their silver and satins | We poor folk are tramping in straw hat and pattens.'

Lamb took William and Dorothy Wordsworth after their return from France in 1802 and in *The Prelude* (1850) Wordsworth remembers the 'chattering monkeys', 'the hurdy gurdy', and the 'children whirling in their roundabouts' at 'The Fair | Holden where martyrs suffered in past time.'

John Betjeman kept a flat at 43 Cloth Fair, situated above a wine bar that now bears his name. He praised the hospital and the churches of St Bartholomew:

> Eight hundred years of compassion and care
> Have hallowed its fountain, stones and Square.
> Pray for us all as we near the gate—
> St Bart the Less and St Bart the Great.

The Lady Chapel of the priory church of **St Bartholomew-the-Great** (Rahere's choir still stands) was used in the 18th c. by a printing works and Benjamin Franklin, who had set up his own press in Philadelphia, worked there for a time after he came to England in 1757.

A brass in the church of **St Bartholomew-the-Less** shows John Shirley (d. 1456) and his wife in the habit of pilgrims. They were buried in the church. Shirley, said to have travelled in many countries, translated from Latin and French and transcribed the works of Chaucer, Lydgate, and others. It is on his authority that some poems are said to be Chaucer's. Thomas Watson, author of *The Tears of Fancie* (1593), sonnets inspired by Ronsard, and by Petrarch, whose equal some consider him, was buried here in 1592. He also wrote Latin versions of Tasso's *Aminta*, which were translated into English without his knowledge. He is Spenser's 'Amyntas' in *Colin Clouts come home againe* (1595). John Lyly, author of *Euphues* (1578) and other works, was buried here in 1606.

SOHO, district between the E end of Oxford St. and Leicester Sq. A plaque on Dickins and Jones's store commemorates Mme de Staël, who lived (1813–14) at 30 **Argyll St.** She was visited by Crabb Robinson, who was helping her with the publication of *De l'Allemagne* (1813), the book which provoked her exile by Napoleon. When Byron visited he met de Rocca, the young Swiss cavalry officer she had married secretly in 1811. Thomas Campbell also visited her here and wrote a sonnet to her.

In *Light on a Dark Horse* (1951), Roy Campbell writes of his escapades at 50 **Beak St.**, off Regent St., where he lived (1920–2) after his marriage at the age of 19. He began *The Flaming Terrapin* (1924) here and reviewed for the *Daily Herald* and the *New Statesman*.

William Blake was born (1757) at 28 Broad St. (now **Broadwick St.**). Most of the street has been rebuilt. An inscription on the wall on the left of steps leading to William Blake House, 8 Marshall St., states that the house is on the site of his birthplace.

The 'Circus', headquarters of the beleaguered British Secret Service in John le Carré's 'Smiley' novels, is housed in an 'Edwardian mausoleum' in **Cambridge Circus**, where George Smiley himself could be found 'stooped over a heap of papers at any hour of day or night in his scruffy throne room on the fifth floor'.

The satirical magazine *Private Eye* is based at 6 **Carlisle St.** Throughout the 1970s and

1980s the magazine published a famous diary column by Auberon Waugh.

In 1810 Crabb Robinson visited an exhibition of Blake's paintings and engravings in **Carnaby St.** This street was restyled in the 1960s as a pedestrian precinct and became a symbol of 'swinging London'.

Some of the characters of Doris Lessing's *The Sweetest Dream* (2001) shoplift regularly; in Geoffrey's case, Foyle's bookshop on the **Charing Cross Rd** is a particular favourite target: 'God bless Foyle's,' he says; 'I've liberated more there than anywhere else in London. A benefactor to humankind, is Foyle's.'

At the foot of Charing Cross Rd is the National Portrait Gallery, whose collection includes likenesses of every major British writer. The very first piece in the collection was the 'Chandos' portrait of Shakespeare.

William Collins lived (1744–9) in the old Kings Sq. Ct, site now part of **Dean St.**, with his mistress. Hester Chapone had lodgings in this street and in 1791 was at no. 17. Thackeray's Lamberts in *The Virginians* (1859) lived here and Dickens's Dr Manette in *A Tale of Two Cities* (1859) lived at no. 10.

Karl and Jenny Marx, after a brief stay at the German Hotel on Leicester St. (now Manzi's restaurant) moved into 64 Dean St. in 1850. They stayed for six months, moving on to 28 Dean St. (Ⓟ, dates incorrect), where the Marx family lived, often in siege-like circumstances, for some six years. A Prussian police spy who gained entry to the house gives an idea of Marx's rather chaotic domestic routine:

> He leads the existence of a real bohemian intellectual. Washing, grooming and changing his linen are things he does rarely, and he likes to get drunk. Though he is often idle for days on end, he will work day and night with tireless endurance when he has a great deal of work to do . . . He often stays up all night, and then lies down fully clothed on the sofa at midday and sleeps till evening, untroubled by the comings and goings of the whole world.

They lost three of their children—Henry, Franziska, and Edgar—while living here.

Elizabeth Inchbald, actress and dramatist, finished her first novel, *A Simple Story* (1791), in a second-floor room of a house in **Frith St.** The two main characters are based on herself and Kemble the actor. Maria Edgeworth was able to forget the author and believe 'in the real existence of all the people' in the novel. Hazlitt died (1830) at no. 6 Ⓟ and opposite was the site of the Commercio (gone), the restaurant where plans for *The Criterion*, a quarterly, were worked out. Richard Church, in his autobiography, mentions dining there in 1921 with T. S. Eliot the editor, Herbert Read, and Bonamy Dobrée, when Richard Aldington came in and said he had decided to leave England.

The crowded late-night café on Frith St. gave Hugo Williams the title of his poem 'Bar Italia'.

Dryden, after moving (1686) from Long Acre, lived at 43 **Gerrard St.** (rebuilt, Ⓟ). He had become a Catholic and was out of favour after

OXFORD STREET

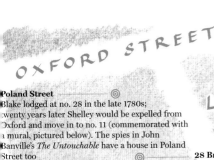

London bus

Poland Street
Blake lodged at no. 28 in the late 1780s; twenty years later Shelley would be expelled from Oxford and move in to no. 11 (commemorated with a mural, pictured below). The spies in John Banville's *The Untouchable* have a house in Poland Street too

61 Greek Street
In this house Thomas De Quincey met the prostitute who features in his *Confessions*

28 Broadwick Street
William Blake was born here (then called Broad Street). The site is now occupied by 8 Marshall Street

The Coach and Horses, Greek Street
Spiritual home to its most loyal patron, columnist Jeffrey Barnard, as well as many other local journalists—most famously the staff of *Private Eye*. Keith Waterhouse would set his play *Jeffrey Barnard Is Unwell* here

CHARING CROSS ROAD

SHAFTESBURY AVENUE

St Giles-in-the-Fields Church, St Giles High St
George Chapman, Andrew Marvell, and James Shirley are all buried here; Chapman's monument is designed by Inigo Jones

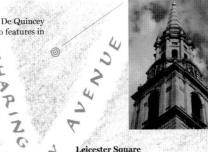

Leicester Square
The Square boasts statues of artists Hogarth and Reynolds (Reynolds lived here, where he was visited by Dr Johnson), as well as one of Shakespeare. Swift had lodgings on the Square too

LONG ACRE

Royal Opera House Covent Garden

St Anne's, Wardour Street
You can pay tribute to essayist William Hazlitt, who's buried here

Eros Piccadilly Circus

Royal Academy

PICCADILLY

REGENT ST

N

PALL MALL

STRAND

Nelson's Column Trafalgar Square

London Eye

RIVER THAMES

43 Gerrard Street
Poet John Dryden lived and died in a house on this site. In Timothy Mo's Chinatown novel *Sour Sweet*, Chen waits tables in a restaurant off Gerrard Street

The Turk's Head, Gerrard Street
The pub which once stood at no. 9 was a favourite meeting place for Dr Johnson and his cronies

National Portrait Gallery
The very first piece in the Gallery's collection was the famous Chandos portrait of Shakespeare; but you'll find pretty much every other significant writer of the last four centuries here too, from Ben Jonson to Zadie Smith

LONDON: Soho

the revolution, when he lost the Laureateship and a government post. His last years were devoted to translations of the classics and to *Fables Ancient & Modern* (1700), a collection of tales from Chaucer, Boccaccio, and Ovid, partly written while staying with friends in the country. He died here in 1700. Dr Johnson's Club, which included Burke, Joshua Reynolds, Goldsmith, Garrick, and Boswell among its members, met (1764–83) at the Turk's Head (gone) at no. 9. Burke lived later at no. 37 (Ⓟ, now a restaurant). Dickens, who, as a boy, visited his uncle in lodgings over Manson's bookshop, wrote about the characters he met there in *Sketches by Boz* (1836–7). His uncle's barber remembered the Napoleonic wars and Mrs Manson lent him books. At the beginning of the 20th c. the Mont Blanc restaurant was one of the meeting places for the Tuesday literary lunches when Edward Thomas, Galsworthy, Norman Douglas, Belloc, and W. H. Davies asembled from the country. Conrad first met Hudson here in 1902.

Now the heart of London's 'Chinatown', Gerrard St.'s Chinese kitchens are the setting for Timothy Mo's exploration of the city's Chinese immigrant community *Sour Sweet* (1982). Chen lives with his family up in Brent, but works in a restaurant kitchen just off Gerrard St., with

> its complex of travel agencies, supermarkets, fortune tellers, quack acupuncturists and Chinese cinema clubs, in a quiet lane whose only establishments were restaurants. At the end of the row was a passage with a double bend, so that what seemed to strangers like a blind alley was in reality a concealed entrance, constructed on the same principle as a crude lobster trap. A sharp right turn after passing an iron bollard took the knowledgeable or intrepid into a gloomy canyon formed by the blind backs of two forty-feet high Georgian terraces. Rubbish filled the alley. At nights rats scrabbled in the piles of rotting vegetable leaves and soggy cardboard boxes. There was a muffled silence in the enclosure. At the other end another series of baffles led, quite suddenly, into the brightness and sound of Leicester Square.

The Regent Palace Hotel on **Glasshouse St.** is the venue for John Betjeman's 'The Flight from Bootle':

> Lonely in the Regent Palace,
> Sipping her 'Banana Blush'
> Lilian lost sight of Alice
> In the honey-coloured rush.

The same hotel occupies the site on which a Neanderthal stops and leans upon his flint-tipped spear in Maureen Duffy's novel *Capital* (1975).

Nearly all the houses in **Golden Sq.** have been refaced. Swift dined at no. 21 with Lord Bolingbroke, to whom Pope dedicated his *Essay on Man* (1733). Lady Mary Wortley Montagu lived at no. 19 and John Reynolds lived at no. 27 in 1832. Smollett's Matthew Bramble lodges here and the hero of Thackeray's *Henry Esmond* visits General Webb here, a vain man who regards the

Churchills as upstarts. Dickens's Ralph Nickleby of *Nicholas Nickleby* also lives in the Square and Newman Noggs, who had 'once been a gentleman', lives nearby 'at the Crown in Silver St.' (gone).

The painter B. R. Haydon had a studio (1808–17) at 41 **Gt Marlborough St.** In his *Autobiography* (1853), published posthumously, he writes of Leigh Hunt, whom he visited in jail, and of Hazlitt, who invited him with Charles and Mary Lamb to the christening of his son. He invited Keats, whom he had met at Leigh Hunt's, to dine here with Cowden Clarke and John Reynolds. On his way home Keats composed the sonnet 'Great spirits now on earth are sojourning', meaning Wordsworth, Hunt, and Haydon. Haydon later took Keats to see the Elgin Marbles (which the nation bought through Haydon's persuasion). Keats, who admired his robust directness, enclosed the sonnet he wrote on them with one to Haydon himself. On another visit here he took a mask of Keats's face. Wordsworth, whom Haydon introduced to Keats, also wrote a sonnet to him and also came here to have a plaster cast made of his head. Haydon's paintings sold at first but later he quarrelled with his patrons (even Sir George Beaumont's mansion had no space for his very large canvases), fell into debt, and killed himself (1846). Another painter, James Northcote, lived for 40 years (1790–1831) in this street. Hazlitt, whose merit as a painter was recognized by Northcote, wrote *Conversations of James Northcote, Esq., R.A.* (1830, republished in 1894 with an essay by Edmund Gosse on Hazlitt as an art critic). Northcote illustrated his own *One Hundred Fables* (1828), and Sir Walter Scott sat for his portrait here in the same year. John Reynolds, Keats's friend, lived (1836–8) at no. 10.

On Gt Marlborough St. once stood the firm of Lane and Newby Ltd, Wholesale Costumiers and Mantle Manufacturers, the family firm of the travel writer Eric Newby. He describes his 10 years as a women's fashion buyer for his father in the 1940s and 1950s in his memoir *Something Wholesale: My Life and Times in the Rag Trade* (1962).

The first English performance of Samuel Beckett's *Waiting for Godot* took place at the Arts Theatre Club on **Gt Newport St.** in 1955.

In 1802 Thomas De Quincey was befriended at 61 **Greek St.** by Ann, the prostitute who saved him from destitution and who appears in *Confessions of an English Opium Eater* (1822). The House of St Barnabas, at no. 1, on the corner of Soho Sq., is often wrongly thought to be the birthplace of William Beckford. The first owner was Richard Beckford, a prosperous Alderman in the City, who died (1756) before his nephew William was born (1759). Douglas Jerrold, author of 'Mrs Caudle's Curtain Lectures' in *Punch* during 1845, was born in this street in 1803. He was the author of the plays *Black Ey'd Susan* (1829) and *The Bride of Ludgate* (1831), amusing and successful comedies, and he edited *Lloyds Weekly Newspaper* from 1852 until his death in 1857.

The interior of the Coach and Horses pub on Greek St., well known as a favourite local for the staff of *Private Eye* magazine and for *The Spectator*'s notoriously dipsomaniacal 'low life' columnist Jeffrey Bernard, was re-created on the stage of a number of London theatres (including the Apollo, the Old Vic, and the Garrick) in Keith Waterhouse's play *Jeffrey Bernard Is Unwell* (1989). Bernard himself lived and died in the small tower block on Berwick Street.

Clive James's fourth volume of memoirs, *North Face of Soho* (2006), sees him making his first forays into the journalist business, and being introduced to Grub St. watering holes by the editor Ian Hamilton:

> The work would have been easier if Hamilton had been less scrupulous. Right there in the Pillars, he would blue-pencil your copy while everybody else watched. Everybody else included his other reviewers and sometimes, hovering dangerously at the rim of the scrum, one or two of the poets whose slim collections I was presuming to hose on. . . . The final work of emendation done, I would go on drinking with Hamilton and the others, buying my round along with them but getting drunk much faster . . .

Arthur Rimbaud and Paul Verlaine came to London in 1872 (they were 18 and 28 respectively) and lodged at 35 **Howland St.** (now gone), off Tottenham Court Rd and later at 8 Gt College St., where a plaque records the fact. They felt lonely and homesick at first and were depressed by the dreariness of the English Sunday. However, they settled down to a regular life of reading and studying English, and Verlaine, who was so happy here that he wished this existence could continue for ever, finished his collection of poems *Romances sans paroles* (1874). They wandered from pub to pub, learning English of great variety, and they tramped throughout London (*Kew, *Pimlico, Whitechapel, and the *City) in order to get to know it thoroughly. Rimbaud left Verlaine in February 1873 to return to his home at Charleville. In the following year he returned to lodgings at 12 Argyll Sq. with his mother and sister Vitalie, who wrote a delightfully unsophisticated account of their stay.

Leicester Sq., formerly Leicester Fields, has statues to Shakespeare, Hogarth, and Joshua Reynolds in the central garden. Swift had lodgings in the Square in 1711. Thomas Holcroft, the son of a shoemaker, was born (1745) in Orange Ct (gone), Leicester Fields. Hannah More in 1774, and Crabbe in 1782, both met Dr Johnson at the house (Fanum House now on site, Ⓟ) in the centre of the W side, where his friend Sir Joshua Reynolds lived for many years. Mrs Inchbald, the actress known as the Muse, who earlier had lodgings in Leicester Ct (gone) returned to the E side opposite Reynolds's house in the late 1790s and stayed until 1803. Each of her many comedies including *Wives As They Were* (1797) and *Lovers' Vows* (1798) was written in a few weeks and their success enabled her to give up acting.

The premises of the *Literary Review*, founded in 1979 and edited for 14 years by Auberon Waugh, stand at 44 **Lexington St.** As the publicity for the magazine has declared, 'the reviewers are usually authors themselves, not just critics'.

From 1950 the novelist Paul Scott spent 10 years of his professional life at the literary agency that became David Higham Associates, 5–8 **Lower John St.**, near Golden Sq. Among the authors he represented were Muriel Spark and John Braine.

Quentin Crisp frequented the Black Cat on **Old Compton St.** in the 1950s: 'In that happier time all was squalor and a silence spangled only with the swish of knives and the tinkle of glass as the windows of the Black Cat got pushed in' (*The Naked Civil Servant*, 1968). Halliday & Son, the 'unusually respectable' second-hand bookshop in Graham Greene's *The Human Factor* (1978), trades on Old Compton St. opposite the more representative 'Books' which 'displayed girlie magazines which nobody was ever seen to buy—they were like a signal in an easy code long broken; they indicated the nature of private wares and interests inside'. The seedier aspects of literary Soho feature in the second part of Edwin Morgan's poem 'London'—'cacti and succulent flagellation havelock and after'—and in Dannie Abse's poems 'Odd' and 'After the Release of Ezra Pound':

> In Soho's square mile of unoriginal sin
> where the fraudulent neon lights haunt,
> but cannot hide, the dinginess of vice . . .

The Restaurant de la Tour Eiffel, formerly on 1 **Percy St.**, was a haunt of Wyndham Lewis and his fellow Vorticists. Lewis created a Vorticist room and, with Ezra Pound, organized a launch party for the iconoclastic magazine *Blast!* in 1914.

William Blake lodged (1785–90) at 28 **Poland St.** He engraved his own drawings to his *Songs of Innocence*, *The Book of Thel*, and *Tiriel* in 1789, and the next year produced his major work *The Marriage of Heaven and Hell*.

Shelley and his friend Hogg found lodgings at no. 11 in March 1811 after their expulsion from *Oxford. Shelley tried inexpertly to appease his father but the break between them proved final.

Victor Maskell, the narrator of John Banville's novel *The Untouchable* (1997), and his friends keep up a bohemian lifestyle at a flat on Poland St.

The pubs on **Rathbone Pl.**—the Black Horse, the Marquess of Granby, the Burglar's Rest, and the Duke of York—were all frequented by Julian Maclaren-Ross, but his regular was the Wheatsheaf (at no. 25), where, propped up nightly in the right-hand corner of the bar, attired in teddy bear coat and dark glasses, a carnation in his buttonhole, he stood throughout the 1940s and 1950s drinking and talking with literary men: Dylan Thomas, John Heath-Stubbs (who has written of the local pubs and their clientele in his memoir *Hindsights*, 1993), the poet-editors Alan Ross

and Prince J. Meary Tambimittu, the artist Gerald Wilde, and a variegated assortment of 'regulars, wits and bums' of the *demi-monde*. The Wheatsheaf provided a model for the 'Hero of Acre' in Anthony Powell's novel sequence *A Dance to the Music of Time* (1951–75), with its 'roving intelligentsia of the saloon bar . . . professional topers, itinerant bores, near criminals'. Maclaren-Ross himself, with his belted overcoat, silver-topped malacca cane, and gifts as a raconteur, was the inspiration for Powell's X. Trapnel, the eloquent, indigent, and egotistical author of *Camel Ride to the Tomb*.

A plaque in the Central Reference Library in **St Martin's St.** states that this was the site of Isaac Newton's house, which later became the home (1774–89) of Dr Burney. Here Fanny Burney wrote *Evelina* (1778), her most successful novel, and *Cecilia* (1782).

William Beckford, author of *Vathek* (1787), was born (1759) at 22 **Soho Sq.**, his father's town house. William Beckford senior, who was twice Lord Mayor and who possessed a colossal fortune, chose the best tutors for his son. Mozart, an 8-year-old prodigy, taught the 5-year-old boy musical exercises, and Alexander Cozens taught him painting and drawing. Cozens was the first to influence Beckford in oriental, Persian, and Arabic studies, which inspired *Vathek*. Beckford, who inherited his father's fortune at the age of 11, spent many years travelling abroad.

Fleur Adcock's poem 'The Soho Hospital for Women' preserves some of her experiences at the hospital at 30 Soho Sq.:

> Strange room, from this angle:
> white door open before me,
> strange bed, mechanical hum, white lights.
> There will be stranger rooms to come.

Hazlitt's gravestone can still be seen in the churchyard (now a garden) of St Anne's, **Wardour St.**, where he was buried (1830). Hester Lynch Salusbury married Henry Thrale here, against her will, in 1763.

SOUTHGATE, district to the N. Eagle Hall (demolished 1940s), in the **High St.**, was the birthplace (1784) of Leigh Hunt.

The novelist Paul Scott was born at 130 **Fox Lane**, Southgate, and educated at Winchmore Hill School. The district provided inspiration for his descriptions of suburban Delhi in his novel series *The Raj Quartet* (1966–75).

SOUTHWARK (pr. 'Sŭtherk), district S of London Bridge.

Old **London Bridge** (gone) was considered one of the great sights of the city. The travel writer Fynes Moryson described it in his *Itinerary* (1617) as 'worthily to be numbered among the miracles of the world' and Spenser praised it in *The Faerie Queene*. Shakespeare alludes to the heads of traitors impaled at each end of the bridge in *Richard III*; Ben Jonson to the suicides occasionally committed there when in *Epicoene* he makes True-Wit wonder that Morose is still alive when there is 'London Bridge at a low fall with a fine leap to hurry

you down the stream'. T. S. Eliot saw a correspondence between the crowds of working people who walked over the bridge and those consigned to Dante's hell:

> Unreal City,
> Under the brown fog of a winter dawn,
> A crowd flowed over London Bridge, so many,
> I had not thought death had undone so many.

Bankside was in Shakespeare's day an area of entertainment with theatres, amusement parks, and a bear garden. Philip Henslowe (d. 1616) managed the Rose Theatre ℗ here from 1592 to 1603. The foundations of the Rose were discovered, amid some controversy, partly excavated in 1989. An exhibition on Park St. interprets the remains (which are preserved under a concrete membrane) and provides a history of the theatre (www.rosetheatre.org.uk). Henslowe employed many dramatists, including Christopher Marlowe, George Chapman, John Webster, Thomas Dekker, Thomas Kyd, and Michael Drayton, and his *Diary* kept during 1592–1609 records their transactions. Shakespeare acted at the Rose. In 1599 the timbers from Burbage's theatre at *Shoreditch were reassembled here as the Globe by Burbage's son Richard, a friend of and fellow actor with Ben Jonson and Shakespeare. Richard Burbage and Shakespeare were one of a number (varying from eight to twelve) of 'sharers', or partners, in the Lord Chamberlain's Company. The foundations of the Globe, partly excavated in 1989, lie under Anchor Ter. on Southwark Bridge Rd. An interpretative panel produced by the Musuem of London stands on Park St. (below), which is also the best place to gain a sense of the theatre's original position. Many of Shakespeare's plays were acted at the Globe including *Hamlet*, *King Lear*, *Macbeth*, *Richard III*—one of Burbage's most popular roles—*As You Like It*, *A Midsummer Night's Dream*, and *Twelfth Night*. The first Globe, 'the wooden O' (the description may refer to the Curtain or Theatre in Shoreditch, but applies just as well to the Globe) with its thatched roof, was burnt down in 1613, when wadding from a prop cannon, fired during a performance of *Henry VIII*, set fire to the thatch. It was rebuilt with a tiled roof the next year.

Following in part in the steps of William Poel and others who had failed in the attempt, the American actor, director, and producer Sam Wanamaker led the campaign to build a reconstruction of the Globe, having founded what became the Shakespeare Globe Trust in 1970. After decades of research into the best design for the theatre (which made timely use of the excavations of the Rose and Globe sites) and the most appropriate materials with which to build it (largely green oak, lime plaster, and thatch), Shakespeare's Globe (www.shakespeares-globe.org) opened its doors in 1997, some 200 yds from the site of the original. Excellent tours of the theatre run daily and a comprehensive exhibition tells the story of the theatre's painstaking reconstruction and gives a vivid account of theatrical life in

William Shakespeare and London

Unlike such contemporaries as Thomas Dekker, Ben Jonson, or Thomas Middleton, all of whom were native Londoners, Shakespeare did not set his comedies in the London of his time. The closest equivalents are to be found in the ancient Ephesus of *The Comedy of Errors*, with its harbour, marketplace, merchants, and courtesan; in the plague-ridden Vienna of *Measure for Measure*, with its taverns, suburban whorehouses, and teeming prison; in the busy seaport of Mytilene in *Pericles*, with its bawds and their seafaring clientele; or in the entrepôt of *The Merchant of Venice*, where 'the trade and profit of the city | Consisteth of all nations'.

Shakespeare was fascinated, rather, by historical London, whose great monuments, still standing in his time, had been the scene of the events enacted in his history plays, which mention or depict murders at the Tower of London, a coronation at Westminster Abbey, a queen's sanctuary in the precincts of the Abbey, and a king's death in the Abbey's chapter-house. They portray public events in the Parliament at Westminster Hall and at the Guildhall, seat of London's municipal government. *Henry VI Part 1* famously places the origin of the Wars of the Roses in the Temple gardens.

He also sets historic scenes in the great London palaces of noblemen—in the garden of the Duke of York in *Henry VI Part 2*, whose palace became Whitehall when Henry VIII seized it from the fallen Cardinal Wolsey in *Henry VIII*, and in the lairs of Richard, Duke of Gloucester, at Baynard's Castle and Crosby House. When the same Richard visited the palace of the Bishop of Ely in Holborn, he noticed good strawberries in the garden.

London's streets were for Shakespeare the scene of happy tumult and dangerous rebellion. Windows crowded with onlookers and 'walls | With painted imagery' greet the coronation procession of Henry IV in *Richard II*. More dangerous is the rebellion of Jack Cade in *Henry VI Part 2*, which Shakespeare follows from its beginnings at Blackheath and Southwark, across London Bridge to Canwick St. and London Stone, to Smithfield, where Cade gives orders to burn the Inns of Court and the Savoy, the palace of John of Gaunt (partly in ruins in Shakespeare's time). In *Henry IV Parts 1 and 2*, Shakespeare immortalized Eastcheap, the site of medieval London's flesh market and home to the Boar's Head tavern, the haunt of Sir John Falstaff and his companions. Memories of Falstaff's youthful escapades with Robert Shallow, who studied law at Clement's Inn, show Shakespeare's familiarity with the disreputable Turnbull St. in Clerkenwell and with the brothel district of St George's Field between Lambeth and Southwark. Falstaff, who bought his horse in Smithfield and hired his manservant Bardolph in Paul's Walk (an aisle in St Paul's Cathedral), attended

WILLIAM SHAKESPEARE BY MARTIN DROESHOUT, FROM THE FRONTISPIECE TO THE FIRST FOLIO OF SHAKESPEARE'S PLAYS, 1623

tournaments at the Tilt-Yard in Westminster and marched in 'Arthur's show', an archery muster, at Mile-End Green, where military assemblies still took place in Shakespeare's time.

The prosperous citizens of London in Shakespeare's plays are by nature conservative. He described them in *Henry IV Part 1* as 'velvet-guards and Sunday citizens' who never stray further than Finsbury on their holidays. The trading classes of London are not prominent on Shakespeare's stage, but his offstage world is populated with unseen characters like 'Master Three-Pile, the Mercer' in *Measure for Measure*, or, from *Henry IV Part 2*, 'Samson Stockfish, the fruiterer' and 'Master Smooth, the silk man', who resided at the sign of the Leopard in Lombard Street. The narrower dimensions of the city's parish life and its officials are probably reflected in the parish constabulary of Dogberry in *Much Ado About Nothing* or in the inept constable Elbow in *Measure for Measure*.

At the opposite end of the social order, *King Lear* shows that Shakespeare was familiar with Bedlam beggars, *Henry V* that he knew St Mary Spital, the East London pesthouse for

London's poorest classes. References in *The Merry Wives of Windsor* and *Henry VIII* show that he knew the debtors' prisons in the Poultry and Bread St. and the Marshalsea in Southwark. He had witnessed spectacles of public punishment, including the marching of prisoners 'two and two, Newgate fashion' mentioned in *Henry IV Part 1*, and the impaling of traitors' heads on the gatehouse of London Bridge in *Richard III*. A reference in *Love's Labour's Lost* shows that he had seen the public gallows at Tyburn, a triangle of horizontal beams mounted on posts.

Of the London theatrical scene there are many allusions, such as the 1599 mention of the 'wooden O', the newly built Globe, in *Henry V*. He returns frequently to the sport of bear-baiting, the din and smell of which must have been sensible to anyone passing through Bankside, and in *The Merry Wives of Windsor* he mentions the famous bear Sackerson, whose chain Master Slender claims to have pulled. His usual route to Bankside seems to have been over London Bridge, since he alludes more than once to the dangerous force of the tide rushing through its arches. But Viola's cry of 'Westward ho!' repeats the phrase with which passengers summoned river transport by boat.

In making his way through the city streets, Shakespeare learned to look with his ears, catching not just the many accents of London voices, but sounds like the midnight chimes of St Clement Danes and the clinking of tavern pewter he mentions in *Henry IV*, the clacking of the beggar's dish in *Measure for Measure*, and the noise of cannon-founding in *Hamlet*. Hotspur's revulsion at the sound of a 'brazen canstick' being turned may suggest Shakespeare's familiarity with the metal-founding trades of Lothbury, which got its name, John Stow alleged, from the 'loathsome noise' of candlesticks and chafing dishes being lathed 'smooth and bright with turning and scrating'.

Shakespeare also learned to smell his way through London. He alludes to 'th'uncleanly savors of a slaughter-house' in *King John* and to the 'melancholy' odour of Moorditch, a portion of the old city moat that served as a drainage ditch to Moorfields, the pleasure-ground just to the north. He may have known the 'reek of a lime-kiln' described in *The Merry Wives of Windsor* from the kilns of Limehouse, between Wapping and Poplar; he certainly enjoyed the sweet smell of 'Bucklersbury in simple time', when the grocers of that district stocked fresh herbs. As a migrant from the countryside who prospered and became famous in the city, Shakespeare understood every provincial Englishman's 'hope to see London once ere I die'.

LAWRENCE MANLEY

❖

Shakespeare's London. Productions of Shakespeare, usually employing clothing and music from the period, run from May to October and there is a range of lively events for all ages throughout the year. The Globe is also an important venue for new writing, and premièred Howard Brenton's *In Extremis* in 2006.

According to tax records, Shakespeare lived in Southwark, perhaps near the bear garden, as did Beaumont and Fletcher. Indeed, if John Aubrey is to be believed, 'They lived together on the Banke side, not far from the play-house, both bachelors; lay together; had one wench in the house between them, which they did so admire; the same cloathes and cloak, &c. between them.' Fletcher and Peele collaborated with Shakespeare and Massinger, and Beaumont with Fletcher, during this very productive time for playwriting. Jonson's *Bartholomew Fayre* (1614) was first acted at the Hope Theatre, which Henslowe opened (1613) as a bear garden where plays could be acted.

In *The House by the Thames* (2006), the historian Gillian Tindall explores the history of 49 Bankside, the house at Cardinal Cap Alley, where (unfortunately) Christopher Wren never lived, whatever the legend may claim.

Borough High St. was the main medieval route from London to Canterbury and the Continent. Southwark is commonly known as 'the Borough'. On the W side of the street just S of the Thames is **Southwark Cathedral**, or the Church of St Saviour and St Mary Overie (or Overy), one of the finest Gothic buildings in London, with many associations with the Elizabethan actors and playwrights on Bankside. In the N aisle is the tomb of John Gower (d. 1408), whose head in the effigy rests on his three main works, *Speculum Meditantis*, *Confessio Amantis*, and *Vox Clamantis*, the last of which gives an account of contemporary life including the Peasants' Revolt. Gower spent his last years in the precincts. Sir Edward Dyer, who had considerable fame as a poet at the end of the 16th c., was buried in the chancel on 11 May 1607. Shakespeare is commemorated by an alabaster effigy (1912) in the S aisle and by stained-glass windows (1954) showing characters from his plays. John Fletcher (d. 1625) and Philip Massinger (d. 1639) have inscriptions on flagstones in the choir. The tomb of Lancelot Andrewes (d. 1626), who as Bishop of Winchester lived in the 13th-c. Winchester Palace (site among the warehouses in Clink St.), is in the S ambulatory. He was one of the translators of the Authorized Version of the Bible.

Keats studied Medicine from 1814 to 1816 at Guy's Hospital on the E side of the street. An idea of the medical conditions he would have known is conveyed by the Old Operating Theatre and Herb Garret on St Thomas St. (www.thegarret.org.uk). At no. 77 the medieval George inn (NT), with a gallery round its courtyard, was rebuilt in 1677 after an extensive fire in Southwark and became a flourishing coaching inn in the 18th and 19th cc., and was mentioned by Dickens in *Little Dorrit* (1855–7).

Shakespeare's plays are occasionally acted in the courtyard in the summer.

The poet and essayist P. J. Kavanagh worked for a period at the post office on Borough High St., where he met Sally, the 'perfect stranger' in the memoir of that name.

Nearby, **White Hart Yard** marks the site of the 15th-c. White Hart inn, mentioned in the *Paston Letters* (written 1440–86), in Shakespeare's *2 Henry VI*, and in Dickens's *Pickwick Papers* (1836–7). The Old Tabard inn is on the corner of **Talbot Yard**, the alley where The Tabard inn (demolished 1629), known to Chaucer's pilgrims, was situated.

The Old Marshalsea, a prison (site near entrance to **Mermaid Ct**), held Ben Jonson, George Chapman, and John Marston when they were imprisoned after writing *Eastward Hoe* (1605), a comedy with a mistimed slight on the Scots. They were soon released through the influence of their powerful friends. George Wither was fined and imprisoned in 1614 for the sedition in *Abuses Stript and Whipt* (1613), and while here wrote *Shepherd's Hunting*, a collection of pastorals in which he sometimes calls himself Philarete. He may also have written the lyric 'Shall I wasting in despair' here as it was first printed in *Fidelia* in 1615, soon after his release. He was again imprisoned here after the publication of *Wither's Motto* (1621), a self-eulogy on 'nec habeo, nec careo, nec curo', in which some hidden satire was suspected. King's Bench prison stood until 1758 near the entrance to **Angel Pl.** Thomas Dekker, always poor, was confined here (1613–19) for debt and

Richard Baxter, interrogated by Judge Jeffreys, was fined and imprisoned (1685–6) for libelling the Church in *Paraphrase of the New Testament* (1685). The Marshalsea prison Ⓟ moved into new buildings near here in 1811 and Dickens, who visited his father during his imprisonment for debt, faithfully depicted 'the crowding ghosts of many miserable years' in scenes in *Little Dorrit* (1855–7).

Nahum Tate, Poet Laureate from 1692 and satirized in *The Dunciad*, was buried (1715) in the **Church of St George the Martyr**. Little Dorrit, christened in the church, was rescued from sleeping on the steps by a kindly verger, and was later married here. She is depicted in a poke bonnet, praying, in the modern stained-glass window in the E end.

Nearby, in Horsemonger Lane (gone), Leigh Hunt was imprisoned in the King's Bench prison for two years (1812–14) for libelling the Prince Regent. He was on friendly terms with the jailer, who allowed him to walk in the garden, and he wrote of his room:

> I papered the walls with a trellis of roses . . . the barred windows I screened with Venetian blinds; I had the ceiling covered with clouds and sky and when my bookcases were set up with their busts, and flowers and a pianoforte made their appearance, perhaps there was not a handsomer room on that side of the water.

He was visited by Byron, Keats, and Charles Lamb, who compared the room to one in a fairy tale. After 1758 the King's Bench prison was transferred to a site near **Scovell Rd**. Tobias Smollett was tried by the King's Bench in 1759 for defaming the character of Admiral Sir Charles Knowles, fined, and imprisoned for three months. He was visited by his friend Goldsmith, who had practised as a doctor in Southwark, by Garrick, and by the publisher John Newbery, for whom he had often worked and who now arranged for him to edit the *British Magazine*. Christopher Smart was confined here for debt from *c*. 1769 to his death in 1771. His decline took the form of praying aloud, which Dr Johnson had no difficulty in accepting, but insolvency was more generally unpalatable. Mrs Charlotte Smith lived in the prison for some months with her children while her husband was a debtor (*c*. 1784). William Combe, who wrote the verses for Rowlandson's satirical drawings about Dr Syntax, was imprisoned for debt here on a number of occasions. Benjamin Robert Haydon was imprisoned here for debt four times between 1822 and 1837, and John Galt on returning from an unsuccessful venture in Canada was here for debt in 1829. The prison closed *c*. 1860.

In September 1816 Keats took lodgings at 8 Dean St. (what remains of the road, now under the railway arch, is called **Stainer St.**) to be near Guy's Hospital, where he was studying. Charles Cowden Clarke, son of his schoolmaster at *Enfield, was now lodging at 6 Little Warren, Clerkenwell, and on a visit there in October, Keats first saw the folio edition of Chapman's translation of Homer. They spent the night reading and discussing this and at dawn Keats walked back to Dean St., where he immediately wrote down the sonnet beginning 'Much have I travell'd in the realms of gold'.

The bust on the Dickens School in **Lant St.** (running between Southwark Bridge Rd and Borough High St.) commemorates his stay in lodgings when his father was a debtor in the Marshalsea. Lant Street is home to an assortment of criminals including Sue Trinder, the heroine of Sarah Waters's novel of the underworld of Victorian London *Fingersmith* (2002).

A plaque at the E end of **Park St.** commemorates the Globe Theatre on Bankside, in which Shakespeare, who acted there, had a share. The brewery is a successor to that owned by Henry Thrale, who lived with his wife, Hester, after their marriage in 1763 to his death in 1782 at their town house in this street (formerly called Deadman's Place). Arthur Murphy, Hester Thrale's 'dear Mur', introduced them to Dr Johnson, who was soon given his own room, where he wrote part of the *Lives of the English Poets* (1779–81). When Henry Thrale stood successfully for Parliament, Johnson, who enjoyed electioneering, wrote his speeches. Mrs Thrale's diaries and notebooks, started here, were published as *Thraliana* (1942). The Anchor Bankside has the 'Thrale Bar', which has what is said to be her portrait.

Laurence Durrell's brief school career in England in the mid-1920s included two years at St Olave's and St Saviour's in Southwark.

The stretch of tube line between Embankment and Elephant and Castle stations on the Bakerloo line, on the morning of 11 January 1995, is the setting for Geoff Ryman's novel *253* (1996), which collects 253 stories (one for each seated passenger plus one for the driver), of 253 words apiece. They begin with driver Taksin Çelikbilekli, no. 1, who looks like Antonio Banderas but in a London Underground uniform, to no. 253, at the end of carriage no. 7, the famous diarist Anne Frank.

SPITALFIELDS, district on N edge of the City. John Huffam, the narrator of Charles Palliser's Victorian pastiche novel *The Quincunx* (1993), follows his associate Mr Digweed down into the sewers through 'an old brick culvert' on Dorset St.

STOKE NEWINGTON, district NE of Islington. Daniel Defoe was educated (*c*. 1670) at the Nonconformist Academy (gone) at **Newington Green**. He was followed (1690–4) by Isaac Watts, whose first hymn, 'Behold the glories of the Lamb', was written about the time he left the school. Defoe lived at Stoke Newington from 1709 to 1729. At first he lived in a house on the N side of **Stoke Newington Church St.** and later he built a house on the site of no. 95 Ⓟ. While living here he wrote *Robinson Crusoe* (1719) and *Moll Flanders* (1722), a novel written in the form of an autobiography of an adventuress. His tombstone, thought to have been removed from his grave in Bunhill Fields when a marble obelisk was erected there, is now in the entrance hall at Stoke Newington District Library.

Thomas Day, author of *The History of Sandford and Merton* (1783–9), lived in Stoke Newington Church St. before he settled in *Anningsley Park in 1781. The house was later divided into nos. 109 and 111, with shopfronts added.

Mary Wollstonecraft (later Godwin), her sister Eliza, and a friend, Fanny Blood, transferred their school from *Islington to Newington Green (site unknown), a few months after its opening in 1783. Mary Wollstonecraft's *Thoughts on the Education of Daughters* (1787) and *Original Stories from Real Life* (1788) arose from the practical experience of teaching here and, when the school failed to provide her with a living, as governess to Lord Kingsborough's children.

Samuel Rogers, poet and friend of Thomas Moore, was born and brought up here. He was a trustee of the Unitarian Church, where he is remembered in a memorial.

John Aikin, a Unitarian who lived here from 1798 to his death in 1822, was attracted to this former village because of its long-established Dissenting community. He wrote most of the volumes of his *General Biography* (1815) in a house (gone) in Stoke Newington Church St., helped in his later years by his daughter Lucy. His sister Anna Barbauld (her life was written by Lucy Aikin) lived at no. 113, opposite his house, from 1802. Her short tales, written for the children at her school in *Palgrave, proved popular. Charles Lamb, who wrote, 'Mrs. Barbauld's stuff has banished all the old classics of the nursery,' may have taken from her the idea that grew into his *Tales from Shakespear* (1807), published by the second Mrs Godwin (whose husband wrote as 'Baldwin'). Mrs Godwin, Mrs Inchbald, and Mrs Barbauld, were called 'the three bald women' by Lamb.

Edgar Allan Poe, who had come from America in 1815 to stay with cousins at *Irvine, was at Bransby's School on the N side of Church St. from 1817 to 1820. A plaque commemorating him is in the entrance hall of Stoke Newington District Library.

In the imaginary borough of 'Romley', located somewhere that is 'optimistically and falsely described by estate agents as "on the borders of Stoke Newington"', is the house of Frieda Haxby—the big old family house known as 'The Mausoleum'. As Margaret Drabble's *The Witch of Exmoor* (1996) opens, Frieda has decided to sell up and leave London, buying herself a falling-apart castle on Exmoor.

STRAND, district between Trafalgar Sq. and the City. George Orwell worked for the BBC at Bush House on **Aldwych** during the Second World War. The difficulty he experienced being allowed to broadcast what he wanted contributed to his conception of the Ministry of Truth in his novel *Nineteen Eighty-Four* (1949). The canteen at Bush House was an inspiration for the canteen in that book.

The **Aldwych Theatre**, once the London home of the Royal Shakespeare Company, was the location of premières of new work by playwrights including Harold Pinter (*The Homecoming* on 3 June 1965) and Tom Stoppard (*Travesties* on 10 June 1974).

Students at the London School of Economics on the N of Aldwych have included the novelists Hilary Mantel (studied Law) and Pat Barker.

Pepys lived (1679–88) at 12 **Buckingham St.** Ⓟ but the house has been altered since his day. In 1688 he moved to no. 14 (rebuilt), which then overlooked the river. He lived here until in 1700 failing health led him to stay with his former clerk and friend at *Clapham Common.

Coleridge stayed at no. 21 during 1799 and Dickens put David Copperfield in a 'set of chambers' at no. 15 with Mrs Crupp, the landlady.

Charing Cross station is on the site of Hungerford Stairs, which led up from the river to the Strand. In his autobiographical novel *David Copperfield* (1849–50), Dickens's own experiences as a boy in Warren's Blacking Factory here are retold by David and set in Blackfriars. Mr Micawber, whom David first met there, set off with his family for their new life in Australia from Hungerford Stairs. 'The last days of the emigrants were spent in a little, dirty, tumbledown public-house, which in those days was close to the stairs, and whose protruding wooden rooms hung over the river.'

Clement's Inn was formerly one of the Inns of Chancery. Hardy worked here for a few weeks in 1870 and wrote a wistful little poem, 'To a Tree in London (Clement's Inn)'.

Heinrich Heine, who visited England for three months in 1827, stayed at 32 **Craven St.** Ⓟ. Benjamin Franklin, who represented the Pennsylvania Assembly (1757–62 and 1764–72) as well as other states, lived at no. 36 Ⓟ. His *Autobiography*, partly written in French, was published in 1868.

Devereux Ct, a narrow street off the Strand, was the site of the Grecian Coffee House, patronized by Addison and Steele and mentioned in *The Spectator*. Harrison Ainsworth, who lodged at no. 6 on first arriving in London in 1824, noted that it was still in existence then.

Essex St. is on the site of the Earl of Leicester's great Tudor house, where Edmund Spenser was one of the household (1578–80) before he left for Ireland. He met Leicester's nephew Philip Sidney here and they formed the Areopagus Club with others. Spenser wrote the sonnets to Rosalind, published *The Shepheards Calender* (1579), and began *The Faerie Queene* here. After Leicester's death in 1588 the house became the home of the 2nd Earl of Essex, brother of Sidney's Stella. Essex, who married Sidney's widow in 1590, was a patron of literature and was praised by Daniel, Chapman, Spenser, and Jonson. On Spenser's return from Ireland (1596–7) he again stayed here and wrote *Prothalamion* (1596) and *View of the Present State of Ireland* (1596). The red-brick arch and steps at the lower end of the street is the old watergate to Essex House, where in *Prothalamion* 'the gentle knights' receive their 'fair brides'.

Essex House was the home (1712–31) of the Cottonian Library, now in the British Library. A plaque on the new Essex Hall, at the Strand end, commemorates Fielding, who lived in the street, and Dr Johnson, who planned a club to meet at the Essex Head (rebuilt). This tavern was kept by a former servant of the Thrales, and Johnson and his friends made rules to meet thrice weekly. Eight years after Johnson's death Boswell recorded that they were still meeting there.

Northumberland St. is the site of Hartshorne Lane, thought to be the birthplace of Ben Jonson (b. 1573), who spent his early years here with his mother and stepfather, a bricklayer, who taught Jonson his trade.

Sir Arthur Conan Doyle's consulting detective, accompanied on many of his exploits by Dr Watson, is commemorated at the Sherlock Holmes pub and restaurant at no. 10, which accommodates a re-creation of the famous sitting room at 221ʙ Baker Street. The *Strand Magazine* published many of the Sherlock Holmes short stories from 1892.

The **Strand** itself is the principal thoroughfare from the West End to the City. A short way from the Trafalgar Sq. end, near Villiers St., is the site of York House, a Tudor residence of the archbishops of York. Francis Bacon, born here in 1561, was befriended by a later occupant, Sir Thomas Egerton, whose household after his second marriage included his wife's young niece Anne More, and John Donne. Donne became Egerton's secretary after his return in 1596 from the Cadiz expedition, where he had been with Egerton's son, whom he had first met at Lincoln's Inn. Egerton's third marriage (1600) to the influential Dowager Countess of Derby might have improved Donne's chances of a place at court but for his rash marriage with the 17-year-old Anne More. This caused his imprisonment and dismissal from Egerton's service. Donne's wife was the subject of many of his love poems throughout her life but at this moment he is said to have written 'John Donne, Anne Donne, Undone'. York House itself was demolished at the end of the 17th c. but Arthur Murphy, who came from school at St Omer aged 16, lodged in the old York House buildings in 1744. Sir John Davies died (1626) at his house in the Strand, during the night after his appointment as Lord Chief Justice had been announced.

Early in the 17th c. Endymion Porter's house in the Strand (site unknown) was a centre for poets and painters including D'Avenant, Dekker, Ben Jonson, and Herrick. The area N of **John Adam St.** is the site of Durham House, the home of the 1st Earl of Essex where *c.* 1576 Philip Sidney met Essex's daughter Penelope Devereux, thought to be the Stella of his collection of sonnets *Astrophel and Stella* (1591), published posthumously. Durham House was later granted by Queen Elizabeth I to Ralegh, who lived there before being sent to the Tower in 1592. Exeter House (site between **Exeter St.** and **Burleigh St.**) was the home of the Earl of Shaftesbury where Locke, the family physician and friend, wrote part of the *Essay Concerning Human Understanding* (1690). The Burleigh St. corner was the site of Exeter Change (Exchange) (demolished 1829), a large building with bookstalls and other stalls on the ground floor, and with a famous menagerie above. 'Parson' Woodforde paid a shilling to see the wild beasts and Mr and Mrs John Dashwood in Jane Austen's *Sense and*

'Until Old Hungerford Stairs were destroyed, I never had the courage to go back to the place where my servitude began,' wrote Dickens, who as a boy had worked in a blacking factory here, now the site of Charing Cross station

Sensibility (1811) took little Harry (whose inheritance was safeguarded at Marianne's and Elinor's expense). Mary Lamb often heard the lions roaring when she walked home along the Strand and Charles Lamb included the Exeter Change in the list of places he rated higher than the Lakes.

Savoy St. and **Lancaster Pl.** are on the site of Savoy Palace, the home of John of Gaunt (Shakespeare's 'time-honoured Lancaster'), which with its outbuildings and gardens stretched from the Strand to the river. Chaucer found a patron in Lancaster, married a retainer of his Duchess, and wrote *The Boke of the Duchesse* on her death.

The Queen's Chapel of the Savoy, rebuilt after a fire in 1864, is in Savoy St. on the site of the original chapel burned by the peasants in 1381 and rebuilt in 1505, and again in the 19th c. Gavin Douglas, author of the allegorical poem *The Palice of Honour* and first translator of the *Aeneid*, who went to the English court in 1517, died of the plague in 1522 and was buried here. Thomas Fuller was a lecturer here in 1642 and again after the Restoration. Pepys, who often met Fuller and formerly had 'a high esteem of his preaching', heard him give 'a poor dry sermon' a few months before his death of 'a sort of fever' in 1661. The Puritan George Wither, who had often been imprisoned on account of his satirical pamphlets, died (1667) in this neighbourhood and was buried here, though he had expressed a wish to return to his birthplace at *Bentworth.

Somerset House is on the site of an earlier royal house where Anne of Denmark, James I's queen, was entertained by a series of masques and pastoral plays by the leading dramatists, often stage-managed by Inigo Jones.

Lamb's poem beginning 'When maidens such as Hester die' refers to Hester Savory (daughter of a goldsmith of the Strand), who died three months after her wedding in 1802.

Blake's workroom at 3 Fountain Ct, Strand, his home from 1821 until his death

William Blake lived from 1821 to his death in 1827, in **Fountain Ct**, an alley once between 103 and 104 The Strand. Crabb Robinson, who saw only two chairs and a bed, called it squalid, but Samuel Palmer, one of the young painters influenced by Blake, disagreed. 'The millionaire's upholsterer can furnish no enrichments like those of Blake's enchanted room,' he wrote, remarking on his 'delightful working corner' with the 'implements ready—tempting to the hand'. The Fountain tavern (℗ on site), formerly at the Strand end of the alley, was frequented by Swift and by those who opposed the policies of the Prime Minister, Walpole. Congreve, author of *Love for Love* (1695) and *The Way of the World* (1700), lived for many years in Surrey St. (site now Arundel Gt Ct). He frequented The Fountain with his friends from the Kit-Cat Club.

The publisher John Chapman, who resembled Byron, had his offices at no. 142 and lived on the floors above with his wife, his children, and their governess. He put up many of his literary friends in the house and Emerson, who visited briefly in 1847, stayed for three months in 1848. In 1851 Chapman persuaded Mary Ann Evans (George Eliot) to board here. She was anxious to increase the small income left her by her father and Chapman needed an assistant to edit the *Westminster Review*. She began to write her name as Marian at this time. Gordon Haight in *George Eliot and John Chapman* (1940) describes how the two women in the house reacted to the arrival of a third. In October 1851 Chapman introduced Miss Evans to George Lewes in Jeff's bookshop in Burlington Arcade (off Piccadilly), and she frequently went with Lewes when he reviewed plays for his journal *The Leader* (1850–66).

The young Hale White was another employee who boarded at no. 142. He found Marian Evans (her family still called her Mary Ann) a stimulating influence who made the menial tasks allotted to him bearable by her interest and encouragement. She was 12 years older than he and he describes her in the quiet back room, sitting 'half sideways to the fire' with her feet over the arm of a chair, correcting proofs. White met many of the literary figures of the day at Chapman's Wednesday evening parties. American visitors to no. 142 at this time included William Bryant, poet and editor of the New York *Evening Post*, and Horace Greeley, founder (1841) of the *New-York Tribune*, and of 'Go West, Young Man!' fame.

The Somerset Coffee House at no. 166 was frequented by Boswell in the 1760s.

Mrs Inchbald, who had been living in a community, welcomed the independence of her lodgings (*c*. 1805–9) with Miss Baillie, a milliner at no. 163 (gone). She was writing the prefaces to the many volumes of *The British Theatre* (1806).

King's College (founded 1829) was attended by Charles and Henry Kingsley, W. S. Gilbert, Walter Besant, and Edwin Arnold. More recent college alumni include the novelists Susan Hill (who graduated in 1963, then returned in 1978

to take up a lectureship there) and Hanif Kureishi (who was there in the mid-1970s studying Philosophy), and later (in 1986) Lawrence Norfolk graduated from King's too.

In Maureen Duffy's novel *Capital* (1975), King's—called 'Queen's' in the novel—employs the historian Emery as a lecturer and the eccentric Meepers—a homeless amateur archaeologist of London's Dark Ages—as a porter. Maureen Duffy was a student at King's in the 1950s, as was the novelist Anita Brookner. Brookner, who is also an art historian, taught at the Courtauld Institute of Art, now accommodated next door at Somerset House, from 1967 to 1988. The Courtauld was once under the directorship of the art historian and spy Anthony Blunt, a model for Victor Maskell in John Banville's novel *The Untouchable* (1997).

St George's Coffee House (gone), between **Devereux Ct** and **Essex St.**, was visited by Shenstone, Arthur Murphy (*c*. 1752), and Walpole. Danes End, behind iron gates, was the home and chambers of Watts-Dunton from 1873. Guests on his sociable Wednesday nights included Swinburne and William Morris.

The narrator of Julian Barnes's *Metroland* (1980) hunts emotions:

> Railway termini gave us weepy farewells and coarse recouplings. That was easy. Churches gave us the vivid deceptions of faith—thought we had to be careful in our manner of observation. Harley Street doorsteps gave us, we believed, the rabbit fears of men about to die.

But their favourite haunt is the **National Gallery** on Trafalgar Sq., for

> examples of pure aesthetic pleasure—although, to be honest, they weren't as frequent, as pure, or as subtle as we'd first hoped. Outrageously often, we thought, the scene was one more appropriate to Waterloo or Victoria: people greeted Monet, or Seurat, or Goya as if they had just stepped off a train—'Well, what a nice surprise. I knew you'd be here, of course, but it's a nice surprise all the same. And my, aren't you looking just as well as ever? Hardly a day older. No really . . .'

The Wren church of **St Clement Danes** (rebuilt after bombing in the Second World War) still has an oranges-and-lemons ceremony, and the bells chime the air of the nursery rhyme. John Lyly was married here in 1583 and Nathaniel Lee (d. 1692) and Thomas Otway (d. 1685) were buried here. Dr Johnson worshipped in the old church and a statue of him, with low reliefs of Boswell and Mrs Thrale on the base, stands outside.

The largest of the maypoles set up at every street corner after the Restoration, according to John Aubrey, stood at the corner of Drury Lane, near the **Church of St Mary-le-Strand**. It was broken by a high wind in 1672 and taken down. The Revd James Bramston (1694?–1744) wrote of it in *Art of Politics*: 'What's not destroyed by Time's devouring hand? | Where's Troy, and where's the Maypole in the Strand?' Sir John Betjeman was instrumental in the restoration of the church.

Dickens often mentions the Strand. The young David Copperfield visits two pudding shops in the vicinity, one near St Martin's Church, where the pudding was dear, and the other in the Strand itself, where the pudding was 'heavy and flabby, with great flat raisins in it, stuck in whole at wide distances apart'. David later stays at the Golden Cross Hotel (gone) with Steerforth. Mr Pickwick and his friends leave London in the *Commodore* coach from the same hotel. Mr Jingle delivers a cautionary tale to the outside passengers about hitting their heads on the low archway. The *Commodore* was the stagecoach Dickens had himself travelled up in from school at *Chatham in 1823. As the only inside passenger he had eaten his sandwiches 'in solitude and dreariness' while the rain lasted the whole journey.

When Baroness Orczy was waiting for a train at the **Temple underground station** in 1901, the character of Sir Percy Blakeney, the hero of *The Scarlet Pimpernel* (1905) and other romances of the French Revolution, came to her mind complete with his elegant hands, his spyglass, and his characteristic speech and laugh. In her autobiography, *Links in the Chain of Life* (1947), she writes that he was her creation alone and that he was not modelled on anyone.

Francis Bacon (b. 1561), essayist and philosopher, and Thomas Holcroft (b. 1745), actor and dramatist, were baptized, and the poet, Tom Moore, was married (1811) in **St Martin-in-the-Fields** (rebuilt 1726), in **Trafalgar Sq.** The following were buried here: Sir John Davies (d. 1626), author of *Nosce Teipsum*, George Farquhar (d. 1707), author of *The Recruiting Officer* and *The Beaux' Stratagem*, and James Smith (d. 1839), co-author of *Rejected Addresses*.

Kipling lived (1889–91) at 43 **Villiers St.** Ⓟ in rooms on the fifth floor, where he wrote *The Light That Failed* (1890), contributed 'Barrack-Room Ballads' to the *National Observer*, and arranged for the publication of *Life's Handicap* (1891), a collection of short stories.

The 'end of the whole "affair" ' is brought back to Maurice Bendrix when he meets Henry Miles at nearby **Victoria Gdns** in Graham Greene's novel *The End of the Affair* (1951):

The gulls flew low over the barges and the shot-tower stood black in the winter light among the ruined warehouses . . . the fruit-sellers cried like animals in the dusk outside the station. It was as if the shutters were going up on the whole world; soon we should all of us be abandoned to our own devices.

Prentis, the narrator of Graham Swift's novel *Shuttlecock* (1981), works as a senior clerk in the 'dead crimes' department of the police archives five minutes' walk from Embankment tube station. In a lane off Villiers Street 'past all the black garbage bags', Michael Frayn imagines the premises of the political pressure group in his novel *Now You Know* (1992).

Dickens published *Household Words* (1850–9) from offices at 16 **Wellington St.** This weekly had contributions from Edward Bulwer-Lytton, Elizabeth Gaskell, William and Mary Howitt, and Wilkie Collins, who collaborated on many stories with Dickens in *Household Words* and in its successor *All the Year Round* (1859–70), which was published from no. 10. *The Leader* (1850–66), founded by George Lewes and Thornton Leigh Hunt, with Spencer and Kinglake on the staff, was published in this street. George Eliot, who lived with Lewes after Mrs Lewes had left him for Thornton Hunt, often helped with the periodical when Lewes was ill.

STRATFORD, district to the E. Johnny, the object of the infatuated narrator's unrequited love in J. R. Ackerley's *We Think the World of You* (1960), lives in Stratford. The narrator's

bus journeys there take him through an 'ugly, stricken landscape' during which he thinks sadly of 'the vanished days when, the figure of Johnny standing at the end of it, this had seemed to me the most exciting journey in the world'. He finds an emotional substitute in Johnny's Alsatian dog Evie, which he inherits.

STREATHAM (pr. 'Strettam'), district to the S. Streatham Park was the country home (now built over) of Henry and Hester Thrale, who married in 1763 and were introduced to Dr Johnson by the playwright Arthur Murphy soon afterwards. Johnson, who had his own room here and conducted chemistry experiments in an oven he had built in the kitchen garden (site behind Thrale Rd), was the most frequent of the visitors, who included Goldsmith, Burke, Murphy, Garrick, Boswell, and Cumberland. Many of these had portraits painted for the library. Giuseppe Baretti was resident Italian tutor (1773–6) to Queeney Thrale, the eldest daughter. Author of an *Italian and English Dictionary* (1760), he also wrote at Johnson's suggestion an account of his travels in Spain and Portugal (1762). Dr Charles Burney came to teach Queeney music and later his daughter Fanny was patronized by Mrs Thrale. Dr Johnson wrote the lines on Henry Thrale's memorial (d. 1781) in the church. Hester married Gabriel Piozzi in 1784 and after Johnson's death wrote *Anecdotes of the Late Samuel Johnson* (1786) on her honeymoon tour of Italy. She also published Johnson's letters (1788). The Piozzis left Streatham Park in 1795.

The winter trees, with their 'sad spring bravery of leaves' provide the inspiration for Alan Brownjohn's poem 'In Crystal Palace Park'.

SURBITON, district to the SW. Richard Jefferies lived (1877–82) at 2 Woodside, now 296 **Ewell Rd** (site later shops near the police station), where he wrote *Nature Near London* (1883).

In 1965 Christina Stead moved from Hawley into a flat at 12a Elmers Ct, Avenue Elmers.

Briefly home to the young Isaiah Berlin, shortly after his family moved to England in 1921, Surbiton receives an even more unlikely visitor in Bernice Rubens's novel *Our Father* (1987), in which Veronica Smiles returns from her intrepid adventures in the Sahara to her Surbiton home; and one morning she goes for an early walk to the local bakery:

The streets were deserted. It would be an hour before the first trains left for the city. She savoured her aloneness as she savoured it in the desert, that appetite of hers that had first lured her to the solitary wastes of the world. So she was slightly irritated to see a figure approach her from the opposite direction. As she ran towards him, nibbling on the crust of the hot bread, she saw that he was God. She pulled up sharply as she reached Him.

'What are you doing in Surbiton?' she asked crossly.

'I am everywhere,' He said.

The booking hall of Temple Station, where Baroness Orczy first thought of Sir Percy Blakeney, the hero of *The Scarlet Pimpernel*

SYDENHAM, district to the SE. The Scottish poet Thomas Campbell lived (1804–22) at **Sydenham Common** in a house with 'green jalousies' and 'white palings' (gone, site thought to be in **Peak Hill**). After writing *Annals of Great Britain* (1807), he planned, with Scott, *Specimens of British Poets*, and, when Scott drew back from the scheme, he went on alone. The work was published in 1819. He also wrote here the poems 'Lord Ullin's Daughter', 'The Soldier's Dream', 'The Turkish Lady', and 'Battle of the Baltic'. Campbell's home life was tragic: one son died here, the other became mentally deranged, and his wife was an invalid. He had some happiness in the visits of his friends George Crabbe, Tom Moore, Samuel Rogers, and Byron. The first three thought of forming a poets' club with him, choosing the name 'The Bees'.

Graham Swift was brought up in Upper Sydenham, and the area is the setting for his first novel, *The Sweet Shop Owner* (1980).

TEDDINGTON, riverside district to the SW. Thomas Traherne lived (1669–74) in the house (gone) of Sir Orlando Bridgeman, Lord Keeper, as his chaplain. The manuscripts of his metaphysical poems, thought at first to be by Vaughan, were recognized and edited by Bertram Dobell (see CREDENHILL). Traherne died here and was buried in St Mary's Church, of which he was rector (1672–4).

In 1857 R. D. Blackmore, who was teaching classics at Twickenham, inherited enough money to build himself a country house in a large garden. He moved in in 1860 and called it Gomer House (site at end of **Doone Close** opposite the station) after a favourite dog. He started a market garden there, specializing in fruit growing, and wrote novels during the winter, including the most popular *Lorna Doone* (1869), *Craddock Nowell* (1866), and *Cripps the Carrier* (1876). He was buried (1900) at Teddington cemetery.

Noel Coward was born at 131 Waldegrave Rd. in 1899 ℗, the family home until 1908.

Thom Gunn's 'Last Days at Teddington' bids farewell to a fondly remembered house and garden:

> How green it was indoors. The thin
> Pale creepers climbed up brick until
> We saw their rolled tongues flicker in
> Across the cracked paint of the sill.

TOOTING, district to the S, near Wandsworth Common. After the publication of *The Return of the Native* (1878), Hardy lived (1878–81) at 1 Arundel Ter., **Trinity Rd** (℗ on no. 172), Upper Tooting, but his stay here was marred by an illness during 1880–1, when *The Trumpet-Major* (1880) was published.

Two of William Trevor's comic early novels, *The Old Boys* (1964) and *The Boarding House* (1965)—'an imposing building that suggested the reign of Victoria but which had been in fact erected at a later date'—are set in imaginary streets in Tooting.

The Granada cinema was a favourite haunt of young Angela Carter, who was brought regularly; from these beginnings film became an important presence in much of her work. The building is now the Gala Bingo Hall.

TWICKENHAM, riverside district to the SW. The philosopher Francis Bacon lived (1595–1605) and perhaps wrote some of his *Essays* (1597) at Twickenham Park, the Tudor house and grounds (now covered by the St Margaret's area) which Lucy, Countess of Bedford, took over after he left. She was the centre of a brilliant circle, and patron of Jonson, Drayton, George Chapman, Samuel Daniel, and Donne, who all wrote poems to her. Donne often stayed here between 1605 and 1610. Sir John Suckling was born in 1609 in a house on the site of the present Kneller Hall at **Whitton**, which in the 19th c. was a government training college for teachers, with F. T. Palgrave its Vice-Principal (1850–5). Palgrave was a friend of Tennyson and talked with him about his plan for a volume of selections from English verse, which became known as *The Golden Treasury*.

Pope leased a villa with gardens to the river in **Crossdeep** in 1719, when he was translating the last volume of the *Iliad*, and he spent much time improving the house and embellishing the gardens. His grotto (in the grounds of St Catherine's Convent) built under the Teddington road to link his gardens on either side, was lined with rock crystals. His ideas, implemented by William Kent and Charles Bridgeman, the landscape architects, impressed others. The fashion for grottoes was taken up by Samuel Richardson and Mrs Delany. Pope's influence on the landscape was also felt at **Marble Hill**, the Palladian villa built (1724–9) for Henrietta Howard, a mistress of George II. Pope advised her on the gardens and wrote to his friend Lord Bathurst for the loan of some sheep to crop the 'new springing grass'. He was often visited by his friends the Scriblerians, Gay, Arbuthnot, Congreve, and Swift, and by Voltaire (in exile 1726–9). Lady Mary Wortley Montagu's residence at Savile House (gone) in **Heath Rd** was short-lived, as their friendship turned to enmity. Pope, who

Drawing by William Kent of Pope in his Grotto at Crossdeep, Twickenham

A view by Paul Sandby of Strawberry Hill, Horace Walpole's Gothic mansion in Twickenham, *c.* 1775

was known as the Wasp of Twickenham, attacked many of his friends in *The Dunciad* (1728), which appeared anonymously. Henry Brooke moved here (to be near Pope, who had admired his poem *Universal Beauty*, 1735) after the success of *Gustavus Vasa* (1739), which had previously been banned. However, he soon settled in *Dublin. Pope, who had erected an obelisk (1732) in the garden to the memory of his mother, died in 1744 and was buried by her side in the parish church. His parents' memorial is on the E wall. His friend William Warburton erected a monument in 1761 on the N wall referring to Pope's desire to be buried here rather than in Westminster Abbey. Horace Walpole commented on the sorry state of the gardens in 1760, and in 1807 another owner razed the villa to the ground and 'blotted out utterly every memorial to the poet'. Today **Pope's Grove** and **Grotto Rd** point to the site. Henry Fielding lived (1743–8) in Back Lane (now **Holly Rd**) and is thought to have written part of *Tom Jones* (1749), here. He was a cousin of Lady Mary Wortley Montagu.

Colley Cibber, actor and dramatist, lived a little upstream from Pope (who lashed him in *Epistle to Dr. Arbuthnot* and *The Dunciad*, 1743) and is thought to have written *The Refusal* (1721) in the cottage later famous as **Strawberry Hill** (now St Mary's University College, Strawberry Hill).

Horace Walpole rented this small coachman's cottage in 5 acres, 300 yds from the river, in 1747. Two years later he bought and began to Gothicize it, after toying with other styles, including the Chinese. He continued to improve it throughout his life so that the house, once small enough to have been 'sent in a letter', eventually had 22 rooms and 46 acres of gardens containing cottages, a little wood, and two cascades. His press, set up in 1757, printed *The Bard* and *The Progress of Poetry* by his friend Thomas Gray and 30 years later some verses by Hannah More. She dined here in 1783 and 'passed as delightful a day as elegant

literature, high breeding, and lively wit can afford'. He also printed some copies of his own play *The Mysterious Mother*, which has never been performed. His earlier novel *The Castle of Otranto, a Gothic Story* (1765) was a great success, 21 editions appearing before the end of the century. Walpole stocked the house with curiosities and opened it to visitors. He died in London and the contents of the house were sold in 1842. The sale lasted a month, and Harrison Ainsworth wrote a preface to the catalogue. Walpole's young friends, with whom he corresponded, Agnes and Mary Berry, lived for a time at Little Strawberry Hill (gone) in the grounds.

From 1929 to 1933 Sean O'Faolain taught at Strawberry Hill after it had been converted to St Mary's Teachers' Training College. He taught for 10 hours a week, which left plenty of time for writing. He developed a friendship with the editor Edward Garnett while working here that led to the publication of his first collection of short stories, *Midsummer Night Madness* (1932). Gavin Ewart included a poem on Strawberry Hill in his collection *Londoners* (1964).

Dickens lived (1838–9) at 2 **Ailsa Pk Villas** (near St Margaret's station *c.* 3–4 m. E) while writing *Nicholas Nickleby*, in which Morleena Kenwigs dines, as did her creator, on 'a cold collation—bottled beer, shrub, and shrimps' on Eel Pie Island (approached by a footbridge from the river bank).

Tennyson lived (1851–3) at Chapel House, **Montpelier Row**, bordering Marble Hill. He wrote 'Ode on the Death of the Duke of Wellington' here, and at such a short distance from London was often visited by his friends, including Thackeray and FitzGerald.

R. D. Blackmore taught classics (1853) at Wellesley House Grammar School, **Hampton Rd** (later Fortescue House School). While here his *Poems by Melanter* and *Epullia* were published, both anonymously.

Walter de la Mare lived (from *c.* 1950) at the end of Montpelier Row at 4 South End House, where he died in 1956.

VAUXHALL GARDENS (pr. 'Vŏxhall), former gardens S of the river. They were a popular resort of London citizens and the fashionable, covering the area about Vauxhall Walk and Kennington Lane, which opened in 1661 and was at first called the New Spring Gardens after the old pleasure ground at Charing Cross. The gardens contained fruit trees in a wild tangle of bushes divided by gravelled walks as well as the 'pretty-contrived plantation' mentioned by Evelyn in his *Diary*. He often visited his friend Samuel Morland, whose house, where he conducted his experiments in pumping water, was near the gardens which later enveloped the site. Pepys was rowed across the Thames by watermen and landed at Vauxhall Stairs. He mentions the 'abundance of roses' and 'the cakes and powdered beef and ale' that refreshed the party before going 'home again by water, with much pleasure'. Sir Roger de Coverley with Mr Spectator also arrived by boat (the land route before the building of Westminster Bridge was very circuitous) and he would have enjoyed himself better had there been 'more nightingales and fewer strumpets'. The popularity of the gardens was revived in 1732 by Jonathan Tyers, who arranged concerts for fashionable music-lovers and controlled the worst excesses of the bucks who caused annoyance to the heroines of both Fielding's *Amelia* and Fanny Burney's *Evelina*.

Lydia in *Humphry Clinker* thought the walks delightful and marvelled at the 'pavilions, lodges, groves, grottos, lawns, temples and cascades', which Matthew Bramble dismissed as a 'composition of baubles, overcharged with paltry ornaments'. The cascade which operated only at set times was the cause of Beau Tibbs's friend's irritation in Goldsmith's *The Citizen of the World* (1762). She wished to see the waterworks but as she feared she would appear lacking in gentility to leave before the music stopped, she waited, and so missed the spectacle. A Rowlandson sketch shows Dr Johnson, Goldsmith, and Hester Thrale at supper in one of the booths while the Regent and Perdita Robinson stand under the orchestra's box. Tom Tyers, then proprietor, was portrayed as Tom Restless by Johnson in *The Idler*. J. H. Reynolds in his sonnet on Vauxhall calls the thinly cut ham 'transparent'. He also mentions the 'soaked silks and wet white satin' caused by watching fireworks 'while it hardly rains'. Arias from Thomas Holcroft's operas were popular here and songs written by Robert Anderson and sung by Master Phelps earned Anderson free admission to the gardens in 1794.

Karl Moritz, a German schoolmaster, mentions in *Travels* (1795) his delight at the gardens and the music, although he thought the women over-bold. Other visitors were Leigh Hunt, and Keats, who wrote the sonnet 'To a Lady seen for a few moments at Vauxhall'. The gardens also included the Rural Downs, among whose tree-studded hillocks was a statue of Milton. Nightingales had always frequented the gardens and Gilbert White, staying with his brother at Lambeth, recorded seeing a green woodpecker and commented on the noise of the owls.

In *Vanity Fair* (1847–8), Captain Dobbin, unhappily escorting two pairs of lovers, hardly noticed any of the sparkling attractions of the gardens because his Amelia went with George. Rebecca Sharp walking with Jos in the dark walks had almost flattered him into a proposal when interrupted by the bell for the fireworks. After that, a bowl of rack punch caused Jos to sing and wink and call Rebecca his 'diddle-diddle-darling' to the amusement of the onlookers, so that the chance of her becoming Mrs Jos Sedley was lost for ever. A final gala was held in 1859 and then the gardens were dismantled.

VICTORIA, district round Victoria station. Ann Radcliffe, whose Gothic novels combined horror, sensibility, and a love of the picturesque, lived (1815–23) at 5 Stafford Row, which was situated where **Bressenden Pl.** joins Buckingham Palace Rd. She influenced many writers including Keats, who called her Mother Radcliffe and used many of her typical adjectives in 'The Eve of St. Agnes'. Byron is said to have modelled his scowl on one of her characters, and Coleridge reviewed *Mysteries of Udolpho* (1794), the novel that Catherine Morland found was no guide to life in Jane Austen's *Northanger Abbey* (1818). Mrs Radcliffe made one journey to Holland and Germany but preferred to live quietly at home as her health was poor and she suffered from asthma. She died here in 1823.

Sue Townsend's satirical novel *The Queen and I* (1992) begins at **Buckingham Palace**, in the presence of the assembled Windsor family; but the action soon moves location, as a republic has just been declared and the family are evicted to 9 Hellebore Close, Flowers Estate. The Queen Mother is given a pensioner's bungalow. 'A bungalow, good. I couldn't manage stairs. Will my staff be living in or out?'

Joseph Conrad took rooms (1893–6) at 17 **Gillingham St.** after returning from the voyages to Australia on which he was first mate and had made the acquaintance of John Galsworthy. While waiting for another ship he continued the novel *Almayer's Folly* (1895) and when this and *The Outcast of the Islands* (1896) were accepted he gave up the merchant navy. He married Jessie George in March 1896 and they spent four months in Brittany.

Thomas Campbell lived (1804) after his marriage, at 25 Upper Eaton St., Pimlico, as **Grosvenor Gdns** was called before it was rebuilt. George Darley, on the staff of the *London Magazine*, published *Sylvia* (1827), a pastoral drama, the year he moved to no. 5. After an interval (1830–9) he returned to no. 27 until 1842. He was then writing for *The Athenaeum*.

Campbell also lived at 8 **Victoria Sq.** Ⓟ, looked after by his niece Mary, for the last four years of his life (1841–4). He worked on *The Pilgrim of Glencoe* (1842), *Frederick the Great* (1842), *Petrarch* (1841), and 'The Child and the Hind'. Margaret Oliphant, who wrote popular tales of Scottish life, lived at no. 14 *c.* 1880, when she published *A Beleaguered City*, a tale of the occult.

Opposite St James's Park tube station on Broadway is **New Scotland Yard**, professional home to P. D. James's detective hero Adam Dalgliesh, a Metropolitan Police commander, who features in a series of her books beginning with *Cover Her Face* (1962).

Sigmund Freud fled Vienna to exile in London in the summer of 1938; he arrived at **Victoria Station** on 6 June. Such was the interest in the great man's arrival that his train had to be diverted to a different platform to avoid the attentions of the waiting press.

WALLINGTON, district SW of Croydon, the country edge of suburbia. Mervyn Peake's boyhood home from 1924 was a large house called Woodcroft at 55 Woodcote Rd, where his father had bought a medical practice on retiring from work in China. Mervyn, who seemed destined to become an artist, went daily to the Croydon School of Art after leaving school, and then progressed to the Royal Academy Schools in London for a five-year course.

WALTHAMSTOW, district to the NE. William Morris was born in 1834 at Elm House (gone), which he left at the age of 6. A plaque commemorating him is on the fire station opposite the site. After the death of his father the Morris family moved to the Water House, so called from a moat in the grounds behind the house, his home from 1848 to 1856. These grounds are now **Lloyd Park**, called after Edward Lloyd, the publisher, a later owner of the Water House whose family donated it to Walthamstow in 1898. The William Morris Gallery was opened in 1950, an event made possible by a gift of works of art by Sir Frank Brangwyn RA (who had worked with Morris in his youth) in association with A. H. Mackmurdo, architect and founder of the Century Guild, who had introduced Brangwyn to Morris. The collections contain material of all aspects of William Morris's work, including a selection of his correspondence, original manuscripts, and a complete set of books printed by the Kelmscott Press. The reference library contains books and periodicals relating to the period and publications by private presses and can be visited by appointment.

WANDSWORTH, district S of the river SE of Putney. Marian Evans (George Eliot) and George Lewes lived from February 1859 to September 1860 at Holly Lodge, South Fields, now 31 Wimbledon Pk Rd Ⓟ. During this time they found a suitable site for the mill in her novel *The Mill on the Floss*, which she finished here.

WANSTEAD, district to the NE. Wanstead House (site on golf course), home of the Earl of Leicester, was the scene of Philip Sidney's masque *Queen of the May*, written for Queen Elizabeth I's visit (1578). Pepys visited the house, and Evelyn in 1683 commented in his *Diary* on 'the prodigious cost in planting of walnut trees . . . and making of fish-ponds' by 'the over growne and suddenly monied' Josiah Child, one time an ordinary merchant's apprentice. Thomas Hood (1799–1845) lived (1832–5) in dilapidated splendour at Lake House (gone), part of the estate, which had a Grinling Gibbons fireplace and peeling plaster. Here he edited the *Comic Annuals* (begun 1830) and wrote the ballad *Tylney Hall* (1834). His son Tom (1835–74) was born there, but soon afterwards the family moved abroad to save money.

WEMBLEY, district to the NW. The travel writer Robert Byron was born at 23 Swinderby Rd on 26 February 1905.

WESTMINSTER, district between Pimlico and the Strand.

In 1895 Thomas Hardy rented a flat in **Ashley Gdns**, Ambrosden St., for a season. Bernard Shaw set the first act of his play *The Philanderer* (1893) here, re-creating the character of the block in a characteristically meticulous piece of scene-setting. Anthony Powell was born in 1905 at no. 44, 'a furnished flat rented for the occasion in one of the several redbrick blocks in that rather depressing area between Victoria Street and the Vauxhall Bridge Rd' (*To Keep the Ball Rolling*, 1983). Nicholas Jenkins, the narrator of his 12-volume novel *A Dance to the Music of Time* (1951–75), eats lunch at the House of Commons, repairing later to the smoking rooms and lobbies, 'suffocating . . . with the omnipresent and congealed essence of public contentions and private egotisms'. In an earlier volume of the same novel, the comic figure Widmerpool is described as living with his mother on Victoria St., in a block of flats near Westminster Cathedral.

Leo Tolstoy listened to Lord Palmerston make a three-hour speech in the Commons during his visit to England in March 1861.

Axe Yard, Whitehall, a court which disappeared in the 18th c., was near today's **King Charles St.** Pepys, born in London in 1633, began his *Diary* here in January 1660, living in a garret with his wife and servant Jane.

William Gifford, editor of the *Anti-Jacobin* and first editor of the *Quarterly Review*, died at his house, 6 **Buckingham Gate**, on 31 December 1826.

Boswell mentions in his memoirs (*London Journal*) the good bargain he had in his lodgings in **Downing St.**, where he spent the year 1763.

James Macpherson, author of poems which he claimed were translations from Ossian, spent his last years in **Fludyer St.** (gone).

Matthew Prior, poet and moderate Tory, lived, from 1706 until sent as a diplomat to

Paris in 1711, at the end of **Gt George St.** near St James's Park.

Auberon Waugh enlisted with the Royal Horse Guards ('the Blues') in 1957 where he inadvertently shot himself in the chest with a machine gun.

Spenser returned from Ireland in 1598 and lodged in **King St.** (gone, site parallel to Whitehall), where he died a month later, in January 1599, some say in poverty.

Crabb Robinson lodged with the Colliers in **Little Smith St.** from 1805 until he moved with them to Hatton Garden in 1810. His *Diary* mentions most of the writers of the time.

Geoffrey Hill's poem 'To the High Court of Parliament' describes the **Palace of Westminster** (Parliament) as 'Barry's and Pugin's grand | dark-lantern above the incumbent Thames'.

Milton lived (1652–60) at a house (gone) on the N side of **Petty France**, where the gardens extended to St James's Park, soon after becoming Latin Secretary (1649) to the new Council of State. The state papers he read provoked the sonnet 'On the Late Massacre in Piedmont'. Also written here were the sonnets on the death of his second wife and 'On his Blindness'. In 1658 he turned again to an early draft of *Paradise Lost*, but at the Restoration in 1660 he was deprived of his office by the Royalist government and went into hiding.

Aaron Hill lived in this street until 1738. He wrote the words for Handel's opera *Rinaldo* (1711), rewrote an earlier play of his own, *Elfrid*, as *Athelwold* (1732), and translated and adapted Voltaire's *Zaïre* as *Zara* (1736). Correspondence with Pope, which followed the satirical exchanges in *The Dunciad* and Hill's *Progress of Wit*, eventually became more friendly.

John Cleland, author of *Fanny Hill* (1748–9) and *Memoirs of a Coxcomb* (1751), died in a house (gone) here in 1789. Hazlitt rented (1812–19) Milton's house from Jeremy Bentham, who lived nearby. Hazlitt's friend the painter Benjamin Robert Haydon mentions in his *Autobiography* (1853) that he 'and I often looked with a longing eye from the windows of the room at the white-haired philosopher in his leafy shelter'. Haydon was invited here to the christening of Hazlitt's son and complained that nothing was arranged and the parson not ordered, yet Charles and Mary Lamb remained unperturbed.

St Margaret's, Westminster was built on the site of an earlier church where Caxton was buried (1491). A memorial brass was erected (1820) to him by bibliophiles, who founded a club named after the Duke of Roxburghe, collector of many volumes printed on Caxton's press. A stained-glass window to Caxton was destroyed by bombing. Skelton, who spent his last years in a house abutting on the Abbey, where the right of sanctuary still existed, keeping him free from Wolsey's reprisals, was buried (1529) by the altar but his alabaster memorial has gone. Sir Walter Ralegh, beheaded nearby (1618), is thought to have been buried here. A memorial window to him,

with an inscription by James Russell Lowell, was donated by Americans. Milton, who married his second wife here (1656) and buried her and their infant child here a year later, also has a memorial window donated by Americans. His inscription is by John Greenleaf Whittier. In 1655 Pepys married the dowerless 15-year-old Elizabeth St Michel, who often appears in his *Diary*, and in 1631 Edmund Waller married an heiress here. Thomas Campbell also married here in 1803. The west porch was built in memory of Frederick Farrar, rector of St Margaret's (1876–95), author of a number of school stories, including *Eric, or, Little by Little* (1858), as well as the popular *Life of Christ* (1874).

Charles Churchill, who was born (1731) in Vine St. (gone), succeeded his father as curate of **St John's Church, Smith Sq.** in 1758. He separated from his wife, with whom he had made a Fleet marriage while still at Westminster School, in 1761, the year he published *The Rosciad*, a satire on actors of the day. Two years later his reckless spending and improprieties caused his parishioners to demand his resignation. Churchill, whom Dr Johnson called a 'blockhead', had become a follower of Wilkes and wrote for his *North Briton*. He was on his way to visit Wilkes in Paris when he died (1764) of a fever.

From 1955 the novelist Angus Wilson kept a flat at nearby **Dolphin Sq.** The Tothill estate and Tothill House, the magnificent baroque mansion very plausibly invented by him in his

last novel, *Setting the World on Fire* (1980), takes its name from Tothill Fields, the land which lay between Westminster Abbey and Millbank and which is now commemorated by **Tothill St.** Not far from here, 102 Lord North St. was the address of the bereaved Meg Eliot in Wilson's *The Middle Age of Mrs Eliot* (1958).

In 1895 Somerset Maugham wrote his first novel, *Liza of Lambeth* (1897), when lodging at 11 **Vincent Sq.** while a medical student.

Westminster Abbey, Collegiate Church of St Peter, dates from the 11th c., when the Benedictine abbey on Thorney Island was refounded by Edward the Confessor. English kings and queens have been crowned here from the time of William the Conqueror in 1066 to Queen Elizabeth II in 1953, and many of them are buried here. Francis Beaumont reflects on this in 'Ode on the Tombs in Westminster Abbey':

> Mortality behold and fear
> What a change of flesh is here!
> Think how many royal bones
> Sleep within this heap of stones:
> Here they lie had realms and lands,
> Who now want strength to stir their hands.

Many writers are buried in the Abbey and others have memorials; most of these are near the S transept, an area now called Poets' Corner. There is a canopied tomb of Chaucer (d. 1400); a tablet to William Tyndale (d. 1536), translator of the Bible; a marble

Poets' Corner, Westminster Abbey, showing memorials to Campbell, Shakespeare, Keats, Shelley, Southey, Burns, Johnson, and Thomson

monument and an effigy to William Thynne (d. 1584), first editor of Chaucer's works; a monument to Spenser (d. 1599), who was buried near Chaucer at the expense of his patron, the Earl of Essex; the grave of Francis Beaumont (d. 1616), playwright and collaborator of John Fletcher; the grave of Hakluyt (d. 1616), ambassador to Paris, Archdeacon of the Abbey, and author of *Principall Navigations, Voyages, and Discoveries of the English Nation*; a monument to Shakespeare (d. 1616) with lines from *The Tempest*; a tablet to Camden (d. 1623), the antiquary; the grave of Drayton (d. 1631) and a monument with lines ascribed by tradition to Ben Jonson; the grave of Ben Jonson (d. 1637) with a medallion; the grave of James Ussher (d. 1656), author of *Annales Veteris et Novi Testamenti*; the grave of Abraham Cowley (d. 1667), author of *The Mistress* and *Pindaric Odes*; the grave of playwright William D'Avenant (d. 1668), said to be Shakespeare's godson; the grave of John Denham (d. 1669), author of *Cooper's Hill*; a bust of Milton (d. 1674); the grave of Edward Hyde, Earl of Clarendon, who died in Rouen in 1674; the grave of Thomas Killigrew (d. 1683), playwright and partner with D'Avenant in the monopoly controlling acting in London; a monument with the lines

The Poets Fate is here in emblem shown:
He asked for Bread and he received a Stone,

commemorating Samuel Butler, who died in poverty (1680); a stained-glass window to Bunyan (d. 1688) with scenes from *The Pilgrim's Progress*; the grave of Aphra Behn (d. 1689), author of *The Rover*; the grave and monument of Dryden (d. 1700); the grave of Nicholas Rowe (d. 1718), dramatist and Poet Laureate (1715–18); the grave and a statue of Addison (d. 1721), creator of 'Sir Roger de Coverley'; the grave of Matthew Prior (d. 1721), author of *Four Dialogues of the Dead*, buried, as he wished, at the feet of Spenser; the grave and a statue of Congreve (d. 1729), author of *The Way of the World*; and the grave of his friend John Gay (d. 1732), author of *The Beggar's Opera*; a statue to James Thomson (d. 1748), author of *The Seasons*; a monument to Isaac Watts (d. 1748), author of 'O God, our help in ages past'; the grave of Aaron Hill (d. 1750), librettist of Handel's *Rinaldo*; a monument to Gray (d. 1771), author of 'Elegy in a Country Churchyard'; a monument with a bust of Goldsmith (d. 1774) and lines by Johnson, erected by fellow members of the Literary Club; the grave of Samuel Foote, actor and dramatist, who died (1777) in Dover; the grave of David Garrick (d. 1779), actor and author of 16 plays, including *The Clandestine Marriage* (with G. Colman the Elder, 1766); the grave and a bust of Johnson himself (d. 1784); the grave of James Macpherson (d. 1796), author of Ossianic poems, who was buried here at his own request; a bust of Burns (d. 1796); the grave of Sheridan (d. 1816), author of *The Rivals*; tablets to Keats (d. 1821), Shelley (d. 1822), and Byron (d. 1824), who all died

abroad; the grave of William Gifford (d. 1826), first editor of the *Quarterly Review*; busts of Scott (d. 1832), Coleridge (d. 1834), and Southey (d. 1843); the grave and a statue of Thomas Campbell (d. 1844), author of *The Pleasures of Hope* and 'Hohenlinden'; a tablet to Henry Francis Lyte (d. 1847), author of 'Abide with me', commemorating the centenary of his death and placed near that of Isaac Watts; a statue of Wordsworth (d. 1850); a tablet to the Brontë sisters: Emily (d. 1848), Anne (d. 1849), and Charlotte (d. 1855), with Emily's line 'with courage to endure'; the grave and bust of Macaulay (d. 1859), author of *Lays of Ancient Rome*; a bust of Thackeray (d. 1863); the grave of Dickens (d. 1870), who had wished to be buried in *Rochester; a bust (unveiled 1934) of Adam Lindsay Gordon (d. 1870), 'National Poet of Australia' and author of *Bush Ballads and Galloping Rhymes*; the grave of Bulwer-Lytton, Lord Lytton (d. 1873), author of *The Last Days of Pompeii*; tablets to George Eliot (Marian Evans, d. 1880) and to Gerard Manley Hopkins (d. 1889), laid in 1975 on the centenary of the shipwreck in the Thames which had caused him to write 'The Wreck of the Deutschland'; the graves and memorials of Browning (d. 1889) and Tennyson (d. 1892); a tablet to Lewis Carroll (C. L. Dodgson, d. 1898) and a medallion to Ruskin (d. 1900), author of *Modern Painters*; a tablet to Henry James (d. 1916); the graves of Hardy (d. 1928), Kipling (d. 1936), and John Masefield (d. 1967); and tablets to Dylan Thomas (d. 1953), T. S. Eliot (d. 1965), and W. H. Auden (d. 1973). Charles Darwin, who died in 1882, is buried in Westminster Abbey too, though this was agreed only after considerable controversy, given how he was perceived by some in high religious circles.

It is the setting of Betjeman's satirical poem 'In Westminster Abbey'.

Westminster Abbey Gatehouse (gone) was used as a prison in the 16th and 17th cc. The lines in Sir Walter Ralegh's Bible found here, which begin 'Even such is Time, that takes in trust | Our youth, our joys, our all we have,' are believed to have been written on the eve of his execution. The Royalist Richard Lovelace, imprisoned in 1642 after presenting the Kentish Petition to the House of Commons, wrote the lyric 'To Althea, from Prison', which contains the lines 'Stone walls do not a prison make, | Nor iron bars a cage.'

Wordsworth's sonnet 'Earth hath not anything to show more fair' was written on 3 September 1802 when he and Dorothy were driving across **Westminster Bridge** in the coach early in the morning on their way to France. It is matched by her description of 'one of nature's own grand spectacles' in her *Journal*.

Westminster School, through the archway from Broad Sanctuary to **Dean's Yard**, was founded *c.* 1560 by Queen Elizabeth I, but the school attached to Westminster Abbey which it superseded was mentioned in the 14th c. The main hall (restored 1950s) was the monks' dormitory. Nicholas Udall (or Uvedale), who

had been the Headmaster of Eton, was Headmaster here from 1554 until his death in 1556. William Camden was usher here from 1575 to 1593 when he was appointed Headmaster. He collected much antiquarian material on his journeys in the vacations for *Britannia* (1586), his survey of the country, and *Annales* (1589), a panegyric on Queen Elizabeth I. Both were translated from Latin into English later. Ashburnham House in Little Dean's Yard, a 17th-c. building now part of the school, once housed the Cottonian Library. In 1731 a fire destroyed some of the manuscripts and in 1753 the library was moved to the British Museum (now in the British Library). Literary pupils at Westminster School include: William Harrison, Richard Hakluyt, William Alabaster, Robert Bruce Cotton, Ben Jonson, Richard Corbett, Giles Fletcher the Younger, George Herbert, Thomas Randolph, William Cartwright, Abraham Cowley, John Locke, John Dryden, Elkanah Settle, Nathaniel Lee, Matthew Prior, Nicholas Rowe, Aaron Hill, John Dyer, Charles Wesley, John Cleland, John Burgoyne, William Cowper, Charles Churchill, George Colman the Elder, Richard Cumberland, Edward Gibbon, Augustus Toplady, the Hon. John Byng, George Colman the Younger, Robert Southey—expelled for writing an essay against flogging—Matthew Gregory Lewis, James Anthony Froude, George Alfred Henty, A. A. Milne, Patrick Hamilton, Angus Wilson, and the poet Michael Hamburger. Hamburger attended Westminster School in late 1930s, describing in his memoir *A Mug's Game* (1973) his endurance, among other things, of the school uniform of 'morning coat, striped trousers, top hat and obligatory umbrella or cane', worn in the face of 'stares, rude or sarcastic comments in tube trains, and the occasional stone aimed at the top hat by less privileged boys in the remaining working-class streets of St John's Wood'.

Bernard Shaw lived 1928–45 at 4 **White-Hall Ct**, between Horse Guards and Northumberland Ave. This was his London pied-à-terre while his home was at *Ayot St Lawrence.

WHITEHALL, street and government district between Parliament Sq. and Trafalgar Sq. **Whitehall**, the enormous rambling palace (gone) which Henry VIII appropriated from the Archbishop of York, embellished and extended by Elizabeth I, was the chief venue for court performances in Shakespeare's time. Dramatic activity at court was most vigorous under James I, who only 10 days after his accession had drawn up letters patent to advertise the royal protection Shakespeare's company, renamed the King's Men, would receive: 'freely to use and exercise the art of playing comedies, tragedies, histories, interludes, morals, pastorals, stage plays as well for the recreation of our loving subjects as for our solace and pleasure'.

During the 1940s Widmerpool, the archetypal comic figure of Anthony Powell's *A Dance to the Music of Time* (1951–75), works in the **Cabinet Offices**, a 'brightly lit dungeon'

Ian Fleming in Room 39 at the Admiralty, Whitehall, during the Second World War

where there 'lurked a sense that no one could spare a word, not a syllable, far less gesture, not of direct value in implementing the matter at hand'. Jenkins, narrator of the novel, also worked at the nearby War Office (now part of the Ministry of Defence), home of, among others, 'the unsleeping sages of Movement Control . . . sightless magicians deprived eternally of the light of the sun' and of Blackhead, a civil servant of legendary bureaucratic obstruction. In 1943 Powell himself was summoned to the subterranean offices under Gt George St. to serve on the Secretariat of the Joint Intelligence Committee following the actions of Denis Capel-Dunn, one of the chief models for Widmerpool.

Ian Fleming worked in naval intelligence in Room 39 of the **Admiralty** building on Whitehall, rising, like his creation James Bond, to the rank of commander. His period here gave him much of the background in political espionage he later exploited and fantasized in the Bond novels.

WIMBLEDON, district to the S. Captain Marryat had a country retreat at a Gothic lodge in Woodhayes Rd from 1839 to 1843.

Robert Graves was born at Red Branch House, **Lauriston Rd**, a place he saw 'only at Christmas and for a day or two at the beginning and end of the other holidays'. London, although only half an hour away, was seldom visited. William Trevor's novel *The Love Department* (1966) is set in Wimbledon.

WINCHMORE HILL, district S of Enfield. Rose Cottage (demolished) in **Vicars Moor Lane** was the home of Thomas Hood from 1829 to 1832, when he began his *Comic Annual* (1830).

WOOLWICH, district to the SE. At the Royal Army Medical Corps, the novelist Jocelyn Brooke re-enlisted after the Second World War as a 'pox-wallah', treating venereal disease.

WORMWOOD SCRUBS, common land to the W, comprising HM prison Wormwood Scrubs. The poet Basil Bunting, refusing military service when he left school, was sent to jail here in 1918 and the Scottish poet Norman MacCaig, a conscientious objector during the Second World War, spent three months of 1941 in the prison.

East of England

East of England

ALDBURY *Hertfordshire*

Old village off the A41, 3 m. NE of Tring. Mrs Humphry Ward lived (1892–1920) at (Great) Stocks, visible behind the house and converted barn of Stocks Farm. The 18th-c. house with its long lime avenue, chosen for its seclusion, had a walled garden, where she wrote. A brutal killing which took place in the village was woven into her novel *Marcella* (1894). She entertained large parties on Sundays; Henry James was a visitor and her young relatives Julian and Aldous Huxley spent many holidays here. In 1908 she moved into her cottage, which she had let to friends, including Bernard Shaw, while Stocks was repaired and altered. Mrs Ward died in London but is buried in the churchyard near the NW corner of the church.

Louis MacNeice spent his last years at 39 Stocks Rd and died there. He was a regular at the Greyhound, where his accustomed chair was under the clock in the public bar.

ALDEBURGH *Suffolk*

Coastal resort, with a music festival in June, on the A12 and A1094, 19 m. NE of Woodbridge. George Crabbe, son of a collector of salt taxes, was born (1755) here, but the house and Slaughden quay, where he worked as a boy in his father's warehouse, have been swallowed up by the sea. Later he practised unrewardingly as a surgeon. The publication of his poems *Inebriety* (1775) and *The Candidate* (1780) brought him little money and many times he went hungry, so he set out for London, where Burke's timely help saved him from starvation. After his ordination in December 1781 he returned to Aldeburgh as curate and then accepted the chaplaincy at Belvoir Castle in 1782. *The Village* (1783), praised by Dr Johnson, who read and revised the manuscript, is a satire on the idealized picture of rural delights popular in drawing rooms and it gives a realistic account of the harsh and squalid lives of the working people of Aldeburgh. After many years away from the town Crabbe returned to the same theme in *The Borough* (1810). In an article in *The Listener* of 29 May 1941 E. M. Forster wrote of Crabbe's preoccupation with Aldeburgh and the sea. It was this article which led Benjamin Britten, whose own childhood was spent by the sea at Lowestoft to the N, to compose the opera *Peter Grimes* (1945), based on a character in *The Borough*. Forster himself was librettist with Eric Crozier of another of Britten's operas, *Billy Budd* (1951), based on the story by Herman Melville. Both operas have been performed at the annual festival in June. Crabbe is commemorated by a bust by Thomas Thurlow

erected in the church in 1947. Visitors in the 19th c. included Wilkie Collins, whose novel *No Name* (1862) has a local setting, and M. R. James, writer of ghost stories, who stayed at Wyndham House, near the church. Others were guests at Strafford House, home of the sociable banker Edward Clodd (1840–1930), founder of the Johnson and Omar Khayyám clubs. Anthony Hope recounts in *Memories and Notes* (1927) how he, Hardy, and James Frazer sailed in Clodd's yacht to visit FitzGerald's grave (see BREDFIELD).

The resort was also the birthplace of the novelist Louis Wilkinson. He wrote a biographical study of the three Powys brothers, *Welsh Ambassadors* (1936), and novels which include *The Buffoon* (1916) and *A Chaste Man* (1917).

ALDERTON *Suffolk*

Village on the B1083, 2 m. from the coast between the Deben and the Ore. Giles Fletcher the Younger was rector here from *c.* 1618 to his death in 1623. He is buried in the church.

AMPTHILL *Bedfordshire*

Old market town on the B530, 8 m. S of Bedford. Horace Walpole, who told one of his correspondents, the Countess of Upper Ossory, 'I dote on Ampthill', often stayed with her at Ampthill Park, where, in the former castle, Catherine of Aragon had been held pending her divorce. Walpole wrote the inscription for the ornate cross erected on the site in the park:

> In days of old, here Ampthill's towers were seen
> The mournful refuge of an injur'd Queen.
> Here flow'd her pure but unavailing tears
> Here blinded Zeal sustained her sinking years.

Hale White, who wrote as 'Mark Rutherford', called the town 'Cowfold' in *The Revolution in Tanner's Lane* (1887). Houghton House, 1 m. N off the A418, was built in 1615 and improved by Inigo Jones for the Countess of Pembroke, patron of many poets. Henry Luttrell, a fashionable wit, in his 'Lines written at Ampthill Park' (1818) mentions the 'roofless walls' and 'Chambers now tenantless'. The three-storey house makes an imposing ruin today on the sandstone ridge. It is said to have been Bunyan's 'House Beautiful' in *The Pilgrim's Progress* (1678).

AMPTON *Suffolk*

Village E off the A134, 5 m. N of Bury St Edmunds. The flint church opposite the red-brick hall has a tablet reading 'Remember Jeremy Collier, M.A. rector of this parish 1679–84 Divine, Historian, Controversialist,

Outlaw, Nonjuring Bishop. Born 23 Sept. 1650, Buried at Old St Pancras, London 26 Apr. 1726. 'He was in the full force of words, a Good Man.' Macaulay.

AUDLEY END *Essex*

Country house on the B1383, W of Saffron Walden, maintained by English Heritage. Sir Philip Sidney accompanied Queen Elizabeth on a progress and stayed with Lord Thomas Howard in 1578 when Gabriel Harvey gave an entertainment. Evelyn, the diarist, who came three times, described the style of the architecture as mixed, on his visit in 1654. Pepys played the flageolet in the cellars in 1677, and the portrait of Lord Sandwich on the staircase was painted for him by Emanuel de Critz from an original by Lely, as Pepys mentions in his *Diary* for 22 Oct. 1660. Vanbrugh made alterations to the Great Hall in 1721 and on his advice the three sides of the outer court were pulled down. The library contains a French *caquetoire* armchair, once belonging to Pope.

AYOT ST LAWRENCE *Hertfordshire*

Village 3 m. NW of Welwyn Garden City, between the A656 and the B651. Bernard Shaw lived here from 1906 until the end of his life, and the way to his home, Shaw's Corner (NT), is well signposted. The house is unchanged since Shaw's time and the ground-floor rooms contain his working equipment as well as many personal relics and pictures of friends and fellow writers such as Sean O'Casey, W. B. Yeats, and Lady Gregory. Hidden from view at the bottom of the garden is the summerhouse where Shaw used to write, sheltered from noise and interruptions. His ashes, with those of his wife, were scattered in the garden.

BACTON *Norfolk*

Village on the B1159. The miller's wife in 'The Reeve's Tale' in *The Canterbury Tales* and Avarice in Langland's *Piers Plowman* invoke the holy cross of Bromholm, once in the 12th-c. priory, now a ruin on the Keswick road. The *Paston Letters* give details of the funeral feast and burial of John Paston (1421–66). Panes of glass had to be removed to let out the 'reke of the torches'. His table tomb was later taken to Paston (2 m. NW).

BARNACK *Cambridgeshire*

Village on the B1443, 7 m. MW of Stamford. Charles Kingsley lived at the rectory from 1824 to 1830, the year his brother Henry was born, and the family moved to Devon. Only part of their house remains by the side of the Victorian rectory (later Kingsley House).

G.B.S. at work in his summerhouse at Shaw's Corner, Ayot St Lawrence

BARNINGHAM WINTER *Norfolk*

Village near Matlask between the A140 and the A148. The manor was a home of the Paston family rebuilt in Jacobean times. The church in the park has memorials.

BARSHAM *Suffolk*

Village on the B1062. The dramatist Sir John Suckling (1609–42), chiefly remembered for 'Why so pale and wan, fond lover?' and other lyrics, inherited the estate and lived briefly at the Hall (gone). Soldiers he recruited were housed in his banqueting hall (later a barn) before going to the Scottish war; their gaudy clothes were later derided in the ballad 'Sir John Suckling's Campaign'. The site of the Hall is down the track between the houses W of the church.

Adrian Bell is buried in the churchyard. A farmer, he wrote a series of charming narratives of English country life, including *Corduroy* (1930), *Silver Ley* (1931), *The Cherry Tree* (1932), *Folly Field* (1933), *Shepherd's Farm* (1939), *Apple Acre* (1942), and *A Suffolk Harvest* (1956), as well as a volume of autobiography, *My Own Master* (1961).

BAWDESWELL *Norfolk*

Village on the A1067 and the B1145, Chaucer's Baldeswelle, where the Reeve Oswald in *The Canterbury Tales* lived.

BECCLES *Suffolk*

Small town on the A146, 16 m. SE of Norwich. Crabbe, who first met Sarah Elmy, the 'Mira' of his poems, when he was an apprentice surgeon, often visited her at Beccles, where she lived with her mother. On his visit in 1780 he worked on *The Village*, a satire on pastoral happiness. Crabbe and Sarah were married at St Michael's Church in 1783.

In 1794 the émigré Chateaubriand, calling himself M. de Combourg, was rescued from penury by the Society of Antiquaries, who employed him to decipher early French manuscripts. He stayed at the King's Head here and spent a romantic interlude at *Bungay.

BEDFORD *Bedfordshire*

County town on the Ouse, where John Bunyan was imprisoned from 1660 to 1672 for preaching without a licence and where he wrote *The Pilgrim's Progress*, *Grace Abounding*, and other works. His spirit lives in the Bunyan Meeting (the Congregational–Baptist church) in Mill St., where he was minister from the end of 1671 until his death in 1688. The present church (built 1849) is the third on the site. Its doors have bronze panels with scenes from *The Pilgrim's Progress* in low relief. Attached to the church, on the site of the barn where Bunyan preached, is an excellent museum containing personal relics and a collection of his works in over 150 languages. The Frank Mott Harrison John Bunyan Collection (library and exhibition devoted to Bunyan) is at the History and Local Studies Library, County Hall Library, Cauldwell St. A bronze statue by Sir Joseph Boehm, given by the 9th Duke of Bedford in 1874, stands at the corner of St Peter's St. and the Broadway. The words of the inscription are taken from *The Pilgrim's Progress*:

> It had its eyes lifted up to heaven
> The best of books in his hand . . .

Bedford was also the birthplace of William Hale White ('Mark Rutherford'). He attended Bedford Modern School and the Bunyan Meeting. Though he left the district as a young man, his books *The Autobiography of Mark Rutherford* (1881) and *Mark Rutherford's Deliverance* (1885) are interesting accounts of the dissenting community in which he grew up. The town also appears as 'Eastthorpe' in his novel *Catharine Furze* (1893). The Essex-born novelist John Fowles was a pupil at Bedford School, before moving on to university studies at *Edinburgh and *Oxford.

BERKHAMSTED *Hertfordshire*

Old town on the A4251. Cowper was born at the rectory on the site of the modern one. It was red brick and had chimneys as tall as the Old Rectory which was built behind it in 1840. Cowper was 7 when his mother died and he was sent away to school.

In 1904 Graham Greene was born at St John's, one of the boarding houses of Berkhamsted School, at which his father was a housemaster and where, as he records in *A Sort of Life* (1971),

> the misery of life started, and the burial ground, long disused, which lay opposite our windows, was separated from our flower-beds by an invisible line, so that every year the gardener would turn up a few scraps of human bone in remaking the herbaceous border.

When Greene's father was promoted to headmaster, the family moved to School House, where Greene was able to read the books in the school library during the holidays. This reading left a profound influence on his life and career. His return to St John's House as a boarder was traumatic:

> I had left civilization behind and entered a savage country of strange customs and inexplicable cruelties: a country in which I was a foreigner and a suspect, quite literally a hunted creature, known to have dubious associates. Was my father not the headmaster? I was like the son of a quisling in a country under occupation.

At the other end of town stood the Hall (gone), where Greene's wealthier cousins lived; one of these, Barbara, accompanied him on the demanding trip across Liberia in 1935 recorded in his *Journey Without Maps*. As an undergraduate, Greene suffered from pathological boredom, and Berkhamsted Common, where as a boy he had imagined himself a hero out of Buchan and in whose trees he had hidden when he ran away from school, was also the scene of his first experiments with Russian roulette:

> I put the muzzle of the revolver into my right ear and pulled the trigger. There was a minute click, and looking down at the chamber I could see that the charge had moved into the firing position. I was out by one. I remember an extraordinary sense of jubilation, as if carnival lights had been switched on in a dark drab street.

Greene was fond of the local countryside, all the more for being on 'the very borders of Metroland', and returned to the scenes of his childhood when he housed Castle, the principal character of *The Human Factor* (1978), in the town, riding his bicycle from the railway station

> across the canal bridge, past the Tudor school, into the High Street, past the grey flint parish church which contained the helmet of a crusader, then up the slope of the Chilterns towards his small semi-detached house in King's Road.

He also returned to Berkhamsted in his last novel, *The Captain and the Enemy* (1988).

BLAXHALL *Suffolk*

Village 8 m. W of Aldeburgh off the B1069. George Ewart Evans, the oral historian, came to live here at School House in 1948 and stayed until 1956, when he moved to Needham Market (1956–62). He later lived at Helmingham (1962–8) in the same county, and at Brooke, near Norwich (1968–88). At Blaxhall, which he called his 'second academy', he began interviewing agricultural workers and writing the series of books which began with *Ask the Fellows Who Cut the Hay* (1956). It was followed by *The Horse in the Furrow* (1960), *The Pattern Under the Plough* (1966), *Where Beards Wag All* (1970), *The Leaping Hare* (with David Thomson, 1972), *The Days That We Have Seen* (1975), *From Mouths of Men* (1976), and *Horse Power and Magic* (1979).

BLETCHLEY *Bedfordshire*

Town now part of Milton Keynes. The novelist Angus Wilson and the poets Henry Reed and Vernon Watkins all worked on the breaking of Enigma and other German codes at Bletchley Park during the Second World War.

BLUNDESTON *Suffolk*

Village off the A12, 4 m. NW of Lowestoft, the birthplace of David Copperfield, though Dickens calls the place 'Blunderstone'. The round church tower has been restored as a memorial to the author, though the high-backed pews, from which Clara Peggotty could look through the window and make sure the house was safe during the service, are no longer there. Thomas Gray, who first met the Revd Norton Nicholls in 1761, used to visit him at the rectory here.

BLUNHAM *Bedfordshire*

Village off the A1, 2 m. NW of Sandy. John Donne, rector (1622–31) while also Dean of St Paul's, paid a yearly visit and stayed in the manor house at the entrance to Park Lane, opposite the church, then used as the rectory. Village tradition tells that he returned to London with a load of cucumbers in his carriage. The church chalice, marked 1626, was Donne's gift.

BLUNTISHAM *Cambridgeshire*

Village on the A1123, 3 m. NE of St Ives. Dorothy Sayers lived (1898–1917) at her father's Georgian rectory on the main road. In 1916, after university, she published her first verse, *Op. 1*, followed two years later by *Catholic Tales*.

BLYTHBURGH *Suffolk*

Small village near the Suffolk coast. Holy Trinity, the large parish church, is known as the 'cathedral of the marshes'. The angels attached to the roof beams were once shot at by Oliver Cromwell's soldiers and inspired Peter Porter's poem 'An Angel in Blythburgh Church'.

BOCKING *Essex*

Village 3 m. S of Braintree. John Gauden was given the living (called a deanery here) in 1641 and retained it throughout the Commonwealth in spite of losing his seat at the Westminster Assembly. He claimed to be the author of *Eikon Basilike*, the account of Charles I's ordeal in 1649, which many thought to be by the King himself.

BOOTON *Norfolk*

Village 1 m. E of Reepham, off the B1145. Whitwell Elwin (1816–1900), born at Thurning Hall, 6 m. NW, was rector (1849–1900). He contributed to the *Quarterly Review*, which he edited from 1853 to 1860. He also edited Pope's works in five volumes (1871–2). The twin-towered Gothic church with carved angels in the roof was built by him after a fire had destroyed the old church.

BRADFIELD COMBUST *Suffolk*

Village on the A134, 5 m. SE of Bury St Edmunds. Arthur Young (1741–1820), the agricultural theorist, lived at Bradfield Hall (rebuilt 1857), which was described by Fanny Burney, a relative, in *Camilla* (1796). She also wrote in her *Diary* (1842) how wretched Young's life was made by his wife, whose language was violent and whose face was so red she looked like a fiend.

BRAINTREE *Essex*

Formerly a wool town, later a nylon weaving centre, on the A131 and the A120. Nicholas Udall (or Uvedale), vicar here from 1537 to 1544, was the author of the earliest-known English comedy, *Ralph Roister Doister*, printed in 1566, but probably first acted by the boys at Eton, where Udall was headmaster from 1534 to 1541.

BRAMPTON *Cambridgeshire*

Village between the A14 and the A1, 2 m. W of Huntingdon. Pepys House, on the E outskirts of the village, was the home of Samuel Pepys's uncle, a cousin of Lord Sandwich, through which connection Pepys had his post at the Admiralty. Pepys's father lived here on his brother's death and Pepys in his *Diary* mentions his visits here.

BRAUGHING *Hertfordshire*

A village between the rivers Rib and Quin. In 1914 H. G. Wells, who lived nearby at *Little Easton, helped set up his lover, the critic and novelist Rebecca West, and their son Anthony at Quinbury, a solid Victorian farmhouse near the village, from which they would explore the local countryside together. In her novel *The Fountain Overflows* (1956), West named the lovable boy Richard Quinbury in memory of happy days spent here with Wells.

BREACHWOOD GREEN *Hertfordshire*

Village on an unclassified road between Whitwell and Luton, 2 m. S of King's Walden. The Baptist Chapel has John Bunyan's pulpit, dated 1658 (originally at nearby Coleman's Green, Bendish). Near the pulpit is a copy of the Geneva Bible (the 'Breeches Bible', 1562), described as 'the Bible of Shakespeare, Milton, Bunyan, and Cromwell . . . [translated by Puritan scholars who fled from this country to Geneva when Mary came to the throne]'.

BREDFIELD *Suffolk*

Village 3 m. N of Woodbridge, off the A12. Edward FitzGerald was born (1809) at The White House (later Bredfield House and then demolished), and he lived until 1838 with his parents at Boulge Hall (1 m. E; burnt 1923 and demolished 1946) leaving only the stables near Boulge church. Boulge can be reached by a track leading off the Debach road. FitzGerald then lived (1838–58) in the single-storey thatched cottage (now Boulge House, altered) where many of his friends visited him. He is buried in Boulge churchyard, where the latest successor of the rose tree from the tomb of Omar Khayyám, planted by his friends in the Omar Khayyám Club in 1893, grows over his grave. The remains of both Fitzgerald's childhood homes are visited by the narrator of W. G. Sebald's novel *The Rings of Saturn* (1998).

BRINKLEY *Cambridgeshire*

Village on the B1052, 5 m. S of Newmarket. Christopher Anstey, poet and satirist, was born (1724) at the rectory, at the end of Lammas Lane, near the Hall.

BRUISYARD *Suffolk*

On the B1120, 5 m. NE of Framlingham, is the turning to the village of Bruisyard. A drive on the W leads to Oakenhill Hall, a tall red-brick house with old chimneys and pointed finials. This was 'Crakenhill', 'the best farm in Bruisyard' of H. W. Freeman's novel of a farming family, *Joseph and his Brethren* (1928).

BUNGAY *Suffolk*

Small town on the B1332, 15 m. SE of Norwich. In 1794 Chateaubriand, a penniless émigré calling himself M. de Combourg, taught French to the young ladies of the district, including Charlotte Ives, a vicar's daughter. Injured in a fall from his horse, he was carried into Bridge House Ⓟ and cared for by the Ives family. He fell in love with the 15-year-old Charlotte and Mrs Ives suggested they should marry and make their home at the vicarage. His confession that he was already married broke the idyll: Mrs Ives fainted and M. de Combourg left the house. He and Charlotte met once more. In 1822 Charlotte, by now Mrs Sutton, sought an audience with Chateaubriand, then French Ambassador in London, to ask a favour for her elder son.

BURY ST EDMUNDS *Suffolk*

Town on the A14 and the A143. The translation in 1840 of Jocelin de Brakelond's 12th-c. chronicle of the abbey prompted Carlyle to describe the town in *Past and Present* (1843). John Lydgate entered the monastery at the age of 15 and was ordained in 1397. Although he became a court poet and was granted lands through the patronage of the 'Good Duke Humphrey' of Gloucester, who died in custody at St Saviour's Hospital (ruined gatehouse in Northgate St.), Lydgate returned to spend many years in the abbey, whose library was one of the largest in the country. The massive Abbey Gateway is now the entrance to public gardens amid the ruins.

In Shakespeare's *2 Henry VI* the king forms a parliament at Bury St Edmunds, and several scenes are set there.

Celia Fiennes visited the newly built Cupola House (later an inn in the Traverse) on her rides, and a plaque records Defoe's stay a few years later in 1704.

Crabb Robinson, a native, lived in Westgate St., where at 15 he first met Catherine Buck, his lifelong correspondent. She married Thomas Clarkson, the abolitionist, and she introduced Crabb Robinson to the literary circle of the Lambs and the Lake Poets, whose activities fill his diary. Edward FitzGerald was at the King Edward VI School (1821–6) with James Spedding, a lifelong friend.

Henry Cockton, author of the comic novels *The Life and Adventures of Valentine Vox the Ventriloquist* (1840) and *Sylvester Sound the Somnambulist* (1844), is commemorated by a plaque in the abbey grounds.

Ouida, author of *Under Two Flags* (1867), was born (1839) at 14 Hospital Rd Ⓟ. Her friends put up a commemorative drinking fountain for animals (now dry and neglected) at the foot of West St., opposite the Spread Eagle. Dickens stayed at the Angel Hotel in 1859 and 1861 on reading tours, and in *The Pickwick Papers* Sam Weller first meets Job Trotter there.

BUXTON *Norfolk*

Village off the B1354, 4 m. SE of Aylsham. Dudwick House (rebuilt), in its park opposite the Black Lion, was the home of Anna Sewell's aunt and uncle, and is thought to be the original of Birtwick Park in *Black Beauty* (1877). Anna Sewell (1820–78) learned to ride when staying as a child with her grandparents at Dudwick Farm. See also LAMAS.

CAISTER CASTLE *Norfolk*

A 15th-c. castle 5 m. NW of Great Yarmouth, built by Sir John Fastolf (Shakespeare's Falstaff), on whose death (1459) it passed to John Paston (1421–66) by a will disputed by other claimants. Many of the *Paston Letters* were written from the castle by John's wife, Margaret, during his absence in London.

CAMBRIDGE *Cambridgeshire*

University town on the A10, founded in the 12th c. on a site first settled by the Romans. Michael Drayton mentions Cambridge as 'my most beloved town' in *Polyolbion* (1622), and Celia Fiennes, on one of her journeys in 1697, comments on all the 'walks with rows of trees and bridges over the river'. She was also interested that the Fellows and gentlemen commoners could have 'a large dining room, a good Chamber and good studdy for £8 a year'. Daniel Defoe in *Tour through Great Britain* (1724–7) honours the University for giving no encouragement to those who would hold scandalous assemblies at unseasonable hours: 'nor is there want of mirth and good company of other kinds'. The River Granta is called the Cam as it flows through the town and the tree-covered grounds connected to the colleges by elegant bridges has become known as the Backs. Charles and Mary Lamb walked here with Crabb Robinson, who mentions it in his *Diary*; Mary Lamb wrote that they were 'walking the whole time—out of one college into another' on their visit in 1815, when they lodged at 11 King's Parade Ⓟ. Charles Lamb, sad that he had missed a university education, wrote a sonnet in which he imagined himself walking about in a gown. The Lambs first met Emma Isola here, whom they later adopted.

Lamb's 'Oxford in the Vacation' was written on his visit to Cambridge in 1820 and combines his memories of both universities. The G.D. of the essay is his friend George Dyer of Emmanuel. Trollope's novel *John Caldigate* (1879) is set partly in Cambridge and partly in the nearby village of Chesterton.

Henry James wrote in *Portraits of Places* (1883) that the Backs show

> the loveliest confusion of gothic windows and ancient trees, of grassy banks and mossy balustrades, of sun-chequered avenues and groves, of lawns and gardens and terraces, of single arched bridges spanning the little stream, which . . . looks as if it had been 'turned on' for ornamental purposes.

In 1907 he accepted the invitation to revisit Cambridge by the young men whom he addressed as 'My dear Cambridge Three', and he stayed two nights at 8 Trumpington St., a tall, narrow house with a walled garden where they sat after meals as the June days were warm, and from where he was taken on a tour of the University. His youthful hosts introduced him to Rupert Brooke, who poled the punt on their excursion on the Cam, and though James later recalled that he was introduced to 'hundreds and hundreds of undergraduates all exactly alike', he was aware at Brooke's death 'of the stupid extinction of . . . so exquisite a being'.

Rose Macaulay, who was born (1881) here, was the daughter of a Fellow of Trinity. The second chapter of *Orphan Island* (1924) describes a don's household in Grange Rd and most of *They Were Defeated* (1932), in which John Cleveland of Christ's and Abraham Cowley of Trinity (see below) appear, is set in 17th-c. Cambridge.

As a child Frances Cornford often visited her Darwin cousins (see Darwin College). After her marriage in 1908 she lived at Conduit Head, off Madingley Rd, and Rupert Brooke, whom she described as 'A Young Apollo golden haired', was one of the undergraduates who visited there. Her first collection of poems was published in 1910, and she mentions the poets at Cambridge over the centuries in 'In the Backs' from *Travelling Home* (1948). One of her most widely known poems was 'To a Fat Lady Seen from a Train' from *Collected Poems* (1954). Her son John Cornford was killed (1936) in the Spanish Civil War, the subject of many of his poems.

The novelist Jean Rhys, lately arrived from Dominica, briefly and unhappily attended the Perse School; the school would appear in her story 'Overture and Beginners Please'.

Phyllis Dorothy James, later the crime novelist P. D. James, moved to Cambridge with her family when she was 11; she studied at Cambridge Girls' High School.

J. B. Priestley, though remembered today for his writing rather than for his political endeavours, did in 1945 stand for Parliament for the Cambridge University seat, as an independent. He lost.

Harold Pinter's *The Birthday Party* gave him his first London production; but the play actually opened first at the Arts Theatre in Cambridge, on 28 April 1958.

An effaced Cambridge is the dystopian setting for L. P. Hartley's post-Third World War novel *Facial Justice* (1960): 'Cambridge—for so the settlement was named—was built on the supposed site of the famous University town, not a vestige of which remained.'

Susan Hill's novel *Air and Angels* (1991) describes a Cambridge of tutorials and boat trips, with the story of a university don who falls in love with a young girl.

Recent Cambridge-educated novelists include Nick Hornby and Jane Rogers.

The poet and novelist John Burnside, who studied English and European Languages at Cambridge College of Arts and Technology in the 1970s, set his novel *The Locust Room* (2001) in the city (rather than the University) of Cambridge of 1975.

In his play *Rock 'n' Roll* (2006), Tom Stoppard moves between Prague and a house in Cambridge, home to Marxist academic Max Morrow.

CHRIST'S COLLEGE (1505). John Leland (or Leyland), who claimed to have saved the manuscripts of 'many good authors' from the monasteries after their dissolution, graduated here in 1522. Gabriel Harvey left after his BA in 1570 to become a Fellow of Pembroke. John Milton, whose fair complexion earned him the nickname 'Lady of Christ's', is said to have had rooms (1625–32) in the first court (refaced). Here he wrote 'Hymn on the Morning of Christ's Nativity' and the sonnet to Shakespeare. His memories of the University are reflected in 'Il Penseroso', written soon after he went down:

> But let my due feet never fail
> To walk the studious cloister's pale,
> And love the high embowéd roof,
> With antique pillars massy proof,
> And storied windows richly dight
> Casting a dim religious light.

The death of Edward King, whose friend he became here, inspired 'Lycidas' (1638). The mulberry tree, traditionally associated with Milton, is still in the Fellows' Garden. John Cleveland, an undergraduate 1627–31, also wrote an elegy on his friend Edward King. Wordsworth, when at *St John's, visited Milton's rooms and drank to his memory, as he records in *The Prelude*.

C. S. Calverley was elected a Fellow in 1858. His 'Ode on Tobacco' from *Verses and Translations* (1862) is written on a bronze plaque on Bacon's tobacconist's shop (rebuilt 1934), which he patronized, on Market Hill. His friends were Walter Besant (1856–9) and W. W. Skeat, Professor of Anglo-Saxon (1878–1912) and editor of *Piers Plowman* (1867–85) and *The Complete Works of Chaucer* (1894–7). There is a plaque to Skeat in the library. Forrest Reid, a novelist influenced by Henry James, was at Christ's College *c.* 1894.

The novelist and scientific administrator C. P. Snow was made a Fellow of Christ's in 1930. He famously clashed with F. R. Leavis (at Downing) after the publication of his celebrated essay 'The Two Cultures'. Three novels in Snow's *Strangers and Brothers* novel sequence (1940–70) are set largely in Cambridge and two in particular—*The Masters* (1951) and *The Affair* (1960)—explore the movements of power in an academic context based on his experience of Christ's.

Snow was tutor in natural sciences to the novelist William Cooper (H. S. Hoff) in the early 1930s. He and Snow became friends and Cooper published a study of Snow's books in 1971. Snow appears disguised as 'Robert' in Cooper's 'Scenes from' novels. The poet Gavin Ewart studied at Christ's in the 1930s. Charles Darwin and Colin Dexter, creators of (respectively) the theory of natural selection and Inspector Morse, are also among the College's alumni. Darwin graduated in 1831, Dexter in 1953.

Near Christ's Pieces stands Penelope Fitzgerald's imaginary 'St Angelicus', the scene of her novel *The Gate of Angels* (1990), and the smallest college in Cambridge:

> Although everything was in miniature, it resembled a fortress, a toy fortress, but a toy of enormous strength, with walls three-and-a-half feet thick, built without rubble. There were no cloisters, no infirmary, no hospice, no welcome (to be honest), to those, strangers or not, arriving from outside, no house apart for the Master, who crowded in on an upper floor along with the Fellows, an arrangement which had caused him to be known in the old days as Master Higgledy-Piggledy.

CLARE COLLEGE (1326), with its picturesque bridge over the Cam, is one of the colleges thought to be 'Soler Hall' of Chaucer's 'The Reeve's Tale' (see Trinity College). Hugh Latimer, who first came to the University in 1500 and was elected a Fellow here in 1511, became noted for his sermons. He was one of the young men bent on reforming the Church (see Jesus College).

Robert Greene received an MA here (1583) after graduating at St John's College. William Whitehead, who was born (1715) in St Botolph's parish and baptized in the 14th-c. church of that name in Trumpington St., studied here and became a Fellow in 1742.

Novelist Sabine Baring-Gould studied here in the 1850s. Siegfried Sassoon started to write poetry as an undergraduate (1904–8). He enlisted on the outbreak of the war in 1914. Students at Clare in the early 1970s included Peter Ackroyd, who graduated with a double first in English.

CORPUS CHRISTI COLLEGE (1352) was formerly called Bene't College from the partly Saxon Church of St Bene't (i.e. Benedict), which was used as the college chapel. The Parker Library houses an outstanding collection of early books and manuscripts, including the Anglo-Saxon Chronicle and the best surviving manuscript of Chaucer's *Troilus and Criseyde*. Members of the College may take visitors to see exhibitions (www.corpus.cam.ac.uk).

Christopher Marlowe had first-floor rooms (*c.* 1578) on the right of 'P' staircase. He graduated MA in 1587, by which time he had already written *Tamburlaine* (1590). John Fletcher, who came up (1593) the year Marlowe was killed in a tavern, is commemorated with him on the wall plaque at the foot of 'O' staircase.

Thomas Fuller, perpetual curate of St Bene't's from 1630, preached the funeral sermon on Thomas Hobson, the well-known carrier, who operated his business from the inn later called The George (gone). Hobson, who appears in Fuller's *Worthies of England* (1662) and is also the subject of two epitaphs by Milton, let out his horses in strict rotation whatever his customer's preference, which gave rise to the phrase 'Hobson's Choice'.

John Cowper Powys and his youngest brother, Llewelyn, were undergraduates here at the turn of the 20th c.

Christopher Isherwood went up to the College with a scholarship to read History in 1924 but, having written lampoons on his sixth-term examination papers, left without a degree. He wrote memorably about his university years in his autobiography *Lions and Shadows* (1938):

> I think that those first two University terms have been amongst the most enjoyable parts of my whole life. I had sufficient money and no worries and as long as I could be together with Chalmers, which was all day and most of the night, the word boredom didn't exist. I was in a continuous state of extreme mental excitement. Every idea we discussed seemed startling and brilliantly new. My official education was, it is true, at a standstill: but Chalmers was educating me all the time.

'Chalmers' was Isherwood's pseudonym for his schoolfriend Edward Upward, with whom he created an elaborate metaphysical fantasy centred on the idea of 'the Other Town', a parallel world suggested by Garret Hostel Bridge (the 'Rats' Hostel') and entered through 'a rusty-hinged little old door in a high blank wall' running along an alley off Silver St. Their private brand of medieval surrealism found permanent expression in *The Mortmere Stories*, of which the best known is Upward's 'The Railway Accident' (written 1928). Certain parts of Isherwood's novel *The Memorial* (1932) are set in Cambridge and reflect his undergraduate career.

DARWIN COLLEGE (1964). A graduate college housed partly in Newnham Grange, the name given to a prosperous corn merchant's house bought by Charles Darwin's son, after his marriage in 1884. *Period Piece* (1952), an entertaining account by Gwen Raverat of her childhood in Newnham Grange, where she was born (1895), gives a picture of her eccentric Darwin uncles and aunts, and her cousin

Magdalene College
Samuel Pepys was a student here; the College's Pepys Library holds the manuscripts of his famous diaries. C. S. Lewis was a Fellow here, 1954-63

St John's College
William Morgan began the first translation of the Bible into Welsh here in the 1560s. Wordsworth studied here; he and Samuel Butler are remembered in portraits in the Hall

Clare College
Siegfried Sassoon, Hugh Latimer, and Robert Greene all studied here; and it may be the 'Soler Hall' of Chaucer's *Canterbury Tales*

Punting on the Cam

Jesus College
Coleridge studied here, 1791-4, though never graduated. He wrote in his *Biographia Literaria* of 'friendly cloisters, and the happy grove of quiet, ever honoured Jesus College'

JESUS LANE

N

NEWMARKET ROAD

Trinity College
Alumni include Dryden, Byron (who kept a pet bear), Nabokov, Thackeray, and Bertrand Russell; also Tennyson, who met Hallam here

Milton's Mulberry Tree

Christ's College
Famous alumni include John Milton; the college gardens house the 'Milton Mulberry Tree' (and a new accommodation block that has been known as 'the Milton Hilton'). Darwin was a student here too

King's College
E. M. Forster studied here and stayed most of his lifetime (and set his novel *Maurice* in Cambridge). Rupert Brooke studied at King's too, as did latterly Salman Rushdie and Zadie Smith; Wordsworth wrote three sonnets about the Chapel

ST ANDREW'S STREET

KING'S PARADE

DOWNING STREET

PARKSIDE

King's College Chapel

Corpus Christi College
This is where Christopher Marlowe studied, and probably where his *Tamburlaine* was written. The College owns a portrait of a young man believed to be Marlowe. His fellow playwright John Fletcher studied here too

Pembroke College
Edmund Spenser and Thomas Gray both studied here. More recently Clive James wrote about his time at Pembroke in his memoir *May Week Was in June*

Parker's Piece

TRUMPINGTON STREET

Fitzwilliam Museum

8 Trumpington Street
Henry James stayed here in 1907, and met Rupert Brooke, who took him punting

LENSFIELD ROAD

Railway Stn.

The Fitzwilliam Museum
The Museum's collection includes a number of William Blake pictures, and manuscripts from Keats (his 'Ode to a Nightingale') and Rupert Brooke ('Grantchester')

Frances (later Cornford), in Cambridge in the decades before and after 1900.

DOWNING COLLEGE (1800).

The critic F. R. Leavis, who was born at 64 Mill Rd, read first History then English at Emmanuel College in the early 1920s and began his professional career as a lecturer at Emmanuel in 1931. He immediately got into trouble with the university authorities and even the Home Office (who viewed him as a 'dangerous crank') for lecturing on Joyce's *Ulysses*, then still under a ban.

Leavis's career at Downing—pursued in collaboration with his wife, the indefatigable Queenie—was often turbulent and fractious, but his influence on the English syllabuses in universities, on what constitutes the 'canon' of English literature, and his conviction that the criticism of literature—the 'common pursuit of true judgement'—is an important and humanizing activity, has been immense.

His lectures influenced several generations of Cambridge undergraduates, including the poet and critic D. J. Enright, who studied under Leavis at Downing in the 1940s and contributed to his highbrow periodical *Scrutiny*, which Leavis edited at his house on Chesterton Rd. Enright's association with Leavis made it difficult for him to find a university job in Britain, which is why he pursued his academic career overseas.

Howard Jacobson took his degree at Downing; he would later return to Cambridge for a spell as a lecturer at Selwyn College. Cambridge college life would appear in Jacobson's novel *Redback* (1987), part of which is set at the fictional Malapert College.

EMMANUEL COLLEGE (1584).

William Law, author of *A Serious Call to a Devout and Holy Life* (1729), a work of great influence in the 18th and 19th cc., became a sizar in 1705 and a Fellow in 1711. He stayed here briefly as he refused to take the oath of allegiance. Richard Hurd, who was elected a Fellow after taking his MA in 1742, wrote *The Polite Arts, or, A dissertation on poetry, painting, music, etc.* (1749). Thomas Percy was granted a DD in 1770, five years after he published the *Reliques*. George Dyer, the friend who often appears in Lamb's *Essays of Elia*, and who wrote a *History of the University and Colleges* (1814), graduated in 1778. Hugh Walpole was an undergraduate here from 1902 to 1905. Michael Frayn studied philosophy at Emmanuel in the 1950s, where he came under the influence of Wittgenstein. Between the writing of novels and plays in the 1970s, Frayn wrote the philosophical work *Constructions* (1974).

FITZWILLIAM MUSEUM.

Museum built (1837–47) to house the bequests of Viscount Fitzwilliam. The picture galleries contain works by Joseph Highmore, the friend of Samuel Richardson, who illustrated his novel *Pamela* (1740), illustrations by Blake, and portraits of Hardy and Shaw. The library has many autograph manuscripts, including Keats's 'Ode to a Nightingale' and Brooke's 'Grantchester', which are sometimes on display (www.fitzmuseum.cam.ac.uk). M. R. James, while Director (1893–1908), catalogued the manuscripts of the Museum and the colleges.

GIRTON COLLEGE (1869).

The novelist Rosamond Lehmann came here on a scholarship to read English in 1919. She was tutored by Sir Arthur Quiller-Couch ('Q') and in 1985 became an honorary fellow of the College. The poet, Blake scholar, and critic Kathleen Raine came up to Girton on a scholarship to read Natural Sciences in 1926, finding accurate Lehmann's portrait of college life in her novel *Dusty Answer*. Raine left with a Third in psychology, but returned to Girton in 1954 as a Research Fellow for five years.

After a prizewinning student career, Queenie Roth was made a Research Fellow of Girton in 1929, the same year in which she married the critic F. R. Leavis (see Downing College).

GONVILLE AND CAIUS (pr. Keys) COLLEGE (1348 and 1557).

Jeremy Taylor, who was born (1613) in the town and baptized in Holy Trinity Church, Market St., was elected a Fellow in 1633, but was summoned to Oxford in 1635. Thomas Shadwell entered in 1656, but left without a degree.

Charles Doughty, chiefly remembered for *Travels in Arabia Deserta* (1888), was an undergraduate from 1861 to 1863. After transferring to Downing College (1800) and some months studying in Norway, he returned to take his degree in 1865.

J. E. Flecker studied (1908–10) Oriental Languages before entering the Consular Service.

JESUS COLLEGE (1496).

Thomas Cranmer was made a Fellow (1515) after studying here. It is said that he, William Tyndale, and Hugh Latimer of Clare used to meet at the Old White Hart Inn (gone) to discuss the reforms they hoped to make in the practices of the Church. Wordsworth begins his sonnet to them with:

Aid, glorious Martyrs, from your fields of light
Our mortal ken!

Laurence Sterne, who came up in 1733 (MA 1740), met here his lifelong friend John Hall (later John Hall-Stevenson, 1718–85), whom he afterwards depicted as Eugenius.

S. T. Coleridge came up in 1791 and after a short interval, when he enlisted in the Dragoons in 1793, remained until 1794. In *Biographia Literaria* (1817), he writes of the 'friendly cloisters, and the happy grove of quiet, ever honoured Jesus College'. The ceiling of the chapel was decorated by William Morris and the glass is by Morris, Burne-Jones, and Madox Brown (late 1860s–1870s). Sir Arthur Quiller-Couch became a Fellow in 1912 when elected to the Chair of English Literature. His published lectures, *On the Art of Writing* (1916) and *On the Art of Reading* (1920), reached a wide public beyond the University.

KING'S COLLEGE (1441).

The view of the chapel and Fellows' Building, familiar from 18th-c. prints, can still be seen from the Backs. Thomas Preston, author of *Cambises, King of Persia* (1569), became a Fellow of King's in 1556 (LL D 1576) before becoming the Master of Trinity Hall. Giles Fletcher the Elder, an undergraduate from 1565 to 1569, became a Fellow in 1568, and John Harington studied here *c.* 1575. Fletcher's *Licia, or, Poemes of Love* was published in 1593. His elder son Phineas, a student from 1605 to 1608, was elected Fellow in 1611. Edmund Waller stayed here for a short time (1620–2) before entering Lincoln's Inn. Horace Walpole studied here (1735–9) and then left for a tour of the Continent with Thomas Gray of Peterhouse, whom he had first met at Eton. Christopher Anstey, a former scholar, became a Fellow *c.* 1743. Most visitors admire the chapel, and John Evelyn in his *Diary* mentions, as well as the beauty of the inside, the wide view that he saw from the roof. Wordsworth, who wrote three sonnets in its praise, describes

the branching roof
Self poised, and scooped into ten thousand cells
Where light and shade repose, where music dwells
Lingering—and wandering on as loth to die . . .

William Johnson won the Chancellor's Medal, by a single vote, in 1843 with his poem 'Plato'. He became a Fellow in 1845 and held his Fellowship while he was master (1846–72) at Eton. On his retirement he took the additional name of Cory. Percy Lubbock was an undergraduate here *c.* 1898.

M. R. James was elected Provost of his old college in 1905. His *Ghost Stories of an Antiquary* (1905) and its sequel (1911) reached a wide public. He became Vice-Chancellor in 1913.

Rupert Brooke had rooms in the Fellows' Building in 1906, but found his first year unexciting. Later he became one of the Apostles (see Trinity College), contributed poems and reviews to the *Cambridge Review*, and joined the Fabian Society. After acting in *Dr Faustus*, he was instrumental in forming the Marlowe Society, still in being as an undergraduate dramatic society. In 1909 he found rooms above the Orchard Tea Rooms in *Grantchester. He wrote a thesis on Webster and was elected a Fellow in 1913.

G. Lowes Dickinson, an undergraduate and Fellow (1886–1920), lived here when he retired. His friend E. M. Forster, who read Classics and History here (1897–1901), became a Fellow in 1927 and had rooms on 'A' staircase from 1946 to his death in 1970. In Forster's novel *The Longest Journey* (1907), he writes of the main character that Cambridge 'had taken and soothed him, and warmed him and had laughed at him a little, saying that he must not be so tragic yet awhile'; a pleasant fate after the rigours of a public school, an institution Forster thought responsible for 'the undeveloped heart', a constant thread in his novels. Lowes Dickinson and Forster were both elected to the

Society of Apostles. The happiness that both men found at the University was described by Forster when he used Lowes Dickinson's autobiographical material to write his *Life* (1934). 'As Cambridge filled up with friends it acquired a magic quality . . . People and books reinforced one another, intelligence joined hands with affection, speculation became passion, and discussion was made profound by love.'

The college is the setting for two novels by King's men: E. F. Benson's *David of King's* (1924) and Shane Leslie's *The Cantab* (1926).

The chapel's 'stonework soars and springs' in Betjeman's 'Sunday Morning, King's Cambridge'. Simon Raven was educated here and recruited as a reviewer for *The Listener* by J. R. Ackerley in the college urinal. King's features as 'Lancaster College' in his novel sequence *Alms for Oblivion* (1960s and 1970s). The novelist J. G. Ballard, after attending the Leys School in Cambridge, came up to King's in the late 1940s, and read Medicine for two years. He spent a great deal of time in the dissecting room.

The playwright and novelist John Arden studied architecture at King's in the early 1950s. Zadie Smith graduated in 1997, by which time she had already secured a publishing deal and considerable publicity for her first novel, *White Teeth* (2000).

MAGDALENE (pr. 'Mawdlin) **COLLEGE** (1542). Samuel Pepys came here from Trinity Hall in 1651 and graduated in 1653. In his *Diary* he writes of his later visits. On one occasion he spent the afternoon drinking immoderately at the Three Tuns and in 1667 he walked into 'the butterys, as a stranger, and there drank my bellyful of their beer, which pleased me as the best I ever drank'. The original diary is one of the manuscripts, books, and prints bequeathed by Pepys to his college and housed in his own bookcases in the Pepys Library in the Second Court. Percy Lubbock, Curator of the Pepys Library (1906–8), wrote a study of Pepys (1909).

Charles Kingsley, an undergraduate here from 1838 to 1842, became Professor of Modern History in 1860. His novel *Alton Locke* (1850) has many scenes in Cambridge. A. C. Benson, Fellow from 1904, was Master 1915–25 and did much to beautify the College, where he wrote *From a College Window* (1906). Vernon Watkins came up in 1924, but cared more about writing poetry than taking a degree and, intolerant of academic criticism, left the following year. C. S. Lewis became a Fellow here, when elected Professor of Medieval and Renaissance English (1954–63). One of his popular children's books, *The Magician's Nephew* (1955), and *Studies in Words* (1960) and *An Experiment in Criticism* (1961), were published during his years here. He died here in 1963.

The Old Library (First Court) contains the Ferrar Papers (see Trinity College) and manuscripts of Hardy, Kipling, and T. S. Eliot, Hon. Fellows whose portraits hang in the Hall. The novelist, editor, and memoirist J. R. Ackerley achieved a Third in English in

1921. In 1925 Sir William Empson won a scholarship to the College and pursued a student career of precocious brilliance here, studying first Mathematics and later English under I. A. Richards. He wrote much of his most famous work, *Seven Types of Ambiguity* (1930), a study of the many levels of meaning in poetry, while still an undergraduate. He was made Bye-Fellow of the College in 1929 but was dismissed after a month for keeping contraceptives in his college rooms and entertaining a woman at a late hour.

NEWNHAM COLLEGE (1875). Katharine Bradley, who later collaborated with her niece to write as 'Michael Field', was one of the first students here. Virginia Woolf's *A Room of One's Own* (1929) is based on the papers she read to the Arts Society at Newnham and the Odtaa at Girton in 1928. The J—H—who appears in the garden of the imaginary college 'Fernham' is Jane Harrison, a Fellow and author of *The Religion of Ancient Greece* (1905). The poet Anne Stevenson was born in Cambridge in 1933, where her father was studying Philosophy with Wittgenstein, and, after a childhood and education in the United States, came back to Cambridge on a Fulbright Scholarship to Newnham College. She describes her response to the city in her poem 'Returning to Cambridge':

> the river is the same—conceited
> historic, full of the young.

The novelists A. S. Byatt and Margaret Drabble both studied at Newnham too.

PEMBROKE COLLEGE (previously Pembroke Hall, 1347). Nicholas Ridley, who may have helped Thomas Cranmer with the Prayer Books of Edward VI, became a Fellow here (*c.* 1524) and is commemorated by Ridley's Walk, a path S of the Master's Lodge.

Edmund Spenser was admitted in 1569 as a sizar, having already written sonnets on themes of Petrarch and Du Bellay and 'Hymnes in honour of Love and Beauty', which he said he wrote in his 'green youth'. He graduated BA in 1573. Gabriel Harvey, the Fellow lecturing in Rhetoric, became his friend and appeared as Hobbinol in *The Shepheards Calender* (1579). Harvey, who also helped Spenser get a place in Leicester's household, carried on fierce disputes with Robert Greene and Richard Nash, and he and Nash came under the wrath of the authorities. Lancelot Andrewes, a student contemporary with Spenser, became Master (1589–1605). Richard Crashaw was a student here (1632–4) before going to Peterhouse as a Fellow.

Christopher Smart, who entered under the Duchess of Cleveland's patronage, became a Classics Scholar in 1742, graduated in 1743, and was elected a Fellow in 1745. His play *A Trip to Cambridge*, acted by his fellow undergraduates, called forth the scorn of Thomas Gray in his *Letters* (1935), 'he acts five parts himself, and one is only sorry that he can't do all the rest'. However, Smart's translation

into elegant Latin of Pope's 'Ode for Music on St Cecilia's Day' pleased the author, and his entries for the Seatonian Prize twice saved him from his creditors, whose presence at one time barricaded him in his room. These poems on a sacred subject also tempered the wrath of the College, who found that while holding a Fellowship for a single man, Smart had not told them of his marriage. His Fellowship was renewed but he sank further into debt and left his college rooms in 1749 and Cambridge in 1755. Gray, who had come to Pembroke from Peterhouse, disapproved of Smart's drinking and extravagance and foretold his end. William Mason, whom Gray had helped to a Fellowship in 1749, also disapproved but collected money for his relief, though he thought Smart's poem *Song to David* (1763) proved he was still mad. Gray spent most of his life in Cambridge and became Professor of History and Modern Languages (1768). In 'Ode to Music' (1769), Gray describes the 'Willowy Camus', 'the level lawn', and 'the cloister dim'. In his *Letters* he emphasizes how much more enjoyable the place is without people. 'It is they, I assure you, that get it an ill name and spoil it all.' Gray had rooms in the Hitcham Building, in the Second Court, from 1756 to 1771, when he died.

Ted Hughes won a scholarship to Pembroke College; national service delayed his taking it up (he first had to spend two years at the Fylingdales radar post—reading, for most of that time); but eventually he did come up to Cambridge in 1951, to study Archaeology and Anthropology. At Cambridge, Hughes and a group of friends launched the *St Botolph's Review*, a poetry magazine; it was launched with a party on 26 February 1956—it was at this party that Hughes met the young American student Sylvia Plath. 'Our magazine was merely an overture | To the night and the party . . .' ('St Botolph's').

After their marriage Hughes and Plath lived at 55 Eltisley Ave., where he wrote and worked as an English and drama teacher. Hughes's *Birthday Letters* (1998) includes the poem '55 Eltisley'.

The novelist Tom Sharpe studied at Pembroke; his time in Cambridge (where after some years abroad he returned to teach, and where he still lives today) has provided the backdrop for all of his most successful fiction. His college of 'Porterhouse' (of *Porterhouse Blue*, 1974) may be fictional, but those who know Cambridge will feel it is nonetheless somehow very familiar; this account of a dinner, for example:

> For two hours the members of Porterhouse were lost to the world, immersed in an ancient ritual that spanned the centuries. The clatter of knives and forks, the clink of glasses, the rustle of napkins and the shuffling feet of the College servants dimmed the present. Outside the Hall the winter wind swept through the streets of Cambridge. Inside all was warmth and conviviality. Along the tables a hundred candles esconced in silver candelabra cast elongated shadows of the crouching waiters across the portraits of past Masters that lined the walls.

Severe or genial, scholars or politicians, the portraits had one thing in common: they were all rubicund and plump. Porterhouse's kitchen was long established.

(In Sharpe's *Wilt* (1976), meanwhile, Henry Wilt teaches at Fenland College of Arts and Technology, a setting quite different from Porterhouse.)

Also at Pembroke was Clive James, whose third volume of memoir, *May Week Was in June* (1990), describes his experiences at this legendary old seat of learning; the very architecture, he thought, was designed to calm any radicalism out of its students:

> the lovely façades, the sweeping lawns, the intricate crannies opening on distant vistas, were meant not just to lull but to disarm: nobody who had once lived in these emollient surroundings would ever again feel sufficiently alienated from society to be anything more troublesome than a reformist. Gradualism was implicit in every carefully repainted coat of arms and battered refectory table . . .

PETERHOUSE (1281), the oldest college. John Skelton is thought to have been attached to Peterhouse. He graduated MA in 1484 and in 1493 became 'poet laureate', at that time a title given to an outstanding student. He is also known to have been at Cambridge in 1504–5. Richard Crashaw, an undergraduate at Pembroke, became a Fellow here (1637–43), but was expelled for refusing to accept the Solemn League and Covenant.

Thomas Gray was here from 1734 to 1738 and again from 1743 to 1756, when a practical joke by some students, who were amused by his dread of fire, caused him to find quarters at Pembroke. His rooms in the Fellows' Building still have the bars he placed at his windows.

Between 1961 and 1963 Kingsley Amis held a lectureship (somewhat unhappily) at Peterhouse; during this time he lived at 9 Madingley Rd; the set-up was described by his son Martin Amis (in his book *Experience*) thus:

> The house on Madingley Road differed from every other don's house in the city: students could be found in it, regularly. They stayed the night. They drove the car. They read or dozed in the garden. They made some of my meals.

QUEENS' COLLEGE (1448). Erasmus Tower in Pump Court contains the rooms occupied (1511–14) by the Dutch humanist Desiderius Erasmus while Lady Margaret Reader in Greek. His *Colloquia* and his *Letters* are the source for details in Scott's *Anne of Geierstein* (1829) and *The Cloister and the Hearth* (1861) by C. Reade. Thomas Fuller, who studied here (1621–8), wrote *History of the University of Cambridge* (1655). The classicist Horace Moule, Thomas Hardy's unhappy friend and mentor, whose life and tragic death exerted an influence on Hardy's *Jude the Obscure*, committed suicide in his college rooms in 1870.

T. H. White, author of the epic *The Once and Future King* (1958, incorporating *The Sword in the Stone* (1939) and *The Goshawk* (1951), came up to read English at Queens' in 1925. He was hard up and made ends meet by taking on tutorial work during the vacations. His detective novel *Darkness at Pemberley* (1933) is set in part at Queens'. Charles Tomlinson, poet, critic, and translator, now an honorary fellow of the College, studied at Queens' in the 1940s. The poet Peter Redgrove won a scholarship to read Natural Sciences at Queens' in 1951, but considered himself a 'barbarian scientist'. After trying unsuccessfully to switch to English, he left without a degree.

Graham Swift came up to read English in 1967.

Stephen Fry was a student here from 1979; he joined the Footlights drama group, where he would meet his comedy partner Hugh Laurie. When he came to feature Cambridge in his debut novel, *The Liar*, Fry would create the fictional St Matthew's College as his setting; but—St Matthew's apart—the Cambridge of *The Liar* is otherwise true to life; this, for instance, is the hero, Adrian, on the University Library:

> Adrian walked through Clare College to the University. The impertinence of the building, as it launched upwards like a rocket, had always annoyed him. Compared to the feminine domed grace of Oxford's Bodleian or London's British Museum, it was hardly a thing of beauty. It strained up like a swollen phallus, trying to penetrate the clouds. The same principle as a Gothic spire, Adrian supposed. But the union of the library and the heavens would be a very secular Word-made-Flesh indeed.

Fry's later novel *Making History* (1996), a counterfactual story set in a world in which Hitler has never been born, begins in Cambridge too.

ST CATHARINE'S COLLEGE (1473). James Shirley came from Oxford to Catz (as it is familiarly known) and graduated (*c.* 1618), when his poem *Narcissus*, written in the style of Shakespeare's *Venus and Adonis*, was published as *Eccho*.

After an interval spent travelling, Malcolm Lowry, an undergraduate 1929–32, came up from the Leys School, where he had written precocious articles for the school magazine. He had visited America, staying with Conrad Aiken, to whom he had written after reading his novel *The Blue Voyage*. Lowry first had rooms in Bateman St. and frequented Roebuck House, where Charlotte Haldane kept open house for aesthetes. His friends drank with him at the Red Cow, The Bath, and The Eagle, and he spent the long vacations with Aiken in *Rye. Lowry's novel *Ultramarine* (1933), which he worked at intermittently here, was accepted in lieu of a thesis by his tutor.

ST JOHN'S COLLEGE (1511). Thomas Wyatt came here at the then usual age of 12 and graduated in 1518, MA 1520. William Morgan, first translator of the whole Bible into Welsh, entered in 1565 and graduated in 1568, MA 1571. It is possible that he may have begun his translation (London, 1588) before leaving Cambridge.

Robert Greene entered as a sizar and graduated in 1579. Thomas Nash wrote that he spent 'seven yere altogether lacking a quarter' in 'the sweetest nurse of learning in all the University', perhaps from 1581 to 1587. He developed an antipathy to Gabriel Harvey of Pembroke, which resulted in a spate of satires on both sides. Nash defended Greene, whom Harvey in *Foure Letters* had called 'The Ape of Euphues', in *Strange Newes* (1593). Robert Herrick was a student here (1613–16) but graduated from Trinity Hall. John Cleveland came here after graduating at Christ's in 1631. He became a Fellow in 1635 and appears in Rose Macaulay's *They Were Defeated* (1932), in which Herrick also features. Many of Cleveland's poems relate to Cambridge. Matthew Prior studied here from 1682 to 1686 and became a Fellow in 1688, but soon left for diplomatic service on the Continent. Charles Churchill is thought to have left the College after it was discovered that he had made a Fleet marriage (see LONDON: CITY) at the age of 18 in 1749. The same year William Mason became an MA and was elected to a Fellowship at Pembroke. William Wordsworth, an undergraduate from 1787 to 1790, wrote his impressions of coming up in *The Prelude* (1850), as he roamed:

> Delighted through the motley spectacle;
> Gowns grave, or gaudy, doctors, students, streets,
> Courts, cloisters, flocks of churches, gateways,
>   towers:
> Migration strange for a stripling of the hills,
> A northern villager.

An inscription can be seen in the college kitchen. Wordsworth's room was on 'F' staircase. He studied Mathematics, but left without a degree.

Henry Kirke White, whose poems impressed Southey and other friends who raised money for him to come up in 1805, died in his rooms in October 1806. He was buried in All Saints' Church (site an open space opposite the gate) but when this was demolished (1865) his memorial was removed to the chapel.

William Barnes kept his name on the college roll for 10 years from 1838 as a 'ten-year-man' and graduated BD in 1850. Samuel Butler entered in 1854, like Barnes intended for the Church, but he quarrelled with his father and emigrated to New Zealand. His first accounts of the country were published in *The Eagle*, the college magazine. Butler's self-portrait is in the Hall, where there are also portraits of Matthew Prior and Wordsworth.

The poet Ted Walker won a scholarship to read Modern Languages at St John's in the 1950s. Frederick Raphael attended the College in the same decade, which provided experiences that are reflected in his novel of a Cambridge generation *The Glittering Prizes* (1976). In Kate Atkinson's novel *Case Histories* (2004), Victor is a Fellow at St John's—and the whole book wanders freely around the town, from college to college, from Parker's Piece to Addenbrooke's Hospital.

SIDNEY SUSSEX COLLEGE (1589). Thomas Rymer, author of *A Short View of Tragedy*, and clergyman Thomas Fuller (formerly at Queens'), were educated here.

TRINITY COLLEGE (1546). This, the largest college, has an ornate fountain (1602) in the Great Court, which was the source of the College's drinking water. The Library, designed by Wren (usually open two hours daily, www.trin.cam.ac.uk), has manuscripts of works by Milton, Byron, Tennyson, Thackeray, and A. E. Housman, and busts of Bacon (Roubiliac) and Tennyson (Woolner), and the statue of Byron (Thorvaldsen) refused by Westminster Abbey. Celia Fiennes praised Grinling Gibbons's work as 'the finest carving in wood in flowers, birds, leaves, figures of all sorts, as ever I saw'. In the ante-chapel of the chapel there are statues of Macaulay and Tennyson.

Soler Hall, of Chaucer's 'The Reeve's Tale', may have been King's Hall, one of the three colleges amalgamated by Henry VIII in his foundation of Trinity College (see Clare College). King Edward III's Gate and King's Hostel remain, W of the chapel. One of the earliest Fellows was Dr John Dee, whose reputation as a magician began with his startling stage effects for a production of Aristophanes' *Peace* in 1546. Shakespeare is thought to have had Dee in mind in creating Prospero in *The Tempest*, written probably *c.* 1611, a few years after Dee's death. George Gascoigne was one of the earliest students and Francis Bacon (1573–5), William Alabaster (*c.* 1582), and Henry Peacham (*c.* 1590) followed before the end of the century. Giles Fletcher the Younger, a student from 1603 to 1606, became Reader in Greek Grammar (1615) and Literature (1618). *Christ's Victory and Triumph* (1610) and many of his allegories were written here. George Herbert entered in 1609, became a Fellow in 1616, and was Public Orator 1619–27. His friend Nicholas Ferrar, of Clare, prompted his decision to leave university life for the Church. The more flamboyant John Suckling was a student (*c.* 1625) for a short time before entering Gray's Inn. Thomas Randolph spent most of his adult life here, first as a student and then (1629–32) as a Fellow, when his reputation as a writer of verse both in English and Latin was made. He left Cambridge for London (1632) and died three years later. His *Aristippus, or, The Jovial Philosopher* (1630) includes an amusing sketch on the rival merits of ale and sack. Andrew Marvell, an undergraduate from 1633 to 1638, contributed to *Musa Cantabrigiensis* (1637), the year Abraham Cowley came up. Cowley lived here for six years until ejected from his Fellowship by the Parliamentarians in 1644. One of his comedies was acted before Prince Charles in 1641 and he speaks of Cambridge with affection in his poem 'On the Death of Mr William Harvey':

> Ye fields of Cambridge, our dear Cambridge, say
> Have ye not seen us walking every day?

> Was there a tree about, which did not know
> The love betwixt us two?
> Henceforth, ye gentle trees, for ever fade,
> Or your sad branches thicker join
> And in some darksome shades combine
> Dark as the grave wherein my friend is laid.

John Dryden (BA 1654) and Nathaniel Lee (BA 1668) were both scholars, who drew on their classical studies for their later dramatic works. Zacharias Conrad von Uffenbach, whose diary was edited, with others, in *Cambridge Under Queen Anne* by J. E. B. Mayor in 1911, visited Richard Bentley, the Master, whom he found 'as well lodged as the queen at St. James's'. Bentley became Master in 1699 at the time his *Dissertation on the Letters of Phalaris* silenced his critics by proving the letters spurious. Echoes of the long controversy occur in Swift's *The Battle of the Books* written in 1697. Bentley, who was satirized by Pope in *The Dunciad*, held the Mastership, in spite of opposition to his despotism, which nominally deprived him of it, until his death in 1742. Laurence Eusden became a Fellow of this, his own college, in 1712, and in 1717 wrote verses celebrating the marriage of the Duke of Newcastle, who had the gift of the Poet Laureateship. Eusden became the Laureate and Pope sharpened his pen to include him in *The Dunciad* (1728). Richard Cumberland, who was born (1732) in the Master's Lodge, became a Fellow for a short while before his marriage.

Lord Byron, who entered in 1805 and had rooms in Nevile's Court, published *Juvenilia* (1807), later called *Hours of Idleness*, which did not find favour in the *Edinburgh Review*. In his *Letters* Byron writes 'I like a College Life extremely . . . I am now most pleasantly situated in Superexcellent Rooms, flanked on one side by my Tutor, on the other by an Old Fellow, both of whom are rather checks to my vivacity.' He kept a tame bear in his rooms.

Dorothy and William Wordsworth stayed (1820) at the Master's Lodge to see their brother Christopher, who had recently been elected Master and who was then Vice-Chancellor. 'All is so quiet and stately both within and without doors,' wrote Dorothy Wordsworth. One evening 'a small but zealous band' of undergraduates was invited to meet the poet, and one of them, John Moultrie (1799–1874), wrote verses about his impressions of Wordsworth, which are quoted in Mary Moorman's biography. Wordsworth later wrote a sonnet on the portrait of Henry VIII by Holbein, then in the Master's Lodge.

T. B. Macaulay, who came up in 1818, became a Fellow in 1824. His first essay, on Milton, was published in the *Edinburgh Review* in 1825. Macaulay's rooms were on 'E' staircase, where Thackeray also lived (1829–30), as did the hero of his novel *Henry Esmond* (1852). Edward FitzGerald, an undergraduate 1827–30, had lodgings at 20 King's Parade Ⓟ. In *Euphranor* (1851), a dialogue on educational systems set in Cambridge, he describes the 'sluggish current' of the Cam, 'which seem'd indeed fitter for the slow merchandise of coal,

than to wash the walls and flow through the groves of Academe'. He was a contemporary of Thackeray, Tennyson, Kinglake, James Spedding, and Monckton Milnes. Tennyson, who won the Chancellor's Medal (1829) with the poem 'Timbuctoo', met Arthur Hallam here, the friend whose death inspired *In Memoriam*. Hallam had rooms in New Court and Tennyson lodged at 59 Trumpington St., now incorporated in Corpus Christi College. Tennyson, Hallam, and Monckton Milnes were among the earliest members of the Society of Apostles, which met weekly in Trinity. Henry Sidgwick, Knightbridge Professor of Philosophy, elected in 1856, wrote: 'Absolute candour was the only duty that the tradition of the Society enforced . . . The greatest subjects were continually debated, but gravity of treatment . . . was not imposed, though sincerity was.'

F. W. Farrar, who came up in 1852, also won the Chancellor's Medal and was an Apostle. He was elected a Fellow in 1856 and he based his novel *Julian Home* (1859) on his life at Cambridge. F. C. Burnand, an undergraduate 1853–6, founded the Cambridge Amateur Dramatic Club in 1855, now in Park St., and wrote humorous sketches and burlesques. In May 1873 F. W. H. Myers, a Fellow interested in psychical research, invited Marian Evans (George Eliot) to visit him. Their talk in the Fellows' Garden was recounted later in Bertrand Russell's *Autobiography*: 'George Eliot told F. W. H. Myers that there is no God, and yet we must be good; and Myers decided that there is a God and yet we need not be good.'

James Frazer came to Trinity in 1875 (Fellow 1879) and remained here, with the exception of a short stay as Professor of Social Anthropology in Liverpool, until his death in 1941. His *Golden Bough* (12 vols, 1890–1915) is a comparative study of the beliefs and religions of mankind.

Lytton Strachey, an undergraduate from 1899 to 1903, settled in attic rooms on 'K' staircase, called mutton-hole corner. After an uncomfortable time at school he found he enjoyed Trinity. With his friends Clive Bell, Leonard Woolf, A. J. Robertson, and Saxon Sydney-Turner he formed a group called the Midnight Society, which met on Saturdays, at midnight, in Clive Bell's rooms. The group, later joined by Thoby Stephen (brother of Virginia, later Woolf), was the precursor of the Bloomsbury Group. Strachey, who won the Chancellor's English Medal, had his first poems published in *The Granta*. A. A. Milne was an undergraduate from 1900 to 1903 and editor of *The Granta* in 1902.

A. E. Housman became a Fellow here when appointed Professor of Latin in 1911. *A Shropshire Lad* (1896) was followed by *Last Poems* in 1922 and, in the year of his death, by *More Poems* (1936). He published a Cambridge lecture, *The Name and Nature of Poetry*, in 1933.

G. M. Trevelyan, who made history a pleasure for the general reader with *English*

Trinity Lane, Cambridge. Vladimir Nabokov spent his student years here in the 1920s

Social History (1942), was Master from 1940 to 1951 and wrote a history of the college.

The novelist Erskine Childers studied here in the early 1890s, where he held opinions about the future of Ireland entirely at variance with those he would hold later in life (when he became Minister of Propaganda for Sinn Fein). Bertrand Russell won a scholarship to Trinity in 1890, and later became a Fellow. His relationship with the college was volatile.

Vladimir Nabokov, exiled from his native Russia after the revolution, studied Slavonic and Romance languages at Trinity in the 1920s and played football for his college. In his autobiography, *Speak, Memory* (1967), he

described his college lodgings as 'intolerably squalid' in comparison with the home he had been forced to leave behind:

> The story of my college years in England is really the story of my trying to become a Russian writer. I had the feeling that Cambridge and all its famed features—venerable elms, blazoned windows, loquacious tower clocks—were of no consequence in themselves but existed merely to frame and support my rich nostalgia.

He also wrote in the same book, with a view to the interest of posterity: 'I do not know if anyone will ever go to Cambridge in search of the imprints which the teat-cleats on my soccer

boots have left.' Nabokov's Cambridge years are reflected in his first novel in English, *The Real Life of Sebastian Knight* (1941).

Thom Gunn studied English at Trinity in the 1950s, coming, like many of his contemporaries, under the spell of F. R. Leavis (see Downing College). He also discovered, in particular, the poetry of Yeats and wrote his first collection of poems while here.

In 1958 Simon Gray came as a research student to Trinity from Dalhousie University, Halifax, Nova Scotia, to pursue research on Henry James. He quickly decided to 'take a few steps down the ladder' to undergraduate status. Cambridge, and particularly his experiences teaching in the Davis School of English, one of the town's foreign language schools, feature in early novels such as *Little Portia* (1967) and in his plays *Quartermaine's Terms* (1981) and *The Common Pursuit* (1984).

The novelist Jonathan Coe took his first degree here.

TRINITY HALL (1350). Raphael Holinshed, the chronicler from whom Shakespeare took the plots of many of his plays, is thought to have spent some time here. He died (*c.* 1580) the same year as Thomas Tusser, whose *Stanzas* (1580) contain the lines about his return to his college:

> When gains were gone, and years grew on,
> And death did cry, from London fly,
> In Cambridge then I found again
> A resting plot;
> In college best of all the rest,
> With thanks to thee, O Trinity!
> Through thee & thine, for me and mine
> Some stay I got.

Many proverbs can be traced to Tusser's *Hundreth Good Pointes of Husbandrie* (1557).

Thomas Preston, author of *A Lamentable Tragedy . . . of the Life of Cambises King of Persia* (1569), became Master in 1584. He died here in 1598 and is buried in the chapel. Robert Herrick came here from St John's College and graduated BA 1617 (MA 1620).

William Hayley was at Trinity Hall from 1763 to 1767. His 'Ode on the Birth of the Prince of Wales', the first of his then popular poems, was published in Cambridge and then reprinted in the *Gentleman's Magazine*.

Edward Bulwer-Lytton came here after a few months at Trinity College. He won the Chancellor's Medal (1825) for a poem, 'Sculpture'.

F. J. Furnivall (BA 1847) was later founder of the Chaucer Society and the Early English Text Society.

Leslie Stephen (an undergraduate 1850–4) was a Fellow from 1854 to 1867. In his *Life* (1885) of his friend and colleague Henry Fawcett he gives a description of the Fellows' Garden, 'which Mr Henry James—a most capable judge—pronounces to be unsurpassed in Europe'.

Ronald Firbank, whose artificial conversation pieces were published between 1915 and 1926, was an undergraduate from

1907 to 1909. He left, without a degree, to spend some years travelling about the Mediterranean. In 1919 J. B. Priestley matriculated at Trinity Hall, to study English and Political Science.

UNIVERSITY LIBRARY. This copyright library includes a large number of manuscripts and early printed books including Caxton's first book, *Recuyell of the Historyes of Troye*, and the first book printed in English (*c.* 1474). Exhibitions are held regularly. (See also Queens' College, above.)

CAMPTON *Bedfordshire*

Village off the A507. Robert Bloomfield is buried outside the E window of the church, which has Dorothy Osborne's family monuments.

CATFIELD *Norfolk*

Village 13 m. NE of Norwich, on the A149. William Cowper spent childhood holidays at the rectory with his uncle Roger Donne, whose daughter Ann became the recipient of many of his letters after her marriage to Thomas Bodham.

CATTAWADE (or CATTIWADE) *Suffolk*

Village on the A137, 9 m. NE of Colchester. Thomas Tusser, while farming here, wrote *Hundreth Good Pointes of Husbandrie* (1557), which, though full of maxims to which many of our proverbs can be traced, proved to have been of little help to him, as he died (1580) a prisoner for debt in London. He is commemorated by a tablet in Manningtree church (1 m. S).

CHADWELL ST MARY *Essex*

Village on the A1089, 2 m. N of Tilbury. Daniel Defoe had a part interest in a tile works at West Tilbury (1 m. E) from 1694 to his imprisonment in Newgate in 1703. He is thought to have lived for part of this time, when he was managing the business, at Sleepers (now a scheduled building), a thatched, wattle and daub farmhouse opposite the church. The house got its name from the days of the pilgrims, who slept here before crossing the Thames at Tilbury. Defoe is also thought to have returned, when in hiding to escape more charges of sedition, as he is traditionally thought to have written part of *Robinson Crusoe* (1719) here. The parish registers list the family name as Foe: Daniel called himself Defoe after 1703.

CHARSFIELD *Suffolk*

Village near Wickham Market. *Akenfield*, Ronald Bythe's intensely detailed study of a Suffolk village in 1969, was based on Charsfield and Blythe's long interviews with local people.

> In Akenfield, evidence of the good life, a tall old church on the hillside, a pub selling the local brew, a pretty stream, a football pitch, a handsome square vicarage with a cedar of Lebanon shading it, a school with jars of tadpoles in the window, three shops with doorbells, a Tudor mansion, half a dozen farms and a lot of quaint cottages, is there for all to recognize.

Blythe wrote the book at French's Farm (now a bed and breakfast) on Charsfield Rd in Debach. It was turned into both a film, directed by Peter Hall, and a television series in 1975.

CHEVELEY *Cambridgeshire*

Village off the B1063, 4 m. SE of Newmarket. When Crabbe was a young apprentice (1768–70) to the surgeon apothecary of Wickhambrook (6 m. S), he delivered some medicines to Cheveley Park, a country house of the Duke of Rutland. Crabbe was amazed at this first contact with riches and elegance. In 'Silford Hall', published posthumously, he writes of a boy's delight at being shown round the house with its picture gallery and other splendours, and in being given a good meal by the housekeeper.

CHICKSANDS *Bedfordshire*

Ministry of Defence Base off the A507 near Shefford. The priory, within the camp, was the home and perhaps the birthplace in 1627 of Dorothy Osborne, whose *Letters* to William Temple tell of the long engagement forced on them by their disobliging families. They met by chance in 1648 in Carisbrooke on their way to St Malo, but were not married until 1654. Recounting her uneventful life at Chicksands, with nothing to look forward to but his letters, she asks him if he remembers the little house on the island of Herm which they saw from the ship on their way to St Malo.

> Shall we go thither? that's next to being out of the world. There we might live like Baucis and Philemon, grow old together in our little cottage, and for our charity to some ship-wrecked strangers, obtain the blessing of dying both at the same time.

S of the priory is the church at Campton with the family chapel where her father was buried. She sometimes wrote her letters while sitting at his bedside during his long illness. The priory was improved by Wyatt in 1813; the cloisters glazed 'with ancient stained glass' and fashionably rough cast. John Byng was reminded of a dairy when he visited in 1791, and feared that in place of meditation he would now think of cream. The grounds were ornamented by a ruined chapel and a cascade.

CHIGWELL *Essex*

Outer suburb NE of London. James Smith (1775–1839), returning here, recalled the area known to him as a schoolboy:

> Abridge her tank and waterfall
> The path beneath Sir Eliab's wall
> 　　I once again am stepping,
> Beyond that round we rarely stirred;
> Loughton we saw—but only heard
> 　　Of Ongar and of Epping.

Ye Olde King's Head is 'The Maypole' in Dickens's *Barnaby Rudge* (1841).

CHRISTCHURCH *Cambridgeshire*

Village in Upwell Fen off the A1101, 11 m. S of Wisbech. Dorothy Sayers spent vacations at the rectory, her parents' home after 1917. Upwell Fen was probably the setting for her detective story involving campanology, *The Nine Tailors* (1934), in which the church of Fenchurch St Paul has an angel roof resembling that of Upwell (4 m. N). On the NE of Upwell Fen, near Denver, she set the imaginary village of Denver Ducis, ancestral home of her detective Lord Peter Wimsey.

COCKFIELD *Suffolk*

Village off the A134, 8 m. SE of Bury St Edmunds. While R. L. Stevenson was staying with his cousin and her husband, Churchill Babington (rector, 1866–89), he met a Cambridge colleague of his, Sidney Colvin. It was to Colvin that Stevenson addressed his *Vailima Letters* (1895) from Samoa.

COLCHESTER *Essex*

Old town on the A12. Crabb Robinson, the diarist, was articled to an attorney here in 1790. Jane and Ann Taylor lived (1796–1811) at 11–12 West Stockwell St. ⓟ, off the High St. by the Town Hall. They wrote *Original Poems for Infant Minds* (1804), *Rhymes for the Nursery* (1806), which included 'Twinkle, twinkle, little star', and *Hymns* (1810).

CROMER *Norfolk*

Coastal resort 21 m. N of Norwich at the junction of the A148 and the A149. The district was popularized by Clement Scott under the name Poppyland and many writers came here as visitors. He is commemorated by a stone horse trough. On nearby Roughton Heath the refugee Albert Einstein was given shelter when he first arrived in England, by the Locker-Lampson family.

Whenever something goes missing in Kazuo Ishiguro's novel *Never Let Me Go* (2005), the protagonists comment that it must be 'in Norfolk', where all lost things apparently go. Eventually a group of them arrange a trip to the seaside at Cromer, to see what they might find.

DARSHAM *Suffolk*

Village and railway station near the Suffolk coast. Blake Morrison's poem 'Darsham' celebrates the places thereabouts:

> We go down to the water and are sand-flies.
> We rejoin the lugworm and the celandine.
> We listen for cathedral bells at Dunwich
> tolling from the graveyards of the sea.

DISS *Norfolk*

Town on the A143 and the A1066, 22 m. NE of Bury St Edmunds, where the poet Skelton was rector from 1498 to his death in 1529. He made his will here but was not permanently resident. The church is the setting of his poem 'Ware the Hawk'.

Sir John Betjeman made a television programme about Diss ('Something About

Diss'), which was broadcast in 1964, and the town provides the terminus of his poem 'A Mind's Journey to Diss'.

DITCHINGHAM *Norfolk*

Village on the B1332, 1 m. N of Bungay. Rider Haggard's wife inherited the square, red-brick Ditchingham House, set back behind a paddock on the main road. He wrote many of his novels here including *Dawn* (1884) and *Eric Brighteyes* (1888), and they settled here from 1889. He is commemorated by a window in the N aisle of the church and the porch was rebuilt by him.

DOWN HALL *Essex*

The estate in Matching Green, S of the A414 from Hatfield Heath, bought by Matthew Prior in 1720 partly with money from the folio edition of his poems (1719) and partly with a gift from Lord Oxford, who owed his liberty in some measure to Prior's loyalty to him when under interrogation in prison. The ballad *Down Hall* (1721), admired by Lamb, is an amusing account of Prior's adventures on his first visit there. He spent his last two years of failing health improving the house and gardens and died while visiting Lord Oxford. Pope spent the Christmas of 1725 at Down Hall, staying on with Bridgman to discuss plans for the landscaping of Marble Hill at Twickenham. Down Hall was rebuilt by Pepys Cockerell in 1870, and has indented panels decorated in the Mughal style. Later a girls' school, it is now a hotel. It overlooks a great expanse of Epping Forest. A thatched summerhouse has a quotation from FitzGerald cut into the panelling.

DUMPLING GREEN *Norfolk*

Hamlet between East Dereham and Yaxham on the B1135. The lane opposite the Jolly Farmers, a thatched house (once a pub) at right angles to the road, leads to the red-brick house, traditionally known as George Borrow's birthplace, said to be his grandparents' farm. However, research reveals that a house 400 yds away was their smallholding.

DUNWICH *Suffolk*

Coastal resort off the B1125, an important port before erosion by the sea. Shakespeare's troupe, the King's Men, played at Dunwich in 1605–6, for which service they were 'laid out for a gratuity' of 6*s*. 8*d*. Some 10 years previously a rival company, the Queen's Men, were 'much discontented' with the same fee. However, Shakespeare's company returned in 1608–9 and 1610–11. There is no record of what they performed.

Edward FitzGerald, who took Carlyle there in 1855, also visited when translating the *Rubáiyát* of Omar Khayyám (1859). Jerome K. Jerome, who spent annual holidays at the turn of the century at Mrs Scarlet's lodgings (she also kept a shop), found that FitzGerald had stayed there. Swinburne's 'By the North Sea' from *Studies in Song* (1880) was inspired by his visit, and Henry James visited in 1879. A

digression on Swinburne's visits to Dunwich features in W. G. Sebald's *The Rings of Saturn* (1998), where the village also forms part of the book's more general meditation on destruction and dissolution.

Edward Thomas finished the first draft of his biography of Richard Jefferies in a coastguard cottage at Minsmere in 1907, high up on 'a heaving moor of heather and close gorse' ½ m. away from where the ruined church had half fallen over the eroded cliff. He often walked on the sands below, sometimes picking up shells and coloured pebbles with a 17-year-old girl who showed him her poems, until he was suddenly confronted by her irate father.

EARLHAM HALL *Norfolk*

Country house 1 m. W of Norwich, now the administrative building of the University of East Anglia, was the home of the Gurney family. *Earlham* (1922) is Percy Lubbock's account of his childhood among his eccentric aunts, uncles, and other relations at the end of the 19th c., which is considered his masterpiece.

EAST DEREHAM *Norfolk*

Town on the A47. Cowper, ill with depression, was brought here by his cousin the Revd John Johnson, with Mrs Unwin (d. 1796) helpless after strokes. They lived in a red-brick house in the marketplace, now replaced by the 19th-c. Memorial Congregational Chapel Ⓟ. Cowper died in 1800 and his memorial in the church has lines by his friend William Hayley.

George Borrow's parents (married here in 1793) were tenants in Norwich St. (now the Co-op) at the time of his birth but tradition holds that his mother returned to her parents in *Dumpling Green for the event.

EAST MERSEA *Essex*

Straggling village in the marshes at the mouth of the Colne, where Baring-Gould was rector from 1870 to 1881. His novel *Mehalah* (1880, reprinted 1969) is set in the local marshes and the main character has been compared to Heathcliff in *Wuthering Heights* (1847).

EAST TUDDENHAM *Norfolk*

Village S of the A47, 8 m. E of East Dereham, where Parson Woodforde dined with his friend the Revd John Du Quesne in the Hall he bought as his vicarage, later Berries Hall, on the Weston road.

ELSTOW *Bedfordshire*

Village on the A6, 3 m. S of Bedford, the home of John Bunyan, who lived here with his parents and, after a brief period of service in the Parliamentary army at Newport Pagnell, as a young married man, practising the trade of tinker. His birthplace, often described as 'at' or 'near' Elstow, is in fact nearer to the hamlet of Harrowden and can be approached from the Harrowden road out of Bedford. A granite block in the fields marks the site of the cottage, and the determined pilgrim can reach it by turning down Old Harrowden Lane and

following the signpost beside the brook. Except in dry weather the going is heavy and the mud can be a chastening reminder of the Slough of Despond.

The village church dates from the foundation of Elstow Abbey in 1078. It was extensively restored in 1880, but the Perpendicular font in which Bunyan was baptized on 30 November 1628 is still there. The Bunyan memorial windows in the N and S aisles illustrating *The Holy War* and *The Pilgrim's Progress* were added in 1880. The Moot Hall on the green, a medieval market hall and manorial court, houses a collection of furniture, books, and documents associated with Bunyan and his time. In the upper room there is a beautiful Chinese lacquer cabinet in which Sir William Temple cherished the letters of Dorothy Osborne, written mainly between 1648 and 1655, before their marriage.

ELY *Cambridgeshire*

Cathedral city on the A10. Alexander Barclay, a Benedictine monk here, translated the *Life of St George* from Latin, and wrote his *Eclogues* (*c*. 1515), moral pastorals anticipating Spenser. Tradition says the monastery, where Hereward the Wake sought sanctuary, was saved in return for his surrender and he was killed outside.

The lofty remains of a ruined Ely Cathedral provide a moment of transcendence in L. P. Hartley's dystopian novel *Facial Justice* (1960).

ESSENDON *Hertfordshire*

Village on the B158, 4 m. E of Hatfield. Beatrix Potter, as a child, used to stay with her grandmother at Camfield Place. She describes the house as 'the place I love best in the world' in her *Journal* (1966), which is illustrated with photographs and some of her drawings.

EUSTON *Suffolk*

Village 3 m. SE of Thetford on the A1088. The Duke of Grafton's estate here was described by Robert Bloomfield in *The Farmer's Boy* (1800):

Round Euston's water'd vale and sloping plains, Where woods and groves in solemn grandeur rise, Where the kite brooding unmolested flies; The woodcock and the painted pheasant race, And skulking foxes destined for the chase.

FELIXSTOWE *Suffolk*

Port and resort on the coast between the Orwell and the Deben. The sea by the long esplanade was the scene of the swim in Meredith's *Lord Ormont and his Aminta* (1894). The town features in 'Felixstowe, or, The Last of her Order', by John Betjeman.

FELSHAM *Suffolk*

Village between Bury St Edmunds and Stowmarket. To satisfy in part his 'extreme visual attachment to the English countryside' Angus Wilson moved to a cottage at Felsham Woodside in 1955, renting it at first only by the week for writing. In *The Wild Garden* (1964), he wrote about the cultivation of its neglected grounds into 'a carefully artificial wild garden', a recurring symbol in his novels. The garden

Angus Wilson in his garden at Felsham Woodside, Suffolk, in 1977

inspired the climactic episode of his fantasy novel *The Old Men at the Zoo* (1961).

FINCHINGFIELD *Essex*

Village 4 m. E of Thaxted. Dodie Smith, author of *I Capture the Castle* (1949) and *The Hundred and One Dalmations* (1956) lived on and off at her cottage, The Barretts, from the 1930s until her death in 1990. From the early 1960s until his death in 2003 Norman Lewis lived at The Parsonage, a medieval house opposite the church. He was drawn to the area not only for its cheapness but also by the 'sour poetry of these landscapes' and the 'settlements where they reared chickens and sold car spare-parts by the sticky wildernesses of the estuarial rivers of this county'.

FORDHAM *Cambridgeshire*

Large village on the A10 and the A1122, 16 m. NE of Cambridge. James Withers came here in 1824 to work for a market gardener and, with the exception of a few years, lived here until his death in 1892. He had been writing for many years before his *Poems* were published (1854), after coming to the notice of his employer. Two other collections followed in 1856 and 1860, and the three volumes were issued as one in 1863. This resulted in a visit to London and an offer of employment there, but Withers refused to live in a town and settled with his wife and four children in a riverside cottage at the foot of the hill below the church, now known as the Poet's Cottage. One of his longer poems was 'Wicken Fen', about a village 4 m. W, which now has the fen preserved in its natural state by the NT. His grave is marked by a tombstone, and a stained-glass window in the church was inscribed to his memory.

FRAMLINGHAM *Suffolk*

Market town at the junction of the B1116 and the B1119. The ruined flint castle with its moat and 13 towers, some having red-brick Tudor chimneys, was the home of the Howards, hosts to Mary Tudor when Jane Grey was declared queen. Henry Howard, Earl of Surrey, who with Thomas Wyatt first used the Italian sonnet form, and, in his translation of the *Aeneid*, blank verse, has an ornate painted alabaster tomb in the church; he was beheaded by Henry VIII. Under Elizabeth, William Alabaster was confined to the castle after having been interrogated in the Tower for being a Catholic.

GRANTCHESTER *Cambridgeshire*

Village 3 m. SW of Cambridge on a cutting of the Granta. Chaucer, who may have been in Cambridge on a parliamentary visit, places 'The Reeve's Tale' from *The Canterbury Tales* at Trumpington Mill on the Granta itself. The mill and its successor (burnt down in 1928) stood above the millpond, now known as Byron's Pool, signposted from the Trumpington Rd. Skelton, while at Cambridge, is thought to have often walked to Trumpington (1 m. E), where the vicar's daughter is said to have copied out his poems for him. Wordsworth visited Chaucer's mill and Tennyson is thought to have had Trumpington Mill in mind as the setting for his poem 'The Miller's Daughter'.

G. A. Henty, novelist and writer of stories for boys, was born at Trumpington (1832).

Rupert Brooke, while an undergraduate, found lodgings at The Orchard (now tearooms) in 1909 with an indulgent landlady.

I have a perfectly glorious time, seeing nobody I know day after day. The room I have opens straight out onto a stone verandah covered with creepers, and a little old garden full of old-fashioned flowers and *crammed* with roses. I work at Shakespeare, read, write all day, and now and then wander in the woods or by the river. I bathe every morning and sometimes by moonlight, have all my meals (chiefly fruit) brought to me out of doors, and am as happy as the day's long.

The popular bathing place was Byron's Pool, named after the poet, who visited from Cambridge. E. M. Forster and Lytton Strachey also stayed at The Orchard when visiting him. He had offered Strachey a room at the Old Vicarage next door, where he wrote:

The garden is a great glory. There is a soft lawn with a sundial and tangled antique flowers abundantly; and a sham ruin, quite in a corner . . . There are trees rather too closely all round; and a mist.

In 1910 Brooke moved into the Old Vicarage, a three-storey house with dormer windows, where his landlady was Mrs Neeve, whose husband kept bees. Brooke's friends (some of whom were later members of the Bloomsbury Group), with whom he used to spend camping holidays, visited him here and would have large breakfast parties on the lawn. While holidaying in Germany his nostalgia for Grantchester led him to write 'The Sentimental Exile', a poem better known as 'The Old Vicarage, Grantchester', which contains the lines:

Oh! there the chestnuts, summer through, Beside the river make for you A tunnel of green gloom, and sleep Deeply above; and green and deep The stream mysterious glides beneath Green as a dream and deep as death.

On his return he was surprised to be greeted by his landlady with the assurance that there was 'honey still for tea'. She had read the poem published in his college magazine.

GREAT DUNMOW *Essex*

Market town at the junction of the A130 and the A120. Harrison Ainsworth's novel *The Flitch of Bacon* (1854) caused the revival, in the Town Hall in 1855, of the ceremony (which he attended) mentioned in *Piers Plowman* and *The Canterbury Tales*, of the award of a side of bacon to a married couple who could swear to have lived in complete harmony for a year and a day. In Chaucer's time the oath was taken at Dunmow Priory, 2½ m. SE, but the custom lapsed in the 18th c. Now a jury awards the prize every fourth year at a ceremony in the park below the Foakes Memorial Hall.

GREAT GLEMHAM *Suffolk*

Village 5 m. SW of Saxmundham off the A12. Crabbe and his wife accepted the offer of Dudley North's large house (gone) in 1796 and remained until 1801. They had hoped to live in *Parham but his wife's relatives resented them.

Rupert Brooke writing in the garden of the Old Vicarage, Grantchester

GREAT LIVERMERE *Suffolk*

Village E of the A134, 6 m. NE of Bury St Edmunds. M. R. James, antiquary and writer of ghost stories, was brought up at the rectory, a large house in grounds opposite the war memorial. His last tale, 'A Vignette', was probably an attempt to record a real supernatural experience he had in the village as a child.

GREAT WIGBOROUGH *Essex*

Village on the B1026, 6 m. E of Tiptree. Stephen Gosson was rector from 1591 to 1600, during which time Philip Sidney's *Apologie for Poetry* was published (1595). This essay, probably written *c.* 1580, was in reply to Gosson's *Schoole of Abuse* (1579), dedicated to Sidney and containing 'a pleasant invective against Poets, Pipers, Players, Jesters and Such like Caterpillers of a Commonwealth'. His church tower was rebuilt after the earthquake in 1884.

GREAT YARMOUTH *Norfolk*

East coast port and resort on the A47. Thomas Nash's *Lenten Stuffe* (1599) is a satire on the town and the smoked herrings for which it is famous. The Royalist poet John Cleveland was imprisoned in 1655, possibly in the jail in Middlegate St., but was released after appealing to Cromwell. The actor and playwright Arthur Murphy (1727–1805), who became a barrister, wrote *The Raffle* while holidaying here after being on the Norfolk circuit (*c.* 1780). John Aikin, perhaps to be near his sister Mrs Barbauld at Palgrave, settled here in 1784 to practise medicine. He wrote *England Delineated*, on national character, and

a memoir on John Howard, whom he had helped with the appendix to his book on prison reform. He had also given up eating sugar as a protest against the slave trade, but he found the Yarmouth people against his liberal ideas and left for London in 1792. James Woodforde (1740–1803) mentions staying at The Wrestlers in Church Plain with his nephew in *Diary of a Country Parson* (1924–31). They walked on the quay and saw the sailors from a Dutch ship wearing 'monstrous large trousers'. They drank wine and gin on a collier, and his nephew was 'highly pleased' with the place.

Anna Sewell, author of *Black Beauty* (1877), was born (1820) in a 17th-c. house (now called Anna Sewell House; Ⓟ) in Church Plain.

F. T. Palgrave was born (1824) at his maternal grandfather's house on the quay, and used to visit it for holidays when he lived in Hampstead. Among his 'Recollections of Childhood' he remembers the garden:

> I love the swing that shook between
> The jawbones of the whale.

George Borrow lived here for his wife's health, first (1853–5) at 169 King St. and then (1856–9) at 37–9 Camperdown Place, later a hotel. Watts Dunton in his autobiography mentions first meeting him swimming in the sea. Dickens set many scenes in *David Copperfield* (1850) in the neighbourhood. Mr Peggotty lived on the shore.

GRESHAM *Norfolk*

Village off the A148, 3 m. SE of Sheringham. The tree-covered hill, once a moated island, ¼ m. S of the church is the site of the castle (built *c.* 1319) inherited by the Pastons, who withstood a siege here in the 15th c.

HARSTON *Cambridgeshire*

Village S of Cambridge. An uncle of Graham Greene's lived in Harston House, and his family spent summer holidays there (without the uncle, who would remove himself to a bachelor flat in Hanover Square). As well as exploring the large garden, the orchard, fountain, stream, and pond with an island (which inspired the short story 'Under the Garden'), Greene discovered at Harston 'quite suddenly' that he could read, which he did secretly in a remote attic. In August 1914 he witnessed, passing through the village, the first troops on their way to the front.

HAWSTEAD *Suffolk*

Village off the A134, 4 m. S of Bury St Edmunds. John Donne wrote *An Anatomie of the World* (1611), the funeral elegy on the 12-year-old daughter of Sir Robert Drury of Hawstead Place (demolished 1827), who died in London and was buried here. Though it is thought Donne never saw Dorothy, he may have heard of her from his sister, who might have been living in the village as her husband was attached to the Drury household. He may also have heard of the family from his friend Joseph Hall, who was urging him to become ordained and who had been chaplain (1601–8) to Lady Drury. The elegy was thankfully accepted by the now childless couple and Donne was asked to join them on their tour of the Continent. The church has the alabaster tomb of the Drury children with an effigy of Dorothy above. There is also a memorial window to Joseph Hall.

HELPSTON *Cambridgeshire*

Village on the B1443, 7 m. E of Stamford. John Clare, born (1793) in a thatched farm labourer's cottage in Woodgate (Ⓟ erected in 1921 by the Peterborough Museum Society), spent his early years on the land. He went to school in the church vestry at Glinton (1 m. E), tried unsuccessfully to become a lawyer's clerk, and in 1809 was hired by the proprietor of the inn next door to the cottage to help in his smallholding. The young men of the village met at a cottage where the Billings brothers lodged in Woodgate, which they called Bachelors' Hall. Clare, whose poems show his close observation of the countryside, transplanted many of the local wild flowers into the garden of the cottage next door to his birthplace, where he made his home with Patty after their marriage in 1820. *Poems Descriptive of Rural Life* (1820) was popular, but though Clare continued to write he was never able to keep his family solvent for long. He suffered many attacks of mental distress, and in 1832 a cottage and smallholding were provided for him in *Northborough. After his death (1864) at Northampton asylum, his body was buried in the churchyard at Helpston as he had wished. A monument was erected opposite the Buttermarket. His grave was visited by Charles Causley, and inspired his macabre poem 'Helpston', in which the poet's face

Stared at me
As clearly as it once stared through
The glass coffin-lid
In the church-side pub on his burial day . . .

The John Clare Society, to study the life and work of the poet, was founded in 1982 at the instigation of the rector (www.johnclare.org.uk).

HERTFORD *Hertfordshire*

Erskine Childers, author of *The Riddle of the Sands*, attended Haileybury College in the 1880s. Alan Ross recalled his 1930s schooldays at Haileybury affectionately in his autobiography *Blindfold Games* (1986).

HIGH BEECH *Essex*

Village off the A104 in Epping Forest. Tennyson lived at Beech House (rebuilt 1850) at the foot of Wellington Hill with his mother and siblings from 1837 to 1840. He was described as 'wandering weirdly up and down the house in the small hours, murmuring poetry to himself; the sisters fond, proud, cultivated, appreciative'. His engagement to Emily Sellwood was accepted by her parents in 1837 though his lack of means and employment caused doubts. Perhaps to allay these Tennyson invested a legacy in a scheme to carve wood by machinery, an enthusiasm of the owner of the asylum, Fairmead (gone), where John Clare was sent in 1837. Tennyson often visited the 'earnest-frothy' Dr Allen there, where Thomas Campbell had found a refuge (1828) for his deranged son, and probably remembered the inmates when writing *Maud* (1855). The wood-carving venture was not successful and the engagement was broken off in 1840, his unhappiness appearing in 'Love and Duty'.

Though Clare felt compelled to escape to his family, in 1841 he had written:

I love the breakneck hills, that headlong go,
And leave me high, and half the world below.
I love to see the Beech Hill mounting high,
The brook without a bridge and nearly dry,
There's Buckets Hill, a place of furze and clouds,
Which evening in a golden blaze enshrouds.

In *Edge of the Orison* (2005), Iain Sinclair traces Clare's escape from the asylum.

Edward Thomas was stationed here in the army in 1915. About his poem to his younger daughter he wrote, 'All the place names are from this part of Essex—which I like more and more.' A year later he installed his family in a cottage where he spent his last Christmas with them before he was killed in France; the novelist Arthur Morrison (1863–1945) was his neighbour.

HIGH LAVER *Essex*

Village on a minor road E of Harlow on the A1025, and W of Fyfield on the B184. John Locke, author of *An Essay Concerning Human Understanding* (1690), lived from 1691 to his death in 1704 at Oates, the home of Sir Francis and Lady Masham. Damaris Masham, educated by her father, a Regius Professor of Hebrew at Cambridge, was influenced by

Locke's philosophy and was a writer of religious works. She read to Locke in his last illness and published an account of him in *The Great Historical Dictionary*. Locke was buried, by his desire with little pomp, in the churchyard. His tomb was enclosed by a railing in 1866 and his epitaph, which he wrote in Latin, is on the churchyard wall.

HILGAY *Norfolk*

Village on the A10, S of Downham Market, where Phineas Fletcher was rector from 1621 to his death in 1650. His chief work was *The Purple Island, or, The Isle of Man* (1633), a poem in ten books in imitation of Spenser. His rectory and much of the church have been rebuilt.

HINGHAM *Norfolk*

Market town 17 m. from Norwich. The narrator of W. G. Sebald's *The Emigrants* (1992) comes to live in the village, renting a flat in the house of the Jewish exile Dr Henry Selwyn, who lives in a flint-built hermitage in the dilapidated garden, 'giving his entire attention . . . to thoughts which on the one hand grew vaguer day by day, and, on the other, grew more precise and unambiguous'.

HINXWORTH *Hertfordshire*

Village lying between Biggleswade and Baldock, just E of the Bedfordshire county line. Bury End, a thatched cottage in Hinxworth, was home to the novelist Monica Dickens, her husband, and horses.

HITCHIN *Hertfordshire*

Market town at the junction of the A505 and the A600. George Chapman, poet, playwright, and translator of Homer, is traditionally thought to have been born in or near the town and a plaque at 35 Tilehouse St. records that he lived there. Also in Tilehouse St. is the Baptist church (rebuilt in 1844) established in 1674 'under the pastoral care of John Bunyan', which contains his chair and a letter written by him.

The poet, novelist, and Milton scholar E. H. Visiak (1878–1972) was educated at Hitchin Grammar School.

HOLLESLEY (pr. 'Hōzli) *Suffolk*

Village 16 m. E of Ipswich, near the mouth of the Ore. Brendan Behan was arrested in 1939 in connection with IRA activities and he was subsequently sent to a Borstal school here. He tells of his experiences in *Borstal Boy* (1958), which was dramatized and first played at the Abbey Theatre in 1967.

HOLT *Norfolk*

Large village on the A148, 10 m. SW of Cromer. W. H. Auden was at Gresham's School (founded 1555) from 1920 to 1925. He called himself a 'typical little highbrow and difficult child' in an essay in *The Old School* (1934) edited by Graham Greene. He also wrote in the same essay: 'The best reason I have for opposing Fascism is that at school I lived in a

Fascist state.' It was while walking in a salt marsh near the school that he first became aware of his vocation as a poet.

In 1918 Stephen Spender was sent to Old School House preparatory school of Gresham's School, where for two years he lived under the shadow of his brother Michael, was bullied by masters and schoolfellows alike, and suffered acute homesickness: 'I was like an animal or a peasant, deprived of his familiar surroundings' (*World Within World*, 1951). He was sent away as unteachable. The unhappy experience provided material for his novel *The Backward Son* (1940).

HONINGHAM (pr. 'Hunningam) *Norfolk*

Village off the A47. 'Parson' Woodforde dined with the MP for Great Yarmouth, Charles Townshend, at the Hall (gone). His *Diary* records that the meal was 'too frenchified in dressing' but 'the drawing room in which we drank Tea etc. was hung with Silk and there were elegant gilded chairs and expensive mirrors'. He won a shilling at loo. The smugglers John and Robert Buck, who supplied 'coniac' and gin to Woodforde, lived at the inn, which was renamed after them.

HONINGTON *Suffolk*

Village on the A1088, 7 m. SE of Thetford. Robert Bloomfield, author of *The Farmer's Boy* (1800), was born in the cottage, later called after him, at the corner of Mill Lane, near the church, in which he is commemorated with a bronze plaque. Bloomfield also wrote 'On Visiting the Place of My Nativity' and a poem on vaccination, his father having died of smallpox when he was a year old. His mother is buried in the churchyard.

HOUGHTON (pr. 'Howton or 'Hōton) HALL *Norfolk*

Country house, *c.* 14 m. NE of King's Lynn, N of the A148 at the New Houghton turn, built by Sir Robert Walpole (1722–31). The house is open to the public (www.houghtonhall.com). In the park is the parish church of St Martin, where Sir Robert and Horace Walpole are buried without memorials.

HUNSTANTON (pr. 'Hŭnston or Hŭn'stanton) *Norfolk*

Summer resort on the A149, on the Wash, 16 m. N of King's Lynn. It is the seaside where the children play in *The Shrimp and the Anemone* (1944), the first novel of the trilogy *Eustace and Hilda* by L. P. Hartley.

Patrick Hamilton, who lived along the coast at *Sheringham, opens *Hangover Square* (1941), his novel of alcohol abuse, hopeless love, and schizophrenia, on the red cliffs at Hunstanton, above 'the vast grey sweep of the Wash under the sombre sky of Christmas afternoon'.

P. G. Wodehouse was a frequent guest of the Le Strange family at Hunstanton Hall in the 1920s. He was particularly fond of the moat:

P. G. Wodehouse in his motor outside Hunstanton Hall, New Year's Day, 1928

I spend most of my time on the moat, which is really a sizeable lake. I'm writing this in a punt with my typewriter on a bed-table wobbling on one of the seats. There is a duck close by which utters occasional quacks that sound like a man with an unpleasant voice saying nasty things in an undertone.

The Octagon, which stands on the island in the middle of the lake, was the imagined location for the rescue by Jeeves and Wooster of the Rt Hon A. B. Fillmer in 'Jeeves and the Impending Doom'. The character of the household was an inspiration for life at Blandings and the Hall itself the basis of Rudge Hall, residence of Bertie Wooster's nemesis, the formidable Aunt Agatha.

HUNTINGDON *Cambridgeshire*

Town on the A14. Hinchingbrooke, the mansion bought from the Cromwell family by the Montagu who married Pepys's great-aunt, became the home of Sir Edward Montagu (later Lord Sandwich), who employed Pepys in his household and later at the Admiralty. As a boy (c. 1644) the diarist spent a short time at the Free School in the High St. (now the Cromwell Museum, www.cambridgeshire.gov.uk, variable opening times). Pepys, who often visited his relatives in the neighbourhood, records being choked by the dust of the rebuilding at Hinchingbrooke (now a wedding and conference venue).

Cowper lodged in the town in 1765, bringing with him the servant who had looked after him at Dr Allen's asylum. At the end of the year he was rescued from housekeeping difficulties by the Unwin family, who invited him to join them in their house ℗ in the High St. (opposite Hartford Rd). Cowper stayed here happily until the sudden death of the Revd Morley Unwin

from a riding accident led him to move with Mrs Unwin, the Mary of his poems, to Olney in 1767. John Clare, making his first journey from his village to London, passed through the town in the coach and was shown Cromwell's birthplace at one end and Cowper's house with its 'melancholy looking garden' at the other. This garden is now obscured by other houses.

HUNTINGFIELD *Suffolk*

Village off the B1117, 4 m. SW of Halesworth. John Paston, who lived at the Hall after marrying the owner's widow, was buried (1575) in the church, which has a painted hammer-beamed roof with gilded angels. This 'gentele man by birth and deedes' is commemorated by a long rhyme which, though difficult to read, is given in full in the church guide.

IPSWICH *Suffolk*

Market town and port on the Orwell, visited by Defoe, who abhorred the 'noisome cookery of whaling'. Clara Reeve, author of Gothic romances, was born (1729) here, daughter of the perpetual curate of St Nicholas' Church. Cobbett visited in 1830 and Dickens stayed at the Great White Horse Hotel in Tavern St., where he set Mr Pickwick's encounter with the lady in yellow curl-papers. *Margaret Catchpole* (1845, reprinted 1930) is the story of a girl who becomes involved with smugglers while in service with the family of the author, Richard Cobbold. Edward FitzGerald was introduced by the vicar of Flowton (5 m. W) to the oriental scholar E. B. Cowell, who had joined his father's business in the town in 1842. Cowell, who went to India in the 1850s, sent FitzGerald the *Rubáiyát* of Omar Khayyám which he translated so successfully into English. Jeremy Collier in the 1660s and Rider Haggard in the

1860s were pupils at Ipswich School. V. S. Pritchett was born above a toyshop at 41 St Nicholas St. in 1900. His father, Walter, ran for a while a declining business as a newsagent and stationer in the town. The family returned to Ipswich for a year in 1910 and lived near Cauldwell Hall Rd, where they tried to dodge Walter Pritchett's creditors.

ISLINGTON *Norfolk*

Village 7 m. SW of King's Lynn off the A47. A turn off the main road near Tilney leads to Church Farm, traditionally the home of the heroine of the ballad 'The Bailiff's Daughter of Islington'.

KENNINGHALL *Norfolk*

Village on the B1113, 9 m. NW of Diss. Place Farm, 2 m. past the church, is the remaining wing of Kenninghall Palace, a home of the Howards, and birthplace of Henry Howard, Earl of Surrey (1517–47). Ploughing uncovered foundations to the N, and the banqueting hall to the S, then used as a barn, was demolished in living memory.

KESSINGLAND *Suffolk*

Coastal resort on the A12, 5 m. S of Lowestoft. Rider Haggard bought (c. 1900) The Grange, a large house on the cliffs formerly a coastguard station (the lane there from Wash Lane is called after him). He named each room after an admiral and made a garden, preventing erosion of the clifftop by planting marram grass. He continued his successful novels with *Pearl-Maiden* (1903) and *Ayesha* (1905), but he also wrote *Rural England* (1902) and *The Poor and the Land* (1905), detailed surveys of the plight of the agricultural workers, for which he was knighted in 1912. He let the house to Kipling for the summer of 1914.

KING'S LYNN *Norfolk*

Port on the Great Ouse, 3 m. S of the Wash, formerly called Lynn and Lynn Episcopi. The mystic Margery Kempe, daughter of John Burnham, a prominent man, was born in Lynn c. 1373. She sailed from the port on her travels to the Continent and to Jerusalem in her search for true faith. She dictated *The Book of Margery Kempe*, an account of her spiritual journey through life, part of which was printed by Wynken de Worde in 1501. It was published by the Early English Text Society in 1940.

John Capgrave was born in Lynn in 1393 and spent many years in the Augustinian Friary here, eventually becoming Provincial of the Order in England. His chronicle of English history, and Lives of St Gilbert of Sempringham and St Catharine of Alexandria, unlike his other works, were written in English.

Eugene Aram was arrested (1758) for murder while a master at the Grammar School, which at that time was in St John's Chapel adjoining St Margaret's Church. His tragedy was the subject of a poem by Thomas Hood in 1831 and of a novel by Lytton in 1832. One of his pupils was Charles Burney, whose sister Fanny was born (1752) either at St Augustine's House in

Chapel St., or at 84 High St. (rebuilt). Fanny, who started writing at the age of 10, spent holidays with her stepmother at the Dower House, near St Margaret's Church, where her father was organist (1751–60), and she wrote in a little cabin in the garden which bordered the river. She recalls in her *Diary* how she was sometimes driven indoors by the damp air or 'the annoying oaths of the watermen'.

KNEBWORTH *Hertfordshire*

Tudor mansion, 3 m. S of Stevenage, off the A1, mostly rebuilt in the Regency Gothic style by the novelist Sir Edward Bulwer-Lytton (1st Baron Lytton) and his mother. He was portrayed as the Hon. Bertie Tremaine in Disraeli's *Endymion* (1880). He and Dickens took part in Jonson's *Everyman in his Humour*, performed here in 1850, and also in his own *Not So Bad As We Seem* (1851). Lytton's later works were written here, including the futuristic *The Coming Race* (1871), published anonymously. The house and grounds (a well-known venue for rock concerts) are open to the public (www.knebworthhouse.com).

LAMAS *Norfolk*

Village E of the B1354, 10 m. N of Norwich, also known as Buxton Lamas. The grave of Anna Sewell, author of *Black Beauty* (1877), is still tended among the Irish yews by the chapel (closed).

LANGHAM *Norfolk*

Village on the B1156, 15 m. W of Cromer. Captain Frederick Marryat moved here after publishing *Masterman Ready* (1841) and lived (1843–8) at Manor Cottage (rebuilt) in Cocksthorpe Rd. He is buried in the churchyard, and a tablet in the church commemorates him.

LAVENHAM *Suffolk*

Village on the A1141 and the B1071, 7 m. NE of Sudbury. The Grange in Shilling St., one of the old timbered houses with an overhanging storey, was the childhood home of Jane and Ann Taylor, authors of verses and tales for the young. Their father, Isaac Taylor, author and engraver, published *Specimens of Gothic Ornaments selected from the Parish Church of Lavenham* in 1796, the year they left for *Colchester.

LEIGH-ON-SEA *Essex*

Seaside town at the western edge of Southend. The critic and novelist Rebecca West lived with Anthony, her son by H. G. Wells, at Southcliffe on Marine Parade. The novelist John Fowles was born here at Leigh, the son of a cigar merchant, on 31 March 1926.

LEIGHTON BROMSWOLD *Cambridgeshire*

Village off the A14, 10 m. NW of Huntingdon. The church was rebuilt during the time George Herbert was prebend, though it is not known whether he ever visited it. His family crest is on one of the lead rainwater pipes. A copy of his poem 'The Elixir', now a popular hymn, is in the church.

LEVERINGTON *Cambridgeshire*

Village 2 m. NW of Wisbech off the A1101. Tradition holds that Oliver Goldsmith stayed at Park Farm on the Gorefield Rd with the Lumpkin family when writing *She Stoops to Conquer* (1773). A pond by the roadside, and a tablet in the church commemorating an Anthony Lumpkin, were two points of evidence for the tradition.

LIDGATE *Suffolk*

Village on the B1063, 7 m. SE of Newmarket. John Lydgate (1370?–1451?), court poet for a time under the patronage of Humphrey of Gloucester, was born at Suffolk House (rebuilt) on the main street. Known as 'the Monk of Bury' (see BURY ST EDMUNDS), he is shown wearing a habit in the brass on the chancel floor.

LITTLE BARFORD *Bedfordshire*

Hamlet off the B1043, 2 m. S of St Neots, birthplace of Nicholas Rowe (1674–1718), dramatist and Poet Laureate, who lived chiefly in London.

LITTLE DUNHAM *Norfolk*

Village off the A47, 6 m. NE of Swaffham. The Revd John Johnson took his cousin the poet Cowper and Mrs Unwin to Dunham Lodge, a large 18th-c. house in a park, in 1795. They stayed here a short time only before moving to *East Dereham.

LITTLE EASTON *Essex*

Village off the A130 and B184, 2 m. NW of Great Dunmow. The road to the church leads beyond the two lakes to The Glebe, the large Georgian house where H. G. Wells lived during the First World War, and where he wrote *Mr. Britling Sees It Through* (1916). After reviewing Wells's novel *Marriage* (1912) in *The Freewoman*, Rebecca West was invited to the house for lunch. They subsequently embarked on a 10-year love affair.

LITTLE GADDESDEN *Hertfordshire*

Village 5 m. N of Berkhamsted on the B5406. The house, traditionally the home of John of Gaddesden (d. 1361), is near the war memorial on the green ℗ opposite the entrance to Ashridge Park. He was an eminent 14th-c. medical writer, who may have been known to Chaucer. In the Prologue to *The Canterbury Tales* (written *c*. 1387–1400), the Doctor of Physic refers to him as 'Gatesden'.

LITTLE GIDDING *Cambridgeshire*

Hamlet 8 m. SW of Norman Cross, off the B660, where Nicholas Ferrar (1592–1637) founded, at the Manor House (gone) in 1625, a family community devoted to prayer and practical works of charity. He was a friend of George Herbert, who sent him the manuscript of his collection of poems before he died. These were published as *The Church* (1633), later becoming known as *The Temple*. The Little Gidding Community worshipped three times a day in the church, which resembles a small college chapel. T. S. Eliot in *Four Quartets* (1944) commemorates the place 'Where prayer has been valid'. Both poets are remembered in the church. 'A Visit to Little Gidding' expresses the poet Patricia Beer's response to the place.

LITTLE HADHAM *Hertfordshire*

Village near Bishop's Stortford. Angus Wilson wrote the story 'Raspberry Jam' (1949) here during a period of mental recuperation. The story launched his literary career.

LITTLEPORT *Cambridgeshire*

Large fenland village on the river Great Ouse. Littleport is a plausible model for 'Gildsey' in Graham Swift's novel *Waterland* (1983), powerfully evocative of the fen country:

> We lived in a lock-keeper's cottage by the River Leem, which flows out of Norfolk into the Great Ouse. And no one needs telling that the land in that part of the world is flat. Flat, with an unrelieved and monotonous flatness, enough of itself, some might say, to drive a man to unquiet and sleep-defeating thoughts.

Lesley Glaister's first novel, *Honour Thy Father* (1990), is also set in the fens.

LITTLE WENHAM *Suffolk*

Small village 8 m. SW of Ipswich, off the A12 W of Capel St Mary. Jane Brewis (née Scrope), for whom Skelton wrote *Phylyp Sparowe*, a lamentation on her pet killed by a cat, lived after her marriage in the old moated manor down the narrow lane by the inn. She died in 1514 and her tomb is in the church here.

LONG MELFORD *Suffolk*

Village stretching for 2 m. along the A134, just N of Sudbury. At the N end the large green is dominated by the Perpendicular church. In the Clopton chantry chapel (*c*. 1496) the ceiling is decorated by verses on a scroll said to be by John Lydgate (d. 1450), one-time monk at Bury St Edmunds. Edmund Blunden, who returned from Hong Kong in 1965, lived at Hall Mill. He died in 1974 and is buried in the churchyard. A souvenir collection of his poems is on sale in the church, for which he wrote a guide. Patricia Beer's 1967 poem 'Concert in Long Melford Church' speaks for itself: 'By each tombstone a well-dressed person | It looks just like the Resurrection.'

LOUGHTON (pr. 'Lauton) *Essex*

Town on the A121, on the NE outskirts of London. Loughton Hall (rebuilt) was the home of Lady Mary Wroth after her marriage in 1604. She was the daughter of Robert Sidney of *Penshurst and she wrote *Urania* (1621) in the style of the *Arcadia* of her uncle Philip Sidney. She was the subject of a poem by George Wither, and a sonnet by George Chapman which prefaced his translation of the *Iliad* (1611).

Arthur Morrison, who settled here soon after his marriage in 1892, wrote the novels of London working-class life *A Child of the Jago* (1896), *To London Town* (1899), and *The Hole in the Wall* (1902). *Cunning Murrell* (1900), a novel about witchcraft in earlier years of the 19th c., is set in Essex. Morrison left Loughton in 1913. W. W. Jacobs, a contemporary of Morrison, lived for some years at The Outlook, Park Hill. He wrote many humorous short stories about the Cockney crews of the barges and small coasters, including *Many Cargoes* (1896), *Short Cruises* (1907), and *Sea Whispers* (1926). He also wrote macabre tales, of which the most gripping, 'The Monkey's Paw', was dramatized.

LOWESTOFT *Suffolk*

Large seaside resort on the A12; fishing and boatbuilding town. Thomas Nash was born here in 1567; his father was the minister, probably a curate. Crabbe, a surgeon-apprentice at Woodbridge, used to ride to Normanston Park, where the Misses Blackwell and Waldron and others, who had formed a small community, had agreed to 'polish' Sara Elmy, his fiancée. After his ordination and their marriage (1783) they revisited Normanston (1790) and Crabbe, who called them his 'Ladies of the Lake', after Lake Lothing, wrote

> Trees may be found and lakes as fair
> Fresh lawns and gardens green:
> But where again the Sister-pair
> Who animate the scene.

Crabbe also heard Wesley preach on this visit.

Conrad first landed in England (1878) here and served on the coaster *Skimmer of the Sea*. Part of Watts-Dunton's *Aylwin* (1898), a romance that features the East Anglian gypsies, takes place in the neighbourhood.

The journeying narrator of W. G. Sebald's *The Rings of Saturn* (1998) stays at the Albion Hotel and reflects on the vanished glamour of the resort, when 'fashionable society swirled to the sound of the orchestra, seemingly borne aloft in a surge of light above the water'.

MACKERY END *Hertfordshire*

Hamlet approached by the road opposite the Cherry Tree Inn in Lower Luton Rd., Wheathampstead, 3 m. E of Harpenden. The Lambs' visits to their great-aunt Gladman at the farmhouse, and the mansion, farmyard, and the sheep-shearing supper, are described by Mary Lamb in *Mrs. Leicester's School* (1808) and by Charles in his essay 'Mackery End' (1820).

MALDON *Essex*

Small port and yachting resort on the Blackwater, 10 m. E of Chelmsford. The Old English poem *The Battle of Maldon* tells of the raid in 991 by the Northmen, who were camped on an island (now Northey Island) in the estuary. The battle was delayed by the rising tide and after a stand by the ealdorman Byrhtnoth and his friend Ælfric, Byrhtnoth was slain with a poisoned spear. The end of the poem, thought to have been written before the close of the century, is missing.

MANNINGTREE *Essex*

Small market town on the river Stour. Essex oxen, which were well known for their size and quality in the 16th c., were immortalized by Shakespeare in *1 Henry IV*, when he made Prince Hal describe Falstaff as 'that huge bombard of sack, that stuffed cloak-bag of guts, that roasted Manningtree ox with the pudding in his belly'. See also CATTAWADE.

MARKYATE *Hertfordshire*

Village (formerly called Market Street) 6 m. NW of Harpenden, bypassed by the A5. William Cowper was sent at the age of 6 to a private boarding school here and endured nearly four years of being teased and bullied before going to Westminster School (1741). The school, situated in the High St., was originally known as The Mermaid, later the Old Vicarage, and 'Cowper's Oak', the tree where he took refuge from being pelted with stones for being 'bookish', is near the field across the way from the Old Vicarage garden.

MATTISHALL *Norfolk*

Village off the A47, 4 m. SE of East Dereham. Mattishall Hall, a red-brick Georgian house in South Green, was the home (then called South Green House) of the Bodhams. Anne Bodham (née Donne) sent her cousin William Cowper the miniature of his mother that inspired the poem 'On the Receipt of My Mother's Picture Out of Norfolk'. The Bodhams were often visited by 'Parson' Woodforde, whose *Diary* includes a description of Thomas Bodham's funeral. The church contains memorials to the Bodhams and other members of the Donne family and to George William Smith, the curate, who took the services at Weston Longville when Woodforde went on holiday.

MAUTBY *Norfolk*

Village 6 m. NW of Great Yarmouth, home of Margaret Mautby, an heiress who married (1440) John Paston. She wrote many of the *Paston Letters*, and was the mother of Margery, who was determined to marry for love in spite of punishments. Margaret Paston returned here when she became a widow. Her funeral (1484) was costly and an elaborate monument was erected in the S aisle of the church, but this was lost when the aisle became ruined.

MAYLAND *Essex*

Small village off the B1018, 8 m. SE of Maldon. John Gauden, Bishop of *Exeter and *Worcester, was born here in 1605 while his father was rector, but the rectory and the church have been rebuilt.

MERTON *Norfolk*

Village 14 m. N of Thetford, off the B1110. The Old Rectory, now called Silverdell, was often visited by Edward FitzGerald while his friend George Crabbe, grandson of the poet, was incumbent. FitzGerald visited in 1883 but was taken ill almost immediately and died here soon afterwards.

MIDDLETON *Suffolk*

Village near the coast, 4 m. SE of Saxmundham. The poet, horticulturalist, and celebrated translator of Hölderlin and Celan, Michael Hamburger, lived in the village until his death in 2007. Much of his poetry, particularly that in *Variations* and the long poem *From a Diary of Non-Events*, bears the influence of his life in rural Suffolk. A visit from his friend W. G. Sebald, whose work Hamburger translated, is recorded in Sebald's *The Rings of Saturn* (1998).

MIDDLETON TOWER *Norfolk*

A 15th-c. gatehouse of the moated manor (rebuilt 1860), off the A47, on a minor road near the railway station, *c*. 6 m. SE of King's Lynn. The gatehouse tower was built by Lord Scales, some of whose letters from Middleton are included in the *Paston Letters*. He had fought with Henry V and when he was killed in London he was succeeded by his daughter, whose husband, Sir Anthony Woodville (or Wydvill), translated some French works, which were printed by Caxton.

MILTON BRYAN *Bedfordshire*

Small village halfway between Milton Keynes and Luton. The novelist Muriel Spark was employed here in the Political Intelligence section of MI6 during the Second World War. She worked on fake radio broadcasts designed to undermine German morale. The station was occasionally visited by Ian Fleming.

MOOR PARK *Hertfordshire*

A 17th-c. mansion (altered by Leoni 1720) off the A404, SE of Rickmansworth, now a golf club. In 1620 the Earl and Countess (née Lucy Harington of Bedford, a patron of many poets) built a new house here and planned the famous gardens. Sir William Temple, the diplomat, occasionally managed to meet Dorothy Osborne here when she visited her cousins. In his essay *Of Gardens* he describes the walks, tree-hung cloisters, and parterres: 'the perfectest figure of a garden I ever saw, either at home or abroad, was that of Moor Park'. When the differences between their families were finally resolved they spent their honeymoon (1654–5) here. In 1680 he renamed the house he bought near *Farnham, Moor Park.

MUNDESLEY (pr. 'Mŭnzli') *Norfolk*

Coastal resort on the B1145. Cowper spent his final years (1795–1800) alternately in his cousin's house in the High St. (now Cowper House) and at *East Dereham, as change was thought to help his depression.

NAVESTOCK *Essex*

Straggling village 4 m. NW of Brentwood off the A128. After leaving Oxford, Swinburne spent the summer of 1859 as the pupil of the Revd William Stubbs, the historian, later

Bishop of Oxford, whom he called 'a very passable parson'. Swinburne showed the first draft of his play *Rosamond* (1860) to Stubbs, who persuaded him to burn it as it was erotic. Stubbs's Victorian–Gothic vicarage, later renamed Marleys, is on the green.

NORTHBOROUGH *Cambridgeshire*

Village on the A15, 7 m. NW of Peterborough. John Clare's poor health caused his patrons to build him a six-room stone cottage (opposite Pingle Lane beyond the church). His income was too small to stock the smallholding but friends gave him a cow and some pigs and he moved in with Patty and the children in 1832. He was irritated by sightseers and had the door put in at the back, from where he could escape when he saw their approach from his study window. *The Rural Muse* was published in 1835 and two years later Clare's mental condition caused his friends to send him to a private asylum. Clare later described his escape and the long walk back to his family, in 'Journey Out of Essex' (*Selected Poems and Prose*, ed. E. Robinson and G. Summerfield, 1967). His freedom was short-lived as his mental distress again caused his removal, this time permanently.

NORTHCHURCH *Hertfordshire*

Village 1 m. NW of Berkhamsted, on the A41. Maria Edgeworth spent her school holidays (1776–80) here with her father, Richard Edgeworth, and stepmother, Honora. After Honora died of consumption in 1780, her father married Honora's sister Elizabeth, and brought her back to the house with the shutters, on the main road, now called Edgeworth House. Richard Edgeworth's friend Thomas Day visited here, after the awkwardness of his having been a suitor of Honora had lessened by her death and his own marriage.

NORWICH *Norfolk*

Cathedral, market, and manufacturing city on the Wensum. An alley off King St. leads to the church (rebuilt after war damage) of Julian, or Juliana (1343–1413), the mystic recluse, whose cell is now a chapel incorporating the original roughcast stones. She wrote *XVI Revelations of Divine Love* here, and at Carrow Abbey (ruins and the rebuilt Prioress's house in Reckitt and Colman Co.'s grounds in Bracondale Rd) was visited by Margery Kempe (b. 1373?), whose search for true belief also took her to Jerusalem. Extracts from the *Book of Margery Kempe* were printed (1501) by Wynken de Worde.

John Skelton, made rector of Diss in 1498, met the young Jane Scrope at Carrow seeking refuge with her sister and mother, whose husband had been executed. Jane's pet sparrow, killed by a cat, inspired Skelton's *Phylyp Sparowe* (*c.* 1542–6).

The Pastons, a merchant family with many castles and manors, also had houses in the town. The Music House (so called because the waits met there) in King St., the 12th-c. home of Jewish merchants, belonged to them in the 15th c. (now called Wensum Lodge; Ⓟ). The Pastons also lived in Crown Court, off the cobbled Elm Hill. They gave money for the rebuilding of St Peter Hungate Church, at the top of the hill, completing the hammerbeam roof with the carved angels in 1460. The Maid's Head, dating from Norman times, is also mentioned in the *Paston Letters*, though the façade is 18th-c. John Bale (1495–1563) was educated by the Carmelites (site of the Friary near Whitefriars Bridge) but later became a Protestant.

Robert Greene, dramatist, poet, and pamphleteer, was born in the city (*c.* 1560) and went to the Grammar School (founded 1250; refounded by Edward VI; enlarged and modernized by Dr Augustus Jessopp, headmaster 1859–79).

Henry Peacham, tutor to the sons of William Howard in 1613–14, spent some time between his travels on the Continent in Howard House Ⓟ in King St., where many of the old houses had riverside gardens. His best-known work, *The Compleat Gentleman*, written for the youngest Howard son, was published in 1622.

Richard Corbett, bishop in 1632, quarrelled with the Strangers, the immigrant weavers, and banned them from his chapel in 1634. His collected poems (1647) were published after his death.

Thomas Browne lived (1637–82) near The Lamb inn (now Henry's Bar and Terrace). *Religio Medici* (1643) was written before he settled here. He was knighted in St Andrew's Hall, once the Blackfriars' church, when Charles II visited the city in 1671. John Evelyn, who stayed with him that year, described Browne's house in his *Diary* as 'A paradise and cabinet of rarities' and wrote about the city, 'The suburbs are large, the prospect sweet, and other amenities, not omitting the flower gardens, which all the inhabitants excel in.' Browne was buried in St Peter Mancroft Church (tablet); his statue stands in the little paved garden below.

George Crabbe was ordained in the Cathedral in 1782. Southey in 1798 visited a group of intellectuals who attended the Octagon Chapel (built 1756) in Colegate. One of them, John Opie, who painted his portrait, was newly married, and the couple lived where Opie St. joins Castle Meadow. Amelia Opie wrote *Father and Daughter* (1801), *Poems* (1802), *Adeline Mowbray* (1804), suggested by a story of Mary Wollstonecraft, and a memoir of her husband (d. 1807). In 1825 she became a Quaker through the influence of the Gurneys, who lived at Gurney Court Ⓟ until *c.* 1786.

The Martineau family (descended from the Strangers) then lived at the Court, where Harriet was born in 1802. She started writing moral tales for children, progressing to *Illustrations of Political Economy* (1832–4), after which she moved to London.

William Taylor (1765–1836), an enthusiast for German literature, which he publicized by his translations, lived in Upper King St. (rebuilt) and later Surrey St. He taught George Borrow German and wrote *Historic Survey of German Poetry* (1828–30). He and Amelia Opie contributed to Southey's *Annual Anthology* (1799–1800).

George Borrow, whose parents' house in Willow Lane is now called Borrow House, attended the Grammar School, and was then

John Clare's cottage at Northborough, showing the back door, by which he could escape from sightseers

Statue of Sir Thomas Browne near St Peter Mancroft Church, Norwich

The creative writing course continued to run at the University, with writers such as Kazuo Ishiguro, Toby Litt, and Tracy Chevalier following in McEwan's footsteps.

Norwich is also the birthplace (1946) of the novelist Philip Pullman, though he didn't grow up in the city; his family travelled through his childhood and settled in Wales when he was 11.

OAKINGTON *Cambridgeshire*

Village off the A14, 8 m. NW of Cambridge. H. E. Bates was posted to the RAF station here in the winter of 1941. In *The World in Ripeness* (1972), he describes the pilots' asides which inspired his short stories 'It's Just the Way It Is' and 'The Sun Rises Twice', published under the pseudonym 'Flying Officer X'.

OBY *Norfolk*

Small village 10 m. NW of Great Yarmouth. Oby is the setting for Sylvia Townsend Warner's novel of medieval convent life *The Corner That Held Them* (1948). The poet George MacBeth lived in the tiny village and published his *Poems from Oby* in 1982. He celebrated his home in 'The Renewal':

> Naked space
>
> Over the cornfields, and the next-door farm,
> Contracts to an oasis with great trees
> That north-east winds can ravage in their rage
>
> And leave still rooted and serene.

ONGAR *Essex*

Village made up of Chipping Ongar on the A128 and High Ongar on the A414, 7 m. E of Epping. Isaac Taylor, the engraver and dissenting minister, moved in 1811 with his children, including Ann and Jane, authors of popular rhymes and hymns for children, to Castle House. Soon after Ann's marriage the family moved to Peaked Farm in 1814, where Jane wrote *Display, a Tale for Young People* (1815), and other works. She was buried (1824) in the chapel graveyard.

ORFORD *Suffolk*

Coastal village on the river Ore. The deserted Secret Weapons Research Establishments on Orfordness are visited by the narrator of W. G. Sebald's *The Rings of Saturn* (1998), the ruined buildings resembling 'temples or pagodas' suggesting 'the remains of our own civilization after its extinction in some future catastrophe'.

OULTON (pr. Ōlton) *Suffolk*

Village 3 m. NW of Lowestoft, just N of Oulton Broad. George Borrow settled at Oulton Cottage (gone), his wife's home on the N bank, after their marriage in 1840. He wrote *The Bible in Spain* (1843) and *Lavengro* (1851) in a summerhouse in the garden. He returned to Oulton in 1874 after his many excursions and died here in 1881. There is a memorial in the church.

OXNEAD *Norfolk*

Hamlet 4 m. SE of Aylsham, off the B1354, near Burgh. William Paston (1378–1444), the

articled to a solicitor for a short time before setting out on his travels. Mousehold Heath, the open space on the NE outskirts, and the gypsies he met there feature in *Lavengro* (1851) and *Romany Rye* (1857), both partly autobiographical. Some Borrow manuscripts are in the Archives Centre located at County Hall.

Mary Sewell, author of popular poems for children, lived (1867–84) at 125 Spixworth Rd, Old Catton. Her daughter Anna kept bees in the garden of the L-shaped house and there wrote *Black Beauty* (1877). A horse trough was erected in Anna's memory by her niece, at the junction of Constitution Hill and St Clement's Hill.

Daisy Ashford, author of *The Young Visiters* (1919), lived here with her husband, James Patrick Devlin, from the 1950s in Woodland Rd, Helston. Three earlier stories, two by Daisy and one by her sister Angela, first published in *Daisy Ashford: Her Book* in 1920, were reissued in 1965 as *Love and Marriage*.

In 1965 the novelist Malcolm Bradbury was given a lectureship at the University of East Anglia, and charged with developing an American Studies course. In 1970 he and Angus Wilson founded the creative writing Masters' course, whose first graduate (indeed, whose only student in the first year) was Ian McEwan. Since its founding the department has employed a number of distinguished teachers, including Rose Tremain, Angela Carter, and Andrew Motion. In addition, the travel writer and novelist Jonathan Raban taught in the English Department in the late 1960s, as did the critic and memoirist Lorna Sage until her death in 2001. The novelist W. G. Sebald taught here from 1970, becoming Professor of European Literature in 1988. He founded the British Centre for Literary Translation at the University in 1989. Bradbury retired from the University in 1995, but remained in Norwich, where he died on 27 November 2000; a memorial service was held in Norwich Cathedral in February 2001.

'Good Judge', one of Fuller's *Worthies*, inherited the manor by marrying Agnes Berry, who wrote many of the *Paston Letters*. One low, red-brick servants' wing of the Tudor house remains. The church has a memorial to Clement Paston, a sea captain (d. 1597).

PALGRAVE *Suffolk*

Village between the A143 and the A1066, 1 m. S of Diss. Palgrave House (gone), where Palgrave School had been in Tudor times, was the home of 'honest Tom Martin' (1697–1771), the antiquary whose collections were published as *The History of Thetford* (1779). Anna Barbauld helped her husband with his school (1774–86) in the same house, which came to be called Barbauld House. She wrote *Hymns in Prose for Children* (1781) and *Evenings at Home*. One pupil was William Taylor, later author of *Historic Survey of German Poetry* (1828–30).

PARHAM *Suffolk*

Village on the B1116, 3 m. SE of Framlingham. Crabbe, a surgeon's apprentice at Woodbridge (1771–5), first met Sara Elmey, the 'Mira' of his early poems, at Ducking Hall (rebuilt), where she was staying with her uncle John Tovell. He returned in 1792, with Sara, his wife, as Tovell's executor and intended to settle, but her relatives' resentment, and the death in quick succession of two of their sons, decided their move. In 1814, after Sara's death, Crabbe spent a day here rambling round the fields and wrote:

> The nightbird's song that sweetly floats
> On this soft gloom—this balmy air
> Brings to the mind her sweeter notes,
> When those dear eyes can shine no more.

PASTON *Norfolk*

Village on the B1159, 9 m. SE of Cromer. It was a home of the Paston family, whose letters, written between *c.* 1420 and 1503, tell of the difficulties of life in the Wars of the Roses, the castle sieges, wrangles with powerful neighbours, and a daughter determined to marry beneath her. The site of their house extends NE of the present Hall (*c.* 1750), but their old flint barn is still near the church. The tomb of John Paston (d. 1466) in the chancel was brought from Bromholm Priory at *Bacton and the ornate effigy of Katherine Paston (d. 1628) has an inscription by John Donne. Selections from the letters, edited by Norman Davis, were published in 1958 and (in modern spelling) in 1963. Part I of a complete edition, *The Paston Letters and Papers of the Fifteenth Century*, edited by Norman Davis, was published in 1971 and Part II in 1976.

PETERBOROUGH *Cambridgeshire*

Industrial and cathedral city on the Nene, 11 m. SE of Stamford. The latest version of the Anglo-Saxon Chronicle, to 1155, was written in the Benedictine abbey, of which the church, built in the early 12th c., has been Peterborough Cathedral since 1541.

L. P. Hartley, who was born (1895) at Whittlesea (or Whittlesey), 5 m. E, spent his youth at Fletton Towers, the family home, in the suburb of Fletton among brick-fields. Hartley wrote *The Killing Bottle* (1932), short stories, and the novels *The Shrimp and the Anemone* (1944), a study of the childhood of a brother and sister, *The Go-Between* (1953), and *The Brickfield* (1964).

There is a collection of John Clare's manuscripts at the City Museum and Art Gallery.

Charles Causley attended a teacher training college in the city, and his early poem 'A Ballad of Katherine of Aragon' was inspired by her tomb in the Cathedral, 'Her lovely breast in a cold stone chest | Under the farmers' boots.'

PLAYFORD *Suffolk*

Village 5 m. NE of Ipswich, off the A12. The red-brick Tudor Hall surrounded by its moat was the home of Thomas Clarkson (1760–1846), the abolitionist. He was visited here by the diarist Crabb Robinson, who had known Catherine Clarkson since their youth in Bury. Haydon, staying here in 1840 to paint the portraits of those in the Anti-Slavery Convention, mentions in his autobiography that the date 1593 was on the house but that parts were older. One of the main rooms had a fireback with this date.

POTTERS BAR *Hertfordshire*

Town 16 m. N of London, latterly notorious for a train crash in May 2002 which killed seven people. Among the passengers on the train was the novelist Nina Bawden, whose husband was killed; Bawden wrote about the event at points 2182A and its aftermath in *Dear Austen* (2005), in which she describes the battles with the corporate 'Snakeheads' she encounters in her fight for justice.

RADWINTER *Essex*

Village 4 m. E of Saffron Walden on the B1053. William Harrison, rector from 1559 to his death in 1593, wrote the *Description of England*, which, with his translation of a *Description of Scotland*, was included in Holinshed's *Chronicles* (1577).

RAMSHOLT *Suffolk*

Small village on the river Deben. Peter Porter evokes the local country around the river in his poem 'At Ramsholt':

> The harvest is in early. Across the paddock,
> where we raise the bull's head with mimic
> bellows, through the salt-dead trees and
>   thatcher's
> rushes, yachts navigate on seeming land.

RENDHAM *Suffolk*

Village on the B1119, 3 m. NW of Saxmundham. Crabbe, who had left Muston to be his wife's uncle's executor, spent 1801 to 1805 at Rendham Grove ℗, known locally as Lady Whincups, then opposite the new parsonage at the bottom of the hill (later at the entrance to Grove Farm).

ROOS HALL *Suffolk*

Tudor house on the B1062, 1 m. W of Beccles, family home of Sir John Suckling (1609–42), who lived mainly at court.

SAFFRON WALDEN *Essex*

Town on the M11, SE of Cambridge. Gabriel Harvey, friend of Spenser and disputant with Roger Greene and Thomas Nashe, was born (1550) in a house in the cattle market. The museum (opened in 1834), near the church, has the carved fireplace showing his father's craft of rope-making, an oak window, and part of a wall painting (*c.* 1580), all from the Harvey home (gone).

ST ALBANS *Hertfordshire*

Town on the A5183 and the A1081, which sprang from Roman Verulamium, whose extensively excavated ruins are on view. The great Norman abbey marks the site where Alban became the first Christian martyr in Britain *c.* 304. Matthew Paris entered the monastery in 1217 and was its chronicler (from 1236 until his death in 1259), expanding his account to include Continental events. The Dissolution swept away all the monastic buildings except the Abbey and its great Gateway, erected in 1365, where the third printing press to be set up in England was working *c.* 1480. *The Boke of St Albans* (1486), printed there by an unnamed 'Scholemaster printer', has generally been attributed to Dame Juliana Berners. She was thought to be a prioress at Sopwell Nunnery, which was ½ m. SE of the Abbey, though only a ruined Elizabethan house remains on the site. It is now thought more likely that the part on hawking was written by Julyan Barnes, as the name was first printed, and the rest by other hands.

Francis Bacon, Lord Chancellor, Baron Verulam, and Viscount St Albans, inherited Gorhambury 2 m. W, and retired there after his impeachment in 1621, to devote himself to science and literature. He reissued his famous *Essays* (1597) in a final form in 1625. He wished to be buried in St Michael's Church and a monument of him, sitting in a characteristic pose, was erected in the chancel by his heir. The present Gorhambury, completed in 1784, has a collection of family books and portraits, but his house is a ruin in the park. James Shirley was master of the Grammar School from 1623 to 1625.

Cowper, during one of his fits of despondency, was looked after here in 1763 by Dr Nathaniel Cotton, who also wrote verses. On his recovery Cowper wrote that he was 'very deep in debt to my little physician of St. Albans'.

Dickens often stayed at the Queen's Hotel in Chequer St. and mentions the brickmakers' cottages on Bernard's Heath in *Bleak House* (1852), but the Georgian building of that name has no connection with him.

Charles Williams, whose parents owned a stationer's shop at 36 Victoria St., was educated at the Grammar School (1899–1902).

ST IVES *Cambridgeshire*

Market town on the Ouse. The critic and novelist Theodore Watts (he added his mother's name of Dunton in 1896) was born in 1832 at the Red House, Market Hill. He was a solicitor's son and after leaving school he joined his father's firm in the house (it is a solicitor's firm again now) until setting up his own practice in London (*c.* 1870). The gypsies he met when driving with his father near Rington and Graylingham woods appear in the romance *Aylwin* (1898).

SAPISTON *Suffolk*

Village off the A1088, 6 m. SE of Thetford. Robert Bloomfield worked from the age of 11 to 15 on the farm of William Austin, a connection of his mother's. Then, too puny for the work, he was apprenticed to his brother, a shoemaker, in London, where he wrote *The Farmer's Boy* (1800) about his life in this neighbourhood. On the green by the church, where the cows were milked and where Austin's farmhouse still stands, Bloomfield's 'shadowing elms' have been cut down. The old church is no longer used but Austin's tombstone and those of his infant children can still be seen in the churchyard. Fakenham nearby, a favourite resort of young Bloomfield and the Austin children, is remembered in the lines:

> The moat remains, the dwelling is no more,
> Its name denotes its melancholy fall
> For village children call the spot Burnt Hall.

SCARNING *Norfolk*

Village on the A47, 3 m. W of East Dereham, where Dr Augustus Jessopp was rector (1879–1911). His book *Arcady for Better for Worse* (1887) has fine descriptions of the district. He lived in The Hall, next to the church. A granite cross marks his grave by the entrance from The Hall to the churchyard and there is a tablet in the church.

SHEFFORD *Bedfordshire*

Small town at the junction of the A507 and the A600. Robert Bloomfield, who lived his last years in great poverty in North Bridge St. Ⓟ, died there in 1823.

SHERINGHAM *Norfolk*

Seaside town in N Norfolk. The novelist and playwright Patrick Hamilton spent his declining, alcoholic years at 3 Martincross, North Street, dying there in 1962. The poet Stephen Spender spent his childhood at The Bluff, a house on the extreme edge of the town on the cliffs. 'My childhood', he wrote in *World Within World* (1951), 'was the nature I remember: the thickness of the grass in the pasture fields, amongst whose roots were to be found heartsease . . . speedwell of a blue as intense as a bead of sky.'

SIZEWELL *Suffolk*

Fishing and holiday village on the Suffolk coast, now well known for its two nuclear power stations. Blake Morrison's impressions of the power station in his poem 'On Sizewell Beach' give way to reflections on a narrowly averted road accident:

> the three of us spared that other life we dream of
> where the worst has already happened
> and we are made to dwell forever on its shore.

SOMERLEYTON *Suffolk*

Model village in NE Suffolk near the river Waveney. On his journey through E Suffolk the narrator of W. G. Sebald's *The Rings of Saturn* (1998) visits Somerleyton Hall, the sumptuous, dreamlike mansion of the entrepreneurial builder Morton Peto, a house where 'those who visited were barely able to tell where the natural ended and the man-made began . . . And how fine a place the house seemed to me now that it was imperceptibly nearing the brink of dissolution and silent oblivion.'

SOUTHEND-ON-SEA *Essex*

Large town and resort on the Thames estuary. In Jane Austen's *Emma* (1816), Mrs John Knightley stoutly declares that her family thoroughly enjoyed their holidays here and that they 'never found the least inconvenience from the mud'.

Disraeli lived at the Tudor mansion of Porters from late 1833 until early 1834 while writing 'The Revolutionary Epic' (1834), an ambitious three-volume poem on the French Revolution which turned out a failure. Writing to his sister he said, 'You could not have a softer clime or sunnier skies than at abused Southend.'

Edwin Arnold wrote *The Light of Asia* (1879), the poem on the life of Buddha which proved very popular, while living at Hamlet House.

Warwick Deeping, author of many popular novels, remembered especially for the best-

seller *Sorrell and Son* (1925), was born (1877) at Prospect House, at the bottom of High St. He lived for many years in the Royal Ter. Some of his novels are set in Southend.

SOUTHWOLD *Suffolk*

Coastal resort, and brewing and market town. Penelope Fitzgerald lived in a converted oyster warehouse in the town in the 1950s. Her experience working in a haunted bookshop in 1957 provided material for her novel *The Bookshop* (1978), where its original becomes 'Hardborough', a kind of 'island between sea and river', where 'every fifty years or so it had lost, as though careless or indifferent to such things, another means of communication'. The narrator of W. G. Sebald's *The Rings of Saturn* (1998) stops at the Sailors' Reading Room here on his journey along the Suffolk coast.

STANFORD-LE-HOPE *Essex*

Village off the A13, 9 m. NE of Tilbury. In 1896 Joseph Conrad and his wife moved to a small house which he called 'a damned jerry-built rabbit hutch'. The next year they moved into Ivy Walls, an Elizabethan farmhouse (gone) on the edge of the village. Conrad felt isolated from intellectual stimulation and welcomed the visits of John Galsworthy, Edward Garnett, and Stephen Crane. On a visit to the Garnetts at Limpsfield he met Ford Madox Hueffer, who persuaded him to move to Postling in 1898.

STEVENAGE *Hertfordshire*

Town off the A1(M), SE of Hitchin, expanded as one of the New Towns after the Second World War. Rooks-nest, beyond the church, off Rectory Lane, Old Town, was E. M. Forster's childhood home. He lived in the large red-brick house until 1893, and the house and the wych elm in the garden are portrayed in *Howards*

The Sailors' Reading Room at Southwold, in which the narrator paused on his journey through Suffolk in W. G. Sebald's *The Rings of Saturn*

End (1910), the novel in which Mrs Wilcox resembles his mother. His sole playmate was the gardener's boy. Forster's sudden removal from his home, when his mother was turned out abruptly, may have inspired his short story 'Ansell', published posthumously, in which a middle-aged academic gives up his Fellowship to make his home with a former gardener's boy.

STISTED (pr. Stīsted) *Essex*

Village between the A120 and the A131, 3 m. NE of Braintree. The Revd Charles Forster, rector 1838–71, was the grandfather of E. M. Forster, whose biography of his great-aunt, *Marianne Thornton* (1956), includes a description of the rectory (now Glebe House, in Rectory Rd), overflowing with laundry and children. The church, restored by Charles Forster, contains a roundel to one of the children, Doanie, who died aged 16.

STOWMARKET *Suffolk*

Town on the A1308, 13 m. NW of Ipswich. The Old Vicarage in Milton Rd was the home from 1628 of Dr Thomas Young, who earlier had tutored John Milton in London. Milton is thought to have visited Young here and to have planted a mulberry tree (gone) in the garden. George Crabbe went to Richard Haddon's school here in 1766, when he was 11, and learned the rudiments of grammar and Latin, but he was mostly self-taught.

STRADBROKE *Suffolk*

Village on the B117, 10 m. SE of Diss. There is a tradition that Robert Grosseteste (d. 1253), Bishop of Lincoln and first Chancellor of Oxford University, was born here. A modern painted effigy of him is at the crossroads.

SUDBURY *Suffolk*

Market town on the A134 and the A131, 16 m. NW of Colchester, thought to be 'Eatanswill', where the parliamentary election takes place in Dickens's *Pickwick Papers* (1837), and where Pickwick and his friends encounter Mrs Leo Hunter, the hostess who likes to meet famous people.

SWAFFHAM (pr. 'Swoffam) *Norfolk*

Market town on the A47 and the A1065. The 15th-c. church contains the Parochial Library, which includes an illuminated Book of Hours (*c.* 1420) and *The Black Book of Swaffham*, an inventory of church rents, donations, and possessions, compiled by Dr John Botright, rector from 1435 to his death in 1474, whose tomb is in the chancel. In 1690 the priest's chamber above the vestry was fitted up to house almost 400 books bequeathed by Sir Henry Spelman the antiquary, born (1560 or 1564) at Congham, a village 9 m. NW. Spelman's library includes *Holinshed's Chronicles* (1577).

SWAFFHAM (pr. 'Swoffam) PRIOR *Cambridgeshire*

Village on the B1102, 9 m. NE of Cambridge. Edwin and Willa Muir, who first translated

Franz Kafka's novels, moved to Priory Cottage in 1956. In a letter to T. S. Eliot, Muir wrote:

> The little house is very charming, and we have fallen in love with it. It is in a pleasant village, and looks out on two ruined church towers, each set on a little knoll of its own; one of them damaged by lightning sometime, and the other by time itself. The neighbours are kind, and the village shop is next door. I confess that sometimes I have a slightly sinking feeling, knowing that now I have nothing to do but write, and must depend upon it. But I feel it will be all right.

The poems Muir wrote here are included in *Collected Poems* (1960), published after he died in Cambridge in January 1959. He is buried in the churchyard. Willa wrote *Living with Ballads* (1965), for which her husband had begun some notes, and then *Belonging* (1968), the story of their life together.

TASBURGH *Norfolk*

Small village 7 m. S of Norwich. A long-time local resident, the novelist and critic Malcolm Bradbury, who died in November 2000, is buried at St Mary's Church.

THAXTED *Essex*

Old wool town on the B184 off the A130, birthplace in 1577 of Samuel Purchas, later rector of St Martin's, Ludgate Hill, London.

The silver hanging lamp in the S chapel of the 14th-c. church is a memorial to A. E. Coppard (d. 1957), short-story writer and poet, who lived at Duton Hill, *c.* 3 m. S.

THEBERTON *Suffolk*

Village on the B1122, 2 m. N of Leiston. C. M. Doughty, author of *Travels in Arabia Deserta* (1888) and *The Dawn in Britain* (6 vols, 1906) was born (1843) at Theberton Hall and is commemorated by a tablet in the thatched church with the round flint tower.

THERFIELD *Hertfordshire*

Village 3 m. SW of Royston, off the A505. The poet William Alabaster, who had been the Earl of Essex's chaplain on the Cadiz expedition (1596), and had been imprisoned by Elizabeth after becoming a Catholic, was given the rich living here in 1614 by James I, whose chaplain he was. The Old Rectory is partly medieval.

THETFORD *Norfolk*

Town on the A10 and the A142. The site of the birthplace of Thomas Paine (1737–1809), author of *The Rights of Man* (1791–2), is the garden of Grey Gables in White Hart St. A gilded statue erected by American friends of the Thomas Paine Society stands outside the Council offices opposite the Bell Hotel. Educated at the Grammar School, Paine worked for his father, a staymaker, before leaving the town when he was 20.

THORNEY *Cambridgeshire*

Fenland village on the A47 and the B1040. Reginald Pecock was forced to resign as Bishop

of *Chichester in 1458 and was sent to live in seclusion here at the Norman abbey, where he died (1460).

Gilbert White, who visited in 1750 to help his uncle, an agent on the Duke of Bedford's estate, wrote here the verses 'Invitation to Selborne', addressed to Hester Mulso, the sister of a friend at Oxford.

THORPE-LE-SOKEN *Essex*

Village on the B1033, 12 m. E of Colchester. Arnold Bennett bought Comarques, a Queen Anne house, opposite the vicarage, midway between this village and Thorpe Green, in 1913, the year *The Regent* was published. He wrote his third Clayhanger novel, *These Twain* (1916), here, bought a yacht, and kept a flat in London. He sold the house in 1920 before separating from his wife.

WAIN WOOD *Hertfordshire*

Wood a few miles S of Hitchin, approached by a footpath from the road from Hitchin to Preston. Among the trees is a natural amphitheatre known as Bunyan's Dell, where people gathered in their hundreds to hear Bunyan preach secretly, knowing that they risked fines or imprisonment or even transportation for defying the law prohibiting such meetings. Services have been held annually in commemoration.

WALBERSWICK *Suffolk*

Coastal village near the Blyth estuary. George Orwell, while staying in the village in 1931, described having seen at 5.20 p.m. on 27 July a ghost disappear behind the masonry in the churchyard, 'a man's figure, small & stooping, & dressed in lightish brown'. The piers of the bridge crossing the river Blyth between Walberswick and Southwold, and which once supported a narrow-gauge railway line bearing a train originally built for the Emperor of China, start a digression on the last years of the Chinese empire in *The Rings of Saturn* (1998), W. G. Sebald's blend of fiction, history, travel, and autobiography.

WALLINGTON *Hertfordshire*

Village on a minor road *c.* 3 m. E of Baldock from the A505. Eric Blair ('George Orwell') rented the former general store here (1936–47) and married his first wife in the village church (1936). He wrote *Homage to Catalonia* (1939) and found ideas for *Animal Farm* (1945) in the local Manor Farm. He left in 1940, but returned for occasional visits.

WALTHAM ABBEY *Essex*

Old town on the A121, surrounding the Norman abbey where King Harold was interred. John Foxe, author of *The Book of Martyrs* (1563), lived here from 1565 but the house has gone. Thomas Fuller, who admired Foxe, was perpetual curate from 1649 to 1658. He married his second wife in 1651, finished his *Church History* (1655) here, and worked on *The Worthies of England* (1662). Sheridan stayed here from August 1772 to April 1773 between escorting Elizabeth Linley to Paris and their marriage.

WALTHAM CROSS *Hertfordshire*

Town on the A121 and the A1010, 1 m. E of Waltham Abbey. Trollope lived at the brick Georgian Waltham House (gone), 'a rickety old place' near the Cross, from 1859 to 1870. This was his most settled home; he enjoyed hunting and found time to write *The Claverings* (1867), *The Last Chronicle of Barset* (1867), and other novels by rising early. On summer evenings his guests sat talking under the cedar tree while 'tobacco smoke went curling up into the night'. At Christmas the same children's games were played here as at Noningsby in *Orley Farm* (1862) and a nephew said later he had only to play commerce to imagine himself a child again.

WARE *Hertfordshire*

Old town on the A1170 and the A119, 3 m. NE of Hertford. The Great Bed of Ware, a richly carved oak bed 10 ft square, was a well-known wonder mentioned in Shakespeare's *Twelfth Night*, Farquhar's *The Recruiting Officer*, and Ben Jonson's *Epicœne*. The bed is thought to have been made for the owner of Ware Park during Queen Elizabeth's reign, when visitors expected to share a bed, and it was rebuilt in an inn in the town in 1650. Guests carved their initials on the oak, the first dated 1653. In the 19th c. it became a spectacle at various inns, where it was displayed for twopence. It can now be seen in the Victoria and Albert Museum in London.

Ware was the unexpected limit of John Gilpin's ride in William Cowper's ballad (1782).

WELWYN (pr. 'Wĕllin') *Hertfordshire*

Village off the A1(M). Edward Young, rector 1730–65, wrote the long poem *The Complaint, or, Night Thoughts, on Life, Death, and Immortality* (1742–5), which became very popular at once. The bluestocking Mrs Chapone, who admired the man and his philosophy, wondered how he could have 'blundered so egregiously as to imagine himself a poet', but Dr Johnson, who included him in *Lives of the English Poets*, wrote that 'with all his defects, he was a man of genius and a poet'. Young married the widowed granddaughter of Charles II, Lady Elizabeth Lee, and bought Guessons Ⓟ, the house opposite the W door of the church. He promoted Welwyn as a spa on his arrival, building the Assembly Rooms (now the cottages behind the garden next to the White Horse in Mill St.) and laying out a bowling green at his own expense. The chalybeate spring still occasionally floods the gardens of the Mill House. John Byng, recording his tour of 1789 in the *Torrington Diaries*, states that 'The Welwyn Assemblies, tho' continued, are not so frequented as formerly.' The W wall of the church has a monument to Young.

A plaque on the White Hart, a former staging post, records that Byron's body rested there for a night on the way for interment at Hucknall (1824).

WELWYN (pr. 'Wĕllin') GARDEN CITY *Hertfordshire*

Satellite town of London, founded in 1920, just S of Welwyn and bypassed by the A1(M). The Scottish novelist James Leslie Mitchell, who wrote as 'Lewis Grassic Gibbon', lived here from 1931 to 1935—the most productive period in his writing career. His greatest achievement was *Sunset Song* (1932), the first novel of a trilogy based on the land of his childhood, in NE Scotland. *Cloud Howe* (1933) and *Grey Granite* (1934) complete the trilogy, which was published in one volume in 1946 under the title *A Scots Quair*. His other novels include *Spartacus* (1933), and among his non-fiction may be mentioned *Niger: The Life of Mungo Park* (1934) and *The Conquest of the Maya* (1934), both published under his own name. Mitchell lived at 107 Handside Lane for his last two years, a period of much happiness before his untimely death in his 34th year.

WEST BRADENHAM *Norfolk*

Village off the A47, 8 m. E of Swaffham. A lane leads S through the village of Little Fransham to a turn marked 'Wood Farm only'. This house on the family estate was the birthplace of Rider Haggard (1856).

WESTMILL *Hertfordshire*

Village off the A10, 4 m. N of Puckeridge. The turning to Cherry Green leads to Button Snap, the little thatched cottage on the hill owned by Charles Lamb from 1812 until he sold it for £50 in 1815. A plaque states that the cottage was acquired from the Royal Society of Arts by the Charles Lamb Society and 'Dedicated to Elia's Memory' on 3 September 1949.

WESTON COLVILLE *Cambridgeshire*

Village on the B1052, 8 m. SW of Newmarket. James Withers, born here in 1812, the only son of a shoemaker, was taught to read and write by his mother and started work on a farm at the age of 10. He returned here for a short time, when his mother paid for his apprenticeship as a shoemaker from a legacy, but after her death he had to take to labouring again. 'My Native Village', from his *Collected Poems* (1863), describes the annual Feast and the shoemaker's shop, where his father, and later he himself, had worked.

WESTON LONGVILLE *Norfolk*

Village off the A1067, 11 m. NW of Norwich where 'Parson' Woodforde was rector (Old Rectory *c.* 1840 on the site) from 1776 to his death in 1803. 'I breakfasted, dined, supped and slept again at home' he prefaces many entries in his *Diary*. He fishes in his pond; goes coursing; doses his household against the Whirligigousticon (malaria) and other agues; reads *Evelina* and *Roderick Random*; meets the female soldier turned pedlar at The Hart (now a private house), from where he also sets out to beat the bounds. He brews beer and by mischance his pigs get drunk; hears 'a thump at

the front door' and finds 'Coniac' and gin. He frequently dines with the Custance family, both at Weston Hall and then after 1781 at their new Weston House, until they leave for Bath. He is buried in the chancel of the church, which has a memorial and his portrait, painted by his nephew Samuel from a crayon drawing made here.

WETHERINGSETT *Suffolk*

Village with timber and plaster houses off the A140, the old Roman Pye Rd, 11 m. S of Diss. Richard Hakluyt was rector here from 1590 until his death in 1616, but he was also made archdeacon of Westminster in 1603 and was therefore not resident during the whole of his rectorship.

WHIPSNADE *Bedfordshire*

Small village perhaps best known now for the eponymous zoo; it was here that a young Gerald Durrell learnt about taking care of animals, being appointed assistant keeper in 1945.

WICKHAMBROOK *Suffolk*

Village off the A143, 10 m. SW of Bury St Edmunds. George Crabbe, after his short period of schooling, was apprenticed (1768) to Mr Smith, a surgeon–apothecary here. He helped on the farm and with the delivery of medicines. One errand was to Cheveley Park (5 m. NW), where he was amazed at the elegance and culture. As a diversion from the dullness of his job he had started to write verse but after two years he rebelled and went home to *Aldeburgh.

WIDFORD *Hertfordshire*

Village on the B180 and the B1004, 5 m. NE of Ware. Blakesware at Wareside (1½ m. W) was the mansion where Mary Field, grandmother of Charles and Mary Lamb, lived as housekeeper to the Plumer family. Charles and his sister sometimes stayed here. Mary remembers the house in some of the tales in *Mrs. Leicester's School* (1808), and Charles refers to his grandmother and Blakesware in 'The Grandame' and his essays 'Blakesmoor in H—' and 'Dream Children'. This last also recalls his love for Ann Simmons, who lived at the cottages called Blenheims (gone, site in field opposite New Blenheims). Their grandmother is buried in the churchyard at Widford. Blakesware (demolished 1830) was on the site of the Blessed Sacrament House, and near the main drive is a road which once led to the mill (of which only a few traces remain) where Charles Lamb slept on a goosefeather bed when visiting the Misses Norris. These were the daughters of his father's friend at the Temple and they ran a school at Goddards in Widford on the Stansted Abbots road. Charles Lamb's visits—he sometimes walked here from Edmonton—used to stop work at the school for the day. The children, eager to fetch him for breakfast, arrived at the mill before he was awake.

WIMPOLE HALL *Cambridgeshire*

Mansion (built 1638–40) between the A603 and the A1198, 10 m. SW of Cambridge. The wings were added to the house by Robert Harley, Earl of Oxford, when he was patron to Matthew Prior, who often visited here from *Down Hall. Prior died here in 1721 and was buried in Westminster Abbey. Pope was another visitor here. Harley's fine library is now in the British Library in London (see LONDON: BLOOMSBURY).

WISBECH *Cambridgeshire*

Town on the A47 and the A1101. The Wisbech and Fenland Museum, near the church, houses the 17th-c. Town Library, the Literary Society's library, and the Chauncey Hare Townshend bequest. Townshend was a friend of Southey and Dickens, and his collection contains the manuscripts of *Great Expectations* and Lewis's *The Monk*, first editions autographed by Dickens, and letters from Swift, Goethe, Burns, Keats, Lamb, Clare, Byron, and others.

William Godwin, philosopher and novelist, was born (1756) here. John Clare travelled to Wisbech by water as a boy for a brief stay when his uncle tried unsuccessfully to get him work in an attorney's office.

WITHAM (pr. 'Witam) *Essex*

Old town on the B1018, bypassed by the A12, 9 m. NE of Chelmsford, possible birthplace of Thomas Campion in 1567. A tablet in the parish church commemorates William Pattisson, who, on his honeymoon, was drowned with his bride in a Pyrenean lake. Crabb Robinson, who saw it happen from the shore, recounted it in his *Diary* (1869).

Dorothy L. Sayers lived from 1929 to her death in 1957 at 24 Newland St. (listed as being of architectural interest), where a plaque was unveiled in 1975 by the Lord Peter Wimsey of

the contemporary dramatizations of her detective novels, two of which, *The Nine Tailors* (1934) and *Busman's Honeymoon* (1936), have an East Anglian setting. Her plays with religious themes include *The Man Born To Be King* (1943), written for the radio, and she also translated Dante's *Inferno* (1949) and *Purgatorio* (1955).

WOODBRIDGE *Suffolk*

Market town on the A12, 8 m. NE of Ipswich. In 1771 George Crabbe was apprenticed to Mr Page, a surgeon-apothecary who employed him chiefly in his dispensary on the bank of the Deben. Crabbe found congenial friends and first met Sara Elmy, his future wife, during this time. Edward FitzGerald, who often came here from Bredfield, met Bernard Barton (1784–1849), friend of Lamb and Southey, and wrote his life, which prefaced the collection of Barton's poems in 1849. FitzGerald married Barton's daughter Lucy in 1860, but separated from her six months later and moved to lodgings over a shop in the marketplace. The 'Wits of Woodbridge', who included FitzGerald, Barton, and Crabbe's grandson, met at the Bull Inn. Tennyson and his son Hallam also stayed at The Bull in 1876 on their visit to FitzGerald at Little Grange, Pytches Rd, his home from 1864 until his death (1883). Members of the Omar Khayyám Club, founded in 1892 by Edward Clodd, often met at The Bull. They sometimes sailed here from Aldeburgh in Clodd's yacht to visit FitzGerald's grave at Boulge. There is a collection of FitzGerald papers and publications at the Public Library in Woodbridge.

WOODCROFT CASTLE *Cambridgeshire*

Private house 1 m. SE of Helpston, on the Etton–Marholm road. Its siege by Cromwell's men inspired Clare's poem 'Woodcroft Castle',

written when he was sent 'to drive plough' here (c. 1809).

WOOLVERSTONE *Suffolk*

Located just S of Ipswich, Woolverstone Hall School, a boarding school established in 1951, numbers the novelist Ian McEwan among its distinguished alumni.

WORTHAM *Suffolk*

Village on the A143, 4 m. SW of Diss, where the Revd Richard Cobbold wrote about smugglers and transportation in the novel *Margaret Catchpole* (1845). The large old rectory is by the new one, on the hill above the church, where he is commemorated.

WREST PARK *Bedfordshire*

Former country estate, 9 m. N of Luton and S of Silsoe on the A6. In the 1620s John Selden was steward to Henry Grey, 9th Earl of Kent, and is thought to have written *Marmora Arundelliana* (1624) at a former house here. He also came here after being released, because of the plague, from imprisonment for supporting protests about tonnage and poundage. John Aubrey's gossip relates that he married the Countess of Kent after the Earl's death. Another member of the household here was Samuel Butler (1612–80), first as page to the Countess and then as secretary. There is a poem 'To My Friend G.N. from Wrest' by Thomas Carew. The gardens (English Heritage), are open to the public.

WYMONDHAM (pr. 'Windam) *Norfolk*

Market town 9 m. SW of Norwich, on the A11. Henry Peacham (1576?–1643?) was the master of the Grammar School from 1617 to 1621. The last edition of his best-known work, *The Compleat Gentleman* (1622), was Johnson's source for the heraldic definitions in his dictionary. The school was held in the 12th-c. Becket's Chapel.

Midlands

Midlands

EAST MIDLANDS

ABNEY *Derbyshire*

Village off the B6001, 3 m. SW of Hathersage. Cockey Farm (½ m. S) was the birthplace in 1750 of William Newton, who became a machinery carpenter. He was known as the 'Peak Minstrel' after his verses came to the attention of the curate of *Eyam.

ALDWINCLE *Northamptonshire*

Village off the A605, 5 m. SW of Oundle, made up of two parishes. The Church of Aldwinkle St Peter has a commemorative window to Thomas Fuller, born (1608) in the rectory (gone). At the other end of the village John Dryden was born (1631) in the Old Rectory, opposite the Church of Aldwinkle All Saints. This, seldom used now, has a memorial tablet. Dryden, whose maternal grandfather held the living here for 40 years, often visited the village.

ALTHORP (pr. 'Awltrop) *Northamptonshire*

Country house 6 m. NW of Northampton on the A428, altered in the late 18th c. Ben Jonson wrote the masque for the entertainment in 1603 of James I's queen on her way S from Scotland after his accession. She was the guest of the Spencer family, whose home it has been since 1508.

ANNESLEY *Nottinghamshire*

Village on the A611, 3 m. W of Newstead Abbey. Byron at 15 fell desperately in love with his cousin Mary Chaworth, who lived at Annesley Hall, 1 m. S, and was already engaged. He used to ride over from *Southwell, and sometimes spent the night here. In 'The Dream' (1816) he tells of his unrequited love and how it ended:

> the one
> To end in madness—both in misery.

His attachment was more poignant because, as he relates in 'The Duel' (1818), his great-uncle killed her grandfather. Byron used to keep his great-uncle's sword by his bed and it is still at Newstead. Her descendants later lived at the Hall.

ASHBOURNE *Derbyshire*

Old town where the A52 and the A515 cross. Sir Thomas Cokayne, author of 'A Treatise of Hunting' (1591), is buried in the parish church. 'Viator' and 'Piscator', who converse in Walton's *The Compleat Angler* (1653), rested at the Talbot Inn, formerly on the site of the Town Hall. Dr Johnson often stayed with his friend Dr John Taylor at The Mansion, a large red-brick house with a pillared porch opposite the old buildings of the Elizabethan Grammar School. He and Boswell stayed later at the Green Man. The peal of St Oswald's church bells inspired Tom Moore at Mayfield 2 m. W to write the lines for his song 'Those Evening Bells'. Elizabeth Gaskell stayed during the 1850s at the 18th-c. Ashbourne Hall, her cousin's home, now the County Library.

ASHBY-DE-LA-ZOUCH *Leicestershire*

Small town and former spa on the A50, 10 m. SE of Burton-upon-Trent off the A511. The castle, a ruin comprising the remains of a Norman keep and 14th- and 15th-c. manor houses, was the scene in 1607 of George Marston's masque, an entertainment given by the Countess of Huntingdon in honour of her mother, the Dowager Countess of Derby, who had arrived from Harefield (see LONDON). The Tournament Field, where many scenes in Scott's *Ivanhoe* (1819) take place, is 1 m. N. Ashby-de-la-Zouch's most famous 20th-c. resident must be Adrian Mole, the hero of the series of comic diaries penned by Sue Townsend. Adrian begins the series in *Leicester but as it develops moves to Ashby, and eventually his beloved Pandora becomes the town's MP.

AULT HUCKNALL *Derbyshire*

Village S off the A617 at Glapwell. Thomas Hobbes (1588–1679), the philosopher, who was tutor to two earls of Devonshire, and spent the last years of his life at Hardwick Hall (1 m. S), is buried in the church. A Latin memorial on the floor of the S chapel records that he was famous at home and abroad.

AYNHO *Northamptonshire*

Stone village on the A4100, birthplace of Shakerley Marmion (1603), author of *The Antiquary* (1641) and other plays. He contributed, with Ben Jonson and Drayton, to *Annalia Dubrensia* (see DOVER'S HILL).

BAG ENDERBY *Lincolnshire*

Small village where Tennyson's father was rector jointly with Somersby (½ m. W). The tall box pews, including the squire's pew where the family sat, have gone.

BEAUVALE PRIORY *Nottinghamshire*

Ruin off the B600 NW of Eastwood, the setting for D. H. Lawrence's historical short story 'A Fragment of Stained Glass'.

BELVOIR (pr. 'Beever) CASTLE *Leicestershire*

Seat of the Duke of Rutland, 7 m. WSW of Grantham. Crabbe was chaplain (1782–8) and he published the realistic *The Village* (1783) while here, though it stemmed from his experiences at Aldeburgh, and *The Newspaper* (1785). After his marriage (1783) he had an apartment in the castle, which was rebuilt by Wyatt in 1816 after a fire.

Disraeli, who was a friend of Lord John Manners (later the 6th Duke), used to stay at the castle and is thought to have made it the 'Beaumanoir' of his novel *Coningsby* (1844).

BERESFORD DALE *Derbyshire*

Part of the Dove valley approached by public footpath from Hartington on the A444, 25 m. SE of Ashbourne. The Beresford family owned land here for centuries and Charles Cotton, a descendant, was born (1630) in the gabled Tudor Hall with the Elizabethan wing (now all demolished) where he entertained Izaak Walton. Together they fished the Dove, resting in the little temple, where their initials are entwined in a monogram over the door. This, built in 1674, is dedicated to the river and its sportsmen. Cotton wrote the second part, on fly-fishing, of the 5th edition of *The Compleat Angler* (1676), *Wonders of the Peak* (1681), and translated Montaigne's *Essays* (1685). Collections of his other works appeared posthumously. He sold the Hall, which he called by the local name, Basford Hall, in his poems, when in debt but was able to live there again when it was bought by a Beresford cousin. The parish church at Alstonfield 2 m. S has the pew, now painted, with the Cotton arms where the two men worshipped. It and the other oak pews were carved in Cotton's father's time.

BLATHERWYCKE *Northamptonshire*

Village off the A43, 8 m. SW of Stamford. Thomas Randolph died, aged 30, while on a visit to his friend Anthony Stafford. While in London, Randolph had written 'An Ode to Anthony Stafford to hasten him into the Country', which contains the lines:

> Come, spur away
> I have no pleasure for a longer stay,
> But must go down
> And leave the chargeable noise of this great town
>   I will the country see
>   Where old simplicity
>   Though hid in gray
>   Dost look more gay
> Than Foppery in plush and scarlet clad.
>   Farewell you city wits that are
>   Almost at civil war—

'Tis time that I grow wise, when all the world
grows mad.

Randolph is buried in the Stafford family vault
in the church, where there is a memorial.

BOSTON *Lincolnshire*

Port and market town on the Witham. A
plaque on the Rum Puncheon Inn states that
John Foxe, martyrologist, was born there in
1516. His *Actes and Monuments* (1563), a
history of the Church, has become known as
the Book of Martyrs. St Botolph's Church,
whose tall tower, a landmark in the fens, is
popularly known as the Boston Stump, has a
stained-glass window commemorating Anne
Bradstreet and Jean Ingelow. The former,
her husband, and her father were part of the
Puritan community who formed the
Massachusetts Bay Company in 1629 and
planned to settle there. They left in 1630 in the
Arbella, formerly Kenelm Digby's privateer.
Anne was the first English woman to write
poetry in America and her verses were
published in London without her knowledge as
The Tenth Muse lately Sprung up in America
(1650).

Jean Ingelow was born (1820) in South St.
near the Haven Bridge. Part of the foundations
of her birthplace forms a low wall round a
shrub garden in her memory. 'High Tide on the
Coast of Lincolnshire 1571' from *Poems* (1863)
is one of her most popular ballads.

Mark Lemon spent his youth at South Place,
the home of his uncle, a hop grower. Some of
Tom Moody's Tales (1863) and his first novel,
about a farmer, stem from his experience here.
He left for London in 1836.

The poet Elizabeth Jennings was born at The
Bungalow on Tower Road, Skirbeck, on 18 July
1926.

BURGHLEY HOUSE
Northamptonshire

Elizabethan country house on the SE outskirts
of Stamford, built for the Cecil family. The 5th
Earl, John Cecil, was host to Dryden during the

summer and autumn of 1696, when he was
translating the Seventh Book of the *Aeneid*,
which he finished here. Celia Fiennes, who
visited *c.* 1700, was impressed with the carvings
and tapestries but affronted by the pictures as
'they were all without garments'. In 1809 John
Clare was taken on for a three-year gardener's
apprenticeship. In his short *Autobiography*
(1831), he tells how some servants managed to
get out of their locked quarters to drink the
strong beer in Tant Baker's Hole in the Wall
tavern. He also saved his meagre wages to buy
one of Abercrombie's popular gardening
manuals but before the year was out he had left
the drunken head gardener and was on his way
to Newark. After the publication of his poems
in 1820 the Marquess, whom Clare had often
seen fishing or shooting in the park when they
were both boys, sent for him to give him a
pension of £50. In 1833 Tennyson wrote 'The
Lord of Burleigh', a true though fairy-story-like
tale of Sarah Hoggins, 'a village maiden', who
married 'a poor landscape painter' expecting to
live in a cottage, only to find herself above her
station. Sarah pined away after six years, but
Tom Moore in 'You remember Ellen' from *Irish
Melodies* (1822), gives her a happy ending.
Hazlitt also told her story in the *New Monthly
Magazine* (1822). Her portrait is in the house.

CANONS ASHBY *Northamptonshire*

Country house, off the B4525, built (1551)
by the Dryden family on the ruins of an
Augustinian Priory. Spenser was thought to
have written part of *The Faerie Queene* in a
room now called after him. His 'Rosalynde' was
a kinswoman of the wife of the owner, Erasmus
Dryden, according to John Aubrey. John
Dryden was related to the owners but it is not
thought he visited often, although his son
Erasmus lived here and is buried in the church.
This, with its massive ironstone tower, is all
that remains of the monastic buildings. Samuel
Richardson used 'Ashby-Canons' as the address
Lucy Selby gives in *Sir Charles Grandison*
(1754).

CLIFTON *Nottinghamshire*

Suburb S of Nottingham on the A453. Clifton
Grove, formerly a country estate, now a public
park with a tree-lined walk above the Trent,
gives the title to a collection of poems (1803) by
Henry Kirke White. He died (1806) soon after
entering Cambridge. His hymn 'Oft in danger,
oft in woe' is still sung.

COLEORTON HALL *Leicestershire*

Mansion (later offices of the National Coal
Board) on the A512, 1 m. NW of the village,
the country home of Sir George Beaumont
(1753–1827), patron of painters and poets.
He lent his new farmhouse, Hall Farm, to
Wordsworth, from November 1806 to June
1807, as Dove Cottage was too small for his
growing family. The mansion was being built
by Dance the Younger, and Wordsworth, who
walked daily in the grounds, was soon occupied
in planning a winter garden of hollies,
cypresses, yews, and box for Lady Beaumont.
Dorothy Wordsworth's letters describe the
farmhouse with its coal fires from Sir George's
pits (mentioned in Corbett's 'Iter Boreale'), and
their walks to Grace Dieu, ancestral home of
the Beaumonts, and recount that her brother
'composes frequently in the grove'. Coleridge,
long awaited, arrived in December with
Hartley, but the easy productive friendship of
*Alfoxton was not recaptured here. Their last
guest was Walter Scott. Under the limes,
painted by Constable, is a decorative urn with
lines to Joshua Reynolds, who stayed here, and
the terrace walk has an inscription to Francis
Beaumont (d. 1616), brother of Sir John, whose
poems were edited (1810) by Sir George, his
direct descendant. Many of Wordsworth's
poems were illustrated by Sir George.

CONINGSBY *Lincolnshire*

Village on the A153 near Tattershall Castle.
Laurence Eusden (1688–1730), whose
appointment as Poet Laureate in 1718 after he
had written a flattering poem to the appointer
caused ridicule, was rector here (1725–30).
Pope called him a drunken parson in *The
Dunciad*. John Dyer, the poet, was rector from
1752 to his death. In the introduction to Dyer's
poems in *British Poets* (1820), John Aikin
suggests he was ordained and 'sat down' on the
livings of Coningsby and Kirkby-on-Bain as a
relief from a dissolute life. The rectory, now
Church Close, where he wrote *The Fleece* (1757)
is next to the church and has a medieval core.
The 'fenny country' did not agree with him and
he complained 'of a lack of books and company'.
He died of a 'gradual decline' in 1758 and was
buried in the church, but no memorial remains.

CORBY *Northamptonshire*

Industrial town N of Kettering. The poet and
novelist John Burnside moved to Corby as a
child in the 1970s when his father took a job at
Stewart's and Lloyd's steelworks. He describes
life here in his memoir *A Lie About My Father*
(2006) and set his novel *Living Nowhere*
(2003) in the town.

Burghley House, Northamptonshire. Dryden finished translating book 7 of the *Aeneid* here

COSSALL *Nottinghamshire*

Village 4 m. SE of Eastwood off the A6096. Church Cottage was the home of Louie Burrows, for a short time D. H. Lawrence's fiancée and a possible model for Ursula Brangwen of *Women in Love* (1920). It was the honeymoon cottage of the Brangwens, but Marsh Farm is no longer there. Will Brangwen was modelled on Louie's father, Alfred, whose carvings are in the church with the family memorial windows.

COTTERSTOCK *Northamptonshire*

Village off the A605, 2 m. N of Oundle. Cotterstock Hall, a 17th-c. house with rounded gables, was the home of Mrs Elmes Steward, the daughter of Dryden's first cousin. In 1698 and 1699 Dryden spent the summers here writing *Fables Ancient and Modern* (1700), adaptations from Boccaccio and Chaucer. He was in failing health and she fed him on venison and marrow puddings.

CROWLAND (or CROYLAND) *Lincolnshire*

Small town off the A47, 10 m. NE of Peterborough, where the half-ruined Norman abbey towers above the fens. Some consider *Gesta Herewardi* to have been a 15th-c. forgery and not written by the 10th-c. monk Ingulf of Croyland as was supposed. It gives an account of the Saxon outlaw Hereward and his resistance to the Normans. Charles Kingsley's novel *Hereward the Wake* (1866) also tells the story of Hereward and his horse Swallow.

DERBY (pr. 'Darby) *Derbyshire*

Industrial town on the Derwent, formerly a Roman settlement and an important Saxon town on the A38 and the A6. Dr Johnson married Mrs Elizabeth Porter at St Werburgh's Church in Friar Gate in 1735, and he and Boswell made later visits. Maria Edgeworth attended Mrs Latuffiere's school here (1775–81) and learned handwriting, French, and embroidery, lessons augmented in the holidays by her father's advanced ideas on education. She accompanied her father in 1813, when he stayed with his friend William Strutt, the inventor of the Belper stove.

Erasmus Darwin, physician and poet, came here on the occasion of his second marriage in 1781. He founded the Derby Philosophical Society. At the end of his life he moved to Breadsall Priory, 2½ m. NE, where he died shortly afterwards in April 1802. Herbert Spencer, who was born (1820) in Exeter St., went to school here until 1833, and then returned as an assistant master (1837), with more interest in natural science than classics. Derby is 'Stoniton' in George Eliot's *Adam Bede* (1859).

DOVEDALE *Derbyshire*

Narrow wooded valley NW of Ashbourne, stretching for 2 m. N from Thorpe (footpath only) through limestone crags. Izaak Walton and Charles Cotton, who both fished the Dove, praised its beauty. Dr Johnson's Happy Valley in *Rasselas* (1759), and George Eliot's Eagle Valley in *Adam Bede* (1859), are thought to have been modelled on Dovedale.

DRONFIELD *Derbyshire*

Small town between Sheffield and Chesterfield. The travel writer, novelist, and essayist Bruce Chatwin was born in Dronfield in 1940.

EASTON MAUDIT *Northamptonshire*

Village off the A509, 11 m. E of Northampton, where Thomas Percy lived as vicar (1756–78). His collection of old ballads was published as *Reliques of Ancient English Poetry* (1765). His house (later the Old Rectory) was visited by Goldsmith, of whom he wrote a memoir (1801), and by Dr Johnson in 1764, when he was completing his edition of Shakespeare's plays and helping Percy with his researches. A bedroom in the house is still known as 'Johnson's Room' and a box and yew walk as 'Johnson's Walk'. A brass on the front pew of the church commemorates his visit.

EASTWOOD *Nottinghamshire*

Small hilltop mining town 9 m. NW of Nottingham. D. H. Lawrence, a miner's son born (1885) at 8a Victoria St. ⓟ, transposed many local scenes into his novels and called the town 'Bestwood' in *Sons and Lovers* (1913), 'Woodhouse' in *The Lost Girl* (1920), and 'Beldover' in *Women in Love* (1920). The Lawrences lived (1887–91) at 28 Garden Rd, the 'Bottoms' of *Sons and Lovers*, restored (1973) by the Association of Young Writers. While living (1891–1902) at 12 Walker St., then on the edge of cornfields, Lawrence attended Beauvale School and in 1898 was its first pupil to win a scholarship to a grammar school. Lawrence described the view from Walker St. as 'the country of my heart'. There was the small Moorgreen colliery where Walter Morel worked in *Sons and Lovers*, Lambclose House, off the B600, the probable model for many of Lawrence's middle-class homes, and Moorgreen Reservoir, then much deeper than today, where a real drowning fatality led to the similar tragedy in Willey Water in *Women in Love*. The reservoir becomes 'Nethermere' in *Sons and Lovers* and *The White Peacock* (1911). His family moved to 97 Lyncroft in 1902, where Lawrence and his friends, who were training as teachers, often met while they were at the British School here. They called themselves the Pagans and no. 97 was the Pagan Headquarters.

ELSTON *Nottinghamshire*

Quiet village E of the A46, 6 m. SW of Newark. Erasmus Darwin was born in 1731 at the Hall (rebuilt in 1837). There are family monuments in the church and his mother built the almshouses in 1744.

EYAM (pr. Eem) *Derbyshire*

Village off the A623, 5 m. SW of Hathersage, which volunteered to isolate itself to contain the plague in 1665. Anna Seward was born (1747) and lived at the vicarage near the church until her father became prebend of Lichfield as well, and they moved there. His curate Peter Cunningham, author of the poems 'Britannia's Naval Triumph' and 'Russian Prophecy', recognized the merit of William Newton, a young machinery carpenter of *Abney. Cunningham introduced Newton to Anna Seward when she visited the parish and she encouraged his writing and got him a mill partnership. The poet Richard Furness (b. 1791), son of a small farmer of Eyam, set up his own business as currier in 1813. After a runaway marriage he moved to Dore (8 m. NE) as a schoolmaster, where he also practised medicine and surgery and superintended the design and building of a new chapel. The satirical *Rag Bag* (1832) was followed by

The kitchen at D. H. Lawrence's birthplace, 8a Victoria St., Eastwood

Medicus-Magus (1836), a long poem with a glossary, on local village life, which was later called *The Astrologer*. He was buried (1857) at Eyam.

FOREMARK *Derbyshire*

Village 2 m. E of Repton. William Stevens became chaplain (1778) to Sir Robert Burdett of Foremark Hall (built 1759–61), now the Preparatory Department of Repton School. Stevens's *Journal* (1965), kept from 1792 to 1800, tells of his weekly journeys from Repton to preach and his irksome dependence on his patron. He met Fanny Coutts here and they fell in love, but her parents prevented their marriage. A miniature of Stevens is in the school and the three-decker pulpit he used is still in the church.

GAINSBOROUGH *Lincolnshire*

Manufacturing and market town on the Trent and the A159, *c.* 20 m. NW of Lincoln. Marian Evans, who wrote as George Eliot, searching for a river capable of producing a flood to cause the tragedy in the novel she was writing, visited the town in 1859. George Lewes wrote, 'We took a boat from Gainsborough and rowed down to the Idle [a tributary joining the Trent at Stockwith, 4 m. N] which we ascended on foot some way, and walked back to Gainsborough.' The title of the novel, *The Mill on the Floss*, was chosen by John Blackwood, the publisher, but though 'St Ogg's' was set on a tributary of the tidal river Trent, descriptions of life at the mill come from Marian Evans's memory of Arbury Mill near her childhood home.

GLOSSOP *Derbyshire*

Market town 13 m. E of Manchester in the Peak District; the novelist Hilary Mantel was born here in 1952.

GRACE DIEU *Leicestershire*

Ivy-clad ruin of an Augustinian priory on the A512, 2 m. E of *Coleorton. Francis Beaumont, the dramatist brother of Sir John Beaumont the poet, was born (1584) at the manor house built in the secularized priory after the Dissolution. His friend Michael Drayton visited him here. The Wordsworths walked here in 1807 while staying at Coleorton, where they would have liked a stream 'bustling through the rocks' as they found here.

GREAT CASTERTON *Rutland*

Village once on the Great North Rd, now bypassed by the A1. John Clare, who called it Bridge Casterton, 'a lovely little town', worked (1817–18) here as a lime burner, sometimes more than the usual 14 hours a day. He spent his wages on buying books and his free time writing verses, collected in 1820 as *Poems Descriptive of Rural Life*. He drank with other lime burners at the Flower Pot (later Stonecroft, a private house) at Tickencote (½ m. N). Clare described the banks of the Gwash as 'very stunt', giving flat-country dwellers the fancy of mountains. He first met Patty Turner, later his wife, here.

HARRINGTON HALL *Lincolnshire*

Large mansion in the village N of the A158, 7 m. NW of Horncastle. In 1834 Alfred Tennyson became acquainted with Rosa Baring, stepdaughter of Admiral Eden, the tenant of the Hall. Her companionship was a solace to him when he and his sister at Somersby (1 m. NE) were suffering after the death of Arthur Hallam. Years later he recalled the walled garden with the raised walk round the walls in *Maud* (1855) and also in 'Roses on the Terrace' from *Demeter and Other Poems* (1889).

HATHERSAGE *Derbyshire*

Village on the A625, 9 m. SW of Sheffield. In 1845 Charlotte Brontë spent a short holiday with her friend Ellen Nussey, who was housekeeping at the vicarage for her brother away on his honeymoon. He had proposed to Charlotte some years before. The Eyre family memorials in the church may have prompted her to choose that name for the heroine of *Jane Eyre* (1847). Opposite the church porch is the grave tended by the Ancient Order of Foresters of Little John of the Robin Hood legends. Tradition says he died in a cottage nearby.

HIGHAM FERRERS *Northamptonshire*

Small market town on the A6 and the A45. The heroine of H. E. Bates's novel *The Sleepless Moon* (1956) lives in the small house on the edge of the churchyard near the 15th-c. Grammar School, and she walks to her wedding in the church. Bates, in his autobiography *The Vanished World* (1969), mentions the prisoner of war he saw here, which gave him the idea for the short story 'The Hessian Prisoner'.

HINCKLEY *Leicestershire*

Town near Nuneaton, approximately equidistant between Leicester and Coventry. A Cold Comfort Farm stands near the town, giving its name to Stella Gibbons's famous parody of the rural novel. The novel itself is set near the fictional village of Howling on the Sussex Downs.

HUCKNALL *Nottinghamshire*

Small town, once called Hucknall Torkard, 7 m. N of Nottingham. The church contains the Byron family vault where the body of Lord Byron, brought back from Greece, was buried in 1824. A high relief of his head surmounts the memorial in the chancel erected by his half-sister Augusta. Thomas Moore, visiting in 1827 while writing the Life of his friend, found the church locked but a small boy climbed through a window and let him in. The King of Greece presented a marble slab in 1881, in recognition of Byron's efforts for Greek freedom. An account of Byron's funeral and the opening of the vault in 1938 is obtainable in the church. A statue of Byron erected in 1903 stands on the front of the Co-operative building near the church.

KEGWORTH *Leicestershire*

Village off the A6, 13 m. SW of Nottingham. Tom Moore lived on the London Rd (now The Cedars) from the spring of 1812 to 1813. He got the house through Lord Moira, from whom he had expected a substantial government post. When he returned in 1827, he called the place 'our wretched barn of a house' but his wife, Bessy, was pleased with the large garden. Moore often walked to Donington Park, Moira's house, where he read in the library.

KETTERING *Northamptonshire*

Manufacturing town on the A6 and the A43, 17 m. NE of Northampton. H. E. Bates was educated at the Grammar School (1916–21). In his autobiography, *The Vanished World* (1969), he writes that the arrival of a wounded ex-officer as his teacher and his reading of *The Red Badge of Courage* (1895) by Stephen Crane combined to give him the desire to write for a living. He left school at 16 to become a reporter on a local newspaper, and he published his first novel, *The Two Sisters* (1926), at 20. The novelist J. L. Carr was an eccentric and popular headmaster at Highfield primary school, getting pupils to put their names in bottles and throw them into the river Ise, marching them through the town reciting A. E. Housman, or conducting assemblies by the railway line. His novel *The Harpole Report* (1972) made use of his experience as a teacher. He threw in his job in the mid-1960s to set himself up as a writer and small publisher. At the back of his house and in the garden shed at 1 Cranleigh Rd he produced, in addition to novels, a range of charming and idiosyncratic pocket books, maps, drawings, and sculpture. A collection of his work is held by Kettering Library.

LANGAR *Nottinghamshire*

Village S of the A52, 12 m. SE of Nottingham. Samuel Butler was born (1835) at the rectory (later Langar House). *The Way of All Flesh* (1903), a satirical and autobiographical novel, paints a grim picture of his youth here before the differences with his father reached the point where he emigrated to New Zealand.

LANGTON BY SPILSBY *Lincolnshire*

Small village 9 m. E of Horncastle, off the A158, the home of the Langton family for 800 years. When Johnson visited his friend Bennet Langton in 1764 he stayed in the Elizabethan manor, which was demolished in 1845. The church, built in 1725, was more recently restored, and the Langton pew where Johnson sat now contains the organ.

LEICESTER *Leicestershire*

Roman settlement, manufacturing city, and county town. Shakespeare's Richard III stays in Leicester before the battle of Bosworth. Shakespeare's company almost certainly performed in the 14th-c. Guildhall on Guildhall Lane.

In 1916 the novelist, scientist, and administrator C. P. Snow entered Alderman

Newton's School on Grange Rd at the age of 11, where he excelled at all subjects except gymnastics and woodwork. Snow was born in 1905 at 40 Richmond Rd. After school he studied at the Leicester, Leicestershire, and Rutland University College (later Leicester University). *Strangers and Brothers* (1940)—renamed *George Passant* in 1970—and *Time of Hope* (1950), the first and second books in his 11-book novel sequence *Strangers and Brothers*, draws upon his early years in a provincial university. In 1964 he became Baron Snow of Leicester. The novelist H. S. Hoff followed in the footsteps of Snow, his *Cambridge tutor and mentor, by teaching at Alderman Newton's in the 1940s, a time which bore fruit when, as 'William Cooper', he came to write his irreverent novel *Scenes from Provincial Life* (1950): 'The school at which I was science-master was desirably situated, right in the middle of the town. By walking only a few yards the masters and boys could find themselves in a café or a public house.' Philip Larkin became an assistant librarian at University College in 1946. He met Monica Jones, a lecturer in the English Department here. From the late 1940s she became his confidante and companion.

In the mid-1950s Colin Dexter (pre-Inspector Morse) spent three years in Leicester teaching at Wyggeston Boys' School, by Victoria Park (now Wyggeston and Queen Elizabeth College).

The novelist and critic Malcolm Bradbury took his first degree at Leicester University, before moving on to London and *Manchester for his postgraduate work.

The novelists Julian Barnes and Sue Townsend were both born in Leicester in 1946. In Townsend's *The Secret Diary of Adrian Mole, Aged 13¾* (1982), the first in a series, Adrian is living in Leicester, where he discovers that deep down he is a misunderstood philosopher–poet, and struggles with delinquent parents, raging hormones, and unrequited love for the beautiful Pandora Braithwaite; the series continues with *The Growing Pains of Adrian Mole* (1984), and a number of successors which eventually see Adrian leaving Leicester for *Ashby, then moving down to London. Unlike Adrian, Townsend still lives in Leicester today.

LINCOLN *Lincolnshire*

Cathedral city at the junction of the A15 and A57. Walter Map or Mapes (*fl.* 1200), author of *De Nugis Curialium*, a collection of essays and tales giving a contemporary account of life in the 12th c., was a canon of the Cathedral. The child martyr 'Little St Hugh' (1246?-55), whose shrine is in the S aisle of the choir, was a favoured subject of poets. He is mentioned in 'The Prioress's Tale' in Chaucer's *The Canterbury Tales*, in Marlowe's *The Jew of Malta*, and in 'The Jew's Daughter', a ballad in Percy's *Reliques*. Robert Grosseteste, notable philosopher and scientist, and author of *Le Chasteau d'amour*, was bishop 1235-53. He was buried in the SE transept of the choir.

The Norman castle figures in the Early English verse romance *Havelok the Dane*.

Elizabeth Penrose (1780-1837), who as 'Mrs Markham' wrote popular histories for young people, died in Minster Yard and was buried in the Cloister Garth. Ada Bayly, the novelist 'Edna Lyall', lived with her sister at 5 Minster Yard, where *Donovan* (1882) and its popular sequel *We Two* (1884) were written; she left Lincoln in 1884.

Tennyson, a native of Lincolnshire, is commemorated by a statue on the green outside the Cathedral. Lincoln Public Library has a permanent display of Tennyson material. The Library also houses the Tennyson Research Centre, a large collection of family books and papers (visits by appointment), (www.lincolnlibrary.com).

The University and library at Lincoln are the academic home of La Motte scholar Maud Bailey, in A. S. Byatt's novel *Possession* (1990).

Penelope Fitzgerald (born Knox), whose grandfather was Bishop of Lincoln, was born at the Old Palace in 1916. She makes oblique reference to her childhood in *The Knox Brothers* (1977), a multiple biography of her father, Eddie, an editor of *Punch*, and her uncles Wilfred, Dilly, and Ronald (the Catholic divine who was also the subject of a biography

by Evelyn Waugh). The train in Anne Stevenson's poem 'Branch Line' travels from Lincoln to Market Rasen, past fields of rape,

> wanton patches the colour of heat
> dropped like cheap tropical skirts
> on the proper wolds.

LOUGHBOROUGH (pr. 'Luffbruh) *Leicestershire*

Manufacturing town on the A6, 11 m. NW of Leicester. John Cleveland, who was born here (*c.* 1613), was educated at the school founded by a charitable bequest, which was held in All Saints' Church. His father was the schoolmaster.

LOUTH *Lincolnshire*

Market town 25 m. NE of Lincoln on the A16 and the A157. Tennyson was at the Grammar School from 1815 to 1820, when his father decided to teach him at home. In 1827 *Poems of Two Brothers*, by Tennyson and his brother Charles, was published by Jacksons in the Market Place.

LUTTERWORTH *Leicestershire*

Market town on the A426, W of the M1 intersection 20. Wycliffe was rector (1374-84)

Statue of Tennyson on Minster Green, Lincoln

and spent his last years here working on the first English translation of the Bible. He died after being taken ill during a service in the church and was carried through what is now Wycliffe's Doorway in the S side of the chancel. He was buried in the churchyard but in 1428 his body was exhumed and burnt, and his ashes cast into the Swift by order of a Papal Commission. Copies of some of his works and a medieval cope, reputedly his, can be seen in the church. A white marble memorial, erected in 1837 under the E window in the S aisle, shows Wycliffe preaching.

MACKWORTH *Derbyshire*

Village on the A52, 3 m. NW of Derby. Samuel Richardson was baptized in the parish church in August 1689, and spent his early years here. It is thought that he was apprenticed to a stationer in Derby before starting his own printing business in London.

MARKET BOSWORTH *Leicestershire*

Small town on the B585, 14 m. W of Leicester and 2 m. N of the battlefield of Bosworth Field, 1485, which brings an end to Richard of Gloucester in Shakespeare's *Richard III*.

In 1731 Samuel Johnson, soon after his father's death, became a master at the Grammar School for a few years. This was called Dixie School, which had been refounded in 1601 with bequests from Sir Wolstan Dixie (1525–94), a Lord Mayor of London. Johnson combined teaching with acting as secretary to a descendant of Sir Wolstan, who lived at Bosworth Hall, visible across the park. Johnson, who also lived at the Hall, often used to visit the Revd Beaumont Dixie at the rectory.

MATLOCK *Derbyshire*

Town at the SE edge of the Peak District. John Betjeman yields to apocalyptic misgivings in 'Matlock Bath':

> In this dark dale I hear the thunder
> Of houses folding with the shocks
> The GRAND PAVILION buckling under
> The weight of the ROMANTIC ROCKS.

MELBOURNE *Derbyshire*

Small town on the B587 off the A514, 9 m. S of Derby. Melbourne Hall, a mainly 17th- and 18th-c. building, was a retreat during the Commonwealth for Richard Baxter, the Nonconformist minister at Kidderminster. He wrote here part of *The Saint's Everlasting Rest* (1650), the book that George Eliot, in *The Mill on the Floss* (1860), makes Mrs Glegg turn to with such relief in times of domestic crisis. Baxter, who has been called an 'irrepressible heresiarch', was a Parliamentarian who did much to restore the monarchy, and then suffered under Charles II and James II.

MIDDLETON-BY-WIRKSWORTH *Derbyshire*

Hillside village on the B5023, 5 m. SW of Matlock. D. H. Lawrence lived from April 1918 to May 1919 at the bungalow Mountain Cottage, built overlooking the gorge. He was writing his 'never-to-be-finished *Studies in Classic American Literature*' and reading Gibbon. He wrote of the country in a letter to Katherine Mansfield in February 1919 and described the different trails in the snow around the cottage:

> beautiful ropes of rabbit prints, trailing away over the brows; heavy hare marks; a fox, so sharp and dainty, going over the wall; birds with two feet that hop; very splendid straight advance of a pheasant . . . little leaping marks of weasels, coming along like a necklace chain of berries; odd little filigree of the field mice; the trail of a mole . . .

Lawrence failed to obtain a grant to help his finances and moved south again with the idea of going abroad.

MOUNT ST MARY'S COLLEGE *Derbyshire*

Jesuit school at Spinkhill, off the A616, 8 m. SE of Sheffield. While Gerard Manley Hopkins was bursar here from October 1877 to April 1878, he wrote 'The Loss of the *Eurydice*', a long poem on a training ship 'with all sail set' that foundered in a gale off the Isle of *Wight.

MUSTON *Leicestershire*

Village off the A52, 6 m. W of Grantham. Crabbe was rector here from 1789 to 1814, with a prolonged absence (1792–1805) in Suffolk. He often combined his new calling with his old profession of doctoring and was well liked in his early days here. He was also in touch with many botanists and made a garden to help his study of rare specimens. His wife had developed a depressive illness after the loss of her two sons and she died here in 1814 and is buried in the chancel ℗. Crabbe exchanged the living for *Trowbridge in the same year. His rectory has been rebuilt.

NEWARK ON TRENT *Nottinghamshire*

Ancient town on the Great North Road, now bypassed by the A1. In 1619 Richard Corbett with some Oxford friends stayed at the 14th-c. White Hart inn on the journey he describes in 'Iter Boreale'. John Cleveland was Judge-Advocate at the Royalist garrison in Newark in 1645–6. While here he wrote *The Character of a London Diurnal* (1647). In Scott's *Heart of Midlothian* Jeanie Deans stayed a night at the Saracen's Head inn (now a bank) on her way to London.

NEWSTEAD ABBEY *Nottinghamshire*

Former Augustinian priory, on the A60, 11 m. N of Nottingham, which became the Byron family home and was inherited by the poet in 1798. He lived here intermittently until forced by debts to sell in 1816.

> Shades of heroes, farewell! your descendant departing
> From the seat of his ancestors, bids you adieu!
> Abroad or at home, your remembrance imparting
> New courage, he'll think upon glory and you.

Thomas Moore, writing his life of Byron (1830), mentions in his *Memoirs* seeing the oak Byron planted and the grave of Boatswain, the favourite dog who died of rabies, subjects of two poems by Byron. Moore's host on this visit in 1827 was Colonel Wildman, Byron's successor, who also entertained Washington Irving in 1832 when he wrote his impressions in *Abbotsford and Newstead Abbey* (1835). Though the old priory church is a ruin, the visitor will no longer find that, as in 'On Leaving Newstead Abbey',

> Through thy battlements Newstead, the hollow winds whistle:
> Thou, the hall of my Fathers art gone to decay;
> In thy once smiling garden, the hemlock and thistle
> Have choak'd up the rose which late bloom'd in the way,

as the Abbey and grounds are well cared for by Nottingham City Council.

NORTHAMPTON *Northamptonshire*

Manufacturing town on the A43 and the A45. Anne Bradstreet, who became the first poet in English in North America, is thought to have been born (*c.* 1613) here. George Dyer, the kindly but absent-minded friend of Charles Lamb, taught at a school here in the 1780s.

In 1841 John Clare, who had previously been cared for in a private institution, was brought to the county asylum here. At first he was able to walk the mile to the town centre where his favourite resting place was under the portico of All Saints' Church. He was well looked after by the staff and his fellow inmates, enjoyed the gardens in summer, and sat in the large window in the winter. His poems reveal the sadness he felt on being abandoned by his family, and on being far from the familiar sights and sounds of home. Some of the many poems written here were published in *The Later Poems of John Clare 1837–1864* (ed. E. Robinson, D. Powell, and M. Grainger, 2 vols, 1984). Mary Mitford gives an account of her visit to him in her *Recollections* (1852). Clare died in 1864 and was buried by his wish in his native *Helpston. There is a collection of his manuscripts in the Public Library in Abington St.

Jerome K. Jerome died (1927) here suddenly while on a motoring holiday. His ashes were buried in the churchyard at *Ewelme.

NOTTINGHAM *Nottinghamshire*

Manufacturing town on the A52 and the A60, well known to Celia Fiennes, who stayed on her rides through England at The Crown and the Blackamoor's Head (both gone). She approved of the beer and compared other towns unfavourably with Nottingham.

In 1656 Charles Cotton married his cousin Isabella Hutchinson at St Mary's Church and Lovelace wrote the poem 'Triumph of Philamore and Amoret' in celebration.

Henry Kirke White was born (1785) in Exchange Alley at his father's butcher's shop (℗ now on new Cheapside). After working at a stocking loom he was employed by lawyers, who encouraged his studies. His determination to be ordained led him to publish *Clifton Grove and Other Poems* (1803) in the hope that the proceeds would pay for his education at Cambridge. The money was insufficient, but his piety and scholarship so impressed the Fellows that he was able to enter St John's. Southey, who believed him a genius, edited his literary remains, of which many editions were published.

Philip Bailey was born (1812) here (Ⓟ on site of Weekday Cross) and lived at Old Basford. The founder of the 'Spasmodic School' (the name given to a contemporary group of poets by William Aytoun), he returned there and wrote *Festus* (1839) after practising at the Bar. Byron, who could not afford to live at Newstead Abbey, lived with his mother in Pelham St. (house gone) in 1798 and later in St James St. Ⓟ. They worshipped in the Unitarian Chapel in High Pavement where Coleridge had preached.

Soon after collaborating on *The Forest Minstrel* (1823) William and Mary Howitt settled in the town, living first above their chemist's shop in a small house in Parliament St., then in 1822 in 'part of a fine old mansion house built by a French architect' in the marketplace 'opposite to the Long Row'. William Howitt wrote a poem on the occasion of Byron's lying-in-state. He and his wife had both joined the large throng but disapproved of the disorderly scenes which continued en route for the interment at Hucknall. In 1831 Wordsworth visited Howitt's chemist's shop when his wife was taken ill on their journey back to the Lakes. Mrs Wordsworth was put to bed in their house and the poet also stayed the night with them. Later in the year the 6 acres of the marketplace were filled with rioters and 'the heaving, raging ocean of agitated life' became 'a headlong torrent leading directly to the Castle', which the Howitts then saw burning. In 1835 Howitt was elected Alderman. The next year they sold the shop and left on a tour of Scotland and the Lakes. They were friends of Joseph Gilbert and his wife, Ann, author of rhymes for the young, who lived in College St. (now offices) and are buried in the cemetery.

John Drinkwater was on the staff (1898–1901) of the Northern Assurance Co. in Victoria St. Ⓟ. D. H. Lawrence was at the High School and became a schoolteacher (1902–6) before taking a 'normal' course at University College (now Nottingham University) (1906–8). The riots in the town form the background of his story 'Goose Fair'.

Graham Greene worked as a sub-editor on the *Nottingham Journal* in 1925. He was converted to Catholicism in Nottingham Cathedral after a period of spiritual tutelage from a Father Trollope. In a dark empty corner of the Cathedral he was baptized, the only witness being a woman who had been dusting the chairs. The city, thinly disguised as 'Nottwich', where everyone 'went to bed early', is dismally conveyed in his early thriller *A Gun for Sale* (1939):

Near the market you changed at a corner from modern chromium offices to little cats'-meat shops, from the luxury of the Metropole to seedy lodgings and the smell of cooking greens. There was no excuse in Nottwich for one half of the world being ignorant of how the other half lived.

The novelist Stanley Middleton, born some 4 m. away in Bulwel in 1919, was educated at High Pavement School (where he later taught) and Nottingham University. Many of his novels are set in the city. The novelist, poet, and playwright Alan Sillitoe was born in Nottingham in 1928, and, like Arthur Seaton, the hero of his novel *Saturday Night and Sunday Morning* (1958), turned a lathe at one of the city's bicycle factories—in Sillitoe's case, Raleigh. The sights and smells of the city are vividly conveyed:

July, August, and summer skies lay over the city, above rows of houses in the western suburbs, backyards burned by the sun with running tar-sores whose antiseptic smell blended with that of dustbins overdue for emptying, drying paint even drier on front doors, rusting knockers and letter-boxes, and withering flowers on windowsills, a summer blue sky up to which smoke from factory-chimneys coiled blackly.

Seaton opens the novel by falling down the stairs of the White Horse pub in Radford. Sillitoe began his career writing short stories for the *Nottingham Weekly Guardian* and half of his 25 works of fiction, including *The Loneliness of the Long Distance Runner* (1959), *Key to the Door* (1961), *The Death of William Posters* (1965), *The Open Door* (1989), *Birthday* (2001), and *A Man of His Time* (2004), are based in and around the city.

Howard Brenton's dystopian *The Churchill Play* was first performed at the Nottingham Playhouse, Wellington Circus, in 1974.

The poet and critic Blake Morrison attended Nottingham University in the 1970s.

OUNDLE *Northamptonshire*

Market town on the river Nene, home since the 16th c. to Oundle School, whose pupils have included the playwright David Edgar.

PICKWORTH *Rutland*

Village E of the A1, 6 m. NW of Stamford. Late in 1817 John Clare worked at Mr Clark's lime kilns, traditionally sited at the entrance to the village, W of the church: their remains can still be seen.

The ruins of the medieval village were the subject of Clare's 'Elegy on the Ruins of Pickworth', and the old church, whose Gothic arch near the classical building of the new church can still be seen, inspired 'On a Sunday Morning'. Clare used to cross the fields to Walk Farm (situated between the village and the Ryhall road and then called Walkherd Lodge),

Where in youth and beauty blooming
Lives sweet Patty of the Vale.

He married Patty in 1820 after the publication of *Poems Descriptive of Rural Life*.

RENISHAW *Derbyshire*

Village on the A6135, 2 m. N of Staveley. The 16th-c. Renishaw Hall, home of Edith and Osbert Sitwell, features in *Left Hand, Right Hand!*, one of the five volumes of Osbert Sitwell's autobiography, 1945–50, which tells of his early life here and the eccentricities of his father, Sir George Sitwell.

REPTON *Derbyshire*

Village on the B5008, 9 m. SW of Derby. W. B. Stevens was appointed usher at Repton School in 1776, and although teaching was 'scholastic slavery' he became headmaster three years later. His second book of poems was published in 1782. His lack of money twice dashed his hopes of a wife and his *Journal* (1965), kept from 1792 to his death in 1800, reveals his obsession with independence. He died and is buried here and the lines on his monument in the church are by Anna Seward, whom he visited at Lichfield.

Towards the end of the First World War, Christopher Isherwood attended the school with Edward Upward. His friendship with Upward—known as 'Chalmers'—and relationship with the history master, Mr Holmes, are warmly recorded in his autobiography *Lions and Shadows* (1938).

Vernon Watkins, poet and scholar, was educated at Repton School from 1920 to 1924 before going to Magdalene College, *Cambridge.

ROCKINGHAM *Northamptonshire*

Village 6 m. N of Kettering on the A6003. Rockingham Castle, a mainly Elizabethan house inside the Norman walls, was the model for Chesney Wold in *Bleak House* (1853). Part of the book was written here while Dickens was staying with his friends the Watsons.

ROTHLEY *Leicestershire*

Village on the A6, 7 m. N of Leicester. The old manor house, home of the Babingtons from 1565 to 1845 (now the Rothley Court Hotel), was the birthplace of Thomas Babington Macaulay (b. 1800). The hotel has a memorial on the lawn commemorating the drafting of the Treaty for the Abolition of Slavery, a cause to which Macaulay's father was dedicated. Macaulay was made Baron Macaulay of Rothley in 1857.

RUSHDEN *Northamptonshire*

Small manufacturing town on the A5028 off the A6, 15 m. SE of Kettering. Robert Herrick visited Rushden Hall in 1623. He wrote 'Panegyric to Sir Lewis Pemberton', the owner, and found him 'good, hospitable and kind'.

H. E. Bates was born here in 1905, and worked in the warehouse of a firm of leather and grindery factors near Rushden Hall. He had time to read at work and he also began to write, 'a conscious hunger' he developed after reading Stephen Crane's novels. His first novel, *The Two Sisters* (1926), was published when he was 20. Bates, who had visited Rushden Hall on his first job on a newspaper, noticed on his way back a tall, proud girl in a cloak lined with scarlet, and later he used this, combined with the Hall, in *Love for Lydia* (1952). Like *The Fallow Land* (1932) and *The Poacher* (1935), this is set locally in the Nene valley.

SEAGRAVE *Leicestershire*

Village W of the A46, the Fosse Way, 10 m. N of Leicester. Robert Burton, who, in the fifth edition of the *Anatomy of Melancholy* (1638), mentions that the village is more barren than neighbouring ones 'yet no place likely yields better aire', was inducted into the living here in 1632. Burton spent most of his time in *Oxford but he visited this parish occasionally, perhaps because it is not far from his brother's home and his own birthplace, at Lindley. He also left some money to Seagrave in his will.

SHAWELL *Leicestershire*

Village off the M1, 5 m. NE of Rugby. Tennyson often stayed at the rectory (now the Old Rectory) after his father's ward Sophie Rawnsley married the rector, Mr Elmhirst. They built a wooden room in the rectory garden, where Tennyson could smoke and work undisturbed at his elegy on his friend Hallam. The eldest Elmhirst daughter was a bridesmaid in 1850 at Tennyson's wedding, conducted by Sophie's brother.

SHIRLEY *Derbyshire*

Village off the A52, 10 m. NW of Derby. John Cowper Powys and his brother Theodore Francis were born at their father's rectory in 1872 and in 1875 respectively. They lived here until their father returned to Dorchester in his native Dorset in 1879.

SOMERSBY *Lincolnshire*

Small village between the A153 and the A158, 7 m. NW of Horncastle. Alfred Tennyson was born (1809) at the rectory, his home until 1837. He and his brothers and sisters suffered from the peculiar position of their father, the elder son disinherited in favour of his younger brother. Tennyson, after a short time at Louth Grammar School, was educated at home by his father and at an early age had written *The Devil and the Lady* in imitation of Elizabethan drama. *Poems by Two Brothers*, a collection of his and his brother Charles's verse, was published in 1827, the year he went to Trinity College, Cambridge. *Poems Chiefly Lyrical* (1830), which contained 'Claribel' and 'Mariana', was followed by a collection in 1833, which included 'The Lotos-Eaters', 'Œnone', and 'Two Voices'. The brothers used to write in an attic reached by a separate stair. A Cambridge friend, Arthur Hallam, visited the rectory and became engaged to Alfred's sister but his sudden death soon afterwards plunged the family into despair. In 1833 Tennyson started a series of elegies to Hallam, which were published many years after the family had left Somersby. Tennyson spent some time visiting *Harrington Hall and then became acquainted with Emily Sellwood, whom he first met in Holywell Wood on the Tetford road. The church, which had a thatched roof in Tennyson's time, has a bust of the poet.

SOUTHWELL *Nottinghamshire*

Small cathedral city NE of Nottingham on the A612. Byron's mother rented Burgage Manor, the white house with the pillared porch on the green, from 1803 to 1808. He spent his holidays here from Harrow, extending them at 15 when he fell so desperately in love with his elder cousin at Chaworth that he wouldn't go back. The Eliza of his early poems, printed at Newark, lived opposite him at The Burgage with her mother and brothers, and told Thomas Moore, who was staying at the Saracen's Head in 1828 preparing his *Life of Byron*, that, after overcoming his shyness, Byron would 'come in and go out at all hours, as it pleased him, and in our house considered himself perfectly at home'. They sang ballads together, a favourite being 'Mary Anne', the name of his cousin. His signature is preserved on the wall.

SOUTH WIGSTON *Leicestershire*

Suburb to the S of the city of Leicester. The Leicester-born novelist Sue Townsend, creator of Adrian Mole, was educated at South Wigston Girls' High School.

SPALDING *Lincolnshire*

Market town on the Welland, 16 m. SW of Boston. In 1709 the antiquary Maurice Johnson founded the Spalding Gentlemen's Society, modelled on the Royal Society. He lived in the Elizabethan Ayscoughfee Hall (altered), now a school and museum. The Society, which has its museum in Broad St., had Pope and Gay among its members.

STAMFORD *Lincolnshire*

Market town bypassed by the A1. John Clare often walked here from Helpston. One of the books he bought for 'little or nothing' at Ned Drury's shop (site opposite Walker's bookshop) was *The Compleat Angler*, but he caught no more fish after reading it than before. Drury's cousin, John Taylor, published Clare's first poems in 1820. Octavius Gilchrist, a grocer, editor of Corbett's *Poems* and a contributor to Leigh Hunt's *Reflector* and the *Quarterly Review*, befriended Clare and conveyed him on his first visit to London. Gilchrist's shop is thought to have been in the High St. opposite the public library. The novelist Colin Dexter, creator of Inspector Morse, was born in Stamford in 1930 and educated at Stamford School.

STATHERN *(pr. Stăt'hern) Leicestershire*

Village S of the A52, 5 m. SW of Belvoir Castle. In 1785 Crabbe was made curate here and lived happily with his wife in the rectory next to the church where their three children were baptized. He met Dr Edmund Cartwright, inventor of the power loom, rector of Goadby Marwood, 6 m. S, and author of a popular poem, *Armine and Elvira* (1772), and accompanied him to Doncaster to see the looms working. In 1787 Crabbe's patron, the Duke of Rutland, died and with the help of the Duchess, who had his sermon on the Duke published, Crabbe was made rector of *Muston in 1789.

STICKNEY *Lincolnshire*

Village on the A16 between Boston and Spilsby, where Paul Verlaine spent a year (1875–6) teaching French, Latin, and drawing on an au pair basis at the Grammar School, where he was known as 'Mr. Mossou'. He had come from prison in Brussels, where he had been sentenced to two years' hard labour for wounding Rimbaud, the young poet with whom he had been living, in an emotional scene. He wrote after his arrival, 'my life is madly calm, and I am so happy about it . . . I have an appalling need of calm.' He found private pupils and made friends, among them Canon Coltman, the rector and a friend of Tennyson. Verlaine used to make translations from *Hymns Ancient and Modern* while walking up and down the playground and these inspired many poems in *Sagesse* (1881). He left in March 1876 as he found the climate too depressing.

TEALBY *Lincolnshire*

Village on the B1203, 4 m. NE of Market Rasen. When Tennyson's uncle inherited Bayons Manor here in 1835, he embellished it with all the conceits of the Gothic style. There were concealed staircases, secret rooms, oriel windows, and crenellated towers, costly enough for a sly story to spread that the son would not be responsible for his father's debts. The tension between the poet's family and Bayons was increased when the novelist Edward Bulwer, later Lord Lytton, who often stayed here, labelled Tennyson a 'School-Miss' and he retaliated with the 'Literary Squabbles' verses. Lytton wrote *The Last of the Barons* (1843) in the Tapestry Room. The house became a ruin after its Victorian heyday and was totally demolished in 1964. The church has Tennyson family memorials.

TETFORD *Lincolnshire*

Village 6 m. NE of Horncastle, off the A158. Johnson when staying at Langton in 1764 came to the White Hart inn to address the Tetford Club, a gathering of neighbouring gentry, and it remains very much as it was then, with its high-backed oak settle.

TISSINGTON *Derbyshire*

Village off the A515, 5 m. N of Ashbourne. In late 1739 Dr Johnson spent a long holiday in Derbyshire visiting local families such as the FitzHerberts of Tissington. In this beautiful village can be seen Tissington Hall, still the home of the FitzHerberts, and the Norman church opposite, containing their memorials.

TITCHMARSH *Northamptonshire*

Village off the A605, 2 m. NE of Thrapston. John Dryden, who was born (1631) at Aldwinkle nearby, grew up in his parents' house (recently identified as Brookside Farm, on the E side of the village) and attended the local school, before going to Westminster School, London, *c.* 1644. The church has memorials to the Pickerings and to Dryden, composed by his cousin Elizabeth Creed. Mrs Creed said that when Dryden returned later in life to see friends and relations in the vicinity, 'he often made us happy by his kind visits and *most delightful conversation*'.

TWYWELL *Northamptonshire*

Stone village off the A14, 3 m. W of Thrapston, where Hester Mulso was born. The Elizabethan manor (gone) in which she wrote 'The Loves of Amoret and Melissa', when only 9, has 'numerous chimnies', trees trained up between the stone mullioned windows, and was near 'a lake overhung with trees'. She became 'nearly mistress of French and Italian' and was proficient enough in Latin to be considered a bluestocking. Dr. Johnson published her letters in *The Rambler* and Samuel Richardson treated her as one of his 'daughters'. She married a Mr. Chapone but was widowed within a year. The churchwarden is custodian of a copy of her *Letters on the Improvement of the Mind* (1774) conceived originally for a favourite niece and then highly esteemed. The house was demolished *c.* 1839.

UNDERWOOD *Nottinghamshire*

Village 9 m. N of Nottingham near the junction of the B600 and the A608, particularly

associated with D. H. Lawrence. Haggs Farm, up a private gated track from Felley Mill Lane, was the home of his friends the Chambers family.

> Whatever I forget, I shall never forget the Haggs—I loved it so. I loved to come to you all, it really was a new life began in me there. . . . Oh, I'd love to be nineteen again, and coming up through the Warren and catching the first glimpse of the buildings.

Miriam in *Sons and Lovers* (1913) is partly modelled on Jessie Chambers. Felley Mill Farm, where he and his friends often walked to, becomes 'Strelley Mill' in *The White Peacock* (1911).

UPPINGHAM *Rutland*

Small market town on the A6003, 7 m. N of Corby. Jeremy Taylor, chaplain to Archbishop Laud and to Charles I, became resident rector here early in 1638. The church still has the pulpit from which he preached and the paten that he gave. He left in the summer of 1642 to join Charles I, who was with his troops.

Uppingham School (founded 1584), which came into prominence as a public school under Edward Thring (1853–87), had Norman Douglas as a pupil in the early 1890s and James Elroy Flecker and Ronald Firbank at the turn of the century. E. W. Hornung, best known as the creator of 'Raffles' in *The Amateur Cracksman* (1899), was also a pupil and wrote a story about the school, entitled

Fathers of Men (1912). More recently the London-born Stephen Fry attended the school, before taking up a degree place at Queens' College, *Cambridge.

WEEDON LOIS *Northamptonshire*

Village off the B4525, 3 m. SE of Moreton Pinkney. The extension to the churchyard contains the grave of Dame Edith Sitwell (1887–1964), with a tombstone by Henry Moore.

WEST BRIDGFORD *Nottinghamshire*

Southern suburb of the city of Nottingham, just to the S of the Trent. A young Malcolm Bradbury moved to *Nottingham with his family in the early 1940s; from 1943 to 1950 Bradbury attended West Bridgford Grammar School.

WIRKSWORTH *Derbyshire*

Small market town on the B5035 and the B5023, 5 m. S of Matlock. Marian Evans, who wrote as George Eliot, occasionally used to visit her aunt, who told her the story that became the germ of the novel *Adam Bede* (1859), in which the main characters bear a resemblance to her aunt and uncle. Marian Evans read Southey's *Life of Wesley* (1820) for help on Methodists, and drew on articles in the *Gentleman's Magazine* for her descriptions of the countryside, Poyser's Farm, and the lead miners of Derbyshire. The town is said to be the 'Snowfield' of the novel.

WEST MIDLANDS

ABBERLEY *Worcestershire*

Village off the A451, SW of Stourport-on-Severn, home of the poet William Walsh, friend of Dryden and Addison, and encourager of the young Pope. All three may have stayed here; Pope was invited in 1707 and a tree-lined path at Abberley Hall is called Addison's Walk. Walsh, an MP, is buried in the Saxon church; his library was auctioned in *c.* 1790 (see STANFORD-ON-TEME), and the house, formerly Abberley Lodge, was rebuilt in the 19th c. and later became a school. Walsh collaborated with Vanbrugh in an adaptation of Molière, and his poems, of which the best-known is 'The Despairing Lover', were published in *Poems* (1716).

ALTON TOWERS *Staffordshire*

House and theme park in hilly, wooded country, *c.* 6 m. W of Ashbourne, well signposted from the B5032 and the B5417. The vast, ornate mansion, now partly ruined and partly converted to entertainment rooms, was a former seat of the Earl of Shrewsbury. Thomas Moore was staying there as Lady Shrewsbury's guest when he visited his old home at *Mayfield in September 1835. In Disraeli's novel *Lothair* (1870), it becomes the magnificent 'Muriel

Towers', the hero's chief seat, where he celebrated his coming of age with boundless pomp and extravagance.

ARELEY KINGS (or ARLEY REGIS) *Worcestershire*

Village just SW of Stourport-on-Severn on the A451. Layamon mentions that he was priest here (*c.* 1200) in *The Brut*, a poem about early Britain retelling the stories of Arthur, Lear, and Cymbeline from Geoffrey of Monmouth's history. A memorial tablet is in the church.

BATTLEFIELD *Shropshire*

Village on the A49, 5 m. N of Shrewsbury. The church, built in 1408, commemorates the battle of Shrewsbury (1403) when Henry IV defeated the rebel Earl of Northumberland, his son Hotspur, and the Earl of Worcester. In Shakespeare's version of the battle in *1 Henry IV* Falstaff plays the valiant braggart when he pretends to have slain Hotspur himself in single combat.

BILSTON *West Midlands*

Industrial town on the A463 on the SE edge of Wolverhampton. Sir Henry Newbolt, elder son of the vicar of St Mary's, the Revd H. F. Newbolt, was born (1862) in Baldwin St., Bradley (area demolished and rebuilt), and baptized at his father's church. The family later

moved into St Mary's vicarage, but the father died in 1866.

BILTON *Warwickshire*

Former village, now a suburb SW of Rugby. Joseph Addison bought the country estate of Bilton Hall in 1713, the year of the success of his tragedy *Cato*. He started to plan gardens and plant avenues, one of which ended at wrought-iron gates (now at Magdalen College, Oxford) ornamented with his initials and those of his wife, the former Countess of Holland and Warwick. A small summerhouse overlooking the stream, where Addison used to sit with his friends to eat the produce of the gardens, was destroyed (*c.* 1968) by vandals.

BIRMINGHAM *West Midlands*

Second largest city in England and centre of an industrial region, Birmingham has three universities and an Anglican and a Catholic cathedral. Dr Johnson lived here for a short while (*c.* 1734) and contributed essays to the *Birmingham Journal*. It was through Edmund Hector, who lived in a house (gone) in Old Square, that Johnson came to translate a French version of Father Lobo's *Voyage to Abyssinia*. This appeared anonymously in 1735, the year he married Mrs Porter, whom he met here. Panelling from Hector's house has been re-erected in Aston Hall (the Jacobean home of the Holte family until the 19th c.). It is thought to be the original of Washington Irving's *Bracebridge Hall* (1822), the title of a collection of his essays which followed his original *Sketch-Book* (1820), which contained 'Rip Van Winkle'. This story was written while he was visiting his brother-in-law in 1818 as a diversion from the worries of a business failure. The house where he stayed has been demolished.

J. H. Newman established the Oratory of St Philip Neri in the Hagley Rd in the SW suburb of Edgbaston in 1847, and a tablet to him is in the memorial church of the Immaculate Conception. J. H. Shorthouse, born in 1834 in Gt Charles St. and educated at a Quaker school here, wrote the novel *John Inglesant*, influenced by Ruskin, at 6 Beaufort Rd (gone) before moving in 1876 to 60 Wellington Rd. He died (1903) there and is buried in Old Edgbaston cemetery. Harriet Martineau, who died in *Ambleside, was buried (1876) in the cemetery on Key Hill. A plaque at 63 Aston Rd North marks the house where Arthur Conan Doyle lived from 1878 to 1881.

J. R. R. Tolkien lived at Hall Green from 1896 to 1900, for what he looked back on as 'the longest-seeming and most formative part of my life'. He was 4 years old when his recently widowed mother brought him and his younger brother to live at 5 Gracewell, a semi-detached brick cottage in the former hamlet of Hall Green, Worcestershire (since 1911 part of Greater Birmingham). The cottage (now 264 Wake Green Rd) is across the way from Sarehole Mill, on Cole Bank Rd (the Outer Ring Rd), which, with its millpond and the valley of the Cole, was a place of enchantment for the two little boys and represented for the adult Tolkien the heart of an unspoiled English countryside and the inspiration for Hobbiton in *The Hobbit* (1937). In 1900 Tolkien went to King Edward VI's School, in New St. in the centre of Birmingham (now at Edgbaston Pk), and the family moved house. As a schoolboy Tolkien lived in several houses in Edgbaston, one being 37 Duchess Rd (gone), where he met his future wife, Edith Bratt, and there is a plaque in his memory on 1 Duchess Pl., Hagley Rd, between Five Ways and the Plough and Harrow.

W. H. Auden moved to the suburb of **Solihull** with his family in 1909, moving in 1918 to the suburb of Harborne, where his house stood on a site now occupied by Harborne Swimming Pool and Fitness Centre Ⓟ. He retained sharp memories of the area, recalling in his poem 'Letter to Lord Byron' childhood journeys from Birmingham to Wolverhampton that helped to develop his taste for the industrial landscape:

> Tramlines and slagheaps, pieces of machinery,
> That was, and still is, my ideal scenery.

The science-fiction novelist John Wyndham was born in Knowle, now in the borough of Solihull, in 1903. He lived here and at Edgbaston, including an address at 239 Hagley Road. After his parents' separation, he was educated at Woodward's Private School in Edgbaston and then (in 1914–15) at Edgbaston High School, where he was bullied.

In the 1920s the novelist Henry Green lived at Stockfield Hall (gone), a large boarding house on Stockfield Road, near Acock's Green, and relished its Balzacian atmosphere. Trains for London and Oxford ran close by the house. 'If I spit on one it will be better than blowing kisses, more in keeping with Birmingham, safer from any suspicion of sentiment.' He worked nearby in the storehouse of the family manufacturing firm of H. Pontifex and Son, situated at the Farringdon Works beside the Grand Union Canal at Tyseley. His novel *Living* (1929) is set in the offices and among the 'wild incidental beauty' of the machine workshops of the fictional Birmingham engineers Dupret & Son, and in the houses of its employees. In 1948–9 the novelist Bernice Rubens was living in Birmingham too, teaching English at the Handsworth Grammar School for Boys.

Francis Brett Young graduated in medicine at the University of Birmingham. The city is the 'North Bromwich' of his novels. Louis MacNeice, who was lecturer in Classics at the University (1930–5), published a collection of *Poems* in his last year here. The novelist, journalist, and polymath Anthony Burgess lectured on phonetics at Birmingham University from 1946 to 1950. The poet D. J. Enright was a tutor at the Extra-Mural Department from 1953 to 1956. The novelist and critic David Lodge studied at the University, where he later returned to spend many years as Professor of Modern English Literature (teaching there from 1976 to 1987). His 'campus novels' include *Changing Places* (1975), *Small World* (1984), and *Nice Work* (1989); they are not set in Birmingham, but in the deeply grey fictional university of 'Rummidge', which, Lodge explains, is 'an imaginary city, with imaginary universities and imaginary factories, inhabited by imaginary people, which occupies, for the purposes of fiction, the space where Birmingham is to be found on maps of the real world'. Lodge's fellow novelist Malcolm Bradbury also spent a few years in the early 1960s lecturing at Birmingham before taking up his post at the University of East Anglia (*Norwich).

The playwright David Edgar and the novelist Jonathan Coe were both born here (in 1948 and 1961, respectively). Coe would set his novel *The Rotters Club* (2000) in 1970s Birmingham, where a group of secondary school pupils at the fictional King William's School in Edgbaston are working on the school magazine; Birmingham also provides part of the setting to his sequel, *The Closed Circle* (2004).

BISHOP'S TACHBROOK
Warwickshire

Village on the B4087, 3 m. S of Leamington Spa. The church has a tablet to W. S. Landor (d. 1864 in Italy), author of *Imaginary Conversations* (1824), whose family lived here.

The E window commemorates Charles Kingsley's widow, who lived at Grove House.

BISHOPSTONE *Herefordshire*

Village off the A438, 6 m. W of Hereford. Wordsworth wrote a sonnet, 'Roman Antiquities Discovered at Bishopstone' (1835), on the uncovering of 'this time-buried pavement'.

BOCKLETON *Worcestershire*

Hamlet on a minor road off the A4112, *c.* 4 m. S of Tenbury Wells. Wordsworth and his wife, Mary, stayed at the vicarage with their friends the Millers in 1845. They walked over to Laysters to see the church (*c.* 1 m. NW) and then across to Wilden Dingle, to admire the view of the Clee Hills. Wordsworth sat down to rest on a flat boulder, which became known as the 'Poet's Stone' and bears the initials 'W W' and 'M W' and the date '1845', which Mr Miller carved on it. The stone is on the S side of a gated road, E of Laysters church (signposted from Laysters Pole on the B4553), but trees now obscure the view. Francis Kilvert stayed at Bockleton vicarage 26 years later and gives a delightful account of the district and the 'Poet's Stone' in his *Diary* (ed. 1969, ii. 73). Bockleton Court, where he dined with his friends the Decies, is now Bockleton Country Study Centre.

BOSBURY *Herefordshire*

Village on the B4220, 5 m. N of Ledbury. The ashes of Ada Ellen Bayly, who wrote as 'Edna Lyall' and who often stayed with her brother, the vicar, were buried (1903) here. The churchyard is thought to be the one which features in her novel *In Spite of All* (1901).

BREDON *Worcestershire*

Village on the B4080 and the B4079, 3 m. NE of Tewkesbury. The church, dating from *c.* 1180, has a tall, graceful spire, immortalized by Masefield in 'All the land from Ludlow Town | To Bredon Church's spire'. In A. E. Housman's 'In summertime on Bredon' (*A Shropshire Lad*, xxi), the bells ring out over Bredon Hill, which rises 2½ m. E. The village is the setting for John Moore's novel *Brensham Village* (1946).

BREDWARDINE *Herefordshire*

Village off the B438, 12 m. NW of Hereford. Francis Kilvert was vicar here from 1877 until his death two years later. His grave in the churchyard is marked with a white marble cross. Selections from the notebooks which he kept from 1870 were published in three volumes (*Diary*, ed. William Plomer, 1938–40; new edn, 1969). The Kilvert Society, formed at Hereford in 1948, arranges local gatherings and expeditions and an annual commemorative service in a church of the 'Kilvert Country' (www.communigate.co.uk/here/kilvertsociety).

BRIDGNORTH *Shropshire*

Old market town on the A442 and the A458, picturesquely situated on the Severn, which

The vicarage, Bredwardine, overlooking the Wye. Francis Kilvert was vicar from 1877 until his death in 1879

divides it into the Low Town on the E bank and the High Town on the W, connected by a steep winding road (the Cartway), flights of steps, and a short inclined railway. The town's earliest literary association is the Hermitage legend (recorded in *The Reliquary*, Oct. 1878) concerning Ethelward (d. 924), brother of King Athelstan and grandson of Alfred the Great. Tradition has it that Ethelward, known only for his love of literature, retired from the world and lived with his books in some sandstone caves until his death. His retreat was originally entered through a small door and seems to have consisted of four rock chambers, one apparently a chapel. Traces of gable roofing and brickwork indicate other caves that were still used for human habitation in the late 19th c.

In the High Town near St Leonard's Church is the small black-and-white timbered house ℗ where 'the learned and eloquent' Richard Baxter lived when he was assistant minister. He dedicated *The Saint's Everlasting Rest* (1650) to the people of Bridgnorth.

Thomas Percy was born (1729) in a handsome house near the bridge, his home until 1756, formerly called Foster's or Forester's Folly, now Bishop Percy's House. He was baptized at St Leonard's Church and at 8 went to Bridgnorth School, then in the School Building (the predecessor of the present Old Grammar School, erected 1784) in the High Churchyard. His publication of *Reliques of Ancient English Poetry* (1765) was instigated by his discovery of an old manuscript, containing ballads, songs, and metrical romances, in the house of Humphrey Pitt in *Shifnal. The books of the Stackhouse Library, formerly housed in the vestry of St Leonard's, were found to be affected with damp in the 1960s and were transferred to the County Library at

Shrewsbury, but Bishop Heber's chair, where he used to write his well-known hymns, remained in the vestry.

Mary Martha Butt (Mrs Sherwood), author of moral stories for children, lived with her widowed mother and sister in the High St. from 1795 until her marriage in 1803. Her novel *Susan Grey* was published in 1802.

BRINSOP *Herefordshire*

Village on the A480, 6 m. NW of Hereford. Dorothy and William Wordsworth sometimes stayed with his wife's brother at Brinsop Court (1 m. N), and when there in 1843, their maid and friend, Jane, fell ill and died. Wordsworth's poems on *Bishopstone and *Ledbury were written here. The Revd Francis Kilvert came over from *Bredwardine in 1879. In his *Diary* (1938–40; new edn, 1969), he mentions 'the grand old manor house and the lawn and the two snow-white swans on the flowing water of the Moat'. He also saw the cedar on the lawn planted by Wordsworth.

BROMSGROVE *Worcestershire*

Town SW of Birmingham. A. E. Housman lived with his parents from 1860 to 1873 at Perry Hall ℗, now a hotel, on the Kidderminster road. He was educated at Bromsgrove School. The poet Geoffrey Hill was born here in 1932, and educated at the County High School, before moving to *Oxford (Keble) to take his university degree.

CHARLECOTE PARK *Warwickshire*

Country house (NT) off the B4086, 4 m. NE of Stratford-upon-Avon. A tradition grew up that Shakespeare, as a young man, was caught poaching deer on the Lucy estate, and when brought before Sir Thomas Lucy, who imposed severe penalties, retaliated with satirical verses, and prudently left the district (*c*. 1585). Sir Thomas Lucy is said to be the model for Justice Shallow. The tradition suffered a setback when it was realized that Charlecote did not have a park in Shakespeare's time but rallied again as a warren, which Charlecote did possess, could have contained roe deer.

CHURCH STRETTON *Shropshire*

Small town below the Long Mynd, 16 m. S of Shrewsbury on the A49. In the S transept of the church there is a memorial to Sarah Smith, author under her pen-name 'Hesba Stretton' of *Jessica's First Prayer* (1866), who spent her childhood in the neighbourhood. The lancet window above has a stained-glass picture of Jessica. The background of her less-known novel *The Children of Claverley* is set in the nearby valley. Church Stretton is the 'Shepwardine' of Mary Webb's novels and the main location of Henry Kingsley's novel *Stretton*.

CLEOBURY (pr. 'Clĭbury) MORTIMER *Shropshire*

Market town on the river Rea, on the A4117 between Ludlow and Kidderminster. A strong claim has been made for it as the birthplace

of the 14th-c. poet William Langland, the reputed author of the allegorical poem *Piers Plowman*. A panel in the church porch has the quotation:

> Holy Church am I, quoth she,
> Thou oughtest me to know
> 'Twas I received thee first
> And then, the Faith, didst teach.
> To me, they brought your sureties
> My bidding to fulfil
> That thou wouldst love me loyally
> Thy whole life through,

and records that, according to tradition, Langland was born at Cleobury Mortimer and educated at the nearby Augustinian monastery of Woodhouse (later a farm) and later at *Great Malvern Priory. The stained glass in the E window was the gift of the Vicar Prebendary Baldwyn Childe in 1875 and shows biblical and allegorical figures and the dreaming poet reclining by the Rea, with the Malvern Hills in the background. A detailed description of the window is given at the W end of the nave.

CLIFFORD CHAMBERS *Warwickshire*

Village off the A3400 2 m. S of Stratford-upon-Avon. The half-timbered Manor House was the home of Anne Goodere on her marriage to Sir Henry Rainsford. She was Michael Drayton's 'Idea' and welcomed him to

> deere Cliffords seat (the place of health and sport)
> Which many a time hath been the Muses' quiet port.

He 'yearly used to come in the summertime to recreate himself' and was treated with syrup of violets by Shakespeare's son-in-law, who prescribed for Lady Rainsford. It is thought Ben Jonson and Donne, who visited her father and sister at Polesworth, came here too. The Manor was burnt down in 1918 and the present red-brick house was designed by Lutyens. Village tradition says that Shakespeare was born in the black-and-white rectory next to the church, his mother staying here because of plague in Stratford. There were certainly Shakespeares in the village, as a John Shakespeare gave a bier to the church in 1608.

CLUN *Shropshire*

Small town in the Clun valley, on the A488 and the B4368, 7 m. N of Knighton. The ruined Norman castle on the hill is thought to be Scott's Garde Douloureuse in *The Betrothed* (1825), where the scene is laid in the Welsh Marches. He possibly wrote part of the novel while staying here. The town is immortalized in A. E. Housman's *A Shropshire Lad* (1896):

> Clunton and Clunbury,
> Clungunford and Clun,
> Are the quietest places
> Under the sun,

though this is probably just Housman's chosen version of a traditional jingle with various alternative adjectives, such as 'prettiest' or 'wickedest'.

The Villa, a substantial house ½ m. N of Castle Hill, on the left-hand side of the A488, is believed to be the prototype of 'Oniton', the Wilcox house in E. M. Forster's *Howards End* (1910).

In the novels of Mary Webb, Clun appears as 'Dysgwlfas-on-the-Wild-Moors'.

The playwright John Osborne and Helen Dawson married in 1978 and moved to Shropshire, settling into village life in Clunton, 2 m. E of Clun. Osborne died at his home, The Hurst, in Clunton on Christmas Eve 1994. He is buried in Clun, at St George's churchyard. The Hurst is now one of the Arvon Foundation's creative writing centres.

COLWALL *Herefordshire*

Large village near the Malvern Hills. W. H. Auden came to teach at the Downs School in Colwall in 1932. His unconventional teaching practice went down well with both pupils and teachers. He helped to found the school magazine, *The Badger*, wrote, composed, and produced a musical revue in which the whole school participated, recycling some of the lyrics in the play he co-wrote with Christopher Isherwood, *The Dog Beneath the Skin* (1935). He lived at the school in a cottage he named in honour of D. H. Lawrence and in the summer slept on the lawn. His poem 'Out on the lawn I lie in bed', dedicated to the headmaster, Geoffrey Hoyland, reflects what he later described elsewhere as 'a vision of agape':

> I felt myself invaded by a power which, though I consented to it, was irresistible and certainly not mine. For the first time in my life I knew exactly—because, thanks to the power, I was doing it—what it means to love one's neighbour as oneself.

COLWICH (pr. 'Collich) *Staffordshire*

Village 8 m. SE of Stafford on the A51 near its junction with the A513. William Somerville, author of *The Chace*, was born at the manor house on 2 September 1675, but the house (which had been rebuilt) was demolished in the 1960s and only the wall and the park gates are left.

CONGREVE *Staffordshire*

Hamlet a little W of Penkridge, 8 m. S of Stafford off the A449, reached by a minor road turning left beyond Cuttlestone Bridge over the Penk. This was the birthplace of Richard Hurd (1720–1808), the farmer's son who became a critic and divine and Bishop of Lichfield and Worcester.

COVENTRY *West Midlands*

Cathedral and manufacturing town 15 m. SE of Birmingham. The Coventry Plays of the 15th and 16th cc. are thought to have been named after the town where they were performed. The legend telling of Lady Godiva's sacrifices for the people of Coventry is mentioned in Drayton's *Polyolbion* (1612–22), and is the subject both of Tennyson's poem, written after a visit in 1840, and of one of Landor's *Imaginary*

Bird Grove, Foleshill Rd, Coventry. The home for eight years of Mary Ann Evans (George Eliot) after her father retired in 1841

Conversations. There is a statue of Lady Godiva in Broadgate.

Mary Ann Evans ('George Eliot'), who went to boarding school at 29 Warwick Row, returned to Coventry in 1841 when her father retired and moved to Bird Grove, Foleshill Rd. She was often invited to Rosehill, Radford Rd, the home of Charles Bray, a manufacturer. He was a freethinker and Miss Evans met other well-educated women there including Rufa Brabant, whose father was acquainted with the publisher John Chapman. Emerson stayed with the Brays on his way from London to Liverpool to return to America and was most impressed with his first meeting with Miss Evans, who surprised him with her decided praise for Rousseau's *Confessions*. The Brays took Mary Ann Evans on a holiday to the Continent as a diversion after her father's death in 1849. Bray was asked to find a translator for Strauss's *Life of Jesus* and when Rufa Brabant was unable to continue with it after her marriage the task came to Mary Ann Evans, who was to have help from Charles's sister-in-law Sara Hennell. Mary Ann Evans completed her own translation in 1846.

Philip Larkin was born at 2 Poultney Rd, Radford, and was taught at King Henry VIII School. In his poem 'I remember, I remember', passing through the city 'by a different line', he evokes an uneventful childhood in the city:

> Our garden, first: where I did not invent
> Blinding theologies of flowers and fruits,
> And wasn't spoken to by an old hat.
> And here we have that splendid family
>
> I never ran to when I got depressed,
> The boys all biceps and the girls all chest,
> Their comic Ford, their farm where I could be
> 'Really myself'.

The Scarborough-born novelist Susan Hill spent part of her education at Coventry Grammar School. The events of Jonathan Coe's early novel *A Touch of Love* (1989) hinge on a conversation that takes place at Coventry's Memorial Park.

CREDENHILL *Herefordshire*

Village on the A480, 5 m. W of Hereford. Thomas Traherne, rector here from 1657 to 1667, but not resident until 1661, was the author of meditations known as the *Centuries*, written for a community in Kington (12 m. NW). Manuscripts of these and of his poetry were discovered on a London bookstall by Bertram Dobell in the winter of 1896 and published as *Centuries of Meditations* (1908) and *Poetical Works* (1903) respectively. Later, further poems were found in manuscript in the British Museum and published as *Poems of Felicity* (1910).

DAWLEY *Shropshire*

Small town, now part of Telford. The town is evoked by the ghost of the famous swimmer, John Betjeman's Captain Webb:

> How Captain Webb the Dawley man
> Captain Webb from Dawley
> Rose rigid and dead from the old canal
> That carries the bricks to Lawley.

DONNINGTON *Shropshire*

Village on a minor road E of the B5060, just W of The Wrekin. Goronwy Owen, the Welsh poet, wrote some of his best poetry while he was master of Donnington School, including 'Cywydd y Farn Fawr'. In 1753 he moved to Walton, near *Liverpool, and in 1755 to *Northolt (London). The first edition of his works (*Goroviana*), published in 1860, was followed by many later editions. There are copies of his letters and poems among the manuscripts in the British Library (see LONDON: ST PANCRAS) and the National Library of Wales (see ABERYSTWYTH).

DROITWICH SPA *Worcestershire*

Town built on large salt deposits. P. G. Wodehouse stayed on more than one occasion at the Chateau Impney Hotel, where he would write notes for his next story in the shallow end of the salt baths. The hotel was the inspiration for Walsingham Hall, the monstrous house of Sir Buckstone Abbott in *Summer Lightning* (1929). 'Whatever may be said of the Victorians, it is pretty well generally admitted that few of them were to be trusted within reach of a trowel and a pile of bricks.'

EDIAL *Staffordshire*

Village *c.* 3 m. SW of Lichfield on the A5190. Edial House (somewhat altered in the early 19th c.) was Dr Johnson's home when he married in 1735 and the place where he opened a private school with the help of his wife's money. The school was not successful and in 1737, accompanied by the young David Garrick, one of his pupils, he set out for London, which was henceforth to be his home.

ELLASTONE *Staffordshire*

Village on the B5032, 5 m. SW of Ashbourne, the 'Hay-slope' of George Eliot's *Adam Bede* (1859). Halfway to Ashbourne and S of the road are the ruins of Calwich Abbey, later farm buildings, a contender with Wootton Lodge on the Farley Rd for her 'Donnithorne Chase'. Calwich (pr. Callich) had been the home of Bernard Granville, who entertained his sister Mrs Delany and also Rousseau from *Wootton Hall. Rousseau, Byron's 'self-torturing sophist', walked in the gardens with his host's niece, the pretty Mary Dewes, who received a stern warning from her aunt about the danger of his ideas. A memorial to Granville (d. 1775) composed by Mrs Delany is on the end wall outside the church.

EVESHAM *Worcestershire*

Market town built on a loop of the river Avon. The poet Geoffrey Grigson and the critic and poet William Empson monitored foreign broadcasts at Wood Norton Hall during the Second World War.

FLADBURY *Worcestershire*

Village *c.* 4 m. NW of Evesham, just S of the A44. E of the crossroads a drive leads uphill to Craycombe House, a dignified Georgian building restored by Francis Brett Young, who lived there from 1932 until the end of the war, when he moved to South Africa. Many of his books were written here, including *White Ladies* (1935).

FOCKBURY *Worcestershire*

Hamlet *c.* 3 m. NW of Bromsgrove, between the A491 and the A448. A. E. Housman was born (1859) in Valley House (now Housmans), a pleasant Georgian building in sheltered grounds. When still an infant he moved with his parents to *Bromsgrove, returning to Fockbury *c.* 1873 to live at the Clock House (called at that time Fockbury House).

GREAT MALVERN *Worcestershire*

Spa on the A449, 10 m. SW of Worcester. William Langland, traditionally the author of the late 14th-c. poem *Piers Plowman*, is thought to have been born at *Colwall to the SW, and educated at the Benedictine monastery here, of which the Abbey church remains. The Malvern Hills at Colwall were perhaps the scene of the dream that inspired his poem.

The mineral waters of the town attracted many visitors but Defoe was more interested in the gold which 'this idle generation' seemed to him too lazy to mine. Thomas Gray, who stayed for a week in 1770, first read *The Deserted Village* here and immediately recognized Goldsmith's worth as a poet. Lord Lytton came for the water cure many times, as did Sydney Dobell, who brought his wife and had 'a charming stroll on the hills with Carlyle'. M. R. James, author of *Ghost Stories of an Antiquary*, initiated the restoration of the Abbey glass (1910). Dikrān Kouyoumdjian (Michael Arlen, 1895–1956) and C. S. Lewis (1898–1963) were at school here.

GREAT WYRLEY *Staffordshire*

Village NW of Walsall in the E of Staffordshire, the site of the 'Great Wyrley outrages', a series of brutal attacks on horses in 1903. While Arthur, one of the two protagonists of Julian Barnes's novel *Arthur and George* (2005), is *Edinburgh-born, the other, George, hails from Great Wyrley, and the famous 'outrages' come to play an important part in the book.

HAGLEY *Worcestershire*

Village 6 m. NE of Kidderminster, bypassed by the A456. Hagley Hall, the home of the Lyttelton family since 1564, rebuilt as a Palladian mansion in the 18th c., is at the end of a cul-de-sac, opposite the church. James Thomson stayed here in 1743 and added lines on Lord Lyttelton and Hagley Park to the text of *Spring* in his revised edition of *The Seasons* (1744). Horace Walpole visited in 1753 and praised the garden ecstatically:

> all manner of beauty; such lawns, such woods, rills, cascades, and a thickness of verdure quite to the summit of the hill, and commanding such a vale of towns and meadows, and woods extending to the Black Mountains in Wales, that I quite forgot my favourite Thames!

Addison, Pope, and Shenstone, all specialists in landscape gardening, visited at one time or another. Dr Johnson came with Mr and Mrs Thrale in 1774 as the guests of the young Lord Lyttelton's uncle, but unhappily they were coldly received and made to feel uncomfortable and unwanted.

There is a good view of the Hall and estate from a track beyond the church that leads uphill for ½ m. to Milton's Seat, a bench in a clearing on the hillside, inscribed with lines from *Paradise Lost*, Book V, perhaps in memory of Walpole's statement that Milton's description of the Garden of Eden was direct inspiration for Hagley Park.

HALESOWEN *West Midlands*

Town on the A458, *c.* 9 m. W of Birmingham. William Shenstone, a minor 18th-c. poet, was born at the Leasowes, an estate on Mucklow Hill, 1½ m. NE of the town, which he inherited in 1745. He spent most of the rest of his life here, writing poetry, corresponding with his friends, and, for which he is best remembered, beautifying his estate in the 'picturesque' manner. The grounds are now partly a golf course and partly a public park, and the clubhouse occupies the 'new house' on the site of Shenstone's home, mentioned by John Byng in the *Torrington Diaries* on his visit in 1781. In the shrubbery near the front door is the grave of Rajah, a favourite dog. There is a memorial to Shenstone in the parish church, in the form of a large urn beside the N wall and an inscription praising his 'native elegance of mind' and 'wit that never gave offence'. A plain tombstone in the churchyard marks his grave. Francis Brett Young, the novelist, is commemorated by a tablet on one of the church pillars, recording his birth (1884) and baptism.

HARTLEBURY *Worcestershire*

Village 4 m. S of Kidderminster on the A449. The dark sandstone castle has been a seat of the bishops of Worcester for over a thousand years. Izaak Walton lived here (1660–2) as Bishop Morley's steward, probably fishing in the moat and nearby rivers. John Gauden, bishop after Morley was translated to Winchester in 1662 taking Walton with him, claimed authorship of *Eikon Basilike* (1649), thought to be by Charles I. Richard Hurd, bishop (1781–1808), whose writings include *Letters on Chivalry and Romance* (1762), left a lasting memorial in his library opened in the castle in 1782. This contains a number of books that once belonged to Pope, including a copy of Chaucer, which he was given at the age of 13.

HARTSHILL *Warwickshire*

Hilltop village on the B4114, 3 m. NW of Nuneaton. A shelter, built (1972) in granite from the quarry nearby, stands on the green to commemorate the birthplace of Michael Drayton (1563–1631). He is thought to have become page at the age of 7 to Sir Henry Goodere at Polesworth. Later he dedicated a series of sonnets, *Ideas Mirror* (1594), to Anthony Cooke, 'his everkind Maecenas', who lived in the manor here.

HEREFORD *Herefordshire*

Ancient cathedral and former county town on the Wye. The poet who called himself John Davies of Hereford, his 'loving and deere mother', was born in the town some time between 1560 and 1565. He was probably educated at the Grammar School, as he went to *Oxford. Thomas Traherne was born (1638) here, the son of a shoemaker. It is thought that after his father's death he was brought up by Philip Traherne, a prosperous innkeeper, who became mayor of the town and sent him to

Oxford. David Garrick was born (1717) in Maylord St. (ⓟ on site of his birthplace).

The Cathedral, built from the 11th to the 13th cc., still retains a large part of the pre-Conquest library in the Archive Chamber. This includes 8th- and 9th-c. manuscripts and thousands of chained books in their old presses, a collection said to be the largest in the world. Parts of the library and an exhibition dedicated to its treasures is open to the public (www.herefordcathedral.org). Walter Map or Mapes (*fl.* 1200), who is thought to have been born in the old county of Herefordshire, was a canon here. A plaque on the wall of the bishop's garden in Gwynne St. marks the site of the traditional birthplace of Nell Gwynne, who is often mentioned by Pepys in his *Diary*.

Arthur Machen (as Arthur Machen-Jones) attended the Cathedral School. Bruce Chatwin made good use of the public library, scouring old volumes of the *Hereford Times* to provide material for his visionary border country novel *On the Black Hill* (1982). Lewis Jones, one of Chatwin's twin protagonists, spends a wretched day in the city.

HERGEST *Herefordshire*

Hamlet off the A44, 2 m. SW of Kington. The Red Book of Hergest, a manuscript of Welsh prose and verse, written between 1375 and 1425, was for many years in the possession of the Vaughan family at Hergest Court (built 1430). It was given to Jesus College, *Oxford, in 1701 and is kept at the Bodleian Library. Lady Charlotte Guest, who had learned Welsh after her marriage in 1833, translated some of the tales (exploits of Welsh knights) together with other legends, including some of King Arthur, which were published under the title *The Mabinogion* (1839–49), from the Welsh *mabinogi*, 'tales of youth'.

Hergest was also the site of the family home of Sir John Clanvowe (1341?–91), now generally regarded as the author of 'The Cuckoo and the Nightingale' (or 'The Boke of Cupide'), wrongly attributed to his friend Chaucer until 1895. Said to be 'one of the prettiest things in medieval English', the poem was rendered into modern English by Wordsworth in 1801.

HODNET *Shropshire*

Small hill town, with many half-timbered houses, *c.* 15 m. NE of Shrewsbury, on the A53 and the A442. The church contains an illustrated Bible printed at Nuremberg in 1479, also Erasmus's New Testament of 1522, and a copy of Bishop Jewel's attack on the Catholic Church (edited by his friend John Garbrand, 1582). A tile in the chancel commemorates Reginald Heber (later bishop), author of 'From Greenland's Icy Mountains' and other hymns, who was vicar here from 1807 to 1823. In the town a lamp-post at the crossroads also serves as a memorial to Heber.

HOPE *Shropshire*

Little village on the A488, *c.* 12 m. SW of Shrewsbury. It lies under the Stiperstones, with ancient Roman lead mines in the vicinity, and was chosen by Mary Webb as the background to her novel *Gone to Earth* (1917).

HOPE END *Herefordshire*

Estate 2 m. N of Ledbury, off the B4124, where Elizabeth Barrett lived from 1809 when she was 3. Her father improved the house (later rebuilt) in the Gothic style to the admiration of fashionable tourists (Princess Victoria was a visitor), until forced to sell in 1832. All but the three eldest of his large family were born here. Elizabeth rode her pony to visit her Greek tutor, the blind Hugh Boyd, subject of some of her poems, and in her *Diary* (1969) tells how much her visits meant. Her father paid for the publication of her poem *Battle of Marathon* (1820) when she was 14. Many of her early poems were inspired by the district, and 'The Lost Bower', set in the wood above the house, 'by an actual fact of my childhood'. In a letter to Miss Mitford in December 1842 she recalled her feelings as 'our old serene green stilness was trodden under foot' when Hope End was open to view before the auction.

HUGHLEY *Shropshire*

Small village off the B4371, in the valley below the N end of Wenlock Edge. Those who know A. E. Housman's poem

> The vane on Hughley steeple
> Veers bright, a far-known sign,

will look in vain, as did the poet's brother Laurence, for the steeple and the suicides' graves. A. E. Housman explained that the place he really meant had an ugly name, so he substituted Hughley: 'I did not apprehend', he wrote, 'that the faithful would be making pilgrimages to these holy places.'

ILAM *Staffordshire*

Small village 4 m. NW of Ashbourne, between the A515 and the A52. The 19th-c. Ilam Hall, now a Youth Hostel, is on the site of an earlier house where Izaak Walton and his friend Charles Cotton often visited Robert Port, who is buried in the church, where his memorial has verses by Cotton. Congreve also stayed with the Port family and is said to have written *The Old Bachelor* (1693) in a grotto in the extensive grounds (NT).

Dr Johnson visited Ilam with the Thrales in 1774, and again in 1779 when he and Boswell walked to see the Manifold rise from its underground journey from Thor's Cave (footpath), but in spite of the evidence of the gardener, who had experimented with corks, Dr Johnson was not convinced. But he thought it 'a place that deserves a visit' even if the stream was too small to come up to his expectation.

IPSLEY *Worcestershire*

Village to the E of Redditch. It is the subject of a trio of poems by Geoffrey Hill, 'In Ipsley Church Lane': 'More than ever I see through painters' eyes . . .'.

KENILWORTH *Warwickshire*

Town on the A429 and the A452. The 12th-c. castle, now ruined, was improved by John of Gaunt and when lived in by the Earl of Leicester was often visited in his school holidays by his nephew Philip Sidney, who was 11 when Queen Elizabeth I paid her first visit. George Gascoigne describes the Queen's last stay (1575) in *The Princely Pleasures of the Court of Kenilworthe*. Scott stayed at the Kings Arms Hotel while writing *Kenilworth* (1821). Edith Cooper, the poet, who wrote in collaboration with Katharine Bradley as 'Michael Field', was born in the town in 1862.

KIDDERMINSTER *Worcestershire*

Manufacturing town on the Stour, 15 m. N of Worcester. Richard Baxter, the Presbyterian minister, lectured here in 1641 before becoming a chaplain to Parliamentary troops. He returned here after writing in retirement *Aphorisms of Justification* (1649) and *The*

Hope End, near Ledbury, as it was when Elizabeth Barrett grew up there

Saint's Everlasting Rest (1650). He moved to London *c.* 1660. His statue, which stood in the main square, now stands in a garden next to the parish church.

KILPECK *Herefordshire*

Village 9 m. from Hereford. The famous Saxon-Norman sculpture in the church inspired Anne Stevenson's 1980 poem 'At Kilpeck Church'.

LEAMINGTON (pr. 'Lemmington') SPA *Warwickshire*

Fashionable health resort in Georgian and Victorian times, 9 m. S of Coventry. Camden, whose family held land here, mentions the medicinal well in *Britannia* (1586).

Ruskin, whose parents were worried about his tubercular symptoms, came here in 1841 to consult Dr Henry Jephson, who subjected him to a regimen of baths and exercise. He stayed first at The Bedford, a fashionable hotel at 15 Leamington Parade, and then moved to 53 Russell Ter., a 'small square brick lodging-house'. He amused himself by writing a fairy tale, *The King of the Golden River*, for the 12-year-old Effie Gray (later his wife), who had been staying with his family.

Dickens gave readings here in 1855 and 1862. The local paper hoped he might attract large audiences, which they regretted were 'not common things in this town'. In *Dombey and Son* (1846–8), Dombey and Major Bagstock meet Mrs Skewton at the pump rooms.

Nathaniel Hawthorne paid three visits to Leamington: in 1895 he stayed briefly at 13 Lansdowne Cres. on his way for a summer trip to the Lake District; from 8 September to 10 November 1857 he rented 10 Lansdowne Circus (later called Hawthorne House), 'one of the coziest nooks in England, or in the World', after resigning his US consulship in Liverpool, and wrote parts of the *English Notebooks*, later to be embodied in *Our Old Home* (1863); and from October 1859 to March 1860 he finished *The Marble Faun* (first pub. in Britain as *Transformation*), which he had begun in *Redcar, Yorkshire. Ambrose Bierce wrote *The Lantern* (1874), a short-lived satirical magazine, while staying here. This was subsidized by the empress Eugénie to help refute attacks on the Emperor.

Lytton Strachey was educated at Leamington College for Boys (later Binswood Hall), Binswood Ave., from the summer of 1894 until April 1897, shortly before going to University College, *Liverpool.

The town provides the peeling stuccoed setting for John Betjeman's 'Death in Leamington':

> Nurse looked at the silent bedstead,
>   At the grey decaying face,
> As the calm of a Leamington ev'ning
>   Drifted into the place.

The poet and critic D. J. Enright was born at Camberwell Ter. in 1920 and educated at Leamington College. Enright, the son of a postman, wrote about his school-leaving in the late 1930s in 'The Terrible Shears':

> How docile the lower orders were
> In those days! Having done
> Unexpectedly well in the School Cert,
> I was advised by the headmaster to leave school
> At once and get a job before they found
> A mistake in the examination results.

LEDBURY *Herefordshire*

Market town on the A449 and A417, 9 m. SW of *Great Malvern, which has a claim to be the birthplace of William Langland. Wordsworth's sonnet 'St. Catherine of Ledbury' (1835) describes the saint's rapture on hearing the bells peal out without human ringers, which she took to be a sign for her to settle here 'Till she exchanged for heaven that happy ground'. John Masefield was born (1878) at The Knapp, a Victorian house on the N edge of the town. The family moved to the Priory, near the centre of the town, when John was 8. After being taught at home by a governess he went to Liverpool in 1891 to become a naval cadet. Some of his *Collected Poems* (1946) refer to the country near Ledbury and to the church, which has 'a golden vane surveying half the shire'. The local secondary school is named after him.

LEIGHTON *Shropshire*

Village on the B4380, S of The Wrekin and above the valley of the Severn. Leighton Lodge was the birthplace of Mary Webb, author of country novels in a Shropshire setting such as *Gone to Earth* (1917) and *Precious Bane* (1924).

LICHFIELD *Staffordshire*

Cathedral city at the junction of the A38 and the A5127. Elias Ashmole, antiquary and Windsor Herald to Charles II, was born (1617) in Breadmarket St., at a house known as Priests' Hall Ⓟ, adjacent to Barclays Bank. He was educated at the Grammar School, an ancient foundation originally situated in St John's St. The building was replaced by the present structure in 1849, but the school itself was moved in 1903 to Borrowcop Hill, to the S of the city. The 17th-c. Schoolmaster's House (now offices) still exists. Another of the school's many distinguished pupils was Joseph Addison, whose father became Dean of the Cathedral in 1643.

George Farquhar stayed at the George Inn in Bird St. Ⓟ in 1705, when he was a lieutenant in the Grenadiers, recruiting troops in Lichfield. The inn is mentioned in *The Beaux' Stratagem* (1707) as the place where Aimwell and Archer arrive to seek the rehabilitation of their fortunes.

Samuel Johnson, the city's most famous son, was born above his father's bookshop in the house at the corner of Breadmarket St. on the Market Sq. and was baptized in St Mary's Church across the way. The house, hardly altered since his father built it in 1707–8, is now an admirable museum containing books and personal relics of Dr Johnson and portraits of relatives and friends (www.lichfield.gov.uk/johnson.ihtml). There is a statue of Johnson in the square, erected in 1838, with three low reliefs on the base

depicting scenes from his life, and another statue, of later date, of James Boswell, his biographer. Johnson had his first English lessons in 1714 at Dame Oliver's School in Dam St., where the site is marked by an inscription. He later went to the Grammar School. He kept a close attachment to Lichfield throughout his life, and he and Boswell used to return for visits and stay at the Three Crowns inn (Ⓟ on the site), two doors from his birthplace. Johnson also frequently stayed at Redcourt House, the 'stately house with a handsome garden' built by his stepdaughter Lucy Porter in Tamworth St., but this has now been demolished. His parents and his brother Nathaniel are buried in St Michael's Church on Greenhill on the E side of the city and the tombstone bears the eloquent Latin epitaph he wrote. The Johnson Society, founded in 1910, aims to encourage the study of the life, works, and times of Dr Johnson; to preserve memorials, books, manuscripts, etc. concerning him; and to share in the annual civic celebration of his birthday (www.lichfieldrambler.co.uk).

David Garrick spent the first 20 years of his life at his father's house in Bird St., the Old Probate Court (Ⓟ on the site). He was educated at the Grammar School before attending Dr Johnson's school at *Edial.

Erasmus Darwin, botanist, physician, and author of the poem *The Botanic Garden* (1789–91), written in heroic couplets in imitation of Pope, lived in a house at the W end of The Close (Ⓟ; the house can still be visited: www.erasmusdarwin.org) from 1756 to 1781 and established a botanical garden nearby. Although his poem, once popular, was later ridiculed, it contains lines of not wholly fantastic prophecy:

> Soon shall thy arm, Unconquered Steam, afar
>   drag the slow barge, or drive the rapid car;
>
> Or on wide waving wings expanded bear
>   the flying chariot through the fields of air.

Anna Seward, a poet known as 'the Swan of Lichfield', lived from 1754 to 1809 at the Bishop's Palace, for a long time the residence of her father, Canon Seward. She was the centre of a literary coterie which included Erasmus Darwin, and was visited by Sir Walter Scott, who published her poems in 1810 with a memoir. She knew Johnson (her portrait is in the Birthplace Museum) and was able to supply Boswell with information for his *Life of Samuel Johnson* (1791). Miss Mitford, however, was less than charitable in a letter of April 1818:

> I wonder [she wrote] by what accident Miss Seward came by her fame. Setting aside her pedantry and presumption, there is no poet male or female who ever clothed so few ideas in so many words. She is all tinkling and tinsel—a sort of Dr Darwin in petticoats.

Nathaniel Hawthorne came to Lichfield in the mid-19th c. partly to see the Cathedral and partly to visit Johnson's birthplace. The agreeable account of his visit can be read in *Our Old Home* (1863). Richard Garnett, one-time Keeper of Printed Books at the British

Museum and author of *The Twilight of the Gods* (1888), a series of classical and oriental fables, was born (1835) in Lichfield.

The city is dominated by 'the Ladies of the Vale', the three graceful spires of the Cathedral, which stands in the quiet Close, surrounded by courtyards and historic buildings of great charm and elegance. Among the numerous statues and memorials in the Cathedral the literary pilgrim can find monuments to Lady Mary Wortley Montagu (discovered with delighted surprise by Hawthorne) and Anna Seward near the W door, and in St Michael's Chapel a bust of Johnson by Westmacott and Johnson's epitaph on Garrick. Richard Hurd, critic and divine, best known for his *Letters on Chivalry and Romance* (1762), was Bishop of Lichfield 1775–81.

The city is the setting for James Fenton's poem 'A Staffordshire Murderer', where

The good weather brings out the murderers
By the Floral Clock, by the footbridge,
The pottery murderers in jackets of prussian blue.

And Penelope Lively's first adult novel, *The Road to Lichfield* (1977), tells the story of Ann Linton, whose father is being taken into a Lichfield nursing home.

LOWER SAPEY *Herefordshire*

Hamlet on the B4203, 6 m. NE of Bromyard. Hatt House, an old farmhouse perched on the hillside on the way to Harpley, was the home of Edmund Seward, with whom Robert Southey stayed in December 1793, falling in love briefly with another guest, Augusta Roberts. 'The snow confined us for six days,' he wrote.

LOWER WICK *Worcestershire*

Village on the outskirts of Worcester, *c.* 2 m. along the A499 to Malvern. Mrs Mary Martha Sherwood, best known for *The History of the Fairchild Family* (1818–47), came to live here on her return from a period spent in India, with her husband, their five children, two adopted Indian orphans, and the motherless child of a distant relative from Brussels. The house, where she said she spent the happiest years of her life, was old and 'marvellously ill-constructed', standing among orchards above the roar and whirl of the mill where the Teme joins the Severn. Henry, her little boy, thought of Worcester as Calcutta and the Teme as the Ganges. Sherwood Lane above the roundabout leads to the site of the house, demolished in 1966 to make way for a housing estate.

LUDLOW *Shropshire*

Picturesque old town bypassed by the A49, on a hill above the junction of the Teme and the Corve. In 1634 Milton's masque *Comus*, with music by Henry Lawes, was performed in the (now roofless) great hall of the castle in celebration of the Earl of Bridgewater's appointment as President of Wales and the Marches. Samuel Butler (1612–80) wrote part of his satire *Hudibras* in his rooms above the 14th-c. castle gateway during the time he was steward to the Earl of Carbery (1661–2).

Stanley Weyman, author of many historical romances, including *Under the Red Robe* (1894), was born at 54 Broad St., where he lived until his marriage in 1895. His novel *The New Rector* (1891) is set in Ludlow. A. E. Housman, though not a native of Shropshire, knew and loved the country near Ludlow and Much Wenlock, and his ashes are buried outside the N door of St Laurence's Church. A tablet on the outer wall of the church commemorates him as Professor of Latin and author of *A Shropshire Lad*:

> Goodnight. Ensured release
> Imperishable peace:
> Have these for yours.

MARTLEY *Worcestershire*

Village 9 m. NW of Worcester on the B4204, with a red sandstone church which has medieval wall paintings and a fine chancel screen. The poet and parodist C. S. Calverley was born in 1831 in a panelled room in one of the oldest rectories lived in by an incumbent. His father, Henry Blayds, who changed his name in 1852, was a curate-in-charge here during the long absence of the rector after a riding accident. The beautiful raftered hall was 'modernized' in Elizabethan times, the addition of a floor giving a bedroom above.

MAYFIELD *Staffordshire*

Village 2 m. W of Ashbourne on the B5032 and the A52. Mayfield Cottage (later Stancliffe Farm, and then named after Moore, off Gallowstree Lane in Upper Mayfield) was the home of Thomas Moore (1813–17), where he wrote the satirical *Twopenny Post Bag* (1813) and the successful *Lalla Rookh* (1817), four tales in verse to entertain a young princess on her journey across India to be married. Moore's young daughter Olivia Byron, called after his friend Lord Byron, died here and is buried in the churchyard. He returned here in 1827 and visited her grave.

MEOLE (pr. Meel) BRACE *Shropshire*

Suburb of Shrewsbury on the A5 and the A49. Mary Webb (then Mary Meredith) lived here before her marriage at her family home, Maesbrook (gone). In 1912 she married Henry Webb in the village church, a 19th-c. building remarkable for its stained-glass windows by Morris and Burne-Jones. A brass plate on one of the pews records that Mary Webb worshipped here, 1902–12.

MINSTERLEY *Shropshire*

Village on the A488, 10 m. SW of Shrewsbury. William Thynne, the first editor of Chaucer's works, died (1546) at his family home, Minsterley Hall, a timber-framed building (now restored) near the church.

NEWCASTLE UNDER LYME *Staffordshire*

Old industrial town on the A34, 3 m. W of Stoke-on-Trent. Sir John Davies (1569–1626), barrister and poet, was MP here in 1614. Mrs

Craik (Dinah Maria Mulock, 1826–87), author of *John Halifax, Gentleman* (1857), came here with her parents in 1831 and lived first in Lower St. and later at 2 (now 7) Mount Pleasant. Arnold Bennett (1867–1931) came to the Middle School, where he became head boy, for the last stage of his education before entering his father's legal practice at 18. The town appears as 'Oldcastle' in his 'Five Towns' novels.

NEWPORT *Shropshire*

Small country town on the A41 and the A518, 8 m. NE of Wellington. The Grammar School (founded 1656) numbers among its famous pupils Thomas Brown (1663–1704), the satirist remembered chiefly for his lines beginning 'I do not like thee, Dr. Fell', and Thomas Percy (1729–1811), who collected the ballads, historical songs, and metrical romances published as *Reliques of Ancient English Poetry* (1765). They both proceeded to Christ Church, *Oxford.

NUNEATON *Warwickshire*

Manufacturing town on the A444. 3m. N of Nuneaton, in the former hamlet of Lindley, was the site of the manor (now Watling St.) where Robert Burton was born (1577); the manor was subsequently replaced by the 18th-c. Lindley Hall; there is now a modern house on the site. Burton went away to school and spent most of his life in *Oxford.

The novelist George Eliot (Mary Ann, or Marian, Evans), born (1819) at Arbury Farm 2 m. SW (now South Farm), lived (1820–41) at Griff House (now a hotel) on the A444. She was baptized at Chilvers Coton (church rebuilt) in Avenue Rd, the 'Shepperton' of *Scenes of Clerical Life*, and attended a dame school in the double-fronted house opposite her home before going to Coventry. Many of her characters and situations were modelled on her experiences here. Her father, agent to the Newdigate family of Arbury Hall, the 'Cheverel Manor' of *Scenes of Clerical Life*, was partly the model for Adam Bede and Caleb Garth; and her mother (d. 1835) partly for Mrs Poyser and Mrs Hackit. Arbury Mill inspired *The Mill on the Floss* (1860), although the scene was changed to the Trent. The town, the 'Milby' in *Janet's Repentance*, has George Eliot Memorial Gardens near the library and a hospital with wards named after her characters. The Nuneaton Museum and Art Gallery displays personal effects of George Eliot and a reconstruction of her London drawing room (www.nuneatonandbedworth.gov.uk).

OLD MILVERTON *Warwickshire*

Village 3 m. NW of Leamington Spa. The grave of Vera Brittain (1893–1970), pacifist and feminist, stands in the churchyard of the parish church of St James. The daughter of a wealthy manufacturer, she was educated at Somerville College, *Oxford, but her studies were interrupted by the First World War, in which her fiancé was killed. Her *Testament of Youth* (1933) is a moving account of her girlhood, her struggle for education, and her experience of the war, in which she served as a nurse. Only

George Eliot and the Midlands

EORGE Eliot's Midlands was always as much an imagined landscape as it was a deeply known and felt one. For while Eliot set at least half her novels in the flat Warwickshire countryside where she spent her childhood, the last time she ever saw it with her own eyes was in 1855 when she made a final visit at the age of 36. The disapproval of Eliot's elder brother Isaac at her recent informal 'marriage' to George Henry Lewes, the London-based author and scientist whose legal wife was still living, meant that she was banned from returning to the much-loved people and places of her youth.

And so it was that in 1857, cooped up in a series of suburban London houses, Eliot sat down to write a series of novels in which she re-created with dwelling detail the rural Warwickshire from which she had been so recently and painfully exiled. So rich is her evocation of the muddy canals, the deep yellow fields, and the busy conviviality of a market town pub that even today, 150 years after she published her first novel, travellers from all over the world flock to see the landscape through which Eliot's best-loved characters including Hetty Sorrel, Maggie Tulliver, and Dorothea Brook once moved.

In her earliest fiction, and still feeling her way as a creative artist, Eliot transplanted her native landscape wholesale into her novels, sometimes with embarrassing consequences. In 'The Sad Fortunes of the Reverend Amos Barton', in *Scenes of Clerical Life* (1858), 'Shepperton Church' with its 'intelligent eye' of a clock, is clearly Chilvers Coton, the church at which she and her family worshipped and where her parents and brother are buried. The magnificently Gothic Arbury Hall, which forms the backdrop to 'Mr Gilfil's Love Story', can still be seen, although now the house is open to the public only on bank holidays. In 'Janet's Repentance', the Red Lion pub where so much of the riotous action was set is easily recognizable as The Bull, although more recently it has been renamed The George Eliot Hotel in honour of Nuneaton's most famous daughter.

So blatant in Eliot's early fiction was this wholesale borrowing of the people and places of her childhood that many local readers recognized themselves and their neighbours and a hunt soon ensued to find out the identity of the real 'George Eliot'. One of the most popular theories circulating in the Midlands and in London in the late 1850s was that 'George Eliot' was a Nuneaton clergyman who had subsequently become a pauper and taken to turning out *romans-à-clef* as a way of scraping a living.

Eliot's next book, *Adam Bede* (1859), was set in Derbyshire, her father's native county. While still a young man Robert Evans had moved south to take up a job as land agent to the Newdegate family of Arbury Hall. As a little girl the young

GEORGE ELIOT BY SIR FREDERIC WILLIAM BURTON, 1865

Mary Ann Evans—Eliot's real name—travelled in her father's gig as he made his daily rounds of the estate. It was now that the wide-eyed child took in her surroundings, making mental pictures of the cottages, the tenant farmers, and the labourers, all of whom would appear years later in her novels.

The Evans family lived at Griff House, a comfortable farmhouse on the Abury Estate, which today is run as a pub. And so, on seven days of the week, you may still walk on the flagstones where Eliot walked for the first thirty years of her life, and sit in the snug study next to the front door from where her father received rent from the Newdegate tenants. And, although the attic is not open to the public, from the outside it is still possible to see the room in which the recalcitrant Maggie Tulliver in Eliot's next book, *The Mill on the Floss* (1860), 'fretted out all her ill-humours' on her long-suffering doll.

As Eliot became more confident in her work as a novelist, she was happy to mix up details from the landscape of her childhood. Thus, although Griff was possibly the model for the Tullivers' 'trimly-kept, comfortable dwelling house as old as the elms and chestnuts that shelter it' in *The Mill on the Floss*, the original for 'Dorlcote Mill' itself was found during a much later trip to the tidal Ouse in Lincolnshire (a flood, of course, being crucial to the story). Likewise, although Raveloe, the setting for *Silas Marner* (1861), may well be based on either Attleborough or Bulkington—two villages neighbouring Griff—the weaver himself comes from an unnamed town much further north.

One of the main themes of Eliot's novels, set mostly from the end of the eighteenth century to the middle of the nineteenth, is the coming of the industrialized world. And perhaps no other part of the British landscape speaks so graphically of the arrival of steam, coal, and iron. On the one hand, the Arbury Estate was part of the ancient forest of Arden. As you walk around the small villages of Griff, Meriden, and Bedworth, the trees you see today are not only the trees that Eliot saw, they are the ones that Shakespeare knew. On the other hand, beneath this rich agricultural soil lay solid coal seams, which the Newdegate family had long exploited as part of their natural inheritance. Robert Evans was himself an expert in mining technology, and the Coventry canal, which ran a few hundred yards from Griff, carried a constant traffic of coal- and stone-laden barges.

This interlinking of town and country, urban and agricultural, allowed the young Eliot to watch while History worked its changes on the landscape. Each year she saw how the country fields became written over by canals, mines, weaving sheds, and, eventually, the railway. And it was this sense of the impermanence of the physical world, and the way in which men and women were left to make sense of the political and social changes which ensued, that Eliot went on to deal with so deftly in her later novels, *Felix Holt* (1866), *The Radical* (1866) and the magnificent *Middlemarch* (1871–1).

KATHRYN HUGHES

❖

one-third of her ashes are buried here; the rest are in Italy. Her husband, Sir George Catlin (1896–1979), shares the same grave.

OSWESTRY *Shropshire*

Ancient border market town on the A483. This was the home for the last 11 years of his life (1569–80) of the Welsh poet William Llŷn, one of the four chief bards of the Caerwys eisteddfod in 1568. His poetry, which was collected by J. C. Morrice (*Barddoniaeth W. Llŷn*, 1908), contains poems of praise of his patrons in many parts of Wales and of a number of clergy, including the bishops of St Asaph and St David's, as well as some fine elegies in memory of other poets. In his will he left his house to his wife and asked to be buried in the churchyard.

Wilfred Owen was born (18 Mar. 1893) at Plas Wilmot, the home that his parents shared with his maternal grandfather. He spent four happy years here before his grandfather died and the family had to sell the house and its contents and move away.

Barbara Pym was born at 72 Willow St. in 1913 and spent much of her childhood at Morda Lodge on Morda Rd, to which her family moved in around 1919.

PENDOCK *Worcestershire*

Village on the B4708, 8 m. W of Tewkesbury. William Symonds, who became the rector in 1845 and inherited Pendock Court shortly afterwards, wrote two historical novels about the district. *Malvern Chase* (1881) is set in the Wars of the Roses, and *Hanley Castle* (1883) during the Civil War.

PERSHORE *Worcestershire*

Small market town on the river Avon. The railway station is the scene of Betjeman's regretful verse 'Pershore Station—or, A Liverish Journey, First Class'.

PLOWDEN HALL *Shropshire*

Home of the Plowden family for many generations, situated *c*. 2 m. E of Lydbury North, between the A489 and the B4385. This splendid old white house is said to be the original of the Hall described at the beginning of J. H. Shorthouse's historical novel *John Inglesant* (1881).

POLESWORTH *Warwickshire*

Village on the B5000, 4 m. E of Tamworth. The red-brick and timbered house (gone), built after the dissolution of the Abbey, was the home of Sir Henry Goodere (1534–95), a patron of Michael Drayton, who it is thought came as a page at the age of 7 and possibly had lessons in the school over the abbey gateway (now a flat). Drayton wrote many poems to Anne the younger daughter, eight years his junior, who, as 'Idea', was the object of his love throughout his life. Goodere was Philip Sidney's cousin, was with him when he died, and present at his funeral. Drayton's 'Lyrick Pieces' to Sir Henry trust that

> They may become John Hewes his lyre
> Which oft at Polesworth by the fire
> Hath made us gravely merry.

One of the old stone fireplaces, with the Goodere crest of a partridge with an ear of corn in its beak, still survives at the vicarage built in 1868 on the site of the house, and John Hewes is mentioned by Hakluyt in a list of those sailing to Virginia in 1584. Drayton's 'Ode to the Virginia Voyage' may have been inspired by Hewes. The second Sir Henry (1571–1627), a nephew, married his cousin Frances, whom Drayton wrote of as 'Panape'. Goodere was the lifelong correspondent of Donne, who officiated at the marriage of his daughter Lucy to Francis Nethersole (memorial in the church) and visited him here. In 1613 Donne wrote 'Good Friday' on leaving Polesworth for *Montgomery.

Ben Jonson's verses to Goodere mention his 'well-made choice of books and friends'.

PRESTON BROCKHURST *Shropshire*

Village on the A49, 10 m. N of Shrewsbury. William Wycherley, Restoration dramatist, was born (1640) at Clive Hall, 1½ m. W. After his education in France and at *Oxford he often returned to Clive Hall, which he inherited on his father's death in 1697.

REDNAL *West Midlands*

Village, now a suburb, 10 m. SW of Birmingham, off the A38. Cardinal Newman (d. 1890) is buried in the graveyard of the country house of the Oratory Fathers.

ROSS-ON-WYE *Herefordshire*

Market town on the A40, situated on high grounds above the river, looking towards the Welsh hills. Inside the Market Hall at the end of the S wall there is a memorial to John Kyrle (1637–1724), the 'Man of Ross', celebrated by Pope in his *Moral Essays*, Epistle III, 'To Lord Bathurst' (1732), concerning the use of riches. Kyrle was a wealthy man who spent nearly all his life in Ross, where he lived in modest style and devoted his surplus income to the public good. Pope, whose poem holds up Kyrle's good works as an example of a rich man's liberality, wrote to a friend (7 June 1732): 'A small exaggeration you must allow me as a poet; yet I was determined the groundwork at least should be *Truth*, which made me so scrupulous in my enquiries.' Kyrle's house, a half-timbered building in the marketplace, became the King's Arms inn after his death and was later converted into shops (Ⓟ and low-relief portrait). His garden, with a summerhouse and curious 'mosaic' made with horses' teeth by the poor whom he patronized, is at the back of what is, at the time of writing, an unoccupied shop. The Prospect, a public garden given by Kyrle to the people of Ross, leads off the churchyard, and the footpath, John Kyrle's Walk, offers fine views of the river and the hills. Kyrle is buried in the chancel of the church.

Coleridge stayed at the King's Arms on his tour of Wales in 1794 and wrote the lines beginning:

> Richer than miser o'er his countless hoards,
> Nobler than kings or king-polluted lords,
> Here dwelt the man of Ross.

Robert Bloomfield lodged at The Swan in the summer of 1807 when touring with friends along the Wye. Dickens met his biographer, John Forster, in the Royal Hotel Ⓟ in September 1867 to discuss his proposed American tour of 1867–8. Forster was not in favour of the project, but Dickens decided to go nevertheless.

From 1920 to 1936 the novelist Peggy Eileen Whistler (1909–58), who wrote under the pen-name Margiad Evans, lived at Lavender Cottage, Bridstow, 3 m. W on A49, and after her marriage in 1940 her home was at nearby Llangarron. The first of her four novels, *Country Dance* (1932), evokes the atmosphere of the Welsh-English border and reflects her perception of all borderlands as places of torn allegiances and incessant strife.

The playwright Dennis Potter moved to Morecambe Lodge in Ross-on-Wye in 1967; he would remain until his death 27 years later. His ashes are buried in St Mary's churchyard.

ROWTON (pr. 'Rauston) *Shropshire*

Village on a minor road W of the A442, 7 m. N of Wellington. Richard Baxter, the Nonconformist divine, son of Richard Baxter of Eaton-Constantine (9 m. S) and Beatrice, daughter of Richard Adeney of Rowton, was born (1615) at his mother's home. It is thought that Mrs Baxter was obliged to return to her parents' house because her husband had 'gambled away' his freehold property and involved himself in debts and difficulties, though he later altered his way of life.

RUGBY *Warwickshire*

Town 12 m. SW of Coventry, on the A428. Rugby School, founded in 1567, came into prominence in the 19th c., when Thomas Arnold became headmaster (1828–42). Literary Rugbeians include W. S. Landor, Thomas Hughes, Matthew Arnold the headmaster's son, Arthur Clough, C. L. Dodgson ('Lewis Carroll'), P. Wyndham Lewis, Arthur Ransome, and Rupert Brooke, born (1887) in Hillmorton Rd, the son of a housemaster. Thomas Hughes's novel *Tom Brown's Schooldays* (1857), by 'An Old Boy', gives a picture of life in the school under Dr Thomas Arnold. Matthew Arnold, who wrote a poem on the school chapel (replaced in 1872 by a building of Butterfield's), taught here for a term in 1845.

SHALLOWFORD *Staffordshire*

Little village on the river Meece, 6 m. NW of Stafford, reached by a turning off the A5013

The Izaak Walton Cottage at Shallowford, where Walton used to stay

near Great Bridgeford. The Izaak Walton Cottage, a charming half-timbered building in a pleasant garden, was originally part of Halfhead Farm, where Izaak Walton used to stay after he retired from business in London. He bequeathed the property, which he is believed to have owned from 1654 onwards, to his native *Stafford for charitable uses. Eventually the farm was sold, and the cottage, admirably restored, was opened as a museum (www.staffordbc.gov.uk).

SHERIFFHALES *Shropshire*

Village *c.* 3 m. N of Shifnal, on the B4379, N of the A5. In the latter part of the 17th c. an academy was held at the Manor House (down a private road W of the village) for the advanced education of those who were barred from university by the Test Act of 1673 on account of their Nonconformist views. The academy was run by the Revd John Woodhouse on a plan devised by Richard Baxter.

SHIFNAL *Shropshire*

Market town on the A464, 12 m. NW of Wolverhampton. Thomas Brown, the satirist, was reputed to have been born (1663) in Shifnal, but the exact location is not known. The parish was formerly a very large one, including several townships, and Brown's birthplace may have been outside the town itself. Thomas Percy owed the publication of his *Reliques of Ancient English Poetry* (1765) to the discovery, while visiting his friend Humphrey Pitt, of an old manuscript (which was being used for lighting fires) containing ballads, songs, and metrical romances. The Pitts lived at Priors Lee Hall in the parish (but not in the town) of Shifnal.

The town, which has many well-preserved half-timbered and Georgian houses, appealed strongly to Dickens and is described by him in *The Old Curiosity Shop* (1841).

SHOTTERY *Warwickshire*

Village 1 m. NW of Stratford-upon-Avon, home of Anne Hathaway, whom Shakespeare married in 1582. A bond giving the names of two men standing surety for Shakespeare's pledge to marry Anne Hathaway can be seen at *Worcester. The Hathaways, yeomen farmers, owned the partly 15th-c. farmhouse until it was bought by the Shakespeare Birthplace Trust in 1892. Much of their furniture is still in the house, formerly larger, but known now as Anne Hathaway's Cottage (www.shakespeare.org.uk).

SHREWSBURY (pr. 'Shrōzbry) *Shropshire*

Historic county town, strikingly situated on rising ground within an almost encircling loop of the Severn, now bypassed by the A5. The town dates from the 5th c., when it became the seat of the princes of Powys. It was conquered at the end of the 8th c. by Offa, King of Mercia, and as a Saxon and then a Norman stronghold it suffered many sieges and plunderings by the Welsh, who were subjugated by Edward I in 1283.

At the top of Pride Hill, opposite the post office, a modern cross (1952, replacing an earlier one) marks the place where the body of Hotspur was hanged, drawn, and quartered after the battle of Shrewsbury, 1403 (see BATTLEFIELD).

George Farquhar wrote *The Recruiting Officer* while staying (1705) at the Raven Hotel (gone) in Castle St., near the Gateway of the Council House. The play, dedicated to 'all friends round the Wrekin', gives a lifelike picture of Shrewsbury at the time of the Restoration and includes an allusion to The Raven itself.

William Hazlitt, who spent most of his youth at *Wem, was within easy reach of Shrewsbury. He picked up a copy of *Paradise Lost* here, and his first 'literary production' was a letter in 1791 to the *Shrewsbury Chronicle*, protesting against the treatment of Joseph Priestley by the Birmingham mob. Hazlitt was a great admirer of Coleridge and in 1798 walked over to Shrewsbury to hear him preach at the Unitarian Chapel, the last occasion on which Coleridge did so, as he shortly afterwards gave up Unitarianism.

John Hamilton Reynolds, poet and friend of Keats, was born (1794) in the town and baptized in St Mary's Church. He went to Shrewsbury School before going on to St Paul's School, London.

Mary Webb (1881–1927), whose novels are set in Shropshire, where she was born and grew up, is buried in Shrewsbury cemetery. In her stories the town is depicted as 'Silverton'.

Charles Darwin was born at The Mount on 12 February 1809, the son of a distinguished local physician, and grandson to Erasmus Darwin and the potter Josiah Wedgwood; he entered Shrewsbury School as a boarder in 1818.

In 1907 Wilfred Owen came with his parents and his brother Harold to live at 1 Cleveland Pl., the house of his paternal grandfather, and then at 71 Monkmoor Rd, called 'Mahim' by his father. Wilfred attended the Technical School before going to *Dunsden in 1911.

Shrewsbury School (founded 1552 by Edward VI) stands on the hill across the river, reached by Kingsland Bridge. The present buildings (1882) superseded the old buildings on the original site opposite the castle (now occupied by the library). Sir Philip Sidney (1554–86) was educated here, and entered school in 1564 on the same day as Sir Fulke Greville, Lord Brooke (1554–1628), his friend and later his biographer. A statue of Sidney was erected (1923) in front of the new school as a memorial to the First World War. Other notable pupils include Frederick William Faber (1814–63), author of devotional books and hymns, remembered especially for 'My God, how wonderful Thou art' and 'Pilgrims of the Night'; Samuel Butler (1835–1902), author of *Erewhon* (1872); Stanley Weyman (1855–1928), author of historical romances; and Nevil Shute Norway (1899–1960), aircraft engineer and (as Nevil Shute) novelist. The school library, which can be seen by arrangement with the librarian, has special collections which include Western medieval manuscripts, among which is a manuscript of the earliest known miracle play in English, and incunabula and other early printed books.

Shrewsbury cakes have long been famous and are celebrated in 'Bloudie Jacke' in *The Ingoldsby Legends* (1840): 'She has given him . . . a Shrewsbury cake, | Of Pailin's own make.'

Simon Raven joined the King's Own Shropshire Light Infantry, garrisoned at Shrewsbury, in 1953. His army experiences furnished material for his novel sequence *Alms for Oblivion* (1964–83).

SNAILBEACH *Shropshire*

Hamlet in the Hope Valley, on a minor road off the A488, *c.* 12 m. SW of Shrewsbury. The little chapel, frequented by the mining community, was the centre of interest in Mary Webb's *Gone to Earth* (1917).

STAFFORD *Staffordshire*

County town on the A34 and the A518. Izaak Walton was born here on 9 August 1593, a plaque on 62/62a Eastgate St. marking the traditional site of his birthplace. He was baptized on 21 September 1593 (the entry in the register is at the County Record Office) in the strangely oriental-looking font in the parish church of St Mary's and is commemorated by a 19th-c. bust on the N wall of the nave.

R. B. Sheridan was MP for Stafford 1780–1806 and used to stay at Chetwynd House, a pleasant Georgian building, at the time of writing a post office Ⓟ, on the corner of Greengate St. and Mill Bank.

The Swan Hotel seems to have been a lively place in 1825 when, according to his account in *Romany Rye* (1857), Borrow appears to have been general superintendent of the stables:

> The inn, of which I had become an inhabitant, was a place of infinite life and bustle . . . And often in after life, when lonely and melancholy, I have called up the time I spent there, and never failed to become cheerful from the recollection.

But with the coming of the railways the old coaching inns declined and when Dickens stayed a night in the town some time in the 1840s he gave a depressed account of what may well have been the Swan, as

> the extinct town inn, the Dodo . . . It provides one with a trackless desert of sitting room . . . and possesses interminable stables at the back— . . . horseless

(see 'A Plated Article' in *Household Words*, 1858). But the pendulum swung again and with the advent of the car it gradually recovered and is now flourishing once more.

The William Salt Library (established 1872) in Eastgate St., and the County Record Office, next door, between them have a valuable collection of books and manuscripts relating to Staffordshire local history.

The poet Carol Ann Duffy came to Stafford at the age of 4 and was brought up in the town. She went to Stafford Girls' High School, where she published *Fleshweathercock* (1973), her first collection of poetry. 'The Laughter of Stafford Girls' High' and 'Stafford Afternoons' evoke childhood times:

> Only there, the afternoons would suddenly pause
> and when I looked up from lacing my shoe
> a long road held no-one, the gardens were empty,
> an ice cream van chimed and dwindled away.

STANFORD-ON-TEME *Worcestershire*

Village on the B4203, 17 m. NW of Worcester. Mrs Sherwood, author of *The Fairchild Family* series (1818–47) and numerous other novels, was the daughter of the Revd George Butt. She was born at the rectory on the hill W of the bridge over the Teme, and her first memory was of 'the half circular window over the hall door'. This part of the house has been demolished and the rest modernized (later the Old Rectory). She describes her happy childhood in her *Life* (1854), recording how pleased she was at her father's purchase for a guinea of a wagonload of books at the auction of William Walsh's library at *Abberley.

STOKE-ON-TRENT *Staffordshire*

City of the Potteries in the N of the county, formed by the federation of the familiarly known 'Five Towns' of Tunstall, Burslem, Hanley, Stoke-on-Trent, and Longton (immortalized by Arnold Bennett's novels and stories as Turnhill, Bursley, Hanbridge, Knype, and Longshaw), which, with Fenton, were united in 1910. Records of literary figures begin with Elijah Fenton, a poet best remembered for his collaboration with Pope in translating the *Odyssey* (1725–6), who was born (1683) at Shelton Old Hall (later an iron- and steelworks), Hanley.

Another native was Mrs Craik (Dinah Maria Mulock), who was born (1826) in the parish of Stoke-on-Trent, at Longfield Cottage (gone), Hartshill, where her father was minister of a small congregation. 'Longfield' appears in *John Halifax, Gentleman* (1857). In 1831 the family moved to *Newcastle under Lyme.

Arnold Bennett, Stoke's most famous author, was born (27 May 1867) in a house and shop formerly at the corner of Hope St. and Hanover St., Hanley (Ⓟ on present building). Later he lived at Dain St., Burslem (1875–6), 175 Newport Lane (1876–8), and 198 Waterloo Rd (1878–80). In 1880 his father moved the family to 205 Waterloo Rd. Bennett began his education (1875) at the infants' school in the Swan Bank Methodist Sunday School (gone) and went on (1876) to the Burslem Endowed School, formerly part of the Wedgwood Institute before it was moved (1880) to Longport Hall (an event referred to in *The Old Wives' Tale*). He entered his father's legal practice at 18, but finding it uncongenial left for London in 1889. The experience and understanding of these 22 years provided the background for 13 novels and three volumes of short stories set in 'the Five Towns', of which the best-known are probably *Anna of the Five Towns* (1902), *The Old Wives' Tale* (1908), *Clayhanger* (1910), and *The Card* (1911). Bennett's topography centres on Burslem, and there is a leaflet, *Arnold Bennett's Bursley Trail*, available from the Stoke-on-Trent City Archives and the Tourist Office. The site of 'The Shambles' and post office (see *The Old Wives' Tale* and *Clayhanger*) was redeveloped in 1960 as an ornamental garden, and a commemorative portrait plaque of Bennett made by the Wedgwoods was erected there in 1962. Moorland Rd leads up the hill from Burslem to the local cemetery, where Bennett's ashes are interred in his mother's grave. Bennett's life and work is celebrated on the

View of Burslem (Arnold Bennett's 'Bursley') from Hanley parish church tower

mezzanine level of Ceramica, an educational centre occupying the old Burslem Town Hall.

H. G. Wells stayed at 18 Victoria St. Ⓟ, Basford, in the spring of 1888. Here he wrote the short story 'The Cone' and the romance *The Chronic Argonauts*, which later became *The Time Machine* (1895).

The poet Charles Tomlinson was born in Stoke in 1927 and was educated at Longton High School. As a child he was influenced by the poetry he heard recited by his parents and grandmother. His home, the town, and the local landscape are evoked in poems such as 'The Boy on the Sick Bed', 'The Marl Pits', 'Gladstone Street', and, especially, 'At Stoke', the well-travelled Tomlinson's tribute to the country of his childhood:

> I have lived in a single landscape. Every tone
>   And turn have had for their ground
> These beginnings in grey-black: a land
>   Too handled to be primary—all the same,
> The first in feeling . . .
> This place, the first to seize on my heart and eye,
>   Has been their hornbook and their history.

The playwright Peter Whelan was born in Stoke in the Potteries; his play *The Bright and Bold Design* (1991) is set in the local 1930s pottery industry, introducing Jessie Frost and her fellow workers at a small pottery firm near Burslem.

STOURBRIDGE *West Midlands*

Old market town on the A458, 12 m. W of Birmingham. The 17-year-old Samuel Johnson spent six months (1726–7) at King Edward VI School. This was then a long, low building behind the headmaster's and usher's houses in the High St. between the two inns, The Vine and the Old Horse. Johnson is thought to have taught the younger boys in return for his board and lodging. The school had a good library and both the headmaster and the usher had been at Oxford University. Johnson's family had many connections in the town and the neighbourhood and Bishop Percy later wrote that Johnson was well entertained by his relatives, who introduced him to prominent people. Johnson wrote many poems on classical themes as well as 'Festina Lente', an exhortation in heroic couplets, and the hymn for the feast of St Simon and St Jude, which contains much 'extatic fury' and shows that he was experimenting with a variety of verse forms. No reason has been found for his sudden return to Lichfield. Some years later, in 1731, he stayed in the town again hoping to be selected for the post of usher, but he was unsuccessful. The school has been rebuilt.

STRATFORD-UPON-AVON *Warwickshire*

Old market town on the A3400, 24 m. SE of Birmingham. According to tradition, Shakespeare was born (1564) in Henley St. in a house owned by his father, a glover and wool merchant, who became an alderman. His mother, Mary (née Arden), came from *Wilmcote. The house known as Shakespeare's Birthplace, half-timbered with lattice windows, was bought by the Shakespeare Birthplace Committees of Stratford and London in 1847 and is in the care of the Shakespeare Birthplace Trust (formed 1866, incorporated 1891). Shakespeare was brought up in the house, which combined living accommodation with his father's shop and workshop. The house convincingly reconstructs the living conditions likely to have been experienced by the young Shakespeare. On his father's death in 1601, the ownership passed to Shakespeare, who, having no need of it for himself or his family, divided the property in two, leasing the larger part to one Lewis Hiccox, who converted it into an inn called The Maidenhead (later the Swan and Maidenhead); the remainder was rented out as a residence which at the time of Shakespeare's death was lived in by Joan Hart, the playwright's sister. The whole property passed to Susanna, his elder daughter, on his death in 1616.

The Birth Room has the signatures of Scott, Carlyle, Isaac Watts, and others scratched on a window pane. Part of the house is furnished as an Elizabethan home, part as the shop and workshop of a glover and wool dealer, and part is a museum housing books, manuscripts, and pictures relating to Shakespeare's life. The pretty garden at the back is planted with flowers, herbs, and trees mentioned in the plays. Not far from the Birthplace stands the Grammar School, where Shakespeare was probably a pupil some time in the 1570s. Shakespeare's desk is reputed (without much authority) to have been the third from the front on the left-hand side. It is a raftered room on the first floor of the Guildhall. Shakespeare could have seen plays acted in the Guildhall by the travelling players of Lord Leicester or Lord Derby.

Shakespeare left Stratford some time between 1585 and 1592 (the so-called 'lost years'), according to a doubtful tradition because of deer-poaching at *Charlecote Park. In 1597 he bought the town's second biggest house, New Place, built for Hugh Clopton, a Lord Mayor of London, *c.* 1483. Shakespeare kept up his Stratford connections while living in London, and his family continued to live at New Place. He died in 1616 and is buried in the parish church by the Avon; the words on the stone over his grave in the chancel are said to be his own:

> Good frend for Iesus sake forbeare,
> To digg the dust encloased heare.
> Bleste be ye man yt spares thes stones,
> And curst be he yt moves my bones.

A monument with a bust by his contemporary Gerard Janssen, or Johnson, a Flemish sculptor working near the Globe in *Southwark is on the wall above the grave. Many visitors have not warmed to this likeness. Dickens's ironical response is fairly representative: 'I have here the counterfeit presentment of a face suggestive above all things of a strong vitality, freshness of spirit and liveliness of disposition.' The scholar J. Dover Wilson described it as the face of a 'self-satisfied pork butcher'. In the 19th c. Shakespeare's American admirers donated two stained-glass windows, one representing the Seven Ages of Man. The graves of his wife, his daughter Susanna, and her husband, the eminent physician Dr Hall (monument), are nearby. His daughter Judith, who married a vintner and lived at the corner of Bridge St. and High St. (now Quiney House, the Information Centre), and her twin, Hamnet (who died at the age of 11), are believed to be buried in the churchyard. Susanna Hall and her husband, who lived in Old Town (now Hall's Croft),

Signature window in the Birth Room at Shakespeare's Birthplace, showing Isaac Watts's name

the headquarters of the Shakespeare Birthplace Trust, which administers the Birthplace, Anne Hathaway's Cottage at *Shottery, the garden at New Place, Hall's Croft, Nash's House, Mary Arden's House, and Harvard House (www.shakespeare.org.uk).

Washington Irving stayed at the Red Horse in Bridge St. *c.* 1818 and wrote about the town in *The Sketch-Book of Geoffrey Crayon, Gent.* (1819–20). He was amused by the memorabilia then on display in the Birthplace:

> There was the shattered stock of the very matchlock with which Shakespeare shot the deer, on his poaching exploit. There, too, was his tobacco-box; which proves that he was a rival smoker to Sir Walter Ralegh; the sword also with which he played Hamlet; and the identical lanthorn with which Friar Laurence discovered Romeo and Juliet at the tomb!

His compatriot Nathaniel Parker Willis, author of two books about his visits to this country, stayed in Irving's room about 10 years later. He reported the landlady's account of her surprise when a guest told her how she had been 'immortalized' in Irving's book. She showed Willis Irving's poker, inscribed with his pseudonym, and a battered copy of the *Sketch-Book*. Irving's chair and the sexton's clock he mentions, both inscribed, can now be seen on the first-floor landing, but the poker has disappeared.

Elizabeth Gaskell, who was at Avonbank School (demolished 1866) near the entrance to the church, wrote an account of Clopton House (1 m. N), which she visited when at school, which William Howitt included in his *Visits to Remarkable Places* (1840); it was her first published work.

The historian G. M. Trevelyan was born (1876) at Welcombe House (now a hotel).

Mary Mackay, who wrote as 'Marie Corelli', settled at Mason Croft (Ⓟ, administered by the Shakespeare Institute of the University of Birmingham) in Church St. in 1901, at the height of her popularity as a romantic novelist. Her pony-chaise drawn by Shetland ponies, her gondola, *The Dream*, on the Avon, and later her Daimler became well known in the town. Her enthusiasm for rescuing old buildings from development was not always welcomed, but Samuel Clemens ('Mark Twain') appreciated her renovation of Harvard House (home of the mother of the founder of Harvard University and an elegant Elizabethan town house now managed by the Birthplace Trust), which he asked her to show him on his visit in 1907. She died at Mason Croft in 1924 and is buried in the cemetery.

The Royal Shakespeare Company has numbered the novelist Margaret Drabble among its acting companies, and Liz Lochhead, David Edgar, and Peter Whelan among its dramatists. Lochhead was writer in residence in 1988, and both Edgar and Whelan premièred a number of their plays there. Edgar's most notable RSC success was his epic adaptation of Dickens's *Nicholas Nickleby* (1980); other works to receive their debut

moved into New Place after Shakespeare's death. Hall's Croft is now handsomely furnished with a fine garden growing many of the herbs mentioned in Hall's medical notebook.

In 1769, 10 years after the demolition of New Place (now a garden) had angered the town, David Garrick organized a commemorative Jubilee attended by many friends, including James Boswell and Arthur Murphy, but marred by rain. Garrick declared the new Shakespeare Hall (now the Town Hall) open and donated a replica, by John Cheere, of the statue by Peter Scheemakers, now over the door. The Garrick inn in High St. commemorates his visit. Nash's House Ⓟ, inherited by Shakespeare's granddaughter, contains Tudor furniture and

items about local history including the Jubilee. A theatre was built in Chapel Lane in 1827, but the first permanent Shakespeare Memorial Theatre, founded by Charles Flower, opened in 1879. This burnt down in 1926 and a worldwide fund made possible the present building (opened 1932), now called the Royal Shakespeare Theatre, currently being redeveloped (due to reopen 2010). The theatre, which has a picture gallery and museum, stands in gardens and overlooks the Avon. The Gower Monument to Shakespeare is nearby. The opening of the Shakespeare Centre, next to the Birthplace, commemorated the 400th anniversary of Shakespeare's birth. The Centre has a public exhibition about Shakespeare's life in Stratford, and a library for students, and is

productions with the RSC include a state-of-the-nation play, *Destiny* (1976), *The Jail Diary of Albie Sachs* (1978), and *Maydays* (1980). Whelan's RSC premières have included *The Accrington Pals* (1981, about a First World War battalion), *School of Night* (1992), and *The Herbal Bed* (1996).

STRENSHAM *Worcestershire*

Village S of the A4104, at the junction of the M5 and the M50. Samuel Butler was born (1612) in a long, low house known later as Butler's Cot (demolished in the 1870s), which his father had leased from Sir John Russell of Strensham Court, for whom he worked, perhaps as secretary. After a few years at Worcester School and having been given his father's 'Law and Latin books', Samuel Butler went as secretary to Thomas Jefferey, a justice, who lived at Earl's Croom (2 m. NW). Jefferey lived in the 16th-c. half-timbered house (altered) opposite the church, and there Butler started his hobby of painting. Two portraits thought to be his are now at the rectory there.

STRETTON HALL *Staffordshire*

Manor house NW of the crossing of the A5 and the A449. After leaving Trinity College *Dublin in 1689, William Congreve came to stay here with his paternal grandfather, Richard. According to tradition, it was under one of the old oaks in the grounds that he wrote the first draft of *The Old Bachelor* (1693), possibly revised later in another version written at *Ilam.

TONG *Shropshire*

Little village on the A41, 10 m. NW of Wolverhampton. The 15th-c. church is remarkable for the number and beauty of its tombs. At the W end of the tomb of Sir Richard Vernon is the miniature effigy of his son George, later Sir George Vernon, reputed to be the 'King of the Peak' in Scott's novel *Peveril of the Peak* (1823). The verses forming the epitaph at the head and foot of Sir Thomas Stanley's tomb were written by Shakespeare, according to Sir William Dugdale (1605–86), antiquarian, and begin:

> Ask who lyes heare, but do not weep,
> He is not dead, he dooth but sleep.

Dickens had the village in mind when he described the place where Little Nell and her grandfather find peace at the end of their wanderings in *The Old Curiosity Shop* (1841), and Cattermole's illustrations are reminiscent of the interior of the church. Outside the S door a sign marks the 'reputed resting-place of Little Nell'.

TRENTHAM GARDENS
Staffordshire

Park and pleasure grounds on the Trent, on the A34 just S of Stoke-on-Trent. Trentham Hall, the mansion, now ruined, was described by Disraeli in his novel *Lothair* (1870) as 'Brentham', the ducal home of the hero's college friend, where the stables had the best riding

horses in England and the guests played croquet on the velvet lawn, watched by the duchess from a Turkish tent.

UPTON UPON SEVERN
Worcestershire

Village on the B4211, 11 m. S of Worcester. The White Lion in the High St. was the hotel where the characters in Henry Fielding's *Tom Jones* (1749) had a disturbed night . . .

UTTOXETER *Staffordshire*

Market town on the A50 and the A518. In the centre of the marketplace a low relief (a replica of that on the base of his statue in Lichfield) on the stone conduit depicts the scene of Dr Johnson's 'penance'. As a youth he once refused to look after his father's bookstall at the market when the latter was ill and the remembrance of this sin of pride caused him to return 50 years later and stand in contrition at the site for a long time, bareheaded in the rain. 'I trust', he said, 'I have propitiated heaven for this only instance, I believe, of contumacy towards my father.'

Nathaniel Hawthorne, in *Our Old Home* (1863), tells how he made a sentimental journey to see the very spot where Johnson had stood, but had to rely on his imagination, as there was no memorial to mark it or person who could tell him. He dined at the Nag's Head (gone) on 'bacon and greens, some mutton chops, juicier and more delectable than all America could serve up at the President's table, and a gooseberry pudding . . . besides a pitcher of foaming ale'—all for 18 pence.

WALSALL *West Midlands*

Manufacturing town E of the M6, NW of Birmingham. Jerome Klapka Jerome, author of the popular novel *Three Men in a Boat* (1889), was born (1859) in a house (later Belsize House) on the corner of Bradford St. and Caldmore Rd Ⓟ. The Jerome K. Jerome Birthplace Museum is housed in two ground-floor rooms, one containing photographs, books, and personal items, and the other refurbished to give an impression of a parlour of the 1850s (open Saturday afternoons, www.jeromekjerome.com). A Jerome K. Jerome Society was founded in 1984 and enquiries should be addressed to the Museum. There is also a collection of Jerome Memorabilia at Walsall Local History Centre, Essex St.

WARWICK *Warwickshire*

Ancient county town on the A41, 11 m. S of Coventry, home of Guy of Warwick, a legendary knight of giant size, who became a hermit. *Guy of Warwick* is a verse romance of the early 14th c. about his exploits in the Holy Land and against the giant Colbrand, the monstrous dun cow, and the winged dragon. He is commemorated at Guy's Cliffe (1¼ m. N) by a 15th-c. chantry erected by Richard de Beauchamp, Earl of Warwick, who claimed to be a descendant, and by a statue by Keith Godwin erected in 1964. In 1449 the last de Beauchamp heiress married Richard Neville,

known as Warwick the Kingmaker, hero of Lytton's *The Last of the Barons* (1843). The kingmaker's large camp kettle is in the Great Hall of Warwick Castle dating from the 14th c.

Richard Corbett mentions Guy of Warwick in 'Iter Boreale', which tells of his visit to the castle in 1619. James I gave Warwick Castle to his Chancellor of the Exchequer, Fulke Greville, whom he made Baron Brooke. Corbett meets Fulke Greville and comments on the beauty of the gardens. Greville, who was born in 1554 at Beauchamp Court (gone), was a friend of Philip Sidney from their school days. They went to Queen Elizabeth's court together and were members of the Areopagus Club. Greville's collected poems, *Caelica*, were influenced by Sidney, whose *Life* (1652) Greville wrote *c.* 1610, though like most of his other work it was not published until after his death. Greville, assassinated by a servant who thought himself excluded from Greville's will, was buried N of the choir in St Mary's Church, in the former Chapter House. The Beauchamp Chapel, S of the choir, contains the ornate tomb of Robert Dudley, Earl of Leicester (d. 1588), who features in Scott's *Kenilworth* (1821). The church also has a bust of W. S. Landor, born (1864) at Ipsley Court, below the East Gate.

John Masefield was a boarder at Warwick School for boys from 1888 to 1890. He first began writing poetry at this time.

Philip Larkin and his parents were evacuated to Coten End, Warwick, after the bombing of Coventry in 1940.

The novelist Jonathan Coe spent some years at Warwick teaching poetry and completing a Ph.D. on Henry Fielding's *Tom Jones*.

WELLINGTON *Shropshire*

Market town, now part of the new town of Telford. Philip Larkin took a job as a district librarian here in 1943, more by accident than inclination. He ran the library single-handed, stamping the books, stoking the boiler, filing reports, and driving vagrants out of the reading room. Larkin's first collection of poems, *The North Ship* (1945), appeared without notice while he was working here, in 1945. He wrote his 'Shropshire labour', the novel *A Girl in Winter* (1947) here, in which he drew on his experience of working in a provincial library. He also embarked on an uneasy love affair with Ruth Bowman, a local sixth-former, to whom he was briefly engaged.

WEM *Shropshire*

Small market town on the B5063 and the B5476, 11 m. N of Shrewsbury. William Hazlitt came here when he was 8 and lived in Noble St. for most of his early years. His father was a Unitarian minister.

WEST MALVERN *Worcestershire*

Village on the B4232, to the W of Great Malvern. Dr Roget, author of *The Thesaurus of English Words and Phrases* (1852), died on his annual holiday at Ashfield House, now 225 West Malvern Rd. He is buried in the churchyard of St James's Church.

The house in Noble St., Wem, where William Hazlitt was brought in 1786 and spent his early years

WESTON-UNDER-LIZARD
Staffordshire

Village close to the Shropshire border between Telford and Stafford. Weston Park has been proposed by the P. G. Wodehouse scholar Norman Murphy as the model for the Blandings estate, whose gardens, as Evelyn Waugh wrote, 'are that original garden from which we are all exiled. All those who know them long to return.'

WILMCOTE (pr. 'Wilmcut)
Warwickshire

Village off the A3400, 4 m. NW of Stratford-upon-Avon. Mary Arden's House, part of the Shakespeare Birthplace Trust, was the birthplace and home until her marriage of Shakespeare's mother. The long, low, half-timbered farmhouse is furnished with Tudor furniture and functions as a 16th-c. working farm (www.shakespeare.org.uk).

WOLVERHAMPTON *West Midlands*

Industrial city on the A41 and the A449, noted for ironworks and all kinds of hardware. The poet Alfred Noyes was born in 1880 in St Mark's Rd Ⓟ, Chapel Ash, ¾ m. from the town centre. He attended Jasper House School, a small school near his home, before going up

to *Oxford in 1898. The novelist Howard Jacobson spent some time as a lecturer at Wolverhampton Polytechnic; in 1983 his debut novel *Coming from Behind* would recount the hilarious trials of Sefton Goldberg, a lecturer at 'Wrottesley Polytechnic'.

WOOTTON *Staffordshire*

Village 6 m. SW of Ashbourne off the B5032. Wootton Hall (somewhat extended and altered in the 19th c.) was lent by Mr Davenport to Jean-Jacques Rousseau and his mistress Thérèse Le Vasseur in 1766 when he was forced to leave France. William Howitt in *Visits to Remarkable Places* (1842) reports that Rousseau dressed in 'Armenian dress, a furred cap, and caftan or long striped robe with a belt', and that he was still remembered by the local people who called him 'Roos Hall' or 'Dross Hall', and who thought his habit of roaming the hills botanizing was peculiar. Many neighbours were sociable, though, including the young Duchess of Portland, who shared his interest in plants, Mrs Delany's brother at Calwich Abbey, who invited him there, and his host, who arranged for his servants to look after him when he himself was in London. Rousseau wrote the major part of his *Confessions* here, but left suddenly, fearing that he was about to be poisoned.

WOOTTON WAWEN (pr. Wawn)
Warwickshire

Village on the A3400, 7 m. NW of Stratford-upon-Avon. The church with its Saxon sanctuary and 11th- to 15th-c. additions has a memorial to the poet of *The Chace* (1735), William Somerville (1675–1742), who lived at Edstone nearby. His poems are about the sports and pastimes of a country squire. The house he lived in has been replaced.

WORCESTER (pr. 'Wŏŏster)
Worcestershire

Cathedral city on the Severn. Florence of Worcester, a Benedictine monk, wrote *Chronicon ex Chronicis*, which was continued by other monks after his death here in 1118. Near the Cathedral is the city's oldest church, St Helen's, where the bond of 1582 pledging two Stratford men to ensure the marriage of 'William Shagspere' and 'Anne Hathwey' can be seen.

Samuel Butler and Samuel Foote were pupils (*c.* 1620 and *c.* 1730 respectively) at King's School, whose hall is the monks' old refectory, a Decorated building on a Norman base.

Bishop Gauden, whose seat was at *Hartlebury Castle, is buried at the W end of the S aisle of the Cathedral. Izaak Walton, who also lived at Hartlebury Castle as Bishop Morley's steward, wrote the inscription on the tablet in the Lady Chapel commemorating his wife, which contains, after a list of her virtues, the anguished aside 'Alas, that she is dead'.

Celia Fiennes writes in her journal (*The Journeys of Celia Fiennes*, ed. Christopher Morris, 1947) that she visited the town on the day William Walsh, the poet from *Abberley, was elected to parliament.

Mrs Henry Wood was born here in 1814. She was Ellen Price, the daughter of a glover, and though she seldom returned after leaving when 20, many of her novels have the city, which she disguises as 'Helstoneleigh', as their background. *Mrs. Halliburton's Troubles* (1862) is about glovers.

Mary Martha Sherwood, who spent most of her life in the neighbourhood with the exception of the years with her husband's regiment in India, was living in Britannia Sq. when she finished the last volume of the popular moral saga *The Fairchild Family* (1847). Many of the novels of Francis Brett Young are set in the neighbourhood. His ashes were interred in the Cathedral, which has tablets commemorating the three local novelists.

The poet John Heath-Stubbs was educated at the Worcester School for the Blind at Whittington in the mid-1930s. The travel writer and novelist Jonathan Raban attended the King's School, Worcester, in the 1950s.

North of England

North of England

NORTH-WEST

ACCRINGTON *Lancashire*

Small Lancashire mill town 18 m. N of Manchester. Manchester-born novelist Jeanette Winterson was adopted and raised here in Accrington, and educated at Accrington Girls' Grammar School; her Pentecostal upbringing in the town appears in her novel *Oranges Are Not the Only Fruit* (1985); in response to a question about the link between her own Accrington childhood and the Lancashire childhood in the book, and whether the novel was autobiographical, Winterson's response was 'No not at all and yes of course.'

AMBLESIDE *Cumbria*

Little town in the vale of the Rothay, 1 m. N of the head of Lake Windermere, on the A593 and the B5285, a busy centre for visitors in the southern Lake District. When William and Dorothy Wordsworth lived at *Grasmere they frequently walked the 12 miles there and back, calling for letters at the post office and taking their own to the post. Mrs Hemans lived at Dove Nest (1829–31), a house *c.* 1½ m. S, signposted up a steep road just N of the Low-wood Hotel and recognizable by its golden dove weathercock, overlooking Windermere, with the woods (NT) on the Wansfell slopes above. She came to know Wordsworth and stayed at *Rydal Mount in 1830 for a fortnight, which his wife, Mary, and her sister Sara found '*long*'. 'Her affectation', said Sara, 'is perfectly unendurable,' but Wordsworth defended her and when she died, in the same year as James Hogg, commemorated her in the 'Extempore Effusion upon the Death of James Hogg' (1835) as 'that holy Spirit, | Sweet as the spring, as ocean deep'.

Matthew Arnold lived for a time at Fox How, a pleasant house built by his father, Dr Arnold of Rugby, on an estate below Loughrigg Fell, on the far side of the Rothay. Wordsworth, a quarter of an hour's walk away at Rydal Mount, had encouraged the Arnolds to settle here and had negotiated the purchase of the land and helped with building plans. Later on Harriet Martineau used to find it a pleasant walk across the fields to visit the Arnolds from her own house, The Knoll, which she had built in 1845. Wordsworth, who was 76 when she first met him, took a great interest in the house, saying that the building of it was the wisest step of her life, 'for the value of the property will be doubled in ten years'. He planted two stone pines in the garden and helped to choose the motto for the sundial, 'Come, Light! Visit me!' The house (preserved as a historic monument) is on the W side of Rydal Rd, down a turning just before Haven Cottage. Charlotte Brontë, who had greatly admired Harriet's novel *Deerbrook* (1839), stayed here for a week in 1850, between the publication of *Shirley* and *Villette*, and met the Arnold family. Matthew Arnold, in 'Haworth Churchyard, 1855', his lament for Charlotte's early death, remembers how he 'saw the meeting | Of two gifted women'. Crabb Robinson, who gave Harriet a marble-mounted sideboard, also visited. She lived here until her death in 1876, a tireless advocate of social reform and an active journalist. She contributed to Dickens's *Household Words*, from its beginning in 1849 until 1857, stories and articles on health and sanitation and various industries, 'grimly bent', as Dickens said, 'on the enlightenment of mankind'. She continued writing for many other periodicals, notably the *Westminster Review* and the *Edinburgh Review*, the *National Anti-Slavery Standard* of New York, and above all the *Daily News*. Her *Complete Guide to the Lakes* was published in 1855.

ASHTON-UNDER-LYNE *Greater Manchester*

Old cotton town 7 m. E of Manchester. The novelist Livi Michael was brought up on an estate in Ashton; in Jane Rogers's novel *Mr Wroe's Virgins* (1991) the town is the home of a religious community.

> Though it has been revealed formerly to others that Britain is to be the centre of His second reign on earth (there are those indeed who argue that the first Jerusalem was builded here) it is only to our Prophet that the exact vicinity of the New Jerusalem has been vouchsafed. It is fitting that it should be Ashton . . .

ASHTON-UPON-MERSEY *Greater Manchester*

Suburb of Manchester, just S of the Mersey on the A56. Stanley Houghton, author of the play *Hindle Wakes* (1912), was born here (1881), probably in Doveston Rd, though the exact location is uncertain.

BALLAUGH *Isle of Man*

Village on the A3, 7 m. W of Ramsey. Hall Caine spent much of his childhood here with his uncle, who was a farmer and butcher, and his grandmother, who told him stories and folk tales of the island, which he later depicted in *The Deemster* (1887) and *The Manxman* (1894).

BIRKENHEAD *Merseyside*

Town on the Wirral, facing Liverpool across the Mersey. The poet Adrian Henri was born here in 1932, at a maternity hospital in Tranmere.

BOLTON *Lancashire*

Former mill town, now a large urban centre within Greater Manchester. The novelist Monica Ali, born in Bangladesh, moved here when her family came over to the UK when she was 3 years old, and spent her childhood here.

BORROWDALE *Cumbria*

Valley of the Derwent, one of the most beautiful of the Lake District dales, which runs 5 m. S from Derwentwater to the village of Seathwaite. Sir Hugh Walpole spent much of the latter part of his life at Brackenburn, an estate on the W side of the valley, and died there on 1 June 1941. His romantic 'saga' of a Lakeland family, *The Herries Chronicle* (*Rogue Herries*, 1930; *Judith Paris*, 1931; *The Fortress*, 1932; and *Vanessa*, 1933), is set in and around Borrowdale.

BOWDON *Greater Manchester*

District adjacent to Altrincham, on the A56, *c.* 15 m. SW of Manchester. Mrs Juliana Horatia Ewing, writer of books for children, came here from Aldershot in 1877 and stayed 1½ years while her husband, Major Ewing, was stationed at Manchester. They lived in the higher part of the town in a semi-detached house which Mrs Ewing refers to as Downs Villa (one of a pair called Downs Villas), later 14 Higher Downs. Mrs Ewing, who began by writing stories for *Aunt Judy's Magazine* (started by her mother, Mrs Gatty), had recently made her name with three long novels written in army quarters at Aldershot: *A Flat Iron for a Farthing* (1870–1), *Six to Sixteen* (1872), and *The Miller's Thumb* (1872–3; later published as *Jan of the Windmill*, 1876).

BRANTWOOD *Cumbria*

House and 200-acre estate 1½ m. from the head of Coniston Water, on the E shore, on an unclassified road off the B5285, the home of John Ruskin from 13 September 1872 until the end of his life (20 Jan. 1900). In the summer of 1871, when he was recovering from a serious illness, he heard that Brantwood was for sale and bought it at once without even seeing it. When he came to inspect the property in September he found 'a mere shed of rotten timber and loose stone', but the view was splendid, 'on the whole', he said, 'the finest I know in Cumberland or Lancashire', and he put in hand extensive repairs, enabling him to occupy his new home the following year. From now on his time was full of intense activity: tours, lectures, writing, sketching. In 1871, when he began *Fors Clavigera*, a series of monthly letters 'to the Workmen and

Labourers of Great Britain', he decided to publish the work himself and by 1873 had transferred all his books to George Allen, a carpenter–wood engraver who became sole publisher, acting directly under him and greatly improving the style and appearance of his works. In 1885 Ruskin began *Praeterita*, his autobiography, and with its completion (on a diminished scale from the original plan) in 1889 his literary and artistic work ended.

The house is open to the public and contains a large number of pictures by Ruskin and his contemporaries together with some of his furniture and part of his library. Also on view are his boat and coach and the harbour which he built with some of his friends. A nature trail through the grounds is divided into two sections, each returning via Ruskin's stone seat overlooking a small waterfall (www.brantwood.org.uk).

BRIDEKIRK *Cumbria*

Small village 2 m. N of Cockermouth, on a minor road off the A595. Thomas Tickell, poet and editor of Addison's works, was born (1686) at the vicarage.

BRIERY CLOSE *Cumbria*

Large house and estate (later a stud farm) *c.* 2 m. SE of Ambleside, on a narrow road leading up from the A591, near the Low-wood Hotel on the NE shore of Lake Windermere. It was formerly the home of Sir James and Lady Kaye-Shuttleworth, where Charlotte Brontë was staying when Elizabeth Gaskell first met her, in August 1850. The meeting is vividly described in Elizabeth Gaskell's *Letters* (1966).

BURY *Lancashire*

N Manchester town between Bolton and Rochdale. Richmal Crompton, creator of the William books for children, was born on Manchester Road on 15 November 1890; her father was a teacher at Bury Grammar School.

BUTTERMERE *Cumbria*

Village at the NW end of Lake Buttermere. Melvin Bragg's novel *The Maid of Buttermere* (1978) is based on the true story (from 1802) of Mary Robinson, an innkeeper's daughter who marries a bigamist. Robinson also features in a Wordsworth poem.

CARLISLE *Cumbria*

City on the Eden, just S of Hadrian's Wall, on the A6 and the A7, once the Roman camp of Luguvallium and former capital of NW England. Thomas Percy, later Bishop of Dromore, was Dean here from 1778 to 1782.

Robert Anderson, the Cumbrian dialect poet, was born (1 Feb. 1770) at Down Side in St Mary's parish and educated first at the charity school run by the dean and chapter and then at the Quaker school under Isaac Ritson. He began to earn his living at 10 as assistant calico printer for his brother and was later apprenticed to a pattern drawer. After five years in London he returned to Carlisle in 1796, fired with ambition to be a poet, and in 1805

published *Cumbrian Ballads*, based on subjects from real life. His 'Lucy Gray', a poetic rendering of a rustic Northumbrian story, probably suggested Wordsworth's poem 'She dwelt among the untrodden ways'. Anderson's *Poetical Works* with his autobiography was published in 1820. He died in Carlisle in 1833 and is buried in the cathedral yard, where a tombstone erected by public subscription marks his grave. There is a marble monument to him in the Cathedral, with a portrait bust in high relief.

Sir Walter Scott married Margaret Charlotte Charpentier (known as Charlotte Carpenter) in the Cathedral in December 1797, having met her only a few months earlier when staying at *Gilsland. The house, 81 Castle St., where she was living with her companion, Miss Jane Nicholson, can still be seen.

CARTMEL FELL *Cumbria*

Parish to the W of the A5074, between the Winster valley and the S end of Windermere. The interesting old church of St Anthony (*c.* 1504) plays an important part in Mrs Humphry Ward's *Helbeck of Bannisdale* (1898). In 1925 Arthur Ransome and his wife, Evgenia, bought Low Ludderburn, an old stone farmhouse at the upper end of the Winster valley, nearly 600 ft above sea level. Here he lived for 10 years, writing, fishing, and sailing. *Swallows and Amazons* (his pet book) was published in 1930, *Swallowdale* in 1931, and *Peter Duck* in 1932.

CHESTER *Cheshire*

Ancient cathedral city on the right bank of the Dee, on the A51. The first literary connection is with William of Malmesbury, the 12th-c. historian who spent most of his life in Malmesbury, but also travelled widely in England. He writes (*c.* 1125):

> Chester is called the City of the Legions because the veterans of the Julian legions were settled there . . . The natives greatly enjoy milk and butter; those who are richer live on meat . . . Goods are exchanged between Chester and Ireland, so that what the nature of the soil lacks, is supplied by the toil of the merchants.

Ranulf Higden, a monk at St Werburgh's, wrote the *Polychronicon* (*c.* 1342) here, a Latin universal history from the Creation to his own time. He is buried in the Cathedral. Another monk of St Werburgh's, Henry Bradshaw (d. 1513), was born in Chester and wrote (*c.* 1500) a lost chronicle of the city and a verse life of St Werburgh, of which five known copies of a 1521 edition survive.

Celia Fiennes enjoyed her visit here in 1698 and gives a good description of the city and its principal buildings and the 'wall all aboute with battlements and a walke all round paved with stone' (*Journeys*, 1947), and Defoe was also interested in the walls, which he found in very good repair, commenting that 'it is a very pleasant walk round the city, upon the walls, and within the battlements, from whence you may see the country round' (*Tour*, 1724–7).

Swift used to travel to and from Ireland by way of Chester and his letters to Esther Johnson (*Journal to Stella*, complete edn 1948) began in 1710, when he stayed at the Yacht Inn on the corner of Nicholas St. His friend Thomas Parnell, poet and archdeacon of Clogher, died (1718) in Chester after falling ill on his journey to Ireland, and is buried at Holy Trinity Church (rebuilt 1865), opposite the corner of Watergate St. and Weaver St. Boswell, writing to Dr Johnson in 1779, expressed his delight in Chester and especially in its feminine society: 'here again I am in a state of much enjoyment. . . . Chester pleases my fancy more than any town I ever saw.'

When De Quincey ran away from Manchester Grammar School in July 1802, he made his way, on foot, to his mother's house, The Priory (gone), 'a miniature priory attached to the walls of the very ancient Anglo-Saxon Church to St. John', once owned by Sir Robert Cotton, the antiquary. After staying here a while he left to wander through Wales, on an allowance from his uncle of a guinea a week, and eventually reached London. In March 1803 he came back briefly 'to rest after the storms' before going to Worcester College, Oxford. The site of The Priory, at the bottom of Nicholas St., was later occupied by the Police Headquarters. A. H. Clough was educated at the King's School (founded by Henry VIII in 1541; formerly in Northgate St.; removed to Wrexham Rd, 1962).

Thomas Hughes, author of *Tom Brown's Schooldays* (1857), was appointed a county court judge in 1882 and came to Chester to be near his circuit. After living for three years in rented houses (11 Stanley Pl. and 2 Sandowne Ter.) he and his wife, Fanny, moved into Uffington House, 16 (now 20) Dee Hills Pk, which they had had built for them, with wrought iron gates embodying the initials TH and FH. This was Hughes's last home (1885–96).

There is an evocative description of Chester in Henry James's *The Ambassadors* (1903).

CLEATOR MOOR *Cumbria*

Small, former iron-working town. The local poet Norman Nicholson wrote of the changing fortunes of the ironworks industry, now suffering an economic slump, now revived only to produce arms, in his poem 'Cleator Moor':

> Every wagon of cold steel
> Is fire to drive a turbine wheel;
> Every knuckle of soft ore
> A bullet in a soldier's ear.

COCKERMOUTH *Cumbria*

Market town on the A5086 at the confluence of the Derwent and the Cocker. William Wordsworth and his sister Dorothy were born (7 Apr. 1770 and 25 Dec. 1771 respectively) in a handsome double-fronted house, now called Wordsworth House and dedicated to the poet's childhood years (NT, www.wordsworthhouse.org.uk), at the W end of the wide High St. The Derwent, flowing past the terrace walk at the foot of the garden, was

Wordsworth House, Cockermouth, Cumbria. The birthplace of William and Dorothy Wordsworth

Wordsworth's lifelong happy memory of his earliest days, the river that, in *The Prelude* (1850),

> loved
> To blend his murmurs with my nurse's song . . .
> And from his fords and shallows sent a voice
> That flowed along my dreams.

He attended the Grammar School, a small building (gone) in the churchyard, for a time in 1776, though regular schooling did not begin until the early summer of 1779, when he went to *Hawkshead Grammar School, but the foundations of a love of poetry were laid at home in his father's library and in learning by heart 'large portions of Shakespeare, Milton, and Spenser'.

R. L. Stevenson visited the town in 1871 and stayed at the Globe Hotel Ⓟ in Main St.

COLTHOUSE *Cumbria*

Hamlet ½ m. E of *Hawkshead, where Wordsworth lodged with Ann Tyson while he was attending Hawkshead Grammar School (1779–87). Although it was formerly thought that the Tysons' cottage, referred to in *The Prelude* (1850), was in Hawkshead, investigations initiated by Mrs Heelis of Sawrey (Beatrix Potter) indicate that Ann Tyson and her husband moved from Hawkshead, where they had kept a shop, to Colthouse *c.* 1773 and made their living by taking schoolboy boarders. It is not certain whether the cottage still exists, but it may have been the present Green End Cottage, and the brook of *The Prelude* (IV. 50–1), which ran 'boxed within our garden', may be the little stream which runs in a channel through the orchard.

CONISTON *Cumbria*

Village near the head of Coniston Water, on the A593 and the B5285. Ruskin is buried in the churchyard, his grave marked by a tall cross of Tilberthwaite stone, designed by his friend W. G. Collingwood. The Ruskin Museum in the village contains a collection of drawings, letters, and other relics, such as his harmonium.

Tennyson spent his honeymoon (1850) at Tent Lodge, at the NE end of the lake, on the road leading to Ruskin's beautifully situated home, Brantwood. The house combines displays of Ruskiniana with those of local history (www.ruskinmuseum.com).

Arthur Ransome came here for holidays as a child, staying at a farm near the lake. In *Swallows and Amazons* (1930), which he began writing in 1929, the imaginary family of children was suggested to him by two girls whom he had seen playing on the lake's shore.

COWAN BRIDGE *Lancashire*

Village on the A65, 2 m. SE of Kirkby Lonsdale. Just N of the old bridge over the Leck is a row of cottages Ⓟ, once part of the Clergy Daughters' School, where Charlotte and Emily Brontë were pupils (1824–5). Their elder sisters Maria and Elizabeth had died of typhus contracted there and Charlotte gives a gloomy picture of the school as 'Lowood' in *Jane Eyre* (1847). The school was moved to Casterton, a few miles N, in 1833.

CREWE *Cheshire*

Railway and engineering town. The novelist William Cooper (H. S. Hoff) was born at 99 Brooklyn St., Monks Coppenhall.

CROSTHWAITE *Cumbria*

Village on the A5074, 27 m. SE of Keswick. Robert Southey is buried in the churchyard, his grave and tombstone recently restored at the expense of the Brazilian government in memory of his *History of Brazil* (1810–19). In the church he has a marble effigy, carved by a young local sculptor, with a poem thought to be by Wordsworth.

DARESBURY (pr. 'Darzbry) *Cheshire*

Village *c.* 4 m. S of Warrington, on the B5356 between the A49 and the A56. Charles Lutwidge Dodgson ('Lewis Carroll') was born (27 Jan. 1832) and lived until 1843 at the Old Parsonage, Newton-by-Daresbury, when his father was vicar of Daresbury. The house, situated on the Glebe Farm *c.* 2 m. S of the church, was burnt down in 1883 and not rebuilt, the site has been acquired by the NT. The foundations of the house are laid out in bricks. A pillar bears a quotation from Dodgson's poem 'The Three Sunsets':

> An island farm 'mid seas of corn
> Swayed by the wandering breath of morn
> The happy spot where I was born.

The place can be reached by turning S from the village, crossing over the M56, bearing left and then right, almost to the end of Morphany Lane. The church has a Lewis Carroll memorial window (1934) at the E end of the Danniell Chapel, depicting the Adoration of the Babe and including the figures of Lewis Carroll and Alice and illustrations from *Alice's Adventures in Wonderland* as heraldic supports. An album listing Lewis Carroll's works and the names of

215

subscribers to the memorial from Great Britain and the US stands below the window on a table made from some of the original oak beams of the church.

DOUGLAS *Isle of Man*

Port and chief town, on the wide bay SE of the island. Wordsworth, accompanied by Crabb Robinson, spent a few days here in 1833. Of the many sonnets he wrote on his tour, three were inspired by the sight of the island from the sea, and one was called 'On Entering Douglas Bay, Isle of Man'. Matthew Arnold enjoyed holidays here, as many thousands have later, and in 1843 wrote 'To a Gipsy Child by the Sea-shore'. T. E. Brown was born (1830) at the Old Grammar School house (gone) in New Bond St., when his father was chaplain of St Matthew's Church (gone) in North Quay. When he was 2 the family moved to Kirk Braddan vicarage (gone), a simple, long, low, whitewashed house, 2½ m. S of Douglas. It was here that he met the men and women from whom he drew the characters in his stories in *Fo'c's'le Yarns* (1881): his father's gardener became 'Old John', and the Revd William Corrin, vicar of Kirk Christ in Rushen nearby, became 'Pazon Gale'. Brown's poem 'Braddan Vicarage', written in England, has the lines:

> I wonder if in that far isle
> Some child is growing now, like me
> When I was child: care pricked, yet healed the
>   while
> With balm of rock and sea.

The Manx Museum in Crellin's Hill has manuscripts and other memorials of T. E. Brown.

Walter Greenwood, writer of *Love on the Dole*, moved into a flat in Douglas in the 1950s and died here in 1974.

Jonathan Raban stopped at the town during the journey around Britain he recorded in his travel book *Coasting* (1986).

> Athol Street in Douglas—a hundred yards or so of seaside stucco and a bad place in a wind—was a smuggler's cove of tinpot banks, off-the-peg companies, avoidance schemes and useful dodges . . . the source of innumerable good wheezes . . . loans, investments, savings and pension plans, all done on the cheap, all, in the smugglers' favourite smooth phrase, 'tax advantageous'.

DROYLSDEN *Greater Manchester*

Town 4 m. E of Manchester city centre. The novelist Livi Michael was a pupil at Fairfield High School.

DUDDON *Cumbria*

River which rises on Wrynose Fell and flows S to the sea near Barrow-in-Furness. Wordsworth wrote, between 1806 and 1820, a series of 34 sonnets to the river, which he had first explored in childhood, when staying with cousins at Broughton. The sonnets proved 'wonderfully popular' and, as Wordsworth realized later, were 'more warmly received' than some of his other work.

ESTHWAITE LODGE *Cumbria*

White Georgian house on a minor road near the W shore of Esthwaite Water, *c*. 1 m. S of Hawkshead. Francis Brett Young spent his summers here between 1928 and 1933 and wrote *The House Under the Water* (1932). Hugh Walpole stayed with him and his wife and finished the Paris section of *Judith Paris* (1931).

FLEETWOOD *Lancashire*

Large seaside resort at the end of the A585, at the mouth of the Wyre. Mrs Molesworth, writer of children's books, spent several summers there in her childhood, when it was only a small, quiet place, and describes it as 'Sandyshore' in *The Rectory Children* (1889). J. R. Ackerley went to school at Rossall School, and reflects upon it in his frank autobiography, *My Father and Myself* (1968):

> I see myself, then, gazing back, as an innocent, rather withdrawn, self-centred boy, more repelled by than attracted to sex, which seemed to me a furtive, guilty, soiling thing, nothing to do with those feelings I had not yet experienced but about which I was already writing a lot of dreadful sentimental verse, called romance and love.

GILSLAND *Cumbria*

Village in the Irthing valley, on the B6318, *c*. 5 m. NW of Haltwhistle. The young Walter Scott, on a tour of the Lakes with his brother and a friend in the summer of 1797, made it (then a sequestered little watering place) their headquarters. One September day they noticed an attractive young woman on horseback and at a ball that night they vied with each other to get presented. She was Charlotte Mary Carpenter, daughter of Jean Charpentier of Lyons, who had died early in the Revolution, and was under the guardianship of Lord Downshire. Scott took her in to supper, fell in love, and after a whirlwind courtship married her in December in Carlisle. The surrounding country forms much of the background to *Guy Mannering* (1815).

GRASMERE *Cumbria*

Village on the W side of the A591, *c*. 1 m. N of the lake of the same name. On the E side of the main road is Town End, where Wordsworth and his sister Dorothy came in December 1799 to 'live in retirement' among their native mountains. Their cottage, formerly an inn known as the Dove and Olive Branch, now called Dove Cottage, at the foot of the hill on the old road to Ambleside, consisted of two rooms downstairs and four upstairs (of which two were very small). At that time there were no buildings between the cottage and the lake and from the 'little nook of mountain-ground' that rose steeply behind they had a view, as Wordsworth wrote to Coleridge, 'of the lake, the church, Helm Crag, and two thirds of the vale'. The little garden was soon stocked with vegetables and flowers; in May, when Dorothy began her *Grasmere Journals*, she spoke of

hoeing the first row of peas, transplanting radishes, and bringing back wild plants from the woods. The *Journals* record the day-to-day life of herself and her beloved William, their walks and observations of everything around them, the local people, the visits of Coleridge and William's sailor brother John, until January 1803, soon after William's marriage to Mary Hutchinson (October 1802). William drew on Dorothy's writings for many of his themes, sometimes for the very words, as in her descriptions of the daffodils near Ullswater, beyond Gowbarrow Park:

> I never saw daffodils so beautiful they grew among the mossy stones about and about them, some rested their heads upon these stones as on a pillow for weariness and the rest tossed and reeled and danced and seemed as if they verily laughed with the wind that blew upon them over the lake, they looked so gay ever glancing ever changing,

which echoes in 'I wandered lonely as a cloud':

> When all at once I saw a crowd,
> A host of golden daffodils;
> Beside the lake, beneath the trees,
> Fluttering and dancing in the breeze. . . .
>
> Ten thousand saw I at a glance,
> Tossing their heads in sprightly dance.
> The waves beside them danced; but they
> Out-did the sparkling waves in glee.

Wordsworth was writing poetry almost from the day they moved in, and Dorothy noted down the details, together with the weather and her domestic chores, as in these entries for March 1802: 'A mild morning. William worked at the Cuckow poem ["To the cuckoo"]. I sewed beside him'; 'While I was getting into bed he wrote the Rainbow ["My heart leaps up"]'; 'A divine morning. At Breakfast Wm wrote part of an ode [*Ode: Intimations of Immortality*]. Mr Olliff sent the dung and Wm went to work in the garden.'

On 4 November 1807 they had a memorable visit from De Quincey, who arrived as escort to Sara Coleridge and her three children. He had already written (at the age of 18) to Wordsworth in admiration of the *Lyrical Ballads*, and was now meeting his hero for the first time. He was 'so modest', wrote Dorothy later, 'and so very shy, that even now I wonder how he ever had the courage to address himself to my brother by letter'. He stayed in the best bedroom of the humblest house he had known as a guest, and was wakened by the eldest Wordsworth child (aged 3), who became a devoted friend. The cottage, small enough on any account for accommodating three people and their frequent visitors, became too cramped when Wordsworth's children numbered three, and the family moved to Allan Bank (NT) in May 1808. This house, on high ground at the foot of Easedale, *c*. 1½ m. NW of Grasmere, was more spacious for their needs—Dorothy wrote of 'the comfort of each having a room of our own'—and in spite of chronically smoking chimneys they settled in happily, with Coleridge and De Quincey as their guests

William Wordsworth and the Lakes

To Wordsworth, Grasmere was, quite simply, home. He never forgot his first glimpse of it from Red Bank at the southern end of the lake:

> Once on the brow of yonder hill I stopped,
> While I was yet a schoolboy (of what age
> I cannot remember, but the hour
> I well remember though the year be gone),
> And with a sudden influx overcome
> At sight of this seclusion, I forgot
> My haste, for hasty had my footsteps been
> As boyish my pursuits—and sighing said:
> 'What happy fortune were it here to live!
> And if I thought of dying, if a thought
> Of mortal separation could come in
> With paradise before me, here to die.'

Wordsworth would not die here, but spent some of his happiest and most productive years in Grasmere. His expectations were formed by Thomas Gray's inspired description of the village as he found it in 1769, viewed from Dunmail Raise at the valley's northern end:

> The bosom of the mountains spreading here into a broad basin discovers in the midst Grasmere water; its margin is hollowed into small bays with bold eminences; some of rock, some of turf, that half-conceal, and vary the figure of the little lake they command: from the shore, a low promontory pushes itself far into the water, and on it stands a white village with the parish church rising in the midst of it . . . Not a single red tile, no gentleman's flaring house, or garden walls, break in upon the repose of this little unsuspected paradise; but all is peace, rusticity, and happy poverty, in its neatest, most becoming attire.

Wordsworth must often have returned while a schoolboy, but it was not until the end of 1799, when he was 29, that he and his sister Dorothy settled at Dove Cottage, five minutes' walk from the centre of the village, on the main Ambleside to Keswick road. They would remain in Grasmere until 1813, when Wordsworth's growing family precipitated a move to a larger house in the neighbouring valley of Rydal.

In those days Dove Cottage had a clear view to the lake, now obscured by a terrace built as part of a ribbon development in the mid-Victorian period. Today the house and its gardens are maintained by the Wordsworth Trust, which also owns the recently built museum and library next door. Despite the many thousands of people who visit the cottage each day, it is still possible, if you venture onto the upper slopes of the garden, to get some idea of how it must have felt for Wordsworth and his sister when they first moved in. 'Embrace me then, ye hills, and close me in!', he was to write—and if you think of those words as you look across the valley from Wordsworth's summerhouse, you can see why he thought that.

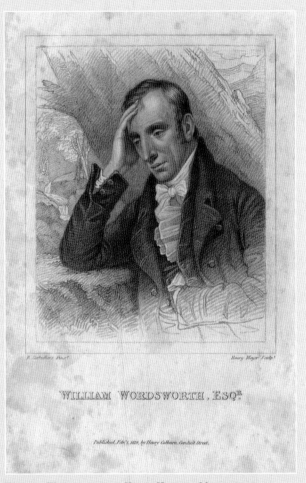

WILLIAM WORDSWORTH BY HENRY HOPPNER MEYER AFTER RICHARD CARRUTHERS, PUBLISHED 1819

He had high hopes of the place, and not just because he had known it since childhood. This was where he hoped to compose 'The Recluse'—the epic poem that would precipitate the millennium, Christ's thousand-year rule on earth. But that exalted ambition was to fail. One reason was his uneasy relation to Grasmere and its inhabitants. Wordsworth was too clear-sighted not to see that, far from representing poverty 'in its neatest, most becoming attire', its denizens were typical of country folk everywhere: he soon heard the voice of a local shepherd made (as he put it) 'An organ for the sounds articulate | Of ribaldry and blasphemy and wrath', and witnessed others subject to 'selfishness and envy and revenge'. He was never entirely at ease with the local people, and they were always a little suspicious of him. 'A man who writes poetry for a living! Whatever next?' Even today, some Grasmerians take more pride in the gingerbread shop and garden centre than they do in the writer whose grave provides an essential stop on every visitor's itinerary.

That may have been why, in his poetry, Wordsworth made Grasmere the forum for confrontations with fallen, suffering humanity. Take, for instance, 'Point Rash-Judgement', in which he describes how, during harvest time, he, Dorothy, and Coleridge went for a leisurely walk round Grasmere Lake, as many visitors do today. They catch sight of a peasant on the far side, holding a fishing rod in his hand.

> We all cried out, that he must be indeed
> An idle man, who thus could lose a day
> Of the mid-harvest, when the labourer's hire
> Is ample, and some little might be stored
> Wherewith to cheer him in the winter time.

But as they approach, they see that the man is sick, 'gaunt and lean, with sunken cheeks | And wasted limbs'. He does not have the strength to labour with the others, and does what little he can to provide for his loved ones. Wordsworth can hardly put into words the shame that fills him at his 'rash judgement'.

Or take his encounter with the leech gatherer, whom he met when walking up the hill immediately behind Dove Cottage. In those days leeches were worth money as a treatment for fevers and infections; leech gatherers stood in cold rivers and ponds waiting for leeches to attach themselves to their legs. But the tale of hardship and suffering related by this old man turns him into an angelic figure:

> Like one whom I had met with in a dream;
> Or like a man from some far region sent,
> To give me human strength, and strong admonishment.

In both cases the encounter seems to have shaken Wordsworth to the core.

Its power as a site of self-analysis and self-questioning was only part of what made Grasmere so important to Wordsworth. For all that unease, Grasmere never lost its power as a sanctuary. It was where he composed the greatest of his long poems, *The Prelude*; where he started his family; and where in 1850 he chose to be buried. It is not hard to see why he fell in love with it: climb Red Bank early in the day, before anyone else, and you find yourself looking down on a 'little unsuspected paradise'.

DUNCAN WU

for the first winter. In March 1809 the Wordsworths took Dove Cottage for the latter and he kept the tenancy until 1834, long after he had moved to Edinburgh with his family.

Dove Cottage now forms part of a complex which constitutes a museum displaying manuscripts, notebooks, and personal relics and presents a lively programme of literary events and exhibitions (www.wordsworth.org.uk).

The Wordsworths left Allan Bank in June 1811 and moved into the old vicarage, a more manageable house, though it turned out to be sadly damp. It stood by the bridge opposite the church. During his last years in Grasmere, Wordsworth completed *The Excursion*. But after the deaths of his two children Catherine and Thomas in 1812, the nearness to the graveyard became too painful and in 1813 they moved to *Rydal Mount. Wordsworth is buried in Grasmere churchyard, near Dorothy (d. 1855), his wife, Mary (d. 1859), and Sara Hutchinson (Mary's sister, d. 1835), and other members of the family lie close by. There is also the grave of Hartley Coleridge and a memorial to Arthur Hugh Clough (who died in Florence, 1861). Eight of the yew trees near the path by the Rothay, which runs by the churchyard wall, were planted by Wordsworth.

There is a monument in the church to Wordsworth, with a profile head by Woolner and a translation of Keble's Latin dedication to Wordsworth of his *Oxford Lectures on Poetry*.

GREEBA CASTLE *Isle of Man*

Large house on the slopes of Greeba Hill, off the Douglas–Peel road, A1, near Crosby. Hall

Caine, the novelist, recommended to write about the Isle of Man by D. G. Rossetti, rented the house, after his success with *The Deemster* (1887), and here started *The Manxman* (1894), which was finished in a boarding house on Marine Parade in Peel. Caine then bought Greeba Castle, which was his home, though he made frequent journeys, until his death here in 1931. For a short while (1901–8) he was a Member of the House of Keys but his reforming zeal, which had appealed to the voters, was short-lived.

HAVERTHWAITE *Cumbria*

Small village in the Leven valley, 3 m. SW of Newby Bridge, on the A590. In 1963 Arthur Ransome made his last home at Hill Top, a house (now a kennels) on a minor road on the edge of the woods, with a splendid view of Furness Fells, *c.* 1½ m. NW of the village.

HAWKSHEAD *Cumbria*

Village on the B5285, NW of the head of Esthwaite Water. Although the village has become much enlarged and caters for many visitors, the heart of it, consisting of picturesque narrow streets and footpaths, is virtually unspoilt. Below the church is the Free Grammar School, founded by Edwin Sandys (later Archbishop of York) of Esthwaite Hall and attended by Wordsworth (1779–87) before he went to Cambridge. The school is now a museum, housing what is believed to be the finest extant library of a medieval grammar school. Wordsworth's desk, with his name carved on it, is still there, and among objects of particular interest is the housekeeping ledger

of Ann Tyson, with whom he lodged after she moved to *Colthouse and to whom reference is made in *The Prelude*. Her cottage near the centre of the village has a plaque that later research has made out of date.

The Beatrix Potter Gallery (NT) in Main St. contains an exhibition of Beatrix Potter's original drawings and illustrations of her children's story books, together with a display telling the story of her life. The building was once the office of her husband, William Heelis.

HOGHTON (pr. 'Hawton) *Lancashire*

Small village *c.* 5 m. SE of Preston, on the A675. On the E side of the road a long, straight drive runs up the hill to Hoghton Tower, a fortified 16th-c. mansion in which Harrison Ainsworth set the last episodes of his novel *The Lancashire Witches* (1848). He deplored its then ruinous condition, but it has since been restored.

HURSTWOOD *Lancashire*

Hamlet at the end of a minor road 3 m. SE of Burnley (or 1 m. NE of a turning to Walk Mill off the A646 SSE of Burnley), lying below Worsthorne Moor and Black Hameldon Hill. Past the Hall a farm track leads to a gabled Elizabethan cottage known as 'Spenser's House'. This was the home of the grandparents of Edmund Spenser, who, though born in London, probably spent much of his boyhood in the district of Burnley, where his father had numerous relatives. After getting his MA at Cambridge in 1576 Spenser came to live at Hurstwood for two years, during which time he fell deeply in love with a beautiful girl who rejected him for a rival. Although her identity is uncertain it has been thought that she was Rose Dyneley, the daughter of a Clitheroe yeoman. She became the Rosalynd of *The Shepheards Calender* (1579), in which Spenser laments his unrequited love, and of *Colin Clouts come home againe* (1595). In 1578 Spenser sadly took a friend's advice to 'quit the bleak and shelterless hills to go down to the warmer and softer south', and left for London, taking the manuscript of *The Shepheards Calender* with him.

HUYTON *Merseyside*

Suburb of E Liverpool. The Liverpool-born playwright Alan Bleasdale was a pupil at St Aloysius Roman Catholic Junior School here in Huyton in the early 1950s.

KESWICK *Cumbria*

Market town and holiday centre on the A591, in the heart of the Lake District, situated on the Greta near the NE shore of Derwentwater. Thomas Gray came here on a Lakeland tour in September 1767 and again two years later, when his letters take the form of a *Journal* written to amuse his friend Dr Thomas Wharton, who had been prevented by illness from accompanying him. He spent six days at Keswick, 'lap'd in Elysium', before proceeding slowly by Ambleside to Kendal.

In the spring of 1794 William and Dorothy Wordsworth stayed about six weeks at Windy Brow, a farmhouse on Latrigg lent by their friends William and Raisley Calvert. Dorothy, enraptured to be with her brother after long separation, recalls how they travelled by coach from Halifax to Kendal and thence on foot: 'I walked with my brother at my side, from Kendal to Grasmere, eighteen miles, and after from Grasmere to Keswick, fifteen miles, through the most delightful country that ever was seen.' After Dorothy left in June to stay with cousins at Rampside on the Furness coast, William spent most of the rest of the year at Keswick, probably at Windy Brow, where Raisley Calvert became seriously ill with the consumption, from which he died in the following January.

Later Coleridge, who was staying with the Wordsworths at Town End, near *Grasmere, in April 1800, found a house to let on the hillside on the W of Keswick, high above the river, with a magnificent view. This was Greta Hall ℗, and he brought his family to live here until 1803, when the damp climate at last proved too much for his tendency to severe colds. He was in constant touch with Wordsworth, the two keeping up a frequent interchange of visits, discussing poetry, and preparing a new edition of *Lyrical Ballads*. During this time Coleridge completed 'Christabel' and wrote 'Dejection: An Ode'. In 1802 Charles Lamb, who only tolerated the country for the sake of his friends, brought his sister Mary to visit Coleridge and they spent three 'delightful weeks'. In the same year Southey came to Keswick and for a time shared Greta Hall with Coleridge, whose wife, Sara, was his sister-in-law. After Coleridge's departure in 1803 Southey stayed on with his

family and in 1809 took possession of the house, where he remained until his death on 21 March 1843. (He is buried in the churchyard of *Crosthwaite, nearby.) During these years he wrote an immense amount of verse and prose, and was a regular contributor to the *Quarterly Review*. He became Poet Laureate in 1813 after Sir Walter Scott had generously declined the honour in his favour. His longer poems include *Madoc* (1805), *The Curse of Kehama* (1810), and *Roderick, the Last of the Goths* (1814), and his *History of Brazil* (1810–19) is still valued. In the winter of 1811–12 Shelley came with Harriet, shortly after their marriage, to stay with Southey and his wife, but found Southey lacking in his earlier reforming enthusiasms, and his wife dull. Shelley returned to Keswick in 1813 and stayed at a house (now called Shelley's Cottage) in Chestnut Hill, where (as on so many other occasions) he alarmed his neighbours by performing chemistry experiments.

Sir Hugh Walpole, who lived at Brackenburn, *Borrowdale, is buried in the SW corner of St John's churchyard, which occupies a commanding position SW of the marketplace.

The Fitz Park Museum in Station Rd (www.dokeswick.com), opposite the entrance to Fitz Park, contains manuscripts of Southey, Wordsworth, and Hugh Walpole, some personal relics, and a bust of Walpole by Epstein.

A short walk from the town along the E shore of Derwentwater leads to the Ruskin Memorial at Friar's Crag (NT), where a plinth bears a low-relief portrait bronze by Lucchesi. When Ruskin was 5½ he spent a few days in the Lake District when travelling with his parents to Scotland, and long after recorded his vivid memory of the spot:

> The first thing which I remember, as an event in life, was being taken by my nurse to the brow of Friar's Crag on Derwent Water; the intense joy mingled with awe, that I had in looking through the hollows in the mossy roots, over the crag into the dark lake, has ever associated itself more or less with all twining roots of trees ever since.

Beatrix Potter stayed near Keswick with her family in 1903 and sketched the lake and St Herbert's Island (the sanctuary of a 7th-c. hermit, NT), which is pictured as Owl Island in *The Tale of Squirrel Nutkin* (1903). The island can be reached by regular boats from Keswick.

Mirehouse, a manor house on the A591, 4½ m. N of Keswick (www.mirehouse.com), dates from the 17th c. and has many literary associations. James Spedding (1808–81), younger son of John Spedding, who inherited the house in 1802, devoted most of his working life to the study of Francis Bacon, whose works he edited (7 vols, 1857–9). The smoking room contains a collection of Bacon's papers and first editions of his works; also a portrait of him by an unknown artist. Tennyson was much attached to the house and in 1835, being hard up, sold his Chancellor's Gold Medal for English verse for £15 to pay for the journey to visit. Here he met Edward FitzGerald and they

became lifelong friends. After his marriage in 1851 Tennyson returned to Mirehouse with his bride. Another regular visitor was Thomas Carlyle, a close friend of Spedding's elder brother Tom. 'Mirehouse was beautiful', he wrote, 'and so were the ways of it.'

KING WILLIAM'S COLLEGE *Isle of Man*

Public school (founded 1668), on the A5. F. W. Farrar and T. E. Brown were contemporaries here in the 1840s. Farrar's school story *Eric, or, Little by Little* (1858), written while he was a master at Harrow, is thought to have been loosely based on his experiences here. Brown, who was a day-boy and lived with his mother and family at Castletown nearby, became Vice-Principal (1858–61).

KNOWSLEY HALL *Merseyside*

Country seat of the Earl of Derby, 8 m. E of Liverpool, just N of the M57. When Shakespeare was a member of the Earl of Leicester's company, which gave two performances at Latham House, near Ormskirk, in July 1587, he probably played here about the same time. Edward Lear was engaged by Lord Stanley (later the 13th Earl) in 1832 to make coloured drawings of the rare birds and animals in his menagerie. Lear became a friend of his patron's grandchildren and entertained them with limericks and other verse which he illustrated himself and published as *A Book of Nonsense* (1846, anonymously; 1861, with more limericks and his own name). Adult society was formal and distinguished. Lear wrote to a friend: 'Nothing I long for half so much as to giggle heartily and to hop on one leg down the Great Gallery—but I dare not.' The grounds are now a safari park. The house is open occasionally (www.knowsley.com).

KNUTSFORD *Cheshire*

Quiet town on the A50 and the A537. Mrs Elizabeth Cleghorn Gaskell (née Stevenson) came here from London when she was just over a year old, after her mother's death, and was brought up by her aunt Mrs Hannah Lumb at Heath House (now Heathwaite House, ℗), a double-fronted brick house on the S side of Knutsford Heath (now Gaskell Ave.). She lived here until her marriage to the Revd William Gaskell in 1832, in the parish church, and attended the Brook St. Unitarian Chapel, which is described in her novel *Ruth* (1853). She is buried in the chapel graveyard, with her husband and two of her daughters. Her best-known novel, *Cranford* (first published in *Household Words*, 1851–3), is a sympathetic portrait of the little town she grew up in and the idiosyncrasies of its inhabitants.

A memorial tower in King St. (erected 1907) displays a bust of Elizabeth Gaskell as a young woman, on the wall facing the street, and a high-relief plaque of her in later life on another side, and gives a list of her works, accompanied by quotations from Job, Thomas à Kempis, Milton, Gladstone, and King Alfred. The King's

Coffee House next door, designed in the rural Italian 18th-c. style, was also built to commemorate Elizabeth Gaskell, with a suitable inscription referring to *Cranford*. The interior, decorated in the contemporary 1907 style, a blend of the Arts and Crafts Movement and Art Nouveau, was a favourite haunt of Galsworthy and other literary and artistic celebrities of the day.

Tatton Park (maintained by Cheshire County Council on behalf of the NT, www.tattonpark.org), 3½ m. N, with over 1,000 acres of deer park and a 19th-c. mansion containing collections of pictures, furniture, and silver, was the original of Cumnor Towers in Elizabeth Gaskell's *Wives and Daughters* (1864–6). It can be entered on foot from the Knutsford gate or by car from the main entrance in Ashley Rd, off the Manchester road.

LAKE DISTRICT *Cumbria*

Area in the Cumbrian Mountains *c*. 35 m. square, occupying large parts of the former counties of Cumberland and Westmorland and the former N part of Lancashire. Its mountains, dales, and lakes form a pattern of great beauty and variety and offer endless scope to naturalists, climbers, and walkers. They were both an inspiration and a way of life to the Lake Poets, Wordsworth, Coleridge, and Southey, who lived and wrote in Grasmere, Keswick, and Ambleside. The terms 'Lake Poets' and 'Lake School' derive from the *Edinburgh Review*, which used 'Lake School' in August 1817, in a derisory context (later the scorn was modified and the terms became current without a derogatory sense). But before these poets were writing Thomas Gray recorded his impressions of the Lake District in his *Journal of a Tour in the Lakes*, embodied in his *Correspondence* (ed. P. Toynbee and L. Whibley, 3 vols, 1935), and William Gilpin, in his series of *Picturesque Tours*, published a *Guide to the Lakes* (1789), which became one of Wordsworth's treasured possessions. Wordsworth's own *Guide Through the Lakes* (1835) was originally written in 1810 as an introduction to J. Wilkinson's *Select Views in Cumberland*.

Wordsworth and his sister Dorothy were natives who stayed for a time in the south of England, but were irresistibly drawn back to the country of their early days and settled there for life, first at Grasmere and then at Rydal Mount, near Ambleside. Coleridge, on the other hand, was drawn there more by devotion to Wordsworth, and after a few years found the climate too damp and left for the south. Southey joined them and put down roots at Keswick for the rest of his life. De Quincey came at 18 as a visitor to Grasmere, a wholly dedicated worshipper of Wordsworth, and maintained his attachment to the district for many years, marrying, acquiring property, writing, but never really settling. He made friends with the ebullient John Wilson of Elleray at Windermere and when the latter moved to Edinburgh he joined him and

abandoned the Lakes for good. Later literary figures have included Harriet Martineau and Matthew Arnold at Ambleside, Ruskin at Brantwood, on Coniston Water, Sir Hugh Walpole at Borrowdale, Beatrix Potter at Near Sawrey, near Esthwaite Water, and Arthur Ransome at Newby Bridge and Haverthwaite. Large areas of the Lake District have become the property of the National Trust, thanks to the tireless efforts of Canon H. D. Rawnsley (1851–1920), vicar of Crosthwaite, 1883–1917. Beatrix Potter (later Mrs William Heelis) was a strong supporter and generous benefactor.

LANCASTER *Lancashire*

Historic town on the tidal Lune, where the A6 crosses by Skerton Bridge. No. 1 High St. was the birthplace (1869) of Laurence Binyon, poet and authority on Far Eastern art, who is remembered especially for his poem 'For the Fallen' (1914): 'They shall grow not old, as we that are left grow old.' The University of Lancaster houses the Ruskin Library, the largest single collection of Ruskin's works. A gallery is open to the public daily (www.lancs.ac.uk).

LEVENS HALL *Cumbria*

Tudor mansion 6 m. S of Kendal, on the A6. Mrs Humphry Ward, granddaughter of Thomas Arnold of Rugby, stayed here during the winter of 1896–7 while writing her novel *Helbeck of Bannisdale* (1898). She used the Hall and Sizergh Castle (2 m. N) as models for 'Bannisdale'.

LIVERPOOL *Merseyside*

Second seaport of England, on the N bank of the estuary of the Mersey. The earliest known reference to Liverpool in a dramatic work occurs in *Fair Em, the Miller's Daughter of Manchester: With the Love of William the Conqueror*, a 'pleasant comedie' containing the lines: 'Since fortune hath thus spitefully crost our hope, let us leave this quest and harken after our King, who is at this daie landed at Lirpoole' (*c*. 1590, anon., though it has been attributed to Shakespeare, who was a member of Lord Strange's company, which performed it).

Defoe, always ready for new experiences in his travels, describes his arrival by ferry from the Wirral:

> You land on the flat shore on the other Side, and must be content to ride thro' the water for some length, not on Horseback, but on the shoulders of some Lancashire Clown, who comes knee-deep to the Boat's side, to truss one up; and then runs away more nimbly than one desires to ride, unless his Trot were easier.

Having arrived dryshod, he was favourably impressed with all he saw, noting not only the 'prodigious Increase of Trade' but also that 'there is no town in England, except London, that can equal Liverpoole for the Fineness of the Streets and Beauty of the Buildings' (*A Tour Through the Whole Island of Great Britain*, 1724–7).

William Roscoe, author of *The Life of Lorenzo de' Medici* (1795) and *The Life and Pontificate of Leo the Tenth* (1805), as well as poems, including the piece for children *The Butterfly's Ball and the Grasshopper's Feast* (1807), was born (8 Mar. 1753) in **Mount Pleasant** (the subject of another poem), and later lived at 51 Lord St., Islington, Allerton Hall, and Lodge Lane, where he died.

Another native was Mrs Felicia Dorothea Hemans (née Browne), the daughter of a merchant, who began writing poetry at an early age and achieved great popularity in her day. She was born (25 Sept. 1793) at 118 **Duke St.** Ⓟ and lived there until the family moved to North Wales *c*. 1800. She had already made her name as a poet (*The Forest Sanctuary*, 1826, was one of her best works) when she returned to Liverpool in 1827 to further the education of her five sons (her husband having settled permanently abroad). She lived in a Georgian house (demolished 1958) on the N side of Wavertree High St., near the junction of Sandown Lane, leaving finally for Dublin in 1831.

Hazlitt briefly visited Liverpool in 1790 and, while staying with a Mrs Tracy, the wife of a West India merchant, saw his first play, *Love in Many Masks*, with the farce *No Song, No Supper*, and wrote his first drama criticism in a letter to his father.

In 1801 De Quincey stayed with his mother at Mrs Best's Cottage, **Everton** (at that time a pleasant little village), and again in 1803, when he first wrote to Wordsworth (31 May), a letter of homage and praise of *Lyrical Ballads*, to which the latter replied briefly and self-deprecatingly (though he wrote again, more fully, the following year when De Quincey was at Oxford). Liverpool fascinated De Quincey by its concourse of strangers from overseas: he called it 'the many-languaged town'.

Washington Irving's literary connection with Liverpool was tenuous, but it could be claimed that a business failure there *c*. 1818 led to the writing of 'Rip Van Winkle' (*The Sketch-Book*, 1820). Irving had joined his brother in the Goree Arcade as a merchant, but the venture failed and he sank into acute depression, which was relieved only by a visit to his brother-in-law at *Birmingham, where he took to writing.

Arthur Hugh Clough was born (1 Jan. 1819) at 9 **Rodney St.** Ⓟ, the son of a cotton merchant, but went to America with his family at the age of 4. He returned to England to be educated at Rugby and Oxford, and was back in Liverpool in 1836 for a time, living at 51 **Vine St.**

When William Cobbett returned in November 1819 from his second visit to America he caused great excitement at the **Custom House** by having the bones of Tom Paine in his luggage. He had exhumed these from a patch of unconsecrated ground near New York, where Paine had been buried (1809), with the intention, advertised in the *Political Register*, of raising money to build a mausoleum to house them in England as an object of pilgrimage, but instead of

Liverpool Playhouse
The oldest repertory theatre in the country; Noël Coward and Gertrude Lawrence first worked together here, and more recently it has featured important new work by, among others, Alan Bleasdale and Willy Russell

Walker Art Gallery

Royal Liver Building

Dale Street
Melville stayed at the White Bear Hotel in 1856 when he was visiting Nathaniel Hawthorne

DALE STREET

VICTORIA STREET

LONDON ROAD

LIME STREET

Lime Street Station

THE STRAND

Cavern Club

HANOVER STREET

RENSHAW STREET

RODNEY STREET

Customs House
William Cobbett turned up here in 1819 with the recently exhumed bones of Thomas Paine. The building has been destroyed; the site is now Chavasse Park

DUKE STREET

Rodney Street
Arthur Hugh Clough was born here in 1819, and lived later at 51 Vine Street. In 1838 Dickens made his first visit to Liverpool with his illustrator, 'Phiz', whose son was an oculist here on Rodney Street

Tate Gallery

PARK LANE

118 Duke Street
Poet Felicia Dorothy Hemans was born here in 1793

Mount Street
Adrian Henri lived here, and died here in 2000. With his fellow 'Mersey Sound' poets Roger McGough and Brian Patten he would be awarded the freedom of the city

RIVER MERSEY

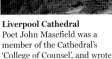

Coburg Docks
Dickens set off for the US from here in 1842, and described the departure at the start of his travelogue *American Notes for General Circulation*

Liverpool Cathedral
Poet John Masefield was a member of the Cathedral's 'College of Counsel', and wrote poems about it

LIVERPOOL

subscriptions he received only ridicule, as in Byron's lines:

> In digging up your bones, Tom Paine,
> Will. Cobbett has done well;
> You visit him on earth again,
> He'll visit you in hell.

Transatlantic visitors continued to come and go throughout the 19th c. Ralph Waldo Emerson, American philosopher and poet, came (1848) to lecture on his second visit to England. His six lectures on 'Representative Men', given at the Mount St. Mechanics Institute, were published in 1850. Herman Melville, American writer of stories of the sea, and remembered especially for his novel *Moby-Dick, or, The Whale* (1851), stayed here for a time in 1837 when a cabin boy on a sailing ship, drawing on his experiences later in his novel *Redburn* (1849). He was back again in 1856 for 10 days, en route for Constantinople, when he stayed at the White Bear Hotel, **Dale St.**, and visited Nathaniel Hawthorne, who was US Consul (1853–7). In *Our Old Home* (1863), Hawthorne describes the Consulate, which he detested, as

> located in Washington Buildings, (a shabby and smoke-stained edifice of four stories high, thus illustriously named in honour of our national establishment) at the lower corner of Brunswick St., contiguous to the Goree Arcade, and in the neighbourhood of some of the oldest docks.

His landlady Mrs Blodget, with whom he lodged in 1853 and in the winter of 1855–6, lived at 153 (formerly 133) Duke St. Mrs Harriet Beecher Stowe came on a visit in 1853 and stayed with Mr Cropper, a brother-in-law of Matthew Arnold, at **Dingle Bank**—'a beautiful little retreat on the banks of the Mersey'.

Dickens was a frequent visitor to the city. He first came in 1838 with Hablot K. Browne ('Phiz', his illustrator), whose son was an oculist in Rodney St. At one time Dickens enrolled as a special constable in order to investigate the 'home industry' of separating the sailors from their money. This, and a description of a workhouse he visited (gone), are recorded in *The Uncommercial Traveller* (1860). He appeared as an actor in benefit performances at various premises, including the Theatre Royal (gone), and over the years, until almost the end of his life, he gave readings of his works to packed houses in the Philharmonic Hall, St George's Hall Concert Room, the Theatre Royal, and elsewhere. *Nicholas Nickleby* (1839) and *Martin Chuzzlewit* (1844) have references to a famous Liverpool character, Sarah Biffin, an armless artist who painted miniatures with a brush in her mouth (she was not legless, as Dickens believed).

The Scottish-born novelist Mrs Margaret Oliphant spent her adolescence in Liverpool, where her father was a Customs official. Her first novel, *Passages in the Life of Mrs. Margaret Maitland* (1849), was written here. Augustine Birrell, critic and essayist, was born (1850) in **Wavertree**, the son of a Baptist

minister, but the house is not recorded. Richard Le Gallienne was born (1866) at 55 Prescot St. and later moved with his family to *Birkenhead. According to one of his publishers 'he looked more like a poet than any man has ever looked before or since'.

Matthew Arnold was in Liverpool in 1888 to meet his daughter on her return from the US when he died suddenly of a heart attack, but there are different accounts of the place and manner of his death: in one it was thought that he collapsed as he was running to catch a tram to the landing stage, where he was to meet his daughter's ship; in another that he strained his heart by jumping over a gate or fence while staying with his brother-in-law at Dingle Bank and died suddenly on his way back from church, but it seems that records are confused. The primary school at Dingle Lane is called after him.

John Masefield was a cadet (1891–4) on the training ship *Conway* (see the description of Liverpool in his semi-autobiographical *New Chum*, 1944). He wrote many poems connected with Liverpool, among them 'The Valediction (Liverpool Docks)' (1902); 'The Wanderer of Liverpool' (about a four-masted 3,000-ton barque laid down in 1890) and 'A Masque of Liverpool' (both 1930); and a poem to mark the opening of the **Cathedral**'s new doors in 1949 (he had a stall in the Cathedral as a member of the College of Counsel). In 1911 the production of John Galsworthy's play *Strife* at Kelly's Theatre (destroyed 1941) led to the emergence of the **Liverpool Playhouse**, the oldest repertory theatre in the country. The first UK performance of Samuel Beckett's *Happy Days* (1974) took place here.

When George Orwell was touring in the N of England in 1935, gathering material for *The Road to Wigan Pier* (1937), he was interested to see some blocks of workers' flats in corporation housing estates (St Andrew's Gdns, **Brownlow Hill**), which struck him as being modelled on the contemporary pioneer flats in Vienna.

Robert Noonan, the house painter of Irish extraction who wrote *The Ragged Trousered Philanthropists* (1914, 1955) under the pen-name 'Robert Tressell', came to Liverpool after leaving *Hastings. He is believed to have died of tuberculosis (1911) and was buried in a pauper's grave in **Walton**.

Two distinguished men of letters had chairs at the **University**: A. C. Bradley, remembered chiefly as a Shakespearian scholar (*Shakespearean Tragedy*, 1904), was Liverpool's first Professor of Literature and History (1882–9), and Sir James Frazer, author of *The Golden Bough* (1890–1915), was Professor of Social Anthropology (1907–22). Lytton Strachey was an undergraduate (1897–9), lodging at 80 Rodney St., but was lonely and unhappily self-conscious about his appearance—he wanted to be a superman, but felt he was a freak. Professor Walter Raleigh, under whom he studied English Literature, recommended him to Trinity College, Cambridge, as a student of remarkable distinction.

The Brown, Picton, and Hornby libraries, containing together more than 200,000 volumes, are housed in the **Central Library** (largely rebuilt since the Second World War) in **William Brown St**. The Hornby Library has a fine autograph collection, including poems by Johnson and Cowper. The Walker Art Gallery next door has a link with D. H. Lawrence. He corresponded at one time with a Liverpool girl called Blanche Jennings, who, in return for a photograph of himself, sent him a reproduction of Maurice Greiffenhagen's *The Idyll*, which belongs to the gallery. The picture is discussed in *The White Peacock* (1911).

Liverpool has had two MPs who were also literary figures: Sir Francis Bacon (1588–92) and William Roscoe (1806–7).

The novelist Barbara Pym was educated at Liverpool College for Girls at **Huyton** (later Huyton College), near Huyton railway station. Her unremarkable schooldays are recalled in *Excellent Women* (1952):

> My heart sank as I recognised the familiar landmarks. I could almost imagine myself a schoolgirl again, arriving at the station on a wet September evening for the autumn term and smelling the antiseptic smell of the newly scrubbed cloakrooms.

The Liverpool-born, Liverpool-educated poets Roger McGough and Brian Patten, along with Adrian Henri, who moved over to the city from Birkenhead in 1957, came to be known as the Liverpool Poets, a dynamic group determined to keep poetry accessible to its public. They collaborated on an anthology, *The Mersey Sound* (1967).

Henri's poems in *The Mersey Sound* included 'Liverpool Poems' and 'Christ's Entry into Liverpool':

> City morning, dandelionseeds blowing from
>   wasteground.
> smell of overgrown privethedges, children's voices
> in the distance, sounds from the river.
> round the corner into Myrtle St. Saturdaymorning
>   shoppers
> headscarves, shoppingbaskets, dogs.
> then
>   down the hill
>   THE SOUND OF TRUMPETS . . .

More than 30 years later Henri was still living in Liverpool, on **Mount St.**; he was granted the freedom of the city on 19 December 2000, and died the next day. The freedom was granted to his fellow Liverpool Poets McGough and Patten the following year.

To be near her lover Adrian Henri the poet Carol Ann Duffy came to the city to read Philosophy at the University of Liverpool in the 1970s. The novelist Barry Unsworth was writer in residence at the University from 1984 to 1985. His inability to write a novel about the city's associations with the slave trade eventually resulted in *Sugar and Rum* (1988)— about a contemporary writer's inability to write about the city's associations with the slave trade. The original subject later bore fruit in his novel *Sacred Hunger* (1992), where the

Liverpool Merchant is built in Liverpool and sets sail for the West Indies. The first part of the novel evokes the streets of the 18th-c. city.

The novelist Beryl Bainbridge was born in Liverpool in 1934, and educated here (at the **Merchant Taylors' School**) and set much of her early work here; the wartime scenes of *The Dressmaker* (1973) take place in the city, and *Young Adolf*, published in 1978, imagines a visit by the young Hitler to Merseyside. Bainbridge's experience working at the Liverpool Repertory Theatre informed the novel *An Awfully Big Adventure* (1989), which is narrated by a Liverpool rep company assistant stage manager during a production of *Peter Pan*.

The novelist Alice Thomas Ellis was born in Liverpool in 1932, and educated at **Liverpool School of Art**. The playwright Alan Bleasdale was born and educated in Liverpool too, in 1946. His TV play *The Boys from the Blackstuff* (1982) examines the lives of unemployed men on Merseyside; in the episode *George's Last Ride*, an ailing George is brought back to the **Albert Docks** where he used to work:

Forty-seven years ago, I stood here, a young bull, and watched my first ship come in . . . They say that memories live longer than dreams . . . But my dreams, those dreams, those dreams of long ago, they still give me some kind of hope and faith in my class . . . I can't believe there is no hope, I can't.

And it is on this spot filled with memories that he dies.

Long Sleddale *Cumbria*

Narrow valley, 7 m. long, off the A6, 4 m. N of Kendal, in which Mrs Humphry Ward set the first part of her novel *Robert Elsmere* (1888), under the name 'Long Whindale'. At the head of the valley, where the road is only a rough track, is Low Sadgill, a lonely farmhouse which became 'High Ghyll', the home of Mary Backhouse, whose illness brings together Catherine and Robert Elsmere.

Lowick *Cumbria*

Small village a few miles S of Coniston Water, on a minor road between the A5084. Arthur Ransome was lord of the manor (1947–9) when he lived at Lowick Hall, a manorial hall dating from Norman times, which he worked on and greatly improved during his short residence.

Manchester *Greater Manchester*

Great commercial city and capital of the cotton-manufacturing district formerly in SE Lancashire; with the opening of the Ship Canal in 1894 the first major inland port in the world. In the Civil War it withstood a Royalist siege in 1642, but in 1715 and again in 1745, when Prince Charles Edward Stuart occupied the town, it showed Jacobite sympathies (see Shenstone's ballad 'Jemmy Dawson'). When it was still known as 'the largest village in the country' it was the home of John Byrom, Jacobite poet and inventor of a system of

shorthand. His loyalties are discreetly worded in 'To an Officer in the Army':

God bless the King, I mean the Faith's Defender;
God bless—no harm in blessing—the Pretender;
But who Pretender is, or who is King,
God bless us all—that's quite another thing.

Byrom wrote the hymn 'Christians awake' for his daughter Dorothy. It was originally entitled 'Christmas Day—for Dolly' and it seems likely that it was sung in the street of the Byrom house in Hanging Ditch in 1750. Byrom was born (1692) in the house now called the Old Wellington inn, in the old marketplace, lived in **St John St.**, and was buried in the Cathedral.

There has been doubt about the birthplace of De Quincey, but according to local records he was born (15 Aug. 1785) in a small house on the corner of the former Tasle St. and **Red Cross St.**, near his father's place of business in the city, on the corner of Cross St. and John Dalton St. (Ⓟ above first-floor window on Cross St. frontage). He was baptized in St Ann's Church nearby and was taken when a few weeks old to The Farm, Moss Side, 'a pretty rustic dwelling'. In 1791 he moved with his family to Green Heys, a large country house (demolished 1852), 2 m. NW of the city centre, built and furnished by his father for *c.* £6,000. After his father's death in 1792 he stayed on with his mother for four years and then, after boarding for a short time with his tutor, the Revd Samuel Hall, followed her to Bath. In 1800 he went to Manchester Grammar School, but found the monotonous routine irksome and, when his guardians refused to remove him, ran away in 1802 and went to Chester (travelling on foot in two days) to stay with his mother. He wrote 'Vision of Sudden Death' in a Manchester tavern.

Charles Swain, an engraver who wrote poetry in his leisure time, was born (1803) in **Every St.**, **off Gt Ancoats St.**, and died at his house, Prestwich Park. He is buried in Prestwich churchyard, with a memorial in the church. Many of his lyrics were set to music, including the popular 'When the Heart Is Young' and 'I cannot mind my wheel, mother'. He also wrote 'Dryburgh Abbey, a Poem on the Death of Sir Walter Scott' (1832). There are portraits of Swain in Salford Museum.

William Harrison Ainsworth, the son of a solicitor, was born (4 Feb. 1805) at 21 (now 57) **King St.** Ⓟ He went to Manchester Grammar School, of which he gave an interesting and accurate account in *Mervyn Clitheroe* (1851). He was articled to a solicitor, but on his father's death in 1824 went to finish his legal education in London, and soon afterwards turned from law to literature. On 15 September 1881, near the end of a prolific writing career, he was entertained by the mayor of Manchester at a banquet in the Town Hall 'as an expression of the high esteem in which he was held by his fellow-townsmen and of his services to literature'.

Elizabeth Gaskell came to Manchester in 1832 after her marriage to William Gaskell, minister of Cross St. Unitarian Chapel and

lecturer on English Literature at Owens College. They lived first at 14 **Dover St.**, Oxford Rd (gone), then (1842–9) at 121 Upper Rumford St. (gone), and finally at 84 **Plymouth Grove** (Ⓟ; currently under restoration, but with occasional open days: www.thegaskellhouse.org), a large family house where visitors were welcomed, including distinguished writers such as Charlotte Brontë, Dickens, Carlyle, and Mrs Harriet Beecher Stowe. *Mary Barton, a Tale of Manchester Life* (1848), her first novel, which brought her immediate success, and *North and South* (published serially in *Household Words*, 1854–5) are stories of industrial life and the struggle as she saw it of working people to obtain their rights. Dickens, who admired her work and shared her interests in social reform, also used a Manchester setting for his novel *Hard Times* (1854). On a visit in 1837 he was introduced by Harrison Ainsworth to a solicitor named Gilbert Winter, at whose home, Stock House (gone) in **Cheetham Hill Rd**, he met William and Daniel Grant, on whom he is said to have modelled the Cheeryble Brothers in *Nicholas Nickleby* (1838–9). He was in Manchester again in 1852, when he visited the Gaskells and was for a time both theatrical manager and actor at the Free Trade Hall. In June 1851 Charlotte Brontë paid her first visit to the Gaskells, for a couple of days on her way home from London. It was very hot and the only thing she made a point of doing was to buy a shawl as a present for Tabby, the old family servant at *Haworth. Before she had met Elizabeth Gaskell, Charlotte Brontë had already stayed in Manchester, where she had brought her father in August 1846 for a cataract operation. They stayed in lodgings at 83 Mount Pleasant, now **Boundary Lane**, Oxford Rd (gone; Ⓟ on site), then a quiet terrace of brick houses, and arranged their own board, about which Charlotte found herself excessively ignorant: 'I can't tell what to order in the way of meat,' she wrote in a letter. It was here that she began *Jane Eyre* (1847), at the very time when *The Professor* (1857, published posthumously) was being rejected by one publisher after another. They returned home at the end of September. In 1853 Elizabeth Gaskell had a visit from Harriet Beecher Stowe, whose anti-slavery novel *Uncle Tom's Cabin* (1852) was creating widespread interest. Mrs Stowe describes the visit 'to the author of *Mary Barton*' in her *Sunny Memories of Foreign Lands* (1854). Mrs Molesworth (Mary Louisa Stewart), writer of children's books, came to Manchester when she was 2 (1841) and stayed until she was married 20 years later. She was a pupil of William Gaskell at Plymouth Grove. Her home, 92 **Rusholme Rd**, is described in *Little Miss Peggy* (1887) and in the beginning of *The Carved Lions* (1895).

George Macdonald, a Congregational minister who turned to literature *c.* 1856 and became a lay member of the Church of England, lived (from 1854) at 3 Camp Ter., **Lower Broughton**, before he moved to London. He wrote numerous novels, including

Elizabeth Gaskell and Manchester

In Elizabeth Gaskell's fiction—and in her *Life of Charlotte Brontë*—particular places function almost as an attribute of character and often provide a subtle moral comment upon the action. Perhaps the most striking example is *North and South* (1855), where contrasting places are integral to the novel's argument. We first meet Margaret Hale in a London drawing room, then in a rose-embowered vicarage, and tramping the glades of the New Forest:

> crushing down the fern with a cruel glee, as she felt it yield to her light foot, and send up the fragrance peculiar to it, out on the broad commons into the warm scented light, seeing multitudes of wild, free, living creatures, revelling in the sunshine, and the herbs and flowers it called forth.

When the Hales move north, Margaret's first impression of Milton (an epic stand-in for Manchester) is the absence of 'warm scented light'. First comes a leaden cloud, then 'the taste and smell of smoke', less a positive scent than 'a loss of the fragrance of grass and herbage'. Her error, as she is whirled into the streets and mills, is to judge the people chiefly in terms of the sombre townscape. It takes time for her to recognize their energy and romance and see through her picturesque image of the South to the harsh dullness of its agricultural life.

Margaret's sense of being wrenched from a free, open life reflects Gaskell's own feelings when she moved to Manchester in 1832 on her marriage to the young Unitarian minister of Cross Street Chapel, William Gaskell. She was shocked by the dirt, disease, and overcrowding, and in 'Lizzie Leigh', her first short story for Dickens's *Household Words*, she followed the life of a prostitute in the dark streets. Feeling that the industrial city was almost a foreign land to the southern middle classes, in *Mary Barton* (1848) she used setting to dramatize the lives of its people, taking her readers into a range of dwellings, each defining its owner: the Bartons' artisan cottage, gradually stripped of its small fineries, like the red lacquer tray; old Alice's basement, hung with healing herbs; Job Legh's room, where *Principia* lies open on the loom, and which seems like a wizard's chamber with its instruments and impaled insects.

Gaskell drives home the novel's moral vision of the gulf between rich and poor by the juxtaposition of the mill owner Carson's fine house and the Davenports' cellar:

> with a grating instead of a window, down which dropped the moisture from pigstyes, and worse abominations. It was not paved; the floor was one mass of bad smelling mud. It had never been used, for there was not an article of furniture in it; nor could a human being, much less a pig, have lived there many days.

This is an inner circle of hell, where the poor 'need only a Dante to describe their woes'. Gaskell knew all sides of

ELIZABETH GASKELL BY GEORGE RICHMOND, 1851

Manchester life, since the Unitarian congregation contained mill owners and professionals, but also ran Sunday schools for workers, and missions to the destitute. But her fondness for the place was always tinged with revulsion: she was pleased to move to her new house at Plymouth Grove, on the fringes of the town, and in later life she spent more and more time away: abroad, in the South, or in the country.

Gaskell had grown up in Knutsford, Cheshire, and she brilliantly re-creates the life of the small country town in *Cranford* (1853), and in the dense texture of *Wives and Daughters* (1866). But her most cherished rural image was her grandparents' farm at Sandlebridge, a few miles away. Staying here in May 1836, she told her sister-in-law:

> Fancy me sitting in an old fashioned parlour 'doors and windows opened wide', with casement window opening into a sunny court all filled with flowers which scent the air with their fragrance—in the very depth of the country—5 miles for the least approach to a town—the song of the birds, the hum of insects, the lowing of cattle the only sounds.

The pastoral ideal is at its most intense in *Cousin Phillis* (1864), where Gaskell makes us feel that we know every field and path around Hope Farm, with its woodpile and byre, its snowy tiles and crimson hearthrug, and the great clock going 'tick-tick' in the stillness of the house. In the overflowing vegetable garden—an Eden-like profusion behind a sheltering wall—roses compete with strawberries, and in the autumn great bushes of Michaelmas daisies, and yellow leaves ready to fall at a puff of air, hang over the great clothes baskets full of apples. The problem, as this story makes all too clear, is that one can never return to such an idyll. Time and human frailty cast us out.

Places are at once detached from human destinies and expressive of them. Gaskell's young heroine Ruth, in the novel of the same name, is seduced amid the Welsh mountains, a landscape of staggering, indifferent grandeur. But when she later encounters her seducer Bellingham, the father of her son, it is on a wide seashore, the margin of the safe land: 'It seemed as if weights were tied to her feet—as if the steadfast rocks receded, as if time stood still—it was so long, so terrible, that path across the reeling sand.' Here we are in an almost Bunyanesque landscape. Place ceases to be a suggestive external setting, and forms the inner landscape of psychic drama, as in *Lois the Witch* (1859), set in New England at the time of the witch trials, where Lois contrasts the safe Warwickshire lanes she has left to 'the great wood with its perpetual movement of branch and bough, and its solemn wail, that came into the very streets of Salem when certain winds blew'.

Gaskell is a realist, allowing us to see and savour every detail of houses, rooms, gardens, and hills. But she is also a Romantic, using place to create a poetic context that carries the underlying themes of her fiction, and painting a rich and varied landscape of the mind. JENNY UGLOW

❖

David Elginbrod (1862), *Alex Forbes* (1865), and *Robert Falconer* (1868), as well as some delightful fairy stories, such as *The Princess and the Goblin* (1872), *At the Back of the North Wind* (1871), and 'The Light Princess'.

Frances Hodgson Burnett, author of some 40 books, but best remembered for *Little Lord Fauntleroy* (1886), was born (24 Nov. 1849) at 141 York St. (later Cheetham Hill Rd) (original house probably demolished) and moved in 1852 to 9 St Luke's Ter. (now 385 Cheetham Hill Rd; Ⓟ). After the death of her father, Edwin Hodgson, in 1853 the family fortunes declined and in 1855 she moved with her family to a house in a poorer district, 19 **Islington Sq.** (gone), Salford, where she lived until they all emigrated (1856) to Knoxville, Tennessee. Another native writer, of a very different kind, was Nathaniel Gould, who left school to enter the tea trade, but became a journalist and, while living in Australia (1884–95), a novelist. Nearly all his novels were about horse racing.

Charles Edward Montague came to Manchester in 1890 as a journalist. He joined the staff of the *Manchester Guardian* and worked for it (except for his years of war service) until his retirement in 1925. His first novel (originally a play, 1900), *A Hind Let Loose* (1910), is an entertaining account of a journalist who writes for two papers of conflicting political views. Montague was made an Hon. D.Litt. of Manchester University in 1926. He was in Manchester for the University Founders' Day celebrations in 1928 when he caught a chill and died at his father-in-law's house, The Firs, Fallowfield, near his old home in **Oak Drive**. He was cremated at the city crematorium and his ashes were taken to *Burford for burial.

John Hay Beith ('Ian Hay'), novelist and playwright, son of a Manchester cotton merchant of Scottish descent, was born (17 Apr. 1876) on the corner of **Wilmslow Rd** and Norman Rd, Rusholme. He began writing novels and plays in 1907 under the pen-name 'Ian Hay' and continued while serving with the British Expeditionary Force in the First World War, when his humorous novels about service conditions were very popular. In all he wrote 27 novels and more than 20 plays, of which the following are perhaps the best known: *Tilly of Bloomsbury* (1919), *The Willing Horse* (1921), *Leave it to Psmith* (with P. G. Wodehouse, 1930), and *The Housemaster* (1936). In the Second World War he was Director of Public Relations at the War Office with the rank of major-general.

Howard Spring came to Manchester from Cardiff and was a journalist on the *Manchester Guardian* from 1915 until 1931, when he moved to London. After his marriage in 1920 he lived at 26 **Hesketh Ave.** Ⓟ, Didsbury, until 1931, and of this period he wrote, 'I came to love Manchester as I have known and loved no other city.' His career as a novelist began with *Shabby Tiger* (1934), followed by a dozen others, of which the best known is *Fame Is the Spur* (1940).

Two late 19th-c. writers were students at Owens College, incorporated (1871) in the **University** and transferred from its original site in Quay St. (Ⓟ on County Court) in 1873; one was the novelist George Gissing, a brilliant student (specializing in Greek and Latin) whose academic career began in 1872 and was cut short because of petty thefts to help a girl he loved; the other was the poet Francis Thompson, who studied Medicine reluctantly (1877–83) and left without a degree. The University Library has a permanent exhibition of editions of their works and also those of Elizabeth Gaskell.

Manchester Grammar School (founded 1515) was moved from its original site beside Chetham's Hospital in 1931 to Birchfields Rd (a continuation of Upper Brook St.), Rusholme. As well as De Quincey and Harrison Ainsworth, mentioned above, its distinguished pupils include William Stanley Houghton, author of the farce *The Dear Departed* (1908) and the more famous *Hindle Wakes* (1912); and Louis Golding, born in Red Bank, Cheetham, whose best-known novels of life in the city were *Magnolia Street* (1931) and *Five Silver Daughters* (1934).

George Orwell stayed at 49 **Brynton Rd**, Longsight, in February 1936 on his way to Wigan, as he recounts in his diary (31 Jan.–25 Mar. 1936). This typescript diary formed the basis of *The Road to Wigan Pier* (1937) and was printed in his *Collected Essays, Journalism, and Letters* (ed. S. Orwell and I. Angus, 1968).

Jane Rogers's novel *The Voyage Home* (2004) moves between Nigeria and England; the principal character, Anne Harrington, is an artist who has an exhibition of her work staged at **Manchester Central Library** in St Peter's Sq.

There are three libraries of special interest near the city centre in addition to the Central Library. The Portico Library in **Mosley St.**, established in 1806 as a social and literary institution, has rare first editions and was mentioned by De Quincey. A plaque records the names of famous readers, including De Quincey, Elizabeth Gaskell, and Peter Mark Roget. The last-named, best known for his *Thesaurus of English Words and Phrases* (1852), was appointed physician to Manchester Infirmary in 1804 and became the Library's first secretary. He was primarily a scientist with leanings to higher mathematics and did not devote his time to the *Thesaurus* until after he retired in 1840. Chetham's Library, near the Cathedral, established in 1653 under the will of Humphrey Chetham (1580–1653), claims to be the oldest free public library in England. It has a special collection of the works of John Byrom. Harrison Ainsworth wrote much of his early work at a table in the bow window, traditionally used by Sir Walter Ralegh. The

John Rylands Library, established in 1900 in Deansgate, was built and endowed by the widow of John Rylands (1801–88) in his memory. Its collection of rare bibles, books, and manuscripts, which includes the Althorp Library of the 5th Earl Spencer, is among the most valuable in the world. It became the John Rylands University Library of Manchester in 1973. It is open for exhibitions (www. library.manchester.ac.uk).

Elias Canetti lived at **Palatine Road** from 1911 to 1913 and attended school on Barlowmoor Rd. His two childhood years in the city are described in the first volume of his autobiography, *The Tongue Set Free* (1977).

The novelist, literary journalist, and composer Anthony Burgess (John Wilson), who has left a colourful account of his Manchester years in the first volume of his autobiography, *Little Wilson, Big God* (1987), was born at **Carisbrook St.**, Harpurley. His mother and sister both died in 1919, victims of the Spanish influenza pandemic, while Burgess lay 'chuckling in [his] cot'. He was moved to live with his aunt in a terraced house on **Delauneys Rd**, Higher Crumpsall. 'Opposite the house', recalled Burgess, 'was a great infirmary where, I learned, people were cut open.' His father played the piano at the Golden Eagle, 'a boozer of Victorian amplitude' on Lodge St., Miles Platting, and married the widowed landlady. Burgess came to live at the pub as a child, sleeping at first in a truckle bed in the room belonging to Harry, the resident barman. His father and stepmother later ran a shop at 21 **Princess Rd**, Moss Side, which sold tobacco and chocolates, its stockroom filled with the 'strong odour of the pinewood of Swan matches'. Burgess went to school at the Xaverian College on Wilmslow Rd in the Rusholme district of the city, and later read English at Manchester University (then the Victorian University of Manchester). His tutor was L. C. Knights, a contributor to F. R. Leavis's journal *Scrutiny* and the author of, among other books on Shakespeare, *How Many Children Had Lady Macbeth?* The novelist Barry Unsworth studied English at Manchester University in the 1950s.

W. G. Sebald came to Manchester as an assistant lecturer at the University in 1966, staying in a hotel on an alley off **Great Bridgewater St.** His desolate impressions of the post-industrial city are conveyed by the narrator of *The Emigrants* (1992): 'I passed a long-disused gasworks, a coal depot, a bonemill, and what seemed the unending cast-iron palisade fence of the Ordsall slaughterhouse, a Gothic castle in liver-coloured brick . . .'. Near Old Trafford he meets the obscure painter and Jewish exile Max Ferber, a man 'closer to dust' than light, air, or water. In 1944 Ferber had stayed at 104 Palatine Rd, where, some 36 years earlier, Ludwig Wittgenstein had also lived.

The novelist and critic Malcolm Bradbury did his Ph.D. at Manchester University, and the playwright David Edgar studied drama here too; in 2007 the novelist Martin Amis was appointed the University's Professor of Creative Writing.

The novelists Howard Jacobson and Livi Michael were both born in Manchester too, in 1942 and 1960, respectively. Michael's novel *Inheritance* (2000) is set on the outskirts of the city.

The Shakespeare Garden in **Platt Fields Park**, Rusholme, near the Grangethorpe Rd turning off Wilmslow Rd, is a quiet place of unique appeal. It is an Elizabethan-style walled garden, with narrow paths between formal beds of flowers and herbs, sheltered by shrubs and trees, and reputedly contains all the plants mentioned in Shakespeare's works and nothing that is not mentioned.

Manchester is the 'Drumble' of Elizabeth Gaskell's *Cranford* (1851–3) and the 'Doomington' of Louis Golding's *Magnolia Street* (1931).

MARPLE *Greater Manchester*

Village now in the SE corner of Greater Manchester. Christopher Isherwood was born at Wybersley Hall, High Lane, in 1904. The house was traditionally used by the elder sons of the Bradshaw-Isherwood family, and was tied to Marple Hall, a large 17th-c. house and the Isherwood family seat. Isherwood's restless and rebellious temperament may be traced in part back to the conservative atmosphere his mother created at the house in the aftermath of the First World War (in which Isherwood's father had been killed). He inherited the Hall in 1940 (while living in California), but passed it on to his brother Richard the following year. It fell into disrepair in the 1950s and was pulled down—an action not at all regretted by Isherwood. The grounds are now occupied by Marple Hall School. Isherwood set parts of *The Memorial* (1932) in a house based on Marple Hall.

MAUGHOLD (pr. 'Măckold) *Isle of Man*

Village 2 m. SE of Ramsey. T. E. Brown, who married his cousin here in 1858, considered it one of the three places dearest to his heart. After he retired as a schoolmaster, he settled at 10 Windsor Mount, Ramsey, a few miles to the E.

During his youth Hall Caine often stayed with his uncle in the Schoolhouse, which had a rounded end like a lighthouse. When he was 17 his uncle died and for almost a year Hall Caine took his uncle's place as schoolmaster. After his death at Greeba Castle, Hall Caine, who had once planned to be buried on the headland, was interred in the churchyard (1931), where a tall Celtic cross, engraved with characters from his novels, was later erected.

MILLOM *Cumbria*

Small former iron-working town on the Duddon estuary. Apart from two years spent in a hospital in Hampshire in the 1930s (where, during treatment for tuberculosis, he had a lung removed) the poet Norman Nicholson spent his whole life in Millom, never moving from his parents' house at 14 St George's Ter.

Ⓟ. He attended the Methodist church as a child, but converted to Anglicanism at the age of 22. His chief subject was the landscape of Cumbria and Millom itself: 'To me Millom is the world. It is society writ small. It is the history of the last century or so, of the first phase of the industrial revolution—of boom and decline.' The old iron-ore industry in and around the town is the subject of criticism and lament in poems such as 'On the Dismantling of Millom Ironworks' and 'Hodbarrow Flooded':

> Old winding towers
> Up-ended float on glass
> Where once the shafts struck down through yielding limestone,
> Black coot and moorhen
> Lay snail-wakes on the water.

Other poems, such as 'Scafell Pike' ('Rock-pie of volcanic lava') and the 'grey millipede on slow stone hooves' that marches over the fells in 'Wall', celebrate more enduring aspects of the Cumbrian scene. Nicholson's boyhood years are vividly recalled in his memoir *Wednesday Early Closing* (1975). His life and work is recorded in a permanent display in the Folk Museum and there is a commemorative stained-glass window with imagery inspired by his poetry in St George's Church.

MORECAMBE *Lancashire*

Seaside resort town on Morecambe Bay. John Osborne spent May and June of 1955 performing in *Seagulls Over Sorrento* at Morecambe; sitting in a deckchair on the pier that summer he wrote much of the play that became *Look Back in Anger*.

NAB FARM *Cumbria*

Farm, also referred to as The Nab or Nab Cottage, on the N shore of Rydal Water, on the A591, *c.* 13 m. W of Rydal Mount. This was the home of Margaret Simpson, whom De Quincey used to visit when he was living at Dove Cottage and whom he married in Grasmere church in February 1817 after she had borne him a child the previous November. Although it was an enduring love match the union incurred the strong disapproval of the Wordsworths, especially Mary and Dorothy, who thought marriage between one of the gentry and a 'low-born woman' quite unsuitable. De Quincey resented their criticism, and his former happy relationship with them, already strained by his cutting down of hedges round Dove Cottage orchard and his increasing addiction to opium, came to an end. He maintained friendly relations with his father-in-law, however, and in 1829 became owner of Nab Farm, where his family were staying, in a complicated mortgage arrangement devised for their mutual benefit. But De Quincey was unable to keep up the payment of interest on the mortgage and in 1833 the farm had to be sold.

NEAR SAWREY *Cumbria*

Quiet village 2 m. SE of Hawkshead on the B5285, between Esthwaite Water and Lake Windermere. Hill Top (NT), behind the Tower

Bank Arms (pictured in *The Tale of Jemima Puddle-Duck*) and out of sight of the road, is the 17th-c. farmhouse bought by Beatrix Potter and bequeathed by her to the National Trust. In the summer of 1896 her parents, with whom she lived in London, had rented a furnished house called Lakeland (now a hotel) in the village, and she explored the neighbourhood with delight. Of Sawrey itself she wrote in her secret journal: 'It is as nearly perfect a little place as I ever lived in' (*The Journal of Beatrix Potter, 1881-1897*, transcribed from her code writings by Leslie Linder, 1966). When Hill Top Farm came on the market a few years later the royalties from *The Tale of Peter Rabbit* (1900), the first of her series of children's books, helped her to buy it, and by degrees her visits there became longer and more frequent until she broke right away from her family and made it her own home, where for the first time in her life she was really happy. Six of the now classic *Tales* are closely connected with Hill Top and Sawrey, especially *Tom Kitten* (1907), *Jemima Puddle-Duck* (1908), and *Samuel Whiskers, or, The Roly-Poly Pudding* (1908), and it is a joy to recognize their familiar features in the much-loved old house and its surroundings. After her marriage in 1913 to William Heelis, her solicitor, Beatrix Potter moved to Castle Cottage, a long, low house across the meadow at the other side of the road. Here she gave up writing and spent the next 30 years of her life concerned with farming matters, breeding sheep, and buying farm property eventually to be made over to the National Trust. Through her generosity and farsightedness over 4,000 acres in some of the most beautiful parts of the Lake District have been preserved for the nation.

OLDHAM *Greater Manchester*

Large town set amid the Pennines. The poet Simon Armitage worked here as a probation officer from 1988, and it has since also been home to the novelist Livi Michael.

PARKGATE *Cheshire*

Village on the B5135 on the W coast of the Dee estuary, former port for Ireland. It was after leaving here that Milton's friend Edward King, lamented in 'Lycidas', was drowned when his ship foundered on the way to Dublin, 10 August 1637. Swift referred to his arrival from Dublin in his first letter to Stella (*Journal to Stella*, 1710-13) from Chester in September 1710: 'I got a fall off my horse riding here from Parkgate, but no hurt; the horse understanding falls very well, and lying quietly till I got up.' De Quincey, writing from Ireland to his sister Jane on 3 September 1800, said:

> We shall sail [from Dublin] by the first Parkgate packet. . . . Parkgate is situated near Chester, on the River Dee, twice as far from Dublin as Holyhead. This passage is very dangerous . . . in general not more than three days . . . but sometimes much longer.

The long stretches of sand, subject to tidal flooding, are the scene of Kingsley's poem 'O Mary go and call the cattle home', which first appeared in his novel *Alton Locke* (1850). The hero hears an old air on the piano, 'wild and plaintive, rising and falling like the swell of an Æolian harp upon a distant breeze', and, searching for words to fit it, is inspired by a painting of the sands at the mouth of the Dee and the story of a girl who was drowned bringing home her father's cattle.

PARTINGTON *Greater Manchester*

Village between Manchester and Liverpool. Karl Forelock, hero of Howard Jacobson's novel *Redback* (1987), is Partington-born, and offers this defence:

> The town of Partington, for those who don't know it, hides itself in shame—pretending to be a village or hamlet—a little way off the East Lancashire Road, exactly equidistant from Manchester and Liverpool, between whom, in my day, it acted as a kind of industrial mediator, receiving the waste from one and passing it on sweetened and palatable to the other. Nothing noxious issued from Manchester or Liverpool without its turning up for treatment in Partington. The rivalry between these two great cities is legendary, but it would have been far worse without Partington. Think of Henry Kissinger keeping Egypt and Israel from each other's throat and you'll get the picture. Except that no one has paid Partington a small fortune for its memoirs.

PEEL *Isle of Man*

Fishing port and resort on the W coast, at the mouth of the Neb. The tower known as Fenella's Tower at Peel Castle was the place where Fenella, the beautiful girl who was pretending to be a deaf mute, jumped into the boat in Scott's *Peveril of the Peak* (1823).

PENRITH *Cumbria*

Old market town on the A6, bypassed by the M6. Wordsworth's mother, Ann Cookson, before her marriage to John Wordsworth, lived in her parents' house in the market square. Her father was a linen-draper and lived over his shop (still a draper's store, now called Arnison's, but rebuilt). As children, William and Dorothy and their brothers used to visit their grandparents and for a time attended a select and old-fashioned little dame school, but the atmosphere of the household was uncongenial and William, who was a high-spirited boy, found his grandparents and his Uncle Kit stern and unsympathetic. After the death of their father (1783) William and his brothers spent their school holidays at Penrith under the supervision of their uncle, who was especially unfriendly to William, with whom he had frequent clashes. Dorothy, who had been living with relations at Halifax after her mother's death in 1778, moved to Penrith in the summer of 1787 and was happy to be with her brothers, especially William, in the holidays. Together they used to explore the countryside, climb Penrith Beacon, and scramble over the ruins of Brougham Castle (1½ m. SE), and they renewed a friendship, begun in their early schooldays, with Mary Hutchinson and her sisters and youngest brother, who, also orphaned, were living with an aunt at Penrith. This friendship laid the foundation of an extraordinarily happy household when William married Mary (1802), and brought her to share his home with Dorothy at *Grasmere.

PRESTON *Lancashire*

Engineering and cotton-weaving city on the A6, with docks on the Ribble. Francis Thompson, a doctor's son, was born (16 Dec. 1859) at 7 Winckley St. (a bronze plaque has a portrait head in relief and a quotation from 'The Hound of Heaven'). He spent his early childhood here before the family moved (1864) to *Ashton-under-Lyne.

ROCHDALE *Greater Manchester*

Large town on the river Roch. In Vikram Seth's novel *An Equal Music* (1999), the main

St Patrick's Isle and Peel Castle, Isle of Man

protagonist, Michael, is from Rochdale. He remarks, 'When I say I come from Rochdale, people in London smile, as if the name itself were amusing. I no longer feel resentful, let alone puzzled by this . . .'.

ROCK FERRY *Merseyside*

Suburb of Birkenhead, on the A41. Nathaniel Hawthorne lived here 1853–5 when US consul at Liverpool, crossing the Mersey to his office by ferry. His house (gone) was in Rock Park, described by his son as 'a damp, winding, verdurous street, protected at each end by a small granite lodge, and studded throughout its length with stuccoed villas'. It was the starting place for many excursions in the Wirral and North Wales, recorded in Hawthorne's *Journal*.

RYDAL *Cumbria*

Little village on the A591, 2 m. NW of Ambleside. Just above the church a steep road leads up to Rydal Mount, the home of Wordsworth from 1813 until his death in 1850. Here he wrote almost half the poems published in his lifetime and established his reputation (he became Poet Laureate in 1843), and here he received visits from countless admirers and many distinguished writers, including Matthew Arnold, Henry Crabb Robinson, Ralph Waldo Emerson, Nathaniel Hawthorne, and William and Mary Howitt. In 1848 Swinburne, aged 11, was taken to visit Wordsworth. The old man treated the boy with kindly understanding and the latter was moved to tears by his parting words: 'I do not think, Algernon, that you will forget me.'

The house, dating from the mid- to late 16th c., was built by one John Keene as a yeoman-style farmhouse and enlarged by later owners in the 18th c. In 1812 it was owned by the le Flemings of Rydal Hall, the adjacent property, who let it to Wordsworth for a peppercorn rent in 1813. From 1969 it was owned by Mrs Mary Wordsworth Henderson, great-great-granddaughter of the poet, and it now belongs to her children and grandchildren, and is open to the public (www.rydalmount.co.uk). Much of the furniture is that used by the Wordsworth family, and William's study contains numerous first editions of his works, including that of *The White Doe of Rylstone*, published soon after he came here from Grasmere. Adjacent is 'Dora's field', which William bought at a time when he feared he might be turned out of Rydal Mount, so that he would be able to build a house on it: however, the tenancy was renewed and he gave the field to his daughter Dora. The 4 acres of fellside garden, with two long terraces and beautiful vistas between the trees, are much as they were when Wordsworth designed them.

SALFORD *Greater Manchester*

Old industrial city separated from Manchester by the river Irwell. In 1903 Walter Greenwood was born on Ellor St. and educated at Langworthy Rd School. His novel, later stage play, *Love on the Dole* (1933) is set in and around Hanky Park, its local streets 'polished by the boots and clogs of many generations', and evokes a Salford of the 1930s, a town of tiny houses, churches, chapels, pawnshops, and pubs; of 'nude, black patches of land, "crofts", as they are called, waterlogged, sterile, bleak and chill'; a place where 'forgetfulness lurks in a mug'. The novel did much in the period to win sympathy for the chronically unemployed. Hanky Park is also the setting for his memoir *There Was a Time* (1967).

SCALEBY CASTLE *Cumbria*

Castle 1 m. S of the village of Scaleby, between the B6264 and the A6071. William Gilpin was born here (4 June 1724), the son of Captain John Bernard Gilpin, and was educated at Carlisle and St Bees before going to Oxford.

SEDBERGH *Cumbria*

Small town at the foot of the Howgill Fells. The playwright and novelist John Arden attended Sedbergh School in the 1940s. Basil Bunting spent his childhood holidays near here at Briggflatts, and the place served as the inspiration for his best-known poem, 'Briggflatts', in which Northumbrian lives and landscapes make themselves heard:

> The moon sits on the fell
> but it will rain.
> Under sacks on the stone
> two children lie,
> hear the horse stale,
> the mason whistle,
> harness mutter to shaft,
> felloe to axle squeak,
> rut thud the rim,
> crushed grit.

The poet's ashes were strewn by the Quaker meeting house in 1985.

SELLAFIELD *Cumbria*

Nuclear power station (earlier called Windscale) near Seascale. The accident in 1957 at the nuclear power station and the secrecy which had surrounded the construction of its 'toadstool towers' angered the Cumbrian poet Norman Nicholson and inspired his poem 'Windscale'.

SILVERDALE *Lancashire*

Village on an unclassified road *c.* 5 m. NW of Carnforth (A6). Elizabeth Gaskell often came from Manchester and stayed at a house known as Lindeth, or Gibraltar Tower, in a secluded position next to Gibraltar Farm. Her study was at the top of the tower, commanding a magnificent view of Morecambe bay, and here she found the much-needed peace and privacy for writing many of her books. 'Abermouth' in *Ruth* (1853) is probably modelled on Silverdale. The village hall is called Gaskell Hall in her memory.

SOUTHPORT *Lancashire*

Well-built seaside resort and residential town on the A565, S of the Ribble estuary. Nathaniel Hawthorne stayed with his family from September 1856 to July 1857 in 'a tall stone-house, fronting on the sands, and styled "Brunswick Terrace"'. Herman paid them a two-day visit there. The sporting novelist Nathaniel Gould (1857–1919) was educated at Strathmore House School. Mary Webb (1881–1927), author of novels set in the background of her native Shropshire, spent two years (1897–9) at Mary Walmesley's school, Longsight, 1 Albert Rd. In 1901 the

Basil Bunting at Briggflatts, Cumbria

The house on Henley St., Stratford-upon-Avon, where Shakespeare was born in 1564 and where he lived until he left Stratford in or around 1585

Bulgarian-born Dikrān Kouyoumdjian (1895–1956) came to live at Southport, first at Rosslare, Park Rd, then Rosslare, 85 Hesketh Rd, and finally 6 Hesketh Rd. He became a naturalized British subject in 1922, taking the name Michael Arlen, and achieved outstanding success with his best-selling novel *The Green Hat* (1924).

THRELKELD *Cumbria*

Lakeland village, E of Keswick. W. H. Auden's family owned a holiday house at Wescoe, near Threlkeld quarry. As he grew up it was the fells and moors of the Pennines that made the greatest impression upon him. Auden's belief that 'rock creates the only truly human landscape' and his lifelong fascination with geology both find expression in his poem 'In Praise of Limestone'.

TUNSTALL *Lancashire*

Village on the A683, 4 m. S of Kirkby Lonsdale. When Charlotte and Emily Brontë were at school at *Cowan Bridge they used to come the 2¼ m. by the 'exposed and hilly road' to attend the parish church, where the Revd. William Carus Wilson, founder of the Clergy Daughters' School (1823), was vicar. After the morning service the girls were given food in the room above the porch. Charlotte depicts Tunstall as 'Brocklebridge' in *Jane Eyre* (1847).

TYNWALD (pr. Tĭnwald) HILL *Isle of Man*

Artificial mound off the A1, near Peel, seat of the old parliament, where new laws and names of officers appointed for the year are still announced in a ceremony held formerly on Midsummer Day, now 5 July. Wordsworth wrote a sonnet on the ceremony ('Tynwald Hill'), which is also described in Hall Caine's *The Deemster* (1887), his most popular novel.

WARRINGTON *Lancashire*

Large town to the E of Liverpool. Born in *Bury (to the NE), Richmal Crompton (author of *Just William* (1922) and its multiple sequels) studied here at St Elphin's Clergy Daughters' School, before moving to Darley Dale in Derbyshire. In 1915 she would return to the school to spend two years as a teacher.

Anthony Burgess was posted to the military hospital at Winwick near Warrington during the Second World War.

WHALLEY (pr. 'Whawli) *Lancashire*

Town on the Calder, on the A59 and the A671. The ruined Cistercian abbey is depicted in Harrison Ainsworth's *The Lancashire Witches* (1848). Ainsworth stayed (1848) with Archdeacon Rushton at the vicarage at Newchurch-in-Pendle, a small village *c.* 6 m. NE, in the Forest of Pendle, while he was gathering material for the novel. Pendle appears in the story as 'Goldshaw'.

Stonyhurst College, a Roman Catholic (Jesuit) school for boys (founded at St Omer,

1594, and transferred here in 1794), is situated 4 m. NW of Whalley, off the B6243. The nucleus of the buildings is the Elizabethan mansion built by Sir Richard Shireburn in 1594–1606. The library contains an ancient manuscript of the Gospels, copies of Froissart's *Chronicles*, and Caxton's version of *The Golden Legend*. Charles Waterton, naturalist and travel writer, Alfred Austin, Poet Laureate 1896–1913, Wilfred Scawen Blunt, who entered the Diplomatic Service from school in 1858, and Sir Arthur Conan Doyle, who went on to Edinburgh University, were educated here. G. M. Hopkins studied scholastic philosophy (1870–1) here before becoming a theology student at *St Beuno's College. After his ordination Hopkins returned to teach classics at Stonyhurst for a short time in 1878 and then from 1882 until 1884. He describes the neighbourhood in his *Journal* (1959).

WHITEFIELD *Greater Manchester*

Town 3 m. S of Bury; it was here that the novelist Howard Jacobson grew up, as a pupil at the Stand Grammar School.

WIDNES *Cheshire*

Industrial town 8 m. E of Liverpool city centre. Alan Bleasdale, dramatist of Liverpool life, studied here at Widnes, at Wade Deacon Grammar School, before going on to teacher training college.

WIGAN *Greater Manchester*

Former mining and mill town. While researching *The Road to Wigan Pier* in February 1936, George Orwell stayed briefly at 72 Warrington Lane, later moving to lodgings above a tripe shop on Darlington Road, where he stayed until March. He records in his letters and diary a fondness for the people and descriptions of walks taken in and around the town: 'Long walk along the canal (one-time site of Wigan Pier) . . . Frightful landscape of slag-heaps and belching chimneys.' Wigan's original pier, a music hall joke, was once an industrial jetty used to load coal onto barges on the Leeds and Liverpool canal. It was broken up in 1929. The Wigan Pier Experience at Wallgate explores the town's industrial past (www.wlct.org).

WIGTON *Cumbria*

Market town on the Solway Plain, on the northern edge of the Lake District. The novelist and broadcaster Melvyn Bragg was born in Wigton in 1939, where he attended Nelson-Thomlinson Grammar School. Many of his novels would feature the town, including *The Cumbrian Trilogy* (1969–80); *The Soldier's Return* (1999), which describes the return in 1946 from Burma to Wigton of soldier Sam Richardson, coming home to his family, and the difficulty he faces adapting to his old Cumbria life; and its sequel, *The Son of War* (2001). Since 1998 he has been Lord Bragg of Wigton.

WINDERMERE *Cumbria*

Popular tourist centre for the Lake District, comprising the combined villages of Bowness, on the E shore of Lake Windermere, and Windermere, on the hillside 1 m. NE, on the A591 and the A592. On the N side of Church St., nearly opposite the railway station, a public footpath leads up the hill through Elleray Wood to Orrest Head, which commands a magnificent view of the lake and mountains. The house of Elleray, now a girls' school reached by a private drive, was once the home of John Wilson (author, under the pen-name 'Christopher North', of many of the *Noctes Ambrosianae* papers in *Blackwood's Magazine*). While still an undergraduate at Oxford, Wilson inherited a fortune and bought the small estate of Elleray. He left the University in 1807 and settled in a small rustic cottage (now Christopher North's Cottage, Old Elleray, situated beside the public footpath), at that time the only dwelling on the estate. He lived here for several years while planning and building the mansion of Elleray, from which, he said, 'The whole course of a noble lake, about 11 miles long, lies subject to your view.' Wilson was a devoted admirer of Wordsworth, whom he first visited at Grasmere in 1807, and one of the first critics to do justice to his poetry. He was also a friend of Southey and Coleridge at Keswick and of De Quincey, who described their first meeting at Wordsworth's house. Wilson was a colourful and athletic figure who became well known for his prowess in sport and sailing as well as his intellectual interests. Harriet Martineau said of him, 'He made others happy by being so intensely happy himself, and when he was mournful none desired to be gay.' When he was at Elleray he wrote a quantity of poetry, published under the title *The Isle of Palms and Other Poems* (1812). In 1815 he suddenly lost most of his money and went to *Edinburgh, but Elleray remained in his possession until 1848, and he was able to return there from time to time. On one of his holidays, in 1825, he entertained Sir Walter Scott and J. G. Lockhart, the highlight of the visit being a regatta on the lake in honour of Scott's 54th birthday, with a procession of more than 50 gaily decorated barges following Wilson's 'flagship'.

WINNINGTON HALL *Cheshire*

Former country house, now a guest home in a chemical factory estate, NW of Northwich. When Ruskin was in the neighbourhood (1859–68), he often stayed here at Margaret Bell's school for girls. He enjoyed the company of the young pupils, whom he called affectionately 'the birds' and who, in spite of their flowing cotton dresses, played cricket and swung dangerously on rope swings. His correspondence with Miss Bell and the girls, some of whom called him 'Bear' or 'Papa', is edited by Van Akin Burd as *The Winnington Letters* (1969).

Derwentwater from the slopes of Cat Bells. The Lake District was both an inspiration and a way of life to Wordsworth, Coleridge, and Southey

YORKSHIRE

ACKWORTH *West Yorkshire*

Village on the river Went in the metropolitan borough of Wakefield. The poet Basil Bunting went to Ackworth, the Quaker school here, from 1912 to 1916.

APPLETON ROEBUCK *North Yorkshire*

Village off the A64, 6 m. E of Tadcaster. Andrew Marvell was tutor (1650–2) to General Fairfax's daughter Mary at Nunappleton House (1½ m. S, rebuilt). In his poem on the house Marvell refers to its origins as a nunnery, where in Tudor times the orphaned heiress, soon to marry the general's great-grandfather, was living. At the Dissolution the nunnery was handed over to the Fairfax family by the Abbess, who had tried to prevent the marriage, and rebuilt with two long wings. Marvell also wrote 'The Garden' here and a poem on the house at Billborow (Bilbrough, N of the A64), where the family lived when the Wharfe and the Oare flooded. Mary became the wife of the Duke of Buckingham, the 'Zimri' of Dryden's *Absalom and Achitophel* (1681). In 1810 the poet Francis Hastings Doyle was born in the house, the home of his grandfather Sir William Milner. Doyle in his *Reminiscences* (1878) calls it an 'ugly place', much altered since Marvell's time.

ASTON *South Yorkshire*

Large village on the A57, 10 m. E of Sheffield. William Mason became rector (1754) and was host to Thomas Gray, who wrote to a friend that he was in 'a wilderness of sweets, an Elysium among the coal-pits, a terrestrial heaven', adding slyly that this was Mason's description, not his own. Mason rebuilt the rectory facing the hills, and Gray, whose pet name for his friend was Skroddles or Scroddles, complained that this sounded as if he was settling in the north and he would burn the rectory down when he came. However, on that visit (1770), his last, he spent an uneventful fortnight with his friend Dr Thomas Wharton. Walpole stayed with Mason in 1792 and visited Roche Abbey (7 m. NE) as Gray too had done. The house, later the Old Rectory, is opposite the church.

BARNSLEY *South Yorkshire*

Large town on the river Dearne. The novelist Barry Hines was brought up near the town, and Barnsley and the countryside around it are the inspiration for *A Kestrel for a Knave* (1968), later filmed on location by Ken Loach as *Kes*:

> Towards the City, a pit chimney and the pit-head winding gear showed above the rooftops, and at the back of the estate was a patchwork of fields, black, and grey, and pale winter green; giving way to a wood, which stood out on the far slope as an ink blot.

The playwright and novelist John Arden was born in Barnsley in 1930.

BINGLEY *West Yorkshire*

A town in the City of Bradford Metropolitan District, some 5 m. N of Bradford. John Braine was assistant librarian at Bingley Public Library (1940–51), and the town is the original of the dismally presented Dufton of Braine's novel *Room at the Top* (1959). Blake Morrison's controversial dialect poem 'The Ballad of the Yorkshire Ripper', telling the story of Peter Sutcliffe, opens in Bingley and follows the Ripper's grisly progress through Yorkshire:

> Ower t'ills o Bingley
> stormclouds clap an drain,
> like opened blood-black blisters
> leakin pus an pain.

BIRSTALL *West Yorkshire*

Town on the A62 and the A643, 6 m. SW of Leeds. Oakwell Hall, now a museum, an old stone house with mullioned windows, was 'Fieldhead' in *Shirley* (1849), the home of Charlotte Brontë's heroine Shirley Keeldar. The Rydings, with its castellated roof, later the premises of the Birstall carpet factory and visible from the gates, was the home of Ellen Nussey, the correspondent and confidante of Charlotte Brontë, whom she first met at school. In *Jane Eyre* (1847), the Rydings became 'Thornfield Hall'. Ellen Nussey is buried in the churchyard here, the 'Briarfield' church of *Shirley*.

BOLTON ABBEY *North Yorkshire*

Augustinian Priory established on the banks of the Wharfe in 1151. The nave is used as the parish church but the choir and the monastic buildings are now in ruins. Wordsworth, who came here first in 1807, wrote *The White Doe of Rylstone* (1815) about a tradition connected with the area.

BOWES *North Yorkshire*

Village on the A66 and the A67, 4 m. SW of Barnard Castle. The boarding school run by William Shaw was one of the places visited by Charles Dickens, when investigating the conditions of pupils housed and taught for the pittance paid by their parents and guardians. Shaw, though no worse than many school owners, becomes Wackford Squeers in *Nicholas Nickleby* (1838–9). His school (later apartments) was the last building in the main street W of the village, where, through the courtyard, a pump, such as described by Dickens at Dotheboys Hall, can still be seen.

BRADFORD *West Yorkshire*

Former wool and textile town (now a city) in the S Pennines. J. B. Priestley was born at 34 Mannheim Rd in Bradford on 13 September 1894; as a teenager he worked briefly as a clerk in a wool company on Swan Arcade. In 1921 he married Pat Tempest at the Westgate Baptist Chapel. In 1929 (by now living in London) he published his most famous novel, *The Good Companions*, in which the city of his birth would feature prominently, though rechristened 'Bruddersford'.

John Braine was born in Bradford in 1922. Thinly disguised as 'Warley', the city whose sky suggests the 'grey of Guiseley sandstone' serves as the background for the life of the restlessly ambitious working-class Joe Lampton, hero of *Room at the Top* (1959) and later of its disaffected sequel, *Life at the Top* (1962). In its suburbs Lampton pursues his rather unimaginative dreams with single-minded ruthlessness: 'I wanted an Aston-Martin, I wanted a three-guinea linen shirt, I wanted a girl with a Riviera suntan—these were my rights, I felt, a signed and sealed legacy.' Bradford and its neighbour Baildon are the bases for the fictional Stradhoughton in Keith Waterhouse's novel *Billy Liar* (1959):

> it was the usual Saturday morning down in town, the fat women rolling along on their bad feet like toy clowns in pudding basins, the grey-faced men reviewing the sporting pinks. Along Market Street, where the new glass-fronted shops spilled out their sagging lengths of plywood and linoleum, there were still the old-fashioned stalls, lining the gutter with small rotten apples and purple tissue paper.

In 1978 Bradford saw a notorious 'wrongful arrest' case involving a young black man called George Lindo, which inspired a Linton Kwesi Johnson poem, 'It Dread inna Inglan':

> dem frame-up George Lindo
> up in Bradford Toun
> but di Bradford Blacks
> dem a rally roun.

BRIDLINGTON *East Riding of Yorkshire*

Coastal resort on the A165 and the A1038. Charlotte Brontë and her friend Ellen Nussey hoped to spend a holiday by the sea here in 1839, but Ellen's brother Henry arranged their accommodation with his friends at Easton House Farm, 2 m. inland. However, the young women walked to Burlington, as Bridlington was then called, and Charlotte Brontë was so overcome at her first sight of the sea that she burst into tears and had to sit down. 'Our visit to Easton was extremely pleasant,' she wrote, and she especially enjoyed the final week, when her host and hostess arranged for their stay in lodgings on the cliff opposite the pier (now the Esplanade). She visited Easton again after her sister Anne's death (1849) and funeral at Scarborough, and for solace spent many hours writing her novel *Shirley* (1849) in the summerhouse.

BROMPTON-BY-SAWDON *North Yorkshire*

Village on the A170, 9 m. SW of Scarborough, where Wordsworth married Mary Hutchinson at the parish church on 4 October 1802. His sister Dorothy had accompanied him the night before, but did not attend the service. The entry in her *Journals* records something of her emotions:

> At a little after 8 o'clock I saw them go . . . towards the Church. William had parted from me upstairs. I gave him the wedding ring—

with how deep a blessing! I took it from my forefinger where I had worn it the whole of the night before—he slipped it again onto my finger and blessed me fervently.

She then threw herself on her bed until the married couple returned, but recovered in time to welcome Mary warmly at the wedding breakfast. Mary was acting as housekeeper for her uncle at Gallows Hill Farm, now screened by trees from the main road a mile towards Scarborough. A copy of the banns and marriage certificate is in the vestry.

CALVERLEY *West Yorkshire*

Town between Shipley and Leeds on the A657. Frederick Faber, the hymn writer who established the London Oratory in 1849, was born (1814) in his grandfather's vicarage (rebuilt) here.

CARLTON MINIOTT *North Yorkshire*

Village 2½ m. W of Thirsk. J. L. Carr, novelist and independent publisher, was born in the village in 1912, the son of a railwayman and Methodist preacher like Mr Ellerbeck in his best-known novel, *A Month in the Country* (1980). His Yorkshire childhood forms the background to this novel, as it does to *How Steeple Sinderby Wanderers Won the F. A. Cup* (1975), which looks back to the local football matches of his youth.

CONISBROUGH (pr. 'Cunnisbŭra) *South Yorkshire*

Town on the A630, 6 m. SW of Doncaster. The Norman castle in Scott's *Ivanhoe* was the home of Athelstane, whom Cedric was disappointed not to find more zealous for the Saxon cause. A young Ted Hughes befriended the gamekeeper's son from the Crookhill estate, whose grounds and wildlife he came to know well through his years of childhood exploration.

COXWOLD *North Yorkshire*

Village off the A19, 8 m. SE of Thirsk. Laurence Sterne acquired the living here in 1760 and divided his time between Shandy Hall Ⓟ, his name for the cottage he improved (the last house in the village well beyond the church), and London society. He finished *Tristram Shandy* (1760–7), and wrote *A Sentimental Journey* (1768) and *Letters to Eliza* (1775) here. He and his wife often visited Newburgh Priory (1 m. E) as guests of Lord Fauconberg, the patron of the living. Shandy Hall, which is open to the public and where his works are on sale, is owned by the Laurence Sterne Trust (www.shandean.org/shandyhall.html), who in 1969 had Sterne's body removed from London and reburied outside the S wall of the nave where his original tombstone now stands.

CROFT-ON-TEES *North Yorkshire*

Village on the A167, 5 m. S of Darlington. C. L. Dodgson ('Lewis Carroll') lived at the rectory (later the Old Rectory) opposite the church as a boy when his father was rector. The garden, where tea was often laid on a long table, is mostly unchanged, though the acacia tree has grown a new trunk. The boy used to do conjuring tricks and write plays for his marionettes while on holiday from Richmond Grammar School (1844–5) and Rugby (1845–50). A bronze tablet has been erected in the church by the village to commemorate him as the author of *Alice's Adventures in Wonderland* (1865). Also in the church is the curtained Milbanke pew, like a small gallery up a winding stair, where tradition says Byron and Annabella Milbanke worshipped on their honeymoon at Halnaby (pr. Hannaby) Hall. The lodge gates and the drive can be seen 1½ m. along the Middleton Tyas road, but the house has gone.

DARFIELD *South Yorkshire*

Small town on the A635, 6 m. SE of Barnsley. The churchyard on the hill has the railed tomb of Ebenezer Elliott (d. 1849), the iron founder and author of *The Village Patriarch* (1829).

DEWSBURY *West Yorkshire*

Town on the A638, 10 m. SW of Leeds. Healds House on Dewsbury Moor (1 m. W) was the new site of Miss Wooler's school on its move from *Mirfield. Charlotte Brontë was a teacher here, and Emily was a pupil but missed her home so much that she left and Anne came in her place. Charlotte remained until 1838.

Dewsbury is the basis of 'Cressley', the fictional town of Stan Barstow's novel *A Kind of Loving* (1960), although it also includes aspects of other West Yorkshire towns such as Wakefield, Horbury, and Barstow's native Ossett.

ECCLESFIELD *South Yorkshire*

Town on the A6135. Margaret Gatty, wife of the incumbent, created *Aunt Judy's Magazine* (1866) and wrote the improving *Parables from Nature* (1855–71). Her daughter Juliana (later Mrs Ewing), was born at the vicarage (gone) and contributed to *Aunt Judy's Magazine*. A tablet in the church commemorates them.

EPWORTH *East Riding of Yorkshire*

Small town on the A161, 16 m. E of Doncaster. The Old Rectory was the boyhood home of John and Charles Wesley. Built in 1709, it replaced the house where they were born, burnt down earlier in the year.

FOSTON-LE-CLAY *North Yorkshire*

Village off the A64, 12 m. NE of York, where Sydney Smith was rector from 1806 to 1828. He might have appointed a curate-in-charge of the parish, but conditions of residence in livings were tightened, so he left London, where he had lectured on moral philosophy to an appreciative audience, and arrived in 1809. Finding the rectory ruinous he stayed at Heslington, York, until his new one was finished in 1814. A brass in the N aisle of the church, erected by public subscription, calls him the 'Friend and Counsellor of his parishioners'.

GIGGLESWICK *North Yorkshire*

Village off the A65, 1 m. NW of Settle. Near here, 1 m. SW of Settle, on the A65 opposite a turning to a farm, is the Ebbing and Flowing Well, which is called a fountain in Drayton's *Polyolbion* (1612–22):

At Giggleswick where I a Fountain can you show,
That eight times in a day is sayd to ebb and flow.

The water comes from under the limestone Giggleswick Scar, which towers above the road.

GOMERSAL *West Yorkshire*

Town, 6 m. SE of Bradford, on the A643 and the A651. Herbert Knowles (1798–1817), a poet of promise, was born here and lived with his

Laurence Sterne's Shandy Hall at Coxwold, North Yorkshire, where *Tristram Shandy* was finished

parents at Pollard Hall. He sent his poem 'The Three Tabernacles' (known as 'Stanzas in Richmond Churchyard', and written when he was at Richmond Grammar School) to Southey. Sadly, he died of a decline a month after Southey had obtained a sizarship for him at St John's, Cambridge. He is buried at Heckmondwike, 2 m. S. The Red House (1660) in Oxford Rd, now a museum, was the home of Charlotte Brontë's friends at Roe Head School, Mary and Martha Taylor, whose family appear in *Shirley* (1849) as the Yorkes and their house as Briarmains. Charlotte Brontë often stayed here between 1831 and 1840 and described the house and local scenes in her novel. Oakwell Hall, *Birstall, was the home of her heroine, and Hartshead and Kirklees Park (where tradition places Robin Hood's grave) were Nunnely. There are restored outbuildings with exhibitions exploring Brontë links. Mary Taylor (Rose Yorke) is buried in the churchyard.

GRETA BRIDGE *North Yorkshire*

Village on the A66, 10 m. NW of Scotch Corner. In 1809 and 1812 Sir Walter Scott stayed at Rokeby Hall here with his friend the MP, classical scholar, and traveller in Greece and Turkey J. B. Morritt. Scott set *Rokeby* (1813) here, his long poem about the Civil War, which contains the songs 'A weary lot is thine, fair maid' and 'Brignal Banks'. Brignall (1 m. SW) is a village on the N side of the river Greta.

GRIMSBY *East Riding of Yorkshire*

Important fishing port on the S bank of the Humber and on the A16. It takes its name from Grim, a Danish fisherman who, in the early 14th-c. verse romance *The Lay of Havelok the Dane*, saves the young prince of Denmark by escaping with him to England. Grim figures in the port's seal.

HALIFAX *West Yorkshire*

Industrial town 8 m. SW of Bradford. The novelist Phyllis Bentley was born at Victoria House in Stanley Rd, 'to the middle of the middle class and an uncertain welcome', but she is mainly associated with 8 Heath Villas, to which the family moved in 1910 and where she remained until moving to The Grange, Warley, in 1963. The West Riding forms the background for many of her novels, which include *Carr* (1929), *Inheritance* (1932), *A Modern Tragedy* (1934), and *Manhold* (1941). Her 'Iredale' is the Colne valley and 'Annotsfield' is based on Halifax and Huddersfield. She also wrote on the Brontës, and published an autobiography, *O Dreams, O Destinations* (1962).

HAMBLETON HILLS *North Yorkshire*

The Wordsworths paused when they reached the highest point on the road (A170) over the hills, where the view inspired William's sonnet 'Dark and more dark the shades of evening fell' and Dorothy's entry in her *Journal*, both describing the same objects silhouetted against the western sky. It was Wordsworth's wedding day, 4 October 1802.

HARROGATE *North Yorkshire*

Town on the A59 and the A61, 17 m. N of Leeds. From the late 16th to the 19th cc. the sulphur and iron in the many springs made the place a fashionable health resort, which was visited by the characters of Smollett's *Humphry Clinker* (1771). In 1816 Elizabeth Hamilton, a novelist brought up in Scotland, persuaded that a warmer climate than Edinburgh would benefit her health, came south but was taken ill on the journey and died here. She was buried in Christ Church (rebuilt 1831), High Harrogate (on the A59, Knaresborough Rd), where the marble tablet placed by her sister to 'one who was the ornament, the instructress and the example of her sex' still remains on the wall of the N aisle.

Karl Marx took a spa cure here with his daughter for some weeks in 1873, enjoying the 'quiet life, breezy air, mineral waters and pleasant walks'.

In one of her greatest and most famous mysteries, Agatha Christie disappeared—herself—in December 1926; she checked herself into Harrogate's Hydropathic Hotel (under the name 'Miss Neale') and it was ten days before she was identified. She claimed afterwards to have no memory of how she came to be there.

HAWORTH (pr. 'Howarth') *West Yorkshire*

Moorland village off the A6033, 4 m. SW of Keighley. Patrick Brontë brought his wife and young family to the parsonage (now the Brontë Parsonage Museum, www.bronte.org.uk) at the top of the village on the edge of the moor in 1820. Mrs Brontë died the next year and her sister took over the care of the six children. After short-lived and unhappy absences for schooling and teaching, the parsonage was their home until their early deaths.

The first publication of the three surviving girls (the oldest two died as a result of privations at a school which later emerged as Lowood) was a collection of poems (1846) which did not sell, under the pseudonym of 'Currer, Ellis, and Acton Bell'. Charlotte then wrote *The Professor*, refused by the publishers, based on her stay in Brussels, where she and Emily were equipping themselves to open their own school at the parsonage. This failed, as no pupils applied. Charlotte's next book, *Jane Eyre* (1847), was an immediate success. Emily's *Wuthering Heights* and Anne's *Agnes Grey* written at the same time were then published; Anne's second novel, *The Tenant of Wildfell Hall*, followed in 1848. A few months later Emily died before the worth of *Wuthering Heights* was acknowledged. Anne died at Scarborough six months after Emily. Charlotte, left alone with her father, finished *Shirley* (1849) and *Villette* (1853) and made the acquaintance of her biographer Elizabeth Gaskell. She also received a proposal of marriage from Mr Nicholls, the curate, but was only allowed to accept him after two years of opposition by her father. They were married in Haworth Church (their certificate is on view), but Charlotte died 9 months later (1855).

The Brontë Society (founded 1893), whose museum started in one room over the Pennybank, was given the parsonage in 1927 and transferred there the next year, which also saw the arrival of Henry Houston Bonnell's collection of Brontëana from Philadelphia. The Society's annual periodical, *Transactions*, contains the first printing of many Brontë documents. Its comprehensive guide to the house, which has been restored to resemble the Brontë home, contains a short history of the family. A leaflet lists the places which influenced their work, including a favourite walk to the Brontë waterfall, Ponden Hall (setting of Thrushcross Grange), and High or Top Withens (ruins), the possible site of *Wuthering Heights*. Elizabeth Gaskell, who visited in 1853, contrasted the bleak aspect of the house outside with the 'snugness and comfort' of the interior. She walked on the moor with Charlotte, who told her stories of the families there which made her think *Wuthering Heights* tame in comparison.

Matthew Arnold's poem 'Haworth Churchyard', written after Charlotte's death, says in error that the grass 'Blows from their graves to thy own' as the Brontës (with the exception of Anne) were buried in the family vault in the church (rebuilt 1881), where a plaque marks the site. A stained-glass window is an American tribute to Charlotte Brontë, and the Memorial Chapel has been added.

Ted Hughes would write several poems inspired by Top Withens, Haworth, and nearby Stanbury, including 'Two Photographs of Top Withens':

> The house is ruinous enough, in my snapshot.
> But most of the roofslabs are in place.
> You sit holding your smile, in one of the
>   sycamores.
> We'd climbed from Stanbury.
> And through all the leaves of the fierce book
> To touch Wuthering Heights—a fouled nest.

HEPTONSTALL *West Yorkshire*

Small village in the Calder Valley, NE of Hebden Bridge, home to Ted Hughes (born in nearby *Mytholmroyd), who would write a number of poems about the village ('Black village of gravestones . . .'). Hughes bought a mill house—Lumb Bank—at Heptonstall Slack (between Heptonstall and Hebden Bridge) in 1969, but soon moved back to Court Green on Dartmoor and leased the house to the Arvon Foundation, who continue to use it as one of their writing centres. One of many writers who have visited the centre has been Alan Brownjohn, whose poem 'Heptonstall February' evokes the local landscape.

Sylvia Plath is buried at Heptonstall cemetery; on various occasions vandals blaming Hughes for her suicide have removed the name 'Hughes' from her tombstone.

The Brontës and Yorkshire

MY sister Emily . . . loved the moors . . . They were far more to her than a mere spectacle; they were what she lived in & by, as much as the wild birds, their tenants, or the heather, their produce. . . . She found in the bleak solitude many and dear delights; and not the least and best loved was— liberty.

The Brontës' region is usually imagined as entirely wild, romantic moorland. This picture was created by the Brontës themselves, and is only partially true. They built it out of their adolescent reading in Sir Walter Scott, and out of a Gothic admiration for the wilder reaches of Shakespeare. Even the word 'wuthering' Emily plucked out of Scott. It is not a local dialect word, except among those who see the mid-Pennines through her eyes. Their wishing it to be so made it seem to be so—for them, and for us.

The Brontë family moved to Haworth in 1820 at a time of dramatic and violent change, yet this barely entered their writing. The first woollen manufactories had been built along moorland streams, and were rapidly and rapaciously expanding, replacing domestic handloom weaving as an industry. This is not the place to enlarge upon the social changes. The point is that the Brontës mostly ignored this, and the alteration to the natural environment. Charlotte Brontë's *Shirley* (1849) takes industry as part of its subject, but it is the industry of the Luddite, Napoleonic period, not the 1840s, and it is typically a love story, with only an underlying frisson of revolution.

So the Brontës' Yorkshire was not exactly what they said it was. It was smelly, dirty, unhealthy, polluted, and darkened with smoke to an extent that we rarely imagine nowadays. It was something that they presumably took for granted and were not interested in for their fictions. Yet I am not surprised that Emily Brontë wrote paeans to the west wind. At the Parsonage, situated on the edge of the town at the top of the hill, the cleanest air would have blown in on a west wind from the hills, while an east wind would have been dire, bringing up not only the domestic smoke but also the sulphurous fumes from the wool combers' shops, where the furnaces roared to heat the combs. It also brought the stench of the middens, the muck heaps of human and animal refuse (no water closets, remember) at the backs of the houses. One of the many unsung achievements of their father, Patrick, was his campaign (finally successful) to move the graveyard, from where its drainage polluted the town springs, to a site half a mile away. It took him years to achieve because of local indifference to such niceties.

Charlotte, first of all through her friends Ellen Nussey and Elizabeth Gaskell, founded the legend of life in a miserable and inhospitable parsonage with this 'misanthropic' father. I have always been surprised by the number of visitors who

THE BRONTË SISTERS BY PATRICK BRANWELL BRONTË, C. 1834

stick to this myth despite what they actually see—that handsome building with its suntrap of a garden reaching to the church wall. Yes, it must have been cramped for that large family (in a way typical enough for the times) and when writing a novel about them I devoted much ingenuity to creating charts of what their sleeping arrangements might have been at various times. But it must have been a busy, happy, and creative house, focused, as with many rural houses, on the kitchen. Emily, surprisingly to some readers, was very domesticated, keen on her baking, and the back door of such a country parsonage must have received a stream of invited or casual visitors—especially as Haworth was not, as today, a dead-end village, but situated on a major thoroughfare crossing the Pennines. Charlotte's famous anecdote of her sister having 'scarcely more knowledge of the peasantry among whom she lived, than a nun has of the country people who sometimes pass her convent gates' is surely disingenuous. I imagine it as more likely that she welcomed strangers and parishioners to the back door of the Parsonage with cakes and home-brewed ale.

In their fiction the Brontë sisters were certainly more interested in the gentry scattered over the West Riding, and in the movements of their own hearts (Charlotte especially, in *Jane Eyre* (1847) and in that most poignant depiction of hopeless love *Villette* (1853)), than in their father's humbler parishioners. But, again, there are exceptions—in Emily's wonderful portrait of Joseph in *Wuthering Heights* (1847), for instance, that prating Methodist serving in a moorland farmstead, a typical figure of the Victorian, Pennine world. It was not so much the 'brownish moors', as they described them in their early writing, as the rich domestic life in the Parsonage, and their wonderful father, that held them captive, always bringing them back from their travels. Above all else that typified their home life were the fantasies they brewed around the dining room table.

All of them enjoyed from childhood onwards an imaginative freedom encouraged by their Rousseau-esque (as he seems to me) father. Their brother Branwell—a hippie before his day—found his freedom also in the Black Bull, in drinking with the local gentry, and in taking laudanum. He was therefore a source of inspiration for Anne in *The Tenant of Wildfell Hall* (1848): Anne who was surely the sanest (and possibly, in part, overlooked for that reason) member of the Brontë family.

But it was Emily especially who was consumed by inner fantasies that were and are, in a special way that it is impossible to define precisely, expressive of the spirit of that darker millstone-grit area of the mid-Pennines. They gave rise to her lurid imaginings: one of her 'liberties', not unrelated to the sense claimed for her upon the moors. But don't expect too much of a *Wuthering Heights* frisson from visiting its supposed model, Top Withens, for even before it was virtually demolished it did not resemble the house we know from the novel. However, the site is terrific.

GLYN HUGHES

HOWDEN *East Riding of Yorkshire*

Small market town 3 m. N of Goole. The critic William Empson was born on his family's estate at Yokefleet Hall in 1906.

HUBBERHOLME *North Yorkshire*

Small village in the Yorkshire Dales about 5½ m. NW of Kettlewell. J. B. Priestley, the proudest of Yorkshireman, described Hubberholme as 'one of the smallest and pleasantest places in the world'. His ashes are now buried in the village's Norman church.

HUDDERSFIELD *West Yorkshire*

Large town 7 m. S of Bradford. The poet Simon Armitage was born here in 1963, and much of his poetry is well rooted in the county of his birth. His 1998 prose collection *All Points North* would include an essay entitled 'Huddersfield Is Hollywood'.

ILKLEY *West Yorkshire*

Spa town in the N of England. Now home to an annual literature festival (the largest and oldest in the north of England), Ilkley was in 1859 also used as a much-needed writers' retreat; when an exhausted Charles Darwin completed work on his *Origin of Species* he came to Ilkley to recover at the spa, and to take refuge from the criticisms he was sure its publication would bring him—he described the period of waiting to hear of the book's reception as being like 'living in Hell'. Today his time here is remembered in the naming of 'Darwin Gardens'.

KINGSTON UPON HULL
(or HULL) *East Riding of Yorkshire*

Port on the Humber, visited by John Taylor, 'the water-poet', who travelled extensively, on his 'merry-wherry-ferry voyage'. Andrew Marvell spent his youth at the vicarage of Holy Trinity Church, where his father was 'lecturer' from 1624 until his death by drowning in the Humber in 1641. Marvell was educated at the Grammar School, then nearby, under his father, who was the Master. Marvell, who left for Cambridge in 1638, later spent much of his life in Hull and was three times elected MP. His statue stands outside the new Grammar School.

William Mason, who had a poetical interest in gardens, was born (1724) at Holy Trinity vicarage while his father was incumbent. A large bronze plaque, erected in Queen's Gdns in 1973, depicts the hero of Defoe's *Robinson Crusoe* (1719), who sailed from the port on his adventures.

The poet Stevie Smith (1902–71) was born here but left for London when she was 5.

Philip Larkin moved to the city in 1955, taking up the post of Librarian at the university library. For some 30 years he ran it with striking efficiency and transformed it, from 'a nice little Shetland pony' into 'a frightful Grand National winner'. His first lodgings in the city were at 11 Oatlands Rd, Cottingham, where his mean room and 'blasted RADIO' provided the *mise-en-scène* for the poem 'Mr Bleaney':

> Bed, upright chair, sixty-watt bulb, no hook
>
> Behind the door, no room for books or bags—
> 'I'll take it.' So it happens that I lie
> Where Mr Bleaney lay, and stub my fags
> On the same saucer-souvenir, and try
>
> Stuffing my ears with cotton-wool, to drown
> The jabbering set he egged her on to buy.

In 1956 he moved to 32 Pearson Pk, where he stayed for 18 years; in 1974 he bought 105 Newland Pk, where he lived until his death in 1985. What is now the Quality Royal Hotel, its 'silence laid like carpet', was the setting for 'Friday Night in the Royal Station Hotel', and railway journeys to and from Hull provided the inspiration for some of his best-known poems, including 'The Whitsun Weddings' and 'Here', in which Larkin's passage through some local undemonstrative countryside 'gathers to the surprise of a large town' and

> a terminate and fishy-smelling
> Pastoral of ships up streets, the slave museum,

Statue of Andrew Marvell, at the corner of Savile St. and George St., Hull

LAW HILL *West Yorkshire*

House 1,000 ft up on Southowram Bank, 3 m. SE of Halifax. Emily Brontë was a teacher here in 1837 when the house was an efficiently run school for girls. She is thought to have been employed for six months but it is possible that she stayed for eighteen. Many of her poems written here have a nostalgia for Haworth, including the lines:

> Awaken on all my dear moorlands
> The wind in its glory and pride,
> O call me from valleys and highlands
> To walk by the hill-river's side! . . .
>
> But lovelier than cornfields all waving
> In emerald and scarlet and gold
> Are the slopes where the north wind is raving
> And the glens where I wandered of old.

The history of the family who previously owned Law Hill and the nearby Walterclough Hall furnished her with the story of *Wuthering Heights* (1847), and one of her fellow teachers was called Earnshaw. Her description of the façade of Wuthering Heights closely resembles High Sunderland Hall (demolished 1950), 1 m. N.

LEEDS *West Yorkshire*

Large industrial city on the river Aire. J. R. R. Tolkien was Reader in English Language at the University of Leeds from 1920 to 1925. He brought out an edition of *Sir Gawain and the Green Knight*, which remained the standard edition throughout the 20th c. and was made a Professor in 1924. His time here coincided with that of the poet and critic Lascelles Abercrombie, who was Professor of English at Leeds from 1923 to 1929. The critic, biographer, and editor of *The Oxford History of English Literature*, Bonamy Dobree (1891–1974), was Professor of English from 1936 to 1955. Peter Redgrove was Gregory Fellow in Poetry at the University from 1962 to 1965. The poet and editor D. J. Enright was a visiting lecturer at the University of Leeds in 1972. Keith Waterhouse, who has described his native city as 'the rhubarb centre of the universe', grew up in Leeds. Like the hero of his comic novel *Billy Liar* (1959), Waterhouse worked as an undertaker's clerk before taking up writing. But Billy Fisher's Stradhoughton is not recognizably Leeds, and the movie based on the novel was filmed in *Bradford and Baildon.

Alan Bennett was born in Leeds in 1934, and educated at Leeds Modern School.

> I don't recall the sixth form in my year being considered outstandingly clever but in 1951, for the first time, the headmaster, who had been at Cambridge himself, made an effort to push some of his university entrants towards the older universities. Snobbery was part of it, I imagine, and by the same token he switched the school from playing soccer to rugger, though since I avoided both this had little impact on me . . .

Bennett would go up to university at *Oxford. Meanwhile, in Harold Pinter's play *The Collector* (1969), Bill crucially either did or didn't go to Leeds last week . . .

Philip Larkin in the stacks at the Brynmor Jones Library, University of Hull, in 1974

> Tattoo-shops, consulates, grim head-scarved wives;
> And out beyond its mortgaged half-built edges
> Fast-shadowed wheat-fields, running high as hedges . . .

The travel writer and novelist Jonathan Raban studied English at the University of Hull from 1960 to 1965. In the meeting with Larkin he records in *Coasting*, he gives an account of the spurious 'library committee' he invented in order to meet Larkin regularly. He returned to Hull to start a postgraduate degree.

The poets Roger McGough, Douglas Dunn, and Tom Paulin were all educated at the University. Dunn worked under Larkin at the Brynmor Jones Library and lived in Terry St., in a Hull suburb. He would give the name 'Terry Street' to his 1969 collection, which included the poems 'New Light on Terry Street', 'Sunday Morning Among the Houses of Terry Street', and 'The Clothes Pit':

> The young women are obsessed with beauty.
> Their old fashioned sewing machines rattle in Terry Street.
> They must keep up, they must keep up . . .
> Three girls go down the street with the summer wind.
> The litter of pop rhetoric blows down Terry Street.
> Bounces past their feet, into their lives.

The poet Tony Harrison was born in Leeds, and educated at Leeds Grammar School and Leeds University, where he studied Classics. One of his best-known poems, *v*, written in 1985 during the miners' strike, is a meditation in a graveyard (on Beeston Hill) that has been vandalized:

> Flying visits once or twice a year,
> and though I'm horrified just who's to blame
> that I find instead of flowers cans of beer
> and more than one grave sprayed with some
>   skin's name?

In his poem 'Hitcher', Simon Armitage describes picking up a hitch-hiker here in Leeds:

> I picked him up in Leeds.
> He was following the sun to west from east
> with just a toothbrush and the good earth for a
>   bed. The truth,
> he said, was blowin' in the wind,
> or round the next bend.

The poet and critic Tom Paulin was also born here in Leeds, in 1949, but his family moved to Belfast while he was still very young.

The Manchester-born novelist Livi Michael took her degree at the University here at Leeds.

LOTHERSDALE *North Yorkshire*

Village off the A629, 5 m. SW of Skipton. The painted posts and entrance gate to Stonegappe Hall are visible from the crossroads above the village. Charlotte Brontë was governess for a few months in 1839 to Mrs Sidgwick's family here, the 'Gateshead Hall' of *Jane Eyre*.

MALHAM TARN *North Yorkshire*

Lake 3 m. N of Malham between the B6479 N of Settle, and the B6160. Charles Kingsley, when a guest at Malham Tarn House (now owned by the Field Studies Council and the NT), is said to have been asked why there were black streaks down the limestone cliffs nearby, and jokingly replied that a chimney sweep must have fallen over them. This gave him the idea from which he wrote *The Water Babies* (1863), where Tom goes over Harthover Fell and Lewthwaite Crag.

The area round the lake is the property of the National Trust and the public has access to the S shore.

MEXBOROUGH *South Yorkshire*

Town on the N bank of the Don. Ted Hughes moved here with his family in 1937, and he attended Schofield Street Junior School. Exploring the Manor Farm at Old Denaby just S of Mexborough inspired his first animal poem, 'The Thought-Fox':

> Cold, delicately as the dark snow,
> A fox's nose touches twig, leaf;
> Two eyes serve a moment, that now
> And again now, and now, and now
> Sets neat prints into the snow . . .

MIRFIELD *West Yorkshire*

Town on the A644, 3 m. SW of Dewsbury. Anne Brontë became a governess to Mrs

The cliffs at Malham, with the black streaks that made Kingsley think of chimney sweeps

Ingham for nine months at Blake Hall (gone). Miss Wooler's School at Roehead to the N was attended by Charlotte (1831–2), who returned as a teacher from 1835 to the end of 1837, while first Emily, who stayed two months only, and then Anne were pupils. Charlotte first met Ellen Nussey and Mary Taylor here, who, with the exception of her sisters, became her closest friends.

MUSCOATES *North Yorkshire*

Hamlet S of the A170, on the Slingsby road, 4¼ m. S of Kirkbymoorside. Muscoates Grange, a stone farmhouse with a tiled roof, was the birthplace of Herbert Read (1893–1968), who in the 1930s published many works of literary and art criticism, and in 1940 *Annals of Innocence and Experience*, his autobiography.

MYTHOLMROYD *West Yorkshire*

Town in the Calder valley 6 m. W of Halifax. Generations of Ted Hughes's family were millworkers in the Calder valley. Hughes himself was born at 1 Aspinall St., Mytholmroyd, on 17 August 1930, and educated at Burnley Road School. His childhood spent fishing in the canal and playing in the nearby woods and farms, and observing wildlife, instilled the fascination for the natural world that would infuse so much of his subsequent work. He celebrated the Calder valley area in his collection *Remains of Elmet* (1979), which included photos by Fay Godwin.

OSSETT *West Yorkshire*

Industrial town halfway between Dewsbury and Wakefield. The novelist Stan Barstow, the author of *A Kind of Loving* (1960), who was born in nearby Horbury in 1928, was brought up in Ossett and educated at Ossett Grammar School. He left to work in the drawing office of an engineering firm.

POCKLINGTON *North Yorkshire*

Small market town, 13 m. E of York. A teenage Tom Stoppard was at boarding school in Pocklington, leaving at 17 to get a job on a local paper in *Bristol.

PONDEN HALL *West Yorkshire*

House 3 m. from Haworth, across the moor beyond Stanbury. Emily Brontë, who found the story for her novel *Wuthering Heights* (1847) when she was a teacher at *Law Hill, set 'Thrushcross Grange', the home of the Lintons, here in her own well-loved moors. The Earnshaws' home, 'Wuthering Heights', is thought to have been placed at the small farmhouse of Top Withens (ruins; see HAWORTH), to the S, not far from the waterfall that is now called the Brontë Waterfall.

PONTEFRACT *West Yorkshire*

Market town now in the borough of Wakefield. The castle at Pontefract (formerly Pomfret) was the scene of the incarceration and death of Shakespeare's Richard II:

> I have been considering how I may compare
> This prison where I live unto the world . . .

Considerable ruins of the castle survive and are open to visitors (www.wakefield.gov.uk). The town is the home of one of John Betjeman's sturdy sirens in his poem 'The Liquorice Fields at Pontefract'.

REDCAR *North Yorkshire*

Seaside resort and racing town. The novelist Jane Gardam was brought up in Coatham, once a separate town, but now a district of Redcar, and educated at Saltburn High School for Girls in the 1930s and 1940s. A number of her novels are set in the area—including *Crusoe's Daughter* (1985), where the yellow house Oversands stands beside Coatham's ancient marsh and grasslands. She has also described the Yorkshire of her childhood in her non-fiction portrait *The Iron Coast* (1994).

RICHMOND *North Yorkshire*

Town on the A6108, 5 m. SW of Scotch Corner, with a ruined castle above the Swale. In 1816 Herbert Knowles, a pupil at the Grammar School, wrote 'The Three Tabernacles', better known as 'Stanzas in Richmond Churchyard' (see GOMERSAL). C. L. Dodgson was also at the Grammar School (1844–6) before going to Rugby. Katharine Bradley and Edith Cooper lived at 1 The Paragon from 1899.

The Georgian theatre in Richmond, transported to Knaresborough, features in John Arden's novel *Jack Juggler and the Emperor's Whore* (1995).

ROBIN HOOD'S BAY
North Yorkshire

Seaside village at the foot of a steep cliff on the B1447, 6 m. SE of Whitby. Leo Walmsley grew up in Robin Hood's Bay, the 'Bramblewick' of his first three novels, *Three Fevers* (1932), *Foreigners* (1935), and *Sally Lunn* (1937), set in this part of his native county.

ROTHERHAM *South Yorkshire*

Industrial town NW of Sheffield. Ebenezer Elliott was born (1781) at the New Foundry, his father's ironworks in the suburb of Masborough. He wrote his first poem, 'Vernal Walk', when 17, and his later *Tales of the Night* (1818) was praised by Southey. In 1821 he set up his own ironworks in *Sheffield. Angela Carter spent much of her early childhood at her maternal grandmother's house in Rotherham, escaping from the bombing raids afflicting the south of the country.

RUDSTON *East Riding of Yorkshire*

Village on the B1253, 6 m. W of Bridlington. Winifred Holtby, author of *South Riding* (1936), the novel set in Yorkshire by which she is best remembered, was born (1898) at the Victorian Rudston House in Long St., where she spent her youth. She is buried in the churchyard and the memorial by the font in the church was erected after her death (1935) by the Winifred Holtby Society.

RYLSTONE *West Yorkshire*

Village on the B6265, 5 m. N of Skipton. *The White Doe of Rylstone* (1815) is the title of Wordsworth's poem about a tragedy of Queen Elizabeth's time, when the survivor of a persecuted Catholic family is visited by the doe she had reared in happier days.

SCARBOROUGH *North Yorkshire*

Resort on the E coast popular since the 18th c. In Smollett's *Humphry Clinker* (1771), the drowning Matthew Bramble was brought safely to the beach. But he was naked and had 'extravagant ideas of decency and decorum', so the party left next day. Sheridan set his comedy *A Trip to Scarborough* (1777) here. In 1849 Anne Brontë died at 2 The Cliff, demolished about 20 years later to make way for the Grand Hotel. She is buried not far from the castle in the detached part of St Mary's churchyard, beyond the ruined part of the church. Charlotte visited the grave in 1852.

Edith Sitwell was born in the family's seaside home, Wood End, by the Crescent. The future of the house's museum status, with its Sitwell Room, containing first editions of the Sitwells' works, is uncertain. Osbert Sitwell's novel *Before the Bombardment* (1926) is set in the town. The novelist Susan Hill—who would visit the Sitwells at Wood End and set her story 'In the Conservatory' here—was born here in 1942 and attended Scarborough Grammar School.

Most of the 70 or so plays written by Sir Alan Ayckbourn—including *Absurd Person Singular* (1974), *The Norman Conquests* (1975),

Bedroom Farce (1977), *Just Between Ourselves* (1978), *A Chorus of Disapproval* (1985), *Man of the Moment* (1990), *Comic Potential* (1999), and *Private Fears in Public Places* (2004)—have been premièred at the Stephen Joseph Theatre on Westborough. Ayckbourn was artistic director of the company from 1970 until his retirement in 2008.

SHEFFIELD *South Yorkshire*

University, cathedral, and steel-manufacturing city on the Don. James Montgomery settled here as clerk to the *Sheffield Register* in 1792. This changed its name to the *Sheffield Iris* and Montgomery became a contributor, editor, and then its owner. He was imprisoned for libel over political articles and wrote *The Wanderer of Switzerland* (1806) and other poems which have fallen into obscurity. His hymns, which include 'Songs of praise the angels sang' and 'Forever with the Lord', remain popular.

Ebenezer Elliott, owner of a successful ironworks (1821–41), took an active interest in literary and political events. His early verse *Tales of the Night* (1818) was praised by Southey, but anger at the 'bread tax' produced *The Village Patriarch* (1829) and the *Corn-Law Rhymes* (1831), by which he is best remembered. A bronze statue (now in Weston Park), paid for by Sheffield working men, was erected (1854) in the marketplace.

In 1876 Ruskin, idealistic superintendent of the Guild of St George, bought 13 acres of land at Abbeydale. 'We will try to make some small piece of English ground, beautiful, peaceful and fruitful. We will have no steam engines upon it, and no railroads.' There were few supporters for this simple life and the land was run as a market garden. Ruskin's collection of paintings, books, illuminated manuscripts, plaster casts, and minerals, which he gave to the Guild, can be seen, handsomely displayed, at the Ruskin Gallery in the Millennium Galleries, Arundel Gate.

W. H. Auden, who loved lead-mining machinery as a child, visited the Blue John mine at Castleton near Sheffield and hoped to become a mining engineer.

The poet George MacBeth was educated at King Edward VII School in the 1940s. Returning to Hull from Oxford by train in his poem 'Dockery and Son', Philip Larkin changed at Sheffield,

> And ate an awful pie, and walked along
> The platform to its end to see the ranged
> Joining and parting lines reflect a strong
> Unhindered moon.

The critic and poet Sir William Empson was Professor of English at the University from 1953 until his retirement in 1971. The novelists Malcolm Bradbury, A. S. Byatt, and Margaret Drabble were born in Sheffield, in 1932, 1936, and 1939, respectively. The Derbyshire-born novelist Hilary Mantel was a student at Sheffield University, where at one point Angela Carter also held a temporary teaching post.

The University of Sheffield Hallam has a prestigious creative writing course whose tutors have included the novelists Livi Michael, Jane Rogers, and Lesley Glaister. A number of Glaister's novels—including *Trick or Treat* (1991), *The Private Parts of Women* (1996), and *Now You See Me* (2002)—are set in Sheffield.

Although his play *The History Boys* (2004), about a group of sixth-formers being prepared for their Oxbridge exams, doesn't exactly specify a setting for the school, Alan Bennett himself has written that 'On the stage the school is vaguely taken to be in Sheffield, and in my head I called it Cutlers' and though there isn't a Cutlers' Grammar School in Sheffield I feel there ought to have been.'

SHERIFF HUTTON *North Yorkshire*

Village 12 m. NE of York, off the A64. The ruined castle (privately owned; no public access, but public footpaths run nearby), within a double moat and with its five storeys visible on the skyline from far away, was granted to the Earl of Surrey, victor of Flodden (1513). Skelton, who celebrated the battle in *Ballade of the Scottyshe Kynge*, spent Christmas (1522) here with Surrey's daughter-in-law Elizabeth (mother of the poet). Her ladies-in-waiting crown him among the great poets in his egotistic *Garlande of Laurell*, probably written here at this time.

SKIPTON *West Yorkshire*

Market town on the A59 and the A65. The Norman castle was repaired (1650–8) by Lady Anne Clifford (born here 1590), who built a new entrance. The poet Samuel Daniel became her tutor here until her marriage in 1609, and she acted in some of his masques performed at court.

SOCKBURN *North Yorkshire*

Village on the Tees, 13 m. N of Northallerton, off the A167. Dorothy Wordsworth wrote that Thomas Hutchinson's home here was 'a pleasant farm on the banks of the Tees' when she, her brother William, and Coleridge stayed with him in 1799 after their tour of Germany. Wordsworth married Hutchinson's sister Mary in 1802, and on a later visit wrote much of *The White Doe of Rylstone* here after seeing Scarsdale and Bolton Abbey.

SPURN HEAD *East Riding of Yorkshire*

Sand and shingle spit forming N bank of the mouth of the Humber estuary. The town of Ravenspur (or Ravenspurn) once stood near here, but succumbed to coastal erosion in the 1500s. Bolingbroke lands here ostensibly to reclaim his father's estates in Shakespeare's *Richard II*, an episode recalled in *1 Henry IV*.

STONEGRAVE *North Yorkshire*

Village 5 m. SE of Helmsley, on the B1257. Stonegrave House was the home for 20 years of Sir Herbert Read (1893–1968), the literary and art critic, whose writings include *In Defence of Shelley* (1935), *Poetry and Anarchism* (1938), collected poems and essays, and his

autobiography, *Annals of Innocence and Experience* (1940). His allegorical novel *The Green Child* (1935) is set in this part of Yorkshire.

SUTTON-ON-THE-FOREST *North Yorkshire*

Village on the B1363, 9 m. N of York. Laurence Sterne held the living here (1738–69), at first staying in York. In 1741 he married Elizabeth Lumley, whose money furnished and repaired the thatched vicarage (rebuilt after a fire) next to the church, where they lived until 1759. Her influence got him the parish of Stillington (2 m. N), to which he walked across the fields to preach in the afternoons after taking morning service here. Stephen Croft of Stillington Hall often entertained him but his other parishioners were not so friendly and were deliberately slow in saving him when he fell through the ice. Sterne went shooting with his pointer (once keeping his congregation waiting while he pursued a covey of partridges), played his fiddle, and painted portraits. His wife became deranged and had to be taken to an asylum. Sterne relieved his loneliness by writing *Tristram Shandy* (1760–7), which he paid to have printed in York and which was an immediate success. After acquiring the additional living of *Coxwold in 1760, he spent much of his time in fashionable circles.

THORNABY-ON-TEES *North Yorkshire*

Small town to the SW of Stockton-on-Tees. The novelist Pat Barker was born here in 1943, and educated at Grangefield Grammar School.

THORNTON *West Yorkshire*

Suburb 4 m. W of Bradford. Brontë Pl., off the B6145, leads to the High St., where a plaque on no. 74 commemorates the births of Charlotte (1816), Branwell (1817), Emily (1818), and Anne (1820) Brontë.

Thornton is the local village in Blake Morrison's poem 'Whinny Moor'.

THORPE GREEN HALL *North Yorkshire*

Mansion in the village of Little Ouseburn, off the A6265, 5 m. NE of Knaresborough. In March 1841 Anne Brontë became governess to the daughters of Mrs Robinson here. In 1843 her brother Branwell joined her as tutor to Edmund Robinson. Branwell, who took opium and was a drunkard, was the model for Arthur Huntingdon in Anne Brontë's novel *The Tenant of Wildfell Hall* (1848). Anne left the Robinsons in June 1845 and Branwell was dismissed a few weeks later. Her first novel, *Agnes Grey* (1847), is about the life of a governess who suffers from both her employers, one a parsimonious manufacturer and the other a fashionable country gentleman.

WAKEFIELD *West Yorkshire*

Industrial town on the A6638, 12 m. S of Leeds. Charles Waterton, naturalist and author of

Wanderings in South America (1825), was born (1782) at nearby Walton Hall and died there (1865). A cross marks his grave on an island in the park lake.

Richard Duke of York meets his end in Wakefield at the hands of Queen Margaret and Clifford in Shakespeare's *3 Henry VI*.

George Gissing, whose father was a chemist, was born (1857) and spent his youth in the house behind the shop in the marketplace at 30 Westgate Ⓟ. The Gissing Trust has restored the house and opened a Centre (1989) for exhibiting Gissing memorabilia (open Saturday afternoons, www.wakefield.gov.uk). George's father, author of two books on the flora of the neighbourhood, died when George was 13, and he and his brothers were sent away to boarding school. Wakefield appears as the heroine's home town in Gissing's novel *A Life's Morning* (1888).

The novelist and playwright David Storey was educated at the Queen Elizabeth Grammar School. To fund his education at the Slade School of Art, he signed a professional contract with Leeds Rugby League Club in 1952. His rugby-playing career provided him with material for *This Sporting Life* (1960), the novel that made his name. The narrator, Arthur Machin, lives in and plays for 'Highfield', based largely on Wakefield. Storey returned to the subject of rugby in his play *The Changing Room* (1972). 'The Place', the old house at the heart of the fictional Beaumont estate in Storey's novel *Radcliffe* (1963), suggests surviving old country houses such as Bretton Hall and Woolley Hall, whose estates have been swallowed up by the growth of Wakefield. After a period writing for the theatre in the 1960s, Storey returned to the region of his childhood with *Saville* (1976).

WHITBY *North Yorkshire*

Old whaling port on the A170, 20 m. NW of Scarborough. The cross commemorating Caedmon, an Anglo-Saxon herdsman, who in a vision suddenly received the power to compose verse, stands on the headland near the abbey he entered *c.* 670. Though other poems have been attributed to him, the hymn on Creation quoted by Bede is the only one thought to have survived.

Mary Linskill (1840–91), novelist, was born at 14 Blackburn's Yard (gone), off Church St. She left the local school at an early age and became a milliner's apprentice. The rector, the Revd W. Keane, encouraged her to read widely and seriously, and after various jobs as a governess she devoted herself to writing. On her father's death in 1874 she assumed responsibility for her mother and sister and they moved to a cottage (later called Clevedon Cottage) in Newholm, and then to a house, later Linskill Cottage, at Spring Vale. In spite of poverty and ill health Mary Linskill wrote 13 volumes as well as eight smaller books, the best-known being *Between the Heather and the Northern Sea* (1884) and *The Haven Under the Hill* (1886). Her readership was discriminating and included Gladstone, who entertained her

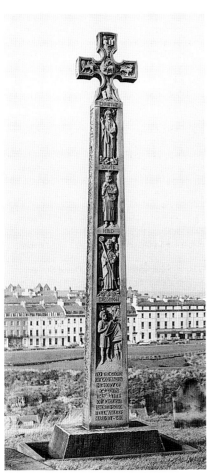

The cross in the churchyard at Whitby commemorating Caedmon

to dinner in London in 1887. She died at home and was buried in the cemetery, her grave marked by a Celtic cross. Her memorial in the old churchyard is inscribed, 'She wrote for all English readers of the lives and home of her own country folk, dwellers between the heather and the Northern Sea'.

C. L. Dodgson stayed in Whitby from July to September 1854, while he was an Oxford undergraduate, at 5 East Ter., the house of Mrs Hunton. His first literary works to have been published are believed to have been those that appeared in the *Whitby Gazette*, a weekly paper for visitors, with a small literary supplement. They consisted of a humorous poem, 'The Lady of the Ladle' (31 Aug.) and a mock-romantic story, 'Wilhelm von Schmitz' (in four instalments, 7–28 Sept.), and were signed 'B.B.' (he had not yet adopted the pen-name 'Lewis Carroll'). The 'Alice' stories were written many years later, but it is thought that the stretch of sands from Whitby North Cliff to Sandsend may have inspired the grief of the Walrus and the Carpenter in *Through the Looking-Glass* (1872), who 'wept like anything to see | Such quantities of sand'.

St Mary's Church has many memorials to the whalers, whom Elizabeth Gaskell, after staying

at 1 Abbey Ter. in 1859, portrayed in *Sylvia's Lovers* (1863), calling the town 'Monkshaven'. Alfred Ainger, preparing to holiday here in the 1890s with his nieces, was advised by Gerald du Maurier

> to see the forty or fifty cobles embark to herring-fish, with all the town, men women and children, pushing the boats off . . . Tell them to walk along the cliffs westward . . . through fields and over stiles till they reach Sylvia Robson's cottage (of course they know Sylvia's Lovers by heart) . . .

James Russell Lowell, American poet and first editor of the *Atlantic Monthly*, was a frequent visitor. He began coming for holidays when he was Minister (ambassador) in London (1880–5) and after his return to America he came back to England several times, visiting Whitby on each occasion. He used to stay at 3 Wellington Ter., West Cliff, with the Misses Gallilee, who, he said, would never let his rooms (the best in the house) so long as there was any chance of his coming. His *Letters* (ed. C. E. Norton, 1893) show his deep attachment to the old town. In August 1887 he wrote,

> A very primitive place it is, and the manners and ways of its people much like those of New England . . . 'Tis a wonderfully picturesque place, with the bleaching bones of its Abbey standing aloof on the bluff, and dominating the country for leagues.

Two years later, on his last visit, he said, 'This is my ninth year at Whitby, and the place loses none of its charm for me,' and, in another letter, 'I am very well . . . A poem even got itself written here, which seems to me to be not altogether bad.'

Bram Stoker knew Whitby well, and the heroine of his horror story *Dracula* (1897) gives a vivid description of the town and the harbour in the chapter headed 'Mina Murray's Journal' when she has come to stay with her friend Lucy Westrena in The Crescent. Her delight in her surroundings is marred by the sinister foreshadowings of Lucy's impending doom, which synchronize with the arrival of the Russian schooner *Demeter*, which runs ashore in a violent storm, manned only by the corpse of the captain, lashed to the wheel. Places described in the novel can be seen from the thoughtfully placed Bram Stoker Memorial Seat at the southern end of the West Cliff.

Leo Walmsley, who grew up in *Robin Hood's Bay, called Whitby 'Burn-harbour' in his novels about local fishermen.

An archaeological dig at Whitby Abbey is the setting for Michel Faber's novel *The Hundred and Ninety-Nine Steps* (2001). The steps rise up the town's East Cliff.

WINESTEAD *East Riding of Yorkshire*

Village off the A1033, 16 m. SE of Hull. Andrew Marvell was born (1621) at the rectory at the Rimswell turn (later the Old Rectory, rebuilt), but when he was 6 his father became 'lecturer' at Holy Trinity Church, Hull, and the family left for the town.

YAFFORTH *North Yorkshire*

Village on the Wiske and the B6271, 2 m. W of Northallerton. Thomas Rymer was born (1641) at the Tudor Old Hall (altered). He was the author of *A Short View of Tragedy* (1692) and editor of 15 volumes of historical documents, *Fœdera* (1704–35). The collection continued after his death (1713).

YORK *North Yorkshire*

Cathedral city on the Ouse, on the A19 and the A64, the Roman Eboracum. Alcuin, author of metrical annals and philosophical works, was born (735) in the city and educated at the Cathedral School, of which he became Master (778). He was later archbishop here but, after meeting Charlemagne, settled on the Continent.

The hero of Scott's *Ivanhoe* (1819), home from the Crusades, is helped by Isaac the Jew, who lived in Castlegate, where Ivanhoe is nursed by Rebecca. The Poet Laureate Laurence Eusden was educated (*c.* 1700) at St Peter's, now in Clifton on the NW, but whose traditions stem from Alcuin's school in the cloister.

Defoe, who makes York the birthplace of Robinson Crusoe, describes the city in *A Tour Through the Whole Island of Great Britain* (1724–7). Elizabeth Robinson, who as Mrs Montagu presided over a fashionable literary salon in London, was born (1720) at the Great House, now the Treasurer's House. Sterne, who married her cousin Elizabeth Lumley after a two-year courtship, also sometimes stayed there, as he was made prebend of the Cathedral in the same year (1741). Later he lodged in Stonegate, where his inamorata Miss Fourmantelle was also staying. *Tristram Shandy* (1760–7), published in Stonegate, though generally popular, was disapproved of in York, as many of the characters, including Dr Slop, were recognized as local people.

The Castle Museum, in the old prison, has the condemned cell where in 1739 Dick Turpin, a leading character in Ainsworth's *Rookwood* (1834), and 20 years later Eugene Aram, subject of a novel by Lytton, spent their last nights before being hanged. In 1811 Shelley, then just married to Harriet Westbrook, stayed with his friend Hogg at 20 Coney St., while trying without success to reconcile his father to the marriage. W. H. Auden, poet, dramatist, and critic, was born in 1907 at 54 Bootham.

The York-born novelist Kate Atkinson set her first novel, *Behind the Scenes at the Museum* (1995), here in her home town in the 1950s; her heroine, Ruby, lives above a pet shop in the run of little streets just under the Minster:

> In this street lived the first printers and the stained-glass craftsmen that filled the windows of the city with coloured light. The Ninth Legion Hispana that conquered the north marched up and down our street, the *via praetoria* of their great fort, before they disappeared into thin air. Guy Fawkes was born here, Dick Turpin was hung a few streets away and Robinson Crusoe, that other great hero, is also a native son of this

city. . . . These streets seethe with history; the building that our Shop occupies is centuries old and its walls tilt and its floors slope like a medieval funhouse. There has been a building on this spot since the Romans were here and needless to say it has its due portion of light-as-air occupants who wreathe themselves around the fixtures and fittings and linger mournfully at our backs . . .

The novelist Margaret Drabble and her sister the novelist A. S. Byatt, both *Sheffield-born, were educated in York, at the Mount School, a Quaker school on Dalton Ter. For the poet Tony Harrison, even the apparently unlikely setting of York railway station has been a worthy subject for a sharp and poignant poem, 'Changing at York'.

NORTH-EAST

ALNWICK (pr. 'Annick) *Northumberland*

NE English market town whose castle, the seat of the Duke of Northumberland, has become more recognizable in recent years as one of the locations for the film versions of J. K. Rowling's Harry Potter books, where it stands in for Hogwarts School of Witchcraft and Wizardry.

BARNARD CASTLE *co. Durham*

Old town 11 m. NW of Scotch Corner, on the A67. Dickens and his illustrator Hablot Browne stayed at the King's Head in 1838 when they were investigating abuses in cheap boarding schools to give authenticity to Dotheboys Hall in *Nicholas Nickleby* (1839). Dickens is said to have been influenced by the clockmaker's shop, then opposite the hotel, in choosing the title *Master Humphrey's Clock* (1840) for his new weekly, in which *The Old Curiosity Shop* (1840–1) and *Barnaby Rudge* (1840–1) appeared.

BAVINGTON *Northumberland*

Village approximately 16 m. N of Hexham. Kathleen Raine, poet, critic, and scholar of William Blake, spent part of her childhood living with an aunt in the village. As a small girl she would sit on a cherished rock and look at the moors and experience, as she put it in her autobiography *The Lion's Mouth* (1977), 'that happiness of finding in all about me the reflected radiance of what I then was—myself.'

CAPHEATON HALL *Northumberland*

Country house 14 m. SW of Morpeth, off the A696, home of the Swinburne family. Algernon Swinburne often spent holidays here at his grandfather's house in the mid-19th c. He used to ride his pony to Cambo, where he was tutored by the rector, and to Wallington, where his friends Sir Walter and Lady Trevelyan lived. Memories of Capheaton occur in *Lesbia Brandon* (1952), the unfinished novel in which Swinburne explores the state of mind of young Bertie at Ensdon, whose library the boy falls upon with 'miscellaneous voracity'.

DARLINGTON *co. Durham*

Industrial town, terminus of the first railway (1825). Ralph Hodgson was born (1871) in Garden St., ran away from school, and later lived in Japan and then in the US, where he died. His poems first appeared in the anthologies called *Georgian Poetry*. He also published short collections entitled *The Last*

Blackbird and Other Lines (1907), *Poems* (1917), and *The Skylark and Other Poems* (1958).

Joseph Malaby Dent, the publisher and founder of Everyman's Library, was born in Archer St. The tenth child of a house painter, his love of books was awakened after he joined a mutual improvement society in the town.

DURHAM *co. Durham*

Cathedral and university city which began on the high peninsula made by the Wear's horseshoe bend, with the building of a church in 995 to safeguard the coffin of St Cuthbert. This coffin (now restored and in the Chapter Library) was carried with them by the monks driven from the monastery at Lindisfarne by fear of Danish raids. The Cathedral, which replaced this church, still retains the Norman 'solidity' remarked on by Dr Johnson. It became the burial place in 1020 of the Venerable Bede, who died (735) at *Jarrow. The words 'Hac sunt in fossa Baedae venerabilis ossa' were carved on his 16th-c. tomb in the Lady Chapel called the Galilee in 1831, but he was first described as venerable in the 9th c.

Dobson's Drie Bobbes, edited by E. A. Horsman (1955), gives a lively account of Dobson's pranks at school and in the town in the middle of the 16th c.

The bishops, once Princes Palatine, lived in the castle (part of the University since 1836), where it is possible that Barnabe Barnes spent some time while his father was bishop (1577–87). Barnes, a younger son, published soon after his return from one of the Earl of Essex's expeditions *Parthenophil and*

Bede's 16th-century tomb in the Lady Chapel of Durham Cathedral

Parthenope, Sonnettes, Madrigals, Elegies and Odes (1593), which made his reputation as a poet, and as one who used the recently introduced sonnet form. His last publication, an anti-popish tragedy, *The Devil's Charter* (1607), is said to have influenced some scenes in Shakespeare's *The Tempest* and *Cymbeline*. Barnes was buried (1609) in the church of St Mary-le-Bow (rebuilt 1668), North Bailey, now disused and dwarfed by university buildings.

Christopher Smart attended Durham School in the 1730s and came to the notice of Henrietta, Duchess of Cleveland, of Raby Castle (off the A688 just E of Staindrop). She invited him to the castle, secured his entry to Cambridge in 1739, and gave him a pension.

Robert Surtees, born (1779) in South Bailey, spent most of his life gathering material for his *History of Durham* (1816–40). The Surtees Society, founded in 1834, the year of his death, concentrates on the literature of the old kingdom of Northumbria. Robert Smith Surtees, a younger son of another family, was educated at Durham School, which he left in 1819 to work in a solicitor's office. The death of his elder brother changed his fortune and he became High Sheriff in 1856. Thomas Jefferson Hogg, whose grandfather had made a fortune in Durham, also attended Durham School, and left for Oxford in 1810.

Sir Walter Scott visited Durham in 1827 and dined at the castle hall at the banquet given by the bishop to honour the Duke of Wellington. The old ballad 'Durham Garland' gave Scott the story for his novel *Guy Mannering* (1815). An inscription on the Prebends Bridge is a quotation from Scott's 'Harold the Dauntless':

> Grey towers of Durham
> Yet well I love thy mixed and massive piles
> Half Church of God, half castle 'gainst the Scot
> And long to roam these venerable aisles
> With records stored of deeds long since forgot.

Edward Bradley was at University College (1843–7) and he took the pseudonym Cuthbert Bede when he wrote his satire of Oxford University life, *The Adventures of Mr. Verdant Green, an Oxford Freshman* (1853–7). John Meade Falkner, whose post as tutor took him to Newcastle in 1883, after leaving Oxford, was drawn to the city, which he later made his home, by his interest in church architecture, archives, and heraldry. He combined these interests with a mystery in his novel *The Nebuly Coat* (1903). He became honorary librarian to the Dean and Chapter and was appointed honorary reader in Palaeography. He lived in Durham from 1892 until 1932 and was at The Divinity House, Palace Green, from 1902 until his death.

Hugh Walpole was a day-boy at Durham School when his father was principal of Bede College.

The critic and memoirist Lorna Sage won a scholarship to Durham University in 1961 and touches on the university years she shared with her husband, Vic, in her memoir *Bad Blood*

(2000). The novelists James Kirkup and Pat Barker studied here too.

FLODDEN FIELD *Northumberland*

The site, 3 m. SE of Coldstream off the A697, was where the battle (1513) took place in the wars between the Scots and the English. It was made the subject of poems and ballads, including *Ballade of the Scottysshe Kynge* (1513) by John Skelton, a ballad by Thomas Deloney, and 'The Flowers of the Forest' by Jane Elliot—a Scottish lament beginning 'I've heard them lilting at the ewe-milking'. Scott's *Marmion, A Tale of Flodden Field* (1808), a poem in six cantos, ends with the battle in which Marmion is killed.

HAMSTERLEY HALL *co. Durham*

Estate off the A694, 12 m. SW of Newcastle, inherited by R. S. Surtees from his father in 1838. Surtees was the creator of Jorrocks, the sporting grocer who became a Master of Foxhounds, and the Hall was probably the original of that described in his novel *Hillingdon Hall* (1845). He was buried (1864) in Ebchester church nearby.

HARTLEPOOL (pr. 'Hartlipool') *co. Durham*

Industrial town and port *c.* 17 m. SE of Durham. Compton Mackenzie was born (1883) in theatrical lodgings in Adelaide St., West Hartlepool. His parents were appearing at the Gaiety Theatre.

HEXHAM *Northumberland*

Market town on the A69, 22 m. W of Newcastle and just S of Hadrian's Wall. W. W. Gibson, friend of Rupert Brooke and the Georgian poets, was born in a bow-windowed Georgian house on Battle Hill. Only the room above the archway, which led to the stables, now remains—next to the post office. He wrote the lines for the fountain (now dry), erected in the marketplace in 1901.

JARROW *Tyne and Wear*

Industrial town on the Tyne, with shipyards and oil installations, formerly the site of the monastery where Bede spent much of his life. The partly 7th-c. St Paul's Church has a chair traditionally said to be his. Bede's Latin history, *Historia Ecclesiastica Gentis Anglorum*, finished in 731, contains the simile likening a man's life to the short span of a sparrow's flight from the dark of the night through a lighted room into the night again, which Wordsworth mentions in 'Persuasion', one of his *Ecclesiastical Sonnets* (1822). Catherine Cookson, who studied at Jarrow, at St Peter's and St Paul's Roman Catholic School at Tyne Docks, would become the area's most celebrated chronicler. Anne Stevenson takes a passage from Bede's *History* as the epigraph to her poem on the modern town in 'Jarrow', with:

> the blue sheet of river
> rusty with ships, the cranes
> against the monks' sky.

KELLOE *co. Durham*

Village off the A177, 7 m. SE of Durham. Elizabeth Barrett was born (1806) at Coxhoe Hall, an 18th-c. mansion (gone, site now in the conifers E of the Kelloe–Coxhoe road near the junction with the B6291) where her parents stayed before moving to their estate at Hope End. A tablet in Kelloe Church states she was 'a great poetess, a noble woman, a devoted wife'.

MIDDLETON ST GEORGE *co. Durham*

Village 2 m. from Darlington. The ex-RAF base near the village, now Durham Tees Valley Airport, is the subject of Alan Brownjohn's poem 'At Middleton St George'.

MORPETH *Northumberland*

Small town on the Wansbeck (or Wensbeck) and the A1. Mark Akenside, who often stayed here as a youth, praised the town in these lines from *The Pleasures of Imagination* (1744):

> O ye Northumbrian shades! which overlook
> The rocky pavement and the mossy falls
> Of solitary WENSBECK's limpid stream,
> How gladly I recall your well-known seats,
> Beloved of old; and that delightful time,
> When all alone, for many a summer's day,
> I wander'd through your calm recesses, led
> In silence, by some powerful hand unseen.

NEWCASTLE UPON TYNE & GATESHEAD *Tyne and Wear*

Newcastle is a port on the A167, and former county town of Northumberland, which grew up round the strategic site chosen by the Romans for a station on Hadrian's Wall and by the Normans for a castle. On the opposite (S) bank of the Tyne to Newcastle, is the town of Gateshead.

Mark Akenside was born (1721) in Butcher Bank (now Akenside Hill). After a short time at the free school, he was sent to a private academy kept by a dissenting minister, a calling he intended to follow, when he set out for Edinburgh at 18.

John Forster, biographer of his friend Charles Dickens, was born (1812) in Gallowgate, where his father was a dairy farmer. He began writing at an early age and while still at the Royal Grammar School had his play *Charles at Tunbridge* performed at Newcastle Theatre in 1828. Another native was Hugh Stowell Scott, son of a shipowner. He went away to school and spent much of his life abroad. His travels gave his historical novels, many of which have a European background, an authentic setting. He wrote as 'Henry Seton Merriman'.

In 1916 a Russian marine engineer named Evgeni Zamyatin (1884–1937) came to Newcastle to supervise the construction of a number of ice-breakers for the then tsarist Russian government. He worked for 18 months at the Armstrong Whitworth shipbuilding yard, and lived for most of this time at 19 Sanderson Rd, Jesmond, and has described how he used to return here from the yard in the evening to check his blueprints of ice-breakers and work on his 'novel about the English—*Islanders*'. This 'novel' is very short, but in its fierce satire on dull middle-class life and manners, enlivened by a few non-conforming rebels, is compelling reading. After his return to Russia in 1917 he wrote *The Fisher of Men*, intended as a continuation of *Islanders*, but in the end not so fully developed. His best-known novel, *We* (1920), was praised by George Orwell, who was interested in 'that kind of book' and kept making notes for one himself some years before his *1984* was published (1948). *We* was not published in Russia, as being too critical of state control of individual freedom, and his work has been strangely neglected in English-speaking countries.

The novelist Rosamond Lehmann moved in 1924 with her first husband to 3 Sydenham Ter., near the Town Moor. She didn't much care for the city's docks and factories or the noise from the trams which ran near the house.

Basil Bunting was born at 27 Denton Rd, Scotswood upon Tyne, in 1900, now on the outskirts of Newcastle. He was educated at the Newcastle upon Tyne Royal Grammar School for two years before being moved to Quaker schools. He studied seamanship at Nellists' Nautical School in the late 1930s. The first reading of his poem 'Briggflatts' (1965) took place at the Morden Tower on Back Stowell St., as did the first reading in Europe of Allan Ginsberg's poem *Kaddish* (1959). The tower has hosted readings by many well-known poets since it opened in 1964. The angel under which readings are given is the subject of Anne Stevenson's poem, 'The Morden Angel':

> Here come those poets again,
> their inelegant wails!
> If only my wings would work.
> If only my smile could talk.

In support of her research into an English working-class family for her novel *Cotters' England* (1967), Christina Stead stayed with the Kelly family at 37 South St. in 1949 (gone). She immersed herself in family life and started writing letters in Tyneside speech. Her friend Annie Dooley (née Kelly) provided the basis

for the heroine, Nelly Cotter, and the book's 'Bridgehead' is a disguised version of Gateshead.

Pat Barker's novel *Border Crossing* (2001) is a contemporary Newcastle novel, whose tension is set up in the very first scene with a suicide attempt, a young man sighted walking into the Tyne: 'His trainers bit into the gravel . . . and then he was slipping and slithering over the rotted timbers of the jetty. He stood, poised, at the end, a black shape smudged with mist . . .'.

Having left Tyneside for the south many years earlier, Catherine Cookson returned in the 1970s; her final home was in Jesmond, at 23 Glastonbury Grove, where she died on 11 June 1998.

The 'Liverpool poet' Adrian Henri studied art at King's College, Newcastle. Today the city is home to the poet Tony Harrison.

Seven Stories, the Centre for Children's Books, is at 30 Lime St., in the Ouseburn Valley (www.sevenstories.org.uk).

NORHAM CASTLE *Northumberland*

Ruined 12th-c. castle on the Tweed, 7 m. SW of Berwick-upon-Tweed. This border stronghold of Durham's Princes Palatine was the setting for the opening scenes of *Marmion* (1808), Scott's long poem about the battle of Flodden in 1513.

NORTON *co. Durham*

Former village now joined to Stockton-on-Tees. Thomas Jefferson Hogg, friend and first biographer of Shelley, was born (1792) at Norton House.

OLD PARK *co. Durham*

Farm on the Wilmington road off the A688, 3 m. NE of Bishop Auckland. Thomas Gray was a visitor in the 1760s to his friend Dr Thomas Wharton, whose experimental farm and gardens were an attraction for the tourists of his day.

ROOKHOPE *co. Durham*

Former Pennine lead-mining and fluospar-mining village. As a 12-year-old, W. H. Auden came to know the abandoned mines and 'most wonderfully desolate' industrial landscape at Rookhope. It inspired a visionary intensity he

was to describe in many essays and poems—notably 'New Year Letter'—throughout his career:

> In Rookhope I was first aware
> Of self and not-self, Death and Dread . . .

SEAHAM *co. Durham*

A coal port off the A19, 6 m. SE of Sunderland. Seaham Hall (now a hotel) was the home of Anne Isabella Milbanke, whose marriage ceremony to Lord Byron took place in the drawing room in January 1815.

SOUTH SHIELDS *Tyne and Wear*

Coastal town at the mouth of the Tyne, on the S bank. The poet James Kirkup was born in South Shields in 1918, and studied at South Shields High School. Kirkup's autobiographical *The Only Child* (1957) offers vivid descriptions of a northern childhood, from birth in 'a two-roomed downstairs flat in Cockburn Street, only a few doors from where my Granny Johnson lived'.

South Shields is now more associated with another writer, though, the novelist Catherine Cookson—indeed, the area now refers to itself as 'Catherine Cookson Country' and the town museum includes a replica of her home. Cookson was born at 5 Leam Lane, on 20 June 1906. Her mother was in service, and young Catherine, in her own words, 'scavenged for wood and coal on the banks of the Tyne'—she called herself 'a child of the Tyne', and her books chart the development of the region where she grew up through the lives of their working-class heroines. She herself took a job at a workhouse laundry in Harton.

WALLINGTON *Northumberland*

Country house (NT), 13 m. W of Morpeth, on the B6342, home of the Trevelyan family since 1777. In the mid-19th c. Ruskin made many visits here. In 1853 he came with his wife and the Pre-Raphaelite painter Millais. His visit in 1857 coincided with that of William Bell Scott, who was painting the new hall, made by covering in the courtyard, where his *St Cuthbert* was being displayed. Ruskin first met Swinburne here riding from his home at *Capheaton to tuition at Cambo rectory.

Wales

Wales

ABER *Gwynedd*

Small village 5 m. E of Bangor on the A55. Here Llywelyn the Great, Prince of Gwynedd, had his court in the early 13th c. His wife, Joan, daughter of the English king John, is said to have had a brief affair with Llywelyn's prisoner the young Marcher lord William de Braose, who was hanged for that reason in 1230. One of the finest plays ever written in Welsh, *Siwan* (1956) by Saunders Lewis, is set at Llywelyn's court.

ABERCYNON (pr. Abbĕr'kŭnnŏn) *Glamorgan*

Former mining village at the confluence of the rivers Cynon and Taff, 4 m. N of Pontypridd on the A470. Here in 1909 the short-story writer, novelist, and oral historian George Ewart Evans was born at Bristol House, Glancynon Ter., next to Calfaria Chapel. The village and valley are lovingly portrayed in his short novel *The Voices of the Children* (1947), his collection of short stories *Let Dogs Delight* (1975), and his autobiography *The Strength of the Hills* (1983).

ABERDARON *Gwynedd*

Fishing village at the end of the Llŷn peninsula. R. S. Thomas was appointed vicar of Aberdaron in 1967. He described life here in all its moods, 'joyful and sad, quiescent and turbulent' in his prose journal *Blwyddyn yn llyn* (A Year in Llŷn, 1990) and the difficulty of his ministry in poems such as 'The Moon in Lleyn':

> Just as though
> choirs had not sung, shells
> have swallowed them; the tide laps
> at the Bible; the bell fetches
> no people to the brittle miracle
> of the bread. The sand is waiting
> for the running back of the grains
> in the wall into its blond
> glass. Religion is over, and
> what will emerge from the body
> of the new moon, no one
> can say.

A memorial in honour of the science-fiction novelist John Wyndham stands at Cwyrt Farm near Aberdaron.

ABEREDW (pr. Abbĕr'ĕdoo) *Powys*

Small village on the B4567, 5 m. SE of Builth Wells, in the valley of the Wye. The rocky, wooded steep inspired Francis Kilvert, in an entry in his *Diary* for 13 April 1875, to rhapsodize thus:

> Oh, Aberedw, Aberedw. Would God I might dwell and die by thee. Oh, Aberedw, Aberedw. I never pass thy enchanted gorge and look up through the magic gateway of thy Rocks without

seeming for a moment to be looking in at the gates of Paradise just left ajar . . . Oh, Aberedw, Aberedw.

ABERGAVENNY *Monmouthshire*

Market town on the A40 at the confluence of the rivers Gavenny and Usk. In the 19th c. it was an important centre in the movement to revive the literary culture of Wales. At the Sun Inn (later the Coach and Horses in Cross St.) the society known as Cymreigyddion y Fenni was inaugurated in 1833. For nearly 30 years the annual eisteddfod attracted many visitors from outside Wales, including the French poet Alphonse de Lamartine in 1839. Here, in 1848, Thomas Stephens won a prize for the essay subsequently published as *The Literature of the Kymry* (1849), which became the authoritative work on Welsh literature throughout Europe.

ABERGELE (pr. Abbĕr'gĕlĕ) *Conwy*

Small coastal resort on the A55, 12 m. E of Llandudno. The Calvinist Methodist minister and writer Robert Ambrose Jones (Emrys ap Iwan) was born at Bryn Aber nearby, and attended the elementary school until he was 14.

ABERGWILI *Carmarthenshire*

Little village on the A40, 2 m. NE of Carmarthen. A minor road leads steeply up to the N and circles round Merlin Hill, where the enchantress Nimue ('The Lady of the Lake') is said to have lured the aged Merlin and buried him deep under a rock. Merlin's Oak, which used to stand in Carmarthen, has been moved to Carmarthen Museum in Tŷ'r Esgob.

ABERYSTWYTH *Cardiganshire*

Seaside resort and university town on Cardigan Bay, on the A487. The National Library of Wales (founded 1907), on a hill E of the town, contains a unique collection of books in the Welsh language or relating to Wales. Among its treasures are the manuscript of the 12th-c. *Black Book of Carmarthen*, the *White Book of Roderick*, and the *Book of Taliesin*. As a copyright library (since 1911) it is entitled to receive new publications issued in Great Britain and Ireland.

Owen Morgan Edwards entered the University College of Wales in 1880, where he excelled in English and History. He proceeded in 1883 to the University of Glasgow and then to Oxford. Robert Williams Parry graduated in English at University College in 1908 and then followed a teaching career until going to University College, Bangor, as an assistant lecturer in 1921.

Thomas Gwynn Jones became a cataloguer in the National Library in 1909. He lived first at Eirlys (now The Vicarage), Y Buarth, moving

later to Hafan in the village of Bow Street, just N of the town. In 1913 he was appointed lecturer in Welsh at University College, and Professor of Welsh Literature in 1919. He retired in 1939 and was awarded an Hon. D.Litt. by the University of Wales and by the University of Ireland. He died at Willow Lawn, Caradog Rd, and was buried in Llanbadarn Rd cemetery. He had begun writing poetry in the 1880s and his first major poem, a satirical work entitled 'Gwlad y Gân' (The Land of Song), appeared first in periodicals and later in a collection called *Gwlad y Gân a Chaniadau Eraill* (The Land of Song and Other Poems) in 1902, in which year he also won the Bangor National Eisteddfod chair with his ode 'Ymadawiad Arthur' (The Passing of Arthur)—a poem which marked the beginning of a new era in Welsh poetry in subject, language, and form. He won the chair again in 1909 with his ode 'Gwlad y Bryniau' (Land of the Hills). Both odes were included in *Detholiad o Ganiadau* (A Selection of Poems). He also published novels, plays, a travel book, and other works.

The Welsh-language poet T. H. Parry-Williams was educated at University College before going to Jesus College, Oxford, in 1909. He returned in 1914 as lecturer in Welsh, and became Professor from 1920 until his retirement in 1952. He was knighted in 1958 and was awarded an Hon. LL D by the University of Wales in 1960. He died at his home, Wern, North Rd, in 1975. D. J. Williams entered University College in 1911 and graduated in Welsh and English before proceeding to Jesus College, Oxford, in 1916.

David Gwenallt Jones, Welsh-language poet, author, and critic, entered University College in 1919, after a two-year imprisonment as a conscientious objector, and graduated with honours in Welsh and English. In 1927 he was appointed lecturer in the Department of Welsh and later became Reader until his retirement in 1967. He lived at Rhyd-y-môr, Ffordd Rheidol, Penparcau, and is buried in Aberystwyth cemetery, where his grave is marked by a specially commissioned stone. He twice won the National Eisteddfod chair: at Swansea (1926) with 'Y Mynach' (The Monk) and in Bangor (1931) with 'Breuddwyd y Bardd' (The Poet's Dream). His first volume of verse *Ysgubau'r Awen* (Sheaves of the Muse, 1939) established his reputation as a major poet and was followed by other collections, *Cnoi Cil* (Ruminating, 1942), *Eples* (Leaven, 1951), *Gwreiddiau* (Roots, 1959), and *Y Coed* (Trees, 1969). The Welsh-language poet Waldo Williams was a student from 1923 to 1927 at University College, where he graduated in English.

Alun Lewis read History here in 1932–5 and his first poem, describing the waking of a ladybird, was published in the college literary magazine, *The Dragon*, to which he also contributed six short stories. His story 'The Wanderers' appeared in the *Welsh Review* (1939). He trained as a teacher and taught at Lewis Boys' School, Pengam, from 1938 to 1940. In 1941 he joined the Officer Cadet Training Unit and was posted to Woodbridge, Suffolk, and then Bovington, Dorset. During this period *Raiders' Dawn and Other Poems* (1942) and a volume of short stories, *The Last Inspection* (1942), were published. He was killed on active service in Burma (1944) and his poems *Ha! Ha! Among the Trumpets* (1945) and previously uncollected short stories *In the Green Tree* (1948) were published posthumously.

Caradoc Evans, who had lived in London during his writing career, returned to his native land in 1939 and spent the rest of his life in and near Aberystwyth, living at Bryn Awelon, New Cross, a village 6 m. SE, on the B4340, and in Aberystwyth, at Queens Square House, and finally at 36a North Parade. He is buried in Horeb Chapel graveyard, New Cross, near the top wall, a little to the right. The inscription on his gravestone reads: 'Bury me lightly so that the small rain may reach my face and the fluttering of the butterfly shall not escape my ear.'

The Marxist poet T. E. Nicholas settled in the town in 1921, practising as a dentist, and lived here at Glascoed in Elm Tree Ave. until his death in 1971. A selection of his political verse (with English prose renderings) appeared in the volume *Tros Ryddid Daear* in 1981.

Goronwy Rees, who was born in Aberystwyth, the son of a minister of the Presbyterian Church, spent his childhood in the town. He returned in 1953 as Principal of the University College, but stayed only four years. His childhood and the stormy course of his principalship are described in his volumes of autobiography, *A Bundle of Sensations* (1960) and *A Chapter of Accidents* (1972).

The poet and translator of Welsh poetry Gwyn Williams (1904–90) lived the last years of his life at 40 Queen St.

BALA *Gwynedd*

Small market town at the head of Llyn Tegid. Jacques Austerlitz, the principal character of W. G. Sebald's last novel, *Austerlitz* (2001), is brought to Britain as a child by one of the Kindertransports to live in Bala with the Calvinist preacher and former missionary Emyr Elias and his wife. The novel describes journeys through the surrounding countryside and life at home: 'The manse was always freezing . . . not just in winter, when the only fire was often in the kitchen stove and the stone floor in the hallway was frequently covered with hoar frost, but in autumn too, and well into spring and the infallibly wet summers.'

BANGOR *Gwynedd*

Cathedral town on the A5, near the mouth of the Menai Straits. John Morris-Jones, scholar,

critic, and Welsh-language poet, attended Friars School from 1876 to 1879. In 1889 he returned to Bangor as lecturer in Welsh at the University College of North Wales, becoming Professor in 1895. His early poetry, collected and published as *Caniadau* in 1907, included original lyrics, translations from Heine, and the stanzas from the Persian of Omar Khayyám. His major work of scholarship, the result of many years' study of the language, was *A Welsh Grammar Historical and Comparative* (1913), which remains the standard grammar on literary Welsh. The language and style of poetry were his great interest, and his book *Cerdd Dafod* (1925) embodies his exhaustive study of traditional Welsh prosody. He was knighted in 1918 and the following year was awarded an Hon. LL D by the University of Glasgow and in 1927 an Hon. D.Litt. from the National University of Ireland.

Albert Evans-Jones (whose bardic name was Cynan), Welsh-language poet and eminent public figure, entered the University College of North Wales in 1913 and graduated in 1916. After serving with the RAMC in Salonika (1916–18) he was minister of the Welsh Presbyterian church at Penmaenmawr from 1920 to 1931. He then returned to Bangor to become lecturer on Welsh literature for the Extra-Mural Department of University College (1931–60). He was closely associated with the National Eisteddfod and the Gorsedd of Bards (for which he was Recorder, 1935–70) and was twice elected (1949 and 1962) for a three-year term as Arch-Druid. In 1961 he was awarded an Hon. D.Litt. by the University of Wales, and in 1969 he was knighted. His large and varied literary output included lyrics, translations, ballads, hymns, sonnets, and two plays, *Hywel Harris* (1932) and *Absalom fy Mab* (Absalom my Son) (1957). A collection of his poems, *Cerddi Cynan*, was published in 1959 (enlarged edn, 1967).

Kate Roberts had a thorough education in literary Welsh at the college when she studied under John Morris-Jones. John Gwilym Jones entered the college after a year as a pupil-teacher. He returned in 1953 as lecturer in Welsh, later as a Reader, and retired in 1971.

The Welsh-language poet Robert Williams Parry was assistant lecturer at University College for the Welsh Department and for extra-mural evening classes from 1921 to 1944. His poetry, largely concerned with nature and the rejection of the industrial scene, was published in two volumes: *Yr Haf a Cherddi Eraill* (Summer and Other Poems, 1924) and *Cerddi'r Gaeaf* (Poems of Winter, 1953). The Welsh-language novelist and poet T. Rowland Hughes graduated in 1925 with first-class honours in English and in 1928 was awarded a University of Wales Fellowship at Jesus College, *Oxford.

R. S. Thomas studied Classics at the University College of North Wales from 1932 to 1935. His lodgings overlooked the river Menai towards Anglesey and his childhood home. He made his way, as he recorded in his

autobiography *Neb* (No-one, 1985), 'like a caterpillar' through the Latin and Greek texts set for his degree.

The poet and critic Alun Llywelyn-Williams was Director of Extra-Mural Studies from 1948 and had a personal Chair at the University from 1975 until his retirement. He lived at Penylan in Belmont Rd and latterly at Cwm Bychan in Ffriddoedd Rd.

The novelist Alice Thomas Ellis was educated at Bangor Grammar School.

BARDSEY *Gwynedd*

Small island 2 m. off the extreme SW tip of the Llŷn peninsula; it is known in Welsh as Ynys Enlli. A monastic community was established in the 6th c. and, according to tradition, some 20,000 saints are buried here. They were eulogized in poems by Lewys Glyn Cothi and Hywel ap Rheinaullt, among others. The island was a place of pilgrimage in the Middle Ages. The religious house was dissolved about 1537, but the island continued to inspire Welsh poets such as T. Gwynn Jones. Among writers who lived on Bardsey was Brenda Chamberlain, whose *Tide Race* (1962) is an account of the excitements and austerity of her life there.

BETHEL *Gwynedd*

Village in the parish of Llanddeiniolen, *c.* 3 m. NE of Caernarfon, on the B4366. The Welsh-language poet William John Gruffydd was born (1881) at Gorffwysfa, where a memorial stone marks his childhood home. He was educated at the village school before going to Caernarfon Grammar School. He is buried at Llanddeiniolen, NE of Bethel, near the yew tree of his most celebrated poem.

BETHESDA *Gwynedd*

Former slate-quarrying town on the E side of the A5, 7 m. SE of Bangor. The Welsh-language poet Robert Williams Parry lived here after his marriage in 1923 at 3 Coetmor Estate. He is buried in Coetmor cemetery, where his tombstone bears a low-relief carving of Y Lôn Goed, a grass track, lined both sides by trees, famed in one of his best-known poems.

The poet and novelist Caradog Prichard was born here at Llwyn Onn in 1904 and the district forms the background for his novel *Un Nos Ola Leuad* (One Moonlit Night, 1961). His grave is in the Anglican section of Coetmor cemetery.

BETWS-YN-RHOS *Conwy*

Village on the B5381, *c.* 10 m. W of St Asaph. Thomas Gwynn Jones was born at Gwyndy Uchaf farm nearby and received elementary education at schools in the neighbourhood as his family moved to other farms. After beginning his career in journalism at *Denbigh he worked in Liverpool, *Caernarfon, and *Mold before settling in *Aberystwyth.

BLAENAU FFESTINIOG *Gwynedd*

Town on the A470, 11 m. NE of Porthmadog. John Cowper Powys moved to 1 Waterloo in 1955 and spent his last years at nearby Manod.

Among the works published while he was here are the novels *Atlantis* (1956), and *All or Nothing* (1960). *Poems* (1964), selected by Kenneth Hopkins, was published the year after his death here.

The Welsh Puritan author Morgan Llwyd was born in 1619 at Cynfal Fawr, a farmhouse 1 m. S of Ffestiniog off the A470. Part of the original house can still be seen and Llwyd's birth here is recorded on a plaque. He was the author of books in both English and Welsh, notably *Llyfr y Tri Aderyn* (The Book of the Three Birds, 1653), a clarion call to the Welsh to prepare themselves for the imminent coming of Christ to reign as King on earth.

BRECON *Powys*

Historic market town in mid Wales. From a monastic room at the top of a medieval tower-house at the nearby village of Scethrog, overlooking meadows and a bend of the river Usk, Bruce Chatwin wrote much of his novel set in the Welsh border country *On the Black Hill* (1982).

BRO GYNIN *Cardiganshire*

Once a farm, 2 m. E of Aberystwyth, in the parish of Llanbadarn Fawr. This has been widely accepted as the birthplace of the 14th-c. Welsh poet Dafydd ap Gwilym. It is reached by following a right-hand turn off the A487 to Penrhyncoch and then left to Salem and finally left again. The remains of the house ℗ can be seen in the grounds of a bungalow. Dafydd ap Gwilym was a supreme master of the Welsh language and of the metrical rules of his time.

BUILTH WELLS *Powys*

Market town on the river Wye at the junction of the A470 and the A483. Here, in 1790, was born Thomas Jefferey Llywelyn Prichard, the author of *The Adventures and Vagaries of Twm Shon Catti* (1824), sometimes said to be the first novel by a Welsh writer in English. He is commemorated by a sculpture in the courtyard of Builth High School.

Hilda Vaughan, who later became the wife of Charles Morgan, was born in 1892 at a house known as The Castle, a small Victorian mansion, in the town. The house is no longer there. Some of her novels are set in Radnorshire, the county with which she is generally associated; they include *The Battle to the Weak* (1925), *Her Father's House* (1930), and *The Invader* (1928).

The poet T. Harri Jones was born at Cwm Crogau, a farm in the Hirnant valley off the B4358 between Newbridge-on-Wye and Llanafan. He emigrated to Australia in 1959 and there made his name as the author of *The Enemy in the Heart* (1957), *Songs of a Mad Prince* (1960), and *The Beast at the Door* (1963). After his death by drowning, his ashes were buried in the churchyard of St Michael's at Llanfihangel Brynpabuan, near the entrance to Cwm Crogau. The hill Allt-y-clych, which figures in many of his poems, overlooks the church. A bust of T. H. Jones is kept at Builth High School.

CAERLEON *Monmouthshire*

Town on the Usk, 3 m. NE of Newport. The name means 'Fortress of the Legion' and the extensive remains of the amphitheatre and barracks of the Roman stronghold of AD 80 are still there. The most impressive description of ancient Caerleon is in the seventh part of Geoffrey of Monmouth's *History of the Kings of Britain*, from which Thomas Love Peacock borrowed in *The Misfortunes of Elphin* (1829). The town is probably the Carlion of Malory's *Le Morte d'Arthur* (1485), where Arthur was crowned and held his court. Tennyson stayed at the Hanbury Arms (℗ inside) in 1856 while gathering material for the Arthurian legends of *Idylls of the King* (1859).

Arthur Machen (born Arthur Llewellyn Jones), writer of mystical, romantic, and macabre stories, who made his name in the First World War as the author of 'The Angels of Mons' in *The Bowmen and Other Legends* (1915), was born at 33 High St. (1863). Soon after his birth he was taken to Llanddewi rectory, not far away, where his father was rector, and spent his boyhood and youth there. His novel *The Hill of Dreams* (1907) describes Caerleon and its environs.

The poet Clifford Dyment spent several happy years at 1 Ashwell Terr. (gone), describing his childhood in his autobiography, *The Railway Game* (1962).

CAERNARFON *Gwynedd*

Ancient county town on the A487, near the SW end of the Menai Strait. It stands on the site of the Roman fort Segontium, which gave the Welsh name Caer Saint. The place features in many early Welsh tales. The offices of the newspaper *Yr Herald Cymraeg* (est. 1855) were situated in the town (now moved to Llandudno Junction), and many prominent Welsh literary figures have worked on the paper including Thomas Gwynn Jones.

William John Gruffydd, Welsh-language poet and author, attended the Grammar School before going to Jesus College, Oxford. After his retirement in 1946 from the chair of Welsh at University College, Cardiff, he lived near Caernarfon for the last eight years of his life.

CAERPHILLY *Monmouthshire*

Industrial town 8 m. N of Cardiff on the A469. The philosopher David Williams was born in 1738 at Waun Waelod, a house later in ruins behind the Old Carpenters' Arms, in the parish of Eglwys Ilan to the W of the town. There is a memorial in the small park, Parc Dafydd Williams, which faces the castle on its S side. Williams attracted the attention of Benjamin Franklin with his *Treatise on Education* (1774), and his *Liturgy on the Universal Principles of Religion and Morality* (1776) was praised by Voltaire and Rousseau. His reputation in France was established by a translation of his *Letters on Political Liberty* (1782), a defence of the American colonists. Ten years later he was awarded the honorary citizenship of France and invited to Paris to help draw up a

constitution for the Girondists. His chief claim to fame in England lies in his establishment of the Royal Literary Fund in 1790.

CAPEL BANGOR *Cardiganshire*

Village 6 m. E of Aberystwyth on the A44. At the farm known as Pwllcenawon, on the bank of the river Rheidol, the essayist Lewis Edwards was born in 1809. He was the founder in 1843 of the influential magazine *Y Traethodydd*. His literary essays appeared in the volume *Traethodau Llenyddol* (1865). There is a bust of the author against the wall of the chapel in the village.

CARDIFF *Glamorgan*

Capital city of Wales, situated on the Taff. William John Gruffydd, Welsh-language poet and author, was an assistant lecturer in Welsh at University College from 1906 to 1915. After serving with the Royal Navy (1915–18) he was appointed to the chair of Welsh, which he held until his retirement in 1946. His literary output was prolific and diverse and included poetry, stories, literary and philosophic essays, criticism, autobiography, and scholarly works. In 1900 he published, with R. Silyn Roberts, a book of lyrics entitled *Telynegion*. His other published poems are included in *Caneuon a Cherddi* (Songs and Poems, 1906), *Ynys yr Hud* (The Enchanted Island, 1923), and *Caniadau* (Poems, 1932). His *History of Welsh Literature* (1450–1600) (1922) and *History of Welsh Prose* (1540–1660) (1926) have become standard works, and his anthology of lyrical poems *Y Flodeugerdd Gymraeg* (1931) is one of the best anthologies in the Welsh language. From 1922 to 1951 he was editor of the literary magazine *Y Llenor*, said to have been the 'most brilliant piece of literary journalism' ever seen in Wales. The autobiographical *Hen Atgofion* (Old Memories, 1936) vividly depicts society in the late 19th c. Gruffydd's home in Cardiff was at 22 Lôn y Dail, Rhiwbina, a northern suburb.

The novelist Howard Spring was born (1889) at 32 Edward St., Canton (now an inner suburb). The street was renamed Albert St. c. 1892, but the house has been demolished. After his father's death Howard left school and worked in a butcher's shop. Later he became an office boy for the *South Wales News* and attended evening classes at University College, which his editor paid for. His childhood in Cardiff is evoked in his book *Heaven Lies About Us* (1939). He became a reporter on the paper and eventually moved to Bradford and then to *Manchester.

The poet Alun Llywelyn-Williams was born in Roath Park in 1913 and brought up at 33 Ninian Rd in that part of the city. He described his boyhood in his autobiography, *Gwanwyn yn y Ddinas* (1975).

Ivor Novello, man of the theatre, was born David Ivor Davies at 95 Cowbridge Rd ℗ in 1893. A few months later the family moved to 11 Cathedral Rd, now the offices of Lloyds Bank and known as Novello House; there is a display of memorabilia in the reception area. He won fame during the First World War as the composer of the song 'Keep the Home Fires Burning' and for the rest of his life enjoyed success as actor and playwright. His greatest triumphs were the musical comedies *Glamorous Night* (1935), *Careless Rapture* (1936), *The Dancing Years* (1939), *Perchance to Dream* (1945), and *King's Rhapsody* (1949).

Children's writer Roald Dahl was born at Villa Marie (now Tŷ Gwyn) in Fairwater Rd in 1916. Three years later the family moved to Tŷ Mynydd in the northern suburb of Radyr, but that house has been demolished. In 1920 they moved to Llandaff, where they lived at Cumberland Lodge, now part of Howells School and where Roald Dahl was educated at the Cathedral School. His childhood is described in *Boy* (1984). The last years of his life were spent at Gipsy Cottage in *Great Missenden.

In 1929 the novelist and playwright Jack Jones came to Rhiwbina and lived above a boot shop on the junction of Heol-y-Bryn and Heol-y-Coed, where he wrote the novels *Rhondda Roundabout* (1934) and *Black Parade* (1935), the first part of an autobiography, *Unfinished Journey* (1937), and a play, *Land of My Fathers* (1937). He moved to a house called Sarandai in 1938, where he lived until 1946, writing the novels *Off to Philadelphia in the Morning* (1947), *Some Trust in Chariots* (1948), and *River Out of Eden* (1951), as well as a further autobiographical instalment, *Me and Mine* (1946). His last home was at 57 Pen-y-dre, where the following novels were written: *Lily of the Valley* (1952), *Lucky Lear* (1952), *Time and the Business* (1953), *Choral Symphony* (1955), and *Come, Night; End Day!* (1956). He died at his home in 1970 and was buried at Pantmawr cemetery. There is a collection of his books and other materials at Rhiwbina Public Library.

T. Rowland Hughes was a producer of feature programmes with the BBC from 1935 to 1945. He had already been acclaimed as a poet before he began writing novels, having won the chair at the National Eisteddfod in 1937 for his ode in strict metres 'Y Ffin' (The Boundary), and in the Radio Eisteddfod of 1940 for his poem 'Pererinion' (Pilgrims). He turned to writing novels when his health was failing. The first, *O Law i Law* (From Hand to Hand, 1943), was enthusiastically received and was followed by four more, published annually. They are largely concerned with life in the slate-quarrying area of North Wales. His collected poems *Cân neu Ddwy* (A Song or Two) were published in 1948. He died at his home in 1948 and was buried in Cathays cemetery, where his gravestone bears the inscription 'Y Dewraf o'n Hawduron' (The Bravest of Our Writers).

The Central Public Library contains a number of old Welsh manuscripts, including the 'Llyfr Aneirin' (Book of Aneirin), a manuscript dating back to *c.* 1265, in which there is the long heroic poem by the 6th-c. poet Aneirin, the 'Gododdin', 1,480 lines dealing with a host of Mynyddawg Mwynfawr and the march of 300 warriors to Catterick to recapture it from the Saxons, as well as three other old poems also ascribed to Aneirin.

The poet John Tripp is commemorated by a bench near Ararat Chapel on the common in the suburb of Whitchurch, where he lived for most of his life at 2 Heol Pen-y-fai. His friend the poet John Ormond lived from 1955 to his death in 1990 at 15 Conway Rd, off Cathedral Rd, in the district of Pontcanna. Both made important contributions to 'the second flowering' of Anglo-Welsh poetry which began in the 1960s.

R. S. Thomas was born at 5 Newfoundland Rd, Llandaff, the son of a seaman. He returned to Llandaff to pursue his theological training at St Michael's College. He found, as he wrote in his autobiography *Neb* (No One, 1985), 'the buildings old-fashioned, the food uninteresting, the chapel nothing but some prefabricated hut and the warden . . . effeminate'. Dannie Abse was born to Jewish parents in Cardiff in 1923, and his work has often looked back on the city—from his autobiography, *A Poet in the Family* (1974), and the autobiographical novels, *Ash on a Young Man's Sleeve* (1954) and *There Was a Young Man from Cardiff* (1991), to the poems 'Leaving Cardiff', 'Last Visit to 198 Cathedral Road', and 'Return to Cardiff':

'Hometown'; well, most admit an affection for a
    city:
grey, tangled streets I cycled on to school, my
    first cigarette
in the back lane, and, fool, my first botched love
    affair.
First everything. Faded torments; self-indulgent
    pity.

Abse has combined writing with his career as a doctor and began his medical training at the Welsh National School of Medicine on the outskirts of the city.

The novelist Bernice Rubens was also born in Cardiff (1928) and educated here, at Cardiff High School for Girls and then reading English at the University of Wales; and the poet Gillian Clarke was born here too, in 1937, as was Iain Sinclair, in 1943.

CARMARTHEN *Carmarthenshire*

Town on the estuary of the Towy. The name is connected with the legendary Merlin, first popularized in Arthurian lore by Geoffrey of Monmouth in his *Historia Regum Britanniae* (1136), the name 'Merlinus' being a Latinized form of the Welsh Merddin or Myrddin, a prophet or seer after whom Carmarthen (or Caerfyrddin) was named. A Welsh version can be found in the 'Llyfr Du Caerfyrddin' (Black Book of Carmarthen), a manuscript rich in ancient Welsh literature, believed to have been copied at the Priory of St John's (now gone) in the 12th c., consisting of dialogues on mythology, theology, history, and literature. A facsimile copy, edited by J. Gwenogvryn Evans (1904–6), was later held in the Public Library.

An important eisteddfod was held in *c.* 1450, probably in Carmarthen Castle, when the work of the bards was discussed and new rules decreed which gave the present classic shape to Welsh traditional metric poetry. Tudur Aled (*fl.* 1480–1526) was present and Dafydd ab Edmwnd (*fl.* 1450–90) won a silver chair. Tudur Aled is believed to have died here and to have been buried in the Friars' graveyard, in the habit of a Grey Friar.

Merlin's Oak, said to have grown from an acorn planted on 19 May 1659 to mark the town's proclamation of Charles II as king, was killed by poison by an early 19th-c. tradesman who disapproved of people gathering under it at all hours of the day and night. The old stump, patched and supported by cement, used to stand at a road junction at the E end of the town, but as traffic increased it became a hazard and was moved to *Abergwili. The prophecy traditionally ascribed to Merlin reads:

    When Merlin's Tree shall tumble down,
    Then shall fall Carmarthen Town.

Sir Richard Steele moved to Carmarthen from Hereford in 1724 and lived in King St. in a house ℗ belonging to the Scurlocks, the family of his second wife, Mary ('dear Prue'). After her death he moved to nearby Llangunnor, returning to Carmarthen after a seizure. He died in King St., and was buried in the Scurlock vault in St Peter's Church ℗.

Sir Lewis Morris, a 19th-c. poet best remembered for *The Epic of Hades* (1876–7), was born in Spilman St.

Ernest Rhys spent holidays at 50 King St., his grandfather's house, which he described in his autobiography, *Wales England Wed* (1940); his father lived at 2 Nott Sq.

After the death of his three brothers in London, the travel writer and novelist Norman Lewis spent much of his childhood living with his three slightly mad aunts in his grandfather's house on Wellfield Rd. His autobiography, *Jackdaw Cake* (1985; reissued as *I Came, I Saw*), recalls a town of 'ugly chapels, of hidden money, psalm-singing and rain'. Water from the reservoir ran down the road outside his house carrying with it fish into the marketplace. Snails, 'curled and striped like little turbans', were everywhere, as were the jackdaws which fed on them. Every Saturday the aunts observed the ceremony of the jackdaw cake:

On Saturday mornings at ten o'clock the cake was fed to the jackdaws. This had been happening for years, so that by half past nine the garden was full of birds, anything up to a hundred of them balancing and singing with a tremendous gleeful outcry on the bushes and the low boughs of the trees. This was the great moment of the week for my aunts, and therefore for me . . . For some hours after this weekly event the atmosphere was one of calm and contentment, and then the laughter and weeping would start again.

The magazine *Wales* was edited and published by Keidrych Rhys during the 1940s from offices in Lammas St. He was born at Bethlehem, near Llandeilo, and lived during the 1940s at Tŷ Gwyn, Llanybri. The poet Tony Curtis was born in Carmarthen in 1946.

Merlin's Oak at Carmarthen, photographed *c.* 1936

twenties left for London and lived thereafter as a writer. The trilogy of novels *Honey and Bread* (1935), *A Time to Laugh* (1937), and *Jubilee Blues* (1938) are set in the district, as are many of his short stories, which were published in his *Collected Stories* in 1955. The Rhys Davies Trust, a charity founded in 1990, perpetuates his memory and sponsors literary projects in Wales.

CLYRO *Powys*

Village on the A438, 2 m. NW of Hay-on-Wye. Francis Kilvert, while curate here (1865–72), lived at Brook House (Ⓟ; formerly Tŷ Dulas), later an art gallery and private home. He kept notebooks (*Diary*, 1938–40; new edn, 1969) in which he recorded the events of the day, his journeys to outlying farms, his grief at the many lives cut short by fatal illness, and his pleasure in the beauties of the countryside.

Conan Doyle stayed at the Baskerville Arms and used the family name in his novel *The Hound of the Baskervilles* (1902).

CORWEN *Denbighshire*

Town on the A5, 11 m. E of Llangollen. John Cowper Powys moved here from Dorchester late in 1934 and lived at 7 Cae Cod. His novel *Maiden Castle*, which he had been writing in Dorchester, was published in 1937. He also wrote the historical novel *Owen Glendower* (1941), *Porius* (1951), a romance of the Dark Ages, *Up and Out* (1957), which contained the short story 'The Mountains of the Moon', and many works of philosophy and criticism. He moved to *Blaenau Ffestiniog in 1955.

COWBRIDGE *Glamorgan*

Market town on the junction of the A48 and the A4222. A shop opposite the Town Hall bears a plaque recording that the poet and antiquary Iolo Morganwg (Edward Williams) had a bookshop there. The poet Alun Lewis was a boarder at the Grammar School from 1926 to 1932, when he was already showing promise as a writer of poetry and short stories.

CRICCIETH *Gwynedd*

Small town on Cardigan Bay. The village features in Robert Graves's satirical poem 'Welsh Incident', with the strange 'things' that come out of the sea caves nearby:

> Things never seen or heard or written about,
> Very strange, un-Welsh, utterly peculiar
> Things.

The poem was inspired by a visit Graves made to the caves with the botanist and mythologist Lloyd Williams and by a railway journey along the (now defunct) Cambrian Railway, during which a Welsh policeman claimed with great seriousness that he had seen a mermaid.

CWMAMAN (pr. Cŏŏmăʹman) *Glamorgan*

Village in a valley just S of Aberdare, off the A4059. Alun Lewis, poet of promise who was killed in the Second World War, was born at 16 Llanwynno Rd Ⓟ on 1 July 1915 and grew up

CHEPSTOW *Monmouthshire*

Old market town and former port on the A48, on the W bank of the Wye, 2 m. above its junction with the Severn. Robert Bloomfield stayed at the Beaufort Arms when he was touring with friends along the Wye and into Wales in the summer of 1807. He describes in *The Banks of Wye* (1811) the 'delightful and social evening' spent after visiting the castle by moonlight and hearing an owl hooting lustily from the battlements. A century and a half later a girl called Joanne Kathleen Rowling, who as J. K. Rowling would achieve extraordinary global success as the author of the Harry Potter boarding school fantasy books, grew up here in Chepstow.

CHIRK *Wrexham*

Small town near Wrexham and Oswestry, 1 m. from the English border. R. S. Thomas was ordained curate here in 1936. He enjoyed exploring the local countryside in the summer, but with the coming of winter experienced *hiraeth* (longing) for Anglesey and the sea.

CLYDACH VALE *Glamorgan*

Former mining village near Tonypandy off the A4119 in the Rhondda valley. Here, in 1897, the novelist Lewis Jones was born at 7 Danycoed Terr., Blaenclydach. At the age of 12 he went to work in the Cambrian Colliery (gone), was married four years later, and spent the rest of his life in the village, latterly at 61 Brynhyfryd St. His two novels *Cwmardy* (1937) and *We Live* (1939) are authentic, passionate accounts of working-class life in the Rhondda during the inter-war years, highly coloured by his Marxism. He died in Cardiff in 1939 and was buried in Trealaw cemetery in his native Rhondda.

Rhys Davies, the short-story writer and novelist, was born in 1901 at 6 Clydach Rd, where his father kept a grocer's shop known as the Royal Stores (later a private house). Opposite stands the Central Hotel, on which the author based the 'Jubilee Arms' that is featured in many of his stories. After leaving Porth Intermediary School, he worked for a while in his father's shop, but in his early

in a time of depression in the mining valleys of S Wales. He went to Glynhafod Elementary School and obtained a scholarship as a boarder at Cowbridge Grammar School. There is a memorial low-relief bust of him in the reference department of Aberdare Public Library. The plaque on the house where he was born bears a quotation from his poem 'The Mountain Over Aberdare':

I watch the clouded years
Rune the rough foreheads of these moody hills
This wet evening in a lost age.

CWMFELINFACH
(pr. Cŏomvĕlĭnvahχ) *Monmouthshire*

Village in the Sirhowy valley, on the A4048, *c.* 4 m. W of Crosskeys. The Calvinistic Methodist minister and poet William Thomas (Islwyn) began preaching at Babell, the chapel here, in 1854 and was ordained in 1859. After his marriage in 1864 he lived at Green Meadow, near the chapel, and then at Y Glyn, which he built himself. He is buried in the chapel burial ground. He was a prolific writer, most of his output being in the form of odes presented for competition at *eisteddfodau*, but he is remembered mainly for his lengthy poem 'Y Storm' (The Storm), which he began to write at the age of 22 after the death of Anne Bowen, to whom he was engaged to be married.

CYNWYL ELFED *Carmarthenshire*

Village 7 m. NW of Carmarthen, on the A484. A signpost by the bridge shows the way to Y Gangell, the birthplace of Dr Elvet Lewis, minister, poet, and hymn writer, crowned bard of the National Eisteddfod of Wales. The tiny cottage is preserved as a national memorial and contains his portrait, bardic chair, and other personal relics. He is buried at Blaen-y-coed, about 1 m. W.

DENBIGH *Denbighshire*

Historic town at the junction of the A525 and the A543, on a hill overlooking the Vale of Clwyd. Kate Roberts married Morris T. Williams in 1928 and in 1935 the couple bought Gwasg Gee, the printing-press founded by Thomas Gee (1815–98), which published the newspaper *Baner ac Amserau Cymru*, and settled in Denbigh at Y Cilgwyn. After her husband's death in 1945 Kate Roberts continued to run the business alone for another 10 years and published *Y Faner*, regularly contributing to its columns on a wide range of subjects. The town is the background to much of her later works. They include *Stryd y Glep* (1949), *Y Byw sy'n Cysgu* (1956), *Y Lôn Wen* (1960), *Tywyll Heno* (1962), *Hyn o Fyd* (1964), and *Tegwch y Bore* (1967). A selection of her earlier short stories, translated into English as *A Summer Day and Other Stories*, was published in 1946. Many of her stories are based on the lives of the people with whom she grew up, their hardships and poverty, and their fortitude. Her lighter side is shown in her stories for and about children, especially *Te yn y Grug* (1959). She is generally regarded as the

most distinguished Welsh prose writer of the 20th c.

Thomas Edwards ('Twm o'r Nant'), the writer of interludes, is buried at Whitchurch in the town and there is a memorial plaque inside the church.

DYLIFE *Powys*

Hamlet 5 m. SW of Pennant off the B4518. On an unclassified road on the slopes of Moel Fadian there is a stone commemorating the writer and broadcaster Wynford Vaughan-Thomas. This was his favourite spot and the view is memorable. The ground was acquired by the Council for the Preservation of Rural Wales, the work of which meant much to the writer. Born in Swansea, he was the author of books about the history and topography of Wales, and of a volume of autobiography, *Trust to Talk* (1980).

EGLWYSFACH *Powys*

Village 4 m. from Machynlleth. R. S. Thomas was vicar here from 1954 to 1967, where 'once every day the tide would come up the river and the tang of the sea could be smelt in the foam' (*Neb*; No-one, 1985). The parish was largely English and middle-class in character, with types of people 'not to his liking as a subject for poetry'.

ELAN VALLEY *Powys*

Narrow valley SW of Rhayader, traversed by the A470, now flooded by the building of a reservoir. In the summer of 1811 Shelley spent some weeks here at Cwm Elan, a house owned by his cousins the Grove family. Shelley returned the next year with his wife, Harriet, and in 'The Retrospect' contrasts the sad time he had the year before with the happiness of

this visit with her. Shelley was also writing part of *Queen Mab* (1813) here. Thomas Grove helped them in their negotiations for a house of their own: this was Nantgwillt, a large house with a ghost and 200 acres, in which they lived while the negotiations were under way, but the lease proved too expensive and they left. Shelley is commemorated by a sculpture at the Elan Valley Visitors' Centre.

Francis Brett Young was fascinated by the engineering enterprise of the reservoir which brought Welsh water to the Midlands and it became the inspiration of his novel *The House Under the Water* (1932).

FISHGUARD *Pembrokeshire*

Town and ferry port at the end of the A40, overlooking Fishguard Bay. After taking degrees in English, David John Williams (1885) was appointed assistant master at the Grammar School, where he remained until his retirement in 1945. He lived at the Bristol Trader (formerly a pub), 49 High St. ℗, where he spent most of his adult life. His earliest literary works, articles, and short stories were collected in *Y Gaseg Ddu* (The Black Mare, ed. J. Gwyn Griffiths, 1970). His two masterpieces are *Hen Dŷ Ffarm* (The Old Farmhouse, 1953) and *Hen Wynebau* (The Old Faces, 1934), imbued with a shrewd and affectionate knowledge of the people and places of his native district. His friend the poet Waldo Williams lived at 1 Plasygamil Rd.

Near Trefaser, 5 m. W of Fishguard, on the coastal path above Pwllderi, there is a memorial to the Welsh poet Dewi Emrys (David Emrys James). He won the Crown at the National Eisteddfod in 1926 and the Chair on four occasions between 1929 and 1948. His most famous poem is 'Pwllderi', written in the

R. S. Thomas at Eglwysfach in 1966

Welsh dialect of northern Pembrokeshire, and a couplet is inscribed on the stone.

FLEMINGSTON (or TREFFLEMIN)
Glamorgan

Village on a minor road above the Thaw valley, *c.* 4 m. SE of Cowbridge. The poet and antiquary Edward Williams (Iolo Morganwg) (1747–1826) grew up here. He did not attend school, but learnt to read by watching his father cutting inscriptions on gravestones, and was taught at home by his mother. At an early age he came under the influence of local bards, who encouraged him to learn the bardic craft and to study Welsh manuscripts. He travelled in North Wales and in 1773 went to London, where he met members of the Society of Gwyneddigion and continued his studies. After his marriage in 1781 he lived for a time at Llandaff and other places before returning to Flemingston, where he settled for the rest of his life. The house where he lived, near the church, has gone and a farmhouse later occupied the site. In 1772 he published an elegy on his poetic teacher Lewis Hopkin, entitled *Dagrau yr Awen* (The Tears of the Muse), and in 1794 two volumes of English poems, *Poems Lyric and Pastoral*. He also wrote many hymns, published as *Salmau yr Eglwys yn yr Anialwch* (The Church Psalms in the Desert). His poetry was very different from that of his contemporaries—*cywyddau* (a Welsh metrical form) directly inspired by Dafydd ap Gwilym. He was an authority on Welsh history and literature, but is perhaps mainly remembered as a remarkable literary forger. He was also the inventor of most of the Gorsedd ritual of the modern Eisteddfod. There is a memorial tablet in the church to him and his son Taliesin ab Iolo.

FLINT *Flintshire*

Town on the estuary of the river Dee and county town of the historic county of Flintshire. Shakespeare, following the Chronicles of Raphael Holinshed, sets the abdication of Richard II and his surrender to Henry Bolingbroke at Flint Castle. The ruins of the castle are open to visitors (www.cadw.wales.gov.uk).

GILFACH GOCH *Glamorgan*

Former mining village 2 m. W of Tonyrefail off the A4093 and on the B4564. Here the novelist Richard Llewellyn (Richard Llewellyn Lloyd) spent childhood holidays at the home of his maternal grandfather. He returned in 1937 to work underground in one of the local pits while gathering material for his best-selling novel *How Green Was My Valley* (1939), which is thought to have been based on the district.

GLYN CEIRIOG *Wrexham*

Village *c.* 3 m. S of Llangollen, reached by a minor road or by the B4500 from Chirk (on the B5070). The Institute and Library are a memorial to John Ceiriog Hughes (1832–87), poet, farmer, and stationmaster on the Cambrian Railway. He wrote lyrics in Welsh, many for setting to traditional airs, and was the author of 'God Bless the Prince of Wales'. His poem *Owain Wyn* (1856) has been acclaimed as the best Welsh pastoral. Adjoining the Institute there is a memorial to George Borrow, who praised the Ceiriog valley in *Wild Wales* (1862).

GLYNLLIFON *Gwynedd*

Mansion on the A499 between Llandwrog and Pontllyfni, 6 m. SW of Caernarfon, in the grounds of which the Writers of Gwynedd scheme was inaugurated in 1990 by Cywaith Cymru (formerly the Welsh Sculpture Trust) in association with the County Council. Some of the sculpture in the park celebrates the major writers associated with the county, including O. M. Edwards, Saunders Lewis, and John Gwilym Jones.

GOLDEN GROVE *Carmarthenshire*

Mansion *c.* 3 m. SW of Llandeilo, just S of the B4300 (also signposted from the A40, 3 m. W of Llandeilo). Jeremy Taylor, who had been Charles I's chaplain and imprisoned after the Royalist defeat at Cardigan, retired here in 1645 and stayed until he moved to *Lisburn in 1658. Many of his best works were written at this time, including *Holy Living* and *Holy Dying* (1650–1) and *The Golden Grove* (a manual of daily prayers, 1655). The mansion on the site of the original building in which he lived later became the Carmarthen Technical and Agricultural College but has since been sold.

GROESLON (pr. 'Groysslön) *Gwynedd*

Small village 5 m. S of Caernarfon, just E of the A487. John Gwilym Jones, dramatist, short-story writer, novelist, and literary critic, was born here, grew up, lived, and died in the house known as Angorfa Ⓟ. After teaching in London (1926–30) he returned to Wales and took a number of teaching posts before being appointed a producer of radio plays with the BBC in Bangor (1949–53). He was later a lecturer at the University College of North Wales, Bangor. His first play, *Y Brodyr* (The Brothers), was published in 1934, and was followed by many more, which increased in subtlety.

HANMER *Flintshire*

Village on the A539, 6 m. W of Whitchurch. Dafydd ab Edmwnd, 15th-c. Welsh poet, was born in the parish and was the owner of Yr Owredd and of other lands in Hanmer, though he spent part of his life at Tre Wepra, Englefield, his mother's old home. He won the silver chair at the famous eisteddfod at *Carmarthen and was regarded as the final authority on language and metre. Most of his poetry consisted of love lyrics and he devised two new metrical forms of extreme complexity-the *Cadwynfyr* ('Short chain') and *Gorchest y Beirdd* ('Bards' masterpiece). His work shows his love of his country and poems of praise and worship in accordance with the duties of a bard. He is buried in Hanmer church.

R. S. Thomas was a curate in the village from 1940 to 1942. The critic Lorna Sage spent her childhood in the vicarage at Hanmer, recalled unflatteringly in her memoir *Bad Blood* (2001):

> Domestic life in the vicarage had a Gothic flavour at odds with the house, which was a modest eighteenth-century building of mellowed brick, with low ceilings, and attics and back stairs for help we didn't have. At the front it looked on to a small square traversed only by visitors and churchgoers. The barred kitchen window faced this way, but in no friendly fashion, and the parlour on the other side of the front door was empty and unused, so the house was turned in on itself, against its nature.

HARLECH *Gwynedd*

Town on the A496, on Tremadoc Bay, dominated by its castle built by Edward I *c.* 1283. In the Mabinogion, Brân, king of Britain, has a court at Harlech. Ellis Wynne, cleric and author, was born (1670/1) at Y Lasynys Ⓟ, a farmhouse (later restored) 2 m. N, on the main road. He was incumbent of Llandanwg, a village on the coast, 2 m. S of Harlech, with the chapelry at nearby Llanbedr, 1704/5–1711. In 1711 he moved to Llanfair-juxta-Harlech, a little further N, and was incumbent there until his death in 1734. He is buried under the altar in the church, which has a memorial window. Ellis Wynne was the author of a Welsh prose classic, *Gweledigaetheu y Bardd Cwsc* (The Visions of the Sleeping Bard, 1703), of which at least three English translations were made.

The poet Siôn Phylip (*c.* 1543–1620) is buried in the churchyard at Llandanwg *c.* 2 m. S of Harlech, off the A496.

Robert Graves spent holidays at Erinfa, Harlech, in the years before the First World War, a place whose countryside 'seemed to be independent of formal nature'. He would venture into the hills behind the town with a wax phonograph to collect Welsh folk songs. He evokes the local country in 'Rocky Acres':

> Time has never journeyed to this lost land,
> Crakeberry and heather bloom out of date,
> The rocks jut, the streams flow singing on either
>   hand,
> Careless if the season be early or late,
> The skies wander overhead, now blue, now
>   slate . . .

Graves was in Harlech when war was declared against Germany, a few days after leaving school. His experience with the Royal Welch Fusiliers is the subject of *Goodbye to All That* (1929). When, 10 years after the war ended, Graves moved to Majorca, he chose to live in a place whose scenery was as close as possible to that around Harlech.

As a boy the novelist Philip Pullman lived in Harlech, where he was a pupil at the Ysgol Ardudwy.

HAVERFORDWEST *Pembrokeshire*

Market town on the Western Cleddau, on the A40 and the A4076. Waldo Williams, Welsh-language poet, was born (1904) at the School House of the Boys' School. He moved with his family to the village of *Mynachlogddu when he was 7.

HAY-ON-WYE *Powys*

A market town on the river Wye lying within the Brecon Beacons National Park. The poet Anne Stevenson founded the Poetry Bookshop in Hay in the mid-1970s. Her poem 'Walking Early by the Wye' recalls her time here:

> I will not forget how the ash trees stood, silvered and still,
> how each soft stone on its near shadow knelt,
> how the sheep became stones where they built their pearled hill.

The town is one of a number (Kington, Knighton, and *Clun being others) that formed the basis for 'Rhulen', the local market town in Bruce Chatwin's *On the Black Hill* (1982). The twin protagonists of the novel live long, isolated lives on their farm 'The Vision', located in the border country, as Chatwin himself said, 'anywhere between South Shropshire and Monmouthshire'. The novel bears the impression of the long visits Chatwin made to the houses of friends in and around the Black Mountains. Chatwin's Black Hill lies at the head of the Olchon valley, which is also the scene of *Resistance* (2007), Owen Sheers's novel imagining a Britain overrun by Nazi Germany.

The more than 30 bookshops in Hay (a town of some 1,900 inhabitants) ensures a regular stream of bibliophile visitors; but the stream turns into a torrent at the end of May every year, when it hosts the massive Hay Festival of Literature and the Arts, which since 1988 has grown into an annual fixture for locals and visitors from around the country and the world. The event was famously described by Bill Clinton as 'the Woodstock of the mind'; Arthur Miller's comment was 'Hay-on-Wye? Is that some kind of sandwich?'

HOLYHEAD *Gwynedd*

Port and town on Holy Island, connected to Anglesey by bridge. R. S. Thomas moved to Holyhead from Cardiff in 1918. His father was a sailor, and his home, as he recorded in his autobiography, *Neb* (No-one, 1985), was surrounded by a sense of the sea, 'its noise, its smell, its ferocity on windy days . . . At night the flashes from the lighthouse would dart through his room like the sails of a windmill.' His love of the natural world grew from a childhood spent exploring the cliffs and beaches of Holy Island.

HOLYWELL *Flintshire*

Town on the A5026, 11 m. E of St Asaph, named after the Holy Well of St Winefride, the most famous healing well in the British Isles and a place of pilgrimage from the 7th c. to the present day. According to legend, Prince Caradoc attempted to seduce Winefride and struck off her head when she ran from him. She was miraculously restored to life by St Beuno, her uncle, and a spring of water gushed from the place where her head had fallen. In the late

15th c. a fine Perpendicular Gothic chapel was built over the well, which was housed in the lofty fan-vaulted crypt. Celia Fiennes described her visit in 1698:

> I saw abundance of devout papists on their knees all round the well . . . there are stone steps for the persons to descend who will bathe themselves in the well; and so they walk along the stream to the other end and then come out but there is nothing to shelter them but are exposed to all the company that are walking about the well . . . they tell of many lamenesses and aches and distempers which are cured by it. . . . They come also to drink the water which they take up where the spring rises . . . (*Journeys*, 1947)

Defoe in 1724 remarked on the 'fine chapel dedicated to this holy Virgin . . . [under which] the water gushes out in a great stream, and the place where it breaks out is formed like a cistern, in which [the pilgrims] bathe', and Dr Johnson, visiting with the Thrales in 1774, noted, like Celia Fiennes, the lack of privacy for bathing: 'the bath is completely and indecently open: a woman bathed while we all looked on'; as well as the copious flow of water that 'yields a 100 tuns of water a minute and all at once becomes a great stream . . . turning a mill within 30 yards of its eruption and in the course of 2 miles 18 mills more'. G. M. Hopkins's poem 'St. Winefred's Well' extols the curative power of the water of

> This dry dene, now no longer dry nor dumb, but moist and musical
> With the uproll and the downcarol of day and night delivering
> Water, which keeps thy name, (for not in rock written,
> But in pale water, frail water, wild rash and reeling water,
> That will not wear a print, that will not stain a pen,
> Thy venerable record, virgin, is recorded)
> Here to this holy well shall pilgrimages be.

Frederick Rolfe lived here from 1895 to 1898 under the name of 'Fr. Austin' (the abbreviation stood for his Christian name—not, as he might have wished to suggest, 'Father'). He wrote for the local magazine, the *Holywell Record*, in which he aired his views and his grievances, and he obtained a commission to paint banners for the shrine. Five of these, representing St Augustine of Canterbury, St George, St Gregory, St Winefride, and St Ignatius of Loyola, may be seen at the Presbytery on request. His emblem of a crow (with reference to his pseudonym 'Baron Corvo') appears as a background detail in the first two.

LAMPETER *Cardiganshire*

University and market town on the A482 c. 25 m. NE of Carmarthen. The humorist Idwal Jones was born at Rhoslwyn in Station Ter.; the house is now the Registry Office of the University of Wales Lampeter. It was his contention that Wales, 'our little country, does not take its humour seriously enough', and he wrote verse, plays, and songs in Welsh which

made many people laugh. They are to be found in the volumes *Cerddi Digri a Rhai Pethau Eraill* (Humorous Poems and Other Things, 1934), *Cerddi Digri Newydd a Phethau o'r Fath* (New Humorous Poems and Similar Things, 1937), and *Ystorïau a Pharodïau* (Stories and Parodies, 1944). His *Pobl yr Ymylon* (People of the Hinterland, 1927) is an argument against respectability. He is buried in the graveyard of Soar Chapel, which faces the common.

LAUGHARNE (pr. Larn) *Carmarthenshire*

Small town on the A4066, on the Taf estuary. Richard Hughes and his wife lived in a house in the grounds of the ruined castle from 1934/5 until the end of 1946. Here he completed the novel *In Hazard* (1938), which had been begun when he was living in Norfolk. It was at his invitation that Dylan Thomas came here with his wife in 1938. They lived first in a two-room cottage in Gosport St. and then at Sea View, near the Town Hall. They left in October and after returning briefly in 1939 and 1940 came back for good in 1949, to live at The Boathouse, a whitewashed, slate-roofed house below the cliff, where Thomas worked in the blue-painted garden shed. The house can be seen from the end of Cliff Rd called Dylan's Walk and now comprises the Dylan Thomas Education and Heritage Centre (www.dylanthomasboathouse.com).

When he first came to Laugharne, Thomas was writing the short stories later published as *Portrait of the Artist as a Young Dog* (1940), and *Quite Early One Morning*, from which his best-known work, *Under Milk Wood* (1954), a play for voices, developed. The town of 'Llareggub' is traditionally associated with Laugharne, where the play has been performed periodically since 1958. Dylan Thomas died on a lecture tour in the US in November 1953 and was brought home for burial in the hillside graveyard of St Martin's Church, where his grave is marked by a plain white wooden cross.

LLANARMON DYFFRYN CEIRIOG (pr. 'Dŭffrĭn 'Kīrĭog) *Wrexham*

Quiet little village in the depths of the Berwyn Mountains, c. 6 m. SW of Llangollen, at the end of the B4500. John Ceiriog Hughes (1832–87), the lyric writer who is commemorated at *Glyn Ceiriog, was born at Penybryn Ⓟ, a long, low farmhouse, high above the bridge.

LLANBADARN FAWR (pr. Vowr) *Powys*

Village 1¼ m. ESE of Aberystwyth (along Northgate St.), originally its parent village. The 13th-c. parish church is the setting of Dafydd ap Gwilym's poem 'The Girls of Llanbadarn'.

LLANBERIS *Gwynedd*

Town on the A4086, at the N end of the Pass of Llanberis. The poet and novelist T. Rowland Hughes was born (1903) at 20 Goodman St. and spent his first nine years there before moving to Angorfa Ⓟ, next to the Baptist Chapel in Well St.

Dylan Thomas and South Wales

EW writers enjoy more fitting memorials than Dylan Thomas at his Boat House in Laugharne, south Carmarthenshire. Jutting out over the Taf estuary in a charmed position that is part of both land and water, and neither, stands his 'sea shaken house | On a breakneck of rocks' ('Prologue'). This was Thomas's home for four years before his early death in New York in November 1953, and the landscape permeated his later writings. From the Boat House, he could gaze out across 'the mussel-pooled and the heron-priested shore' ('Poem in October') to the low, green-crested Llanstephan peninsula, where he spent long periods as a boy. Southwards, towards the sea, stood St John's Hill, where 'The hawk on fire hangs still' and, below it, the 'Crystal harbour vale | Where the sea cobbles sail' ('Over St John's Hill'). On a bright day, it is tranquil and near-perfect, a mixture of bubbling life and inert mass, testament to the distinctive Dylan Thomas message of animate existence hurrying towards its inevitable end. Somewhere, in his mind's eye, he could no doubt see his alter ego, Nogood Boyo, fishing from his boat the *Zanzibar* and musing: 'I want to be good Boyo, but nobody'll let me' (*Under Milk Wood*).

Each day Thomas would climb the forty-one steps which led from the Boat House's wooden veranda to the overhead cliff walk, and make his way, past the nondescript shed where he worked, to the pub, Brown's. Instinctively he had chosen an unusual town, with Georgian architecture and eccentric customs, and its legacy as one of only two places in Britain with its own constitution. From his regular drink-fuelled conversations at Brown's, he concocted his brilliant radio play *Under Milk Wood* (which in an early draft was called *The Town That Was Mad*).

But this was not where Thomas started his life. His early years were spent in the very different environs of the Swansea suburbs, where he was born in October 1914 at 5 Cwmdonkin Drive in the Uplands, to the W of the city, looking out over the Bristol Channel. His first forays into the world were in the adjacent Cwmdonkin Park, remembered in his story 'Pamela, Edith and Arnold', and also, after a passage of time, in his poem 'The Hunchback in the Park', 'A solitary mister | Propped between trees and water' (that image of the juxtaposition of solid and liquid again).

The Uplands were generally English-speaking. But, like many people in Swansea, Thomas had family in Carmarthenshire. As a boy he often went to stay with relations around Llanbryi and Llangain in the Llanstephan peninsula. One was his aunt Annie Jones, whose death at her farm, Fern Hill, in 1933 he commemorated in his sardonic poem 'After the Funeral'. He later recalled the physical surroundings in his breezy 'Fern Hill', with its memorable opening, 'Now as I was young and easy under the apple

DYLAN THOMAS PHOTOGRAPHED BY FRANCIS REISS FOR *PICTURE POST*, 1946

boughs'. The experience put him in touch with Welsh language and culture, and infused his short stories—some accessible, like 'A Visit to Grandpa's', others experimental, such as 'The Tree'.

As a young reporter on the *South Wales Evening Post* he started to explore his native town. He also ventured further afield, to the Mumbles, a small port to the W, and beyond into the untouched Gower peninsula, where he explored his personal communion with nature in experimental poems such as his ecological anthem 'The force that through the green fuse drives the flower'. The Gower's natural beauty provided a vivid backdrop to his stories: for example, Rhossili Bay's 'very long golden beach' and its mile-long promontory Worm's Head, where Thomas and a friend were cut off by the tide in 'Who Do You Wish Was With Us'?

As he became more sophisticated, Thomas was drawn to the conviviality of the Kardomah café, a former Congregational church on Wind St. in the centre of Swansea, where he met fellow artists and writers, who became known collectively as the Kardomah boys. He would recall in *Return Journey*, a later piece for BBC radio, how they would talk about 'music and poetry and painting and politics, Einstein and Epstein, Stravinsky and Greta Garbo, death and religion, Picasso and girls'.

In 1934, when he was 20 and Swansea seemed provincial, he decamped to London. His experience of the capital was largely defined by its pubs, particularly those in Soho, such as the Fitzroy and the Wheatsheaf, his haunts when working as a film scriptwriter during the war and for the BBC afterwards. He also wrote some fine war verse, such as 'Ceremony After a Fire Raid', while his unfinished *Adventures in the Skin Trade* offers an amusing perspective on London in the 1930s.

His wife, Caitlin, preferred to stay away from the capital, particularly during the war, when her family was growing. So the Thomases shuffled between Hampshire, Gloucestershire, and, after the war, Oxfordshire, where, after a short sojourn in the historian A. J. P. Taylor's summerhouse in the grounds of Magdalen College, they lived in the village of South Leigh, near Eynsham.

More significant artistically were their wartime stays in Cardiganshire in west Wales. In 1942 they took a house at Talsarn in the Aeron valley, where their daughter Aeronwy was conceived. They also rented a bungalow in the bustling fishing port of New Quay, where Thomas played with some early ideas for *Under Milk Wood*—a cause of friction between this community and Laugharne as to which can be described as the model for Llareggub in Thomas's play. Living in Wales convinced Thomas that this was where his roots lay. So, when he tired of the daily grind of English existence, he looked to re-establish himself in Laugharne, which he had first visited and enthused about on 'a hopeless fallen angel of a day' in 1934. His parents, who had retired, followed him to live in the same town.

It is a delightful paradox that this self-confessed 'boily boy' from the suburbs could write so evocatively about the countryside. But Thomas's chameleon-like ability to move between settings and cultures lay at the heart of his genius. With his grounding in Welsh rhythms of language and nature, he brought new vitality to English poetry.

ANDREW LYCETT

LLANBRYNMAIR *Powys*

Village 5 m. off Cemmaes Rd on the A470. Here in 1800 the Radical writer Samuel Roberts was born in the chapel house of Yr Hen Gapel (The Old Chapel). He was brought up at a nearby farm known as Diosg.

The poet Iorwerth C. Peate, who became the first Curator of the Welsh Folk Museum at St Fagans, near Cardiff, was born at Glan-llyn, Pandy Rhiwsaeson, 2 m. N of the village. The district is lovingly evoked in many of his poems; they are to be found in the volumes *Y Cawg Aur* (1928), *Plu'r Gweunydd* (1933), *Y Deyrnas Goll* (1947), and in a volume of his selected poems, *Canu Chwarter Ganrif* (1957).

LLANDAFF *Glamorgan*

Cathedral town 2¼ m. NW of Cardiff, of which it is practically a suburb. Geoffrey of Monmouth (1100?–54), chronicler and author of *Historia Regum Britanniae* (first printed 1508), the principal source of the stories of King Arthur and the Knights of the Round Table, was made archdeacon of the 12th-c. Cathedral *c.* 1140. He was appointed Bishop of St Asaph in 1152, but died at Llandaff before entering his diocese.

William Morgan, first translator of the Bible into Welsh, was consecrated bishop here in 1595. He was translated to *St Asaph in 1601.

Many of the windows and decorations in the Cathedral are Pre-Raphaelite, and Swinburne, Burne-Jones, and William Morris and his wife were models for the figures in the Rossetti Triptych (1856–64), illustrating the Seed of David.

LLANDDEUSANT (pr. Llăn'thaysănt) *Powys*

Village 7 m. S of Llandovery off the A4069. The novelist Richard Vaughan (Ernest Lewis Thomas) was born at Blaenllechach, a farm in the upper reaches of the Llechach valley, in 1904. His novels *Moulded in Earth* (1951), *Who Rideth So Wild* (1952), and *Son of Justin* (1955) are set in the district of the Black Mountain.

LLANDEGLA *Wrexham*

Village *c.* 10 m. W of Wrexham at the junction of the A5104 and the A525. The Welsh prose writer Edward Tegla Davies was born at Yr Hen Giât ℗ in Pen Stryt in 1880. Many of his books, such as *Hunangofiant Tomi* (Tommy's Autobiography, 1912) and *Nedw* (1922), are humorous tales about boys. His novel *Gŵr Pen y Bryn* (The Man of Pen y Bryn, 1923), translated as *The Master of Pen y Bryn* (1975), describes the spiritual conversion of a well-to-do farmer during the Tithe Wars of the 1880s and is set in the district.

LLANDOUGH (pr. Llăn'dō) *Glamorgan*

Village in the Vale of Glamorgan, overlooking Cardiff. Dannie Abse commemorates the last stage of his father's life in his moving poem 'In Llandough Hospital':

> I grasp his hand so fine, so mild,
> which still is warm surprisingly,
> not a handshake either, father,
> but as I used to when a child.

LLANDOVERY (pr. Llăn'dŭv-vrĭ) *Carmarthenshire*

Market town on the A40, 13 m. NE of Llandeilo, in the Vale of Towy. Rhys Prichard ('Yr Hen Ficer') was probably born at Old Neuadd, now 33 High St. He built Neuadd Newydd (gone) on a site near the Blue Bell inn, now partly occupied by the Assembly Rooms. Vicar Prichard obtained the living of Llandovery in 1602 and lived here until 1614, when he became chaplain to the Earl of Essex.

He wrote a large number of verses about the Christian life, which were published under the title *Cannwyll y Cymry* (The Candle of the Welsh) in 1681. This book took its place in the affection of the common people with a Welsh translation of Bunyan's *Pilgrim's Progress*.

William Williams (known as 'Williams Pantycelyn' or simply 'Pantycelyn'), prolific writer of hymns and poems as well as a number of prose works, was born (1717) at Cefn-Coed, a farmhouse just N of Pentre-tŷ-gwyn, a hamlet 3 m. E of Llandovery. He became one of the chief leaders of the Methodist movement in Wales and was the author of nearly 90 works between 1744 and 1791. After his marriage *c.* 1748 he came to live at his mother's old home, Pantycelyn, a farmhouse a little to the E of Pentre-tŷ-gwyn. His wide range of published work written here includes two long poems, *Golwg ar Deyrnas Crist* (A View of Christ's Kingdom, 1756), an attempt to evaluate the divine purpose in the Creation, and *Bywyd a Marwolaeth Theomemphus* (The Life and Death of Theomemphus, 1764), a study of the soul's progress in the world. William Williams is buried in the churchyard of Llanfair-ar-y-Bryn, just outside Llandovery, on the A483. He is commemorated by the Pantycelyn Memorial Chapel in the centre of the town.

George Borrow stayed at the Castle Hotel on his travels through Wales, recounted in *Wild Wales* (1862), and his four-poster bed in the room named after him is still in use.

LLANDUDNO (pr. Llăn'dĭdnō) *Conwy*

Popular seaside resort in North Wales on the A470 and the A546. When Matthew Arnold took his family there for a holiday in 1864 he found inspiration for his essay *On the Study of Celtic Literature* (1864). 'All interests are here,' he wrote, '—Celts, Romans, Saxons, Druidism,

Middle Ages, Caer, Castle, Cromlech, Abbey,— and this glorious sea and mountains with it all.' He stayed at 10 St George's Cres. (4–24 August), his visit coinciding with the Eisteddfod, which he describes in the essay.

About the same time C. L. Dodgson ('Lewis Carroll') is believed to have visited Dean Liddell of Christ Church, Oxford, at his summer residence, Pen Morfa, on the West Shore, now part of the Gogarth Abbey Hotel. Sir William Richmond (1842–1921), whose portrait of the three Liddell daughters *The Three Graces* hangs in the Tate Gallery, said that part of *Alice in Wonderland* (1865) was written at Pen Morfa and read aloud in the evenings to the family and guests including Matthew Arnold and Gladstone. Dodgson is commemorated by a statue of the White Rabbit at the end of the Model Yacht Pond and by a marble font, given by children, in the Church of Our Saviour.

LLANFAIR-MATHAFARN-EITHAF (pr. Llănvīr-Matha'varn-'Aythăv)
Anglesey

Parish to the S of Llanallgo, just W of the A5025 from the Menai Bridge to Amlwch. The poet Goronwy Owen, whose father and grandfather (a tinker) were both rhymers and genealogists, was born in a cottage here, possibly in the family home, Y Dafarn Goch. After education at Llanallgo, Pwllheli, and Bangor, which led to a scholarship at Jesus College, Oxford, he was ordained in 1746 and appointed curate of Llanfair-Mathafarn-Eithaf, which gave him the opportunity of meeting the poets and antiquaries of Anglesey. Later he moved to Oswestry, *Donnington, Shropshire, and *Northolt, London. He produced translations and adaptations from classical languages, a few imitations of the old Welsh poets, and addresses to and elegies on his friends. His best-known poems are 'Cywydd y Farn Fawr' (The Last Judgement), 'Bonedd a Chyneddfau'r Awen' (The Lineage and Attributes of the Muse), 'Cywydd yn ateb Huw'r Bardd Coch' (Cywydd in Answer to Huw the Red Poet), and 'Cywydd y Gem neu'r Maen Gwerthfawr' (The Gem or the Precious Stone). There is a memorial tablet in Bangor Cathedral.

LLANFAIR-PWLL (pr. 'Llănvīr-'pŏŏll)
Anglesey

Village on the A5, 2 m. W of the Menai Bridge. John Morris-Jones, scholar and Welsh-language poet, came to live here as a child in 1868 and attended the elementary school before proceeding to Friars School, *Bangor, in 1876. After his marriage in 1897 he lived for most of his life at Tŷ Coch in Llanfair-pwll. He died in 1929 and is buried in the village cemetery.

LLANFAIR TALHAIARN
(pr. 'Llănvīr Tăl'hĭărn) *Conwy*

Village at the junction of the A548 and the A544, 5 m. S of Abergele. Here, in 1810, the poet John Jones was born at The Harp inn (renamed Hafod-y-gân), near the church. Apprenticed as a youth to an architect, in 1851

he was employed by Sir Joseph Paxton as superintendent of the construction of the Crystal Palace. He won fame, under his bardic name Talhaiarn, as a writer of songs, many of which became extremely popular. Returning to Wales in 1865, and suffering from severe arthritis, he died by his own hand in the tavern which had been his home. He is buried in the churchyard where, on his grave, is to be seen a profile of him which is similar to the one above the door of Hafod-y-gân.

LLANFECHAIN (pr. Llănvĕ'χīn) *Powys*

Small village on the B4393 *c.* 10 m. SW of Oswestry off the A495. Here the novelist James Hanley lived between 1940 and 1964; he had previously lived at Tŷ-nant, Merionethshire. During his residence in Wales (34 years in all), he wrote four novels with Welsh settings: *Don Quixote Drowned* (1953), *The Welsh Sonata* (1954), *Another World* (1971), and *A Kingdom* (1978).

LLANFIHANGEL-AR-ARTH
(pr. Llănvī'hăngel-) *Carmarthenshire*

Village on the B4459, 4 m. E of Llandysul, on the A486. David Caradoc Evans, novelist and short-story writer, who wrote as Caradoc Evans, was born (1878) at Pantycroy. The district and that of Rhydlewis, *c.* 8 m. NW, where he grew up and attended the board school, were fiercely satirized in his writings and offended many people in his homeland. After apprenticeship to a draper in Carmarthen he went to London in 1901 and later entered journalism. His first collection of short stories, *My People*, was published in 1915, followed by *Capel Sion* (1916) and *My Neighbours* (1919). He also wrote a play, *Taffy* (1923), which caused riots when it was produced in London, and novels, including *Nothing to Pay* (1930) and *Wasps* (1934).

LLANFIHANGEL TRE'R BEIRDD (pr. Llănvī'hăngel Trair Bairth)
Anglesey

Hamlet on a minor road 2 m. E of Llanerchymedd in Anglesey. Here the four Morris brothers, antiquaries and writers, were born in the first decade of the 18th c. The most gifted was the eldest, Lewis (1701–65), who was born at the farm known as Tyddyn Melys ℗. Behind Pentreriannell, another farm nearby, there is a monument to the four brothers, erected by the Honourable Society of Cymmrodorion, which was founded by Richard (1703–79) in 1751. The letters of the Morris brothers and their circle are a rich source of information about the literary life of Wales in their day. George Borrow, who was a great admirer, had much to say about them in *Wild Wales* (1862), although some of his details are not quite correct.

LLANFIHANGEL-YNG-NGWYNFA (pr. Llănvī'hăngel-ŏŏng-ngw'ŏŏnva) *Powys*

Village on the B4382, 4 m. S of the B4393 from Llanfyllin to Lake Vyrnwy. There is a

monument in the churchyard to Ann Griffiths, whose hymns, transmitted by oral tradition, are regarded as a unique and valuable part of Welsh literature. These hymns were published in various 19th-c. anthologies and collected by O. M. Edwards in *Gwaith Ann Griffiths* (The Work of Ann Griffiths) in the series of Welsh classics Cyfres y Fil in 1905. Ann Griffiths (née Thomas) was born (1776) at Dolwar Fach, *c.* 2½ m. S. The hamlet of Dolanog (*c.* 1 m. further S), where she received rudimentary education, has an Ann Griffiths Memorial Chapel.

LLANFROTHEN (pr. Llăn'vrŏthĕn) *Gwynedd*

Village on the B4410, just N of the western end of the Vale of Ffestiniog. While he was a student at Oxford (1919–22), Richard Hughes came to live with his mother at Garreg Fawr, a cottage nearby. At this time he was writing poems, plays, articles, and book reviews. His first novel, *A High Wind in Jamaica* (1929), was begun here. After the first draft of the first chapter he went abroad and eventually finished it in Connecticut (published in New York as *The Innocent Voyage*).

LLANFYNYDD (pr. Llăn'vŭnnĭth) *Carmarthenshire*

Village on a tributary of the Towy, *c.* 10 m. NW of Llandeilo, approached by narrow twisting roads through wooded country. John Dyer, who later lived at Aberglasney House, Llangathen, was born (1699) here and baptized in the parish church.

LLANGAIN (pr. Llăn'gīn) *Carmarthenshire*

Small village on the B4312, 4 m. SW of Carmarthen. The farm known as Fernhill, situated nearly 1 m. from the village (turn right off the road to Llanstephan), belonged to the aunt and uncle of Dylan Thomas, who spent holidays here. Two of his most famous poems, 'After the Funeral' (written in memory of his aunt, Ann Jones) and 'Fern Hill', and the short story 'The Peaches', are set here.

LLANGATHEN *Carmarthenshire*

Village in the Vale of the Towy, off the A40 *c.* 4 m. W of Llandeilo. Aberglasney House, below the village, was the home of the 18th-c. poet John Dyer, whose poem *Grongar Hill* (1726) celebrates the nearby hill and the surrounding country seen from the summit. The landmarks in the poem can be recognized today and one can still 'Hear the thrush, while all is still | Within the groves of Grongar Hill', but the blackthorn tree under which Dyer wrote, pictured in the frontispiece to the 1941 edition, has disappeared. The house, probably built around portions of a 16th-c. mansion belonging to Bishop Anthony Rudd of St David's, has long been derelict.

LLANGOLLEN (pr. Llăn'gŏllĕn) *Denbighshire*

Picturesque resort in the valley of the Dee, on the A5. Hazlitt describes his visit to 'this delightful spot' in the essay 'On Going a Journey' in *Table-Talk* (1821–2), when he dined at the inn on his birthday (10 Apr. 1798) off a bottle of sherry and a cold chicken. For 50 years it was the home of the eccentric 'Ladies of Llangollen', Lady Eleanor Butler (1739–1829) and the Hon. Sarah Ponsonby (1755–1831), who lived at Plas Newydd, an elaborately decorated house standing in extensive grounds on the hillside above the town. They were ardent admirers of Rousseau and read *La Nouvelle Héloïse* aloud, but their literary interests also ranged widely and they constantly sought to 'improve' themselves. Among their many visitors were Southey and his wife and Hannah More and her sister Patty in 1811, Wordsworth (who wrote a sonnet in the grounds) in 1824, and Sir Walter Scott and his son-in-law John Lockhart in 1825. Lockhart, writing to his wife, Sophia, says:

> your papa was waylaid by the celebrated 'Ladies' . . . who having been one or both crossed in love, foreswore all dreams of matrimony in the heyday of youth, beauty, and fashion, and selected this charming spot for the repose of their now time-honoured virginity.

Borrow was too late to see the Ladies, but was shown round the house in 1854 by a guide who remembered them well.

Browning spent the autumn of 1886 at the Hand Hotel with his sister Sarianna (who was convalescing), to be near his old friends Sir Theodore and Lady Martin of Bryntisilio, 3 m. away. Sir Theodore had said that 'a word to the hostess of the Hand Hotel was scarcely needed to secure every attention for the poet and his sister, for she was one of his readers'.

On the Eglwyseg escarpment above Llangollen, *c.* 3 m. N of the town, on the mountain road known as Panorama Walk, there is a monument commemorating the Welsh poet I. D. Hooson, at a spot where his ashes were scattered in 1948. He was born, lived, and died at Victoria House, Market St. Ⓟ, in nearby Rhoslannerchrugog. His poems, written for children, are among the most delightful of their kind in Welsh and are still great favourites as recitation pieces. They are to be found in *Cerddi a Baledi* (1936) and in the posthumous volume *Y Gwin a Cherddi Eraill* (1948).

LLANGRANNOG *Cardiganshire*

Small seaside village on the B4334 *c.* 12 m. SW of Aberaeron off the A487. One of the farms near the village, known as Y Cilie, is famous as the home of a family of country poets. The father, Jeremiah Jones (1855–1902), was a blacksmith and farmer, and his wife, Mary, bore him 12 children. Six of their seven sons vied with each other in bardic contests from an early age. The literary talent of this extraordinary family, known in Welsh as Bois y Cilie, persists in the third and fourth generation. A selection of the verse written by the Cilie poets was published as *Awen Ysgafn y Cilie* (ed. Gerallt Jones, 1976).

LLANGRISTIOLUS *Anglesey*

Village off the B4422, 3 m. SW of Llangefni in Anglesey. Here the writer Ifan Gruffydd (1896–1971) was born and spent most of his life, latterly at Tros-y-Ffordd Ⓟ. His two volumes of autobiography, *Gŵr o Baradwys* (The Man from Paradise, 1963) and *Tân yn y Siambar* (Fire in the Chamber, 1966) are vivid portraits of Anglesey country life from 1900 to 1935. After the author's death J. Elwyn Hughes edited a volume of his stories, together with commemorative essays by some of his friends, under the title *Cribinion* (1971).

LLANGUNNOR *Carmarthenshire*

Scattered parish *c.* 2 m. E of Carmarthen, on the B4300. Richard Steele retired here and lived at a farmhouse called Ty-Gwyn (or White House), a property belonging to his wife's family on the slope of the hill. From here he could look up the Towy valley to the distant view of Grongar Hill, celebrated by his friend John Dyer. *The Conscious Lovers* is traditionally supposed to have been written, at least in part, in an arbour in the orchard and first acted at Ty-Gwyn by friends of Steele. The house was demolished in the early 19th c., but a farmhouse of the same name later occupied the site. The little church on the top of the hill commemorates Steele in an eloquent stone tablet above the font.

Sir Lewis Morris, a 19th-c. poet, born at Carmarthen, is buried in the churchyard according to his wish:

> Let me at last be laid
> On that hillside I know, which scans the vale,
> Beneath the thick yew's shade
> For shelter, when the rains and winds prevail.

LLANRHAEADR-YM-MOCHNANT (pr. Llăn'rīader-ŭm-'Mŏχnănt) *Powys*

Village on the B4580, *c.* 6 m. N of Llanfyllin. William Morgan, first translator of the Bible into Welsh, was vicar here from 1578 to 1595. During this period he completed the translation, which he may have begun before leaving Cambridge. It was published in London in 1588, an event of outstanding literary significance. Morgan combined the vigour and purity of the medieval Welsh bardic tradition with a new flexibility and wider range of expression, and his translation marks the beginning of modern Welsh literature.

LLANRWST (pr. Llăn'rōost) *Conwy*

Market town on the right bank of the Conway, on the A470. This was the home for most of his life of William Salesbury, scholar and chief translator of the first version of the New Testament in Welsh. He was a Hebrew, Greek, and Latin scholar, and was also proficient in modern languages, but he was above all a Welsh scholar and man of letters. One of his best-known books is a collection of Welsh proverbs, *Oll Synnwyr pen Kembero ygyd* (The Sum of All Welsh Wisdom, *c.* 1547). The ruins of his home, Plas Isa, were formerly

to be seen near the station, but nothing now remains.

The poet and novelist T. Glynne Davies was born at Llanrwst in 1926. His novel *Marged* (1974) traces the history of his family over the span of 100 years. He was born at 64 Denbigh St. and brought up from the age of 5 at 3 School Bank Ter.

LLANSANNAN *Denbighshire*

Village on the A544, in the Aled valley. Tudur Aled, a bard of great distinction, who flourished between 1480 and 1526, was born in the parish. It is not known where he was educated, nor when he first began to write poetry, but it is clear that he was steeped in Welsh traditions. The Welsh scholar William Salesbury was born (1520?) at a house named Cae Du, near Llansannan, and a memorial, by W. Goscombe John, to him and Tudur Aled, together with other local celebrities, stands in the middle of the village.

LLANSANTFFRAED

(pr. Llănsănt'frīd) *Powys*

Village on the A40, 6 m. SE of Brecon. Henry Vaughan was born (1621) in the parish at a house called Newton (sometimes Newton-by-Usk; in Welsh, Trenewydd), near Scethrog. The present-day Newton Farm was probably built out of the ruins and on the site of his birthplace. This was his lifelong home, except for the years (1632–8) at *Oxford and London, and probably a short period of soldiering, and from here he practised medicine both locally and further afield. In *Silex Scintillans* (1650,

Emblematic frontispiece to *Silex Scintillans* (1650), by Henry Vaughan. Llansantffraed was his lifelong home

1655), his collection of religious and mystical poetry, he calls himself 'Silurist', by association with his beloved county of Brecon, anciently inhabited by the Silures tribe. He is buried outside the E wall of the church, with a tombstone bearing a Latin epitaph composed by himself. The church (rebuilt in the 19th c.) has a memorial tablet. Siegfried Sassoon writes movingly in 'At the Grave of Henry Vaughan' (*Collected Poems 1908-1956*):

> Here sleeps the Silurist; the loved physician;
> The face that left no portraiture behind; . . .
>
> Here faith and mercy, wisdom and humility
> (Whose influence shall prevail for evermore)
> Shine. And this lowly grave tells Heaven's tranquillity.
> And here stand I, a suppliant at the door.

LLANSAWEL (pr. Llăn'săwĕl)
Carmarthenshire

Village at the junction of the B4310 and the B4337, to the W of the Llandovery–Lampeter road. The Welsh-language prose writer David John Williams was born (1885) at Penrhiw Fawr, a farm in the parish which is now an inaccessible ruin on forestry land. When he was 6 he moved with his family to Abernant ℗, a smaller farm near Rhydcymerau, a few miles NW, and lived there until he left at 16 to work in the Rhondda coal mines. Later, having been a student first at Aberystwyth and then at Oxford, he became a schoolteacher. He was a prolific writer on a variety of subjects from his university days, but his first published work of note did not appear until 1934, when he was a master at Fishguard County School (1919–45): a series of sketches of characters of his native district, *Hen Wynebau* (Old Faces). This was followed by collections of short stories, *Storïau'r Tir Glas* (Stories of the Green Pasture, 1936), *Storïau'r Tir Coch* (Stories of the Ploughland, 1941), and *Storïau'r Tir Du* (Stories of the Black Earth, 1949). His last literary works were volumes of autobiography, *Hen Dŷ Ffarm* (The Old Farmhouse, 1953) and *Yn Chwech ar Hugain Oed* (At Twenty-Six Years of Age, 1959), and, like all his writings, are based on the local country, its traditions, and its people. D. J. Williams died in the chapel at Rhydcymerau in 1970 and was buried in the adjoining cemetery, where a memorial stone marks his grave.

LLANTHONY (pr. Llăn'thŏnny)
Monmouthshire

Small village in the Honddu valley, 10 m. N of Abergavenny, reached by turning off the A465 at Llanfihangel Crucorney. The ruined Augustinian priory, now in the care of Cadw, was bought *c.* 1807 by Walter Savage Landor, who planned to develop the estate and live as a model country gentleman. He was refused permission to restore the Priory, but managed to live in the building occupying the W range, now a hotel. He married Julia Thuillier in 1811 and they frequently entertained Southey and his wife, but in 1814, having quarrelled with his neighbours and the country people, Landor left

Llanthony Priory in the 19th century and the building, subsequently an inn, where W. S. Landor lived

Llanthony and his mother took over the management of the estate.

David Jones, poet and artist, is closely associated with the hamlet of Capel-y-ffin, 3½ m. further up the valley. Here he joined the sculptor Eric Gill from 1924 to 1927 and did much of his painting at the nearby monastery. An everyday experience is remembered in *In Parenthesis* (1937), his first book, written in prose and free verse, based on his experiences in the First World War:

> The water in the trench-drain ran as fast as stream in Nant Honddu in the early months, when you go to get milk from Pen-y-maes.

LLANTYSILIO *Denbighshire*

Small village off the A5, 2 m. NW of *Llangollen. The church, in the fields above the river, has a brass tablet on the S wall in memory of Browning, who, though not usually a regular churchgoer, attended services here during his stay at Llangollen in 1886.

LLANUWCHLLYN (pr. Llăn'ūχhlĭn)
Gwynedd

Village on the A494, 1 m. SW of Bala Lake. Owen Morgan Edwards, Welsh prose

writer and scholar, was born (1858) at Coed-y-pry. After a rudimentary early education he entered Bala Calvinistic Methodist College, and then proceeded to University College, Aberystwyth, and later to Oxford. He returned to Wales in 1907 when he was appointed first Chief Inspector of Schools under the new Welsh Education Department. He was knighted in 1916, and in 1918 became an honorary D.Litt. of the University of Wales. His extensive literary output was written in Welsh for the benefit of the ordinary people of Wales, and included *Yn y Wlad* (In the Country, 1921), *Er Mwyn Cymru* (For the Sake of Wales, 1922), and, most attractive of his works, *Cartrefi Cymru* (The Homes of Wales, 1896). He also founded the periodical *Cymru* (Wales) in 1891, for which he wrote the history of Wales and her literature and famous men, and which he continued to edit for the rest of his life. He also established the more purely literary periodical *Y Llenor* (The Writer, 1895–8), and another for non-Welsh-speaking readers, *Wales*. He died in 1920 and is buried at Pandy cemetery, Llanuwchllyn. A statue of him by R. L. Gapper stands in the village.

LLANWRTYD (pr. Llăn'ŏortĭd) *Powys*

Small town 14 m. W of Builth Wells on the A483. The farmhouse known as Cefn-brith Ⓟ *c.* 3 m. SE on the northern slope of Mynydd Eppynt was the birthplace in 1563 of John Penry, the Puritan pamphleteer. He was suspected of being the author of the Martin Marprelate tracts (1588–9), directed against the institution of episcopacy, which mocked the foibles and corruption of the bishops of the Church of England. Betrayed and arrested in London, Penry was indicted under the Act of Uniformity and executed at the age of 30.

LLANYSTUMDWY *Gwynedd*

Village W of Criccieth, a coastal town in NW Wales, once home to the British prime minister David Lloyd George. Llanystumdwy is now the site of Ty Newydd, the National Writers' Centre for Wales. The Welsh poet Gillian Clarke was one of the founders of the Centre, and is president of the Taliesin Trust, which manages it.

LLEDROD *Cardiganshire*

Village on the A485, 10 m. SE of Aberystwyth. Here the Welsh poet Evan Evans (Ieuan Fardd or Ieuan Brydydd Hir), one of the great classicists of the 18th c., was born at Cynhawdref, a farm in the parish, in 1731. He spent most of his tempestuous life in the district ('incorrigibly addicted' to strong drink, observed Samuel Johnson), and there is a memorial tablet in the church, but his burial place is unknown.

MANAFON *Powys*

Rural village near Welshpool. R. S. Thomas was rector here from 1942 to 1954. It was in Manafon, 'a church, a school, a public house and a shop', that he first began to study the Welsh language, where he published his first three volumes of poetry, *The Stones of the Field* (1946), *An Acre of Land* (1952), and *The Minister* (1953), and where, in poems such as 'The Welsh Hill Country', he started writing about the harsh life of rural Wales:

> Too far for you to see
> The fluke and the foot-rot and the fat maggot
> Gnawing the skin from the small bones.
> The sheep are grazing at Bwlch-y-Fedwen,
> Arranged romantically in the usual manner
> On a bleak background of bald stone.

MANORBIER *Pembrokeshire*

Village near the coast, on the B4585, just S of the A4139 Pembroke–Tenby road. The picturesque ruined castle was the birthplace of the chronicler and travel writer Giraldus Cambrensis (Gerald de Barri, 1146?–1200?). His most important work was *Itinerarium*, a description of the topography of Wales in which he described Manorbier as the pleasantest spot in the country.

MENAI BRIDGE *Anglesey*

Small town on the A5 and A545, at the Anglesey end of the Menai suspension bridge.

Manorbier Castle, Pembrokeshire, where the 12th-century chronicler Giraldus Cambrensis was born

This was the home of Albert Evans-Jones (Cynan), Welsh-language poet and eminent public figure, who lived at Penmaen, Ffordd Cynan, from 1937 until his death in 1970. He was buried at St Tysilio's Church, Church Island, in the Strait, reached by a causeway from the Holyhead road.

The monumental lions on the Britannia Bridge were celebrated by John Evans (1826–88), known in Welsh as Y Bardd Cocos (The Cockle Poet), who was famous for the unintentional humour of his doggerel in which meaning was neglected for the sake of rhyme. He described them thus:

> Four fat lions
> Without any hair,
> Two on this side
> And two over there.

He, too, is buried at St Tysilio's.

MERTHYR TYDFIL *Monmouthshire*

Industrial town on the A4060, in the Taff valley. Lady Charlotte Guest (1812–95), the first translator of the medieval Welsh tales known as the Mabinogion (3 vols, 1846), lived at Dowlais House after her marriage in 1835 to Sir Josiah John Guest, the ironmaster. The house has been demolished.

Thomas Stephens (1821–75), the literary critic and author of *The Literature of the Kymry* (1849), kept a chemist's shop at 133 High St., near Hope Chapel. Jack Jones, novelist and playwright, was born (1884) at Tai Harri Blawd, a row of cottages (gone) near Pontmorlais. He attended St David's Church School (gone) until he was 12 and then went to work at Cwm pit (closed). He joined the army at 17 and after serving abroad he returned to Merthyr, married, and lived for a time in Park Place and Milton Place.

MILFORD HAVEN *Pembrokeshire*

Ex-whaling town and port. The Earl of Richmond is reported as landing a force at Milford in Shakespeare's *Richard III*. The town also provides a rendezvous for Leonatus and Imogen in *Cymbeline*.

MOLD *Flintshire*

Former county town of Flintshire, situated on the Alyn, on the A494 and the A541. The Welsh-language novelist Daniel Owen was born (1836) at Maes-y-dref (the house is gone, but a commemorative stone marks the site). Owen received little education and at the age of 12 was apprenticed to a tailor. He began to preach in 1864 and studied for two years (1865–7) at the Calvinistic College at *Bala, but had to return home to look after his mother and sister. He worked as a tailor, first for his old master and then in his own business, and was encouraged in literary interests by the Revd Roger Edwards. His novels, which first appeared serially in periodicals, are mainly studies of Welsh life as it revolved round the chapel, and are famous for their characterization and wealth of detail as well as humour. His three major works are *Rhys Lewis* (1865), *Enoc Huws* (1891), and *Gwen Tomos* (1894). Other prose works include a collection of short stories, *Straeon y Pentan* (1894). Owen is buried in Mold public cemetery. The Daniel Owen Centre in Earl St. contains a small museum, and a statue in his memory stands outside the building.

MONTGOMERY *Powys*

Village, formerly the county town of Montgomeryshire, on the B4385, B4386, and B4388, 9 m. S of Welshpool. George Herbert, the brother of Edward Herbert, 1st Baron

257

Herbert of Cherbury (1583–1648), was born (1593) either in the now ruined castle or in the town. Donne, who was a lifelong friend of their mother, Lady Magdalen Herbert, stayed at the castle in 1613, but his poem 'The Primrose, being at Montgomery Castle' is thought to have been written earlier. The poem 'Good Friday 1613 Riding Westward' was written on his way here from *Polesworth.

The novelist and short-story writer Geraint Goodwin lived here at the end of his life, from November 1939 to October 1941, at Bowling Green Cottage. His last short stories, included in *The Collected Stories of Geraint Goodwin* (ed. R. Mathias and S. Adams, 1976), were written here. He is buried in the parish churchyard of St Nicholas.

MOSTYN *Flintshire*

Village on the A548 3 m. NW of Holywell. The playwright Emlyn Williams (1905–87) was born at 1 James Ter., Pen-y-ffordd, and christened at Gwynfa Chapel. He was brought up at the White Lion inn, known locally as Pen-y-maes, at the top of the low hill in the nearby village of Glanrafon. When he was 10 his family went to live at 1 Mainstone Cottages, Berthengam, Trelogan, another village in the same district. In 1917, when his father found employment at Summers's steelworks, they moved again, to 314a High St., very close to the railway in Connah's Quay. The play *The Corn Is Green* (1938) is based on the author's experiences while a pupil at Holywell County School and *The Druid's Rest* (1944), set in the fictitious village of Tan-y-maes, is a dramatic re-creation of Glanrafon.

In the nearby village of Whitford the naturalist and antiquary Thomas Pennant was born in 1726. Downing, the house where he was born, was destroyed by fire in 1922. He is chiefly remembered for his *Tours in Wales* (2 vols, 1778, 1781), one of the earliest and best surveys of North Wales.

MUMBLES *Glamorgan*

Seaside resort near Swansea. Here, on 27 January 1883, Maggie and Jessie Ace, daughters of the lighthouse keeper, waded into the stormy sea during the shipwreck of the *Prinz Albert* and pulled men to safety with their scarves. This act of bravery was celebrated in a stirring ballad by Clement Scott, 'The Women of Mumbles Head', which became a favourite piece for recitation in school and music hall.

MYNACHLOGDDU (pr. 'M'năχ'lŏgthē) *Pembrokeshire*

Small village in the Preseli mountains *c.* 12 m. S of Cardigan, to the W of the A478. Waldo Williams lived here as a boy (1911–15) when his father was headmaster of the village school. The fact that Welsh was the first language of the inhabitants proved a decisive influence on Waldo's future writing. After graduating at the University College of Wales, Aberystwyth, he held various teaching appointments, but his stand as a conscientious objector and his refusal to pay income tax as a protest against

conscription brought him into conflict with the authorities and he was twice in prison. Most of his poetry was written in the 1940s, when he was moving from one place to another, but it derives its inspiration chiefly from the Preseli area. His one volume of poetry, *Dail Pren* (Leaves of a Tree), was published in 1956, and in the same year he also contributed 20 poems to *Cerddi'r Plant* (Children's Poems). A commemorative stone to Waldo was unveiled near the village in 1978.

NANMOR *Gwynedd*

Small village *c.* 3 m. S of Beddgelert, on the E side of the A487. This was the birthplace of Dafydd Nanmor, a 15th-c. Welsh poet, whose love lyrics to a local married woman, Gwen o'r Ddôl, caused his banishment from the district at an early age. He wrote poems of praise and eulogy in honour of patrons in South Wales, and is believed to have been buried in Whitland (Y Ty Gwyn ar Daf), Dyfed. He was fond of puzzles and abstruse questions and wrote on astronomy, astrology, and weather signs in the medium of bardic measures, and he also imitated in Welsh an early Latin palindrome ('Sator arepo tenet opera rotas'). His *Poetical Works*, edited by T. Roberts and I. Williams, were published in 1923.

NEWCASTLE EMLYN *Carmarthenshire*

Small town on the river Teifi 10 m. E of Cardigan on the A484. Here, in Bridge St., the romantic novelist Allen Raine (Anne Adaliza Evans) was born in 1836. At the age of 40 she married Beynon Puddicombe at Penrhyn church, Tresaith, a seaside village 12 m. to the N. From 1900 they lived at Bronmôr, a large house above the village, and there she wrote the immensely popular novels *A Welsh Witch* (1902), *Hearts of Wales* (1905), and *Queen of the Rushes* (1906). Her grave is at the top end of Penrhyn churchyard.

NEWPORT *Monmouthshire*

Industrial city and seaport on the estuary of the Usk. W. H. Davies records in *The Autobiography of a Super-Tramp* (1908) that he was born on 20 April 1871 at the Church House inn, 14 Portland St. (off Commercial Rd, near the docks), and in 1938 attended the unveiling of a plaque on the house to this effect. In 1941 (soon after his death) the discovery of his birth certificate showed that his memory had been unreliable and that he had in fact been born on 3 July 1871 at 6 Portland St. (gone). When he was 3 his father died and he went to live with his grandparents at the Church House, moving with them on their retirement first to 38 Raglan St. and later to Upper Lewis St. He disliked school and benefited more from his own wide reading than from lessons. After his grandfather's death his grandmother apprenticed him to a picture framer, but he became restless and left for work in Bristol. He set sail for America in June 1893. On the junction of Hill St. and Commercial St. in the town's shopping centre there is an

allegorical sculpture by Paul Bothwell-Kincaid, erected in 1990, which is inscribed with the famous couplet from Davies's poem 'Leisure':

> What is this life if, full of care,
> We have no time to stand and stare?

St Julian's parish church, on the Caerleon side of the town, was built on a site given by Ronald Firbank. On the E wall is a large crucifix which he presented in memory of his parents, Sir Thomas and Lady Firbank, and beneath it is a memorial stone inscribed with a request for prayers for the donor, who died (1926) six months before the church was finished. Firbank had visited Newport *c.* 1904 to look for the former home of his paternal grandparents, Firbank House, but found that it had fallen into disrepair. The grounds of the ruined house have been developed as St Julian's Estate.

The few remains of Gwern-y-Clepa, the home in the 14th c. of Ifor ap Llywelyn, friend and patron of Dafydd ap Gwilym, can be seen among the trees about 2 m. to the W of Newport and 1 m. from the village of Bassaleg. The poet wrote verse in praise of his patron, whom he called Ifor Hael (the Generous). Four centuries later Edward Williams (Iolo Morganwg) and Evan Evans (Ieuan Brydydd Hir) visited the spot and the latter was inspired to write the poem 'Llys Ifor Hael', in which he lamented the loss of patronage to Welsh poets (trans.):

> A poor sight the hall of Ifor Hael—mounds
> In a swamp are lying,
> Thorn and blasted thistle own it,
> Bramble where was greatness.

NEWTON NOTTAGE *Glamorgan*

Little village on the A4106, 1 m. NE of Porthcawl. R. D. Blackmore, whose mother died when he was a baby, was cared for by his aunt Mary Frances Knight, probably at Nottage Court, her home here before her marriage to the Revd Richard Gordon, and later at *Elsfield. About 2½ m. NW of Newton Nottage, across the sand dunes, stands Sker House, a tall Elizabethan building, which was the inspiration for Blackmore's *The Maid of Sker* (1872), which he wrote on one of his many visits to his uncle at Nottage Court.

NEWTOWN *Powys*

Town on the A483 and the A489, an agricultural and sheep-raising centre, between the hilly slopes of the Severn valley. Robert Owen, the utopian socialist and author, was born here in 1771 and returned to the town to die in 1858. The Robert Owen wing of the Public Library was built at the expense of the Co-operative Union in 1903 and the statue in the town's centre was erected in 1956. A museum devoted to his memory was opened in 1983. Owen's best-known work, *A New View of Society* (1813), dedicated to William Wilberforce, was the last influential statement of a rationalist doctrine to be published in England and his autobiography (1857) is valuable for its account of working-class movements.

Geraint Goodwin, novelist and short-story writer, was born (1903) at 43 Commercial St., in the parish of Llanllwchaearn. He spent his boyhood at Forest Villa, New Rd, and also lived there from 1920 to 1924 while working for the *Montgomeryshire Express* before he went to London. Newtown is the setting for his novels *The Heyday in the Blood* (1936), *Watch for the Morning* (1938), and *Come Michaelmas* (1939), and for several of his short stories, and most of his work is rooted in the surrounding countryside.

OGMORE-BY-SEA *Glamorgan*

Seaside village in the Vale of Glamorgan, 20 m. W of Cardiff. Dannie Abse's poem 'At Ogmore-by-Sea this August Evening' recalls the poet's relationship with his father:

I'm at your favourite place where once you held
a bending rod and taught me how to bait
the ragworm hooks. Here, Father, here, tonight
we'll catch a bass or two, or dabs, or cod.

OYSTERMOUTH *Glamorgan*

Village 5 m. SW of Swansea on the road to the Mumbles. On the W side of All Saints' churchyard is the grave of Dr Thomas Bowdler, whose *Family Shakespeare* (1818), an expurgated edition 'in which those words and expressions are omitted which cannot with propriety be read aloud in a family', gave rise to the verb 'to bowdlerize'.

PANDY *Monmouthshire*

Village on the A465, 6 m. N of Abergavenny. Raymond Williams, the social historian, critic, and novelist, was born in 1921 at Llwyn Derw, situated behind Glannant House in the old part of the village near the Lancaster Arms. The signal box where his father worked is no longer there. From 1932 to 1939 Williams attended the King Henry VIII Grammar School (now community theatre workshops) in Abergavenny. His novel *Border Country* (1960) is set in his native district, as is the posthumous *People of the Black Mountains* (1989). He died in 1988 and was buried at Clodock in the churchyard of St Clydawg on the road to Longtown, on the other side of the road from the church.

PANTASAPH *Flintshire*

Village off the A55, *c.* 3 m. W of Holywell. Francis Thompson lived (1893-7) near the Franciscan monastery. He stayed at various places, including the old post office (gone), the last being Aloysius Cottage (formerly Craecas), up the hill to the N. Most of the poems in *New Poems* (1897) were written here.

PENARTH *Glamorgan*

Town 4 m. from Cardiff, of which it is a dormitory. The Welsh-language writer Saunders Lewis (1893-1985) lived at Bryn-y-mor in Westbourne Rd after his appointment to a lecturer's post in the Welsh Department of University College, Cardiff, in 1952. The poet, literary historian, dramatist, and critic Saunders Lewis is generally regarded as the greatest Welsh literary figure of the 20th c. In 1925 he was the founder of the Welsh Nationalist Party (later Plaid Cymru). He wrote some 20 plays, notably *Buchedd Garmon* (The Life of Germanus, 1937), *Blodeuwedd* (The Woman of Flowers, 1948), and *Brad* (Treachery, 1958), as well as two novels and a substantial body of literary criticism. All his writings are informed by a love of Wales seen in the context of European Catholic Christendom. He is buried in the Roman Catholic cemetery at Penarth.

PEN-ONN *Denbighshire*

Farm in the parish of Llancarfan, on a minor road off the B4266, *c.* 5 m. NW of Barry. This was the birthplace of Edward Williams (Iolo Morganwg), poet and antiquary, the son of a stonemason. The house where he was born no longer stands and it is thought that Bryn Iolo, a modern bungalow, may have been built on the site. At an early age Iolo moved with his parents to the neighbouring village of *Flemingston.

PENRHYNDEUDRAETH *Gwynedd*

Small town on the A487 E of Porthmadog. The philosopher and logician Bertrand Russell (3rd Earl Russell), who won the Nobel Prize for Literature in 1950, lived from 1954 until his death in 1970 at Plas Penrhyn, *c.* 1½ m. W just off the main road near Minffordd. It offered not only solitude but also an outlook over the Glaslyn estuary and a sight of Snowdon. He continued to write prolifically and vigorously here, well into his nineties and up to his death.

PONTARDAWE *Glamorgan*

Village on the A4067, 9 m. NE of Swansea. David Gwenallt Jones, Welsh-language poet, author, and critic, was born (1899) in Wesley Ter. Ⓟ, but moved at an early age with his family to the nearby village of Alltwen, overlooking the Swansea valley. In the open-air theatre in Ynysderw a memorial fountain commemorates David Gwenallt Jones, together with Professor T. J. Morgan (1907-86) and Tom Ellis Lewis (1900-78), who were both prominent literary figures. In 1989 a plaque was unveiled to commemorate Thomas Jones (1910-79), Professor of Welsh at the University College of Wales, Aberystwyth, notable especially for his translation of the Mabinogion into English (1948) in collaboration with Gwyn Jones.

PONTERWYD (pr. Pontĕr'wĭd) *Cardiganshire*

Village on the Rheidol, 12 m. E of Aberystwyth on the A44. George Borrow stayed at the inn (now the George Borrow inn) on his tour of Wales in the summer and autumn of 1854. He gives an account of his travels in *Wild Wales* (1862).

PONTYPRIDD *Glamorgan*

Industrial town at the confluence of the rivers Taff and Rhondda on the A470. Here, in 1856, the words of 'Hen Wlad fy Nhadau' (Old Land of My Fathers), which later became the Welsh national anthem, were written by Evan James (1809-78); his son James composed the music. They owned a wool factory in Mill St., where a plaque commemorates them. The nearby Welsh school is named after Evan James. A bronze monument to father and son, the work of Sir Goscombe John, was erected in Ynys Angharad Park, on the eastern bank of the Taff, in 1930. The town is now home to the University of Glamorgan, where the poet Tony Curtis has been Professor of Poetry and Creative Writing since the late 1980s.

PORTH *Glamorgan*

Industrial town at the confluence of the Rhondda Fawr and Rhondda Fach on the A4058, 4 m. NW of Pontypridd. Gwyn Thomas (1913-81), novelist and playwright, was born and brought up at 196 High St. Ⓟ, Cymmer, in the direction of Trebanog. He attended Porth County School (1924-30) and after studying at St Edmund Hall, Oxford, taught Spanish and French at Cardigan (1940-2) and Barry (1942-62). But Porth remained the centre of his world and Rhondda society is vividly and often hilariously portrayed in his novels. They include *The Dark Philosophers* (1946), *The Alone to the Alone* (1947), *The World Cannot Hear You* (1950), *A Frost on My Frolic* (1953), and *A Point of Order* (1956). His ashes were scattered at Llanwynno on the hill between the rivers Rhondda Fach and Cynon, near the Brynffynon Arms, one of his favourite spots.

PORTHMADOG *Gwynedd*

Small town and seaside resort on the estuary of the river Glaslyn and at the junction of the A487 and A497. Here, in 1867, the poet Eifion Wyn (Eliseus Williams) was born at 10 Garth Ter. Ⓟ. He was a teacher in the town and later clerk and accountant to the North Wales Slate Company. His reputation as a lyricist was won with the volume *Telynegion Maes a Mor* (1906), which contains a number of poems still famous as recitation pieces, and some of his hymns are still popular. The primary school is named after him. He was buried in the village of Chwilog *c.* 9 m. E on the B4354, where the monument on his grave was unveiled by David Lloyd George in 1934.

R. S. Thomas, who moved into a house at the nearby village of Pentrefelin with his second wife in 1999, worshipped at St John's Church. He received the Cymrodorion Medal at his home shortly before his death in September 2000. A slate marks the place where his ashes are buried in the churchyard.

PORTH NEIGWL *Gwynedd*

Stretch of coast and beach known as 'Hell's Mouth'. R. S. Thomas retired here to 'Sarn Rhiw' in the grounds of Plas yn Rhiw.

PORT TALBOT *Glamorgan*

Welsh industrial town, celebrated by the poet Gillian Clarke in her poem 'A Heron at Port Talbot':

259

Snow falls on the cooling towers
delicately settling on cranes.
Machinery's old bones whiten; death
settles with its rusts, its erosions . . .

The steel town's sulphurs billow
like dirty washing. The sky stains
with steely inks and fires, chemical
rustings, salt-grains, sand under snow.

And the bird comes, a surveyor
calculating space between old workings
and the mountain hinterland, archangel
come to re-open the heron-roads . . .

PRESTATYN *Denbighshire*

Seaside resort in the old county of
Denbighshire. The town's allure and the girl
who advertises it are disrespectfully subverted
in Philip Larkin's poem 'Sunny Prestatyn'.

PWLLHELI (pr. Po͝ollhēlē) *Gwynedd*

Market town on the A497, on the N coast of
Cardigan Bay. The Welsh-language poet and
dramatist Albert Evans-Jones (Cynan) was
born at Liverpool House (now a stationer Ⓟ),
Penlan St. He attended Pwllheli Elementary
School and Pwllheli County School before
going to college at *Bangor. His literary
interests were cultivated from an early age and
he had already won several local eisteddfod
prizes when his poem 'Mab y Bwthyn' (The
Cottager's Son) gained him the National
Eisteddfod crown at Caernarfon in 1921.
Ffynnon Felin Bach, a well where as a boy he
used to draw water for his grandmother, is
mentioned in 'Mab y Bwthyn' and now has a
commemorative tablet, inscribed with a
quotation from the poem. The well is on the left
as one leaves the town along Lôn Llŷn. Much of
Evans-Jones's work derives its inspiration from
the area in which he grew up. He was made a
Freeman of Pwllheli in 1963.

At Penyberth, a farmhouse near Penrhos
c. 2 m. W of Pwllheli on the A499, there is a
memorial to Saunders Lewis, D. J. Williams,
and Lewis Valentine, the three Welsh
Nationalists who committed a token act of
arson at an RAF bombing school that was
being built here in 1936. The house was
significant in the Welsh cultural tradition in
that it was the home of a Recusant family in the
16th and early 17th cc. There was widespread
opposition to the bombing school in Wales and
the incident had a deep influence on many
writers such as R. Williams Parry.

RESOLVEN *Glamorgan*

Former mining village 6 m. NE of Neath on the
B4434. Bert Lewis Coombes (1894–1974) came
here from Madley, Herefordshire, in 1912 and
spent the rest of his life in the village, working
as a collier in the local pit. His first book, *These
Poor Hands* (1939), was praised by J. B.
Priestley and Cyril Connolly and is generally
considered to be among the most authentic
accounts ever written about mining.
Encouraged by John Lehmann, the author
went on to write *Those Clouded Hills* (1944)
and *Miners' Day* (1945), both of which describe
the harsh conditions prevailing in the mines of
South Wales during the years between the
world wars.

RHEWL (pr. 'Hrĕo͝ol) *Denbighshire*

Village 2 m. NW of Ruthin, on the A525. The
Calvinist minister and writer Robert Ambrose
Jones, known as Emrys ap Iwan, spent the last
years of his life (1900–6) and is buried here.
He was a tireless writer to the Press and as a
literary critic he sought to trace the mainstream
of Welsh classical prose tradition and restore
the simplicity and purity he found there. He
studied at *Bala Calvinistic Methodist College,
visited the Continent frequently, and was
ordained at *Mold in 1883. His Welsh
grammar appeared in 1881, and his sermons
were first published in 1906 (*Homiliau*, ed.
Ezra Roberts), followed by further collections
and reprints. Three volumes of his writings
were published by the Welsh Book Club
(1937–40), and much of his unpublished
work, including his translation of Renan's
Job, is in the National Library of Wales,
Aberystwyth.

RHOSGADFAN (pr. Rōs'gadvan) *Gwynedd*

Village *c*. 5 m. S of Caernarfon, between
the A487 and the A4085. Kate Roberts
(1891–1985), novelist, short-story writer, and
literary journalist, was born and brought up
here at Cae'r Gors Ⓟ; the house is now a
heritage centre. Generally considered to be the
greatest writer of fiction in Welsh, she was the
author of some 15 novels and collections of
short stories, notably *Traed mewn Cyffion* (Feet
in Chains, 1936), *Y Byw sy'n Cysgu* (The Living
Dead, 1956) and *Te yn y Grug* (Tea in the
Heather, 1959). Much of her early work deals
with her native district at a time when the
slate-quarrying industry was in its heyday,
while her later novels often portray old people
living alone in a harsh modern world. On the
moorland road above the village, Y Lon Wen,
there is a memorial at a spot often mentioned
in her writing, with splendid views N and NW.

RHYD-DDU (pr. 'Rŭdthē) *Gwynedd*

Village on the A4085, situated on the upper
Gwyrfai at the W foot of Snowdon. The Welsh-
language poet and essayist T. H. Parry-
Williams was born (1887) at the school house
Ⓟ and educated at the village school, where his
father was headmaster. These buildings have
been converted by the county council into a
residential centre, Canolfan Rhyd-ddu, which
houses a permanent exhibition of the life
and work of Parry-Williams. He first won
recognition as a poet by gaining both chair and
crown at the National Eisteddfod at Wrexham
(1912) and at Bangor (1915). His first published
work, *Ysgrifau* (Essays), appeared in 1928,
followed by *Cerddi* (Poems, 1931), *Olion*
(Vestiges, 1935), *Synfyfyrion* (Meditations,
1937), *Lloffion* (Gleanings, 1942), *O'r Pedwar
Gwynt* (Out of the Four Winds, 1957), and
Pensynnu (Musing, 1966). An anthology
from previous volumes, *Detholiad o Gerddi*
(A Selection of Poems), was published in 1972.

The influence of his native Snowdonia
predominates in his work, which is
characterized by great flexibility of style, in the
use of majestic literary language and the words
and idioms of common speech. His later poetry
was written in the form of the *rhigwm*, or
sequence of irregular rhyming couplets. He
wrote some of the finest sonnets in Welsh, and
was also the first Welsh writer to make
extensive use of the essay form. Parry-Williams
was Professor of Welsh at *Aberystwyth, and
received many honours, including a knighthood
in 1958. He was President of the Court of the
Royal National Eisteddfod of Wales (1955–67)
and President of the Honourable Society of
Cymmrodorion (1961–9).

RHYL *Denbighshire*

Welsh seaside town at the mouth of the river
Clwyd. The poet Adrian Henri's family moved
here in 1938, where he attended St Asaph
Grammar School.

RHYMNEY (pr. 'Rŭmnĭ) *Monmouthshire*

Colliery and iron-working town on the A469, at
the head of the Rhymney valley. The poet Idris
Davies was born (1905) at 16 Field St. (gone),
into a mining family. He was educated at
Rhymney, Loughborough Training College, the
University of Nottingham, and the University
of London. After working as a miner (1919–26),
he taught in various primary schools in
England and Wales, and finally, from 1947
until his death, at Cwmsyfiog Primary School,
Rhymney. He died in 1953 at 7 Victoria Rd,
and is buried in the public cemetery. There is
a plaque to his memory in Rhymney Public
Library. The mood of Idris Davies's poetry is
best captured, perhaps, W of Rhymney at
the Cairns (Old Bent Iron Beacon), which
commands a panoramic view of the Rhymney
valley. He is the poet par excellence of
industrial South Wales between the wars. His
poems were published as *Collected Poems of
Idris Davies*, edited by Islwyn Jenkins (1972).

ST ASAPH *Denbighshire*

Small cathedral city on the A55 and the A525,
6 m. N of Denbigh. In 1601 Bishop William
Morgan, first translator of the Bible into
Welsh, came from the see of Llandaf to that of
St Asaph. He died in 1604 and is buried in the
Cathedral, beneath the throne in the presbytery.
There is a memorial to him and other
translators on the N side of the Cathedral.

Mrs Felicia Hemans, a poet of great
popularity in her day, and admired by
Wordsworth, now perhaps best remembered
for 'Casabianca', lived as a girl (1809–12) and
again, after her marriage and a brief stay at
Daventry, until 1825 at Bronwylfa, a large
house on the hillside NE of the town. It was
replaced by a later building, which could be
seen from 'Mrs. Hemans' Bridge', where she
used to sit and write her poetry. The bridge,
no longer spanning the diverted Elwy, can be
reached by leaving St Asaph by Chester St.,
crossing the dual carriageway, and turning
left along a narrow lane. Mrs Hemans is

Dylan Thomas's writing desk in his shed at the Boathouse, Laugharne, Carmarthenshire. Thomas wrote *Under Milk Wood* here

IN THIS HOVSE
SIR WALTER SCOTT
LIVED FROM 1802 TO 1808

commemorated in the Cathedral by a tablet in the S aisle and a window in the N wall of the chancel. A lock of her hair and a book of her poems are on view in the cathedral museum, which also contains various books of historic interest from the cathedral library (now mainly housed at Aberystwyth) and autograph letters from Dickens, Charles Darwin, Thackeray, and Trollope.

ST BEUNO'S (pr. 'Bīnōw's) COLLEGE *Denbighshire*

Jesuit seminary on the E slopes of the Vale of Clwyd, ¾ m. N of the village of *Tremeirchion. Gerard Manley Hopkins entered the college as a theology student in August 1874, and it was here that he wrote 'The Wreck of the Deutschland', in the early part of 1876, a long, profoundly religious poem in the form of a Pindaric ode, inspired by the disaster which had occurred the previous December. In 1877, his last year at St Beuno's, he wrote a number of sonnets concerned with objects of nature as his discerning eye saw them, including 'The Windhover', and 'Pied Beauty', which begins 'Glory be to God for dappled things—'. He was ordained priest in September and moved to Mount St Mary's College in Derbyshire.

ST DAVID'S *Pembrokeshire*

Smallest cathedral city in Great Britain, on the westernmost bend of the A487, *c.* 1 m. from the sea. Giraldus Cambrensis (Gerald de Barri), chronicler and travel writer, gives an entertaining account of the see in 1188. He was twice elected bishop (1176 and 1198) but failed to obtain consecration, probably because the English feared that he would make the Welsh Church independent of Canterbury. He was buried here *c.* 1223 and an effigy in the S choir aisle of the Cathedral has been suggested as possibly his.

ST FAGANS *Glamorgan*

Village 4 m. W of Cardiff off the A4232. The Welsh Folk Museum, a branch of the National Museum of Wales, was established here in 1948 in the castle, which was the gift of the 3rd Earl of Plymouth. Its first curator was the poet Iorwerth C. Peate (1901–82). His ashes, with those of his wife, Nansi, are buried in the graveyard of Penrhiw Chapel, which, like many other buildings, has been rebuilt in the Museum's grounds.

SARN MELLTEYRN (pr. Melltirn) *Gwynedd*

Village on the B4413, 6 m. NE of Aberdaron. Roy Campbell and his wife, Mary, lived (1922–4) at Ty Corn, an old cottage they thought had been a stable, not far from the sea. While Campbell finished *The Flaming Terrapin* (1924) and their daughter Tess was born, they were supported by his father. In *Light on a Dark Horse* (1951), Campbell writes how well he got on with the local people, who admired his bravery in rowing the doctor to an urgent case on the nearby island during a heavy storm.

STRATA FLORIDA ABBEY *Cardiganshire*

Situated to the E of the B4343 Tregaron-Devil's Bridge road, near the village of Pontrhydfendigaid, the now ruined Abbey was once one of the most celebrated monasteries in Wales, and the burial place of princes of the house of Dinefwr. There is a tablet inside the walls in memory of the poet Dafydd ap Gwilym, who is traditionally believed to be buried under a yew tree in the graveyard outside the monastery (though *Talley Abbey has a rival claim to his grave).

SWANSEA *Glamorgan*

Large seaport and metal-working town on the NW shore of Swansea Bay, at the mouth of the Tawe. Richard Savage, whose biography appears in Dr Johnson's *Lives of the English Poets* (1781), lived here from 1739 to 1740, in Barber's Court, off Orchard St. (site later occupied by a large store), having left London to escape his creditors. He had published a moderately successful play, *The Bastard* (1728), and a long moral and descriptive poem entitled *The Wanderer* (1729), which was praised by Johnson, but his financial state was chronically precarious and he was forced to move on again, this time to *Bristol.

Walter Savage Landor wrote his epic poem *Gebir* (1798) while staying here, influenced, it seems, by his reading of an Arabian romance by Clara Reeve, which he had borrowed from the Swansea Library. During his visit he met Lord Aylmer, father of Rose, his early love, whose death at the age of 20 he lamented in the elegy 'Rose Aylmer'.

Julia Ann Hatton (1764–1838), known as Ann of Swansea, the sister of Sarah Siddons, settled here in 1799 after taking a lease of Swansea Bathing House. Besides a dozen novels and two volumes of verse, she wrote a play, *Zaffine, or, The Knight of the Burning Cross*, in which Edmund Kean acted in Swansea in 1810.

Amy Elizabeth Dillwyn (1845–1935) was born in Swansea and lived most of her life here. After her father's death in 1892 she managed the Dillwyn Spelter Works, her unorthodox views and way of life bringing her a reputation for eccentricity. She was a literary critic of some standing and her review of *Treasure Island* (1883) for *The Spectator* helped to discover the talent of Robert Louis Stevenson. The first of her six novels, *The Rebecca Rioter* (1880), is set in the Swansea area.

Dylan Thomas was born (27 Oct. 1914) at 5 Cwmdonkin Drive, on the west side of the town, known as the Uplands, and spent his first 20 years in Swansea. He was a delicate child and had somewhat erratic schooling before going to the Grammar School at the age of 10. (The school suffered damage by firebombs in 1941 and was rebuilt in another part of the town and renamed Bishop Gore School.) Much of the background of his early life is described in the semi-autobiographical *Portrait of the Artist as a Young Dog* (1940) and in *A Child's*

Christmas in Wales (first published in the US in *Harper's Bazaar*, 1950; in the UK as a book, 1968). He left school in 1931 and got a job with the *South Wales Daily Post* (now the *South Wales Evening Post*). During the next three years he wrote the poems published in *Eighteen Poems* in 1934, the year after his first visit to London, when his reputation as a poet was steadily growing. Although Cwmdonkin Drive remained his home for another two years, he made frequent visits to London, meeting new people and extending his literary acquaintance. In early 1936 he completed *Twenty-Five Poems*, which was published in the autumn and aroused much controversial criticism, including warm praise from Edith Sitwell. The same year he moved to London and cut his ties with Swansea. A simple carved stone monument in his memory has been erected in Cwmdonkin Park, where he played as a child. It is inscribed with a quotation from his poem 'Fern Hill':

> Oh as I was young and easy in the mercy of his means,
> > Time held me green and dying
> > Though I sang in my chains like the sea.

There is a statue of the poet on Dylan Thomas Square, near the Dylan Thomas Theatre, in the Maritime Quarter of Swansea; the theatre has a mural commemorating Thomas. In nearby Abernethy Sq. stands a sculpture depicting Captain Catione of the characters in *Under Milk Wood* (1954).

Vernon Watkins, poet and friend of Dylan Thomas, was educated at Swansea Grammar School for a year (1915–16) before going to a preparatory school in Essex and then to *Repton. He lived with his parents from 1931 to 1941 at Heatherslade (now Heatherslade Café), Pennard Cliffs, 8 m. SW of Swansea, where he wrote *Ballad of the Mari Lwyd and Other Poems* (1941), as well as three long poems in *The Lamp and the Veil* (1945) and some of the ballads in *The Death Bell* (1954). After serving in the RAF he married (1946) and settled at The Garth, Pennard Cliffs, for the rest of his life. Here he wrote the poems in *The Lady with the Unicorn* (1948) and all his subsequent work, and also edited a collection of letters from Dylan Thomas to himself (1957). For most of his life he worked at Lloyds Bank in St Helen's Rd, Swansea. He died at Seattle, US, when a visiting lecturer on modern poetry, and his ashes were brought back and scattered over the sea at Pennard Cliffs. A tablet in his memory on the N wall of Pennard church reads:

> Death cannot steal the light
> Which love has kindled
> Nor the years change it.

Kingsley Amis lectured at University College from the autumn of 1949, and for the rest of his life was a regular visitor to the city. His *The Old Devils* (1986) explores how Wales has changed over the years, as Alun Weaver and his wife return after many years away, and are reunited with all the people who never left. It was here in Swansea on one of his frequent summer

Kingsley Amis in Swansea in 1958

holidays that Amis had a fall and a stroke, in August 1995; he died two months later.

The poet Tony Curtis studied English at University College.

TALGARREG *Cardiganshire*

Village 7 m. SE of New Quay on the B4338. The cottage ℗ where Dewi Emrys (David Emrys James) spent his last years stands opposite the Glanyrafon Arms. The poet is buried in the graveyard of Pisgah Chapel.

The poet Thomas Jacob Thomas was born at Sarnicol, a house *c.* 2 m. W at the junction of two minor roads in the direction of Capel Cynon. A slate plaque is set into a stone wall that forms a gatepost to a barnyard belonging to the farm, Allt Maen. Sarnicol, now a ruin, stands in a field *c.* 500 yds away on the other side of the crossroads.

TALLEY ABBEY *Carmarthenshire*

Remains of a Premonstratensian monastery 8 m. N of Llandeilo in the valley of the Dulais, on the B4302. It has a rival claim (not generally acknowledged) to *Strata Florida Abbey as the burial place of Dafydd ap Gwilym, and a memorial stone to the poet was erected in 1984.

TALSARNAU *Gwynedd*

Village on the A496, between Harlech and Maentwrog; also the name of the surrounding area, in the parish of Llanfihangel-y-Traethau, consisting of various small hamlets and farms. Richard Hughes was staying at Harlech for his school holidays in 1916 when he discovered a one-room cottage which he proceeded to rent out of his pocket money. The cottage, Ysgol Fach, on the estate of Maeyneuadd, can be seen from the mountain road, 2½ m. above the village. Most of his early verse was written here and was published in various literary magazines, and much of it is included in his first book, *Gipsy-Night and Other Poems* (1922). Hughes returned to Talsarnau in 1947, with his wife and family, after leaving *Laugharne and settled at Môr Edrin, a house on the shores of the Dwyryd estuary, opposite Portmeirion. Here he began to write his long historical novel *The Human Predicament*. The first volume, *The Fox in the Attic*, was published in 1961 and was followed by the second, *The Wooden Shepherdess*, in 1973. He had written 12 chapters of the third volume at the time of his death. He died at his home on 28 April 1976 and is buried in the beautiful churchyard of the church at Llanfihangel-y-Traethau on the Ynys, where he had been churchwarden.

TALWRN *Anglesey*

Village on Anglesey *c.* 3 m. NE of Llangefni on the B5109. The poet Gruffudd ab yr Ynad Coch (Son of the Red Judge) was born in the parish of Llanddyfnan in the 13th c. He is renowned in Wales for his elegy to Llywelyn ap Gruffudd, the last prince of independent Wales, killed by the forces of Edward I in 1282. A memorial, erected in 1991, stands on the village square.

TAL-Y-SARN *Conwy*

Village on the B4418, *c.* 8 m. S of Caernarfon. The Welsh-language poet Robert Williams Parry was born (1884) at Rhiwafon ℗ and there is a memorial to him in the centre of the village. He first made his name when he won the National Eisteddfod chair at Colwyn Bay in 1911 with his poem 'Yr Haf' (Summer), and though he soon abandoned this form of romantic medievalism he is still known as Bardd yr Haf (the Poet of Summer).

TENBY *Pembrokeshire*

Seaside resort on the W side of Carmarthen Bay, on the A478 and the A4139, situated on a rocky promontory overlooking two sandy bays. The town dates from the 12th c., when it was a settlement of Flemish cloth workers. Giraldus Cambrensis was rector of the parish church (the predecessor of the present Church of St Mary) from 1172 to 1175. Edmund Gosse, in *Father and Son* (1907), refers to his seventh birthday spent here 'in an ecstasy of happiness'. The expenses of the holiday were paid by his father's fees for a class in marine biology.

Talley Abbey, Carmarthenshire, which rivals Strata Florida in claiming the burial place of Dafydd ap Gwilym. Photograph taken in 1932

Walter Savage Landor, who was in love with Nancy Jones, a young lady of Tenby, immortalized her as Ione in his poems.

Soon after the Second World War the travel writer and novelist Norman Lewis moved to the town on medical advice and lived a solitary life at St Catherine's Fort, situated on top of a rock some 30 yds offshore in the bay and built in the 1860s to protect the Pembrokeshire coast from French invasion. He wrote in the central redoubt of the banqueting hall: 'Here I escaped the worst of the gale's shindy, although the living rooms reverberated and clanked endlessly and the wind whimpered through keyholes and round the edges of loose-fitting panes of glass.'

TINTERN ABBEY *Monmouthshire*

Ruined Cistercian abbey (founded 1131, rebuilt 13th and 14th cc., and suppressed by Henry VIII, 1536), situated on grassland in a bend of the Wye, with wooded hills above, *c*. 5 m. N of Chepstow, on the A466. Wordsworth and his sister Dorothy visited the Abbey in July 1798, after leaving *Alfoxton and before going to Germany. Wordsworth wanted to revisit the hills and valleys of Wales, which he had explored in 1793. He and Dorothy left *Bristol after spending a few days with Joseph Cottle, crossed the Severn by ferry, and walked up the Wye valley as far as Goodrich Castle. They spent a night at Tintern on the way and, after walking back to Chepstow, returned to Tintern for a second night before going back all the way to Bristol by boat. Wordsworth's poem 'Lines Composed a Few Miles Above Tintern Abbey, on Revisiting the Banks of the Wye during a Tour, July 13, 1798' was composed after leaving

Tintern, completed on his return to Bristol, and taken to Cottle for publication in *Lyrical Ballads* (1798).

Sydney Dobell made a journey to Tintern Abbey with some friends in 1858 and wrote a sonnet about it.

TRAWSFYNYDD (pr. Trows'vŭnĭth) *Gwynedd*

Village on the W side of the A470 near its junction with the A4212. A bronze statue commemorates the poet Ellis Humphrey Evans ('Hedd Wyn'), portrayed as a shepherd, who was born nearby. He worked on his father's farm before enlisting with the Royal Welsh Fusiliers in the First World War, when he was killed in action at Pilkem Ridge on 31 July 1917. He was posthumously awarded the bardic chair at the National Eisteddfod at Birkenhead in September 1917 for his *awdl* (a long poem in traditional metres) entitled *Yr Arwr* (The Hero), which relates the myth of Prometheus to Christian symbolism. The announcement of his death was received with great emotion by the audience and the empty chair was draped in black for the ceremony.

TREALAW *Glamorgan*

Former mining village in the valley of the Rhondda Fawr on the A4058, 2 m. NW of Porth. The poet and dramatist James Kitchener Davies lived from 1940 until his death in 1952 at Aeron in Brithweunydd; from 1926 he had lived at 136 Kenry St. in Tonypandy. A well-known militant on behalf of Plaid Cymru, he was a teacher of Welsh at Pentre Secondary School. His long poem 'Sŵn y Gwynt sy'n Chwythu' (The Sound of the Blowing Wind),

broadcast by the BBC while the poet was on his deathbed, is one of the finest long poems in the Welsh language. The writer was buried at Llethr Ddu cemetery near his home.

TREFOR (pr. 'Trēvor) *Anglesey*

Village in the parish of Llandrygarn in Anglesey, at the crossing of the B5109 and the B5112. The scholar and Welsh-language poet John Morris-Jones was born here in 1864. At the age of 4 he moved with his family to *Llanfair-pwll.

TREGARON *Cardiganshire*

Village on the junction of the A485 and the B4343, 14 m. S of Aberystwyth and 11 m. NE of Lampeter. The poet and dramatist James Kitchener Davies was born in 1902 at Llain in the district of Llwyn-piod, to the W of the village. The croft is now a ruin. Davies's verse play *Meini Gwagedd* (Stones of Emptiness, 1945) is set in Cors Caron, the nearby bog. The writer is commemorated by a plaque on the wall of Llwynpiod Chapel, just off the B4578.

TREGYNON *Powys*

Village on the B4389, 6 m. N of Newtown. At Gregynog Hall (now a University of Wales residential centre) a private press was founded in 1923 by the sisters Gwendoline and Margaret Davies, the granddaughters of the industrialist David Davies of Llandinam. Its chairman was the civil servant Thomas Jones (1870–1955) and its Controllers were Robert Ashwin Maynard, William McCance, Loyd Haberley, and James Wardrop. Among those who illustrated Gregynog books were Blair Hughes Stanton and Agnes Miller Parker. The press was revived as Gwasg Gregynog by the University in 1974 and since then it has published books by R. S. Thomas, R. Williams Parry, Francis Kilvert, Kate Roberts, Dylan Thomas, and William Williams (Pantycelyn). The press workshops are open to visitors by prior arrangement.

TRELLECK *Monmouthshire*

Historic village near Monmouth. Bertrand Russell was born at Ravenscroft, Trelleck in 1872.

TREMADOG *Gwynedd*

Village, 1 m. N of Porthmadog on the A487, laid out by W. A. Madocks in 1810 but never developed into the town he envisaged. Madocks's philanthropy in building a causeway to reclaim land in the estuary of the Glaslyn inspired Shelley to help him to raise the money. Shelley and Harriet, his wife, rented Tan-yr-Allt, a house belonging to Mr Madocks, from the autumn of 1812 until February 1813, when intruders fired shots at him one evening and the Shelleys left the neighbourhood. The reasons for the attack are obscure but might have arisen out of local resentment of Shelley's political views.

T. E. Lawrence, who became known as 'Lawrence of Arabia' after his exploits during the First World War, recounted in *Seven Pillars of Wisdom* (1926), was born at Woodlands Ⓟ in 1888.

TREMEIRCHION *Denbighshire*

Straggling hillside village overlooking the Vale of Clwyd, a few miles SE of St Asaph, off the A55. A tablet on the N side of the chancel in the little church commemorates Hester Lynch Piozzi, 'Dr. Johnson's Mrs. Thrale', who was buried (1821) in a vault then outside the church, but since covered by the N transept, built later. The only child of John Salusbury, she grew up at the family home, Bach-y-Graig (gone), a 16th-c. mansion of pyramidal shape, topped by a cupola, which nestled at the foot of Dymeirchion (now spelt Tremeirchion) Hill on the edge of a wood. When she revisited it in 1774 with her husband, Henry Thrale, and Dr Johnson, she was saddened to find the place in a dilapidated state, as was the church, which Johnson noted was 'in a dismal condition, the seats all tumbling about, the Altar rail falling'. After her husband's death (1781) Mrs Thrale married Gabriel Piozzi (1784) and they decided to build a house at Tremeirchion, near the top of the hill, with a fine view of the valley and distant Snowdonia. The house, built as an Italian villa, was called Brynbella (Welsh *Bryn*, hill; Italian *bella*, beautiful) and in 1795 became their home for the rest of their lives. In 1800 Gabriel Piozzi renovated Bach-y-graig for a tenant and a few years later undertook extensive additions and repairs to the church. Mrs Piozzi wrote in September 1803 to her daughter Queeney that they were 'paving, glazing, slating it etc.' and providing a new pulpit, desk, and cloths.

TREORCHY *Glamorgan*

Former mining village on the A4061 in the valley of the Rhondda Fawr. Here, in 1878, the poet Ben Bowen was born at 126 High St. Ⓟ. At the age of 12 he became a collier at the Ty'n-y-bedw colliery (closed) and later trained for the Baptist ministry in Cardiff. In poor health, he showed great promise as a poet, but was excommunicated for heresy by Moriah, the chapel to which he belonged at Ton Pentre. He died at the age of 24 and was buried in the cemetery at Treorchy, where his gravestone bears the epitaph (in Welsh), 'He talked too much about Wales and Eternity'—the complaint of an adjudicator at the National Eisteddfod. The plaque which commemorates him at 6 Victoria St., Ton Pentre, his sister's home, where he died, is inscribed with his *englyn* 'Cystudd' (Affliction).

Euros Bowen (1904–88), one of the most accomplished Welsh poets of the 20th c., belonged to the same family as Ben Bowen. He was born at 112 High St., Treorchy.

TRE-TALIESIN *Cardiganshire*

Village on the A487, *c.* 9 m. NE of Aberystwyth. A footpath leads 1 m. E to Bedd Taliesin, an ancient stone tomb traditionally regarded as the grave of Taliesin (*fl.* 550), reputedly the greatest of the Welsh bards, but probably a mythical personage. He is first mentioned in *Saxon Genealogies*, appended to the *Historia Britonum c.* 690. Much poetry, probably of later date, has been ascribed to him, and the 14th-c. Book of Taliesin is a collection of poems by different authors and of different dates. Taliesin figures prominently in Peacock's *The*

Misfortunes of Elphin (1829) and is mentioned in Tennyson's *Idylls of the King* (1859) as a member of the Round Table.

TŶ MAWR WYBRNANT (pr. Tē Mah-oōr OŌēbrnănt) (or GWYBRNANT) *Conwy*

House (NT) at the head of the Wybrnant valley, 3 m. SW of Betws-y-Coed. This was the birthplace of Bishop William Morgan, first translator of the complete Bible into Welsh. There is a memorial window to him in the church at Penmachno, the nearest village.

WREXHAM *Wrexham*

Industrial town and conurbation in North Wales. Robert Graves trained here with the Royal Welch Fusiliers. He was billeted with a Welsh solicitor, who, as he records in *Goodbye to All That* (1929), wore

three wigs, with hair of progressive lengths. After wearing the medium-sized hair for a few days, he would put on the long-haired wig, and say that, dear him! he really ought to get a hair-cut. Then he would leave the house and, in a public lavatory perhaps, or wayside copse, change into the short-haired wig, which he wore until he thought it time to change to the medium once more.

YNYS-DDU (pr. Ŭnĭsthē) *Gwynedd*

Village on the A487, in the Sirhowy valley, *c.* 10 m. WNW of Newport. Tŷ'r Agent near here was the birthplace of William Thomas (Islwyn), minister and poet.

Scotland

Scotland

ABBOTSFORD *Borders*

Home (1812–32) of Sir Walter Scott, who transformed the little farm of Clartyhole, once belonging to the monks of Melrose, who forded the Tweed nearby, into the large estate. When Maria Edgeworth, who first met Scott in Edinburgh, stayed here in August 1823 the new house, started in 1818, was almost complete. Lockhart, in the *Memoirs* (1837–8) of his father-in-law, recalls their enjoyment of the picnic at Thomas the Rhymer's waterfall in the glen. Scott, in his General Preface to the 'Waverley' novels (1829), written here, said he tried to introduce 'Scotland's natives in a more favourable light than hitherto' as Maria Edgeworth had done for Ireland. He entertained many literary friends here, including Washington Irving, Thomas Moore, who, in 1825, was flattered to be the sole guest, and Wordsworth. The house contains Scott's library, family portraits, a large collection of weapons and armour, much of his furniture, and miscellaneous items relating to Scottish history donated by friends, including Joseph Train of *Castle Douglas. Scott was cared for in the dining room during his long illness and he died there in 1832. N. P. Willis, the American writer, visited soon afterwards, and asked, in *Pencillings by the Way* (1835), 'why does not Scotland buy Abbotsford?' The house is now carefully tended by Scott's descendants (www.scottsabbotsford.co.uk).

ABERDEEN *Aberdeenshire*

The 'granite city' on the Don and the Dee, a cathedral and university city and prosperous port on the NE coast of Scotland. John Barbour was born here a few years after Robert the Bruce's victory over the English at Bannockburn (1314). He became Archbishop of Aberdeen in 1357 and was made a member of the Scottish royal household by Robert II. The king commissioned Barbour to write *The Bruce*, a narrative poem in octosyllabic couplets comprising 20 books and 13,550 lines, the full text of which was published in 1616.

William Dunbar, who accompanied Queen Margaret on her tour of the north, described her visit here in 1511 in *The Queenis Progress at Aberdeen*. She was Margaret Tudor, the 'Rose' of his *Thrissil and the Rois* (1503), which he wrote on her marriage to James IV. Thomas Urquhart was (*c.* 1628) at King's College (founded 1494) in Old Aberdeen before leaving on a long tour of the Continent. Arthur Johnston, 'the Scottish Ovid', who had spent over 20 years studying in Italy and France, was appointed (1637) Rector of the University soon after his return. He wrote *Musae Aulicae* (1637),

translated the Psalms, and edited *Delitiae Poetarum Scotorum* (1637), Latin poems by Scots. He died in 1641. John Arbuthnot went to Marischal College aged 14 in 1682, before attending medical school in St Andrews. John Skinner was only 13 when he obtained a bursary (1735) to Marischal College. When Burns was here on his tour in 1787 he met Skinner's son, who was the Bishop of Aberdeen. The encounter led to a correspondence, sometimes in rhyme, between Burns and the elder Skinner which resulted in some of

Skinner's songs, which Burns thought among the best in Scotland, being published. Skinner retired to stay with his son at the medieval Bishop's Gate, where he died 12 days later (1807).

James Beattie was at Marischal College (1749–53) and returned to study Divinity there. He taught at the Grammar School from 1758, and in 1760 was invited to become Professor of Moral Philosophy and to join the select literary society called the Wise Club. *Original Poems and Translations* (1761) led to a correspondence and friendship with Gray in

Sir Walter Scott's study at Abbotsford

1765. His *Essay on Truth* (1770) and the poem *The Minstrel* (bk I, 1771) brought him the acquaintance of Dr Johnson, whom he visited in London. Boswell successfully enlisted Beattie's help in persuading Johnson to undertake their tour of the Highlands, though Beattie was not in Aberdeen when they arrived. Johnson found the professors disappointing— 'they had not started a single mawkin [hare] for us to pursue'—and he and Boswell were relieved to sit quietly at the New Inn (gone), where they were staying. They were also disappointed at not being able to find a single copy of Arthur Johnston's poems in the bookshops. Beattie, whom Mrs Thrale said she would have chosen if she were to marry again, died in Crown Court, Upper Kirkgate, and is buried in St Nicholas's churchyard. James Macpherson, a contemporary of Beattie's at the University, came under Johnson's censure for not handing to the professors the manuscripts from which he said he translated *Fingal* (1762).

The poet and classical scholar Ewan MacLachlan entered King's College with a scholarship in 1796, when Beattie encouraged him in his studies. MacLachlan later attended the Divinity Hall with a view to becoming a minister in the Church of Scotland. He was a schoolmaster at the Grammar School and librarian to King's College, but finally left Aberdeen on account of ill health. He is buried in Ardgour in Argyll and Bute. He helped to compile the first Gaelic–English dictionary and translated into Gaelic seven books and a fragment of the *Iliad*. He wrote much verse in Latin and in Gaelic, including *Metrical Effusions* (1816) and *Elegy to Professor James Beattie* (1803).

The 6-year-old Byron attended the Grammar School in Old Town (1794–8) after his father had died and his mother, whose fortune had been dissipated, took lodgings in the town. Byron said later that his love of mountainous country stemmed from his childhood here. A statue in Skene St. in the gardens of the Grammar School commemorates him. William Thom was born (1798?) in Sinclairs Close, Justice Port (gone), and became a weaver. After hard times he settled at Inverurie and had 'The Blind Boy's Pranks' accepted by *The Aberdeen Herald* in 1841. This created enough interest for the publication of *Rhymes and Recollections* (1844), after which he enjoyed a brief period of acclaim in London. George Macdonald went to 'Byron's old school' and King's College (1840–5). Most of his life was spent in England but he occasionally returned to the area to collect legends and Gaelic tales, which he used in his fairy stories. Marion Angus lived with her sister and invalid mother at Zoar, a cottage with a corner fireplace in Springfield Rd, Hazlehead, after her father's death. She was over 50 when she published her first collection, *The Lilt and Other Verses* (1922), here. Many of her poems have the sadness of old ballads like 'Mary's Song':

> My beloved sall hae this he'rt tae break,
> Reid, reid wine and the barley cake,

> A he'rt tae break, and a mou' tae kiss
> Tho' he be nae mine, as I am his.

Other poems were collected in *Tinker's Road* (1924), *Sun and Candlelight* (1927), and *Lost Country and Other Verses* (1937).

When Eric Linklater was at the Grammar School from 1913 to 1916 he felt that Byron's statue, seen through the window, 'undid the schoolroom teaching that Literature must be a solemn thing'. In 1919 he returned to his medical studies, which he had begun at the University, and then changed to read English. After some years abroad he became an assistant lecturer (1927–8) until he gained a bursary to America. After his success as a novelist he was elected Rector of the University (1945–8).

The poet Iain Crichton Smith left his home on Lewis to study English at the University in 1945, the first time he had ever left the island on which he had grown up. He returned in 1980 as creative writing fellow. Aberdeen's modern status as an oil city, and the fragile prosperity that goes with it, are the subjects of Blake Morrison's poem 'Proserpina in the Oilfields' and of Anne Stevenson's 'Aberdeen':

> Poor girl.
> She's got to marry oil.
> Nobody who loves her wants to save her.

ABERFELDY *Perth and Kinross*

Town on the A924 and the A9, 14 m. SW of Pitlochry. Robert Burns is thought to have written 'The Birks of Aberfeldy', beginning 'Now summer blinks on flowery braes', at the Falls of Moness (1 m. SW) on the Urlar Burn. A footpath leads to the spot.

ABERFOYLE *Stirlingshire*

Village off the A81, 27 m. N of Glasgow, at the entrance to The Trossachs. A plough hangs in a tree opposite a hotel to recall the incident in Scott's *Rob Roy* (1817) when Bailie Nichol Jarvie (after whom the hotel is named) met the outlaw.

ACHMELVICH *Highland*

Settlement 3 m. W of Lochinver in Scotland's highland region. Norman MacCaig spent holidays in a cottage here and in many lyrical and witty poems celebrated the landscape, wildlife, and people of the surrounding parish of Assynt. In 'Clachtoll' he found local correspondences for Persephone, Perseus, and Icarus, where 'one decorum binds the sounds | Of crafting lands and fishing grounds'. 'A Man in Assynt' laments the oppression and depopulation of the local country, a place with which MacCaig had pursued:

> a love-affair, so nearly human
> we even have quarrels.—
> When I intrude too confidently
> it rebuffs me with a wind like a hand
> or puts in my way
> a quaking bog or a loch
> where no loch should be. Or I turn stonily
> away, refusing to notice
> the rouged rocks, the mascara
> under a dripping ledge, even
> the tossed, the stony limbs waiting.

ALEXANDRIA *Dunbartonshire*

Village in the Vale of Leven on the A82, NW of Dumbarton, called after a member of the Smollett family of Bonhill nearby. Cameron House, now a hotel, at the S end of Loch

Norman MacCaig's retreat, Achmelvich, near Lochinver

Lomond, became the family home after 1763. In 1766 Tobias Smollett stayed with his cousin James at Bonhill, which he had last seen in 1739, and he took pleasure in revisiting the scenes of his youth. The house eventually fell into disrepair and was demolished. In 1773 Johnson and Boswell stayed at Cameron House on their Highland tour and Johnson said, 'We have had more solid talk here than any place that we have been.' Their host was the same James Smollett who was preparing to erect an ornate classical column to commemorate his cousin, who had died in Italy in 1771. The first design proved too costly and a simpler Tuscan column, brought from Glasgow, was erected at Renton (1 m. S), where it now stands behind the railings on the site of the school playground on the main road. The square plinth carries a Latin obituary, which Johnson helped to revise.

ALFORD *Aberdeenshire*

Small town 26 m. W of Aberdeen on the A944. Here in 1864 the Scots vernacular poet Charles Murray was born. Although he spent the greater part of his life in South Africa, working as an engineer with a gold-mining company, and returned to Scotland only in 1924, he wrote much about the scenes of his boyhood and his native place, as in *Hamewith* (1900) and *A Sough o' War* (1917). The Murray Park was opened in Alford in 1956.

ALLOWAY *Ayrshire*

Village on the B7024, 1½ m. S of Ayr. Robert Burns was born (1759) in the thatched single-room cottage with the barn and cowshed built by his father. The cottage is now at the centre of the extensive Burns Heritage Park

(www.burnsheritagepark.com). The museum at the rear of the cottage has original Burns letters, songs, and other relics. Just S the monument, built in 1820 by public subscriptions raised by Boswell's son, stands in gardens overlooking the old Brig o' Doon, where Burns's Tam o' Shanter on his grey mare outstripped the warlocks and hags. When Burns was 6, the family moved to Mt Oliphant Farm (1½ m. S), where he became his father's main help and an efficient ploughman. He was taught at Alloway School by John Murdoch and followed him to the Grammar School at Ayr when he moved there.

ALTRIVE LAKE *Borders*

Valley of a former lake, now drained, joining the Yarrow Water, where the B709 runs S from the *Gordon Arms on the A708. James Hogg, after earlier unsuccessful attempts at farming, followed by some years in Edinburgh, was granted Moss End Farm, later called Eldinhope, here (1815) at a nominal rent by the Duke of Buccleuch. After his marriage (1820) to Margaret Phillips he took a nine-year lease of Mount Benger Farm, a little further N, on the strength of her promised dowry, but this turned out to be disastrously expensive to run. He spent the rest of his life at Altrive, farming and writing. His best-known novel, *The Confessions of a Justified Sinner*, was published in 1824.

AMHUINNSUIDHE (pr. 'Avïnsuey) *Highland*

House on the N shore of West Loch Tarbert, on the B887, which J. M. Barrie rented in the spring of 1912. He heard here the Kilmeny legend of the girl who was taken and then returned by the fairies. He said that this was the place 'where we caught Mary Rose', the heroine of his play *Mary Rose* (1920), where the second act is set on an island in the Hebrides.

ANNAN *Dumfries and Galloway*

Small town at the mouth of the Annan which flows into the Solway Firth. Thomas Carlyle was educated at Annan Academy (now the Old Grammar School), described later by him as Hinterschlag Gymnasium in *Sartor Resartus*, a partly autobiographical work, which first appeared in *Fraser's Magazine* in 1833–4.

ANSTRUTHER (pr. 'Anster) *Fife*

Fishing port on the N bank of the Firth of Forth. William Tennant (1784–1848) was born in the High St. of Anstruther Easter, probably in an easterly extension of the present street, demolished in the late 19th c. It was a narrow building next door to an old tavern known as the Smugglers Howff. Tennant, later Professor of Oriental Languages at St Andrews, was schoolmaster here and wrote *Anster Fair* (1812), a long poem on the courting of Maggie Lauder, who lived in East Green in the 16th c. He is buried in the churchyard near the NE corner of the church; the obelisk has a Latin

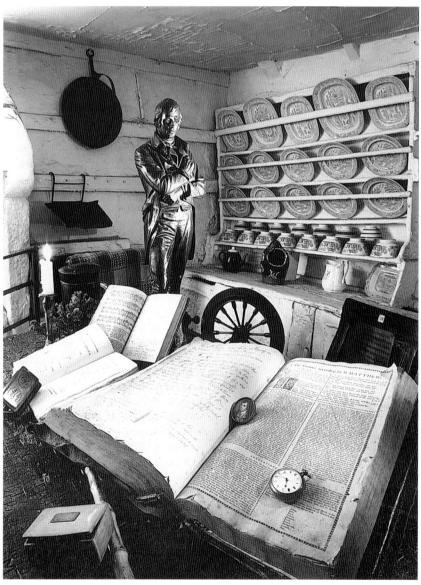

The kitchen at Burns Cottage, Alloway, showing various relics

inscription. R. L. Stevenson spent some time (1868) at Cunzie House Ⓟ in Crail Rd. In 'Random Memories' from *Across the Plains* (1892), he says he 'lodged with Bailie Brown in a room filled with dry rose-leaves' during his practical training to be an engineer, and in the evenings wrote 'Voces Fidelium', dramatic verse dialogues.

ARBROATH *Angus*

Old port and resort on the A92, 17 m. NE of Dundee. Scott called it 'Fairport' in *The Antiquary* (1816), 'the chief favourite among all his novels', and it was 'Redlintie' in J. M. Barrie's *Sentimental Tommy* (1896). Marion Angus spent the early part of her life here, while her father was the United Presbyterian minister. After his death she moved to Aberdeen, where her first poems were published, but she returned here at the end of her life to live with a friend. She died aged 80 in 1946, and her ashes were scattered in the sea off Elliot's Point. *Selected Poems*, which has a personal memoir by Helen B. Cruickshank, was published in 1950.

ARBUTHNOTT *Aberdeenshire*

Village on the B967, 12 m. SW of Stonehaven. John Arbuthnot, creator of John Bull and a close friend of Swift, was born (1667) here, two years after his father became the minister of the 13th-c. church. His family were from the Aberdeenshire branch of the Arbuthnotts of Arbuthnott House and spelt their name with one 't'.

James Leslie Mitchell, who made his name under the pen-name 'Lewis Grassic Gibbon', spent his early years at his birthplace, the farm of Hillhead of Segget, near Auchterless in Aberdeenshire, and moved in 1909 with his family to the small farm of Bloomfield, near Arbuthnott. The work on the land was hard and unrewarding, and in *Scottish Scene* (essays and short stories written with Hugh MacDiarmid in 1934) he says he formed 'a very bitter detestation for all this life on the land and the folk upon it'. His best-known novels, based on the agricultural district around Arbuthnott called the Howe of the Mearns, form the trilogy *A Scots Quair* (1946): *Sunset Song* (1932), *Cloud Howe* (1933), and *Grey Granite* (1934). Mitchell is buried in the SW corner of the churchyard.

ARDNAMURCHAN *Highland*

Coastal village off the A861, N of the Island of Mull. The Gaelic poet Alexander Macdonald, son of the Episcopalian minister here, was employed by the Society for the Promotion of Christian Knowledge in 1729, and produced a Gaelic–English dictionary for them in 1741. He remained a teacher until 1745, when he supported the Jacobite rebellion and was commissioned into the Clanranald Regiment. About this time he was converted to Roman Catholicism. A collection of his poetry, in which he supports not only the Jacobite cause but also the interests of the Gaelic-speaking Scots, was published in 1751 under the title *Ais-eridh na*

Sean Chànain (Resurrection of the Ancient Scottish Tongue).

ARDOCH *Perth and Kinross*

Estate on the Clyde, NW of Dumbarton, inherited in 1772 by Robert Graham. He had lived in Jamaica for some years and had married a Scots girl there, and he found the massive walls and small windows of the 17th-c. house uncomfortable, so he built the present Ardoch House, which looks over the Firth of Clyde (on the A814) in the Georgian colonial style. It was their home until after his father's death, when he moved back to his birthplace at Gartmore in 1777. His grandson Robert Cunninghame Graham, who wrote his biography, called *Doughty Deeds* after his best-remembered ballad, came to live in the house in 1903. He had spent his youth in South America, and his adventures there, and later in N America, formed the background of many of his books written here. His friend A. F. Tschiffely, who wrote (1933) an account of his own journey on horseback from Buenos Aires to Washington, which was later called *Tschiffely's Ride*, visited him here and wrote his biography *Don Roberto* (1937). A plaque on the house was given by his South American friends and a bronze of him on horseback, by Weiss, stands in the garden.

ARISAIG *Highland*

Village on the A830 *c*. 7 m. S of Mallaig. The Gaelic poet Alexander Macdonald returned to the district of Moidart *c*. 1752 and lived near Arisaig until the end of his life. His most famous poem, *Birlinn Chlann Ragnahill* (*The Birlinn of Clanranald*, trans. Hugh MacDiarmid, 1935), describes a voyage from South Uist to Carrickfergus in Ireland. He also wrote nature poems, including *Ode to Summer* and *In Praise of Morag*. He is commemorated by a clock in the tower of Arisaig Catholic church. His grave is on Eilean Finnan, an islet in Loch Shiel, to the SE.

ARRAN *Ayrshire*

Island on the W side of the Firth of Clyde. The dramatist Robert McLellan lived here from 1938 to 1985. He wrote in Scots about Scotland, most notably in *Jamie the Saxt* (1937). The island is the setting for his dramatic poem *Sweet Largie Bay* (1956) and his poem for television *Arran Burn* (1965).

ASHIESTIEL *Borders*

The house which Sir Walter Scott rented (1804–12) when he was Sheriff of Selkirk stands among trees on the slopes of Ashiestiel Hill, overlooking the Tweed. While he was here he published his first important original work, *The Lay of the Last Minstrel* (1805), a romantic poem in six cantos, followed by *Marmion, A Tale of Flodden Field* (1808) and *The Lady of the Lake* (1810). He also began *Waverley* (1814), his first novel. The house is not open to the public, but can be seen from across the river where the A72 from Peebles turns NE for Clovenfords.

ATHELSTANEFORD *Lothian*

Village 3 m. NE of Haddington off the A1. Robert Blair was minister here (1731–46) and is buried in the churchyard. His long poem *The Grave* (1743) is a discussion of death. The Blair Monument, erected in 1857, stands in front of the village hall.

Blair's successor as minister of Athelstaneford was John Home, who lived at Home House. After the sensational success of his verse-drama *Douglas* in Edinburgh in 1756, he had to resign his ministry because the Church of Scotland feared that people might shift their allegiance from the pulpit to the stage. A plaque in the church porch commemorates Home.

AUCHINLECK (pr. 'Awkinlek) *Ayrshire*

Mining village on the A76, 14 m. SE of Kilmarnock. The Second Keep, built in 1612 (3 m. W), was Boswell's family home until 1762, when his father's new house was finished. This, sometimes called Place Affleck, was where he spent some time after his marriage to Margaret Montgomerie in 1769, and where he entertained Dr Johnson on his tour in 1773. Boswell and his wife are buried in the family mausoleum next to the church in the village. The house is open on very occasional open days and is available for holiday lets from the Landmark Trust (www.landmarktrust.org.uk).

AUCHTERARDER *Perth and Kinross*

Small town 15 m. SW of Perth off the A9. James Kennaway was born at Kenwood Park, a stone house facing SE to the Ochil Hills. His novel *Household Ghosts* (1961) is set in Strathearn, the valley in which the village lies. His father, Charles Gray Kennaway, who settled in Auchterarder in 1921, wrote *Gentleman Adventurer*, a novel about the life of Charles Hay between the Jacobite risings of 1715 and 1745.

AYR *Ayrshire*

Large W coast resort 12 m. SW of Kilmarnock. Robert Burns, who was born 1½ m. S, was baptized at the Auld Kirk. He mentions the old and new (rebuilt 1877) bridges in his poem 'The Brigs of Ayr'. The Tam O'Shanter Museum in the High St. was formerly a brewhouse to which Burns's Tam, really Douglas Graham of Shanter, supplied malted grain. There is a statue of Burns by G. A. Lawson in Burns Statue Sq.

George Douglas Brown, who went to Ayr Academy in the 1880s, and made his name (as 'George Douglas') with the realistic novel *The House with the Green Shutters* (1901), is buried at Ayr.

BALAVIL *Highland*

Mansion, formerly called Belleville, built 3 m. NE of Kingussie on the site of Raits Castle by James Macpherson after the success of his long poems *Fingal* (1762) and *Temora* (1763), which purported to be translations from the Gaelic bard Ossian.

BALMORAL CASTLE *Aberdeenshire*

Castle and estate once owned by Queen
Victoria and her consort Prince Albert, and
which remains a summer residence for royalty
to this day. In an unlikely piece of casting, the
novelist Kazuo Ishiguro worked here during his
gap year before beginning university, as grouse
beater for the Queen Mother.

BALNAKEIL BAY *Highland*

Bay near the NW tip of the British Isles
reached by the A838. An obelisk by the ruined
Durness Old Church commemorates Robert
Mackay, the Gaelic poet known as Rob Donn
(*c.* 1715–78), who was born in Strathmore. He
spent some time in the army and then became
cowman to Lord Reay. Although Rob Donn
was illiterate, his interest in poetry was fostered
by the minister of Durness and he may have
been influenced by the work of Alexander Pope.
After Rob Donn's death his poems were
collected by a group of local ministers and the
first of several editions was published in 1829,
entitled *Poems in the Gaelic Language by
Robert Mackay*. His poetry shows an
abundance of wit and insight, including *Ode
to Prince Charlie*, *The Dream*, *Elegies*, and
Seagull's Song.

BALQUHIDDER (pr. Băl'whidder) *Stirlingshire*

Small village 2 m. from the A84 SW of Loch
Earn. Near the ruins of two earlier churches
is the family grave of Robert Campbell or
Macgregor (1671–1734), Scott's *Rob Roy*
(1817). He and his wife and two sons lie under
three stone slabs roughly cut with patterns
looking older than the 18th c. After a career
embellished over the years like Robin Hood's,
he died in his bed at Inverlochlarig (house
gone) 6 m. W. His son Robin Oig, who married
here in 1751, confronts Alan Breck in a duel in
Stevenson's *Kidnapped* (1886), both agreeing
to a contest with pipes in place of weapons.
Wordsworth wrote a poem about visiting Rob
Roy's grave:

> A famous man is Robin Hood,
> The English ballad-singer's joy!
> And Scotland has a thief as good,
> An outlaw of as daring mood;
> She has her brave Rob Roy!

Sue Townsend's Adrian Mole was less
impressed: 'Went to see Rob Roy's grave. Saw
it, came back.'
  The Gaelic poet Dugald Buchanan (Dùghall
Bochanan) was born (1716) on the farm of
Ardoch, nearby. After a rudimentary education
at the local school he left at 14 to live in Stirling
and then Edinburgh for the next four years.
He then returned to his native parish and
became converted to an evangelical form of
Christianity, which led to a licence to preach in
1753. Alasdair Alpin MacGregor (1889–1970),
who wrote many books on the Highlands and
Islands, is commemorated on his father's
tombstone here, which states that his ashes
were scattered in the Hebrides.

BARNS HOUSE *Borders*

Old mansion, 3 m. SW of Peebles, reached by
a rough signposted road from Kirkton in the
Manor Valley. The house, situated by the river,
near a ruined tower, was the setting for John
Buchan's novel *John Burnet of Barns* (1898).

BARRA *Highland*

Island named after St Finnbar, where Compton
Mackenzie lived during the Second World War.
He set the scene of his novel *Whisky Galore*
(1947) on Eriskay, a smaller island NE across
the Sound of Barra. His body was brought here
for burial after his death in 1972; his grave is
near the ruined church and chapel of St Barr,
Eoligarry.

BEN DORAN *Dumfries and Galloway*

Mountain (3,524 ft) 3 m. SE of Loch Tulla.
It is celebrated by the Gaelic poet Duncan
Ban MacIntyre in the poem 'Moladh Beinn
Dòbrain' ('The Praise of Ben Doran', trans.
Hugh MacDiarmid, 1840).

BEN NEVIS *Highland*

Highest peak in the British Isles, a few miles
SE of Fort William. Keats climbed it on his tour
in 1819 with his friend Charles Armitage Brown
and wrote a sonnet on the summit.

BIEL *Lanarkshire*

Mansion, on Biel Water, *c.* 4 m. SW of Dunbar,
in a private estate off the B6370. It has been
held in some accounts that this was the
birthplace of William Dunbar (*c.* 1460–*c.* 1520),
known as 'the chief of ancient Scottish poets' or
'one of the Scottish Chaucerians', author of *The
Thrissil and the Rois* (1503) and *The Twa
Maryit Women and the Wedo* (*c.* 1508), but
there is no strong evidence that he was of the
family of the Dunbars of Biel or, as has been
suggested, the grandson of Sir Patrick Dunbar,
who came into possession of the lands in 1420.
It is, however, extremely likely that he was a
native of East Lothian.

BIGGAR *Lanarkshire*

Town on the A702, 18 m. SW of Peebles. John
Brown, physician and author of *Rab and his
Friends* (1895, see PENICUIK), was born (1810)
at the manse here. From 1951 until his death in
1978 the poet Hugh MacDiarmid (Christopher
Murray Grieve) lived with his wife, Valda, at
Brownsbank Cottage, Candymill.

BIRNAM *Perth and Kinross*

A summer resort near Dunkeld. On Terrace
Walk, which follows the right bank of the Tay
below Birnam, are some old trees, reputed to
be survivors of the original forest where in
Shakespeare's *Macbeth* Malcolm ordered: 'Let
every soldier hew him down a bough and bear't
before him.' *Dunsinane Hill is NW of the
village.

BLACK DWARF'S COTTAGE *Borders*

Cottage on a narrow road beyond Kirkton,
overlooking the Manor Water, *c.* 3½ m. SW of
Peebles off the A72. This was the home of
David Ritchie, the sinister-looking dwarf of
legendary strength who was the hero of Scott's
The Black Dwarf (1816). The present cottage,
bearing the inscription 'D.R. 1802', was built by
the laird of Woodhouse to replace the original
one where Ritchie lived when Scott visited him
in 1797. His 3 ft 10 in.-high doorway has been
preserved (one of normal size having been
added when his sister came to live with him).
He died in 1811 and was buried in Kirkton
Manor graveyard. An inscribed gravestone was
put up in 1845 by W. and R. Chambers of
Peebles. Scott used to stay at Hallyards, on the
Manor Water, and a statue of Ritchie stands in
the grounds.

BOARHILLS *Fife*

Coastal settlement. The mussel flats and
'barnacled, embossed, | stacked rocks' are
evoked in Anne Stevenson's 1975 poem 'With
My Sons at Boarhills'.

BORGUE *Dumfries and Galloway*

Village on the B727, 5 m. SW of Kirkcudbright,
birthplace of William Nicholson (1782–1849),
the pedlar known as the 'Galloway Poet'.
Encouragement from Hogg led to the
publication of *Tales in Verse and Miscellaneous
Poems* (1814). A relief portrait at the school he
attended shows him playing the pipes.

BOTHWELL *Lanarkshire*

Village N of Hamilton on the B7071, 12 m. SE
of Glasgow. Joanna Baillie, poet and dramatist,
whose father was the minister, was born here
in 1762. There is a monument to her in the
grounds of the parish church.

BOWDEN *Borders*

Village on the B6398, 2 m. S of Melrose and
6 m. E of Selkirk (N of the A699). The poet
Thomas Aird was born here (1802), under the
shadow of the Eildon Hills, and educated first
by his father and then at the village school
before going on to study in Edinburgh.

BROUGHTON *Borders*

Village on the A701, W of Peebles. John
Buchan and his sister Anna, who wrote as 'O.
Douglas', spent many holidays at The Green,
their grandparents' home. It was 'Woodilee' in
his novel *Witch Wood* (1927), and she wrote
Penny Plain (1913) while staying here. The
John Buchan Centre, opened in 1983 in the
Free Church, houses an exhibition of books,
photographs, and other memorabilia
(www.johnbuchansociety.co.uk).

BUTE, ISLE OF *Argyll and Bute*

An island on the lower Firth of Clyde. Maria
Tambini, the 13-year-old 'girl with the giant
voice' in Andrew O'Hagan's novel *Personality*
(2003), lives at 120 Victoria Street, Rothesay,
above the family café and chip shop, 'its front
window filled with giant boxes of chocolates
covered in reproduction Renoirs'.

CALLANDER *Stirlingshire*

Busy holiday centre at the foot of the Highlands, on the A84, *c.* 14 m. NW of Stirling. Dugald Buchanan, Gaelic poet, is buried at Little Leny, nearby.

CASTLE DOUGLAS *Dumfries and Galloway*

Small town, a farming and tourist centre, at the N end of Carlingwark Loch, 13 m. SW of Dumfries. Joseph Train, the antiquary, who gave Scott much material for his historical novels, lived here and is commemorated by a plaque in the Town Hall. Lockhart, in his *Life of Scott* (1837–8), quotes Scott as saying, 'if ever a catalogue of the museum of Abbotsford shall appear, no single contributor, most assuredly, will fill so large a space as Mr Train'. Train heard the ballad 'Durham Garland' sung here by a woman whose family kept the words in their memory by singing it frequently. He was buried in 1852 at Kirton, 2 m. S.

CAWDOR *Highland*

The castle and the title of Thane of Cawdor were promised to Shakespeare's Macbeth by the witches. It disputes with the castles at *Inverness and *Glamis the distinction of being the location of Duncan's murder, but the handsome 15th-c. castle (www.cawdorcastle.com) is a building of a much later date.

CELLARDYKE *Fife*

Village on the East Neuk, near Anstruther. John Burnside lived in the village in the 1990s, visited Anstruther as a child, and at the time of writing lives near Pittenweem. Many of his poems and novels express his response to Fife and the coastal villages of the East Neuk. The 'small fishing town' of Coldhaven in his novel *The Devil's Footprints* (2007) is one such place.

CLOVENFORDS *Borders*

Village on the A72, 3 m. W of Galashiels. There is a statue of Sir Walter Scott outside the inn where he used to stay after he was appointed Sheriff of Selkirkshire (Dec. 1799) and before he moved to *Ashiestiel. The church has a memorial window to him.

COWDENBEATH *Fife*

Former coal-mining town near Dunfermline. The poet and novelist John Burnside was born and brought up in Cowdenbeath. He describes his early life here in the memoir *A Lie About My Father* (2006). After living in England for many years, Burnside returned to Fife, which has provided the subject and inspiration for much of his poetry.

CRAIGENPUTTOCK *Dumfries and Galloway*

Moorland farm, 7 m. W up the glen from Dunscore, inherited by Carlyle's wife, Jane Welsh, and lived in by them (1828–34). He contributed articles on German literature to periodicals and wrote *Sartor Resartus* (1833–4) while here.

CRAIGLOCKHART *Lothian*

Suburb to the SW of Edinburgh. During the First World War, Wilfred Owen and Siegfried Sassoon met as patients at the Craiglockhart War Hospital, *c.* 3 m. S of Princes St. Owen had been sent back from the front in France in June 1917, suffering from nervous exhaustion, and was transferred from a hospital in Southampton to Craiglockhart for treatment and observation. Sassoon arrived a few weeks later, a medical board having found him in need of medical attention after he had made public a protest to his commanding officer against the prolongation of the war.

Pat Barker's *Regeneration* trilogy (*Regeneration*, 1991; *The Eye of the Door*, 1993; *The Ghost Road*, 1995) is set largely in the hospital, where Sassoon is among the shell-shocked patients brought to see the army psychologist Rivers: 'nobody arriving at Craiglockhart for the first time could fail to be daunted by the sheer gloomy, cavernous bulk of the place'. Craiglockhart, originally built as a 'hydropathic hotel' or 'hydro' in 1880, became a military hospital in 1916 and is now part of the Napier University campus.

CRAMOND ISLAND *Lothian*

Island off Edinburgh in the Firth of Forth, facing across the water to the village of Cramond. The Scottish poet Kathleen Jamie has written a poem named after the island, describing crossing the causeway:

> Most who choose the causeway cross
> for a handful of years
> turning back before the tide
> cuts them off . . .

CRIEFF *Perth and Kinross*

Town on the Earn and the A85, 17 m. W of Perth, birthplace (1705) of David Mallet (really Malloch), who spent most of his life in London. Charles Reade spent many holidays at his brother's house from 1838 to 1848. His love affair here is thought to have inspired the romance *Christie Johnson* (1853).

CROMARTY *Highland*

Town at the E of the Firth of Cromarty, on the A832, NE of Inverness. Cromartie House is on the site of Cromarty Tower, birthplace of Thomas Urquhart (b. 1611), and where he was living (1645–50) when he joined the rising at Inverness to proclaim Charles II king in 1649. The next year Charles landed in the Firth and Urquhart followed him to Worcester, and after the battle was imprisoned in the Tower of London. He was allowed to return here on parole (1652–3) and some of his translations of Rabelais were published in 1653, and others posthumously in 1693. He died abroad in 1660. *Collections of Miscellaneous Treatises* was published in 1774 and 1834. One, 'Ekskubalauron', includes his account in 'Vindication of the Honour of Scotland' of 'the Admirable Crichton'. He is commemorated by a plaque in the Old Kirk.

The cottage in which Hugh Miller, the geologist and journalist, was born in 1802 is in Church St. The last remaining thatched cottage in Cromarty, it was opened to the public in 1892 and acquired by the NTS in 1938. There is a new building, Miller House, in which can be seen original manuscripts and fossils, as well as the tartan plaid he wore in Edinburgh as editor of *The Witness*, the evangelical weekly he ran from 1840 until his death by suicide in 1856. A stonemason from the age of 17, he combined his trade with a study of natural history and a devotion to literature. His most celebrated book is the collection of essays *The Old Red Sandstone* (1841).

CULLEN *Moray*

Small fishing port on the A98, E of Lossiemouth. In 1773, on their tour of Scotland, Dr Johnson and Boswell breakfasted here; dried haddock was served but Johnson refused the dish. George Macdonald stayed in a house in Grant St. (later a tearoom) in 1873 and he called the place 'Portlossie' in his novel *Malcolm* (1875).

CUPAR *Fife*

Market town 8 m. W of St Andrews on the A91. Sir David Lindsay of the Mount was the author of *The Thrie Estatis*, performed before the Scottish court at Linlithgow in 1540 and generally regarded as Scotland's greatest dramatic work.

DALILEA *Borders*

Hamlet in the district of Moidart, at the end of a minor road off the A72 on the SW shore of Loch Shiel. This was the birthplace of the Gaelic poet Alexander Macdonald (Alasdair Mac Mhaighstir Alasdair) (1700?–70?), son of an Episcopalian minister. Little is known of his early life, though he may have studied at Glasgow University. He became a schoolmaster at *Ardnamurchan.

DALKEITH *Lothian*

Historic town and administrative centre of Midlothian. Edwin Muir was appointed Warden of Newbattle Abbey, a college for working-class men, in 1950. The poet and novelist George Mackay Brown studied here under Muir's mentorship in the 1950s. The support of Muir, a fellow Orcadian, was important in Mackay Brown's decision to pursue a literary career.

DALSWINTON *Dumfries and Galloway*

Village 8 m. N of Dumfries, off the A76. Burns visited the progressive landowner Patrick Miller here and dined in both the old and the improved new mansion. He rented Ellisland (1789) from Miller through his factor, whose son, the poet Alan Cunningham, was born (1784) at Blackwood (rebuilt). Cunningham was apprenticed to a stonemason brother but devoted his time to literature, educating himself at the library of the pastor at Quarrelwood (1½ m. E, manse and church later a private house), a village of weavers with independent minds. In 1804 he walked to

Mitchelstack and met Hogg, the 'Ettrick Shepherd'. His first ballads were published in Cromek's *Remains of Nithsdale and Galloway Song* (1810). His best-remembered poem is 'A Wet Sheet and a Flowing Sea' from *Songs of Scotland, Ancient and Modern* (1825), collected when he was in London.

DENHOLM *Borders*

Village 5 m. NE of Hawick on the A698. John Leyden (1775–1811), poet and orientalist, was born in a thatched cottage Ⓟ near the village green and was educated at home until he was 9. He then attended the village school at nearby Kirkton and went on to Edinburgh University, to become a distinguished linguist. He assisted Sir Walter Scott in compiling *Minstrelsy of the Scottish Border* (1802–3) and also edited *Scottish Descriptive Poems* (1802). Later he went to India and became linguistic adviser to the government. He died in Java and is commemorated by a monument in the centre of Denholm green.

James Murray (1837–1915), lexicographer, was born in a cottage (later a shop) facing the green. He wrote *The Dialect of the Southern Counties of Scotland* (1873) and was the first editor of the *Oxford English Dictionary* from 1879 to 1915.

DEVIL'S BEEF TUB *Dumfries and Galloway*

Deep depression in the hills, 4 m. N of Moffat, visible from the A701. Scott uses this hollow for the scene of the daring escape of the Laird of Summertrees in *Redgauntlet* (1824).

DOUNE *Stirlingshire*

Small town on the A84. The 14th-c. castle was owned later by the 'Bonnie Earl of Moray' of the ballad. He died mysteriously at Donibristle in 1592.

> Oh! lang will his Lady
> Look o'er the Castle Doune,
> Ere she see the Earl of Moray
> Come sounding thro' the toon.

Scott, who stayed at Newton of Doune, the house known locally as 'Old Newton', describes in *Waverley* (1814), traditionally written in the top room of the tower, the escape of prisoners captured during the Jacobite rising of 1745. One of the seven, still confined in February 1746, was John Home, later author of the romantic tragedy *Douglas* (1756), who got safely away carrying a companion injured when their improvised rope broke.

DOWNIE *Aberdeenshire*

Estate on Loch Crinan on the Sound of Jura, W of Lochgilphead, where in 1796 Thomas Campbell stayed as tutor to Sir William Napier's 8-year-old son. His favourite walk was to the opposite end of the bay, called Poet's Hill. He started to write his long poem *The Pleasures of Hope* (1798) here, which has the lines:

> What though my wingèd hours of bliss have been,
> Like angel-visits, few and far between?

DRYBURGH ABBEY *Borders*

Ruined abbey set in a bend of the Tweed among beautiful trees, 7 m. SE of Melrose, signposted from the B6404 N of St Boswells and from the B6356 *c.* 5 m. S of Earlston. The abbey lands belonged to Sir Walter Scott's great-grandfather, but the inheritance passed from his descendants, leaving them only the right to 'stretch their bones' in the abbey. Scott is buried in St Mary's aisle. Near Bemersyde, *c.* 2 m. N on the B6356, is 'Scott's View', where he often went to look across the Tweed to the Eildon Hills, and where it is said that on the day of his funeral his hearse rested briefly when his horses stopped as they had so often done before. J. G. Lockhart, Scott's son-in-law and first biographer, is also buried at Dryburgh Abbey.

DUMBARTON *Dunbartonshire*

County town 20 m. NW of Glasgow on the A82. Tobias Smollett was educated at the Grammar School, situated in his day on what became the site of the parish church at the bottom of Church St. His novel *Roderick Random* (1748) contains a horrific account of a Scottish school, despite the fact that he was taught by John Love, a kindly man who abhorred corporal punishment.

The novelist Archibald Joseph Cronin lived as a boy at Willowbrook next to Miller's farm in what is now Roundriding Rd, and attended Dumbarton Academy at the E foot of Church St. His maternal grandfather owned a hatter's shop at 145 High St. and it is thought that he is portrayed as the domestic tyrant James Brodie in Cronin's *Hatter's Castle* (1931). Cronin, who later worked as a doctor in S Wales, became a prolific and popular author with novels such as *The Citadel* (1937), *The Stars Look Down* (1941), and *The Spanish Gardener* (1950); he was also the creator of the television series *Dr Finlay's Casebook*.

DUMFRIES *Dumfries and Galloway*

Old county town on the A75, where Burns settled in 1791 after giving up farming. He lived first in Bank St. (house gone) and then in Mill Vennel, renamed Burns St. His house is now a museum and is complemented by the large Burns Centre on Mill Rd (www.dumfriesmuseum.demon.co.uk). During his last years, which he spent collecting Scottish songs, he was worried over the health of his children and his own increasing weakness, for which strenuous remedies were recommended by his doctor. He frequented The Globe and the Hole in the Wall in Queensberry Sq. with his friends, and his pew in St Michael's Church is marked with a tablet. He died of rheumatic fever in 1796 and was buried in St Michael's churchyard.

Wordsworth's 'At the Grave of Burns' describes it as 'grass grown' and his sister Dorothy in her *Journal* writes in 1803, 'The churchyard is full of . . . expensive monuments in all sorts of fantastic shapes—obelisk wise, pillar wise . . .', and these are still there today.

In 1808 Robert Anderson made a detour on his way to work in Ireland and visited Burns's widow, who let him sit in the poet's chair. He wrote 'The Mountain Boy' and 'The Vale of Elva' on the journey. In 1815 Burns was reinterred in a mausoleum like a little domed temple which Keats wrote was 'not very much to my taste'. He wrote a sonnet, 'On visiting the tomb of Burns', and 'Meg Merrilees', about the gipsy 'tall as Amazon', also mentioned by Scott in *Guy Mannering*. Thomas Aird became editor (1835–63) of the *Dumfriesshire and Galloway Herald* and lived in the town until his death in 1876. He was buried near Burns's tomb. J. M. Barrie (1860–1937) was educated at the Academy, and the Burgh Museum in the Observatory has some of his and Burns's manuscripts.

DUNBEATH *Highland*

Village on the A9, overlooking Dunbeath Bay. This was the birthplace of Neil Gunn and the setting of his novels *Morning Tide* (1931), *Highland River* (1937), and *The Silver Darlings* (1941).

DUNDEE *Angus*

Port and university city on the Firth of Tay, 22 m. E of Perth. Robert Fergusson was educated at the Grammar School, leaving in 1765.

In 1815 Thomas Hood, emaciated after a series of illnesses, came by sea to recuperate at his aunt's house Ⓟ in Nethergate. His uncle was the owner of the brig *Hope*, and the 16-year-old boy spent much time with the sailors on Craig Pier. Alexander Elliot in *Hood in Scotland* (1885) tells how his sense of fun enabled him to entertain his aunt during an illness. The imaginary side-glances and hand-claspings that he described while watching the churchgoers from her window may have outraged her sense of decorum but she was soon asking him to 'keek oot again, Tam'. Later he had lodgings in Overgate, and he may have worked as an engraver. The manuscript of *The Dundee Guide*, which he wrote in imitation of Anstey's *New Bath Guide*, was lost, and *The Bandit*, also written here, is reminiscent of Scott. Hood returned home, his health temporarily improved, in 1817.

William Thom died in poverty here in 1848. His grave has a memorial in the Western Cemetery.

William McGonagall lived for many years in Paton's Lane and worked as a carpet weaver. His first collection of verses appeared in 1877 and *Poetic Gems* (1890) includes 'Tay Bridge'. Bathos, irrelevant material, and disjointed rhythms have caused him to be known as the best bad poet.

In 1974 the novelist Kate Atkinson took an English degree at Dundee University; she later taught here too. The University of Dundee would feature in her novel *Emotionally Weird* (2000).

> Martha was still in culture shock, having come to Dundee thinking it was part of a Scotland that was built out of lochs and mountains and

decorated with moorland and waterfalls, and every so often you could see a pained look cross her face when she had to negotiate a piece of shoddy modern architecture, a gas-lit close, or a hollow-eyed and abandoned jute mill.

Though Atkinson carefully includes an insistent disclaimer to the effect that the University of Dundee in the book ('and especially the departments of English and Philosophy') bear only 'little resemblance' to real life.

Douglas Dunn wrote a poem entitled 'Leaving Dundee', about a return home and a poignant farewell to his lately dead wife:

Down there, over the green and the railway yards,
Across the broad, rain-misted, subtle Tay,
The road home trickles to a house, a door.
She spoke of what I might do 'afterwards'.
'Go, somewhere else.' I went north to Dundee.
Tomorrow I won't live here any more,
Nor leave alone. *My love, say you'll come with me.*

Anne Stevenson noticed 'Eddies of strong air | swarm up old tenements' in her poem 'Night Wind, Dundee'.

DUNFERMLINE *Fife*

Town across the Firth of Forth from Edinburgh, and one-time Scottish capital; more recently the birthplace (on 16 Feb. 1954) of the novelist Iain Banks.

DUNOON *Argyll and Bute*

Resort on the W shore of the Firth of Clyde, on the A815. A statue on the front commemorates Mary Campbell, the subject of Burns's poems 'Highland Mary' and 'To Mary-in Heaven'. She was born at Auchnamore nearby, met Burns while she was a dairymaid at the house he called 'the castle of Montgomery', and died of typhus before she could accompany him in emigrating to the West Indies.

DUNSINANE *Perth and Kinross*

Hill on the outskirts of the village of Collace, near Dundee. The witches in Shakespeare's *Macbeth* foretold that Macbeth would never be vanquished until 'Great Birnam Wood to high Dunsinane Hill shall come against him'. The remains of two early forts on the hill suggest the original of Macbeth's Dunsinane. *Birnam is to the NE.

DUNSYRE *Lanarkshire*

Village 7 m. from Carnwath. The concrete poet and artist Ian Hamilton Finlay and his partner, Susan, moved to Stonypath Farm in 1966, where he worked prolifically on works that combine poetry with the visual arts—poem cards, posters, booklets, and small objects. He renamed the farm 'Little Sparta' and over the next 25 years, with Susan's help and the example of Roman gardens and the ideas of Rousseau and the Presocratic philosophers, turned the grounds into a poet–philosopher's garden, mixing wild flowers, stone inscriptions, sundials, and broken columns. During certain periods of the year it is possible to visit the garden, which is now run by a trust (www.littlesparta.co.uk).

ECCLEFECHAN *Dumfries and Galloway*

Village off the A74(M), 6 m. S of Lockerbie. Thomas Carlyle's birthplace (NTS) has many relics of the historian and his parents. Carlyle (1795–1881) was at school here before going to Annan Academy. He is buried beside his parents and a statue to him was erected in the village in 1927.

EDINBURGH *Lothian*

Capital of Scotland, cathedral and university city on the S bank of the Firth of Forth, named after the 6th-c. king of Northumbria, Edwin, who built his fortress high on the precipitous crag of volcanic rock which underlies the city. The castle dominates historic Old Edinburgh, or the Royal Mile, which stretches E to Holyrood Palace and Abbey at the foot of the slope. Above Princes St. in the valley the elegant and spacious 18th-c. New Town rises northwards. The literary associations of the city are so manifold that only its distinguished native writers and the more significant of its vast number of residents and visitors can be accounted for here.

Gavin Douglas (1474?–1522), poet and bishop, was provost of St Giles in 1501 and lived at a palace in the Cowgate. He wrote two allegorical poems, *The Palice of Honour* (1553?) and *King Hart* (first printed 1786), and, with his translation of the *Aeneid* (1553), was the earliest translator of the classics into English.

William Drummond of Hawthornden (1585–1649), sometimes called 'the Scottish Petrarch', was educated at the High School and at the University. His library is housed in the University Library, George Sq.

Allan Ramsay (1686–1758) came to Edinburgh in 1701 as a wig maker's apprentice and stayed to make his name as a poet and bookseller. In 1718 he opened a bookshop and by 1720 was publishing books for sale 'at the sign of the Mercury, opposite the head of Niddry's Wynd [now Niddry St.]', the house (gone) where he lived and carried on his business until 1726. While he was here he began the *Tea Table Miscellany* (1724–32), a collection of new Scots songs set to old melodies, and his best-known work, *The Gentle Shepherd* (a pastoral drama, 1725). He moved to another shop in 1726, in the Luckenbooths (gone) in the High St., near St Giles, and here changed his sign of Mercury to that of the heads of Ben Jonson and Drummond of Hawthornden. Two years later he began the first circulating library in Scotland, which was looked at askance by certain sober-minded people as a potential source of lewd and profane reading for the young. Ramsay retired to a house of his own design on Castle Hill, nicknamed the 'Goose Pie' on account of its curious octagonal shape, now (somewhat altered by his son, Allan Ramsay the painter, 1713–84), part of a picturesque group of houses beneath the Castle Esplanade. There is a statue of the elder Ramsay in Princes St. Gardens and

a monument to him in Greyfriars churchyard, on the S wall of the church.

John Gay (1685–1732) enjoyed Ramsay's acquaintance when he came to Edinburgh in 1729 as secretary to the eccentric Duchess of Queensberry. Gay's musical play *Polly* (a sequel to *The Beggar's Opera*) had just been banned in London by the Lord Chamberlain, and 'her mad Grace' had swept him up to Edinburgh to stay at Queensberry House (now part of the Scottish Parliament) in the Canongate. Gay and Ramsay used to meet at an inn called Jenny Ha's Change House (gone) for wine and conversation.

David Hume (1711–76), historian and philosopher, was born in Edinburgh and educated at the University. At the age of 40 he moved into the first home of his own, in Riddle's Close, 322 High St. He was appointed Keeper of the Advocates' Library in 1752, the year he wrote his *Political Discourses*, and while here probably began the *History of Great Britain* (1754–61), which he continued after his removal to Jack's Land (now 229), Canongate, an old four-storey building entered from Little Jack's Close. In 1762 he had apartments in James Court (destroyed by fire) off the Lawnmarket (later occupied by Boswell) and finally built himself an imposing house at the corner of St Andrew Sq. and St David St., where he ended his days. He was buried in the Calton old burial ground, by the SE corner of Waterloo Pl., in a tomb designed by Robert Adam, visible from many parts of the city.

Tobias Smollett (1721–71) stayed with his sister in 1766, in the second flat of 182 Canongate, over the archway leading into St John St. The apartments are reached by a turret staircase in the house now 22 St John St. Ⓟ. Smollett, in the character of Matthew Bramble, describes the city and its notable authors in *Humphry Clinker* (1771).

William Falconer (1732–69) was born in Edinburgh, the son of a barber, and became a sailor. He wrote *The Shipwreck* (1762, revised 1764 and 1769), a poem in three cantos recounting the wreck of a ship off the coast of Greece, which had considerable vogue in its day. He also compiled a useful *Universal Marine Dictionary* (1769).

James Boswell (1740–95), Dr Johnson's biographer, was the son of Lord Auchinleck, a judge of the Court of Session, and was born in Blair's Land, Parliament Sq., where he lived until he was 9. He was educated at a private school and then the High School, and entered the University at 13. He studied law in Edinburgh, Glasgow, and Utrecht, and practised as an advocate, but his interest lay in the direction of politics and literature. Having made the acquaintance of Dr Johnson in London he received him on the latter's arrival in Edinburgh in 1773 (see below). Boswell had apartments in James Court, off the Lawnmarket, previously occupied by David Hume (see above), and for a time he rented the house of his uncle Dr Boswell, S of the Meadows, for £15 a year, now 15a Meadow Pl. and the only one of his Edinburgh homes still

EDINBURGH

Picardy Place
There's a statue of Sherlock Holmes here, to commemorate Arthur Conan Doyle, born near this site

Holyrood House ➤➤

Scottish National Portrait Gallery
Find likenesses of your favourite Scottish writers here: Scott, Burns, David Hume, Adam Smith, Boswell, and many others

Rose Street
The Rose Street pubs were frequented by all the major twentieth-century Scottish poets: Ian MacDiarmid, George Mackay Brown, Iain Crichton Smith, Sorley MacLean, Sidney Goodsir Smith

QUEEN STREET

HANOVER ST

Scott Monument
A Gothic memorial to the great author of *Ivanhoe* and *Waverley*, Sir Walter Scott

Heart of Midlothian
The title of Scott's novel refers to the Old Tolbooth prison commemorated with a mosaic on the pavement on this site. It would give its name to the local football club

YORK PLACE

Charlotte Square
Home to the city's annual International Book Festival, one of the largest events of its kind in the world

PRINCES STREET

National Gallery of Scotland

HIGH STREET

SOUTH BRIDGE

Writers' Museum
Exploring the life and work of Walter Scott, Robert Burns, and Robert Louis Stevenson

LOTHIAN ROAD

Edinburgh Castle

WEST PORT

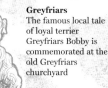

Greyfriars
The famous local tale of loyal terrier Greyfriars Bobby is commemorated at the old Greyfriars churchyard

College Wynd
Walter Scott was born here in 1771

Greyfriars Bobby

Nicolson Street
Nicolson's café on Nicolson Street is said to have been J. K. Rowling's favourite spot for writing when working on the first Harry Potter book

LAURISTON PLACE

Edinburgh University
Students here included current Edinburgh resident Ian Rankin, who spent his time working on his Ph.D. thesis of another Edinburgh writer, Muriel Spark. Novelist Alexander McCall Smith is a Professor of Medical Law here. Rankin, McCall Smith, and Harry Potter author J. K. Rowling now live close to one another on what has been dubbed 'Writers' Block'

standing. The entrance is in a narrow lane behind a derelict church, but the house is obscured by a high wall. He inherited the family house at *Auchinleck on his father's death in 1782.

Dr Johnson (1709–84) first visited Edinburgh in August 1773 at the outset of his tour of the Hebrides with Boswell. He stayed four days at the White Horse Inn (Ⓟ on site) in Boyd's Close (gone), St Mary's Wynd (now St Mary's St.), and was shown the sights by Boswell. On their return from the Hebrides, Johnson stayed about a fortnight with Boswell and his wife and met and enjoyed the hospitality of many distinguished members of society. Boswell's father, Lord Auchinleck, failed to appreciate his qualities, however, and was scathing about his son's attachment to 'an auld dominie', and Mrs Boswell felt provoked to utter her famous comment, 'I have often seen a bear led by a man but never till now have I seen a man led by a bear.'

Henry Mackenzie (1745–1831), author of the once popular novel *The Man of Feeling* (1771), cherished by Burns as one of his 'bosom favourites' books, was born in Libberton Wynd, which ran between the Lawnmarket and the Cowgate, where George IV Bridge now stands. He was educated at the High School and the University, and lived in many different places in Edinburgh, ending his days at 6 Heriot Row, facing Queen St. Gdns. He is buried in the Greyfriars churchyard on the N side of the terrace.

Robert Fergusson (1750–74) was born at Cap Feather Close off the High St. (site now built over on the E side of the North Bridge). He was educated at a small school in Niddry's Wynd and then at the High School before going on to the Grammar School at Dundee and St Andrews University, with the object of reading for the ministry. After his father's death, however, he left the University without a degree and turned his thoughts to literature. He took a job in a law office to help to support his mother, and began writing poetry, and it was as a writer of Scots poetry, especially of the life and manners of his contemporary Edinburgh, that he excelled. In 1773 *Poems by Robert Fergusson* was published, containing his best Scots poems to date and a promise of even better to come. But he began to suffer fits of depression, aggravated by bouts of dissipation, and was removed to the Bedlam (or Mad House, as it was known) of the city, where he died on 16 October 1774. Burns's tribute to him was:

> My elder brother in misfortune
> By far my elder brother in the Muse.

Fergusson was buried in the Canongate cemetery, in a grave on the W side of the church, not far from the gateway, marked by a headstone erected and inscribed by Burns 12 years later.

George Crabbe (1755–1832) visited Edinburgh in August 1822 at the invitation of Sir Walter Scott. He arrived during the preparations for the visit of George IV, met the Highland chieftains at Scott's house, and

attended a levee on 17 August at which the King appeared in a 'Stewart tartan'. Crabbe, like Scott, composed lines in honour of the royal occasion.

Elizabeth Hamilton (1756–1816), a novelist who was brought up in Stirlingshire and later moved to London, stayed for a time in Edinburgh in the West Lodge, where she wrote her most notable book, *The Cottagers of Glenburnie* (1808). Maria Edgeworth, who had corresponded with her after reading her *Memoirs of Modern Philosophers* (1800), met her here during her visit in the winter of 1803–4.

Robert Burns (1759–96) came to Edinburgh in 1786 after the success of the Kilmarnock edition of his poems published that August, in order to arrange for a second impression. He set out from Kilmarnock on a borrowed pony and arrived two days later at his lodgings in Baxter's Close (house long ago demolished, but Ⓟ over the Lawnmarket entrance to Lady Stair's Close). He had a letter of introduction to the Earl of Glencairn, who proved to be an ideal patron and helped to launch him in fashionable and literary circles. Burns played up to his role of 'ploughman poet' and charmed society with his conversation and vitality. The Edinburgh edition of his poems sold 3,000 copies and early the next year Burns toured the Borders with some of his new friends, returning the following winter to stay in the house of a schoolmaster on the SW corner of St James's Sq. in the New Town. Here he worked on the production of the second volume of the *Scots Musical Museum*, a collection of songs including many written by himself. In December he met Mrs Maclehose, a young society woman of poetic aspirations whose husband was abroad, and fell deeply in love. She became the 'Clarinda' of a passionate correspondence and the subject of his poem 'Ae fond kiss', and treasured the memory of their relationship long after his letters had dwindled away after his return home in February 1789. There is a monument to Burns on the S side of Regent Rd.

Sir Walter Scott was born on 15 August 1771 in a house at the top of College Wynd, which led from the Cowgate to the college buildings and has now become part of Guthrie St. (Ⓟ on 8 Chambers St. records the site as 'near this spot'). The family moved in 1774 to 25 George Sq. Ⓟ and here Walter lived until 1797. He and his brothers received their early education from a tutor and in October 1779 he went to the High School for four years, before entering the University to study law. He passed his final examinations and qualified as an advocate in 1792. After his marriage to Charlotte Carpenter in December 1797 he brought her to lodgings at 108 George St., moving from there to 10 South Castle St., and a few months later to 39 Castle St. (Ⓟ and statuette of his seated figure above the door), where they lived for the next 28 years and where Scott wrote most of the 'Waverley' novels. After the crash of James Ballantyne's printing and publishing business in which he was a partner Scott left the house on 15 March

1826 and, apart from the time spent at his home at *Abbotsford, stayed in various lodgings in the city when he needed to be at the court. He retired from the court in 1830 and settled at Abbotsford for the last two years of his life. The Scott Monument (1844) in East Princes St. Gardens has a statue of Scott and his dog Maida by Steell under the canopy of a 200-ft spire, with niches containing 64 figures of characters from his works.

James Hogg (the 'Ettrick Shepherd', 1770–1835) had first met Scott when the latter was collecting material for his *Minstrelsy of the Scottish Border* in 1802, as he and his mother knew many of the old Border ballads, and in 1803 he came to Edinburgh as Scott's guest and astonished Mrs Scott by his unsophisticated manners. Scott remained his friend until the end of his life, encouraging and advising him in his literary work and finding help for him when he was short of money. Hogg later returned to stay in lodgings in Ann St. (obliterated by new buildings W of North St.) and then at the Harrow Inn near the Grassmarket (the remains of which constitute an irregular row of old gabled houses, 46–54 Candlemaker Row). He wrote 'The Forest Minstrel' in 1810, dedicated to the Countess of Dalkeith, who gave him £100. In 1812 he was living in Deanhaugh St. in the NW suburbs, where he completed *The Queen's Wake* (1813), a poem about Mary Queen of Scots and a bardic competition at Holyrood, which made his reputation as a poet. But he is best remembered today for the strange and terrifying novel *The Private Memoirs and Confessions of a Justified Sinner* (1824), published at first anonymously because, said Hogg, 'it being a story replete with horrors, after I had written it I durst not venture to put my name to it', but more probably because he guessed it would offend the Calvinists. The setting is largely in Calvinist Edinburgh of the late 17th and early 18th cc. and there is a vivid description of the Brocken spectre, seen from the summit of Arthur's Seat.

Francis Jeffrey, Lord Jeffrey (1773–1850), advocate, judge, and a leading literary figure of his time, was born at 7 Charles St. and educated at the High School and University. He began married life (1801) at 18 Buccleuch Pl. Ⓟ and it was here that he and Henry Brougham discussed Sydney Smith's proposal for a liberal magazine, the *Edinburgh Review*, launched in 1802. The *Review* was an immediate success and, under Jeffrey's editorship (1803–29), reached the status of an institution. Jeffrey moved in 1802 to 62 Queen St., then to 92 George St. (1810), and finally to a mansion at 24 Moray Pl. Jeffrey's friend the Revd Sydney Smith (1771–1845), who persuaded him and Brougham to take up his suggestion of the *Edinburgh Review*, came to Edinburgh in 1798 as a private tutor and lodged at 38 Hanover St. for about a year. He stayed in the city until 1803, moving to 19 Queen St. for a while and then, after his marriage in 1800, to 46 George St. After he returned to London he continued to keep up his connection with the *Review*.

Sir Walter Scott and Scotland

SCOTT is usually acknowledged as the father of the historical novel but he might be called the father of the geographical novel too. The Gothic novels of Ann Radcliffe use extended descriptions of scenery but the effect is undermined by the knowledge that she never visited the countries where her fiction is set. Not so with Scott, who repeatedly assures the reader that his places are real, and he has seen them himself. To the thirtieth chapter of *Rob Roy* (1817), when the hero emerges from his miserable sleeping quarters to view Aberfoil (as Scott spells it) after his first night in the Scottish Highlands, Scott attached a note that 'the Clachan of Aberfoil now affords a very comfortable little inn' and that the reader 'will find himself in the vicinity of the Rev Dr Patrick Grahame . . . whose urbanity in communicating information on the subject of national antiquities, is scarce exceeded even by the stores of legendary lore which he has accumulated'. But in a later edition Scott added an update: 'The respectable clergyman alluded to has been dead for some years.' The reader cannot fail to infer that Scott has personally visited the scene he describes in the novel, and such assurances are scattered through the rest of his work, especially that set in Scotland.

Scott was born in Edinburgh and there, in what he called 'mine own romantic town', he got his education and his profession. In his earliest years, however, he contracted the illness that left him permanently lame and, to recover, was sent to his grandparents' farm at Sandyknowe, in the Borders near Smailholm and its ancient tower-house. There he learnt, mainly from his grandmother, the legends of the Scott family and became enthused by the romance of the Border reivers and the violence and supernatural of the ballads, which he would go on to collect in his first major publication, *The Minstrelsy of the Scottish Border* (1802–3). Though he became Clerk to the Court of Session in Edinburgh, his vacations were spent on forays into the Borders and the Highlands, in quest of folklore and history, and he managed to combine his profession with his heritage by becoming Sheriff-depute of Selkirkshire in 1799.

No wonder then that his first major poem, *The Lay of the Last Minstrel* (1805), is woven around Borders landscape, with copious use of place names and central use of the ruins of Melrose Abbey in a scene both topographical and Gothic. Scott foreshadows his later novels in the combination of a journey through accurately described countryside, decorated with local allusions and anecdotes, and striking use of individual locations, to whose fame he adds the literary colouring of his romantic imagination. The effect on the public was strong and lasting. *The Lady of the Lake* (1810) so enthralled readers with its vision of the Trossachs that they soon became the tourist attraction they remain to this day,

SIR WALTER SCOTT BY SIR EDWIN HENRY LANDSEER, C. 1824

with steamer trips on Loch Katrine past Ellen's Isle, named after the poem's heroine. Scotland became through Scott the 'land of the mountain and the flood' he eulogizes as 'meet nurse for a poetic child' in *Marmion* (1808).

When, in 1814, feeling the rising power of Byron, Scott turned from verse to prose and published *Waverley* (1814), he began the series of over 30 novels, most set in Scotland, that carry on the combination of fiction and geography found in his poems. *Waverley*, a novel of the 1745 Jacobite rebellion, presents the principal factions involved not just as historical forces but also as geographical ones. The hero's introduction to the Highlands is via the Lowlands and the contrast between them. His journey goes back in time but also through different cultures. Scott is heir to Enlightenment views of the progress of society through key stages. Behind the tartan and claymores he indicates the problem facing Fergus MacIvor, his Highland chief, of maintaining a populous clan in a land where resources are scarce and traditionally supplemented by cattle-rustling and blackmail that the modern British state will no longer

View of Glen Coe. Much of the action in Robert Louis Stevenson's *Kidnapped* takes place around the glen

tolerate. Scott's sense of place can be full of nostalgia, with his commemoration of past events and his notes on relics and ruins, but the converse is that his is not a static but a dynamic vision. Places are as subject to change as the people who live there.

The economic sinews of Scott's anatomy of Scotland are perhaps most evident in *Rob Roy*, where again a young Englishman ventures into remote glens, this time just before the 1715 rebellion, and with a loquacious guide, the Glasgow merchant Bailie Nicol Jarvie. While Frank Osbaldistone, with his poetical pretensions, gives way to somewhat anachronistic feelings of the sublime and the beautiful, Mr Jarvie reminds the reader of the economic facts of life behind the clan turmoils they find themselves in. When, near the end of their adventures, they sail down Loch Lomond, Frank muses that he 'could have consented to live and die a lonely hermit in one of the romantic and beautiful islands amongst which our boat glided', but simultaneously the Bailie is

speculating on draining the lake for farming, leaving just enough water for the passage of coal barges.

The 'Waverley' novels cover the length and breadth of Scotland, from the Solway Firth in *Redgauntlet* (1824) to Shetland in *The Pirate* (1821), from Inveraray in *A Legend of Montrose* (1819) to the places in the titles of *The Fair Maid of Perth* (1828) and *The Bride of Lammermoor* (1819), and of course the Edinburgh of *The Heart of Midlothian* (1818). It is as though Scott followed a programme of novelizing in turn every major region of Scotland. Modern detractors have tried to ridicule the result by naming it 'Scottland', a land of make-believe, but there is truth even in derision and Scott's image of his native land is still a powerful part of the Scottish scene. Certainly his successors—Stevenson, Buchan, Neil Munro and regional novelists like Lewis Grassic Gibbon and Neil Gunn—often seem to be left colouring in the few blank spaces left in the map of Scotland that Sir Walter drew.

CHRISTOPHER MACLACHLAN

❖

Thomas Campbell (1777–1844), one of Scott's regular correspondents, studied law at the University in 1796, but only briefly, as he found it 'dull and unprofitable'. He spent the winter of 1797 teaching Greek and Latin to private pupils, and taking long walks over Arthur's Seat while completing his poem *The Pleasures of Hope*, which had tremendous success when published in Edinburgh the following year. The familiar line ''Tis distance lends enchantment to the view' is supposed to have been written on Calton Hill. Campbell at that time had lodgings in Alison Sq. (gone). He settled his parents in a house that he bought on St John's Hill and, after leaving for London in 1802, used to return there for later Edinburgh visits.

Susan Edmonstone Ferrier (1782–1854) was born in Edinburgh, the daughter of James Ferrier, Writer to the Signet and a colleague of Scott. She lived in her parents' home between Morningside and Edinburgh town, keeping house for her father after her mother's death in 1797. Her home at 25 George St. is now part of the George Hotel. She began writing at an early age, her first novel, *Marriage*, being written in 1810 though not published until 1818. It was followed by *The Inheritance* (1824) and *Destiny* (1831), and all three give entertaining accounts of the friction of fashionable and literary Scottish middle-class society. She was a frequent visitor at Scott's home, where she was always welcome. She is buried in St Cuthbert's churchyard, behind St John's Church, at the W end of Princes St.

Thomas De Quincey (1785–1859) had already contributed to *Blackwood's Magazine* (the Tory rival to the *Edinburgh Review*) when he moved to Edinburgh in 1828. *Blackwood's* published the first part of his 'On Murder as one of the Fine Arts' in 1827 and De Quincey continued to be an occasional contributor until 1849. He also wrote for the *Edinburgh Literary*

Gazette. He lived in Great King St., in Forres St., and at Duddingston, before settling until the end of his days at 42 Lothian St. (gone). But he was improvident and had a large family to support, and the necessity of evading his creditors drove him from time to time to take up residence in the Sanctuary in Holyrood, in one of the 'houses of refuge' where debtors could live, situated within 100 yds of the front of Holyrood Palace. The little community within the Sanctuary was under the jurisdiction of the Baron Bailie of Holyrood, appointed by the Hereditary Keeper of the Palace. With the abolition of imprisonment for debt in 1880 the need for sanctuary ended. The Sanctuary building is now a gift shop. De Quincey was a regular opium taker, but he was well liked for his quiet manner, the excellence of his conversation, and his beautiful voice. He was a friend of John Wilson (see below) from their Lake District days and when he called on him one evening at 29 Ann St. he was invited to stay the night—and remained, a welcome addition to the household, for nearly a year. He is buried in St Cuthbert's churchyard.

John Wilson (1785–1854), a distinguished scholar and athlete, came to Edinburgh from Windermere in 1812 and was called to the Bar, but never practised. He wrote verse, which was well received, and as 'Christopher North' contributed regularly to *Blackwood's Magazine* until the mid-1830s, and is remembered especially for the *Noctes Ambrosianae*, a series of topical, critical, poetical, and convivial dialogues which were supposed to take place in Ambrose's tavern (long gone and whereabouts not known). James Hogg in particular became famous as the 'Ettrick Shepherd' in the *Noctes*. Wilson became Professor of Moral Philosophy at the University in 1820. He lived at 53 Castle St. and in 1819 moved to 29 Ann St., a house of great charm, near the Water of Leith. In 1826 he moved to 6 Gloucester Pl. (Ⓟ, now the

Christopher North House Hotel), where he died.

Thomas Carlyle (1795–1881) first came to Edinburgh in 1809 to study for the ministry, walking from his home at *Ecclefechan in three days. He left the University in 1813 without taking a degree and returned to teach mathematics at his old school at Annan. In 1817 he came back to Edinburgh to begin his theological course, but had doubts about his vocation and abandoned it for a literary career, which started with contributing articles to an encyclopedia. After his marriage to Jane Welsh (1826) he lived at 21 Comely Bank Ⓟ for two years, where Francis Jeffrey was a frequent visitor, 'much taken', Carlyle wrote, 'with my little Jeannie, as well he might be, one of the brightest, cleverest creatures in the whole world'. Carlyle was elected Lord Rector of the University 1865–6.

William Motherwell (1797–1835), poet and collector of ballads, was educated at the High School. With Hogg he issued an edition of Burns's works in 1834–5.

Robert Chambers (1802–71), publisher, editor, and miscellaneous writer, founded with his brother William (1800–83) the publishing firm of W. and R. Chambers of Edinburgh and in 1832 issued a popular weekly educational magazine, *Chambers's Edinburgh Journal*. They also published *Chambers's Encyclopaedia* (begun 1859, completed 1868, and followed by numerous later editions). William became Lord Provost, 1865–9.

Marjory Fleming (1803–11), the child prodigy born at *Kirkcaldy, wrote some of her Journals while staying at 1 North Charlotte St. with her aunt Mrs Keith and the cousin (her 'dear Isa') who acted as her teacher and corrected her work.

George Borrow (1803–81) went to the High School at the time his father was quartered at the castle as an army officer, and *Lavengro*

Stromness Harbour, Orkney. The town was the home of George Mackay Brown for most of his life

(1851) recounts the fights that used to occur between boys of Old Edinburgh and the New Town.

Dr John Brown (1810–82), physician and author of *Rab and his Friends* (1859), was educated at the High School and the University. He practised medicine in Edinburgh for most of his life and from 1850 until his death lived at 23 Rutland St. The house, now offices, has a memorial to him carved in the stonework of the wall to the left of the front window.

William Aytoun (1813–65), poet and humorist, was born in Edinburgh and educated at the Academy and the University. He divided his time between law and literature, joining Blackwood's staff in 1844, and becoming Professor of Belles-Lettres at the University in 1845 and Sheriff of Orkney in 1850. He is remembered chiefly for the *Bon Gaultier Ballads* (1845), a collection of parodies and light verse which he published jointly with Sir Theodore Martin (1816–1909), another Edinburgh native. Martin was educated at the High School and University and practised as a solicitor in Edinburgh before going to London in 1846. He contributed to *Tait's* and *Fraser's* magazines before collaborating with Aytoun.

Robert Michael Ballantyne (1825–94), also a native of Edinburgh, went to Canada as a young man and worked as a clerk in the Hudson's Bay Company before turning to literature. He returned to take up a partnership with the publishing firm of Thomas Constable, and wrote one of the best known of his popular stories for boys, *The Young Fur Traders* (1855), while living in Edinburgh.

Alexander Smith (1829–67), poet and essayist, was made secretary to the University in 1854. He met Sydney Dobell in the same year and collaborated with him on 'Sonnets on the War'. He is buried in Warriston cemetery on the N side of the city, his grave marked by a tall Celtic cross with his portrait in low relief.

Andrew Lang (1844–1912), a native of *Selkirk, was educated at the Edinburgh Academy before going to St Andrews University.

George Edward Bateman Saintsbury (1845–1933), critic and author of many works on English and European literature, was Professor of Rhetoric and English Literature at the University from 1895 to 1915. He lived at Murrayfield House and from 1900 until he retired at 2 Eton Ter.

Robert Louis Stevenson (1850–94) was a native who grew up in Edinburgh and in spite of long absences abroad retained his memories and love of the city to the end of his life. He was born at 8 Howard Pl. (Ⓟ; the mementoes formerly kept here when the house was a museum have been transferred to the Writers' Museum at Lady Stair's House—see below) and was baptized Robert Lewis Balfour Stevenson after his maternal grandfather (he adopted Louis as his middle name while he was a student). In 1857 the Stevensons moved to 17 Heriot Row on the N side of the New Town (now a hospitality venue), their home for the

next 30 years. Incidents and scenes of his childhood, including 'Leerie', the lamplighter, are contained in *A Child's Garden of Verses*, published in 1885 while he was in *Bournemouth, and dedicated to 'Cummy', his pet name for Alison Cunningham, his beloved nurse and lifelong mentor. Robert was a delicate boy and his attendance at various schools was irregular on account of frequent illness. He went to the Academy for a time between the ages of 11 and 12, but his education was mainly at Mr Robert Thompson's school in Frederick St. He entered the University in 1867 to study engineering at his father's wish, but later changed to law and qualified as an advocate. He was called to the Bar in July 1875, but left for France shortly after, and gradually turned to literature as a career. *Treasure Island* (1883), his most popular work, began as a story told to his stepson on holiday at Braemar and was first published as a serial. Two unfinished novels, his masterpiece, *Weir of Hermiston* (1896), and *St Ives* (1898), were set largely in Edinburgh. Stevenson came back to Edinburgh in 1880, but ill health took him away again, and after his father's death in 1887 he returned briefly for the last time, before sailing for America with his wife and mother. He finally settled in Samoa, where he died. There is a commemorative tablet in St Giles's Cathedral bearing the lines from his tomb on Mount Vaea:

> Under the wide and starry sky
> Dig the grave and let me lie.

Kenneth Grahame (1859–1932) was an Edinburgh native whose ties with the city were broken at an early age. He was born at 30 Castle St. (Ⓟ records him simply as the author of *The Golden Age*—the book that first made his name), but after his mother's death when he was a young child he went to live with his grandmother at *Cookham Dean and spent the rest of his life in England.

His contemporary Arthur Conan Doyle (1859–1930) was born at 11 Picardy Pl. (demolished 1969) and in 1876 went to the University to study medicine. He attended the lectures of Dr Joseph Bell, a man of remarkable deductive powers who inspired the creation of the inimitable Sherlock Holmes. Conan Doyle went to Southsea (see Portsmouth) in 1882 to practise as a doctor, and at the same time began his career as a writer.

James Matthew Barrie (1860–1937) entered the University in 1878 and lodged with a Mrs Edwards at 3 Great King St. Ⓟ. After taking his MA in 1882 he worked as a journalist on the *Nottingham Journal* before going to London to make his career. In 1930 he became Chancellor of the University.

Compton Mackenzie (1883–1972), prolific novelist and writer on many topics, spent much of his last decade at 31 Drummond Pl., wintering in Edinburgh and spending summers in the south of France. He completed the last volumes of his autobiography, *My Life and Times* (1963–71), during this time. He was Lord Rector of the University 1931–4.

The poet Helen B. Cruickshank, friend of Hugh MacDiarmid and secretary of Scottish PEN, lived until 1973 at Dinnieduff, 4 Hillview Terr., Corstophine.

After settling at Biggar in 1951, MacDiarmid was a frequent visitor to Edinburgh, often staying with Helen B. Cruickshank. Among the public houses he drank at were The Abbotsford in Rose St., the Café Royal in West Register St., and Milne's Bar in Hanover St. The last-named, the poet's 'favourite howss', has a display of memorabilia and a painted sign outside.

At 4 Nelson St. a plaque put there by the Saltire Society in 1983 marks the home of Robert Garioch, who was born in Edinburgh. His friend Sidney Goodsir Smith lived at 25 Drummond Pl., where there is a plaque with a relief of the poet's head. Born in New Zealand, Smith arrived in Edinburgh at the age of 12. The city is present in much of his work, notably *Under the Eildon Tree* (1948), *The Vision of the Prodigal Son* (1960), *Kynd Kittock's Land* (1965), and the novel *Carotid Cornucopius* (1964).

The critic and novelist Rebecca West (then called Cicily Fairfield) lived as a child at 2 Hope Park Sq. and 24 Buccleugh Pl. The square was the location of Ellen's house in her novel *The Judge* (1922): 'the queerest place, hardly forty paces across, on three sides of which small squat houses sat closely with a quarrelling air'. Both houses are now part of Edinburgh University. She was educated at George Watson's Ladies' College in George Sq. from 1904 to 1907, where she was fond of Mr Budge, the English master. She rarely looked back on her Edinburgh childhood, which was associated with the hardship that followed her father's death, and spoke of the 'Scottish blight that ruined my early life'.

Norman MacCaig was born in 1910 at 53 East London St. and was educated at the Royal High School and at the University, where he studied Classics and where, in 1967, he was to become its first Fellow in Creative Writing. He taught at the Primary School in *Craiglockhart and later became headmaster of Inch Primary School, Liberton, in the south of the city. He lived in Broughton St. He wrote many poems about Edinburgh, some of them, such as 'Edinburgh Courtyard in July', capturing a mood or a moment (in this case of tenement life); others, such as 'Old Edinburgh', expressing the competing claims of the city's brilliant and violent past. 'Nude in a Fountain'—'pudicity herself in shameless stone | In an unlikely world of shells and roses'—is a meditation on the fountain beside Princes St., under the castle. 'Botanic Gardens' playfully reveals the poetic absurdity of the city's garden paradise, with its 'keeper with a hating face' and where 'Frost and sun lie in one bed. | Winter-famished, summer-fed.'

MacCaig was one of a group of poets—which included Hugh MacDiarmid, Sorley MacLean (who lived for a time in nearby Queen St.), Sidney Goodsir Smith, Robert Garioch, and George Mackay Brown—who frequented

Milne's Bar and other pubs in Rose St. in the 1950s and 1960s. George Mackay Brown, studying Gerard Manley Hopkins for a postgraduate degree at the University, was one of a number of poets to write poems for and letters to Stella Cartwright, the 'Muse of Rose Street'.

Sorley MacLean graduated from Edinburgh University with a First in English in 1933, returning in 1973 as a Fellow in Creative Writing. He taught at Boroughmuir High School in 1939, returning in 1943 when he was invalided out of North Africa during the Second World War. In the same year the book of Gaelic love poems that made his name, *Dain do Eimhir agus Dain Eile* (Poems to Emhir and Other Poems), was published.

The novelist and poet Muriel Spark was born and spent the first years of her life at 160 Bruntsfield Pl., Morningside. She attended James Gillespie's High School for Girls on Lauderdale St. in the 1930s, the model for Marcia Blaine School for Girls in her novel *The Prime of Miss Jean Brodie* (1961):

> Marcia Blaine School for Girls was a day school which had been partially endowed in the middle of the nineteenth century by the wealthy widow of an Edinburgh bookbinder. She had been an admirer of Garibaldi before she died. Her manly portrait hung in the great hall, and was honoured every Founder's Day by a bunch of hard-wearing flowers such as chrysanthemums or dahlias. These were placed in a vase beneath the portrait, upon a lectern which also held an open Bible with the text underlined in red ink, 'O where shall I find a virtuous woman, for her price is above rubies.'

Miss Brodie herself was modelled to some extent on Miss Christina Kay, 'that character in search of an author', as Spark described her in her autobiography *Curriculum Vitae* (1992), into whose hands she fell at the age of 11. She later enrolled herself at Heriot Watt College (now a university) to complete her education. The College's 'reputation for practical and businesslike teaching' helped to shape Spark's characteristically economical prose. She went on to work at the Hill School at 35 Colinton Rd, Murchiston (where she was paid in shorthand and typing lessons), and later at the office of Smalls' department store at 106 Princes St.

The poet, novelist, and essayist P. J. Kavanagh lived at Advocates' Close in the Royal Mile while appearing in the Edinburgh Festival as Mortimer in Marlowe's *Edward II*, and expressed in his memoir *The Perfect Stranger* (1966) his love for 'that dark festering area, a stews since the eighteenth century—stinking of violence and history'.

Bruce Chatwin came to study Archaeology at the University in 1966. In spite of carrying off a prize in his first year, he found academic life tiresome and left after only two years.

John James Todd, the silent-film maker hero of William Boyd's novel *The New Confessions* (1987), is brought up in fictional Kelpie's Court, a tenement at the end of a wynd off Lawnmarket.

The novelist Irvine Welsh was born in Edinburgh in 1958 and grew up in Muirhouse, a suburb to the NW of the city, before taking an MBA at Herriot-Watt University. He worked briefly for Edinburgh District Council, before publishing his novel *Trainspotting* (1993), an energetic, hard-hitting look at the 1980s Edinburgh drugs scene, peopled by unemployed heroin addicts and dealers. Set on the estates of Edinburgh and Leith, and rich with thick Leith dialogue, the book looks beyond the city's attractive tourist centre, its international arts festivals, and heritage trails to expose a darker side to Edinburgh life. The 'trainspotting' of the title refers to a scene at Leith station, a 'barren, desolate hangar' where there hasn't been a train for years. The characters reappear in Welsh's later book *Porno* (2002), and much of Welsh's other work has an Edinburgh setting too (for example, *Filth* (1998), the story of a corrupt Edinburgh policeman, or *Glue* (2001), about growing up on an Edinburgh estate).

The Fife-born novelist Ian Rankin studied at Beath Senior High School and at the University of Edinburgh, and he still lives in the city. His 'Rebus' crime novels, beginning with *Knots and Crosses* (1987), show his readers the darkness and violence hidden behind the city's smart façades, which is all the tourists see:

> They were never interested in the housing-estates around this central husk. They never ventured into Pilton or Niddrie or Oxgangs to make an arrest in a piss-drenched tenement; they were not moved by Leith's pushers and junkies, the deft-handed corruption of city gents, the petty thefts of a society pushed so far into materialism that stealing was the only answer to what they thought of as their needs . . .

Rankin has said that he wrote the 'Rebus' books originally 'hoping to make sense of the city of Edinburgh', and the books are indeed very specifically grounded here, with countless references to real locations—Princes St., Fleshmarket Close, Morningside, the Public Library, etc.—peppering every story; Rebus himself lives in Marchmont (exactly opposite where Rankin himself lived as a student at 24 Arden St.). In 2007 Ian Rankin was appointed Deputy Lieutenant of Edinburgh.

Another current Edinburgh resident is J. K. Rowling, who famously wrote several chapters of the first Harry Potter book at an Edinburgh café; then living in Leith, Rowling spent her days writing at what was then Nicolson's café (now a Chinese restaurant), on the first floor of 6a Nicolson St., on the corner with Drummond St. Ⓟ. (According to the rags-to-riches version of the story, as a single mother on benefits, spending her days in the café was a cheaper alternative to keeping her Leith flat heated, but Rowling has since denied that this was her motivation.) A decade later (and having sold more than 300 million books) Rowling would write the last sentence of the seventh and final book in room 652 of Edinburgh's exclusive Balmoral Hotel—now known inevitably as the Harry Potter suite. She

marked the completion of the series with a piece of graffiti on the marble bust decorating the room.

Edinburgh's reputation as a seat of learning and home of philosophers, poets, novelists, and critics has attracted an endless stream of visitors with literary interests, and it seems a matter of chance that some visits have been recorded and others forgotten. A few writers who came only briefly, such as Johnson, and Crabbe, who was the guest of Scott, have been mentioned above: one or two others are added here.

Maria Edgeworth (1768–1849) met Elizabeth Hamilton (see above) when she visited Edinburgh with her father in 1803, and kept in touch with her afterwards by correspondence. She came again 20 years later and visited Sir Walter Scott before setting out on a tour of the Highlands.

Percy Bysshe Shelley (1792–1822) married the 16-year-old Harriet here in 1811, just after he had been sent down from Oxford. They stayed for a short time at 60 George St. and, returning the following year, at 36 Frederick St.

Charlotte Brontë (1816–55) was charmed by her brief visit in July 1850. She contrasted Edinburgh with London in two of her letters: 'Edinburgh compared to London is like a vivid page of history compared to a huge dull treatise on political economy'; and London to her is 'a great rumbling, rambling, heavy Epic—compared to Edinburgh, a lyric, brief, bright, clear and vital as a flash of lightning'.

Sydney Dobell (1824–74), one of the members of the so-called 'Spasmodic School' of poets ridiculed by William Aytoun, visited Edinburgh with his wife while they were staying at Lasswade in 1854. They went out to Granton by the Firth of Forth, on the N edge of the city, and were amazed at the violence of the storm: 'The great waves charged the parapet above the beach in long separate lines and came over like a regiment of white lions, all mane and tail.'

FESTIVAL AND FRINGE, the collection of arts festivals held in Edinburgh annually in August. It was at the Edinburgh Fringe that 'Beyond the Fringe' was discovered in 1960, with a pool of talent that included the playwright Alan Bennett. Six years later the National Theatre's literary manager Kenneth Tynan was at the Fringe and stumbled across a new play by a playwright who had yet to have his work produced professionally, and Tynan had it brought to London, to open at the National—the play was *Rosencrantz and Guildenstern Are Dead*, the playwright Tom Stoppard. Since 1983 Charlotte Sq. has been home to the Edinburgh International Book Festival, the largest event of its kind in the world, which takes place annually in August to coincide with the city's other arts festivals. The festivals provide the backdrop for a chapter of Irvine Welsh's *Trainspotting* (1993), as well as for the vicious road-rage incident that sparks off Kate Atkinson's detective mystery *One Good Turn* (2006).

LYCEUM THEATRE. The Scottish playwright Liz Lochhead translated Molière's *Tartuffe* into Glaswegian vernacular. It opened at the Edinburgh Royal Lyceum in 1989.

NATIONAL LIBRARY OF SCOTLAND, E side of George IV Bridge, one of the largest libraries in Britain, developed from the Advocates' Library (founded 1682). It became a copyright library in 1710 and took its present name in 1925. It possesses an extensive collection of illuminated manuscripts and specimens of early printing, and, among papers illustrating Scottish history, literature, and life, are letters and papers of Hume, Boswell, Burns, Stevenson, Scott, and Carlyle.

OLD TOLBOOTH, Parliament Sq. The site of this historic building (1466–1817), which finally became a prison known as the 'Heart of Midlothian', is marked by decorative cobbles on the pavement near St Giles's Cathedral. It was the setting for the opening of Scott's novel *The Heart of Midlothian* (1818).

ROYAL HIGH SCHOOL. The school traces its origin from the Abbey School, founded in 1128, though the first actual building was not recorded until 1503. It became a grammar school in 1517 and later a 'hie schule', housed in the garden of the Blackfriars monastery, at the end of Infirmary St. near the High School Wynd. This school, which became known as the Royal High School in 1590, was superseded in 1777 by the new High School (the building is known as the Old Infirmary and is now part of the University Geography Dept.), which in turn moved to new premises (1825–9) in Regent Rd (now the City Art Centre), and in 1968 to East Barnton Ave. in the NW of the city.

UNIVERSITY OF EDINBURGH (Old College), South Bridge, founded in 1583 by the town council as the 'Town's College' and later known as the 'College of James VI', and eventually the 'University of Edinburgh'. The present building was designed by Robert Adam in 1789 and completed by W. H. Playfair in 1834. SW are the New University Buildings of 1884, and mid-20th-c. buildings occupy the S and E sides of George Sq. The University Library in George Sq. contains manuscripts of Scottish literature and two important collections of books: Drummond of Hawthornden (16th-c. literature) and Halliwell-Phillipps (Shakespeare). Alexander Anderson, the railway poet known as 'Surfaceman', was assistant librarian 1880–3 and 1886–1909.

Apart from the scholars mentioned above, the list of distinguished writers who attended the University includes the following: James Thomson (1700–48), who came to study Divinity, but cared more for poetry and left for London; David Mallet (or Malloch, 1705?–65); Mark Akenside (1721–70), a brilliant medical student; Oliver Goldsmith (1730?–74), who also studied medicine (1752–4) and is said to

have lived in College Wynd (now Guthrie St.); James Macpherson (1736–96); Thomas Aird (1802–76), poet and friend of Carlyle; William Archer (1856–1924); Alexander Balloch Grosart (1827–99); and John Davidson (1857–1909). Oliver Wendell Holmes (1809–94) received an honorary degree here in 1886. Kathleen Jamie took a Philosophy degree at Edinburgh.

In 1825 Charles Darwin—like his father and grandfather before him—came up to Edinburgh to study Medicine. Darwin managed two years before his queasiness (about surgery in particular) got the better of him, and he left in April 1827 without a degree.

THE WRITERS' MUSEUM, Lady Stair's Close, between the Lawnmarket and the Mound. The house was built in 1622 by Sir William Gray and became the home of Elizabeth, 1st Countess of Stair, in 1719. It was presented to the city by the Earl of Rosebery in 1907 and now houses collections concerning the lives and works of Burns, Scott, and Stevenson: Burns's writing desk, Scott's chessboard and the press on which the 'Waverley' novels were printed, and a particularly rich Stevenson collection. Inscriptions in Makers' Court outside commemorate Scottish writers from the 14th c. to the present.

EDNAM *Borders*

Village on the B6461, *c.* 2 m. N of Kelso. James Thomson was born (1700) in the former manse and is commemorated by a monument on Ferney Hill nearby.

The bridge over the Eden Water has a plaque (1952) commemorating Henry Francis Lyte, author of 'Abide with me', who was born (1793) in a nearby house.

EIGG, ISLE OF *Highland*

Small member of the Inner Hebrides. Sir Walter Scott visited the island in search of the Massacre Cave, where in 1577 members of clan MacDonald were smoked to death by members of clan McLeod. Sir Steven Runciman, the Hellenist and historian of the Crusades and Byzantium, whose family bought Eigg in 1926, entertained the Greek poet and Nobel laureate Giorgios Seferis on the island in the 1930s. His visits inspired Edwin Morgan's poem 'Seferis on Eigg', which also touches on

> the silent cave
> where Walter Scott, that tawdry Ulysses,
> purloined a suffocated clansman's skull.

ELDERSLIE *Renfrewshire*

Village, 3 m. W of Paisley, off the A761, the traditional birthplace of Sir William Wallace. John MacDougall Hay (1881–1919) was minister here from 1909 to the end of his life. His first and most successful novel, *Gillespie*, was completed here and published in 1914. His son, George Campbell Hay (1915–84), was born at The Manse.

ELGIN *Moray*

Town and cathedral city 6 m. S of Lossiemouth on the A941. The poet Andrew Young was born in the station master's house Ⓟ on the site where the railway station now stands; his father was the station master here. Young was educated at Edinburgh University, where he studied Theology, and, after 24 years as a Presbyterian minister, entered the Church of England as vicar of Stonegate, Sussex, in 1939. He lived the rest of his life in Sussex, latterly in the village of Yapton, near Chichester, where he was a canon of the Cathedral. The publication of his *Collected Poems* in 1936 (2nd edn, 1960) confirmed his reputation as a poet in the tradition of Thomas Traherne and Henry Vaughan, able to combine description of the English countryside with interpretation of it from a steadfastly Christian point of view. He also published books on botany, history, and folklore, notably *The Poet and the Landscape* (1962), a series of portraits of British pastoral poets as seen in their rural settings.

The novelist William Boyd attended Gordonstoun School in the 1960s. His experience here has provided material for the television plays *Good and Bad at Games* (1983) and *Dutch Girls* (1985) and for the First World War battalion in his novel *The New Confessions* (1987). He has written frankly about the conditions of public school life in his essay collection *Bamboo* (2006).

ELLEN'S ISLE *Stirlingshire*

Island at S end of Loch Katrine where Scott set some of *The Lady of the Lake* (1810). N. P. Willis tells in his *Pencillings by the Way* (1835) how his coach party was entertained by its guide:

> There . . . gentlemen and ladies, is where Fitz-James blow'd his bugle, and waited for the light Shallop of Ellen Douglas; and here where you landed and came up them steps, is where she brought him to the bower, and the very tree's still there—as you see me tak' hold of it—and over the hill yonder, is where the gallant gray giv' out, and breathed his last, and (will you turn round if you please, them that likes) yonders where Fitz-James met Red Murdoch that killed Blanche of Devon, and right across the water swim young Greme that disdained the regular boat, and I s'pose on the lower step set the old Harper and Ellen many a time, a'watching for Douglas . . .

The island is passed by the SS *Sir Walter Scott* on its way from Trossachs pier to Stronachlachar.

ELLISLAND *Dumfries and Galloway*

Farm on the A76, 6 m. N of Dumfries, on the bank of the Nith. In 1789 Robert Burns leased the farm, which he intended to improve with new methods, but when these proved unprofitable he was forced to work as an excise man. The poem 'To Mary—in Heaven', about the dead Mary Campbell, and 'Tam o' Shanter' were written here, and he also collected here many songs for James Johnson's *Scots Musical*

Museum (1787–1803), including 'Auld Lang Syne' and 'A Red, Red Rose'. Burns's health was not improved by the bizarre medical methods of the time or by his anxiety about the frailty of his children. It is thought his heart was affected by rheumatic fever in his childhood: he died in 1796 and was buried in Dumfries. Part of the farmhouse now contains Burnsiana (www.ellislandfarm.co.uk).

ETTRICK *Borders*

Hamlet on Ettrick Water, on a minor road turning off the B709 at Ramseycleuch. A 20-ft red Corsehill monument carrying a bronze portrait medallion marks the birthplace (long demolished) of James Hogg, 'the Ettrick Shepherd'. He is buried in the churchyard, near the grave of Tibbie Shiel (see TIBBIE SHIEL'S INN).

FAILFORDE *Ayrshire*

Village on the B743, 3 m. E of Mauchline. A path from the bridge leads to the monument marking the spot where Burns and Mary Campbell took their last farewell of each other on 14 May 1786.

> That sacred hour can I forget
> Can I forget the hallowed grove
> Where by the winding Ayr we met
> To live one day of parting love.

FALKIRK *Stirlingshire*

Industrial town on the A803, SW of Stirling. Bantaskyne, SW of the town, was the scene of a battle in January 1746 in which the retreating Young Pretender inflicted a severe repulse on the pursuing Government forces. Duncan Ban MacIntyre fought in the battle and describes the action in a poem.

Robert Burns visited the town twice in 1787 in order to see the Carron Ironworks (now closed). He stayed at the Cross Keys Inn, now 187 High St. Ⓟ.

Falkirk's local poet Robert Buchanan (1835–75) is commemorated by a monument in the cemetery.

FALLS OF BRUAR *Perth and Kinross*

Falls 3 m. W of Blair Atholl on the A9. Robert Burns visited the scene in 1787 and, finding the water falling through bare rocks, wrote 'The Humble Petition of Bruar Water' to the Duke of Atholl, who responded by planting firs. Though these trees have now gone, later plantings still keep the place green.

FALLS OF LEDARD *Perth and Kinross*

Falls at the W of Loch Ard, off the B829, which Scott describes in his novel *Waverley* (1814).

FORTH BRIDGE *Lothian*

Cantilever rail bridge 9 m. W of Edinburgh, crossing the Firth of Forth to Fife. Repainting the Forth Bridge has become proverbial of a Sisyphean task, as by the time the great job is done it already is time to start it again at the other end. In Tom Stoppard's play *Albert's Bridge* (1967), young Albert is charged with the task of painting the Forth Bridge (the 'Clufton Bay Bridge') single-handed. He's embarking on what is estimated will be an eight-year cycle (by which time it'll be ready for him to start over), armed with a very useful Philosophy degree.

FOULSHIELS *Borders*

Hamlet on the A708, *c.* 3 m. W of Selkirk, in the Yarrow valley. On the opposite side of the road to Newark Castle is the dilapidated cottage Ⓟ where Mungo Park was born (1771). It was here that he compiled most of the narrative of *Travels in the Interior of Africa* (1799).

GAIRLOCH *Highland*

Village on the E coast of Loch Gairloch, at the junction of the A832 and the B8021. The poet William Ross was a schoolmaster here and wrote many tender lyrics, especially to a young lady from Lewis, who did not reciprocate his love. He was a fine classical scholar and also an accomplished fiddler and flautist, but died of tuberculosis in 1790, when he was only 28. He is buried in Gairloch, a simple stone marking his grave. His poems include *Love Songs*, *In Praise of Whisky*, and *Ode to Summer*.

GALASHIELS *Borders*

Town on the A72, 6 m. N of Selkirk. A plaque erected in the wall on the outskirts E of the town, on the road to Abbotsford, states that Sir Walter Scott's carriage, bringing him home in 1832 after a journey abroad in search of health, paused at its usual stopping place to let the paralysed man see his favourite view of his home across the Tweed.

GARTMORE *Stirlingshire*

Village off the A81, 3 m. S of Aberfoyle. Gartmore House, looking over Flander's Moss to the Lake of Menteith, was the birthplace of Robert Graham (1735–97), who, having gone at 17 to Jamaica, returned on inheriting *Ardoch in 1772. His father and elder brother having died, he moved to Gartmore in 1777, where he wrote the lyrics, including 'If doughty deeds my lady please', for which he is best remembered. He became MP for Stirlingshire, was twice elected Rector of Glasgow University, and in 1791, on inheriting Finlaystone across the Clyde, the seat of the Glencairns, his mother's family, added Cunninghame to his name. He was buried with his wife and young son in the walled burial ground.

His grandson, R. B. Cunninghame Graham, often known as 'Don Roberto' from his Spanish upbringing in South America, came here on inheriting the encumbered estate in 1885, and wrote *Father Archangel of Scotland* (1896), a collection of short stories, with his wife, Gabriela de la Balmondière, the poet. He left here for Ardoch in 1903 and later sold the house, which changed hands once or twice and was bought in 1984 by an American-based biblical research ministry as their European training centre. The memorial to Don Roberto

and his horse Pampa (NTS), formerly at Dumbarton, was transferred here in 1981.

GASK HOUSE *Perth and Kinross*

Country house 2 m. W of the A9, 9 m. NE of Gleneagles, in the Strathearn area. Caroline Nairne, née Oliphant, was born (1766) here and her family had Jacobite sympathies. She married (1806) a cousin, whose rights were restored to him a few years before his death when he became Lord Nairne of Nairne. Lady Nairne, the author of numerous popular ballads including 'The Land o' the Leal', 'Will ye no come back again?', and 'Caller Herrin', which were published in *Lays from Strathearn* (1846), came back to live in her family home after the death of her husband and only son, and was buried in the chapel (1845).

GATEHOUSE OF FLEET *Dumfries and Galloway*

Small town on the B727 off the A75 at the head of Fleet Bay, 9 m. NW of Kirkcudbright. In 1793, on an August evening walk, Robert Burns composed the lines beginning 'Scots wha hae wi' Wallace bled' to the tune of Bruce's marching song at Bannockburn. The air, which he said always brought tears to his eyes, warmed him to such 'a pitch of enthusiasm on the theme of Liberty and Independance' that he wrote the words with the struggle for liberty then taking place in France also in mind. Burns is traditionally said to have written down the lines in a room, still pointed out, at the Murray Arms Hotel here.

Dorothy L. Sayers and her husband stayed at the Anwoth Hotel on the first of her holidays in this area, when she was writing *The Three Red Herrings* (1931). In the book Lord Peter Wimsey stayed in a rented cottage in Blue Gate Close, Kirkcudbright.

GLAMIS *Perth and Kinross*

Village 4 m. from Kirriemuir. Shakespeare's Macbeth was Thane of Glamis and the castle is sometimes claimed as the place of Duncan's murder (without much foundation as Shakespeare places it in *Inverness). Glamis Castle (www.glamis-castle.co.uk), has its origins in the 11th c., although most of the existing building is of the 17th. Duncan's Hall, its oldest part, commemorates the event, though even the historical Duncan was never killed at the real Glamis.

GLASGOW *Lanarkshire*

Ancient industrial, university city and port on the Clyde. The site of the University, founded in the 15th c., probably with Robert Henryson among the founders, and moved to Gilmorehill in 1870, is now covered by the Goods Station in the High St.

Adam Smith, a student here, became Professor of Logic in 1751 and of Moral Philosophy the next year. His studies here culminated in his great work *The Wealth of Nations* (1776), written after he retired to *Kirkcaldy. He was elected Lord Rector in 1787.

GLASGOW

University
It schooled Adam Smith, John Knox, and Thomas Campbell, among others; more recently novelist Andrew O'Hagan. Edwin Morgan was Professor of English here in the 1970s; novelists Alasdair Gray and James Kelman and poet–playwright Liz Lochhead have all taught creative writing here

18 Park Circus
This is the sinister setting for Alasdair Gray's *Frankenstein*-inspired novel *Poor Things*

79 Renfield Street
Thomas De Quincey rented rooms here 1841–7

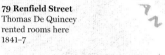

St Joseph's
Gerard Manley Hopkins was priest here in 1881

School of Art

RSAMD

McLellan Galleries
This is the place to go to visit the famous Nasmyth portrait of Robert Burns

George Square
Among the statues here are likenesses of Burns, Scott (though his links to the city are in fact very tenuous), and Thomas Campbell

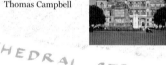

City Chambers
George Square

Central Station

Tolbooth Steeple

215 High Street
Thomas Campbell was born here in 1777 (there's a plaque on the wall of the house today)

Nearby is Gallowgate, where Dr Johnson and Boswell stayed at the Saracen's Head inn (now shops, but the building still stands at the corner of Saracen Lane) at the end of their tour of the Highlands in 1773. They were presented to some of the professors at the University but Boswell says in his account that 'we had not much conversation' because they 'did not venture to expose themselves much to the battery of cannon' they knew Johnson would use.

In 1772 Joanna Baillie, daughter of the minister at Hamilton nearby, was sent to school in Glasgow when she was about 10. In 1776 her father became Professor of Divinity at the University, where the family lived. Soon after her father's death in 1778, she moved to her brother's house in London with her mother and sisters, where she began her writing career.

Thomas Campbell was born (1777) at 215 High St. (Ⓟ on site). He attended the University, of which he was subsequently elected Lord Rector three times.

William Motherwell, who wrote the popular ballad 'Jeanie Morrison' at the age of 14, was born (1797) at 117 High St. Ⓟ. He left the city after university but settled here again in 1830, when he became editor of *The Courier*. *Poems, Narrative and Lyrical* (1832), in which 'Jeanie Morrison' was published, was followed in 1835 by the edition of Burns's works in which he collaborated with James Hogg. He died in the same year and his grave in the Necropolis is marked with a monument.

J. G. Lockhart lived here as a child while his father was minister of the College Kirk. He went to the High School for a short while and at 13 in 1809 he entered the University. He is commemorated by a plaque at 40 Charlotte St.

In 1816 Carlyle made the acquaintance of Edward Irving, founder of the Catholic Apostolic Church, who lived at 34 Kent St. Ⓟ. Carlyle's wife, Jane Welsh, whom he married in 1826, had been a pupil of Irving's.

David Wingate, born (1828) at Cowglen, followed his father into the mines at the age of 9. He published *Poems and Songs* (1862) and *Annie Weir* (1866) and then studied at the Glasgow School of Mines. Later he became manager at collieries nearby. He contributed to *Blackwood's*, and published two more collections of poems. He died at Mount Cottage, Tollcross, in 1892.

William Black, who was born (1841) in Trongate and went to the School of Art, became a clerk with a firm of bookbinders in Jamaica St. He wrote his first novel, *James Merle*, here, but it was not published until he went to London in 1864. Some parts of his novel *A Daughter of Heth* (1871) are set in the city.

De Quincey rented rooms at 79 Renfield St. from 1841 to 1847 though he rarely used them. He had first stayed with Professor John Nichol at The Old College, the former site of the University of Glasgow, and then took rooms in the High St. opposite. Nichol remembered that he often visited the Observatory and that he was 'writing for all sorts of things'. In 1848 his landlady at Rotten Row had nothing to

complain about apart from his poor appetite. He was then contributing to *Tait's Magazine*.

Robert Buchanan lived with his parents at 9 Oakfield Ter. and went to the High School and the University (1856–8). In 1859 his father, who was editor of *The Sentinel* (which had offices in Howard St.), went bankrupt and the next year the 19-year-old Robert Buchanan set out for London with a few pounds in his pocket.

Hugh MacDonald, who lived at Bridgeton, wrote dialect verses for *The Citizen*, *The Sentinel*, and the *Glasgow Times* while on their staffs (1849–58). He became editor (1858) of the *Morning Journal* until his death in 1860. Articles in these journals were collected as *Rambles Round Glasgow* and *Days at the Coast*. He is commemorated by a fountain on Glasgow Green.

MacDonald was a friend of Alexander Smith, a young lace pattern designer whose poetry, first published in the *Weekly Citizen*, soon reached a wider public. *A Life Drama and Other Poems* (1853), published when he was 23, procured him the post of Secretary to the University of Edinburgh and the entrée to the literary world, where he was satirized in *Firmilian* by William Aytoun, who dubbed him a member of the 'Spasmodic School'. In Smith's chapter on Glasgow in *A Summer in Skye* (1865), he writes of Tannahill's indelible association with *Gleniffer Braes and of MacDonald's with the Clyde. In his own poem 'Glasgow' in *City Poems* (1857), he uses country images to describe the town:

> Instead of shores where ocean beats
> I hear the ebb and flow of streets,

and thinks of the Clyde,

> Between the huddled gloom of masts
> Silent as pines unvexed by blasts.

In *Alfred Hagart's Household* (1866), a largely autobiographical novel, Glasgow is 'Hawkhead'.

After Bret Harte's exciting days in the goldfields were over he became American consul at 35 Burnbank Gdns from 1880 until his appointment came to an end with a change of administration in 1885.

William Sharp attended Glasgow Academy and the University (1866–74) and then worked in a lawyer's office (1874–6). He went abroad for health reasons and visited Scotland rarely but wrote many mystical novels and Celtic tales under the name Fiona Macleod. This secret was kept until after his death in Sicily in 1905.

Gerard Manley Hopkins was a priest at St Joseph's Church in 1881. He visited Loch Lomond in September of that year and wrote the poem 'Inversnaid', an expression of his delight in the wildness of nature.

Owen Morgan Edwards spent one session (1883–4) at the University, reading Philosophy under Edward Caird, before going to Balliol College, *Oxford. A. C. Bradley, the Shakespearian scholar, was Professor of English from 1890 to 1900.

John Buchan and his sister Anna lived at 34 Queen Mary Ave., Crosshill, when their family

came to Glasgow in 1888. John attended Hutchesons' Grammar School (founded 1650, moved to Crossmyloof 1959, an old building since demolished) and won a bursary to Glasgow University in 1892. His first novel, *Sir Quixote of the Moors* (1895), was begun in his last few weeks at college, and published the same year. The Gorbals Die-Hards, who appear in *Huntingtower* (1922) and *Castle Gay* (1930), were based on some boys in the Sunday school class he took at his father's church. Anna went to school at Queen's Park Academy, then to Hutchesons' Girls' School, and lastly to a small private school. Under her pen-name O. Douglas she gives a picture of a Glasgow family in *The Setons* (1917).

J. J. Bell, whose book *I Remember* (1932) describes the Glasgow of his youth in the 1880s, was born (1871) at Bothwell Ter. (gone), Hillhead, and went to Kelvinside Academy and the University. The sketches he wrote in the Glasgow dialect for the *Evening Times* became best-sellers when they appeared in book form as *Wee MacGreegor* (1902), and successive volumes.

John Watson, the pastor who wrote as 'Ian Maclaren', published *St Jude's* (1907), Glasgow sketches. He died on a lecture tour of the US after being elected President of the National Free Church Council in 1907.

Neil Munro, best remembered for his historical novels of the Highlands, was also editor (1918–27) of the *Glasgow Evening Times* and author of *The Clyde: River and Firth* (1907). *The Brave Days* is an account of Edwardian Glasgow.

Catherine Carswell was born (1879) in Renfrew St. and, after university, studied music abroad. In 1907 she became dramatic and literary critic of the *Glasgow Herald* until she reviewed D. H. Lawrence's novel *The Rainbow* (1915), then banned as obscene. She wrote two novels in the 1920s and two controversial studies, a life of Burns (1930) and *The Savage Pilgrimage* (1932) about her friend D. H. Lawrence. Her unfinished autobiography *Lying Awake* (1950) was published after her death in 1946.

In *One Way of Living* (1939), O. H. Mavor, who took the pseudonym 'James Bridie' from his grandparents, describes his childhood at the then countrified East Kilbride, and his schooldays at Miss Carter's, the High School and Glasgow Academy, while living at 110 Armadale St., Dennistoun. After qualifying as a doctor at the University and subsequent war service, he settled in Langside Ave. and bought a practice nearby. His popular plays written in Glasgow include *The Anatomist* (1931), *Tobias and the Angel* (1931), and *A Sleeping Clergyman* (1933).

In 1901, when the poet Edwin Muir was 14, his family moved to Glasgow from Orkney. His youth in Glasgow was unhappy. His father, two brothers, and mother all died within the space of a few years and he suffered a series of uncongenial jobs—in a beer-bottling firm, as a clerk in a bone factory at Greenock, and in a shipbuilding office in Renfrew. He saw his move from the Eden of Orkney to the fallen world of Glasgow in mythic terms:

> I was born before the Industrial Revolution . . . Then in 1751 I set out from Orkney to Glasgow. When I arrived I found that it was not 1751, but 1901, and that a hundred and fifty years had been burned up in my two days' journey.

Iain Crichton Smith was born at 8 Lewis Street in 1928. He moved with his parents to the Isle of Lewis two years later.

The visits of Poe, De Quincey, and Hopkins inspired poems by Edwin Morgan, appointed Glasgow's first Poet Laureate in 1999 and, since 2004, the first Scots Makar. Morgan was born in Rutherglen in 1920, then a town south of Glasgow but now officially absorbed by the city. He was taught at Glasgow High School and is particularly associated with the University, which he entered in 1937, graduated from in 1947 (after service in the Second World War) and where he taught until his retirement in 1980. He has written many poems about his native city, including the sequence *Glasgow Sonnets* (1972), where 'the great sick Clyde shivers in its bed', 'The Second Life' with its thoughts by Bingham's Ponds, the moving 'Death in Duke Street', 'The Gorbals Mosque', and, perhaps his best-known poem, 'The Starlings in George Square':

> Sundown on the high stonefields!
> The darkening roofscape stirs—
> thick—alive with starlings
> gathered singing in the square—
> like a shower of arrows they cross
> the flash of western window,
> they bead the wires with jet,
> they nestle preening by the lamps
> and shine, sidling by the lamps
> and sing, shining, they stir
> the homeward hurrying crowds.

John Arden's play *Armstrong's Long Goodnight* (1964) was first performed at the Citizens' Theatre, 119 Gorbals St.

The novelist William Boyd studied English and Philosophy at Glasgow University in the 1970s; Ian Hamilton Finlay studied briefly at the Glasgow School of Art at 167 Renfrew St. in 1940. The novelist Andrew O'Hagan, a native of Kilwinning in Ayrshire, studied at the University of Strathclyde in the 1980s. The Motherwell-born poet and playwright Liz Lochhead was also a student at the School of Art, and subsequently worked as a teacher in the city too.

In his poem 'Anniversaries', Douglas Dunn remembers his late wife, and the days

> when I walked with you first, my love,
> In Roukenglen and Kelvingrove,
> Inchinnan's beech-wood avenue.

Meanwhile,

> Glaswegian starlings fly
> In their black cape, a fluttered noise,
> Ornithological hurrahs
> From spires in the November sky . . .

The novelist Alasdair Gray was born in Riddrie, Glasgow, in 1934, and attended Whitehill Secondary School and Glasgow School of Art. His novel *Poor Things* (1992) is a collection of documents telling a Glasgow-based story with echoes of *Frankenstein*, centred around a house at 18 Park Circus. In the work for which he is most famous, *Lanark* (1981), Gray fragments the story of Duncan Thaw's post-war Glasgow boyhood (school in Whitehill, etc.) and mixes it in with the story of quite another world, a fantastical reinvention of the city as 'Unthank'.

The novelist and short-story writer James Kelman was born in Glasgow in 1946, and studied at the University of Strathclyde. Most of his writing is set in urban Glasgow, often written in dense and energetic local vernacular, as in his *How Late It Was, How Late* (1994), the story of a construction worker and small-time shoplifter who finds himself suddenly having gone blind. *A Disaffection* (1989) sees the Glasgow schoolteacher Patrick Doyle discovering just how disaffected he has become and attempting somehow to make his escape. With Alasdair Gray, Kelman was from 2001 joint Professor of Creative Writing at Strathclyde.

The poet and novelist Jackie Kay, born in Edinburgh in 1961, was brought up in Glasgow. In her novel *Trumpet* (1998), the Highlandman's Umbrella at Central Station is a regular meeting place for the jazz trumpeter Joss Moody, pretending to be a man, and the woman she/he later marries.

Among the statues in George Sq. in the centre of the city are those of Robert Burns, Thomas Campbell, and Sir Walter Scott.

GLEN AFFRIC *Highland*

Valley at the end of the A831, *c.* 25 m. SW of Inverness. Neil Gunn, whose novels *Morning Tide* (1931), *Highland River* (1937), *Young Art and Old Hector* (1942), and *The Well at World's End* (1951) describe the Highland way of life, lived at the end of a mountain road in this valley after resigning from the Civil Service in 1937.

GLEN COE *Stirlingshire*

Valley through steep mountains traversed by the A801 from the village of Glencoe to the desolate Rannoch Moor. The legendary Gaelic bard Ossian (Oisin), son of Fingal (Finn), is said to have been born here in the 3rd c. In 1763 James Macpherson published *Temora*, an epic in eight books purporting to be translations of Ossian. The work was much admired, though some, including Dr Johnson, were sceptical about the existence of originals of such antiquity. After Macpherson's death in 1796 an investigation found he had embellished his free translation of old Gaelic legends with additions of his own.

The sudden massacre in 1692 of Macdonalds by Campbells, who had been living in their midst, called forth the poem by Scott, written in 1814, which begins:

> O tell me Harper, wherefore flow
> Thy wayward notes of wail and woe,
> Far down the desert of Glencoe,
> Where none may list their melody?

Thomas Campbell's *Pilgrim of Glencoe*, a long poem about the reconciliation between a Campbell and a Macdonald in 1715, and William Aytoun's 'Widow of Glencoe', also tell of the treachery.

The Gaelic poet Allan MacDougall ('Ailean Dall', 1750–1829) was born here. He was originally a tailor, but is said to have acquired his nickname (meaning 'Blind Allan') after a rival blinded him with a needle. He was encouraged to write poetry by the schoolmaster–poet Ewan Maclachlan and Colonel MacDonald of Glengarry, who became his patron. Titles of his poems include *Shepherd's Ode*, *Complaint of the Women*, and *Ode to Whisky*. He was buried at Kilfillan on the Caledonian Canal.

Much of Stevenson's *Kidnapped* (1886) takes place in this area and 'Rannoch by Glencoe' is the title of a poem by T. S. Eliot.

GLENCORSE OLD CHURCH *Lothian*

Little ruined church with a frail wooden steeple and remarkable 17th- and 18th-c. gravestones, reached by a steep lane off a minor road beside the Glencorse Burn, *c.* 7 m. S of the centre of Edinburgh, between the A701 and the A702. R. L. Stevenson used to worship here and set his novel *The Body Snatchers* (1881) in the church.

GLENELG *Highland*

Village on the E shore of Glenelg Bay at the mouth of the Glenmore River. Roderick Morrison (1646–1725?), 'the Blind Harpist', spent most of his adult life here, in a rent-free cottage provided by his patron, Chief John MacLeod of Harris.

GLEN FINGLAS *Stirlingshire*

Valley N of Brig o' Turk on the A821, scene of Scott's ballad 'Glenfinlas, or, Lord Ronald's Coronach'. The striking scenery in this glen was the background for the portrait of Ruskin painted by Millais in 1853.

GLENIFFER BRAES *Renfrewshire*

These hills near Paisley, reached by the B775, were a favourite walk of the weaver–poet Robert Tannahill, who wrote the lines:

> Keen blows the wind on the braes o' Gleniffer
> The auld castle turrets are covered wi' snaw.
> How changed frae the time when I met wi' my lover.
> Among the broom bushes on Stanley green shaw.

Stanley Castle no longer has a wooded hillside, as it now rises from the dammed loch forming the waterworks. Open-air concerts held here by the Tannahill Choir from 1876 to 1883 provided money for his memorial statue in Paisley Abbey grounds.

Hugh MacDonald (1817–60), whose popular verses appeared first in Glasgow papers, is commemorated at the well in Robertson Park here. A medallion with his head in relief is on the fountain erected in 1883, which has the verse:

The bonnie wee well on the Breist of the Brae
Where the hare steals to drink in the gloamin'
 sae gray
Where the wild moorlan' birds dip their nebs
 and tak' wing
And the lark weets his whistle ere mounting to
 sing.

GLEN ORCHY *Argyll and Bute*

Valley of the river Orchy, which flows SW from
Bridge of Orchy to the NE end of Loch Awe.
The B8074 runs beside its E bank from the A82
to the A85. This was the birthplace of Duncan
Ban MacIntyre (Donnchadh Bàn Mac an
t-Saoir, 1724–1812), one of the greatest of the
Gaelic poets. After fighting unwillingly at the
Battle of *Falkirk, he worked as a gamekeeper
and forester, and his close touch with nature is
shown in much of his poetry, in particular in
the best-known poems, *Oran Coire a'
cheathaich* (Song of the Misty Corrie) and 'The
Praise of Ben Doran'. Other works include
Lament to Colin Campbell of Glenure and *In
Praise of Edinburgh*, as well as love poems,
satires, and drinking songs. Although illiterate,
MacIntyre had a good friend in the minister's
son, who wrote down his poems and prepared
them for publication in 1768. At Monument
Hill, 2 m. SW on the old Inveraray road, there
is a granite temple which commemorates the
poet.

GLENSHIEL *Highland*

Valley traversed by the A87, *c.* 5 m. NE of
Lochalsh. In 1773 Dr Johnson rode through
with Boswell on their way to Skye. Soon after
passing the site of the battle of 1719, they
stopped to let the horses feed on the rich grass.
Johnson describes the scene in his *Journey to
the Western Islands* (1775), where he wrote that
he 'first conceived the thought of this narration'
at this spot.

GORDON ARMS *Borders*

Hotel (formerly an inn) at the crossroads of the
A702 and the B7059, in the Yarrow valley. It
was here and hereabouts that Sir Walter Scott
traditionally met James Hogg, 'the Ettrick
Shepherd', who spent most of his life at Altrive
and Mount Benger nearby. A plaque records
that they met and parted here for the last time
in the autumn of 1830.

GREENOCK *Renfrewshire*

Clydeside shipbuilding town and port on the
A8. Jean Adam, daughter of a ship's captain,
was born (1710) at Cartsdyke, now part of the
town. She is said to have become interested in
poetry with the help of the minister, whose
children she was teaching. *Poems* (1734) was
published by subscription and she then set up a
school for girls. This failed, and after becoming
a pedlar she was forced to beg. She was
admitted to the workhouse hospital in Glasgow
two days before she died (1765). She is thought
by some to have written the ballad 'The Sailor's
Wife', because of her acquaintance with Collin
and Jean Campbell, a ship's captain and his
wife from Cartsdyke, and because of the

descriptions of the housewife's many tasks,
which might spring more readily to the
thoughts of a woman than of a man. However,
the poem is more often said to be by William
Mickle.

In 1786 Mary Campbell, Burns's 'Highland
Mary', whom he hoped to marry before
emigrating, died here of typhus and was buried
in the churchyard at the West Kirk with her
brother, from whom she caught the disease.
The church was rebuilt in the 19th c. and the
coffins reinterred in the new cemetery at
Nelson St. West, where a monument stands
among the rhododendrons and pines on the
hillside. John Galt, author of *Annals of the
Parish* (1821), arrived in the town with his
parents when he was 10. After some years as a
clerk in the Customs House he went to London
in 1804. He returned in 1834 and lived in West
Blackhall St. Ⓟ, where he became paralysed
and died (1839). He is buried in the old
cemetery in Inverkip St. Ⓟ.

GRETNA GREEN *Dumfries and Galloway*

Village on the Scottish side of the border, 10 m.
NW of Carlisle, off the A74, formerly famous
for its instant marriages. Scottish law
recognized that a declaration of intent to
marry made by two people before witnesses
constituted a legal marriage. This appealed to
runaway couples from England for whom
lengthy negotiations were not desired,
especially after 1753, when an Act of
Parliament made such marriages in the Fleet
prison illegal. In Jane Austen's *Pride and
Prejudice* (1813), Lydia's sisters are torn
between the worry of her future if she had
indeed gone to Gretna with such a feckless
extravagant as Wickham, and the shame her
present association with him would bring on
the family if she had not. In *Mansfield Park*
(1814), the conduct of Julia, who had 'gone to
Scotland' with Yates, was a mere imprudence in
contrast with her sister's adultery.

GREY MARE'S TAIL, THE *Dumfries and Galloway*

Waterfall (NTS) *c.* 8 m. NE of Moffat, near the
A708, where the waters of Loch Skeen fall over
200 ft to flow into Moffat Water. It is described
by Scott in the introduction to Canto II of
Marmion (1808), and the wild scenery of the
mountainous tract above Moffat, which he
loved to explore by hill pony, features in *Old
Mortality* (1816). A level footpath leads to a
viewpoint of the falls. For those with suitable
outdoor clothing and footwear, a rough, steep
path goes past the top of the waterfall and
beyond to Loch Skene.

HARRIS, ISLE OF *Highland*

Southern portion of the largest island of the
Outer Hebrides. Norman MacCaig visited the
island and in his poem 'Harris, East Side'
notices that

> The narrow bay
> Has a knuckle of houses and a nail of sand
> By which the sea hangs grimly to the land.

HAWTHORNDEN *Lothian*

Mansion on the banks of the North Esk, the
'cavern'd Hawthornden' of Scott's ballad
'Rosabelle', *c.* 7 m. S of Edinburgh, reached
from the A768. William Drummond of
Hawthornden was born (1585) in the old 15th-
16th-c. manor and in 1638 restored it for his
own use 'that he might rest in honourable
leisure', as recorded on a panel on the main S
wall. Ben Jonson, who had journeyed from
London to Edinburgh on foot in 1618, paid him
a visit at the old house, staying for three weeks
and draining his cellar dry. Drummond, author
of *The History of Scotland, 1423–1542* (1655),
The Cypresse Grove, a prose meditation on
death (1623), and a number of poems, left a
manuscript record of the visit, *Ben Jonson's
Conversations with William Drummond, 1619*
(published 1833). Ruth Fainlight contemplates
the house and its view in her poem 'In
Drummond's Room'.

HELENSBURGH *Argyll and Bute*

Town and resort, at the entrance to Gare Loch,
on the Firth of Clyde. Neil Munro, author of
popular dialect tales including *The Vital Spark*
(1906), and of the historical novel *John
Splendid* (1898), lived at Craigendoran, S of the
town.

C. Day-Lewis mentions in his autobiography,
The Buried Day (1960), his arrival at Larchfield
Academy, a small preparatory school, in the
autumn of 1928 to teach English. After a little
over a year he was succeeded by W. H. Auden,
who taught the poet and artist Ian Hamilton
Finlay. The school provides much of the setting
for his long fantasy poem *The Orators* (1932).

Marion Angus, Scots poet and ballad writer,
spent the winter of 1931 here and invited
Auden to visit her. She wrote to a friend that he
read 'yards and yards' of his poems, 'not one
line of which I could understand. I thought to
myself, is this the new poetry? It sounds like a
voice from another planet.' George Blake, who
succeeded Neil Munro as literary editor of the
Glasgow Evening News, settled here in 1932
and used the town as the background for *Down
to the Sea* (1937) and other novels about the
shipbuilders of the Clyde. O. H. Mavor, who
wrote as 'James Bridie', lived at Rockbank after
retiring from his medical practice in Glasgow.
His later plays include *Mr. Bolfry* (1943) and
Daphne Laureola (1949).

HUNTLY *Aberdeenshire*

Town on the A97, *c.* 40 m. NW of Aberdeen.
George Macdonald was born (1824) at Upper
Pirriesmill, a farmhouse just beyond the level
crossing by Bleachfield St. This was the home
of his grandparents, who appear as characters
in his novels *Alec Forbes* (1865) and *Robert
Falconer* (1868). The river Bogie runs nearby
and the old mill still stands by the bridge.
Macdonald, who describes the surroundings in
his poem 'The Hills', often returned and his
fairy stories owe much to the tales, half
remembered from his childhood, which he
sought out on these visits.

INCHCAILLOCH *Highland*

Wooded island, whose name means Island of
the Old Women, at the SE end of Loch Lomond
opposite the village of Balmaha. In Scott's *The
Lady of the Lake* (1810), the poem about an
escapade of the disguised James V, a fiery cross
is made from sacred yew trees growing here.

INCHCAPE ROCK *Fife*

Lighthouse rock E of the Tay estuary, also
known as the Bell Rock. Robert Southey's poem
'The Inchcape Rock' recounts the exploits of Sir
Ralph the Rover. R. M. Ballantyne spent two
weeks on the rock before writing his adventure
story *The Lighthouse* (1865).

INCHINNAN *Renfrewshire*

Small village in the W outskirts of Glasgow,
where the poet Douglas Dunn was born in
1942.

INCHMAHOME *Stirlingshire*

Ruined priory on the largest island in the Lake
of Menteith, off the A81, 7 m. SW of Callander.
R. B. Cunninghame Graham, who could see the
island (which can be reached by ferry) from his
home at *Gartmore, chose to be buried here
and his body was brought from Buenos Aires,
where he died (1936).

INNERLEITHEN *Borders*

Busy little town on the A72, 6 m. SE of Peebles.
Scott, who knew it as a straggling village of
thatched and whitewashed cottages, is said
to have laid the scene of *St Ronan's Well*
(1823) here, and soon afterwards it gained a
reputation as a popular watering place. The
waters can still be sampled, and there is a
Visitor Centre, which is open in the summer.

Emma Tennant was brought up at The Glen,
described by her as 'a fake baronial castle'. Her
novel *Wild Nights* (1979) and her memoir
Strangers (1998) draw on memories of an
eccentric aristocratic childhood at the house.

INVERARAY *Argyll and Bute*

Town at the NW of Loch Fyne, on the A83 and
the A819. Inveraray Castle (½ m. N), the seat of
the Campbells, earls and later dukes of Argyll,
is described by Boswell in *Journal of a Tour of
the Hebrides* (1785), an account of his journey
with Dr Johnson in 1773. Matthew Lewis, often
called 'Monk Lewis' after his Gothic novel *The
Monk*, which became very popular in 1796,
stayed at the castle on many occasions. It was
here in 1798 that he first met Scott, whose
poetry he influenced. He dedicated *Romantic
Tales* (1808) to Lady Charlotte Campbell, the
daughter of his host. Alexander Smith stayed
here on his visits to *Skye and in *A Summer in
Skye* (1865) he wrote that he climbed a nearby
hill and saw the town appear like a miniature.
Scott's *A Legend of Montrose* (1819), a novel
about Montrose and his rival the Covenanter
Archibald Campbell, the 8th Earl, was said by
Smith 'to haunt you at Inveraray', where a
fierce battle took place in 1644. Neil Munro,
who was born (1864) in the town, set here part

of his novel *John Splendid* (1898), which also
relates the Covenanters' struggle against the
Highland clans. He is commemorated by a
memorial in Glen Aray, N of the town. In
Stevenson's *Catriona* (1893), David Balfour
attends the trial here of James of the Glens.

INVERKIRKAIG *Highland*

Coastal village near Lochinver at the mouth of
the river Kirkaig. The poet Anne Stevenson
evokes the place in 'Inverkirkaig', where, under
the flight of fighter planes, 'the salmon leaps
and falls'.

INVERNESS *Highland*

City at the mouth of the river Ness as it flows
into the Moray Firth and self-styled 'capital of
the Highlands'. Shakespeare places several of
the early scenes of *Macbeth*, including the
murder of Duncan, at Macbeth's castle at
Inverness:

> This castle hath a pleasant seat; the air
> Nimbly and sweetly recommends itself
> Unto our gentle senses.

The present building, located on the site or
perhaps to the west of an earlier fort, is 19th-c.
Macbeth was Thane of *Cawdor, which is
nearby and also has a castle.

INVERSNAID *Stirlingshire*

Village at the NE end of Loch Lomond, landing
stage of the Inveruglas ferry. Wordsworth, his
sister Dorothy, and Coleridge set out in 1803 to
walk to Loch Katrine, 7 m. E. On their return
they were given dinner in the ferryman's house
by his young daughter, Wordsworth's
'Highland Girl':

> For I methinks, till I grow old
> As fair before me shall behold
> As I do now the Cabin small
> The Lake, the Bay, the Waterfall
> And thee, the spirit of them all.

Crabb Robinson, finding his arrangements for
the ferry had broken down, was rowed across
by Old Andrew, a frail old man. On mentioning
this to Wordsworth later he was amazed to find
that he had inspired Wordsworth's poem on
the Brownie. Gerard Manley Hopkins's poem
'Inversnaid' begins:

> This darksome burn, horseback brown,
> His rollrock highroad roaring down,
> In coop and in comb the fleece of his foam
> Flutes and low to the lake falls home.

INVERURIE *Aberdeenshire*

Town on the A96, 16 m. NW of Aberdeen.
Arthur Johnston, the 'Scottish Ovid', was born
(1587) at Caskieben Castle (now part of Keith
Hall). He left the town as a youth for the
Medical School at Padua. William Thom
settled here in 1840, though it is not certain
whether he worked at a loom in the cottage
where he lived in North St. (rebuilt, Ⓟ removed
to the Public Library) or in a weaving shop
nearby. He had been out of work for three years
following a slump in America and had taken to
the road with his family. He earned a few pence

by playing a flute but they often had to sleep by
the roadside where he also had to bury the baby
that died in its mother's arms. In 1841 his poem
'The Blind Boy's Pranks' was accepted by the
Aberdeen Herald and was well received. His
*Rhymes and Recollections of a Handloom
Weaver* (1844) led to his leaving for London,
where for a time he was befriended by Lady
Blessington.

IONA *Argyll and Bute*

Small island, off the SW of Mull, where
Columba founded a monastery *c.* 563 in which
it is thought the 8th-c. Book of Kells (see
KELLS) was compiled, and where subsequently
many kings and princes were buried, including
Duncan, according to Shakespeare's *Macbeth*.
In St Oran's Chapel (built 1080 and restored) is
the Tomb of Lord Ronald, the subject of Scott's
poem *The Lord of the Isles* (1815), about Bruce's
campaign in 1307. Johnson and Boswell both
recorded their visits to Iona, to which they give
the Gaelic name Icolmkill. Boswell quotes
Johnson's 'sublime passage' 'That man is little
to be envied, whose patriotism would not gain
force upon the plain of Marathon, or whose
piety would not grow warmer among the ruins
of Iona.'

IRONGRAY *Dumfries and Galloway*

Village 1½ m. S of the B729, 4 m. NW of
Dumfries. A flat stone near the E porch of the
church was donated 'by the author of Waverley'
to Helen Walker (d. 1791), who had the
qualities Scott invested in his imaginary
character Jeanie Deans.

IRVINE *Ayrshire*

Port on the W coast, 12 m. N of Ayr. James
Montgomery was born (1771) in the house later
called Montgomery House, in Montgomery
St. and now demolished. He was the son of a
pastor of the Moravian Brethren and his hymns
remain popular today. Burns lodged (1781–2)
at 4 Glasgow Vennel Ⓟ while learning flax
dressing, and then moved to lodgings in the
High St., where he became very ill with
pleurisy. He lost all his possessions when the
house caught fire after he had celebrated
Hogmanay with his friends and he moved back
to Glasgow Vennel. He spent seven months
here and is commemorated by a statue on
Irvine Moor. John Galt, whose father was a sea
captain, was born (1779) in the High St. (the
site was later a bank). The scene of Galt's novel
Annals of the Parish (1821) is set in Dreghorn
(2 m. E) and the surrounding villages. Galt's
family moved to Greenock when he was 10 and
other Galt relatives moved into the house. It
was with them that their young cousin Edgar
Allan Poe came to stay in 1815, and attended
the Royal School.

ISLAY *Lanarkshire*

Southernmost island of the Inner Hebrides.
The Scottish Gaelic poet William Livingstone
(1808–70) was born on the island and became
a tailor by trade. Most of his poetry is highly
patriotic (he was one of the earliest advocates

Inveraray Castle, visited by Boswell and Johnson, 'Monk' Lewis, and Sir Walter Scott. Stevenson set part of *Catriona* in the town

of home rule in Scotland). His best-known poem is probably *The Norsemen in Islay*. The island has also been home to novelist Bernard MacLaverty, who would use it as a setting for his 1997 novel *Grace Notes*.

JEDBURGH *Borders*

Ancient royal burgh, on the A68, situated on the Jed Water. James Thomson was educated at the Grammar School, at that time (early 18th c.) part of the old abbey. Burns stayed at 27 Canongate on a visit in 1787, but the house has gone. Scott was a frequent visitor and it was here that he made his first appearance as an advocate, successfully pleading for a noted poacher and sheep stealer. He visited the Wordsworths in September 1803, when they were staying at 5 Abbey Close Ⓟ, and read to them in the evening from the unpublished manuscript of *The Lay of the Last Minstrel*.

JEMIMAVILLE *Highland*

Small town 5 m. E of Cromarty on the B9163. From 1959 until her death in 1976 the novelist Jane Duncan lived at the Old Barn. Her father's home, a croft called The Colony (now renamed) is the Reachfast of 19 of her novels known as the My Friends series, which represents for the narrator, Janet Sandison (a name used by the author as a pseudonym), a symbol of childhood's innocence in an increasingly ugly world.

JURA *Argyll and Bute*

Island of the Inner Hebrides, S of Mull. George Orwell (Eric Blair) lived at Barnhill from 1946 to 1949, the year his novel *Nineteen Eighty-Four*, on the horrors of totalitarianism, was published. He left the island to go into hospital as he was ill with tuberculosis, and he died in 1950.

KELSO *Borders*

Town with a fine Georgian market square, on the banks of the Teviot and the Tweed. In 1783 Walter Scott attended the old Grammar School then on the site of the nave of the Norman abbey, which still has impressive ruins. Part of his family lived at Garden Cottage, later added to and renamed Waverley Lodge, but he lived with his favourite uncle, Captain Robert Scott, at Rosebank nearby, a property that he inherited on his uncle's death. Scott invested the money from the sale of Rosebank in the printing business of his old schoolfellow here, James Ballantyne.

KILMARNOCK *Ayrshire*

Manufacturing town, bypassed by the A77, 14 m. NE of Ayr. *Poems Chiefly in the Scottish Dialect* (1786), Burns's collection of poems which first brought him recognition, was published here. The site of Wilson's printing shop in Star Inn Close is marked with a granite slab. The Laigh Kirk near the Cross was the setting for 'The Ordination', but Tam Samson's house in London Rd and the Angel Inn (Begbies) in Market Lane have gone. In Kay Park a Victorian tower commemorates Burns

and has a fine view. The spiral stair climbs past two rooms containing books, tape recordings, and portraits. One portrait is of the poet and essayist Alexander Smith, born here (1829, site unknown). In Smith's autobiographical novel *Alfred Hagart's Household* (1866), Kilmarnock is called Spiggleton.

KILWINNING *Ayrshire*

Historic missionary town known as 'the Crossroads of Ayrshire'. The novelist Andrew O'Hagan was born in the town in 1968.

KINGSHOUSE INN *Highland*

Inn on the old road through Glen Coe, now just off the A82. Campbell soldiers are said to have met here before the massacre in 1692. Neil Munro describes the place in his novel *John Splendid* (1898).

KINLOCH RANNOCH *Perth and Kinross*

Village at the E end of Loch Rannoch on the B846. The Gaelic poet Dugald Buchanan (1716–68) was schoolmaster here and lived here until the end of his life. His surviving poems (1767) are all religious and include 'The Day of Judgement', 'The Skull', 'The Dream', and 'Winter'. He also assisted in the production of the first edition of the Gaelic New Testament (1768). He is commemorated by an obelisk in the village. He was buried at Little Leny, near Callander.

KINNESSWOOD *Perth and Kinross*

Village 5 m. E of Kinross on the A911. The poet Michael Bruce was born here in 1746 in a cottage that is now maintained by a trust. His best-known poem is 'Ode to the Cuckoo'. He died of consumption at the age of 21 and was buried in Portmoak churchyard on the E side of Loch Leven, where there is a monument to him and where, since 1935, annual memorial services have been held.

KIRKANDREWS *Dumfries and Galloway*

Hamlet 2 m. W of *Borgue on the Carrick road. William Nicholson, 'the Galloway poet', was buried (1849) in the old churchyard overlooking Wigtown Bay.

KIRKCALDY *Fife*

Port on the A92. Adam Smith (1723–90), son of the Comptroller of Customs, was born at 220 High St. (Ⓟ on site) and educated at the burgh school. He returned to the town in 1766 and devoted his time to the study of economic theory, supported by a pension from the Duke of Buccleuch, whom he had tutored on the Continent. *The Wealth of Nations* was published 10 years later.

Marjory Fleming (1803–11) was born at 130 High St. (rebuilt), then a three-storey house with a garden through an archway. Her journal, written while staying with an aunt and corrected by her cousin, was first edited by H. B. Farnie as *Pet Marjorie* (1858), and later popularized (1863) by Dr John Brown, who

drew a sentimental picture of her sitting on Scott's knee. Though neither Scott nor Marjory mention each other, their meeting was not denied by her sister. *The Complete Marjory Fleming*, with a facsimile of the journals, was edited by Frank Sidgwick in 1934. She died after an attack of measles and is buried in Abbotshall churchyard; her life-size effigy shows the journal open on her knee. Raith Park, where she often played, is now a public park.

Carlyle lived in Kirk Wynd off the High St. in 1816, when appointed a master at the burgh school. A plaque on the wall of the Fife Free Press car park nearby commemorates him and Adam Smith on the site of the school. Anna Buchan ('O. Douglas'), younger sister of John Buchan, was born at the manse at Pathhead, now joined to Kirkcaldy but then a separate town. Her autobiography *Unforgettable, Unforgotten* (1943) describes her happy childhood with her brothers, their large garden (now built over), and their delight in Scott's 'Rosabelle'. The heroine of this ballad lived in Ravenscraig Castle, just N of the town, and was drowned crossing 'the stormy firth'.

KIRKCONNEL *Dumfries and Galloway*

Mining village on the A76. Alexander Anderson (1845–1909), born here, became a platelayer (1862) and published *A Song of Labour and Other Poems* (1873) under the pseudonym 'Surfaceman'. Encouraged by Carlyle, he became assistant librarian at Edinburgh University. There is a monument in the churchyard at the top of the village, where he is buried.

KIRKOSWALD *Ayrshire*

Village on the A77, 13 m. SW of Ayr. Burns studied surveying and mensuration here (1775), sleeping at Ballochniel Farm (1 m. S), where his uncle worked. The nightmare ride in 'Tam O' Shanter' ended here. Tam and his 'ancient drouthy cronie' were modelled on Douglas Graham and John Davidson, who are both buried in the churchyard. They were all friends of the souter (cobbler) and met at his house (Souter Johnnie's House, NTS), which now contains Burnsiana and cobbler's tools.

KIRRIEMUIR *Angus*

Town on the A926 and A928, *c.* 20 m. N of Dundee. J. M. Barrie was born (1860) at 9 Brechin Rd (NTS), which now houses personal relics and mementoes. His father was a handloom weaver like the occupants of many of the other houses in the road. Most of his stories of the town, which he called Thrums, a weaving term, came from his mother, whose life he told in *Margaret Ogilvy* (1896). Her family had been members of the Auld Licht Kirk (demolished 1893) in Bank St., from which he took the name of his first collection of sketches, *Auld Licht Idylls* (1888). Her pastor there became Mr Carfrae in *The Little Minister* (1891). In 1872, after two years in Forfar, the Barries settled at the ivy-covered Strathview (now modernized), but it was the cottage

Souter Johnnie's House at Kirkoswald, the home of John Davidson. The life-size figures in the garden represent the Souter, Tam, the Innkeeper, and his wife

opposite that became known as the House on the Brae of *A Window in Thrums* (1889). The Den, a ravine now a public park, is mentioned in *Sentimental Tommy* (1896). Barrie, who went to London in 1884, often visited his parents here. He is buried with them on the W side of the cemetery near the manse.

KIRROUGHTREE *Dunbartonshire*

Former country house now a hotel on the A712, 2 m. NE of Newton Stewart. It was the home of Patrick Heron, the MP, with whom Burns stayed in 1794 and 1795. He had expectations that Heron would help to further his career and he wrote the verses known as the 'Heron Election Ballads'.

LAGGAN *Highland*

Village N of Loch Lochy on the A82. In 1779 the minister, James Grant, who was also chaplain at Fort Augustus, married Anne, the daughter of the barrack master at the garrison there. Her *Letters from the Mountains* (1803), published after his death to enable their son to join the East India Company, were in the Romantic tradition and proved popular. Anne Grant had spent her adolescence in Albany, America, and was friendly with Dutch settlers there and her *Memoirs of an American Lady* (1808) stems from that time.

LANGHOLM *Dumfries and Galloway*

Small town 15 m. NW of Gretna Green, where the A7 crosses the Esk. William Mickle (1735–88), poet and translator, was born at Wauchope Manse, the last house in the town on the Lockerbie road. A tablet on the Town Hall recalls that 'he was the author of 'Cumnor Hall' and 'There's Nae Luck aboot the Hoose'.

It is said that at 13 he read *The Faerie Queene* and decided to be a poet.

Christopher Murray Grieve, author and journalist, who wrote under the pseudonym Hugh MacDiarmid, was born (1892) in Arkinholm Ter., moved with his family in 1896 to Henry St., and then in 1899 to a house in Library Bldgs, Parliament Sq., behind the post office Ⓟ. He attended the primary department of Langholm Academy and in 1908 left for Broughton Student Centre in Edinburgh. After his father's death in 1911 he went to S Wales as a journalist. In his autobiography, *Lucky Poet* (1943), he says:

My boyhood was an incredibly happy one. Langholm . . . has supplied all my subsequent poetry with a tremendous wealth of sensuous satisfaction, a teeming gratitude of reminiscence, and . . . an immense reservoir to draw upon. My earliest impressions are of . . . great forests, of honey-scented hills, and moorlands infinitely rich in little-appreciated beauties of flowering, of animal and insect life, of strange and subtle relationships of water and light.

Later he became a controversial figure in his home town on account of his Scottish nationalism and communist sympathies, and there was dispute over the siting of the MacDiarmid Memorial Sculpture, a bronze monument by Jake Harvey, cast in the form of an open book, which was eventually installed at Whita Yett, near the town. MacDiarmid was buried in Langholm cemetery on 13 September 1978. His gravestone bears a quotation from his masterpiece, *A Drunk Man Looks at the Thistle* (1926):

I'll ha'e nae hauf-way hoose, but aye be whaur
Extremes meet—it's the only way I ken
To dodge the curst conceit o' bein' richt
That damns the vast majority o' men.

His Complete Poems 1920–1976 (ed. Michael Grieve and W. R. Aitken) appeared posthumously in 1978.

LARGO *Fife*

Village on the A915, comprising Upper and Lower Largo. The latter, on the coast, was the birthplace of Alexander Selkirk (1676), the prototype of Defoe's *Robinson Crusoe* (1719). His thatched cottage on the shore has given way to a street of houses, and on one a statue of Crusoe stares out to sea.

LASSWADE *Lothian*

Village in the Esk Valley, *c.* 6 m. SE of Edinburgh. William Drummond of Hawthornden, who lived in the mansion 2½ m. SW, is buried in the churchyard. Sir Walter Scott used to stay at Lasswade Cottage (enlarged) in the summers of 1798–1804, and the village is possibly the 'Gandercleugh' of Jedediah Cleishbotham, the fictitious schoolmaster and parish clerk who was supposed to have sold *Tales of My Landlord* (1817–31) for publication.

In 1840 De Quincey settled at Mavis Bush (now De Quincey Cottage), Polton, 2 m. SW of Lasswade, on the Hawthornden road, and this, apart from periods in Edinburgh and Glasgow, became his home for the rest of his life.

LAURENCEKIRK *Aberdeenshire*

Chief town in the district of Howe of the Mearns. James Beattie, the poet who became Professor of Moral Philosophy, was born (1835) near the town, where his father was a farmer and shopkeeper. Dr Johnson and Boswell stopped here on their Highland journey (1773) while Boswell arranged a visit to Lord Monboddo. The inn where they stayed was furnished by Lord Gardenstone with a library for travellers. The remains of the books are in the University Library, Dundee. In *The Journal of a Tour of the Hebrides* (1774), Boswell writes of the town and the improvements that Lord Gardenstone is making by 'building a manufacturing village', a project of which he approves, though he remarks that Lord Gardenstone is as fond of it as if he had 'founded Thebes'.

LAURIESTON *Aberdeenshire*

Village on the A762, 9 m. SE of New Galloway. A tall cairn at the N of the village commemorates Samuel Rutherford Crockett, poet and novelist of the Kailyard School, admired by R. L. Stevenson, whose poem dedicated to Crockett is quoted on the cairn. Crockett was born (1859) at the farmhouse of Little Duchrae on the A762, 1 m. S of Mossdale. His first two novels, *The Lilac Sunbonnet* and *The Raiders*, both published in 1894 and set locally, were so successful that he gave up the ministry and devoted himself to writing. He died at Tarascon in France and is buried at Balmaghie churchyard (a left turn by the bridge 3 m. E on the B795). His memorial is included at the foot of a tombstone to Isabella Young, 20 yds from the gate.

LEADHILLS *Lanarkshire*

Village on the B797 in the Lowther Hills, 7 m. SW of Crawford. Allan Ramsay, author of *The Gentle Shepherd* (1725), was born near here. His father was manager of Lord Hopetoun's lead mines, and after his death his mother married a farmer in the same neighbourhood. Allan Ramsay was sent to Crawford School and then, after his mother's death, was apprenticed (1701) to a wig maker in Edinburgh.

LEWIS, ISLE OF *Highland*

Roderick Morrison ('An Clàrsair Dall', 1646–1725?), Gaelic poet, was born on the island. His nickname, meaning 'the Blind Harpist', refers to the loss of his sight through smallpox. He became the family harpist to Chief John MacLeod of Harris and Dunvegan and composed several airs, as well as an elegy for his patron. He is buried on the Isle of Lewis.

The ship carrying the travel writer Robert Byron, who was on his way to Iran to spy against the Russians, was torpedoed by a German U-boat off the island's principal town of Stornoway in 1941.

Iain Crichton Smith's childhood was spent at Upper Bayble, 7 m. from Stornoway. He spoke Gaelic until he began primary school in the village, where he was taught solely in English. He gained a scholarship to the Nicolson Institute in the town. Moving, as he wrote, 'between two worlds—the world of school and the world of the village', Crichton Smith spent a somewhat alienated childhood. His relationship with his mother's Free Presbyterianism and what he saw as its repressive and joyless ways is the more or less explicit subject of many of his poems, such as 'Poem of Lewis' or the well-known 'The Law and the Grace'. Landscape and stern faith collide in the passages on Lewis in his autobiographical poem 'A Life':

> Bibles
> are open in the churchyards, marbly white,
> and the sea sighs towards the gravestones. On
>   the moors
> the heather is wine-red and the lochs
> teem with unhunted fish. The sky
> is an eternal blue and God drowses
> momently from his justice.

Crichton Smith's 1969 prose story *The Last Summer* is a veiled account of his childhood on the island. His poem 'Lolaire' describes the tragedy of 1919, when a ship conveying 300 Lewismen struck a rock off Stornoway.

LOCHABER *Highland*

District around Fort William and birthplace of John Macdonald (Iain Lom, *c.* 1625–1707), poet and warrior. He was active in politics, supporting the cause of the Duke of Montrose against that of the Duke of Argyll in the civil wars of the 1640s. His best-known poem, *The Battle of Inverlochy*, describes the rout of Argyll's forces by those of Montrose in 1645. He is buried in the Braes of Lochaber in Cill Choiril graveyard.

Ewan MacLachlan (Eòghan MacLachlainn, 1775–1822), poet and translator, who became the foremost Celtic scholar of his day, was born on the farm of Coiruanan. After a rudimentary education at Fort William he was a private tutor to several families and at the same time studied Greek and Latin, winning a scholarship to *Aberdeen University.

Mary Cameron MacKellar (1834–90), a Highland poet, was born in Lochaber, near Fort William. She published *Poems and Songs* in 1881.

LOCHINVER *Highland*

Coastal village beneath Mount Suilven in Sutherland's Assynt district. Norman MacCaig spent holidays at nearby *Achmelvich and wrote many poems about the local country and its people. 'Midnight, Lochinver' captures the quiet seafront with characteristic lyricism and wit:

> A lounging fishbox raised
> Its broad nose to the moon. With groans
> And shouts the steep burn drowned itself;
> And sighs were soft among the stones.

He captured the village and the distinctive mountain nearby in 'Climbing Suilven':

> Parishes dwindle. But my parish is
> That tuft, this stone
> And the cramped quarters of my flesh and bone.

The poem is quoted on a plaque commemorating MacCaig on Kirkaig Bridge.

LOCHLEA (pr. Lŏχ'lĭ) *Ayrshire*

Farm 2 m. NW of Mauchline, off the B744, where Burns and his brothers and sisters lived with their parents from 1777 to their father's death in 1784. Some of the poems and songs he wrote here were collected in *Poems Chiefly in the Scottish Dialect* (1786). Burns left to study flax dressing in 1781 as the farm could not provide a living for so many people, and on his return he found his father gravely ill and the farm failing.

LOCH LEVEN (pr. 'Lēvĕn) CASTLE *Stirlingshire*

Ruined 14th-c. castle on an island in the loch. Mary Queen of Scots was imprisoned here in 1567 and escaped in 1568. Scott's novel *The Abbot* (1820) is based on this episode and the battle which followed.

LOGIEALMOND (pr. Lōgĭ'ahmond) *Perth and Kinross*

District by the river Almond, NW of Perth. John Watson, Free Church minister here (1875–7), who wrote as 'Ian Maclaren', calls the area 'Drumtochty' in his stories of rural life, *Beside the Bonnie Brier Bush* (1894). Kinloch, near Blairgowrie, where Watson spent his college vacations, also has a claim to be 'Drumtochty'. These tales in the Kailyard tradition were popular in America and in translation on the Continent.

LONGSIDE *Aberdeenshire*

Village 6 m. W of Peterhead on the A950. John Skinner, the Episcopalian minister here from 1742 until a few days before his death in 1807, lived in a cottage in Linshart, where he wrote songs, poems, and a translation of the Psalms into Latin. He had not thought of publishing the songs until his son met Burns, who proved persuasive. Burns declared 'The Reel of Tullochgorum' the 'best Scotch song Scotland ever saw'. 'The Ewie wi' the Crookit Horn' and 'Tune Your Fiddle' were others included in James Johnson's *The Scots Musical Museum* (1839). Skinner's *Songs and Poems* (1859) were collected posthumously. He died in his son's house in Aberdeen, and is buried here.

MAUCHLINE (pr. 'Mŏχlĭn) *Ayrshire*

Village on the A76, 9 m. SE of Kilmarnock, which Burns often visited when he was living (1777–89) at *Lochlea and *Mossgiel. He fell in love with Jean Armour, daughter of a master mason who found him ineligible. He also met the lawyer Gavin Hamilton here, at whose house next to the 15th-c. Mauchline Tower he at last married Jean Armour in 1788. They rented a room in Castle St. (which now forms the centre of the Burns House Museum), and Poosie Nansie's tavern (still an inn) in Loudoun St. features in 'The Jolly Beggars'. The churchyard has a plan showing the graves of four of Burns's children and of many characters mentioned in his poems. It is also the setting for 'The Holy Fair', a satire on the annual gathering for Communion. The church, where Burns was often punished for his misdemeanours, has been rebuilt.

MAYBOLE *Ayrshire*

Hilltop town on the A77, 9 m. SW of Ayr. Walter Kennedy, the late 15th-c. poet and rival of William Dunbar, whose *The Flyting of Dunbar and Kennedy* (1508) contained some of Kennedy's poems, is thought to have been Provost of Maybole *c.* 1594. The Kennedys were earls of Cassilis in the 15th and 16th cc. and their castle here (restored and now offices) may have been the home of the Countess of Cassilis, heroine of the ballad 'Gypsy Laddie'. This early Scottish ballad was associated with the exploits of Johnny Faa, recognized as lord and earl by James V and later hanged. It was in the 18th c. that a Countess of Cassilis was first associated with the ballad which, in an English version, has her say:

> Oh! What care I for thy goosefeather bed
> With the sheet turned down so bravely-o.
>
> Oh! What care I for my new wedded lord,
> I'm off with the raggle-taggle gypsies-o.

MELROSE *Borders*

Small town below the Eildon Hills on the S bank of the Tweed, renowned for its abbey founded in 1136 for Cistercian monks from Rievaulx. After a chequered history, no real restoration has taken place since the mid-16th c., but the ruins are very fine. In 1803 Sir Walter Scott took Wordsworth and his sister Dorothy to see it and later described it in *The Lay of the Last Minstrel* (1805; II. i) in the lines beginning:

> If thou would'st view fair Melrose aright,
> Go visit it by the pale moonlight.

Scott based the monastery of Kennaquhair in *The Monastery* (1820) and its sequel *The Abbot* (1820) on Melrose.

MINTO *Borders*

Village off the A698, 7 m. NE of Hawick. Minto House, in an estate to the N, was the birthplace of Jane (sometimes Jean) Elliot (1727–1805), third daughter of Sir Gilbert Elliot, and author of the most popular version of the old lament for Flodden, 'The Flowers of the Forest', which begins 'I've heard them lilting at the ewe-milking'. Robert Burns thought 'the gentry were no longer capable of writing true ballads, but they could and did write true folk-songs, as witness Jean Elliot's "The Flowers of the Forest"'.

MONTROSE *Angus*

Small town 38 m. S of Aberdeen on the A92. It was here, during the decade 1919–29, that Hugh MacDiarmid (Christopher Murray Grieve) spent one of the most creative periods of his life, writing *Sangschaw* (1925), *Penny Wheep* (1926), and *A Drunk Man Looks at the Thistle* (1926). He was employed on the editorial staff of the *Montrose Review*, then situated in a close off the High St. Ⓟ, and lived in lodgings with his first wife, Peggy, at 19 Kincardine St. and 12 White's Pl. before moving into a council house at 16 Links Ave., an address that was to become the 'headquarters' of the Scottish Literary Renaissance.

MOSSGIEL *Ayrshire*

The farm (rebuilt) 1 m. N of Mauchline on the Tarbolton road, rented by Robert Burns and his brother Gilbert from Gavin Hamilton, a fellow Freemason, after their father's death in 1784. Burns wrote much of his best work at a table under the skylight in the attic he shared with his brother. The mouse he disturbed with his plough, the daisy, and 'poor Maillie', the old sheep who had fallen on her back, all encountered during his work on the farm, were the subjects of the verses he wrote down at night. *Poems Chiefly in the Scottish Dialect* (1786) was published in Kilmarnock to provide the passage money for him and Mary Campbell, 'Highland Mary', to emigrate, but its success and her death kept him in Scotland. Jean Armour, whose name had so often been linked to his in searing reproofs from the pulpit at Mauchline, became his wife in 1788, and the whole family left the farm the next year.

MOTHERWELL *Lanarkshire*

Large steel-producing town SE of Glasgow. The playwright and poet Liz Lochhead was born here in 1947.

MULL *Highland*

Island off the W coast of Scotland, where the Gaelic poet Mary MacLeod was banished for a time (see RODEL).

Dr Johnson and Boswell visited Mull on their tour in 1773. They landed at Tobermory and rode, with some difficulty as bridles were scarce and streams were high, to visit Sir Allan Maclean on Inch Kenneth.

In the summer of 1795 Thomas Campbell became a tutor at Sunipol (*c.* 8 m. W of Tobermory) where he wrote 'The Exile of Erin'. Ulva (island off mid-west Mull) was the destination hoped for in the escape of Lord Ullin's daughter in Campbell's ballad, and 'Lochgyle' his name for Loch-na-Keal, which divides it from Mull, where to Lord Ullin's horror:

> The waters wild went o'er his child,
> And he was left lamenting.

Keats walked across Mull in 1818 with his friend John Reynolds, whose spectacles caused much interest in such an isolated region. They found the 37-m.-long track hard walking as it was boggy.

Dugald MacPhail (1818–87), a Gaelic poet, was born in Strathcoil, at the head of Loch Spelve in the SE part of the island. A memorial records his poem 'An t'Eilean Mulach', an exile's song written while he was in Newcastle.

Erraid, off the SW tip of Mull, is the island where David Balfour in *Kidnapped* (1886) thought himself stranded.

Sorley MacLean taught at Tobermory Secondary School 1937–8. He found the island—the ancestral home of clan Maclean—depressing. Mull is the basis for the unnamed island in Alan Warner's novel *These Demented Lands* (1998).

NEIDPATH CASTLE *Borders*

A 13th-c. castle on the A72, 1 m. W of Peebles, on a steep hillside above the Tweed. Walter Scott, who often visited the castle, and Thomas Campbell both wrote ballads entitled 'The Maid of Neidpath' about the tragedy of the girl so altered by illness that her lover passed her by, and broke her heart.

NEWARK CASTLE *Ayrshire*

The remains of this 15th-c. royal hunting seat stand in a dominating position above the Yarrow, *c.* 3 m. W of Selkirk. The castle is in the Bowhill estate of the Buccleuch family and is reached by a narrow road off the B7039 immediately after crossing the bridge from the A708. Here, in 'Newark's stately tower' Scott laid the scene of *The Lay of the Last Minstrel* (1805), where the minstrel recited the lay to the Duchess of Buccleuch after the execution of her husband in 1685.

NEW CUMNOCK *Ayrshire*

Village on the A76 where Afton Water joins the Nith. A cairn beside the road above the Afton, on a turn off the B741, was erected by the New Cumnock Burns Club for their Golden Jubilee 1973, to commemorate Burns's song 'Flow gently, sweet Afton'.

NORTH KESSOCK *Highland*

Village on the N of the Firth of Beauly, with a ferry link to Inverness. Dalcraig, 2 m. SW of the B9161 on the way to Redcastle, was the last home of Neil Gunn (d. 1973), whose novels, including *The Silver Darlings* (1941) and *The Green Isle of the Great Deep* (1944), describe the harshness of the life of the coast and of the Highlands.

OBAN *Argyll and Bute*

Resort on the A85 and W coast port for Mull and the Islands. Dr Johnson and Boswell landed here in 1773 after a fine crossing from Mull and next day over a leisurely breakfast they talked of Goldsmith's poem *The Traveller*.

Robert Buchanan lived (1866–74) at the White House on the Hill (later Soraba Lodge, 1 m. S). He attacked the Pre-Raphaelite poets in 'The Fleshly School of Poetry', an article published in the *Contemporary Review* (1871) and wrote *The North Coast and Other Poems* (1868), novels, and plays.

Iain Crichton Smith published his first book of poetry, *The Long River* (1955), while teaching at Oban High School. He lived here until 1982 and reflected upon, among other things, its special light in his autobiographical poem *A Life*:

> The sea is sheaves
> of endless blue on blue and lucid crowns
> of jellyfish drift lazily. No one drowns
> in this amazing light. The War Memorial burns.
> One soldier helps another through the stone.

It was while driving from Glasgow to Oban that Crichton Smith came across the three deer by the roadside that inspired the poet's own favourite, the long poem *Deer on the High Hills* (1960): 'It was icy January and there they were | like debutantes on a smooth ballroom floor.' He wrote his best-known prose work, *Consider the Lilies* (1968), about an old woman's resistance to the Highland clearances, while teaching here. He left in 1977 to take up a full-time writing career.

The novelist Alan Warner is from Connel, a few miles N of Oban. His novels *Morvern Callar* (1995) and *The Sopranos* (1998) are set largely in a West Highland coastal town based on Oban (in *The Sopranos* known as 'Port').

OCHILTREE *Ayrshire*

Hillside village on the A70, W of Auchinleck, birthplace of George Douglas Brown. It is the 'Barbie' of his sombre novel *The House with the Green Shutters* (1901), written under the pseudonym 'George Douglas', whose realism was in sharp contrast to popular sentimental accounts of the simple life of the poor in Scotland. His house Ⓟ in the main street at the top of the village is at the time of writing in the process of being converted into a pub to be named the Green Shutters.

OLD DAILLY *Ayrshire*

Hamlet on the B734, 3 m. E of Girvan. The Pre-Raphaelite poet and painter William Bell Scott (1811–90) was an annual summer guest of Miss Alice Boyd at Penkill Castle, where his illustrations of James I's *Kingis Quair* decorate the stairs. The Penwhapple, which runs through the grounds, was the subject of his sonnets 'The Old Scottish Home', 'Outside the Temple', and 'Lost Love'. Alice Boyd, a painter herself, invited D. G. Rossetti and his sister Christina here. Rossetti, prevented by eye trouble from painting, returned to writing while staying here (1868–9) with Scott, and began 'The Stream's Secret' in a cave in the gardens. Scott designed a new hall for Penkill (*c.* 1883), where he died. He is buried in the church (Ⓟ; ruins) and Swinburne contributed memorial verses to *The Athenaeum*.

ORKNEY ISLANDS *Orkney*

Group of islands off the N coast of Scotland. Edwin Muir was born (1887) at The Folly (gone), a farm his father rented in Deerness parish on Mainland, and moved when he was 2 to the Bu, the biggest farm on the island of Wyre, NW of Deerness. Here he spent six happy years before the landlord repossessed the farm and the family moved to Garth, 4 m. S of Kirkwall, where he attended the Burgh School. In 1901 the Muirs moved to Glasgow. Muir found the move from rural Orkney to industrial Glasgow highly traumatic. Although he only returned for holidays, the Orkneys remained a focal point throughout his life. The Wyre Heritage Centre devotes a portion of its exhibition space to Muir's connections with the island.

Eric Linklater used, from his earliest years, to spend his summer holidays in Orkney. After his marriage in 1933 he came to live in Merkister House, Harray, in the West Mainland, remaining there until 1947. At the beginning of the Second World War he commanded the defences in Orkney, and founded the first newspaper for the troops anywhere in Britain. He died in 1974 and is buried in Harray parish churchyard. His novels *White Man's Saga* (1929) and *Magnus Merriman* (1934) are set partially in the islands.

George Mackay Brown was born on Victoria St., Stromness, and went to school in Stromness Academy, where a sympathetic teacher introduced him to the poetry of Auden, Pound, MacDiarmid, and Eliot. Otherwise he disliked school, a period later evoked in his novel *Beside the Ocean of Time* (1994) and poems such as 'Island School':

> A boy leaves a small house
> Of sea light. He leaves
> The sea smells, creel
> And limpet and cod.

In 1968 he moved to 3 Mayburn Ct Ⓟ, his 'watchtower', from which he could see the fishing boats and watch the sea's 'tremulous silk' come into Hamnavoe, the old Viking name for the town harbour, and his own poetic label for Stromness:

> Although the fleet from Hamnavoe
> Drew heavy nets
> Off Noup Head, in a squall of rain,
> Turning in slow

> Gull-haunted circles near the three-mile
> line,
> And mouthing cod
> Went iced and salted into slippery crates,
> One skipper heard and bowed his head.

The resilience of the islanders and the rhythm of natural life on the islands form the background to all his poems, stories, and novels. His best known novel, *Greenvoe* (1972), is set on the fictional Orcadian island of Hellyn, in which the permanence of island life is threatened by 'Operation Black Star', a mysterious nuclear development. 'The essence of Orkney's magic is silence, loneliness and the deep marvellous rhythm of sea and land, darkness and light.' He lived at Mayburn Ct until his death in 1996, enduring tuberculosis and depression (the 'black bird') throughout his life, but writing prolifically—poems, stories, novels, and a weekly column for *The Orcadian*. By the late 1960s he had become famous and sought to deter literary pilgrims during his (morning) writing hours by pinning a notice to the door saying he was busy or out.

PAISLEY *Renfrewshire*

Industrial town on the W of Glasgow. Alexander Wilson, born here in 1766, became a weaver like his father. In 1791 he published his first volume of poems, which contained 'Watty and Meg', and then emigrated to America, where he became a schoolmaster near Philadelphia. *The Foresters* (1805), a collection of nature poems, led to his commission for *American Ornithology* (1808–14), a study unfinished at his death (1813). He is commemorated by a statue near Paisley Abbey.

Robert Tannahill, also a weaver, was born (1774) in Castle St., where the house has a plaque with the lines:

> Here Nature first wak'd me to rapture and love
> And taught me her beauties to sing.

Nearby at 11 Queen St. is the thatched cottage where he lived from childhood to his death (1810). Most of *Poems and Songs* (1807) had first appeared in Glasgow journals. Tannahill founded a club with a group of friends which met to discuss poetry and music at The Sun tavern, 12 High St., where James Hogg was their guest. A depressive illness and worry over the delay of a second edition of his poems led to his suicide in the millstream, known now as Tannahill's Pool, just visible through the railings in Maxwelton St. He is buried in the cemetery. Open-air concerts on Gleniffer Braes, his favourite walk, raised money for his statue erected in 1883 near the Abbey.

John Wilson ('Christopher North'), son of a rich manufacturer, was born (1785) at 63 High St. and educated at the Grammar School. William Motherwell, while Sheriff-Clerk depute of Renfrewshire (1819–29), published a collection of Scottish ballads, *Minstrelsy, Ancient and Modern* (1827), for which he wrote a historical introduction. He also became editor (1828–30) of the *Paisley Advertiser*.

The novelist William Sharp (1855–95) was born at 4 Garthland Pl. (gone), near Garthland

Lane off the Glasgow Rd, and spent the first 13 years of his life in the town. As 'Fiona Macleod', a pseudonym he adopted in 1894, he became one of the writers associated with the Celtic Twilight.

PEEBLES *Borders*

Quiet country town on the Tweed, on the A72 and the A703. Robert Chambers (1802–71), who with his brother William (1800–83) founded the publishing firm of W. and R. Chambers, Edinburgh, renowned for its encyclopedia and dictionaries, and wrote a number of books on Scottish history, biography, and literature, was a native and spent his early years here. The brothers were born in a small house Ⓟ in Biggiesknowe, over the bridge and to the right, with a garden running down to the river. The Chambers Institute, High St., was their gift to the town. At the E end of High St., on the S side, a plaque records a building erected on the site of the surgery of Mungo Park (1771–1806), the surgeon, explorer, and author of *Travels in the Interior of Africa* (1799). He settled here as a surgeon in 1801 but was out of his element, and in 1805 set off again for Africa, to explore the Niger.

Bank House, on the corner of High St. near the bridge, was the home of Anna Buchan ('O. Douglas'), author of many novels. Peebles appears as 'Priorsford' in a novel of that name (1932), as well as in several others. She describes the life of her family here in *Unforgettable, Unforgotten* (1943).

PENICUIK (pr. 'Pennycŏok) *Lothian*

Town on the Esk, 8 m. S of Edinburgh, on the A701. Allan Ramsay (1686–1758) is commemorated by an obelisk in the grounds of Penicuik House (burnt down in 1899, but now under restoration).

Samuel Rutherford Crockett (1860–1914) was a minister of the Free Church of Scotland here from 1886 to 1895, when he relinquished the ministry to devote himself to writing. He published a book of poems, *Dulce Cor*, in 1887, which attracted the attention of R. L. Stevenson and led to a friendship between the two men. Crockett's collection of short stories of Scottish provincial life *The Stickit Minister* (1893), dedicated to Stevenson, was immediately popular and was followed by the successful novels *The Raiders* (1894), *The Lilac Sunbonnet* (1894), and many others. He lived at Bank House, in Penicuik estate, overlooking the Esk, where he amassed a substantial library, and enjoyed visits from J. M. Barrie, R. L. Stevenson, and Andrew Lang. He moved to Torwood Villa, near Peebles, in 1906.

In the nave of the old church there is a memorial, surmounted by a dog's head in relief, to James Noble, the Howgate carrier, and his wife, Ailie, who are buried in the churchyard. They and their dog Rab lived at Howgate, a hamlet to the SE, and are immortalized in Dr John Brown's story *Rab and His Friends* (1859).

The Martello tower at Sandycove, near Dublin, where James Joyce stayed briefly in 1904. It features in *Ulysses* and now houses a Joyce museum

PERTH *Perth and Kinross*

Large town and tourist centre on the Tay, once the capital of Scotland. The house of the heroine of Scott's *The Fair Maid of Perth* (1828), at the corner of Blackfriars Wynd, was rebuilt in its old style late in the 19th c. and became a craft and curio shop. The City Chambers contain late 19th-c. stained-glass windows of scenes from the novel. Scott describes the Battle of the Clans (1396) fought on the North Inch (now a park) between picked warriors of two rival clans and watched by King Robert and his queen as if at a tournament.

Royal guests stayed at Blackfriars Monastery (then between Athol Pl. and Carpenter St.), where Simon Glover and his daughter the Fair Maid worshipped. It was at Blackfriars that Robert's son King James I was assassinated (1437). His poem *The Kingis Quair*, or King's Book, an account of his courtship of his wife, written *c.* 1424 while a prisoner in England, is used by Rossetti in 'The King's Tragedy' included in *Ballads and Sonnets* (1881). The narrator, Catherine Douglas (Kate Barlass), tells of the events leading to her vain attempt to bar the door with her arm to save the King. James was buried in the Charter House, which he had founded in 1425 (site S of the hospital in King St.). A plaque near the corner of St John St. and South St. states that the site of the house of Gavin Douglas, Bishop of Dunkeld (1516–20), can be seen through the archway, 'pend', there. He was the first translator of the classics into English with the *Aeneid* (1553).

John Ruskin spent many holidays as a boy with his parents in Perth, sometimes staying in Main St., Bridgend (house gone), E of the Tay, and sometimes at 10 Rose Ter. Ⓟ, overlooking North Inch. He married Euphemia (Effie) Gray, whose parents had taken over Ruskin's grandfather's house, Bowerswell (later an old people's home), N of the river. His mother felt unable to attend the wedding there. Ruskin's parents were first cousins; his grandfather had killed himself at Bowerswell, and his mother had an aversion to the house.

The theatre critic William Archer was born (1856) in Perth (house unknown); his family left for Norway soon afterwards. John Buchan was born (1875) at the manse in York Pl. The house is now divided in two and a plaque marks no. 20. William Soutar was born (1898) in Perth and lived with his parents at 27 Wilson St. Ⓟ from 1924 until his death in 1943. His poems, judged as some of the best of the Scottish revival, appeared regularly from 1931. A posthumous collection of previously uncollected, and mostly unpublished, poems appeared in 1948 as *Collected Poems*. He kept diaries from 1930, when he became bedridden, and these were published as *Diaries of a Dying Man* (1954), from the title he gave to his last one, kept from July to October 1943, when he died.

PLOCKTON *Highland*

Highland village on Loch Carron. Sorley MacLean was appointed headmaster of the High School in 1956, where he taught every subject and sought a proper recognition for Gaelic in the school curriculum. Some of his forebears were from the region, a fact he celebrated in 'Going Westwards', a poem whose immediate context was the North Africa campaign:

> *de Mhathanaich Loch Aills' nan geurlann,*
> *agus fir m'ainme—có bu tréine*
> *nuair dh'fhadadh uabhar an léirchreach?*

> (of the sharp-sword Mathesons of Lochalsh; and the men of my name—who were braver when their ruinous pride was kindled?)

RAASAY, ISLE OF *Highland*

Island between Skye and the mainland. The Gaelic poet Sorley MacLean was born in the village of Oscaig in 1911, into a family of traditional singers and pipers. He went to school over the Sound in Portree and later lived on Skye, in the Braes district. The violent and melancholy history of Raasay—and particularly the Clearances following 1843, which destroyed the communities of Hallaig and Screapadal 'facing Applecross and the sun' on the eastern side of the island—provided the subject for some of Maclean's most memorable and elegiac poetry, which he wrote in Gaelic and usually translated into English himself—such as 'The Woods of Raasay' and the haunting 'Hallaig':

> The window is nailed and boarded
> through which I saw the West
> and my love is at the Burn of Hallaig,
> a birch tree, and she has always been

> between Inver and Milk Hollow,
> here and there about Baile-chuirn:
> she is a birch, a hazel,
> a straight, slender young rowan.

Maclean more than anyone else was responsible for sparking the 20th-c. renaissance in Gaelic literature, making the language serve universal ideas and interests that went far beyond his own corner of Scotland. He was also instrumental in promoting the teaching of Gaelic in Scottish schools.

RODEL *Highland*

Village on the S tip of the island, at the end of the A859. The Gaelic poet Mary MacLeod (Màiri nighean Alasdair Ruaidh, *c.* 1615–*c.* 1707) was born here. She was banished for a time to the Island of Scarba for allegedly insulting her patron in a poem. She composed many love songs and elegies as well as panegyrics which were composed to be sung. *The Gaelic Songs of Mary MacLeod*, ed. J. C. Watson, was published in 1934. She was said to have been much given to 'gossip, snuff and whisky'. She is buried at Rodel.

ROSSLYN CHAPEL *Lothian*

15th-c. chapel, in the village of Roslin 7 m. S of Edinburgh, built by Sir William Sinclair (or St Clair), of 'the lordly line of high St Clair'. Legend states that the Sinclairs were buried in their armour instead of coffins, and that a red glare over Roslin would foretell disaster, as Scott mentions in his ballad 'Rosabelle' (see KIRKCALDY):

> Seem'd all on fire that chapel proud,
> Where Roslin's chiefs uncoffin'd lie,
> Each Baron for a sable shroud,
> Sheath'd in his iron panoply.

The chapel's place at the climax of Dan Brown's 2003 publishing phenomenon, *The Da Vinci Code*, has brought upon it a somewhat overwhelming attention in recent years. The novel is more accurate in its account of the chapel's astonishing decorative scheme than in its assertions that the building was designed by the Knights Templar 'as an exact architectural blueprint of Solomon's Temple

The remains of Brochel Castle, Raasay. The island's ruins and deserted villages feature in the poetry of Sorley MacLean, who was born here

Ben Bulben, Sligo, the mountain praised by W. B. Yeats in his poem 'Under Ben Bulben'. The poet is buried at nearby Drumcliff

in Jerusalem' or that the Holy Grail was once hidden here. Open throughout the year (www.rosslynchapel.org.uk).

St Andrews *Fife*

Ancient university town and E coast resort, famous for its golf course. Andrew of Wyntoun was a canon-regular of the Cathedral (ruins) about the last quarter of the 14th c. and author of *The Orygynale Cronykil*. The chronicle, perhaps begun here, was probably mainly written at *St Serf's Inch.

William Dunbar is thought to have been at the University *c.* 1480 before obtaining a place at the court of James IV. David Lindsay (or Lyndsay), who was a student here *c.* 1515, was, like Dunbar, involved with the education of the young James V, to whom many of his poems continued to give advice and exhortation. Gavin (or Gawain) Douglas, a son of the 5th Earl of Angus, studied here (1489–94) and was appointed archbishop here in 1514. Challenged by a rival faction, he was imprisoned in the castle (ruins) until allowed to accept the bishopric of Dunkeld, which he was offered by Queen Margaret. John Mair (Major) taught Logic and Philosophy from 1522 to 1525. In his Latin *History of Greater Britain* (1521), he advocated union of the two countries. After returning from Paris he was appointed (1533) Provost of St Salvator's College, where he spent the rest of his life and died in 1550. Mair, whose writings were all in Latin, was said by Rabelais to have written an account of the making of black puddings, 'De modo faciendi boudinos'. Robert Aytoun graduated from the University in 1588 and also went to Paris. His poems were written in Latin, French, or English. He is said to have written 'Old Long Syne', which may have suggested 'Auld Lang Syne' to Burns. John Arbuthnot, after deciding not to go into the Church like his father, graduated MD here in 1696.

Robert Fergusson studied (1765–8) here before settling as a clerk in *Edinburgh, having had to give up his hope of reading Divinity after his father's death. Dr Johnson and Boswell stayed here on their tour in 1773. They had supper at Glass's tavern and then went in 'procession to St. Leonard's College, the landlord walking before us with a candle, and the waiter with a lantern'. Dr Watson provided them with 'very comfortable and genteel accommodation'. They walked over the ruins of the Cathedral, looked at the old castle, and were well entertained at dinner by the professors. William Tennant, a schoolmaster at *Anstruther, was Professor of Oriental Languages (1834–48) at his old university. Andrew Lang, who was educated here before going to Balliol, returned here and lived at 8 Gibson Pl. He died at Banchory in 1912 and his grave in the East Cemetery at St Andrews has a Celtic cross.

Edwin Muir and his wife, Willa (who had been a student at St Andrews University), moved here from *Hampstead in 1935. They lived at Castlelea, The Scores, until 1938 and then in Queen's Gardens. Here Muir wrote

Scottish Journey (1935), *The Story and the Fable* (1940), the first version of his *Autobiography* (1954), and *Scott and Scotland*, his controversial study that advanced the idea that Scotland can only achieve a national literature by writing in English. He also continued translating and was a reviewer for *The Scotsman*. In 1941 he became a lecturer for the British Council and moved to Edinburgh in 1942.

St Mary's Loch *Borders*

Lake to the W of Ettrick Forest, beside the A708 (Selkirk–Moffat road), Scott's 'lone St. Mary's silent lake' of *Marmion* (introduction to Canto II). His note on this line reads: 'This beautiful sheet of water forms the reservoir from which the Yarrow takes its source. . . . In the winter it is still frequented by flights of wild swans; hence my friend Mr. Wordsworth's lines':

> The swan on sweet St. Mary's lake
> Floats double, swan and shadow

(written in fact before Wordsworth had been there himself, in 'Yarrow Unvisited', in *Memorials of a Tour in Scotland*, 1803).

St Serf's Inch *Stirlingshire*

Island in Loch Leven with åthe ruins of the priory of Augustinian canons, which superseded a Celtic settlement. Andrew of Wyntoun, prior until his death *c.* 1420, probably wrote here the major part of *The Orygynale Cronykil*, a metrical record of Scottish history from the beginning of the world to the accession of James I. It includes the story of Macbeth, Macduff, and the witches, later used by Shakespeare. It was published in 1795 from the manuscript in the Royal Library.

Sandaig *Highland*

Small bay on the Sound of Sleat, *c.* 5 m. SW of Glenelg, reached by a rough track through Forestry Commission land, below the Armisdale road, near a bridge over a rocky stream. This is the place that Gavin Maxwell called Camusfeàrna in *Ring of Bright Water* (1960), which he wrote while he was living at a cottage on the edge of the bay. He describes the pet otters who shared his home, and the wild creatures of the district. In 1968 the cottage was burnt down and Maxwell put up a memorial to Edal, who died in the fire:

> Edal, the otter of Ring of Bright Water,
> 1958–1968.
> Whatever joy she gave to you, give back to nature.

Maxwell died the following year and his ashes are buried under a slab of rock marking the site of the cottage.

The poet Kathleen's Raine's disastrous love for Maxwell (who was homosexual) brought her to Sandaig in the 1950s and the landscape of Wester Ross inspired many of her poems and the title of Maxwell's best-known book was taken from Raine's 'The Marriage of Psyche': 'He has married me with a ring, a ring of bright water | whose ripples travel from the heart

of the sea . . .'. The facts of their unhappy relationship—including the curse that she put on Maxwell when he turned her out of the house during a storm in 1956 (and then had the horror of seeing apparently fulfilled)—are laid out with brutal honesty in her autobiography *The Lion's Mouth* (1977).

Scalpay *Highland*

An island in the Outer Hebrides, 330 yds from Harris. Norman MacCaig, whose mother came from Scalpay, visited the island, and in his poem 'Wreck', wrote of a hulk stranded in the bay, 'hung like a hall with seaweed' and taking aboard twice every day 'a cargo of the tide'.

Selkirk *Borders*

Ancient Royal Burgh on the A7 and the A708, overlooking Yarrow Water. On the hill approaching the W side of the Market Place a wall plaque marks the site of Old Forest inn, where Burns stayed when he wrote his 'Epistle to Willie Creech' (the publisher of the 2nd edn of his poems) on 13 May 1787. In the High St. there is a statue of Mungo Park, the explorer and author of *Travels in the Interior of Africa* (1799), who was born at *Foulshiels. The museum has some relics of his expeditions to Sumatra and the Niger. Sir Walter Scott, who was Sheriff of Selkirkshire from 1800 until his death in 1832, is commemorated by a statue in the Market Place, outside the Court House, where he administered justice. Andrew Lang was born (1844) in a house now called Viewfield and attended the Grammar School before going to Edinburgh Academy.

Shotts *Lanarkshire*

Former mining town halfway between Edinburgh and Glasgow. George MacBeth was born at Hill Rd in 1932.

Skye *Highland*

Island off the W of Scotland reached by ferries from Mallaig and Kyle of Lochalsh.

Dr Johnson and Boswell both give accounts of their month's stay in 1773. They were entertained by the Macdonalds at Kingsburgh (rebuilt), when Flora Macdonald described her adventures during Prince Charles Edward's escape, and Johnson slept in the Prince's bed. Johnson and Boswell also stayed at Broadford with the Mackinnons at Coire Chatachan (now an outbuilding of the farm), which Johnson called Coriatachan and described as being 'very pleasantly situated between two brooks, with one of the highest hills of the island behind it'. Johnson was impressed with the hospitality given without payment on the island. He and Boswell also stayed 10 days at Dunvegan Castle, in the NW of the island, home of the Macleods, which dates back to the 14th c. (open to the public: www.dunvegancastle.com). They saw the drinking horn (still on view) of Rory More, the 16th chief, which Boswell said held 'a bottle and a half'.

The Gaelic poet William Ross (1762–90) was born at Broadford and educated at Forres, Morayshire. He later settled in *Gairloch.

Alexander Smith often spent holidays in Skye, his wife's home, after their marriage in 1857. His *A Summer in Skye* (1865) describes the locality with digressions on the associations it recalls. R. L. Stevenson wrote the song, popularly called 'The Skye Boat Song', published in *Songs of Travel* (1896) after his death.

Sorley MacLean went to school at the High School in Portree, returning to teach briefly in 1934. In 1970 he came back to Skye and lived at The Braes, in a house with a magnificent view over the Sound of Raasay:

> tha mi de dh'fhir mhór' a' Bhràighe,
> de Chloinn Mhic Ghille Chaluim threubhaich
>
> (I am of the big men of the Braes,
> of the heroic Raasay MacLeods).

His poetry is rooted in the island and in neighbouring *Raasay. The Cuillin mountains of Skye are the subject of his long unfinished poem *An Cuilithionn* ('The Cuillin'), which for Maclean were symbols of both destruction and desolation and the beauty and indomitable qualities of the human spirit. He drew a parallel between the islanders who suffered exile and poverty on Skye, particularly during the Highland Clearances of the mid-19th century, and the suffering of those caught up in the Spanish Civil War.

SLAINS CASTLE *Aberdeenshire*

Extensive ruins, off the A975, 8 m. S of Peterhead, of a house (built 1664) which replaced the earlier castle (site 4 m. S). Dr Johnson and Boswell mention staying here in 1773 with the Earl and Countess of Errol. They sat in the bow window looking out across the sea, and also made a visit to the Bullers of Buchan, a collapsed sea cave nearby.

SMA' GLEN *Perth and Kinross*

High valley between Crieff and Amulree on the A822, traditionally the burial place of Ossian, the 3rd-c. legendary bard. Wordsworth passed through the glen in 1803 and wrote:

> In this still place, remote from men
> Sleeps Ossian, in the Narrow Glen.

SMAILHOLM *Borders*

Village on the B6397, 6 m. NW of Kelso. Walter Scott came here at the age of 3 to stay at his grandfather's farm, Sandyknowe, to recuperate from an illness that left him permanently lame. Here he listened to tales of the Borders related by his grandmother and aunt, and here his lifelong attachment to the life and romance of the Border country was first formed. There is a Scott memorial window in the church.

To the SW stands Smailholm Tower, built in 1533 on a hilltop near a small loch and commanding splendid views. It appears in the third canto of Scott's *Marmion* and in 'The Eve of St. John'. The tower has been restored and is open all year (www.historic-scotland.gov.uk).

SOUTH QUEENSFERRY *Lothian*

Town at the S end of the Forth road bridge. Near the ferry jetty, formerly the main way across the Firth of Forth, is Hawes Inn, which Scott mentions in *The Antiquary* (1816), and where David Balfour's abduction is planned in Stevenson's *Kidnapped* (1886).

STIRLING *Stirlingshire*

Ancient burgh (now a city) on the Forth, on the A9 and the A811. The ludicrous attempt of John Damian, alchemist, physician, and favourite of James IV, to fly to France from the ramparts of Stirling Castle with the aid of wings made of chicken feathers was made the subject of two poems by William Dunbar, 'A Ballat of the Friar of Tungland' and 'Lucina Shyning in Silence of the Nycht', and one, written nearly five centuries later, by Edwin Morgan, 'At Stirling Castle, 1507'.

William Alexander (1567?–1640), the poet, built Argyll's Lodging (*c.* 1632) in Castle Wynd, an ornate house round a courtyard behind tall iron gates, after he became Secretary of State. It is now a museum. He wrote *Aurora* (1604) and *Recreations with the Muses* (1637), which include love lyrics, and a number of tragedies. He was a friend of Drummond of Hawthornden and was made Earl of Stirling in 1633. Burns, visiting the Highlands, stayed at James Wingate's inn in 1787, now the Golden Lion Hotel. His statue stands in Albert Place.

George Robert Gleig (1796–1888), novelist and biographer, was born at 81 Baker St. (site later part of a small public garden) and was educated at the Grammar School. Alexander Balloch Grosart (1827–99), who edited reprints of rare works, was born here. The Fife-born novelist Iain Banks was educated at Stirling University.

STRATHMORE *Perth and Kinross*

Valley stretching from Coupar Angus in the SW to Howe of the Mearns in the NE. Violet Jacob (née Erskine) wrote about this area in her dialect poems including *Songs of Angus* (1915)

and *The Northern Lights* (1927). She wrote about her family in *The Lairds of Dun* (1931), which gives an account of the House of Dun, her birthplace (4 m. W of Montrose), built in 1730 by Robert Adam. In 'The Lang Road' she describes the men absent in the war:

> Below the braes o' heather and far alang the glen,
> The road runs southward, southward, that grips
> the souls of men,
> There's mony a lad will ne'er come back amang
> his ain to lie
> An' its lang, lang, waitin' till the time gangs by.

STRATHYRE *Stirlingshire*

Small village on the A84, in the valley, with Strathyre Forest on the hills above, described by Sir Walter Scott in *The Lady of the Lake* (1810) and *A Legend of Montrose* (1819).

SWANSTON *Lothian*

Small village of tidy thatched cottages on the edge of the Pentlands, now within the city of Edinburgh, *c.* 6 m. S from the centre, and reached by Swanston Rd off Oxgangs Rd (B701), 1 m. W from Coniston Rd (A702). Swanston Cottage, now a private home, was the holiday home of R. L. Stevenson (1867–81; 'secluded Swanston, lapped in a fold of the Pentlands'). The village figures in his unfinished novel *St Ives* (New York, 1897; London, 1898; completed by Sir Arthur Quiller-Couch), and the Pentland moorland is associated with *Weir of Hermiston*, his unfinished masterpiece (1896).

On the slope of the village green is a seat in memory of the poet and critic Edwin Muir, given by his friends to mark the place where he liked to linger and meditate.

TANTALLON CASTLE *Lothian*

Massive red sandstone castle on a cliff promontory overlooking the sea, near the A198, 3 m. E of North Berwick. The castle, which dates from *c.* 1375, was a stronghold of the Douglases and features in Scott's *Marmion* (1808) and in Stevenson's *Catriona* (1893).

Tantallon Castle, Lothian, from the east. The 14th-century fortress features in Scott's *Marmion* and Stevenson's *Catriona*

The poet Gavin Douglas (c. 1474–1522), who became Bishop of Dunkeld in 1515, was a member of this family.

TARBERT *Argyll and Bute*

Small resort and fishing port at the head of East Loch Tarbert off the A83. John MacDougall Hay (1881–1919), novelist and minister, was born in Heatherknowe and educated at the local school before going to Glasgow University. Tarbert was the setting, which appears as 'Brieston', in his novel *Gillespie* (1914).

His son George Campbell Hay (1915–84) was brought up here after his father's death. He became a distinguished poet in Gaelic, Scots, and English, and a collection of his poems, *Wind on Loch Fyne* (1948), celebrates scenes associated with Tarbert. His best-known English poem, 'The Old Fisherman', with its plaintive refrain 'my dancing days for fishing are over', has been set to music by Francis George Scott. His finest poetry is in Gaelic, especially *Mochtàr is Dùghall* (Mokhtar and Dougall), a long poem published in 1982. After service during the Second World War in North Africa and the Middle East he suffered a breakdown in mental and physical health and became a semi-invalid. At the end of his life he returned to Tarbert, living for a while at Breaclarach before going to Edinburgh, where he died.

TARBOLTON *Ayrshire*

Village on the B730, 6 m. W of Mauchline, frequented by Robert Burns while living (1777–89) at *Lochlea and *Mossgiel. He joined in the social life of the village at the hall attached to an inn, now called the Bachelors' Club (NTS, open afternoons) from the literary and debating society of that name that he and his friends founded there in 1780. Burns joined the Freemasons, who also met at the hall, but after a dispute their two lodges, which had united, separated again and Burns and the St James's Lodge met at another inn, James Manson's (site nearby marked with a stone). He addressed a poem to this lodge. Dr Hornbook's house ('Death and Dr. Hornbook') is near the churchyard, and Willie's Mill ('Epitaph on William Muir') is at the E of the village. The opening lines of 'Highland Mary',

Ye banks and braes and streams around
The castle of Montgomery,

refer to the nearby Coilford House (burnt down 1960s) where Mary Campbell, who came from the Highlands, was a dairymaid when she first met Burns. He planned to emigrate to the West Indies with her but she died of typhus.

TAYNUILT *Argyll and Bute*

Coastal village on the river Nant. The poet Iain Crichton Smith lived and died at Tigh-na-Fuaran, where he spent perhaps the happiest years of his life, recording in his collection *The Village* (1989) local children building a snowman, washing on the line 'like paintings', or the cries of the market traders 'who have to live, don't they, | just like us'.

TAYPORT *Fife*

Town near Dundee at the NE tip of Fife. Tayport, the town that 'stumbles downhill to untidy mudflats', is the setting for Anne Stevenson's 1975 poem 'The Mudtower'.

TIBBIE SHIEL'S INN *Borders*

Old fishing inn (now a hotel) on the isthmus between St Mary's Loch and the Loch of Lowes, 100 yds from the A708 (Selkirk–Moffat road). It was run by Tibbie Richardson, better known as 'Shiel', from 1824, when she was widowed, until her death in 1878 in her 96th year. It owed its fame initially to Robert Chambers, who stayed there while collecting material about the Yarrow for his *Picture of Scotland* (1827), and wrote about the 'small, neat house, kept by a decent shepherd's widow, who lets her spare room . . . and can provide her lodgers with as wholesome and agreeable country fare as may anywhere be found'. The inn was a favourite haunt of James Hogg, 'the Ettrick Shepherd', whom John Wilson quotes in *Noctes Ambrosianae* as saying: 'A wren's nest round and theekit wi' moss—sae is Tibbie's', and it became famous as a meeting place for the literati of Edinburgh, such as Wilson, Scott, and De Quincey. Carlyle came as a student, tramping from Edinburgh to Ecclefechan, and R. L. Stevenson as a youth in 1867. The pleasant dining room has many mementoes and contemporary engravings, and Tibbie's visitors' book is a remarkable record of the number and character of her patrons. Across the road is a monument to Hogg, with his dog Hector—a fulfilment of his wish for a memorial in 'a quiet spot fornent Tibbie's dwelling'.

TILQUILLIE CASTLE *Aberdeenshire*

Country house off the A974, 2 m. SE of Banchory. Norman Douglas was born here in 1868. His reminiscences, *Looking Back* (1932), state that he spent little time on the estate after leaving to study in Karlsruhe (c. 1886). He lived in Capri when he left the Foreign Service, and wrote there his most successful novel, *South Wind* (1917).

TROSSACHS, THE *Stirlingshire*

The country between Loch Achray and Loch Katrine, so called from the Gaelic word meaning 'bristly', a wild area covered with oak, birch, and rowan trees, bog-myrtle, and heather. Dorothy Wordsworth, who thought the word meant 'many hills', records in her *Journals* (1897) how she and William pleased the boatman on Loch Katrine in 1803 by exclaiming at the grandeur of the scenery as he rowed, while Coleridge strode along the lakeside to keep warm. Wordsworth, who had difficulty in finding any shelter for the night, called the area 'Untouched, unbreathed upon' in his sonnet. Parts of Scott's poem *The Lady of the Lake* (1810), and his novel *Rob Roy* (1817), are set here. One of the islands in Loch Katrine is called *Ellen's Isle after Ellen Douglas, the heroine of *The Lady of the Lake*.

WALLYFORD *Lothian*

Village on the A6094, SE of Musselburgh. Margaret Oliphant Wilson was born (1828) here, though in her *Autobiography* (1899, reprinted 1974) she writes that she 'remembered nothing' about the place. However, she returned after her marriage in 1852 to her cousin Francis Oliphant, and she set the scene of her short story 'Isabel Dysart' here.

WHALSAY *Shetland*

Island off E coast of Mainland. Hugh MacDiarmid (Christopher Murray Grieve) lived here from 1933 to 1942 with his second wife, Valda, and their son Michael. They rented a cottage (now derelict), at Sodom overlooking the Linga Sound. In another cottage nearby (later an office) the poet wrote parts of the *Cornish Heroic Song for Valda Trevlyn* and his autobiography, *Lucky Poet* (1943).

YARROW WATER *Borders*

River that rises above *St Mary's Loch and flows through splendid scenery in the once wild and wooded Ettrick Forest to join the Tweed 3 m. NE of *Selkirk. It had a strong appeal for Wordsworth even before he saw it, and he celebrated it three times in poems. The first poem, 'Yarrow Unvisited', was written in the autumn of 1803 after he and Dorothy and Coleridge had made a six-week tour of Scotland, during which they met Scott at Lasswade and stayed in his company at Melrose later. They came near to the Yarrow but left without seeing it and the poem expresses the sensation of a delight to be treasured for later enjoyment. It is also closely associated with the Wordsworths' new-found friendship with Scott. The second poem, 'Yarrow Visited', was written in 1814 after Wordsworth's second tour of Scotland, this time with his wife, Mary, their son John (aged 11), and Mary's sister Sara. They met James Hogg, who became their guide, taking them to the source of the Yarrow and back by St Mary's Loch and Newark Castle. The third poem, 'Yarrow Revisited', was written in the autumn of 1831, a few days after Wordsworth's second visit to the Yarrow, when he and his daughter Dora were staying with Scott at *Abbotsford. Scott, now frail and ageing, accompanied Wordsworth to Newark Castle and, in spite of the sadness that this was almost certain to be their last meeting, Wordsworth recollected the occasion as a 'day of happy hours'.

Ireland

Ireland

ULSTER (INCLUDING NORTHERN IRELAND)

BALLINDERRY *Antrim*

The village of Lower Ballinderry is near the SE corner of Lough Neagh, on the B12 Lurgan–Glenavy road, and 1 m. WNW, by Lough Beg (or Portmore Lough), are the remains of Ballinderry First Church (or Portmore Church), where Jeremy Taylor used to preach to a small congregation before he became Bishop of Dromore. He had taken refuge from the Cromwellians in Lord Conway's house of Portmore, nearby, and it was here that he wrote (1659) the preface to *Ductor Dubitantium*, dedicated to Charles II. Sallow Island in the lough was one of his favourite retreats. Ballinderry Middle Church, 1½ m. E, was built (1666–8) for him at the end of his life and, thanks to 19th-c. restoration, contains well-preserved original church furniture.

BALLYSHANNON *Donegal*

Town on the N15, situated on the Erne where the estuary opens onto Donegal Bay. William Allingham, poet and editor (1874–9) of *Fraser's Magazine*, remembered especially for 'Up the airy mountain, | Down the rushy glen' (see KILLYBEGS) and 'Four ducks on a pond', was born here when his father was a busy merchant and shipowner. He describes his birthplace ℗, in the Mall, as 'a little house, the most westerly of a row of three, in a street running down to the harbour'. He went to Wray's School, Church Lane, and then to boarding school in 1837 at Killieshandra, Cavan, until he was 14, when he began working at the Provincial Bank, where his father had become manager. A commemorative bust by Vincent Breen was unveiled outside the bank (later the Allied Irish Bank) in 1971. He left in 1846 to train as a customs officer and had various appointments in Ireland and England before leaving the service in 1870. He died in London and his ashes were brought to Ballyshannon for burial in the Church of Ireland cemetery. The bridge, named after him, has a memorial tablet.

BELFAST *Antrim*

Capital of N Ireland (since 1921), seaport, shipbuilding, industrial, and university city, situated on the Lagan, at the head of Belfast Lough. Its literary connections are mainly with those writers who were born here, but there is a dearth of monuments or places of pilgrimage. The earliest writer of interest was Dr William Drennan (1754–1820), a poet and the first president of the United Irishmen, as well as a founder of the Belfast Academical Institution. He was a native of Belfast, the son of a minister of the First Presbyterian church, Rosemary St., and is remembered as the first to call Ireland 'the Emerald Isle', in a poem of 1795. A collection of his verse and prose, *Fugitive Pieces*, was published in 1815. A memorial inscription above his grave can be seen in the Clifton St. cemetery (the New Burying Ground (1797) of the Belfast Charitable Society), on the N edge of the city centre.

Robert Anderson (1770–1833), a poet from Carlisle, came to Belfast in 1808 to work as a pattern drawer in Brookfield, near the grange of Doagh, on the Islekelly, a little N of Belfast. After two years he went to the Carnmoney (later Mossley) Cotton Printing Works, where he worked until the death of his employer, David Bigger, in 1818. He lived with Thomas and Andrew Stewart, at Springtown, in the townland of Ballyyearl, and during this time wrote a number of verses, of which many appeared in the *Belfast News-Letter* and *Commercial Chronicle*, as well as in a collection of *Poems on Various Subjects* (Belfast, 1810).

The poet and antiquary Sir Samuel Ferguson (1810–86) was born at 23 High St. (site later occupied by a restaurant), but later moved to Dublin.

When Anthony Trollope was working for the Post Office in Ireland he was promoted to the position of surveyor in 1853 and sent to Belfast for 18 months to take postal charge of the northern counties. He and his family took lodgings in Belfast (possibly in Lisburn Rd) for a while and then moved to Whiteabbey, a suburban coastal town N of the city, where he completed *The Warden* (1855), the first of the Barsetshire novels and the first of his novels to meet with success.

Canon J. O. Hannay ('George A. Birmingham') (1865–1950) was born at 75 University Rd ℗, now owned by Queen's University.

Forrest Reid (1875–1947) was born at 20 Montcharles and was educated at the Royal Belfast Academical Institution. He lived at 13 Ormiston Cres. ℗ from 1924 to the end of his life. C. S. Lewis (1898–1963), was born at 47 Dundela Ave. (now replaced by a block of flats), and recounts in his autobiography, *Surprised by Joy* (1955), that he and his elder brother grew up in a semi-detached villa where they wrote and illustrated stories of 'Animal-Land'. In 1905 they moved to a new house, 54 (now 76) Circular Rd, on the outskirts of the city, which 'looked down over wide fields to Belfast Lough and across it to the long mountain line of the Antrim shore'. Louis MacNeice

(1907–63) and W. R. Rodgers (1909–69) were also natives of Belfast.

Between finishing at Trinity College Dublin and leaving for Paris the following year, Samuel Beckett spent an unhappy six months in 1928 teaching at Campbell College.

In 1950 Philip Larkin came to work as the sub-librarian at Queen's University. His poetic career took off in Belfast, and many of his best-known poems were written in the city, including 'Lines on a Young Lady's Photograph Album', 'Church Going', and 'Toads':

> Why should I let the toad *work*
> Squat on my life
> Can't I use my wit as a pitchfork
> And drive the brute off?

Michael Longley was brought up in the Malone district of Belfast and, like his fellow poet Derek Mahon, attended the Royal Belfast Academical Institution in the 1950s. In the mid-1960s Longley and Seamus Heaney encountered other young poets at meetings of the Belfast Group, a poets' workshop held at the home of the academic Philip Hobsbaum at 4 Fitzwilliam Street. After studying at Trinity College Dublin, Longley returned to Belfast to teach for a period at his old school, Mahon to teach at Belfast High School. The novelist and short-story writer Bernard MacLaverty was born in Belfast in 1942, and read English at Queen's University; much of his work would deal with sectarian violence in Ulster. The experience of growing up in Belfast in the late 1960s is brought to life in his *The Anatomy School* (2001).

Like MacLaverty, the poet Ciaran Carson was born in Belfast (in 1948) and educated at Queen's University, and his poems chronicle life in the city; his collection *Belfast Confetti* (1989) celebrates in poetry and prose the city where he still lives, beginning with the poem 'Turn Again': 'There is a map of the city which shows the bridge that was never built. | A map which shows the bridge that collapsed; the streets that never existed . . .'. In 2003 Carson was appointed Director of the Seamus Heaney Centre for Poetry, based at Queen's. Heaney himself spent time at Queen's both as a student and as a lecturer, where his students included the English student and promising young poet Paul Muldoon.

The poet and critic Tom Paulin was brought up in Belfast too (though born over the water in *Leeds), where his father was a grammar school headmaster; many of his poems would touch on Ulster politics and violence.

> Its retributions work like clockwork.
> Along murdering miles of terrace-houses
> Where someone is saying, 'I am angry,

I am frightened, I am justified.
Every favour, I must repay with interest,
Any slight against myself, the least slip,
Must be balanced out by an exact revenge.

('Under the Eyes')

The playwright Brian Friel trained at the St Joseph's Teaching College in Belfast, and spent a decade (1950–60) working as a teacher before embarking on his writing career.

BUNCRANA *Donegal*

Largest town in Inishowen, 7 m. from the city of Derry. The playwright Frank McGuinness was born here in 1953, and spent his childhood close to the Donegal–Londonderry border.

CARRICKFERGUS *Antrim*

Small port and market town of great antiquity on the A2, 12 m. NE of Belfast on the N shore of Belfast Lough, renowned for its magnificent castle. William Congreve came to live here when he was 8, when his father, who had been stationed as an infantry lieutenant at Youghal, was transferred to the garrison at Carrickfergus for three years (1678–81). At that time it was a busy port, 'filled with English sailors, rough and jovial fellows', remembrance of whom may have accounted for the character of Sailor Ben, the 'absolute Sea-Wit' of *Love for Love* (1695). Louis MacNeice spent his childhood here at his father's rectory, as he relates in his unfinished autobiography, *The Strings Are False* (1965). Aspects of MacNeice's childhood were adopted for the character of Victor Maskell, the narrator of John Banville's novel *The Untouchable* (1997), where the town is named 'Carrickdrum'.

CARROWDORE *Down*

Small village on the Ards peninsula. Louis MacNeice is buried in the churchyard. His premature death was a blow to, among others, a younger generation of poets born in Northern Ireland: Seamus Heaney, Michael Longley, and Derek Mahon. After a visit to the grave, all three wrote elegies to MacNeice. When they were next together, as Michael Longley has recorded:

Mahon took from his pocket 'In Carrowdore Churchyard' and read it aloud. Heaney started to recite his poem, then crumpled it up. I wisely decided then and there not to make the attempt. Mahon had produced the definitive elegy.

CASTLEDAWSON *Londonderry*

Village 4 m. from the NW shore of Lough Neagh. Seamus Heaney was born in the family farmhouse outside Castledawson in 1939, and brought up nearby at Newbridge (attending Anahorish Primary School) and Bellaghy. His poems about the area would include 'Mossbawn' (the name of the farm where he was born), 'A Lough Neagh Sequence', and 'Anahorish':

My 'place of clear water',
the first hill in the world
where springs washed into
the shiny grass

and darkened cobbles
in the bed of the lane.

CASTLEDERG *Tyrone*

Small woollen-manufacturing town on the B72, 12 m. SW of Strabane, on the Derg. After her marriage in 1850 Mrs Cecil Frances Alexander lived at Derg Lodge in the remote parish of Trienamongan (or Termonamongan), 6 m. W. In 1853 she published *Narrative Hymns for Village Schools*, which included the well-known 'Jesus calls us; o'er the tumult'.

CLANDEBOYE *Down*

Seat of the Marquess of Dufferin and Ava, just S of the A2 Belfast–Bangor road and 1 m. S of Crawfordsburn. At the S end of the demesne is Helen's Tower, erected (1861) by the 1st Marquess in memory of his mother, Helen, Lady Dufferin. The top storey contains verses by Lady Dufferin to her son on his coming of age, inscribed in gold, and lower down are plaques with verses by Tennyson, Browning, and Kipling. Lady Dufferin is remembered by her poem 'The Lament of the Irish Immigrant', published with her songs in 1894. The stile referred to in the poem is at Killyleagh graveyard on Strangford Lough, *c.* 30 m. S.

CLOGHER *Tyrone*

Village on the A4, at the head of the Clogher Valley. Thomas Parnell (1679–1718), poet and scholar, was archdeacon of the Cathedral (rebuilt in 1818) from 1706 to 1716. He was a friend of Swift and of Pope (to whose *Iliad* he contributed an introductory essay) and author of 'The Night Piece on Death', 'The Hymn to Contentment', and 'The Hermit', published in *Poems on Several Occasions* (ed. Pope, 1722). His lines in 'Elegy to an Old Beauty' have become proverbial:

And all that's madly wild, or oddly gay
We call it only Pretty Fanny's way.

CLONES *Monahan*

Small town in the Irish border country. The novelist Patrick McCabe was born here in 1955, and the unnamed small-town setting of his novel *Butcher Boy* (1992) may be inspired by his birthplace.

DESERTMARTIN *Londonderry*

Village between Draperstown and Magherafelt, the subject of a poem by Tom Paulin:

At noon, in the dead centre of a faith,
Between Draperstown and Magherafelt,
This bitter village shows the flag
In a baked absolute September light.
Here the Word has withered to a few
Parched certainties, and the charred stubble
Tightens like a black belt, a crop of Bibles.

DONAGHMORE *Tyrone*

Village on the B43, 3 m. NW of Dungannon. The Revd Charles Wolfe was rector here (1818–21), but resigned on account of ill health. He is remembered for his poem 'The Burial of Sir John Moore', published anonymously in the *Newry Telegraph* (1817) and immediately acclaimed. It was attributed to Byron, among others, before its authorship was known.

DONEGORE *Antrim*

Hamlet 3 m. E of Antrim on the N side of the B95. Sir Samuel Ferguson (1810–86), poet and antiquary, is buried in the old churchyard, once the site of an ancient ecclesiastical settlement.

DROMORE *Down*

Cathedral and market town on the A1 and the B2. Jeremy Taylor (1613–67), appointed Bishop of Down and Connor in 1660, received the further See of Dromore in 1661 and built the core of the present cathedral, to replace the medieval cathedral burnt down in 1641. He was buried in a vault beneath the altar. Thomas Percy, editor of *Reliques of Ancient English Poetry* (1765), was bishop from 1782 until his death in 1811 and carried out a major restoration and enlargement of the cathedral in 1808. He is buried in the transept.

DUNGIVEN *Londonderry*

Village on the A6, 10 m. S of Limavady. John Mitchel (1815–75), nationalist, journalist, and author, was born at Camnish, nearby, where his father was Unitarian minister.

ENNISKILLEN *Fermanagh*

County town, on the A4 and the A46, situated on an island in the Erne, between Upper and Lower Lough Erne. Portora Royal School, 1 m. NW, is an 18th-c. building incorporating the school founded by James I in 1608. Among its pupils were Henry Francis Lyte, Oscar Wilde, and Samuel Beckett, who was better known as a rugby player, swimmer, and cricketer than a scholar.

GLENGORMLEY *Antrim*

A town once near, now absorbed by, Belfast. The poet Derek Mahon was brought up here and the funeral of his uncle, 'buried on a blustery day above the sea' at nearby Carnmoney churchyard, is recorded in 'My Wicked Uncle'. The suburb's 'terrier-taming, garden-watering' qualities are described in his early poem 'Glengormley'.

GLENTIES *Donegal*

Small town near the NW Irish coast, NW of the Blue Stack Mountains. the playwright Brian Friel lives nearby, and it has been suggested that this town is the model for the village of Ballybeg (Baile Beag), in which much of his work is set. In *Translations* (1980), a company of Royal Engineers arrive in this Irish-speaking community and need the Gaelic place names rendered into English; and in *Dancing at Lughnasa* (1990) the Ballybeg home of the Mundy sisters is the backdrop for the Lughnasa Festival (marking the harvesting weeks); *Dancing at Lughnasa* was filmed in 1998.

INNISKEEN *Monaghan*

Village on a minor road off the N53. The poet Patrick Kavanagh was born here (1904) in the townland of Mucker, the son of a cobbler and farmer. After a minimal education he was expected to follow these occupations, but he showed no aptitude for either, preferring to write poetry in the attic. After publishing his first book, *Ploughman and Other Poems* (1936), he left home for good, to make his way as a freelance journalist and poet. He died in 1967 and was buried at Inniskeen.

KILLYBEGS *Donegal*

Fishing port on an inlet of Donegal Bay, on the R263. It was here in January 1849, while on Customs duty, that William Allingham wrote 'The Fairies':

> Up the airy mountain,
> Down the rushy glen,
> We daren't go a-hunting,
> For fear of little men.

KILROOT *Antrim*

Village near the coast, *c.* 3 m. NE of Carrickfergus, just off the A2. Jonathan Swift had his first living here after his ordination in 1695 and stayed until 1696. His home, where he wrote *A Tale of a Tub* (1704), was demolished after a fire in 1959 and the church is now ruined.

LISBURN *Antrim*

Cathedral and manufacturing city on the Lagan, 8 m. SW of Belfast, on the M1. In Christ Church, cathedral (CI) of the diocese of Connor, there is a memorial to Jeremy Taylor, Bishop of Down and Connor (1661–7), who spent the last six years of his life here.

LONDONDERRY (or DERRY) *Londonderry*

Historic port, naval base, and garrison town on the W bank of the Foyle, at the junction of the A2, A5, and A6. George Farquhar was born (1678) in Shipquay St. and attended the Free School (founded 1617, and succeeded by Foyle College in 1814), formerly situated not far from Magee University College in Northland Rd. George Berkeley was appointed Dean of the Protestant cathedral (founded 1633) in 1724, but left for America with plans for founding a missionary college in Bermuda (1728–32), which he had to abandon for want of support. Mrs Cecil Frances Alexander, author of 'All things bright and beautiful' and other hymns, came here in 1867 when her husband became bishop. She died at the palace in 1895 and is buried in the city cemetery. Joyce Cary (1888–1957), the novelist, was a native of Londonderry.

Seamus Deane attended St Columb's College on Buncrana Rd, Derry. His novel *Reading in the Dark* (1997) is set in the city, and centres on the burnt-out distillery near the Bogside:

> To reach the ruins of the distillery, we had only to cross Blucher Street, go along Eglinton Terrace, across the mouth of the Bogside, with the city abattoir on our left . . . There, vast and red-bricked, blackened and gaunt, was the distillery, taking up a whole block of territory. The black stumps of its roof-timbers poked into the sky.

Seamus Deane was one of the directors, with Seamus Heaney, Tom Paulin, David

Hammond, and, later, Thomas Kilroy, of Field Day, the theatre company founded by Brian Friel and Stephen Rea in 1980 to provide an artistic response to the politics and violence of Northern Ireland. Performances took place in the Guildhall.

In 1994 Colm Tóibín published *Bad Blood*, his account of a walk he took along the Irish border, the tense strip of land running between Derry and Newry, and the people he met—on both side of the border, and both sides of the conflict—along the way. He begins in Derry, walking out towards the border

> on a beautiful, cloudless afternoon, past the broken-down public houses, past the abandoned shirt factory and the new housing estates and the sailing boats on the Foyle. It was Saturday. I was wearing a rucksack. When I crossed the border I would turn right and take the road to Lifford. In half an hour I would be in the Republic of Ireland . . .

LOUGH DERG *Donegal*

Station Island in the middle of Lough Derg is a place of pilgrimage that provides the chief setting for Sean O'Faolain's story 'Lovers of the Lake' and lends its name to a long poem (and a collection of poetry) by Seamus Heaney.

LURGAN *Armagh*

Town on the A3 and the A26, 3 m. NE of Craigavon. George William Russell (1867–1935), poet and artist, familiarly known as 'Æ', was born in William St. and was educated in the town until he was *c.* 10, when he moved to Dublin with his family.

MARKETHILL *Armagh*

Little market town on the A28, 7 m. SE of Armagh. Gosford Castle, 1 m. N, a 19th-c. Norman-style mansion, is near the site of the former Manor House where Dean Swift used to visit Sir Arthur Acheson, Bt (later Earl of Gosford), after Stella's death. His 'walk', 'chair', and 'well' are still pointed out in the Demesne.

In 1940 Anthony Powell was sent on detachment to the Divisional Tactical School at the castle, an experience reflected in *The Valley of Bones*, one of the wartime novels of his sequence *A Dance to the Music of Time* (1951–74).

MOY *Tyrone*

Village on the Blackwater river. The poet Paul Muldoon grew up nearby, and the landscape around Moy would recur in much of his early, more rural work, as well as in his 2002 collection *Moy Sand and Gravel*.

MULLAGH *Cavan*

Village at the junction of the R191 and R194, *c.* 5½ m. SE of Virginia. Rantavan House, *c.* 1 m. SW, is the birthplace of Henry Brooke (1703–83). In 1774 he retired to a summerhouse (later a stable) he had erected at Corfad (or Longfield) in Mullagh parish. He died in Dublin and was buried beside the ruined church of Teampull Ceallaigh near Mullagh (his grave is unmarked).

NEWRY *Down*

Seaport and manufacturing city at the head of Carlingford Lough on the A2. John Mitchel, leader of the Young Ireland movement and editor of *The Nation*, whose *Jail Journal, or, Five Years in British Prisons* (1856) gives an account of his transportation for sedition, is buried in the Unitarian (First Presbyterian) churchyard, Old Meetinghouse Green, High St.

OMAGH *Tyrone*

County town of Co. Tyrone, 16 m. E of the Irish border. The playwright Brian Friel was born here in 1929; brought up a Catholic outsider in a Protestant region, many of Friel's plays would deal with the clash of cultures and faiths.

PORTADOWN *Armagh*

Town on the river Bann, where poet Paul Muldoon was born in 1951.

PORTRUSH *Antrim*

Small coastal town on the Ramore Head peninsula. Derek Mahon has evoked the town and its coast in 'The Chinese Restaurant in Portrush' and 'North Wind: Portrush':

> The shops open at nine
> As they have always done,
> The wrapped-up bourgeoisie
> Hardened by wind and sea;
> The newspapers are late
> But the milk shines in its crate.

PORTSTEWART *Londonderry*

Pleasantly situated little seaside resort on the A2, 3 m. W of Portrush. Charles Lever, the novelist, was employed here in 1832 as a dispensary doctor when a young married man, and rented a small house called Verandah Cottage. He soon became popular and his lively temperament and unconventional ways earned him the nickname of 'Dr Quicksilver'. While he was here he began contributing to the *Dublin University Magazine*, which he later edited, his novel *Harry Lorrequer* first appearing there in instalments beginning in 1837. He left for an appointment in Brussels in May 1837.

PROLUSK (or PRILLISK) *Tyrone*

Hamlet 2 m. NW of Clogher (on the A4). The novelist and folklorist William Carleton was born here, the youngest of a peasant family of 14, and grew up in the district. He is remembered especially for his short stories, based on his own experiences and sympathies, which were collected under the title *Traits and Stories of the Irish Peasantry* (1830, 2nd ser. 1833), and for the novel *Fardorougha the Miser* (1837).

RATHLIN *Antrim*

Island 6 m. from the mainland and the most northerly inhabited island off the coast of Northern Ireland. Derek Mahon's poem 'Rathlin' touches on the island's famous population of seabirds, its infamous massacre of 1575, and one of its lighthouses:

> But here they are through with history—
> Custodians of a lone light which repeats
> One simple statement to the turbulent sea.

SPRINGHILL *Londonderry*

Manor house (NT.) 1 m. SE of Moneymore, a Plantation town on the A29, 5 m. NE of Cookstown. The house was built in the latter half of the 17th c., with later additions, and is an example of the fortified manor house built by the settlers in Ulster. Formerly the home of the Lenox Conynghams, it was bequeathed to the National Trust in 1957. The library contained early editions of Gerard's *Herball* (1597), Ralegh's *History of the World* (1614), and Hobbes's *Leviathan* (1651).

STRABANE *Tyrone*

Border town on the A5, situated on the Mourne near where it unites with the Finn to become the Foyle. Mrs Cecil Frances Alexander (née Humphreys) lived at Milltown House (now the main building of the Grammar School) from 1833 until her marriage in 1850. She published her *Hymns for Little Children* (1848) here, which includes 'All things bright and beautiful', 'There is a green hill far away', and 'Once in Royal David's city'. In 1860 she came to live at Camus Rectory, 3 m. S, when her husband, the Revd William Alexander, became rector. While she was here she edited *The Sunday Book of Poetry* (1864), a selection of poems by various authors, for the *Golden Treasury Series*. In 1867 she moved to Londonderry when her husband became bishop.

The novelist and comic journalist Brian O'Nolan ('Flann O'Brien') was born at 15 Bowling Green on 5 October 1911. The Brian O'Nolan housing estate honours his association with the town.

UPPER FAHAN *Donegal*

Parish, part of the little resort of Fahan on the E shore of Lough Swilley, 7 m. NW of Londonderry. Mrs Cecil Frances Alexander, hymn writer remembered especially for 'All things bright and beautiful', 'There is a green hill far away', and 'Once in royal David's city', lived here from 1855 to 1860, when her husband, the Revd William Alexander, was rector. The church has a chancel in her memory.

VIRGINIA *Cavan*

Pleasant little market town on the N3, on the N shore of Lake Ramor. Quilca House, *c.* 1 m. NE, was once the home of the Revd Thomas Sheridan, a friend of Jonathan Swift, who spent many summers here as his guest. Swift wrote the greater part of *Gulliver's Travels* here, and it is said that his Brobdingnagian farmer was modelled on a Mr Doughty, a local man of unusually large proportions. A landmark nearby is known as Stella's Bower. Richard Brinsley Sheridan, the grandson of Thomas, spent the greater part of his youth at the family home at Quilca.

CONNACHT

ACHILL *Mayo*

Island off the west coast of Ireland and Ireland's largest island. The German novelist Heinrich Böll visited the island in the 1950s and 1960s, and wrote his entertaining *Irish Journal* (1957) here. He later returned with his wife and bought a cottage in Dugort (now an artists' retreat). Graham Greene also stayed on the island in the late 1940s with his mistress Catherine Walston. He relished its remoteness and wrote much of *The Heart of the Matter* (1948) and the beginning of *The End of the Affair* (1951) here. Derek Mahon evokes the island, 'thrush and plover, | Wild thyme and sea-thrift', in his poem 'Achill'.

ARAN ISLANDS *Galway*

Three islands, Inishmore (Great Island), Inishmaan (Middle Island), and Inisheer (Eastern Island), lying NW–SE across the mouth of Galway Bay, *c.* 30 m. from Galway. They are rich in archaeological remains from pre-Christian, early Christian, and medieval times. Although communication with the mainland is easier than it used to be, much of the traditional way of life continues and its inhabitants still speak Irish as well as English. J. M. Synge came here in 1898 at the suggestion of W. B. Yeats and returned for several weeks at a time each summer or autumn until 1902. He used to live in a cottage on Inishmaan, with a family named MacDonagh, whose son Martin helped to teach him Irish. The account of his life there and the stories of islanders who became his friends were published in *The Aran Islands*, with illustrations by Jack B. Yeats, in 1907. Synge regarded the book as his first serious piece of work. 'In writing out the talk of the people and their stories', he said, 'I learned to write the peasant dialect and dialogue which I use in my plays . . . *The Aran Islands* throws a good deal of light on my plays.' His play *Riders to the Sea* (1905) is set in Inishmaan.

Liam O'Flaherty was born at Gort na gCapell in 1896 and went to Oatquarter School. The islands are evoked in his novel *Skerrett* (1932), in which Skerrett, a domineering teacher from the mainland, comes to work on the isle of 'Nara'. After a visit here, Michael Longley in his poem 'Leaving Inishmore' writes of an 'island awash in wave and anthem'.

The islands can be reached from Galway by the motor vessels *Naomh Eanna* and *Galway Bay*, daily in the height of the season and on a more limited schedule in the off-season. There are also daily sailings from Rossaveal, 23 m. W of Galway (can be reached by minibus).There are also daily flights by Aer Arann from Galway.

BALLINA *Mayo*

The largest town in Co. Mayo. The river Moy, which flows through the town, features in Paul Durcan's poem 'Ballina, Co. Mayo', where 'in summertime young men and old men | Stand on the bridge watching the waters flow under them, under the arches'.

BALLINAMORE *Leitrim*

As a young child the novelist John McGahern lived in a bungalow beside a forge, a mile outside Ballinamore.

CARRIGSKEEWAUN *Mayo*

Townland near Kilgeever. The landscape here is closely associated with the poet Michael Longley, and he has written many poems about its plants and wildlife:

> Home is a hollow between the waves,
> A clump of nettles, feathery winds,
> And memory no longer than a day
> When the animals come back to me
> From the townland of Carrigskeewaun,
> From a page lit by the Milky Way.

('Remembering Carrigskeewaun')

The focus of Longley's Co. Mayo poems may be the natural world, but the poet, who was brought up in *Belfast, has described them as also among his most political: 'I want the light from Carrigskeewaun to irradiate the northern darkness.'

'An Islander of Inishmaan', a photograph by J. M. Synge of Martin MacDonagh

CLONFERT *Galway*

Ancient ecclesiastical settlement 5 m. NW of Banagher, off the R356. St Brendan the Navigator (484–577) founded a monastery here in 558–64, destroyed and rebuilt several times since, and finally transformed into an Augustinian priory. St Brendan's roving life gave rise to many legends in medieval literature, based on the *Navigatio Sancti Brendani*, of which *The Voyage of St Brendan* is a versified Anglo-Norman form. He is buried at Clonfert, and the partly ruined Protestant cathedral, renowned for its magnificent Romanesque W door, is named after him. In 1771 Richard Cumberland, son of the Bishop of Clonfert, stayed at the palace (burnt down in the 20th c.) while he was writing *The West Indian*, a sentimental comedy produced at Covent Garden the same year, which had a long and outstandingly successful run.

COLLOONEY *Sligo*

Village on the N4, 7 m. S of Sligo, at the junction of the Owenmore and the Unshin. Yeats's 'Ballad of Father O'Hart' (published in *Crossways*, 1889) commemorates Father John, the 'old priest of Collooney', who died in 1793, whose story he learnt from Father O'Rorke of nearby Ballysadare and Kilvarnet.

COOLE PARK *Galway*

The woods and lake of Coole lie 22 m. NW of Gort, off the N18. The house, where Lady Gregory lived from the time of her marriage in 1880 until her death in 1932, was pulled down in 1941 and only the garden walls and ruins of the stable block are left. The grounds are in the care of the National Parks and Wildlife Service, and the Autograph Tree, a copper beech inscribed with the initials of distinguished visitors, including those of Bernard Shaw and W. B. Yeats, still stands beside a box-hedged walk in the garden. In *Coole* (MS, 1931; ed. C. Smythe, 1971), Lady Gregory describes the house in detail, especially the drawing room, where she wrote plays, journals, articles, and folk tales, and typed to Yeats's dictation, and where she kept her letters from writers and artists. She tells how Shaw used to play the piano and sing little folk songs, and how Masefield stayed for a while, 'a shy devotee of

Yeats, a maker of ballads of the sea'; but, most of all, the writer connected with Coole is Yeats, who came first in 1898 and was nursed back to health from sickness, making it his home for many years and working in a room looking towards the lake, a time remembered in his poem 'The Wild Swans at Coole' (1919). In 'Coole Park, 1929' Yeats anticipates the passing of the house and its owner:

> I meditate upon a swallow's flight,
> Upon an aged woman and her house . . .
>
> Here, traveller, scholar, poet, take your stand
> When all those rooms and passages are gone,
> When nettles wave upon a shapeless mound
> And saplings root among the broken stone,
> And dedicate—eyes bent upon the ground,
> Back turned upon the brightness of the sun
> And all the sensuality of the shade—
> A moment's memory to that laurelled head.

COOTEHALL *Roscommon*

Village on the Shannon, just to the Roscommon side of the Roscommon–Leitrim line, close to Leitrim village. The novelist John McGahern's father was a sergeant at the Cootehall barracks, so as he grew up young John would spent his summer holidays here. Some of his experiences would feed into his 1962 novel *The Barracks*; writing in his *Memoir* (2005) McGahern would explain that

> The setting and the rituals of barrack life are replicated in the novel, but the characters are all imagined. The sergeant in the novel bears hardly any resemblance to my father. He is relatively uncomplicated and far more attractive.

DRUMCLIFF *Sligo*

Hamlet on the N15, at the head of Drumcliff Bay, SW of Ben Bulben and 4 m. N of Sligo. W. B. Yeats is buried in the graveyard of the Protestant church where his grandfather was rector (1811–46), in the heart of the countryside he loved so much. He died in France on 28 January 1939, but in 1948 his remains were brought back and buried, as he had wished, 'under bare Ben Bulben's head'. His epitaph is from 'Under Ben Bulben', written at the very end of his life:

> Cast a cold Eye
> On Life, on Death.
> Horseman, pass by!

4 m. NE a minor road leads to Lissadell House on the N side of Drumcliff Bay. This has been the home of the Gore-Booths since 1834 and was the birthplace of the Arctic explorer Sir Henry Gore-Booth (1843–1900) and of his daughters Eva (1870–1926), a poet, and Constance (1884–1927), who as Countess Markievicz took an active part in the Easter rising, 1916. W. B. Yeats visited them in 1894 and long afterwards wrote about their beauty and aspirations:

> The light of evening, Lissadell,
> Great windows open to the south,
> Two girls in silk kimonos, both
> Beautiful, one a gazelle.

Part of the Autograph Tree at Coole Park, Galway, on which Lady Gregory's guests carved their initials. Those of Bernard Shaw, W. B. Yeats, and Sean O'Casey can clearly be seen

The house is open to the public (www.lissadellhouse.com).

DURRAS HOUSE *Galway*

House, now a Youth Hostel Ⓟ, on the W side of Kinvarra Bay, off the N67, 2 m. NW of Kinvarra. At the end of the 19th c. it was the property of Count Florimond de Basterot (1836–1904), a friend of W. B. Yeats and Lady Gregory, who joined him and his cousin Edward Martyn here in talks which first broached the idea of a national theatre.

ELPHIN *Roscommon*

Small town on the R368, 9 m. SW of Carrick-on-Shannon. Oliver Goldsmith's maternal grandmother lived at Ardnagowan nearby, the finest house in the district except for the Bishop's Palace, and it was here that he may have been born (10 Nov. 1730?) (though other accounts of his birth maintain that his mother was at *Pallas at that time). At 8 years old he attended the Diocesan School under the Revd Michael Griffin for a short while, staying with his uncle John at Ballyoughter, near Ardnagowan, before being transferred to another school, at Athlone.

FRENCHPARK *Roscommon*

Hamlet on the N5 and R361, 9 m. NE of Castlerea. Douglas Hyde, poet and Gaelic scholar and one of the founders of the Abbey Theatre, was born (1860) at the rectory. After an academic life in Dublin he retired from his professorship of Modern Irish at University College and came to live at Ratra House, which had been bought for him by public subscription, but he was recalled to Dublin to become first President of the Republic of Ireland (1938–45). He is buried in Frenchpark churchyard.

GALWAY *Galway*

Cathedral and university town, situated at the NE corner of Galway Bay, at the end of the N6 and several other main roads. Frank Harris (1856–1931), journalist, biographer, and miscellaneous writer, was born in Galway of Welsh parentage, but after being educated at the Royal School, Armagh, ran away to America at the age of 16 and became a cowboy. Later he went to London (*c.* 1883) and began his journalistic career on the *Evening News*. Another native of the city, Pádraig Ó Conaire (1882–1928), writer in Irish of essays and short stories, is commemorated in Eyre Sq. by a statue by Albert Power, which shows him seated informally in a setting of rocks and plants.

The modern cathedral, on the W bank of the Corrib, was built on the site of the old county gaol where Wilfrid Scawen Blunt was imprisoned in 1887 for organizing a mass protest meeting of the oppressed tenants on the notorious Clanricarde estates (near Portumna). He described his experiences in *In Vinculis* (1889).

The dramatist and novelist Walter Macken was born in Galway in 1916. His greatest success came with his historical trilogy *Seek the Fair Land* (1959), *The Silent People* (1962), and *The Scorching Wind* (1964). Many of his plays had long runs at the Abbey Theatre, where he also worked as an actor. He died suddenly at his home in Menlo, Galway, in 1967.

Niall Williams's novel *Four Letters of Love* (1997) is set in part in and around the city.

GORT *Galway*

Market town in the plain, on the N18, 15 m. SW of Loughrea. On a minor road a few miles NE, signposted from the N66, is Thoor Ballylee, the 16th-c. castle keep beside a river bridge, formerly the property of Lady Gregory of Coole, which Yeats bought for £35 in 1917, soon after his marriage, and restored as a summer home. It was here that he wrote the *Tower* poems (1928) and the *Winding Stair* poems (1933). On the wall are inscribed his lines:

> I, the poet William Yeats,
> With old mill-boards and sea-green slates,
> And smithy work from the Gort forge,
> Restored this tower for my wife George;
> And may these characters remain
> When all is ruin once again.

After his death the tower did in fact become ruinous, but has since been repaired by Bord Failte Eireann and was opened by Padraic Colum in 1965 as a Yeats museum (www.gortonline.com). Near the castle was the home of Mary Hynes, the miller's daughter loved by Blind Raftery, whom Yeats speaks of in 'The Tower'.

P. J. Kavanagh wrote 'with a tinker's coal | My small and grateful name' in his poem recording a visit to Gort, 'Yeats' Tower'.

INNISFREE *Sligo*

Small island near the SE shore of Lough Gill, the beautiful 5-m.-long lake SE of Sligo. The island, immortalized in Yeats's 'The Lake Isle of Innisfree', can be reached by boat from the shore, at the end of a narrow lane leading N from the R286, 2 m. W of the little town of Dromahair. Further W, near the SW end of the lake, where the main road runs by the shore, is Dooney Rock, also celebrated by Yeats, in 'The Fiddler of Dooney', which commands a splendid view of Lough Gill and its many islands.

KILLEENEN *Galway*

Hamlet 4 m. W of Craughwell, off the N6 (Galway–Loughrea road). In the neglected cemetery is the grave of Antoine Ó Reachtabhra (1784–1834), the poet known as 'Blind Raftery'.

KNOCKNAREA *Sligo*

Mountain (1,078 ft high), 6 m. W of Sligo, crowned by Miosgán Meva (NM), traditionally the tomb of Queen Maeve, a passage-grave-type cairn 200 ft in diameter and 34 ft high, Yeats's 'cairn-heaped grassy hill | Where passionate Maeve is stony-still'. On the S side is Knocknarea Glen, a deep wooded ravine ⅔ m. long. The mountain and many of the surrounding features celebrated in legend are referred to by Yeats in several of his early poems, e.g. 'The Wanderings of Oisin' (1889).

LOUGH CARRA *Mayo*

Lake lying to the E of the N84, between Castlebar and Ballinrobe. On the NE shore, off an unclassified road, are the burnt-out ruins of Moore Hall, where George Moore was born (1852) and spent most of his early life. The scenes of his boyhood are vividly depicted in his novel *The Lake* (1905). After his death in London his ashes were brought to Ireland and buried in a cist on Castle Island, within sight of his birthplace, with a memorial tablet on a cairn built of stones from the ancient castle on the island.

RENVYLE (or RINVYLE) *Galway*

Promontory on the N coast of Connemara, reached by a minor road, 3 m. from Letterfrack, on the N59. Renvyle House Hotel, near the beach, belonged for many years to Oliver St John Gogarty, who entertained Yeats (who felt the spirits of the house unfriendly), Shaw, Augustus John, and other artistic and political friends. Gogarty was buried, close to his beloved Renvyle, in Ballinakill cemetery near Moyard. The epitaph on the gravestone for him and his wife, Neenie, is taken from his poem 'Non Dolet':

> Our friends go with us as we go
> Down the long path where beauty wends,
> Where all we love foregathers, so
> Why should we fear to join our friends?

The history of Renvyle House is recorded in J. A. Lidwill's *A Seagrey House* (1987).

SLIGO *Sligo*

Market town and port, beautifully situated on the Garavogue, between Lough Gill and the sea, at the junction of the N4, the N15, and the N16. As a boy W. B. Yeats spent many holidays here with his maternal grandparents, the dour and difficult old merchant William Pollexfen and his kind and gracious wife, Elizabeth. They lived at Merville, a big house with 60 acres of land on the edge of the town, until the 1880s, when they moved, first to Charlemont, overlooking the harbour, and later to a smaller place called Rathedmond. Yeats and his brother Jack and his two sisters loved Sligo and became deeply attached to the country round—a rich store of legend and folklore for the young poet (see especially COLLOONEY, INNISFREE, and KNOCKNAREA). There is a small permanent exhibition at the Yeats Memorial Building near Hyde Bridge and a second exhibition of Yeatsiana in the Yeats Room at the Sligo Museum and Library on Stephen Street.

Eneas McNulty, the tragic wanderer of Sebastian Barry's novel *The Whereabouts of Eneas McNulty* (1998), owns 'a little room . . . in the middle of the lonesome town, at the back of John Street, in the third house from the end'.

Sligo is now home to the novelist Patrick McCabe.

TUAM *Galway*

Small town N of Galway city. The poet George MacBeth lived at Moyne Park and died here in 1992.

TULLIRA (or TULIRA) CASTLE *Galway*

Mansion *c.* 5 m. N of Gort, E of the N18 to Galway. The house, rebuilt (1882) in a so-called 'Tudor' style which W. B. Yeats found very unpleasing, was the home of Edward Martyn, poet, playwright, patron of the arts, and a founder of the Irish Literary Theatre. His many friends included Yeats, Lady Gregory, and George Moore (in whose autobiographical *Hail and Farewell* (1911–14) he figures prominently). Martyn was a descendant of a wealthy Catholic landowning family and his mother was determined that he should fulfil his role as one of the principal local landlords. He spent lavishly on her rebuilding projects, but to her disappointment refused to contemplate marriage. He bequeathed his entire library to the Carmelites in Clarendon St., Dublin, and gave instructions (which were duly carried out) that after his death his body should be used for dissection by medical students and his remains buried in a pauper's grave.

WESTPORT *Mayo*

Market town and small seaport on the N59 and the N5, beautifully situated on the banks of the Carrowbeg, which flows into the SE corner of Clew Bay. Westport House, a modernized early Georgian mansion (the seat of the Marquess of Sligo), stands at the W end of the town (open to the public, www.westporthouse.ie). De Quincey stayed here in 1800 with his friend Lord Westport after they had been together in *Dublin.

Thackeray was delighted with his visit on his Irish tour of 1842. 'Nature', he said in *The Irish Sketch Book* (1843),

> has done much for this pretty town of Westport; and after Nature, the traveller ought to be greatful to Lord Sligo, who has done a great deal too. In the first place he has established one of the prettiest, comfortablest inns in Ireland . . . Secondly, Lord Sligo has given up, for the use of the townspeople, a beautiful little pleasure-ground about his house.

Canon J. O. Hannay ('George A. Birmingham') was rector here from 1892 to 1913 and began his prolific writing career with *The Spirit and Origin of Christian Monasticism* (1903). He then turned to novels and established his popularity with *Spanish Gold* (1908), followed by *Lalage's Lovers* (1911), *The Major's Niece* (1911), and *The Inviolable Sanctuary* (1912), the beginning of a long and steady output. Westport and scenes of Mayo provided much of his local colour.

Croagh Patric, the pilgrimage mountain known locally as 'the Reek', appears in Paul Durcan's poem 'O Westport in the Light of Asia Minor', the title poem of his first book of poetry.

LEINSTER

ANNAMOE *Wicklow*

Village on the R755 between Bray and Rathdrum. Laurence Sterne had a remarkable adventure here as a child, which he describes in *Memoirs of the Life and Family of the late Rev. Laurence Sterne* (1775). During the frequent travelling of his childhood he stayed in 1721 with Mr Fetherston, a relation of his mother's, at his parsonage at Annamoe ('Animo'), and fell into the mill-race while the mill was working and was rescued unhurt, to the amazement of 'hundreds of the common people [who] flocked to see me'. The mill, now ruined, is just N of the bridge.

ARDAGH *Longford*

Village in pleasant wooded country, 4 m. SW of Edgeworthstown, on a minor road off the N55. Ardagh House, later a convent, is reputedly the place where Goldsmith, returning home from school at the age of 16, put up for the night under the misapprehension that it was an inn. The owner, Mr Fetherston, and his wife and daughter deliberately played up to his mistake and it was not until the next morning that the truth was revealed. The incident suggested the plot for *She Stoops to Conquer, or, The Mistakes of a Night* (1773).

ASHFORD *Wicklow*

Village 4 m. NW of Wicklow on the N11. About 2 m. W in the Devil's Glen are the extensive ruins of Glanmore Castle (part of which was later restored as a restaurant), built by Francis Synge, J. M. Synge's great-grandfather, at the beginning of the 19th c. It was the family seat, built to resemble a castle, on an estate which stretched for 10 m. across Wicklow. Synge was taken there when a year old and visited again in the summer of 1889, when his uncle's widow owned it and it was already falling into decay—a symbol of the decline of a once proud class.

AVOCA, VALE OF *Wicklow*

2 m. N of the village of Avoca on the R755 between Rathdrum and Woodenbridge is the First Meeting of the Waters, where the rivers Avonmore and Avonbeg join. Steps lead down beside the Lion Bridge to a paved garden with an enchanting view, and a bust of Thomas Moore, 'Ireland's National Poet', stands near the stump of the old tree under which he is said to have composed his poem 'The Meeting of the Waters' in 1807.

BALLITORE *Kildare*

Village near the W edge of the Wicklow Mountains, on a minor road W off the N9, 8 m. N of Castledermot. It was once a Quaker settlement and its school (gone), founded in 1726 by Abraham Shackleton, a Yorkshireman, had Edmund Burke among its pupils from 1741 to 1744.

BANAGHER *Offaly*

Village on the E bank of the Shannon, 8 m. NW of Birr, on the R439. Anthony Trollope was stationed here in 1841 (his lodgings have gone), when he first came to Ireland as a Post Office surveyor, and decided to try his hand at novel-writing in order to supplement his income. His first two novels, *The Macdermots of Ballycloran*

The Post Office at Banagher, where Trollope was stationed when he began writing novels

(1847) and *The Kellys and the O'Kellys* (1848), were realistic stories of Irish life, but achieved little success.

Charlotte Brontë, who married her father's curate, the Revd Arthur Bell Nicholls, in 1854, spent part of her honeymoon here. Mr Nicholls, who had been brought up at Cuba House by a schoolmaster uncle, stayed on at Haworth after Charlotte's early death, but eventually returned to Ireland when her father died. He held several curacies, remarried, and finally settled at Banagher for the rest of his life (d. 1906).

BECTIVE *Meath*

House and dissolved abbey complex on the W bank of the Boyne. The father of the short-story writer Mary Lavin came over from the US to work as overseer at Bective House when his daughter was 14. The house was empty for most of the year and only opened up in the hunting season. Lavin nurtured her love of rural Ireland and of literature here, roaming the long solitary passageways and reading Russian novels. Later in life she returned to live at the Abbey Farm, adjoining the Bective estate, dividing her time between Bective and bohemian Dublin. The stories in her first collection, *Tales from Bective Bridge* (1942), convey her response to rural Co. Meath.

BLACKWATER *Wexford*

Village on the E Wexford coast, 10 m. NE of Wexford county town, the setting for Colm Tóibín's novel *The Blackwater Lightship* (1999).

BORRIS *Carlow*

A small town on the river Barrow. P. J. Kavanagh, having taken up 'ancestor-hunting: an interest as sudden | As middle age', records a visit to the seat of the MacMurrough Kavanagh dynasty in his poem 'Borris House, Co. Carlow'. The house is open to visiting groups by prior arrangement.

BRAY *Wicklow*

Busy town and seaside resort 13 m. SE of Dublin off the M11. James Joyce's family home from 1888 to 1891 was 1 Martello Ter., next to a disused public bathhouse, one of a row of three-storey balconied houses at right angles to the Promenade at the far end from Bray Head. Joyce's father had settled here in the hope, as he used to say, that the train fare would keep his wife's relatives away. It was here that the young Joyce used to spend his school holidays from *Clongowes Wood College, and his memories of the surrounding area, the sea and the high sea wall, and the walks round Bray Head, were used in the early part of his autobiographical novel *A Portrait of the Artist as a Young Man* (1914–15). The dining room, where Joyce was first allowed to join his elders for dinner while the younger brothers and sisters waited in the nursery, was the setting for the famous Christmas dinner and the fierce argument over Parnell.

CELBRIDGE *Kildare*

Village on the R403, 13 m. W of Dublin, situated on the Liffey. Celbridge Abbey (now owned by a religious order) was the home of Swift's 'Vanessa', Esther Vanhomrigh (1690–1723), the daughter of a Dutch merchant who came over with William III and provisioned his troops. After meeting and falling in love with Swift in London she returned to Celbridge to be near him when he was in Dublin, and built a rustic bower where they could meet. Swift often rode over to see her, but on the last occasion (in 1723), enraged by her suspicion that he had secretly married Stella (Esther Johnson), he bade her an angry farewell. She died soon afterwards and was buried at Celbridge. Swift's poem 'Cadenus and Vanessa', the story of their relationship (written in 1713), was published after her death, at her request. A seat under the rocks by the river is known as 'Swift's Seat'. The grounds are usually open to the public in the spring and summer.

CHAPELIZOD *Dublin*

Suburban village on the Liffey, 3 m. W of Dublin, on the N4. The name is said to derive from Iseult (or Isolde, or Isoud), in Arthurian legend the sister (or daughter) of Moraunt, King of Ireland, slain by Tristram. The village is the scene of Le Fanu's novel *The House by the Churchyard* (1863), and the place where the Liffey becomes Anna Livia Plurabelle in Joyce's *Finnegans Wake* (1939).

CLANE *Kildare*

Village on the R403, 21 m. W of Dublin. Blackhall House, 1 m. S, was the birthplace of the Revd Charles Wolfe, author of 'The Burial of Sir John Moore'.

CLONGOWES WOOD COLLEGE *Kildare*

Jesuit boarding school (founded 1814), *c.* 1 m. N of Clane, off the R407 Kilcock–Naas road. Francis Sylvester Mahony ('Father Prout') was educated here, as was James Joyce, who portrayed some of his school experiences in *A Portrait of the Artist as a Young Man* (1914–15).

DALKEY (pr. 'Dawky) *Dublin*

Coastal resort and residential district off N11, 9 m. SE of Dublin, for which it was formerly the port and centre of commerce. At the top of the hill, commanding views of Dublin Bay from Dalkey Island to Howth Head and of Killiney Bay from the Island to Bray Head, is Torca Cottage ℗, the summer home of Bernard Shaw and his family from 1866 to 1874. G.B.S. was happy to get away from the dull surroundings of their Dublin house and remembered later: 'I had a moment of ecstatic happiness in my childhood when my mother told me that we were going to live in Dalkey.' He learnt to swim in Killiney Bay. The Shaws were poor and would not have been able to rent such a pleasant place if it had not been for the financial help given by George Vandaleur Lee,

a colourful member of the Shaw ménage at that time, who taught Mrs Shaw singing and influenced the musical taste of the young G.B.S. Lennox Robinson, playwright and director of the Abbey Theatre, lived during the 1920s at Sorrento Cottage, Sorrento Ter.

The Dalkey Archive (1964), Flann O'Brien's comic fantasy novel about James Joyce, St Augustine, and St Ignatius Loyola, is set in and around Vico Rd, where O'Brien's friend Niall Sheridan lived. The character of the resort is subtly evoked in O'Brien's characteristic comic style:

> Dalkey is a little town maybe twelve miles south of Dublin on the shore. It is an unlikely town, huddled, quiet, pretending to be asleep. Its streets are narrow, not quite self-evident as streets and with meetings which seem accidental. Small shops look closed but are open. Dalkey looks like a humble settlement which must, a traveller feels, be next door to some place of the first importance and distinction. And it is—vestibule of a heavenly conspection.

DUBLIN *Dublin*

Capital of the Republic of Ireland, a cathedral and university city and port situated on the Liffey at the head of Dublin Bay. Its site as a human settlement dates from prehistoric times and it was a community of some consequence when the Vikings invaded and established themselves in the 9th and 10th cc. It was enlarged and fortified by the Anglo-Normans in the 12th c. and acknowledged Henry VIII as King of Ireland in the 16th c. But its chief heritage of architecture and literature dates from the early 18th c. and in spite of recent changes it is this that gives it its predominant character. Because of its richness in literary associations the following account has been planned in three parts in order to make reference easy. First come the writers who were natives, regardless of whether they stayed or left; and the writers who came as schoolboys or students or professional men or visitors, however long or short their stay, in so far as it was significant; and then the buildings and institutions which have some connection with literature or literary people.

The first distinguished literary native of Dublin to write in English is Richard Stanyhurst (1547–1618), historian and translator of Virgil, son of the Recorder of Dublin. After graduating at Oxford he studied law for a time and then, diverted by history and literature, returned to Ireland accompanied by Edmund Campion, the Jesuit, as his tutor. He contributed a general description of Ireland and a history of Ireland during the reign of Henry VIII to Holinshed's *Chronicles* (vol. i, 1577). He emigrated to the Low Countries in 1579, where he translated the first four books of the *Aeneid* (Leiden, 1582), a grotesquely prosaic paraphrase of the Latin.

Edmund Spenser arrived in Dublin in November 1580 as secretary to Lord Grey de Wilton, newly appointed Lord Deputy, and the following year was made Clerk of the Irish Court of Chancery, a post which he held for

DUBLIN

85 Upper Dorset Street
Sean O'Casey was born here in 1880

Belvedere House, North Great George's Street
Joyce went to school in this Jesuit college, and describes it in *Portrait of the Artist as a Young Man*

Gate Theatre

James Joyce Centre, 35 North Great George's Street
A museum exploring and commemorating all things James Joyce

Dublin Writers Museum, Parnell Square
A museum commemorating the history of Irish literature: writers like Swift, Joyce, Wilde, Beckett, Yeats, and Shaw

Abbey Theatre
Founded in 1904 by poet W. B. Yeats and patron Lady Gregory, for over a century it has championed Irish writers like O'Casey and Synge, often to considerable controversy (for the former's *The Plough and the Stars* and the latter's *Playboy of the Western World*, in particular)

North Earl Street
There's a statue of Joyce here, hat tilted at a rakish angle

St Mary's Church, Mary Street
Sean O'Casey was baptized in this church in 1880

DORSET STREET

PARNELL STREET

O'CONNELL ST

CAPEL ST

ABBEY STREET

ARRAN QUAY

MERCHANTS QUAY

RIVER

CUSTOM HOUSE QUAY

LIFFEY

Ha'penny Bridge

Trinity College
Students here have included Oliver Goldsmith, Samuel Beckett, William Congreve, and Edmund Burke. Burke and Goldsmith are commemorated in statues at the entrance gateway

21 Westland Row
Oscar Wilde was born here, in 1854. There's a statue close by at the NE corner of Merrion Square

Christ Church Cathedral

GRAFTON ST

NASSAU STREET

St Patrick's Cathedral
Jonathan Swift was Dean of St Patrick's for over 30 years; today there are countless reminders of his association with the Cathedral, including his writing desk and memorials to him and to his beloved 'Stella'

Dublin Castle

7 Hoey's Court, off Castle Street
Jonathan Swift was born here in 1667

National Library of Ireland
Containing over half a million books and a famous domed reading room that makes an appearance in Joyce's *Ulysses*

National Gallery

Newman House, 85–86 St Stephen's Green
Formerly part of the Catholic University of Ireland, Gerard Manley Hopkins was a professor here (his study can still be seen) and Joyce a student. Joyce and Yeats are among those commemorated by statues on the Green

Merrion Square
Yeats lived at no. 52 East, then 82 South; Sheridan Le Fanu at what is now 7 South; and George Russell (Æ) at 84 South

MERRION ROW

PATRICK STREET

Shaw birthplace, Synge Street
Visit the house (now 33 Synge Street) where Bernard Shaw was born in 1856

nearly six years before becoming 'undertaker' for the settlement of Munster and moving to his estate of Kilcolman near *Doneraile. He had just begun writing *The Faerie Queene*, of which the first three books were completed at Kilcolman and taken to London in 1589 for printing.

John Davies (1569–1626), barrister and poet, came to Ireland as Solicitor-General in November 1603 and was knighted in December. In 1606 he was promoted to Attorney-General for Ireland and Sergeant-at-Arms, and became Speaker of the Irish parliament in 1613. During this time he wrote *A Discourse of the true reasons why Ireland has never been entirely subdued till the beginning of His Majesty's reign* (1612). He returned to England in 1619.

The playwright James Shirley (1596–1616) came to Dublin in 1636 when London theatres were closed on account of the plague. He wrote plays (*St Patrick for Ireland*, *The Royal Master*, and others) for the newly opened St Werburgh Theatre before returning to London in 1640.

Sir John Denham (1615–69), poet and playwright, remembered especially for his topographical poem *Cooper's Hill* (1642), was born in Dublin when his father was chief Baron of the Exchequer in Ireland, but after his education at Oxford does not appear to have returned to his birthplace. He served the Royalist cause in the Civil War and spent some years abroad before the Restoration.

Thomas Southerne (1660–1746), dramatist, author of the successful plays *The Fatal Marriage* (1694) and *Oroonoko* (1695), was born in the Oxmantown Rd area and educated at Trinity College, but went to the Middle Temple to study law and spent the rest of his life in London.

One of Dublin's greatest citizens, Jonathan Swift, was born (30 Nov. 1667) at 7 Hoey's Ct (gone), at the corner of Werburgh St. and Ship St. The pub that once displayed his bust has also gone, but a plaque at the corner of Ship St. near the castle gate records the position of his birthplace. He was educated at Kilkenny Grammar School before entering Trinity College, where he was publicly censured for bad behaviour and neglect of study, obtaining his degree only by 'special grace'. After some years in England as secretary to Sir William Temple (see FARNHAM) he returned to Ireland and was ordained (1694), receiving the small prebend of Kilroot and later, after Temple's death in 1699, the living of *Laracor. In 1713, disappointed in his hopes of an English bishopric, he became Dean of St Patrick's Cathedral and spent the remaining 32 years of his life in Dublin. This was the period of his major literary output: in addition to his immortal satire *Gulliver's Travels* (1726), he wrote a great number of tracts and pamphlets on politics, Irish affairs (such as *The Drapier's Letters* of 1724, which prevented the introduction of 'Wood's Half-pence', a supply of copper coins which could have ruined the Irish economy), religious matters, and social life (satirized in *A Complete Collection of Polite and Ingenious Conversation*, 1738), as well as miscellaneous verses, and letters to Bolingbroke, Pope, Gay, Arbuthnot, and others. In *Verses on the Death of Dr. Swift* (1731), he imagines how the news of his death will be received:

> Poor POPE will grieve a Month; and GAY
> A Week; and ARBUTHNOT a Day . . .

and reviews his life and principles:

> Fair LIBERTY was all his Cry;
> For her he stood prepared to die;

Towards the end of his life he suffered acutely from a form of vertigo (now thought to be Ménière's disease) which was followed by periods of insanity. He died in 1745 and was buried in St Patrick's Cathedral (see below). His deanery is now part of a police station in Bride St., and its successor, built in 1781, is entered from Upper Kevin St.

Richard Steele, whose English father was married to a woman of an old Irish family, was born (1672) in Bull Alley, just N of St Patrick's Cathedral. He left Dublin at the age of 13, to be educated at Charterhouse and Oxford, and later to follow a literary career in London, but the effect of his early upbringing was apparently evident enough for Thackeray to describe him as 'undoubtedly an Irishman'.

Thomas Parnell (1679–1718), poet and scholar, who became Archdeacon of *Clogher, was born in Dublin, but his birthplace is not recorded. He was educated at Trinity College.

William Congreve came to Trinity College from school at Kilkenny (as did Swift, just before him) in 1686, leaving for England in 1689 when James II was persecuting the Protestants and so caused Trinity to be closed for a time. George Farquhar entered Trinity in 1694 as a sizar (a student receiving an allowance in exchange for menial duties), but the story goes that he was expelled for making a profane joke. He then served in the army for a time before becoming an actor, but gave up the latter career after accidentally wounding a fellow player in a duelling scene. He turned instead to writing comedies (of which *The Recruiting Officer* (1706) and *The Beaux' Stratagem* (1707) were the most successful), living mostly in London, where he died in poverty.

Thomas Tickell (1686–1740), a poet who enjoyed the patronage of Addison, first visited Dublin in 1710 with him when the latter was secretary to Wharton, the newly appointed Lord Lieutenant of Ireland. Addison lost office the next year with the fall of the Whigs, but after the death of Queen Anne was restored to his old secretaryship (1715) and provided Tickell with employment under him. After Addison's death in 1719 Tickell edited his works (4 vols, 1721), prefacing the first volume with his finest poem, 'On the Death of Mr. Addison', and *c.* 1723 he migrated to Ireland for good, settling at Glasnevin. He became secretary to the Lords Justices of Ireland, and enjoyed the friendship of Swift. His house is now within the beautiful Botanic Gardens (founded 1795), which occupy his former demesne. Tickell is buried at Glasnevin and has a memorial in the church.

Mrs Delany (1700–88), whose letters and diaries brilliantly reflect the literary and social circles of the 18th c., first came to Ireland in 1731, being then Mrs Pendarves, the young widow of Alexander Pendarves. She stayed at the newly built house of Dr Clayton, Bishop of Killala, 80 St Stephen's Green (now part of Iveagh House), from which she made many excursions, entertainingly described, and one in particular that affected her future life—to Delville at Glasnevin. This was Dr Delany's house, which became her home after her marriage to him in 1743. The house, where Swift was a frequent visitor, has gone, as have its once characteristic adjuncts: the orange trees, bowling green, grotto, temples, rustic bridges, and paddocks of deer and cattle, and the site is now occupied by the Bon Secours Hospital.

Henry Brooke (1703–83), author of the curious Rousseau-inspired novel *The Fool of Quality* (1766–72), was educated at a school in Dublin run by Dr Thomas Sheridan, grandfather of R. B. Sheridan and friend of Swift. He entered Trinity in 1720, studied law in London, and returned to Dublin as a practising lawyer. Later he spent some more time in London and then came back to settle in Dublin for the rest of his life.

Edmund Burke was born (1729) at 12 Arran Quay (house gone), the son of a Protestant father and a Catholic mother. After attending a Quaker school at *Ballitore he went to Trinity College and subsequently to the Middle Temple (1750). Among the causes he espoused was the emancipation of Irish trade, the Irish parliament, and the Irish Catholics. His statue, by John Foley, stands in the forecourt of Trinity College.

Edmond Malone (1741–1812), critic and Shakespearian scholar, was born in Dublin and educated at Trinity College. He studied law in London and was called to the Irish Bar soon after 1767, but gave up a promising legal career for a life in London, where he joined Dr Johnson's circle and devoted himself to literature.

Oliver Goldsmith entered Trinity in 1744 as a sizar. He was short of money, especially after his father's death in 1747, but his tutor was unsympathetic and beat him when he broke in on a party with which the young man was celebrating his winning of a 30-shilling-a-year exhibition. Humiliated and hopeless, Goldsmith ran away to Cork, where his brother helped him to reconcile himself to his situation, so that he eventually returned to take his degree in 1749. His statue by John Henry Foley stands at the entrance to Trinity.

Richard Brinsley Sheridan was born (1751) at 12 Upper Dorset St. Ⓟ. His father was Thomas Sheridan, an actor and manager of the old Theatre Royal, and his mother, Frances, a playwright. He received his basic education from his father and from the age of 7 until 8½ attended Samuel Whyte's Academy, which formerly stood on the site of 79 Grafton St. He then joined his parents, who had moved to London, and never returned to his native city, though it always remained a cherished memory.

Thomas Moore, poet and songwriter, was born at a house on the site of 12 Aungier St., at the corner of Little Longford St. ℗. He too attended Whyte's Academy and then proceeded to Trinity College, being one of the first Catholics to be admitted. He began writing poetry at an early age and made a name for himself in Dublin society as a singer and musician. After graduating in 1799 he went to London to study law. He published a volume of *Poetical Works* in 1801 and won himself the title of Ireland's national songwriter with the publication of *Irish Melodies* (1807–35). A statue of him (regarded as 'utterly unworthy') stands on College Green, at the junction of Westmoreland St. and College St.; it features in Joyce's *Ulysses*. A collection of his manuscripts can be seen at the Royal Irish Academy Library, Dawson St.

George Croly (1780–1860), author and divine, was born in Dublin (the site is unrecorded) and educated at Trinity College, which he entered at 15. He was ordained in 1804 and after holding a curacy in the North of Ireland went to London *c.* 1810, where he made his name with a tragedy, *Catiline* (1822), and a romance, *Salathiel* (1829), based on the legend of the Wandering Jew. Byron called him 'the Revd. Rowley Powley' (*Don Juan*, XI. 57).

Charles Robert Maturin (1782–1824), writer of novels of mystery and horror, was born in Dublin of Huguenot descent. He was educated at Trinity College, took orders, and for a time kept a school. He combined a clerical career with the writing of stories and plays, and his first novel, *The Fatal Revenge* (1807), excited the admiration of Scott and was followed by *The Wild Irish Boy* (1808) and *The Milesian Chief* (1811). In 1816 his tragedy *Bertram*, sponsored by Byron, was successfully produced at Drury Lane, but later plays were failures and he returned to novel-writing. His 'Gothic' novel *Melmoth the Wanderer* (1820) is a masterpiece of the genre. Maturin was curate of St Peter's, Aungier St., and lived at 37 York St., where he gained a reputation for bizarre behaviour and eccentric dress that increased with the years.

Mrs Anna Brownell Jameson (1794–1860) was a Dubliner by birth, but left the city when she was only 4, when her family moved to England. Her father, D. Brownell Murphy, was a miniature painter and when she turned to literature after her marriage she specialized to a great extent in subjects connected with art (*Hand Book to the Galleries of Art in London*, 1842; *Early Italian Painters*, 1845; *Sacred and Legendary Art*, 1848), but the book by which she is best remembered is *Shakespeare's Heroines* (formerly entitled *Characteristics of Women*, 1832).

George Darley (1795–1846), poet, critic, and mathematician, was born and educated in Dublin. He spent five years at Trinity College (1815–20), but became estranged from his family, who opposed his wish for a literary

career, and went to London in 1822, in which year his blank-verse poem *The Errors of Ecstasie* was published. He wrote for the *London Magazine* and later joined the staff of *The Athenaeum*. He edited the plays of Beaumont and Fletcher.

Samuel Lover, novelist and songwriter, was born (24 Feb. 1797) at 60 Grafton St. He was educated privately and lived for a time at 9 D'Olier St., having left home to become an artist. He also developed a gift for writing songs and was befriended by Thomas Moore, in whose honour he had sung a tribute of his own composition at a banquet. He went to London in 1835 and in addition to painting and songwriting began to write novels, later returning to live in Dublin. He is remembered especially for the novels *Rory O'More* (developed from a ballad, 1836) and *Handy Andy* (1842), a rollicking burlesque of Irish life. He published his *Songs and Ballads* in 1839, and was associated with Dickens in the founding of *Bentley's Miscellany* (1837).

Anna Maria Hall (née Fielding, 1800–81), novelist, was born and brought up in Dublin and though she left Ireland at 15 she turned her early experiences to good account in several of her successful books, such as *Sketches of Irish Character* (1829), *Lights and Shadows of Irish Life* (1838), and *The White Boy* (1845), which were widely enjoyed in England. Her style in describing rural life has been compared to Mary Russell Mitford's.

James Clarence Mangan, poet, was born (1 May 1803) at 3 Fishamble St. (house gone, but ℗ on site), the son of a poor shopkeeper. He was brilliant at school, receiving most of his education from a priest who encouraged him to learn several languages, but he had to earn money from an early age to help to support his family and his life was shadowed by poverty. He worked as a lawyer's clerk and in Trinity College library, and contributed poems and translations to the *Dublin University Magazine* and *The Nation*. He wrote versions of old Irish songs by studying prose translations of the Gaelic, and his hymn to Ireland 'My Dark Rosaleen' is still remembered. He never achieved the success and recognition that might have been his, and his death from cholera on 20 June 1849 was probably hastened by an addiction to opium. He lived for much of his life at 3 Lord Edward St. ℗. A bust of him by Oliver Sheppard stands in St Stephen's Green Park.

In 1800 De Quincey visited Dublin with his friend Lord Westport. They stayed at the latter's house in Sackville (now O'Connell) St. and attended the last sitting of the House of Lords, described by De Quincey in his *Autobiographic Sketches* (1853–4). After the Act of Union (1800) the handsome 18th-c. Parliament House on College Green was adapted for use as the Bank of Ireland.

Marguerite Power, who married Charles John Gardiner, Earl of Blessington, in 1818 after the end of her first unhappy marriage, lived for a time in Dublin. The Gardiner family house in Henrietta St. (now part of a convent)

where she held her salons is one of a number of especially fine Georgian houses which distinguish this once fashionable district.

A woman writer of a very different kind was her contemporary Mrs Felicia Hemans (1793–1835), a poet greatly extolled in her day (she was the author of the much-parodied 'Casabianca', or 'The boy stood on the burning deck'), who came to Dublin in 1831 to live with her brother, first at 36 Merrion Row and then at 21 Dawson St., where she died. She is buried at St Anne's Church (CI).

Charles James Lever, novelist, was born on 31 August 1806 in the North Strand (now Amiens St.) at the corner of North Cope St. (now Talbot St.) and studied medicine at Trinity College and Steven's Hospital. He practised as a doctor in various parts of Ireland and turned to literature as an extra source of income. He published his first novel, *Harry Lorrequer*, in the *Dublin University Magazine* (which he later edited) in 1837 and thereafter wrote a novel a year, gaining great popularity for the vogue of breezy stories of Irish squires and peasants, the English garrison, and the sporting life. He spent much of his time abroad, but was frequently in Dublin and entertained his literary friends at Templeogue House, his home for many years, now in the suburb of Templeogue, S of Dublin on the Terenure–Tallaght road. Lever was parodied by his friend Thackeray in *Novels by Eminent Hands* (1856).

Sir Samuel Ferguson (1810–86), distinguished poet and antiquary, was educated at Trinity College and lived in Dublin after being called to the Bar in 1838. He contributed poetry to the *Dublin University Magazine*, and lived for many years at 20 North Gt George's St., hospitably receiving writers and their friends. In 1867 he became Deputy Keeper of the Records of Ireland and lived latterly at *Howth.

Joseph Sheridan Le Fanu, great-grandnephew of R. B. Sheridan, was born (23 Aug. 1814) at the Royal Hibernian Military School (now St Mary's Hospital), on the S side of Phoenix Park, above the Liffey, where his father was chaplain. He was educated privately and at Trinity College, where he began contributing to the *Dublin University Magazine*, which he eventually owned. He was called to the Bar in 1839 but did not practise, having already begun to make his name as a writer especially of ballads (such as *Shamus O'Brien*, 1837), which became immensely popular. But he is remembered as a master of the macabre and the supernatural, especially in the novels *The House by the Churchyard* (1863) and *Uncle Silas* (1864), and the collection of stories in *In a Glass Darkly* (1872). He lived at 45 Lower Dominick St. and later at 18 (now 70, ℗) Merrion Sq., where he died (7 Feb. 1873).

Mrs Cecil Frances Alexander (née Humphreys), author of 'All things bright and beautiful' and other hymns, was born (1818) at 25 Eccles St. and lived in Dublin until 1825.

Another Dublin native who left at an early age was Dionysius ('Dion') Lardner Boucicault

The Old Library at Trinity College Dublin, which houses Ireland's greatest collection of books and manuscripts

(*c.* 1820–90), who was educated at University College School, London, and became a skilful adapter of plays and novels by other hands. His early play *London Assurance* (1841) was a great success and was followed by many others including adaptations from the French and those with Irish settings, such as the famous *The Colleen Bawn* (1860), adapted from Gerald Griffin's *The Collegians* (1829), *Arrah-na-Pogue* (1864), and *The Shaughraun* (1874).

Sir Walter Scott visited Dublin briefly but memorably at the outset of his tour of Ireland in July 1825. He stayed in St Stephen's Green with his son, an army officer, and was surprised and touched by the warmth of the public welcome he received. He visited St Patrick's deanery and other places as a pilgrim paying homage to Swift and found that wherever he went he himself was the object of honour and acclaim. Notables called on him, he was cheered in the streets, and almost mobbed in the theatre.

Thackeray stayed with his friend Charles Lever at Templeogue House (see above) during his Irish tour of 1842, and his *Irish Sketch Book* (under the pseudonym 'Michael Angelo Titmarsh', 1843) gives a most readable account of his experiences in Dublin as well as the rest of Ireland.

His admirer Anthony Trollope, who had had various Post Office appointments in Ireland and was making his name as a novelist, came in 1854 from Belfast to Dublin, where he met his future wife. After their marriage and the birth of two sons they settled at 5 Seaview Ter. (off Ailesbury Rd), Donnybrook (now a suburb on the Dublin–Bray road), until their departure for England in 1859.

The historian William E. H. Lecky was born in Newtown Park, near Dublin, and educated at Trinity College, where his statue (by Sir William Goscombe John) stands beside the campanile. His principal work is *The History of England in the Eighteenth Century* (1878–90), in which the last volumes concern the history of Ireland and are designed to refute the misstatements of Froude. Lecky was MP for the University from 1895 to 1902, strongly pro-Irish in his sympathies, though an opponent of Home Rule.

Alfred Perceval Graves (1846–1931), school inspector who published many volumes of Irish songs and ballads, was born at 12 Fitzwilliam Sq. and educated at Trinity College. He was the author of the popular song 'Father O'Flynn', written in 1875 and first published in *The Spectator*.

Bram (Abraham) Stoker (1847–1912), author of the supreme horror story *Dracula* (1897), was born at 15 Marino Cres. in the NE suburb of Clontarf. He worked as a civil servant in Dublin (1867–77) and published *The Duties of Clerks of Petty Sessions* (1878) before becoming touring manager and secretary to Henry Irving.

Oscar Wilde was born (16 Oct. 1854) at 21 Westland Row Ⓟ and later moved to 1 Merrion Sq. Ⓟ with his father, Sir William, an eye surgeon, and his mother, who contributed patriotic poems to *The Nation* under the name

'Speranza'. The house is owned by American College Dublin and, as the Oscar Wilde Museum, is open for group visits (www.amcd.ie). Wilde was at Trinity College before going on to Magdalen College, Oxford, in 1874.

Bernard Shaw was born (1856) at 3 (now 33, Ⓟ) Synge St. The plaque was erected by a local dustman at his own expense, with the wording by Shaw himself. He was baptized at St Bride's Church (now secularized) by the Revd W. G. Carroll, his uncle by marriage, who, when the sponsor arrived for the ceremony drunk and incapable, ordered the sexton to take his place, just as though, according to Shaw, 'he would have ordered him to put coal on the fire'. His education began with a governess at home and was continued at the Wesley Connexional School (later Wesley College) on St Stephen's Green, then at a school in Aungier St., and lastly (for six months only) at the Central Model School in Marlborough St., opposite St Mary's Pro-Cathedral. He took a job at 15 in an estate agency in Molesworth St. and five years later (1876) left Dublin to join his mother in London, where she had settled to follow her musical career. He did not return to Ireland for *c.* 30 years, and then only for occasional visits.

W. B. Yeats, one of the great figures of the Irish literary revival, was born (13 June 1865) at Georgeville, 5 Sandymount Ave., ½ m. from Sandymount Castle, where his uncle was then living. His family moved to London when he was 3 and he did not return to Dublin until he was 15, when he attended the High School at 40 Harcourt St. and then studied art at the National College of Art in Kildare St. After a few years at 10 Ashfield Ter. in the suburb of Harold's Cross the Yeats family went back to London again and he had no settled home in Ireland until after his marriage in 1917, when he bought the old tower at Ballylee (see GORT). After 1922 he lived for a few years at 82 Merrion Sq. Ⓟ and later at a flat at 42 Fitzwilliam Sq. His last move was to Riversdale House in the suburb of Rathfarnham, S of Dublin.

J. M. Synge was born (16 Apr. 1871) at 2 Newtown Villas Ⓟ, Rathfarnham. His father died the following year and his mother moved with her five children to 4 Orwell Pk, Rathgar, *c.* 2 m. nearer the city. Synge was a delicate boy and after four years of irregular schooling, first at Mr Herrick's Classical and English School at 4 Leeson St. and then at Bray, he was taught by a tutor at home. He studied at Trinity College (1888–92), but said that he gained little as his time was almost wholly devoted to playing the violin and attending lectures at the Royal Academy of Music. He went to Coblenz in 1893 to study music, but gave up the idea of a musical career and turned instead to literature. After writing and studying in Paris he took Yeats's advice and visited the Aran Islands and the West of Ireland and drew on his experiences for his prose writings and his plays. By the time *The Aran Islands* was published (1907) he had already made his name as a dramatist with *In the Shadow of the Glen*

(1903), *Riders to the Sea* (1904), *The Well of the Saints* (1905), and his great comedy, produced in the teeth of opposition and rioting at the Abbey Theatre, *The Playboy of the Western World* (1907). His last years, spent in or near Dublin, were clouded by illness and he died at 130 Northumberland Rd on 24 March 1909.

Oliver St John Gogarty, surgeon, poet, and writer of entertaining memoirs, was born (17 Aug. 1878) at 5 Parnell Sq. Ⓟ. He studied medicine at Trinity College and became a fashionable surgeon in Dublin. Yeats had a high opinion of his poetry, and included 17 of his poems in *The Oxford Book of Modern Verse*, but he is best remembered for his autobiographical account of Ireland in the 1920s, *As I Was Going Down Sackville Street* (1937; taking his title from an old ballad; the 18th-c. Sackville St., originally Drogheda St., is now O'Connell St.). Gogarty was at one time a friend of James Joyce and figures as the 'Stately, plump Buck Mulligan' in *Ulysses*. He lived at 15 Ely Pl., formerly the home of John Wilson Croker (1780–1857), editor of Boswell's *Life of Johnson*, and now rebuilt to house the Royal Hibernian Academy and art gallery. Gogarty spent much of the latter part of his life in the US.

Patrick Pearse, poet, short-story writer, patriot, and schoolmaster, was born (10 Nov. 1879) at 27 Pearse St. (then Great Brunswick St.) Ⓟ. He was educated at University College and after qualifying as a barrister devoted himself to encouraging the development of literature in Irish. He was active in the Gaelic League and established a school for teaching the Irish language, St Enda's College (Coláiste Éinne), which he moved to Rathfarnham in 1910, at the Hermitage, down Whitechurch Rd. Pearse was executed on 3 May 1916 for his part in leading the Easter rising.

Sean O'Casey was born (30 Mar. 1880) at 85 Upper Dorset St., a large house, which his father, Michael Casey, a clerk in the Society for Church Missions, rented and probably sublet. The boy was baptized 'John' in St Mary's Church (CI) by the Revd T. R. S. Collins, who appears in O'Casey's autobiographies as part of the composite figure the Revd T. R. S. Hunter. The family moved *c.* 1881 or 1882 to 9 Innisfallen Parade, and when Sean was 5 he went to St Mary's Infant School, 20 Lower Dominick St., where his sister Bella taught. After his father's death in 1886 the family moved twice, coming to 25 Hawthorne Ter. in 1889, a small but pleasant cottage in NE Dublin from which Sean probably attended St Barnabas's School, though his autobiographical *I Knock at the Door* (1939) is rather obscure about his schooling. His school attendance was irregular on account of an eye disease which afflicted him from an early age and dogged him throughout his life, but Bella used to help him out at home. Then, at 14, he began work as a labourer, as described in his autobiography (though dates are lacking and proper names are altered). In 1897 he moved with his mother and three brothers to a flat at 18 Abercorn Rd, near St Barnabas's Church (CI), which he attended for many years. He taught himself Irish, joined the Gaelic League, and was inducted into the Irish Republican Brotherhood. His mother died in 1918 and he left the flat two years later. His early plays *The Shadow of a Gunman* (1925), *Juno and the Paycock* (1925), and *The Plough and the Stars* (1926), based on his experience of Dublin in the years of the 'Troubles', show a strong sense of tragic irony as well as humour, but the fierce critical attacks aroused by the last play drove him from Ireland and from 1926 he spent the rest of his life in England.

George Moore was a visitor to Dublin before settling there in 1901. He stayed in St Stephen's Green at the Shelbourne Hotel, which figures in his novel *A Drama in Muslin* (1886). After some years in London he returned to Ireland and, encouraged by Yeats and Edward Martyn to take part in the Irish literary revival, he settled at 4 Ely Pl., with a small garden across the street. House and garden both figure in his trilogy of Dublin reminiscences, *Hail and Farewell* (1911–14), written largely at his later house, 4 Upper Merrion St.

George William Russell (1867–1935; known as 'Æ' or 'AE' because of an early pseudonym, 'Æon', which a printer's compositor contracted to the diphthong alone) poet, journalist, and painter, came to Dublin with his family from the North of Ireland when he was *c.* 10 and was educated at Rathmines School and at the Metropolitan School of Art, where he met Yeats. He worked for Sir Horace Plunkett in the Irish Agricultural Organization, 84 Merrion Sq., and for many years was editor of the *Irish Homestead* (merged with the *Irish Statesman* in 1923), his office becoming a well-known port of call for literary visitors. His first poems, *Homeward: Songs by the Way* (1894), combine mysticism and Irish mythology and were well received. His play *Deirdre* (1902) was a forerunner of the poetic drama associated with the Irish National Theatre. Æ lived in a modest house in Rathgar, famous for his literary evenings. He left for England in 1932. A ceremony to mark the restoration of his grave and the erection of a new headstone was held in Mount Jerome cemetery in 1980.

James Joyce was born (2 Feb. 1882) at 41 Brighton Sq. Ⓟ, between Rathgar and Terenure, to the S of Dublin. His family were constantly moving house and only a few of the more significant addresses are recorded here. They were at 23 Castlewood Ave., Rathmines (1884–7), before moving to *Bray, while Joyce was a boarder at *Clongowes Wood College. In 1893 he went to Belvedere College for five years, a Jesuit school in Gt Denmark St., where he contemplated but abandoned a vocation to the priesthood. The school figures in *A Portrait of the Artist as a Young Man* (1914–15). Part of this time the family were living at 13 North Richmond St. and many of their neighbours turn up in Joyce's writings: 'North Richmond Street was a quiet street . . . the houses, conscious of decent lives within them, gazed at one another with brown imperturbable faces . . .'. Joyce went on to University College,

where he graduated in modern languages in 1902. No. 8 Royal Ter. (now Inverness Ter.), Fairview, was one of a number of houses in that area in which the Joyce family lived about that time. Although Joyce began his writing career while still an undergraduate, his works were not published until after he left Dublin. After graduating he went to Paris, returning in 1903 when his mother was dying, and then, except for one or two brief visits later, spent the rest of his life in Paris, Trieste, and Zurich. His first published work was a volume of verse, *Chamber Music* (1907), followed by *Dubliners* (1914), shrewd and often touching short stories of unheroic Dublin people. *Ulysses*, his most widely read novel, with its minutely detailed picture of Dublin in 1904, was published in Paris in 1922. A map showing the setting of the 18 episodes of the book can be obtained from the Dublin Writers Museum, the James Joyce Centre, and the James Joyce Museum at *Sandycove. A restored 18th-c. town house at 35 North Gt George's St. now houses the James Joyce Centre, offering a lively programme of lectures and exhibitions (www.jamesjoyce.ie).

Joyce boasted that if Dublin were destroyed it could be rebuilt in detail from his works. His friend and contemporary the poet and novelist James Stephens was born in a poor part of Dublin (his birthplace is not recorded) in 1882 (or possibly earlier) and was largely self-educated. His talent for writing was discovered by 'Æ' (G. W. Russell), who helped him to publish his first book of poems, *Insurrections* (1909). Stephens helped to found the *Irish Review* in 1911 and the following year published *The Crock of Gold*, the prose fantasy by which he is best remembered. He was Registrar of the National Gallery from 1919 to 1924.

Brendan Behan (1923–64), author in Irish and English, was born at 14 Russell St. Ⓟ and educated by the French Sisters of Charity,

North William St. He joined the IRA in 1937 and was arrested in Liverpool and sentenced to three years in Borstal and, on his return to Dublin, to 14 years (of which he served six) by a military court in 1942. He depicts life in an Irish prison in his first play, *The Quare Fellow* (1956), and his own early life in the autobiographical novel *Borstal Boy* (1958). The London success of *The Hostage* (1959), the English version of his Irish play *An Giall* (1958), won him an international reputation.

Liam O'Flaherty was educated at University College Dublin. The dark side of the city is atmospherically portrayed in his classic thriller *The Informer* (1925).

Samuel Beckett was first educated at Earlsfort House School, near Harcourt St., from about 1915 to 1919. He later attended Trinity College from 1923 to 1927, living in rooms in New Sq. He was an outstanding student, leaving with a First Class degree and a gold medal in French. He met the beautiful and vivacious Ethna McCarthy here and embarked upon an unhappy, unreciprocated love affair. She was the inspiration for his poems 'Alba' and 'Yoke of Liberty' and also for the much later monologue *Krapp's Last Tape* (1958). Beckett returned to Trinity to teach French in 1930. It proved a short tenure. He hated the self-exposure of the lecture hall and also disliked 'teaching others what he did not know himself', and put a swift end to 'this hateful comedy of lecturing'. Beckett lived at 6 Clare St. while teaching at Trinity and wrote *More Pricks than Kicks* (1934) and the beginning of *Murphy* (1938) in the top floor of his father's office building, Beckett and Metcalf, Quantity Surveyors.

Brian O'Nolan ('Flann O'Brien') lived as a child at 25 Hubert Pl., beside the leafy Grand Canal celebrated in Patrick Kavanagh's 'Canal Side Walk'. O'Brien's novel *The Hard Life*

The garret at 6 Clare St., Dublin, where Samuel Beckett lived and wrote in the 1930s

James Joyce and Dublin

ALTHOUGH James Joyce spent most of his life and almost his entire literary career outside his native city, his works are set in Dublin and describe the city with almost obsessive meticulousness. Of his masterpiece *Ulysses* (1922), which he wrote over a period of seven years in Paris, Trieste, and Zurich, he is recorded as saying 'I want . . . to write a novel about Dublin so complete that if the city one day suddenly disappeared from the earth, it could be reconstructed out of my book.' Dublin is not simply a backdrop to the stories, but a character and an active influence. Joyce, who announced his intention of presenting Dublin to the world, described the city somewhat caustically as 'the centre of paralysis' and envisioned it as a labyrinth in which its citizens were trapped by their own 'hemiplegia of the will'. The characters in *Dubliners* (1914) dream of escaping the narrowness of their existence but consistently fail to break free. In *A Portrait of the Artist as a Young Man* (1916), Joyce's autobiographical novel, he recalls his family's move to the centre of Dublin and the process of city life as 'a new and complex sensation'. A passage in the fifth section of the novel describes Stephen Dedalus's morning walk across the city to his lectures, in which he associates landmarks along the route with the writers whom he studies.

Ulysses was planned in 18 episodes, each with its own style, technique, specified time of day, and particular location in or near the city. Joyce, who used street maps, newspapers, and *Thom's Directory* to back up his detailed memory of Dublin as it was on 16 June 1904, went to considerable lengths to choreograph the movements and meetings of his characters over the course of a single day. The framework of the novel is based on Homer's *Odyssey*, and the progress of Leopold Bloom from his home in Eccles Street to a series of real-life locations finds its correspondences felicitously enough in the episodes of Odysseus' adventures. Sweny's pharmacy in Lincoln Place becomes the island of the drug-dulled Lotus Eaters; Glasnevin cemetery is Hades, the realm of the dead; Aeolus, controller of the winds, has his kingdom in a newspaper office; and the Cyclops, a one-eyed giant who devours visitors in a cave, is represented by a belligerent nationalist swilling pints in Barney Kiernan's pub. The longest and most extraordinary episode appropriately transposes the island of the enchantress Circe, where men are turned to beasts, to Dublin's notorious brothel quarter.

The real and stultifying Dublin of Joyce's earlier works is transformed in *Ulysses* into a world of immense possibility, where the dingy and unremarkable can also be significant and symbolic. Having placed Dublin on the map of the world in *Ulysses*, Joyce reversed the process in *Finnegans Wake* (1939) to place the map of the world in Dublin. His last and

JAMES JOYCE BY JACQUES-ÉMILE BLANCHE, 1935

most complex novel localizes the whole of human history and mythology in the landscape and environs of Dublin. Everything from the fall of Adam to the battle of Waterloo is swept into the story of a Dublin publican and his wife, living in Chapelizod on the fringes of Phoenix Park (whose name itself is consistent with Joyce's theme of circularity, resurrection, and constant renewal). In a world in which the local and the universal merge, landmarks such as the Wellington Monument, the magazine fort, and 'Howth Castle and Environs' take on multiple levels of significance.

The Dublin of Joyce's works is frozen in the year 1904, the period when he last lived there. By the time *Ulysses* was published in 1922, the physical centre of the city, and Irish society generally, had been transformed by war, rebellion, and the emergence of a new state. The picture he gives of a decayed provincial capital was not received well at the time in Ireland, where his countrymen were more concerned with the future than the past. Nowadays it is a popular mistake to think of 'Joyce's Dublin' as a nostalgic reconstruction of a picture-postcard era, complete with horse-cabs, parasols, and straw boaters—the trappings generally associated with the annual Bloomsday festivities on 16 June—or a celebration of the city's colourful pub culture. Joyce's writings do not flatter 'dear, dirty Dublin'. They include spits and sewage, disease-ridden brothels, and poor food, and the pubs generate more bad feeling than good conversation. The priests and politicians who were to be honoured as the founders of the state get little respect from Joyce, and the great cultural nationalist movement of the time is dismissed by him as inward-looking and parochial, a net for catching souls. For all this, Dublin was to inspire Joyce like none of the other European cities where he spent his life. His works put the city on a plane with Homer's Mediterranean and biblical Jerusalem.

Joyce's picture of Dublin is a selective one, limited mainly to the parts frequented by himself and by middle-class, mostly Catholic, Dubliners. He is familiar with theatres, churches, and pubs, brothels and pawnbrokers, cheap restaurants and small shops, statues and bridges, and all the minor furniture of the city. The places associated with him which managed to survive to more appreciative times have now been accorded a sacred significance. A trail of plaques follows the route of the eighth episode of *Ulysses*; at least half a dozen of his residences, and as many more of the buildings featured in his works, have been similarly marked; innumerable pubs claim the honour of his acquaintance. Every Bloomsday (and throughout the year) pilgrims flock to Dublin to retrace the footsteps of Joyce's characters and to reconstruct, in their own imaginations, the city preserved in his books—a phenomenon possibly unique in literary appreciation.

ROBERT NICHOLSON

(1961) was set in a house on Wilton Pl., the next terrace along the canal. Details of O'Brien's home life at Hubert Pl. were distortedly reflected in the novel (including the antics and ambitions of 'the Brother'), as was (more derisively) the author's education at the Christian Brothers' School on Synge St. In 1927 the family moved to 4 Avoca Terr., after which O'Brien attended the more prestigious Blackrock College. They stayed here for 20 years, in which period O'Brien wrote, among other things, *At Swim-Two-Birds* (1939) and *The Third Policeman* (1939–40, posthumously pub. 1967). *At Swim-Two-Birds* reflects aspects of his student life at University College—including drinking sessions at Grogan's, a pub on Lower Leeson St.—where he proved himself a brilliant extempore speaker in the Literary and Historical Society. After graduation O'Brien worked as a civil servant in the Department of Local Government at the Custom House: the access he gained to administrative life in Ireland provided much material for 'Cruiskeen Lawn', his famous comic column in the *Irish Times*. In 1953 the political content of his column became too much for his employers and he was fired. He also lived at 81 Merrion Ave. and 10 Belmont Ave. (in Donnybrook).

The novelist Iris Murdoch was born at 59 Blessington St. in 1919 but left Dublin as a child and spent the rest of her life in England. But she would return to the city as the setting for her 1965 novel *The Red and the Green*, set at the time of the 1916 Easter rising.

The poet Patrick Kavanagh first visited Dublin in December 1931, tramping his way in hobnailed boots, with only 3*s*. 4½*d*. in his pocket. In his autobiographical *The Green Fool* (1938), he describes his attempts to meet the literary figures of the day, but only succeeds in calling on Æ, who talked a great deal and gave him a pile of books but not a bite to eat; Kavanagh was home again in two days. He

returned to Dublin in 1939 and existed precariously as a freelance journalist and poet until he made his name with the long poem *The Great Hunger* (1942), followed by *A Soul for Sale* (1947) and *Tarry Flynn* (1948), a novel about rural life. A collection of poems, *Come Dance with Kitty Stobling*, and *Collected Poems* were published in 1960 and 1964 respectively. Kavanagh is commemorated by a stone bench near the canal locks at Baggot St. Bridge, where he often used to sit. This answers the request in his poem 'Lines written on a seat on the Grand Canal, Dublin':

O commemorate me where there is water,
Canal water preferably, so stilly
Greeny at the heart of summer. . . .
O commemorate me with no hero-courageous
Tomb—just a canal-bank seat for the passer-by.

In 1923 V. S. Pritchett lived in a temperance hotel in Harcourt St. while trying to report on the Civil War. 'In two years of Ireland, I faded away to a wanness in that languid climate and was rarely able to get up before eleven in the morning. I became sensitive, snobbish and fey.' This did not prevent him from meeting many of the major literary figures of 1920s Dublin—including O'Casey, Æ, and Yeats (who at that time kept an armed guard in his house to whom he would read detective stories 'to train them in their profession')—and 'revelled in the Abbey theatre'. He wrote perceptively and affectionately about the city in his second book of autobiography, *Midnight Oil* (1971), and in his travel book *Dublin: A Portrait* (1967).

Pritchett's fellow short-story writer Mary Lavin was educated at Loreto College, St Stephen's Green, in the 1920s and later returned for a period to teach French. She studied literature at University College Dublin and wrote her first short story, 'Miss Holland', on the back of a draft of her Ph.D. dissertation on Virginia Woolf. She lived most of her

writing life, when not in *Bective, Co. Meath, at 11 Lad Lane, near Fitzwilliam Pl. The setting of her famous story 'In a Café' was based on the Clog, a café which once stood on South King St.

The novelist and short-story writer William Trevor studied history at Trinity in the late 1940s. The Belfast poets Michael Longley and Derek Mahon were both undergraduates at Trinity in the early 1960s. The novelist Patrick McCabe trained to be a teacher at St Patrick's Training College before working as a teacher in London. He would choose a Dublin school as the setting for his 1995 novel *The Dead School*. The Nobel Prizewinning poet Seamus Heaney, born in Co. Derry, now lives in Dublin.

The novelist Roddy Doyle was born in Dublin in 1958. After completing his studies he worked as a teacher at Greendale Community School in Kilbarrack in the city's Northside. He has now written a number of novels portraying life in the fictional Northside suburb of Barrytown, believed to be modelled on Kilbarrack. Among the books are *The Commitments* (1987), *The Snapper* (1990), and *The Van* (1991), which together make up 'The Barrytown Trilogy'. In *The Commitments*—since made into a popular film—Barrytown resident Jimmy Rabbitte decides to form a soul band (which meets to rehearse in the garage of Joey The Lips' mother near Killester); the sequels deal with the continuing trials of the Rabbitte family. The trilogy was followed in 1993 by *Paddy Clark Ha Ha Ha* (the world of the late 1960s seen through the eyes of a 10-year-old boy on a Barrytown estate); *The Woman Who Walked into Doors* (1996, set in contemporary Dublin); and *A Star Called Henry* (1999), a historical novel set in the city's slums in the troubled early years of the 20th c.

The poet Thomas Kinsella was also a student of University College, and the streets—particularly the nocturnal streets—of Dublin have featured a good deal in his poetry:

Phoenix St., Bow Lane, Ely Pl., Westland Row. Baggot St., where the poet lived for a time in the 1950s, is the setting for his celebrated poem 'Baggot Street Deserta':

> The window is wide
> On a crawling arch of stars, and the night
> Reacts faintly to the mathematic
> Passion of a cello suite
> Plotting the quiet of my attic.

The so-called 'great Lockout', when Dublin employers attempted to break the unions in 1913, and which began on O'Connell St. (then Sackville St.), lies at the heart of James Plunkett's novel *Strumpet City* (1969). In his novel *Farewell Companions* (1977), Cornelius Moloney's pub stands at 144 High St., up the road from the premises of his friend the librarian O'Sheehan.

The poet Paul Durcan was educated at Gonzaga College, Dublin. His poem 'Phoenix Park Vespers' contemplates love and time:

> Under the exceedingly lonely conifers of the
>   Phoenix Park,
> Under their blunt cones and amidst their
>   piercing needles,
> I squatted down and wept.

The monument in the park to Éamon de Valéra features in Durcan's 'Making Love Outside Áras an Uachtaráin'.

Sebastian Barry was born in Dublin and educated at Trinity College in the 1970s. Dublin Castle is at the heart of his play *The Steward of Christendom* (1995) and a hospital room in the charitable infirmary on Jervis Street (now closed) was the setting for his play *Our Lady of Sligo* (1998).

ABBEY THEATRE, Marlborough St. Erected by Miss A. E. Horniman of Manchester, a friend and admirer of W. B. Yeats, to provide a permanent home for the Fays' National Theatre Company, which had been producing his plays. It incorporated the hall of the Mechanics' Institute in Abbey St. (formerly the site of the old Theatre Royal, burnt down in 1880) and an adjoining building, and opened in 1904 with Yeats's *On Baile's Strand* and Lady Gregory's *Spreading the News*. Yeats and Lady Gregory were the initial directors, and dramatists whose plays helped to make the theatre world-famous include J. M. Synge, Lennox Robinson (who succeeded Yeats as manager in 1910 and became director in 1923), and Sean O'Casey. In 1951 the theatre was accidentally burnt down and the company played in the Queen's Theatre until the rebuilt Abbey was opened in 1966.

In Samuel Beckett's novel *Murphy* (1938), Murphy desires his ashes to be disposed of in the theatre lavatory ('necessary house') and 'the chain to be pulled upon them, if possible during the performance of a piece, the whole to be executed without ceremony or show of grief'.

ARCHBISHOP MARSH'S LIBRARY, St Patrick's Close. Built in 1701 by Archbishop Marsh, the first public library in Ireland and one of the earliest in the British Isles. There are four main collections, consisting of 25,000 books relating to the 16th, 17th, and early 18th cc., the most important being that of the library of Edward Stillingfleet (1635–99), Bishop of Worcester, which contains books printed by some of the earliest English printers. There are also *c.* 300 manuscripts, including a volume of the Lives of the Irish Saints (*c.* 1400) in Latin. A small book of Elizabethan poetry contains a poem to Queen Elizabeth by Sir Walter Ralegh. There are interesting mementoes of Jonathan Swift, who was a governor of the library, including his copy of Clarendon's *History of the Rebellion*, with extensive annotations. Swift's death mask and some of his autograph writings are also on view, and the table at which he wrote *Gulliver's Travels* and *The Drapier's Letters*. James Joyce's signature can be seen for 19 and 22 October 1902 and the *Ulysses* reference to the 'stagnant bay in Marsh's Library'.

CHARLEMONT HOUSE, in Palace Row, on the N side of Parnell Sq., formerly the mansion of the Earl of Charlemont, since 1930 the Municipal Gallery of Modern Art (now called the 'Hugh Lane'). The portraits include those of Æ, Lady Gregory, and Douglas Hyde. Yeats's poem 'The Municipal Gallery Revisited', evokes the period of Ireland's political and literary revival.

CHESTER BEATTY LIBRARY, 20 Shrewsbury Rd, established in 1952 by Sir Alfred Chester Beatty (1875–1968). The Library contains oriental and Western manuscripts, bindings, colour prints, etc., housed in two galleries. Its treasures include the earliest known manuscripts of the New Testament (AD 200–50) and the 1259–60 manuscript of the *Rubáiyát* of Omar Khayyám.

CHRIST CHURCH CATHEDRAL. In a house beside the Cathedral lives Gretta, the lover of Willie Dunne in Sebastian Barry's novel *A Long Long Way* (2005): 'It was horribly dark because the house was squeezed in against Christ Church, and the windows on each landing looked like those dim paintings in old churches, lurking in the holy, lightless air.'

DOLPHIN'S BARN. The fictional Thaddeus Street, location of the old hotel, with its faded gilt and 'balding maroon carpet' in William Trevor's novel *Mrs Eckdorf in O'Neill's Hotel* (1969), is placed near Cork St. and Bond St. in the Dolphin's Barn area of the city.

DUBLIN WRITERS MUSEUM, 18 Parnell Sq. A comprehensive museum devoted to the last 300 years of Dublin's literary history housed in a sumptuous Georgian mansion. The Museum includes an outstanding collection of first and early editions of Irish classics, correspondence, portraits, and a diverting range of literary paraphernalia, from Samuel Beckett's telephone and Mary Lavin's teddy bear to Lady Gregory's lorgnette (www.writersmuseum.com).

MOUNT JEROME CEMETERY, Harold's Cross, a suburb S of the Grand Canal, between Rathmines and Kimmage. It includes Dublin's largest Protestant burial ground, where the following are buried: Thomas Davis (1814–45), Joseph Sheridan Le Fanu (1814–73), William E. H. Lecky (1838–1903), Edmund Dowden (1843–1913), G. W. Russell ('Æ', 1867–1935), and J. M. Synge (1871–1909).

NATIONAL GALLERY, Merrion Sq., erected in memory of William Dargan (1799–1867), benefactor of the arts. Bernard Shaw, whose statue by Troubetzkoy stands near the entrance, bequeathed one-third of his estate to the Gallery. The numerous portraits of literary figures include those of James Joyce, George Moore, and W. B. Yeats.

NATIONAL LIBRARY, Kildare St. (built 1885–90). It has important collections of books, manuscripts, prints, drawings, and historical archives.

THE PALACE BAR on Fleet St. was frequented by many of the well-known figures of 20th-c. literary life in Dublin, including Patrick Kavanagh and Brian O'Nolan. Cyril Connolly, brought to the bar by John Betjeman in 1941, thought the place 'as warm and friendly as an alligator tank'. Betjeman worked at the British High Commission as a press attaché 1941–3, where his job was to try and sway a neutral Ireland in favour of the British. He wrote reports on Irish politics, including the IRA. One division of the IRA planned to assassinate him, but the attempt was called off because his poetry was said to have been liked by the IRA's head of civilian intelligence.

ROYAL IRISH ACADEMY, ACADEMY HOUSE, 19 Dawson St. (founded 1783; royal charter 1785). The library of the Academy, Ireland's foremost learned society, houses a

Flann O'Brien (Brian O'Nolan) at the Palace Bar, Dublin

noteworthy collection of Irish manuscripts, which includes the *Cathac*, a 6th-7th-c. manuscript of the Psalter, possibly by St Columcille; *Lebor na hUidre*, the *Book of the Dun Cow*, an 11th–12th-c. codex; and the Stowe Missal, an 8th–9th-c. Mass book.

ST PATRICK'S CATHEDRAL, Patrick St. (a church rebuilt 1191 on the site of a pre-Norman church, granted cathedral status 1213, and generally restored 1864–9). Swift's grave is in the S aisle, beside that of 'Stella' (Esther Johnson, 1681–1728), and nearby is his monument to her and a bust of him by Patrick Cunningham (1775), the gift of Swift's publisher. Swift's famous Latin epitaph composed by himself is over the door of the robing room, accompanied by Yeats's translation and lines by Pope. His pulpit stands in the NW corner of the N transept. Other monuments include those to Samuel Lover (N aisle), Charles Wolfe (S transept), and Sir Samuel Ferguson (S aisle).

ST PATRICK'S HOSPITAL, Bow Lane, James's St. (1749–57). The hospital, now a psychiatric centre, was founded by Swift:

> He gave the little wealth he had
> To build a house for fools and mad;
> To show by one satiric touch,
> No nation wanted it so much.

It has an interesting collection of Swift relics.
Derek Mahon, his 'bits and pieces making a home from home', describes a stay in the hospital in 'Dawn at St Patrick's'.

TRINITY COLLEGE, College Green (founded 1592 by Elizabeth I). 'The College of the Holy and Undivided Trinity' was a Protestant establishment from which Catholics were excluded from taking degrees until 1793. On the S side of Library Sq. is the library (1712–32), which houses Ireland's greatest collection of books, manuscripts, and historical papers. The many treasures on view in the splendid Long Room on the first floor include the Book of Durrow, a 7th-c. illuminated gospel book; the Book of Kells (later 8th c.), the most famous of the illuminated gospel books, from the monastery of Kells, Co. Meath, but possibly compiled at St Columba's monastery at Iona; and the Garland of Howth (8th–9th c.), a gospel book from Ireland's Eye, a little island just N of *Howth. Among the many busts lining the aisle is one of Swift by Roubiliac.

Apart from the scholars mentioned above, the list of distinguished writers who attended the College includes the following: James Ussher (1581–1656), a foundation scholar who later became Archbishop of Armagh, and bequeathed his collection of books and manuscripts to the College; Roger Boyle, 1st Earl of Orrery (1621–79); Nahum Tate (1652–1715); George Berkeley (1685–1753); Charles Wolfe (1791–1823); William Maginn (1793–1842); John Wilson Croker (1780–1857); Thomas Davis (1814–45); Aubrey de Vere (1814–1902); John Mitchel (1818–75); Edward Dowden (1843–1913), who became Professor of English Literature here in 1867; and James Owen Hannay ('George A. Birmingham', 1865–1950), who became a canon of St Patrick's. Iain Sinclair, who would become known as a chronicler of the 'psychogeography' of London, actually did his studies here at Trinity, Dublin.

UNIVERSITY COLLEGE, Belfield, Stillorgan Rd, 3 m. SE of the city centre. The main part of the College has moved from Earlsfort Ter. (which houses the faculties of Medicine and Architecture). The College is part of the National University of Ireland, tracing its origin to the Catholic University of 1851, founded at 82–7 College Green. Nos 85 and 86 (Newman House) were joined together in 1853 to form the Catholic University of Ireland, with John Henry Newman as the first rector. In 1852 the College was administered by the Jesuit Fathers and, as University College, housed at nos 84–6.

It was at Newman House that Gerard Manley Hopkins SJ spent an unhappy period as Professor of Classics, 1884–9 (he died of typhoid fever in 1889 and was buried in the Jesuit plot at Glasnevin cemetery). His original study has been re-created as it was when he was here. Patrick Pearse was a student at the College, as was, from 1899 to 1902, James Joyce, who set scenes from *A Portrait of the Artist as a Young Man* here—notably in the Physics Theatre, the venue for the 'tundish' dialogue between Stephen Dedalus and the Dean of Studies. In 1908 it became a college of the new nondenominational National University of Ireland. Thomas MacDonagh, poet and co-founder of Edward Martyn's Irish Theatre, was a lecturer in English Literature here in 1914. Newman House is usually open for guided tours in the afternoons during the summer.

The Dublin-born novelist John McGahern and the Donegal playwright Frank McGuinness were both educated here; in 1997 McGuinness returned to the College as writer in residence. Colm Tóibín studied here too, gaining a degree in History and English. Dublin appears frequently in Tóibín's novels; though they are more frequently set in Co. Wexford, there's often a magnetic pull exerted by the big city—it is from here, the Four Courts, that the judge in *The Heather Blazing* (1992) tries to escape to a quieter rural life on the Wexford coast; in *The South* (1990) it is here that Katherine, an Irish Protestant living in Spain, returns to be reunited with her son.

DYSART CASTLE *Kilkenny*

The site of the now ruined castle is on the W bank of the Nore, 2 m. SE of Thomastown, a small market town on the N9 Kilkenny–New Ross road. This was once the home of the Berkeley family and the birthplace of the philosopher and bishop George Berkeley (1685–1753).

EDGEWORTHSTOWN
(or MOSTRIM) *Longford*

Small town in the Irish midlands at the junction of the N4 and the N55. Goldsmith went to school here (1741–5) under the Revd Patrick Hughes, an old friend of his father's, and learnt to enjoy the Latin poets and historians. From this school (gone) he went to Dublin for his entrance examinations to Trinity College. Edgeworthstown was the ancestral home of Maria Edgeworth, where she came with her father and stepmother in 1782 and settled for the rest of her life. It was here that she wrote her early stories for children (*The Parent's Assistant*, 1796) and, with her father, educational books such as *Practical Education* (1798), followed by novels, of which the first and most famous was *Castle Rackrent* (1800). Sir Walter Scott in his tour of Ireland enjoyed a happy visit here in the summer of 1825, and Wordsworth stayed for two days in September 1829, when he found 'the authoress . . . very lively'. Edgeworthstown House, still with its original pillared porch and square entrance hall, has been modernized and extended to form a nursing home run by the Sisters of Mercy. Maria Edgeworth and her father, Richard Lovell Edgeworth, are buried in St John's churchyard, and there are memorials inside the church (Ⓟ at the church gate).

ENNISCORTHY *Wexford*

Town on the river Slaney, 15 m. N of the county town of Wexford. Enniscorthy is the birthplace of the novelist Colm Tóibín, who uses the area as the setting for many of his works. In *The Heather Blazing* (1992) and *The Blackwater Lightship* (1999), the characters read the *Enniscorthy Echo*, scenes are lit by the beams of the Tuskar lighthouse, and families live in old houses on the Wexford coast, on the crumbling cliffs that look down onto the beach. And those of Tóibín's characters who do not live here are often those who once did and have now moved away, as in the case of Katherine in *The South* (1990), whose mother has also once moved away from here, after the family house was burnt down during the Troubles.

Thomas Kinsella, who met and courted his wife at the hospital here, wrote 'Another September' while staying at St John's Manor, 'all toil | Locked fast inside a dream with iron gates'. The battle of Vinegar Hill (1798), which took place near (and in) the town, is alluded to in Kinsella's ballad 'In the Ringwood'.

FORGNEY *Longford*

Village on the R392, 2 m. E of Ballymahon. The village church has a memorial window to Oliver Goldsmith, who was baptized there.

FOXROCK *Dublin*

Formerly a village near, now a suburb of, Dublin. Samuel Beckett was born at Cooldrinagh, Kerrymount Ave., where the signature of the young Beckett is carved in the panelling of the hall and stairway. It was the place of the bruising relationship with his dominant mother. His relationship with his father was more congenial. Beckett was fond of walking in the district as a boy:

> If there is a paradise, father is still striding along in his old clothes with his dog. At night, when I can't sleep, I do the old walks again and stand beside him again one Xmas morning in the fields near Glencullen, listening to the chapel bells. (letter to Susan Mannering, 1955)

FRESHFORD *Kilkenny*

Village 6 m. SW of Ballyragget. John Bale, author of *Kynge Johan* (1538), which has some claim to be the first historical drama in English, was made Bishop of Ossory and lived at Uppercourt House here. His life is the subject of John Arden's novel *The Books of Bale* (1988).

GLENDALOUGH *Wicklow*

'The Valley of the Two Lakes', 1 m. W of Laragh on the R756. This picturesque glen is associated with the life and legends of St Kevin, who came as a hermit in the 6th c. Beyond the ruins of the Seven Churches there is a hole in the rock, near the shore of the upper lake, known as St Kevin's Bed, which Sir Walter Scott visited on his tour of Ireland in 1825. According to Lockhart, who accompanied him, he insisted on making his way to it, where a fall of 30 or 40 ft would mean plunging into deep water, 'in spite of all remonstrances, crawling along the precipice. He succeeded and got in— the first lame man that ever tried it.'

Erskine Childers, author of *The Riddle of the Sands* (1903), an enduring and remarkably prophetic novel of political espionage, was born at Glendalough House. After a conventional Anglo-Irish upbringing, Childers turned to the cause of Irish independence, worked for Sinn Fein as propaganda minister, and in 1922 sought refuge from Free State troops at Glendalough. He was taken from the house to Beggars Bush Barracks in Dublin, where he faced a firing squad.

GLENMALURE *Wicklow*

Deep gorge through which the Avonbeg flows from the SE slopes of the Wicklow Mountains to join the Avonmore in the Vale of *Avoca. This wild and picturesque place was the setting for Synge's play *In the Shadow of the Glen* (1903).

HOWTH (pr. Hōth) *Dublin*

Fishing port and pleasant suburban resort 10 m. NE of Dublin, on the N side of Howth Head, the great hilly promontory guarding the E approach to Dublin Bay. Sir Samuel Ferguson (1810–86) lived here at Strand Lodge in the latter part of his life and was profoundly interested in local archaeology and legends. His poem 'Aideen's Grave' concerns the fine dolmen in the castle demesne, and 'The Cromlech of Howth' describes the cairn on Shelmartin (or Hill of Howth), supposedly the burial place of the 1st-c. king Crimthan. W. B. Yeats lived here with his family on their return to Ireland in 1881, first at Balscadden Cottage and later at Island View.

The novelist and Irish Nationalist Erskine Childers ran guns for the Irish Volunteers into Howth in his yacht *Asgard* in July 1914. The weapons were later used in the Easter rising. Derek Mahon looks over the water in his poem 'Beyond Howth Head':

> And here I close; for look, across
> dark waves where bell-buoys dimly toss
> the Baily winks beyond Howth Head
> and sleep calls from the silent bed;
> while the moon drags her kindred stones
> among the rocks and the strict bones
> of the drowned, and I put out the light
> on shadows of the encroaching night.

INISTIOGUE *Kilkenny*

Village on the river Nore. The picturesque village, the river, and nearby Woodstock, the burnt-out mansion of the Tighe family, its grounds 'a flitting-place | for ragged feeling, old angers and rumours', inspired Thomas Kinsella's 'Tao and Unfitness at Inistiogue on the River Nore'.

KELLS (or CEANANNUS MÓR) *Meath*

Market town near the Blackwater, on the N3 and the N52. It is celebrated especially for the Columban monastery, which for long treasured the Book of Kells, an illuminated gospel book of the late 8th c., probably written in Iona and brought to Kells when the monks of Iona sought refuge here from the Norse invaders of the early 9th c. The Book of Kells is now in Trinity College Dublin, and of the monastery there survive only five high crosses, St Columcille's House, a round tower, and a few other fragments.

KILKENNY *Westmeath*

Historic cathedral and market town and capital of the county, situated on the Nore, on the junction of the N10 and the N76. Kilkenny College (the Grammar School), a Protestant boarding school founded (1666) by the first Duke of Ormonde, is on the E side of Lower John St., across the river from the castle. Among many distinguished literary men educated here were Jonathan Swift, William Congreve, George Farquhar, and George Berkeley. The original building, superseded by the present one, which dates from 1782, is described in John Banim's novel *The Fetches* (1825) as being of irregular and straggling design, 'having partly a monastic physiognomy'. John Banim (1798–1842), novelist, dramatist, and poet, is remembered chiefly for his pictures of Irish life in *Tales by the O'Hara Family* (1825), in some of which he collaborated with his brother Michael (1796–1874), who was also a novelist. They were both natives of Kilkenny.

In the Parade, opposite the castle, are the premises of the old Private Theatre (later Revenue Commission offices), where Gay's musical play *Polly* (1729) was first performed (it had been banned by the Lord Chamberlain in England), and where Thomas Moore acted in 1808, 1809, and 1810. Moore's roles were chiefly singing ones, but he also wrote and spoke the prologues. He fell in love with Bessy Dyke, a 14-year-old actress who played Lady Godiva in a farce in which he acted, and whom he married in London in 1811. He returned in 1823, when he wrote that he 'dined and slept at Kilkenny, at our old club-house now turned into an inn' and 'walked with Lord L[ansdowne] about the town, and recollected the days of my courtship, when I used to walk with Bessy on the banks of the river'.

The castle, splendidly situated above the W bank of the Nore, was the seat of the powerful Butler family from the 14th c. until 1935, when it became the property of the city. It was the home of Lady Eleanor Butler, who, with her

The chapel at Glendalough, Wicklow, sacred to St Kevin and visited by Sir Walter Scott. Glendalough House was the home of Erskine Childers

315

friend the Hon. Sarah Ponsonby, emigrated to Wales in 1778 in the teeth of family opposition (see LLANGOLLEN).

Many of the events in John Arden's novel *The Books of Bale* (1998) take place in Kilkenny.

KILKENNY WEST *Kilkenny*

Small village *c*. 9 m. NE of Athlone, off the N55, where Oliver Goldsmith's father, the Revd Charles Goldsmith, was first assistant and then successor to his wife's uncle the Revd Mr Green, the curate-in-charge. The church is usually taken to be 'The decent church that topt the neighbouring hill' in *The Deserted Village* (1770).

LARACOR *Meath*

Village on the R158, 2 m. S of Trim. Swift came here in 1700 as rector of the parish and remained, with frequent absences in London and *Dublin, until his appointment as Dean of St Patrick's in Dublin. Only fragments of his Glebe House remain, NW of the church which replaced his, but which still has the altar plate he used. Many of his tracts and satires were written here, including the *Argument to Prove the Inconvenience of Abolishing Christianity* (1708) and also part of the *Journal to Stella* (1766, 1768). Stella (Esther Johnson) came in 1701 to be near him and lived with her friend Mrs Dingley at a house (now ruined, known as Stella's Cottage) a little N, near the gates of Knightsbrook House. The willows bordering the stream where the three of them used to walk are the descendants of those planted by Swift. He kept the living until the end of his life, but seldom returned after he had become dean.

LISSOY *Westmeath*

Small village on the N55, 6 m. SW of Ballymahon. Goldsmith grew up here after his father had moved from Pallas to become curate-in-charge of Kilkenny West, and the ruined parsonage may still be seen. Goldsmith's first lessons began when he was 3, with Mrs Elizabeth Delap, who thought him one of the dullest pupils she had ever taught, though she lived to be proud of him. At the age of 6 he went to the village school, under Thomas Byrne, identified as the schoolmaster of *The Deserted Village* (1770) in the lines: 'A man severe he was, and stern to view; | I knew him well, and every truant knew.' It was at this time that Goldsmith contracted smallpox, which left him scarred for life. Lissoy has been regarded as the 'sweet Auburn' of *The Deserted Village* and many of the features, such as 'the never-failing brook', 'the busy mill', and 'the decent Church that topped the neighbouring hill', can

be matched with local landmarks. It is possible that Goldsmith drew on happy childhood memories for the idyllic scenes in the poem (see also NUNEHAM COURTENAY).

LONGFORD *Longford*

County town at the junction of the N4, N5, and N63. Padraic Colum, poet and playwright, whose father was the Workhouse Master, was born here in 1881.

MALAHIDE CASTLE *Dublin*

Castle SW of the village of Malahide, 13 m. NE of Dublin, the home of the Talbot family for over 800 years. A store of James Boswell's private papers was brought here by Emily Boswell, a direct descendant, who married the 5th Lord Talbot de Malahide. In the 1930s and 1940s further caches of documents and journals were discovered and stimulated the demand for a life of Boswell. The complicated story of the Malahide papers is told in *The Treasure of Auchinleck*, by David Buchanan (1975).

PALLAS *Longford*

Hamlet in the parish of Forgney, 2 m. E of Ballymahon, at the end of a minor road off the R392. The Revd Charles Goldsmith, father of Oliver Goldsmith, rented a dilapidated farmhouse here, farmed the nearby fields, and assisted at the local church of Kilkenny West. Oliver is thought to have been born, probably in 1730, on 10 November, at Pallas, though he may have been born at his maternal grandmother's house, Ardnagowan, near Elphin, where his mother was staying about this time. When he was about 2 his family moved to *Lissoy. The Pallas building has been demolished, but the site can be reached by a stile and footpath.

SANDYCOVE *Dublin*

Coastal resort just SE of Dun Laoghaire. Signposts to 'James Joyce's Tower' indicate the Martello tower, one of a series of defences against the threat of Napoleonic invasion, which figures in the first chapter of *Ulysses* (1922). Joyce stayed there briefly in September 1904 and it now houses a museum. The collection includes portraits, photographs, letters, and personal possessions of Joyce, including his tie and wallet, and his cabin trunk, guitar, and famous cane, some of them donated by close friends such as Samuel Beckett and Sylvia Beach, the first publisher of *Ulysses*. There are first and rare editions of his work, including the deluxe edition of *Ulysses* with illustrations by Henri Matisse and a page of the original manuscript notes for *Finnegans*

Wake. The museum also includes a range of the ordinary or unusual items—a Clongowes pandybat, a Plumtree's pot—which Joyce's imagination was to transform into the stuff of myth.

SLANE *Meath*

Small town in the valley of the Boyne, situated under the lee of Slane Hill, which towers above it, 9 m. W of Drogheda, on the N51. Francis Ledwidge (1891–1917), a poet of great promise, was born here and worked for a time on the land. He served with the British Forces in the First World War and was killed in Flanders. *Songs of the Field* (1915) and *Songs of Peace* (1916) were published in his lifetime; his *Complete Poems*, with a preface by Lord Dunsany, in 1919.

STILLORGAN *Dublin*

Formerly a village near, now a suburb of, Dublin. Samuel Beckett attended the kindergarten and Flann O'Brien (Brian O'Nolan) lived in a bungalow in the town on 21 Waltersland Rd.

TAGHMON (pr. Tah'mōn) *Wexford*

Village on the R738, 9 m. W of Wexford. Henry Francis Lyte, remembered especially as the author of 'Abide with me', was curate here after his ordination in 1815 until 1816. A memorial tablet was erected in the church on the centenary of his birth.

TULLAMORE *Offaly*

Distillery and county town. As a child, Brian O'Nolan ('Flann O'Brien') lived at The Beeches, a large house at Cappincur, 2 m. from Tullamore. The local distillery, Loaches of Kilbeggan, often replenished the 'Crock', Mr Collopy's whiskey jar in O'Brien's comic novel *The Hard Life* (1961).

WEXFORD *Wexford*

County town and former seaport at the mouth of the Slaney. The novelist John Banville was born in Wexford in 1945. He attended the Christian Brothers School and St Peter's College, Wexford, in the 1950s and 1960s. Somewhere on the coast of Co. Wexford, at the end of a peninsula beside the fictional town of Kilnalough, stands the Majestic Hotel in J. G. Farrell's novel *Troubles* (1970). Its incinerated condition at the opening of the book, with its 'great number of cast-iron bathtubs . . . and a simply prodigious number of basins and lavatory bowls', is taken up in Derek Mahon's famous poem 'A Disused Shed in County Wexford', imagined 'deep in the grounds of a burnt-out hotel' and dedicated to Farrell.

MUNSTER

ASKEATON *Limerick*

Small market town 16 m. W of Limerick on the N69, medieval stronghold of the Earls of Desmond. In the graveyard of the Protestant parish church, which is built into the remains of the ruined St Mary's Augustinian priory, is the grave of the poet Aubrey de Vere, who lived at *Curragh Chase 5 m. away.

AWBEG RIVER *Cork*

A clear, shallow river that rises in the Ballyhoura Hills (the ridge continuing W of the Galtee Mountains) and flows by Kilcolman Castle and *Doneraile to join the Blackwater E of Mallow. The Awbeg is Spenser's 'Mulla' in *Colin Clouts come home againe* (written at Kilcolman, 1591; published London, 1595), where Colin Clout sat

> Under the foote of *Mole* that mountain hore,
> Keeping my sheepe amongst the cooly shade,
> Of the greene alders by the *Mulla's* shore . . .

The name 'Mulla' was suggested by the 'Mullach' of Cill na Mullach, the Irish name of Buttevant, a small market town beside the Awbeg, *c.* 2 m. from Kilcolman Castle:

> Mulla, the daughter of old Mole so hight
> The nymph which of that water course hath charge,
> That springing out of Mole, doth run down right
> To Buttevant, where spreading forth at large
> It giveth name unto that auncient cittie
> Which Kilnemullah clepéd is of old.

The Mole represents the Ballyhouras in general, and in Spenser's story the Mulla was loved by the river Bregog, which also rises there and so far as can be traced empties into the Awbeg and the Blackwater. The name 'Bregog' means 'deceitful' and is appropriate to the river's way of disappearing underground and reappearing as a meandering stream, broken by pools and scattered across the countryside. This accounts for the legend of the Bregog hiding and then visiting the Mulla secretly, in defiance of her father, old Mole, who forbade the marriage and in his rage threw down stones from the hills into Bregog's course. Wherever the Bregog may be found today, its banks are littered with rocks. The Mulla is mentioned again in *Epithalamion* (1595), written at Kilcolman to celebrate the poet's marriage with Elizabeth Boyle:

> Ye nymphs of Mulla, which with careful heed
> The silver scaly trouts do tend full well,
> And greedy pikes which use therein to feed
> Those trouts and pikes all others do excel.

BALLINCOLLIG *Cork*

Village on the N22 *c.* 5 m. W of Cork, just S of the Lee. James Thomson (1834–82) came here to teach in 1851 and met Charles Bradlaugh (1833–91), the controversial advocate of free thought, who became his lifelong friend. Thomson's most famous poem, 'The City of Dreadful Night', was published (1874) in

Bradlaugh's weekly paper, *The National Reformer*.

BALLYDAVID *Kerry*

Village on the Dingle peninsula. A description of the detritus around the shore provides the opening for Thomas Kinsella's poem 'Ballydavid Pier':

> The Angelus. Faint bell-notes
> From some church in the distance
> Tremble over the water.
> It is nothing. The vacant harbour
> Is filling; it will empty.

BALLYLANEEN *Waterford*

Village on the R677, halfway between Kilmacthomas and the coastal village of Bunmahon. The Gaelic poet Tadhg Gaelach Ó Súilleabháin (1715–95) is buried in the churchyard, with a Latin epitaph by his friend Donnchadh Rua Mac Conmara.

BANDON *Cork*

Market town on the N71, 19 m. SW of Cork. William Hazlitt came here at the age of 18 months when his father, an outspoken advocate of American independence, came to Ireland and was Presbyterian minister in Bandon for 3½ years, before taking his family to America in 1783. Lennox Robinson, dramatist and a manager and then director of the Abbey Theatre, Dublin, was educated at Bandon Grammar School.

BLASKET ISLANDS *Kerry*

Group of islands off the SW tip of the Dingle peninsula, the most westerly point of Europe. The largest, the Great Blasket, was inhabited until the mid-20th c. by a hardy, independent, Irish-speaking line of men and women, whose way of life is vividly described by Robin Flower in *The Western Island* (1944) and in Maurice O'Sullivan's *Twenty Years A-Growing* (1953), Tomás O'Crohan's *The Islandman* (1937), and Peig Sayers's *An Old Woman's Reflections* (1962), autobiographies written in Irish (later translated) by people born and bred on the island. O'Crohan's *The Islandman* was parodied by Flann O'Brien in his comic novel *An Béal Bocht*—or *The Poor Mouth: A Bad Story About the Hard Life* (1941).

The population supported themselves by fishing and on the produce of their fields and flocks, but as the islanders made more contact with the mainland, so their numbers diminished by emigration and those who remained found it impossible to make a living. In 1953 the last inhabitants left, but a few houses have been restored for visitors. The Great Blasket can be visited from the quay at Dunquin on Blasket Sound, just N of Dunmore Head.

BOWEN'S COURT *Cork*

Former 18th-c. mansion, home of the Bowen family who were granted land by Cromwell, 1½ m. W of Kildorrery on the N73 and NW of Farahy village. Elizabeth Bowen was brought

up here but went to school in England. She inherited the house from her father in 1928 and wrote its history *Bowen's Court* (1942). She and her husband came to live here in 1952, but after his death shortly afterwards the house was too large for her and she sold it in 1960 to a neighbour. He later demolished it. She was buried, at her wish, in Kildorrery church in the grounds (1973). Large Anglo-Irish family houses suggestive of Bowen's Court appear in much of her fiction, including the doomed Danielstown in *The Last September* (1929) and the dilapidated Montefort in *A World of Love* (1955).

CASHEL *Tipperary*

Small historic market town. The novelist Liam O'Flaherty won a scholarship to Rockwell College in 1908 and studied here for four years.

CASTLEGREGORY *Kerry*

Village on the N side of the Dingle peninsula, overlooking Tralee Bay, 19 m. W of Tralee. It takes its name from Gregory Hoare, a tenant-in-chief of the Desmonds, who built a castle here in the early 16th c. In 1580 his son Black Hugh, deeming it prudent to show loyalty to the English Queen, entertained Sir Walter Ralegh and Edmund Spenser, who were leading a company of Lord Grey's army to attack the Spanish and Italian garrison at Fort-del-Oro at Smerwick. An account of the feast is given in *In the Kingdom of Kerry*, by Richard Hayward (1950). The castle stood at the SE end of the village, but nothing is left except some stones built into several of the houses and the remains of an inscribed arch from the castle doorway.

CASTLETOWNSHEND (or BAILE AN CHAISLEÁIN) *Cork*

Village at the end of the R596, 5 m. SE of Skibbereen, on the W shore of Castle Haven. When Swift was staying at *Unionhall in 1723 he used to come over by rowing boat from Glandore Harbour and tradition has it that he composed the Latin poem *Carberiae Rupes* in the ruined tower near the harbour, and that he named one of the houses in the village Laputa (later called Ahakista). Castletownshend was the home of Edith Œnone Somerville, who collaborated with her cousin Violet Martin ('Martin Ross') in writing travel books, essays, sporting books, and children's picture books, and is remembered especially for *Some Experiences of an Irish R.M.* (1899) and *Further Experiences of an Irish R.M.* (1908), entertaining stories written in the ascendancy tradition of the big house and foxhunting, and for the sensitive novel *The Real Charlotte* (1894). Edith Somerville lived nearly all her life at Drishane, the Georgian family mansion at the entrance to the village, and died at Tally House, a little further on. The main street goes steeply down to the harbour, circumventing two tall sycamores, which she referred to as 'walled in their barbaric stone flower pot, the distraction of the village'. The Protestant church of St Barrahane, on a hill overlooking

The pier at Dunquin, from which the boat leaves for Great Blasket. Island life was chronicled by Tomás O'Crohan and parodied by Flann O'Brien

the estuary, contains memorials to Edith Somerville, including bronze chandeliers and a tablet on the N wall presented by American admirers. The holy table was given by her in memory of Violet Martin, who predeceased her by 34 years. They are buried in the churchyard in adjacent graves.

CLONMEL *Tipperary*

Ancient, formerly walled town on the N24, situated in the beautiful valley of the Suir. Laurence Sterne was born here (24 Nov. 1713), traditionally in Mary St. (formerly Our Lady's St.), when his father, an army subaltern, was temporarily stationed in the town.

Marguerite Power, later Countess of Blessington (1789–1846), came to live here at the age of 8, and a secluded part of the river near the weir where she used to bathe, known as 'Lady Blessington's bath', can be seen from the path S of the river, a little E of Old Bridge Rd. She spent much time on the Continent and wrote travel books and novels, but is remembered especially for her *Journal of Conversations with Lord Byron* (1832). George Borrow attended the former Grammar School (later the County Engineering Headquarters), just outside the West Gate, for a few months in 1815, when his father was stationed in the town

as an army officer, and it was here that he first began to learn Irish. Anthony Trollope lived in lodgings in Anne St. in 1844–5 while working as a Post Office inspector. The former Post Office building became a chemist's shop, next to the Provincial Bank in O'Connell St.

CLOUGHJORDAN *Tipperary*

Village at junction of R490 and R491, 6 m. SE of Borrisokane. Thomas MacDonagh, poet and co-founder of Edward Martyn's Irish Theatre (1914), was born in a house in the main street. He was one of the signatories of the Proclamation of the Irish Republic in 1916 and was executed after the Easter Rising.

CLOYNE *Cork*

Village on the R629, 6 m. SE of Midleton. George Berkeley was bishop from 1734 to 1753 and the small cathedral of St Colman, built on older foundations *c.* 1250 and subsequently much altered, has a recumbent alabaster statue of him by Bruce Joy in the N transept. According to the brass tablet on the wall, 'England, Ireland, Scotland and America contributed to the memorial'. His most important philosophical works, *A New Theory of Vision* (1709), *The Principles of Human Knowledge* (1710), and *Three Dialogues between*

Hylas and Philonous (1713), were written in his youth. While he was at Cloyne he published *Siris: A Chain of Philosophical Reflections and Inquiries Concerning the Virtues of Tar-Water* (1744), a work of philosophy in the widest sense, dealing with the action and reaction of the soul and the body. Locally he is remembered for his saintly qualities and for his generosity and medical aid to the poor of Cloyne in difficult times.

COBH (pr. Cove) *Cork*

Cathedral town (called Queenstown, 1849–1922) on Great Island on the N side of Cork Harbour, the principal port for transatlantic liners, reached by the R624 from Carrigtohill on the N25 from Cork. John Tobin (1770–1804), a dramatist whose first successful play, *The Honey Moon*, was produced a few weeks after his death, is buried in the churchyard near the crossroads, 1 m. N, in an unmarked grave. Tobin had sailed for the West Indies in search of health, but died on the first day out and was brought back to Cobh for burial. The Revd Charles Wolfe, author of 'The Burial of Sir John Moore After Corunna' (1817), is buried in the same churchyard, in the NW corner of the ruined church, in a flat-topped grave overgrown with brambles.

CORK *Cork*

Port, university, and cathedral city, situated on the Lee at the head of a long and beautiful estuary on the S coast. The river flows through the city in two main channels, spanned by several bridges, described by Spenser, who was appointed High Sheriff of Cork in 1598, as

> The spreading Lee, that like an island fayre
> Encloseth Corke with his divided flood.

(*The Faerie Queene*, IV. ii)

The Protestant church of Christ Church, between Grand Parade and South Main St., is on the site of the city's second medieval church (demolished 1717), where in 1594 Spenser is thought to have married Elizabeth Boyle, for whom he wrote *Epithalamion* (1595) in celebration of the occasion.

Arthur Murphy, playwright, actor, and friend of Dr Johnson, worked as a merchant's clerk in Cork in 1747 before going to London, where he settled.

Several distinguished writers have been born in Cork, though many of their birthplaces are not recorded. They include James Sheridan Knowles (1784–1862), a dramatist who studied medicine before turning to literature, author of several plays and a popular ballad, *The Welsh Harper*, which attracted the attention of Hazlitt; William Maginn (1793–1842), one of the early contributors (under the pen-name 'Ensign O'Doherty') to *Blackwood's Edinburgh Magazine* and the founder of *Fraser's Magazine* (1830), in which he published his 'Homeric Ballads'; Thomas Crofton Croker (1798–1854), antiquarian and friend of Maginn, born in Buckingham Sq. In spite of a lack of formal education Croker devoted himself from an early age to the study of Irish songs and legends which he collected while rambling in S Ireland, published in *Researches in the South of Ireland* (1824), *The Fairy Legends and Traditions of the South of Ireland* (1825), his best-known work, which was admired by Scott, and *Legends of the Lakes* (1829), later republished as *A Guide to the Lakes* (1831) and *Killarney Legends* (1876). After an apprenticeship at 16 to Lecky and Marchant, a firm of Quaker merchants, he went to London (1818) to work as an Admiralty clerk, made his name as a folklorist, and in 1827 became a member of the Society of Antiquaries. He helped to found the Camden and Percy societies. Scott remembered him as 'little as a dwarf, keen-eyed as a hawk, and of easy, prepossessing manners'. Francis Sylvester Mahony (1804–66), author, under his pen-name 'Father Prout', of many entertaining papers and poems contributed to *Fraser's Magazine* (1834–6) and *Bentley's Miscellany* (1837), was also a native of Cork. He is best remembered for his lines on the celebrated bells of the church of St Anne's, Shandon (CI):

> With deep affection,
> And recollection,
> I often think of
>   Those Shandon bells.
> 'Tis the bells of Shandon,

> That sound so grand on
> The pleasant waters
>   Of the River Lee.

The bells hang in the elegant clock tower of St Anne's Church, which stands on the hillside N of the river, above Pope's Quay. Mahony, who lived nearly all his life in Cork, is buried in the churchyard. Justin McCarthy (1830–1912), historian and novelist, was born in Cork, the son of the clerk to the city magistrates, and at 17 was a reporter on the *Cork Examiner*. He is best remembered for his historical works, especially *A History of Our Own Times* (1879; with additions, 1905). He also wrote novels, of which the best known are *Dear Lady Disdain* (1875) and *Miss Misanthrope* (1878). Edward Dowden (1843–1913), poet and Shakespearian scholar, also a native, was the son of a Cork merchant and landowner, and went to Queen's College (now University College) before going to Dublin. Daniel Corkery (1878–1964), dramatist, was born at 2 Auburn Villas, near the top of Gardiner's Hill, on the NE side of the city. His plays include *The Labour*, *The Yellow Bittern*, and *Fohnam the Sculptor*, but he is remembered principally for his literary studies *The Study of Irish Literature* and *The Hidden Ireland* (1925). He also wrote a novel, *The Threshold of Quiet* (1917). He spent most of his life in Cork and was Professor of English Literature at University College until he retired (1947).

Robert Gibbings (1889–1958), wood engraver and author, was born and brought up in Cork, 'the loveliest city in the world', as he calls it in *Lovely Is the Lee* (1944). He was educated at Cork Grammar School and University College, where he was a medical student for two years before leaving to study art at the local academy, under Harry Scully RHA, and later at the Slade in London. He returned to Cork in 1943 and spent seven months in the west of the county, gathering material for *Lovely Is the Lee* and *Sweet Cork, of Thee* (1951), illustrated by his own woodcuts.

Michael O'Donovan (1903–66), widely known by his pen-name, 'Frank O'Connor', was born in Douglas St., but his earliest memories were of 251 Blarney St., a small cottage at the top of the hill, where he lived until he was 5 or 6, when his parents moved to 8 Harrington's Sq., near Dillon's Cross, NW of Gardiner's Hill. He was educated at the Christian Brothers' School, where he was taught by Daniel Corkery, who inspired him to learn Gaelic. His work includes novels, plays, and criticism, but he is best known for his short stories: 'Bones of Contention' (1936), *The Common Chord* (1947), 'Traveller's Samples' (1950), and others. He was also a Gaelic scholar and *Kings, Lords, and Commons* (1961) is an anthology of translations from the Irish. His autobiography, *An Only Child* (New York, 1958; London, 1961), gives a vivid picture of Cork in the early 1900s. A portrait bust of him stands in the Public Library in Grand Parade.

The short-story writer Sean O'Faoláin was born and brought up over a pub at 16 Half Moon St., not far from the Cork Opera House, for which his mother took visiting artistes as weekly lodgers:

> I gazed in awe at their exotic belongings—the travelling clock in red leather, the whiskey bottle with the patent lock, photographs of themselves and their friends in silver frames, all signed, their specially ordered bits of outlandish food on the sideboard . . .

He was educated at the Lancasterian National School ('even as a building it was crazy') and subsequently the Presentation Brothers' College—the 'Pres'—where his 'unhappiness was chronic and suppressed'. He went on to University College, Cork, which, though tiny, served him well: 'How constricted my whole subsequent life might have been in some dead-end, menial job if I had not for those years enclaved myself in this slightly absurd Lilliput!' He joined the Irish Volunteers, a forerunner of the IRA, and during his eight student years rose within its ranks, ending up as Director of Publicity in Cork during the civil war. O'Faolain records his part in the Republican struggle and the loss of his youthful idealism in his autobiography, *Vive Moi!* (1964). The city features in O'Faoláin's stories, including, memorably, 'The Old Master', in which the huge, facetious, lazy bachelor John Aloysius Gonzaga O'Sullivan works in the law library of the Courthouse. The poet Paul Durcan studied Archaeology and Modern History at University College, Cork, after a period in London when he tried to establish himself as a poet.

The novelist and short-story writer William Trevor is a native of Co. Cork, and recalls with affection visits to the city in his memoir *Excursions in the Real World* (1993). 'Willie Quinton', the narrator of his novel *Fools of Fortune* (1983), lives at the top of St Patrick's Hill, and is sent to a Protestant school on the other side of the city. Somewhere in Co. Cork stands the subject of Derek Mahon's poem 'A Garage in Co. Cork', with its

>   mound
> Of never-used cement, the curious faces,
> the soft-drink ads and the uneven ground
> Rainbowed with oily puddles, where a snail
> Had scrawled its slimy, phosphorescent trail.

Visitors to the city have praised or abused it. Arthur Young found it reminiscent of a Dutch town with its pleasant waterways, and Thomas Moore delighted in the 'sort of sea avenue up to the town, with beautiful banks on either side studded over with tasteful villas'. Thackeray thought it disappointing and was dismayed by its shabbiness and idle populace. Sir Walter Scott, however, on his Irish tour of 1825, was very favourably impressed by his visit and the city reciprocated by presenting him with the freedom of Cork.

CROOM *Limerick*

Small market town on the N20, 10 m. N of Ráthluirc, situated on the Maigue. Seán Ó Tuama, a Gaelic poet who had been a member of the 'Court of Poetry' that was held at the farm of Seán Clarách Mac Domhnaill (see RÁTHLUIRC), was an innkeeper at Mungret Gate, near the Fair Green. After Mac Domhnaill's death in 1754 he invited local poets, including Aindrias Mac Craith, to his own 'Court', which continued to meet at intervals. He is buried in Croom churchyard.

CURRAGH CHASE *Limerick*

Demesne 5 m. SE of Askeaton, on a minor road between the N69 and the N21. The poet Aubrey de Vere was born (10 Jan. 1814) in the family house (burnt down in 1941). He was educated privately and at Trinity College Dublin, and made many literary friends in England, where he often stayed. Tennyson, whom he visited several times, at *Farringford and *Haslemere, spent a month with him at Curragh Chase in 1848. De Vere published *The Waldenses and Other Poems* in 1842, and his voluminous works include *The Legends of St Patrick* (1872), *Critical Essays* (1887-9), and *Recollections* (1897). He died here (21 Jan. 1902) and was buried at *Askeaton.

DONERAILE *Cork*

Attractive small town on the R522, 2 m. E of Buttevant off the N20, situated on the Awbeg. It was part of the 3,000-acre estate granted to Edmund Spenser after the crushing of the Desmond rebellion in 1586, together with the ruined stronghold of Kilcolman (3 m. N). Spenser came from *Dublin, where he had been Clerk to the Irish Court of Chancery, to live at Kilcolman in 1587 and was visited two years later by Sir Walter Ralegh, who encouraged him to bring the newly completed first three books of *The Faerie Queene* to London, for publication in 1590. Spenser returned to Kilcolman the following year and wrote the pastoral allegory *Colin Clouts come home againe* (printed 1595), dedicated to Ralegh. In 1594 he married Elizabeth Boyle, for whom he wrote the *Amoretti* sonnets and *Epithalamion* (both printed in 1595). After another visit to London, when he published the next three books of *The Faerie Queene* (1596), he was back once more at Kilcolman, but was forced to leave when his home was attacked and burnt down, and it is possible that some unpublished manuscripts of *The Faerie Queene* were lost in the fire. The ruined tower of Kilcolman Castle, near the 'rushy lake' of *Epithalamion*, is now in the grounds of the Kilcolman Wildfowl Refuge. It is probable that Spenser did not live in the castle itself, but in a house nearby, all trace of which has gone.

Canon Sheehan, author of *Luke Delmege*, *My New Curate*, *Lisheen*, and other novels of Irish life, especially in Co. Cork, was parish priest of Doneraile from 1895 until his death in 1913. He lived in a house overlooking the river and is commemorated by a statue by Francis Doyle-Jones in front of his church.

DOUGLAS *Cork*

Suburban village on the N28, 5 m. SE of Cork. This was the birthplace of Esmé Stuart Lennox Robinson (1886-1958), playwright, director of the Abbey Theatre, and co-editor of *The Oxford Book of Irish Verse* (1958).

DURRUS *Cork*

Village on the R591, 7 m. SW of Bantry. The novelist J. G. Farrell is buried in the graveyard of the Protestant church of St James, overlooking Friendly Cove, Dunmanus Bay. His manuscripts can be seen in the Library of Trinity College *Dublin.

ENNIS *Clare*

Busy market town on the Fergus, on the N18 and the N85. The poet Thomas Dermody, called by his biographer J. G. Raymond 'Ireland's most erratic genius', was born here (17 Jan. 1775; house gone), the son of a schoolmaster. He was a precocious boy, taught classics in his father's school from the age of 9, and wrote much poetry, including 'Monody on the Death of Chatterton', before he was 12. A born rebel, he ran away to *Dublin, worked in a bookshop, and published his first book of poems in 1792, but rejected a chance of going to Trinity College, and enlisted in the army. Later he lapsed into irregular ways, which led to his early death in London. Lines from his poem 'Enthusiast' match his uneven personality:

> He who such polish'd lines so well could form,
> Was Passion's slave, was Indiscretion's child:
> Now earth-enamour'd, grov'ling with the worm;
> Now seraph-plum'd, the wonderful, the wild.

The Harp of Erin (2 vols, 1807) contains his complete poetical works.

Sean O'Faolain came in 1924 to teach for a year or so at the Christian Brothers' School. A fellow teacher and lodger provided an object lesson in a dead-end teaching life and he got out as soon as he could.

ENNISTYMON *Clare*

Small market town and holiday resort on the Cullenagh, on the N67 and the N85. Brian Merriman, author of *The Midnight Court*, is thought to have been born here *c.* 1749, but the exact place is unrecorded. See FEAKLE.

FEAKLE *Clare*

Secluded little village on the R461 and R468, near the foothills of the Slieve Aughty Mountains. Brian Merriman (Brian Mac Giolla-Meidhre, 1749/1757?-1805), poet and schoolmaster, is buried in the old churchyard. His grave is unmarked, but there is a bronze plaque, designed by Seamus Murphy, on the outer wall (unveiled 1967). He was a native of Clare, possibly of Ennistymon, and lived at Feakle, earning his living as a hedge school teacher and working a small farm (for which he won a premium in 1796 for the quality of his flax). The work for which he is remembered is *Cúirt an mheádhon oidhche* (The Midnight Court, 1780), a long poem that has been described as 'a rhythmical bacchanalia' and has been published in several English translations from the Irish, notably by Frank O'Connor

(1945), Lord Longford (1949), and David Marcus (1953).

FERMOY *Cork*

Town on the river Blackwater. 'Kilneagh', the Anglo-Irish house depicted by William Trevor in his tragic novel *Fools of Fortune* (1983), and destroyed by the Black and Tans, is imagined as standing near Fermoy.

GARINISH ISLAND (or ILNACULLIN) *Cork*

Island off the W shore of Glengarriff Harbour, accessible by boat (March-October) from the harbour. Formerly privately owned and landscaped (1910-13) and containing attractive Italian and Japanese gardens, classical temples, and exotic plants, it is now state property. Bernard Shaw visited the island when he was staying at Glengarriff in 1923, and wrote part of *Saint Joan* (1924) there. 'During that year', he said, 'I was at Glengarriff from the 18th July to the 15th August, and at Parknasilla [Kerry] from the 15th August to the 18th September, working at the play all the time . . . But the play was neither begun nor finished in Eire. A good deal of it was written in rapidly moving trains between King's Cross and Hatfield . . .'.

KILCROHANE *Cork*

Village on the N shore of Dunmanus Bay, 10 m. SW of Durrus, on a minor road off the R591. J. G. Farrell lived near here in the 1970s in a small stone-built house 2 m. N, overlooking Bantry Bay. He had already made his name as a novelist with *Troubles* (1970; G. Faber Memorial Prize), *The Siege of Krishnapur* (1973; Booker Prize), and *The Singapore Grip* (1978), and was working on his half-finished novel *The Hill Station*, when he was tragically drowned while fishing off the rocks nearby. *The Hill Station*, edited by John Spurling, was published in 1981 together with Farrell's Indian diary of 1971. His manuscripts have been given to the Library of Trinity College *Dublin.

KILFENORA *Clare*

Small village and old monastic settlement at the southern tip of Co. Clare's karst landscape region, the Burren. The village is the home of the subject of Paul Durcan's poem 'The Kilfenora Teaboy':

> I'm the Kilfenora teaboy
> And I'm not so very young,
> But though the land is going to pieces
> I will not take up the gun . . .

KILLARNEY *Kerry*

Market town and tourist centre on the N22 and the N71 situated near lakes and mountains of great beauty. Many writers, from the early 19th c. on, have visited the town and made expeditions in the surrounding country. Sir Walter Scott, on his tour of Ireland in 1825, considered the Upper Lake (*c.* 5 m. SW of the town) the grandest sight he had ever seen, and Tennyson, who visited Killarney while he was staying with Aubrey de Vere at *Curragh Chase, wrote the lyric 'The splendour falls on castle walls' (for the 3rd edn of *The Princess*, 1853) when he heard a bugle blown beneath 'The Eagle's Nest' and 'eight distinct echoes'. Hugh Kelly, author of the comedies *False Delicacy* (1768), *A Word for the Wise* (1770), and *The School for Wives* (1773), was born (1739) in Killarney, but went to London (1760) to make his name.

A memorial to the Four Kerry Poets, designed by Seamus Murphy, was unveiled at Martyr's Hill on 15 August 1940 (a further ceremony following at *Muckross on the same day). The memorial, moved for road redevelopment, has been re-erected at the old entrance to the railway nearby. The statue symbolizes the tradition of the free spirit of Ireland which was handed from one to another of these poets who wrote between the early 17th and late 18th cc.: Pierce Ferriter (d. 1653), who 'stands for all that is heroic in Irish history'. He was said to have

composed poetry with one eye on Irish character, Irish manners and customs; the other on the Catholic refinement which distinguished the poetical literature of Europe in the Middle Ages. . . . He lamented with great dignity the Cromwellian transplantation and transportation decrees which affected rich and poor in Ireland.

Geoffrey O'Donoghue (d. 1677) is remembered for 'his lofty courage and intelligent verse which kept alive the spirit of independence among a people fast becoming entangled in a web of slavery'. He was succeeded by Aodhgan O'Rahilly (d. 1728), who flourished in the early 18th c., in whose verse 'the noble qualities of Ireland's chieftains and people' were kept alive at a time when the Catholic Church was suppressed and had to work in secret. Eoghan Ruadh O'Sullivan (d. 1784) was a popular poet of noble birth. It was said of him that 'he dignified labour by his sparkling genius, his wit and humour relieved the tedium of the winter nights'.

KILLIMER (pr. Ki'līmer) *Clare*

Small village on the N shore of the Shannon estuary, the terminus of the car ferry from Tarbert on the S shore. About 1 m. E, on the road to Knock, is the little churchyard of Burrane, the burial place of Ellen Hanley, the 'Colleen Bawn', on whose tragic story Gerald Griffin based his novel *The Collegians* (1829). She is buried in the same grave as Peter O'Connell, a professor of languages and literature, who found her body after she had been drowned in the Shannon by her husband in 1819. The flat gravestone, protected from souvenir hunters by a concrete casing, lies in the old churchyard *c.* 8 ft above the road and opposite the gate to the new churchyard below. The facts and the fiction of the story of the Colleen Bawn are told by William MacLysaght in *Death Sails the Shannon* (1953; new edn, 1970).

KILMACTHOMAS *Waterford*

Village on the Mahon, *c.* 16 m. SW of Waterford, off the N25. The Gaelic poets

Tadhg Gaelach Ó Súilleabháin (1715–95) and Donnchadh Rúa Mac Conmara (d. 1814) lived and worked here for some time and are strongly associated with the neighbourhood.

KILMALLOCK *Limerick*

Small market town on the R512, 6 m. NE of Ráthluirc (Charleville). Aindrias Mac Craith (An Mangaire Súgach), a celebrated 18th-c. Gaelic poet, is buried in the graveyard of the ruined collegiate parish church of SS Peter and Paul (NM), in the grave of the Hawthorne family, at the W side of the S door.

KILNABOY *Clare*

Church on the Burren (see KILFENORA). The poet Michael Longley describes the exhibitionist sculpture over the door of the ruined church at Kilnaboy in 'Sheela-na-gig', the product of 'a stonemason deflowering stone'.

KILTUMPER *Clare*

Townland near Kilmihil. The novelist Niall Williams lives here and has co-written with his wife, Christine Breen, four non-fiction books about life on the townland.

KINSALE *Cork*

Coastal town approximately 15 m. S of Cork at the mouth of the river Bandon. The poet Derek Mahon lives in the town, works 'at [his] sea-lit, fort-view desk | in the turf-smoky dusk' ('Dawn at St Patrick's'), and contemplates its 'shining windows, a future forbidden to no-one' ('Kinsale').

KNOCKBRETT (or KNOCKBRIT) *Tipperary*

Village on the R692, halfway between Cashel and Fethard. Marguerite Power, later Countess of Blessington, was born here (1 Sept. 1789), the daughter of a farmer and agent, and spent her first eight years here before moving to *Clonmel.

LAURAGH *Kerry*

Village on the R571 on the S side of the Kenmare River, near the turning for the Healy Pass. Derreen House, on a small peninsula where the coast road for Kenmare turns off the main road, was rented by J. A. Froude, the historian, from the 5th Marquess of Lansdowne in 1867 and 1869–70, when he began his controversial work *The English in Ireland in the Eighteenth Century* (3 vols, 1872–4). Froude's Seat, above the Middle Walk in the beautiful grounds planted by Lord Lansdowne about this time, commands a fine view of the estuary and distant mountains. While he was here Froude gathered information and local colour for his romance *The Two Chiefs of Dunboy* (1889).

LIMERICK *Limerick*

County town on the river Shannon. The experience of growing up in a Limerick slum is described in the first volume of Frank McCourt's grim but funny memoir *Angela's Ashes* (1996).

MALLOW *Cork*

Busy market town on the Blackwater, on the N20 and the N72, famous as a spa in the 18th c., when it was known as the 'Irish Bath'. People came from all over the country to drink the waters, and the notorious young gallants, the 'Rakes of Mallow', gathered here for their uproarious meetings, but by the time Sir Walter Scott visited (1825) on his Irish tour it was losing its fashionable reputation. The original Spa House (now the Energy Agency Office, Cork County Council) can be seen on the E side of Spa Walk, on the Fermoy road.

Thomas Osborne Davis (1814–45), poet and leader of the Young Ireland movement, was born at 72 Thomas Davis St. Ⓟ. At the age of 4 he moved with his family to live in Dublin. Canon Sheehan (1852–1913) was born in William O'Brien St., near the Main St. corner Ⓟ, and the stained-glass windows behind the altar in St Mary's Church are a memorial to him. Anthony Trollope lived at Bank Place when he was working here as a Post Office surveyor (1845–51). He was trying his hand at novel-writing at this time, but had not yet achieved success. Mrs Henry Wood lived here for some time at Rock Cottage.

MITCHELSTOWN *Cork*

Market town in a valley between the Kilworth and Galty mountains. The novelist and short-story writer William Trevor was born in the town in 1928. In *Excursions in the Real World* (1993), he describes his earliest memories as those of Co. Cork, 'of sunshine and weeds in a garden at Mitchelstown, Civic Guards in the barracks next door, a tarred gate; of dark limestone steps in Youghal, and a backyard tap in Skibbereen'. He has set much of his fiction—including the novels *Fools of Fortune* (1983), *Reading Turgenev* (1991), and *The Story of Lucy Gault* (2002)—in houses and villages near small towns in East Cork.

MUCKROSS *Kerry*

Small village on the N71, 2 m. S of Killarney. Muckross Abbey (NM) was founded for Franciscan friars in 1440 by Donald MacCarthy on the site of an earlier religious settlement. The ruins of the buildings demolished by Cromwell's troops in 1652 are preserved in a beautiful park-like setting. Among the many tombs in the church is a memorial tablet to the Four Kerry Poets of the 17th and 18th cc.: Pierce Ferriter, Geoffrey O'Donoghue, Aodhgan O'Rahilly, and Eoghan Ruadh O'Sullivan (see KILLARNEY). Sir Walter Scott visited the Abbey during his tour of Ireland in 1825.

At the other side of the main road a lane runs up behind the post office to Killeaghy Hill, where a small, tree-ringed burial ground overlooks the Killarney lakes. Somewhere in the tangle of undergrowth is the grave of Rudolph Erich Raspe, German expatriate and mineralogist, who compiled *Baron Munchausen's Narrative of his Marvellous Travels and Campaigns in Russia* (1785) while working as a mining engineer in Cornwall. Raspe subsequently went to Scotland and became estate surveyor of land that he 'planted' with samples of rich ore. On revealing his 'finds' to the landowner he was handsomely rewarded, and left for Ireland before the trickery could be exposed. He became manager of copper mines in Killarney and may well have had new schemes in his head when he contracted typhoid fever and died at Muckross in 1794.

MULLINAHONE *Tipperary*

Village on the R690, 13 m. SW of Kilkenny. Charles Kickham (1828–82), poet, novelist, and patriot, spent the greater part of his life here. The house where he lived, in Fethard St., is marked by a plaque, and a Celtic cross stands over his grave, which bears an epitaph by the celebrated Fenian and friend of Yeats, John O'Leary. Kickham's best novel, *Knocknagow* (1879), is based on rural life in this part of Tipperary. He is thought to have been born at Cnoicin a'Ghabba, 'The Smith's Hillock' (later called Mocklershill), 4 m. E of Cashel.

NEWTOWN *Waterford*

Little village 2 m. NE of Kilmacthomas, just N of the N25. The Gaelic poet Donnchadh Rúa Mac Conmara (d. 1814) is buried in the graveyard.

RÁTHLUIRC *Cork*

Market town, long known as Charleville (so named in honour of Charles II), NW of the Ballyhoura Hills, on the N20 and R515. In the ruined church of Ballysallagh, ¼ m. SSE, is the grave, bearing a Latin epitaph, of Seán Clárach Mac Domhnaill (1691–1754), a Gaelic poet whose works include a translation of Homer. His farm at Kiltoohig, on the west side of the town, became a meeting place (known as a 'Court of Poetry') for other poets, including Seán Ó Tuama (1706–75) and Eoghan Ruadh O'Sullivan (d. 1784).

SCATTERY ISLAND *Clare*

Early pilgrimage centre in the Shannon estuary. In Niall Williams's novel *The Fall of Light* (2001), the Foley family, uprooted by the Irish famine, settle on this island.

SMERWICK *Kerry*

Village on the W shore of Smerwick Harbour, an extensive and beautiful inlet at the NW extremity of the Dingle peninsula. In 1579 invading Spaniards, accompanied by a papal

nuncio, built a fort (Fort-del-Oro) here, to support the Desmond rebellion. The following year the garrison, reinforced by about 600 Italians, was bombarded and ruthlessly massacred by English troops under Lord Grey. Ralegh and Spenser are said to have taken part in the affair, but this has been disputed. Kingsley describes it in *Westward Ho!* (1855), where the hero, Amyas Leigh, takes Don Guzman, a Spanish captain, prisoner. On the W side of the little peninsula, near the Three Sisters rocks, is Ferriter's Castle, whose last owner was Pierce Ferriter, the soldier-poet, commemorated at *Killarney and *Muckross.

TIPPERARY *Tipperary*

Market town and manufacturing centre on the Ara, in the Golden Vale (or Vein), on the N24 and the N74. In Main St. there is a fine statue (by John Hughes, 1898) of Charles Kickham, the poet, novelist, and patriot.

TUAMGRANEY *Clare*

Village in E Clare, known for the antiquity of its church and its chipboard factory. The novelist Edna O'Brien was born at Dewsboro House between Tuamgraney and Scariff. She was educated locally at the National School in Scariff and the Convent of Mercy at Loughreu (which provided some of the background to her first novel, *The Country Girls*, 1960). In *Mother Ireland* (1976), a collection of illustrated essays that combine personal history with the history and customs of Ireland, she described life in her home village as 'enclosed, fervid and catastrophic', but elsewhere with vivid sensuality and affection, particularly in *The Country Girls* (later banned in Ireland):

> The sun was not yet up, and the lawn was speckled with daisies that were fast asleep. There was dew everywhere. The grass below my window, the hedge around it, the rusty paling wire beyond that, and the big outer field were each touched with a delicate, wandering mist. And the leaves and the trees were bathed in the mist, and the trees looked unreal, like trees in a dream.

Rural Co. Clare also provides the setting for her novel *A Pagan Place* (1970).

UNIONHALL *Cork*

Village in the parish of Myross on the S coast, halfway between Skibbereen and Ross Carbery. On the E side of a narrow road up the hill beyond the Protestant parish church of Myross, double gates open onto a drive through the beautiful garden of the former Rock Cottage

(later The Glebe), the rectory where Dean Swift stayed in the summer of 1723, when he left Dublin after Vanessa's death for a three or four months' visit to the south of Ireland. It is not certain with whom he stayed, but the original house still stands, with later additions, overlooking Glandore Harbour, from which, Charles Smith says (in *The Ancient and Present State of the County and City of Cork*, 1750), Swift 'often diverted himself in making little voyages on the coast . . . towards Baltimore; and the excursions occasioned his Latin poem *Carberiae Rupes* ['the Rocks of Carbery']'. According to the Somerville family records, Swift wrote the poem in a ruined tower, known as 'Swift's Tower', at *Castletownshend.

YOUGHAL (pr. Yŏoall) *Cork*

Old market town and port on the W side of the Blackwater estuary, on the N25. Sir Walter Ralegh, who was a commander in Queen Elizabeth's army in Munster, was granted 42,000 acres of land in the counties of Cork and Waterford, which included the town of Youghal. He was appointed mayor, 1588–9, and lived for a time at Myrtle Grove, an Elizabethan gabled house standing in private grounds to the N of St Mary's Church. It is possible that Spenser, who had been writing *The Faerie Queene* at Kilcolman, near *Doneraile, visited Ralegh here and discussed the poem with him. In 1602 Ralegh sold Myrtle Grove, among his other estates, to Richard Boyle, later Earl of Cork.

William Congreve lived in Youghal as a child and probably received his first schooling here. His father had obtained a commission as lieutenant in the infantry and was stationed with the garrison of what was then a thriving seaport from 1674 to 1678, when he was transferred to *Carrickfergus.

Bernard and Norah in Sean O'Faolain's short story 'The Patriot' spend their honeymoon in the town and watch the night 'so blue and lovely where it sank down, darker and darker, over the masts and brown sails of the fishing smacks in the harbour, and far in the distance the peaked mountains that Bernard knew so well'.

William Trevor visited the town as a boy and recalls in *Excursions in the Real World* the 'dark limestone steps . . . to a narrow house, cocked up high, blank windows staring out to sea, valerian in every crevice where it can find a foothold'. He has set some of his fiction— including *The Story of Lucy Gault* (2002)—in houses and villages near Youghal.

INDEX OF WRITERS

All places referred to have entries in the main text. References to titles of works are indicated by page numbers and columns (a, b, *and* c) in parentheses.

B

Baron Corvo. *See* Rolfe, Frederick William.

Barrett, Elizabeth. *See* Browning, Elizabeth Barrett.

Barrie, Sir James Matthew (1860–1937), journalist, short-story writer, and playwright; b. Kirriemuir; educ. Dumfries and Edinburgh; lives in London (Kensington: Gloucester Rd) 1895–8, (Bayswater: Bayswater Rd) 1902–9, (Adelphi: Robert St.) 1909–37; visits Meredith in Mickleham; stays in Amhuinnsuidhe 1912; country cottage in Farnham; buried in Kirriemuir; commemorated in London (Kensington Gdns). *Auld Licht Idylls* 1888 (288c), *A Window in Thrums* 1889 (288c–289a), *The Little Minister* 1891 (288c), *Sentimental Tommy* 1896 (130c, 269a, 289a), *Margaret Ogilvy* 1896 (130c, 288c), *Peter Pan* 1904 (54a, 98a, 130a), *What Every Woman Knows* 1908 (130c), *Mary Rose* 1920 (268c).

Barry, Sebastian (1955–), playwright, novelist, and poet: b. Dublin; educ. Dublin (Trinity College) 1970s. *The Steward of Christendom* 1995 (313a), *Our Lady of Sligo* 1998 (313a), *The Whereabouts of Eneas McNulty* 1998 (303c), *A Long Long Way* 2005 (313b).

Barstow, Stan (1928–), novelist: educ. Ossett. *A Kind of Loving* 1960 (231c, 237a).

Barton, Bernard (1784–1849), poet: lives in Woodbridge. *Poems* 1849 (186c).

Basse (or **Bas**), **William** (1583?–1653), poet: lives in Moreton (Oxfordshire). *Sword and Buckler, or, Serving Man's Defence* 1602, *Three Pastoral Elegies* 1602, 'Epitaph on Shakespeare', 'Angler's Song' (63c).

Bates, Herbert Ernest ('**Flying Officer X**') (1905–74), novelist and short-story writer: b. Rushden; educ. Kettering; frequents Higham Ferrers; lives in Little Chart 1931–74; in RAF at Oakington 1941, at Tangmere 1942. *The Two Sisters* 1926 (191c, 194c), *The Fallow Land* 1932 (61b, 195a), *The Poacher* 1935 (61b, 195a), *Fair Stood the Wind for France* 1944 (61b, 88a), *The Purple Plain* 1947, *The Jacaranda Tree* 1949 (61b), 'It's Just the Way It Is', 'The Sun Rises Twice' (181c), *Love for Lydia* 1952 (61b, 195a), *The Sleepless Moon* 1956 (191b), 'The Hessian Prisoner' (191b), *The Vanished World* 1969 (61a, 191b, 191c), *The Blossoming World* 1971 (61a), *The World in Ripeness* 1972 (61a, 181c), the Larkin family stories (61b).

Bawden, Nina (1925–), novelist: educ. Ilford and Oxford (Somerville); victim of train crash at Potters Bar 2002; lives London (Islington). *Family Money* 1991 (127a), *Dear Austen* 2005 (182b).

Baxter, Richard (1615–91), Presbyterian minister: b. Rowton; assistant minister in Bridgnorth; minister in Kidderminster 1641; devises rules for the academy in Sheriffhales; lives in retirement in Melbourne; imprisoned in London (Southwark: King's Bench) 1685–6; commemorated by a statue in Kidderminster. *Aphorisms of Justification* 1649 (201c), *The Saint's Everlasting Rest* 1650 (193a, 198a, 201c–202a), *Paraphrase of the New Testament* 1685 (150a).

Bayly, Ada Ellen ('**Edna Lyall**') (1857–1903), novelist: spends holidays at Farnham; lives in Lincoln, in Eastbourne 1884–1903; buried in Bosbury. *Donovan* 1882 (192b), *We Two* 1884 (51b, 54a, 192b), *Doreen* 1889 (51b), *To Right the Wrong* 1894 (54a), *In Spite of All* 1901 (197c), *The Hinderers* 1902 (51b).

Beattie, James (1735–1803), poet and philosopher: b. Laurencekirk; educ. Aberdeen; Professor of Moral Philosophy at Aberdeen 1760–1803; buried in Aberdeen. *Original Poems and Translations* 1761 (266c), *Essay on Truth* 1770 (267a), *The Minstrel* bk I 1771 (267a).

Beaumont, Francis (1584–1616), poet and playwright: b. Grace Dieu; educ. Oxford (Pembroke College); enters the Inner Temple, London (City: Temple) 1600; lives in London (Southwark: Bankside); frequents Mermaid tavern (City: Bread St.); buried in London (Westminster Abbey); commemorated in Coleorton Hall. 'Ode on the Tombs in Westminster Abbey' (157c).

Beckett, Samuel Barclay (1906–89), playwright, novelist, and poet: b. Foxrock, Co. Dublin; educ. Stillorgan, Earlsfort House School, Dublin 1915–19, Enniskillen 1920–3, and Dublin (Trinity College) 1923–7; teaches French at Campbell College, Belfast (1927–8), at Trinity College, Dublin (1930–1); lives in Dublin (6 Clare St.), Chelsea (48 Paulton's Sq.) 1933–5; treated at Tavistock Clinic, London 1934–5; secretly marries in Folkestone 1961. *More Pricks than Kicks* 1934 (310c), *Murphy* 1936 (103b, 106c, 310c, 313a), *Waiting for Godot* 1955 (146b), *Krapp's Last Tape* 1958 (107c, 310c), *Endgame* 1958 (107c), *Happy Days* 1961 (222b).

Beckford, William (1759–1844), novelist and travel writer: b. London (Soho: Soho Sq.); inherits Fonthill Abbey 1770; lives in Bath 1822–44: buried in Bath. *Vathek* 1787 (21a, 147b), *Dreams, Waking Thoughts and Incidents* 1834, *Recollections of an Excursion to the Monasteries of Alcobaça and Batalha* 1835 (6a).

Beddoes, Thomas Lovell (1803–49), poet and playwright: b. Bristol (Clifton); educ. Bath, London (City: Charterhouse), and Oxford (Pembroke College). *The Improvisatore* 1821, *The Bride's Tragedy* 1822, *Death's Jest Book* 1850 (76a).

Bede (or **Baeda**) (673–735), historian and scholar: lives in monastery at Jarrow; buried in Durham. *Historia Ecclesiastica Gentis Anglorum* 731 (241b).

Bede, Cuthbert. *See* Bradley, Edward.

Beer, Patricia (1919–99), poet, memoirist, and novelist: b. Exmouth; educ. Exmouth, Exeter (University) in late 1930s, and Oxford (St Hugh's College) 1941; teaches at Goldsmith's College, London; lives in Upottery 1964–9. 'A Visit to Little Gidding' (178c), 'Concert in Long Melford Church' (178c), 'On the Cobb at Lyme Regis' (24c), 'Parson Hawker's Farewell' (26b), 'Group of Islands' (32b), *Mrs Beer's House* 1968 (20c), *Moon's Ottery* 1978 (36c).

Beerbohm, Sir Max (1872–1956), novelist, essayist, critic, and caricaturist: b. London (Kensington: Palace Gardens Ter.); educ. Godalming (Charterhouse) and Oxford (Merton College); lives in London (Marylebone: Upper Berkeley St.) 1893–1910; visits Swinburne in London (Putney: Putney Hill) 1899; broadcasts in London (Marylebone: Langham Pl.); buried in London (City: St Paul's Cathedral); commemorated in Oxford (Merton College). *The Works of Max Beerbohm* 1896 (135c), *More* 1899 (135c), 'No. 2 The Pines' 1899 (139b), *Yet Again* 1909 (135c), *Zuleika Dobson* 1911 (74a, 135c), 'In the Shades' 1915 (111b), *Mainly on the Air* 1946, 1957 (134c).

Behan, Brendan (1923–64), playwright: b. and educ. Dublin; in Borstal school in Hollesley; in prison in Dublin. *The Quare Fellow* 1956 (310c), *Borstal Boy* 1958 (176b, 310c), *The Hostage* (*An Giall*) 1958 (310c).

Behn, Mrs Aphra (or **Ayfara**, or **Astrea**) (1640–89), playwright and novelist: baptized in Harbledown; buried in London (Westminster Abbey). *The Rover* 1677 (158a), *Oroonoko* 1688 (57a).

Beith, John Hay ('**Ian Hay**') (1876–1952), novelist: b. Manchester. *Tilly of Bloomsbury* 1919, *The Willing Horse* 1921, *Leave it to Psmith* 1930, *The Housemaster* 1936 (225b).

Bell, Acton. *See* Brontë, Anne.

Bell, Adrian (1901–80), novelist: buried at Barsham. *Corduroy* 1930, *Silver Ley* 1931, *The Cherry Tree* 1932, *Folly Field* 1933, *Shepherd's Farm* 1939, *Apple Acre* 1942, *A Suffolk Harvest* 1956, *My Own Master* 1961 (162a–b).

Bell, Currer. *See* Brontë, Charlotte.

Bell, Ellis. *See* Brontë, Emily Jane.

Bell, John Joy (1871–1934), writer of humorous sketches: b. and educ. Glasgow. *Wee MacGreegor* 1902 (283c), *I Remember* 1932 (283c).

Belloc, Joseph Hilary Pierre (**Hilaire Belloc**) (1870–1953), poet, novelist, essayist, and historian: educ. Oxford (Balliol College); lives in London (Chelsea: Cheyne Walk) *c.* 1900–6, Shipley 1906–53; meets friends in London (Soho: Gerrard St.); walks to Duncton Hill; visits Limpsfield; buried in West Grinstead; memorial in Shipley. 'To the Balliol Men Still in Africa' (69b), 'The South Country' (84c), *The Four Men* 1912 (40c, 51a).

Bennett, Alan (1934–), playwright: b. Leeds; educ. Leeds and Oxford (Exeter College); Beyond the Fringe discovered 1960 in Edinburgh; lectures in Oxford; lives in London (Camden). *The Lady in the Van* 1990 (105a), *The Laying On of Hands* 2001 (144a), *The History Boys* 2004 (71c, 238a).

Bennett, Enoch Arnold (1867–1931), novelist: b. and lives in Stoke-on-Trent; educ. Stoke-on-Trent and Newcastle under Lyme; lives in Thorpe-Le-Soken 1913–20, London (Chelsea: Cadogan Sq.) 1923–30, (Marylebone: Marylebone Rd) 1930–1; friendship with Eden Phillpotts in Torquay; buried in Stoke-on-Trent; commemorated in the public gardens in Stoke-on-Trent. *Anna of the Five Towns* 1902 (203c), *The Old Wives' Tale* 1908 (207c), *Clayhanger* 1910 (44a, 207c), *Hilda Lessways* 1911 (44a), *The Card* 1911 (207c), *The Matador of the Five Towns* 1912 (207c), *The Regent* 1913 (184c), *These Twain* 1916 (184c), *Riceyman Steps* 1923 (105b, 116a).

Benson, Arthur Christopher (1862–1925), essayist and critic: lives in Cambridge as Fellow 1904 and Master 1915–25 of Magdalene College; commemorated in Rye. *From a College Window* 1906 (168a).

Benson, Edward Frederic (1867–1940), novelist: educ. Marlborough and Cambridge (King's College); lives in Rye. *David Blaize* 1915 (25c), *David of King's* 1924 (168a), the Lucia books, *As We Were* 1930, *As We Are* 1932 (82c).

Bentley, Phyllis (1894–1977), novelist: b. Halifax; educ. Cheltenham 1910–14. *Carr* 1929, *Inheritance* 1932, *A Modern Tragedy* 1934, *Manhold* 1941, *O Dreams, O Destinations* 1962 (232a).

Bentley, Richard (1662–1742), scholar and critic: lives in Cambridge (Trinity College), Master 1699–1742. *Dissertation on the Letters of Phalaris* 1699 (170b).

Berkeley, George (1685–1753), philosopher and theologian: b. Dysart Castle; educ. Kilkenny and Dublin (Trinity College); Dean of Londonderry 1724; Bishop of Cloyne 1734–53. *A New Theory of Vision* 1709, *The Principles of Human Knowledge* 1710, *Hylas and Philonous* 1713, *Siris: A Chain of Philosophical Reflections and Inquiries Concerning the Virtues of Tar-Water* 1744 (318b).

Berlin, Isaiah (1909–97), philosopher: lives London (Surbiton); educ. St Paul's School, London (City) and Oxford (Corpus Christi); lectureships at Oxford (All Souls, New, and Wolfson colleges); m., lives outside Oxford; d. Oxford.

Bernard, Jeffrey (1932–97), journalist: lives and drinks London (Soho). *Jeffrey Bernard Is Unwell* 1989 (146c).

Berners, Gerald Hugh Tyrwhitt-Wilson, 14th Baron (1883–1950), novelist, musician, and painter: educ. Eton; lives in Faringdon 1931–50. *First Childhood* 1934, *The Camel* 1936, *Far From the Madding War* 1941 (53b), *A Distant Prospect* 1945 (52c, 53b).

Besant, Sir Walter (1836–1901), novelist and historian: b. Portsmouth; educ. London (Strand: King's College, The Strand) and Cambridge (Christ's College) 1856–9; lives in London (Hampstead: Frognal Gdns) 1896–1901; memorial in London (City: St Paul's Cathedral). *By Celia's Arbour* 1878 (80b), *The Chaplain of the Fleet* 1881 (110b), *Armorel of Lyonesse* 1890 (32a).

Betham-Edwards, Matilda (1838–1919), novelist: lives in Hastings. *Kitty* 1870 (58a).

Betjeman, Sir John (1906–84), poet, architectural writer, and broadcaster: b. 52 Parliament Hill Mansions, London (Hampstead); childhood in Highgate; educ. Highgate, Oxford (Dragon School), Marlborough 1920s, and Oxford (Magdalen College) 1925–8; teaches in Gerrard's Cross; lives in Uffington 1930s; works in London (Bloomsbury), at High Commission, Dublin 1941–3, at the Admiralty,

Buchan, John, 1st Baron Tweedsmuir (*cont'd*)
Broughton; marries in London (Mayfair); lives in
London (Marylebone: Portland Pl.) 1913–19; stays
in Broadstairs 1914; lives in Elsfield 1919–35; buried
in Elsfield. *Sir Quixote of the Moors* 1895 (283c),
John Burnet of Barns 1898 (270b), *The Thirty-Nine
Steps* 1915 (44c, 60a, 135a), *Huntingtower* 1922
(283c), *Midwinter* 1923 (51c), *Witch Wood* 1927
(270c), *Castle Gay* 1930 (283c), *Memory Hold-the-
Door* 1940 (70a).

Buchanan, Dugald (**Dùghall Bochanan**) (1716–68),
Scottish Gaelic poet: b. near Balquhidder;
schoolmaster at Kinloch Rannoch; d. at Kinloch
Rannoch; buried near Callander; commemorated by
obelisk at Kinloch Rannoch. 'Day of Judgement',
'The Skull', 'The Dream', 1st edn Gaelic New
Testament (asst. ed.) (288b).

Buchanan, Robert (1835–75), poet: commemorated
at Falkirk.

Buchanan, Robert Williams (1841–1901), critic, poet,
and novelist: educ. and lives in Glasgow, in Oban
1866–74. *The North Coast and Other Poems* 1868,
'The Fleshly School of Poetry' 1871 (291c).

Bunting, Basil (1900–85), poet: b. Scotswood upon
Tyne; educ. Ackworth 1912–16; childhood holidays
at Sedbergh; imprisoned in Wormwood Scrubs
and Winchester 1918–19; studies seamanship at
Nellists' Nautical School, Newcastle, 1938; first
performance of 'Briggflatts' at Morden Tower,
Newcastle, 1965; ashes strewn by Briggflatts Quaker
meeting house, Sedburgh. 'Briggflatts' (228b–c).

Bunyan, John (1628–88), Nonconformist preacher
and writer: b. nr Elstow; baptized in Elstow;
preaches and is imprisoned in Bedford; his pulpit
preserved in Breachwood Green; preaches in Wain
Wood and Hitchin; buried in London (Finsbury:
Bunhill Fields); commemorated in Westminster
Abbey and Bedford. *Grace Abounding* 1666 (162c),
The Pilgrim's Progress 1678 (161b, 162c, 173c, 253c),
The Holy War 1682 (173c).

Burgess, Anthony (1917–93), novelist, critic,
memoirist, and composer: b. and educ. Manchester;
educ. Manchester (University); childhood in
Manchester (Higher Crumpsall); parents run shop
in Moss Side; posted to Warrington during the
Second World War; teaches in Birmingham (Central
Advisory Council for Forces Education) 1946–50,
in Banbury (Grammar School) early 1950s, in
Birmingham (University); buys dresses in
Tunbridge Wells 1961; lives in Hove 1959–60,
Etchingham, Sussex late 1960s and 1970s. *A
Clockwork Orange* 1962 (89c), the Enderby novels
1962, 1963, 1968, 1984 (44b, 52b), *Little Wilson, Big
God* 1987 (41a, 226a), *A Dead Man in Deptford* 1993
(117c).

Burgoyne, Sir John (1722–92), general and
playwright: educ. London (Westminster School);
lives in London (Mayfair: Hertford St.). *The Maid
of the Oaks* 1774, *The Heiress* 1786 (137b).

Burke, Edmund (1729–97), statesman and orator: b.
Dublin; educ. Ballitore and Dublin; enters Middle
Temple, London (City: Temple) 1750; visits Bath
1756; frequents Dr Johnson's literary club, London
(Soho: Gerrard St.); buys estate in Beaconsfield
1768; lives in London (Soho: Gerrard St.); elected
MP for Bristol 1774; stays in Bristol (Henbury);
buried in Beaconsfield; commemorated by statue in
Bristol.

Burnand, Sir Francis Cowley (1836–1917), editor
of *Punch* 1880–1906: educ. Cambridge (Trinity
College).

Burnett, Mrs Frances Eliza Hodgson (née **Hodgson**)
(1849–1924), novelist: b. Manchester; lives in
Rolvenden 1880–1901. *Little Lord Fauntleroy* 1886
(82a, 225a), *The Secret Garden* 1911 (82a).

Burney, Frances (**Fanny**) (**Mme D'Arblay**)
(1752–1840), novelist: b. King's Lynn; visits Bristol
(Hotwells) 1767; educ. and lives in London
(Holborn: Queen's Sq.) 1770–4, (Soho: St Martin's
St.) 1774–86; visits Brighton and London
(Chessington) 1770s, Tunbridge Wells, Devizes
1780, Batheaston, Teignmouth 1773, 1778, 1793;

lives in Windsor and London (Kew) 1786–91; visits
Nuneham Courtenay 1786, Cheltenham 1788,
Weymouth 1789, Saltram House 1789; m. in
Mickleham 1793; lives in Great Bookham 1793–6,
Mickleham 1796–1802, Bath 1815–18, London
(Mayfair: Bolton St.) 1818–28; buried in Bath.
Evelina 1778, reprinted 1962 (3b, 11c, 89c, 106a,
108a, 147b, 155c), *Cecilia* 1782 (147b), *Camilla* 1796
(56c, 63a, 89c, 163c), *Diary and Letters* 1778–1840,
1842–6 (13c, 37a, 43c, 64c, 93a, 136b).

Burns, Robert (1759–96), poet: b. and lives in
Alloway; baptized and educ. in Ayr; studies in
Kirkoswald 1775; lives in Lochlea 1777–84; studies
in Irvine 1781–2; frequents Tarbolton and
Mauchline; lives in Mossgiel 1784–9; visits Failford
1786, Kilmarnock 1786, Edinburgh 1786, Aberfeldy
1787, Falkirk 1787, Falls of Bruar 1787, Jedburgh
1787, Stirling 1787, Selkirk 1787, and Dalswinton;
lives in Ellisland 1789–91; visits Kirroughtree 1794
and 1795; lives 1791–6 and is buried in Dumfries;
commemorated in Ayr, Failford, Stirling, Irvine,
Edinburgh, New Cumnock, and London
(Westminster Abbey). *Poems Chiefly in the Scottish
Dialect* 1786 (288a, 290b, 291a), 'The Jolly Beggars',
'The Holy Fair' (290c), 'The Ordination' (288a),
'Epistle to Willie Creech' (294c), 'Ae fond kiss'
(275b), 'Epitaph on William Muir', 'Death and Dr.
Hornbook' (296a), 'Highland Mary' (273a, 285b,
291a, 296a), 'The Birks of Aberfeldy' (267b),
'Humble Petition of Bruar Water' (281a), 'Tam o'
Shanter' (268c, 269c, 280c, 288c), 'To Mary—in
Heaven' (273a, 280c), 'A Red, Red Rose', 'Auld
Lang Syne' (281a), *Scots Musical Museum* (275b,
280c–281a, 290c), 'Heron Election Ballads' (289a),
'Flow gently, sweet Afton' (291b), 'The Brigs of Ayr'
(269c).

Burnside, John (1955–), poet, novelist, and
memoirist: b. Cowdenbeath; lives in Corby 1970s;
educ. Cambridge (Cambridge College of Arts and
Technology) 1970s; lives in Cellardyke. *The Hoop*
1988, 'At Owlpen', 'Uley, Glos', 'A Calendar for the
Parish of Bagpath' (36b), *The Locust Room* 2001
(165a), *Living Nowhere* 2003 (189c), *A Lie About
My Father* 2006 (189c, 271a), *The Devil's Footprints*
2007 (271a).

Burroughs, William (1914–97), novelist: lives
London (St James's) 1966–73. *The Wild Boys* 1971
(141a).

Burton, Sir Richard Francis (1821–90), Arabic
scholar and traveller: prob. b. Torquay; educ.
London (Richmond: Little Green) and Oxford
(Trinity College); buried in London (Richmond).
Pilgrimage to Mecca 1855–6 (35c), *The Lusiads*
(trans.) 1880–4 (55a, 140b), *The Arabian Nights,
or, The Thousand and One Nights* (trans.) 1885–8
(8b, 140b), *Pentamerone* (trans.) (140b).

Burton, Robert (1577–1640), theologian: b. Lindley;
moves from Lindley to Nuneaton; educ. Nuneaton
and Oxford (Brasenose College) 1593–9; Fellow and
rector at Oxford (Christ Church) 1599–1640; rector
of Seagrave 1632–40; buried and has a memorial
in Oxford (Christ Church). *Anatomy of Melancholy*
1621–51 (70b, 195a).

Butler, Samuel (1612–80), satirist and poet: b.
Strensham; educ. Worcester; lives in Wrest Park,
in Ludlow 1661–2, in London (Covent Garden:
Rose St.); frequents Will's Coffee House in Bow St.
(Covent Garden); commemorated in Westminster
Abbey (Westminster). *Hudibras* (3 pts) 1662–78
(116c, 203a).

Butler, Samuel (1835–1902), satirist and novelist: b.
Langar; educ. Shrewsbury and Cambridge (St John's
College) 1854–9; lives in London (City: Clifford's
Inn) 1864–1902; visits Downe 1872. *Erewhon* 1872
(109c, 207a), *Unconscious Memory* 1880 (50c),
Erewhon Revisited 1901 (109c), *The Way of All Flesh*
1903 (109c, 191c).

Byatt, Antonia Susan (1936–), novelist: b. Sheffield;
educ. York and Cambridge (Newnham); lectures in
London (Bloomsbury: University College). *The Virgin
in the Garden* 1978 (14b), *Possession* 1990 (142a,
192b), 'On the Day that E. M. Forster Died' (142a).

Byng, Hon. John, 5th Viscount Torrington
(1742–1813), diarist: educ. London (Westminster
School); lives in London (Marylebone: Duke St.);
visits Halesowen 1781, Welwyn 1789, Mereworth
1790, Chicksands 1791, Bibury 1794. *The Torrington
Diaries* 1934, reprinted 1970 (63a, 134a, 185a,
200c).

Byrom, John (1692–1763), Jacobite poet and
hymn writer: b. Manchester; educ. London (City:
Merchant Taylors' School, Suffolk Lane); lives and
is buried in Manchester. 'Christians awake', 'To an
Officer in the Army' (223b).

Byron, George Gordon, 6th Baron (1788–1824),
poet: b. and baptized in London (Marylebone:
Holles St. and St Marylebone parish church); educ.
Aberdeen, London (Harrow on the Hill) 1801–5, and
Cambridge (Trinity College); swims at Grantchester;
lives in Nottingham 1798, Southwell 1803–8; visits
Annesley 1803; lives in Newstead Abbey 1808–16;
lodges in London (Mayfair: Albany, St James's:
St James's St., Pall Mall, and Bennet St.) 1812–13;
attends Coleridge's lectures in London (City: Crane
Court) 1813; visits Hastings 1814; m. in Seaham
1815; honeymoon in Croft-on-Tees; visits Leigh
Hunt in London (Marylebone: Lisson Grove) 1815;
embarks at Dover 1816; funeral cortège in Welwyn
and Nottingham; buried in Hucknall; memoirs
burnt in London (Mayfair: Albemarle St.);
commemorated in Hucknall, Cambridge (Trinity
College), and London (Hyde Park and Westminster
Abbey). *Juvenilia* 1807 later called *Hours of Idleness*
(170b), 'Lines Written Beneath an Elm' 1807 (123b),
Childe Harold 1812 (136a, 142b), *The Giaour* 1813,
The Bride of Abydos 1813, *The Corsair* 1814 (141a),
'The Dream' 1816 (188a), 'The Duel' 1818 (141b,
188a), *Mazeppa* 1819 (132c), 'To an Oak at
Newstead', 'Inscription on the Monument of a
Newfoundland Dog', 'On Leaving Newstead Abbey'
(193c), *Correspondence*, ed. J. Murray, 1922 (10a,
123b, 170b).

Byron, Robert (1905–41), travel writer: b. London
(Wembley); educ. Eton and Oxford (Merton
College) early 1920s; killed off Isle of Lewis 1941.

C

Caedmon (*fl.* 670), poet: enters monastery at Whitby
c. 670. Hymn on the Creation (238c).

Caine, Sir Thomas Henry Hall (1853–1931), novelist:
childhood at Ballaugh; teaches in Maughold
1870–1; lives in Greeba Castle 1887–1931; looks
after D. G. Rossetti at Birchington; buried in
Maughold. *The Deemster* 1887 (213b, 218b, 229b),
The Manxman 1894 (213b, 218b).

Calverley, Charles Stuart ('**C.S.C.**') (1831–84), poet
and parodist: b. Martley; educ. Marlborough,
London (Harrow on the Hill), Oxford (Balliol
College), and Cambridge (Christ's College). *Verses
and Translations* 1862 (165a).

Camden, William (1551–1623), antiquary and
historian: educ. London (City: Christ's Hospital,
Newgate St., and St Paul's School) and Oxford
(Christ Church); usher 1575–93, then headmaster,
in London (Westminster: Westminster School);
buried in London (Westminster Abbey). *Britannia*
1586 (158c, 202a), *Annales* 1589 (158c).

Campbell, Ignatius Roy (1901–57), South African
poet: visits Oxford (Wadham College); lives in
London (Soho: Beak St.) 1920–2, Sarn Mellteyrn
1922–4. *The Flaming Terrapin* 1924, *Light on a
Dark Horse* 1951 (144b, 261a).

Campbell, Thomas (1777–1844), poet: b. and educ.
Glasgow; tutor in Mull 1795, Downie 1796; lives in
Edinburgh 1796–1802; m. in London (Westminster:
St Margaret's) 1803; lives in London (Victoria:
Grosvenor Gdns) 1804, (Sydenham) 1804–22,
(Holborn: Lincoln's Inn Fields) *c.* 1828–32; visits
Mme de Staël in London (Soho: Argyll St.) 1813–14;
advocates foundation of University College London
(Bloomsbury) 1826–8; visits Hastings 1831–2;
lives in London (St James's: Duke St.) 1832–40,

Cotton, Sir Robert Bruce (1571–1631), antiquary and collector of manuscripts: educ. London (Westminster School); lives in Chester; collection presented to British Museum, London (Bloomsbury) 1702.

Coverdale, Miles (1488–1568), translator of the Bible: Bishop of Exeter 1551–3; rector of St Magnus the Martyr, London (City: Lower Thames St.) 1563–6, and buried there; commemorated in Paignton.

Coward, Sir Noël Pierce (1899–1972), playwright: b. London (Teddington); lives in London (Belgravia: Gerald Rd) mid-1930s–mid-1950s. *Cavalcade* 1931, *Present Indicative* 1937, *This Happy Breed* 1943, *Future Indefinite* 1954 (98c–100a).

Cowley, Abraham (1618–67), poet: educ. in London (Westminster School) and Cambridge (Trinity College); moves to Oxford (St John's College) 1644–6; lives in Chertsey, London (Barnes: Barn Elms Pk) 1663–5; visits Great Tew; buried in London (Westminster Abbey). 'On the Death of Mr. William Harvey' (170a–b).

Cowley, Mrs Hannah (née Parkhouse) (1743–1809), playwright and poet: b. Tiverton; d. and buried in Tiverton. *The Runaway* 1776, *The Belle's Stratagem* 1780, *A Bold Stroke for a Husband* 1783 (34c).

Cowper, William (1731–1800), poet: b. Berkhamsted; educ. Markyate and London (Westminster School); childhood holidays in Catfield; enters Middle Temple, London (City: Temple) 1748; attends Church of St George the Martyr (Holborn: Queen St.); lodges in London (Bloomsbury: Russell Sq.) early 1750s; in asylum in St Albans 1763–5; lives in Huntingdon 1765, Olney 1767–86; visits Gayhurst 1779; lives in Weston Underwood 1786–95; visits Eartham 1792; lives in Little Dunham 1795, Mundesley, and East Dereham 1795–1800; buried in East Dereham; memorials in London (Edmonton) and Olney. *Olney Hymns* (with Newton) 1779 (64c, 111c), *Poems* 1782 (65a–b), *John Gilpin* 1782 (65b, 118c, 185a), *The Task* 1784 (65a, 65b), *Letters* 1803 (65a), 'On Receipt of My Mother's Picture Out of Norfolk' (179b), 'To Mary', 'The Yardley Oak' (92a).

Crabbe, George (1755–1832), poet: b. Aldeburgh; educ. Stowmarket; apprenticed in Wickhambrook 1768; visits Cheveley 1796; apprenticed in Woodbridge 1771; works in Aldeburgh 1775; visits Beaconsfield 1781; ordained in Norwich 1782; chaplain at Belvoir Castle 1782–8; rector of Frome St Quintin 1783; m. in Beccles 1783; curate in Stathern 1785–9; lives in Muston 1789–92; visits Aldeburgh and Lowestoft 1790; lives in Parham 1792, Great Glemham 1796–1801, Rendham 1801–5, Muston 1805–14, Trowbridge 1814–32; visits London (St James's: Bury St. and Kensington: Holland House) 1817, Edinburgh 1822, Longleat 1824, Bath 1826, Hastings 1830, Bristol 1831; d. Merton; buried in Trowbridge; commemorated in Aldeburgh. *Inebriety* 1775, *The Candidate* 1780 (161a), *The Village* 1783 (161a, 162b, 188c), *The Newspaper* 1785 (188c), *The Borough* 1810 (161a), *Tales of the Hall* 1819 (36a).

Craigie, Pearl Mary Teresa ('**John Oliver Hobbes**') (1867–1906), novelist and playwright: lives in Ventnor. *Some Emotions and a Moral* 1891, *The Ambassador* 1898, *Robert Orange* 1902 (90c–91a).

Craik, Mrs Dinah Maria (née Mulock) (1826–87), novelist: b. Stoke-on-Trent; lives in Newcastle under Lyme 1831, London (Hampstead: North End) 1857, (Bromley) 1865–87; d. in London (Bromley); buried in London (Keston); memorial in Tewkesbury. *John Halifax, Gentleman* 1875 (34c, 104a, 122c, 132a, 203b–c, 207c).

Crane, Stephen (1871–1900), American novelist and poet: lives in Oxted 1897, Rye 1899. *The Red Badge of Courage* 1895 (43c, 79b), *The Open Boat* 1898, *The Monster* 1899 (79b).

Cranmer, Thomas (1489–1556), biblical scholar and Archbishop of Canterbury: Fellow at Cambridge (Jesus College) 1515; stands trial in Oxford (St Mary the Virgin) 1554; burnt at the stake in Oxford (see Martyrs' Memorial) 1556.

Crashaw, Richard (1612?–49), poet: educ. London (City: Charterhouse) and Cambridge (Pembroke College); Fellow at Cambridge (Peterhouse College) 1637–43.

Crayon, Geoffrey. *See* Irving, Washington.

Crocker, Charles (1797–1861), poet: b. and lives in Chichester; apprenticed to a shoemaker; becomes sexton at Cathedral 1845; buried in subdeanery graveyard.

Crockett, Samuel Rutherford (1860–1914), poet, novelist, and minister: b. nr Laurieston; lives in Penicuik 1886–95; buried nr Laurieston. *Dulce Cor* 1887 (292c), *The Stickit Minister* 1893 (292c), *The Raiders* 1894, *The Lilac Sunbonnet* 1894 (289c, 292c).

Croker, John Wilson (1780–1857), editor and essayist and a founder of the *Quarterly Review*: educ. Dublin (Trinity College).

Croker, Thomas Crofton (1798–1854), antiquarian and folklorist: b. Cork; lives in Cork until 1818. *Researches in the South of Ireland* 1824, *The Fairy Legends and Traditions of the South of Ireland* 1825, *Legends of the Lakes* 1829, republished as *A Guide to the Lakes* 1831, *Killarney Legends* 1876 (319a).

Croly, George (1780–1860), novelist, poet, and playwright: b. and educ. Dublin. *Catiline* 1822, *Salathiel* 1829 (308a).

Crompton, Richmal (1890–1969), children's writer: b. Bury; educ. Warrington (and subsequently teaches here) and London (Holloway); lives and works in Bromley 1917–53; lives in Chislehurst from 1953; buried in Eltham. *Just William* 1922 (104a, 108b, 229a).

Cronin, Archibald Joseph (1896–1981), novelist: lives at Dunbarton. *Hatter's Castle* 1931, *The Citadel* 1937, *The Stars Look Down* 1941, *The Spanish Gardener* 1950, *Dr Finlay's Casebook* (272b).

Crossley-Holland, Kevin (1941–), poet and children's writer: educ. Bryanston and Oxford (St Edmund's Hall).

Cruickshank, Helen Burness (1886–1975), poet: lives in Edinburgh.

Cumberland, Richard (1732–1811), playwright and novelist: b. Cambridge (Trinity College); educ. in London (Westminster School) and Cambridge (Trinity College); Fellow at Cambridge (Trinity College); stays in Clonfert 1771, London (Marylebone: Queen Anne St.) c. 1771; settles in Tunbridge Wells. *The West Indian* 1771 (123b, 135b, 302a).

Cunningham, Alan (1784–1842), poet: b. and self-educated nr Dalswinton. 'A Wet Sheet and a Flowing Sea' (272a).

Cunningham, Peter (d. 1805), poet: curate at Eyam. 'Britannia's Naval Triumph', 'Russian Prophecy' (190c).

Cunninghame Graham, Robert (1735–97), poet: b. Gartmore; inherits Ardoch 1772; returns to Gartmore 1777; buried in Gartmore. 'If doughty deeds my lady please' (281b).

Cunninghame Graham, Robert Bontine (1852–1936), short-story writer and essayist: educ. London (Harrow on the Hill); lives in Gartmore 1885–1903, Ardoch 1903; imprisoned in London (Islington: Pentonville) 1887; visits Limpsfield; attends Conrad's funeral in Canterbury; buried in Inchmahome. *Father Archangel of Scotland* 1896 (281b), 'Sursum Corda' in *Success* 1902 (129a), *Doughty Deeds* (269b), 'Inveni Portum' in *Redeemed* 1927 (46a, 86a).

Curtis, Tony (1946–), poet: b. Carmarthen; educ. Swansea; Professor at University of Glamorgan (Pontypridd).

Cynan. *See* Evans-Jones, Sir Albert.

D

Dafydd ab Edmwnd (*fl.* 1450–90), gentleman and bardic master: b. Hanmer; wins silver chair at Carmarthen eisteddfod c. 1450; buried in Hanmer 1490.

Dafydd ap Gwilym (*fl.* 1340–70), poet: b. Bro-Gynin; visits Gwern-y-Clepa (Newport, Gwent); buried Strata Florida Abbey (or Talley Abbey). 'The Girls of Llanbadarn' (251c).

Dafydd Nanmor (15th c.), Welsh poet: b. Nanmor; believed to be buried in Whitland. *Poetical Works*, ed. T. Roberts and I. Williams, 1923 (258b).

Dahl, Roald (1916–90), children's author: b. Cardiff. lives, dies, buried Great Missenden.

Daniel, Samuel (1562–1619), poet and playwright: b. probably nr Taunton; educ. Oxford (Hertford College); visits Titchfield, London (Twickenham: Twickenham Park); lives in Beckington 1610–19; buried in Beckington.

Darley, George (1795–1846), poet, critic, and editor of plays of Beaumont and Fletcher: b. and educ. Dublin; leaves Dublin for London 1822; lives in London (Victoria: Grosvenor Gdns) 1827, 1830–9. *Sylvia* 1827 (156a), *Thomas à Becket: A Dramatic Chronicle* 1840 (46a).

Darwin, Charles (1809–82), naturalist: b. Shrewsbury; educ. Shrewsbury, Edinburgh, and Cambridge (Christ's); lives in Downe; rests in Ilkley; buried in Westminster Abbey (London: Westminster). *On the Origin of Species* 1859 (50c, 234a).

Darwin, Erasmus (1731–1802), physician and poet: b. Elston; lives in Lichfield 1756–81; settles in Derby 1781. *The Botanic Garden* 1789–91 (202c).

Daudet, Alphonse (1840–97), French novelist: visits Mickleham and London (Mayfair: Dover St.) 1895.

D'Avenant, Sir William (1606–68), playwright and poet: b. Oxford; educ. Oxford (Lincoln College); theatre manager in London (Covent Garden: Catherine St.); knighted in Gloucester 1643; imprisoned in Cowes 1650, London (City: the Tower) 1650–2; buried in London (Westminster Abbey). *The Tragedy of Albovine* 1629 (72b), *Gondibert* 1651 (49a).

Davidson, John (1857–1909), poet and playwright: educ. Edinburgh (University); visits Dymchurch, nr St Mary in the Marsh; frequents Ye Olde Cheshire Cheese (Rhymers' Club) in London (City: Fleet St.); spends last years in Penzance; drowned nr Penzance. 'In Romney Marsh' (83a), *Fleet Street Eclogues* 1893 (111a).

Davies, David Ivor ('**Ivor Novello**') (1893–1951), songwriter and playwright: b. Cardiff. 'Keep the Home Fires Burning', *Glamorous Night* 1935, *Careless Rapture* 1936, *The Dancing Years* 1939, *Perchance to Dream* 1945, *King's Rhapsody* 1949 (247a).

Davies, Edward Tegla (1880–1967), novelist: b. Llandegla. *Hunangofiant Tomi* 1912, *Nedw* 1922, *Gŵr Pen y Bryn* 1923 (253b).

Davies, Idris (1905–53), poet: b., lives, and is buried in Rhymney. *Collected Poems of Idris Davies*, ed. I. Jenkins, 1972 (260c).

Davies, James Kitchener (1902–52), poet and playwright: b. nr Tregaron; lives, d., and is buried at Trealaw. *Meini Gwagedd* 1945, 'Sŵn y Gwynt sy'n Chwythu' 1952 (263b).

Davies, John ('**John Davies of Hereford**') (b. 1560–5?, d. 1618), poet and writing master: b. and prob. educ. Hereford; buried in London (City: St Dunstan-in-the-West, Fleet St.).

Davies, Sir John (1569–1626), barrister and poet: b. Chicksgrove; educ. Winchester and Oxford (The Queen's College); enters Middle Temple, London (City: Temple) 1587; knighted in Dublin 1603; MP for Newcastle under Lyme 1614; d. London (Strand: The Strand), buried in St Martin-in-the-Fields (Strand: Trafalgar Sq.). *Nosce Teipsum* 1599 (76a, 153a), *The Lottery* 1602 (123b), *A Discourse on the true reasons why Ireland has never been entirely subdued till the beginning of His Majesty's reign* 1612 (307a).

Davies, Rhys (1901–78), short-story writer and novelist: b. Clydach Vale. *Honey and Bread* 1935, *A Time to Laugh* 1937, *Jubilee Blues* 1938, *Collected Stories* 1955 (248c).

Davies, Thomas Glynne (1926–88), poet and
novelist: b. Llanrwst. *Marged* 1974 (255c).

Davies, William Henry (1871–1940), poet: b.
Newport (Gwent); visits Limpsfield and buys a
cottage there; lives in Sevenoaks Weald; lodges in
London (Bloomsbury: Great Russell St.) 1916–22;
visits Edward Marsh in London (Holborn); lives
in Nailsworth 1931–40. *The Autobiography of a
Super-Tramp* 1908 (26c, 83c, 102c, 258b).

Davis, Thomas Osborne (1814–45), ballad writer
and a founder of *The Nation* newspaper: b. Mallow;
educ. Dublin (Trinity College); buried in Dublin
(Mount Jerome cemetery).

Dawkins, Richard MacGillivray (1871–1955), Greek
scholar: Fellow at Oxford (Exeter College) 1922–39
(Hon. Fellow 1939–55); d. Oxford. *Forty-Five
Stories from the Dodecanese* 1950, *Modern Greek
Folk Tales* 1952, *Norman Douglas* 1952 (71c).

Day, Thomas (1748–89), social reformer and novelist:
educ. London (City: Charterhouse) and Oxford
(Corpus Christi College); lives in Anningsley Park;
lives in London (Stoke Newington: Church St.);
buried in Wargrave. *The History of Sandford and
Merton* 1783–9 (40c, 71b, 91b, 150c).

Day-Lewis, Cecil (**'Nicholas Blake'**) (1904–72), poet
and novelist: educ. Sherborne and Oxford (Wadham
College); teaches in Oxford 1927–8, Helensburgh
1928–30, Cheltenham 1930–5; lives nr Cheltenham
1932–8, in Musbury 1938; Professor of Poetry at
Oxford (Wadham) 1951–5; lives in London
(Greenwich: Crooms Hill) 1958–72; buried in
Stinsford. *Country Comets* 1928 (79a), *The Magnetic
Mountain* 1933, *A Question of Proof* 1935, *Collected
Poems 1929–36* 1938 (14a), *The Buried Day* 1960
(26b, 79a, 120a, 285c), *The Gate and Other Poems*
1962, *The Room and Other Poems* 1965, *Whispering
Roots* 1970 (120a).

Deane, Seamus (1940–), poet and novelist: educ.
Derry; works in Derry. *Reading in the Dark* 1997
(300a).

Deeping, George Warwick (1877–1950), novelist: b.
Southend-on-Sea. *Sorrell and Son* 1925 (183b–c).

Defoe, Daniel (1660?–1731), journalist and novelist:
educ. London (Stoke Newington: Newington
Green); manages business in Chadwell St Mary
1694–1703; imprisoned in London (City: Newgate
St.) 1703; stays in Bury St Edmunds 1704; lives
in London (Stoke Newington: Stoke Newington
Church St.) from 1709; visits Bristol, Cambridge,
Chester, Chichester, Dartmouth, Exeter, Great
Malvern, Holywell, Ipswich, Liverpool, Tunbridge
Wells, York; d. London (City: Ropemaker St.) and
buried in Bunhill Fields (Finsbury), gravestone at
Stoke Newington. *The Shortest Way with Dissenters*
1702, *The Review* 1704–13, *Hymn to the Pillory*
1704 (112b), *Robinson Crusoe* 1719 (10a, 150b, 172a,
234b, 239c, 289c), *Moll Flanders* 1722 (150b), *A
Tour Through the Whole Island of Great Britain*
1724–7, ed. G. D. H. Cole, 1927 (89a, 164b, 220b,
239c).

de la Mare, Walter (**'Walter Ramal'**) (1873–1956),
poet and novelist: lives in London (Anerley)
1899–1925, (Twickenham: Montpelier Row)
c. 1950–6; visits Edward Marsh in London
(Holborn); buried in London (City: St Paul's
Cathedral). *Songs of Childhood* 1902, *Henry Brocken*
1904, *The Listeners and Other Poems* 1912, *Memoirs
of a Midget* 1921 (97b).

Delany, Mrs Mary (**Mrs Pendarves**, née **Granville**)
(1700–88), letter writer and diarist: lives in
Buckland 1715; m. Alexander Pendarves in Longleat
1717; lives in Penryn 1717–21; visits Cirencester,
Dublin 1731–3; m. Dr Delany and lives in Dublin
1743; visits Ellastone; lives in London (St James's:
St James's Pl.) 1770–*c.* 1785. *Autobiography and
Correspondence* 1861–2 (121c, 141c, 307c).

Deloney, Thomas (1543–1600), ballad writer and
novelist: author of a poem on Henry II's 'fair
Rosamond' in *The Garland of Good Will* 1631
(93b).

Denham, Sir John (1615–68), poet and playwright:
b. Dublin; educ. Oxford (Trinity College); enters

Lincoln's Inn, London (Holborn) 1634, called to
the Bar 1639; lives in Egham; buried in London
(Westminster Abbey). *Cooper's Hill* 1642 (51c, 158a,
307a).

Dent, Joseph Malaby (1849–1926), publisher: b.
Darlington. Everyman's Library (240b).

De Quincey, Thomas (1785–1859), essayist: b. and
spends early years in Manchester; educ. Bath,
Manchester, and London (Worcester College); lives
in Bath 1796–9; visits Dublin and Westport 1800;
stays in Liverpool 1801, Chester 1802, London
(Soho: Greek St.) 1802, Liverpool 1803; visits
Grasmere, Nab Farm, Bristol (Hotwells) 1807;
meets Coleridge in Bridgwater 1807; stays in
Grasmere 1808–9; rents Dove Cottage, Grasmere
1809–34; m. in Grasmere (see Nab Farm) 1817;
stays in London (Covent Garden: Tavistock St.)
1821; owns Nab Farm 1829–33; frequents
Edinburgh 1822–59; settles in Lasswade 1840;
rents rooms in Glasgow 1841–7; buried in
Edinburgh. 'Vision of Sudden Death' (223b),
Confessions of an English Opium Eater 1821–2
(117b, 146b), 'On Murder as One of the Fine Arts'
1827 (10c, 277a), *Suspiria de Profundis* 1847 (79a).

Dermody, Thomas (1775–1802), poet: b. Ennis;
teaches Classics at Ennis for some years from 1784.
'Monody on the Death of Chatterton', 'Enthusiast', in
The Harp of Erin 1807 (320b).

De Vere, Aubrey (1814–1902), poet: b. Curragh
Chase; educ. Dublin (Trinity College); lives and
dies in Curragh Chase; buried in Askeaton. *The
Waldenses and Other Poems* 1842, *The Legends
of St. Patrick* 1872, *Critical Essays* 1887–9,
Recollections 1897 (320a).

Dexter, Colin (1930–), novelist: b. Stamford; educ.
Cambridge (Christ's); teaches in Leicester; lives in
Oxford. *Last Bus to Woodstock* 1975 (70a–b), *The
Secret of Annexe 3* 1986 (68a), *The Jewel That Was
Ours* 1991 (70b), *The Daughters of Cain* 1994 (70b),
The Remorseful Day 2000 (72a).

Dibdin, Charles (1745–1814), playwright and
songwriter: b. and spends early years in
Southampton; lives in London (Soho: Charlotte St.)
1805–10, (Camden Town: Arlington Row);
memorial in Southampton. *History of the Stage*
1795, 'Tom Bowling' (85b, 104c), 'Poor Jack' (85b),
'The Round Robin' (104c).

Dickens, Charles (1812–70), novelist: b. Portsmouth;
educ. and lives in Chatham 1817–21; lives in London
(Camden Town: Bayham St.) 1823–4; works as
clerk in London (Holborn: Gray's Inn) 1827; posts
first story in London (City: Fleet St.); lives in
London (Marylebone: Bentinck St.) 1833–4; m.
in London (Chelsea: St Luke's) 1836; honeymoons
in Chalk 1836; frequents Rochester, Cobham (Kent);
lives in London (Holborn: Holborn) 1834–7,
(Holborn: Doughty St.) 1837–9, (Twickenham: Ailsa
Park Villas) 1838–9, (Marylebone: Marylebone Rd)
1839–51, (Belgravia: Chester Row); establishes his
parents in Alphington 1839–43; visits London
(Richmond) 1836, 1839, Pickwick 1835, Manchester
1837, 1852, Brighton 1837, 1848, Bowes, Liverpool
1838 and later, Barnard Castle 1838, Bath 1840,
Stafford 1840s, Bonchurch 1849, Bristol (Clifton)
1851, Dover 1852, Leamington Spa 1855, 1862, Bury
St Edmunds 1859, 1861, Clovelly 1861, Chertsey,
Ipswich, Ross-on-Wye 1867; performs in plays
at Knebworth 1850, 1851; lives in London
(Bloomsbury: Tavistock Sq.) 1851–60; buys house in
Gad's Hill 1856; lives in Gad's Hill 1860–70; lodges
in London (Kensington: Hyde Park Gate) 1862,
(Marylebone: Gloucester Pl.) 1865; d. in Gad's Hill;
buried in London (Westminster Abbey). *Sketches by
Boz* 1835–6, 1836–7 (117a, 125b, 133a, 133c, 142a,
146a), *The Pickwick Papers* 1836–7 (7a, 20b, 28b,
44c, 48c, 62a, 110b, 111c, 124c, 125b, 140b, 149c,
184a), *Oliver Twist* 1838 (47c, 124c, 140b), *Nicholas
Nickleby* 1839 (16b–c, 44c, 80b, 124c, 140c, 146b,
155b, 209c, 222a, 223c, 230b, 240a), *Master
Humphrey's Clock* 1840–1 (240a), *The Old Curiosity
Shop* 1840–1 (44c, 133a, 134a, 206c, 210a, 240a),
Barnaby Rudge 1841 (44c, 124c, 134a, 172b, 240a),

A Christmas Carol 1843 (134a), *Martin Chuzzlewit*
1843–4 (47c, 114a, 129a, 134a, 222a), *The Chimes*
1844 (110c), *Dombey and Son* 1848 (43c, 134a,
202a), *David Copperfield* 1849–50 (43a, 44c, 46a,
46c, 109a, 140c, 151a, 153a, 163b, 175b), *Bleak House*
1852–3 (3c, 44c, 50c, 103b, 126a, 182c, 194c), *Hard
Times* 1854 (103b, 223c), *Little Dorrit* 1857 (54c,
103b, 149b, 150a), *A Tale of Two Cities* 1859 (103b,
139b, 144c), *Great Expectations* 1861 (43a, 46c, 49a,
55b, 81c, 103b), *Our Mutual Friend* 1865 (55b),
Edwin Drood 1870 (55b, 81c), *Bentley's Miscellany*
1837–9 (ed.) (88a, 137b, 308b), *American Notes*
1842 (134a), *Household Words* 1850–9, *All the Year
Round* 1859–70 (153b), *Mr. Nightingale's Diary*
(a play privately printed) 1851 (11a, 103b), 'A Plated
Article' in *Household Words* reprinted 1858 (207b),
The Uncommercial Traveller 1860 (47a, 55b, 81c,
222a), 'The Holly Tree' in *Christmas Stories* 1871
(46c), 'A Message from the Sea' in *Christmas Stories*
(with Wilkie Collins) 1871 (15b), *Mudfog Papers*
1880 (81c), 'Bound for the Great Salt Lake' (143a).
• SEE ALSO FEATURE ENTRY (128–9).

Dickens, Monica (1915–92), novelist: b. London
(Bayswater); educ. St Paul's Girls' School (London:
City) and Central School of Speech and Drama
(London: Hampstead); works as a nurse in
Windsor; lives in Hinxworth; spends last years
in Brightwalton. *One Pair of Hands* 1939 (93a),
One Pair of Feet 1942 (93a).

Dickinson, Goldsworthy Lowes (1862–1932), pacifist
and critic: educ. Cambridge (King's College), Fellow
1886–1920; lives in London (Kensington: Edwardes
Sq.) and Cambridge (King's College).

Digby, Sir Kenelm (1603–65), writer and diplomat:
b. Gayhurst; educ. Oxford (Worcester College); lives
and d. in London (Covent Garden).

Dillwyn, Amy Elizabeth (1845–1935), novelist: b. and
lives in Swansea. *The Rebecca Rioter* 1880 (261b).

Disraeli, Benjamin, 1st Earl of Beaconsfield
(1804–81), statesman and novelist: b. London
(Holborn: Theobald's Rd); enters Lincoln's Inn,
London (Holborn) 1824; stays in Southend-on-Sea
1833–4; m. in London (Mayfair: St George's,
Hanover Sq.) 1839; visits Belvoir Castle; lives in
Hughenden 1848–81; visits Bournemouth 1874–5;
d. in London (Mayfair: Curzon St.); buried in
Hughenden. 'The Revolutionary Epic' 1834 (183b),
Coningsby 1844 (50b, 188c), *Tancred* 1847 (59a),
Lothair 1870 (59a, 196a–b, 210a), *Endymion* 1880
(43b, 59a, 137a, 178a).

D'Israeli, Isaac (1766–1848), miscellaneous writer:
lives in Bradenham. *Curiosities of Literature* 1791
(43b).

Dobell, Sydney Thompson (1824–74), poet: b.
Cranbrook; lives in Hucclecote 1846–8, Cheltenham
1848–53; visits Edinburgh 1854, Tintern Abbey
1858, Great Malvern; spends last years nr
Painswick; buried in Painswick. *The Roman* 1850
(14a, 23b), *Balder* 1854 (14a), 'Sonnets on the War'
(with Alexander Smith) 1855 (278a).

Dobrée, Bonamy (1891–1974), critic, biographer, and
editor: teaches in Leeds 1936–55.

Dobson, Henry Austin (1840–1921), poet and critic:
b. Plymouth. *Eighteenth Century Vignettes* 1892,
1894, 1896.

Doctor Mirabilis. *See* Bacon, Roger.

Dodgson, Charles Lutwidge (**'Lewis Carroll'**)
(1832–98), scholar and writer for children: b.
Daresbury; lives in Croft-on-Tees 1843; educ.
Richmond, Rugby, and Oxford (Christ Church);
lives in Oxford (Christ Church); vacations in Whitby
1854, Llandudno 1864, Guildford from 1868, and
Eastbourne 1877–87; visits Brighton 1874–87
and Hastings; d. Guildford; commemorated in
Llandudno and London (Westminster Abbey). 'The
Lady of the Ladle', 'Wilhelm von Schmitz' 1854
(239a), *Alice's Adventures in Wonderland* 1865 (42b,
51b, 54a, 61c, 71a, 215c, 254a), *Through the Looking
Glass* 1872 (71a, 239a), 'The Three Sunsets'
(215c–216a).

Dolben, Digby Mackworth (1848–67), poet: educ.
Eton. *Poems*, ed. R. Bridges, 1915 (52c).

F

Furness, Richard (1791–1857), poet: b. Eyam; lives in Eyam 1813–21 and is buried there. *Rag Bag* 1832, *Medicus-Magus* 1836 (190c–191a).

Furnivall, Frederick James (1825–1910), scholar and founder of the Early English Text Society: b. Egham; educ. Cambridge (Trinity Hall).

G

Galsworthy, John (1867–1933), novelist and playwright: b. London (Kingston upon Thames); educ. Bournemouth, London (Harrow on the Hill), and Oxford (New College); called to the Bar from Lincoln's Inn, London (Holborn) 1890; m. in London (Mayfair: St George's, Hanover Sq.) 1904; spends summers at Manaton 1904–19; visits Limpsfield; lives in London (Adelphi: Adelphi Ter.) 1912–18; refuses knighthood in Littlehampton 1918; lives in London (Hampstead: Admiral's Walk) 1918–33; spends much time at his country house in Bury 1920–33; d. in London (Hampstead: Admiral's Walk); ashes scattered nr Bury. *The Man of Property* 1906 (61a), *The Country House* 1907, *Fraternity* 1909 (25b), *Strife* 1911 (222b), *Saint's Progress* 1919 (61b), *The Forsyte Saga* 1922 (121a, 132b), *A Modern Comedy* 1929 (121a), *Life and Letters* by H. V. Marrot 1935 (25b).

Galt, John (1779–1839), novelist: b. Irvine; spends adolescence at Greenock; imprisoned in London (Southwark: King's Bench prison, Scovell Rd) 1829; retires to Greenock 1834–9; buried in Greenock. *Annals of the Parish* 1821, reprinted 1967 (285b, 286c).

Gardam, Jane (1928–), novelist: b. Redcar; educ. Saltburn 1930s and 1940s. *Crusoe's Daughter* 1985 (237a), *The Iron Coast* 1994 (237a), *Faith Fox* 1996 (54a), *Old Filth* 2005 (114c).

Garioch, Robert (1909–81), poet: b. Edinburgh.

Garnett, Constance (1861–1946), translator of Russian classics: lives in Limpsfield from 1896.

Garnett, Richard (1835–1906), miscellaneous writer: b. Lichfield; official at the British Museum, London (Bloomsbury) 1875–99. *The Twilight of the Gods* 1888 (202c–203a).

Garrick, David (1717–79), actor and playwright: b. Hereford; educ. Lichfield and Edial; lives in Lichfield and London (Adelphi: Adelphi Ter.); buys house in London (Hampton) 1754; buried in London (Westminster Abbey); memorial in Lichfield Cathedral. *The Clandestine Marriage* (with G. Colman the Elder) 1766 (141a, 158a).

Garrod, Heathcote William (1878–1960), critic, scholar, and poet: Fellow and Professor of Poetry at Oxford (Merton College); buried in St Cross churchyard, Oxford. *Oxford Poems* 1912 (74a).

Gascoigne, George (1525?–77), poet: educ. Cambridge (Trinity College); enters Gray's Inn, London (Holborn); accompanies Queen Elizabeth I to Kenilworth 1575. *The Princely Pleasures of the Court of Kenilworthe* 1575 (201c), *The Queen's Majestie's Entertainment at Woodstock* 1575 (93c).

Gaskell, Mrs Elizabeth Cleghorn (née **Stevenson**) (1810–65), novelist and author of *The Life of Charlotte Brontë* (1857): b. London (Chelsea: Cheyne Walk); educ. Stratford-upon-Avon; lives and is m. in Knutsford 1832; lives in Manchester from 1832; meets Charlotte Brontë at Briery Close 1850; visits Ashbourne 1850s, Haworth 1853, Whitby 1859; lodges at Silverdale; buys house and d. at Holybourne; buried in Knutsford. Chapter on Stratford-upon-Avon in W. Howitt's *Visits to Remarkable Places* 1840 (209c), *Mary Barton* 1848 (223c), *Ruth* 1853 (219c, 228c), *Cranford* 1853 (219c, 226b), *North and South* 1855 (223c), *Sylvia's Lovers* 1863 (239a–b), *Wives and Daughters* 1864–6 (58c, 220a), *Letters*, ed. J. A. V. Chapple and A. Pollard, 1966 (214a).

• SEE ALSO FEATURE ENTRY (224–5).

Gatty, Mrs Margaret (1809–73), writer for children: lives in Ecclesfield. *Aunt Judy's Magazine* est. 1866, *Parables from Nature* 1855–71 (231c).

Gauden, Dr John (1605–62), theologian: b. Mayland; educ. Oxford (Wadham College); incumbent of Bocking 1641–60; Bishop of Exeter 1660–2, of Worcester 1662; lives in Hartlebury 1662; buried in Worcester. *Eikon Basilike* 1649 (163b, 200c).

Gay, John (1685–1732), poet and playwright: b. and educ. Barnstaple; secretary to the Duchess of Monmouth in London (Chelsea: Lawrence St.) *c.* 1714; visits Cirencester 1718, Bath 1721, 1724, Tunbridge Wells 1723, Amesbury 1728, Edinburgh 1729, Rousham; lives in London (Richmond); d. in London (Mayfair: Old Burlington St.) and buried in Westminster Abbey. *The Captives* 1724 (89b), *The Beggar's Opera* 1728 (2c, 63b, 158a, 273c), *Polly* 1729 (273c, 315c).

Geoffrey of Monmouth (1100?–54), theologian and chronicler: studies at Oxford *c.* 1129; describes Caerleon; Archdeacon of Llandaf *c.* 1140; d. Llandaf. *Historia Regum Britanniae* 1136, printed 1508 (246b, 247b, 253a).

Gerard, John (1545–1612), herbalist and barber-surgeon: *Herball or generall Historie of Plantes* 1597 (301a).

Gerhardie, William (1895–1977), novelist: educ. Oxford (Worcester College); passes flat of Arnold Bennett 1931; lives in London (Marylebone) 1931–77. *Futility* 1922 (79b, 134b), *The Polyglots* 1925 (134b), *Memoirs of a Polyglot* (79b, 133b, 134b).

Gibbings, Robert John (1889–1958), wood engraver and travel writer: b. and educ. Cork; lives and is buried in Long Wittenham. *Sweet Thames Run Softly* 1940 (61b), *Lovely Is the Lee* 1944, *Sweet Cork, of Thee* 1951 (319b), *Till I End My Song* 1957 (61b).

Gibbon, Edward (1737–94), historian: b. London (Putney); educ. London (Westminster School) and Oxford (Magdalen College); lives in Buriton 1758–72; in the Militia at Cranbrook and Sissinghurst Castle 1760; lives in London (St James's: Pall Mall) 1769, (Marylebone: Bentinck St.) 1773–83; visits Fletching 1793, Bath 1793; d. in London (St James's: St James's St.); buried in Fletching. *History of the Decline and Fall of the Roman Empire* 1776–88 (45b, 141c), *Memoirs of My Life and Writings (Autobiography)* 1796 (116c, 133c, 139a), *Miscellaneous Works* 1796 (54c).

Gibbon, Lewis Grassic. See Mitchell, James Leslie.

Gibbons, Stella (1902–89), novelist: b. London (Kentish Town); educ. Edgware (North London Collegiate) and London (Bloomsbury: University College); lives in London (Hampstead) 1927–89; works in London (Covent Garden) 1930s. *Cold Comfort Farm* 1932 (116b, 118b).

Gibson, Wilfrid Wilson (1878–1962), poet: b. Hexham; lives in Dymock 1914, London (Hampstead: Nassington Rd) 1934–9; visits Edward Marsh in London (Holborn). 'The Old Nail Shop' (19a–b), *Collected Poems (1905–25)* 1926 (122b), *The Golden Room* 1928 (19b), *Within Four Walls* 1950 (122b).

Gifford, William (1756–1826), poet, critic, and classical scholar: b. Ashburton; educ. Ashburton and Oxford (Exeter College); spends last years and d. in London (Westminster: Buckingham Gate); buried in Westminster Abbey. *The Baviad, The Maeviad, The Anti-Jacobin* (ed.) (156c), *Quarterly Review* (ed.) 1809–25 (2c, 136a, 156c).

Gilbert, Mrs Joseph (née **Ann Taylor**) (1782–1866), author of rhymes and stories for children: spends childhood in Lavenham until 1796; lives in Colchester 1796–1811, Ongar 1811 until m. 1814; lives in Nottingham and is buried there. *Original Poems for Infant Minds* 1804, *Rhymes for the Nursery* 1806, and *Hymns* 1810 (all with her sister Jane) (17c).

Gilbert, Sir William Schwenck (1836–1911), poet and writer of comic operas: educ. London (Strand: King's College, The Strand); lives in London (Kensington: Harrington Gdns) 1883–90, (Harrow Weald) 1890–1911, (Belgravia: Eaton Sq.) 1907–11; d. and is buried in London (Harrow Weald). *Princess Ida* 1884, *The Mikado* 1885, *Ruddigore*

1887, *The Yeomen of the Guard* 1888, *The Gondoliers* 1889 (130c), *Fallen Fairies* 1909, *The Hooligans* 1911 (98c).

Gilpin, William (1724–1804), writer and illustrator of tours: b. Scaleby Castle; educ. Oxford (The Queen's College); vicar of Boldre 1777–1804; tours the Lake District; visits Nuneham Courtenay; buried in Boldre. *Latimer* 1755, *Wycliffe* 1765, and *Cranmer* 1784 (76b), *Remarks on Forest Scenery* 1791 (43a), *Guide to the Lakes* 1789 (220a), *Picturesque Tours* 1782 (43a, 220a).

Giraldus Cambrensis (Gerald de Barri) (1146?–1223?), travel writer and chronicler: b. Manorbier; rector of Tenby 1172–5; elected Bishop of St David's; buried in St David's. *Itinerarium* (257a).

Gissing, George Robert (1857–1903), novelist: b. Wakefield; educ. Manchester; lives in London (Bloomsbury: Colville Pl.) 1878, (Chelsea: Oakley Gdns) 1882–4, (Marylebone: Cornwall Residences) 1884–90; visits Meredith at Mickleham; lives in Exeter 1891, Dorking 1898. *The Unclassed* 1884, *Isabel Clarendon* 1886, *Demos: A Story of English Socialism* 1886, *Thyrza* 1887 (133c), *A Life's Morning* 1888 (133c, 238c), *The Nether World* 1889, *The Emancipated* 1890 (133c), *New Grub Street* 1891 (111a), *Born in Exile* 1892 (20a), *The Private Papers of Henry Ryecroft* 1903 (20a, 101c).

Glaister, Lesley (1956–), novelist: teaches in Sheffield. *Honour Thy Father* 1990 (178c), *Trick or Treat* 1991 (238a), *The Private Parts of Women* 1996 (238a), *Now You See Me* 2002 (238a).

Glanvill, Joseph (1636–80), theologian: b. Plymouth; educ. Oxford (Exeter College); rector of the Abbey Church, Bath 1666; buried in Bath. *The Vanity of Dogmatizing* 1661 (71b), *Sadducismus Triumphatus* 1666 (3a).

Gleig, George Robert (1796–1888), novelist, essayist, and biographer: b. Stirling; educ. Oxford (Magdalen Hall). *The Subaltern* 1826 (73b).

Godley, Alfred Denis (1856–1925), poet and classical scholar: Fellow at Oxford (Magdalen College) 1883–1912, and Public Orator 1910–25. *Verses to Order* 1892, *Lyra Frivola* 1899, *Second Things* 1902, *The Casual Ward* 1912, *Fifty Poems* 1927 (73a).

Godolphin, Sidney (1610–43), poet: b. Godolphin House; visits Great Tew; killed in Chagford.

Godwin, Mrs Mary. See Wollstonecraft, Mary.

Godwin, William (1756–1836), philosopher and novelist: b. Wisbech; attends Coleridge's lectures in London (City: Crane Court); buried in London (St. Pancras); reburied in Bournemouth. *Enquiry Concerning Political Justice* 1793 (8b, 142c), *The Adventures of Caleb Williams* 1794 (142c).

Gogarty, Oliver St John (1878–1957), poet, playwright, and surgeon: b. and educ. Dublin; entertains at Renvyle; buried nr Renvyle. *As I Was Going Down Sackville Street* 1937 (309c).

Golding, Louis (1895–1958), novelist: b. Manchester; educ. Manchester and Oxford (The Queen's College); lives and d. in London (St John's Wood). *Magnolia Street* 1931, *Five Silver Daughters* 1934 (225c).

Golding, Sir William (1911–93), novelist, memoirist, and critic: b. Newquay; childhood in Marlborough; educ. Marlborough 1920s and Oxford (Brasenose College) 1930s; teaches at Maidstone Grammar School for Boys from 1938, at Bishop Wordsworth's School, Salisbury 1940–62; lives at Ebble Thatch, Bowerchalke, nr Salisbury 1940–6, 1958–85, and in Perranarworthal, Cornwall 1985–93. *Lord of the Flies* 1954 (24c, 31c), *The Spire* 1964 (8c, 31b), *Darkness Visible* 1979 (8c), *Rites of Passage* 1980 (8c, 28b), *Close Quarters* 1987 (28b), *Fire Down Below* 1989 (28b).

Goldsmith, Oliver (1730?–74), poet, playwright, and novelist: b. Pallas or Elphin; baptized in Forgney; lives when a boy in Lissoy and frequents Kilkenny West; educ. Lissoy, Elphin, Edgeworthstown, and Dublin; spends night in Ardagh; studies medicine in Edinburgh (University) 1752–4; lives in London (City: Green Arbour Ct) 1759–60, (City: Fleet St.,

H

Haggard, Sir Henry Rider (1856–1925), novelist: b. West Bradenham; educ. Garsington and Ipswich; called to the Bar in Lincoln's Inn, London (Holborn) 1884; lives in London (Hammersmith: Gunterstone Rd) 1885–8; settles in Ditchingham 1889; buys house at Kessingland *c.* 1900; winters in Hastings after the First World War; commemorated in Ditchingham. *Dawn* 1884 (173a), *King Solomon's Mines* 1885 (55b, 120b), *Eric Brighteyes* 1888 (173a), *Rural England* 1902, *Pearl-Maiden* 1903, *Ayesha* 1905, *The Poor and the Land* 1905 (177c).

Hakluyt, Richard (1553?–1616), narrator of voyages and translator: educ. London (Westminster School) and Oxford (Christ Church); prebend of Bristol Cathedral 1586; rector of Wetheringsett 1590–1616; buried in London (Westminster Abbey). *Principall Navigations, Voiages, and Discoveries of the English Nation* 1589, enlarged 3 vols 1598–1600 (158a).

Hall, Anna Maria (née **Fielding**) (1800–81), novelist: b. and brought up in Dublin. *Sketches of Irish Character* 1829, *Lights and Shadows of Irish Life* 1838, *The White Boy* 1845 (308b).

Hall, Radclyffe (1883–1943), novelist: buried in London (Highgate cemetery). *The Well of Loneliness* 1928 (124a–b).

Hamburger, Michael (1924–2007), poet, translator, and critic: educ. London (Westminster) and Oxford (Christ Church) 1940s; lives in Middleton. *A Mug's Game* 1973 (71a, 158c), *Variations* 1981 (179c), *From a Diary of Non-Events* 2002 (179c).

Hamilton, Elizabeth (1756–1816), novelist: lives and writes in Edinburgh and Bath; d. and buried in Harrogate. *Memoirs of Modern Philosophers* 1800 (3b, 275b), *The Cottagers of Glenburnie* 1808 (275b).

Hamilton, Patrick (1904–62), novelist and playwright: b. Brighton and Hove; childhood in Hove; educ. Hassocks and London (Hammersmith and Westminster); lives in Sheringham 1950s and 1960s. *The Midnight Bell* 1929 (100a), *Twenty Thousand Streets Under the Sky* 1935 (108b, 118b, 134a), *Hangover Square* 1941 (44b, 61c, 118b, 176c), *The Slaves of Solitude* 1946 (58b), *The West Pier* 1951 (44a–b).

Hanley, James (1901–85), novelist: lives at Llanfechain 1940–64. *Don Quixote Drowned* 1953, *The Welsh Sonata* 1954, *Another World* 1971, *A Kingdom* 1978 (254b).

Hannay, Canon James Owen (**'George A. Birmingham'**) (1865–1950), novelist: b. Belfast; educ. Dublin; rector of Westport 1892–1913, of Mells 1924–34; commemorated in Mells. *The Spirit and Origin of Christian Monasticism* 1903, *Spanish Gold* 1908, *Lalage's Lovers* 1911, *The Major's Niece* 1911, *The Inviolable Sanctuary* 1912 (304c).

Hardy, Thomas (1840–1928), novelist and poet: b. Higher Bockhampton; educ. Dorchester; apprenticed to architect in London (Adelphi: Adelphi Ter.) 1862–7; works in London (Strand: Clement's Inn) 1870; visits St Juliot 1870; m. in London (Paddington: Elgin Ave.) 1874; lives in Sturminster Newton 1878, London (Tooting) 1878–81, Wimborne 1881–3, Dorchester 1885–1928; visits Bonchurch 1910, Plymouth 1913, Oxford (The Queen's College) 1920, 1922; buried in London (Westminster Abbey) and his heart buried in Stinsford; commemorated in Dorchester and Stinsford. *Under the Greenwood Tree* 1872 (23b, 33b), *A Pair of Blue Eyes* 1873 (7c, 30c), *Far from the Madding Crowd* 1874 (23b, 29b), *The Return of the Native* 1878 (34a, 154a), *The Trumpet-Major* 1880 (29b, 37a, 154a), *Two on a Tower* 1882 (37c), *The Mayor of Casterbridge* 1886 (17b), *The Woodlanders* 1887 (32c), *Tess of the D'Urbervilles* 1891 (7a, 8b, 33c, 34a, 37c–38a, 92c), *A Group of Noble Dames* 1891 (32c), *Jude the Obscure* 1895 (32b, 54b, 60c, 67c, 81b, 91b, 169a), *The Well-Beloved* 1897 (19b, 29b), *The Dynasts* 1903–8 (76b), 'Domicilium' 1850s (23a), 'A Church Romance' 1835, 'Afternoon Service at Mellstock'

1850 (33b), 'To a Tree in London' 1870 (151a), 'Copying Architecture in an Old Minster' (37c), 'A Singer Asleep' 1910 (43a), 'The West-of-Wessex Girl' 1913 (29a).

• SEE ALSO FEATURE ENTRY (18–19).

Harington, Sir John (1561–1612), poet and translator: educ. Eton and Cambridge (King's College); lives in Kelston. *Orlando Furioso* (trans.) 1591, *Nugae Antiquae* 1769 (23b–c).

Harris, Frank (1856–1931), journalist and miscellaneous writer: b. Galway.

Harrison, Tony (1937–), poet: b. and educ. Leeds; lives in Newcastle. 'v' (236a), 'Kensal Green Cemetery' (130a), 'Changing at York' (240c).

Harrison, William (1534–93), topographical writer: educ. London (Westminster School); rector of Radwinter 1559–93. *Description of England, Description of Scotland* (trans.) in Holinshed's *Chronicles* 1577 (182b).

Harrison, William (1665–1713), poet: educ. Oxford (New College), Fellow at Oxford (New College) 1706–13. 'Woodstock Park' (74b, 93c).

Harte, Francis Bret (**'Bret Harte'**) (1836–1902), American novelist: US Consul in Glasgow 1880–5; buried in Frimley. *The Luck of Roaring Camp* 1870 (55a).

Hartley, Leslie Poles (1895–1972), novelist: b. nr Peterborough; educ. London (Harrow) and Oxford (Balliol College); spends youth in Peterborough; visits Oxford (Wadham College). *The Killing Bottle* 1932 (182b), *The Shrimp and the Anemone* 1944 (176c, 182b), *Eustace and Hilda* 1947 (176c), *The Go-Between* 1953 (182b), *Facial Justice* 1960 (165a), *The Brickfield* 1964 (182b).

Harvey, Frederick William (1888–1957), poet: brought up at Minsterworth. *Collected Poems* 1983 (26a).

Harvey, Gabriel (1545?–1630), poet and critic: b. Saffron Walden; educ. Cambridge (Christ's College); Fellow at Cambridge (Pembroke College) 1570; entertains Queen Elizabeth I at Audley End.

Hatton, Julia Ann (**'Ann of Swansea'**) (1764–1838), poet and playwright: settles in Swansea. *Zaffine, or, The Knight of the Burning Cross* 1810 (261b).

Hawker, Robert Stephen (1803–75), poet and antiquary: b. Plymouth; educ. Oxford (Pembroke and Magdalen colleges); vicar of Morwenstow 1835–74; buried in Plymouth. 'The Song of the Western Men' 1825 (26b, 73a), 'Pompeii' 1827 (73a), *The Quest of the Sangraal* 1863 (26b).

Hawkins, Sir Anthony Hope (**'Anthony Hope'**) (1863–1933), novelist: educ. Marlborough and Oxford (Balliol College); called to the Bar in Middle Temple, London (City: Temple) 1887; lives in London (Bloomsbury: Bedford Sq.) 1903–17; lives and d. in Walton on the Hill; buried in Leatherhead. *The Prisoner of Zenda* 1894 (101a, 114a), *Memories and Notes* 1927 (91a–b, 161b).

Hawthorne, Nathaniel (1804–64), American novelist: US Consul in Liverpool 1853–7; lives in Rock Ferry 1853–7; visits Bath, Lichfield, Woodstock, Uttoxeter; lives in London (Blackheath) 1856, Southport; visits Green Arbour Ct (London: City), Leamington 1858. *The Scarlet Letter* 1850 (100c), *Our Old Home* 1863, reprinted 1970 (93c, 100c, 111b, 120c, 202a, 202c, 210b, 222a), *Journal* in *Passages from the English Notebooks* 1870, reprinted 1962 (202a).

Hay, George Campbell (1915–84), poet: b. Elderslie; brought up at Tarbert. *Wind on Loch Fyne* 1948, *Mochtàr is Dùghall* 1982 (296a).

'Hay, Ian'. See Beith, John Hay.

Hay, John MacDougall (1881–1919), novelist: b. Tarbert; minister at Elderslie. *Gillespie* 1914 (280b, 296a).

Haydon, Benjamin Robert (1786–1846), painter, critic, memoirist, and friend of Keats: lives in London (Soho: Great Marlborough St.) 1808–17; stays in Hastings, Playford 1840, Walmer. *Lectures on Painting and Design* (1846), *Autobiography* 1853 (91a, 146b, 157a).

Hayley, William (1745–1820), poet and biographer: b. Chichester; educ. Cambridge (Trinity Hall); enters Middle Temple, London (City: Temple) 1766; lives in London (Holborn: Great Queen St.) *c.* 1770, Eartham, Felpham; d. and is buried in Felpham. 'Ode on the Birth of the Prince of Wales' (171c), *Ballads founded on Anecdotes of Animals* 1805 (54b).

Hazlitt, William (1778–1830), critic and essayist: b. Maidstone; early years at Bandon and Wem; educ. London (Hackney); frequents Shrewsbury; visits Liverpool 1790, Nether Stowey, Lynmouth 1797, Llangollen 1798; m. in London (Holborn Circus: St Andrew's) 1808; lives in Winterslow from 1808; d. London (Soho: Frith St.) and buried in St Anne's (Soho: Wardour St.). Letter to the *Shrewsbury Chronicle* 1791 (207a), *Memoirs of Thomas Holcroft* (ed.) 1816, 'Farewell to Essay Writing', *Winterslow* 1839 (37c), 'On Going a Journey' in *Table-Talk* 1821–2 (255a).

Heaney, Seamus (1939–), poet: b. and brought up at Castledawson; educ. and teaches in Belfast (Queen's University); Professor of Poetry at Oxford; lives in Dublin. 'Mossbawn' (299a), 'A Lough Neagh Sequence' (299a), 'Anahorish' (299a), 'Station Island' (300b).

Hearne, Thomas (1678–1735), antiquary: educ. Oxford (St Edmund Hall); visits Ditchley; buried in Oxford. *Reliquiae Bodleianae* 1703 (76c), *Remarks and Collections*, ed. C. E. Doble, D. W. Rannie, *et al.*, 11 vols 1885–1921 (50a, 76c).

Heath-Stubbs, John (1918–2006), poet, memoirist, and critic: educ. Bembridge, Worcester mid-1930s, and Oxford (The Queen's College) late 1930s; teaches at Oxford (Merton College); drinks in London (Soho: Rathbone Pl.); lives in Zennor. 'To the Mermaid at Zennor' (38c), *Hindsights* 1993 (42a, 147a).

Heber, Reginald (1783–1826), hymn writer: educ. at Oxford (Brasenose College); vicar of Hodnet 1807–23; his chair preserved at Bridgnorth. 'From Greenland's Icy Mountains' (69c, 201a).

Hedd Wyn. See Evans, Ellis Humphrey.

Heine, Heinrich (1797–1856), German poet: visits London (Strand: Craven St.) 1827.

Hemans, Mrs Felicia Dorothea (née **Browne**) (1793–1835), poet: b. and spends early years in Liverpool; lives in St Asaph 1809–12, 1812–25; returns to Liverpool 1827–31; visits Ambleside 1829–31; lives in Dublin 1831–5; commemorated in St Asaph. 'Casabianca' (260c, 308a), *The Forest Sanctuary* 1826 (220c).

Henley, William Ernest (1849–1903), poet and critic: b. and educ. Gloucester; lives in London (Muswell Hill) 1896–9; memorial in London (City: St Paul's Cathedral).

Henri, Adrian (1932–2000), poet: b. Birkenhead; educ. Rhyl and Newcastle; lives and d. in Liverpool. *The Mersey Sound* 1967 (222c), 'Liverpool Poems' (222c), 'Christ's Entry into Liverpool' (222c).

Henryson (or **Henderson**), **Robert** (1430?–1506), Scottish poet: probably a founder of Glasgow University.

Henslowe, Philip (d. 1616), theatrical manager: manages theatres in London (Southwark: Bankside; Finsbury: Fortune St.; Dulwich). *Diary* 1592–1609 (118a, 119b, 147c).

Henty, George Alfred (1832–1902), writer of boys' stories and novelist: b. Grantchester; educ. London (Westminster School); lives in London (Battersea: Lavender Gdns); d. Weymouth; buried in London (Kensington: Brompton cemetery). *With Clive in India* 1884, *With Moore at Corunna* 1898, *With Buller in Natal* 1901 (97c).

Herbert, George (1593–1633), poet: b. Montgomery; educ. London (Westminster School) and Cambridge (Trinity College); Fellow at Cambridge (Trinity College) 1616 and Public Orator 1619–27; prebend of Leighton Bromswold; visits Dauntsey; rector of Bemerton 1630–2; buried in Bemerton and commemorated in Little Gidding. *The Temple* 1633 (7a, 178c), 'The Elixir' (178b).

Herrick, Robert (1591–1674), poet: apprenticed to his uncle in London (City: Wood St.) *c.* 1604–14; educ. Cambridge (St John's College and Trinity Hall); vicar of Dean Prior 1629–47, 1662–74; buried in Dean Prior. *Noble Numbers* 1647, *Hesperides* 1648, *Poetical Works*, ed. L. C. Martin, 1956 (16c).

Herzen, Alexander (1812–70), political writer and memoirist: lives in London (Putney, Regent's Park). *My Past and Thoughts* 1867 (140a).

Hewlett, Maurice (1861–1923), novelist, poet, and essayist: lives and d. in Broad Chalke. *The Song of the Plow* 1916, *Wiltshire Essays* 1921 (12b).

Hickey, William (1749–1830), writer of memoirs: lives in Beaconsfield from 1809. *The Memoirs of William Hickey*, ed. A. Spencer 1913–25, ed. P. Quennell 1960, 1975 (41b).

Higden, Ranulf (d. 1364), chronicler: monk at Chester and buried in the Cathedral. *Polychronicon c.* 1342 (20b, 214b).

Hill, Aaron (1685–1750), poet and playwright: educ. London (Westminster School); lives in London (Westminster: Petty France); associated with Theatre Royal (Covent Garden: Catherine St.); buried in Westminster Abbey. *Rinaldo* libretto 1711, *Athelwold* 1732, *Zara* 1736 (157a).

Hill, Geoffrey (1932–), poet: b. Bromsgrove; educ. Oxford (Keble College). 'To the High Court of Parliament' (157a), 'In Ipsley Church Lane' (201c).

Hill, Susan (1942–), novelist: b. Scarborough; educ. Scarborough, Coventry, and London (Strand: King's College); lives in Chipping Campden. *A Change for the Better* 1969 (51b), 'In the Conservatory' 1973 (237b), *Air and Angels* 1991 (165a).

Hines, Barry (1939–), novelist: childhood in Barnsley. *A Kestrel for a Knave* 1968 (230a).

Hoban, Russell (1925–), novelist. *Turtle Diary* 1975 (140a), *Riddley Walker* 1980 (46b, 55a, 81a).

Hobbes, John Oliver. See Craigie, Pearl Mary Teresa.

Hobbes, Thomas (1588–1679), philosopher: b. Malmesbury; educ. Oxford (Magdalen Hall); visits Great Tew; spends last years and is buried in Ault Hucknall. *Leviathan* 1651 (73b, 301a).

Hocking, Joseph (1860–1937), minister and novelist: b. St Stephen.

Hocking, Silas Kitto (1850–1935), novelist: b. St Stephen. *Alec Green* 1878 (31a).

Hodgson, Ralph (1871–1962), poet: b. Darlington. *The Last Blackbird and Other Lines* 1907, *Poems* 1917, *The Skylark and Other Poems* 1958 (240b).

Hogg, James ('the Ettrick Shepherd') (1770–1835), poet and novelist: b. Ettrick; stays at Edinburgh 1803 and later; granted farm in Altrive Lake 1815, his main home for the rest of his life; frequents Tibbie Shiel's Inn; meets Scott at Gordon Arms; buried in Ettrick; monument nr Tibbie Shiel's Inn. 'The Forest Minstrel' 1810, *The Queen's Wake* 1813, *The Private Memoirs and Confessions of a Justified Sinner* 1824 (268c, 275c).

Hogg, Thomas Jefferson (1792–1862), friend and biographer of Shelley: b. Norton; educ. Durham and Oxford (University College). 'Posthumous Fragments of Margaret Nicholson' (with Shelley) (78c).

Holcroft, Thomas (1745–1809), actor and playwright: b. London (Soho: Leicester Sq.); baptized at St Martin-in-the-Fields (Strand: Trafalgar Sq.); works in Mayfair (South Audley St.) as a boy; lives in Marylebone (Marylebone St.) 1780s; d. in Marylebone (Clipstone St.) and buried at Marylebone parish church. *Le Mariage de Figaro* (trans.) 1784 (137c).

Holinshed, Raphael (d. 1580), chronicler: educ. Cambridge (Trinity Hall). *Chronicles* 1577 (54b, 111c, 182b, 305c).

Hollis, Maurice Christopher (1902–77), historian and biographer: lives many years in Mells; d. in Mells. *Foreigners Aren't Fools* 1936 (25c), *Foreigners Aren't Knaves* 1939, *Death of a Gentleman* 1943, *A Study of George Orwell* 1956, *The Seven Ages* 1974, *Oxford in the Twenties* 1976 (25c).

Holtby, Winifred (1898–1935), novelist: b. Rudston; educ. Oxford (Somerville College); buried in Rudston. *The Land of Green Ginger* 1927, *Poor Caroline* 1931, *Virginia Woolf: A Critical Study* 1932 (77c), *South Riding* 1936 (77c, 237b).

Home, John (1722–1808), minister, poet, and playwright: minister at Athelstaneford 1746; imprisoned in Doune 1745–6. *Douglas* 1756 (272a).

Hood, Thomas (1799–1845), poet and journalist: b. London (City: Poultry); lives in London (Islington: Essex St.); convalesces in Dundee 1815–17; spends honeymoon in Hastings 1825; lives in London (Adelphi) 1827, (Winchmore Hill) 1829–32, (Wanstead) 1832–5, (St John's Wood: Elm Tree Rd and Finchley Rd) 1841–5; buried in London (Kensal Green cemetery). *The Bandit* (272c), *Comic Annual* 1830 (156c, 159c), *Eugene Aram* 1831 (177c), *Tylney Hall* 1834 (156c), *New Monthly* 1841–3, *Hood's Magazine* 1843–4 (142b), *The Song of the Shirt* 1843 (109b, 129c, 142b).

Hooker, Richard (1553/4?–1600), theologian: b. Exeter; educ. Oxford (Corpus Christi College); rector of Boscombe 1591–5, of Bishopsbourne 1595–1600; buried in Bishopsbourne; memorial statue in Exeter. *Laws of Ecclesiastical Polity* 1594 (7c), 1597 (42c).

Hoosan, Isaac Daniel (1880–1948), poet: b., lives, and dies at Rhosllannerchrugog (Llangollen); commemorated nr Llangollen. *Cerddi a Baledi* 1936, *Y Gwin a Cherddi Eraill* 1948 (255a).

Hope, Anthony. See Hawkins, Sir Anthony Hope.

Hopkins, Gerard Manley (1844–89), priest and poet: educ. London (Highgate: see Highgate High St.) and Oxford (Balliol College); studies at Stonyhurst College, nr Whalley 1870–1, at St Beuno's College 1874–7; ordained priest 1877 and becomes bursar at Mount St Mary's College 1877–8; curate in Oxford (see Balliol College) 1878; teaches at Stonyhurst College 1878, 1882–4; priest at Glasgow 1881; Professor of Classics at Dublin (University College) 1884–9; buried in Dublin (see University College); memorials in London (Westminster Abbey) and Haslemere. 'Duns Scotus's Oxford', 'Heaven-Haven' 1866 (69a), 'The Wreck of the Deutschland' 1876, 'The Windhover' 1877, 'Pied Beauty' 1877 (261a), 'The Loss of the Eurydice' 1878 (193b), 'Binsey Poplars Felled' 1879 (42b), 'St. Winefred's Well' 1879 (251b), 'Inversnaid' 1881 (283b, 286b), *Journal* 1959 (229b).

Hornby, Nick (1957–), novelist: b. Redhill; educ. Cambridge. *Fever Pitch* 1992 (129b), *High Fidelity* 1995 (126b).

Horne Tooke, John (1736–1812), philologist. *The Diversions of Purley* 1786 (117c).

Hornung, Ernest William (1866–1921), novelist: educ. Uppingham. *The Amateur Cracksman* 1899, *Fathers of Men* 1912 (196b–c).

Houghton, William Stanley (1881–1913), playwright: b. Ashton-upon-Mersey; educ. Manchester Grammar School. *The Dear Departed* 1908, *Hindle Wakes* 1912 (213b, 225c).

Housman, Alfred Edward (1859–1936), poet: b. Fockbury; lives in Bromsgrove 1860–73; educ. Bromsgrove and Oxford (St John's College); lives in London (Highgate: North Rd) 1886–1905, (Pinner) 1905–11; Professor of Latin at Cambridge and Fellow (Trinity College) 1911; buried in Ludlow. *A Shropshire Lad* 1896 (124b, 170c, 198c, 203b), *Last Poems* 1922, *The Name and Nature of Poetry* 1933, *More Poems* 1936 (170c), 'The Vane on Hughley Steeple' (201b).

Howitt, William (1792–1897), miscellaneous writer: lives with his wife, Mary (1799–1888), in Nottingham 1822–35, Esher 1835–70. *The Forest Minstrel* (with Mary Howitt) 1823 (194a, 275c), *Rural Life in England* 1836 (52a), *Visits to Remarkable Places* 1840, 1842 (52a, 209c, 211b).

Hudson, William Henry (1841–1922), naturalist and novelist of American birth: lives in London (Kensington: St Luke's Rd) 1886–1922; visits Limpsfield, Brockenhurst 1903, Zennor 1906–7; buried in Worthing; memorial in London (Hyde Park). *Birds in London* 1898, *Birds and Man*

1901 (126c), *Hampshire Days* 1903 (44c), *Green Mansions* 1904 (126c, 131c), *The Land's End: A Naturalist's Impressions in West Cornwall* 1908 (38b), *A Shepherd's Life* 1910 (62c), *Adventures Among Birds* 1913 (126c).

Hueffer, Ford Madox. See Ford, Ford Madox.

Hughes, John Ceiriog (1832–87), lyric writer: b. Llanarmon Dyffryn Ceiriog; memorial in Glyn Ceiriog. *Owain Wyn* 1856, 'God Bless the Prince of Wales' (250a–b).

Hughes, Richard Arthur Warren (1900–76), novelist and poet: educ. Godalming (Charterhouse) and Oxford (Oriel College); rents cottage at Talsarnau 1916; lives nr Llanfrothen 1919–24, in Laugharne 1934/5–1946, Talsarnau 1947–76; Hon. Fellow at Oxford (Oriel College) 1975; buried in Talsarnau. *The Sisters' Tragedy* 1922 (75c), *Gipsy-Night and Other Poems* 1922 (262c), *A High Wind in Jamaica* 1929 (254c), *In Hazard* 1938 (251c), *The Human Predicament*, vol. i, *The Fox in the Attic* 1961, vol. ii, *The Wooden Shepherdess* 1973 (262c).

Hughes, Ted (1930–98), poet: b. Mytholmroyd; family moves to Mexborough; childhood in Conisbrough; educ. Cambridge (Pembroke) and founds St Botolph's Review; lives in Cambridge and London (Bloomsbury); works at London Zoo (London: Regent's Park); marries in London (Bloomsbury); moves with Plath to London (Chalk Farm); moves to North Tawton; lives in Heptonstall; ashes scattered on Dartmoor (North Tawton). 'The Thought-Fox' (236a), *Remains of Elmet* 1979 (236c), 'Two Photographs of Top Withens' (232c), 'Error' (27a).

Hughes, Thomas (1822–96), novelist: b. Uffington; educ. Rugby and Oxford (Oriel College); enters Lincoln's Inn, London (Holborn) 1845, Inner Temple (City: Temple) 1848; revisits Uffington 1857; lives in Chester 1882–96; d. Brighton; memorial in Uffington. *Tom Brown's Schooldays* 1857 (90a, 206a), *The Scouring of the White Horse* 1859 (90a), *Tom Brown at Oxford* 1861 (75b).

Hughes, Thomas Rowland (1903–49), Welsh-language novelist and poet: b. Llanberis; educ. Bangor (University College of North Wales); B.Litt. at Oxford (Jesus College) 1928; lives in Cardiff 1935–49; buried in Cardiff. 'Y Ffin' (The Boundary) 1937, 'Pererinion' (Pilgrims) 1940, *O Law i Law* (From Hand to Hand) 1943, *Cân neu Ddwy* (A Song or Two) 1948 (247a).

Hugo, Victor (1802–85), French poet and novelist: lives in St Luke's 1852–5, St Peter Port 1855–70; commemorated in St Peter Port. *Les Châtiments* 1853 (30c), *Les Misérables* 1862, *Littérature et philosophie mêlées* 1864, *Chansons des rues et des bois* 1865, *Les Travailleurs de la mer* 1866 (30c).

Hume, David (1711–76), historian and philosopher: b. and educ. Edinburgh; lives in Edinburgh and is Keeper of the Advocates' Library 1752; buried in Edinburgh. *Political Discourses* 1752, *History of Great Britain* 1754–61 (273c).

Hunt, James Henry Leigh (1784–1859), essayist and poet: b. London (Southgate); educ. London (City: Christ's Hospital, Newgate St.); visits Hastings 1812; imprisoned in London (Southwark: Horsemonger Lane jail, Borough High St.) 1812–14; lives in Hampstead (Vale of Health) 1815, Marylebone (Lisson Grove) 1815–17; visits Marlow 1817; lives in London (Chelsea: Upper Cheyne Row) 1833–40, (Hammersmith: Rowan Rd) 1853–9; buried in London (Kensal Green cemetery). *The Story of Rimini* 1816 (57c).

Hurd, Richard (1720–1808), critic and divine: b. Congreve; educ. Cambridge (Emmanuel College); Bishop of Lichfield 1775–81, Bishop of Worcester 1781–1808; lives in Hartlebury 1781–1808. *The Polite Arts, or, A dissertation on poetry, painting, music, etc.* 1749 (167a), *Letters on Chivalry and Romance* 1762 (200c, 203a).

Hurdis, James (1763–1801), poet: b. Bishopstone (East Sussex): educ. Chichester and Oxford (Magdalen College); curate at Burwash 1785–9;

Hurdis, James (*cont'd*)
Fellow of Magdalen College, Oxford 1786; vicar of Bishopstone 1791; meets Cowper at Eartham 1792; buried in Bishopstone. *The Village Curate* 1788 (45b, 73a), *The Favourite Village* 1800 (42c).

Hutchinson, Arthur Stuart Menteith (1879–1971), novelist: makes his last home at Crowborough. *If Winter Comes* 1920 (44a).

Huxley, Aldous Leonard (1894–1963), novelist and essayist: educ. Eton and Oxford (Balliol College); visits Garsington 1915; lives in London (Hampstead: Bracknell Gdns) 1917; teaches at Eton 1917–19; lives in London (Hampstead: Hampstead Hill Gdns) 1919–20. *Defeat of Youth* 1918 (121a), *Leda and Other Poems* 1920 (52c, 121c), *Limbo* 1920 (121c), *Crome Yellow* 1921 (41c, 55c, 88b), *Eyeless in Gaza* 1936 (69b).

Hyde, Douglas (1860–1949), poet, historian, and statesman: b. Frenchpark, and retires here after an academic life.

Hyde, Edward. See Clarendon, Edward Hyde, 1st Earl of.

Hywel ap Rheinallt (*fl.* 1461–1506), poet: eulogizes saints of Bardsey.

I

Ieuan Fardd or **Ieuan Brydydd Hir.** See Evans, Evan.

Inchbald, Mrs Elizabeth (née **Simpson**) (1753–1821), novelist, actress, and playwright: acts in Bristol 1772; lives in London (Covent Garden: Russell St.) 1788, (Soho: Frith St.) 1791, (Soho: Leicester Sq.) 1790s–1803, (Strand: The Strand) *c.* 1805–9. *Such Things Are* 1788 (117a), *A Simple Story* 1791 (177c), *Wives As They Were* 1797 (146c), *Lovers' Vows* 1798 (3c, 146c), prefaces to *The British Theatre* 1806–9 (152b).

Ingelow, Jean (1820–97), novelist and poet: b. Boston. 'High Tide on the Coast of Lincolnshire 1571' in *Poems* 1863 (189a).

Iolo Morganwg. See Williams, Edward.

Irving, Washington (**'Geoffrey Crayon'**) (1783–1859), American essayist and historian: visits Abbotsford, Stratford-upon-Avon, Bromham, London (Kensington: Holland House); suffers business failure in Liverpool 1818; visits Birmingham 1818, Newstead Abbey 1832. 'Rip Van Winkle' in *The Sketch-Book* 1820 (197a, 209c, 220c), *Bracebridge Hall* 1822 (197a), *Abbotsford and Newstead Abbey* 1835 (193c).

Isherwood, Christopher (1904–86), novelist, playwright, memoirist, and critic: b. Marple; educ. Hindhead (meets W. H. Auden), Repton, Cambridge (Corpus Christi College) 1924–7, and London (Camberwell: King's College Hospital); stays in the Scilly Isles; works in London (Shepherd's Bush) mid-1930s. *The Memorial* 1932 (165c, 226b), *The Dog Beneath the Skin* 1935 (199a), *Mr Norris Changes Trains* 1935 (104c), *Lions and Shadows* 1938 (32b, 58c, 165c, 194c), *Goodbye to Berlin* 1939 (104c), *Journey to a War* 1939 (71a), *Prater Violet* 1946 (143a), *Christopher and His Kind* 1976 (104c).

Ishiguro, Kazuo (1954–), novelist: educ. Canterbury and Norwich (University of East Anglia); works at Balmoral. *The Remains of the Day* 1989 (31c, 37a), *Never Let Me Go* 2005 (172c).

Islwyn. See Thomas, William.

J

Jacob, Violet (née **Erskine**) (1863–1946), poet and novelist: b. and lives in Strathmore. 'The Lang Road' in *Songs of Angus* 1915, *The Northern Lights* 1927, *The Lairds of Dun* 1931 (295c).

Jacobs, William Wymark (1863–1943), short-story writer: lives in Loughton; visits Ewelme. *Many Cargoes* 1896, *Short Cruises* 1907, *Sea Whispers* 1926, 'The Monkey's Paw' (179a).

Jacobson, Howard (1942–), novelist: b. Manchester; educ. Whitefield and Cambridge (Downing College); lectures at Wolverhampton Polytechnic and Cambridge (Selwyn College). *Coming from Behind* 1983 (211b), *Peeping Tom* 1984 (7c), *Redback* 1987 (167a, 227b), *No More Mr Nice Guy* 1998 (14a–b), *The Making of Henry* 2004 (142b–c).

James I (1394–1437), King of Scotland and poet: imprisoned in London (City: The Tower) and Windsor Castle; assassinated in Perth. *The Kingis Quair* 1783 (93a, 115a, 292a, 293a).

James, Clive (1939–), broadcaster and memoirist: lives in London (Hampstead); educ. Cambridge (Pembroke College); works as a journalist in London (Soho). *Falling Towards England* 1985 (121c), *May Week Was in June* 1990 (169a), *North Face of Soho* 2006 (146c).

James, David Emrys (**'Dewi Emrys'**) (1881–1952), poet: lives and is buried at Talgarreg; commemorated nr Fishguard.

James, Evan (1809–78), poet: lives at Pontypridd. 'Hen Wlad fy Nhadau' 1856 (259b–c).

James, Henry (1843–1916), novelist of American birth: lives in London (Mayfair: Bolton St.) 1876–85; visits Dover, Hastings, Oxford, Dunwich, Witley, Cambridge; lives and winters in London (Kensington: De Vere Gdns) 1886–96; visits St Ives (Cornwall) 1894; stays in Torquay 1895; visits Mickleham 1895; lives in Rye 1896–1916; winters in London (Chelsea: Cheyne Walk) 1912–16 and d. there; memorials in Westminster Abbey and Chelsea Old Church. *A Passionate Pilgrim* 1875 (67c), *The Europeans* 1878, *Daisy Miller* 1879, *Washington Square* 1881, *The Portrait of a Lady* 1881 (136b–c), *Portraits of Places* 1883 (58a, 67c, 164c), *The Princess Casamassima* 1886 (136c), *The Bostonians* 1886 (50c), *The Tragic Muse* 1890, 'The Altar of the Dead' 1895 (67c), *What Maisie Knew* 1897 (130b), *The Spoils of Poynton* 1897 (35b, 82b), *The Wings of the Dove* 1902 (82c, 130b), *The Ambassadors* 1903 (35b, 82c, 214c), *The Golden Bowl* 1904 (82c), 'Sir Edmund Orme' (44a).

James, Montague Rhodes (1862–1936), antiquary and short-story writer: b. Goodnestone; brought up in Great Livermere; educ. Cambridge (King's College), Director of Fitzwilliam Museum, Cambridge 1893–1908; initiates restoration of Abbey glass at Great Malvern 1910; Provost of King's College, Cambridge 1905; Provost of Eton 1918; visits Aldeburgh. *Ghost Stories of an Antiquary* 1905 (56b, 167c, 200b).

James, Phyllis Dorothy (1920–), novelist: b. Oxford; moves to Cambridge as a child; titled Baroness James of Holland Park. *Cover Her Face* 1962 (156b), *The Maul and the Pear Tree* 1971 (143a), *Innocent Blood* 1980 (139a).

Jameson, Mrs Anna Brownell (1794–1860), essayist and critic: b. and lives early years in Dublin. *Shakespeare's Heroines* 1832 (308a).

Jamie, Kathleen (1962–), poet: educ. Edinburgh. 'Cramond Island' (271b).

Jefferies, Richard (1848–87), novelist and naturalist: b. Coates; lives in London (Surbiton) 1877–82, Brighton 1885, Crowborough 1884–6; d. in Goring-by-Sea; buried in Worthing; bust in Salisbury Cathedral. *Round About a Great Estate* 1880, *Bevis* 1882 (15b), *Nature Near London* 1883 (153c), *Field and Hedgerow* 1889 (49b), *The Old House at Coate* 1948 (15b).

Jeffrey, Francis, Lord Jeffrey (1773–1850), co-founder and editor of the *Edinburgh Review* (1802–29): b. and lives in Edinburgh; educ. Edinburgh High School and University.

Jennings, Elizabeth (1926–2001), poet: b. Boston; educ. Oxford (St Anne's College); lives and d. in Oxford.

Jerome, Jerome Klapka (1859–1927), novelist and playwright: b. Walsall; educ. in London (Marylebone); lives nr Ewelme from 1887, in London (Chelsea: Chelsea Gdns) *c.* 1888–9, (Bloomsbury: Tavistock Pl.) 1889; visits Clifton Hampden, Dunwich; d. in Northampton; buried in Ewelme. *Three Men in a Boat* 1889 (48b, 53a, 79b, 103b, 105b, 210b), *Idle Thoughts of an Idle Fellow* 1889, *The Passing of the Third Floor Back* 1907 (103b), *My Life and Times* 1926 (139a).

Jerrold, Douglas William (1803–57), playwright and poet: b. London (Soho: Greek St.); buried in London (Kensal Green cemetery). *Black Ey'd Susan* 1829, *The Bride of Ludgate* 1831, 'Mrs. Caudle's Curtain Lectures' in *Punch* 1845, *Lloyds Weekly Newspaper* (ed.) 1852–7 (146b).

Jessopp, Augustus (1823–1914), topographical writer: headmaster of Norwich Grammar School; rector of Scarning 1879–1911. *Arcady for Better for Worse* 1887 (183a).

Jewel, John (1522–71), bishop and Anglican apologist: b. Berrynarbor; rector of Sunningwell *c.* 1550–2. *Apologia Ecclesia Anglicanae* 1562 (7b).

Johnson, Linton Kwesi (1952–), poet: lives in London (Brixton); writer in residence in London (Lambeth). 'Five Nights of Bleeding' (104a), 'Yout Scene' (104a), 'Di Great Insohreckshan' (104a), 'New Craas Massakah' (118a), 'It Dread inna Inglan' (230c).

Johnson, Lionel Pigot (1867–1902), poet: educ. Oxford (New College); lives in London and frequents the Rhymer's Club (City: Fleet St.). 'Oxford' in *Poems* 1895 (74c).

Johnson, Samuel (1709–84), lexicographer, critic, and poet: b. Lichfield; educ. Lichfield, Stourbridge, and Oxford (Pembroke College); teaches in Market Bosworth 1731; lives in Birmingham *c.* 1734; m. in Derby 1735; runs private school in Edial 1735–7; spends holidays at Tissington 1739; lives in London (Hampstead: Frognal) 1745, (City: Gough Sq.) 1749–50, (Holborn: Staple Inn) 1759–60, (City: Gough Sq., Johnson's Ct) 1765–76; visits Elsfield 1754; frequents clubs and coffee houses (Chelsea: Lawrence St. and Cheyne Walk), (Soho: Gerrard St.), (Strand: Essex St.), (City: Fleet St., Mitre tavern); visits Garrick (Adelphi), Goldsmith (Fleet St.: Wine Office Ct); frequents the Thrale's home (Southwark: Park St.) 1763–82, (Streatham) 1763–84; visits Thomas Percy, Easton Maudit 1764; tours Scotland 1773, visiting Edinburgh, Auchinleck, St Andrews, Inveraray, Alexandria, Aberdeen, Slains Castle, Cullen, Oban, Skye, Mull, Glenshiel, Iona, Laurencekirk, Glasgow; visits Ashbourne, Great Torrington, Langton by Spilsby, Tetford, Hagley, Brighton, Bath, Beaconsfield, Bristol, Saltram House, Tremeirchion, Henley, Oxford (Trinity and University colleges), Ilam, Uttoxeter; d. London (City: Fleet St.); buried in Westminster Abbey; statues in St Paul's Cathedral, at St Clement Danes (Strand), and Lichfield. *Birmingham Journal* essays 1734–5, *Voyage to Abyssinia* (trans.) 1735 (196c), *The Vanity of Human Wishes* 1749 (121b), *The Rambler* (ed.) 1750–2, *A Dictionary of the English Language* 1755 (111a), *The Idler* (ed.) 1758–60 (111b, 155c), *Rasselas* 1759 (111b, 126b, 190b–c), *A Journey to the Western Islands of Scotland* 1775 (285a), *Lives of the English Poets* 1779–81 (28c, 185a, 261b).

Johnson, William. See Cory, William Johnson.

Johnston, Arthur (**'the Scottish Ovid'**) (1587–1641), doctor and Latin poet: b. Inverurie; Rector of Aberdeen University 1637–41. *Musae Aulicae* 1637, *Delitiae Poetarum Scotorum* (ed.) 1637 (266a).

Jones, David Gwenallt (1899–1968), Welsh-language poet, author, and critic: b. Pontardawe; educ. Aberystwyth (University College of Wales); lecturer and Reader in Welsh at Aberystwyth 1927–67; lives in Aberystwyth 1927–68 and is buried there; commemorated in Pontardawe. 'Y Mynach' (The Monk) 1926, 'Breuddwyd y Bardd' (The Poet's Dream) 1931, *Ysgubau'r Awen* (Sheaves of the Muse) 1939, *Cnoi Cil* (Ruminating) 1942, *Eples* (Leaven) 1951, *Gwreiddiau* (Roots) 1959, *Y Coed* (Trees) 1969 (244c).

Jones, Idwal (1895–1937), humorist and playwright: b. and buried at Lampeter. *Pobl yr Ymylon* (People of the Hinterland) 1927, *Cerddi Digri a Rhai Pethau*

M

Mangan, James Clarence (1803–49), poet: b., lives, and d. in Dublin; commemorated in Dublin. Contributions to the *Dublin University Magazine* and *The Nation*, 'My Dark Rosaleen' (308b).

Mansfield, Katherine (*pseudonym of* **Kathleen Mansfield Beauchamp**) (1888–1923), short-story writer: educ. and lives in London (Marylebone: Harley St.) 1903–6; lives in London (St John's Wood: Acacia Rd) 1915; visits Garsington; visits D. H. Lawrence in Zennor 1916; lives in Mylor 1916; m. John Middleton Murry and lives in London (Hampstead: East Heath Rd) 1918. *The Signature* (142b), *Journal*, ed. J. Middleton Murry, 1927 (121b). *Bliss and Other Stories* 1920, *The Garden Party* 1922.

Mantel, Hilary (1952–), novelist: b. Glossop; educ. Sheffield and London School of Economics (London: Strand).

Map (*or* **Mapes**), **Walter** (*fl.* 1200), chronicler: archdeacon in Oxford 1197; canon in Lincoln and Hereford. *De Nugis Curialium* (192a).

Markham, Mrs. *See* Penrose, Elizabeth.

Marlowe, Christopher (1564–93), playwright: b. and baptized in Canterbury; educ. Canterbury and Cambridge (Corpus Christi College); frequents the Mermaid tavern in London (City: Bread St.); killed and buried in London (Deptford); commemorated in Canterbury, Cambridge, and Deptford. *Tamburlaine* 1590, *Edward II* 1594, 'The Passionate Shepherd to his Love', beginning 'Come live with me and be my love' in *The Passionate Pilgrim* 1599, *The Tragedy of Dr. Faustus* 1604 (117c, 119b), *The Jew of Malta* 1633 (119b, 192a).

Marmion, Shakerley (1603–39), poet and playwright: b. Aynho; educ. Oxford (Wadham College); visits Dover's Hill for the Cotswold Games. *The Antiquary* 1641 (188b), contributions to *Annalia Dubrensia* 1636 (17c, 188b).

Marryat, Captain Frederick (1792–1848), novelist: educ. in London (Enfield); lives in London (Marylebone: Spanish Pl.) 1841–3, (Wimbledon) 1839–43; lives for a time in Lymington; settles in Langham 1843–8; d. and is commemorated in Langham. *Mr. Midshipman Easy* 1836, *Masterman Ready* 1841 (135b, 178a), *The Children of the New Forest* 1847 (61b).

Marsh, Edward (1872–1953), classicist and scholar: lives in London (Holborn) 1899–1940. *Georgian Poetry* 1912–21, *A Memoir of Rupert Brooke* 1918 (125a).

Marston, John (1575?–1634), playwright and poet, author of *The Dutch Courtezan* (1605) and *Sophonisba* (1606): educ. Oxford (Brasenose College) 1591–4; enters Middle Temple, London (City: Temple); company playwright for Paul's Boys, London (City: St Paul's); imprisoned in London (Southwark: Old Marshalsea, Borough High St., Mermaid Ct) *c.* 1605; rector of Christchurch (Dorset) 1616–31; buried in London (City: Temple Church). *The Malcontent* 1604, *Eastward Hoe* (with Jonson and Chapman) 1605 (149c).

Martin, Sir Theodore ('**Bon Gaultier**') (1816–1909), poet and humorist: b. and educ. Edinburgh; practises as solicitor in Edinburgh before leaving for London 1846. Contributions to *Tait's Magazine* and *Fraser's Magazine*, *Bon Gaultier Ballads* (with W. E. Aytoun) 1845 (278a).

Martin, Thomas ('**honest Tom Martin of Palgrave**') (1697–1771), antiquary: lives in Palgrave 1723–71. *The History of Thetford* 1779 (183a).

Martin, Violet Florence ('**Martin Ross**') (1862–1915), novelist with her cousin Edith Somerville, as 'Somerville and Ross'; lives, d., and is commemorated in Castletownshend. *The Real Charlotte* 1894, *Some Experience of an Irish R.M.* 1899, *Further Experiences of an Irish R.M.* 1908 (317c).

Martineau, Harriet (1802–76), novelist and political economist: b. Norwich; lives in Ambleside 1845–76; first meets Charlotte Brontë in London (Bayswater: Westbourne St.) 1849; buried in Birmingham. *Illustrations of Political Economy* 1832–4 (180c), *Deerbrook* 1839 (98b, 213b), *Complete Guide to the Lakes* 1855 (213b), *Autobiography* 1877 (98b).

Martyn, Edward (1859–1924), poet, playwright, and patron of the arts: educ. Oxford (Christ Church); lives in Tullira; promotes the idea of the Irish national theatre at Durras House. *The Heather Field* 1899.

Marvell, Andrew (1621–78), poet: b. Winestead; educ. Kingston upon Hull and Cambridge (Trinity College) 1633–8; tutor in Appleton Roebuck 1650–2; lives in London (Highgate: Waterlow Park); buried in London (Bloomsbury: St Giles-in-the-Fields Church); commemorated in Kingston upon Hull. 'The Garden', 'Upon Appleton House' (230a).

Marx, Karl (1818–83), political writer and philosopher: lives in London (Chelsea) 1849, (Soho) 1850–5, (Kentish Town) 1855–74; works in London (Bloomsbury: British Museum); children buried in London (Tottenham Ct Rd); takes holidays or spa cures at Harrogate 1873, St Helier 1879, Ramsgate 1850s and 1860s; buried in Highgate cemetery. *Das Kapital* 1967 (101a).

Masefield, John (1878–1967), Poet Laureate and novelist: b. Ledbury; educ. Warwick; cadet in Liverpool 1891–4; stays in Great Hampden 1909–13; lives in London (Hampstead: Well Walk) 1913–17; stays nr Wallingford 1914–17; lives in Oxford 1917–33, Sapperton 1933–9; visits Coole Park; lives at Clifton Hampden 1939–67; ashes deposited, and commemorated, in London (Westminster Abbey). 'The Valediction (Liverpool Docks)' 1902 (222b), *The Everlasting Mercy* 1911 (56c), *The Widow in the Bye Street* 1912, *Dauber* 1913, 'August 1914', *Lollington Downs and Other Poems* 1917 (91a), *Reynard the Fox* 1919, *Sard Harker* 1924, *Odtaa* 1926 (68a), 'The Wanderer of Liverpool' 1930, 'A Masque of Liverpool' 1930 (222b), *Eggs and Baker* 1935, *The Square Peg* 1937 (32a), *New Chum* 1944 (48b, 222b), *The Badon Parchments* 1947 (22a, 48b), 'All the land from Ludlow Town' (197c).

Mason, Alfred Edward Woodley (1865–1948), novelist: educ. in London (Dulwich College).

Mason, William (1724–97), poet and friend of Thomas Gray: b. Kingston upon Hull; educ. Cambridge (St John's College); Fellow at Cambridge (Pembroke College); rector of Aston 1754–97; visits Nuneham Courtenay. *Isis* 1748 (78a), *The English Garden* 1772–81 (64c), 'Caractacus' (35c).

Massinger, Philip (1583–1640), playwright: baptized in Salisbury; educ. Oxford (Merton College); boyhood in Wilton; writes for theatres in London (Southwark: Bankside); buried in Southwark Cathedral. *The Duke of Milan* 1623, *A New Way to Pay Old Debts* 1633.

Maturin, Charles Robert (1782–1824), novelist: b., educ., and lives in Dublin. *The Fatal Revenge* 1807, *The Wild Irish Boy* 1808, *The Milesian Chief* 1811, *Bertram* 1816, *Melmoth the Wanderer* 1820 (308a).

Maugham, William Somerset (1874–1965), novelist, playwright, and short-story writer: educ. Canterbury; lives in Whitstable, London (Westminster: Vincent Sq.) 1895, (Mayfair: Chesterfield St.) 1911–19; ashes placed in wall of Maugham Library, Canterbury. *Liza of Lambeth* 1897 (46b, 157c), *Of Human Bondage* 1915 (44a, 46b, 92a), *The Circle* 1921, *The Breadwinner* 1930 (136c), *Cakes and Ale* 1930 (92a), *For Services Rendered* 1932 (136c), *Catalina* 1948 (46b), *Complete Short Stories* 3 vols 1951, *Collected Plays* 3 vols 1952, *Selected Novels* 3 vols 1953 (136c).

Mavor, Osborne Henry ('**James Bridie**') (1888–1951), playwright: spends childhood, educ., and practises medicine in Glasgow; lives in Helensburgh. *The Anatomist* 1931, *Tobias and the Angel* 1931, *A Sleeping Clergyman* 1933, *One Way of Living* 1939 (283c), *Mr Bolfry* 1943, *Daphne Laureola* 1949 (285c).

Maxwell, Gavin (1914–69), writer, especially on wildlife: lives intermittently in Sandaig 1949–69; buried in Sandaig. *Ring of Bright Water* 1960 (294b).

Maxwell, Glyn (1962–), poet: educ. Oxford (Worcester College) 1980s.

Melville, Herman (1819–91), American novelist: visits Liverpool 1837, 1856; visits Nathaniel Hawthorne at Southport 1857. *Redburn* 1849, *Moby-Dick, or, The Whale* 1851 (222a), *Billy Budd* written *c.* 1890, published 1924 (161a).

Meredith, George (1828–1909), novelist and poet: b. Portsmouth; lives in London (Belgravia: Ebury St.) 1849, Shepperton 1853–8, London (Chelsea: Hobury St.) 1858–9, Esher 1859–67; stays in London (Chelsea: Cheyne Walk) 1861–2; lives in Mickleham 1867–1909; buried in Dorking. *The Ordeal of Richard Feverel* 1859 (106b), *Evan Harrington* 1861 (52b, 80b, 106b), *Poems of the English Roadside* 1862, *Modern Love* 1862 (52b), *Beauchamp's Career* 1876 (52a, 86a), *Diana of the Crossways* 1885 (63a), *Lord Ormont and his Aminta* 1894 (173c), *The Amazing Marriage* 1895 (63b).

Merriman (*or* **Merryman**), **Brian** (**Brian Mac Giolla Meidhre**) (*c.* 1749–1805), Irish poet: b. Ennistymon; lives and is buried in Feakle. *The Midnight Court* (*Cúirt an mheádhon oídhche*) 1780 (320b).

Merriman, Henry Seton. *See* Scott, Hugh Stowell.

Meynell, Alice (1847–1922), poet: lives in London (Bayswater: Palace Ct) 1890–1905; arranges care of Francis Thompson in Storrington. *The Rhythm of Life* 1893, *The Colour of Life* 1896, *The Spirit of Peace* 1898 (95c).

Michael, Livi (1960–), novelist: b. Manchester; brought up in Ashton-under-Lyne; educ. Droylsden and Leeds; teaches in Sheffield (University of Sheffield Hallam); lives in Oldham. *Inheritance* 2000 (226b).

Mickle, William Julius (1735–88), poet and translator: b. Langholm; lives, m., and is buried in Forest Hill. *The Lusiads* (trans.) 1775 (55a), 'Cumnor Hall' 1784 (49b, 55a, 289a), 'There's Nae Luck Aboot the Hoose' (The Sailor's Wife) (285b–c, 289a).

Middleton, Stanley (1919–), novelist: b. Bulwel, Nottingham; educ. Nottingham; teaches at High Pavement School, Nottingham.

Middleton, Thomas (1570–1627), poet and playwright: educ. Oxford (The Queen's College); enters Gray's Inn, London (Holborn) 1593; lives in London (Newington) 1609–27; buried in Newington. *The Wisdom of Soloman Paraphrased* 1597, *Micro-Cynicon* 1599, *The Ghost of Lucrece* 1600 (76a), *A Chaste Maid in Cheapside* 1612 (109c, 138a), *Women Beware Women* 1657 (138a).

Miller, Lady Anna (1741–81), verse writer and literary hostess: lives in Batheaston 1766–81; buried in Bath.

Miller, Hugh (1802–56), geologist and writer: b. Cromarty. *The Old Red Sandstone* 1841 (271c).

Milman, Henry Hart (1791–1868), poet and historian: educ. and a Fellow at Oxford (Brasenose College); Professor of Poetry at Oxford 1821; Dean of St Paul's Cathedral, London (City) 1849–68 and commemorated there. 'Apollo Belvedere' 1812, *Fazio* 1815, *Samor, the Lord of the Bright City* 1818 (70a), *Annals of St Paul's Cathedral* 1868 (113a–b).

Milne, Alan Alexander (1882–1956), playwright and children's author: educ. London (Westminster School) and Cambridge (Trinity College); lives in London (Chelsea: Mallord St.) 1920s–1940; country home at Hartfield 1925–56. *Mr. Pim Passes By* 1919, *The Truth About Blayds* 1921, *The Dover Road* 1922, *When We Were Very Young* 1924 (106c), *Winnie-the-Pooh* 1926 (57b, 106c), *Now We Are Six* 1927 (57b, 106c), *The House at Pooh Corner* 1938 (57b, 106c).

Milnes, Richard Monckton, 1st Baron Houghton (1809–85), first biographer of Keats: educ. Cambridge (Trinity College); lives in London (St James's: Pall Mall) from 1837. *Tribute* 1836, *Life and Letters of Keats* 1848 (141b).

Q

R

Radcliffe, Mrs Ann (née **Ward**) (1764–1823), novelist: lives in London (Victoria: Bressenden Pl.) 1815–23; buried in London (Bayswater: Hyde Park Pl.). *Mysteries of Udolpho* 1794, reprinted 1970 (156a).

Raine, Allen. *See* Evans, Anne Adaliza.

Raine, Kathleen (1908–2003), poet, scholar, and memoirist: b. London (Ilford); childhood in Bavington, Northumberland; educ. Ilford and Cambridge (Girton College); later Fellow; lives in London (Chelsea) 1940s, where meets Gavin Maxwell; meets writers in Hampstead; lives in Sandaig 1950s. 'The Marriage of Psyche' (294b–c), *The Lion's Mouth* 1977 (240a, 294c).

Ralegh, Sir Walter (1552?–1618), historian and poet: b. East Budleigh; educ. Oxford (Oriel College) and Middle Temple, London (City: Temple); frequents Gray's Inn, London (Holborn); in army in Ireland and entertained at Castlegregory 1580; reputed to have been in action at Smerwick 1580; holds court at Padstow 1585; lives at Youghal 1588–9; imprisoned in London (City: Tower) 1592; leases castle at Sherborne 1592, owns it 1599 and builds new one; establishes club at Mermaid tavern, London (City: Bread St.) *c.* 1603; tried for treason and condemned to death at Winchester 1603; imprisoned in London (City: Tower) 1603–16; beheaded and buried in London (Westminster: nr St Margaret's) 1618; his Bible kept in London (Westminster Abbey Gatehouse). *History of the World* 1614, 1634 (37c, 115a, 301a), Poem to Queen Elizabeth (313b), Will 1597 (32c), Speech from the scaffold (92c).

Ramal, Walter. *See* de la Mare, Walter.

Ramée, Marie Louise de la (**'Ouida'**) (1839–1908), novelist: b. Bury St Edmunds; lives in London (Hammersmith: Ravenscourt Sq.) 1857–66, (Marylebone: Welbeck St. and Langham Pl.) 1867–70. *Granville de Vigne* 1863, *Strathmore* 1865, *Under Two Flags* 1867 (120c, 135c, 164b).

Ramsay, Allan (1686–1758), poet: b. Leadhills; educ. Crawford; m. in Leadhills; wigmaker's apprentice in Edinburgh 1701; becomes bookseller 1718 and publisher 1720 in Edinburgh; buried in London (Marylebone: Marylebone High St.); memorials in Edinburgh and Penicuik. *Tea Table Miscellany* 1724–32, *The Gentle Shepherd* 1725 (273b, 290a).

Randolph, Thomas (1605–35), writer of English and Latin verse: educ. London (Westminster School) and Cambridge (Trinity College); Fellow at Cambridge (Trinity College) 1629–32; frequents The Devil tavern, London (City: Fleet St.); buried in Blatherwycke. *Aristippus, or, The Jovial Philosopher* 1630 (170a), 'An Ode to Anthony Stafford to Hasten him into the Country' (188c–189a).

Rankin, Ian (1960–), novelist: educ. and lives in Edinburgh. *Knots and Crosses* 1987 (279b).

Ransome, Arthur (1884–1967), writer of stories for children: educ. at Rugby; spends holiday at Coniston; lives nr Cartmel Fell 1925–35; lives in Lowick 1947–9; spends last years at Haverthwaite. *Swallows and Amazons* 1930, *Swallowdale* 1931, *Peter Duck* 1932 (214b).

Raphael, Frederick (1931–), novelist and screenwriter: educ. Cambridge (St John's College). *The Glittering Prizes* 1976 (169c).

Raspe, Rudolph Erich (1737–94), mineralogist and compiler of Baron Munchausen's stories: buried in Muckross. *Baron Munchausen's Narrative of his Marvellous Travels and Campaigns in Russia* 1785 (321c–322a).

Rattigan, Terence (1911–77), playwright: b. London (Kensington); educ. Cobham (Surrey), London (Harrow), and Oxford (Trinity College); lives in Brighton; ashes buried in London (Kensal Green). *First Episode* 1934 (78b), *French Without Tears* 1936 (78b), *The Winslow Boy* 1946 (130b), *The Browning Version* 1948 (130b).

Raven, Simon (1927–2001), novelist and memoirist: b. London (Mayfair); educ. Camberley, Burnham-on-Sea, Godalming, and Cambridge (King's College), where recruited for *The Listener*; joins the army in Shrewsbury 1953; lives in Deal 1961–95; last years in London (City: Charterhouse). *Boys Will Be Boys* 1963 (56a), *Alms for Oblivion* 1964–83 (49c, 56a, 207a), *Shadows on the Grass* 1982 (56a).

Raverat, Gwen (née **Gwendolen Mary Darwin**) (1885–1957), writer and wood engraver: b. Cambridge (see Darwin College); spends holidays at Downe until 1896. *Period Piece* 1952 (50c–51a, 165c).

Read, Sir Herbert (1893–1968), poet and critic: b. Muscoates; lives in Stonegrave. *The Green Child* 1935, *In Defence of Shelley* 1935, *Poetry and Anarchism* 1938 (238a), *Annals of Innocence and Experience* 1940 (236b, 238b).

Reade, Charles (1814–84), novelist and playwright: b. Ipsden; educ. Oxford (Magdalen College); enters Lincoln's Inn, London (Holborn) 1835; Fellow at Oxford (Magdalen College) 1838; spends holidays in Crieff 1838–48; lives in London (Mayfair: Bolton Row) 1856–68, (Hyde Park: Albert Ter.) 1869–79, (Hammersmith: Uxbridge Rd) 1882–4; memorial in London (City: St Paul's Cathedral). *Peg Woffington* 1852 (73a), *Christie Johnson* 1853 (271b), *It Is Never Too Late to Mend* 1856 (136a–b), *The Cloister and the Hearth* 1861 (73a, 136b, 169a), *Hard Cash* 1863 (127a, 136b), *Griffith Gaunt* 1866 (126c, 136b), *A Terrible Temptation* 1871 (127a).

Redgrove, Peter (1923–2003), poet: b. London (Kingston); educ. Taunton and Cambridge (Queens' College); teaches in Leeds (University) 1962–5; m. Penelope Shuttle; teaches in Falmouth (School of Art) 1966–83; lives in Falmouth; ashes scattered at Maenporth beach. 'The Idea of Entropy at Maenporth Beach' (20c), 'Elderhouse' (20c).

Rees, Goronwy (1909–70), essayist and novelist: b. Aberystwyth. *A Bundle of Sensations* 1960, *A Chapter of Accidents* 1972 (245a).

Reeve, Clara (1729–1807), novelist: b. Ipswich. *The Champion of Virtue, a Gothic Story* 1777, later called *The Old English Baron*, reprinted 1967.

Reid, Forrest (1875–1947), novelist: b. Belfast; educ. Belfast and Cambridge (Christ's College). *Uncle Stephen* 1931, and *Young Tom* 1944.

Reynolds, John Hamilton (1796–1852), poet and friend of Keats: b. Shrewsbury; educ. Shrewsbury and London (City: St Paul's School); lives in London (Soho: Golden Sq.) 1832, (Soho: Great Marlborough St.) 1836–8; appointed clerk to County Court in Newport (Isle of Wight) 1846; d. and is buried in Newport.

Rhys, Ernest (1859–1946), poet and novelist: spends holidays in Carmarthen; lives in London (Hampstead: Vale of Health) 1880s, (Chelsea: Cheyne Walk) 1886; meets Yeats in London (Woburn Pl.); founds Rhymers' Club with Yeats at Ye Olde Cheshire Cheese, Wine Office Ct (City: Fleet St.) 1891; visits Steep *c.* 1913–16. *Wales England Wed* 1940 (247c).

Rhys, Jean (1890–1979), novelist: attends school in Cambridge; lives in London (Bromley and Beckenham) 1945–60; spends time in Holloway prison (London: Holloway); spends last 20 years of her life nr Crediton (at Cheriton Fitzpaine); d. Exeter. 'Overture and Beginners Please' (164c), *After Leaving Mr Mackenzie* 1930 (103b), *Voyage in the Dark* 1934 (105a), 'Before the Deluge' (105a), 'Let Them Call It Jazz' (126b), *Smile Please* 1979 (20b).

Rhys, Keidrych (1915–87), poet and editor: publishes *Wales* in Carmarthen 1940s.

Richardson, Dorothy Miller (1873–1957), novelist: b. Abingdon; lives in London (Bloomsbury: Endsleigh St.) 1896–1906, (Bloomsbury: Woburn Pl.) 1906, (Bloomsbury: Endsleigh St.) 1907–11, St Ives (Cornwall) 1912, Trevone and London (St John's Wood: Queen's Ter.) 1916–38. *Pointed Roofs* 1915 (30c), *Pilgrimage* 1915–38 (36a, 142b), *Honeycomb* 1917 (142b).

Richardson, Henry Handel. *See* Robertson, Mrs John G.

Richardson, Samuel (1689–1761), novelist: baptized in Mackworth; educ. London (City: Christ's Hospital, Newgate St.); has printing works in London (City: Fleet St.); lives in London (Fulham: North End Cres.) 1739–54; visits Bath 1740s; lives in London (Fulham: Parson's Green) 1754–61; buried in St Bride's, London (City: Fleet St.). *Pamela, or, Virtue Rewarded* 1740, *Clarissa* 1747–8 (156b), *Sir Charles Grandison* 1753–4 (119c, 189b).

Rickman, Thomas (**'Clio'**) (1761–1834), poet, satirist, and bookseller: b. Lewes; becomes friend of Tom Paine in Lewes. *Black Dwarf* (contributions) (60c).

Ridley, Nicholas (1500?–55), theologian and bishop: Fellow at Cambridge (Pembroke College) *c.* 1524; stands trial in Oxford (St Mary the Virgin) 1554; burnt at the stake in Oxford (Martyrs' Memorial) 1555.

Rimbaud, Arthur (1854–91), French poet: lives in London (Soho: Howland St.) 1872–3, (Lambeth: Stamford St.) 1874. *Jeunesse* (132c).

Roberts, Kate (1891–1985), novelist, short-story writer, and literary journalist: b. and brought up at Rhosgadfan; educ. Bangor; settles in Denbigh. *A Summer Day and Other Stories* 1946, *Stryd y Glep* 1949, *Y Byw sy'n Cysgu* 1956, *Te yn y Grug* 1959, *Y Lôn Wen* 1960, *Tywyll Heno* 1962, *Hyn o Fyd* 1964, *Tegwch y Bore* 1967 (249a–b).

Roberts, Samuel (1800–85), radical writer: b. Llanbrynmair.

Robertson, Mrs John G. (née **Ethel Florence Lindesay Richardson**, **'Henry Handel Richardson'**) (1870–1946), Australian-born novelist: lives in London (Chalk Farm: Regent's Park Rd) 1910–34, Hastings 1930–46; takes holidays at Lyme Regis. *The Fortunes of Richard Mahony* 1930 (24c, 105b), *The Young Cosima* 1941 (58b).

Robinson, Esmé Stuart Lennox (1886–1958), playwright and editor: b. Douglas (Cork): educ. Bandon; manager of the Abbey Theatre, Dublin 1910; director 1923; lives in Dalkey 1920s. *The Oxford Book of Irish Verse* (co-ed.) 1958 (320a–b).

Robinson, Henry Crabb (1775–1867), diarist and letter writer: b. and grows up in Bury St Edmunds; articled to attorney in Colchester 1790; lives in London (Westminster: Little Smith St.) 1805–10, (Holborn: Hatton Garden) 1810; attends Coleridge's lectures (City: Crane Ct) 1813; visits Mme de Staël (Soho: Argyll St.) 1813–14; advocates foundation of University College London (Bloomsbury) 1826–8; visits Cambridge 1815, Douglas (Isle of Man) 1833, Ambleside, and Playford; lives in London (Bloomsbury: Russell Sq.) 1839–67; buried in London (Highgate cemetery). *Diary, Reminiscences and Correspondence* 3 vols 1869 (164a–b, 125b, 157a, 186a).

Robinson, Mary (née **Darby**, **'Perdita'**) (1758–1800), actress, novelist, and poet: b. and educ. Bristol. Poems in *Annual Anthology*, ed. Southey, 1799–1800 (12a).

Rochester, 2nd Earl of. *See* Wilmot, John.

Rodgers, William Robert (1909–69), poet: b. Belfast, visits Binsey.

Rogers, Jane (1952–), novelist: educ. Cambridge; teaches in London (Hackney) and Sheffield (University of Sheffield Hallam). *Mr Wroe's Virgins* 1991 (213b), *The Voyage Home* 2004 (225c).

Rogers, Samuel (1763–1855), poet: b. and brought up in London (Stoke Newington); lives and entertains in London (St James's: St James's Pl.) 1803–55; attends Coleridge's lectures (City: Crane Ct) 1813; visits Gore House (Kensington: Kensington Gore) and Holland House (Kensington); visits Tom Moore in Bromham; buried in London (Hornsey). *The Pleasures of Memory* 1792, *Recollections of the Table Talk of Samuel Rogers*, ed. A. Dyce, 1856, *Recollections* 1859 (141c).

Roget, Peter Mark (1779–1869), physician and scholar: works as doctor in Bristol (Hotwells) 1799; physician in Manchester Infirmary 1804 and first secretary of the Portico Library in Manchester; lives

Scott, Sir Walter (*cont'd*)
286a, 295c, 296c), 'A weary lot is thine, fair maid' and 'Brignal Banks' in *Rokeby* 1813 (232a), *The Lord of the Isles* 1815 (286c), 'Glenfinlas or Lord Ronald's Coronach' (284c), 'Glencoe' in Thomson's *Select Melodies* 1814 (284b), 'The Maid of Neidpath' (291b), *Waverley* 1814 (266a, 269b, 272a, 275b, 281a), *Guy Mannering* 1815 (216b, 241a, 272c), *The Antiquary* 1816 (269a, 295b), *The Black Dwarf* (270c), and *Old Mortality* 1816 (285b), first titles in the series *Tales of My Landlord* (136a, 289c), *Rob Roy* 1817 (267c, 270a, 296c), *The Heart of Midlothian* 1818 (140c, 193b, 280a), *A Legend of Montrose* 1819 (286a, 295c), *Ivanhoe* 1819 (188b, 231a, 239c), *The Abbot* 1820 (290b, 291a), *Kenilworth* 1821 (49b, 77c, 90a, 113a, 201c, 210c), *Peveril of the Peak* 1823 (115b, 210a, 227b), *St Ronan's Well* 1823 (286a), *Redgauntlet* 1824 (272a), *The Betrothed* 1825 (198c), *Woodstock* 1826 (50a, 93c), *St. Valentine's Day, or, The Fair Maid of Perth* 1828 (293a), *Anne of Geierstein* 1829 (169a), 'The Eve of St. John' (295a), contributions to the *Quarterly Review* (136a).
  • SEE ALSO FEATURE ENTRY (276–7).
Scott, William Bell (1811–90), poet and painter: annual guest at Old Dailly; paints murals at Wallington; lives in London (Chelsea: Cheyne Walk); d. and is buried in Old Dailly. 'The Old Scottish Home', 'Outside the Temple', 'Lost Love' (291c–292a), 'Bellevue House' (106b).
Sebald, W. G. (1944–2001), novelist and translator: lives in Manchester; teaches in Manchester (University of Manchester) 1966–70, in Norwich (University of East Anglia) 1970–2001; visits Michael Hamburger at Middleton. *The Emigrants* 1992 (176b, 226a), *The Rings of Saturn* 1998 (164a, 173b, 179a, 179c, 181c, 183b, 183c, 184c), *Vertigo* 1999 (111c–112a), *Austerlitz* 2001 (101b, 112a, 245a).
Sedley, Sir Charles (1639?–1701), poet, playwright, and wit: educ. Oxford (Wadham College) 1656; stays with Dryden in Charlton 1665–6; takes the waters with Charles Sackville and Nell Gwynne in Epsom 1668; frequents The Cock tavern in London (Covent Garden: Bow St.); spends last years in London (Hampstead: Haverstock Hill). *The Mulberry Garden* acted 1668, *Bellamira* acted 1687.
Seferis, Giorgios (1900–71), Greek poet: visits Isle of Eigg 1930s.
Selden, John (1584–1654), jurist and antiquary, author of *Table Talk* (1689): b. nr Worthing; educ. Chichester and Oxford (Hertford College); enters Clifford's Inn, London (City: Clifford's Inn) 1602; frequents the Mermaid tavern (City: Bread St.); lives at Wrest Park; buried in London (City: Temple Church); bequeaths books and manuscripts to the Bodleian (Oxford: Bodleian Library). *Marmora Arundelliana* 1624 (186c).
Self, Will (1961–), novelist: educ. Oxford (Exeter). *Great Apes* 1997 (72a), *The Book of Dave* 2006 (121a).
Seth, Vikram (1952–), novelist and poet: educ. Tonbridge and Oxford (Corpus Christi). *An Equal Music* 1999 (126c, 135a, 135c, 227c–228a).
Settle, Elkanah (1648–1724), playwright: educ. London (Westminster School) and Oxford (Trinity College); appointed City poet, London (City: Guildhall) 1691; writes sketches for Bartholomew Fair (Smithfield); lives 1718–24 and is buried in the Charterhouse (City: Charterhouse Sq.). *Cambyses, King of Persia* 1666 (78a), *The Siege of Troy* 1707 (144a).
Seward, Anna ('the Swan of Lichfield') (1747–1809), poet and letter writer: b. Eyam; lives in Lichfield 1754–1809; visits Bath, Cowslip Green 1791, Eartham 1792 and 1796; writes epitaphs on Lady Miller of Batheaston at Bath and on W. B. Stevens at Repton. *Louisa* 1782 (51a).
Sewell, Anna (1820–78), novelist: b. Great Yarmouth; spends childhood holidays in Buxton; lives in Norwich 1867–78; buried in Lamas; memorial in Norwich. *Black Beauty* 1877 (164b, 175b, 178a, 181a).

Sewell, Mrs Mary (1797–1884), poet: lives in Norwich 1867–84. *Homely Ballads* 1858, *Mother's Last Words* 1860, *Our Father's Care* 1861.
Shadwell, Thomas (1642?–92), playwright and Poet Laureate: educ. Cambridge (Gonville and Caius College) 1656; enters Middle Temple, London (City: Temple); buried in Chelsea Old Church (Chelsea: Cheyne Walk). *Epsom Wells* 1673 (52a).
Shakespeare, William (1564–1616), actor, poet, and playwright: b. Stratford-upon-Avon (see also Clifford Chambers); educ. and lives to *c.* 1585 in Stratford-upon-Avon; m. Anne Hathaway of Shottery (see also Worcester) 1582; poaches deer in Charlecote Park 1585; lives in London (City: Bishopsgate) from 1596; court performances in London (Greenwich and Whitehall); books sold and registered in London (City: St Paul's, Stationers' Ct); frequents Titchfield; visits Wilton 1603; company performs at Maidstone, Dunwich, and Barnstaple 1605–6 and at Leicester; frequents The Mitre tavern and The Mermaid in London (City: Fleet St. and Bread St.), acts at the Theatre and the Curtain (Shoreditch: Curtain Rd), at the Rose and the Globe (Southwark: Bankside), and at Blackfriars Playhouse Theatre (City: Blackfriars), possibly lives in Silver St. (City: Aldermanbury); censored by Master of the Revels (Clerkenwell); buys property in London (City: Blackfriars) 1613; acting colleagues buried in London (Shoreditch); spends last years, d., and is buried in Stratford-upon-Avon; credited with the epitaph to Thomas Stanley in Tong; commemorated by a flower garden in Manchester, in London (City: Aldermanbury, Southwark Cathedral, Westminster Abbey), by the Royal Shakespeare Memorial Theatre in Stratford-upon-Avon, and by the reconstructed Globe theatre (Shakespeare's Globe) in London (Southwark: Bankside). *1, 2,* and *3 Henry IV* 1590–2 (97c, 109b, 114c, 149c, 164a, 238c), *St Irvyne* 1810 (52c), 'The Necessity of Atheism' 1811 (78c), 'The Retrospect' 1812, *Queen Mab* 1813 (249c), *Alastor, or, The Spirit of Solitude* 1816 (42c), *The Revolt of Islam* 1818 (62b), 'Ode to the West Wind' (69c), 'Stanzas in a Summer Evening Churchyard' (24b).
Sir Thomas More 1591–3 (109c, 142c), *Venus and Adonis* printed 1593 (69c, 143b), *The Rape of Lucrece* printed 1594 (143b), *The Comedy of Errors* 1594, printed 1623 (125a), *Richard III* 1594, printed 1597 (109a, 110b, 111b, 113b, 115b, 124c, 147b, 147c, 191c, 193a, 257c), *Love's Labour's Lost* 1595, printed 1598, (89a), *A Midsummer Night's Dream* 1595/6, printed 1600 (147c), *Richard II* (7a, 237a, 238a, 250a), *1* and *2 Henry IV* 1597, printed 1598 (55a, 111c, 112b, 179b, 196b, 238a), *Henry V*, *The Passionate Pilgrim* 1599 (89a), *The Merry Wives of Windsor* 1599–1600, *As You Like It c.* 1600, printed 1623 (37b, 109c, 117c, 147c), *Hamlet c.* 1600 (147c), *Twelfth Night* 1600–1, printed 1623 (113c, 147c, 185a), *Hamlet* 1603 (147c), *Macbeth c.* 1606 (147c, 270b, 271a, 273a, 286b, 286c), *King Lear* 1608 (50b, 108c, 147c), *Sonnets* 1609, *A Lover's Complaint* 1609 (89a), *Cymbeline* 1609–10, printed 1623 (109a, 241a, 257c).
  • SEE ALSO FEATURE ENTRY (148–9).
Sharp, William ('Fiona Macleod') (1855–95), novelist and critic: b. Paisley; author of *The Mountain Lovers* (1895) and *The Sin Eater* (1895): educ. and works in Glasgow.
Sharpe, Tom (1928–), novelist: educ. Lancing and Cambridge (Pembroke); teaches and lives in Cambridge. *Porterhouse Blue* 1974 (168c), *Wilt* 1976 (169a).
Shaw, George Bernard (1856–1950), playwright and critic: b. and educ. Dublin; holidays in Dalkey 1866–74; lives in London (Bloomsbury: Fitzroy Sq.) 1887–98 and m. 1898, (Adelphi: Adelphi Ter.) 1899–1927, (Westminster: Whitehall Ct) 1928–45, Ayot St Lawrence 1906–50; visits Garinish Island 1923, Coole Park, Rinvyle, Limpsfield; frequents Old Wyldes in London (Hampstead Garden Suburb); his plays performed at the Royal Court Theatre in London (Chelsea: Sloane Sq.); commemorated in Dublin and Ayot St Lawrence. *Widowers' Houses* (with William Archer) 1892, *Mrs Warren's Profession* 1893, *Arms and the Man* 1894, *Candida* 1894 (101c, 107b), *The Devil's Disciple* 1900 (137b), *Man and Superman* 1903, *Major Barbara* 1905

(97a, 107b), *Pygmalion* 1916 (116c), *Saint Joan* 1924 (320c).
Sheehan, Patrick Augustine (1852–1913), novelist: b. Mallow; works in Exeter 1875–7; priest in Doneraile 1895–1913; commemorated in Mallow and Doneraile. *Luke Delmege, My New Curate* 1898, *Lisheen* 1907 (320a).
Sheers, Owen (1974–), poet and novelist. *Resistance* 2007 (251a).
Shelley, Mary Wollstonecraft (née **Godwin**) (1797–1851), novelist: exchanges vows of love with Shelley in London (St Pancras) 1814; lives in Bishopsgate 1815; accompanies Shelley and Peacock on the river to Lechlade; lives with Shelley in Bath 1816; after marriage with Shelley lives in Marlow 1817–18; last years in London (Belgravia: Chester Sq.); buried in Bournemouth. *Frankenstein, or, The Modern Prometheus* 1818 (8b, 62b, 284b).
Shelley, Percy Bysshe (1792–1822), poet: b. Warnham; educ. Eton and Oxford (University College); lodges in London (Soho: Poland St.) 1811; stays in the Elan Valley 1811 and 1812; m. Harriet Westbrook in Edinburgh 1811; stays in York 1811, Keswick 1811–12; lodges in Lynmouth 1812, Tremadoc 1812–13; rents house in Keswick 1813, Easthampstead 1814; regularizes Scottish marriage in London (Mayfair: St George's Church) 1814; exchanges vows of love with Mary Godwin in London (St Pancras) 1814; lives with Mary in Bishopsgate 1815; visits Leigh Hunt (Hampstead: Vale of Health); rows up river to Lechlade 1815; visits Peacock in Marlow 1816; lives with Mary in Bath 1816; after marriage with Mary lives in Marlow 1817–18; his heart buried in Bournemouth; commemorated in Christchurch (Dorset), Oxford (University College), and London (Westminster Abbey). *Original Poetry* (with his sister) 1810 (91c), *Zastrozzi* 1810, *St Irvyne* 1810 (52c), 'The Necessity of Atheism' 1811 (78c), 'The Retrospect' 1812, *Queen Mab* 1813 (249c), *Alastor, or, The Spirit of Solitude* 1816 (42c), *The Revolt of Islam* 1818 (62b), 'Ode to the West Wind' (69c), 'Stanzas in a Summer Evening Churchyard' (24b).
Shenstone, William (1714–63), poet and landscape gardener: b. and lives in Halesowen; educ. Oxford (Pembroke College); visits Henley, Hagley, London (Strand: The Strand); buried in Halesowen.
Sheridan, Richard Brinsley (1751–1816), playwright and MP: b. Dublin; spends youth in Virginia; educ. London (Harrow on the Hill) 1762–8; lives in Bath 1770–2; stays in Waltham Abbey 1772–3; m. and lives in London (Marylebone: Marylebone parish church and Orchard St.) 1773, (Harrow on the Hill) 1781; MP for Stafford 1780–1806; visits Bristol (Hotwells) 1787, 1792; lives in London (Mayfair: Hertford St.) 1795; manages Drury Lane (Covent Garden: Catherine St.); lives in Polesden Lacey 1796–1802, Leatherhead 1808, London (Mayfair: Savile Row) 1811–16; buried in London (Westminster Abbey). *The Rivals* 1775 (3b, 123b, 135a, 137c), *The Duenna* 1775 (135a), *The School for Scandal* 1777 (123b, 137c), *A Trip to Scarborough* 1777 (237b), *Speeches* 5 vols 1816 (137c).
Sherriff, Robert Cedric (1896–1975), playwright and novelist: educ. Oxford (New College); stays in Ringmore; lives in Esher 1929–75. *Journey's End* 1929 (30a, 74c), *Badger's Green* 1930, *The Fortnight in September* 1931, *Windfall* 1933, *Home at Seven* 1950, *King John's Treasure* 1954, *A Shred of Evidence* 1960, *The Wells of St Mary's* 1962, *No Leading Lady* 1968 (52b).
Sherwood, Mrs Mary Martha (née **Butt**) (1775–1851), novelist: b. Stanford-on-Teme; educ. Reading; lives at Bridgnorth 1795–1803; visits Bath 1801; lives in Lower Wick. *Susan Grey* 1802 (3b), *The History of the Fairchild Family* 1818–47 (3b, 81a, 203a), *Life, chiefly autobiographical*, ed. S. Kelly, 1854 (207c).
Shirley, James (1596–1666), playwright: educ. London (City: Merchant Taylors' School, Suffolk Lane), Oxford (St John's College), and Cambridge (St Catharine's College); teaches in St Albans

Cambridge (Trinity College); lives at Roos Hall and estate in Barsham. 'Why so pale and wan, fond lover?' (162a).

Surrey, Henry Howard, Earl of (1517?–47), poet: b. Kenninghall; condemned to death for treason in London (City: Guildhall) 1547; buried and commemorated in Framlingham. *Songs and Sonnets*, ed. R. Tottel, 1557 (110b, 174b), *Aeneid* (trans.) (174b).

Surtees, Robert (1779–1834), antiquary and topographer: b. Durham. *History of Durham* 1816–40 (241a).

Surtees, Robert Smith (1803–64), writer of humorous sporting novels and founder of the *New Sporting Magazine*: educ. Durham; lives at Hamsterley Hall; High Sheriff of Durham 1856; d. Brighton; buried nr Hamsterley Hall. *Hillingdon Hall* 1845 (241b).

Swain, Charles (1803–74), poet and engraver: b. Manchester; lives and is buried in Prestwich, nr Manchester. 'When the Heart Is Young', 'I cannot mind my wheel, mother', 'Dryburgh Abbey, a Poem on the Death of Sir Walter Scott' (223b).

Swift, Graham (1949–), novelist: educ. London (Dulwich) and Cambridge (Queens' College) 1967–70; childhood in London (Sydenham). *The Sweet Shop Owner* 1980 (154a), *Shuttlecock* 1981 (153b), *Waterland* 1983 (178c), *Last Orders* 1996 (46b, 47b, 62a–b, 81c, 100b).

Swift, Jonathan (1667–1745), satirist: b. Dublin; educ. Kilkenny and Dublin; secretary *c.* 1690–4 to Sir William Temple nr Farnham; incumbent of Kilroot 1695–6, of Laracor 1700–45; writes to 'Stella' from Parkgate and Chester 1710; visits Letcombe Bassett 1714; lodges in London (St James's: Bury St.) 1710, 1713, 1726, (Soho: Leicester Sq.) 1711; patronizes the Thatched House Tavern (St James's: St James's St.), and The Fountain tavern (Strand: The Strand); spends summers in Virginia; Dean of St Patrick's, Dublin 1713–45; visits Pope in London (Twickenham); visits Celbridge, Unionhall, and Castletownshend 1723, Cirencester 1726, Bibury, and Markethill; d. and is buried in Dublin; commemorated in Dublin, Celbridge, and Markethill. *The Battle of the Books* 1704 (53c, 170b), *A Tale of a Tub* 1704 (53c, 141a, 300a), 'Cadenus and Vanessa' 1713 (305b), *The Drapier's Letters* 1724 (313b), *Gulliver's Travels* 1726 (301c, 307a, 313b), *Verses on the Death of Dr. Swift* 1731 (307b), *A Complete Collection of Polite and Ingenious Conversation* 1738 (307a–b), *Carberiae Rupes* (317c, 322c), *Journal to Stella*, ed. Harold Williams, 2 vols 1948 (53c, 214c, 227a, 316a), *The Correspondence of Swift*, ed. Harold Williams, 5 vols 1963–5 (307a–b).

Swinburne, Algernon Charles (1837–1909), poet: b. London (Belgravia: Chester St.); spends youth in Bonchurch and at Capheaton Hall; visits Wordsworth in Rydal 1848; frequents Wallington; educ. Eton and Oxford (Balliol College); is tutored in Navestock 1859; visits Meredith in Esher 1859; lives in London (Belgravia: Grosvenor Pl.) 1860–1, with Rossetti (Chelsea: Cheyne Walk) 1862–4; visits Tintagel 1864; stays with parents in Shiplake 1865–79; lives in London (Belgravia: Wilton Cres.) 1865, (Marylebone: Dorset St.) 1865–70; is visited by Mallarmé and lives in London 1872–5 and 1877–8 (Bloomsbury: Great James St.), visits Dunwich; visits Sark 1876; visits St Peter Port 1876, 1882; lives in London (Putney) 1879–1909; buried in Bonchurch. *The Queen Mother and Rosamond. Two Plays* 1860 (69a, 100a, 180a), 'Queen Yseult' (69a), *Atalanta in Calydon* 1865 (34c, 100a), *Chastelard* 1865 (100a), 'Laus Veneris' (52b, 134a), 'Dolores', 'A Litany' in *Poems and Ballads* 1866, *A Song of Italy* 1867 (134a), 'By the North Sea' in *Studies in Song* 1880 (173a), *Tristram of Lyonesse* 1882, 'On the Cliffs' (84c), *Letters*, ed. C. Y. Lang, 6 vols 1959–62 (43a).

Symonds, John Addington (1840–93), poet, translator, essayist, and critic: b. Bristol (Clifton);

educ. London (Harrow on the Hill) and Oxford (Balliol College) 1862; m. 1864 and lives in Hastings; lives in Bristol 1868–80; visits Sutton Court. 'Clifton and a Lad's Love' in *In the Key of Blue* 1893 (11a, 34a), *Letters* 1907 (11a).

Symonds, William Samuel (1818–87), novelist: rector of Pendock. *Malvern Chase* 1881, *Hanley Castle* 1883 (205a).

Synge, John Millington (1871–1909), playwright: b., educ., lives, and d. in Dublin; visits Ashford (Wicklow) 1872, 1889, Aran Islands 1898–1902; buried in Dublin (Mount Jerome cemetery). *In the Shadow of the Glen* 1903 (309b–c, 315b), *Riders to the Sea* 1904 (301b, 309c), *The Well of the Saints* 1905 (309c), *The Playboy of the Western World* 1907 (309c).

T

Tagore, Sir Rabindranath (1861–1941), Indian poet and playwright: lives in London (Hampstead: Vale of Health) 1912. *Gitanjali* 1912 (123a).

Taliesin (*fl.* 550), reputed Welsh bard: buried, according to tradition, at Tre-Taliesin. *Book of Taliesin* 14th c. (244b, 264b).

Tannahill, Robert (1774–1810), poet and songwriter: b. and lives in Paisley; frequents Gleniffer Braes; d. and buried in Paisley; commemorated in Paisley. *Poems and Songs* 1807 (292b), 'Keen blows the wind on the braes o' Gleniffer' (284c).

Tate, Nahum (1652–1715), playwright and Poet Laureate: educ. Dublin (Trinity College); buried in London (Southwark: Borough High St., Church of St George the Martyr).

Taylor, Ann. *See* Gilbert, Mrs Joseph.

Taylor, Sir Henry (1800–86), dramatic poet: lives in London (Marylebone: Blandford Sq.); visits Lady Ashburton nr New Alresford; buried at Bournemouth. *Philip van Artevelde* 1834 (64a, 133c).

Taylor, Isaac (1759–1829), dissenting minister and engraver: lives in Lavenham, Colchester 1796–1811, Ongar 1811–29. *Specimens of Gothic Ornaments Selected from the Parish Church of Lavenham* 1796 (178a).

Taylor, Jane (1783–1824), author of rhymes and stories for children: spends childhood in Lavenham until 1796; lives in Colchester 1796–1811, Ongar 1811–24; buried in Ongar. *Original Poems for Infant Minds* 1804, 'Twinkle, twinkle, little star' in *Rhymes for the Nursery* 1806, and *Hymns* 1810 (all with her sister Ann) (172c), *Display, a Tale for Young People* 1815 (181c).

Taylor, Jeremy (1613–67), devotional writer and bishop: b. Cambridge; educ. Cambridge (Gonville and Caius); Fellow at Cambridge (Gonville and Caius) 1633; Fellow at Oxford (All Souls) 1635 and preaches at the University Church; rector of Uppingham 1638–42; graduates DD at Oxford (Brasenose College) 1642; retires after imprisonment following Royalist defeat in Cardigan to Golden Grove 1645–58; preaches in Ballinderry while staying nearby 1658–9; as Bishop of Down and Connor receives additional *See* of Dromore 1661 and rebuilds Cathedral; lives in Lisburn 1661–7; buried in Dromore; memorials in Ballinderry and Lisburn. *Holy Living* and *Holy Dying* 1650–1, *The Golden Grove* 1655 (250b), *Ductor Dubitantium* 1659 (298a).

Taylor, John ('the water-poet') (1580–1653), poet and traveller: b. and educ. Gloucester; lives in Oxford (Oriel College) 1625, 1645; visits Kingston upon Hull.

Taylor, William (1765–1836), man of letters and translator of German authors: educ. Palgrave; lives in Norwich. *Historic Survey of German Poetry* 1828–30, poems in *Annual Anthology*, ed. Southey, 1799–1800 (180c).

Tennant, Emma (1937–), novelist: childhood in Innerleithen; educ. London (Hammersmith) 1950s. *Wild Nights* 1979 (286a), *Queen of Stones* 1982

(24c), *Strangers and Sisters* 1990 (38c), *Strangers* 1998 (286a).

Tennant, William (1784–1848), poet and scholar: b. Anstruther; educ. St Andrews; teaches in Anstruther; educ. St Andrews; teaches in Anstruther; Professor of Oriental Languages in St Andrews 1838–48; buried in Anstruther. *Anster Fair* 1812 (268c).

Tennyson, Alfred, 1st Baron Tennyson (1809–92), Poet Laureate: b. Somersby; educ. Louth, Somersby, and Cambridge (Trinity College); visits Harrington Hall 1834; visits Mirehouse (Keswick) and meets Edward Fitzgerald; lives in High Beech 1837–40; visits Torquay 1838; frequently stays in Shawell; visits Tealby, Curragh Chase 1848, Killarney 1848, New Alresford; m. in Shiplake 1850; visits Coniston and Clevedon on honeymoon 1850; lives in London (Twickenham: Montpelier Row) 1851–3, Farringford from 1853 for many years; visits Swainston Hall, Caerleon, Shottermill, Woodbridge; builds Aldworth in Haslemere 1868, his home for the rest of his life; stays with Froude in Salcombe 1889; d. Haslemere; buried in London (Westminster Abbey); memorials in Haslemere, Lincoln, Somersby, and nr Farringford. 'The Devil and the Lady', *Poems by Two Brothers* (with his brother Charles) 1827 (195a), 'Timbuctoo' 1829 (170c), *Poems Chiefly Lyrical* 1830, 'The Lotos-Eaters', 'Œnone', and 'Two Voices', in *Poems* 1833 (195a), 'The Lord of Burleigh' 1833 (189b), 'Love and Duty' *c.* 1840 (176a), 'Break, break, break' (15a), *In Memoriam* 1850 (14a, 15a, 84b–c, 170c), 'Ode on the Death of the Duke of Wellington' 1852 (155b), 'The splendour falls on castle walls' in *The Princess*, 3rd edn 1853 (62a, 320c–321a), *The Charge of the Light Brigade* 1854 (54a), *Maud* 1855 (54a, 87c, 141b, 176a, 191b), *The Idylls of the King* 1859, 1869 (19a, 22a, 34c, 54a, 246b, 264b–c), *Enoch Arden* 1864 (54a), *Becket* 1884 (46a, 93b–c), *Locksley Hall Sixty Years After* 1886 (54a), 'Roses on the Terrace' in *Demeter and Other Poems* 1889 (191b), 'Swainston' (87c), 'Verses at Clandeboye' (299b), 'The Miller's Daughter' (174b), 'Crossing the Bar' (31b).

Thackeray, William Makepeace (1811–63), novelist: educ. London (Chiswick and City: Charterhouse) and Cambridge (Trinity College); stays in Tunbridge Wells 1825; enters Middle Temple, London (City: Temple) 1831; visits Dickens at Furnival's Inn in London (Holborn: Holborn) 1836; lives in London (Bloomsbury: Coram St.) 1837—early 1840s, (St James's: St James's St.) 1840s; visits Dublin, Cork, and Westport 1842, Clevedon; lives in London (Kensington: Young St.) 1846–53, (Kensington: Onslow Sq.) 1853–60; visits Brighton 1851, Bath 1857, Tunbridge Wells 1860; lives in London (Kensington: Palace Green) 1861–3; buried in Kensal Green cemetery (Kensal Green); bust in Westminster Abbey. *The Yellowplush Papers* 1837 (136a), *The Irish Sketch Book* 1843 (304b, 309a), *Jeames's Diary* 1845 and *The Snobs of England* 1847 in *Punch* (110a–b), *Vanity Fair* 1848 (15a, 44a, 101c, 103a, 108b, 116c, 131c, 136a, 156a), *The Luck of Barry Lyndon* 1844 (142b), *The History of Pendennis* 1848–50 (20b, 27c, 33a, 131c), *The History of Henry Esmond* 1852 (15a, 116b–c, 131c, 146a–b, 170b), *The Newcomes* 1853–5 (56a, 109b, 116c, 131c), *The Virginians* 1857–9 (131c, 144c), *The Adventures of Philip* 1861–2 (126a, 131c), *The Roundabout Papers* 1860–3 (89c, 131c), 'Tunbridge Toys' in *The Roundabout Papers* 1863 (89c), *Denis Duval* 1864–7 (83a).

Theroux, Paul (1941–), travel writer, novelist, short-story writer, and memoirist. *The Family Arsenal* 1976 (118a), *The Consul's File* 1977 (100a), *The London Embassy* 1982 (100a), *The Kingdom by the Sea* 1983 (44c).

Thom, William (1798?–1848), poet: b. Aberdeen; lives and works as a weaver in Inverurie 1840–4; d. and buried in Dundee. 'The Blind Boy's Pranks' in *Aberdeen Herald* 1841, *Rhymes and Recollections of a Handloom Weaver* 1844 (286c).

Thomas, Donald Michael (1935–), poet, novelist, and translator: educ. Redruth and Oxford (New College) 1955–8. 'The Logan Rock' (35c), 'Botallack' (8a), *Birthstone* 1983 (25a).

Thomas, Dylan Marlais (1914–53), poet: b. and educ. Swansea; lives in Swansea until 1936; spends holidays nr Llangain; visits London (Hampstead: Parliament Hill) 1930s; stays in Laugharne 1938, 1939, 1940; visits Oxford 1945–6, Binsey; settles in Laugharne 1949–53; buried in Laugharne; commemorated in Swansea and London (Westminster Abbey); book published by Gregynog Press at Tregynon. 'After the Funeral', 'Fern Hill' (254c), *Eighteen Poems* 1934 (261c), *Twenty-Five Poems* 1936 (21c), *Portrait of the Artist as a Young Dog* 1940 (251c, 261b–c), *Deaths and Entrances* 1946 (68b), *Under Milk Wood* 1954 (251c, 261c), *Adventures in the Skin Trade* 1955 (122c), *A Child's Christmas in Wales* 1968 (261b–c).
• SEE ALSO FEATURE ENTRY (252–3).

Thomas, Ernest Lewis ('**Richard Vaughan**') (1904–83), novelist: b. nr Llanddeusant. *Moulded in Earth* 1951, *Who Rideth So Wild* 1952, *Son of Justin* 1955 (253b).

Thomas, Gwyn (1913–81), novelist: b. and brought up at Porth. *The Dark Philosophers* 1946, *The Alone to the Alone* 1947, *The World Cannot Hear You* 1950, *A Frost on My Frolic* 1953, *A Point of Order* 1956 (259c).

Thomas, Philip Edward (1878–1917), poet, critic, and topographical writer: educ. London (City: St Paul's School) and Oxford (Lincoln College); visits Limpsfield; lodges in London (Battersea: Shelgate Rd) 1900; lives in Bearsted 1901–4, Sevenoaks Weald 1904–6, in and nr Steep 1906–16; stays nr Dunwich 1907, in Dymock 1914; stationed in the army at High Beech 1915–16; memorials at Steep and Eastbury. *Horae Solitariae* 1902 (41c), *Oxford* 1903 (72b), *Rose Acre Papers* 1904 (41c), *Richard Jefferies* 1909 (173b), *The Happy-Go-Lucky Morgans* 1913 (97c), 'Adlestrop' (2a), 'Wind and Mist' (86c–87a).

Thomas, Ronald Stuart (1913–2000), poet and memoirist: b. Cardiff (Llandaff); moves to Holyhead 1918; educ. Bangor 1932–5; ordained curate at Chirk 1936, at Hanmer 1940–2; rector at Manafon 1942–54; vicar in Eglwys-fach 1954–67; appointed vicar of Aberdaron 1967; retires to Porth Neigwl and Porthmadog; buried in Porthmadog. *The Stones of the Field* 1946 (257a), *An Acre of Land* 1952 (257a), *The Minister* 1953 (257a), *Neb* (No One) 1985 (245c, 247b, 249b, 251a), *Blwyddyn yn Llyn* (A Year in Lyn) 1990 (244a), 'The Welsh Hill Country' (257a), ' The Moon in Lleyn' (244a).

Thomas, Thomas Jacob (**Sarnicol**) (1873–1945), poet: b. nr Talgarreg.

Thomas, William (**Islwyn**) (1832–78), Calvinist Methodist minister and poet: b. nr Ynys-ddu; lives in Cwmfelinfach 1864–78; buried in Cwmfelinfach. 'Y Storm' (249a).

Thompson, Flora (née **Flora Jane Timms**) (1876–1947), novelist: b. Juniper Hill; educ. Cotisford; works in Fringford post office 1890–6; lives in Grayshott 1896–1900, Dartmouth 1928–40, Brixham 1940–7. *Lark Rise* 1939 (16b), *Over to Candleford* 1941 (16b), *Candleford Green* 1943 (12b, 55a): these three books published together as *Lark Rise to Candleford* 1945 (49a, 59c), *Still Glides the Stream* 1948 (12b), *Heatherley* in *A Country Calendar and Other Writings*, ed. M. Lane, 1979 (56b).

Thompson, Francis (1859–1907), poet: b. and spends early years in Preston; studies medicine in Manchester 1877–83; stays in Storrington, Pantasaph 1893–7, visits Southwater 1907; buried in London (Kensal Green cemetery). 'The Hound of Heaven' in *Poems* 1893 (87b, 227c), *New Poems* 1897 (259a).

Thomson, James (1700–84), poet: b. Ednam; educ. Jedburgh and Edinburgh (University); lives in London (Richmond: Kew Foot Lane) 1736–48; visits Marlborough, Hagley 1743; buried in London (Richmond: Richmond parish church);

commemorated nr Ednam and in London (Westminster Abbey). *Summer* 1727 (140a), *Spring* 1728 (25b, 200b), *The Seasons* 1730, revised 1744 (25b, 132a, 140a, 158a, 200b), *The Castle of Indolence* 1748.

Thomson, James (1834–82), poet: teaches in Ballincollig from 1851. 'The City of Dreadful Night' in *The National Reformer* 1874 (317a–b).

Thorpe, Adam (1956–), novelist. *Ulverton* 1992 (64a).

Thrale, Mrs Hester Lynch (née **Salusbury**, *later* **Mrs Piozzi**) (1741–1821), friend of Dr Johnson, diarist, and letter writer: spends childhood in Tremeirchion; m. Henry Thrale at St Anne's, London (Soho: Wardour St.) 1763; lives in London (Southwark: Park St.) 1763–82, (Streatham) 1763–95; visits, with Dr Johnson, Brighton 1770s, Beaconsfield, Hagley, Holywell, Tremeirchion, and Ilam 1774; visits, with Fanny Burney, Devizes 1780, Bath, and Tunbridge Wells; lives 1783–4 and m. Gabriel Piozzi in Bath; settles in Tremeirchion 1795; lives in Bath 1814–20, Penzance 1820–1; last months at Bristol (Clifton); buried in Tremeirchion; commemorated in London on Dr Johnson's monument at St Clement Danes (Strand: The Strand), and Clink St. (Southwark: Park St.). *Anecdotes of the Late Samuel Johnson* 1786, *Letters of Samuel Johnson, with Mrs. Thrale's genuine letters to him* 1788, ed. R. W. Chapman, 3 vols 1952 (150b), *Thraliana: The Diary of Mrs. Thrale, 1776–1809*, ed. K. C. Balderstone, 2 vols 1942, 1951 (150b).

Thynne, William (d. 1546), editor of Chaucer's works: lives in London (Erith); d. at Minsterley; buried in All Hallows Barking (City: Tower of London); commemorated in Westminster Abbey.

Tickell, Thomas (1686–1740), poet: b. Bridekirk; educ. Oxford (The Queen's College); obtains post under Addison in Dublin 1710; elected Professor of Poetry, Oxford (The Queen's College) 1711; settles, *c.* 1723, and is buried in Dublin. 'Oxford' 1707, *On the Prospect of Peace* 1712 (221b), 'On the Death of Mr. Addison' in Addison's *Works* (ed.) 4 vols 1721 (76b).

Tindall, Gillian (1938–), novelist and historian: educ. Oxford. *The Fields Beneath* 1977 (132a), *The Man Who Drew London* 2002 (129b), *The House by the Thames* 2006 (149a).

Tobin, John (1770–1804), playwright, author of *The Curfew* (1807) and *The School for Authors* (1808): buried in Cobh. *The Honey Moon* 1805 (318c).

Tóibín, Colm (1955–), novelist: b. Enniscorthy; educ. Dublin. *The South* 1990 (314b, 314c), *The Heather Blazing* 1992 (314b, 314c), *Bad Blood* 1994 (300b), *The Blackwater Lightship* 1999 (305a, 314c), *The Master* 2004 (141a–b).

Tolkien, John Ronald Reuel (1892–1973), scholar and novelist: educ. Birmingham and Oxford (Exeter College); lives in Birmingham 1896–1910; Fellow and Professor of Anglo-Saxon at Oxford (Pembroke College) 1926–45, Felllow and Professor of English Language and Literature (Merton College) 1945–59. *The Hobbit* 1937 (76a, 197a), *Beowulf: The Monsters and the Critics* 1936 (76a), *The Lord of the Rings* 1955 (74a).

Tolstoy, Count Leo (1828–1910), Russian novelist, short-story writer, and critic: visits school in Chelsea; hears Dickens read in Piccadilly; visits House of Commons 1861.

Tomlinson, Charles (1927–), poet: b. Stoke on Trent; educ. Stoke (Longton) and Cambridge (Queens' College) 1940s; teaches in Bristol; lives in Wotton-under-Edge. 'The Boy on the Sick Bed' (208a), 'The Marl Pits' (208a), 'Gladstone Street' (208a), 'At Stoke' (208a).

Toplady, Augustus Montague (1740–78), author of *Psalms and Hymns for Private Worship* (1776): b. Farnham; educ. London (Westminster School); vicar of Broadhembury 1768–78; shelters from a storm in Burrington Combe. 'Rock of Ages, cleft for me' 1775 (12b, 12c, 54a).

Townsend, Sue (1946–), novelist: b. Leicester, educ. South Wigston; lives in Leicester. *The Secret Diary*

of Adrian Mole . . . 1992 (101b, 188b, 192a, 195b, 270a), *The Growing Pains of Adrian Mole* 1984 (192a), *The Queen and I* 1992 (115b, 156a).

Toynbee, Arnold Joseph (1889–1975), historian: educ. at Winchester; Fellow at Oxford (Balliol College) 1912–15, hon. Fellow from 1957. *A Study of History* 12 vols 1934–61, *Acquaintances* 1967 (69b).

Traherne, Thomas (1638?–74), poet: b. Hereford; educ. Oxford (Brasenose College); rector of Credenhill 1657–67; chaplain to Sir Orlando Bridgeman 1669–74 and rector 1672–4 in London (Teddington), d. and is buried in Teddington. *Poetical Works*, ed. B. Dobell, 1903 (154a, 199c), *Centuries of Meditations*, ed. B. Dobell, 1908, *Poems of Felicity*, ed. H. I. Bell, 1910 (199c).

Train, Joseph (1779–1852), antiquary, poet, and friend of Sir Walter Scott: lives, is buried, and commemorated in Castle Douglas.

Trelawny, Edward John (1792–1881), friend of Shelley: lives in London (Belgravia: Eaton Sq.) 1838. *Adventures of a Younger Son* 1831, *Records of Shelley, Byron, and the Author* 1858 (98c).

Tressell, Robert. See Noonan, Robert.

Trevelyan, George Macaulay (1876–1962), historian: b. Stratford-upon-Avon; educ. London (Harrow on the Hill); Master of Trinity College, Cambridge 1940–51. *English Social History* 1942, illustrated edn, 4 vols 1949–52 (170c–171a).

Trevor, William (1928–), novelist, short-story writer, and memoirist: b. Mitchelstown; educ. Dublin (Trinity College) late 1940s; visits Youghal as child; visits Cork as child. *The Old Boys* 1964 (154a), *The Boarding House* 1965 (154a), *The Love Department* 1967 (159c), *Mrs Eckdorf in O'Neill's Hotel* 1969 (313b), *Fools of Fortune* 1983 (319c, 320c, 321c), *Reading Turgenev* 1991 (320c), *Excursions in the Real World* 1993 (319c, 321c, 322c), *The Story of Lucy Gault* 2002 (321c, 322c).

Tripp, John (1927–86), poet: lives in Cardiff.

Trollope, Anthony (1815–82), novelist: b. London (Bloomsbury: Keppel St.); educ. Winchester and London (Harrow on the Hill); Post Office official in Banagher 1841, Clonmel 1844–5, Mallow 1845–51, Belfast 1853–4; visits Salisbury; lives in Dublin 1854–9, Waltham Cross 1859–70, London (Marylebone: Montagu Sq.) 1872–80, South Harting 1880–2; d. London (Marylebone: Welbeck St.); buried in London (Kensal Green cemetery). *The Macdermots of Ballycloran* 1847, *The Kellys and the O'Kellys* 1848 (304c–305a), *The Warden* 1855 (31b, 92c, 298b), *Orley Farm* 1862 (123c, 185a), *The Claverings* 1867, *The Last Chronicle of Barset* 1867 (185a), *The Eustace Diamonds* 1873 (135a), *John Caldigate* 1879 (164c), *Autobiography* 1883 (31b).

Tschiffely, Aimé Felix (1895–1950), travel writer: visits Cunninghame Graham in Ardoch 1936. *From Southern Cross to Pole Star* 1933, later edns called *Tschiffely's Ride, Don Roberto* 1937 (269b).

Tudur Aled (*fl.* 1480–1526), Welsh poet: b. Llansannan; believed to have died and been buried in Carmarthen; commemorated in Llansannan.

Turgenev, Ivan Sergeyevich (1818–83), Russian novelist: stays in Ventnor 1860; visits George Eliot in London (Regent's Park: Lodge Rd) 1878. *Fathers and Sons* 1862 (90c).

Turner, Thomas (1729–93), diarist: keeps a shop at East Hoathly. *The Diary of a Georgian Shopkeeper*, ed. G. H. Jennings, 1979 (51c).

Tusser, Thomas (1524?–80), poet: educ. Cambridge (Trinity Hall); farms in Cattawade; memorial in Manningtree nr Cattawade. *Hundreth Good Pointes of Husbandrie* 1557 (171c, 172a), *Stanzas* 1580 (171c).

Twain, Mark. See Clemens, Samuel Langhorne.

Twm o'r Nant. See Edwards, Thomas.

Tyndale, William (d. 1536), translator of the Bible into English: educ. at Oxford (Magdalen Hall); preacher in London (City: St Dunstan-in-the-West, Fleet St.) 1523–4; commemorated in London (Westminster Abbey) and North Nibley.

U

Udall (*or* **Uvedale**), **Nicholas** (1505–56), playwright and scholar: educ. Winchester and Oxford (Corpus Christi College); headmaster of Eton 1534–41, Westminster School, London (Westminster) 1554–6; rector of Braintree 1537–44. *Ralph Roister Doister* 1566 (52b, 163c).

Unsworth, Barry (1930–), novelist: educ. Manchester 1950s; writer in residence at the University of Liverpool 1984–5. *Sugar and Rum* 1988 (222c), *Sacred Hunger* 1992 (222c–223a), *Losing Nelson* (1999).

Upward, Edward (1903–), short-story writer, novelist, and political writer: ed. Repton (meets Christopher Isherwood) and Cambridge (Corpus Christi College); visits Scilly Isles 1926. 'The Railway Accident' 1928 (165c), *The Mortmere Stories* 1994 (165c).

Urquhart (*or* **Urchard**), **Sir Thomas** (1611–60), translator of Rabelais: b. Cromarty; educ. Aberdeen *c.* 1628; lives in Cromarty 1645–50, 1652–3. 'Ekskubalauron' in *Collections of Miscellaneous Treatises* 1774, 1834 (271b).

Ussher, James (1581–1656), scholar, archbishop, and historian: educ. Dublin (Trinity College); buried in London (Westminster Abbey); bequeaths his books and manuscripts to Trinity College Dublin. *Annales Veteris et Novi Testamenti* 1650–4.

V

Vachell, Horace Annesley (1861–1955), novelist and playwright: educ. London (Harrow on the Hill); lives in Widcombe 1927–52. *The Hill* 1905 (37a–b, 123c), *Quinney's* 1914, *Fellow Travellers* 1923, *Methuselah's Diary* 1950 (37b).

Vanbrugh, Sir John (1664–1726), playwright and architect: designs Blenheim Palace in Woodstock 1705; makes alterations at Audley End 1721; member of the Kit-Cat Club in London (Barnes: Barn Elms Park), (Hampstead: Heath Rd); buried in St Stephen Walbrook (City: Poultry). *The Relapse*, *The Provok'd Wife* 1697, *The Country House* 1705, *The Confederacy* 1705 (93c).

Vaughan, Henry ('**the Silurist**') (1621–95), poet and physician, author of the poem 'They are all gone into the world of light': b. Llansantffraed; educ. Oxford (Jesus College); practises medicine, d., and is buried in Llansantffraed. *Silex Scintillans* 1650, 1655 (255c–256a).

Vaughan, Hilda (1892–1985), novelist: b. Builth Wells. *The Battle to the Weak* 1925, *The Invader* 1928, *Her Father's House* 1930 (246a).

Vaughan, Richard. *See* Thomas, Ernest Lewis.

Vaughan-Thomas, Wynford (1908–87), author and broadcaster: commemorated at Dylife. *Trust to Talk* 1980 (249b).

Verlaine, Paul (1844–96), French poet: lodges with Rimbaud in London (Soho: Howland St.) 1872–3, (Lambeth: Stamford St.) 1874; teaches in Stickney 1875–6, Bournemouth 1876–7. *Romances sans paroles* 1874 (146c), *Sagesse* 1881 (8a, 195c), 'La Mer est plus belle', 'Bournemouth' in *Amour* 1888, *Amour, Bonheur* 1891, *Liturgies intimes* 1892 (8a).

Visiak, E. H. (1878–1972), poet, novelist, and Milton scholar: educ. Hitchin.

Voltaire (**François Marie Arouet**) (1694–1778), French playwright, essayist, novelist, and poet: visits Pope when in exile in London (Twickenham: Crossdeep) 1726–9. *Zaïre* 1732, *Essai sur les mœurs* 1756, *Candide* 1759.

W

Waddell, Helen (1889–1965), medieval scholar and novelist: Research Fellow at Oxford (Somerville College) 1920–2. *Peter Abelard* 1933 (78a).

Walker, Ted (1934–2004), poet and playwright: b. Lancing; educ. Steyning and Cambridge (St John's College); teaches in Chichester (High School) 1960s; lives in Hunston from early 1960s. *Fox on a Barn Door* 1965 (59a, 60b), *The High Path* 1983 (60b), 'On the Sea Wall', 'The Skate Fishers', 'Breakwaters' (60b).

Wallace, Edgar (1875–1932), novelist: b. in London (Greenwich); lives in London (Deptford); commemorated in London (Ludgate Circus). *Sanders of the River* (118a).

Waller, Edmund (1606–87), poet: b. Coleshill; educ. Cambridge (King's College) 1620–2; lives in Beaconsfield 1624–87; m. in London (Westminster: St Margaret's) 1631; courts 'Sacharissa' at Penshurst Place; buried in Beaconsfield. 'On My Lady Dorothy Sidney's Picture', 'At Penshurst', 'To the Servant of a Fair Lady' (79c).

Walmsley, Leo (1892–1966), novelist: lives in Robin Hood's Bay; frequents Whitby. *Three Fevers* 1932, *Foreigners* 1935, *Sally Lunn* 1937 (237b).

Walpole, Horace, 4th Earl of Orford (1717–97), poet, novelist, collector, and letter writer: b. and lives in London (St James's: Arlington St.) 1717–79; educ. Cambridge (King's College) 1735–9; lives at his country house, London (Twickenham) 1747–97, his town house (Mayfair: Berkeley Sq.) 1779–97; visits Ampthill, Hagley 1753, Bath and Batheaston 1766; Nuneham Courtenay, Rousham, Aston, London (Chelsea: Ranelagh Gardens), St George's Coffee House (Strand: The Strand), Schomberg House (St James's: Pall Mall); d. in London (Mayfair: Berkeley Sq.); buried nr Houghton Hall. *The Castle of Otranto, a Gothic Story* 1765, *The Mysterious Mother* (155b), *Letters*, ed. Mrs Paget Toynbee, 16 vols 1903–5, Yale edn of *Correspondence c.* 50 vols 1937– (3a, 6b, 161b).

Walpole, Sir Hugh (1884–1941), novelist: educ. Canterbury, Durham, and Cambridge (Emmanuel College) 1902–5; teaches at Epsom 1908; stays in St Ives (Cornwall) 1912 and Esthwaite Lodge; holiday cottage at Polperro 1912–21; spends last years and d. in Borrowdale; buried and commemorated in Keswick. *The Green Mirror* 1916 (29a), *The Cathedral* 1922, *The Old Ladies* 1924, *Harmer John* 1926 (36b), *The Herries Chronicle: Rogue Herries* 1930 (213c), *Judith Paris* 1931 (213c, 216b), *The Fortress* 1932, *Vanessa* 1933 (213c).

Walsh, William (1663–1708), poet and critic: lives, d., and is buried in Abberley; MP for Worcester. 'The Despairing Lover' in *Poems* 1716 (196a).

Walton, Izaak (1593–1683), angler and biographer: b. and baptized in Stafford; lives in London (City: Fleet St.); m. in Canterbury 1626; attends Magdalen Herbert's funeral in Chelsea Old Church, London (Chelsea: Cheyne Walk); retires to Shallowford; lives in Hartlebury 1660–2; writes his wife's epitaph in Worcester; goes fishing in Dovedale; stays with his friend Cotton in Beresford Dale; visits Ilam; lives in Farnham; spends last years, d., and is buried in Winchester; commemorated in Shallowford, Stafford, Winchester, and London (City: St Dunstan-in-the-West, Fleet St.). *The Compleat Angler* 1653 (110c, 188a, 188c, 195b), *The Life of Mr. Rich Hooker* 1665, *The Life of Mr. George Herbert* 1670 (53c).

Ward, Artemus. *See* Browne, Charles Farrar.

Ward, Mrs Humphry (née **Mary Augusta Arnold**) (1851–1920), novelist: lives in Oxford 1872–81, London (Bloomsbury: Russell Sq.) 1881–91; stays at Peper Harow 1882, Borough Farm 1883–90; meets Gladstone in Oxford 1888; lives in London (Belgravia: Grosvenor Pl.) 1891–1919, Aldbury 1892–1920; stays at Levens Hall 1896–7; visits Hastings, the church at Cartmel Fell is featured in her novel *Helbeck of Bannisdale* 1898; buried in Aldbury. *Robert Elsmere* 1888 (43a–b, 67b, 69a, 80a, 223a), *Marcella* 1894 (161a), *Helbeck of Bannisdale* 1898 (214b, 220b).

Warner, Alan (1964–), novelist: b. nr Oban. *Morvern Caller* 1995 (291c), *The Sopranos* 1998 (291c), *These Demented Lands* 1998 (291b).

Warner, (Nora) Sylvia Townsend (1893–1978), novelist, short-story writer, and poet: b. London (Harrow on the Hill); educ. Harrow; visits T. F. Powys and meets Valentine Ackland at East Chaldon 1922; lives Frome Vauchurch from 1937; buried at St Nicholas's Church, East Chaldon. *Mr Fortune's Maggot* 1927 (13b), *The Corner That Held Them* 1948 (22a, 181c).

Warton, Thomas (1728–90), Poet Laureate and literary historian: educ. Oxford (Trinity College); Fellow at Oxford 1751–90; rector of Kiddington 1771–90. *The Pleasures of Melancholy* 1747, *The Triumphs of Isis* 1749, *The Union* (ed.) 1753, *Observations on the Faerie Queene of Spenser* 1754, *A Companion to the Guide* 1760, *The Oxford Sausage* (ed.) 1764 (78a), *History of Kiddington* 1783 (59c), 'Verses on Sir Joshua Reynold's Painted Window at New College' 1789 (74b–c).

Waterhouse, Keith (1929–), novelist and journalist: b. Leeds. *Billy Liar* 1959 (230c, 235c), *Jeffrey Bernard Is Unwell* 1989 (146c).

Waters, Sarah (1966–), novelist. *Affinity* 1999 (138c), *Fingersmith* 2002 (62c, 150b), *The Night Watch* 2006 (98a).

Waterton, Charles (1782–1865), naturalist and author: b. Wakefield; educ. Whalley (Stonyhurst College); d. Wakefield. *Wanderings in South America* 1825 (238b–c).

Watkins, Vernon Phillips (1906–67), poet and lecturer: educ. Swansea, Repton, and Cambridge (Magdalene College) 1924–5; lecturer in Swansea; lives in Pennard Cliffs nr Swansea 1931–41, 1946–67. *Ballad of the Mari Lwyd and Other Poems* 1941, *The Lamp and the Veil* 1945, *The Lady with the Unicorn* 1948, *The Death Bell* 1954, *Letters to Vernon Watkins by Dylan Thomas* (ed.) 1957 (261c).

Watson, John ('**Ian Maclaren**') (1850–1907), novelist and short-story writer: pastor in Logiealmond 1875–7. *Beside the Bonnie Brier Bush* 1894 (290b), *St. Jude's* 1907 (283c).

Watson, Thomas (1557?–92), poet and translator: buried in London (Smithfield: St Bartholomew-the-Less). Tasso's *Aminta* (trans.) 1585, *The Tears of Fancie* 1593 (144b).

Watts, Isaac (1674–1748), hymn writer: b. Southampton; educ. Southampton and London (Stoke Newington); buried in London (Finsbury: Bunhill Fields); commemorated in London (Westminster Abbey) and Southampton. 'Behold the glories of the Lamb' (150b), 'O God, our help in ages past', 'When I survey the wondrous cross', 'Jesus shall reign where'er the sun' (85b).

Watts-Dunton, Walter Theodore (1832–1914), novelist and critic: b. St Ives (Cambridgeshire); lives in London (Bloomsbury: Great James St.) 1872–3; visits Kelmscott; lives in Danes End, London (Strand: The Strand) 1873; visits Shiplake 1879; lives in London (Putney) 1879–1914. *Aylwin* 1898 (59c, 179a, 183a).

Waugh, Auberon (1939–2001), journalist, editor, and novelist: b. Dulverton; childhood in Stinchcombe and Combe Florey (returns 1971); educ. Downside and Oxford (Christ Church), rusticated 1959; commissioned into Royal Horse Guards, London (Westminster) 1957; writes for *Private Eye* and edits *Literary Review* in London (Soho); lives in Chilton Foliat. *Will This Do?* 1991 (19a, 32b–c).

Waugh, Evelyn Arthur St John (1903–66), novelist: b. London (Hampstead: Hillfield Rd); educ. Lancing and Oxford (Hertford College); frequents Beckley; teaches in Aston Clinton 1925–7; lives in London (Islington: Canonbury Sq.) 1928, Mells 1930, Stinchcombe 1937–56; stays in Chagford 1944; lives in Combe Florey; buried in Combe Florey. *Rossetti: His Life and Works* 1928 (41c), *Decline and Fall* 1928 (41a, 122a), *Edmund Campion* 1935 (25c, 72a), *Brideshead Revisited* 1945 (13a, 72a, 74a), *The Loved One* 1948, *Helena* 1950, *Men at Arms* 1952, *Officers and Gentlemen* 1955, *The Ordeal of Gilbert Pinfold* 1957 (33b), *The Life of Ronald Knox* 1959 (72a), *Unconditional Surrender* 1961 (15c), *A Little Learning* 1964 (60b, 72a), *Sword of Honour* 1965 (15c).

Wyndham, John (**John Wyndham Parkes Lucas Beynon Harris**) (*cont'd*)
lives in London (Bloomsbury) and Petersfield; memorial in Aberdaron. *The Day of the Triffids* 1951 (92a, 100c), *The Kraken Wakes* 1953 (100c), *The Midwich Cuckoos* 1957 (100c), *The Trouble with Lichen* 1960 (100c).

Wynne, Elizabeth Lady Fremantle (1779–1857), diarist: lives in Swanbourne. *The Wynne Diaries*, ed. A. Fremantle, 3 vols 1935–40 (87c).

Wynne, Ellis (1670/1–1734), Welsh cleric and author: b. nr Harlech; educ. Oxford (Jesus College) 1691/2; incumbent nr Harlech 1704/5–1734; buried nr Harlech. *Gweledigaetheu y Bardd Cwsc* (The Visions of the Sleeping Bard) 1703 (250c).

Wyntoun, Andrew of (1350?–1420?), historian: canon-regular in St Andrews; prior in St Serf's Inch to 1420? *The Orygynale Cronykil* 1795 (294a, 294b).

Y

Yeats, William Butler (1865–1939), poet and playwright: b. Dublin; educ. London (Hammersmith: Godolphin Boys' School, Iffley Rd) and Dublin; lives in London (Chalk Farm: Fitzroy Rd) 1867–74, (Kensington: Edith Rd) 1874–6, (Chiswick: Woodstock Rd) 1879–81; lives in Howth 1881; holidays in Sligo; lives in London (Chiswick: Blenheim Rd) 1888–95; founds the Rhymers' Club (City: Fleet St.) 1891; visits Lissadell, Dublin 1894; lives in Bloomsbury (Woburn Pl.) 1895–1919; rents cottage in Coleman's Hatch 1912–13; buys Thoor Ballylee nr Gort 1917; lives in Oxford, Shillingford, and Thame 1921; visits Coole Park, Durras House, Tullira Castle, Rinvyle, Steyning, and Withyham; buried in Drumcliff. *The Wanderings of Oisin and Other Poems* 1889 (303b–c), 'Ballad of Father O'Hart' in *Crossways* 1889 (302a–b), *The Wind Among the Reeds* 1899, *Cathleen ni Hoolihan* 1902, *On Baile's Strand* 1904, *Deirdre* 1907, *The Green Helmet and Other Poems* 1910 (103c), *Seven Poems and a Fragment* 1922 (84b), *The Wild Swans at Coole* 1919, 'Coole Park, 1929' (302c), *The Tower* 1928, *The Winding Stair* 1933 (303b), 'The Lake Isle of Innisfree', 'The Fiddler of Dooney' (303b), 'Meditations in Time of Civil War' (84b), 'Under Ben Bulben' (302c), 'Purgatory' in *Last Poems and Two Plays* 1940 (87a), 'The Municipal Gallery Revisited' (313b).

Yonge, Charlotte Mary (1823–1901), novelist: b., lives, and is buried in Otterbourne; commemorated in Winchester. *The Heir of Redclyffe* 1853 (65b, c).

Young, Andrew (1885–1971), poet: b. and commemorated at Elgin. *Collected Poems* 1936, 1960 (280c).

Young, Arthur (1741–1820), agricultural theorist: lives in Bradfield Combust; visits Cork. *Tour in Ireland* 1780, *Travels in France* 1792.

Young, Edward (1683–1765), poet: b. Upham; educ. Winchester; Fellow in Law at Oxford (All Souls College) 1708; rector of Welwyn 1730–65; frequents Tunbridge Wells; commemorated in Welwyn. *The Complaint, or, Night Thoughts on Life, Death, and Immortality* 1741–5 (89b, 90b, 185a).

Young, Francis Brett (1884–1954), physician, novelist, and poet: b. Halesowen; educ. Birmingham (University); practises medicine in Brixham 1907–14; spends summers at Esthwaite Lodge 1928–33; visits the Elan Valley; lives in Fladbury 1932–c. 1945; buried in Worcester; commemorated in Worcester and Halesowen. *Deep Sea* 1914, *The Dark Tower* 1914 (12a–b), *The House Under the Water* 1932 (216b, 249c), *White Ladies* 1935 (200a).

Young, Robert ('**Rabin Hill**') (1811–1908), tailor and poet: b., lives, d., and is buried in Sturminster Newton. 'Rabin Hill's Visit to the Railway' 1861 (34a).

Z

Zamyatin, Evgeny (1884–1937), Russian author and marine engineer: lives in Newcastle upon Tyne 1916–17. *Islanders* 1917, *The Fisher of Men* 1918, *We* 1920 (242a).

Zangwill, Israel (1864–1926), playwright and novelist: founder and first president of the International Jewish Territorial Organization: visits Ewelme; commemorated in London (Bethnal Green: Old Ford Rd). *Children of the Ghetto* 1892 (53b, 100b–c), *The Melting Pot* 1908 (100c).

INDEX OF PLACES

Index of Places

PICTURE ACKNOWLEDGEMENTS

The publishers are grateful to the following for their permission to reproduce the photographs. Although every effort has been made to contact copyright holders, it has not been possible in every case and we apologise for any that have been omitted. Should the copyright holders wish to contact us after publication, we would be happy to include an acknowledgement in subsequent reprints.

Maps & illustrations by John Taylor

4 Photo Tom Hickman
4 Photo Tom Hickman
4 Photo Carrie Hickman
4 Photo Carrie Hickman
5 © National Portrait Gallery, London
9 © Ian M Butterfield/Alamy
9 David Carton/Fotolibra
9 The Georgian House, a branch of the City of Bristol Museum and Art Gallery
13 Dorset Natural History and Archaeological Society
15 The National Trust
17 Dorset County Museum
18 © National Portrait Gallery, London
20 britainonview.com
opposite 20 britainonview/David Sellman
opposite 21 © NTPL/Andreas von Einsiedel
21 Reproduced by permission of the Dean and Chapter of Exeter
24 © Mark Gerson/National Portrait Gallery, London
30 © Alain Le Garsmeur/Corbis
31 The National Trust
33 Photo by Kurt Hutton/Picture Post/Getty Images
opposite 36 © NTPL/Rupert Truman
opposite 37 © stephen bond/Alamy
47 britainonview.com
47 britainonview.com
50 The Ditchley Foundation
opposite 52 © NTPL/Fay Godwin
opposite 53 Matt Cardy/Stringer/Getty Images News
55 © National Portrait Gallery, London
62 © Hulton-Deutsch Collection/Corbis
65 britainonview.com
65 Hulton Archive/Getty Images
66 Billett Potter
66 britainonview.com
66 Photo John Taylor
66 The Master and Fellows of University College, Oxford
opposite 68 © Paul Seheult/Eye Ubiquitous/Corbis
opposite 69 © NTPL/Rupert Truman
74 Billett Potter
75 Oxfordshire County Coucil Photographic Archive
77 © Bassouls Sophie/Corbis Sygma
80 Portsmouth Central Library
82 pf MS Am 1094. By permission of the Houghton Library, Harvard University.
83 pf MS Eng731.11. By permission of the Houghton Library, Harvard University.
opposite 84 © Angelo Hornak/Corbis
opposite 85 © Oxford Picture Library/Alamy
86 Photo: Private Collection. Reproduced by permission of Pollinger Limited and the proprietor
88 © National Portrait Gallery, London
89 Reproduced by permission of English Heritage. NMR
90 The National Trust
99 © Jon Arnold Images/Alamy
99 © Steve Atkins/Alamy

99 © Eric Nathan/Alamy
99 © Alex Segre/Alamy
100 AF Kersting
opposite 100 britainonview.com
opposite 101 © Michael Nicholson/Corbis
102 Haywood Magee/Stringer/Hulton Archive/Getty Images
105 © Jeremy Horner/Corbis
105 The National Trust
107 © National Portrait Gallery, London
113 © Angelo Hornak/Corbis
114 AF Kersting
115 Ashmolean Museum, Oxford
opposite 116 © NTPL/Nadia Mackenzie
opposite 117 britainonview.com
119 Hulton Archive/Stringer/Getty Images
127 V&A Images/Victoria and Albert Museum
128 Hulton Archive/Getty Images
opposite 133 The British Library
136 © Bettmann/Corbis
143 © Alex Segre/Alamy
145 © Pete Millson/Alamy
145 © National Portrait Gallery, London
145 Nick Robins
145 Nick Robins
151 © Private Collection/The Bridgeman Art Library
153 London Transport Museum © Transport for London
154 Photo: Courthald Institute of Art. © Devonshire Collection, Chatsworth. Reproduced by permission of Chatsworth Settlement Trustees
155 Courtesy Nottingham City Museums and Galleries: Nottingham Castle
157 britainonview.com
159 Andrew Lycett, Ian Fleming, Weidenfeld & Nicholson, a division of The Orion Publishing Group. Photo from the collection of Andrew Lycett
162 Manuscript dept., British Library of Political and Economic Science
opposite 164 © Eric Nathan/Alamy
opposite 165 Collections/Malcolm Crowthers
166 © Nikreates/Alamy
166 © Corpus Christi College, Cambridge, UK/The Bridgeman Art Library
166 britainonview.com
171 Neil Grant/Alamy
174 © Paul Joyce/National Portrait Gallery, London
175 Brooke Trustees and King's College, Cambridge. RCB/Ph/127
177 Photo by Sasha/Getty Images
180 britainonview.com
opposite 180 © Edifice/Corbis
opposite 181 © Ian Goodrick/Alamy
181 photograph G. E. Hammond
183 www.visitsouthwold.co.uk
189 britainonview.com
190 Image courtesy of D.H. Lawrence Heritage, Broxtowe Borough Council
192 From the Local Studies Collection, Lincoln Central Library, by courtesy of Lincolnshire County Council
198 britainonview.com
201 Reproduced by kind permission of the Master and Fellows of Balliol College
204 © National Portrait Gallery, London
206 Stafford Borough Council
208 Times Newspapers
209 The Shakespeare Birthplace Trust

211 britainonview.com
215 britainonview.com
217 © National Portrait Gallery, London
221 © Andy Marshall/Alamy
221 Ron Jones/Merseyside Photo Library
221 Ron Jones/Merseyside Photo Library
221 TopFoto.co.uk
224 © National Portrait Gallery, London
227 britainonview.com
228 Reproduced from the photograph by Derek Smith in the Basil Bunting Poetry Archive, Durham University Library, copyright the Archive
opposite 228 britainonview/David Sellman
opposite 229 britainonview/Joe Cornish
231 AF Kersting
233 © National Portrait Gallery, London
234 britainonview.com
235 © Estate of Fay Godwin/National Portrait Gallery, London
240 Durham Cathedral
opposite 244 © Andy Marshall/Alamy
opposite 245 britainonview.com
248 © National Museum of Wales
249 John Hedgecoe Studio
252 Hulton Archive/Getty Images
255 The British Library
256 V&A Images/Victoria and Albert Museum
257 britainonview.com
opposite 260 © Farrell Grehan/Corbis
opposite 261 britainonview.com
262 Slim Aarons/Stringer/Hulton Archive/Getty Images
263 © National Museum of Wales
266 britainonview.com
267 britainonview/Joe Cornish
268 britainonview.com
274 britainonview/Ingrid Rasmussen
274 Neil Dixon
274 © Brand X Pictures/PunchStock
276 © National Portrait Gallery, London
opposite 276 britainonview.com/Roz Gordo
opposite 277 © Lawson Wood/Corbis
282 © Popperfoto/Alamy
282 © BL Images Ltd/Alamy
282 © G. Richardson/Robert Harding World Imagery/Corbis
287 © BL Images Ltd/Alamy
289 Reproduced by kind permission of The National Trust for Scotland
opposite 292 Liam Blake/The Irish Image Collection
opposite 293 Liam Blake/The Irish Image Collection
293 © WildCountry/Corbis
295 © Crown Copyright, 2006, Historic Scotland Images
301 Board of Trinity College, Dublin
302 Fáilte Ireland Photographic
304 Mr A. Brennan
306 Robert Harding Picture Library Ltd/Alamy
306 © Michael St. Maur Sheil/Corbis
306 Christina Gascoigne/ Robert Harding World Imagery/Getty Images
opposite 308 © Bruno Barbier/Robert Harding World Imagery/Corbis
opposite 309 Connie Coleman/ Photographer's Choice/Getty Images
310 David H. Davison/Davison & Associates
311 © National Portrait Gallery, London
313 Picture Post/Stringer/Hulton Archive/Getty Images